VM
771
.08
1987

Outboard motor
service manual

$14.95

DATE			

**BUSINESS/SCIENCE/TECHNOLOGY
DIVISION**

OUTBOARD MOTOR SERVICE MANUAL

Volume 2
Covers Motors 30 Horsepower & Above
(10th Edition)

Chrysler	Johnson	Suzuki
Evinrude	Mariner	Tohatsu
Force	Mercury	Yamaha
	Sea King	

Published by
INTERTEC PUBLISHING CORPORATION
P.O. BOX 12901 OVERLAND PARK, KS 66212

Cover photograph courtesy of Johnson Outboards.

©Copyright 1987 by Intertec Publishing Corp. Printed in the United States of America
Library of Congress Catalog Card Number 86-83161

CONTENTS

DUAL DIMENSIONS

This service manual provides specifications in both the Metric (SI) and U.S. Customary systems of measurement on some models. The first specification is given in the measuring system used during manufacture, while the second specification (given in parenthesis) is the converted measurement. For instance, a specification of "0.28 mm (0.011 inch)" would indicate that the equipment was manufactured using the metric system of measurement and the U.S. equivalent of 0.28 mm is 0.011 inch.

DESIGN FUNDAMENTALS
OPERATING PRINCIPLES

ENGINE TYPES

The power source for the outboard motor does not differ basically from that used to power automobiles, farm or garden tractors, lawn mowers, or many other items of power equipment in use today. All are technically known as "Internal Combustion, Reciprocating Engines."

The source of power is heat formed by the burning of a combustible mixture of petroleum products and air. In a reciprocating engine, this burning takes place in a closed cylinder containing a piston. Expansion resulting from the heat of combustion applies pressure on the piston to turn a shaft by means of a crank and connecting rod.

The fuel mixture may be ignited by means of an electric spark (Otto Cycle Engine) or by the heat of compression (Diesel Cycle). The complete series of events which must take place in order for the engine to run may occur in one revolution of the crankshaft (referred to as Two-Stroke Cycle), or in two revolutions of the crankshaft (Four-Stroke Cycle).

OTTO CYCLE, In a spark ignited engine, a series of five events are required in order to provide power. This series of events are called the **Cycle** (or Work Cycle) and is repeated in each cylinder as long as work is done. The series of events which comprise the work cycle are as follows:

1. The mixture of fuel and air is pushed or drawn into the cylinder, by reducing cylinder pressure to less than the outside pressure, or by applying an initial, higher pressure to the fuel charge.
2. The mixture is compressed, or reduced in volume.
3. The mixture is ignited by a timed electric spark.
4. The burning fuel:air mixture expands, forcing the piston down, thus converting the generated chemical energy into mechanical power.
5. The burned gases are exhausted from the cylinder so that a new cycle can begin.

The series of events comprising the work cycle are commonly referred to as INTAKE, COMPRESSION, IGNITION, EXPANSION (POWER) and EXHAUST.

DIESEL CYCLE. The Diesel Cycle differs from the Otto Cycle in that air alone is drawn into the cylinder during the intake period, then compressed to a much greater degree. The air is heated by compression. Instead of an electric spark, a finely atomized charge of fuel is injected into the combustion chamber where it combines with the heated air and ignites spontaneously. The power and exhaust strokes are almost identical to those of the Otto Cycle.

FOUR-STROKE CYCLE. In a reciprocating engine, each movement of the piston (in or out) in the cylinder is referred to as a Stroke. Thus, one complete revolution of the engine crankshaft accompanies two strokes of the piston.

The most simple and efficient engine design from the standpoint of fuel and exhaust gas mixture movement is the Four-Stroke Cycle shown schematically in fig. 1-1. The first event of the work cycle coincides with the first stroke of the piston as shown at "A". Downward movement of the piston draws a fresh charge of the fuel:air mixture into the cylinder. View "B" shows the compression of the fuel mixture which occurs during the second stroke of the cycle. Ignition occurs at about the time the piston reaches the top of the cylinder on the compression stroke, resulting in the expansion of the burning fuel:air mixture, and in the power stroke as shown at "C". The fourth stroke of the cycle empties the cylinder of the burned gases as shown at "D", and the cylinder is ready for the beginning of another work cycle.

The fact that a full stroke of the piston is available for each major mechanical event of the cycle is ideal, from the standpoint of efficiency, and four-stroke engines are generally most economical where fuel costs alone are considered.

The four-stroke cycle requires a more complicated system of valving, which adds materially to the weight and original cost of the engine. This fact, coupled with the fact that two revolutions of the crankshaft are required for each power stroke, causes the two-stroke engine to compare more favorably when horsepower to weight ratio is considered; and because of the weight advantage, the two-stroke engine has probably reached its highest degree of development for outboard motor use.

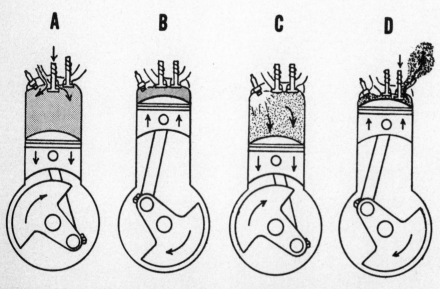

A   B   C   D

Fig. 1-1—Schematic view of a typical four-stroke cycle engine showing basic principles of operation. Two revolutions of the crankshaft are required to complete the cycle. The first, or INTAKE stroke is shown at "A". As the piston moves downward in cylinder the intake valve is opened allowing a combustible mixture of fuel and air to enter cylinder. The intake valve closes as the piston moves upward in the second, or COMPRESSION stroke as shown in "B." The compressed charge is ignited, and expansion of the burning mixture forces the piston down in the POWER stroke "C". The exhaust valve opens as the piston moves upward in the fourth, or EXHAUST stroke "D", and the cylinder is cleared of burned gases for the beginning of another cycle.

TWO-STROKE CYCLE. In a two-stroke cycle engine, the five events of intake, compression, ignition, power and exhaust must take place in two strokes of the piston; or one revolution of the crankshaft. Thus, a compressed fuel charge is fired each time the piston reaches the top of the cylinder, and each downward stroke is a power stroke. In order to accomplish this, the initial pressure of the incoming fuel-air mixture must be raised to a point somewhat higher than the lowest pressure existing in the cylinder, or a fresh charge of fuel could not be admitted and the engine would not run. This elevation of pressure requires the use of an air pump, or compressor, of approximately the same volume as the cylinder itself. Coincidentally, such an air pump is available with a minimum of additional parts, cost, or friction losses by utilizing the opposite side of the piston and cylinder as the pump. Such engines are called "Crankcase Scavenged," and are almost universally used in the outboard motor industry.

Individual cylinders are often combined and connected in series to the shaft to increase power output. Engine operation is also smoothed by increasing the number of power impulses per crankshaft revolution. A single cylinder, four-stroke cycle engine (with only one power impulse for two shaft revolutions) must have a heavy flywheel to store and deliver the developed energy between power strokes. Increasing the number of cylinders to two, three or four enables the design engineer to increase engine power without a corresponding increase in engine weight.

Figure 1-2 shows a schematic view of the crankcase scavenged, reed valve type, two-stroke cycle engine commonly used. The general sequence of events required for operation is as follows: As the piston moves outward from the crankshaft as shown in view "B", the volume of the closed crankcase is enlarged and the pressure lowered, causing air to be drawn through the carburetor (C), where it is mixed with fuel. This mixture is then drawn through the reed valve (R) and into the crankcase. At the same time, a previous charge of fuel is being compressed between head of piston and closed end of cylinder as shown by the darkened area. As the piston approaches top center, a timed spark ignites the compressed fuel charge and the resultant expansion moves the piston downward on the power stroke. The reed valve (R) closes, and downward movement of piston compresses the next fuel charge in the crankcase as shown in view "A". When the piston nears the bottom of its stroke, the crown of piston uncovers the exhaust port (EX)

in cylinder wall, allowing the combustion products and remaining pressure to escape as shown by the wavy arrow. Further downward movement of piston opens the transfer port (TP) leading from the crankcase to cylinder; and the then higher crankcase pressure forces the compressed fuel:air mixture through

transfer port into the cylinder. The baffle which is built into crown of piston deflects the incoming charge upward, and most of the remaining exhaust gases are driven from the combustion chamber by this fresh charge. Two-stroke cycle, crankcase scavenged engines are sometimes produced with a

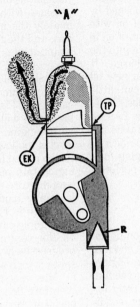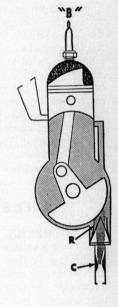

Fig. 1-2—Schematic view of two-stroke cycle, crankcase scavenged engine used in most outboard motors. The same series of events shown in Fig. 1-1 takes place in one revolution of the crankshaft by using the crankcase as a scavenging pump.

C. Carburetor
R. Reed valve
TP. Transfer port
EX. Exhaust port

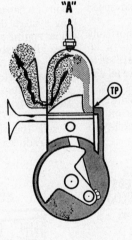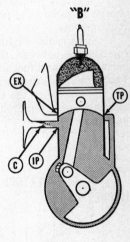

Fig. 1-3—Two-stroke cycle, three port engine. Principles are similar to reed valve or rotary valve types except that a third, intake port is located in cylinder wall and opened and closed by the piston skirt.

C. Carburetor
EX. Exhaust port
IP. Intake port
TP. Transfer port

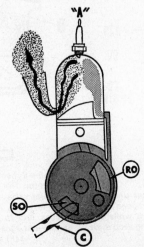

Fig. 1-4—Two-stroke cycle rotary valve engine. The incoming fuel charge is controlled by a rotary valve attached to the crankshaft. The opening in valve (RO) and crankcase (SO) align at the proper time to admit a fresh charge, then close to allow initial crankcase compression.

C. Carburetor
RO. Opening in rotating member
SO. Opening in crankcase wall

Engine Fundamentals

OUTBOARD MOTOR

fuel induction system other than the inlet reed valve. Although they are not extensively used in outboard motor manufacture, they are mentioned in passing and illustrated schematically in Fig. 1-3 and Fig. 1-4.

In the crankcase scavenged engine, most of the friction parts requiring lubrication are located in the fuel intake system. Lubrication is accomplished by mixing the required amount of oil with the fuel, so that a small amount of oil in the form of a fine mist is drawn into the crankcase with each fuel charge. It should be pointed out that the new oil brought into the crankcase can little more than supplement the losses, therefore it is necessary that the friction parts be well lubricated at the time the engine is started. The use of too much oil in the fuel mixture results in plug fouling, excessive carbon, and poor performance, as well as being wasteful.

FUEL SYSTEM

CARBURETOR. The function of the carburetor is to atomize the fuel and mix it with the air flowing into the engine. The carburetor must also meter the fuel to provide the proper fuel:air ratio for the different engine operating conditions, and the proper density of total charge to satisfy the power and speed requirements.

A gasoline-air mixture is normally combustible between the limits of 25 parts air to 1 part fuel, and 8 parts air to 1 part fuel. Because much of the fuel will not vaporize when the engine is cold, a rich mixture is required for cold starting. The exact ratio will depend on the temperature and the volatility (ability to vaporize) of the fuel.

Carburetor operation is based on the venturi principle, in which a gas or liquid flowing through a restriction (venturi) will increase in speed and decrease in pressure, acting in much the same way as water passing through the nozzle of a garden hose. Refer to Fig. 1-5.

An extension tube (nozzle) from the fuel reservoir is inserted into the air passage with the opening at approximately the narrowest part of the venturi, and the fuel level in the reservoir is maintained at just below the opening of the nozzle. When air passes through the venturi, fuel spills over into the air stream in amounts relative to the pressure drop. If the level in fuel bowl is too high, fuel will spill over into carburetor when engine is not operating. If fuel level is too low, a sufficient amount may not be pulled into the the air stream during certain periods of operation, and a lean mixture could result. The fuel level is usually maintained by means of a float as shown in Fig. 1-6.

A simple carburetor which relies only on the venturi principle will supply a progressively richer mixture as engine speed is increased, and will not run at all at idle speeds. The carburetor must therefore be modified if the engine is to perform at varying speeds. The first step in modification is usually the addition of a separate fuel mixing and metering system designed to operate only at slow engine speeds. A fairly representative idle system is shown schematically in Fig. 1-7. An idle passage is drilled in the carburetor body as shown, leading from the fuel chamber to the air horn at the approximate location of the throttle valve (1). When the throttle valve is closed, the air flow is almost shut off. This reduces the pressure in the inlet

manifold, and therefore the density of the charge in the combustion chamber. The pressure drop at the venturi which is shown in Fig. 1-5 ceases to exist, and fuel cannot be drawn from the main fuel nozzle. The high manifold vacuum above the throttle valve (1 – Fig. 1-7) draws fuel up the idle passage through idle jet (5) then through primary idle orifice (2) into the intake manifold. At the same time, air is being drawn through the secondary idle orifice (3) and air metering orifice (4) to mix with the fuel in the idle passage. The sizes of the two orifices (2 and 3) and the idle jet (5) are carefully calculated and controlled. The amount of air passing through metering orifice (4) can be adjusted by the idle mixture adjusting needle (6) to obtain the desired fuel:air mixture for smooth idle.

When throttle valve (1) is opened slightly to a fast idle position (as indicated by the broken lines) both the primary and secondary idle orifices (2 and 3) are subjected to high manifold vacuum. The incoming flow of air through secondary orifice (3) is cut off, which increases the speed of fuel flow through idle jet (5). This supplies the additional fuel needed to properly mix with the greater volume of air passing around the throttle butterfly valve. As the throttle valve is further opened and edge of valve moves away from the idle orifices, the idle fuel system ceases to operate and fuel mixture is again controlled by the venturi of the main fuel system.

In many applications, the main fuel system and idle system will supply the fuel requirements for all operating conditions. In other cases, an additional economizer system is incorporated,

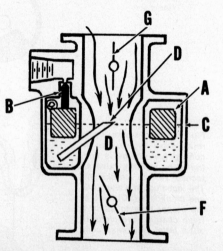

Fig. 1-5—Schematic view of venturi principle. Right hand figures show how air speed is increased by the restriction (venturi) while left hand figures show the accompanying drop in air pressure.

Fig. 1-6—Schematic view of a simple float-type carburetor. The buoyancy of float (A) closes the fuel inlet valve (B) to maintain the fuel at a constant level (C). The pressure drop in the venturi causes fuel to flow out nozzle (D) which protrudes just above the fuel level. Throttle valve is at (F) and choke valve at (G)

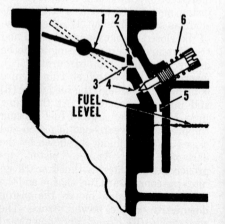

Fig. 1-7—The addition of a separate idle fuel system permits delivery of a correct fuel mixture over a wider range of engine speeds.

1. Throttle valve	4. Air metering orifice
2. Upper idle orifice	5. Idle fuel jet
3. Lower idle orifice	6. Idle mixture level

6

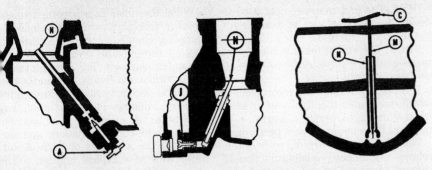

Fig. 1-8—The main fuel metering system may be of many types. Three typical systems are shown. In the left-hand view, the maximum fuel flow through nozzle (N) may be adjusted by the mixture needle (A). In the center view, maximum fuel flow is controlled by the carefully calibrated fixed jet (J). In the right-hand view, the stepped metering needle (M) is moved vertically by a cam (C) on throttle shaft, thus limiting maximum flow to predetermined amounts which vary with throttle setting.

which provides a leaner fuel-air mixture for part throttle operation. Accelerator pumps or an accelerating well which are usually needed for automotive operation are not normally used on outboard motors.

An accelerator pump can be used, however. The accelerator pump can be lever operated or spring operated and vacuum controlled. The purpose of an accelerator pump is to provide an additional charge of fuel at the moment of throttle opening, before balance is restored to the high speed fuel system.

High speed mixture adjustment is controlled by a fixed jet, a fuel adjustment needle, or by a stepped metering rod which is synchronized with the throttle valve. Refer to Fig. 1-8 for a schematic view of the systems.

The basic design of diaphragm type carburetors is shown in Fig. 1-9. Fuel is delivered to inlet (1) by gravity with fuel tank above carburetor, or under pressure from a fuel pump. Atmospheric pressure is maintained on lower side of diaphragm (D) through vent hole (V). When choke plate (C) is closed and engine is cranked, or when engine is running, pressure at orifice (O) is less than atmospheric pressure; this low pressure, or vacuum, is transmitted to fuel chamber (F) above diaphragm through nozzle channel (N). The higher (atmospheric) pressure at lower side of diaphragm will then push the diaphragm upward compressing spring (S) and allowing inlet valve (IV) to open and fuel will flow into the fuel chamber. Some diaphragm type carburetors are equipped with an internal fuel pump.

REED VALVES. The inlet reed (or leaf) valve is essentially a check valve which permits the air-fuel mixture to move in only one direction through the engine. It traps the fuel charge in the crankcase, permitting the inlet pressure to be raised high enough to allow a full charge to enter the cylinder against the remaining exhaust pressure during the short period of time the transfer ports are open. The ideal design for the valve is one which offers the least possible resistance to the flow of gases entering

the crankcase, but completely seals off any flow back through the carburetor during the downward stroke of the piston.

FUEL PUMP. All but the smallest motors normally use a remote fuel tank from which fuel is pumped to the carburetor. Most two-stroke motors use the pulsating, pressure and vacuum impulses in one crankcase to operate the fuel pump. Refer to Fig. 1-10. Operation is as follows:

When the piston moves upward in the cylinder as shown in view "A", a vacuum is created on the back side of diaphragm "D". As the diaphragm moves away from the fuel chamber, inlet check valve (5) opens against the pressure of spring (6) to admit fuel from tank as shown by arrow. When the piston moves downward as shown in view "B", the diaphragm moves into the fuel chamber, causing the inlet check valve to close. The outlet check valve (4) opens and fuel flows to the carburetor. When the carburetor float chamber becomes full and carburetor inlet valve closes, the fuel pump diaphragm will remain in approximately the position shown in "A", but will maintain pressure on carburetor fuel line until additional fuel is required.

On some of the larger motors, a two stage fuel pump of similar construction is connected to two separate crankcases of the motor.

On four-stroke cycle engines, the pump diaphragm is spring loaded in one direction and lever operated in the other. The lever may be actuated by any means, the most common being an eccentric cam on the engine camshaft. As the cam turns, the diaphragm pulsates in much the same way as that described for the pressure-vacuum unit. The strength of the diaphragm return spring determines the standby fuel pressure which will be maintained at the carburetor.

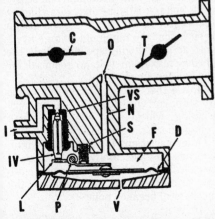

Fig. 1-9—Cross-section drawing of basic design diaphragm type carburetor. Atmospheric pressure actuates diaphragm (D).

C. Choke	N. Nozzle
D. Diaphragm	O. Orifice
F. Fuel chamber	P. Pivot pin
I. Fuel inlet	S. Spring
IV. Inlet valve needle	T. Throttle
L. Lever	V. Vent
	VS. Valve seat

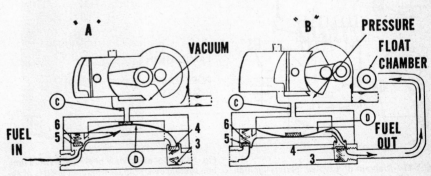

Fig. 1-10—Schematic view of a typical, crankcase operated, diaphragm type fuel pump. Pressure and vacuum pulsations from crankcase pass through connection (C) to rear of diaphragm (D) which induces a pumping action on fuel line as shown.

3. Valve spring	5. Inlet check valve
4. Outlet check valve	6. Valve spring

IGNITION SYSTEM

The timed spark which ignites the fuel charge in the cylinder may be supplied by either a magneto or battery ignition system. To better understand the operation of the components and the differences and similarities of the two systems, they will be combined in this section and the functions of the various units explained and compared.

IGNITION SYSTEM THEORY. In the modern ignition system, a relatively weak electric current of 6 to 12 volts and 2 to 5 amperes is transformed into a momentary charge of minute amperage and extremely high (10,000-25,000) voltage, capable of jumping the spark plug gap in the cylinder and igniting the fuel charge.

To understand the ignition system theory, electricity can be thought of as a stream of electrons flowing through a conductor. The pressure of the stream can be increased by restricting volume, or the volume increased by reducing the resistance to movement, but the total amount of power cannot be increased except by employing additional outside force. The current has an inertia of motion and resists being stopped once it has started flowing. If the circuit is broken suddenly, the force will tend to pile up temporarily, attempting to convert the speed of flow into energy.

A short list of useful electrical terms and a brief explanation of their meanings is as follows:

AMPERE. The unit of measurement used to designate the amount, or quantity of flow of an electrical current.

OHM. The unit measurement used to designate the resistance of a conductor to the flow of current.

VOLT. The unit of measurement used to designate the force, or pressure of an electrical current

WATT. The unit of measurement which designates the abillty of an electrical current to perform work; or to measure the amount of work performed.

The four terms are directly interrelated, one ampere equaling the flow of current produced by one volt against a resistance of one ohm. One watt designates the work potential of one ampere at one volt in one second.

BATTERY IGNITION

Fig. 1–11 shows a very simple battery ignition circuit for a single cylinder engine. The system uses breaker points to control the time of ignition. The system may be called a "total loss ignition" if there is no provision for recharging the battery while the engine is running and the intensity of the spark will diminish as the battery's electromotive Force (emF) is reduced.

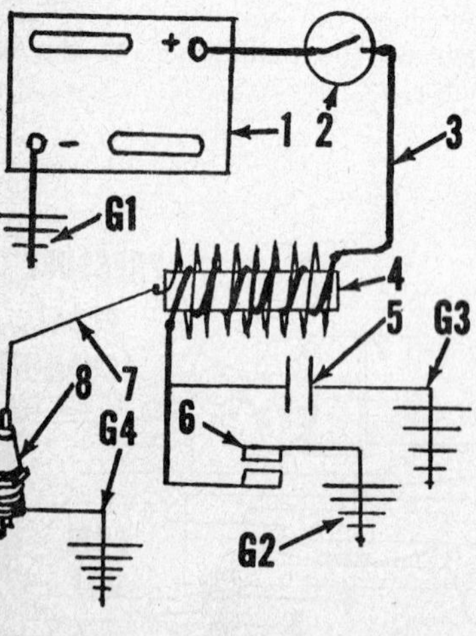

When the timer cam is turned so that breaker (contact) points are closed, a complete circuit is completed from the battery through the breaker points, to the coil primary winding, through the ignition switch and finally back to the battery. The electricity flowing through the primary winding of the ignition coil establishes a magnetic field concentrated in the core laminations and surrounding the windings of wire. A cutaway view of a typical ignition coil is shown in Fig. 1-12. The cam is mechanically connected to rotate a specific amount in relation to the crankshaft. At the proper time, the cam will push the breaker points apart, opening the circuit and preventing current from flowing through the primary windings. The interruption stops the flow of current quickly which causes the magnetic field surrounding the primary windings to collapse. Stopping the magnetic field does not cause the field to fade away, but results in a very fast movement from around the coil windings and through the metal lamination, back to the center of the coil primary windings. As the magnetic field collapses, it quickly passes (cuts) through the primary and secondary windings creating an emf as high as 250 volts in the primary and up to 25,000 volts in the secondary windings. The condenser, which is wired parallel with the breaker points absorbs the self-induced current in the primary circuit, then discharges this current when the breaker points close.

Due to resistance of the primary winding, a certain period of time is required for maximum primary current flow after the breaker contact points are closed. At high engine speeds, the points remain closed for a smaller interval of time, hence the primary current does not build up to the maximum and secondary voltage is somewhat less than at low engine speed. However, coil design is such that the minimum voltage available at high engine speed exceeds the normal maximum voltage required for the ignition spark.

Notice that the ignition switch opens to stop current flow to the primary winding which also stops the high voltage necessary for ignition.

Other variations for this battery ignition are possible. Many use solid state electrical components to open and close the primary circuit in place of the mechanical breaker points.

MAGNETO IGNITION

Two of the principal reasons for utilizing a magneto ignition in place of a battery ignition are: Reduced weight and minimum dependence on other systems for ignition.

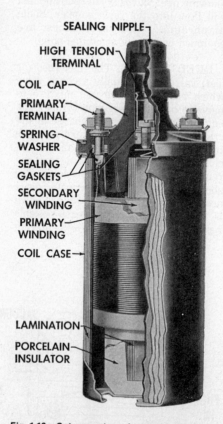

SEALING NIPPLE

HIGH TENSION TERMINAL

COIL CAP

PRIMARY TERMINAL

SPRING WASHER

SEALING GASKETS

SECONDARY WINDING

PRIMARY WINDING

COIL CASE

LAMINATION

PORCELAIN INSULATOR

Fig. 1-11—Diagram of a typical battery ignition system. Refer to text for principles of operation.

1. Battery
2. Ignition switch
3. Primary circuit
4. Ignition coil
5. Condenser
6. Contact points
7. Secondary circuit
8. Spark plug

G1 through G4. Ground connections

Fig. 1-12—Cut-away view of typical battery ignition system coil. Primary winding consists of approximately 200-250 turns (loops) of heavier wire; secondary winding consists of several thousand turns of fine wire. Laminations concentrate the magnetic lines of force and increase efficiency of the coil.

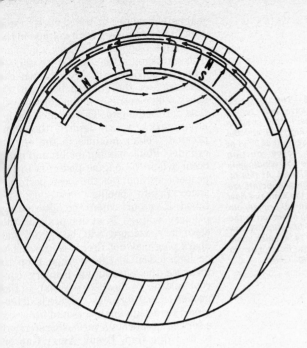

Fig. 1-13—Cut-away view of typical engine flywheel used with flywheel magneto type ignition system. The permanent magnets are usually cast into the flywheel. For flywheel type magnetos having the ignition coil and core mounted to outside of flywheel, magnets would be flush with outer diameter of flywheel.

coil windings and the breaker points which have now been closed by action of the cam.

At the instant the movement of the lines of force cutting through the coil winding sections is at the maximum rate, the maximum flow of current is obtained in the primary circuit. At this time, the cam opens the breaker points interrupting the primary circuit and, for an instant, the flow of current is absorbed by the condenser as illustrated in Fig. 1-16. An emf is also induced in the secondary coil windings, but the voltage is not sufficient to cause current to flow across the spark plug gap.

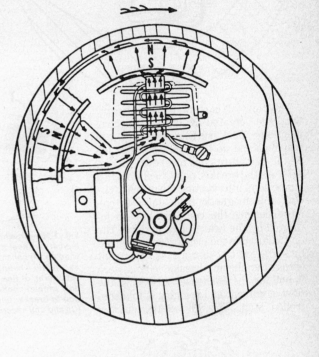

Fig. 1-14—View showing flywheel turned to a position so lines of force of the permanent magnets are concentrated in the left and center core legs and are interlocking the coil windings.

Flywheel Magneto With Breaker Points

Refer to Fig. 1-13 for a cut-away view of a typical flywheel. The arrows indicate lines of force (flux) of the permanent magnets which are carried by the flywheel. As indicated by the arrows, direction of force of the magnetic field is from the north pole (N) of the left magnet to the south pole (S) of the right magnet.

Figs. 1-14, 1-15, 1-16 and 1-17 illustrate the operational cycle of the flywheel type magneto. In Fig. 1-14 the flywheel magnets are located over the left and center legs of the armature (ignition coil) core. As the magnets moved into this position, their magnetic field was attracted by the armature core and a potential voltage (emf) was induced in the coil windings. However, this emf was not sufficient to cause current to flow across the spark plug electrode gap in the high tension circuit and the points were open in the primary circuit.

In Fig. 1-15, the flywheel magnets have moved to a new position to where there magnetic field is being attracted by the center and right legs of the armature core, and is being withdrawn from the left and center legs. As indicated by the heavy black arrows, the lines of force are cutting up through the section of coil windings between the left and center legs of the armature and are cutting down through the coil windings section between the center and right legs. If the left hand rule is applied to the lines of force cutting through the coil sections, it is seen that the resulting emf induced in the primary circuit will cause a current to flow through the primary

Fig. 1-15—View showing flywheel turned to a position so that lines of force of the permanent magnets are being withdrawn from the left and center core legs and are being attracted by the center and right core legs. While this event is happening, the lines of force are cutting up through the coil windings section between the left and center legs and are cutting down through the section between the right and center legs as indicated by the heavy black arrows. As the breaker points are now closed by the cam, a current is induced in the primary ignition circuit as the lines of force cut through the coil windings.

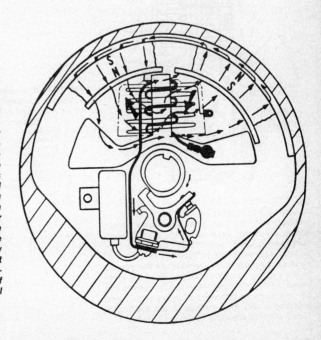

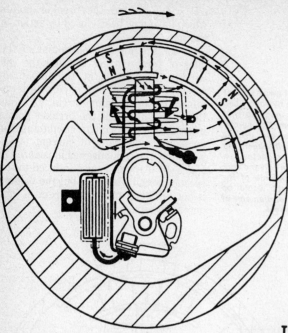

Refer now to Fig. 1-17.

Fig. 1-16—The flywheel magnets have now turned slightly past the position shown in Fig. 1-15 and the rate of movement of lines of magnetic force cutting through the coil windings is at the maximum. At this instant, the breaker points are opened by the cam and flow of current in the primary circuit is being absorbed by the condenser, bringing the flow of current to a quick, controlled stop. Refer now to Fig. 1-17.

The flow of current in the primary windings created a strong electromagnetic field surrounding the coil windings and up through the center leg of the armature core as shown in Fig. 1-17. As the breaker points were opened by the cam, interrupting the primary circuit, this magnetic field starts to collapse cutting the coil windings as indicated by the heavy black arrows. The emf induced in the primary circuit would be sufficient to cause a flow of current across the opening breaker points were it not for the condenser absorbing the flow of current and bringing it to a controlled stop. This allows the electro-

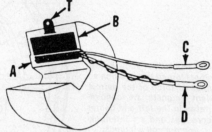

Fig. 1-18—Drawing showing construction of a typical flywheel magneto ignition coil. Primary winding (A) consists of about 200 turns of wire. Secondary winding (B) consists of several thousand turns of fine wire. Coil primary and secondary ground connection is (D); primary connection to breaker point and condenser terminal is (C); and coil secondary (high tension) terminal is (T).

magnetic field to collapse at such a rapid rate to induce a very high voltage in the coil high tension or secondary windings. This voltage, often 10,000 to 25,000 volts, is sufficient to break down the resistance of the air gap between the spark plug electrodes and a current will flow across the gap. This creates the ignition spark which ignites the compressed fuel-air mixture in the engine cylinder. Point opening (or timing) must occur when the engine piston is in the proper position for the best performance. Point opening must also be timed to occur when the alternating primary voltage is at its peak or the secondary voltage will be weak and spark plug may not fire. It is impossible or impractical in the average shop to measure the alternating primary current relative to flywheel position, so the proper timing for peak voltage is determined by design engineers and becomes a service specification variously referrmd to as **Edge Gap, Break Away Gap** or **Pole Shoe Break.**

Flywheel Magnetos Without Breaker Points

BREAKERLESS SYSTEM. The solid state (breakerless) magneto ignition system may operate on the same basic principles as the conventional type flywheel magneto previously described. The main difference is that the breaker contact points are replaced by a solid state electronic Gate Controlled Switch (GCS) which has no moving parts. Since, in a conventional system breaker points are closed for a longer period of crank-

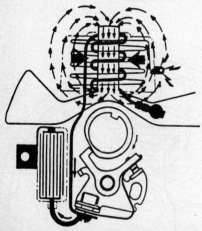

Fig. 1-17—View showing magneto ignition coil, condenser and breaker points at same instant as illustrated in Fig. 1-16, however, arrows shown above illustrate lines of force of the electromagnetic field established by current in primary coil windings rather than the lines of force of the permanent magnets. As the current in the primary circuit ceases to flow, the electromagnetic field collapses rapidly, cutting the coil windings as indicated by heavy arrows and inducing a very high voltage in the secondary coil winding resulting in the ignition spark.

Fig. 1-19—Exploded view of a typical flywheel magneto of the type used on outboard motors.

1. Condenser
2. Contact points
3. Magneto coil
4. Stator plate
5. Coil laminations
6. Washers
7. Mounting adapter
8. Friction washer
9. Throttle control cam
10. Spacer

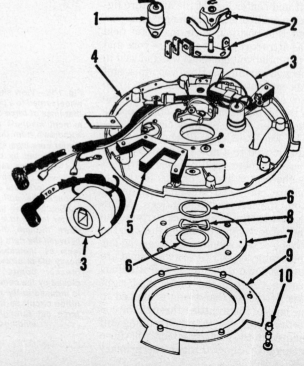

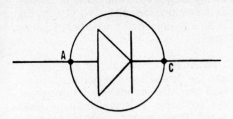

Fig. 1-20—In a diagram of an electrical circuit, the diode is represented by the symbol shown above. The diode will allow current to flow in one direction only, from cathode (C) to anode (A).

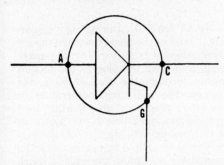

Fig. 1-21—The symbol used for a Gate controlled Switch (GCS) in an electrical diagram is shown above. The GCS will permit current to flow from cathode (C) to anode (A) when "turned on" by a positive electrical charge at gate (G) terminal.

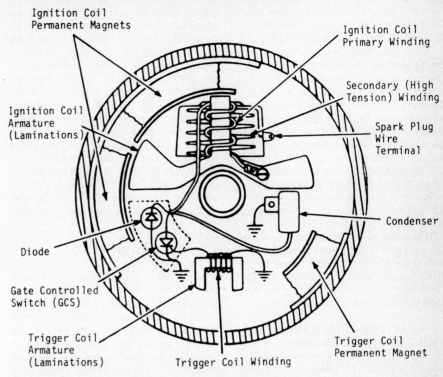

Fig. 1-22—Schematic diagram of typical breakerless magneto igniton system. Refer to Figs. 1-23, 1-24 and 1-25 for schemtic views of operating cycle.

shaft rotation than is the "GCS", a diode has been added to the circuit to provide the same characteristics as closed breaker points.

The same basic principles for electromagnetic induction of electricity and formation of magnetic fields by electrical current as outlined for the conventional flywheel type magneto also apply to the solid state magneto. Therefore the principles of the different components (diode and GCS) will complete the operating principles of the solid state magneto.

The diode is represented in wiring diagrams by the symbol shown in Fig. 1-20. The diode is an electronic device that will permit passage of electrical current (electrons) in one direction only. In electrical schematic diagrams, electron flow is sometimes opposite to direction arrow part of symbol is pointing.

The symbol shown in Fig. 1-21 is used to represent the gate controlled switch (GCS) in wiring diagrams. The GCS acts as a switch to permit passage of current from cathode (C) terminal to anode (A) terminal when in "ON" state and will not permit electric current to flow when in "OFF" state. The GCS can be turned "ON" by a positive surge of electricity at the gate (G) terminal and will remain "ON" as long as current remains positive at the gate terminal or as long as current is flowing through the GCS from cathode (C) terminal to anode (A) terminal.

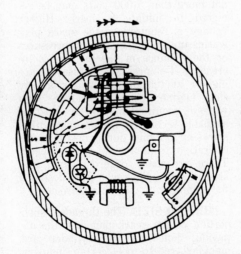

Fig. 1-23—View showing flywheel of breakerless magneto system at instant of rotation where lines of force of ignition coil magnets are being drawn into left and center legs of magneto armature. The diode (see Fig. 1-20) acts as a closed set of breaker points in completing the primary ignition circuit at this time.

The basic components and wiring diagram for the solid state breakerless magneto are shown schematically in Fig. 1-22. In Fig. 1-23, the magneto rotor (flywheel) is turning and the ignition coil magnets have just moved into position so that their lines of force are cutting the ignition coil windings and producing a negative surge of current in the primary windings. The diode allows current to flow and action is same as conventional magneto with breaker

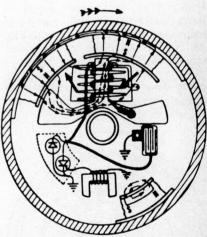

Fig. 1-24—Flywheel is turning to point where magnetic flux lines through armature center leg will reverse direction and current through primary coil circuit will reverse. As current reverses, diode which was previously conducting will shut off and there will be no current. When magnetic flux lines have reversed in armature center leg, voltage potential will again build up, but since GCS is in "OFF" state, no current will flow. To prevent excessive voltage build up, the condenser acts as a buffer.

points closed. As rotor (flywheel) continues to turn as shown in Fig. 1-24, direction of magnetic flux lines will reverse in the armature center leg. Direction of current will change in the primary coil circuit and the previously conducting diode will be shut off. At this point, neither diode is conducting. Voltage begins to build up as rotor continues to turn the condenser and acts as a buffer to prevent excessive voltage build up at the GCS before it is triggered.

When the rotor reaches the approximate position shown in Fig. 1-25, maximum flux density has been achieved in the center leg of the armature. At this time the GCS is triggered. Triggering is accomplished by the triggering coil armature moving into the field of a permanent magnet which induces a positive voltage on the gate of the GCS. Primary coil current flow results in the formation of an electro-magnetic field around the primary coil which inducts a voltage of sufficient potential in the secondary coil windings to "fire" the spark plug.

When the rotor (flywheel) has moved the magnets past the armature, the GCS will cease to conduct and revert to the "OFF" state until it is triggered. The condenser will discharge during the time that the GCS was conducting.

CAPACITOR DISCHARGE SYSTEM. The capacitor discharge (CD) ignition system may use a permanent magnet rotor (flywheel) to induce a current in a coil, but unlike the conventional flywheel magneto and solid state breakerless magneto described previously, the current is stored in a capacitor (condenser). Then the stored current is discharged through a transformer coil to create the ignition spark. Refer to Fig. 1-26 for a schematic of a typical capacitor discharge ignition system.

As the permanent flywheel magnets pass by the input generating coil (1), the current produced charges capacitor (6).

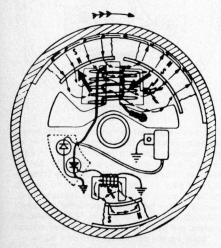

Fig. 1-25—With flywheel in the approximate position shown, maximum voltage potential is present in windings of primary coil. At this time the triggering coil armature has moved into the field of a permanent magnet and a positive voltage is induced on the gate of the GCS. The GCS is triggered and primary coil current flows resulting in the formation of an electromagnetic field around the primary coil which inducts a voltage of sufficient potential in the secondary windings to "fire" the spark plug.

Only half of the generated current passes through diode (3) to charge the capacitor. Reverse current is blocked by diode (3) but passes through Zener diode (2) to complete the reverse circuit. Zener diode (2) also limits maximum voltage of the forward current. As the flywheel continues to turn and magnets pass the trigger coil (4), a small amount of electrical current is generated. This current opens the gate controlled switch (5) allowing the capacitor to discharge through the pulse transformer (7). The rapid voltage rise in the transformer primary coil induces a high voltage secondary current which forms the ignition spark when it jumps the spark plug gap.

SPARK PLUG

In any spark ignition engine, the spark plug provides the means for igniting the compressed fuel-air mixture in the cylinder. Before an electric charge can move across an air gap, the intervening air must be charged with electricity, or ionized. The spark plug gap becomes more easily ionized if the spark plug ground (G4 – Fig. 1-11) is of negative polarity. If the spark plug is properly gapped and the system is not shorted, not more than 7,000 volts may be required to initiate a spark. Higher voltage is required as the spark plug warms up, or if compression pressures or the distance of the air gap is increased. Compression pressures are highest at full throttle and relatively slow engine speeds, therefore, high voltage requirements or a lack of available secondary voltage most often shows up as a miss during maximum acceleration from a slow engine speed. There are many different types and sizes of spark plugs which are designed for a number of specific requirements.

THREAD SIZE. The threaded, shell portion of the spark plug and the attaching holes in the cylinder are manufactured to meet certain industry established standards. The diameter is referred to as "Thread Size." Those com-

Fig. 1-26—Schematic diagram of a typical capacitor discharge ignition system.

1. Generating coil
2. Zener diode
3. Diode
4. Trigger coil
5. Gate controlled switch
6. Capacitor
7. Pulse transformer (coil)
8. Spark plug

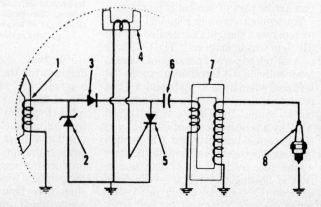

monly used are: 10 mm, 14 mm, 18 mm, 7/8 inch and 1/2 inch pipe. The 14 mm plug is almost universal for outboard motor use.

REACH. The length of the thread, and the thread depth in cylinder head or wall are also standardized throughout the industry. This dimension is measured from gasket seat of head to cylinder end of thread. Four different reach plugs commonly used are: 3/8 inch, 7/16 inch, 1/2 inch and 3/4 inch. The first two mentioned are the only ones commonly used in outboard motors.

HEAT RANGE. During engine operation, part of the heat generated during combustion is transferred to the spark plug, and from the plug to the coolant water through the shell threads and gasket. The operating temperature of the spark plug plays an important part in the engine operation. If too much heat is retained by the plug, the fuel-air mixture may be ignited by contact with the heated surface before the ignition spark occurs. If not enough heat is retained, partially burned combustion products (soot, carbon and oil) may build up on the plug tip resulting in "fouling" or shorting out of the plug. If this happens, the secondary current is dissipated uselessly as it is generated instead of bridging the plug gap as a useful spark, and the engine will misfire.

The operating temperature of the plug tip can be controlled, within limits, by altering the length of the path the heat must follow to reach the threads and gasket of the plug. Thus, a plug with a short, stubby insulator around the center electrode will run cooler than one with a long, slim insulator. Most plugs in the more popular sizes are available in a number of heat ranges which are interchangeable within the group. The proper heat range is determined by engine design and the type of service. Like most other elements of design, the plug type installed as original equipment is usually a compromise and is either the most suitable plug for average condi-

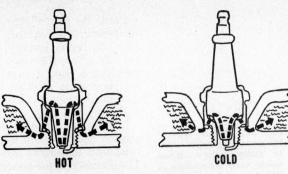

Fig. 1-27—Spark plug tip temperature is controlled by the length of the path heat must travel to reach the coolant medium.

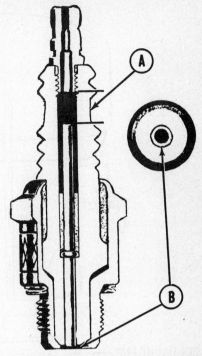

Fig. 1-29—A specially designed surface gap plug offers exceptional freedom from carbon fouling. Features include an air gap (A) in the center element and a circular gap (B) which burns clean. Special voltages are required, and the plug is not interchangeable with other types.

ions; or the best plug to meet the two xtremes of service expected. No one park plug, however, can be ideally uited for long periods of slow-speed peration such as trolling, and still be he best possible type for high-speed peration. Refer to SPARK PLUG ERVICING, in SERVICE FUNDA-MENTALS section, for additional information on spark plug selection.

SPECIAL TYPES. Sometimes, engine design features or operating conditions call for special plug types designed for a particular purpose. Special types include SHIELDED PLUGS which are extensively used for inboard marine applications and RESISTOR PLUGS, with built-in resitance. Of special interest when dealing with outboard motors is the two-stroke spark plug shown in the left hand view, Fig. 1-28. In the design of this plug, the ground electrode is shortened so its end aligns with center of insulated electrode rather than completely overlapping as with the conventional plug. This feature reduces the possibility of the gap bridging over by carbon formations. A second special type designed for outboard motor use is the SURFACE GAP plug shown in Fig. 1-29. This spark plug was engineered by Champion Spark Plug Company for use in high-output motors. This plug is capable of efficient operation over a wide range of conditions. It cannot however, be interchanged with a conventional spark plug.

COOLING SYSTEM

The cooling system on most motors consists of a water intake located on the lower motor leg, a coolant pump, and in many cases, a thermostat to control the coolant temperature. As with all internal combustion engines, the cooling system must be designed to maintain a satisfactory operating temperature, rather than the coolest possible temperature. This is made additionally

difficult in the case of the outboard motor because the coolant liquid is not contained in a separate reservoir where coolant temperature can be controlled. Because the temperature of the incoming liquid cannot be controlled, the only possible means of regulating the operating temperature is by the control of the amount of coolant flowing in the system.

On most outboard motors, the flow is held at a relatively constant level regardless of engine speed, by the design of the coolant pump. Refer to Fig. 1-30. At slow engine speeds the rubber impeller blades follow the contour of the offset housing as shown by the solid line. The pump functions as a positive displacement pump, drawing water in (IN) as area between impeller blades increases. Water is forced into outlet passage (OUT) and up into power head as area decreases. As engine speed increases, pump rotative speed and water pressure forces impeller blade away from outside of housing as shown by the

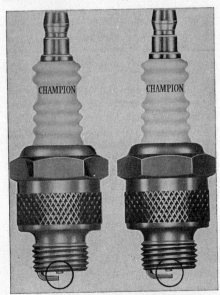

Fig. 1-28—The two stroke plug shown at left, is one of the more important special types in the outboard motor industry.

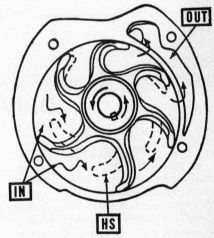

Fig. 1-30—Schematic view of the rubber impeller type water pump which maintains an approximately equal volume of coolant flow at most operating speeds. Water is drawn into pump (IN) as area between vanes increases and is forced into power head (OUT) as area decreases. At high speeds (HS) the blades remain curved and pump operates mostly by centrifugal action.

broken lines (HS). At full speed, the pump operates almost entirely as a centrifugal pump.

Later production motors often use a thermostat to assist in maintaining an efficient operating temperature. The thermostat may recirculate the coolant

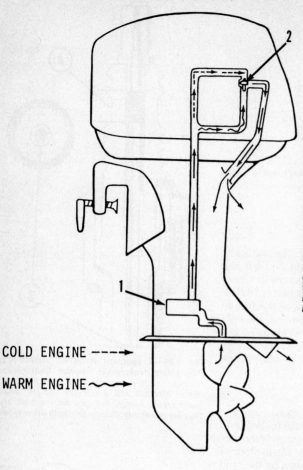

Fig. 1-31—Bypass type of thermostat operation used in some motors. When power head temperature is below normal the thermostat (2) closes coolant outlet through power head and opens the bypass outlet. Coolant flow then follows course shown by broken arrows. As operating temperature is reached, thermostat opens coolant passages through power head and closes bypass. The coolant then flows through power head as shown by wavy arrow. The coolant pump is in lower unit as shown by (1).

COLD ENGINE ---→

WARM ENGINE ～～→

water in the power head until operatin: temperature is reached, then open t allow the heated liquid to be exhauste or, may bypass the power head with th circulated liquid until operatin temperature is reached, then circulat coolant through block. Refer to Fig 1-31.

In almost all liquid-cooled motors, th coolant liquid passes from the powe head into the engine exhaust system The entrance of the water cools the ex haust stream and the exhaust housing which is usually part of the lower moto leg.

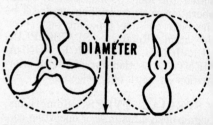

DIAMETER

Fig. 1-32—The proper method of measuring the diameter of a two-blade and three-blade propeller is as shown.

DRIVE UNIT FUNDAMENTALS

PROPELLER

An outboard motor propeller moves a boat through the water in somewhat the same manner that a wood screw passes through a piece of wood. Propellers are rated by diameter, pitch and the number of blades; diameter being the distance across a circle described by blade tips as shown in Fig. 1-32, and pitch the forward thrust imparted in one revolution of the propeller as shown by Fig. 1-33. The correct propeller diameter is determined by motor design, especially the items of horsepower and propeller shaft gear ratio, and should usually not be changed from that recommended by the manufacturer. Propeller pitch is more nearly comparable to the transmission gear ratio of an automobile and should be individually selected to suit the conditions of boat design and usage.

Efficiency is greatest when the propeller operates with only moderate slippage, the actual amount depending to a

certain degree upon the application. Normal slippage on a racing hull may be as low as 10 percent, while a slow speed hull may normally be allowed 50-60 percent.

NOTE: Slippage is the difference between the distance a boat actually moves forward with each turn of the propeller, and the theoretical distance indicated by the pitch. For example, a boat equipped with a 12-inch (30.5 cm) pitch propeller which moves forward 9 inches (22.9 cm) with each revolution of the propeller shaft has 25 percent slippage.

The potential speed of a boat depends as much on the design of the boat as upon the power of the motor. Although there are many individual types, most boats will fall into one of two broad categories: (A) the displacement hull; and (B) the planing hull. Refer to Fig. 1-34. When not moving, any boat will displace its own weight in water. A displacement

hull will run at nearly the standing depth when under way. A planing hull will ride up on the water as shown at (2) as it approaches cruising speed, offering much less resistance to the forward movement.

A displacement hull is the only logical design for slow moving boats which cannot attain planing speed. They are also more stable in rough water and ride somewhat easier than a planing hull. A displacement hull requires a minimum pitch propeller as shown at (A – Fig. 1-33). A three-blade propeller offering maximum thrust area is usually used.

Speed is as important as power in the efficient operation of a planing hull. Maximum resistance is encountered as the boat moves into planing position, and peak slippage occurs at that time. Once planing position has been attained, forward speed will increase to the limits imposed by propeller speed and pitch. A two-blade propeller is capable of attaining a somewhat faster forward speed

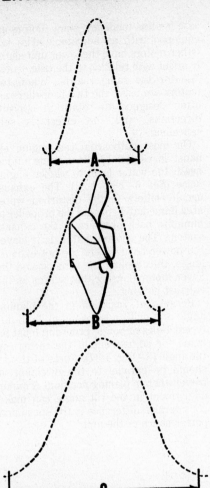

Fig. 1-33—Propeller pitch indicates the theoretical forward movement in one revolution of propeller if there were no slippage. Flat pitch propellers (A) can be likened to low gear in an automobile; while extreme pitch (C) is similar to high gear or overdrive.

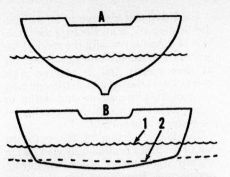

Fig. 1-34—Outboard hulls fall into two general classes; the displacement hull shown at (A) and the planing hull shown at (B). In the displacement hull, the waterline is about the same height on hull when boat is at anchor or under way. The planing hull (B) rises in the water as speed increases, and in extreme conditions barely touches the water surface.

A. Displacement hull
B. Planing hull
1. Standing waterline
2. Planing waterline

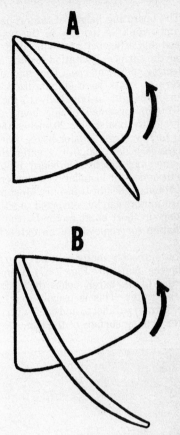

Fig. 1-35—The propeller pitch may be at a constant angle as shown at (A); or of a varying angle (cupped) as shown at (B).

than a three-blade propeller of the same pitch. Planing hulls require a longer pitch propeller, falling somewhere between that shown at (B) and (C), Fig. 1-33.

A propeller is not ideally suited to the same boat and motor under all operating conditions. If a light runabout with a small motor is used to pull a water skier, a lower pitch propeller may be required. The same holds true of a moderate horsepower motor when pulling two or more skiers. A three-blade propeller is usually preferable for water skiing. Top speed may be somewhat reduced over that of a comparable two-blade unit, but performance will usually be improved.

There is no set rule for matching a propeller, boat and motor. The general practice is to select a propeller which will allow the properly tuned and adjusted motor to run in the recommended operating speed range at wide-open throttle. Too little propeller pitch will

cause motor to over-speed, while too much pitch will not allow the motor to reach the proper speed.

Outboard motor propellers are usually made of aluminum or bronze, although some plastic propellers have been made. Stainless steel is sometimes used for racing propellers.

Propellers may be designed with a constant, flat pitch throughout the entire length of the blade as shown at "A"–Fig. 1-35, or with a cupped blade which increases in pitch toward the trailing edge as shown at "B". The flat blade propellers operate efficiently only at relatively slow rotative speeds. Above a certain critical speed, water is moved from the blade area faster than additional water can flow into the area behind the blades, causing "cavitation" and erratic behavior. The extreme turbulence and shock waves caused by cavitation rapidly reduces operating efficiency. The critical speed varies with propeller diameter, the traveling speed of the blade tips being the determining factor. Propeller shape also affects the critical speed, as does any obstruction ahead of the propeller which diverts the water flow. A propeller with curved blades is usually designed for higher speed operation than one with flat blades.

GEARCASE AND LOWER HOUSING

The power head delivers power to a drive shaft which is geared to turn a propeller shaft, thus delivering thrust to propel the boat. The gears, shafts and supporting bearings are contained in a lightweight housing or gearcase. In early motors and in some of today's trolling motors, the power transmitted was small. In today's larger motors, how-

ever, speed and pressure is considerable, requiring precision construction and close attention to bearing and gear clearances.

In spite of the necessity for strength and rigidity, the gearcase must interfere as little as possible with the smooth flow of water to the propeller. This is especially important at the higher speeds where propeller cavitation is a problem. To perform efficiently, the gearcase must be kept as small as possible and well streamlined, as shown in Fig. 1-36 and Fig. 1-37.

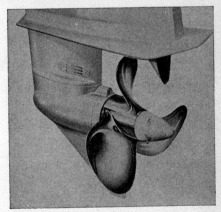

Fig. 1-36—High power, high performance lower unit showing streamlined configuration to eliminate drag and improve the performance.

The operating height of the propeller is important. If too low in the water, speed and efficiency are reduced; if too near the surface, cavitation results, also affecting performance. The manufacturers of boats have standardized the transom height to nominally 15 inches (38.1 cm) for small fishing boats and light utility boats; and 20 inches (50.8 cm) for the larger, faster boats. Actual height is usually slightly greater than the nominal height. Outboard motors are designed for installation on either of the standard height transoms. Most outboard motors can be converted to either a long or short shaft motor by the installation (or removal) of an extension kit.

An outboard motor should operate with the plate (5 – Fig. 1-37) running parallel to and barely below the surface of the water. This is usually (but not necessarily) parallel to and even with the lower planing surface of the hull.

The lower unit also serves as the rudder to steer the boat. Because the direction of thrust turns with the rudder, the system is unusually efficient, especially at slow speeds and in reverse. This makes the outboard unit extremely easy to maneuver in and around docks or other places where maneuverablity at slow speed is important.

The lower portion of the outboard motor propeller continuously operates in slightly less disturbed water than the upper portion. Because of this, the lower portion of the propeller has a tendency to walk the stern of the boat in a direction opposite to its movement. Thus, if a motor is equipped with a propeller which rotates counterclockwise (A – Fig. 1-38), the stern of the boat will move to port as shown by arrow "C"; and boat will pull to starboard when set on a dead ahead course. The opposite will occur if motor is equipped with a propeller rotating clockwise as shown at (B). To compen-

sate for this tendency, some motors are equipped with an adjustable trim tab. Other motors have the lower unit slightly offset with relation to the true centerline for the same reason. When two motors are used, the two propellers are often designed to rotate in opposite directions, and the effect is self-cancelling.

On most outboards, the engine exhaust is vented to the outside underneath the water level to silence engine noise (See 6 – Fig. 1-27). The exhaust usually enters in the disturbed water area immediately behind the propeller to minimize back pressure in the exhaust system. The coolant water as it leaves the power head enters the hot exhaust gases, thus cooling the exhaust and the lower motor housing that serves as the exhaust housing.

Because of variation in the planing angle and built-in transom angle in different types of boats, provision must be made for adjustment of the thrust, or tilt angle (3 – Fig. 1-37). Force of thrust should be parallel to the direction of travel when in planing position. A minor adjustment in the tilt angle can make considerable difference in the speed and performance of the unit.

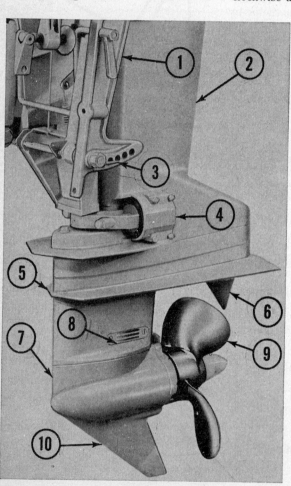

Fig. 1-37—Lower unit, attaching brackets and associated parts showing nomenclature.
1. Stern brackets
2. Lower motor leg
3. Tilt pin
4. Shock mount
5. Antiventilation plate
6. Exhaust outlet
7. Gearcase
8. Water inlet
9. Propeller
10. Skeg

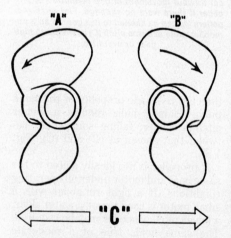

Fig. 1-38—Propellers may be of counterclockwise rotation as shown at "A" or clockwise rotation as shown at "B". The rotation of the propeller has a tendency to pull the stern of the boat off-course in the direction shown by arrow "C".

SERVICE FUNDAMENTALS
PERIODIC SERVICING

Many of the troubles related to outboard motors will be much easier to repair if noticed before they result in extensive damage and sometimes the lack of proper servicing is the primary cause of failure. The following service and inspection schedule can be used as a guide. If the motor is operated under severe conditions, the intervals should be shortened.

NOTE: This schedule of mid-season service, off-season storage and pre-season preparations is taken from the Marine Service Manual of Recommended Practices which is copyrighted by the Boating Industry Association.

MID-SEASON (OR EVERY 50 HOURS)

1. Drain and flush gearcase. Refill to correct level using manufacturer's recommended lubricant.
2. Remove and clean fuel filter bowl. Replace fuel bowl element. Always use new filter bowl gasket.
3. Clean and regap spark plugs to recommended gap. Replace worn or burnt spark plugs. (Use new gaskets and torque plugs to manufacturer's recommendations).
4. Check propeller for correct pitch. Replace if propeller is worn, chipped or badly bent.
5. Lubricate all grease fittings, using manufacturer's recommended lubricant.
6. Check remote control box, cables and wiring harness.
7. Check steering controls; lubricate mechanical steering.
8. Lubricate all carburetor and magneto linkages with manufacturer's recommended lubricant.
9. Adjust tension on magneto and/or generator drive belts.
10. Clean and coat battery terminals with grease.
11. Check water pump and thermostat operation.
12. Check breaker points' condition and timing.
13. Check carburetor and ignition synchronization.
14. Check carburetor adjustment.

OFF-SEASON STORAGE

Operate motor in test tank, or on boat, at part throttle with shift lever in neutral. Rapidly inject rust preventative oil (with pump type oil can) into carburetor air intake, or intakes, until motor is smoking profusely. Stop motor immediately to prevent burning oil out of cylinders. This will lubricate and protect internal parts of powerhead while motor is in storage. If motor was last operated in salt water, run it in fresh water before preparing it for storage.

1. Place motor on a stand in normal upright position. Remove motor cover.
2. Retard throttle all the way and disconnect spark plug leads. Manually rotate motor flywheel several times to draing the water from water pump.
3. Drain carburetor float chamber. Remove fuel filter bowl – drain, clean and replace filter element and gasket.
4. Clean and lubricate electric starter drive mechanism.
5. Completely drain and clean fuel tank.
6. Remove propeller and check for condition and pitch. Clean and liberally lubricate propeller shaft. Replace propeller drive pin if bent or worn. Replace propeller using new cotter pin or tab lockwasher.
7. Drain and refill gearcase, using the manufacturers recommended lubricant.

8. Wipe over entire external motor surface with a clean cloth soaked in light oil.
9. Store in an upright position in a dry, well-ventilated room. To prevent accidental starting, leave spark plug leads disconnected.
10. Remove battery from boat and keep it charged while in storage.

PRE-SEASON PREPARATION

1. Remove, clean, inspect and properly gap spark plugs. Replace defective plugs. (Use new gaskets and torque plugs to manufacturer's recommendations.)
2. Remove oil level plug from gearcase and check for proper oil level.
3. Thoroughly clean and refinish surfaces as required.
4. Check battery for full charge and clean terminals. Clean and inspect battery cable connections. Check polarity before installing battery cables. Cover cable connections with grease to prevent corrosion.
5. If possible, run motor in test tank prior to installing on boat. Check water pump and thermostat operation.

Proper maintenance is important.

SALT WATER CARE

Motors that are operated in salt water require some special care to combat the possibility of corrosion resulting from such use. If possible, tilt motor out of water and flush cooling system and outside of lower unit with fresh water immediately after each use.

Special care is needed if motor is used in salt water.

The aluminum-silicon alloys used for outboard motor castings are relatively resistant to corrosion from oxidation but are very susceptible to galvanic action and the resultant corrosion if unprotected.

Oxidation is the destruction of a useful form of metal resulting from a chemical combination of the element with oxygen. Although oxidation can occur under water, the most favorable environment is the atmosphere under extreme conditions of warmth and humidity. Rust is an iron oxide and the best known example of oxidation. The oxidation of aluminum leaves a white, powdery coating on the surface of the metal which protects it from further oxidation, and aluminum can withstand years of exposure to the atmosphere without harmful effect.

Briefly described, galvanic action is an electrical process where atoms of one metal are carried in a solution and deposited on the surface of a dissimilar metal. Chrome or nickel plating are controlled forms of galvanic action. Each metallic element has a particular degree of susceptibility to galvanic corrosion, and pure aluminum is second only to magnesium in this scale. The aluminum alloys are somewhat less susceptible than pure metal, and galvanic action can be effectively stopped by painting or other surface protection. Aluminum parts are protected by a process known as anodizing, which deposits a hard, protective coating of aluminum oxide over the surface. The anodized surface is impervious to corrosion from any source, but is only effective if unbroken. Scratches or abrasion can expose the unprotected metal.

Galvanic action is more prevalent in salt water because of the presence of minerals in the water which makes it more effective as a conductor. The action can be hastened by the presence of stray electric currents, and batteries or other sources of electricity should be disconnected when not in use. Some protection is offered by attaching a small block of more susceptible metal in the water near the part to be protected. This small block then becomes the target of galvanic action and is consumed, but the valuable part is spared.

All motors, but especially those use in salt water, should have an adequat coverage of approved paint. Paint bond well to an anodized aluminum surface but is difficult to apply to uncoate aluminum. Use only an approved pain applied according to instructions.

WARNING: Most manufacturers do no recommend the use of antifouling pain on any part of the motor. Antifouling paints contain mercury or copper which can cause galvanic corrosion in the presence of aluminum.

TROUBLE-SHOOTING

Intelligent service is normally divided into two basic functions; that of determining the cause of trouble, and correcting the trouble after cause has been determined. The cause may be obvious in many cases, where broken, worn or damaged parts are apparent. Repair in these cases becomes merely a matter of renewal and adjustment. Many of the performance problems, however, are not so apparent and the first task of the experienced service technician is that of determining the cause.

The experienced serviceman generally develops and follows a logical sequence in trouble-shooting which will most likely lead him quickly to the source of trouble. Some of the points to check may not be applicable to certain outboard motors.

NOTE: This sequence (items 1 through 27) is taken from the Marine Service Manual or Recommended Practices which is copyrighted by the Boating Industry Association.

1. Manual starter rope pulls out, but pawls do not engage.
   A. Friction spring bent or burred.
   B. Excess grease on pawls or spring.
   C. Pawls bent or burred.

Develop an orderly procedure when trouble-shooting.

2. Starter rope does not return.
   A. Recoil spring broken or binding.
   B. Starter housing bent.
   C. Loose or missing parts.

3. Clattering manual starter.
   A. Friction spring bent or burred.
   B. Starter housing bent.
   C. Excess grease on pawls or spring.
   D. Dry starter spindle.

4. Electric starter inoperative.
   A. Loose or corroded connections or ground.
   B. Starting circuit safety switch open, or out of adjustment.
   C. Under capacity or weak battery or corroded battery terminals.
   D. Faulty starter solenoid.
   E. Moisture in electric starter motor.
   F. Broken or worn brushes in starter motor.
   G. Faulty fields.
   H. Faulty armature.
   I. Broken wire in harness or connector.
   J. Faulty starter key or push button switch.
   K. Worn or frayed insulation.

5. Electric starter does not engage but solenoid clicks.
   A. Loose or corroded connections or ground.
   B. Weak battery.
   C. Faulty starter solenoid.
   D. Broken wire in electric harness.
   E. Loose or stripped post on starter motor.
   F. See steps in number 4.

6. Hard to start or won't start.
   A. Empty gas tank.
   B. Gas tank air vent not open.
   C. Fuel lines kinked or severely pinched.
   D. Water or dirt in fuel system.
   E. Clogged fuel filter or screens.
   F. Motor not being choked to start.
   G. Engine not primed – pump primer system.
   H. Carburetor adjustments too lean (not allowing enough fuel to start engine).
   I. Timing and sychronizing out of adjustment.
   J. Manual choke linkage bent – auto choke out of adjustment.
   K. Spark plugs improperly gapped, dirty or broken.
   L. Fuel tank primer inoperative (pressurized system).
   M. Ignition points improperly gapped, burned or dirty.

N. Loose, broken wire or frayed insulation in electrical system.
O. Reed valves not seating or stuck shut.
P. Weak coil or condenser.
Q. Faulty gaskets.
R. Cracked distributor cap or rotor.
S. Loose fuel connector.
T. Electronic ignition component malfunction.

7. Low speed miss or motor won't idle smoothly and slowly enough.
   A. Too much oil – too little oil.
   B. Timing and sychronizing out of adjustment.
   C. Carburetor idle adjustment (mixture lean or rich).
   D. Ignition points improper (gap, worn or fouled).
   E. Weak coil or condenser.
   F. Loose or broken ignition wires.
   G. Loose or worn magneto plate.
   H. Spark plugs (improper gap or dirty).
   I. Head gasket, reed plate gasket (blown or leaking).
   J. Reed valve standing open or stuck shut.
   K. Plugged crankcase bleeder, check valves, or lines.
   L. Leaking crankcase halves.
   M. Leaking crankcase seals (top or bottom.)
   N. Exhaust gases returning through intake manifold.
   O. Electronic ignition component malfunction.

8. High speed miss or intermittent spark.
   A. Spark plugs improperly gapped or dirty.
   B. Loose, leaking or broken ignition wires.
   C. Breaker points (improper gap or dirty; worn cam or cam follower).
   D. Weak coil or condenser.
   E. Water in fuel.
   F. Leaking head gasket or exhaust cover gasket.
   G. Spark plug heat range incorrect.
   H. Engine improperly timed.
   I. Carbon or fouled combustion chambers.
   J. Magneto or distributor poorly grounded.
   K. Distributor oiler wick bad.
   L. Electronic ignition component malfunction.

9. Coughs, spits, slows.
   A. Idle or high speed needles set too lean.
   B. Carburetor not synchronized.

C. Leaking gaskets in induction system.
D. Obstructed fuel passages.
E. Float level set too low.
F. Improperly seated or broken reeds.
G. Fuel pump pressure line ruptured.
H. Fuel pump (punctured diaphragm), check valves stuck open or closed, fuel lines leak.
I. Poor fuel tank pressure (pressurized system).
J. Worn or leaking fuel connector.

10. Vibrates excessively or runs rough and smokes.
    A. Idle or high speed needles set too rich.
    B. Too much oil mixed with gas.
    C. Carburetor not synchronized with ignition properly.
    D. Choke not opening properly.
    E. Float level too high.
    F. Air passage to carburetor obstructed.
    G. Bleeder valves or passages plugged.
    H. Transom bracket clamps loose on transom.
    I. Prop out of balance.
    J. Broken motor mount.
    K. Exhaust gases getting inside motor cover.
    L. Poor ignition – see number 8.

11. Runs well, idles well for a short period, then slows down and stops.
    A. Weeds or other debris on lower unit or propeller.
    B. Insufficient cooling water.
    C. Carburetor, fuel pump, filter or screens dirty.
    D. Bleeder valves or passages plugged.
    E. Lower unit bind (lack of lubrication or bent.)
    F. Gas tank air vent not open.
    G. Not enough oil in gas.
    H. Combustion chambers and spark plugs fouled, causing preignition.
    I. Spark plug heat range too high or too low.
    J. Wrong propeller (preignition).
    K. Slow speed adjustment too rich or too lean.

12. Won't start, kicks back, backfires into lower unit.
    A. Spark plug wires reversed.
    B. Flywheel key sheared.
    C. Distributor belt timing off (magneto or battery ignition.)
    D. Timing and synchronizing out of adjustment.
    E. Reed valves not seating or broken.

13. No acceleration, low top Rpm.
    A. Improper carburetor adjustments.
    B. Improper timing and synchronization.
    C. Spark plugs (improper gap or dirty).
    D. Ignition system malfunction.
    E. Faulty coil or condenser.
    F. Loose, leaking or broken ignition wires.
    G. Reed valves not properly seated or broken.
    H. Blown head or exhaust cover gasket.
    I. Weeds on lower unit or propeller.
    J. Incorrect propeller.
    K. Insufficient oil in gas.
    L. Insufficient oil in lower unit.
    M. Fuel restrictions.
    N. Scored cylinder – stuck rings.
    O. Marine growth, hooks, rockers or change in load of boat.
    P. Sticky magneto plate.
    Q. Carbon build-up on piston head at deflector.

14. No acceleration, idles well but when put to full power dies down.
    A. High or low speed needle set too lean.
    B. Dirt or packing behind needles and seats.
    C. High speed nozzle obstructed.
    D. Float level too low.
    E. Choke partly closed.
    F. Improper timing and synchronization.
    G. Fuel lines or passages obstructed.
    H. Fuel filter obstructed. Fuel pump not supplying enough fuel.
    I. Not enough oil in gas.
    J. Breaker points improperly gapped or dirty.
    K. Bent gearcase or exhaust tube.

15. Engine runs at high speed only by using hand primer.
    A. Carburetor adjustments.
    B. Dirt or packing behind needles and seat.
    C. Fuel lines or passages obstructed.
    D. Fuel line leaks.
    E. Fuel pump not supplying enough fuel.
    F. Float level too low.
    G. Fuel filter obstructed.
    H. Fuel tank or connector at fault.

16. No power under heavy load.
    A. Wrong propeller.
    B. Weeds or other debris on lower unit or propeller.
    C. Breaker points improperly gapped or dirty.
    D. Stator plate loose.

    E. Ignition timing over advanced or late.
    F. Faulty carburetion and/or faulty ignition.
    G. Prop hub slips.
    H. Scored cylinders or rings stuck.
    I. Carbon build up on piston head at deflector.

17. Cranks over extremely easy on one or more cylinders.
    A. Low compression.
       1. Worn or broken rings.
       2. Scored cylinder or pistons.
       3. Blown head gasket.
       4. Loose spark plugs.
       5. Loose head bolts.
       6. Crankcase halves improperly sealed.
       7. Burned piston.

18. Engine won't crank over.
    A. Manual start lock improperly adjusted.
    B. Pistons rusted to cylinder wall.
    C. Lower unit gears, prop shaft rusted or broken.
    D. Broken connecting rod, crankshaft or driveshaft.
    E. Coil heels binding on flywheel.
    F. Engine improperly assembled.

19. Motor overheats.
    A. Motor not deep enough in water.
    B. Not enough oil in gas or improperly mixed.
    C. Bad thermostat.
    D. Seals or gaskets (burned, cracked or broken).
    E. Impeller key not in place or broken.
    F. Plugged water inlet, outlet or cavity.
    G. Obstruction in water passages.
    H. Broken, pinched or leaking water lines.
    I. Improper ignition timing.
    J. Motor not assembled properly.
    K. Shorted heat light wiring.
    L. Bad water pump impeller, plate, housing or seal.

20. Motor stops suddenly, freezes up.
    A. No oil in gas, or no gas.
    B. Insufficient cooling water.
    C. No lubricant in gearcase.
    D. Rusted cylinder or crankshaft.
    E. Bent or broken rod, crankshaft, drive shaft, prop shaft, stuck piston.
    F. Bad water pump or plugged water passages.

21. Motor knocks excessively.
    A. Too much or not enough oil in gas.
    B. Worn or loose bearings, pistons, rods or wrists pins.
    C. Over advanced ignition timing.
    D. Carbon in combustion chambers and exhaust ports.

    E. Manual starter not centered.
    F. Flywheel nut loose.
    G. Flywheel hitting coil heels.
    H. Bent shift rod (vibrating against exhaust tube).
    I. Loose assemblies, bolts or screws.

22. Generator will not charge.
    A. Battery condition.
    B. Connections loose or dirty.
    C. Drive belt loose or broken.
    D. Faulty regulator or cutout relay.
    E. Field fuse or fusible wire in regulator blown.
    F. Generator not polarized (dc generators).
    G. Open generator windings.
    H. Worn or sticking brushes and/or slip rings.
    I. Faulty rectifier diodes (ac generators).
    J. Faulty ammeter.

23. Low generator output and a low battery.
    A. High resistance at battery terminals.
    B. High resistance in charging circuit.
    C. Faulty ammeter.
    D. Low regulator setting.
    E. Faulty rectifier diodes (ac generators).
    F. Faulty generator.

24. Excessive battery charging.
    A. Regulator set too high.
    B. Regulator contacts stuck.
    C. Regulator voltage winding open.
    D. Regulator improperly grounded.
    E. High resistance in field coil.
    F. Regulator improperly mounted.

25. Excessive fuel consumption.
    A. Hole in fuel pump diaphragm.
    B. Deteriorated carburetor gaskets.
    C. Altered or wrong fixed jets.
    D. Jets improperly adjusted.
    E. Carburetor casting porous.
    F. Float level too high.
    G. Loose distributor pulley.

26. Shifter dog jumps.
    A. Worn shifter dog or worn gear dogs.
    B. Worn linkage.
    C. Remote control adjustment.
    D. Gearcase loose or sprung.
    E. Exhaust housing bent.
    F. Linkage out of adjustment.

27. Electric shift inoperative or slips.
    A. Improper remote control installation.
    B. Faulty coils.
    C. Faulty springs.
    D. Faulty clutch and gear.
    E. Faulty bearings.
    F. Wrong lubricant.
    G. Loose or sprung gearcase.
    H. Shorted wiring.

SPECIAL NOTES ON TROUBLE-SHOOTING

AIR-COOLED MOTORS. Overheating, low power and several other problems on air-cooled motors can sometimes be traced to improper cooling. Make certain that all shrouds are in place before starting motor. Check for dirt or debris accumulated on or between cooling fins. Broken cooling fins can sometimes cause a localized "hot spot."

SPARK PLUG APPEARANCE DIAGNOSIS. The appearance of a spark plug will be altered by use, and an examination of the plug tip can contribute useful information which may assist in obtaining better spark plug life. It must be remembered that the contributing factors differ in two-stroke and four-stroke engine operation and, although the appearance of two spark plugs may be similar, the corrective measures may depend on whether the engine is of two-stroke or four-stroke design. Fig. 2-1 through Fig. 2-6 are provided by Champion Spark Plug Company to illustrate typical observed conditions in two-stroke engines. Listed also are the probable causes and suggested corrective measures.

GENERAL MAINTENANCE

LUBRICATION

Refer to each motor's individual section for recommended type and amount of lubricant used for power head (engine) and gearcase.

FUEL: OIL RATIO. Most two-stroke cycle engines are lubricated by oil that is mixed with the fuel. It is important that the manufacturer's recommended type of oil and fuel:oil ratio be closely followed. Excessive oil or improper fuel type oil will cause low power, plug fouling and excessive carbon build-up. Insufficient amount of oil will result in inadequate lubrication and rapid internal damage. The recommended ratios and type of oil are listed in LUBRICATION paragraph for each motor. Oil should be mixed with gasoline in a separate container before it is poured into the fuel tank. Unleaded gasoline such as marine white should be used when possible. The following table may be useful in mixing the correct ratio.

RATIO	Gasoline	Oil
10:1	.63 Gallon	½ Pint
14:1	.88 Gallon	½ Pint
15:1	.94 Gallon	½ Pint
16:1	1.00 Gallon	½ Pint
20:1	1.25 Gallons	½ Pint
22:1	1.38 Gallons	½ Pint
24:1	1.50 Gallons	½ Pint
25:1	1.56 Gallons	½ Pint
50:1	3.13 Gallons	½ Pint
100:1	6.25 Gallons	½ Pint
10:1	5 U.S. Gallons	4 Pints 64 Fl. Oz.
14:1	5 U.S. Gallons	3 Pints 45¾ Fl. Oz.
15:1	5 U.S. Gallons	2¾ Pints 42½ Fl. Oz.
16:1	5 U.S. Gallons	2½ Pints 40 Fl. Oz.
20:1	5 U.S. Gallons	2 Pints 32 Fl. Oz.
22:1	5 U.S. Gallons	1¾ Pints 29 Fl. Oz.
24:1	3 U.S. Gallons	1 Pint 16 Fl. Oz.
25:1	4 U.S. Gallons	1¼ Pints 20½ Fl. Oz.
50:1	3 U.S. Gallons	½ Pint 7¾ Fl. Oz.
100:1	3 U.S. Gallons	¼ Pint 4 Fl. Oz.

SPARK PLUGS

The recommended type of spark plug, heat range and electrode gap is listed in the CONDENSER SERVICE DATA table for the individual motor. Under light loads or low speed (trolling), a spark plug of the same size with a higher (hotter) heat range may be installed. If subjected to heavy loads or high speed, a colder plug may be necessary.

The spark plug electrode gap should be adjusted on most plugs by bending the ground electrode. Refer to Fig. 2-7. Some spark plugs have an electrode gap which is not adjustable.

Before a plug is cleaned with abrasive, it should be thoroughly degreased with a nonoily solvent and air-dried to prevent a build up of abrasive in recess of plug.

After plug is cleaned by abrasive, and before gap is set, the electrode surfaces between the grounded and insulated electrodes should be cleaned and returned as nearly as possible to original shape by filing with a point file. Failure to properly dress the points can result in high secondary voltage requirements, and misfire of the plugs.

Spark plugs are usually cleaned by abrasive action commonly referred to as "sand blasting." Actually, ordinary sand is not used, but a special abrasive which is nonconductive to electricity even when melted, thus the abrasive cannot short out the plug current. Extreme care should be used in cleaning the plugs after sand blasting, because any particles of abrasive left on the plug may cause damage to piston rings, piston or cylinder walls.

Fig. 2-1—Two-stroke cycle engine plug of correct heat range. Insulators light tan to gray with few deposits. Electrodes not burned.

Fig. 2-2—Damp or wet black carbon coating over entire firing end of plug. Could be caused by prolonged trolling, rich carburetor mixture, too much oil in fuel, crankcase bleed passage plugged, or low ignition voltage. Could also be caused by incorrect heat range (too cold) for operating conditions. Correct the defects or install a hotter plug.

Fig. 2-3—Electrodes badly eroded, deposits white or light gray and gritty, insulator has "blistered" appearance. Could be caused by lean carburetor mixture, fast timing, overloading, or improperly operating cooling system. Could also be caused by incorrect heat range (too hot) for operating conditions. Check timing, carburetor adjustment and cooling system. If recommended operating speed cannot be obtained after tune-up, install flatter pitch propeller. If timing, carburetor adjustment, cooling system and engine speed are correct, install a colder plug.

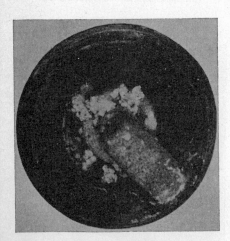

Fig. 2-4—Gray, metallic aluminum deposits on plug. This condition is caused by internal engine damage. Engine should be overhauled and cause of damage corrected.

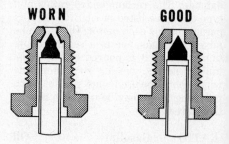

Fig. 2-5—Core bridging from center electrode to shell. Fused deposits sometimes have the appearance of tiny beads or glasslike bubbles. Caused by excessive combustion chamber deposits which in turn could be the result of; excessive carbon from prolonged usage; use of improper oil or incorrect fuel:oil ratio; high speed operation immediately following prolonged trolling.

CARBURETOR

The bulk of carburetor service consists of cleaning, inspection and adjustment. After considerable service it may become necessary to overhaul the carburetor and renew worn parts to restore original operating efficiency. Although carburetor condition affects engine operating economy and power, the ignition system and engine compression must also be considered to determine and correct causes. Also, make certain that the fuel:oil ratio is correct and that fuel is fresh (not last year's).

CLEANING AND INSPECTION.

Before dismantling carburetor for cleaning and inspection, clean all external surfaces and remove accumulated dirt and grease. If fuel starvation is suspected, all filters in carburetor, fuel pump and/or tank should be inspected. Because of inadequate fuel handling methods, rust and other foreign matter may sometimes block or partially block these filters. Under no circumstances

Fig. 2-6—Gap bridging. Usually results from the same causes outlined in Fig. 2-5.

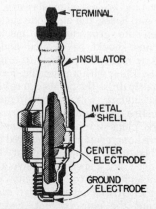

Fig. 2-7—Cross-sectional view of spark plug showing construction and nomenclature.

should these filters be removed from the fuel system. If filters are removed, the blockage will most likely occur within the carburetor and cleaning will be frequent and more difficult.

Refer to appropriate motor repair section for carburetor exploded or cross sectional views. Disassemble the carburetor and note any discrepancies which may cause a malfunction.

Wear of the fuel inlet needle, needle seat, or the float linkage can cause a change in carburetor fuel level and possible flooding. Fuel inlet needle and seat are usually furnished as a matched set, and should be renewed if a groove is noticeable in the valve; or if neoprene seat is damaged on models so equipped. On models with brass seat and tapered steel valve needle, install seat, drop needle into position; then tap outer end of needle with a small hammer to even the seat.

Carburetor flooding can sometimes be caused by a loose fuel valve seat, loose nozzle, cracked carburetor body or binding float. Consider all of these possibilities when service is indicated.

When reassembling, be sure float level (or fuel level) is properly adjusted as listed in the CARBURETOR paragraph of the appropriate motor repair section.

Except for improper fuel, the most common cause of carburetor malfunction is the formation of gum and varnish which plugs or partially plugs the small drillings or calibrated orifices within the

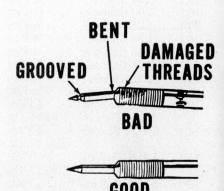

Fig. 2-9—Mixture adjustment needles should be renewed if damaged as shown at top. Never attempt to straighten a bent needle.

carburetor which control fuel flow. This build-up can be of two types, the most common being the gradual accumulation of hard varnish, sometimes mixed with dirt, which slowly builds up on all fuel system surfaces after long use. Over a period of time these deposits change the balance (calibration) of the carburetor or assist in completely blocking some small passsages making carburetor removal necessary. To do a thorough job of cleaning, the carburetor must be completely disassembled, the parts cleaned as recommended by the manufacturer, then the passages blown out with compressed air. It is impractical in most instances to attempt to clean the small passages with needles or wires, although this method is recommended by some. Exercise extreme caution to prevent enlarging passages and be sure that no hidden cross passages are plugged.

A second type of gum is formed by the decomposition of gasoline which is allowed to stand for long periods of time without being used. This form of gum can completely plug the carburetor passages, often causing the fuel inlet valve to stick. Preservative additives have been developed for gasoline which lessens the danger from this type of damage, but the fuel system including the carburetor should be drained when not is use to prevent such damage. This gum can only be loosened by prolonged soaking in a carbon dissolving solvent. Sometimes gum or varnish builds up around the throttle shaft causing the throttle to stick.

Wear damage is slight on the outboard motor carburetor. The throttle valve is not subject to frequent movement or dust abrasion, so wear of throttle valve, shaft and seals is usually negligible. If the throttle shaft does not move freely, check for gum or varnish buildup around shaft. The orifice of metering jets is subject to wear from prolonged use, but such wear cannot be detected by ordinary means. Because the jets are relatively inexpensive, it is common practice to renew them whenever carburetor is disassembled rather than to take a chance on the amount of wear.

Allied to wear damage, but usually from a different cause, is the groove around the tapered point of the mixture adjustment needle valves on carburetors so equipped. Refer to Fig. 2-9. This groove is usuallly caused by carelessness or ignorance, and is the result of bottoming the needle too tightly in the adjustment orifice. A groove on needle prevents the fine gradation of adjustment usually required of a metering needle, making it impossible to make and hold the correct mixture adjustment. When a damaged needle is found, it

should be discarded and a new part installed. It should be noted, however, the seat for the needle valve may also be damaged and accurate adjustment may not be possible even with a new needle. When adjusting the valve, always screw the needle down only lightly with the fingers until it bottoms, then back the needle out the number of turns suggested in the individual motor service sections.

ADJUSTMENT. Before attempting to adjust the carburetor, make certain that fuel used is fresh and contains the proper amount and recommended type of oil. Also, make certain that engine compression or ignition system is not the real problem. Check fuel system for air or fuel leaks and clean all of the fuel system filters. When adjusting the carburetor, make certain that exhaust fumes are properly vented and not allowed to be drawn into engine. Also, use the correct test wheel (or propeller) and do not allow motor to overheat.

Carburetor should be adjusted at the altitude that motor is to be operated. At high elevations, because the air is less dense, the main fuel adjustment on some carburetors should be set leaner than at sea level. Some carburetors have a high speed (main) adjustment needle and have a fixed main jet. On models with adjustment needle, the initial setting is listed in the individual motor section. On carburetors with fixed jets available in various sizes, the standard size is listed. At higher altitudes it may be necessary to install a main jet with smaller metering hole (orifice). In some cases, a propeller with less pitch should be installed to permit the recommended high rpm.

To adjust, first obtain the initial setting recommended in the individual motor section.

NOTE: Be careful when turning needles in and do not force, or damage to needle and/or seat may result.

Generally the initial setting for adjusting needles is too rich but should

allow motor to start. Run the motor until it reaches normal operating temperature, then adjust needles until fuel mixture is correct throughout entire range of rpm. It is preferable to set mixtures slightly rich. If mixture is too lean, motor may overheat and result in serious damage. If a "flat spot" or "4-cycling" condition cannot be corrected by adjusting carburetor, check synchronization between ignition timing advance and carburetor throttle opening as outlined in SPEED CONTROL LINKAGE section for individual motors.

SPEED CONTROL LINKAGE

The speed control on most outboard motors advances the ignition timing and opens the carburetor throttle valve as the handle is moved to the fast position. To provide correct operation, the throttle valve must be opened exactly the right amount as the ignition timing is changed. Refer to the motor repair section for models which have adjustments to synchronize "throttle" opening with the ignition timing.

A "flat spot" or "4-cycling" condition that cannot be corrected by adjusting carburetor (fuel mixture) is usually caused by incorrect throttle to ignition synchronization and/or ignition system malfunction.

REED VALVES

On two-stroke cycle motors, the incoming fuel-air mixture must be compressed in order for the mixture to properly reach the engine cylinder. On engines utilizing reed type carburetor to crankcase intake valve, a bent or broken reed may not allow compression build up in the crankcase. This condition is usually most noticeable at low speed. Thus, if such an engine seems otherwise OK, remove and inspect the reed valve unit. Refer to appropriate repair section in this manual for information on individual models.

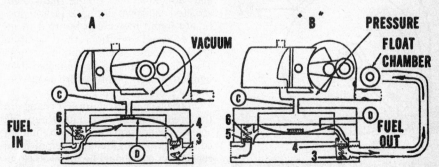

Fig. 2-10—Schematic view of a typical, crankcase operated, diaphragm type fuel pump. Pressure and vacuum pulsations from crankcase pass through connection (C) to rear of diaphragm (D) which induces a pumping action on fuel line as shown.

FUEL PUMP

Diaphragm type fuel pumps can be operated mechanically, electrically or by the vacuum and pressure pulsations in the two-stroke cycle engine crankcase. Refer to Fig. 2-10. Vacuum in the crankcase draws the diaphragm (D) in, pulling fuel past the inlet check valve (5) as shown in view "A". As the piston moves down in the cylinder, pressure is created in the crankcase. The pressure is directed to the back of diaphragm via passage (C) and diaphragm is forced out and trapped fuel is directed to the carburetor past the outlet check valve (4) as shown in view "B".

Passage (C) must be properly sealed. On some motors, the fuel pump is attached directly to the crankcase and passage (C) is sealed with a gasket. Other motors use a hose between the crankcase and fuel pump. Fuel lines (hoses) must not leak air or fuel and fuel filters should be clean. The check valves (4 & 5) should be correctly installed and not leak.

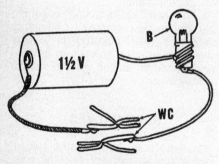

Fig. 2-11—A light can be easily constructed as shown for checking continuity. Bulb (B) should light when wire clamps (WC) are touching.

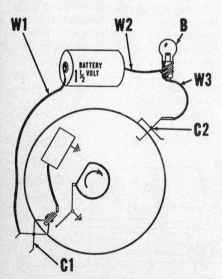

Fig. 2-12—Drawing of typical installation for checking breaker points. Coil wire should be disconnected from terminal before clamp (C1) is connected.

IGNITION SYSTEM

For a quick test of the ignition system, remove the spark plug and hold the spark plug wire with an insulated tool about 1/8-1/4 inch (3.17-6.35 mm) away from cylinder head. Have someone spin the motor and note the condition of spark. Although spark may not be visible in bright daylight, a distinct snap will be noted as the spark jumps gap. On breaker point models, If spark is weak or erratic, adjust breaker point gap and be sure to note point condition. If spark is weak although points are in good condition and properly adjusted, examine the condition of point, condenser and coil wiring, and the insulation on the magneto coils. On all models, look for broken or worn insulation or broken wires. Also check for loose or corroded connections. On models with electronic ignition control, if no external damage is noted, then refer to appropriate model section for electronic ignition control component testing. On motors equipped with a stop switch, check condition of switch and associated wiring. Renew any parts which are damaged or in poor condition.

IGNITION TIMING. On most motors, the ignition timing is advanced as the speed control handle is moved to the fast position. Refer to the SPEED CONTROL LINKAGE section for synchronizing throttle opening to the ignition timing.

Some motors have fixed ignition timing and engine speed is changed only by changing the carburetor throttle valve opening. Fixed ignition timing is usually adjustable but does not change with engine running. Refer to the appropriate motor section for method of adjusting the fixed ignition timing.

On two cylinder motors, ignition timing should be synchronized to fire the cylinders evenly. Refer to the individual motor section for method of checking and adjusting. A timing light constructed as shown in Fig. 2-11 or a continuity (ohm) meter can be used to indicate exact position that ignition breaker points open (ignition occurs). The coil wire must be disconnected from ignition breaker points before using continuity meter (or light).

On breaker point motors, a change in the breaker point (maximum) gap will change the ignition timing. Recommended breaker point gap listed in individual repair sections should be followed closely. Loss of power, loss of speed, "flat spot" and/or overheating may be caused by incorrect breaker point gap.

BREAKER POINTS. Breaker points are usually located under the flywheel. Holes are sometimes provided in the flywheel for checking and adjusting however, flywheel usually must be removed for renewal of ignition points.

Using a small screwdriver, separate and inspect condition of contacts. If burned or deeply pitted, points should be renewed. If contacts are clean to grayish in color, disconnect coil lead wire from breaker point terminal. Connect one lead (C1–Fig. 2-12) to the insulated breaker point terminal and the other (C2) to engine (ground). Light should burn with points closed and go out with points open. If light does not burn, little or no contact is indicated and points should be cleaned or renewed and contact maximum gap should be reset.

NOTE: IN some cases, new breaker point contact surfaces may be coated with oil or wax.

If light does not go out when points are opened, timing light is not connected properly or breaker point insulation is defective.

Adjust breaker point gap as follows unless manufacturer specifies adjusting breaker gap to obtain correct ignition timing. First, turn engine so that points are closed to be sure that the contact surfaces are in alignment and seat squarely. Then turn engine so that breaker point opening is maximum and adjust breaker gap to manufacturer's specification. Be sure to recheck gap after tightening breaker point base retaining screws.

CONDENSER. To check condition of the condenser without special test equipment, proceed as follows: The condenser case and wire should be visually checked for any obvious damage. Remove condenser, then connect one end of test lamp (Fig. 2-11) to terminal at end of condenser wire and other end to condenser case. If light goes on, condenser is shorted and should be renewed. It is usually a good practice to renew condenser when new breaker points are installed. If breaker points become pitted rapidly, condenser is usually faulty.

IGNITION COIL. If a coil tester is available, condition of coil can be checked. Sometimes, an ignition coil may perform satisfactorily when cold but fail after engine has run for some time and coil is hot. Check coil when hot if this condition is indicated.

MAGNETO AIR GAP. To fully concentrate the magnetic field of the flywheel, magnets pass as closely to the armature core as possible without danger of metal-to-metal contact. The clearance between the flywheel magnets and the legs of the armature core is called the armature air gap.

On magnetos where the armature and high tension coil are located outside of the flywheel rim, adjustment of the armature air gap is made as follows: Turn the engine so the flywheel magnets are located directly under the legs of the armature core and check the clearance between the armature core and flywheel magnets. If the measured clearance is not within manufacturer's specifications, loosen the armature mounting screws and place shims at thickness equal to minumum air gap specification between the magnets and armature core. The magnets will pull the armature core against the shim stock. Tighten the armature core mounting screws, remove the shim stock and turn the engine through several revolutions to be sure the flywheel does not contact the armature core.

Where the armature core is located under or behind the flywheel, the following methods may be used to check and adjust armature air gap: On some engines, slots or openings are provided in the flywheel through which the armature air gap can be checked. Some engine manufacturers provide a cutaway flywheel or a positioning ring that can be used to correctly set the armature air gap.

Another method of checking the armature air gap is to remove the flywheel and place a layer of plastic tape equal to the minimum specified air gap over the legs of the armature core. Reinstall flywheel and turn engine through several revolutions and remove flywheel; no evidence of contact between the flywheel magnets and plastic tape should be noticed. Then cover the legs of the armature core with a layer of tape of thickness equal to the maximum specified air gap, then reinstall flywheel and turn engine through several revolutions. Indication of the flywheel magnets contacting the plastic tape should be noticed after the flywheel is again removed. If the magnets contact the first thin layer of tape applied to the armature core legs, or if they do not contact the second thicker layer of tape, armature air gap is not within specifications and should be adjusted.

NOTE: Before loosening armature core mounting screws, inscribe a mark on mounting plate against edge of armature core so adjustment of air gap can be gauged.

MAGNETO EDGE GAP. The point of maximum acceleration of the movement of the flywheel magnetic field through the high tension coil (and therefore, the point of maximum current induced in the primary coil windings) occurs when the trailing edge of the flywheel magnet is slightly past the left hand leg of the armature core. The exact point of maximum primary current is determined by using electrical measuring devices, the distance between the trailing edge of the flywheel magnet and the leg of the armature core at this point is measured and becomes a service specification. This distance, which is stated either in thousandths of an inch or in degrees of flywheel rotation, is called the Edge Gap or "E" Gap.

For maximum strength of the ignition spark, the breaker points should just start to open when the flywheel magnets are at the specified edge gap position. Usually, edge gap is nonadjustable and will be maintained at the proper dimension if the contact breaker points are adjusted to the recommeded gap and the correct breaker cam is installed. However, magneto edge gap can change (and spark intensity thereby reduced) due to the following:

a. Flywheel drive key sheared.
b. Flywheel drive key worn (loose).
c. Keyway in flywheel or crankshaft worn (oversized).
d. Loose flywheel retaining nut which can also cause any above listed difficulty.
e. Excessive wear on breaker cam.
f. Breaker cam loose or improperly installed on crankshaft.
g. Excessive wear on breaker point rubbing block so points cannot be properly adjusted.

COOLING SYSTEM

When cooling system problems are suspected, first check the water inlet for partial or complete stoppage. If water inlet is clear, refer to the appropriate section and check condition of pump, water passages, gaskets, sealing surfaces and thermostat (if so equipped).

The following conditions can cause motor to overheat with cooling system operating properly.

1. Incorrect type of oil or incorrect fuel-oil ratio.
2. Fuel mixture too lean.
3. Clogged exhaust or exhaust leaking into cooling system.
4. Incorrect ignition timing.
5. Throttle not correctly synchronized to ignition advance.

6. Motor overloaded.
7. Incorrect propeller.
8. Missing or bent shields, fins or blower housing. (On air cooled models, never attempt to run engine without all shields in place).

Various types of temperature indicating devices (including heat sensitive sticks or crayons) are available for checking the operating temperature.

WATER PUMP. Most motors use a rubber impeller type water pump. Refer to Fig. 2-13. At slow engine speed, the impeller blades follow the contour of the offset housing as shown by the solid lines. With this type pump, the impeller blades may be damaged (or completely broken off) if turned in opposite direction of normal rotation. If impeller is damaged, all water passages should be cleaned. Some water passages may be blocked and result in overheating of the blocked area.

GENERATING SYSTEMS

Refer to the individual motor section for explanation of generating system used. Some motors use a combined starter-generator unit, others use combined flywheel alternator – flywheel magneto and others use a belt driven, automotive type generator.

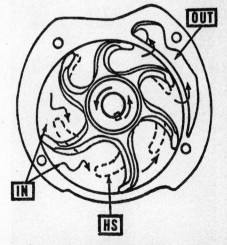

Fig. 2-13—Drawing of impeller type pump. Water is drawn into pump (IN) as area between vanes increases and is forced into power head (OUT) as area decreases. At high speeds the blades remain curved as shown by the broken lines (HS) and pump operates mostly by centrifugal action. Blades may be broken or damaged if turned in reverse of normal direction of rotation.

GENERAL REPAIRS

Because of the close tolerance of the interior parts, cleanliness is of utmost importance. It is suggested that the exterior of the motor and all nearby areas be absolutely clean before any repair is started. Manufacturer's recommended torque values for tightening screw fasteners should be followed closely. The soft threads in aluminum castings are often damaged by carelessness in overtightening fasteners or in attempting to loosen or remove seized fasteners.

Commonly recommended tightening torques, for common screw sizes, are listed below. These recommendations should be followed if specific recommendations are not given in the individual service sections.

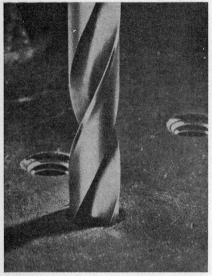

Fig. 2-14—First step in repairing damaged threads is to drill out old threads using exact size drill recommended in instructions provided with thread repair kit. Drill all the way through an open hole or all the way to bottom of blind hole, making sure hole is straight and that centerline of hole is not moved in drilling process. (Series of photos provided by Heli-Coil Corp., Danbury, Conn.)

SCREW SIZE	TORQUE
#4	4-6 in.-lbs.
	(0.5-0.7 N·m)
#6	8-11 in.-lbs.
	(0.9-1.2 N·m)
#8	15-20 in.-lbs.
	(1.7-2.3 N·m)
#10	25-35 in.-lbs.
	(2.8-3.9 N·m)
#12	35-40 in.-lbs.
	(3.9-4.5 N·m)
¼ inch	60-80 in.-lbs.
	(6.8-9 N·m)
5/16 inch	120-140 in.-lbs.
	(13.5-15.8 N·m)
3/8 inch	220-240 in.-lbs.
	(24.8-27.1 N·m)
7/16, ½ inch	340-360 in.-lbs.
	(38.4-40.7 N·m)

Aluminum offers unusual resistance to oxidation. This factor combined with the necessary lightness, makes it an ideal construction material for outboard motors. Aluminum is a relatively soft material, however, and cannot be used for all applications. Shafts, gears, bearings and fasteners (such as bolts, nuts, etc.) must be made of steel or other more rugged material. The presence of dissimilar metals brings the additional danger of destruction or seizure of parts due to galvanic action. The dangers are not insurmountable, but must be recognized and kept constantly in mind when performing service on any motor. Remain doubly alert when servicing motors used in salt water. This problem is carefully considered by the manufacturer when selecting materials for construction. Substitution of bolts, nuts or small components other than those recommended by manufacturer is to be avoided whenever possible. Protective or insulating coatings of sealants, paint, and waterproof grease should be used in assembly wherever possible to prevent corrosion or seizure, and to facilitate future disassembly. If the entrance of air and water can be completely eliminated, dangers are much lessened. Outer surfaces of the aluminum castings are probably anodized, which offers excellent protection against deterioration or damage. This thin coating is easily damaged, however, and cannot be renewed at shop level. Avoid scratches, abrasion and rough handling as much as possible, and protect with an approved touch-up paint when assembly is completed.

REPAIRING DAMAGED THREADS

Damaged threads in castings can be repaired by use of thread repair kits which are recommended by a number of manufacturers. Use of thread repair kits is not difficult, but instructions must be carefully followed. Refer to Figs. 2-14 through 2-16 which illustrate the use of thread repair kits manufactured by the Heli-Coil Corporation, Danbury, Connecticut.

Heli-Coil thread repair kits are available through the parts departments of most engine and equipment manufacturers. The thread inserts are available in all National Coarse (USS) sizes from number 4 to 1½ inch. National Fine (SAE) sizes from number 6 to 1½ inch and metric sizes 5 MM X 0.9 MM, 6 MM X 1.0 MM, 8 MM X 1.25 MM, 10 MM X 1.50 MM and 12 MM X 1.25 MM. Also, sizes for repairing 14MM and 18MM spark plug ports are available.

Fig. 2-15—Special drill taps are provided which are the correct size for OUTSIDE of the insert. A standard size tap cannot be substituted.

Fig. 2-16—Shown is the insert and a completed repair. Special tools are provided in kit for installation, together with the necessary instructions.

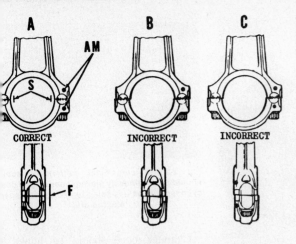

Fig. 2-17—Most connecting rods are provided with marks (AM) which should be aligned as shown in view "A". Bearing surface (S) and sides (F) should be smooth and all machine marks on rod and cap should be perfectly aligned. If cap is reversed as shown in view "B", bearing surface will not be smooth and marks will not be aligned. If incorrect rod cap is installed, machined surfaces will not be smooth even if marks on rod and cap are aligned as shown in view "C".

DISASSEMBLY AND ASSEMBLY

Outboard motors, especially the smaller types, are relatively simple in construction. The larger, more powerful units remain simple in design for the most part, but sometimes offer additional problems in disassembly and assembly.

Two or more identical pistons, rings, connectings rods and bearings may be used in a motor, but parts should never be interchanged when reassembling. As parts are removed, they should all be marked to identify the correct position. All wearing parts seat to the mating parts during operation. If parts are mixed during reassembly, a new wear pattern is established and early failure may result. Connecting rods are made with the cap and only this one cap will fit the rod perfectly. Refer to Fig. 2-17. If the original cap is incorrectly installed as shown in view "B"–Fig. 2-17) or if another rod cap is installed (View "C"–Fig. 2-17), the bearing surface will not be smooth and true. Most connecting rods have raised marks (AM) on rod and cap to facilitate reassembly. Some manufacturers machine the rod as one piece and fracture (break) the cap away. The broken joint will fit together perfectly only when correctly installed.

A given amount of heat applied to aluminum will cause it to expand a greater amount than will steel under similar conditions. Because of the different expansion characteristics, heat is usually recommended for easy installation of bearings, pins, etc., in aluminum or magnesium castings. Sometimes, heat can be used to free parts that are seized or where an interference fit is used. Heat, therefore, becomes a service tool and the application of heat, one of the required service techniques. An open flame is not usually advised because it destroys the paint and other protective coatings and because a uniform and controlled temperature with open flame is difficult to obtain. Methods commonly used for heating are: 1. In oil or water, 2. With a heat lamp, 3. Electric hot plate, 4. In an oven or kiln. See Fig. 2-18. The use of hot water or oil gives a fairly accurate temperature control but is somewhat limited as to the size and type of part that can be handled. Thermal crayons are available which can be used to determine the temperature of a heated part. These crayons melt when the part reaches specified temperature, and a number of crayons for different temperatures are available Temperature indicating crayons are usually available at welding equipment supply houses.

The crankcase and inlet manifold must be completely sealed against both vacuum and pressure. Exhaust manifold and cylinder head must be sealed against water leakage and pressure. Mating surfaces of water inlet, and exhaust areas between power head and lower unit must form a tight seal.

When disassembled, it is recommended that all gasket surfaces, and mating surfaces without gaskets, be carefully checked for nicks, burrs and warped surfaces which might interfere with a tight seal. The cylinder head, cylinder head cover, head end of cylinder block, and some mating surfaces of manifolds and crankcase may be checked, and lapped if necessary, to provide a smooth surface. Flat surfaces can be lapped by using a surface plate or a smooth piece of plate glass, and a sheet of fine sandpaper or lapping compound. Use a figure-eight motion with minimum pressure, and remove only enough metal to eliminate the imperfection. Finish lap using lapping compound or worn emery cloth. Thoroughly clean the parts with new oil on a clean, soft rag, then wash with soapsuds and clean rags.

Mating surfaces of crankcase halves may be checked on the lapping block, and high spots or nicks removed, but surface must not be lowered. Bearing clearances must not be lessened by removing metal from the joint. If extreme care is used, a slightly damaged crankcase may be salvaged in this manner.

Gaskets and sealing surfaces should be lighly and carefully coated with an approved gasket cement or sealing compound unless the contrary is stated. Make sure entire surface is coated, but avoid letting excesss cement squeeze out into crankcase, bearings or other passages.

PISTON, RINGS, PIN AND CYLINDER

When servicing pistons, rings and cylinders, it is important that all recommended tolerances be closely observed. Parts that are damaged should be carefully examined to determine the cause. A scored piston as shown in Fig. 2-19 is obviously not a result of normal wear and if the cause is not corrected, new parts may be similarly damaged in a short time. Piston scoring can be caused by overheating, improper fuel:oil mixture, carburetor out of adjustment, in-

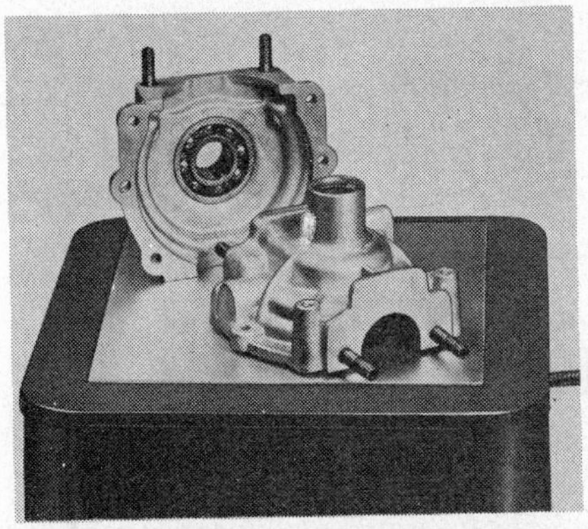

Fig. 2-18—Heat can be used efficiently as a disassembly and assembly tool. Heating crankcase halves on electric hot plate (above) will allow bearings to be easily removed.

Fig. 2-19—If parts are excessively damaged, cause should be determined and corrected before returning motor to service.

Fig. 2-20—Gap between ends of ring should be within recommended limits.

Fig. 2-22—Ring side clearance in groove should be measured with gage as shown. Clearance should be within recommended limits and the same all the way around piston.

Fig. 2-23—A cross-hatch pattern as show should be obtained by moving hone up and dow cylinder bore as it is being turned by slow spee electric drill.

correct ignition timing and/or speed control linkage not correctly adjusted.

Before installing new piston rings, check ring end gap as follows: Position the ring near the top of cylinder bore. The bottom of piston (skirt) should be used to slide the ring in cylinder to locate ring squarely in bore. Measure the gap between end of ring using a feeler gage as shown in Fig. 2-20. Slide the ring down in the cylinder to the area of transfer and exhaust ports and again measure gap. Rings may break if end gap is too tight at any point; but, will not seal properly if gap is too wide. Variation in gap indicates cylinder wear (usually near the ports).

Ring grooves in the piston should be carefully cleaned and examined. Use caution when cleaning to prevent damage to piston. Carelessness can result in poor motor performance and possibly extensive internal engine damage. Refer to Fig. 2-21. When installing rings on piston, expand only far enough to slip over the piston and **do not twist rings.** After installing rings on piston, use feeler gage to measure ring side clearance in groove as shown in Fig. 2-22. Excessive side clearance will prevent an effective seal and may cause rings to break.

Cylinder bore should be honed t remove glaze from cylinder walls befor installing new piston rings. Ridge at to and bottom of ring travel should b removed by honing. If ridge is no removed, new rings may catch enoug to bend the ring lands as shown a (G-Fig. 2-21). The finished cylinde should have light cross-hatched patter as shown in Fig. 2-23. After honing wash cylinder assembly with soap an water to remove all traces of abrasive After cylinder is dry, swab cylinder bor with oil making sure that it is absolutel clean.

Some manufacturers have oversiz piston and ring sets available for use i repairing engines in which the cylinde bore is 'excessively worn and standard size piston and rings cannnot be used. I care and approved procedures are used in oversizing the cylinder bore, installa tion of an oversize piston and ring se should result in a highly satisfactory overhaul.

The cylinder bore may be oversized by using either a boring bar or a hone however, if a boring bar is used it is usually recommended the cylinder bore be finished with a hone. Refer to Fig. 2-23. Before attempting to rebore or

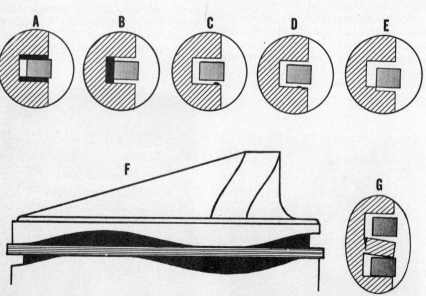

Fig. 2-21—Piston ring grooves must be clean and not damaged to provide a good seal.

A. Carbon on sides of groove may cause ring to stick in groove.
B. Carbon on bottom (back) of groove may prevent rings from compressing.
C. Small pieces of carbon & (C) or nicks (D) in
D. groove will prevent a good seal.
E. If groove is worn as shown, renew the piston.
F. If groove is not straight, renew piston.
G. Renew piston if ring land is bent.

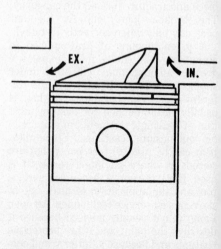

Fig. 2-24—Deflector type piston must be installed with long sloping side toward exhaust port and inlet deflector on transfer port side.

hone the cylinder to oversize, carefully measure the cylinder bore to be sure that new, standard size piston and rings will not fit within tolerance. Also, it may be possible that the cylinder is excessively worn or damaged and that reboring or honing to largest oversize will not clean up the worn or scored surface.

When assembling piston to connecting rod, observe special precautions outlined in the individual motor sections. Deflector type pistons must be installed with long sloping side toward exhaust port and the inlet deflector toward the transfer ports as shown in Fig. 2-24. If connecting rod has an oil hole at piston pin or crankpin end, hole should be toward top of motor. If piston pin has one closed end, it is normally installed toward exhaust port side of piston.

CONNECTING ROD, CRANKSHAFT AND BEARINGS

Before detaching connecting rods from crankshaft, mark rods and caps for correct assembly to each other and to proper cylinder. Most damage to ball and roller bearings is evident after visual inspection and turning the assembled bearing by hand. If bearing shows evidence of overheating, renew the complete assembly. On models with plain (bushing) bearings, check the crankpin and main bearing journals for wear with a micrometer. Crankshaft journals will usually wear out-of-round with most wear on side that takes the force of power stroke (strokes). If main bearing clearances are excessive, new crankcase seals may not be able to prevent pressure from blowing fuel and oil around crankshaft. All crankcase seals should be renewed when crankshaft, connecting rods and bearings are serviced.

SUBMERGED MOTOR

Almost all motors except small fishing motors are equipped for bolting to the transom. If motor is securely fastened by bolting, water damage cannot occur unless boat is swamped, overturned, or sunk. A safety chain will assist in the recovery of a small motor which vibrates loose and falls overboard. The same arrangement on a large motor could be dangerous, as the transom could be knocked out of boat by a wild motor.

There is a danger from two types of damage when a motor has been submerged. If motor was running when dropped, mechanical damage can result from the inability of water to compress. If mechanical damage is avoided, corrosive action can start almost immediately, especially in salt water.

Problems may develop if motor is dropped overboard.

Corrosion damage is most apt to occur after the motor has been removed from the water as corrosive action is greatest in the presence of heat and oxygen. In case of mechanical damage or for salt water submersion even where no actual damage exists, complete disassembly of the power head is indicated. In addition to the necesssary hand tools, fresh water under pressure, and alcohol and oil should be available. Proper care of a submerged motor, therefore, usually indicates that the motor be brought in to a suitable shop for service. If considerable time must elapse before service can be performed, it is best to keep motor submerged in fresh water, adding ice, if available, to keep the water cool. If fresh water is not available, motor is better off submerged in salt water than brought out to air dry.

If an attempt is to be made to run the motor without disassembly, remove the cowling and rinse off any silt or sand. Remove the spark plugs, carburetor and reed valve, if possible; then turn motor over slowly with starter to pump any water out of power head. Blow water from the magneto, spark plugs and wiring. Pour or spray alcohol into the crankcase and cylinders, trying to cover as many of the metal surfaces as possible. the alcohol will combine with the water remaining in the engine, allowing it to be removed by flushing out, and later by evaporation. Disassemble and clean the carburetor, fuel pump, fuel lines and tank and refill with a fresh fuel:oil mixture. If a spray gun is available, spray a new coating of oil in the crankcases and spark plug holes. After motor is reassembled, it should start if magneto coils are not shorted out by moisture. Do not dry magneto parts in an oven. Excess heat will damage insulation. Check for silt in cooling system inlet before attempting to start the motor. If motor is started, it should be run for at least thirty minutes after it is warm, to give the remaining drops of water an opportunity to evaporate and disappear. The most likely points of corrosion damage are the main bearings and crankshaft journals, especially the lower one, as water drains into these parts and cannot be drained out or thrown out by centrifugal force. Even one drop of water can cause etching of the crankshaft or needle roller which will cause noise and early failure if bearings are of this type.

If silt or sand is present, in cases of salt water submersion, or where mechanical damage exists, the motor should be disassembled and cleaned. The corrosion factors of salt water or the presence of silt will cause early failure and are almost impossible to remove by flushing.

If the motor is to be disassembled, speed is essential, and the motor should be protected as much as possible from corrosion until disassembly is begun. Submersion in some type of liquid will inhibit corrosion temporarily. If several hours must elapse before disassembly can be started, keeping the parts submerged may limit the damage. In the case of large motors where complete submersion would be difficult, remove power head from lower unit and submerge the power head only. Remove the electrical units if tools are available. Alcohol offers the best protection if available. There is no special advantage of oil over fresh water if disassembly is to take place within 24 hours, and it most certainly should.

When motor is disassembled, scrub the parts thoroughly in hot, soapy water and air dry, then immerse in oil or spray with an oil mist until parts are completely coated. Ball or roller bearings which cannot be disassembled for cleaning should be renewed if their condition is at all questionable. It is very difficult to be sure that all traces of silt are removed from such bearings, and renewal at this time is usually cheaper than risking early failure.

CHRYSLER

US MARINE CORP.
105 Marine Drive
Hartford, Wisconsin 53027

CHRYSLER 30 AND 35 HP

30 HP Models

Year Produced	Model
1973, 1974 . . . . 302HA, 302BA, 303HA, 303BA, 304HA, 304BA, 305HA, 305BA	
1975 . . . . 302HB, 302BB, 303HB, 303BB, 304HB, 304BB, 305HB, 305BB, 306HA, 306BA, 307HA, 307BA	
1979 . . . . 302H9C, 302B9C, 303H9C, 303B9C, 306H9B, 306B9B, 307H9B, 307B9B	
1980 . . . . 306H0C, 305B0C, 307H0C, 307B0C	
1981 . . . . 307H1D, 307B1D	
1982 . . . . 307H2E, 307B2E	

35 HP Models

Year Produced	Model
1976, 1977 . . . . 350HK, 350BK, 351HK, 351BK, 356HK, 356BK, 357HK, 357BK	
1978 . . . . 350H8L, 350B8L, 351H8L, 351B8L, 356H8M, 356B8M, 357H8M, 357B8M	
1983 . . . . 357H3N, 357B3N, 357R3P	
1984 . . . . 357H4, 357B4	

CONDENSED SERVICE DATA

TUNE-UP	30 HP (Prior to 1976)	30 HP (After 1978)	35 HP
Hp/rpm	30/5000	30/4750	35/5000
Bore – Inches	2.8125	3.00	3.00
Stroke – Inches	2.414	2.414	2.414
Number of Cylinders	2	2	2
Displacement – Cu. In.	29.99	34.10	34.10
Compression at Cranking Speed (Average)	125-135 psi	125-135 psi	120-130 psi
Spark Plug:			
Champion	L4J	L4J	L4J
Electrode Gap – Inches	0.030	0.030	0.030
Magneto:			
Point Gap – Inches	†0.020	See text	†0.020
Timing	See text	See text	See text
Carburetor:			
Make	Tillotson	Tillotson	Tillotson
Model	WB	WB	WB
Fuel:Oil Ratio	**50:1	**50:1	**50:1

†Breaker point gap is 0.015 inch for models 306HA, 306BA, 307HA, 307BA, 356HK, 356BK, 357HK and 357BK. Models 356H8M, 356B8M, 357H8M and 357B8M are equipped with a breakerless ignition system.
**Fuel:oil ratio should be 25:1 for break-in period.

SIZES – CLEARANCES	30 HP (Prior to 1976)	30 HP (After 1978)	35 HP
Piston Ring End Gap:			
Top Ring		0.006-0.016 in.	
Bottom Ring		0.004-0.014 in.	
Piston to Cylinder Clearance		0.0060-0.0095 in.	
Piston Pin Diameter		0.50000-0.50015 in.	
Crankshaft Journal Diameters:			
Upper Main		1.3774-1.3780 in.	
Center Main		1.3446-1.3451 in.	
Lower Main		0.9849-0.9853 in.	
Crankpin		1.1391-1.1395 in.	

TIGHTENING TORQUES (All Values in Inch-Pounds)	30 HP (Prior to 1976)	30 HP (After 1978)	35 HP
Cylinder Head	225	190	225
Flywheel Nut	540	720	540
Spark Plug	120-180	120-180	120-180
Connecting Rod Screws	165-175	180-190	165-175
No. 10-24	30	30	30
No. 10-32	35	35	35
No. 12-24	45	45	45
1/4-20	70	70	70
5/16-18	160	160	160
3/8-16	270	270	270

LUBRICATION

The power head is lubricated by oil mixed with the fuel. For normal service after break-in, mix 1/6 pint of two-stroke engine oil with each gallon of gasoline. The recommended ratio is one third (1/3) pint of oil per gallon of gasoline for severe service and during break-in. Manufacturer recommends no-lead automotive gasoline although regular or premium gasoline may be used if octane rating is 85 or higher. Gasoline and oil should be thoroughly mixed.

The lower unit gears and bearings are lubricated by oil contained in the gearcase. Only non-corrosive, leaded, EP90, outboard gear oil such as "Chrysler Outboard Gear Lube" should be used. The gearcase should be drained and refilled every 30 hours. Maintain fluid at level of upper (vent) plug.

To fill gearcase, have motor in upright position and fill through lower hole in side of gearcase until fluid reaches level of upper vent plug hole. Reinstall and tighten both plugs securely, using new gaskets if necessary, to assure a water tight seal.

FUEL SYSTEM

CARBURETOR. A Tillotson WB type carburetor is used on all models. Refer to Fig. C7-1 for an exploded view of the carburetor.

Initial setting of idle mixture screw (10 – Fig. C7-1) is 1 1/4 turns out from a lightly seated position. Final adjustment of carburetor should be made with engine at normal operating temperature and with outboard in forward gear. Standard main jet size is 0.068 inch on 30 hp motors prior to 1979 and 0.064 inch on 30 hp motors after 1978. Standard main jet on 35 hp motors is 0.066 inch. Standard main jet sizes should be correct for operation below 1250 ft. altitude.

To check float level, remove float bowl and invert carburetor. Side of float nearest main jet should be parallel with gasket surface of carburetor. Adjust float level by bending float tang.

Install throttle plate (1 – Fig. C7-1) so that notch is up and chamfer is towards flange end of carburetor.

SPEED CONTROL LINKAGE. Ignition timing and throttle opening on all models must be synchronized so that throttle is opened as timing is advanced.

To synchronize linkage, first check ignition timing to be sure it is set correctly as outlined in IGNITION TIMING section. Disconnect link (L – Fig. C7-2) from magneto control lever and with throttle closed, turn eccentric screw (S) until roller (R) is exactly centered over mark (M) on throttle cam (C). Reconnect link (L) to magneto contol lever and rotate magneto stator ring until it is against full advance stop. Upper mark (AM) on throttle cam should now be aligned with

roller (R). Disconnect link (L) and turn link ends to adjust length of link so that mark (AM) and roller are aligned when stator is at full advance. Turn throttle stop screw in steering handle shaft on models with manual starter so that screw provides a positive stop just as stator plate reaches full advance stop.

Idle speed in forward gear should be 550-650 rpm on manual start models. Adjust idle of manual start models by turning idle speed screw on side of steering handle. Idle speed in forward gear should be 650-750 rpm on electric start models. Adjust idle speed of electric start models by turning idle speed screw (I – Fig. C7-3) adjacent to exhaust port covers.

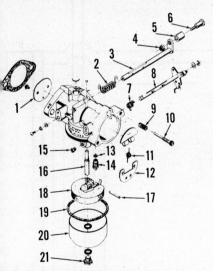

Fig. C7-1—Exploded view of typical Tillotson model WB carburetor.

1. Throttle plate
2. Spring
3. Throttle shaft
4. Nut
5. Roller
6. Eccentric screw
7. Spring
8. Choke shaft
9. Spring
10. Idle mixture screw
11. Spring
12. Choke plate
13. Gasket
14. Fuel inlet valve
15. High speed jet
16. Main nozzle
17. Float pin
18. Float
19. Gasket
20. Float bowl
21. Bowl retaining screw

Fig. C7-2—View of throttle cam and linkage. Refer to text for adjustment.

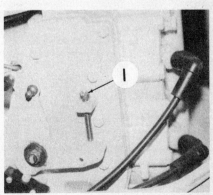

Fig. C7-3—View of idle speed screw (I) used on models with electric starter. Idle speed should be 650-750 rpm with unit in forward gear.

REED VALVES.
All models are equipped with a "V" type reed valve. The reed plate is located between the intake manifold and crankcase. Remove carburetor and intake manifold for access to reed valve.

Renew reeds if petals are broken, cracked, warped or bent. Never attempt to bend a reed petal in an effort to improve performance, nor attempt to straighten a damaged reed. Never install a bent or damaged reed. Seating surface of reed plate should be smooth and flat. Install reeds so that petals are centered over openings. Assembled reeds may stand open to a maximum of 0.010 inch at tip end. Reed stop setting should be 9/32 inch when measured from tip of reed stop to reed plate.

PUDDLE DRAIN VALVE.
Models prior to 1981 are equipped with a puddle drain valve located in the hose from the bottom of the crankcase cover to the bottom of the transfer port cover. The puddle valve is designed to remove puddled fuel from the crankcase, thus providing smooth operation at all speeds and lessening the possibility of spark plug fouling.

To check operation of puddle valve, disconnect hose ends and blow through each end of hose. Puddle valve should pass air when blowing through crank-

case cover end of hose but not when blowing through transfer port end of hose. Remove puddle valve from hose if it does not operate correctly. Install new puddle valve in hose approximately one inch from end of hose with small hole in puddle valve towards short end of hose. Attach hose to engine with puddle valve end of hose connected to crankcase cover.

FUEL PUMP.
All models are equipped with a two-stage diaphragm type fuel pump which is actuated by pressure and vacuum pulsations from the engine crankcases.

NOTE: Either stage of the fuel pump operating independently may permit the motor to run, but not at peak performance.

To remove fuel pump, disconnedt fuel hoses to pump and unscrew six cap screws which retain fuel pump body. Check valves are renewable but be sure a new check valve is needed before removing old check valve as it will be damaged during removal. Unscrew the two retaining screws to remove center check valve. The two outer check valve must be driven out from below. Refer to Fig. C7-5 for view of correct check valve installation. Install check valves care

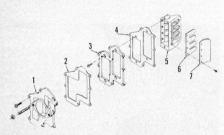

Fig. C7-4—Exploded view of reed valve assembly.

1. Inlet manifold
2. Gasket
3. Adapter plate
4. Gasket
5. Reed body
6. Reed petals
7. Reed stop

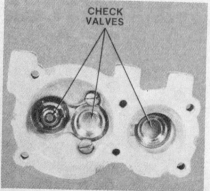

Fig. C7-5—Fuel pump check valves must be installed as shown for proper operation of fuel pump.

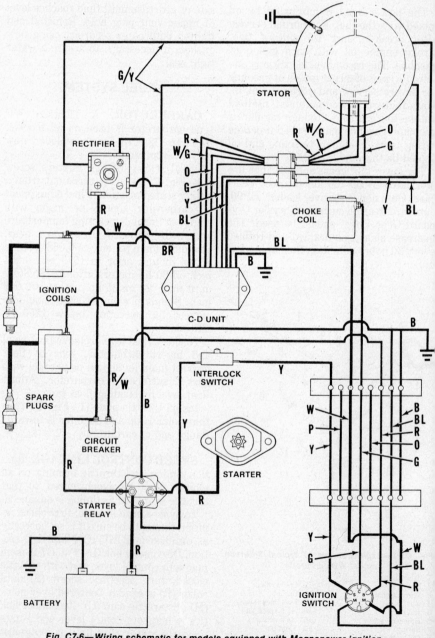

Fig. C7-6—Wiring schematic for models equipped with Magnapower ignition.

B. Black
BL. Blue
G. Green
O. Orange
P. Purple
R. Red
W. White
Y. Yellow

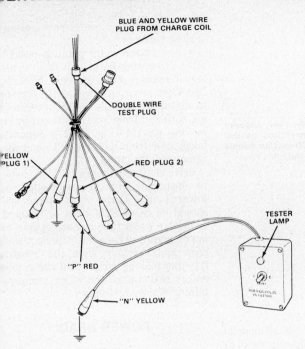

Fig. C7-7—Tester connections for checking low voltage output of charge coils.

fully to prevent damage. Inspect diaphragm and renew diaphragm if cracked, torn or badly distorted.

IGNITION

Magnapower Models

These models are equipped with a breakerless, capacitor discharge ignition system. Note wiring diagram in Fig.C7-6. Tapered bore of flywheel and crankshaft end must be clean, dry and smooth before installing flywheel. Renew a chipped or cracked flywheel. Flywheel and crankshaft tapers may be cleaned by using fine valve grinding compound. Apply grinding compound to tapers and rotate flywheel back and forth approximately one quarter turn. Do not spin flywheel on crankshaft. Clean flywheel and crankshaft tapers throughly. Tighten flywheel nut to 45 ft.-lbs. torque.

If ignition malfunction occurs, use Chrysler tool T8953, plug adapter set T11201 and number 22 tester with load coil from tool T8996 and refer to following troubleshooting procedure:

Check and make sure ignition malfunction is not due to spark plug or ignition coil failure. If spark is absent at both cylinders, check condition of charge coil as follows: Separate the blue and yellow wire connection between charge coil and CD ignition module and attach double wire plug adapter to wire plug from charge coil as shown in Fig. C7-7. Attach red (P) lead from tester number 22 to red sleeved adapter wire marked "Plug 2." Attach yellow (N) lead of number 22 tester and yellow sleeved adapter wire marked "Plug 1" to engine

ground. Place tester switch in number 2 position and crank engine. If tester lamp does not light, low voltage windings of charge coil are defective and stator should be renewed. If lamp lights, continue charge coil test by disconnecting yellow sleeved wire adapter from engine

ground and attaching it to red (P) lead of T8953 tester as shown in Fig. C7-8. Attach yellow (N) lead of T8953 tester to engine ground. Turn tester switch to position 10 and crank engine. If tester lamp does not light, high voltage windings of charge coil are defective and stator should be renewed. If lamp lights, charge coil operation is satisfactory and trigger coil and CD ignition module circuits for each cylinder must be checked. Remove tester and plug adapter set, then reconnect blue and yellow wire plugs.

Separate the four-wire connection between CD ignition module and trigger coil and attach four wire plug adapter to wire plug from trigger coil as shown in Fig. C7-9. Attach red (P) lead from tester number 22 to red sleeved adapter wire marked "Trigger 1 Pos." and yellow (N) lead to yellow sleeved adapter wire marked "Trigger 1 Neg." Place switch of tester in number 1 position and crank engine. Trigger coil operation is satisfactory if tester lamp lights. Renew trigger housing if tester lamp does not light.

To check operation of number 2 cylinder trigger coil, repeat test procedure for number 1 cylinder trigger coil

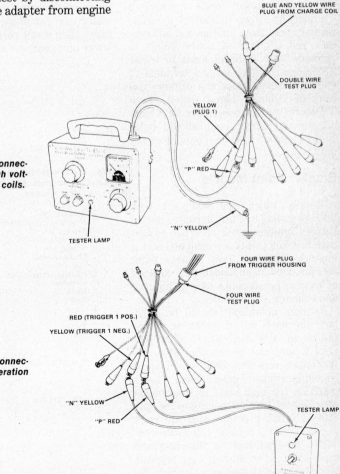

Fig. C7-8—Tester connections for checking high voltage output of charge coils.

Fig. C7-9—Tester connections for checking operation of trigger coil.

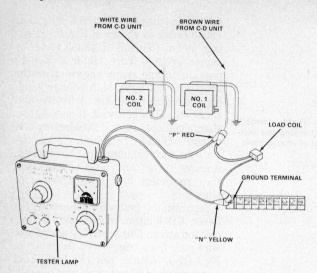

WHITE WIRE FROM C-D UNIT

BROWN WIRE FROM C-D UNIT

NO. 2 COIL

NO. 1 COIL

LOAD COIL

"P" RED

GROUND TERMINAL

"N" YELLOW

TESTER LAMP

Fig. C7-10—View showing tester connections needed to check CD ignition module output.

tion of water pump, water passages and sealing surfaces.

Access to the water pump is possible after separating lower unit from motor leg. Remove motor leg covers. Unscrew fasteners securing drive shaft housing to motor leg and disconnect intermediate shift rod from lower shift rod by removing pin (11–Fig. C7-24). Separate lower unit from motor leg. Unbolt and remove water pump.

Drive shaft seal (3–Fig. C7-24) should be installed with spring loaded lip towards top. Drive shaft spline seal should be renewed if hard or cracked. Lubricate water tube seal and splines on upper end of drive shaft. Connect shift rods and carefully slide the housing together making certain that water tube enters seal. Install the water pump retaining screws and nuts.

but connect red (P) lead of tester to red sleeved adapter wire marked "Trigger 2 Pos." and yellow (N) lead to yellow sleeved adapter wire marked "Trigger 2 Neg."

To check ignition module performance for each cylinder, connect yellow (N) lead from tester T8953 to ground terminal of engine terminal block (Fig. C7-10). Disconnect white (number 2 cylinder) or brown (number 1 cylinder) primary lead from ignition coil and connect red (P) lead of tester T8953 to primary lead. Connect leads of tester T8996 load coil to ground terminal of engine terminal block and primary coil lead of cylinder being tested. Turn T8953 tester dial to number 50. Crank engine and tester lamp should light. Renew ignition module if lamp does not light.

Breaker Point Models

Motors which are equipped with breaker points and an alternator have a battery ignition while all other motors with breaker points are equipped with a magneto ignition. Two breaker point sets are used on all models with each set of breaker points controlling ignition for one cylinder.

Breaker point gap should be 0.020 inch for each set of points except as noted in CONDENSED SERVICE DATA, and can be adjusted after the flywheel is removed. Both sets of points should be adjusted exactly alike. Place a mark on the high point of the breaker cam and set breaker point gap for both sets of breaker points with the mark aligned with the breaker point rub block.

The tapered bore in flywheel and tapered end of crankshaft must be clean, dry and smooth before installing flywheel. Tighten flywheel nut to 45 ft.-lbs.

Spark plug electrode gap on all models should be 0.030 inch. Recommended spark plug is Champion L4J.

COOLING SYSTEM

WATER PUMP. All motors are equipped with a rubber impeller type water pump. When cooling system problems are encountered, first check the water inlet for plugging or partial stoppage, then if not corrected, remove the lower unit gearcase and check the condi-

Fig. C7-11—Wiring schematic for models with battery ignition.

1. Alternator
2. Breaker plate
3. Neutral interlock switch
4. Top ignition coil
5. Bottom ignition coil
6. Starter relay
7. Choke solenoid
8. Circuit breaker
9. Electric starter motor
10. Rectifier
B. Black
BL. Blue
G. Green
O. Orange
P. Purple
R. Red
W. White
Y. Yellow

POWER HEAD

R&R AND OVERHAUL. To remove the power head, mount the outboard motor on a stand and remove the engine cove. Disconnect choke rod from carburetor. Detach magneto control shaft gear (13–Fig. C7-13) from magneto control shaft (13–Fig. C7-14) on manual start models. Remove bushing (12) and detach magneto control shaft from control shaft link (31–Fig. C7-17). Loosen set screw in collar (3–Fig. C7-14) and

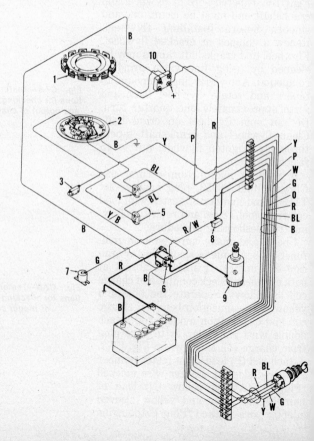

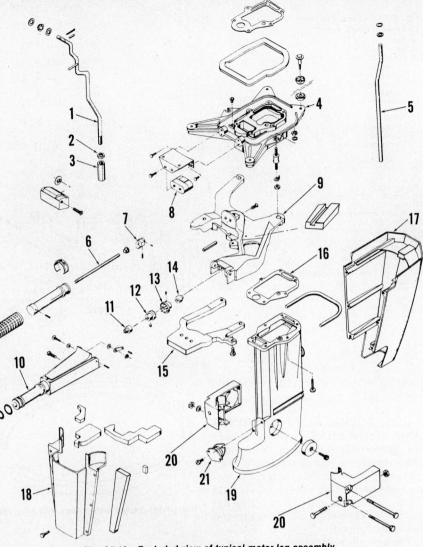

Fig. C7-13—Exploded view of typical motor leg assembly.

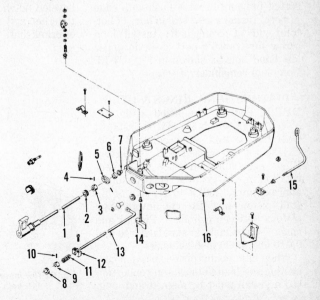

Fig. C7-15—Cylinder head cap screws should be tightened in the sequence shown above.

1. Uppper shift rod
2. Locknut
3. Coupler
4. Spacer plate
5. Water tube
6. Steering handle shaft
7. Throttle stop
8. Upper thrust mount
9. Kingpin plate
10. Steering handle
11. Bushing
12. Steering handle gear
13. Magneto control shaft gear
14. Bushing
15. Carrying handle
16. Exhaust gasket
17. Rear motor leg cover
18. Front motor leg cover
19. Motor leg
20. Lower shock mount cover
21. Lower thrust pad

and remove starter and ignition assemblies from upper end of crankshaft. Unbolt and remove upper bearing cage and cylinder head. Remove reed valve assembly and transfer port cover. Unscrew cylinder to crankcase screws (two screws are in reed cavity) and using a suitable pry point separate cylinder and crankcase. Do not pry at machined mating surfaces between cylinder and crankcase.

Crankshaft, pistons and bearings are now accessible for removal and overhaul as outlined in the appropriate following paragraphs. Assemble as outlined in the ASSEMBLY paragraph.

ASSEMBLY. When reassembling, make sure all joint and gasket surfaces are clean, free from nicks and burrs,

remove gear shift knob and shaft (1) on manual start models. On electric start models, disconnect battery leads, red lead from upper terminal of starter relay and black lead from crankcase. On all models, unscrew nut retaining shift lever (20–Fig. C7-17) and detach gear shift linkage from lever. Remove lower shock mount covers, lower thrust pad (21–Fig. C7-13) at front of motor leg and shock and lower nuts of the two studs between the kingpin plate (9) and spacer plate (4). Unscrew motor leg cover bolts and remove rear motor leg cover. Engage reverse lock and pull motor back enough to allow removal of front motor leg cover. Unscrew power head bolts and remove power head.

To disassemble power head, remove seal in bore of bottom end of crankshaft

Fig. C7-14—Exploded view of manual start model support plate assembly.

1. Gear shift knob & shaft
2. Grommet
3. Collar
4. Set screw
5. Gear shift lever
6. Spacer
7. Bushing
8. Grommet
9. Retainer
10. Set screw
11. Spring
12. Bushing
13. Magneto control shaft
14. Latch pin
15. Choke rod
16. Support plate

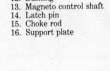

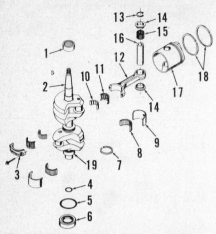

Fig. C7-16—Exploded view of crankshaft assembly.

1. Roller bearing
2. Crankshaft
3. Rod cap
4. Seal
5. "O" ring
6. Seal
7. Seal ring
8. Bearing rollers
9. Bearing liner
10. Bearing rollers
11. Bearing cage
12. Connecting rod
13. Snap ring
14. Spacer
15. Needle bearing
16. Piston pin
17. Piston
18. Piston rings
19. Ball bearing

Fig. C7-17—Exploded view of cylinder block assembly.

1. Seal
2. Bearing cage
3. Gasket
4. Stator ring
5. Crankcase seal
6. Exhaust cover
7. Gasket
8. Exhaust plate
9. Gasket
10. Cylinder block
11. Lower crankcase
12. Dowel pin
13. Thermostat cover
14. Plug
15. Cylinder head
16. Gasket
17. Drain hose
18. Gasket
19. Transfer port cover
20. Gear shift lever
21. Starter interlock rod
22. Bushing retainer
23. Interlock lever pin
24. Bushing
25. Shift interlock lever
26. Shift interlock rod
27. Throttle cam
28. Throttle link
29. Magneto stator link
30. Magneto control lever
31. Magneto control link

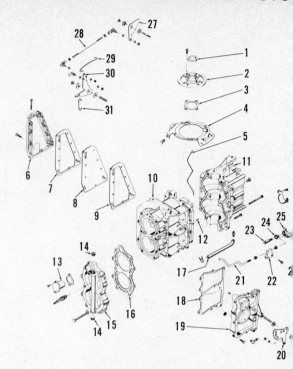

warped surfaces or hardened cement or carbon. The crankcase and inlet manifold must be completely sealed against both vacuum and pressure. Exhaust manifold and cylinder head must be sealed against both vacuum and pressure. Exhaust manifold and cylinder head must be sealed against water leakage and pressure. Mating surfaces of exhaust areas between power head and motor leg must form a tight seal.

Sparingly apply a coating of sealant to mating surfaces of cylinder and crankcase. Tighten crankcase screws in a spiral pattern starting with center screws. Tighten cylinder head screws in sequence shown in Fig. C7-15. Install seal (6–Fig. C7-16) with "O" ring end inserted first until seal is flush with edge of bore. Install a new seal in bore of bottom end of crankshaft. Install long screw for transfer port cover in upper left hand hole as shown in Fig. C7-18. Complete remainder of assembly.

PISTONS, PINS, RINGS & CYLINDERS. Pistons are fitted with two piston rings which should be installed with the beveled inner edge (B–Fig. C7-19) toward closed end of piston. Rings are pinned in place to prevent rotation in ring grooves. Heat piston to approximately 200°F to remove or install piston pin. Do not interchange pistons between cylinders. Pistons and rings are available in standard size and 0.010 and 0.030 inch oversizes.

When assembling piston, pin and connecting rod, match marks on connecting rod and cap must be aligned and long,

tapering side of piston must be towards exhaust port.

CONNECTING RODS, BEARINGS AND CRANKSHAFT. Before detaching connecting rods from crankshaft, mark connecting rod and cap for correct reassembly to each other and in the correct cylinder. The needle rollers and cages at crankpin end of connecting rod should be kept with the assembly and not interchanged.

The bearing rollers and cages used in the connecting rods and the rollers and liners in the center main bearing are available only as a set for each bearing. The complete assembly should be installed whenever renewal is indicated. Connecting rod bearing cages have beveled notches which must be installed together and toward top (flywheel) end of crankshaft. Match marks on connect-

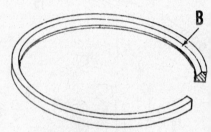

Fig. C7-19—Install piston rings with bevel (B) top.

ing rod and cap must be on same side a shown in Fig. C7-20. Connecting rod i fractured to provide an uneven surfac between rod and cap. Be sure rod an cap are properly meshed before tighter ing rod screws.

Inspect condition of seal ring (7–Fig C7-16) and carefully install ring i crankshaft groove. Seal ring (7) mus prevent leakage between cylinders and defective seal will result in poor engin performance.

Fig. C7-18—Install long cap screw (L) in upper left hole of transfer port cover.

Fig. C7-20—Match marks on connecting rod and rod cap must be on same side and toward flywheel end of crankshaft.

Illustrations Courtesy Ch

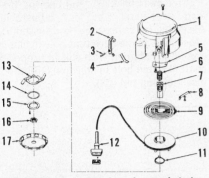

Fig. C7-21—Exploded view of manual starter.

1. Starter housing
2. Interlock lever
3. Pin
4. Spring
5. Plate
6. Spring
7. Rope guide
8. Housing liner
9. Rewind spring
10. Rope & pulley
11. Spring
12. Handle
13. Pawl plate
14. Shims
15. Retainer
16. Flywheel nut
17. Starter cup

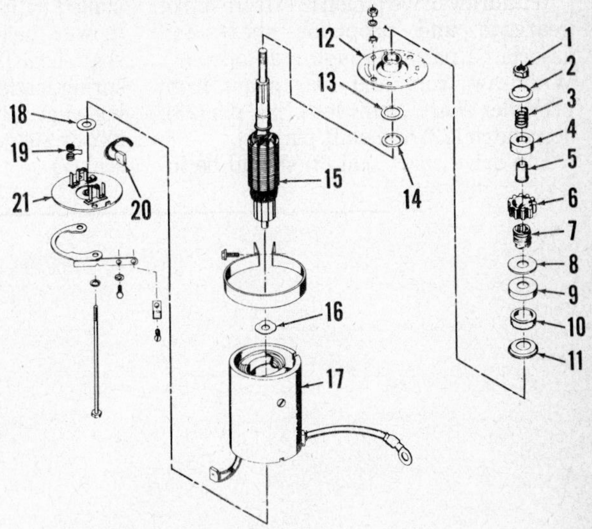

Fig. C7-22—Exploded view of electric starter motor.

1. Nut
2. Stop cup
3. Spring
4. Pinion cup
5. Sleeve
6. Pinion
7. Screw shaft
8. Washer
9. Cushion cup
10. Cushion
11. Thrust cup
12. End plate
13. Thrust washer
14. Shim
15. Armature
16. Thrust washer
17. Housing
18. Thrust washer
19. Spring
20. Brushes
21. Brush plate

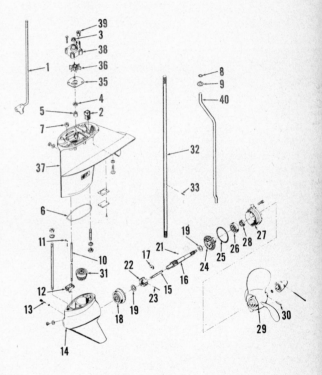

Fig. C7-24—Exploded view of lower unit.

1. Shift rod
2. Water screen
3. Drive shaft seal
4. Seal
5. Bushing
6. Gasket
7. Seal
8. Seal
9. Washer
10. Shift rod
11. Pin
12. Shift arm
13. Pivot pin
14. Gearcase
15. Shift pin
16. Propeller shaft
17. Yoke
18. Front gear & bushing
19. Thrust washer
21. Ball
22. Dog clutch
23. Spring pin
24. Rear gear
25. Cage seal
26. Bearing
27. Bearing cage
28. Seal
29. Propeller
30. Propeller pin
31. Drive pinion & bearing
32. Drive shaft
33. Water pump drive pin
35. Back plate
36. Impeller
37. Drive shaft housing
38. Pump body
39. Grommet
40. Water tube

Before installing crankshaft in crankcase, install bearing liner (9) over dowel pin and place fourteen bearing rollers (8) in liner with a suitable grease to hold rollers in place. Install crankshaft and position remaining sixteen bearing rollers around crank journal. Place remaining bearing liner over rollers so that liner ends dovetail. Upper main bearing (1) should stand ⅛ inch higher than surface of crankcase.

MANUAL STARTER

Refer to Fig. C7-21 for an exploded view of manual starter. To disassemble starter, remove starter from engine, unscrew retainer (15) screws and remove retainer, shims (14), pawl plate (13) and spring (11). Remove rope handle, press interlock lever and allow rope to rewind into starter housing. Press interlock lever and remove rope and pulley (10). If necessary, remove rewind spring.

Install rewind spring in housing with spring wound in counterclockwise direction from outer end of spring. Wind rope on pulley in counterclockwise direction as viewed with pulley in housing. Insert rope through slot of pulley with about nine inches of rope extending from slot. Install rope pulley in housing and place pawl spring (11) on rope pulley with ends pointing up. Install pawl plate (13) with pawl side toward pulley and engage slots with pawl spring (11) ends. Install three shims (0.006, 0.007 and 0.010 inch) and retainer (15). Turn rope pulley approximately two turns counterclockwise to preload rewind spring and pass end of rope through rope guide of starter housing. Attach rope handle and pull rope until it is fully extended. It should still be possible to rotate rope pulley a slight amount after rope is extended to prevent damage to rewind spring.

PROPELLER

Propellers for normal use have three blades and are equipped with a thrust pin to prevent damage. Various pitch propellers are available and should be selected to provide full throttle operation within the recommended limits of 4500-5500 rpm on models prior to 1979 and 4250-5250 rpm on 1979 and later models. Propellers other than those designed for the motor should not be used.

LOWER UNIT

R&R AND OVERHAUL. To remove the lower unit, refer to WATER PUMP section. Drain the gearcase and secure gearcase skeg in a vise. Disassemble and remove the drive shaft and water pump assembly. Remove propeller nut, pin (30 – Fig. C7-24) and propeller (29). Carefully clean exposed end of propeller shaft and remove the two screws securing propeller shaft bearing cage (27) to gearcase. Rotate the bearing cage approximately ½-turn until tabs are accessible from the sides; then using a soft hammer, gently tap the bearing cage rearward out of gearcase. Remove the gearcase rear retaining stud nut by working through propeller shaft opening. Unscrew gearcase front retaining stud nut, then lift off drive shaft housing (37).

Withdraw drive pinion (31) from top of gearcase and propeller shaft and associated parts through rear opening. Withdraw front and rear gears from propeller shaft. Remove spring pin (23), dog clutch (22) and shift pin (15).

The drive shaft seal (3) should be in-stalled with spring loaded lip toward top (power head). Rubber coated side of shaft seal (28) should be installed with spring loaded lip toward outside of bear-ing cage (27). Sparingly apply Loctite 222 or 262 to outer diameter of shift rod seal (7).

Drive gear backlash and bearing pre-load are fixed and not adjustable. Assemble by reversing the disassembly procedure. Make sure that hole in clutch dog (22) is aligned with slot in propeller shaft (16) and hole in shift pin (15); then, insert spring pin (23).

CHRYSLER
35, 45, 50 AND 55 HP

Year Produced	35 HP	45 HP	50 HP	55 HP
1969	35*†	45*†	.....	55*†
1970	35*§	45*§	.....	55*§
1971	35*§	45*§	.....	55*§
1972	35*§	45*§	.....	55*§
1973	35*§	45*§	.....	55*§
1974	35*§	45*§	.....	55*§
1975	35*§	45*§	.....	55*§
1976	.....	45*§	.....	.....
1977	.....	45*§	.....	.....
1978	.....	45*§	.....	.....
1979	35*§	45*§	.....	.....
1980	35*§	45*§	.....	.....
1981	35*§	45*§	50*§	.....
1982	.....	45*§	50*§	.....
1983	.....	45*§	50*§	.....
1984	.....	45*§	50*§	.....

*Variation Code:
0 – Standard shaft, manual starter.
1 – Long shaft, manual starter.
2 – Standard shaft, manual starter, with tiller.
3 – Long shaft, manual starter, with tiller.
4 – Standard shaft, electric starter.
5 – Long shaft, electric starter.

6 – Standard shaft, electric starter, with alternator.
7 – Long shaft, electric starter, with alternator.
8 – Same as number 6 except with "Magnapower" ignition.
9 – Same as number 7 except with "Magnapower" ignition.

†Production Code Before 1970:
1, 3 & 5 – USA models.
2, 4 & 6 – Canada models.

§Production Code Beginning in 1970: HA, HB, HC, HD, HE, HF, HG, HH, HJ, HK, HL, HM & HN – USA models. BA, BB, BC, BD, BE, BF, BG, BH, BJ, BK, BL & BN – Canada models.

CONDENSED SERVICE DATA

TUNE-UP	35 HP	45 HP	50 HP	55 HP
Hp/rpm	35/4750	45/5000	50/5000	55/5250
Bore – Inches	3	3⅛	3-3/16	3-3/16
Stroke – Inches	2.54	2.75	2.80	2.80
Number of Cylinders	2	2	2	2
Displacement – Cu. In.	35.9	42.18	44.7	44.7
Compression at Cranking Speed (Average)	95-105 psi	115-125 psi	135-150 psi	145-155 psi
Spark Plug:				
Champion (1969-1977)	L4J	L4J*	.....	L4J*
(1978-1981)	L4J	UL4J	UL4J	.....
(1982-1984)	.....	UL81J	UL4J	.....
Electrode Gap – In.	0.030	0.030	.....	0.030
Ignition:				
Point Gap – In.	0.020§	0.020§	0.015	0.020§
Timing	See Text	See Text	See Text	See Text
Carburetor:				
Make	Tillotson	Tillotson	Tillotson	Tillotson
Model	WB	WB	WB	WB
Fuel:Oil Ratio	**50:1	**50:1	**50:1	**50:1

*A UL-18V Champion spark plug is used on models with "Magnapower" capacitor discharge ignition.
**Use 25:1 fuel:oil ratio for first 10 hours and for severe service.
§Breaker point gap should be 0.015 inch on models with battery ignition or "Magnapower" ignition.

SIZES—CLEARANCES

	35 HP	45 HP	50 HP	55 HP
Piston Ring End Gap		0.006-0.016 in.		0.008-0.015 in.
Piston Ring Groove Width		0.0645-0.0655 in.		
Piston to Cylinder Clearance	0.005 in.	0.0038-0.007 in.	0.005-0.007 in.	0.005 in.
Piston Pin:				
Diameter		0.6875-0.68765 in.		
Clearance (Rod)		Needle Bearing		
Clearance (Piston)		0.00025 in. tight to 0.0002 in. loose		
Crankshaft Journal Diameters:				
Upper Main Bearing		1.1815-1.1820 in.		.....
Center Main Bearing		1.1388-1.1392 in.		.....
Lower Main Bearing		1.1245-1.1250 in.		.....
Crankpin		1.1391-1.1395 in.		.....

TIGHTENING TORQUES
(All Values in Inch-Pounds Unless Noted)

	35 HP	45 HP	50 HP	55 HP
Connecting Rod (1969-1979)	165-175	165-175	.....	165-175
(1980-1984)	180-190	180-190	180-190	.....
Cylinder Head	270***	270***	270***	270***
Flywheel Nut	80 Ft.-Lbs.	80 Ft.-Lbs.	80 Ft.-Lbs.	80 Ft.-Lbs.
Main Bearing Bolts	270	270	270	270
Standard Screws:				
6-32	9	9	9	9
10-24	30	30	30	30
10-32	35	35	35	35
12-24	45	45	45	45
¼-20	70	70	70	70
5/16-18	160	160	160	160
⅜-16	270	270	270	270

***Refer to text for tightening cylinder head screws.

LUBRICATION

The power head is lubricated by oil mixed with the fuel. One-third (⅓) pint of two-cycle or Outboard Motor Oil should be mixed with each gallon of gasoline. The amount of oil in the fuel may be reduced after the first 10 hours of operation (motor is broken in), provided the highest quality SAE 30 Outboard Motor Oil is used and motor is subjected to normal service only. The minimum recommended fuel-oil ratio is 50:1, or half the normally recommended amount of oil. If the amount of oil is reduced, fuel and oil must be thoroughly mixed and idle mixture carefully adjusted to make sure any error is on the "Rich" side.

Manufacturer recommends using no-lead automotive gasoline in motors with less than 55 hp although regular or premium gasoline with octane rating of 85 or greater may also be used. Regular or premium automotive gasoline with octane rating of 85 or greater must be used in motors with more than 54 hp.

The lower unit gears and bearings are lubricated by oil contained in the gearcase. A non-corrosive, leaded, Extreme Pressure SAE 90 Gear Oil, such as "Chrysler Special Purpose Gear Lube" should be used. DO NOT use a hypoid type lubricant. The gearcase should be drained and refilled every 100 hours or once each year, and fluid maintained at the level of upper (vent) plug opening.

To fill the gearcase, position motor in an upright position and fill through lower plug hole on starboard side of gearcase until lubricant reaches level of upper vent plug opening. Reinstall and tighten both plugs, using new gaskets if necessary, to assure a water tight seal.

FUEL SYSTEM

CARBURETOR. Tillotson type WB carburetors are used. Refer to Fig. C8-1. Normal initial setting is one turn open for idle mixture adjustment needle (12). Fixed jet (3) controls high speed mixture. The carburetor model number is stamped on the mounting flange. Float level is 13/32 inch from float to gasket surface (Fig. C8-2). Care must be used in selecting the high speed fixed jet (3). A fixed jet which is too small will result in a lean mixture and possible damage to power head. Jet may be identified by the diameter (in thousandths of an inch) stamped on the visible end of an installed jet. Optional jets are available which will improve performance when

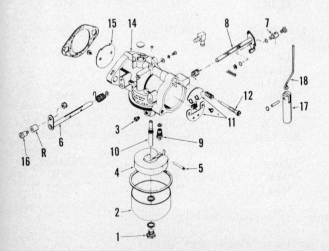

Fig. C8-1 — Exploded view of Tillotson WB type carburetor.

R. Roller
1. Bowl retaining screw
2. Fuel bowl
3. High speed jet
4. Float
5. Float pivot shaft
6. Throttle shaft
7. Connector
8. Choke shaft
9. Inlet needle and seat
10. Main nozzle
11. Choke plate
12. Idle mixture needle
14. Throttle body
15. Throttle plate
16. Eccentric screw
17. Choke solenoid plunger
18. Rod

Illustrations Courtesy Chrysler

motor is used in high-altitude locations;
optional jet sizes and recommended
altitudes are as follows:

35 HP (WB-3A)

Altitude	Jet Size	Part Number
Standard	0.084	014302

35 HP (WB-3C)

Altitude	Jet Size	Part Number
Sea Level-1250 ft.	0.0785	014306
1250-3750 ft.	0.070	013430
3750-6250 ft.	0.068	013967
6250-8250 ft.	0.062	014187

35 HP (WB-12A)

Altitude	Jet Size	Part Number
Sea Level-1250 ft.	0.074	014303
1250-3750 ft.	0.072	015026
3750-6250 ft.	0.070	013430
6250-8250 ft.	0.068	013967

35 HP (WB-12B)

Altitude	Jet Size	Part Number
Sea Level-1250 ft.	0.074	014303
1250-3750 ft.	0.072	015026
3750-6250 ft.	0.070	013430
6250-8250 ft.	0.068	013967

35 HP (WB-17A)

Altitude	Jet Size	Part Number
Sea Level-1250 ft.	0.090	015406
1250-3750 ft.	0.088	013193
3750-6250 ft.	0.086	013949
6250-8250 ft.	0.084	014302

35 HP (WB-17A with "X" stamped on mount flange)

Altitude	Jet Size	Part Number
Standard	0.098	014152

35 HP (WB-17C)

Altitude	Jet Size	Part Number
Sea Level-1250 ft.	0.090	015406
1250-3750 ft.	0.088	013193
3750-6250 ft.	0.086	013949
6250-8250 ft.	0.084	014302

45 HP (WB-4A)

Altitude	Jet Size	Part Number
Standard	0.096	012947

45 HP (WB-4C)

Altitude	Jet Size	Part Number
Sea Level-1250 ft.	0.086	013949
1250-3750 ft.	0.0785	014306
3750-6250 ft.	0.074	014303
6250-8250 ft.	0.068	013967

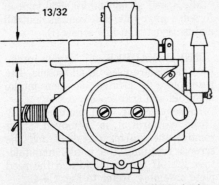

Fig. C8-2 — Correct float level is 13/32 inch when measured as shown between float and gasket surface.

45 HP (WB-11A & WB-11B)

Altitude	Jet Size	Part Number
Sea Level-1250 ft.	0.082	014109
1250-3750 ft.	0.080	013194
3750-6250 ft.	0.0785	014306
6250-8250 ft.	0.076	013191

45 HP (WB-16A)

Altitude	Jet Size	Part Number
Sea Level-1250 ft.	0.086	013949
1250-3750 ft.	0.084	014302
3750-6250 ft.	0.082	014109
6250-8250 ft.	0.080	013194

45 HP (WB-16A with "X" stamped on mount flange)

Altitude	Jet Size	Part Number
Standard	0.088	013193

45 HP (WB-16C)

Altitude	Jet Size	Part Number
Sea Level-1250 ft.	0.090	015406
1250-3750 ft.	0.088	013193
3750-6250 ft.	0.086	013949
6250-8250 ft.	0.084	014302

45 & 50 HP (WB-16D)

Altitude	Jet Size	Part Number
Sea Level-1250 ft.	0.084	014302
1250-3750 ft.	0.082	014109
3750-6250 ft.	0.080	013194
6250-8250 ft.	0.078	014306

55 HP (WB-5A)

Altitude	Jet Size	Part Number
Standard	0.089	013367

55 HP (WB-5B)

Altitude	Jet Size	Part Number
Sea Level-1250 ft.	0.092	014152
1250-3750 ft.	0.084	014302
3750-6250 ft.	0.076	013191
6250-8250 ft.	0.074	014303

55 HP (WB-7A & WB-7B)

Altitude	Jet Size	Part Number
Sea Level-1250 ft.	0.086	013949
1250-3750 ft.	0.084	014302
3750-6250 ft.	0.082	014109
6250-8250 ft.	0.080	013194

55 HP (WB-15A)

Altitude	Jet Size	Part Number
Sea Level-1250 ft.	0.088	013193
1250-3750 ft.	0.086	013949
3750-6250 ft.	0.084	014302
6250-8250 ft.	0.082	014109

55 HP (WB-15A with "X" stamped on mount flange)

Altitude	Jet Size	Part Number
Standard	0.090	015406

55 HP (WB-15C)

Altitude	Jet Size	Part Number
Sea Level-1250 ft.	0.0937	014191
1250-3750 ft.	0.092	014109
3750-6250 ft.	0.090	015406
6250-8250 ft.	0.088	013193

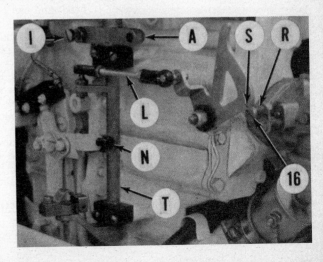

Fig. C8-3 — Throttle linkage typical of all models. Refer to text for method of checking and adjusting.

A. High speed stop
I. Idle stop
L. Throttle link
N. Neutral stop screw
R. Roller
S. Scribed line
T. Tower shaft
16. Eccentric screw

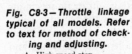

Illustrations Courtesy Chrysler

55 HP (WB-27A)

Altitude	Jet Size	Part Number
Sea Level-1250 ft.	0.066	014188
1250-3750 ft.	0.064	014108
3750-6250 ft.	0.062	014187
6250-8250 ft.	0.060	014186

NOTE: Be sure that proper jet is installed before motor is used at a lower altitude.

Choke is properly adjusted when choke plate (11 – Fig. C8-1) is 0.010-0.040 inch open when choke is engaged. On electric choke models, bottom plunger (17) in solenoid and adjust choke plunger rod (18) in connector (7) as required. On manual choke models, pull choke knob and adjust cable in connector at carburetor as required. On all models, make certain choke plate is free and returns to full open position.

SPEED CONTROL LINKAGE. On all models, ignition timing advance and throttle opening must be synchronized so that throttle is opened as timing is advanced.

To synchronize the linkage, first make certain that ignition timing is correctly set as outlined in IGNITION TIMING paragraph. Shift to forward gear and disconnect link (L – Fig. C8-3) from tower shaft (T). With carburetor throttle closed, turn the eccentric screw (16) until roller (R) is exactly centered over the scribed line (S). Move the tower shaft (T) to full advance position and move the throttle cam until carburetor throttle is completely open. Vary the length of link (L) until the ball joint connector will just attach. Snap the ball joint connector onto ball stud and check maximum speed in neutral. Maximum rpm in neutral is approximately 1800 rpm and on late models, is adjusted at neutral stop screw (N). Early models have a non-adjustable neutral stop linkage.

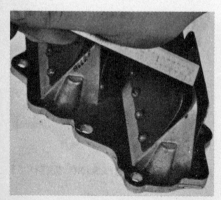

Fig. C8-4 — Reed stop setting should be 9/32 inch when measured as shown. Holes in stops and petals are elongated and should be positioned as shown by arrows for maximum overlap.

Idle speed should be 700-800 rpm in forward gear (800-900 rpm in neutral) and is adjusted at idle screw (I).

REED VALVES. "V" type intake reed valves are used on all models. The reed plate is located between intake manifold and crankcase.

To remove the reed plate assembly after carburetor is removed, first remove the starter assembly and the screws retaining the intake manifold; then lift off the manifold and the reed plate assembly. Refer to Fig. C8-4.

Reed valve must be smooth and even with no sharp bends or broken reeds. Assembled reeds may stand open a maximum of 0.010 inch at tip end. Check seating visually.

Reed stop setting should be 9/32-inch when measured as shown in Fig. C8-4. Renew reeds if petals are broken, cracked, warped or bent. Never attempt to bend a reed petal in an effort to improve performance; nor attempt to straighten a damaged reed. Never install a bent or damaged reed. Seating surface of reed plate should be smooth and flat. When installing reed petals and stops, proceed as follows: Install reed petals, stop, and the four retaining screws leaving screws loose. Slide the reed petals as far as possible toward mounting flange of reed plate and reed stops out toward tip of "Vee" as far as possible as indicated by arrows in Fig. C8-4. Position reed petals and reed stops as outlined to provide maximum overlap; then, tighten the retaining screws.

PUDDLE DRAIN VALVES. All models are equipped with a puddle drain system designed to remove any liquid fuel or oil which might build up in the crankcase; thus providing smoother operation at all speeds and lessening the possibility of spark plug fouling during slow speed operation.

The puddle drain valve housing is located on the starboard side of power head, and can be removed as shown in Fig. C8-5. The reed-type puddle drain valve petals must seat lightly and evenly against valve plate. Reed stops should be adjusted to 0.017-0.023 inch clearance at the tip. Blow out drain passages with compressed air while housing is off.

Later models are equipped with a recirculating puddle drain system. Fluid accumulated in puddle drain during slow speed operation is reintroduced to the cylinders once engine is returned to cruising speed. Inspect hoses and check valves when unit is disassembled.

FUEL PUMP. All models are equipped with a diaphragm type fuel pump which is actuated by pressure and

Fig. C8-5 — View of puddle drain housing removed.

vacuum pulsations from both crankcases as shown in Fig. C8-6. The two stages operate alternately as shown.

NOTE: Either stage operating independently may permit the motor to run, but not at peak performance.

Most fuel pump service can be performed without removing the assembly from power head. Disconnect the pulse hoses and remove the retaining cap screws; then lift off the pump cover and diaphragm. Remove the sediment bowl and strainer. First stage inlet check valve can be driven out from below, using a ½-inch diameter drift. First stage outlet check valve can be lifted out after removing the retaining screws. The check valves must be installed to permit fuel to flow in the proper direction as shown. To renew the second stage outlet check valve, it is first necessary to remove pump body from power head, remove outlet fuel elbow and drive the check valve out from below. Check valve will be damaged, and a new unit must be

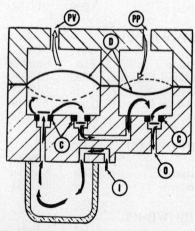

Fig. C8-6 — Cross sectional view of the two stage fuel pump. Broken lines indicate position of diaphragm when pulse pressure and vacuum are reversed.

C. Check valves
D. Diaphragm
I. Fuel inlet
O. Fuel outlet
PP. Pulse pressure
PV. Pulse vacuum

Fig. C8-7 — Special tool is available for positioning piston at correct timing position. Refer to text for proper tool usage.

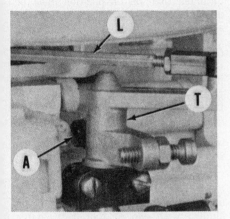

Fig. C8-8 — Full advance stop (A) on tower shaft (T) should contact housing before adjusting link (L) when setting ignition timing.

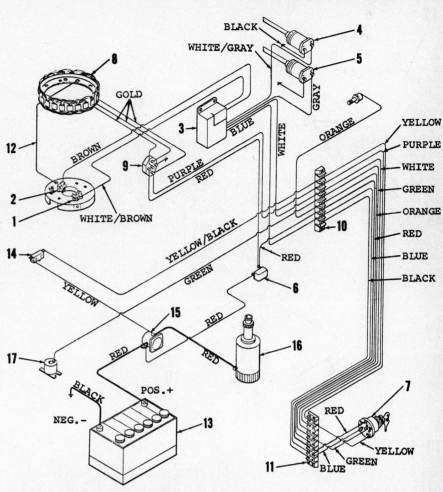

Fig. C8-9 — Wiring diagram for 45 and 55 hp motors with "Magnapower" ignition system. Yellow wires are for starting system, purple for charging, white for tachometer, green for choke, orange for heat indicator, red for battery positive, blue for ignition and black for ground. Note wiring diagram for later model rectifier in Fig. C8-12.

1. Breaker points for top cylinder
2. Breaker points for bottom cylinder
3. Ignition capacitor discharge module
4. Coil for top cylinder
5. Coil for bottom cylinder
6. Circuit breaker
7. Ignition and start switch
8. Alternator stator
9. Rectifier
10. Terminal block at motor
11. Terminal block at dashboard
12. Alternator ground
13. Battery
14. Neutral interlock switch
15. Starter solenoid
16. Starter motor
17. Choke solenoid

installed. DO NOT remove the valve unless renewal is indicated. Install new valve carefully, using an 11/16-inch diameter punch.

Renew the diaphragm if cracked, torn, or badly distorted. Install check valves carefully to prevent damage, and reassemble by reversing the disassembly procedure.

IGNITION SYSTEM

Thirty-five horsepower motors may be equipped with a magneto ignition or a battery ignition with a flywheel mounted alternator. Forty-five and fifty-five horsepower models may be equipped with magneto ignition, battery ignition with a flywheel mounted alternator or "Magnapower" capacitor discharge ignition. Fifty horsepower models are equipped with battery ignition and flywheel mounted alternator only. Refer to the appropriate following paragraphs after determining type of ignition used.

All Models

R&R FLYWHEEL. A special puller (Chrysler Part Number T-8948-1) is used to remove the flywheel on late model units. Pulling bosses are provided on the flywheel for puller installation.

NOTE: Models with alternators must have the three screws that secure the emergency starter collar removed, as well as the emergency starter collar. Make certain that aligning marks on flywheel and emergency starter collar are matched when reassembling.

Flywheels may be removed from models without puller bosses by using a special knockout nut (Chrysler Part Number T-2910). Install the tool and apply upward pressure to rim of flywheel, then bump the tool sharply with a hammer to loosen flywheel from tapered portion of crankshaft.

The manufacturer recommends that mating surfaces of flywheel and crankshaft be lapped before flywheel is reinstalled. If evidence of working exists proceed as follows:

Remove the flywheel key and apply a light coating of valve grinding or lapping compound to tapered portion of crankshaft. Install the flywheel without the key or crankshaft nut and rotate flywheel gently back and forth about ¼-turn. Move flywheel 90° and repeat the operation. Lift off the flywheel, wipe off excess lapping compound and carefully examine crankshaft. A minimum of 90% surface contact should be indicated by the polished surface; continue lapping only if insufficient contact is evident. Thoroughly clean the crankshaft and flywheel bore to remove all traces of lapping compound, then clean both surfaces with a non-oily solvent.

Reinstall crankshaft key and flywheel, then tighten flywheel nut to torque indicated in CONDENSED SERVICE DATA table.

POINT ADJUSTMENT. Breaker point gap should be 0.020 inch for models with magneto ignition and 0.015

magneto ignition models when setting piston position with Chrysler special tool T-8938 or 32° BTDC on all other models when setting piston position with Chrysler special tool T-2937-1. When setting piston position with a dial indicator, the equivalent reading should be 0.210 in. BTDC on 35 and 45 hp magneto ignition models or 0.281 in. BTDC on all other models. To adjust ignition timing, breaker point gap must first be carefully adjusted as previously outlined, then piston position must be accurately determined using a Chrysler special tool or a dial indicator as follows:

To determine piston position using Chrysler special tool (Fig. C8-7), thread the tool body into top spark plug opening. Insert the gage rod into tool body, rotate the crankshaft and carefully position top piston at exactly TDC.

NOTE: Gage rod should be installed with the double scribed line end or the 25-55 HP marked end out.

With the top piston at TDC, thread timing tool body in or out as necessary until the inner scribed line on gage rod is aligned with end of tool body. After gage body is correctly positioned, turn the crankshaft clockwise almost one complete revolution while applying pressure to end of gage rod. Stop the crankshaft just as the first (outer) scribed line on rod aligns with tool body. The crankshaft should be at correct position BTDC for maximum ignition advance timing.

To determine piston position using a dial indicator, insert dial indicator into top spark plug opening, then rotate crankshaft and carefully position piston at exactly TDC. Zero the dial indicator, then turn crankshaft clockwise almost one complete revolution stopping crankshaft just as dial indicator reads desired specification. The crankshaft should be at correct position BTDC for maximum ignition advance timing.

With the crankshaft correctly positioned and breaker point gap properly adjusted, connect one lead from timing test light (with battery) or ohmmeter to the breaker point terminal of number one cylinder and ground other test lead to motor. On magneto models, it may be necessary to disconnect coil ground and condenser and prevent them from contacting engine ground. Move the speed control from slow toward fast (maximum advance) speed position and observe the test light or ohmmeter. The breaker points should just open (test light goes off or ohmmeter registers infinite resistance) when the speed control reaches maximum ignition advance. If the breaker points do not open, shorten rod (L—Fig. C8-8) or if breaker points open too soon, lengthen rod (L).

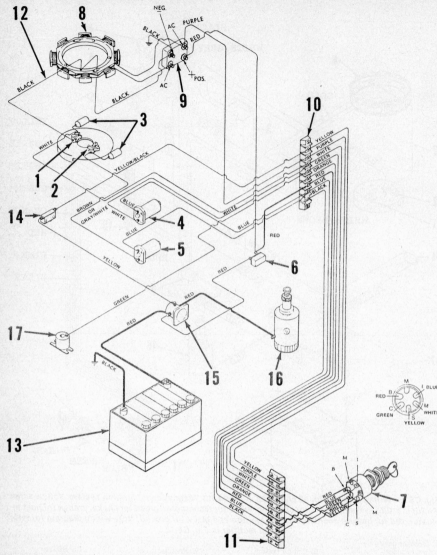

Fig. C8-10—Wiring diagram for models equipped with battery ignition and flywheel mounted alternator.

1. Breaker points for top cylinder
2. Breaker points for bottom cylinder
3. Condensers
4. Coil for top cylinder
5. Coil for bottom cylinder
6. Circuit breaker
7. Ignition and start switch
8. Alternator stator
9. Rectifier
10. Terminal block at motor
11. Terminal block at dashboard
12. Alternator ground
13. Battery
14. Neutral interlock switch
15. Starter solenoid
16. Starter motor
17. Choke solenoid

inch for all other models. Both sets of points must be adjusted as nearly alike as possible.

NOTE: Point gap variation of 0.0015 inch will change ignition timing one degree.

To adjust the points, first remove the flywheel as previously outlined. Turn crankshaft clockwise until the rub block on one set of points is resting on high point of breaker cam approximately 10° from first point of maximum opening. Mark the exact location of rub block contact for use in adjusting the other set of points. Loosen breaker point mounting screws and adjust point gap until a

slight drag exists using a 0.020 inch feeler gage for models with magneto ignition and 0.015 inch feeler gage for all other models.

Turn crankshaft until the previously installed mark on breaker cam is aligned with the rub block on the other set of points and adjust the other set of points in the same manner.

NOTE: If mid-range of breaker plate movement is used, final positioning can be made by moving the speed control handle to correctly position the rub block at the same point of breaker cam.

IGNITION TIMING. Crankshaft timing should be 28° BTDC on 35 and 45 hp

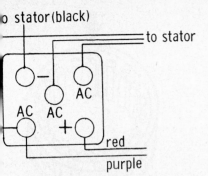

Fig. C8-11 — Wiring diagram for rectifier used with three-phase alternator.

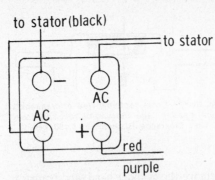

Fig. C8-12 — Wiring diagram for rectifier used on later models.

Magnapower Models

TROUBLESHOOTING. Use only approved procedures when testing to prevent damage to components. The fuel system should be checked to make certain that faulty running is not caused by incorrect fuel mixture or contaminated fuel.

CHECKING FOR SPARK. Remove the spark plugs and attach spark plug leads to a spark gap tester. With all wiring attached, attempt to start motor using the electric starter.

NOTE: Two conventional spark plugs (such as Champion L4J) with ground electrodes removed can be used to check for spark. Make certain that test plug shell is grounded against power head when checking.

If good regular spark occurs at tester (or test plugs), check fuel system and spark plugs. Also, make certain that wires from breaker points (1 & 2 – Fig. C8-9) to CD ignition module (3), from CD ignition module to ignition coils (4 and 5) and from coils to spark plugs are correct to provide spark to the proper cylinder.

If spark does not occur at tester (or test plugs), make certain that the small black wires on ignition coils (4 and 5) are attached to the negative (–) terminals and are securely grounded to the coil clamp screws. Also check continuity of the spark plug wires. If test plugs still do not spark, proceed with following checks.

WIRING. Engine missing, surging or failure to start can be caused by loose connections, corroded connections or short circuits. Electrical system components may also be damaged by faulty connections or short circuits.

Attach one lead of voltmeter or 12 volt test light (such as Chrysler part T-2951) to the terminal (10 – Fig. C8-9) where the blue wires are attached. Ground the other test lead to the metal case (housing) of the CD ignition module unit (3). Turn the ignition switch ON and observe the test light or voltmeter. If the test light glows, current is available to the

CD ignition module. If checking with a voltmeter, voltage should be the same as available at the battery.

If test light does not glow or voltmeter indicates zero or low voltage, check the circuit breaker (6). If the circuit breaker is not faulty, check for broken wires, loose connections, faulty ignition switch or improper ground. Make certain that the CD ignition module (3) is properly grounded. Mounting surfaces on bracket and CD ignition module must be free of all paint and the mounting bracket to motor ground wire must provide a good ground connection. Check the ground strap between power head and support plate. Before proceeding with remaining tests, make certain current is available to the CD ignition module.

BREAKER POINTS. The breaker points are used to trigger the ignition system. Failure of breaker points to make contact (open circuit) or failure to break contact (short circuit) will prevent ignition just as in conventional magneto or battery ignition systems.

Remove the flywheel and check condition and gap of the breaker points as outlined in the preceding POINT ADJUSTMENT paragraphs. Check condition of all wires, making certain that ground wire from breaker plate to the alternator stator has good contact,

Fig. C8-13 — Removing thermostat from cylinder head. "Vee" slot should point up when thermostat is installed.

especially at the stator end. Varnish should be scraped from stator before attaching ground wire. Check the BROWN and the WHITE/BROWN wires for short circuit to ground, for loose connections and for broken wire. Refer to IGNITION TIMING paragraphs and Fig. C8-9. Make certain that breaker point wires and coil wires are properly connected to provide spark to the correct cylinder.

IGNITION COILS AND CD IGNITION MODULE. If the preceding checks do not indicate any malfunctions, the ignition coils can be tested using an ignition tester available from Chrysler or several other sources, including the following:

Graham-Lee Electronics, Inc.
4220 Central Ave. N.E.
Minneapolis, Minn. 55421

Merc-O-Tronic Instruments Corp.
215 Branch St.
Almont, Mich. 48003

An alternate method of checking is possible as follows:

Connect one lead of a 12-volt test light (such as Chrysler part number T-2951) to each of the two primary terminals of one ignition coil. Turn ignition switch to the ON position, attempt to start motor with the electric starter and observe test light.

NOTE: After checking one of the ignition coils, connect the 12-volt test light to the primary terminals of the other coil and check the coil.

If the 12-volt test light flashes but spark did not occur at the test plug as tested in the CHECKING FOR SPARK paragraphs, the coil or attaching wires are faulty.

NOTE: The test plug connected to the tension spark plug wire will not fire with test light connected across the primary terminals. Inspect the black ground wire from negative (–) terminal of coil to the coil clamp screw and the high tension spark plug wire.

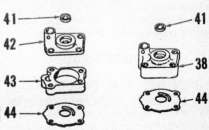

Fig. C8-14 — Variations of water pump bodies used on some models. Refer also to Fig. C8-23.

38. Water pump body
41. Seal
42. Cover
43. Pump housing
44. Back plate

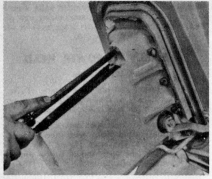

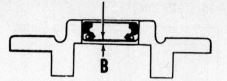

Fig. C8-16 — Cross sectional view of crankshaft upper bearing cage showing correct seal location. Clearance (B) should be 0.150 inch.

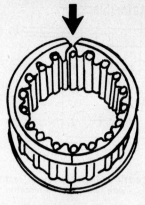

Fig. C8-18 — When installing needle bearing cages, make sure beveled ends (arrow) are together and to the top.

If the 12-volt test light does not flash, when connected to the coil primary terminals, make certain that current is available to the CD ignition module as outlined in WIRING paragraphs. Make certain that breaker points and associated wires are not faulty as outlined in the BREAKER POINTS paragraphs in the TROUBLESHOOTING section. If current is still not available to the coil primary terminals, the CD ignition module should be renewed.

COOLING SYSTEM

THERMOSTAT. The thermostat is located beneath a separate housing on top, rear face of cylinder head as shown in Fig. C8-13. When installing the thermostat, position with "Vee" slot in visible end up as shown. Power head will overheat if run without thermostat installed.

WATER PUMP. All motors are equipped with a rubber impeller type water pump. Refer to Figs. C8-14 and C8-23. The water pump is mounted in the lower unit drive shaft housing (upper gearcase).

When cooling system problems are encountered, first check the thermostat to see that it is operating properly. Check the water inlet for plugging or partial stoppage, then if trouble is not corrected, remove the lower unit gearcase as outlined in LOWER UNIT section, and check the condition of water pump, water passages and sealing surfaces.

POWER HEAD

REMOVE AND DISASSEMBLE. To overhaul the power head, clamp the motor on a stand or support and remove the engine cover (shroud) and motor leg covers. Remove the starter, flywheel and magneto or alternator; fuel pump, carburetor and intake manifold. Disconnect all interfering wiring and linkage.

Remove the cylinder head, and transfer port and exhaust covers if major repairs are required. Remove the power head attaching screws and lift off the cylinder block, crankshaft and associated parts as a unit.

NOTE: One of the power head attaching screws is located underneath the rear exhaust cover as shown in Fig. C8-15. Cover must be removed for access to the screw.

To disassemble the power head, unbolt and remove the upper bearing cage; then unbolt and remove the crankcase front half. Pry slots are provided adjacent to retaining dowels for separating the crankcase; DO NOT pry on machined mating surfaces of cylinder block and crankcase front half.

Crankshaft, pistons and bearings are now accessible for removal and overhaul as outlined in the appropriate following paragraphs. Assemble as outlined in the ASSEMBLY paragraph.

ASSEMBLY. When reassembling, make sure all joint and gasket surfaces are clean, free from nicks and burrs, warped surfaces or hardened cement or carbon. The crankcase and inlet manifolds must be completely sealed against both vacuum and pressure. Exhaust manifold and cylinder head must be sealed against water leakage and pressure. Mating surfaces of exhaust areas between power head and motor leg must form a tight seal.

Install crankshaft making certain upper, center and lower main bearings are properly positioned over main bearing locating pins in cylinder block. The crankshaft upper seal should be installed with LOWER edge 0.150 inch from bearing counterbore as shown at (B – Fig. C8-16).

Apply 3M-EC750 Sealer to mating surfaces of crankcase in areas adjacent to upper and center main bearings and lower crankshaft seal. Do not apply sealer to areas outside of crankcase seal groove. Immediately install crankcase half and tighten main bearing bolts to 270 in.-lbs. torque. Make sure crankshaft turns freely before proceeding with assembly.

When installing cylinder head, coat the first ¾-inch of screw threads with anti-seize lubricant or equivalent. Tighten the retaining cap screws progressively from the center outward first to 75 in.-lbs. torque, then in 50 in.-lb. increments until final torque of 270 in.-lbs. is achieved. After motor has been test run and cooled, retorque screws to 270 in.-lbs.

PISTONS, PINS, RINGS & CYLINDERS. Pistons on 35, 45 and early 55 hp models are fitted with three rings, while 50 and late 55 hp model pistons have two piston rings. Piston rings should be installed with the beveled inner edge toward closed end of piston. Rings are pinned in place to prevent rotation in ring grooves.

The piston pin is a tight fit in piston bores and rides in a roller bearing in connecting rod. Special tool, part number T-2990, should be used when removing or installing piston pin. When assembling piston, pin and connecting rod, make sure long, tapering side of piston

Fig. C8-17 — Correlation marks (M) and oil hole (H) should be toward the top when connecting rod is installed.

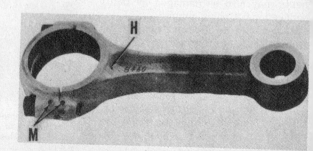

toward exhaust side of cylinder and correlation marks (M – Fig. C8-17) or bevel cut on rod are toward top (flywheel) end of crankshaft. Install piston pin retaining clips with sharp

edge out or if bowed retaining rings are used, install with convex side toward piston pin. All friction surfaces should be lubricated with new engine oil when assembling.

Pistons are available in standard sizes on all models and in oversizes on some models.

CONNECTING RODS, BEARINGS AND CRANKSHAFT. Before detaching connecting rods from crankshaft, make certain that rod and cap are properly marked for correct assembly to

each other and in the correct cylinder. The needle rollers and cages at crankpin end of connecting rod should be kept with the assembly and not interchanged.

The bearing rollers and cages used in the two connecting rods and center main bearings are available only as a set which contains the rollers and cage halves for one bearing. The complete assembly should be installed whenever renewal is indicated. Bearing cages have beveled match marks as shown by arrow, Fig. C8-18. Match marks must be installed together and toward top (flywheel) end of crankshaft.

A non-fibrous grease can be used to hold loose needle bearing in position during assembly. All friction surfaces should be lubricated with new engine oil. Check frequently as power head is being assembled, for binding or locking of the moving parts. If binding occurs, remove the cause before proceeding with the assembly. When assembling, follow the procedures outlined in the ASSEMBLY paragraphs. Tightening torques are given in the CONDENSED SERVICE DATA tables.

MANUAL STARTER

Refer to Fig. C8-19 or Fig. C8-20 for exploded views of the recoil starter assembly. Starter pinion (3) engages a starter ring gear on the flywheel.

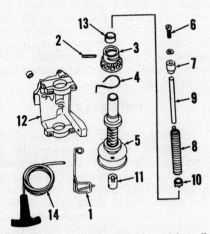

Fig. C8-19 – Exploded view of early model recoil starter assembly. Pinion (3) meshes with teeth on flywheel.

1. Rope guide	8. Recoil spring
2. Drive pin	9. Guide post
3. Pinion	10. Retainer
4. Pinion spring	11. Retainer extension
5. Starter spool	12. Mounting bracket
6. Lock screw	13. Interlock guide
7. Spring drive	14. Rope

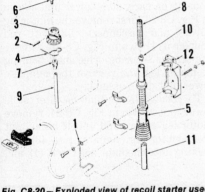

Fig. C8-20 – Exploded view of recoil starter used on late models. Refer to Fig. C8-19 for parts identification.

Fig. C8-21 – View showing tool (T3139) used to preload the recoil spring.

Fig. C8-22 – Disconnect the shift rod coupler before attempting to remove gearcase.

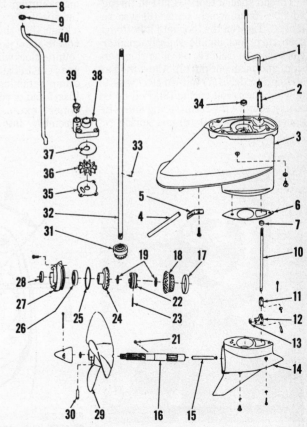

1. Shift rod	21. Ball
2. Nut	22. Dog clutch
3. Drive shaft housing	23. Spring pin
4. Inlet water tube	24. Rear gear
5. Inlet plate	25. Cage seal
6. Gasket	26. Bearing
7. Seal	27. Bearing cage
8. Seal	28. Seal
9. Washer	29. Propeller
10. Shift rod	30. Propeller pin
11. Link	31. Drive pinion
12. Shift arm	32. Drive shaft
13. Yoke	33. Drive pin
14. Gearcase	34. Shaft seal
15. Shift pin	35. Back plate
16. Propeller shaft	36. Impeller
17. Bearing cup	37. Top plate
18. Front gear	38. Pump body
19. Thrust washer	39. Grommet
	40. Water tube

Fig. C8-23 – Exploded view of typical early lower unit and associated parts. Refer also to Fig. C8-14 for other types of water pumps. Refer to Fig. C8-24 for later type lower unit.

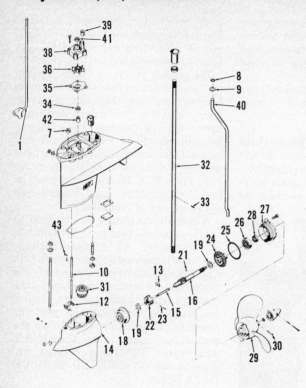

Fig. C8-24—Exploded view of lower unit used on later models. Refer to Fig. C8-23 for parts identification except for: 41. Drive shaft seal; 42. Upper drive shaft bearing; 43. Pin.

Secure rope guide with remaining clamp screw. Thread rope through support plate and install starter handle. With recoil spring and drive pinion (3) installed, use the special tool to wind the recoil spring counterclockwise 8½ turns. Align the holes in pinion (3), spool (5) and spring drive (7); then install the drive pin (2). Remove the tool and secure the pin with the locking screw (6). Recoil spring cavity should be partially filled with Lubriplate or similar grease when reassembling.

PROPELLER

The propellers for normal use have three blades and are protected by a cushioning-slip clutch. Various propellers are available and should be selected to provide full throttle operation within the recommended limits of 4500-5000 rpm for 1969 55 hp motors; 5000-5500 rpm for 1970 and later 55 hp motors; 4400-5100 rpm for 35 hp motors; 4500-5500 rpm for 45 and 50 hp motors. Propellers other than those designed for the motor should not be used.

LOWER UNIT

R&R AND OVERHAUL. To remove the lower unit gearcase and drive shaft housing on early style lower unit shown in Fig. C8-23, first remove the motor leg covers and disconnect the shift rod coupler as shown in Fig. C8-22, remove the screws securing drive shaft housing to motor leg and remove the complete lower unit drive assembly.

To remove lower unit on later style lower unit shown in Fig. C8-24, remove motor leg covers and unbolt lower unit from motor leg. Remove pin (43) connecting intermediate shift rod (1) and

To disassemble the starter, first remove the engine cover, then remove screw (6) in top of starter shaft.

NOTE: This screw locks pin (2) in place.

Thread special tool T3139-1 in threaded hole from which screw (6) was removed. Tighten the tool until it bottoms; then turn tool handle slightly counterclockwise to relieve recoil spring tension, and push out pin (2). Allow the tool and spring drive (7) to turn clockwise to unwind the recoil spring (8). Pull up on tool to remove the recoil spring and components. Guide post (9) and spring re-

tainer (10) can be lifted out after recoil spring is removed.

Recoil spring, pinion (3) or associated parts can be renewed at this time. To renew the starter rope, remove clamps on mounting bracket (12) then remove the spool. Tie one end of starter rope in a knot, then thread the free end through hole in spool (5). Wind rope around spool counterclockwise as viewed from the top and reinstall assembly leaving the inside clamp retaining screw out at this time. Insert end of rope guide (1) in hole on retainer extension (11), then insert assembly into bottom of spool (5).

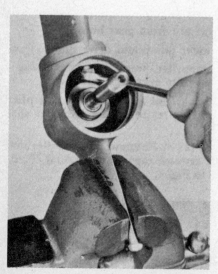

Fig. C8-25—Gearcase rear nut is accessible through propeller shaft opening as shown.

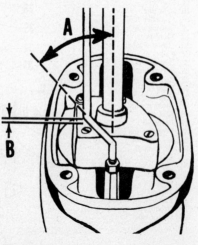

Fig. C8-26—Before tightening shift rod locknut on early units, angle (A) should be 28° with a minimum clearance (B) of 1/16-inch. Refer to text.

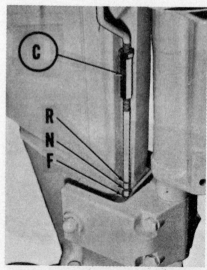

Fig. C8-27—Check the shift linkage adjustment by marking detent positions as shown. Refer to text.

wer shift rod (10). Separate lower unit rom motor leg.

Drain the gearcase and secure gearase skeg in a vise. Disassemble and renove the drive shaft and water pump ssembly (32 through 38 – Fig. C8-23 or C8-24). Remove propeller nut, pin (30) nd propeller (29). Carefully clean exosed end of propeller shaft and remove he two screws securing propeller shaft earing cage (27) to gearcase. Rotate he bearing cage approximately ½-turn ntil tabs are accessible from the sides; hen using a soft hammer, gently tap the earing cage rearward out of gearcase. Remove the gearcase rear retaining tud nut working through propeller haft opening as shown in Fig. C8-25. Remove shift rod (1 – Fig. C8-23 or C8-24), nut (2 – Fig. C8-23) and the gear-

case front retaining stud nut, then lift off drive shaft housing.

Withdraw drive pinion (31) from top of gearcase and propeller shaft and associated parts through rear opening. Withdraw front and rear gears from propeller shaft. Remove spring pin (23), clutch dog (22) and shift pin (15).

The drive shaft seal (34) should be installed with spring loaded lip toward top (power head). Propeller shaft seal (28) should be installed with spring loaded lip toward outside of bearing cage (27).

Drive gear backlash and bearing preload are fixed and not adjustable. Assemble by reversing the disassembly procedure. Make sure that hole in dog clutch (22) is aligned with slot in propeller shaft (16) and hole in shift pin (15); then, insert spring pin (23).

When reinstalling shift rod (1 – Fig. C8-23) refer to Fig. C8-26. Upper end of shift rod must point to rear, starboard, so that angle (A) from housing centerline is approximately 28 degrees; and bend of rod must clear pump housing (B) approximately 1/16-inch, when shifted to lowermost (forward detent) position.

After early stage lower unit is installed, refer to Fig. C8-27 and adjust the shift linkage coupling as follows: Using the shift lever, move the linkage through Forward, Neutral and Reverse detent positions and mark the intermediate shift link where it emerges from motor leg as shown at (F, N & R). If marks are not equally spaced (caused by interference in linkage), adjust by means of the turnbuckle connector (C) until interference is removed.

CHRYSLER 55, 60 AND 65 HP

55 HP Models

Year Produced	Models
1977	558HH, 558BH, 559HH, 559BH, 558HJ, 558BJ, 559HJ, 559BJ
1978	558HK, 558BK, 559HK, 559BK
1979	558H9L, 558B9L, 559H9L, 559B9L
1980	559H0M, 559B0M, 559H0N
1981	559H1N, 559B1N
1982	559H2P, 559B2P
1983	559H3R, 559B3R, 559V3S

60 HP Models

Year Produced	Models
1974, 1975, 1976	608HA, 608BA, 609HA, 609BA
1984	608H4, 608B4

65 HP Models

Year Produced	Models
1977	659HA, 659BA
1978	659H8B, 659B8B

CONDENSED SERVICE DATA

TUNE-UP

Hp/rpm	55/5000
	60 & 65/5250
Bore-Inches	3.375
Stroke-Inches	2.80
Number of Cylinders	2
Displacement-Cu. In.	49.9
Compression at Cranking Speed (Average)	150-165 psi
Spark Plug:	
Champion (1974-1980)	UL18V
(1981-1984)	L20V
Ignition:	
Point Gap	Breakerless
Timing	See Text
Carburetor:	
Make	Tillotson
Model	WB
Fuel:Oil Ratio	50:1

*Use 25:1 fuel:oil ratio for first 10 hours and for severe service.
**Publication not authorized by manufacturer.
***Refer to text for tightening cylinder head screws.

SIZES-CLEARANCES

Piston rings:	
End Gap	**
Side Clearance	**
Piston to Cylinder:	
Clearance	**
Piston Pin:	
Diameter	**
Clearance (Rod)	**
Crankshaft Bearing	
Clearance	Roller Bearing

TIGHTENING TORQUES
(All Values in Inch-Pounds Unless Noted)

Connecting Rod	270-280
Cylinder Head	225***
Flywheel Nut	90 Ft.-Lbs.
Main Bearing Bolts	270
Standard Screws:	
10-24	30
10-32	25
12-24	45
1/4-20	70
5/16-18	160
3/8-16	270

LUBRICATION

The power head is lubricated by oil mixed with the fuel. One-third (1/3) pint of two-stroke or Outboard Motor Oil should be mixed with each gallon of gasoline. The amount of oil in the fuel may be reduced after the first 10 hours of operation (motor is broken in), provided BIA certified TC-W or TC-2 oil is used and motor is subjected to normal service only. The minimum recommended fuel:oil ratio is 50:1, or half the normally recommended amount of oil. If the amount of oil is reduced, fuel and oil must be thoroughly mixed and idle mixture carefully adjusted to make sure any error is on the "Rich" side.

Regular grade automotive gasoline is recommended if octane rating is 85 or higher. Premium grade gasoline may be used if regular is not available.

Extreme Pressure SAE 90 Gear Oil, such as "Chrysler Special Purpose Gear Lube" should be used. DO NOT use a hypoid type lubricant. The gearcase should be drained and refilled every 100 hours or once each year, and fluid maintained at the level of upper (vent) plug opening.

To fill the gearcase, have motor in an upright position and fill through lower plug hole on starboard side of gearcase until lubricant reaches level of upper vent plug opening. Reinstall and tighten both plugs, using new gaskets if necessary, to assure a water tight seal.

FUEL SYSTEM

CARBURETOR. Tillotson carburetors are used on all models. Tillotson

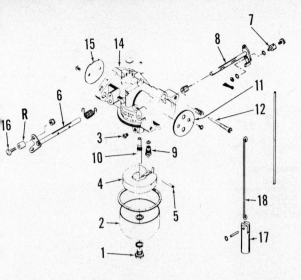

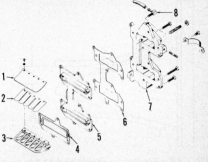

Fig. C9-1 – Exploded view of typical Tillotson WB model carburetor.

1. Bowl retaining screw
2. Fuel bowl
3. High speed jet
4. Float
5. Float pivot shaft
6. Throttle shaft
7. Choke link connector
8. Choke shaft
9. Inlet needle and seat
10. Main nozzle
11. Choke plate
12. Idle mixture needle
14. Throttle body
15. Throttle plate
16. Eccentric screw

Fig. C9-4 – Exploded view of inlet manifold and reed valve assembly.

1. Reed stop
2. Reed petals
3. Reed body
4. Gasket
5. Adapter plate
6. Gasket
7. Inlet manifold
8. By-pass check valve

WB29A carburetors are used on 65 hp models while WB23A carburetors are used on early 60 hp models and WB27A carburetors are used on later 60 hp models. Tillotson WB27A or WB27B carburetors are used on 55 hp models. Normal initial setting is one turn open for idle mixture adjustment needle (12 – Fig. C9-1). Standard high speed jet (3) sizes for sea level operation are: WB23A-0.070; WB27A, WB27B-0.066; WB29A-0.068.

Care must be used in selecting the high speed fixed jet (3 – Fig. C9-1). A fixed jet which is too small will result in a lean mixture and possible damage to power head. Jet may be identified by the diameter (in thousandths of an inch) stamped on visible end of installed jet. Optional jets are available which will improve performance when motor is used in high-altitude locations.

Float level (L – Fig. C9-2) should be 13/32 inch.

Throttle plates in carburetors must be synchronized to obtain maximum performance. Detach throttle link from tower shaft and rotate cam plate away from throttle roller on carburetor. Remove "E" ring from throttle arm of upper carburetor and detach end of throttle tie bar from upper carburetor

arm. Loosen tie bar screw (S – Fig. C9-3). Throttle plates should be closed in both carburetors. Attach upper end of tie bar to upper carburetor arm and tighten tie bar screw. Check to be sure throttle plates are closed. Attach throttle link to tower shaft.

SPEED CONTROL LINKAGE. On all models, ignition timing advance and throttle opening must be synchronized so that throttle is opened as timing is advanced.

To synchronize the linkage, first make certain that ignition timing is correctly set as outlined in IGNITION TIMING paragraph. Shift to forward gear and disconnect throttle link (L – Fig. C9-3) from tower shaft (T). With carburetor throttle closed, turn the eccentric screw (16) until roller (R) is exactly centered

over the scribed mark (M). Move the tower shaft (T) to full advance position and move the throttle cam until carburetor throttle is completely open. Vary the length of link (L) until the ball joint connector will just attach. Snap the ball joint connector onto ball stud and check maximum speed in neutral. If maximum rpm in neutral is not 1800-2500 rpm, it may be necessary to readjust speed control linkage.

Idle speed should be 700-800 rpm in forward gear (800-900 rpm in neutral) and is adjusted at idle screw (I – Fig. C9-3).

REED VALVES. "Vee" type intake reed valves are used on all models. The reed plate is located between intake manifold and crankcase and may be removed after removing carburetors.

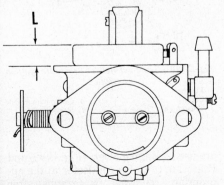

Fig. C9-2 – Float level (L) should be 13/32 inch.

Fig. C9-3 – View of tower shaft and carburetor linkage.

A. High speed stop
I. Idle speed screw
L. Throttle link
M. Cam mark
R. Roller
S. Screw
T. Tower shaft
16. Eccentric screw
19. Ignition timing rod

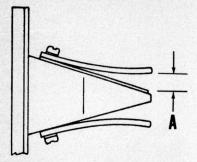

Fig. C9-5 — Reed stops should be 0.27-0.29 inch (A) from seating surface of reed block.

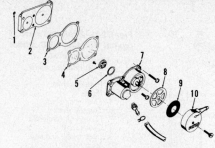

Fig. C9-7 — Exploded view of fuel pump.

1. Seal
2. Base
3. Gasket
4. Diaphragm
5. Check valve
6. Gasket
7. Pump housing
8. Gasket
9. Filter
10. Fuel filter inlet

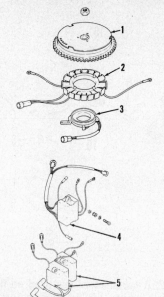

Fig. C9-9 — Exploded view of Magnapower II ignition system. Inset (9A) shows regulator/rectifier used on models after 1976.

1. Flywheel
2. Timing decal
3. Timing ring retainer
4. Timing ring
5. Trigger module bracket
6. Trigger module clip
7. Trigger module
8. Capacitors
9. Regulator/rectifier
10. Alternator
11. Bearing cage & seal
12. CD ignition module

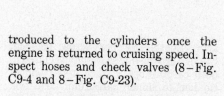

Fig. C9-6 — Cross sectional view of the two stage fuel pump used on all models. Broken lines indicate position of diaphragm when pulse pressure and vacuum are reversed.

C. Check valve
D. Diaphragm
I. Fuel inlet
O. Fuel outlet
PP. Pulse pressure
PV. Pulse vacuum

troduced to the cylinders once the engine is returned to cruising speed. Inspect hoses and check valves (8 – Fig. C9-4 and 8 – Fig. C9-23).

FUEL PUMP. All models are equipped with a diaphragm type fuel pump which is actuated by pressure and vacuum pulsations from both crankcases. The two stages operate alternately as shown.

NOTE: Either stage operating independently may permit the motor to run, but not at peak performance.

Most fuel pump service can be performed without removing the assembly from power head. Disconnect the pulse hoses and remove the retaining cap screws; then lift off the pump cover and diaphragm. Remove the sediment bowl and strainer. First stage inlet check valve can be driven out from below, using a ½-inch diameter drift. First stage outlet check valve can be lifted out after removing the retaining screws. The check valves must be installed to permit fuel to flow in the proper direction as shown in Fig. C9-6. To renew the second stage outlet check valve, it is first necessary to remove pump body from power head, remove outlet fuel elbow and drive the check valve out from below. Check valve will be damaged, and a new unit must be installed. DO NOT remove the valve unless renewal is indicated. Install new valve carefully, using an 11/16-inch diameter punch.

Renew the diaphragm if cracked or torn, or badly distorted. Install check valves carefully to prevent damage, and reassemble by reversing the disassembly procedure.

Reed valve must be smooth and even, with no sharp bends or broken reeds. Assembled reeds may stand open a maximum of 0.010 inch at tip end. Check seating visually.

Reed stop setting should be 0.27-0.29 inch (A – Fig. C9-5). Renew reeds if petals are broken, cracked, warped or bent. Never attempt to bend a reed petal in an effort to improve performance; nor attempt to straighten a damaged reed. Never install a bent or damaged reed. Seating surface of reed plate should be smooth and flat.

BY-PASS VALVES. All models are equipped with a by-pass drain system designed to remove any liquid fuel or oil which might build up in the crankcase; thus providing smoother operation at all speeds and lessening the possibility of spark plug fouling during slow speed operation.

The by-pass system is a recirculating type. Fluid accumulated in the crankcase during slow speed operation is rein-

IGNITION SYSTEM

All models are equipped with a breakerless, capacitor discharge ignition system. Two types of ignition systems

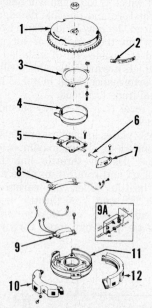

Fig. C9-10 — Exploded view of Prestolite ignition system.

1. Flywheel
2. Stator
3. Trigger coil
4. CD ignition module
5. Ignition coils

are used, "Magnapower" (Fig. C9-9) and Prestolite (Fig. C9-10). Refer to the appropriate following paragraphs after determining type of ignition used.

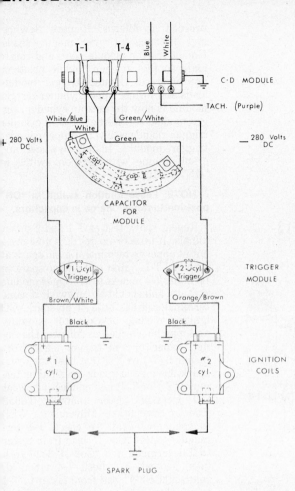

CAPACITOR
FOR
MODULE

Fig. C9-11—Schematic of Magnapower II ignition system.

Place lower unit in water and connect a suitable power timing light or Chrysler timing light number T8978 to upper spark plug. With engine in fully retarded position, crank engine with starter and note timing marks. If timing marks are not within three degrees of TDC, repeat static timing procedure. To check advanced ignition timing, run engine at 5000 to 5500 rpm with timing light connected to upper spark plug and note timing marks. Turn timing rod (19—Fig. C9-3) between tower shaft and timing ring arm to adjust advanced ignition timing.

NOTE: Engine should be stopped when turning ignition timing rod.

Magnapower Models

TROUBLESHOOTING. If ignition malfunction is suspected, install test plugs in place of the spark plugs and observe spark while engine is being cranked with starter. If ignition spark is satisfactory, install plugs known to be good and run engine to check performance. If engine miss or failure to start is due to ignition malfunction and not faulty spark plugs, proceed as follows: Detach spark plug wires from spark plugs. Crank engine with ignition switch in "ON" position to charge capacitors. Using a suitable insulated tool such as a plastic handled screwdriver, ground flywheel to terminal (T-1 – Fig. C9-12) and then ground flywheel to terminal (T-4). If a good spark is present at both terminals, then the CD ignition module and capacitors are good. To check upper cylinder trigger module, connect "Coil N" lead from Chrysler CD ignition tester number T8953 (Electro-Specialties, Milwaukee, Wis.) to a good ground and

All Models

R&R FLYWHEEL. A special puller (Chrysler part number T-8948-1) is used to remove the flywheel. Pulling bosses are provided on the flywheel for puller installation. Flywheel should be renewed if flywheel is chipped or cracked as an unbalanced condition may be produced.

The manufacturer recommends that mating surfaces of flywheel and crankshaft be lapped before flywheel is reinstalled. If evidence of working exists proceed as follows:

Remove the flywheel key and apply a light coating of valve grinding or lapping compound to tapered portion of crankshaft. Install the flywheel without the key or crankshaft nut and rotate flywheel gently back and forth about ¼-turn. Move flywheel 90° and repeat the operation. Lift off the flywheel, wipe off excess lapping compound and carefully examine crankshaft. A minimum of 90% surface contact should be indicated by the polished surface; continue lapping only if insufficient contact is evident. Thoroughly clean the crankshaft and flywheel bore to remove all traces of lapping compound, then clean both surfaces with a non-oily solvent.

Reinstall crankshaft key and flywheel, then tighten flywheel nut to torque indicated in CONDENSED SERVICE DATA table.

IGNITION TIMING. Remove both spark plugs and thread body of special timing gage (Chrysler part number TA-2937-1) into top spark plug opening. Insert the gage rod into tool body, rotate the crankshaft and carefully position top piston at exactly TDC.

NOTE: Gage rod should be installed with "25 through 55" end out.

With the top piston at TDC, thread timing tool body in or out as necessary until the inner scribed line on gage rod is aligned with end of tool body. After gage body is correctly positioned, turn the crankshaft clockwise almost one complete revolution while applying pressure to end of gage rod. Stop the crankshaft just as the first (outer) scribed line on rod aligns with tool body.

Piston should be positioned at 32 degrees BTDC and timing mark on carburetor adapter flange should be aligned with 32 degree mark on flywheel timing decal. If marks do not align, install a new decal or make new marks on flywheel.

Fig. C9-12—View of CD module showing location of (T-1) and (T-4) terminals.

proceed as follows: Remove flywheel and disconnect trigger module leads. Unbolt trigger module plate and rotate plate so that trigger module positions are reversed. Connect trigger module leads and former upper cylinder trigger module is now the bottom cylinder trigger module and former bottom cylinder trigger module is now the upper cylinder trigger module. Install flywheel and crank engine with ignition switch in "ON" position.

NOTE: Leave ignition switch in "ON" position to retain charge in capacitors.

Repeat spark test at T-1 and T-4 terminals. If little or no spark is now present at opposite terminal, **i.e.** no spark at terminal T-1 in first test and no spark at terminal T-4 in next test, trigger module is faulty and should be renewed. If same terminal still has little or no spark, CD ignition module or capacitor is faulty and may be checked as follows: Disconnect capacitor and trigger leads from terminal (T-1 or T-4) that has little or no spark. Connect a spade terminal or terminal (T-1 or T-4) and connect Chrysler CD ignition tester number T8953 (Electro-Specialties, Milwaukee, Wis.) to spade terminal. To check T-1 terminal, connect "Coil P" lead from tester to T-1 terminal and "Coil N" lead to a good ground. To check T-4 terminal, connect "Coil N" lead from tester to T-4 terminal and "Coil P" lead to a good ground. Set dial of tester to "50" and crank engine. If tester lights, CD ignition module is good and capacitor module should be renewed. If tester does not light, CD ignition module is faulty and should be renewed.

Prestolite Models

TROUBLESHOOTING. Use only approved procedures when testing to prevent damage to components. The fuel system should be checked to make cer-

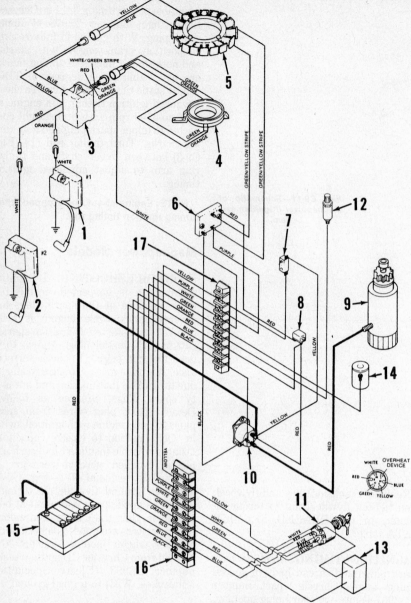

Fig. C9-13 — Wiring diagram for motors with Prestolite ignition system.

1. Ignition coil for top cylinder
2. Ignition coil for bottom cylinder
3. CD ignition module
4. Trigger coil
5. Stator
6. Regulator/rectifier
7. Neutral interlock switch
8. Circuit breaker
9. Starter
10. Starter solenoid
11. Ignition switch
12. Heat indicator
13. Overheat warning device
14. Choke solenoid
15. Battery
16. Terminal block at dashboard
17. Terminal block at motor

connect "Coil P" lead from CD tester to positive (+) terminal of upper cylinder ignition coil. Set dial of tester to "65" and crank engine. If lamp lights on tester, trigger module is operating correctly. If lamp does not light, renew trigger module. To check operation of bottom cylinder trigger module, connect "Coil P" lead of CD ignition tester to a good ground and connect "Coil N" lead to negative (−) terminal of bottom cylinder ignition coil. Repeat test procedure used for upper cylinder trigger module.

If little or no spark was present when T-1 and T-4 terminals were tested, note which terminal had little or no spark and

Fig. C9-14 — Tester connections for checking voltage output of charge coil.

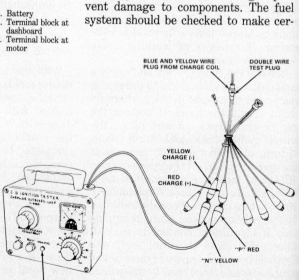

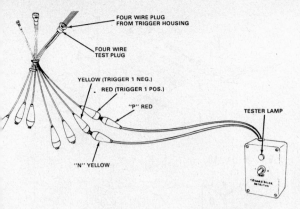

FOUR WIRE PLUG FROM TRIGGER HOUSING

FOUR WIRE TEST PLUG

YELLOW (TRIGGER 1 NEG.)

RED (TRIGGER 1 POS.)

"P" RED

"N" YELLOW

TESTER LAMP

Fig. C9-15 — Tester connections for checking trigger coil operation.

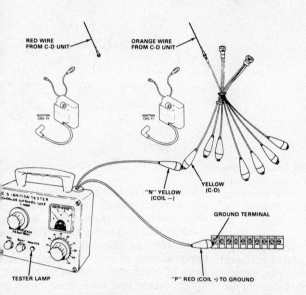

RED WIRE FROM C-D UNIT

ORANGE WIRE FROM C-D UNIT

IGNITION COIL #2

IGNITION COIL #1

"N" YELLOW (COIL —)

YELLOW (C-D)

GROUND TERMINAL

TESTER LAMP

"P" RED (COIL +) TO GROUND

Fig. C9-16 — View showing tester connections needed to check CD ignition module output.

ain that faulty running is not caused by ncorrect fuel mixture or contaminated uel. If ignition malfunction is uspected, use Chrysler tool T8953, plug dapter set T11237 and number 22 ester. Check and make sure ignition nalfunction is not due to spark plug or gnition coil failure. Install test plugs in place of the spark plugs and observe spark while engine is being cranked with starter. If spark is absent at both cylinders, check condition of charge coil as follows:

Separate the blue and yellow wire connection between charge coil (stator) and CD ignition module and attach double wire plug adapter to wire plug from charge coil as shown in Fig. C9-14. Attach red (P) lead from T8953 tester to red sleeved adapter wire marked Charge (+). Attach yellow (N) lead of tester to yellow sleeved adapter wire marked Charge (—). Turn tester switch to position 60 and crank engine. If tester lamp does not light, charge coil is defective and stator should be renewed. If lamp lights, charge coil operation is satisfactory and trigger coil and CD ignition module circuits for each cylinder

must be checked. Remove tester and plug adapter set, then reconnect blue and yellow wire plugs.

Separate the four-wire connection between CD ignition module and trigger coil and attach four-wire plug adapter to

wire plug from trigger coil as shown in Fig. C9-15. Attach red (P) lead from number 22 tester to red sleeved adapter wire marked Trigger 1 Pos. and yellow (N) lead to yellow sleeved adapter wire marked Trigger 1 Neg. Place switch of tester in number 1 position and crank engine. Trigger coil operation is satisfactory if tester lamp lights. Renew trigger housing if tester lamp does not light.

To check operation of number 2 cylinder trigger coil, repeat test procedure for number 1 cylinder trigger coil but connect red (P) lead of tester to red sleeved adapter wire marked Trigger 2 Pos. and yellow (N) tester lead to yellow sleeved adapter wire marked Trigger 2 Neg.

To check CD ignition module performance for each cylinder, separate primary lead connections between CD ignition module and ignition coils. Connect single wire adapter to orange (number 1 cylinder) or red (number 2 cylinder) wire from CD ignition module (Fig. C9-16), then attach yellow (N) lead of T8953 tester to yellow sleeved adapter wire marked C-D. Attach red (P) tester lead to ground terminal of engine terminal block. Turn tester switch to position 60 and crank engine. Renew CD module if tester lamp does not light.

COOLING SYSTEM

The thermostat is located in the cylinder head and is accessible after removing engine covers surrounding engine. All models are equipped with a rubber impeller type water pump. Water pump is mounted in lower unit drive shaft housing.

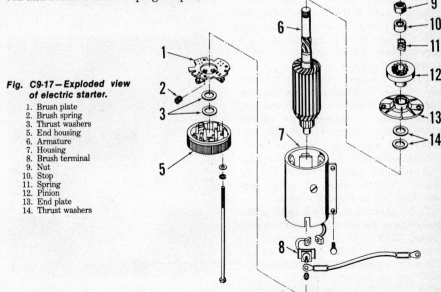

Fig. C9-17 — Exploded view of electric starter.

1. Brush plate
2. Brush spring
3. Thrust washers
4. End housing
5. Housing
6. Armature
7. Housing
8. Brush terminal
9. Nut
10. Stop
11. Spring
12. Pinion
13. End plate
14. Thrust washers

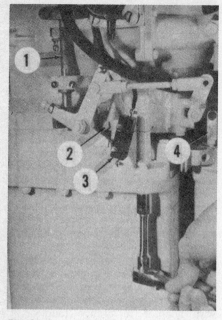

Fig. C9-18—View of right side of power head showing location of tower shaft (1), interlock switch bracket (2), interlock switch (3) and upper shift rod (4).

Fig. C9-19—Exploded view of motor leg assembly.

1. King pin
2. Spacer plate
3. Upper shift rod
4. Exhaust tube
5. Motor leg
6. Lower shock mount cover
8. Pivot bolt
9. Lock bar
10. Stern bracket
11. Link
12. Swivel bracket
13. Bearing
14. Spacer
15. Tilt stop
16. Stern bracket

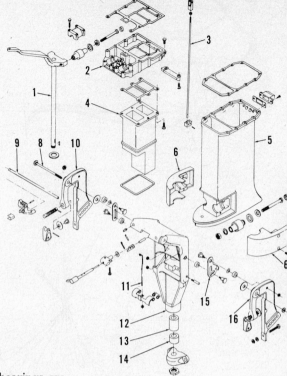

When cooling system problems are encountered, first check the thermostat to see that it is operating properly. Check the water inlet for plugging or partial stoppage, then if trouble is not corrected, remove the lower unit gearcase as outlined in LOWER UNIT section, and check the condition of water pump, water passages and sealing surfaces.

POWER HEAD

REMOVE AND DISASSEMBLE. Cylinder head may be removed without removing power head. Refer to CYLINDER HEAD section for cylinder head removal.

To remove power head, remove engine covers and disconnect fuel line from fuel pump. Disconnect upper shift rod (4 – Fig. C9-18) from shift arm. Unscrew power head retaining nuts and lift power head off spacer plate.

To gain access to short block assembly, remove flywheel and ignition, carburetors, carburetor adapter and reed valve. Remove starter motor, starter relay, circuit breaker, exhaust port cover and fuel pump. Remove tower-shaft (1 – Fig. C9-18), gear shift linkage and interlock switch bracket (2). Remove remote cable bracket and stabilizer bar at front of engine.

To disassemble the power head, unbolt and remove the upper and lower bearing cages; then unbolt and remove the crankcase front half. Pry slots are provided for separating the crankcase; DO NOT pry on machined mating surfaces of cylinder block and crankcase front half.

Crankshaft, pistons and bearings are now accessible for removal and overhaul as outlined in the appropriate following paragraphs. Assemble as outlined in the ASSEMBLY paragraph.

ASSEMBLY. When reassembling, make sure all joint and gasket surfaces are clean and free from nicks, burrs, warped surfaces, hardened cement or carbon. The crankcase and inlet manifolds must be completely sealed against both vacuum and pressure. Exhaust manifold and cylinder head must be sealed against water leakage and pressure. Mating surfaces of exhaust areas between power head and spacer plate must form a tight seal.

Install crankshaft making certain upper and center main bearings are properly positioned over main bearing locating pins in cylinder block. With new crankcase seal installed in seal groove, apply a suitable sealer to mating surfaces of crankcase in areas adjacent to upper, center and lower main bearings and around main bearing bolt holes. Immediately install crankcase front half and tighten main bearing bolts to 270 in.-lbs. torque. Make sure crankshaft turns freely before proceeding with assembly.

Renew outer "O" ring (21 – Fig. C9-22) and seals (20 and 23) in lower bearing cage (22) as required. Press small diameter seal (23), with spring loaded lip away from crankshaft, into bearing cage until it bottoms. Press large diameter

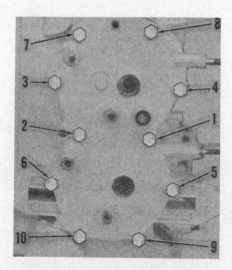

Fig. C9-20—View showing cylinder head bolt tightening sequence.

match marks

Fig. C9-21—Match marks on rod and cap should be aligned and toward top of engine.

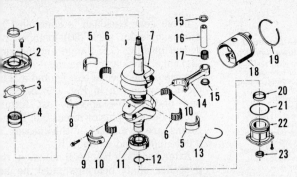

Fig. C9-22—Exploded view of piston and crankshaft assemblies.

Seal
Upper bearing cage
Gasket
Roller bearing

5. Bearing outer race
6. Bearing and cage
7. Crankshaft
8. Crankcase seal

9. Rod cap
10. Bearing and cage
11. Ball bearing
12. Snap ring
13. Snap ring
14. Connecting rod
15. Spacer
16. Piston pin
17. Needle bearing
18. Piston
19. Piston ring
20. Seal
21. Seal
22. Lower bearing cage
23. Seal

eal (20), with spring loaded lip toward rankshaft, into bearing cage until seal 0.009-0.012 inch below cage surface.

CYLINDER HEAD. To remove cyl- der head, remove covers surrounding ngine. Remove ignition coils, spark lugs and thermostat. Unscrew cylinder ead screws and separate cylinder head rom engine. Unscrew cylinder head over screws and water temperature witch and separate cylinder head cover nd cylinder head.

Apply an anti-seize liquid to cylinder ead screws and tighten in sequence hown in Fig. C9-20. Tighten screws to n initial torque reading of 70 in.-lbs. nd then tighten in increments of 50 n.-lbs. until a final torque reading of 225 n.-lbs. is attained.

PISTONS, PINS, RINGS & CYLIN- DERS. Pistons are equipped with two iston rings which are pinned in place to revent rotation. Piston pin rides in oller bearing in small end of connecting od.

On early models, assemble piston, pin nd connecting rod with long tapering ide of piston crown toward exhaust side f cylinder and alignment marks (Fig. C9-21) toward the top end of crankshaft.

On late models, disassembly of piston, in and rod for repair is not required as omponents are renewable only as a omplete unit.

CONNECTING RODS, BEARINGS AND CRANKSHAFT. Before detach- ing connecting rods from crankshaft, make certain that rod and cap are prop- erly marked for correct assembly to each other and in the correct cylinder. The needle rollers and cages at crankpin end of connecting rod should be kept with the assembly and not interchanged.

The bearing rollers and cages used in the two connecting rods and center main bearing are available only as a set which contains the cages and rollers for one bearing. Center main bearing outer

races are held together by snap ring (13—Fig. C9-22).

To install connecting rod on crank- shaft, apply a light coating of a suitable grease to connecting rod and install bearing cage half and seven bearing rollers in rod. Position rod and bearing against crankpin and install remaining bearing cage and nine bearing rollers on crankpin. Install rod cap being sure match marks are aligned and rod and cap are properly meshed before tighten- ing screws: Connecting rod and cap will be flush when rod and cap are meshed correctly.

PROPELLER

Standard propeller for 55, 60 and 65 hp models has three blades and is de-

signed for right-hand rotation. Diameter of propeller for 55 and 60 hp models is 11½ inches with a 12-inch pitch while 65 hp propeller has 10-inch diameter and 13-inch pitch.

LOWER UNIT

60 Hp And Early 55 Hp Models

R&R AND OVERHAUL. To remove lower unit from motor leg, unscrew six bolts securing lower unit to motor leg, remove pin (14—Fig. C9-24) connecting intermediate shift rod and lower shift rod (15) and separate lower unit from motor leg.

Drain gearcase and secure gearcase skeg in a vise. Disassemble and remove water pump assembly (1 through 6). Re- move propeller nut, pin and propeller. Carefully clean exposed end of propeller shaft and remove the two screws secur- ing propeller shaft bearing cage (34) to gearcase. Remove bearing cage with Chrysler tool number T8948 or a suitable puller. Unscrew stud nuts and separate gearcase and drive shaft hous- ing. Drive shaft and drive pinion (19) will remain with drive shaft housing. Thread a 5/16-inch lag screw into top of shift rod seal (10) and press against bottom of screw to remove seal from housing. Unscrew drive pinion (19) retaining screw and separate pinion from drive shaft. Press drive shaft out of drive shaft housing then press upper drive shaft bearing cup out of housing.

Fig. C9-23—Exploded view of cylinder block assembly.

1. Exhaust port cover
2. Gasket
3. Exhaust port plate
4. Gasket
5. Cylinder block
6. Seal
7. Front crankcase half
8. By-pass check valve
9. Dowel pin
10. Ignition timing rod
11. Tower shaft
12. Throttle link
13. Shift link
14. Gasket
15. Cylinder head
16. Gasket
17. Thermostat cover
18. Gasket
19. Thermostat
20. Grommet
21. Thermoswitch
22. Cylinder head cover

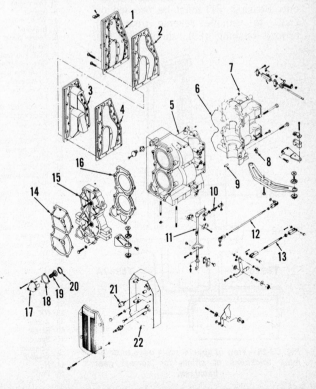

Illustrations Courtesy Chrysler

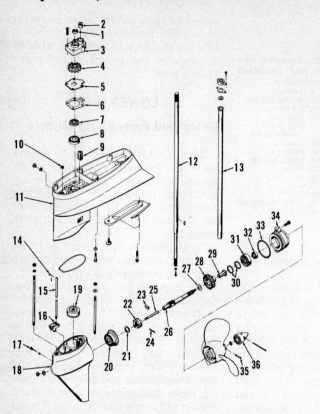

Fig. C9-24 — Exploded view of lower unit.

1. Drive shaft seal
2. Water tube seal
3. Water pump housing
4. Impeller
5. Back plate
6. Gasket
7. Drive shaft seal
8. Bearing
9. Water inlet screen
10. Shift rod seal
11. Drive shaft housing
12. Drive shaft
13. Water tube
14. Shift rod pin
15. Lower shift rod
16. Pivot coupling
17. Pivot pin
18. Gearcase
19. Drive pinion & bearing
20. Forward gear & bearing
21. Thrust washer
22. Shift coupling
23. Shift yoke
24. Shift pin
25. Shift shaft
26. Propeller shaft
27. Thrust washer
28. Reverse gear
29. Bushing
30. Shims
31. Bearing
32. Seal
33. "O" ring
34. Bearing cage
35. Shear pin
36. Nut

Drive gear backlash is controlled b means of shim pack (30) installed b tween bushing (29) flange and bearin (31) cone. Backlash adjustment require the use of the special test jig and dial i dicator as shown in Fig. C9-25. Sha end play in the special test fixtur should be zero, plus or minus 0.001 inch Shims are available in thicknesses 0.005, 0.006 and 0.008 inch.

After backlash has been adjusted, th propeller shaft bearings must be a justed by varying the thickness of fron thrust washer (21 – Fig. C9-24). Th bearings should be adjusted t 0.004-0.006 inch end play. Thru washers are available in thicknesse from 0.056 inch to 0.086 inch in 0.00 inch increments. To measure the bea ing adjustment, assemble propelle shaft components (20 through 34) excep yoke (23) and "O" ring (33) in gearcase Install a 0.056 inch thrust washer (21 Measure propeller shaft end play.

To assemble the propeller shaft, refe to Fig. C9-24. Slide the shift couplin (22) onto propeller shaft with hole i coupling aligned with slot in shaft. Pos tion shift shaft (25) inside propeller shaf and align hole with hole in coupling Drive pin (24) through holes in coupling propeller shaft and shift shaft. Insta pivot coupling (16), pivot pin (17) an lower shift rod (15). Slide the forwar gear (20) and bearing cone on front en

Withdraw propeller shaft and associated parts.

NOTE: Shift yoke (23) will be free to drop when propeller shaft is removed. Do not lose the yoke.

Slip the forward gear and bearing assembly (20) from the propeller shaft. Shift coupling (22) and shift shaft (25) can be removed after driving pin (24) out. Bearing (31) must be pressed off shaft to remove reverse gear (28), bronze bushing (29), shims (30) and

thrust washer (27). Keep the thrust washers (21 & 27) with their respective gears. The washers are similar but NOT interchangeable.

Fig. C9-26 — Exploded view of lower drive unit used on 65 hp and late 55 hp models.

1. Water tube seal
2. Drive shaft seal
3. Spacer
4. Water pump housing
5. Impeller
6. Lower plate
7. Gasket
8. Shift rod seal
9. Gearcase cover
10. Drive shaft seal
11. Cover seals
12. Crush ring
13. Pin
14. Lower shift rod
15. Pivot coupling
16. Pivot pin
17. Gearcase
18. Exhaust snout
19. Drive pinion
20. Nut
21. Bearing cup
22. Forward gear & bearing
23. Shim
24. Shift coupling
25. Shift pin
26. Shift shaft
27. Shift yoke
28. Propeller shaft
29. Reverse gear
30. Thrust bearing
31. Thrust washer
32. Retainer clips
33. Bearing & cage
34. "O" ring
35. Spool
36. "O" ring
37. Seal
38. "O" ring
39. Anode
40. Screw
41. Spacer
42. Propeller
43. Washer
44. Nut
45. Pin
46. Prop extension
47. Bracket
48. Seal
49. Grommet
50. Water tub
51. Bearing
52. Shim
53. Drive sha

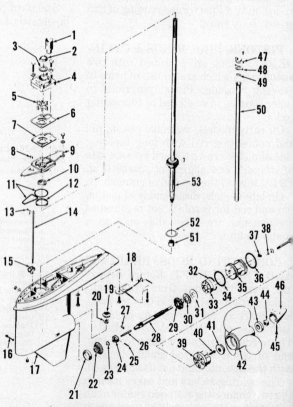

T8982B

T8982

T8924   **T8982A**

Fig. C9-25 — View of special tools used to determine thickness of shims for correct gear backlash.

propeller shaft and position the yoke
3) in front slot of shift shaft (25). Care-
lly slide the assembled propeller shaft
to gearcase housing making sure that
bs of shift yoke (23) engage both
rked slots in pivot coupling (16). Care-
lly install bearing cage using new seal
2) and "O" ring (33). Assemble drive
aft, drive pinion and bearings in drive
aft housing (11). Apply Loctite 271 or
0 to drive pinion retaining screw
reads. Tighten pinion retaining screw
drive shaft just turns freely without
nding. Tap on screw to be sure bear-
gs are seated and retighten screw.

Be sure to install shift rod pin (14)
ter mating drive shaft housing with
otor leg.

5 Hp And Late 55 Hp Models

R&R AND OVERHAUL. Remove
wer front shock mount cover and re-
ove shift rod pin (13–Fig. C9-26).
nscrew six screws and separate gearase from motor leg. Drain lubricant and
emove propeller and exhaust snout
8).

Disassemble and remove water pump
components (1 through 7). Turn shift rod
(14) counterclockwise until disengaged
from pivot coupling (15) and remove rod.
Remove cover (9) and anode (39). Remove screws securing bearing spool (35)
and using a suitable puller withdraw
spool from gearcase. Remove retaining
clips (32), bearing and cage (33), thrust
washer (31), thrust bearing (30) and
reverse gear (29). Withdraw propeller
shaft (28) with components (22 through
27). Unscrew pinion nut (20), withdraw
drive shaft (53) and remove pinion gear
(19). Unscrew pivot pin (16) and remove
pivot coupling (15).

Use the following procedure to check
reverse gear backlash: Install a 0.050
inch spacer (Chrysler T8997) in place of
shims (52). Install forward gear and
bearing (22), drive shaft (53), pinion gear
(19) and nut (20). Tighten nut (20) to 600
in.-lbs. Insert Chrysler shim tool number
T8997B in forward gear (22) so flat portion of tool is towards pinion gear (19).
Pull up on drive shaft and using a feeler
gage measure gap between large OD of
tool and pinion gear. Subtract measured

gap from 0.055 inch (0.050 inch spacer
plus 0.005 inch desired backlash) to obtain thickness of shim pack (52). Remove
0.050 inch shim, install shim pack (52)
and repeat above procedure. Gap between pinion gear (19) and large OD of
shim tool should be 0.004-0.006 inch.

To check propeller shaft end play, install components (21 through 32) and
bearing spool (35). Shim (23) should be
thinnest available (0.054 inch). Do not install "O" rings on spool. Tighten spool retaining screws to 150 in.-lbs. Measure
end play of propeller shaft and install
shims (23) necessary to obtain
0.009-0.011 inch end play.

To reassemble lower unit, reverse disassembly procedure. Tighten pinion nut
(20) to 600 in.-lbs. Install seal (37) with
lip towards propeller. "O" rings (34 & 36)
have different diameters and must be installed correctly on bearing spool (35).
Chamfered end of spool is installed first.
Tighten bearing spool (35) retaining
screws to 150 in.-lbs. Install seals (8 &
10) with lip towards gearcase. Tighten
cover (9) to 70 in.-lbs. Install seal (2) with
lip towards power head.

CHRYSLER

3 AND 4 CYLINDER
MODELS

Year Produced	70 hp	75 hp	85 hp	90 hp	100 hp	105 hp
1969	70*†	.....	85*†	.....	.....	105*†
1970	70*§	.....	85*§	.....	.....	105*§
1971	70*§	.....	85*§	.....	.....	105*§
1972	70*§	.....	85*§	.....	.....	105*§
1973	70*§	.....	85*§	.....	.....	105*§
1974	.....	75*§	.....	90*§	.....	105*§
1975	.....	75*§	.....	90*§	.....	105*§
1976	.....	75*§	.....	90*§	.....	105*§
1977	.....	75*§	.....	90*§	.....	105*§
1978	.....	75*§	85*§	.....	.....	105*§
1979	70*§	75*§	85*§	.....	100*§	.....
1980	70*§	75*§	85*§	.....	100*§	.....
1981	.....	75*§	85*§	.....	100*§	.....
1982	.....	75*§	85*§	.....	.....	105*§
1983	.....	75*§	85*§	90*§	100*§	.....
1984	.....	75*§	85*§	90*§	100*§	.....

Year Produced	115 hp	120 hp	125 hp	130 hp	135 hp	140 hp	150 hp
1969	.....	.....	.....	.....	.....	.....	.....
1970	.....	120*§	.....	.....	135*§	.....	.....
1971	.....	120*§	.....	.....	135*§	.....	.....
1972	.....	120*§	.....	130*§	.....	.....	150*§
1973	.....	120*§	.....	130*§	.....	.....	150*§
1974	.....	120*§	.....	.....	135*§	.....	150*§
1975	.....	120*§	.....	.....	135*§	.....	150*§
1976	.....	120*§	.....	.....	135*§	.....	150*§
1977	.....	120*§	.....	.....	135*§	.....	.....
1978	115*§	.....	.....	.....	.....	140*§	.....
1979	115*§	.....	.....	.....	.....	140*§	.....
1980	115*§	.....	.....	.....	.....	140*§	.....
1981	115*§	.....	125*§	.....	.....	140*§	.....
1982	115*§	.....	125*§	.....	.....	140*§	.....
1983	115*§	.....	.....	.....	.....	140*§	.....
1984	115*§	.....	.....	.....	.....	140*§	.....

*Variation Code:
0 – Standard shaft, manual starter.
1 – Long shaft, manual starter.
2 – Standard shaft, manual starter, with tiller.
3 – Long shaft, manual starter, with tiller.
4 – Standard shift, electric starter.
5 – Long shaft, electric starter.
6 – Standard shaft, electric starter, with alternator.
7 – Long shaft, electric starter, with alternator.
8 – Same as number 6 except with "Magnapower" ignition.
9 – Same as number 7 except with "Magnapower" ignition.

†Production Code Before 1970:
1, 3 & 5 – USA Models.
2, 4 & 6 – Canada Models

§Production Code for 1970 and Later:
HA, HB, HC, HD, HE, HF, HG, HJ & HN – USA Models; BA, BB, BC, BD, BE, BF, BG, BJ, & BN – Canada Models

CONDENSED SERVICE DATA

	70, 75, 85, 90 HP	100, 105, 120, 130 HP 135 HP (1970-1971) 150 HP (1972-1975)	125 HP	115 HP 135 HP (1974-1977) 150 HP (1976)	140 HP
TUNE-UP					
Hp/rpm	70/4750 75/4750 85/5000 90/5000	100 & 105/5000 120 & 130/5250 135 & 150/5400	125/5000	115 & 135/5000 150/5400	140/5250
Bore – Inches	3.3125	3.3125	3.3125	3.375	3.375
Stroke – Inches	*2.80	2.80	2.875	2.80	2.875
Number of Cylinders	3	4	4	4	4
Displacement – Cu. In.	*72.39	96.55	99.23	99.8	103
Spark Plug:					
Champion	L20V	L20V	L20V	L20V	L20V
Electrode Gap	Surface Gap	Surface Gap	Surface Gap	Surface Gap	Surface Gap
Ignition:					
Point Gap	See Text	See Text	See Text	See Text	See Text
Firing Order	1-2-3	1-3-2-4	1-3-2-4	1-3-2-4	1-3-2-4
Carburetor:					
Make	Tillotson	Tillotson	Tillotson	Tillotson	Tillotson
Model	WB	WB	WB	WB	WB
Fuel:Oil Ratio	50:1	50:1	50:1	50:1	50:1

*Performance 85 hp models have a 2.70 in. stroke and a 69.81 cu. in. displacement.

SIZES – CLEARANCES

Piston Ring End Gap	†0.006-0.016 in.
Piston Ring Groove Width	†0.0645-0.0655 in.
Piston to Cylinder Clearance . . .	0.0075-0.0103 in. 0.006.0.008 in.
Piston Pin:	
Diameter	0.68750-0.68765 in.
Clearance (Rod)	Needle Bearing
Clearance (Piston)	0.00005 in. tight to 0.00040 in. loose
Crankshaft Journal Diameters:	
Upper Main Bearing	1.3789-1.3793 in.
Center Main Bearing	1.3748-1.3752 in.
Lower Main Bearing	1.2495-1.2500 in.
Crankpin	1.1391-1.1395 in.

†A semi-keystone top piston ring is used on 140 hp models and has an end gap of 0.004-0.014 in. Refer to text to check top ring groove wear.

TIGHTENING TORQUES
(All Values in Inch-Pounds Unless Otherwise Noted)

Connecting Rod (1969-1978)	170
(1979-1984)	185
Cylinder Head	225
Flywheel Nut	90 Ft.-Lbs.
Crankcase	270
Standard Screws:	
10-24	30
10-32	35
12-24	45
¼-20	70
5/16-28	160
⅜-16	270

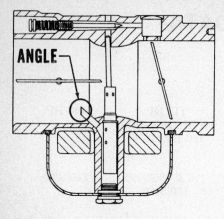

Fig. C10-1—Cross section of WB-2A carburetors showing two different types of air bleed tubes. Angle cut type requires a larger main jet and can be viewed through choke bore. Square cut type is shown at bottom.

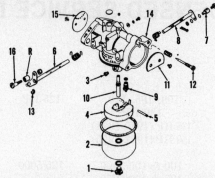

Fig. C10-2—Exploded view of typical Tillotson WB model carburetor. Type TC carburetors are similar.

1. Bowl retaining screw	9. Inlet needle and seat	
2. Fuel bowl	10. Main nozzle	
3. High speed jet	11. Choke plate	
4. Float	12. Idle mixture needle	
5. Float pivot shaft	13. Snap ring	
6. Throttle shaft	14. Throttle body	
7. Choke link connector	15. Throttle plate	
8. Choke shaft	16. Eccentric screw	

LUBRICATION

The power head is lubricated by oil mixed with the fuel. One-third (⅓) pint of two-stroke engine oil should be mixed with each gallon of gasoline. The amount of oil in the fuel may be reduced after motor is well broken in (at least 10 hours of operation), provided BIA certified TC-W or TC-2 oil is used. The minimum, recommended fuel:oil ratio is 50:1, or one (1) pint of oil for each six (6) gallons of fuel. If the oil amount is reduced, it is extremely important that fuel and oil be thoroughly mixed, that idle mixture adjusting screws be carefully checked to make sure any error of adjustment is on the "Rich" side, and that the recommended high speed jets are used. Regular grade leaded automotive gasoline is recommended. If regular is not available, use a good grade of premium gasoline.

The lower unit gears and bearings are lubricated by oil contained in the gearcase. Only a non-corrosive, leaded outboard, gear oil, EP90 such as "Chrysler Marine Gear Lube" or equivalent should be used. The gearcase should be drained

and refilled every 100 hours or once each year, and fluid maintained at the level of the upper (vent) plug hole.

To fill the gearcase, have the motor in upright position and fill through the lower plug hole in starboard side of gearcase until fluid reaches level of upper vent plug. Reinstall and tighten both plugs securely, using new gaskets if necessary, to assure a water tight seal.

FUEL SYSTEM

CARBURETOR. Tillotson type WB and TC carburetors are used. Refer to Fig. C10-2. The carburetor model number is stamped on the mounting flange. Three carburetors are used on 3-cylinder models. Two carburetors are used on 4-cylinder models.

NOTE: On 3-cylinder motors, make certain that all three carburetors used are the same model number. On 4-cylinder models, both carburetors must be the same model. If WB-2A carburetors are used, both idle bleed tubes should be the same. Refer to Fig. C10-1. On early 3-cylinder models, the choke return spring on choke shaft should be removed from the lower carburetor.

Normal initial setting is one turn open for idle mixture adjustment needle (12 – Fig. C10-2). Fixed jet (3) controls high speed mixture. Idle mixture must be readjusted under load, after motor is warm, for best slow speed performance. Idle mixture needle for all carburetors must be adjusted as nearly as possible for equal performance and all main jets (3) must be the same size.

Care must be used in selecting the high speed fixed jet (3 – Fig. C10-2). A fixed jet which is too small will result in

a lean mixture and possible damage to power head. Jet may be identified by the diameter (in thousandths of an inch) stamped on visible end of installed jet. Optional jets are available which will improve performance when motor is used in high-altitude locations; optional jet and recommended altitudes are as follows:

70 HP (WB-1C)

Altitude	Jet Size	Part Number
Sea Level-1500 ft.	0.070	013430
1500-3000 ft.	0.066	014188
3000-4500 ft.	0.064	014108
4500-6000 ft.	0.062	014187
Above 6000 ft.	0.060	014186

70 HP (WB-8A, WB-8B, WB-8C, WB-26B & WB-31A) Except Models 709H9A & 709B9A

Altitude	Jet Size	Part Number
Sea Level-1500 ft.	0.062	014187
1500-3000 ft.	0.060	014186
3000-4500 ft.	0.058	015337
4500-6000 ft.	0.056	015338
Above 6000 ft.	0.054	015339

70 HP (WB-26B) Models 709H9A & 709B9A

Altitude	Jet Size	Part Number
Sea Level-1500 ft.	0.066	014188
1500-3000 ft.	0.064	014108
3000-4500 ft.	0.062	014187
4500-6000 ft.	0.060	014186
Above 6000 ft.	0.058	015337

75 HP (WB-22A)

Altitude	Jet Size	Part Number
Sea Level-1500 ft.	0.064	014108
1500-3000 ft.	0.062	014187
3000-4500 ft.	0.060	014186
4500-6000 ft.	0.058	015337
Above 6000 ft.	0.056	015338

75 HP (WB-26B)

Altitude	Jet Size	Part Number
Sea Level-1500 ft.	0.066	014188
1500-3000 ft.	0.064	014108
3000-4500 ft.	0.062	014187
4500-6000 ft.	0.060	014186
Above 6000 ft.	0.058	015337

85 HP (WB-6A)

Altitude	Jet Size	Part Number
Sea Level-1500 ft.	0.074	014303
1500-3000 ft.	0.072	015026
3000-4500 ft.	0.070	013430
4500-6000 ft.	0.068	013967
Above 6000 ft.	0.066	014188

85 HP (WB-9A, WB-9B & WB-9D)

Altitude	Jet Size	Part Number
Sea Level-1500 ft.	0.064	014108
1500-3000 ft.	0.062	014187
3000-4500 ft.	0.060	014186
4500-6000 ft.	0.058	015337
Above 6000 ft.	0.056	015338

85 HP (WB-21C)

Altitude	Jet Size	Part Number
Sea Level-1500 ft.	0.072	015026
1500-3000 ft.	0.070	013430
3000-4500 ft.	0.068	013967
4500-6000 ft.	0.066	014188
Above 6000 ft.	0.064	014108

90 HP (WB-21A)

Altitude	Jet Size	Part Number
Sea Level-1500 ft.	0.074	014303
1500-3000 ft.	0.072	015026
3000-4500 ft.	0.070	013430
4500-6000 ft.	0.068	013967
Above 6000 ft.	0.066	014188

100 HP (WB-24B)

Altitude	Jet Size	Part Number
Sea Level-1500 ft.	0.080	013194
1500-3000 ft.	0.078	014306
3000-4500 ft.	0.076	013191
4500-6000 ft.	0.074	014303
Above 6000 ft.	0.072	015026

105 HP (WB-2C and WB-10B)

Altitude	Jet Size	Part Number
Sea Level-1500 ft.	0.088	013193
1500-3000 ft.	0.084	014302
3000-4500 ft.	0.082	014109
4500-6000 ft.	0.080	013194
Above 6000 ft.	0.0785	014306

105 HP (WB-10D & WB-10E)

Altitude	Jet Size	Part Number
Sea Level-1500 ft.	0.084	014302
1500-3000 ft.	0.082	014109
3000-4500 ft.	0.080	013194
4500-6000 ft.	0.0785	014306
Above 6000 ft.	0.076	013191

105 HP (WB-24A)

Altitude	Jet Size	Part Number
Sea Level-1500 ft.	0.078	014306
1500-3000 ft.	0.076	013191
3000-4500 ft.	0.074	014303
4500-6000 ft.	0.072	015026
Above 6000 ft.	0.070	013430

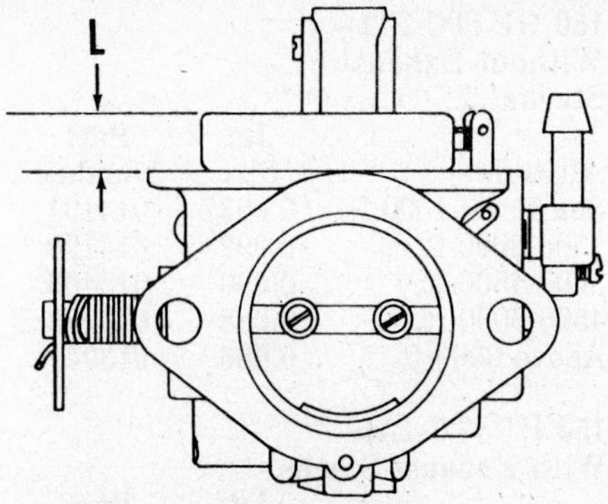

Fig. C10-3—Float level (L) should be 13/32 inch for WB and TC carburetors.

105 HP (WB-24B)

Altitude	Jet Size	Part Number
Sea Level-1500 ft.	0.080	013194
1500-3000 ft.	0.078	014306
3000-4500 ft.	0.076	013191
4500-6000 ft.	0.074	014303
Above 6000 ft.	0.072	015026

115 HP (WB-25B)

Altitude	Jet Size	Part Number
Sea Level-1500 ft.	0.086	013949
1500-3000 ft.	0.084	014302
3000-4500 ft.	0.082	014109
4500-6000 ft.	0.080	013194
Above 6000 ft.	0.078	014306

115 HP (TC-6B)

Altitude	Jet Size	Part Number
Sea Level-1500 ft.	0.0937	014191
1500-3000 ft.	0.092	014190
3000-4500 ft.	0.090	015406
4500-6000 ft.	0.088	013193
Above 6000 ft.	0.086	013949

115 HP (TC-7A)

Altitude	Jet Size	Part Number
Sea Level-1250 ft.	0.090	015406
1250-3750 ft.	0.088	013193
3750-6250 ft.	0.086	013949
6250-8250 ft.	0.084	014302
Above 6000 ft.	0.082	014109

120 HP (WB-13A)

Altitude	Jet Size	Part Number
Sea Level-1500 ft.	0.088	013193
1500-3000 ft.	0.086	013949
3000-4500 ft.	0.084	014302
4500-6000 ft.	0.082	014109
Above 6000 ft.	0.080	013194

120 HP (WB-13C & WB-13D)

Altitude	Jet Size	Part Number
Sea Level-1500 ft.	0.088	013193
1500-3000 ft.	0.086	013949
3000-4500 ft.	0.084	014302
4500-6000 ft.	0.082	014109
Above 6000 ft.	0.080	013194

120 HP (WB-25A)

Altitude	Jet Size	Part Number
Sea Level-1500 ft.	0.080	014302
1500-3000 ft.	0.082	014109
3000-4500 ft.	0.080	013194
4500-6000 ft.	0.078	014306
Above 6000 ft.	0.076	013191

120 HP (WB-25B)

Altitude	Jet Size	Part Number
Sea Level-1500 ft.	0.086	013949
1500-3000 ft.	0.084	014302
3000-4500 ft.	0.082	014109
4500-6000 ft.	0.080	013194
Above 6000 ft.	0.078	014306

125 HP (TC-6B)

Altitude	Jet Size	Number Number
Sea Level-1500 ft.	0.0937	014191
1500-3000 ft.	0.092	014190
3000-4500 ft.	0.090	015406
4500-6000 ft.	0.088	013193
Above 6000 ft.	0.086	013949

130 HP (TC-1A & TC-1B)

Altitude	Jet Size	Number Number
Sea Level-1500 ft.	0.0937	014191
1500-3000 ft.	0.092	014190
3000-4500 ft.	0.090	015406
4500-6000 ft.	0.088	013193
Above 6000 ft.	0.086	013949

135 HP (WB-14B)— Without Exhaust Stacks

Altitude	Jet Size	Part Number
Sea Level-1500 ft.	0.092	014190
1500-3000 ft.	0.090	015406
3000-4500 ft.	0.088	013193
4500-6000 ft.	0.086	013949
Above 6000 ft.	0.084	014302

135 HP (WB-14B)— With Exhaust Stacks

Altitude	Jet Size	Part Number
Sea Level-1500 ft.	0.0937	014191
1500-3000 ft.	0.092	014190
3000-4500 ft.	0.090	015406
4500-6000 ft.	0.088	013193
Above 6000 ft.	0.086	013949

135 HP (TC-5A)

Altitude	Jet Size	Part Number
Sea Level-1500 ft.	0.0937	014191
1500-3000 ft.	0.092	014190
3000-4500 ft.	0.090	015406
4500-6000 ft.	0.088	013193
Above 6000 ft.	0.086	013949

135 HP (TC-5C)

Altitude	Jet Size	Part Number
Sea Level-1500 ft.	0.096	012947
1500-3000 ft.	0.0937	014191
3000-4500 ft.	0.092	014190
4500-6000 ft.	0.090	015406
Above 6000 ft.	0.088	013193

140 HP (TC-5E)

Altitude	Jet Size	Part Number
Sea Level-1500 ft.	0.096	012947
1500-3000 ft.	0.0937	014191
3000-4500 ft.	0.092	014190
4500-6000 ft.	0.090	015406
Above 6000 ft.	0.088	013193

150 HP (TC-1A)— Without Exhaust Stacks

Altitude	Jet Size	Part Number
Sea Level-1500 ft.	0.0937	014191
1500-3000 ft.	0.092	014190
3000-4500 ft.	0.090	015406
4500-6000 ft.	0.088	013193
Above 6000 ft.	0.086	013949

150 HP (TC-1A)— With Exhaust Stacks

Altitude	Jet Size	Part Number
Standard	0.106	016246

Float level (L – Fig. C10-3) should be 13/32-inch for WB and TC carburetors.

Throttle plates in carburetors must be synchronized to obtain maximum performance. The throttle cam (C – Fig. C10-4) actuates only one carburetor. The rod connecting the other carburetor (or carburetors on 3-cylinder models) must be adjusted to open the other carburtor exactly the same amount. On 3-cylinder models, the adjusting clamp screws (A) are on the connecting link near the top and bottom carburetors. On 4-cylinder models, the adjuster is located near the top carburetor.

SPEED CONTROL LINKAGE. On all models, ignition timing advance and throttle opening must be synchronized so that throttle is opened as timing is advanced. If incorrect, the power head may overheat, lack power and will usually not accelerate smoothly.

To synchronize the linkage, first make certain that ignition timing is correctly set as outlined in IGNITION TIMING paragraph.

Disconnect the throttle rod (TR – Fig. C10-5) and move the throttle cam (C – Fig. 4) until mark on cam is aligned with center of roller as shown. Loosen

locknut on roller and turn the eccentric screw until the cam just contacts the roller when index mark is aligned with center of roller. Tighten the locknut. Move the speed control to the maximum speed position and adjust the length of throttle rod (TR – Fig. C10-5) so that it can be connected when carburetor throttles are at maximum opening. Recheck adjustments after connecting throttle rod to make certain that the vertical control shaft contacts the maximum speed stop at the same time carburetor throttles are completely opened.

REED VALVES. "Vee" type intake reed valves are located between the inlet manifold and the crankcase for each cylinder. To remove the reed valve, it is necessary to remove the carburetors and inlet manifold (7 – Fig. C10-7 or C10-8). On 3-cylinder models, all three reed valve assemblies (1, 2 & 3) are attached to plate (5). On 4-cylinder models, two reed valve assemblies (1, 2 & 3) are attached to each plate (5). Spacer plate (S) is used on 3-cylinder 85 hp models and late 4-cylinder models.

Seating surface of reed valve body (3) must be smooth and reed petals (2) must not be bent, broken or cracked. Assembled reed petals may stand open a maximum of 0.010 inch at tip end. Check seating visually. Reed stop setting should be measured as shown in Fig. C10-9. Stop should be 0.281 inch on all models without spacer plate (S) and 0.310 inch on models with spacer plate.

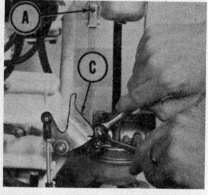

Fig. C10-4—The throttle cam (C) should just contact throttle roller when the index line is aligned with center of roller. Throttle plates should all open and close exactly alike by adjusting at screws (A).

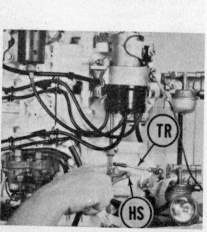

Fig. C10-5—Refer to text for adjusting speed control linkage. High speed stop screw (HS) is used on early models.

Fig. C10-7—Exploded view of inlet manifold and reed valve assembly used on three cylinder models. Refer to Fig. C10-8 for legend.

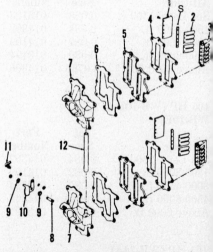

Fig. C10-8—Exploded view of inlet manifolds and reed valve assemblies used on four cylinder models.

S. Spacer plate
1. Reed stop
2. Reed petals
3. Reed body
4. Gasket
5. Adapter plate
6. Gasket
7. Inlet manifold
8. Stud
9. Bushing halves
10. Throttle cam
11. Rod end (ball joint)
12. Balance tube (105 hp)

PUDDLE DRAIN VALVES. The puddle drain valves are designed to remove any liquid fuel or oil which might build up in the crankcase; thus providing smoother operation.

The puddle drain valve is located on the starboard side of power head as shown in Fig. C10-10 or C10-11. The reed type valve petals (4) must seat tightly and evenly against valve plate (5). Reed stops (3) should be adjusted to 0.017-0.023 clearance at tip. Make certain that screens (6) are in place in valve plate.

On four-cylinder models, one-way check valves are located in drain hoses (8 – Fig. C10-11). Check to make certain that air will pass freely through both hoses toward "T" fitting (9), but will not pass from fitting to either of the hoses (8).

FUEL PUMP. A two-stage diaphragm type fuel pump is used which is actuated by pressure and vacuum pulsations picked up from the two lower cylinder crankcases. Refer to Fig. C10-12. The two stages operate alternately as shown.

NOTE: Either stage operating independently may permit the motor to run, but not at peak performance.

Most fuel pump service can be performed without removing the assembly from power head. Disconnect the pulse hoses and remove the retaining cap screws; then lift off the pump cover and diaphragm. Remove the sediment bowl and strainer. First stage inlet check valve can be driven out from below, using a ½-inch diameter drift. First stage outlet check valve can be lifted out after removing the retaining screws. The check valves must be installed to permit fuel to flow in the proper direction as shown. To renew the second stage outlet check valve, it is first necessary to remove pump body from power head, remove outlet fuel elbow and drive the check valve out from below. Check valve will be damaged, and a new unit must be installed. DO NOT remove the valve unless renewal is indicated. Install new valve carefully, using an 11/16-inch diameter punch.

Renew the diaphragm if cracked, torn or badly distorted. Install check valves carefully to prevent damage, and reassemble by reversing the disassembly procedure.

IGNITION SYSTEM

All models are equipped with a Magnapower capacitor discharge ignition system except the 125 hp models which are equipped with a Prestolite ignition system. Three different Magnapower ignition systems have been used; Delta, Magnapower II and Motorola and may be identified by the location and type of regulator/rectifier on the engine. Models equipped with a Magnapower (Delta) ignition system have a flat plate type of rectifier (A or B – Fig. C10-13) located adjacent to the distributor. Models equipped with a Magnapower II

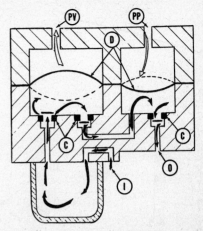

Fig. C10-12 – Cross sectional view of the two stage fuel pump used. Broken lines indicate position of diaphragm when pulse pressure and vacuum are reversed.

C. Check valves
D. Diaphragm
I. Fuel inlet
O. Fuel outlet
PP. Pulse pressure
PV. Pulse vacuum

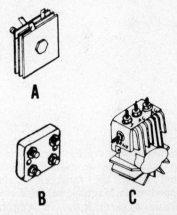

Fig. C10-13 – Magnapower ignition systems may be identified by type of rectifier. Flat rectifiers (A and B) are used on Magnapower (Delta) ignition systems while finned aluminum regulator/rectifiers (C) are used on Magnapower (Motorola) systems. Magnapower II regulator/rectifier is located under the flywheel.

Fig. C10-9 – Reed stops should be 9/32-inch from seating surface of reed block.

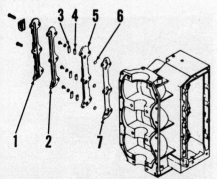

Fig. C10-10 – View of puddle drain valve assembly used on 3-cylinder models. Refer to Fig. C10-11.

1. Cover
2. Gasket
3. Valve stop
4. Valve reed
5. Valve plate
6. Screen
7. Gasket
8. Hoses
9. "Tee" fitting

Fig. C10-11 – Exploded view of puddle drain system used on 4-cylinder models. Hoses (8) contain one way check valves and must be installed so that fluid will pass only in direction of arrows.

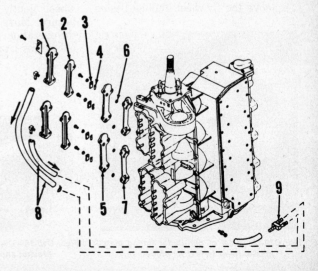

Illustrations Courtesy Chrysler

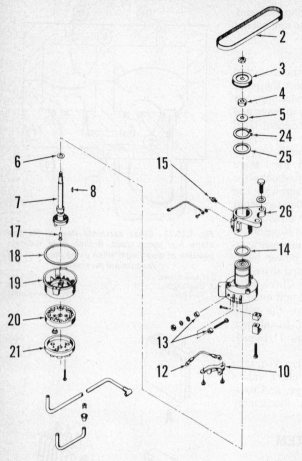

Fig. C10-14 — Exploded view of distributor and bracket assembly. Breakerless ignition distributor is similar but has a trigger in place of breaker points (10).

2. Drive belt
3. Pulley
4. Spacer
5. Thrust washer
6. Spacer
7. Shaft and rotor
8. Key
10. Breaker points
12. Wire
13. Insulators
14. Shims
15. Grease fitting
17. Brush
18. Gasket
19. Distributor cap
20. Seal
21. Cover
24. Snap ring
25. Thrust washer
26. Bracket

fully examine crankshaft. A minimum of 80% surface contact should be indicated by the polished surface; continue lapping only if insufficient contact is evident. Thoroughly clean the crankshaft and flywheel bore to remove all traces of lapping compound, then clean both surfaces with a non-oily solvent.

On models equipped with distributor, slip timing belt off distributor and position belt away from crankshaft so flywheel may be installed without binding timing belt. After installing flywheel, set distributor timing and adjust timing belt tension as outlined in ignition timing section.

On all models, reinstall crankshaft key and flywheel, then tighten flywheel nut to 90 ft.-lbs. torque.

Models With Distributor

DISTRIBUTOR DRIVE BELT. To renew distributor drive belt (2—Fig. C10-14), first loosen distributor retaining cap screws and slip belt off drive pulley (3). Refer to R&R FLYWHEEL section, then remove flywheel, install new drive belt and reinstall flywheel.

Set top cylinder at TDC by aligning "0°" or "TDC" mark on flywheel with "I" or index mark on pointer. Turn distributor pulley until the match mark (Fig. C10-15) on pulley is toward flywheel and install the drive belt. Belt should be tightened until slight (one pound) force will deflect belt 1/4-inch. If belt is too tight, the speed control linkage may bind. After installation is complete, adjust timing as outlined in IGNITION TIMING section.

DISTRIBUTOR. On breaker point models, point gap should be 0.013-0.015 inch for 3-cylinder motors; 0.009-0.011 inch for 4-cylinder motors. Distributor should be removed for breaker point renewal.

ignition system have the regulator/rectifier encased in a molded housing located under the flywheel. Models equipped with a Magnapower (Motorola) ignition system have a regulator/rectifier in a finned aluminum housing (C) located adjacent to the distributor. Refer to the appropriate following paragraphs after determining type of ignition used.

All Models

R&R FLYWHEEL. A special puller (Chrysler part number T-8948-1) is used to remove the flywheel. Pulling bosses

are provided on the flywheel for puller installation. Flywheel should be renewed if flywheel is chipped or cracked as an unbalanced condition may be produced.

The manufacturer recommends that mating surfaces of flywheel and crankshaft be lapped before flywheel is reinstalled. If evidence of working exists proceed as follows:

Remove the flywheel key and apply a light coating of valve grinding or lapping compound to tapered portion of crankshaft. Install the flywheel without the key or crankshaft nut and rotate flywheel gently back and forth about 1/4-turn. Move flywheel 90° and repeat the operation. Lift off the flywheel, wipe off excess lapping compound and care-

Fig. C10-15 — View of distributor timing match marks. Refer to text for procedure.

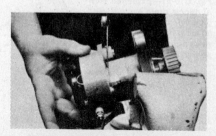

Fig. C10-16 — Distributor body end play in bracket should be 0.001-0.005 inch.

Fig. C10-17 — Refer to text for speed control linkage adjustment.

Illustrations Courtesy Chrysler

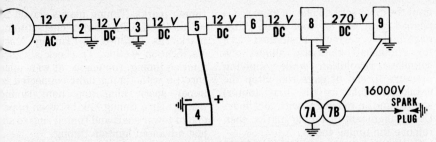

Fig. C10-18—Basic drawing showing flow of current for the Magnapower (Delta) ignition system. Checking for current between the various components should indicate where current flow stops, if a malfunction exists.

		7A. Distributor breaker points	
Alternator	4. Battery		
Rectifier	5. Circuit breaker	7B. Distributor rotor and cap	8. CD ignition module
Trip regulator	6. Ignition switch		9. Ignition coil

Check distributor operation as follows: Position top cylinder at TDC by aligning appropriate mark on flywheel with index mark on timing pointer. Loosen distributor mounting cap screws and slip drive belt off pulley. Install test plugs in place of spark plugs, then switch ignition on. Observe spark while rotating distributor drive pulley. If spark is satisfactory at all cylinders, then no further testing is required. If spark is available to some but not all cylinders, check condition of distributor cap and spark plug wires. If spark is absent at all cylinders, check for spark from coil by inserting a test wire in coil tower and hold the other end of test wire ½-inch from engine ground. Rotate distributor pulley and observe spark. If spark is evident, check for defective coil wire, distributor cap and/or rotor. If spark is absent, check condition of

breaker points on models so equipped and preamplifier on breakerless models.

A general inspection of components may be accomplished by removing the distributor cap without removing the distributor from motor. Check condition and gap of breaker points on models so equipped and for loose carbon from brush (17—Fig. C10-14) that may collect around points causing misfiring. Distributor should be cleaned of carbon after every 50 hours of operation. Inspect rotor and distributor cap for cracks or other damage. Check condition of distributor ground wires. All paint must be removed from areas where ground wires are attached. Check distributor lead wires for short circuits to ground, loose connections and for broken wire.

On breakerless models, check preamplifier operation using a suitable volt-

meter. Remove the white/black stripe wire from distributor terminal and connect voltmeter negative lead to terminal. Connect voltmeter positive lead to remaining distributor terminal that has the blue wire attached. Turn ignition switch on, then slowly rotate distributor drive pulley. Preamplifier operation should be considered satisfactory if voltmeter reads battery voltage every time the closed portion of rotor passes preamplifier and no voltage every time open portion of rotor passes preamplifier.

When overhauling, end play of distributor in bracket should be measured with feeler gage as shown in Fig. C10-16. End play should be within limits of 0.001-0.005 inch. Rotor is available only as a unit with the distributor shaft (7—Fig. C10-14). Distributor shaft bearings are included in housing. After installing distributor assembly, refer to DISTRIBUTOR DRIVE BELT section for distributor timing and belt adjustment procedure.

IGNITION TIMING. Crankshaft timing should be 32° BTDC on 135 hp models manufactured after 1971, all 100, 105 and 115 hp models and all 3-cylinder models. When setting piston position with a dial indicator, the equivalent reading should be 0.278 in. BTDC except on performance 85 hp models with 2.70 in. stroke which should have a 0.266 in. dial indicator equivalent.

Crankshaft timing should be 30° BTDC on 135 hp models manufactured prior to 1972 and all 140 and 150 hp models. When setting piston position with a dial indicator, the equivalent reading should be 0.254 in. BTDC on 140 hp models and 0.246 in. BTDC on all other models.

Crankshaft timing should be 34° BTDC on all 120 and 130 hp models. When setting piston position with a dial indicator, the equivalent reading should be 0.312 in. BTDC.

Adjust Ignition Timing. To adjust ignition timing on breaker point models, first refer to preceding timing specification paragraphs, then make certain breaker points are correctly gapped and are in good (or new) condition. Turn the flywheel until the 36° mark on flywheel is aligned with the "–2" mark on timing pointer of 120 and 130 hp models, "–6" mark on 135 and 150 hp models, and "–4" mark on all other models. Connect one lead of a continuity (test) light to the white primary lead wire on distributor and ground other lead to power head. Move speed control lever to the maximum speed position and observe the test light. Loosen locknut (L—Fig. C10-17) and turn the control rod (R)

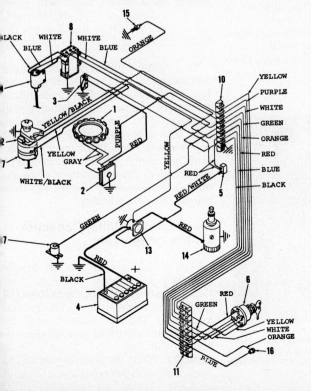

Fig. C10-19—Wiring diagram for Magnapower (Delta) ignition models showing location and color of wires.

1. Alternator stator
2. Bridge rectifier
3. Trip regulator
4. Battery
5. Circuit breaker
6. Ignition-start switch
7. Distributor
8. CD ignition module
9. Coil
10. Terminal block on motor
11. Terminal block at dashboard
12. Starting safety switch
13. Starter solenoid
14. Starter motor
15. Heat indicator sending unit
16. Overheat indicator light
17. Choke solenoid

counterclockwise until breaker points just open as indicated by light going out and tighten locknut (L). Check carburetor synchronization and speed control linkage adjustment as outlined in FUEL SYSTEM section.

To adjust ignition timing on breakerless models, first refer to preceding timing specification paragraphs. Two methods of adjusting breakerless models may be used. One method is to immerse outboard in water and connect a suitable power timing light or Chrysler timing light number T8978 to upper spark plug. With engine throttle in full retard position, crank engine with starter and note timing marks. Timing marks should be within 3° of TDC. If not, check timing marks as outlined in Timing Mark Verification section. To check advance ignition timing, run engine at wide open throttle with timing light connected to upper spark plug and note timing marks. Turn timing link between upper end of tower shaft and distributor to adjust advance ignition timing.

The other method is to static time the engine using a voltmeter. Disconnect the battery, then remove the white/black stripe wire from distributor terminal and connect voltmeter negative lead to terminal. Connect voltmeter positive lead to remaining distributor terminal that has the blue wire attached. Position flywheel so required degree mark on flywheel timing decal (see preceding timing specification paragraphs) is aligned with index mark on timing pointer. Reconnect the battery and turn ignition switch on. With engine throttle at full advance position, turn timing link until voltmeter reads battery voltage. Check adjustment by deflecting play in distributor drive belt. Voltmeter reading should fluctuate from no voltage to battery voltage.

Timing Mark Verification. If the validity of engine timing marks is questioned, verify marks after accurately determining piston position using special timing gage (Chrysler part number TA-2937-1) or a dial indicator as follows:

Disconnect the battery and remove all spark plugs. To determine piston position using special timing gage, thread the tool body into top spark plug opening. Insert the gage rod into tool body, rotate the crankshaft and carefully position piston at exactly TDC.

NOTE: On breaker point models, gage rod should be installed with "70 & up" end out. On breakerless models, gage rod should be installed with "25 through 55" end out.

With the top piston at TDC, thread timing tool body in or out as necessary

until the inner scribed line on gage rod is aligned with end of tool body. After gage body is correctly positioned, turn the crankshaft clockwise almost one complete revolution while applying pressure to end of gage rod. Stop the crankshaft just as the first (outer) scribed line on rod aligns with tool body. Check alignment of timing marks, then remove the timing tool.

On breaker point models, the "36°" mark in flywheel should align with the "I" mark on timing pointer. If incorrect, relocate the pointer.

On breakerless models, the "32°" mark on flywheel timing decal should align with index mark on timing pointer. If incorrect, relocate the pointer or install a new flywheel timing decal.

To determine piston position using a dial indicator, insert dial indicator into top spark plug opening, then rotate crankshaft and carefully position piston at exactly TDC. Zero the dial indicator, then turn crankshaft clockwise almost one complete revolution stopping crankshaft just as dial indicator reads desired specification. Check alignment of timing marks as previously described, then remove the dial indicator.

Models Without Distributor

IGNITION TIMING. Crankshaft timing should be 32° BTDC on all models. When setting piston position with a dial indicator, the equivalent reading should be 0.287 in. BTDC on 125 hp models and 0.278 in. BTDC on all other models.

Adjust Ignition Timing. To adjust ignition timing, first immerse outboard in water and connect a suitable power timing light or Chrysler timing light number T8978 to upper spark plug. With engine throttle in full retard position, crank engine with starter and note

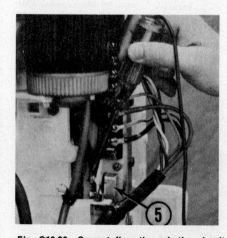

Fig. C10-20—Current flow through the circuit breaker (5) can be checked using a Chrysler test light (T-2951) or voltmeter. Be sure to check both terminals.

timing marks. Timing marks should be within 2° of TDC. If not, check timing marks as outlined in Timing Mark Verification section. To check advance ignition timing, run engine at wide open throttle with timing light connected to upper spark plug and note timing marks. Turn timing link between upper end of tower shaft and timing ring to adjust advanced ignition timing.

NOTE: Engine throttle should be returned to retarded position and engine stopped before turning ignition timing link.

Timing Mark Verification. If the validity of engine timing marks is questioned, verify marks after accurately determining piston position using special timing gage, (Chrysler part number TA-2937-1) or a dial indicator as follows: Disconnect the battery and remove all spark plugs. To determine piston position using special timing gage, thread the tool body into top spark plug opening. Insert the gage rod with "25 through 55" end out, into tool body. Rotate the crankshaft and carefully position piston at exactly TDC. With the top piston at TDC, thread timing tool body in or out as necessary until the inner scribed line on gage rod is aligned with end of tool body. After gage body is correctly positioned, turn the crankshaft clockwise almost one complete revolution while applying pressure to end of gage rod. Stop the crankshaft just as the first (outer) scribed line on rod aligns with tool body. Check alignment of timing marks. The "32°" mark on flywheel timing decal should align with index mark on timing pointer. If incorrect, relocate the pointer or install a new flywheel timing decal. Remove the timing tool.

To determine piston position using a dial indicator, insert dial indicator into top spark plug opening, then rotate crankshaft and carefully position piston at exactly TDC. Zero the dial indicator, then turn crankshaft clockwise almost one complete revolution stopping crankshaft just as dial indicator reads desired specification. Check alignment of timing marks as previously described, then remove the dial indicator.

Magnapower (Delta) Capacitor Discharge Ignition

The ignition system can be briefly described as follows: Refer to Fig. C10-18. Battery or charging voltage (12 volts DC) is delivered to the CD ignition module (8). The CD ignition module increases this voltage (12 volts) to approximately 270 volts and stores it in a capacitor. When the breaker points (7A) open, a signal is delivered to the CD igni-

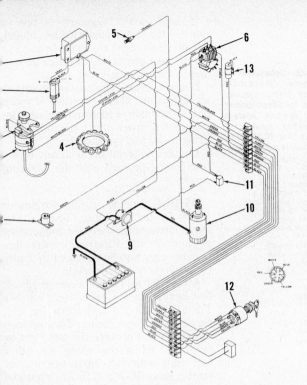

Fig. C10-22—Wiring diagram of early type Magnapower (Motorola) breaker point ignition system. Refer to Fig. C10-23 for parts identification.

tion module to release the 270 volts from the capacitor into the primary winding of coil (9). The coil again increases the voltage to approximately 16000 volts (or whatever is required to fire the spark plug). A wire from the coil to distributor cap and rotor (7B) delivers the secondary voltage (16000 volts) and as the rotor turns, it directs the voltage to the various spark plug wires.

Refer to the following paragraphs for locating trouble and servicing the "Magnapower" ignition system.

TROUBLESHOOTING. Use only approved procedures when testing to prevent damage to components. The fuel system should be checked to make certain that faulty running or failure to start is not caused by incorrect fuel mixture or contaminated fuel.

CHECKING FOR SPARK. A spark gap tester can be used to determine whether the ignition system is delivering current to the spark plugs. The tester is attached to the spark plug leads and grounded to the power head the same as for testing conventional magneto or battery ignition systems. Attempt to start motor with electric starter.

NOTE: Conventional spark plugs (such as Champion J4J) with ground electrodes removed can be used to check for spark. Make certain that shells of test plugs are properly grounded to power head when checking.

If spark occurs regularly at one or more of the tester points (or test plugs), but does not occur regularly or at all at certain test points, check tester ground and the spark plug wires.

If spark occurs regularly and evenly at all test points, check condition of spark plugs, condition of fuel (and mixture), installation of spark plug leads for correct firing order and ignition timing.

If spark does not occur at any of the test points, proceed with the following checks.

WIRING. Engine missing, surging or failure to start or run can be caused by loose connections, corroded connections or short circuits. Electrical system components may also be damaged by faulty connections or short circuits.

Attach one lead of voltmeter or 12 volt test light (such as Chrysler part number T-2951) to the blue wire terminal at top of CD ignition module (8 – Fig. C10-19) and ground other test lead to the metal case (housing) of the CD ignition module. Turn the ignition switch on and observe the test light or voltmeter. If the test light glows, current is available to the CD ignition module. If checking with a voltmeter, voltage should be the same as available at the battery.

If test light does not glow or voltmeter indicates zero or low voltage, check the circuit breaker (5) and trip regulator (3). If the circuit breaker and trip regulator are not faulty, check for broken wires, loose connections, faulty ignition switch or improper ground. A ground wire is used between housing of CD ignition module (8) and power head. Before checking the remaining ignition system components, make certain that current is available to the CD ignition module.

CIRCUIT BREAKER. A 12-volt test light (such as Chrysler part number T-2951) or voltmeter is required for checking. Attach one test lead (Neg. lead of voltmeter) to a suitable ground on the motor. Touch other test lead to each of the two terminals of circuit breaker as shown in Fig. C10-20. If current is available at one of the terminals but not at the other terminal, the circuit breaker is faulty. If the circuit breaker clicks OFF and ON, there is a short circuit in the wiring. Battery voltage should be available at both terminals of circuit breaker.

TRIP REGULATOR. A test light with battery (such as Chrysler part number T-2938) or ohmmeter is required for testing the trip regulator (3 – Fig. C10-19). Attach one lead of test light or ohmmeter to each of the two terminals on trip regulator; then, reverse the test leads. Current should pass through the trip regulator with one connection and not when test leads are reversed. Also, make certain that the red wire from the rectifier (2) is attached to terminal of trip regulator which is identified by a yellow washer. The red wire from circuit breaker (5) should be attached to the top terminal of trip regulator, identified by a red washer.

DISTRIBUTOR AND BREAKER POINTS. The breaker points are used to trigger the ignition system. Failure of breaker points to make contact (open circuit) or failure to break contact (short circuit) will prevent ignition just as in conventional magneto or battery ignition systems. Refer to preceding DISTRIBUTOR section for service information.

IGNITION COIL AND C-D UNIT. Check the installation of the coil. The black wire from terminal stud on side of CD ignition module should be connected to "G" terminal of coil. The blue wire from CD ignition module should be connected to "+" terminal of coil. The white wire from CD ignition module should be attached to the "−" terminal of coil. Also, make certain that white/black (breaker point wire), white and blue wires are correctly attached to terminals at top of CD ignition module as shown in Fig. C10-19.

The ignition coils can be tested using an ignition tester available from Chrysler or several other sources, including the following:

GRAHAM-LEE ELECTRONICS, INC.
4220 Central Ave. N.E.
Minneapolis, Minn. 55421

MERC-O-TRONIC INSTRUMENTS CORP.
215 Branch St.
Almont, Mich. 48003

Illustrations Courtesy Chrysler

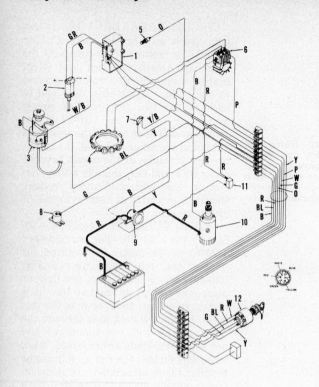

Fig. C10-23—Schematic of Magnapower (Motorola) breakerless ignition system. Schematic for Magnapower (Motorola) ignition system with breaker points is similar but blue (BL) lead to distributor is not used.

1. CD module
2. Ignition coil
3. Distributor
4. Alternator
5. Thermoswitch
6. Regulator/rectifier
7. Interlock switch
8. Choke solenoid
9. Starter relay
10. Starter
11. Circuit breaker
12. Ignition switch
B. Black
BL. Blue
G. Green
GR. Gray
O. Orange
P. Purple
R. Red
W. White
Y. Yellow

If spark occurs regularly at one or more of the tester points (or test plugs), but does not occur regularly or at all at certain test points, check tester ground and the spark plug wires.

If spark occurs regularly and evenly at all test points, check condition of spark plugs, condition of fuel (and mixture), installation of spark plug leads for correct firing order and ignition timing.

If spark does not occur at any of the test points, proceed with the following checks.

WIRING. Engine missing, surging or failure to start or run can be caused by loose connections, corroded connections or short circuits. Electrical system components may also be damaged by faulty connections or short circuits.

Attach one lead of voltmeter or 12 volt test light (such as Chrysler part number T-2951) to ground and check for continuity in ignition wiring. Turn ignition switch on and observe the test light or voltmeter when contacting the other test lead with the input terminal of starter relay (9 – Fig. C10-23), input and output terminals on circuit breaker (11), "B" and "I" terminals on ignition switch (12), red wire connections between ignition switch and CD ignition module and blue wire connections between ignition switch and distributor. Voltmeter should read battery voltage or test light should glow at each test point. Broken wires, loose connections, faulty ignition switch or circuit breaker may be isolated and repaired if test is conducted in sequence.

If the coil is not faulty and all other tests do not indicate a malfunction, renew the CD ignition module. It is important that all other tests are satisfactory before renewing the CD ignition module.

Magnapower (Motorola) Capacitor Discharge Ignition System

Some models are equipped with a Magnapower (Motorola) capacitor discharge ignition system. Three variations of the Motorola ignition system have been used. The first ignition system (Fig. C10-22) has breaker points and an external capacitor. the second and third ignition systems (Fig. C10-23) are similar with the third ignition system using a preamplifier in place of breaker points for a breakerless ignition system.

Troubleshooting and servicing procedures will be for breakerless ignition models but will also apply to breaker point models.

TROUBLESHOOTING. Use only approved procedures when testing to prevent damage to components. The fuel system should be checked to make certain that faulty running or failure to start is not caused by incorrect fuel mixture or contaminated fuel.

CHECKING FOR SPARK. A spark gap tester can be used to determine whether the ignition system is delivering current to the spark plugs. The tester is attached to the spark plug leads and

grounded to the power head the same as for testing conventional magneto or battery ignition systems. Attempt to start motor with electric starter.

NOTE: Conventional spark plugs (such as Champion J4J) with ground electrodes removed can be used to check for spark. Make certain that shells of test plugs are properly grounded to power head when checking.

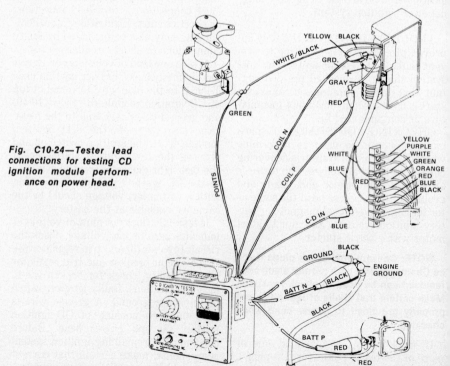

Fig. C10-24—Tester lead connections for testing CD ignition module performance on power head.

Illustrations Courtesy Chrysler

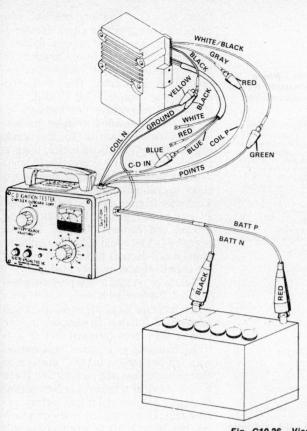

Fig. C10-25—Tester lead connections for testing CD module performance if CD module has been removed from power head.

fails to shut off, CD ignition module is defective and should be renewed. If lamp shuts off, alternately depress test and reset buttons at least 5 times to check for intermittent CD ignition module operation. If lamp fails to turn on then off each time, renew CD ignition module. Repeat test procedure and compare indicator switch position reading when test lamp lights with first test. If indicator switch position varies more than 2 points between tests, CD ignition module is defective and should be renewed.

After conducting CD ignition module tests at 12 volts, set battery voltage adjustment switch to obtain a 9-volt reading on voltmeter and repeat entire test sequence using 65 instead of 80 as minimum indicator switch position when test lamp lights.

DISTRIBUTOR AND COIL. All models are equipped with a distributor which contains breaker points on early models and is breakerless on later models. Refer to preceding DISTRIB-

STARTING SYSTEM. Ignition malfunction may also be due to low voltage when starting. Check cranking voltage by attaching voltmeter test leads to engine ground and input side of starter relay. Disconnect spark plug wires to prevent starting and engage electric starter. A minimum reading of 9 volts is required for proper operation of ignition system during starting. If voltage is less than minimum, check and repair starting system as required.

CD IGNITION MODULE. Perform CD ignition module test using Chrysler CD ignition tester number T8953 (Electro-Specialties, Milwaukee, Wis.). Attach tester leads to CD ignition module and ignition wiring as shown in Fig. C10-24 connecting 12-volt power lead (BATT P) last. If CD ignition module has been removed from power head, make tester lead connections as shown in Fig. C10-25. Turn battery voltage adjustment switch as required to obtain a 12-volt reading on voltmeter. Turn indicator switch to position 100, then slowly turn indicator switch counterclockwise while working test button 2-3 times per second until tester lamp lights. Note indicator switch position, if test lamp does not light on or before position 80 and CD ignition module is properly grounded, then CD module is defective and should be renewed. Depress reset button to shut off tester lamp. If lamp

Fig. C10-26—View showing location of Magnapower II CD module (B), regulator/rectifier (C) and alternator (A). Trigger modules (1, 2, 3, & 4) are numbered according to their respective engine cylinders. Location of terminals. (T-1 and T-4) is also shown.

Fig. C10-27—Schematic of Magnapower II ignition system.

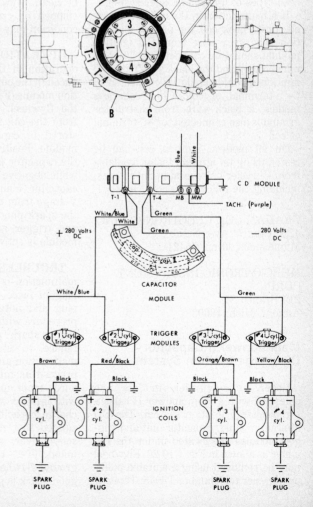

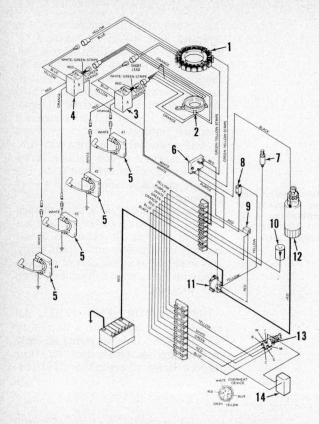

Fig. C10-28—Wiring diagram of Prestolite breakerless ignition system.

1. Stator
2. Trigger coil
3. CD ignition module for no. 1 and no. 2 cylinders
4. CD ignition module for no. 3 and no. 4 cylinders
5. Ignition coils
6. Regulator/rectifier
7. Heat indicator
8. Neutral interlock switch
9. Circuit breaker
10. Choke solenoid
11. Starter solenoid
12. Starter
13. Ignition switch
14. Overheat warning device

UTOR section for service information on both types of ignition breaker systems.

If a malfunction in the coil is suspected, first check coil for proper installation. The gray wire from CD ignition module should be connected to "+" terminal of coil and the black wire from CD ignition module should be connected to "−" terminal of coil. On breakerless models, a black wire from distributor ground is also connected to "−" terminal of coil.

On all models, ignition coil can be tested using an ignition tester available from Chrysler or several other sources, including the following:

GRAHAM-LEE ELECTRONICS, INC.
4220 Central Ave. N.E.
Minneapolis, Minn. 55421

MERC-O-TRONIC INSTRUMENTS CORP.
215 Branch St.
Almont, Mich. 48003

Magnapower II Capacitor Discharge Ignition System

Later four-cylinder models are equipped with a Magnapower II capacitor discharge ignition system. The CD ignition module, capacitor unit and trigger modules are located under the flywheel as shown in Fig. C10-26. Flywheel may be removed using a suitable puller or Chrysler tool number T8948. Taper of crankshaft end and flywheel bore must be clean. Flywheel should be renewed if chipped or cracked as an unbalanced condition may be produced.

OPERATION. Voltage necessary for operation of the ignition system is induced in the coil windings of the CD ignition module (Fig. C10-27) by a magnet in the flywheel. The alternating current from the coil windings is rectified and stored in capacitors in the capacitor module. Positive 280 volts is stored by the capacitor connected to terminal T-1 while negative 280 volts is stored by the capacitor connected to terminal T-4. Voltage from the capacitor is applied to the spark plug through the ignition coil and trigger module when the trigger module is activated by the flywheel.

TROUBLESHOOTING. If ignition malfunction is suspected, install a test plug in place of number 1 (top) spark plug and note spark at plug. Repeat procedure with other cylinders to locate faulty spark plug. If engine miss or failure to start is due to ignition malfunction and not faulty spark plugs, proceed as follows: Detach spark plug wires from spark plugs. Crank engine with ignition switch in "ON" position to charge capacitors. Using a suitably insulated tool such as a plastic handled screwdriver, ground flywheel to terminal (T-1–Fig. C10-27) and then ground flywheel to terminal (T-4). If a good spark is present at both terminals, then the CD ignition module and capacitors are good. To check number 1 or number 2 cylinder trigger module, connect "Coil N" lead from Chrysler CD ignition tester number T8953 (Electro-Specialties, Milwaukee, Wis.) to a good ground and connect "Coil I" lead from CD tester to positive (+) terminal of number 1 or number 2 cylinder ignition coil. Set dial of tester to "65" and crank engine. If lamp lights on tester, trigger module is operating correctly. If lamp does not light, renew trigger module. To check operation of number 3 or number 4 cylinder trigger module, connect "Coil P" lead of CD ignition tester to a good ground and connect "Coil N" lead to negative (−) terminal of bottom cylinder ignition coil. Repeat test procedure used for upper cylinder trigger module.

If little or no spark was present when T-1 and T-4 terminals were tested, note which terminal had little or no spark and proceed as follows: Disconnect trigger module lead from terminal (T-1 or T-4) which had little or no arc. Crank engine with ignition switch in "ON" position to charge capacitors and recheck arc. If arc is now good to terminal, inspect wiring to trigger module and if satisfactory, renew trigger module on cylinder which was misfiring. If arc to terminal was still weak or absent, CD ignition module or capacitor is faulty and may be checked as follows: Disconnect capacitor and trigger leads from terminal (T-1 or T-4) that has little or no spark. Connect a spade terminal to terminal (T-1 or T-4) and connect Chrysler CD ignition tester number T8953 (Electro-Specialties, Milwaukee, Wis.) to spade terminal. To check T-1 terminal, connect "Coil P" lead from tester to T-1 terminal and "Coil N" lead to a good ground. To check T-4 terminal, connect "Coil N" lead from tester T-4 terminal and "Coil P" lead to a good ground. Set dial of tester to "50" and crank engine. If tester lights, CD ignition module is good and capacitor module should be renewed. If tester does not light, CD ignition module is faulty and should be renewed.

Prestolite Models

All 125 hp models are equipped with a Prestolite capacitor discharge ignition system. Voltage necessary for ignition system operation is induced in the windings of the stator (1–Fig. C10-28) by a magnet in the flywheel which develops 225 volts AC. The alternating current from the stator windings is fed to the CD ignition modules (3 and 4) and rectified, then the 225 volts DC is stored in capacitors. Voltage from the capacitors is released to the ignition coils (5) when timing magnets in the flywheel cause the trigger module to close the circuit.

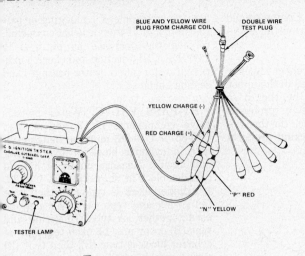

Fig. C10-29—Tester lead connections for checking voltage output of charge coil.

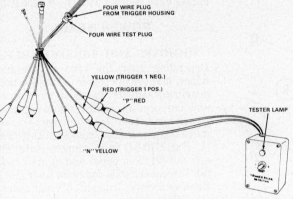

Fig. C10-30—Tester lead connections for checking trigger coil operation.

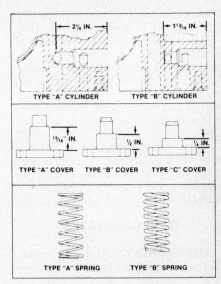

Fig. C10-32—Water by-pass valve components must be matched to hole in cylinder block. Refer to text.

The voltage is then stepped up to 25,000-32,000 volts in the ignition coils and applied to the spark plugs.

TROUBLESHOOTING. Use only approved procedures when testing to prevent damage to components. The fuel system should be checked to make certain that faulty running is not caused by incorrect fuel mixture or contaminated fuel. If ignition malfunction is suspected, use Chrysler tool T8953, plug adapter set T11237, number 22 tester from ignition tester set T8996 and suitable timing light such as Chrysler timing light T8978. Check and make sure ignition malfunction is not due to spark plug or ignition coil failure. Install test plugs in place of the spark plugs and observe spark while engine is being cranked with starter. If spark is absent at both cylinders, check condition of charge coil as follows:

Separate the blue and yellow wire connection between charge coil (stator) and CD ignition module and attach double wire plug adapter to wire plug from charge coil as shown in Fig. C10-29. Attach red (P) lead from T8953 tester to red sleeved adapter wire marked "Charge (+)." Attach yellow (N) lead of tester to yellow sleeved adapter wire marked "Charge (−)." Turn tester

switch to position 50 and crank engine. If tester lamp does not light, charge coil is defective and stator should be renewed. If lamp lights, charge coil operation is satisfactory and trigger coil and CD ignition module circuits for each cylinder must be checked. Remove tester and plug adapter set, then reconnect blue and yellow wire plugs.

To check operation of number 1 and number 2 cylinder trigger coil, separate the four-wire connection between CD ignition module and trigger coil and attach

four-wire plug adapter to wire plug from trigger coil as shown in Fig. C10-30. Attach red (P) lead from number 22 tester to red sleeved adapter wire marked "Trigger 1 Pos." and yellow (N) tester lead to yellow sleeved adapter wire marked "Trigger 1 Neg." Place switch of tester in number 1 position and crank engine. Trigger coil operation is satisfactory if tester lamp lights. Renew trigger housing if tester lamp does not light.

To check operation of number 3 and number 4 cylinder trigger coil, repeat test procedure for number 1 and number 2 cylinder trigger coil but connect red (P) tester lead to red sleeved adapter wire marked "Trigger 2 Pos." and yellow (N) tester lead to yellow sleeved adapter wire marked "Trigger 2 Neg."

To check CD ignition module performance for number 1 and number 3 ignition coils, separate primary lead connectors between CD ignition modules and ignition coils. Connect single wire adapter to

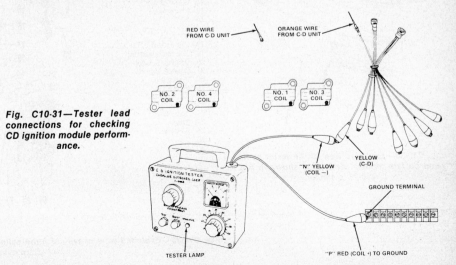

Fig. C10-31—Tester lead connections for checking CD ignition module performance.

orange (number 1 or number 3 cylinder) wire from CD ignition module (Fig. C10-31), then attach yellow (N) lead of T8953 tester to yellow sleeved adapter wire marked C-D. Attach red (P) tester lead to ground terminal of engine terminal block. Turn tester switch to position 60 and crank engine. Renew CD ignition module if tester lamp does not light.

Repeat CD ignition module performance test for number 2 and number 4 ignition coils, by connecting single wire adapter to red (number 2 or number 4 cylinder) wire from CD ignition module.

COOLING SYSTEM

THERMOSTAT. The cooling system thermostat is located beneath a cover on top of the cylinder head. Engine should not be run without a thermostat as engine may overheat.

WATER PUMP. The rubber impeller type water pump is located in the upper gearcase and is driven by the drive shaft. When cooling system problems are encountered, first check the thermostat to see that it is working properly and the water inlet for plugging or partial stoppage. If trouble is not corrected, remove the gearcase as outlined in LOWER UNIT section and check condition of water pump, water passages and sealing surfaces.

BY-PASS VALVE. Water by-pass valve components (7, 8 and 9 – Fig. C10-35 or C10-36) must be matched to hole in cylinder block or overheating may result. Measure depth of hole in cylinder block as shown in Fig. C10-32. If cylinder block is type (A), then type (A) spring and type (A) cover may be used together, or type (B) spring and type (B) cover may be used together. If cylinder block is type (B), then type (B) spring must be used with cover type (C).

POWER HEAD

REMOVE AND DISASSEMBLE. Depending upon the type of maintenance, it is usually easier to remove the distributor, starter, flywheel, alternator and carburetors before removing the power head from the motor leg. To remove the power head, remove all screws (1 – Fig. C10-34) from support plate (8) and nut (2) from upper end of shift rod (9). Disconnect shift rod from lever (10). Remove screws (3) and lift off rear cover (11). Remove screws (4) and nuts (5), then carefully lift power head from the lower unit. Remove screws (6) and stud nuts (7) and remove the exhaust tube (12) and spacer plate (13) from power head.

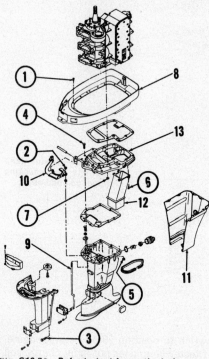

Fig. C10-34—Refer to text for method of removing the power head.

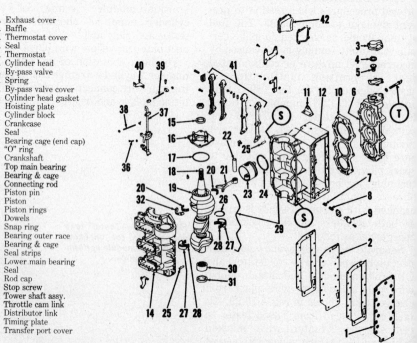

1. Exhaust cover
2. Baffle
3. Thermostat cover
4. Seal
5. Thermostat
6. Cylinder head
7. By-pass valve
8. Spring
9. By-pass valve cover
10. Cylinder head gasket
11. Hoisting plate
12. Cylinder block
13. Crankcase
14. Seal
15. Bearing cage (end cap)
16. "O" ring
17. Crankshaft
18. Top main bearing
19. Bearing & cage
20. Connecting rod
21. Piston pin
22. Piston
23. Piston rings
24. Dowels
25. Snap ring
26. Bearing outer race
27. Bearing & cage
28. Seal strips
29. Lower main bearing
30. Seal
31. Rod cap
32. Stop screw
36. Tower shaft assy.
37. Throttle cam link
38. Distributor link
39. Timing plate
40. Transfer port cover

Fig. C10-35 – Exploded view of typical three cylinder power head. Refer to Fig. C10-10 for puddle drain system (41).

Fig. C10-33—Exploded view of the water pump used on late models. Early type shown in Fig. C10-36 is similar.

1. Drive shaft
2. Impeller drive key
3. Pump housing
4. Impeller
5. Back plate
6. Gasket
7. Drive shaft seal (lower)
9. Snap ring
10. Bearing cone
11. Bearing cup
53. Water line seal
54. Drive shaft seal (upper)

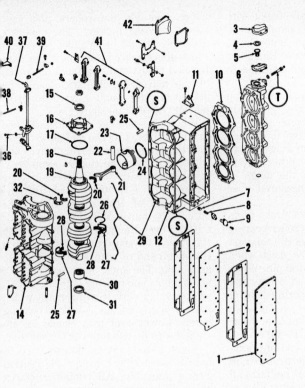

Fig. C10-36—Exploded view of typical four-cylinder power head assembly. Refer to Fig. C10-11 for puddle drain system (41).

1. Exhaust cover
2. Baffle
3. Thermostat cover
4. Seal
5. Thermostat
6. Cylinder head
7. By-pass valve
8. Spring
9. By-pass valve cover
10. Cylinder head gasket
11. Hoisting plate
12. Cylinder block
14. Crankcase half
15. Seal
16. Bearing cage (end cap)
17. "O" ring
18. Crankshaft
19. Top main bearing
20. Bearing & cage
21. Connecting rod
22. Piston pin
23. Piston
24. Piston rings
25. Dowels
26. Snap ring
27. Bearing outer race
28. Bearing & cage
29. Seal strips
30. Lower main bearing
31. Seal
32. Rod cap
36. Stop screw
37. Tower shaft assy.
38. Throttle cam link
39. Distributor link
40. Timing plate
41. Transfer port cover

Clean oil, grease and fingerprints from outer race of upper main bearing (19) and its bore in crankcase.

NOTE: If alcohol or other flammable solvent is used for cleaning, make certain that area is well ventilated and free from sparks, open flames and electrical equipment.

Apply a light coat of "Loctite" to upper bearing bore in cylinder with all main bearings installed. Outer races of center main bearings (27) and lower main bearings (30) should be turned until the bearing locating pins engage holes in the outer races. Position end gaps of crankshaft sealing rings toward crankcase (14). Install the upper bearing cage (16) without seal (15) or "O" ring (17) and tighten the two screws attaching cage to the cylinder. The lower end of crankshaft can be temporarily attached using two screws and a wood block as shown in Fig. C10-37. The upper bearing cage (16—Fig. C10-35 or C10-36) and the wood block will hold the crankshaft in position while connecting rods and pistons are being installed.

Install piston and connecting rod assemblies making certain that long sloping side of piston is toward exhaust side of cylinder and match marks (M—Fig. C10-38) on connecting rod are up toward top of motor (flywheel end). Install the connecting rod bearing cage halves in connecting rod with the ground matching marks on corners together and up toward top of motor (flywheel end of crankshaft). Position bearing rollers in the cages and install rod cap with match marks (M—Fig. C10-38) together. Connecting rod screws should be tightened to 180 in.-lbs. torque.

Remove the upper bearing cage (16—Fig. C10-35 and Fig. C10-36) and the wood block (WB—Fig. C10-37). Install the crankcase seal strips (29—Fig. C10-35 or C10-36) in grooves, then apply 3M-EC750 sealer to mating surfaces of crankcase in areas adjacent to upper and

Refer to Fig. C10-35 or C10-36 and remove the cylinder head (6). Remove the exhaust cover (1), plate (2), transfer port covers (42), by-pass valve (7, 8 and 9) and puddle drain assembly (41) for cleaning. The crankcase front half (14) can be removed after removing all of the retaining stud nuts and screws including those attaching the bearing cage (16). The crankcase halves are positioned with dowel pins (25) and can be separated by prying at the two slots (S). Use extreme care to prevent damage to the crankshaft and do not pry anywhere except the slots provided.

Before removing connecting rods, piston or crankshaft, mark the parts (32, 20, 21, 22 and 23) for correct assembly to each other and in the correct cylinder. Parts (27 and 28) of the center main bearings must be marked for correct assembly to the main bearing journal from which they were removed. Separation of these parts can be easily accomplished with seven containers marked to indicate the correct position.

Refer to the appropriate following paragraphs for service and assembly instructions for crankshaft, connecting rods, pistons, and bearings.

ASSEMBLY. Before assembling, make certain that all joint and gasket surfaces are clean, free from nicks, burrs, warped surfaces or hardened sealer or carbon. The crankcase must be completely sealed against both pressure and vacuum. Exhaust cover and cylinder

head must be sealed against water leakage pressure. Mating surfaces between power head, lower unit and the spacer plate (13—Fig. C10-34) must form a tight seal.

Refer to the appropriate paragraphs for assembling the piston rings to pistons, pistons to connecting rods and main bearings to the crankshaft.

NOTE: It is extremely important that parts (20, 21, 22, 23, 24, 26, 27, 28 and 32—Fig. C10-35 or C10-36) are installed in the same location from which they were removed if the old parts are reinstalled. If parts are intermixed or installed in wrong location, early failure may result.

Fig. C10-37—The crankshaft can be held in position while installing the connecting rods and pistons using a wood block (WB) at lower end and bearing cage at upper end.

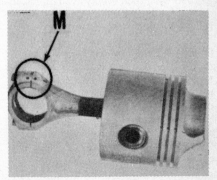

Fig. C10-38—Match marks (M) on rod and cap should be aligned and toward top of motor. The long, tapering side of piston should be toward exhaust ports in cylinder.

Illustrations Courtesy Chrysler

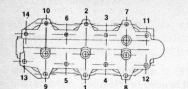

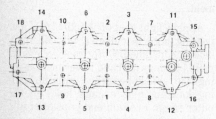

Fig. C10-39—To prevent damage, tighten cylinder head retaining screws in sequence shown to the torque values recommended in text.

center main bearings and lower crankshaft seal. Do not apply sealer to areas outside of crankshaft seal groove. Coat the upper main bearing bore in front crankcase half (14) with "Loctite" and position the crankcase over the cylinder and crankshaft.

NOTE: Make certain that holes in center and lower main bearing races correctly engage the locating dowels in cylinder.

A suitable sealant should be used on threads of screws and studs that attach crankcase halves together and screws and nuts should be tightened to 270 inch-pounds torque. Install new seal (15) in bearing cage (16) with lip down (toward lower unit). Install upper bearing cage and seal assembly using new "O" ring (17) and tighten the four retaining screws to 70 inch-pounds torque.

When installing the cylinder head, coat the first ¾-inch of screw threads with "Permatex #2" or equivalent. Tighten the retaining screws in sequence shoqn in Fig. C10-39 first evenly to 75 in.-lbs., then evenly in 50 in.-lbs. increments until final torque setting is reached. Final torque setting is 225 in.-lbs. for 5/16-18 cap screws and 270 in.-lbs. for 3/8-16 cap screws. After motor has been test run and cooled, retorque screws to final setting. On models so equipped, the thermoswitch is installed at (T—Fig. C10-35 or C10-36). On later models with cylinder head cover, apply a silicone rubber sealant to mating milled surfaces of head and cover.

PISTONS, PINS, RINGS AND CYLINDERS. On 115, 125 and 140 hp models, pistons are fitted with two rings

while all other models are fitted with three rings. Piston rings should be installed with the beveled inner edge toward closed end of piston. Rings are pinned in place to prevent rotation in ring grooves.

On 140 hp models, a semi-keystone top piston ring is used. Top ring groove in piston for semi-keystone ring is measured for wear using two 0.060 inch diameter pins inserted in ring groove directly opposite each other. Ring groove should be within the limits of 3.347-3.351 inch when measured over pins.

The piston pin is a tight press fit in piston bores and rides in a roller bearing in connecting rod. The special tool, part number T-2990, should be used when removing or installing piston pin. When assembling piston, pin and connecting rod, make sure long, tapering side of piston is assembled for installation toward exhaust side of cylinder and correlation marks (M—Fig. C10-38) on rod are toward top (flywheel) end of crankshaft. Piston pin must be centered in connecting rod bore so that neither end of pin will extend through piston boss as rod is moved from side to side. All friction surfaces should be lubricated with new engine oil when assembling.

CONNECTING RODS, BEARINGS, AND CRANKSHAFT. Before detaching connecting rods from crankshaft, make certain that rod and cap are properly marked for correct assembly to each other and in the correct cylinder. It is important that parts (20, 21, 22, 23, 24, 26, 27, 28 and 32—Fig. C10-35 or C10-36) are installed in the same location from which they were removed if the old parts are reinstalled. If parts are intermixed or if assembled in wrong location, early failure may result.

The crankshaft upper main bearing is renewable. Place upper main bearing on crankshaft with lettered side towards flywheel, then using a suitable press, install bearing flush to within 0.001 inch of bearing seat.

The bearing roller and cages used in the connecting rods and center main bearings are available only as a set

which contains the rollers and cage halves for one bearing. The complete assembly should be installed whenever renewal is required. Bearing cages have beveled match marks ground on corner of cage halves. Match marks must be installed together and toward top (flywheel) end of crankshaft.

When assembling crankshaft and main bearings, proceed as follows: Position the center main bearing halves and rollers (28) over the correct main bearing journal with the notches in cage halves (Fig. C10-40) toward top (flywheel) end of crankshaft. Install the outer race halves (27—Fig. C10-35 or C10-36) over the cage and rollers with the groove for snap ring (26) toward top (flywheel) end of crankshaft and install snap ring. The lower main bearing (30) and center main bearing outer races (27) are provided with locating holes which must properly engage dowels in bearing bores. Lower seal (31) should be installed with lip down toward lower unit.

A non-fibrous grease can be used to hold loose needle bearings in position during assembly. All friction surfaces should be lubricated with new engine oil. Check frequently as power head is being assembled, for binding or locking of the moving parts. If binding occurs, remove the cause before proceeding with the assembly. When assembling, follow the procedures outlined in the ASSEMBLY paragraphs.

PROPELLER

Propellers for normal use are protected by a cushioning-slip clutch. Both two- and three-blade propellers are used. Solid-hub, high-speed propellers are available, but are not intended for general use. Various pitch propellers are available and should be selected to provide full throttle operation within the recommended limits of 4500-5100 rpm on 70 and 75 hp motors; 4500-5500 rpm on 85, 90, 100, 105, 115 and 125 hp motors; 5000-5500 rpm for 120, 130 and 140 hp motors; 5200-5600 rpm for 135

Fig. C10-40—The center main bearing cage halves are provided with match marks which should be toward flywheel end of crankshaft.

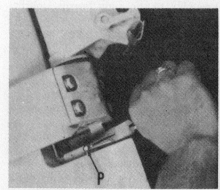

Fig. C10-41—The lower shift rod is attached to the upper rod with a pin shown at (P).

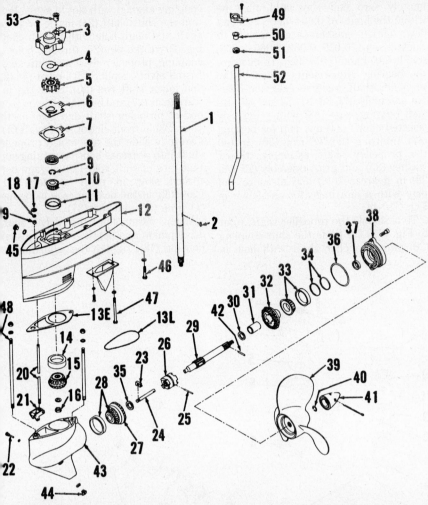

Fig. C10-42 — Exploded view of drive shaft housing, gearcase and associated parts. Late motors use three studs (48) and seal ring (13L). Earlier motors use two studs (48) and gasket (13E). Refer to Fig. C10-33 for exploded view of water pump used on late models.

1. Drive shaft	15. Bearing cone & drive pinion	28. Bearing cup & cone	41. Nut
2. Water pump key	16. Nut	29. Propeller shaft	42. Shear pin
3. Water pump housing	17. Seal retainer	30. Thrust washer	43. Gearcase housing
4. Top plate	18. Spacer	31. Bearing	44. Filler plug
5. Impeller	19. Shift rod seal	32. Reverse gear	45. Vent plug
6. Back plate	20. Shift rod	33. Bearing cup & cone	46. Screws (6 used)
7. Gasket	21. Pivot coupling	34. Shims	47. Screw
8. Drive shaft seal	22. Pivot pin	35. Thrust washer	48. Stud
9. Snap ring	23. Shift yoke	36. "O" ring	49. Water tube bracket
10. Bearing cone	24. Shift shaft	37. Seal	50. Seal
11. Bearing cup	25. Shift pin	38. Bearing cage	51. Grommet
12. Drive shaft housing	26. Shift coupling	39. Propeller	52. Water tube
14. Bearing cup	27. Forward gear	40. Nut seal	53. Water tube seal

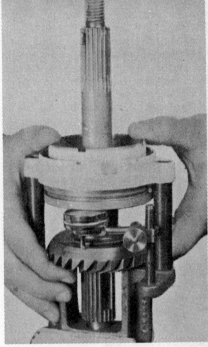

Fig. C10-43 — Special test fixture and dial indicator are used to adjust reverse gear position (backlash).

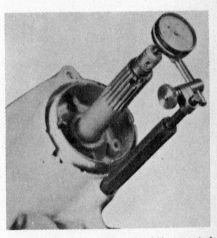

Fig. C10-44 — A dial indicator should be mounted for measuring propeller shaft end play.

and 150 hp motors. Propellers other than those designed for the motor should not be used.

LOWER UNIT

All 90 Hp Models, All 75 Hp Models Prior to 1980 and All Other Models Prior to 1977

R&R AND OVERHAUL. To remove the lower unit gearcase and drive shaft housing from the lower motor leg, remove the pin connecting the upper and lower shift rod (Fig. C10-41). Remove screws (46 and 47 – Fig. C10-42) which attach the drive shaft

housing to lower motor leg and withdraw the complete lower unit drive assembly from the motor leg.

Disassemble and remove the water pump (3 through 7). Remove the propeller and shear pin, and remove any rust or burrs from exposed end of propeller shaft. Remove the stud nuts retaining gearcase housing to driveshaft (upper gearcase) housing.

NOTE: Early motors use two studs (48); late motors use three studs.

Remove shift rod (20); then remove the lower unit gearcase (43). Drive shaft (1), drive pinion (15) and bearings will remain in the drive shaft housing.

Remove the two screws retaining the propeller shaft bearing cage (38) to gearcase, rotate the cage slightly, then tap on ears of cage with a soft hammer to remove the cage. Propeller shaft and associated parts may now be withdrawn.

NOTE: Shift yoke (23) will be free to drop when propeller shaft is removed. Do not lose the yoke.

Slip the forward gear and bearing assembly (27) from the propeller shaft. Shift coupling (26) and shift shaft (24) can be removed after driving pin (25) out. Reverse gear (32) and bearings (31 and 33) can be removed from propeller shaft at the same time using a press.

Keep the thrust washers (30 and 35) with their respective gears. The washers are similar but NOT interchangeable.

Drive gear backlash is controlled by means of shim pack (34) installed between bearing cup (33) and bearing cage (38). Backlash adjustment requires the use of the special test jig (part number J9362) and dial indicator as shown in Fig. C10-43. Shaft end play in the special test fixture should be zero, plus or minus 0.001 inch. Shims are available in thicknesses of 0.006, 0.007 and 0.008 inch.

After backlash has been adjusted, the propeller shaft bearings must be adjusted by varying the thickness of front thrust washer (35–Fig. C10-42). The bearings should be adjusted to approx-

imately zero end play, and must be within the limits of 0.004-0.006 inch end play. Thrust washers are available in thicknesses of 0.059, 0.062, 0.065, 0.068, 0.071, 0.074 and 0.077 inch. To measure the bearing adjustment, assemble the propeller shaft, reverse gear and bearing assembly (29, 30, 31, 32 and 33). Install bearing cage (38) with previously selected shims (34) and cup for bearing (33), omitting the "O" ring (36). Install the propeller shaft assembly, thrust washer (35) and gear assembly (27 and 28) in gearcase (43) and measure end play with a dial indicator as shown in Fig. C10-44.

To assemble the propeller shaft, refer to Fig. C10-42. Slide the shift coupling (26) onto propeller shaft with hole in

coupling aligned with slot in shaft. Position the shift shaft (24) inside propelle shaft and align hole with hole in coup ing. Drive the pin (25) through holes i coupling, propeller shaft and shift shaf Install pivot coupling (21), pivot pin (2 and lower shift rod (20). Slide the for ward gear (27) and bearing cone on fron end of propeller shaft and position th yoke (23) in front slot of shift shaft (24 Carefully slide the assembled propelle shaft into gearcase housing making sur that tabs of shift yoke (23) engage bot forked slots in pivot coupling (21 Carefully install bearing cage using ne "O" ring (36) and seal (37).

When assembling the drive shaf drive pinion and bearings in drive shaf housing (12), tighten the adjusting nu

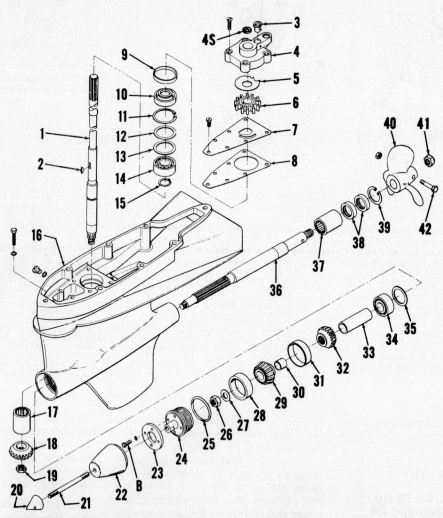

Fig. C10-45 – Exploded view of the racing lower unit. Top plate (5) is not used on all models.

1. Drive shaft	12. Washer	22. Nose cone	34. Ball bearing
2. Impeller drive key	13. Shims (0.006-steel;	23. Retainer	35. Shims (0.006-steel;
3. Water tube seal	0.007-brass; 0.010-	24. Bearing cup	0.007-brass; 0.010-
4. Water pump housing	black)	25. "O" ring	black)
4S. Drive shaft seal	14. Ball bearing	26. Nut	36. Propeller shaft
5. Top plate	15. Snap ring	27. Washer	37. Needle bearing
6. Impeller	16. Gear housing	28. Bearing cup	38. Seals
7. Lower plate	17. Needle bearing	29. Bearing cone	39. Snap ring
8. Gasket	18. Drive pinion	30. Sleeve	40. Propeller
9. Sleeve	19. Nut	31. Sleeve	41. Nut
10. Seal	20. Nose cone nut	32. Driven gear	42. Shear bolt
11. Snap ring	21. Stud	33. Spacer	

16) finger tight and back off to the first castellation; then install the cotter pin.

After completing the assembly of gearcase to the drive shaft housing (12) and drive shaft housing to the lower motor leg, install the shift rod pin (P – Fig. C10-41).

All Other Models

R&R AND OVERHAUL. Remove lower front shock mount cover and remove shift rod pin (13 – Fig. C10-46). Unscrew six screws and separate gearcase from motor leg. Drain lubricant and remove propeller and exhaust snout (18).

Remove spline seal (55) and retainer (54). Disassemble and remove water pump components (1 through 7). Turn shift rod (14) counterclockwise until disengaged from pivot coupling (15) and remove rod. Remove cover (9) and anode (39). Remove screws securing bearing spool (35) and using a suitable puller withdraw spool from gearcase. Remove retaining clips (32), bearing and cage (33), thrust washer (31), thrust bearing (30) and reverse gear (29). Withdraw propeller shaft (28) with components (22 through 27). Unscrew pinion nut (20), withdraw drive shaft (53) and remove pinion gear (19). Unscrew pivot pin (16) and remove pivot coupling (15).

Use the following procedure to check reverse gear backlash: Install a 0.050 inch spacer (Chrysler T8997) in place of shims (52). Install forward gear and bearing (22), drive shaft (53), pinion gear (19) and nut (20). Tighten nut (20) to 85 ft.-lbs. Insert Chrysler shim tool number T8997B in forward gear (22) so flat portion of tool is towards pinion gear (19). Pull up on drive shaft and using a feeler gage measure gap between large OD of tool and pinion gear. Subtract measured gap from 0.055 inch (0.050 inch spacer plus 0.005 inch desired backlash) to obtain thickness of shim pack (52). Remove 0.050 inch shim, install shim pack (52) and repeat above procedure. Gap between pinion gear (19) and large OD of shim tool should be 0.004-0.006 inch.

To check propeller shaft end play, install components (21 through 32) and bearing spool (35). Shim (23) should be thinnest available (0.054 inch). Do not install "O" rings on spool. Tighten spool retaining screws to 150 in.-lbs. Measure end play of propeller shaft and install shims (23) necessary to obtain 0.009-0.011 inch end play.

To reassemble lower unit, reverse disassembly procedure. Tighten pinion nut (20) to 85 ft.-lbs. Install seal (37) with lip towards propeller. "O" rings (34 and 36) have different diameters and must be installed correctly on bearing spool (35). Chamfered end of spool is installed first. Tighten bearing spool (35) retaining screws to 150 in.-lbs. Install seals (8 and 10) with lip towards gearcase. Tighten cover (9) to 70 in.-lbs. Install seal (2) with lip towards power head. Install seal (55) with ridged end towards power head.

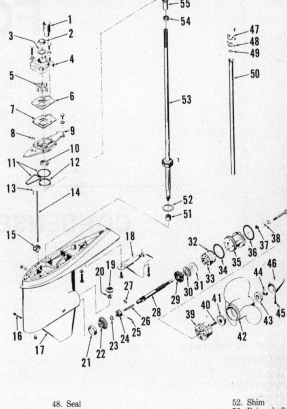

Fig. C10-46 – Exploded view of lower drive unit used on models after 1976.

1. Water tube seal
2. Drive shaft seal
3. Spacer
4. Water pump housing
5. Impeller
6. Lower plate
7. Gasket
8. Shift rod seal
9. Gearcase cover
10. Drive shaft seal
11. Cover seals
12. Crush ring
13. Pin
14. Lower shift rod
15. Pivot coupling
16. Pivot pin
17. Gearcase
18. Exhaust snout
19. Drive pinion
20. Nut
21. Bearing cup
22. Forward gear & bearing
23. Shim
24. Shift coupling
25. Shift pin
26. Shift shaft
27. Shift yoke
28. Propeller shaft
29. Reverse gear
30. Thrust bearing
31. Thrust washer
32. Retainer
33. Bearing & cage
34. "O" ring
35. Spool
36. "O" ring
37. Seal
38. "O" ring
39. Anode
40. Screw
41. Spacer
42. Propeller
43. Washer
44. Nut
45. Pin
46. Prop extension
47. Bracket
48. Seal
49. Grommet
50. Water tube
51. Bearing
52. Shim
53. Drive shaft
54. Seal retainer
55. Seal

FORCE

US MARINE CORP.
105 Marine Drive
Hartford, WI 53027

35 HP

CONDENSED SERVICE DATA

TUNE-UP

Hp/rpm	35/5000
Bore	3 in.
	(76.2 mm)
Stroke	2.414 in.
	(61.3 mm)
Number of Cylinders	2
Displacement	34.1 cu. in.
	(559 cc)
Compression at Cranking Speed (Average)	125-135 psi
	(862.5-931.5 kPa)

Spark Plug:
Champion	L4J
Electrode Gap	0.030 in.
	(0.76 mm)
Ignition Type	CDI

Carburetor:
Make	Tillotson
Model	WB
Fuel:Oil Ratio	50:1

SIZES—CLEARANCES—CAPACITIES

Piston Ring End Gap:
Top Ring	0.006-0.016 in.
	(0.15-0.41 mm)
Bottom Ring	0.004-0.014 in.
	(0.10-0.36 mm)
Piston to Cylinder Clearance	0.0060-0.0095 in.
	(0.152-0.241 mm)
Piston Pin Diameter	0.50000-0.50015 in.
	(12.7000-12.7038 mm)

SIZES—CLEARANCES—CAPACITIES CONT.

Crankshaft Journal Diameters:
Upper Main	1.3774-1.3780 in.
	(34.986-35.001 mm)
Center Main	1.3446-1.3451 in.
	(34.153-34.165 mm)
Lower Main	0.9849-0.9853 in.
	(25.016-25.027 mm)
Crankpin	1.1391-1.1395 in.
	(28.933-28.943 mm)
Gearcase Oil Capacity	12 oz.
	(355 mL)

TIGHTENING TORQUES

Cylinder Head	190 in.-lbs.
	(21.5 N·m)
Flywheel Nut	55-65 ft.-lbs.
	(74.8-88.4 N·m)

Standard Screws:
10-24	30 in.-lbs.
	(3.4 N·m)
10-32	35 in.-lbs.
	(4 N·m)
12-24	45 in.-lbs.
	(5.1 N·m)
1/4-20	70 in.-lbs.
	(7.9 N·m)
5/16-18	160 in.-lbs.
	(18.1 N·m)
3/8-16	270 in.-lbs.
	(30.5 N·m)

LUBRICATION

The power head is lubricated by oil mixed with the fuel. For normal service after break-in, mix 1/6 pint of US Marine Outboard oil or a BIA TC-W certified oil with each gallon of gasoline. The recommended ratio is one-third (1/3) pint of oil per gallon of gasoline for severe service and during break-in. Manufacturer recommends no-lead automotive gasoline although regular or premium gasoline may be used if octane rating is 85 or higher. Gasoline and oil should be thoroughly mixed.

The lower unit gears and bearings are lubricated by oil contained in the gearcase. Recommended gearcase oil is US Marine Outboard Gear Lube or a suitable noncorrosive EP 90 outboard gear oil. The gearcase should be drained and refilled every 100 hours or at least once per season prior to storage. Maintain fluid at level of upper (vent) plug.

To fill gearcase, have motor in an upright position and fill through lower hole in side of gearcase until fluid reaches level of upper (vent) plug hole. Reinstall and tighten both plugs securely, using new gaskets if necessary, to assure a water tight seal.

FUEL SYSTEM

CARBURETOR. A Tillotson WB
pe carburetor is used. Refer to Fig.
5-1 for an exploded view of the car-
uretor.

Initial setting of idle mixture screw
0) is 1¼ turns out from a lightly seated
osition. Final adjustment of car-
uretor should be made with engine at
ormal operating temperature and with
tboard motor in forward gear. Stand-
rd main jet size is 0.066 inch.

To check float level, remove float bowl
nd invert carburetor. Bottom side of
oat should be parallel with gasket sur-
ce of carburetor. Adjust float level by
ending float tang.

Intall throttle plate (1) so notch is up
nd marked side is toward flange end of
arburetor.

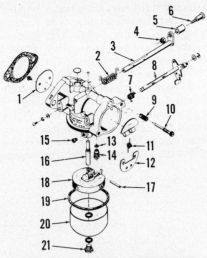

Fig. F5-1—Exoploded view of Tillotson WB carburetor.

1. Throttle plate	12. Choke plate
2. Spring	13. Gasket
3. Throttle shaft	14. Fuel inlet valve assy.
4. Nut	15. High speed jet
5. Roller	16. Main nozzle
6. Eccentric screw	17. Float pin
7. Spring	18. Float
8. Choke shaft	19. Gasket
9. Spring	20. Float bowl
10. Idle mixture screw	21. Bowl retaining screw
11. Spring	

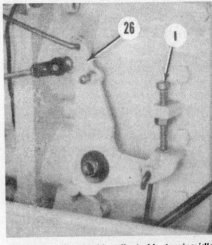

Fig. F5-3—Idle speed is adjusted by turning idle
speed screw (I). Magneto control lever (26) is
identified.

SPEED CONTROL LINKAGE. Igni-
ion timing and throttle opening on all
models must be synchronized so throttle
s opened as timing is advanced.

To synchronize linkage, first check ig-
ition timing to be sure it is set correctly
s outlined in IGNITION TIMING sec-
ion. Disconnect link (L – Fig. F5-2) from
magneto control lever (T – Fig. F5-3)
nd with throttle closed, turn eccentric
crew (S – Fig. F5-2) until roller (R) is
xactly centered over mark (M) on throt-
le cam (C). Reconnect link (L) to
magneto control lever and rotate magneto stator ring until it is against full advance stop. Upper mark (AM) on throt-
le cam should now be aligned with roller
R). Disconnect link (L) and turn link
nds to adjust length of link so mark
AM) and roller are aligned when stator
s at full advance.

Adjust idle speed to a maximum 750
rpm in forward gear by turning idle
speed screw (I – Fig. F5-3) adjacent to
exhasut port covers.

REED VALVES. A "V" type reed
valve is used. The reed plate is located
between the intake manifold and crankcase. Remove carburetor and intake
manifold for access to reed valve.

Renew reeds if petals are broken,
cracked, warped or bent. Never attempt
to bend a reed petal in an effort to improve performance, nor attempt to
straighten a damaged reed. Never install a bent or damaged reed. Seating
surface of reed plate should be smooth
and flat. Install reeds so petals are
centered over openings. Assembled
reeds may stand open to a maximum of
0.010 inch (0.25 mm) at tip end. Reed
stop setting should be 9/32 inch (7.14
mm) when measured from tip of reed
stop to reed plate.

Fig. F5-2 – View of throttle cam and linkage.
Refer to text for identification of components
and adjustment procedures.

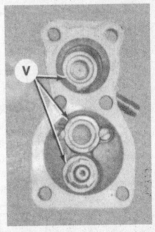

Fig. F5-4—Fuel pump check valves (V) must be
installed as shown for proper operation of fuel
pump.

FUEL PUMP. All models are
equipped with a two-stage diaphragm
type fuel pump which is actuated by
pressure and vacuum pulsations from
the engine crankcases.

**NOTE: Either stage of the fuel pump
operating independently may permit the
motor to run, but not at peak performance.**

To remove fuel pump, disconnect fuel
hoses to pump and unscrew six cap
screws which retain fuel pump body.
Check valves are renewable, but be sure
a new check valve is needed before
removing old check valve as it will be
damaged during removal. Unscrew the
two retaining screws to remove center
check valve. The two outer check valves
must be driven out from below. Check
valves (V – Fig. F5-4) must be correctly
installed as shown. Install check valves
carefully to prevent damage. Inspect

diaphragm and renew diaphragm if
cracked, torn or badly distorted.

IGNITION

A breakerless, capacitor discharge ignition system is used. Note wiring
diagram in Fig. F5-5. Tapered bore of
flywheel and crankshaft end must be
clean, dry and smooth before installing
flywheel. Renew a chipped or cracked
flywheel. Flywheel and crankshaft
tapers may be cleaned by using fine
valve grinding compound. Apply grinding compound to tapers and rotate
flywheel back and forth approximately
one-quarter turn. Do not spin flywheel
on crankshaft. Clean flywheel and
crankshaft tapers thoroughly. Tighten
flywheel nut to 55-65 ft.-lbs. (74.8-88.4
N·m).

If ignition malfunction occurs, use
tester tool T8953, plug adapter set

T11201 and number 22 tester with load coil from tool T8996 and refer to following trouble-shooting procedures:

Check and make sure ignition malfunction is not due to spark plug or ignition coil failure. If spark is absent at both cylinders, check condition of charge coil as follows: Separate the blue and yellow wire connection between charge coil and CD ignition module and attach double wire plug adapter to wire plug from charge coil as shown in Fig. F5-6.

Attach red (P) lead from tester number 22 to red sleeved adapter wire marked "Plug 2." Attach yellow (N) lead of number 22 tester and yellow sleeved adapter wire marked "Plug 1" to engine ground. Place tester switch in number 2 position and crank engine. If tester lamp does not light, low voltage windings of charge coil are defective and stator should be renewed. If lamp lights, continue charge coil test by disconnecting yellow sleeved wire adapter from engine

ground and attaching it to red (P) lead of T8953 tester as shown in Fig. F5-7. Attach yellow (N) lead of T8953 tester to engine ground. Turn tester switch to position 10 and crank engine. If tester lamp does not light, high voltage windings of charge coil are defective and stator should be renewed. If lamp lights, charge coil operation is satisfactory and trigger coil and CD ignition module circuits for each cylinder must be checked. Remove tester and plug adapter set then reconnect blue and yellow wire plugs.

Separate the four wire connection between CD ignition module and trigger coil and attach four-wire plug adapter to wire plug from trigger coil as shown in Fig. F5-8. Attach red (P) lead from tester number 22 to red sleeved adapter wire marked "Trigger 1 Pos." and yellow (N) lead to yellow sleeved adapter wire marked "Trigger 1 Neg." Place switch of tester in number 1 position and crank engine. Trigger coil operation is satisfactory if tester lamp lights. Renew trigger housing if tester lamp does not light.

To check operation of number 2 cylinder trigger coil, repeat test procedure for number 1 cylinder trigger coil but connect red (P) lead of tester to red sleeved adapter wire marked "Trigger 2 Pos." and yellow (N) lead to yellow sleeve adapter wire marked "Trigger 2 Neg."

To check ignition module performance for each cylinder, connect yellow (N) lead from tester T8953 to ground terminal of engine terminal block (Fig. F5-9). Disconnect white (number 2 cylinder) or brown (number 1 cylinder) primary lead from ignition coil and connect red (P) lead of tester T8953 to primary lead. Connect leads of tester T8996 load coil to ground terminal of engine terminal block and primary coil lead of cylinder being tested. Turn T8953 tester dial to number 50. Crank engine and tester lamp should light. Renew ignition module if lamp does not light.

COOLING SYSTEM

WATER PUMP. All motors are equipped with a rubber impeller type water pump. When cooling system problems are encountered, first check the water inlet for plugging or partial stoppage. Then if not corrected, remove the lower unit gearcase and check the condition of water pump, water passages and sealing surfaces.

Access to the water pump is possible after separating lower unit from motor leg. Remove motor leg covers. Unscrew fasteners securing drive shaft housing to motor leg and disconnect intermediate shift rod from lower shift rod

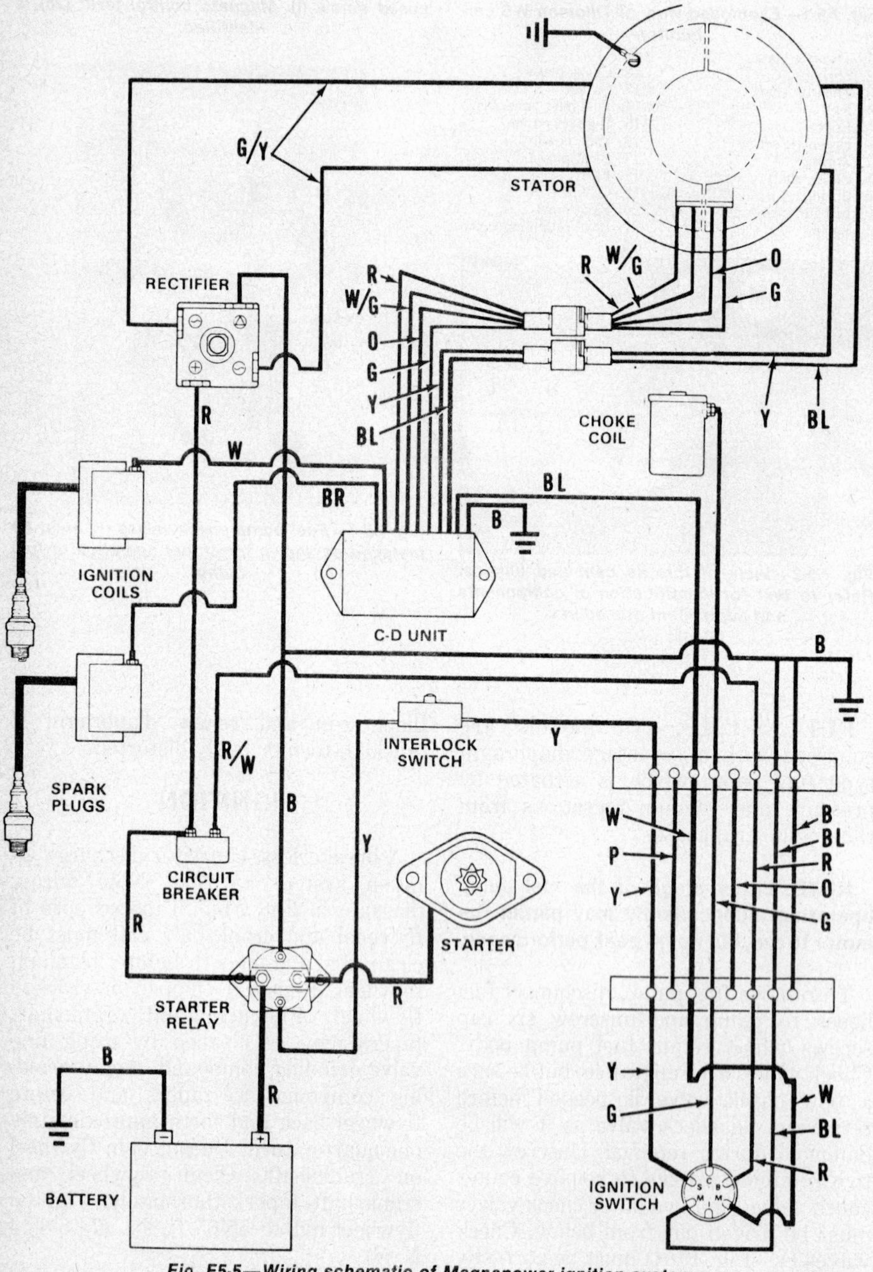

Fig. F5-5—Wiring schematic of Magnapower ignition system.

B. Black	O. Orange	R. Red	Y. Yellow
G. Green	P. Purple	W. White	BL. Blue

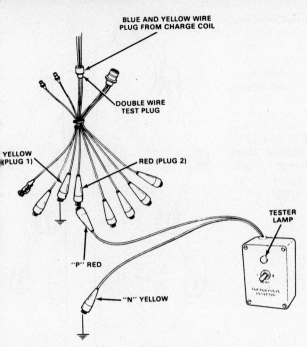

Fig. F5-6 — Tester connections for checking low voltage output of charge coils.

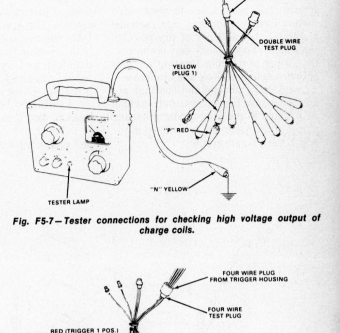

Fig. F5-7 — Tester connections for checking high voltage output of charge coils.

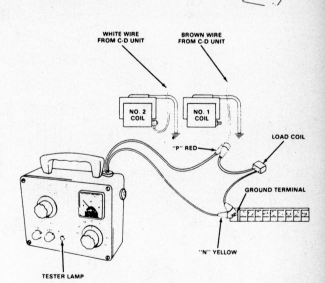

Fig. F5-8 — Tester connections for checking operation of trigger coil.

Fig. F5-9 — View showing tester connections needed to check CD ignition module output.

by removing pin (13 – Fig. F5-16). Separate lower unit from motor leg. Unbolt and remove water pump.

Drive shaft seal (3) should be installed with spring loaded lip towards top. Drive shaft spline seal should be renewed if hard or cracked. Lubricate water tube seal and splines on upper end of drive shaft. Connect shift rods and carefully slide motor leg and drive shaft housing together making certain that water tube enters seal. Complete reassembly in reverse order of disassembly.

POWER HEAD

R&R AND OVERHAUL. To remove the power head, mount the outboard motor on a suitable stand and remove the engine cover. Disconnect the red battery lead from upper terminal of starter relay. Disconnect choke solenoid lead. Remove emergency hand starter assembly. Remove electric starter bracket, interlock switch and any other electrical wiring or component that will interfere with power head removal. Label all wires for correct reassembly. Remove flywheel and stator with ignition and alternator components. Remove fuel pump, carburetor and reed valve assembly. Detach shift linkage and throttle control linkage as needed. Remove lower shock mount covers, lower thrust pad (21 – Fig. F5-10) at front of motor leg and shock and lower nuts of the two studs between the kingpin and plate (9) and spacer plate (4).

Unscrew motor leg cover bolts and remove rear motor leg cover. Engage reverse lock and pull outboard motor back enough to allow removal of front motor leg cover. Unscrew power head

retaining screws and withdraw power head.

To disassemble power head, remove seal in bore of bottom end of crankshaft. Unbolt and remove upper bearing cage and cylinder head. Remove transfer port cover, exhaust cover and exhaust plate. Unscrew cylinder block to crankcase screws (two screws are in reed valve cavity). Drive out locating pins, then use a suitable tool and pry at pry point to separate cylinder block and crankcase. Do not pry at machined mating surfaces between cylinder block and crankcase.

Crankshaft, pistons and bearings are now accessible for removal and overhaul as outlined in the appropriate following paragraphs. Assemble as outlined in the ASSEMBLY paragraph.

ASSEMBLY. When reassembling, make sure all joint and gasket surfaces are clean, free from nicks and burrs, warped surfaces or hardened cement or carbon. The crankcase and inlet manifolds must be completely sealed against both vacuum and pressure. Exhaust manifold and cylinder head must be sealed against both vacuum and pressure. Exhaust manifold and cylinder head must be sealed against water leakage and pressure. Mating surfaces of exhaust areas between power head and motor leg must form a tight seal.

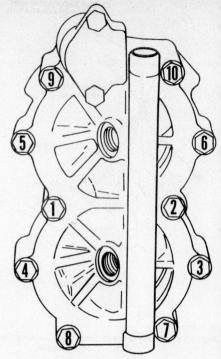

Fig. F5-11—Tighten cylinder head cap screws in the sequence shown.

Sparingly apply a coating of sealant to mating surfaces of cylinder block and crankcase. Tighten crankcase screws in a spiral pattern starting with center screws. Tighten cylinder head screws in sequence shown in Fig. F5-11. Install seal (6 – Fig. F2-12) with "O" ring end inserted first until seal is 0.030 inch (0.76 mm) above edge of bore. Install a new seal in bore of bottom end of crankshaft. Install long screw for transfer port cover in upper left-hand hole as identified by (H) in Fig. F5-13. Complete remainder of assembly.

PISTONS, PINS, RINGS & CYLINDERS. Pistons are fitted with two piston rings which should be installed with the beveled inner edge (B – Fig. F5-14) toward top of piston. Piston ring end gap for top ring should be 0.006-0.016 inch (0.15-0.41 mm) and 0.004-0.014 inch (0.10-0.36 mm) for bottom ring. Rings are pinned in place to prevent rotation in ring grooves. Piston must be heated to install piston pin. Do not interchange pistons between cylinders. Piston to cylinder clearance should be 0.0060-0.0095 inch (0.152-0.241 mm).

When assembling piston, pin and connecting rod, match marks on connecting rod and cap must be aligned and long, tapering side of piston must be towards exhaust port.

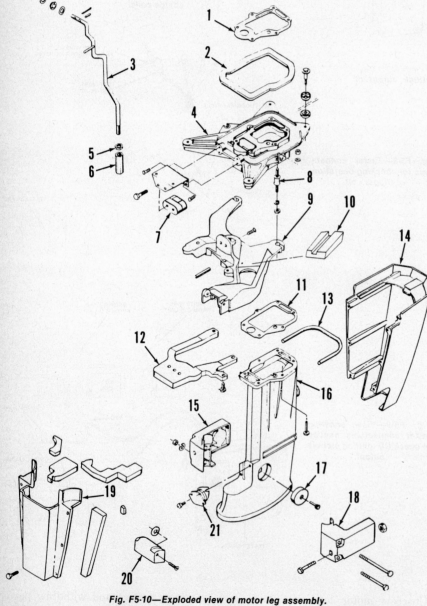

Fig. F5-10—Exploded view of motor leg assembly.

1. Gasket	7. Upper thrust mount	13. Seal
2. Seal	8. Stud	14. Rear motor leg cover
3. Upper shift rod	9. Kingpin plate	15. Shock mount cover (Starboard)
4. Spacer plate	10. Pad	16. Motor leg
5. Locknut	11. Gasket	17. Shock mount
6. Coupler	12. Carrying handle	18. Shock mount cover (Port)
		19. Front motor leg cover
		20. Cover
		21. Thrust pad

CONNECTING RODS, BEARINGS AND CRANKSHAFT. Before detaching connecting rods from crankshaft, mark connecting rod and cap for correct assembly to each other and in the correct cylinder. The needle rollers and cages at crankpin end of connecting rod should be kept with the assembly and not interchanged.

The bearing rollers and cages used in the connecting rods and the rollers and liners in the center main bearing are available only as a set for each bearing. The complete assembly should be installed whenever renewal is indicated. Connecting rod bearing cages have beveled notches which must be installed together and toward top (flywheel) end of crankshaft. Match marks stamped on connecting rod and cap must be on the same side. Connecting rod is fractured to provide an uneven surface between rod and cap. Be sure rod and cap are properly meshed before tightening rod screws.

Inspect condition of seal ring (7 – Fig. F5-12) and carefully install ring in crankshaft groove. Seal ring (7) must prevent leakage between cylinders and a defective seal will result in poor engine performance.

Before installing crankshaft in crankcase, install bearing liner (9) over dowel

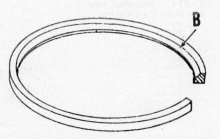

Fig. F5-14—Install piston rings with bevel (B) toward top of piston crown.

pin and place fourteen bearing rollers (8) in liner with a suitable grease to hold rollers in place. Install crankshaft and position remaining sixteen bearing rollers around crankshaft journal. Place remaining bearing liner over rollers so liner ends dovetail. Upper main bearing (1) should stand 1/8 inch (3.17 mm) higher than surface of crankcase.

ELECTRIC STARTER

Electric starter motor shown in Fig. F5-17 is used. Renew any components which are damaged or excessively worn.

A neutral interlock switch is used so engine will start in neutral but not in forward or reverse position. Make sure neutral interlock switch is properly adjusted.

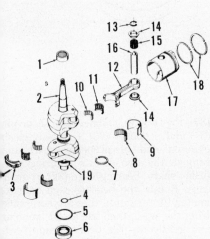

Fig. F5-12—Exploded view of crankshaft assembly.

1. Roller bearing	11. Bearing cage
2. Crankshaft	12. Connecting rod
3. Rod cap	13. Snap ring
4. Seal	14. Spacer
5. "O" ring	15. Needle bearing
6. Seal	16. Piston pin
7. Seal ring	17. Piston
8. Bearing rollers	18. Piston rings
9. Bearing liner	19. Ball bearing
10. Bearing rollers	

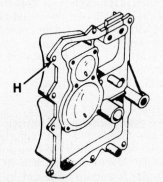

Fig. F5-13—Install long cap screw in upper left-hand hole (H) of transfer port cover.

Fig. F5-15—Exploded view of cylinder block assembly.

1. Seal	9. Gasket	16. Gasket	23. Shift interlock lever
2. Bearing cage	10. Cylinder block	17. Plug	24. Pivot fitting
3. Gasket	11. Crankcase	18. Gasket	25. Shift interlock rod
4. Stator ring	12. Dowel pin	19. Transfer port cover	26. Magneto control lever
5. Crankcase seal	13. Thermostat cover	20. Spring	27. Magneto stator link
6. Exhaust cover	14. Gasket	21. Detent ball	28. Throttle link
7. Gasket	15. Cylinder head	22. Gear shift lever	29. Throttle cam
8. Exhaust plate			

PROPELLER

Propellers for normal use have three blades and are equipped with a shear pin to prevent damage. Various pitch propellers are available and should be selected to provide full throttle operation within the recommended limits of 4250-5250 rpm. Propellers other than those designed for the motor should not be used.

LOWER UNIT

R&R AND OVERHAUL. To remove the lower unit, refer to WATER PUMP section. Drain the gearcase and secure gearcase skeg in a vise. Disassemble and remove the drive shaft and water pump assembly. Remove the cotter pin

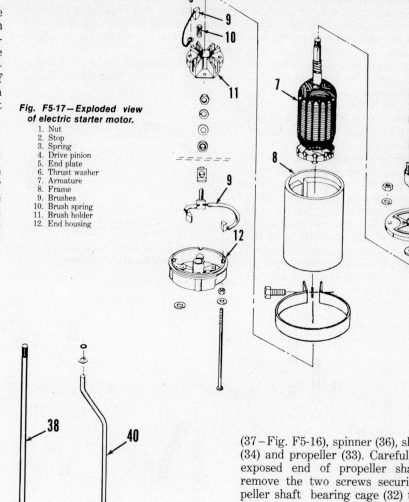

Fig. F5-17 — Exploded view of electric starter motor.

1. Nut
2. Stop
3. Spring
4. Drive pinion
5. End plate
6. Thrust washer
7. Armature
8. Frame
9. Brushes
10. Brush spring
11. Brush holder
12. End housing

Fig. F5-16 — Exploded view of lower unit.

1. Shift rod	11. Drive shaft housing	21. Dog clutch	31. Seal
2. Grommet	12. Seal	22. Spring pin	32. Bearing cage
3. Drive shaft seal	13. Pin	23. Yoke	33. Propeller
4. Pump body	14. Shift rod	24. Shift pin	34. Shear pin
5. Impeller	15. Pinion gear & bearing	25. Propeller shaft	35. Seal
6. Back plate	16. Shift arm	26. Ball	36. Spinner
7. Seal	17. Pivot pin	27. Thrust washer	37. Cotter pin
8. Bushing	18. Gearcase	28. Rear gear	38. Drive shaft
9. Water screen	19. Front gear & bearing	29. "O" ring	39. Impeller drive pin
10. Seal	20. Thrust washer	30. Bearing	40. Water tube

(37 – Fig. F5-16), spinner (36), shear pin (34) and propeller (33). Carefully clean exposed end of propeller shaft and remove the two screws securing propeller shaft bearing cage (32) to gearcase. Rotate the bearing cage approximately ½ turn until tabs are accessible from the sides, then use a soft hammer and gently tap the bearing cage rearward out of gearcase. Remove the gearcase rear retaining stud nut by working through propeller shaft opening. Unscrew gearcase front retaining stud nut, then lift off drive shaft housing (11).

Withdraw drive pinion (15) from top of gearcase and propeller shaft and associated parts through rear opening. Withdraw front and rear gears from propeller shaft. Remove spring pin (22), dog clutch (21) and shift pin (24).

The drive shaft seal (3) should be installed with spring loaded lip toward top (power head). Rubber coated side of shaft seal (31) should be installed with spring loaded lip toward outside of bearing cage (32). Sparingly apply Loctite 222 or 262 to outer diameter of shift rod seal (10).

Drive gear backlash and bearing preload are fixed and not adjustable. Assemble by reversing the disassembly procedure. Make sure that hole in dog clutch (21) is aligned with slot in propeller shaft (25) and hole in shift pin (24), then insert spring pin (22).

FORCE 50 HP

CONDENSED SERVICE DATA

TUNE-UP

Hp/rpm	50/5000
Bore	3-3/16 in.
	(82.6 mm)
Stroke	2.8 in.
	(71.1 mm)
Number of Cylinders	2
Displacement	44.7 cu. in.
	(733 cc)
Compression at Cranking Speed	
(Average)	135-150 psi
	(931.5-1035 kPa)
Spark Plug:	
Champion	L4J
Electrode Gap	0.030 in.
	(0.76 mm)
Breaker Point Gap	0.015 in.
	(0.38 mm)
Carburetor:	
Make	Tillotson
Model	WB
Fuel:Oil Ratio	50:1

SIZES—CLEARANCES—CAPACITIES

Piston Ring End Gap	0.006-0.016 in.
	(0.15-0.41 mm)
Piston Ring Groove Width	0.0645-0.0655 in.
	(1.638-1.664 mm)
Piston to Cylinder Clearance	0.004-0.007 in.
	(0.102-0.178 mm)
Piston Pin Diameter	0.50000-0.50015 in.
	(12.7000-12.7038 mm)
Crankshaft Journal Diameters:	
Upper Main	1.1815-1.1820 in.
	(30.010-30.023 mm)

SIZES—CLEARANCES—CAPACITIES CONT.

Center Main	1.1388-1.1392 in.
	(28.926-28.936 mm)
Lower Main	1.1245-1.1250 in.
	(28.562-28.575 mm)
Crankpin	1.1391-1.1395 in.
	(28.933-28.943 mm)
Gearcase Oil Capacity	12 oz.
	(355 mL)

TIGHTENING TORQUES

Cylinder Head	270 in.-lbs.
	(30.5 N·m)
Flywheel Nut	80 ft.-lbs.
	(108.8 N·m)
Connecting Rod	180-190 in.-lbs.
	(20.3-21.5 N·m)
Main Bearing Screws	270 in.-lbs.
	(30.5 N·m)
Standard Screws:	
10-24	30 in.-lbs.
	(3.4 N·m)
10-32	35 in.-lbs.
	(4 N·m)
12-24	45 in.-lbs.
	(5.1 N·m)
1/4-20	70 in.-lbs.
	(7.9 N·m)
5/16-18	160 in.-lbs.
	(18.1 N·m)
3/8-16	270 in.-lbs.
	(30.5 N·m)

LUBRICATION

The power head is lubricated by oil mixed with the fuel. For normal service after break-in, mix 1/6 pint of US Marine Outboard oil or a BIA TC-W certified oil with each gallon of gasoline. The recommended ratio is one-third (1/3) pint of oil per gallon of gasoline for severe service and during break-in. Manufacturer recommends no-lead automotive gasoline although regular or premium gasoline may be used if octane rating is 85 or higher. Gasoline and oil should be thoroughly mixed.

The lower unit gears and bearings are lubricated by oil contained in the gearcase. Recommended gearcase oil is US Marine Outboard Gear Lube or a suitable noncorrosive EP 90 outboard gear oil. The gearcase should be drained and refilled every 100 hours or at least once per season prior to storage. Maintain fluid at level of upper (vent) plug.

To fill gearcase, have motor in an upright position and fill through hole in side of gearcase until fluid reaches level of upper (vent) plug hole. Reinstall and tighten both plugs securely, using new gaskets if necessary, to assure a water tight seal.

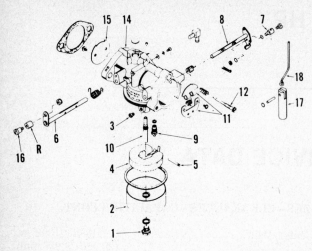

Fig. F6-1 — Exploded view of Tillotson WB type carburetor.

R. Roller
1. Bowl retaining screw
2. Fuel bowl
3. High speed jet
4. Float
5. Float pivot shaft
6. Throttle shaft
7. Connector
8. Choke shaft
9. Inlet needle & seat
10. Main nozzle
11. Choke plate
12. Idle mixture needle
14. Body
15. Throttle plate
16. Eccentric screw
17. Choke solenoid plunger
18. Rod

Fig. F6-2 — Correct float level is 13/32 inch (10.3 mm) when measured as shown between float and gasket surface.

FUEL SYSTEM

CARBURETOR. A Tillotson WB type carburetor is used. Refer to Fig. F6-1 for an exploded view of the carburetor.

Initial setting of idle mixture screw (10) is 1 turn out from a lightly seated position. Final adjustment of carburetor should be made with engine at normal operating temperature and with outboard motor in forward gear. Standard main jet size is 0.084 inch.

To check float level, remove float bowl and invert carburetor. Refer to Fig. F6-2. Bottom side of float should be a distance of 13/32 inch (10.3 mm) from float bowl gasket surface. Adjust float level by bending float tang.

SPEED CONTROL LINKAGE. Ignition timing advance and throttle opening must be synchronized so throttle is opened as timing is advanced.

To synchronize the linkage, first make sure that ignition timing is correctly set as outlined in IGNITION TIMING section. Shift to forward gear position and disconnect link (L—Fig. F6-3) from tower shaft (T). With carburetor throttle closed, turn eccentric screw (16) until roller (R) is exactly centered over scrib-ed line (S). Move tower shaft (T) to full advance position and move the throttle cam until carburetor throttle is completely open. Vary the length of link (L) until the ball joint connector will just attach. Snap the ball joint connector onto ball stud and check maximum speed in neutral. Maximum rpm in neutral should be approximately 1800 rpm and is adjusted at neutral stop screw (N).

Idle speed screw should be 700-800 rpm in forward gear (800-900 rpm in neutral) and is adjusted at idle screw (I).

REED VALVES. "V" type intake reed valves are used. The reed plate is located between intake manifold and crankcase.

To remove the reed plate assembly after carburetor is removed, first remove the electric starter assembly and the screws retaining the intake manifold. Then lift off the intake manifold and the reed plate assembly.

Reed valve must be smooth and even with no sharp bends or broken reeds. Assembled reeds may stand open a maximum of 0.010 inch (0.255 mm) at tip end. Check seating visually.

Reed stop setting should be 9/32 inch (7.1 mm) when measured as shown in

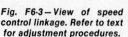

Fig. F6-3 — View of speed control linkage. Refer to text for adjustment procedures.

A. High speed stop
I. Idle stop
L. Throttle link
N. Neutral stop screw
R. Roller
S. Scribed line
T. Tower shaft
16. Eccentric screw

Fig. F6-4. Renew reeds if petals are broken, cracked, warped or bent. Never attempt to bend a reed petal in an effort to improve performance, nor attempt to straighten a damaged reed. Never install a bent of damaged reed. Seating surface of reed plate should be smooth and flat. When installing reed petals and stops, proceed as follows: Install reed petals, stop and the four retaining screws leaving screws loose. Slide the reed petals as far as possible toward mounting flange of reed plate and reed stops out as far as possible toward tip of "V." Position reed petals and reed stops as outlined to provide maximum overlap. A minimum overlap of 0.040 inch (1.01 mm) is required. Tighten the retaining screws to secure position.

PUDDLE DRAIN VALVES. The puddle drain system is designed to remove any liquid fuel or oil which might collect in the crankcase, thus providing smoother operation at all speeds and lessening the possibility of spark plug fouling during slow speed operation.

The puddle drain valve housing is located on the starboard side of the power head and the puddle drain valve components can be disassembled as shown in Fig. F6-5. The reed-type puddle drain valve petals must seat lightly and evenly against valve plate. Reed stops should be adjusted to 0.017-0.023 inch (0.43-0.58 mm) clearance at the tip. Blow out drain passages with compressed air while housing is off.

FUEL PUMP. All models are equipped with a two-stage diaphragm type fuel pump which is actuated by pressure and vacuum pulsations from the engine crankcases.

NOTE: Either stage of the fuel pump operating independently may permit the motor to run, but not at peak performance.

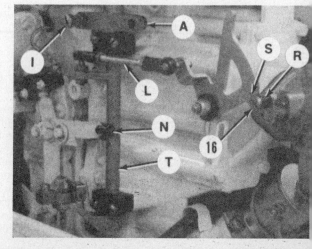

Illustrations Courtesy US Marine Corp.

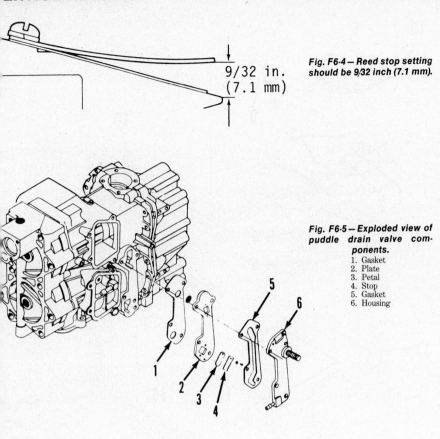

Fig. F6-4 — Reed stop setting should be 9/32 inch (7.1 mm).

Fig. F6-5 — Exploded view of puddle drain valve components.
1. Gasket
2. Plate
3. Petal
4. Stop
5. Gasket
6. Housing

mm). Both sets of points must be adjusted as nearly alike as possible.

NOTE: Point gap variation of 0.0015 inch (0.038 mm) will change ignition timing one degree.

To adjust the points, first remove the flywheel as previously outlined. Turn crankshaft clockwise until the rub block on one set of points is aligned with mark on breaker cam. Loosen breaker point mounting screws and adjust point gap until a slight drag exists using a 0.015 inch (0.38 mm) feeler gage.

Turn crankshaft until mark on breaker cam is aligned with the rub block on the other set of points and adjust the other set of points in the same manner.

IGNITION TIMING. Crankshaft timing should be 32° BTDC when setting piston position with special tool T-2937-1. When setting piston position with a dial indicator, the equivalent reading should be 0.281 inch (7.14 mm) BTDC. To adjust ignition timing, breaker point gap must first be carefully adjusted as previously outlined, then piston position must be accurately determined using special tool or a dial indicator as follows:

To remove fuel pump, disconnect fuel hoses to pump and unscrew six cap screws which retain fuel pump body. Check valves are renewable, but be sure a new check valve is needed before removing old check valve as it will be damaged during removal. Unscrew the two retaining screws to remove center check valve. The two outer check valves must be driven out from below. Check valves (V – Fig. F6-6) must be correctly installed as shown. Install check valves carefully to prevent damage. Inspect diaphragm and renew diaphragm if cracked, torn or badly distorted.

IGNITION

A battery ignition with a flywheel mounted alternator is used.

R&R FLYWHEEL. A special puller (Part T-8948-1) should be used to remove the flywheel. Threaded holes are provided in the flywheel for installation of three puller screws.

NOTE: The three screws that secure the emergency starter collar must be removed, as well as the emergency starter collar. Make certain that aligning marks on flywheel and emergency starter collar are matched when reassembling.

Correctly position a large screwdriver or pry bar and apply upward pressure (Do Not apply excessive pressure) to rim of flywheel. Then bump jackscrew of puller sharply with a hammer to loosen flywheel from tapered portion of crankshaft.

The manufacturer recommends that mating surfaces of flywheel and crankshaft be lapped before flywheel is reinstalled. If evidence of working exists, proceed as follows:

Remove the flywheel key and apply a light coating of valve grinding or lapping compound to tapered portion of crankshaft. Install the flywheel without the key or crankshaft nut and rotate flywheel gently back and forth about ¼ turn. Move flywheel 90° and repeat the procedure. Lift off the flywheel, wipe off excess lapping compound and carefully examine crankshaft. A minimum of 90 percent surface contact should be indicated by the polished surface. Continue lapping only if insufficient contact is evident. Thoroughly clean the crankshaft and flywheel bore to remove all traces of lapping compound, then clean both surfaces with a non-oily solvent.

Reinstall crankshaft key and flywheel, then tighten flywheel nut to 80 ft.-lbs. (108.8 N·m).

POINT ADJUSTMENT. Breaker point gap should be 0.015 inch (0.38

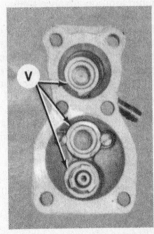

Fig. F6-6 — Fuel pump check valves (V) must be installed as shown for proper operation of fuel pump.

Fig. F6-7 — Special tool is available for positioning piston at correct timing position. Refer to text for proper tool usage.

To determine piston position using special tool T-2937-1 (Fig. F6-7), thread the tool body into top spark plug opening. Insert the gage rod into tool body, rotate the crankshaft and carefully position piston at exactly TDC.

NOTE: Gage rod should be installed with the double scribed line end on the 25-55 HP marked end out.

With the top piston at TDC, thread timing tool body in or out as necessary until the inner scribed line on gage rod is aligned with end of tool body. After gage body is correctly positioned, turn the crankshaft clockwise almost one complete revolution while applying pressure to end of gage rod. Stop the crankshaft just as the first (outer) scribed line on rod aligns with tool body. The crankshaft should be at correct position BTDC for maximum ignition advance timing.

To determine piston position using a dial indicator, insert dial indicator needle into top spark plug opening, then rotate crankshaft and carefully position piston at exactly TDC. Zero the dial indicator, then turn crankshaft clockwise almost one complete revolution stopping crankshaft just as a dial indicator reads 0.281 inch (7.14 mm). The crankshaft should be at correct position BTDC for maximum ignition advance timing.

With the crankshaft correctly positioned and breaker point gaps properly adjusted, connect one lead from timing test light (with battery) or an ohmmeter to the breaker point terminal of number one cylinder and ground other test lead to motor. Move the speed control from slow toward fast (maximum advance) speed position and observe the test light or ohmmeter. The breaker points should just open (test light goes off or ohmmeter registers infinite resistance) when the speed control reaches maximum ignition advance. If the breaker points do not open, shorten rod (L – Fig. F6-8) or if breaker points open too soon, length rod (L).

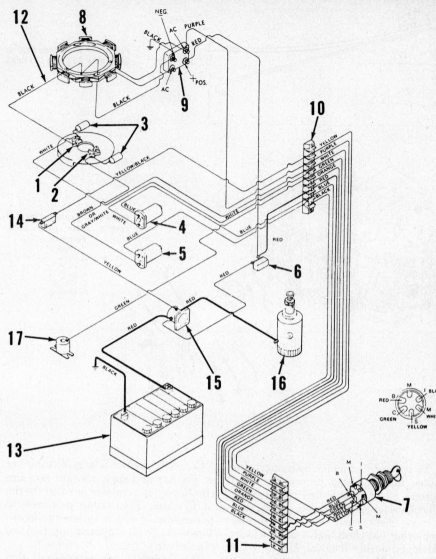

Fig. F6-9 — Wiring diagram of battery ignition and flywheel mounted alternator.

1. Breaker points for top cylinder
2. Breaker points for bottom cylinder
3. Condensers
4. Coil for top cylinder
5. Coil for bottom cylinder
6. Circuit breaker
7. Ignition & start switch
8. Alternator stator
9. Rectifier
10. Terminal block at motor
11. Terminal block at dashboard
12. Alternator groun
13. Battery
14. Neutral interlock switch

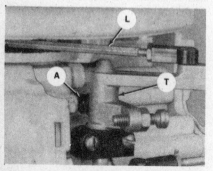

Fig. F6-8 — Full advance stop (A) on tower shaft (T) should contact housing before adjusting link (L) when setting ignition timing.

COOLING SYSTEM

THERMOSTAT. The thermostat is located beneath a separate housing on top, rear face of cylinder head. Remove cover (14 – Fig. F6-10) to gain access to thermostat (16). Install new thermostat as shown in figure.

WATER PUMP. All motors are equipped with a rubber impeller type water pump. Refer to Fig. F6-16. The water pump is mounted on top the lower unit drive shaft housing.

When cooling system problems are encountered, first check the water inlet for plugging or partial stoppage. Then if

trouble is not corrected, remove the lower unit gearcase as outlined in LOWER UNIT section, and check the condition of water pump, water passages and sealing surfaces.

POWER HEAD

REMOVE AND DISASSEMBLE. To overhaul the power head, clamp the outboard motor on a stand or support and remove the engine cover and motor leg covers. Remove the starter collar, flywheel, alternator, fuel pump, carburetor and intake manifold. Disconnect all interfering wiring and linkage. Remove the cylinder head, and transfer

rt and exhaust covers if major repairs
e required. Remove the power head
aching screws and lift off the cylinder
ck, crankshaft and associated parts
a unit.

**NOTE: One of the power head attaching
rews is located underneath the rear ex-
ust cover as shown in Fig. F6-11. Cover
ust be removed for access to the screw.**

Fig. F6-11 — Rear exhaust cover must be removed from motor leg for access to power head rear attaching screw.

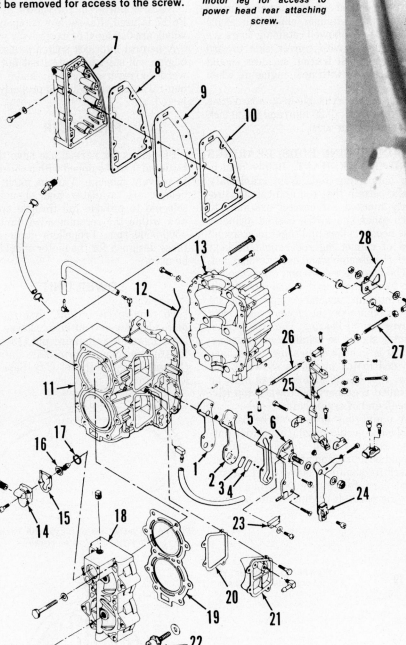

Fig. F6-10 — Exploded view of cylinder block assembly.

To disassemble the power head, unbolt
and remove the upper bearing cage;
then unbolt and remove the crankcase
front half. Pry slots are provided adjacent to retaining dowels for separating
the crankcase. DO NOT pry on machined mating surfaces of cylinder block
and crankcase front half.

Crankshaft, pistons and bearings are
now accessible for removal and overhaul
as outlined in the appropriate following
paragraphs. Assemble as outlined in the
ASSEMBLY paragraph.

ASSEMBLY. When reassembling,
make sure all joint and gasket surfaces
are clean, free from nicks and burrs,
warped surfaces or hardened cement or
carbon. The crankcase and inlet manifolds must be completely sealed against
both vacuum and pressure. Exhaust
manifold and cylinder head must be
sealed against water leakage and
pressure. Mating surfaces of exhaust
areas between power head and motor
leg must form a tight seal.

Install crankshaft making certain upper, center and lower main bearings are
properly positioned over main bearing
locating pins in cylinder block.

Install new crankcase to cylinder block
seals (12 – Fig. F6-10). Apply a suitable
sealant to mating surfaces of crankcase
in areas adjacent to upper and center
main bearings and lower crankshaft
seal. Do not apply sealant to areas outside of crankcase seal groove. Immediately install crankcase half and
tighten main bearing screws to 270
in.-lbs. (30.5 N·m). Make sure
crankshaft turns freely before proceeding with assembly.

1. Gasket
2. Plate
3. Petal
4. Stop
5. Gasket
6. Housing
7. Exhaust cover
8. Gasket
9. Exhaust plate
10. Gasket
11. Cylinder block
12. Seal
13. Crankcase
14. Thermostat housing
15. Gasket
16. Thermostat
17. Seal
18. Cylinder head
19. Gasket
20. Gasket
21. Transfer port
22. Thermoswitch
23. Neutral interlock switch
24. Shift arm
25. Tower shaft
26. Spark control link
27. Throttle link
28. Throttle cam

When installing cylinder head, coat the first ¾ inch (19.05 mm) of screw threads with antiseize lubricant. Follow tightening sequence shown in Fig. F6-12 and torque the cylinder head cap screws first to 75 in.-lbs. (8.5 N·m), then in 50 in.-lbs. (5.6 N·m) increments until final torque of 270 in.-lbs. (30.5 N·m) is obtained. After outboard motor has been test run and cooled, retorque screws to 270 in.-lbs. (30.5 N·m).

PISTONS, PINS, RINGS & CYLINDERS. Pistons are fitted with two piston rings which should be installed with the beveled inner edge (B–Fig. F6-14) toward top of piston. Piston ring end gap for both rings should be 0.006-0.016 inch (0.15-0.41 mm). Rings are pinned in place to prevent rotation in ring grooves. Do not interchange pistons between cylinders. Piston to cylinder clearance should be 0.004-0.007 inch (0.102-0.178 mm).

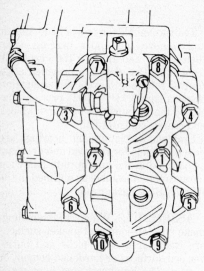

Fig. F6-12—Tighten cylinder head cap screws in the sequence shown.

The piston pin is a tight fit in piston bores and rides in a roller bearing in connecting rod. Special tool T-2990 should be used when removing or installing piston pin. When assembling piston, pin and connecting rod, make sure long, tapering side of piston is toward exhaust side of cylinder and match marks or bevel cut on rod are toward top (flywheel) end of crankshaft. Install piston pin retaining clips with sharp edge out or if bowed retaining rings are used, install with convex side toward piston pin. All friction surfaces should be lubricated with new engine oil when assembling.

Pistons are available in standard sizes and 0.010 inch (0.25 mm) and 0.030 inch (0.76 mm) oversizes.

CONNECTING RODS, BEARINGS AND CRANKSHAFT. Before detaching connecting rods from crankshaft, make certain that rod and cap are properly marked for correct assembly to each other and in the correct cylinder. The needle rollers and cages at crankpin end of connecting rod should be kept with the assembly and not interchanged.

The bearing rollers and cages used in the two connecting rods and center main bearings are available only as a set which contains the rollers and cage halves for one bearing. The complete assembly should be installed whenever renewal is indicated. Bearing cages have beveled match marks as shown by arrow, Fig. F6-15. Match marks must be installed together and toward top (flywheel) end of crankshaft.

A nonfibrous grease can be used to hold loose needle bearing in position during assembly. All friction surfaces should be lubricated with new engine oil. Check frequently as power head is being assembled, for binding or locking of the moving parts. If binding occurs, remove

the cause before proceeding with th assembly. When assembling, follow th procedures outlined in the ASSEMBL paragraphs. Tightening torques ar given in the CONDENSED SERVIC DATA tables.

ELECTRIC STARTER

Electric starter motor shown in Fi F6-17 is used. Renew any component which are damaged or excessively wor

A neutral interlock switch is used s engine will start in neutral but not fo ward or reverse position. Make sur neutral interlock switch is properly a justed.

PROPELLER

Propellers for normal use have thre blades and are equipped with a shear p to prevent damage. Various pitch pr pellers are available and should b selected to provide full throttle opera tion within the recommended limits o 4500-5500 rpm. Propellers other tha those designed for the motor should n be used.

LOWER UNIT

To remove lower unit, first remov motor leg covers and unbolt lower un from motor leg. Remove pin (13–Fig F6-16) connecting intermediate shift ro (1) and lower shift rod (14). Separat lower unit from motor leg.

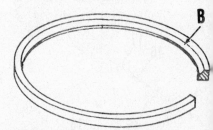

Fig. F6-14—Install piston rings with bevel (B toward top of piston crown.

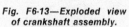

Fig. F6-13—Exploded view of crankshaft assembly.

1. Seal
2. Bearing cage
3. Gasket
4. Crankshaft assy.
5. Ball bearing
6. Bearing rollers & cage half
7. Bearing liner
8. Seal ring
9. Lower main bearing
10. Seal
11. Bearing rollers & cage half
12. Rod cap
13. Connecting rod
14. Needle bearing
15. Piston pin
16. Spacer
17. Snap ring
18. Piston
19. Piston ring (2)

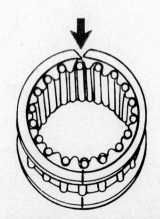

Fig. F6-15—When installing bearing cages make sure beveled ends (arrow) are together an toward top (flywheel) end of crankshaft.

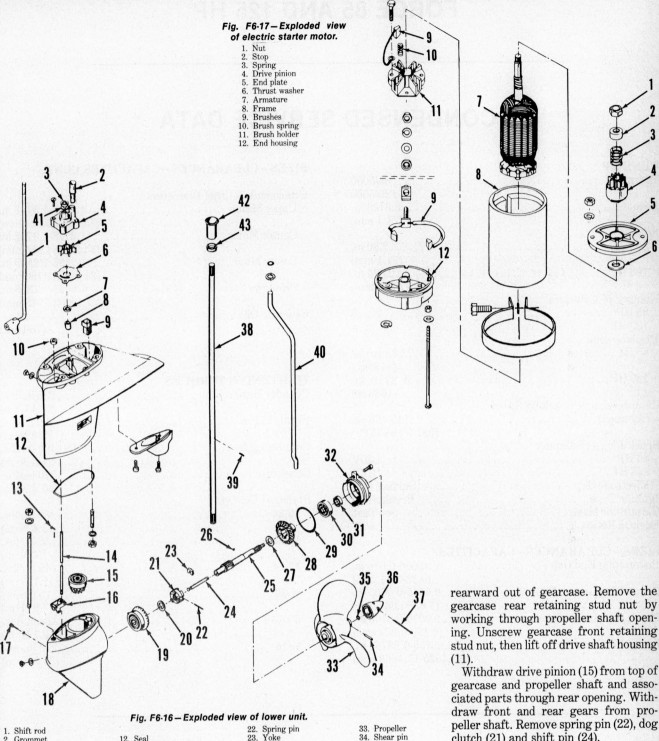

Fig. F6-17 — Exploded view of electric starter motor.

1. Nut
2. Stop
3. Spring
4. Drive pinion
5. End plate
6. Thrust washer
7. Armature
8. Frame
9. Brushes
10. Brush spring
11. Brush holder
12. End housing

Fig. F6-16 — Exploded view of lower unit.

1. Shift rod	12. Seal	22. Spring pin	33. Propeller
2. Grommet	13. Pin	23. Yoke	34. Shear pin
3. Drive shaft seal	14. Shift rod	24. Shift pin	35. Seal
4. Pump body	15. Pinion gear & bearing	25. Propeller shaft	36. Spinner
5. Impeller	16. Shift arm	26. Ball	37. Cotter pin
6. Back plate	17. Pivot pin	27. Thrust washer	38. Drive shaft
7. Seal	18. Gearcase	28. Rear gear	39. Impeller drive pin
8. Bushing	19. Front gear & bearing	29. "O" ring	40. Water tube
9. Water screen	20. Thrust washer	30. Bearing	41. Disc
10. Seal	21. Dog clutch	31. Seal	42. Seal
11. Drive shaft housing		32. Bearing cage	43. Retainer

Drain the gearcase and secure gearcase skeg in a vise. Disassemble and remove the drive shaft and water pump assembly. Remove cotter pin (37), spinner (36), shear pin (34) and propeller (33). Carefully clean exposed end of propeller shaft and remove the two screws securing propeller shaft bearing cage (32) to gearcase. Rotate the bearing cage approximately ½ turn until tabs are accessible from the sides, then use a soft hammer and gently tap the bearing cage

rearward out of gearcase. Remove the gearcase rear retaining stud nut by working through propeller shaft opening. Unscrew gearcase front retaining stud nut, then lift off drive shaft housing (11).

Withdraw drive pinion (15) from top of gearcase and propeller shaft and associated parts through rear opening. Withdraw front and rear gears from propeller shaft. Remove spring pin (22), dog clutch (21) and shift pin (24).

The drive shaft seal (3) should be installed with spring loaded lip toward top (power head). Rubber coated side of shaft seal (31) should be installed with spring loaded lip toward outside of bearing cage (32).

Drive gear backlash and bearing preload are fixed and not adjustable. Assemble by reversing the disassembly procedure. Make sure that hole in dog clutch (21) is aligned with slot in propeller shaft (25) and hole in shift pin (24), then insert spring pin (22).

FORCE 85 AND 125 HP

CONDENSED SERVICE DATA

TUNE-UP

Hp/rpm......................................85/5000

125/5000

Bore.......................................3.3125 in.

(84.1 mm)

Stroke:

85 HP.....................................2.80 in.

(71.1 mm)

125 HP....................................2.875 in.

(73.02 mm)

Number of Cylinders:

85 HP...3

125 HP..4

Displacement:

85 HP..................................72.39 cu. in.

(1186 cc)

125 HP.................................99.23 cu. in.

(1626 cc)

Compression at Cranking Speed

(Average)..............................145-165 psi

(931.5-1035 kPa)

Spark Plug – Champion:

85 HP.......................................L20V

125 HP.....................................UL18V

Electrode Gap........................Surface Gap

Ignition Type........................Breakerless

Carburetor Make........................See Text

Fuel:Oil Ratio...............................50:1

SIZES – CLEARANCES – CAPACITIES

Piston Ring End Gap...................0.006-0.016 in.

(0.15-0.41 mm)

Piston Ring Groove Width............0.0645-0.0655 in.

(1.638-l.664 mm)

Piston to Cylinder Clearance...........0.0075-0.0103 in.

(0.190-0.262 mm)

Piston Pin Diameter.............0.68750-0.68765 in.

(17.4625-17.4663 mm)

SIZES – CLEARANCES – CAPACITIES CONT.

Crankshaft Journal Diameters:

Upper Main........................1.3789-1.3793 in.

(35.024-35.034 mm)

Center Mains......................1.3748-1.3752 in.

(34.920-34.930 mm)

Lower Main........................1.2495-1.2500 in.

(31.737-31.750 mm)

Crankpin..........................1.1391-1.1395 in.

(28.933-28.943 mm)

Gearcase Oil Capacity.........................26 oz.

(769 mL)

TIGHTENING TORQUES

Cylinder Head.........................225 in.-lbs.

(25.4 N·m)

Flywheel Nut...........................90 ft.-lbs.

(122.4 N·m)

Connecting Rod.......................180-190 in.-lbs.

(20.3-21.5 N·m)

Crankcase.............................270 in.-lbs.

(30.5 N·m)

Standard Screws:

10-24................................30 in.-lbs.

(3.4 N·m)

10-32................................35 in.-lbs.

(4 N·m)

12-24................................45 in.-lbs.

(5.1 N·m)

¼-20.................................70 in.-lbs.

(7.9 N·m)

5/16-18..............................160 in.-lbs.

(18.1 N·m)

⅜-16.................................270 in.-lbs.

(30.5 N·m)

LUBRICATION

The power head is lubricated by oil mixed with the fuel. For normal service after break-in, mix 1/6 pint of US Marine Outboard oil or a BIA TC-W certified oil with each gallon of gasoline. The recommended ratio is one-third (⅓) pint of oil per gallon of gasoline for severe service and during break-in. Manufacturer recommends regular lead-ed automotive gasoline. If regular is not available, use a good grade of premium gasoline. No-lead gasoline may be used if octane rating is 85 or higher. Gasoline and oil should be thoroughly mixed.

The lower unit gears and bearings are lubricated by oil contained in the gearcase. Recommended gearcase oil is US Marine Outboard Gear Lube or a suitable noncorrosive EP 90 outboard gear oil. The gearcase should be drained and refilled every 100 hours or at least once per season prior to storage. Maintain fluid level of "VENT" plug hole.

To fill gearcase, have motor in an upright position and add oil through "FILL" plug hole located on starboard side of gearcase until fluid reaches level of "VENT" plug hole. Reinstall and tighten both plugs securely, using new gaskets if necessary, to assure a water tight seal.

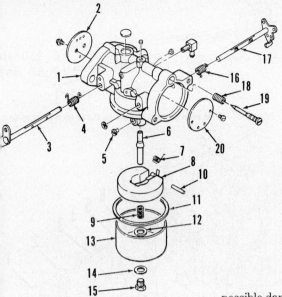

Fig. F7-1 – Exploded view of typical Tillotson type carburetor. Walbro type carburetor is similar.

1. Body
2. Throttle plate
3. Throttle shaft
4. Spring
5. Main jet
6. Main nozzle
7. Spring
8. Float
9. Spring
10. Float pin
11. Gasket
12. Gasket
13. Float bowl
14. Gasket
15. Bowl retaining screw
16. Spring
17. Choke shaft
18. Spring
19. Idle mixture needle
20. Choke plate

FUEL SYSTEM

CARBURETOR. A Tillotson or Walbro type carburetor is used. Refer to Fig. F7-1 for an exploded view of a Tillotson type carburetor. Walbro type carburetor is similar. Three carburetors are used on 85 hp models and two carburetors are used on 125 hp models.

NOTE: The carburetor model number is stamped on the mounting flange. Make sure that all carburetors used are the same type and model number.

Initial setting of idle mixture adjustment needle (19) is 1 turn out from a lightly seated position. Main jet (5) controls high speed mixture. Idle mixture must be readjusted under load, after motor is warm, for best slow speed performance. Idle mixture needle for all carburetors must be adjusted as nearly alike as possible for equal performance and all main jets (5) must be the same size.

Care must be used in selecting the main jet (5). A main jet which is too small will result in a lean mixture and

possible damage to power head. Jet may be identified by the diameter (in thousandths of an inch) stamped on visible end of installed jet. The standard main jet size is 0.72 inch on 85 hp models and 0.937 inch on 125 hp models. Optional jets are available which will improve performance when motor is used high-altitude locations.

To check float level, remove float bowl and invert carburetor. Refer to Fig. F7-2. Bottom side of float should be a distance of 13/32 inch (10.3 mm) from float bowl gasket surface. Adjust float level by bending float tang.

Throttle plates in carburetors must be synchronized to obtain maximum performance. The tie bar connecting the three carburetors on 85 hp models must be adjusted so all three carburetors open the same amount at exactly the same time. The adjusting clamp screws are on the connecting link near the top and bottom carburetors. The tie bar connecting the two carburetors on 125 hp models must be adjusted so both carburetors open the same amount at exactly the same time. The adjusting clamp screw is

on the connecting link near the bottom carburetor.

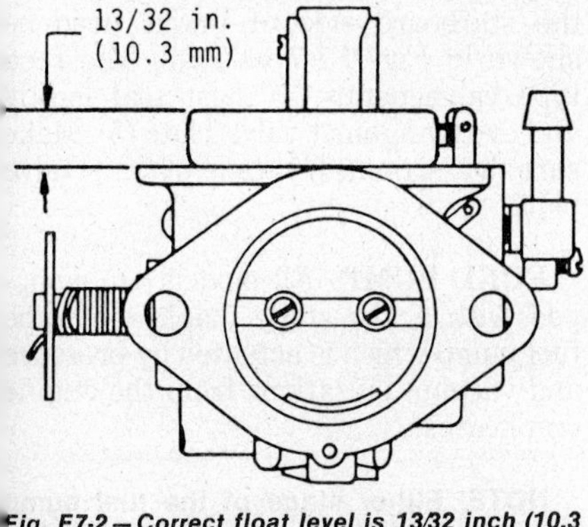

SPEED CONTROL LINKAGE. Ignition timing advance and throttle opening must be synchronized so throttle is opened as timing is advanced. If incorrect, the power head may overheat, lack power and will usually not accelerate smoothly.

To synchronize the linkage, first make certain that ignition timing is correctly set as outlined in IGNITION TIMING section.

Disconnect the throttle rod (TR–Fig. F7-3) and move throttle cam (C) until mark (M) on cam is aligned with center of roller (R).

NOTE: If throttle cam (C) has two marks (M), roller (R) should be centered between marks.

Loosen locknut on roller (R) and turn the eccentric screw (S) until the cam just contacts the roller when mark (M) or marks are positioned as previously outlined. Tighten the locknut. Move the speed control to the maximum speed position and adjust the length of throttle rod (TR) so rod can be connected when carburetor throttles are at maximum opening. Recheck adjustments after connecting throttle rod to make certain that the vertical control shaft contacts the maximum speed stop at the same time carburetor throttles are completely opened.

REED VALVES. "V" type intake reed valves are located between the inlet manifold and the crankcase for each cylinder. To remove the reed valve, it is necessary to remove the carburetors and inlet manifold (1–Fig. F7-4 or Fig. F7-5). On 85 hp models, all three reed valve assemblies are attached to adapter plate (3). On 125 hp models, two reed valve assemblies are attached to each adapter plate (3).

Fig. F7-3 – Refer to text for adjusting speed control linkage.

C. Throttle cam
M. Mark
R. Roller
S. Eccentric screw
TR. Throttle rod

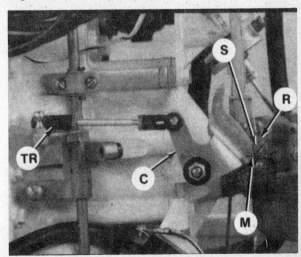

Fig. F7-2 – Correct float level is 13/32 inch (10.3 mm) when measured as shown between float and gasket surface.

13/32 in.
(10.3 mm)

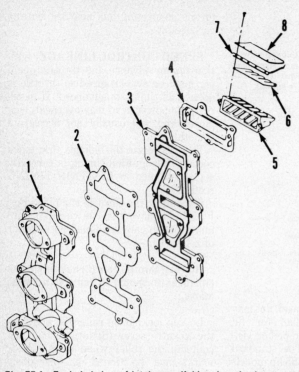

Fig. F7-4 — Exploded view of intake manifold and reed valve assembly used on 85 hp models.

1. Intake manifold
2. Gasket
3. Adapter plate
4. Gasket
5. Reed body
6. Reed petals
7. Spacer
8. Reed stop

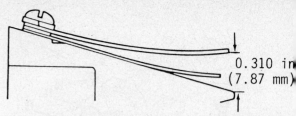

Fig. F7-6 — Reed stop setting should be 0.310 inch (7.87 mm).

0.310 in
(7.87 mm)

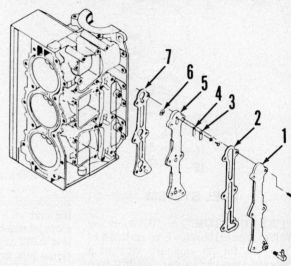

Fig. F7-7 — Exploded view of puddle drain valve components on 85 h[p] models.

1. Housing
2. Gasket
3. Stop
4. Petal
5. Plate
6. Scree[n]
7. Gask[et]

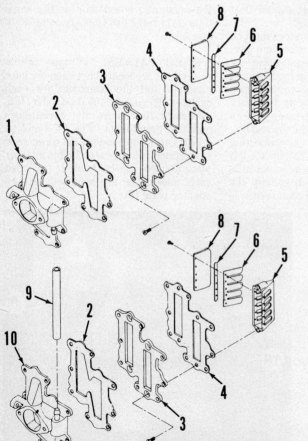

Fig. F7-5 — Exploded view of intake manifolds and reed valve assembly used on 125 hp models.

1. Upper intake manifold
2. Gasket
3. Adapter plate
4. Gasket
5. Reed body
6. Reed petals
7. Spacer
8. Reed stop
9. Balance tube
10. Lower intake manifold

Seating surface of reed valve body (5[)] must be smooth and reed petals (6) mus[t] not be bent, broken or cracked. Assem[m]bled reed petals may stand open a max[i]imum of 0.010 inch (0.255 mm) at ti[p] end. Check seating visually. Reed sto[p] setting should be 0.310 inch (7.87 mm[)] when measured as shown in Fig. F7-6[.] When installing reed petals, a minimum overlap of 0.040 inch (1.01 mm) is re[-]quired.

PUDDLE DRAIN VALVES. The[ ] puddle drain valves are designed t[o] remove any liquid fuel or oil which migh[t] build up in the crankcase, thus providing smoother operation at all speeds an[d] lessening the possibility of spark plu[g] fouling during slow speed operation.

The puddle drain valve is located o[n] the starboard side of power head a[s] shown in Fig. F7-7 or F7-8. The ree[d] type valve petals (4) must seat lightl[y] and evenly against valve plate (5). Mak[e] sure that screens (6) are in place in valv[e] plate.

FUEL PUMP. All models are equip[-]ped with a two-stage diaphragm typ[e] fuel pump which is actuated by pressur[e] and vacuum pulsations from the engin[e] crankcases.

NOTE: Either stage of the fuel pump[,] operating independently may permit the motor to run, but not at peak performance[.]

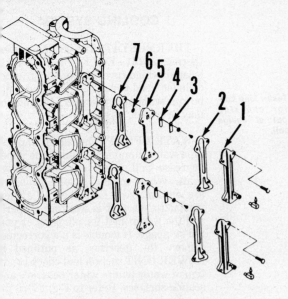

Fig. F7-8 – Exploded view of puddle drain valve components on 125 hp models. Refer to Fig. F7-7 for identification of components.

To adjust ignition timing, first immerse lower unit of outboard motor in water and connect timing light T8978 or a suitable power timing light to upper spark plug. With engine throttle in full retard position, crank engine with starter and note timing. Index mark on carburetor adapter flange should be within 2° of TDC mark on flywheel. If not, adjust timing link (L – Fig. F7-10). To check advance ignition timing, run engine at wide-open throttle with timing light connected to upper spark plug and note timing. Timing pointer should align with 32° BTDC mark on flywheel. Turn timing link (L) to adjust advanced ignition timing.

NOTE: Engine throttle should be returned to retarded position and engine stopped before turning ignition timing link.

To remove fuel pump, disconnect fuel oses to pump and unscrew six cap screws which retain fuel pump body. Check valves are renewable, but be sure a new check valve is needed before removing old check valve as it will be damaged during removal. Unscrew the wo retaining screws to remove center check valve. The two outer check valves must be driven out from below. Check valves (V – Fig. F7-9) must be correctly nstalled as shown. Install check valves carefully to prevent damage. Inspect diaphragm and renew diaphragm if cracked, torn or badly distorted.

IGNITION

A Prestolite ignition system is used on 85 and 125 hp models.

R&R FLYWHEEL. A special puller (Part T-8948-1) should be used to remove the flywheel. Threaded holes are provided in the flywheel for installation of three puller screws.

Remove nut securing flywheel to crankshaft and install puller assembly. Rotate puller jackscrew to apply pulling pressure. Then bump jackscrew sharply with a hammer to loosen flywheel from tapered portion of crankshaft.

The manufacturer recommends that mating surfaces of flywheel and crankshaft be lapped before flywheel is reinstalled. If evidence of working exists, proceed as follows:

Remove the flywheel key and apply a light coating of valve grinding or lapping compound to tapered portion of crankshaft. Install the flywheel without the key or crankshaft nut and rotate flywheel gently back and forth about ¼ turn. Move flywheel 90° and repeat the procedure. Lift off the flywheel, wipe off excess lapping compound and carefully examine crankshaft. A minimum of 80 percent surface contact should be indicated by the polished surface. Continue lapping only if insufficient contact is evident. Thoroughly clean the crankshaft and flywheel bore to remove all traces of lapping compound, then clean both surfaces with a non-oily solvent.

Reinstall crankshaft key and flywheel, then tighten flywheel nut to 90 ft.-lbs. (122.4 N·m).

IGNITION TIMING. Crankshaft timing should be 32° BTDC with engine running at wide-open throttle.

TROUBLESHOOTING. Use only approved procedures when testing ignition system to prevent damage to components. The fuel system should be checked to make certain that faulty running is not caused by incorrect fuel mixture or contaminated fuel. If ignition malfunction is suspected, use tool T8953, plug adapter set T11237, number 22 tester from ignition tester set T8996 and timing light T8978 or a suitable power timing light. Check and make sure ignition malfunction is not due to spark plug or ignition coil failure. Install test plugs in place of the spark plugs and observe spark while engine is being cranked with starter. If spark is absent at one or more plugs, check condition of charge coil as follows:

Separate the blue and yellow wire connection between charge coil (stator) and CD ignition module and attach double wire plug adapter to wire from charge coil as shown in Fig. F7-11. Attach red (P) lead from T8953 tester to red sleeved adapter wire marked "Charge (+)." Attach yellow (N) lead of tester to yellow sleeved adapter wire marked "Charge (–)." Turn tester switch to position 50 and crank engine. If tester lamp does not light, charge coil is defective and stator should be renewed. If lamp lights, charge coil operation is satisfactory and trigger coil and CD ignition module circuits for each cylinder must be checked.

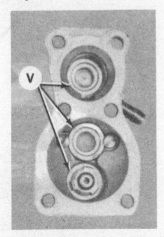

Fig. F7-9 – Fuel pump check valves (V) must be installed as shown for proper operation of fuel pump.

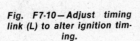

Fig. F7-10 – Adjust timing link (L) to alter ignition timing.

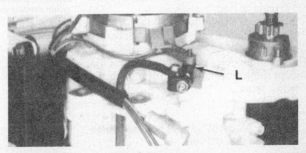

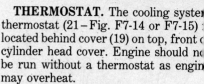

Blue and Yellow Wire
Plug From Charge Coil

Double Wire
Test Plug

Yellow Charge (-)

Red Charge(+)

"P" Red

"N" Yellow

Tester Lamp

Fig. F7-11 — Tester lead connections for checking voltage output of charge coil.

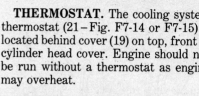

Four Wire Plug
From Tigger Housing

Four Wire Test Plug

Yellow (Trigger 1 Neg.)
Red (Trigger 1 Pos.)
"P" Red

Tester Lamp

"N" Yellow

Fig. F7-12 — Tester lead connections for checking trigger coil operation.

Remove tester and plug adapter set, then reconnect blue and yellow wire plugs.

To check operation of trigger coil, separate the four-wire connection between CD ignition module and trigger coil and attach four-wire plug adapter to wire plug from trigger coil as shown in Fig. F7-12. Attach red (P) lead from number 22 tester to red sleeved adapter wire marked "Trigger 1 Pos." and yellow (N) tester lead to yellow sleeved adapter wire marked "Trigger 1 Neg." Place switch of tester in number 1 position and crank engine. Trigger coil operation is satisfactory if tester lamp lights. Renew trigger housing if tester lamp does not light. Repeat the previous test procedure but connect red (P) tester lead to red sleeved adapter wire marked "Trigger 2 Pos." and yellow (N) tester lead to yellow sleeved adapter wire marked "Trigger 2 Neg."

To check CD ignition module performance, proceed as follows: Separate primary lead connectors between CD ignition modules and ignition coils. Connect single wire adapter to orange or red wire from CD ignition module (Fig. F7-13).

NOTE: Model 85 hp does not use orange lead from rear CD unit.

Then attach yellow (N) lead of T8953 tester to yellow sleeved adapter wire marked "C-D." Attach red (P) tester lead to ground terminal of engine terminal block. Turn tester switch to position 60 and crank engine. Renew CD ignition module if tester lamp does not light. Repeat CD ignition module performance test for remaining cylinders.

COOLING SYSTEM

THERMOSTAT. The cooling syste thermostat (21 – Fig. F7-14 or F7-15) located behind cover (19) on top, front o cylinder head cover. Engine should no be run without a thermostat as engin may overheat.

WATER PUMP. The rubber impelle type water pump is located in the uppe gearcase and is driven by the driv shaft. When cooling system problem are encountered, first check the the mostat to see that is working properl and the water inlet for plugging or par tial stoppage. If trouble is not correctec remove the gearcase as outlined i LOWER UNIT section and check cond tion of water pump, water passages an sealing surfaces. Refer to Fig. F7-20 fo an exploded view of water pum assembly.

POWER HEAD

REMOVE AND DISASSEMBLE
Depending upon the type of main tenance, removal of the ignition com ponents, starter, flywheel, alternator carburetors and linkage and fuel pum prior to power head removal will eas operation. To remove power head remove support plate retaining screw. and withdraw. Remove screws and lif off rear motor leg cover. Detach any components or wiring that will interfere with power head removal. Remov screws and nuts securing power head then carefully lift power head fron lower unit. Remove screws and stud nuts to remove exhaust tube and space plate from power head.

Refer to Fig. F7-14 or F7-15 and re move cylinder head cover (23) and cylin

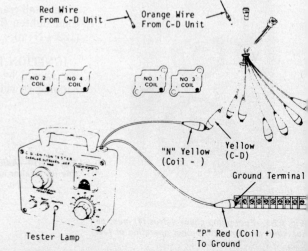

Red Wire
From C-D Unit

Orange Wire
From C-D Unit

NO 2
COIL

NO 4
COIL

NO 1
COIL

NO 3
COIL

"N" Yellow
(Coil -)

Yellow
(C-D)

Ground Terminal

Tester Lamp

"P" Red (Coil +)
To Ground

Fig. F7-13 — Tester lead connections for checking CD ignition module performance.

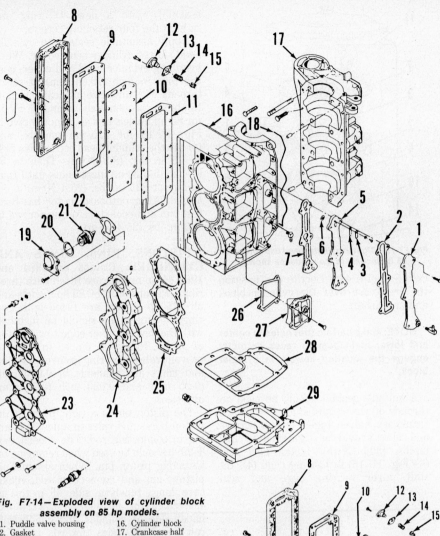

the correct cylinder. Center main bearings must be marked for correct assembly to the main bearing journal from which they were removed.

Refer to the appropriate following paragraphs for service and assembly instructions for crankshaft, connecting rods, pistons and bearings.

ASSEMBLY. Before assembling, make certain that all joint and gasket surfaces are clean, free from nicks, burrs, warped surfaces or hardened sealer or carbon. The crankcase must be completely sealed against both pressure and vacuum. Exhaust cover and cylinder head must be sealed against water leakage pressure. Mating surfaces between power head, lower unit and spacer plate must form a tight seal.

Refer to the appropriate paragraphs for assembling the piston rings to pistons, pistons to connecting rods and main bearings to the crankshaft.

NOTE: It is extremely important that each cylinders parts are installed in the same location from which they were removed if the old parts are reinstalled. If parts are intermixed or installed in wrong location, early failure may result.

Fig. F7-14—Exploded view of cylinder block assembly on 85 hp models.

1. Puddle valve housing
2. Gasket
3. Stop
4. Petal
5. Plate
6. Screen
7. Gasket
8. Exhaust cover
9. Gasket
10. Baffle
11. Gasket
12. Bypass valve cover
13. Gasket
14. Spring
15. Bypass valve
16. Cylinder block
17. Crankcase half
18. Seal strip
19. Thermostat cover
20. Seal
21. Thermostat
22. Gasket
23. Cylinder head cover
24. Cylinder head
25. Cylinder head gasket
26. Gasket
27. Transfer port cover
28. Gasket
29. Spacer plate

der head (24). Remove exhaust cover (8), plate (10), transfer port covers (27), bypass valve (12, 14 and 15) and puddle drain assembly for cleaning. The crankcase front half (17) can be removed after removing all of the retaining stud nuts and screws including those attaching the crankshaft bearing cage. The crankcase halves are positioned with dowel pins and can be separated by prying at the two mating surface pry points. Use extreme care to prevent damage to the crankshaft and do not pry anywhere except the pry points provided.

Before removing connecting rods, piston or crankshaft, mark components for correct assembly to each other and in

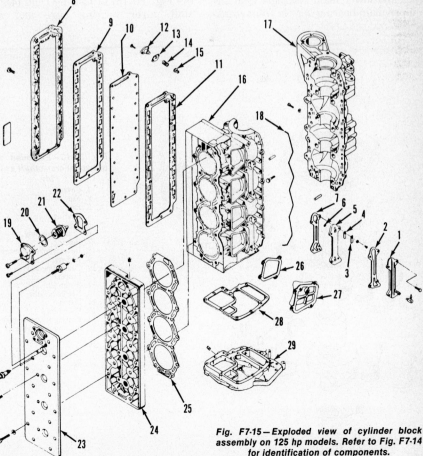

Fig. F7-15—Exploded view of cylinder block assembly on 125 hp models. Refer to Fig. F7-14 for identification of components.

99

Install piston and connecting rod assemblies in the correct cylinder making certain that long sloping side of piston is toward exhaust side of cylinder.

Clean oil, grease and fingerprints from outer race of upper main bearing (7 – Fig. F7-16) and bearing bore in crankcase.

NOTE: If alchohol or other flammable solvent is used for cleaning, make certain that area is well ventilated and free from sparks, open flames and electrical equipment.

Apply a light coating of Loctite to upper bearing bore in cylinder and position crankshaft in cylinder with all main bearings installed. Outer bearing races (17) and lower main bearing (20) should be turned until the bearing locating pins engage holes in the outer races. Position end gaps of crankshaft sealing rings (19) toward crankcase half.

Install the connecting rod bearing cage halves and rollers. Install rod cap with match marks together. Connecting rod screws should be tightened to 180-190 in.-lbs. (20.3-21.5 N·m).

Install crankcase seal strips (18 – Fig. F7-14 or F7-15) in grooves, then apply a suitable sealer inside seal groove and on both sides of seal groove in areas of upper and lower main bearings. Coat the upper main bearing bore in front crank-

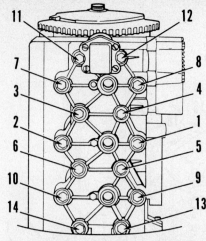

Fig. F7-17 — Tighten cylinder head cap screws on 85 hp models in the sequence shown.

case half (14) with Loctite and position the crankcase over the cylinder block and crankshaft.

NOTE: Make certain that holes in center and lower main bearing races correctly engage the locating dowels in cylinder block.

A suitable sealant should be used on threads of screws and studs that attach crankcase halves together and screws and nuts should be tightened to 270 in.-lbs. (30.5 N·m). Install new seal (3 – Fig. F7-16) in bearing cage (4). Install upper bearing cage and seal

assembly with a new "O" ring and tighten the four retaining screws.

Apply a suitable sealant to cylinder head side of cylinder head cover. When installing cylinder head and cover, coat the first ¾ inch (19.05 mm) of screw threads with antiseize lubricant. Follow tightening sequence shown in Fig. F7-17 for 85 hp models and sequence shown in Fig. F7-18 for 125 hp models, and torque the cylinder head cap screws first to 75 in.-lbs. (8.5 N·m). Then in 50 in.-lbs. (5.6 N·m) increments until final torque of 225 in.-lbs. (25.4 N·m) is obtained. After outboard motor has been test run and cooled, retorque screws to 225 in.-lbs. (25.4 N·m).

PISTONS, PINS, RINGS AND CYLINDERS. Pistons on 1984 and 1985 85 hp models are fitted with three rings. Pistons on 1986 85 hp models and all 125 hp models are fitted with two rings. Piston rings should be installed with the beveled inner edge towards top of piston. Rings are pinned in place to prevent rotation in ring grooves. Pistons and rings are available in 0.010 inch (0.25 mm) and 0.030 inch (0.76 mm) oversizes.

The piston pin is a tight press fit in piston bores and rides in a needle bearing in connecting rod. The special tool T-2990 should be used when removing or installing piston pin. When assembling piston, pin and connecting rod, make sure long, tapering side of piston is assembled for installation toward exhaust side of cylinder and connecting rod bevel cut faces towards top (flywheel) end of crankshaft.

All friction surfaces should be lubricated with new engine oil during assembly.

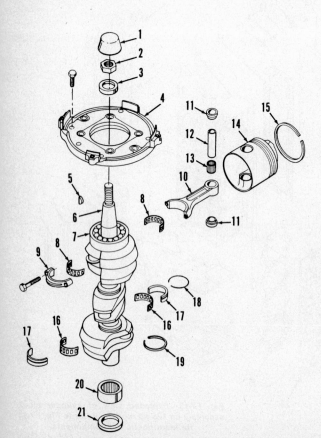

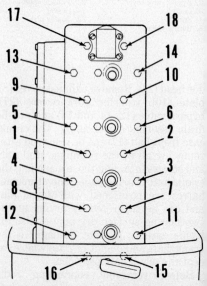

Fig. F7-16 — Exploded view of typical crankshaft assembly.

1. Cover
2. Nut
3. Seal
4. Bearing cage
5. Key
6. Crankshaft assy.
7. Bearing
8. Bearing rollers & cage half
9. Rod cap
10. Connecting rod
11. Spacer
12. Piston pin
13. Needle bearing
14. Piston
15. Piston ring
16. Bearing rollers & cage half
17. Bearing outer race
18. Snap ring
19. Seal ring
20. Lower main bearing
21. Seal

Fig. F7-18 — Tighten cylinder head cap screws on 125 hp models in the sequence shown.

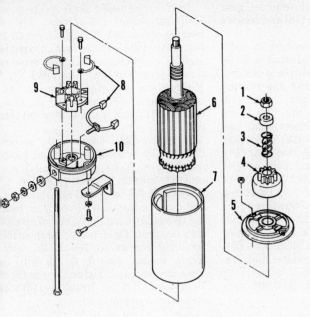

A neutral interlock switch is used so engine will start in neutral but not in forward or reverse position. Make sure neutral interlock switch is properly adjusted.

Fig. F7-19 — Exploded view of electric starter motor.

1. Nut
2. Stop
3. Spring
4. Drive pinion
5. End plate
6. Armature
7. Frame
8. Brushes
9. Brush holder
10. End housing

PROPELLER

Propellers for normal use have three blades and are protected by a cushioning slip clutch. Various pitch propellers are available and should be selected to provide full throttle operation within the recommended limits of 4500-5500 rpm. Propellers other than those designed for the motor should not be used.

CONNECTING RODS, BEARINGS AND CRANKSHAFT.

Before detaching connecting rods from crankshaft, make certain that rod and cap are properly marked for correct assembly to each other and in the correct cylinder. It is important that each cylinders parts are installed in the same location from which they were removed if the old parts are reinstalled. If parts are intermixed or installed in wrong location, early failure may result.

The crankshaft upper main bearing is renewable. Place upper main bearing on crankshaft with lettered side towards flywheel, then using a suitable press, install bearing flush to within 0.001 inch (0.02 mm) of bearing seat.

The bearing roller and cages used in the connecting rods and center main bearings are available only as a set which contains the rollers and cage halves for one bearing. The complete assembly should be installed whenever renewal is required.

A nonfibrous grease can be used to hold loose needle bearings in position during assembly. All friction surfaces should be lubricated with new engine oil. Check frequently as power head is being assembled, for binding or locking of the moving parts. If binding occurs, remove the cause before proceeding with the assembly. When assembling, follow the procedures outlined in the ASSEMBLY paragraphs.

ELECTRIC STARTER

Electric starter motor shown in Fig. F7-19 is used. Renew any components which are damaged or excessively worn.

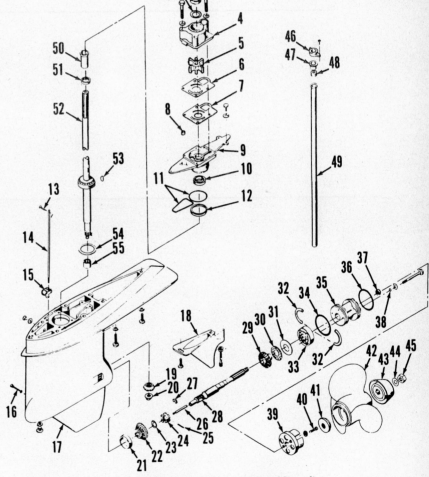

Fig. F7-20 — Exploded view of lower drive unit.

1. Water tube seal	15. Pivot coupling	28. Propeller shaft	42. Propeller
2. Drive shaft seal	16. Pivot pin	29. Reverse gear	43. Washer
3. Spacer	17. Gearcase	30. Thrust bearing	44. Washer
4. Water pump housing	18. Exhaust snout	31. Thrust washer	45. Nut
5. Impeller	19. Drive pinion	32. Retainer clips	46. Bracket
6. Lower plate	20. Nut	33. Bearing & cage	47. Seal
7. Gasket	21. Bearing cup	34. "O" ring	48. Grommet
8. Shift rod seal	22. Forward gear & bearing	35. Spool	49. Water tube
9. Gearcase cover	23. Shim	36. "O" ring	50. Seal
10. Drive shaft seal	24. Shift coupling	37. Seal	51. Retainer
11. Cover seals	25. Shift pin	38. "O" ring	52. Drive shaft
12. Crush ring	26. Shift shaft	39. Anode	53. Impeller drive key
13. Pin	27. Shift yoke	40. Screw	54. Shim
14. Lower shift rod		41. Spacer	55. Bearing

LOWER UNIT

R&R AND OVERHAUL. Remove shift rod pin (13 – Fig. F7-20). Remove exhaust snout (18) and unscrew seven screws to separate gearcase from motor leg. Drain lubricant and remove propeller.

Disassemble and remove water pump components (1 through 7). Turn shift rod (14) counterclockwise until disengaged from pivot coupling (15) and remove rod. Remove cover (9) and anode (39). Remove screws securing bearing spool (35) and using a suitable puller withdraw spool from gearcase. Remove retaining clips (32), bearing and cage (33), thrust washer (31), thrust bearing (30) and reverse gear (29). Withdraw propeller shaft (28) with components (22 through 27). Unscrew pinion nut (20), withdraw

drive shaft (52) and remove pinion gear (19). Unscrew pivot pin (16) and remove pivot coupling (15).

Use the following procedure to check reverse gear backlash: Install a 0.050 inch spacer (tool T8997) in place of shims (54). Install forward gear and bearing (22), drive shaft (52), pinion gear (19) and nut (20). Tighten nut (20) to 85 ft.-lbs. (115.6 N·m). Insert shim tool T8997A in forward gear (22) so flat portion of tool is towards pinion gear (19). Pull up on drive shaft and using a feeler gage measure gap between large OD of tool and pinion gear. Subtract measured gap from 0.055 inch (0.050-spacer plus 0.005 inch desired backlash) to obtain thickness of shim pack (54). Remove 0.050 inch shim, install shim pack (54) and repeat above procedure. Gap between pinion gear (19) and large OD of shim tool should be 0.004-0.006 inch (0.10-0.15 mm).

To check propeller shaft end play, install components (21 through 32) and bearing spool (35). Shim (23) should be thinnest available (0.054 inch). Do not install "O" rings on spool. Tighten spool retaining screws to 160 in.-lbs. (18.1 N·m). Measure end play of propeller shaft and install shims (23) necessary to obtain 0.009-0.011 inch (0.23-0.28 mm) end play.

To reassemble lower unit, reverse disassembly procedure. Tighten pinion nut (20) to 85 ft.-lbs. (115.6 N·m). Install seal (37) with lip towards propeller. "O" rings (34 & 36) have different diameters and must be installed correctly on bearing spool (35). Chamfered end of spool is installed first. Tighten bearing spool (35) retaining screws to 160 in.-lbs. (18. N·m). Install seals (8 & 10) with lip towards gearcase. Tighten cover (9) to 70 in.-lbs. (7.9 N·m). Install seal (2) with lip towards power head.

MARINER

MARINER INTERNATIONAL CO.
1939 Pioneer Rd.
Fond du Lac, Wisconsin 54935

MARINER 30 HP

CONDENSED SERVICE DATA

NOTE: Metric fasteners are used throughout outboard motor.

TUNE-UP

Hp/rpm	30/4500-5500
Bore	72 mm
	(2.84 in.)
Stroke	61 mm
	(2.40 in.)
Number of Cylinders	2
Displacement	496 cc
	(30.3 cu. in.)
Spark Plug—NGK	B7HS
Electrode Gap	0.5-0.6 mm
	(0.020-0.024 in.)
Ignition	CDI
Idle Speed (in gear)	600-700 rpm
Fuel:Oil Ratio	50:1

SIZES—CLEARANCES

Piston Ring End Gap	0.2-0.4 mm
	(0.008-0.016 in.)
Lower Piston Ring Side Clearance	0.04-0.08 mm
	(0.0016-0.0032 in.)
Piston Skirt Clearance	0.060-0.065 mm
	(0.0024-0.0026 in.)
Crankshaft Runout—Max.	0.03 mm
	(0.0012 in.)

SIZES—CLEARANCES CONT.

Connecting Rod Small End Shake:	
Standard	0.8 mm
	(0.03 in.)
Limit	2.0 mm
	(0.08 in.)

TIGHTENING TORQUES

Crankcase	24.5-34 N·m
	(18-25 ft.-lbs.)
Cylinder Head	24.5-34 N·m
	(18-25 ft.-lbs.)
Flywheel	149.6-170 N·m
	(110-125 ft.-lbs.)
Standard Screws:	
4 mm	2.3 N·m
	(20 in.-lbs.)
5 mm	4.3-6.6 N·m
	(38-58 in.-lbs.)
6 mm	6.6-10.8 N·m
	(58-96 in.-lbs.)
8 mm	13.6-21.8 N·m
	(10-16 ft.-lbs.)
10 mm	27.2-44.9 N·m
	(20-33 ft.-lbs.)
12 mm	35.4-50.3 N·m
	(26-37 ft.-lbs.)

LUBRICATION

The power head is lubricated by oil mixed with the fuel. Fuel should be regular leaded, low lead or unleaded gasoline with a minimum pump octane rating of 86. Recommended oil is Quicksilver Formula 50-D Outboard Lubricant. Normal fuel:oil ratio is 50:1; during engine break-in fuel:oil ratio should be 25:1.

Lower unit gears and bearings are lubricated by oil contained in the gearcase. Recommended oil is Mariner Super Duty Gear Lube. Lubricant is drained by removing vent and drain plugs in the gearcase. Refill through drain plug hole until oil has reached level of vent plug hole.

FUEL SYSTEM

CARBURETOR. Refer to Fig. MR16-1 for an exploded view of carburetor. Use the standard carburetor jet sizes as recommended by the manufacturer for normal operation when used at altitudes of 2500 feet (750 m) and less. Main jet (15–Fig. MR16-1) size should be reduced from standard recommenda-

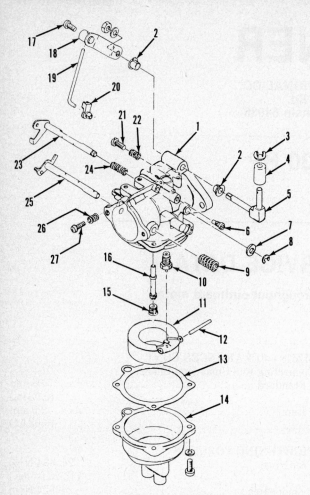

Fig. MR16-1 – Exploded view of carburetor.

1. Body
2. Bushing
3. Clip
4. Cam follower roller
5. Cam follower
6. Pilot jet
7. Washer
8. Clip
9. Spring
10. Fuel inlet valve
11. Float
12. Pin
13. Gasket
14. Float bowl
15. Main jet
16. Main nozzle
17. Screw
18. Throttle arm
19. Link
20. Link keeper
21. Idle mixture screw
22. Spring
23. Throttle shaft
24. Spring
25. Choke shaft
26. Spring
27. Idle speed screw

Fig. MR16-4 – View showing early type fuel pump assembly. Late type fuel pump assembly can be identified by ribs on the inlet and outlet nozzle. Late type fuel pump uses reed type check valves instead of umbrella type check valves (11 and 12) as used on early type fuel pump.

1. Gasket	
2. Base	11. Outlet check valve
3. Gasket	12. Inlet check valve
4. Diaphragm	13. Gasket
5. Spring plate	14. Retainer
6. Spring	15. Gasket
7. Gasket	16. Diaphragm
8. Body	17. Spring plate
9. Retainer	18. Spring
10. Gasket	19. Cover

tion by one size for altitudes of 2500 to 5000 feet (750 to 1500 m), two sizes for altitudes of 5000 to 7500 feet (1500 to 2250 m) and three sizes for altitudes of 7500 feet (2250 m) and up. Initial adjustment of idle mixture screw (21) is 1-3/8 to

2 turns out from a lightly seated position. Recommended idle speed is 600-700 rpm (in gear) with the engine at normal operating temperature.

To determine the float level, remove the carburetor and float bowl (14). Invert carburetor body (1) and slowly raise float (11). Note whether float (11) is parallel with surface of carburetor body when needle of fuel valve (10) just breaks contact with float (11) tang. If not, adjust float (11) tang until proper float level is obtained.

FUEL FILTER. A fuel filter assembly (1 – Fig. MR16-3) is connected between fuel supply line (2) and fuel pump inlet line (3). With the engine stopped, periodically unscrew fuel filter cup (7) from filter base (4) and withdraw filter element (6), "O" ring (5) and gasket (8). Clean cup (7) and filter element (6) in a suitable solvent and blow dry with clean compressed air. Inspect filter element (6). If excessive blockage or damage is noted, renew element.

Reassembly is reverse order of disassembly. Renew "O" ring (5) and gasket (8) during reassembly.

FUEL PUMP. The diaphragm type fuel pump is located on the port side of

the engine. Refer to Fig. MR16-4 for an exploded view of fuel pump. Alternating pressure and vacuum pulsations in the crankcase actuates the diaphragm and check valves in the pump.

NOTE: Early type fuel pump assembly uses umbrella type check valves and late type fuel pump assembly uses reed valve type check valves.

Make certain that all gaskets, diaphragms and check valves are in good condition when reassembling unit. Coat gasket (1) with a nonhardening type gasket sealer making certain that passage in center is not blocked with gasket sealer.

REED VALVE. The reed valve assembly is located between the intake manifold and crankcase. Refer to Fig. MR16-6 for a view of reed valve assembly.

Cracked, warped, chipped or bent reed petals will impair operation and should be renewed. Do not attempt to straighten or repair bent or damaged reed petals. Reed petals should seat smoothly against reed plate along their entire length. Reassemble reed stops and reed petals on chamfered side of reed plate (3). Position reed petals so index marks (B – Fig. MR16-7) are show-

Fig. MR16-3 – Exploded view of fuel filter assembly, fuel hoses and mounting bracket.

1. Fuel filter assy.
2. Fuel supply line
3. Fuel pump inlet line
4. Filter base
5. "O" ring
6. Filter element
7. Cup
8. Gasket

g between petals. Note that index mark consists of two dots on later models. Height (A) of reed stop should e 5.4 mm (0.21 in.). On later models, he manufacturer does not recommend he adjustment of reed stop height (A). Renew reed stop if height adjustment is ncorrect or damage is noted.

SPEED CONTROL LINKAGE. To ynchronize ignition and throttle control inkage, first make sure the ignition timng has been correctly adjusted. Detach magneto base plate control rod (3–Fig. MR16-9) and blockout lever control rod 1). Measure length of magneto base plate control rod from joint center to oint center and adjust to a length of 59.2-70.0 mm (2.58-2.90 in.), then reconnect control rod. Position gear shift ever in "NEUTRAL."

Turn twist grip to full throttle posiion. Loosen locknuts (N) and turn conrol cable adjustment (A) until cable slack is 1-2 mm (0.039-0.079 in.), then ighten locknuts.

Fig. MR16-9 – View of blockout lever control rod (1), blockout lever (2) and stator base plate control rod (3). Locknuts (N) and adjuster (A) are used to adjust cable slack. Refer to text.

With the twist grip held in the full throttle position, push magneto base plate to full advance position. Measure length of blockout lever control rod (1) from joint center to joint center and adjust to a length of 91.5 mm (3.6 in.), then reconnect control rod. Blockout lever (2) should contact bottom cowling stopper when twist grip is turned to the full throttle position with the magneto base plate fully advanced and the gear shift lever is in "NEUTRAL" position. If not, readjust blockout lever control rod (1) until the proper adjustment is obtained.

IGNITION

All models are equipped with a capacitor discharge ignition (CDI)

system. If engine malfunction is noted and the ignition system is suspected, make sure the spark plugs and all electrical connections are tight before proceeding to troubleshooting the CD ignition system.

Proceed as follows to test CDI system components: Refer to Fig. MR16-11. To test ignition coil, disconnect black wire (B) and orange wire (O) at connectors and spark plug boots from spark plugs. Use a suitable ohmmeter and connect red tester lead to orange wire (O) and black tester lead to black wire (B). The primary winding resistance reading should be 0.08-0.10 ohms. Connect rod tester lead to terminal end in one spark plug boot and black tester lead to terminal end in remaining spark plug boot. The secondary winding resistance reading should be 3,475-4,025 ohms. Use a suitable coil tester or tester Model 9800 Magneto Analyzer to perform a power test. Connect tester leads as outlined in tester's handbook. A steady spark should jump a 5 mm (13/64 in.) gap when a current value of 1.7-2.1 amperes is applied. A surface insulation test can be performed using a suitable coil tester or tester Model 9800 Magneto Analyzer and following tester's handbook.

To check source (charge) coil, disconnect black wire (B) and brown wire (Br) at connectors leading from magneto base plate. Use a suitable ohmmeter and connect red tester lead to brown wire (Br) and black tester lead to black wire (B). DO NOT rotate flywheel while making test. The ohmmeter should read 121-147 ohms. Reconnect wires after completing test.

To check pulser (trigger) coil, disconnect white wire with red tracer (W/R) at connector leading from magneto base plate and black wire (B) at back of CDI unit. Use a suitable ohmmeter and con-

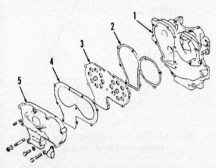

Fig. MR16-6 – Exploded view of reed valve and intake manifold assembly.

1. Crankcase half
2. Gasket
3. Reed valve assy.
4. Gasket
5. Intake manifold

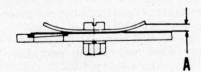

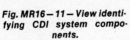

Fig. MR16–11 – View identifying CDI system components.

1. CDI module
2. Charge coil
3. Pulser coil
4. Lighting coil
5. Stop switch
6. Ignition coil
7. Spark plugs

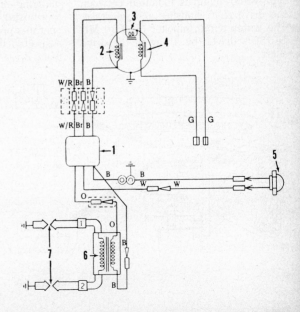

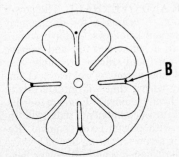

Fig. MR16-7 – Height (A) of reed stop should be 5.4 mm (0.21 in.). Make sure marks (B) are aligned between reed petals when reassembling unit.

Red Test Lead \ Black Test Lead	CDI UNIT LEADS				
CDI UNIT LEADS (Red)	White	Black	Brown	White w/Red	Orange
White	A	B	B	B	B
Black	C	A	D	B	J
Brown	E	F	A	B	J
White w/Red	G	H	I	A	J
Orange	B	B	B	B	A

Fig. MR16-12—Use chart and values listed below to test condition of CD ignition module. Before making test (J), connect CDI module's orange wire and black wire together. Then disconnect wires and perform desired test.

A. Zero
B. Infinity
C. 9,000-19,000 ohms
D. 2,000-6,000 ohms
E. 80,000-160,000 ohms
F. 70,000-150,000 ohms
G. 33,000-63,000 ohms
H. 7,000-17,000 ohms
I. 15,000-35,000 ohms
J. Tester needle should show deflection then return toward infinite resistance

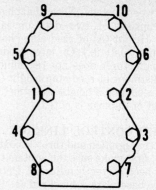

Fig. MR16-17—Tighten crankcase screws in sequence shown above.

nect red tester lead to white wire with red tracer (W/R) and black tester lead to black wire (B). DO NOT rotate flywheel while making test. The ohmmeter should read 12.6-15.4 ohms.

To test CDI module, first disconnect all wires at connectors and remove CDI module from outboard motor. Use a suitable ohmmeter and refer to Fig. MF16-12. With reference to chart, perform CDI module resistance tests.

Renew any components that are not within the manufacturer's recommended limits.

To check ignition timing, rotate flywheel so the timing pointer (TP–Fig. MR 16-13) is aligned with 25° BTDC mark on flywheel. Rotate stator plate so stop bracket tab (T) is against timing pointer. The stamped mark on the stator plate should be aligned with 0° (TDC) mark (5° BTDC mark on Work 30 model) on flywheel. Adjust timing by loosening stop bracket retaining screws and relocating bracket.

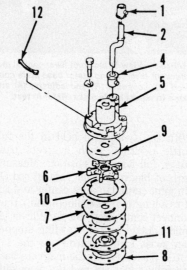

Fig. MR16-15—Exploded view of later type water pump assembly.

1. Seal
2. Water tube
4. Seal
5. Pump housing
6. Impeller
7. Plate
8. Gasket
9. Liner
10. Gasket
11. Base
12. Spacer

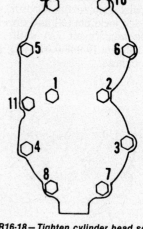

Fig. MR16-18—Tighten cylinder head screws in sequence shown above.

COOLING SYSTEM

WATER PUMP. A rubber impeller type water pump is mounted between the drive shaft housing and gearcase. The water pump impeller (6–Fig. MR 16-15) is driven by a key in the drive shaft.

When cooling system problems are encountered, first check water inlet for plugging or partial stoppage. Be sure thermostat located in cylinder head operates properly. If the water pump is suspected defective, separate gearcase from drive shaft housing and inspect

pump. Make sure all seals and mating surfaces are in good condition and water passages are unobstructed. Check impeller (6) and plate (7) for excessive wear. When reassembling, coat gasket surfaces with a thin coating of Perfect Seal.

POWER HEAD

R&R AND OVERHAUL. The power head can be removed for disassembly and overhaul as follows: Clamp outboard motor to a suitable stand and remove engine cowl and starter assembly. Disconnect speed control cables, fuel line and any wiring that will interfere with power head removal. Remove or disconnect any component that will interfere with power head removal. Remove six screws securing power head to drive shaft housing and lift power head free. Remove flywheel, ignition components, carburetor, intake manifold

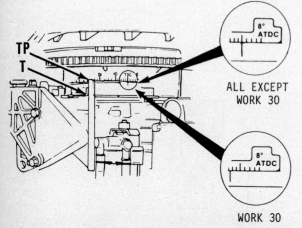

Fig. MR16-13—Full advance occurs when stop bracket tab (T) contacts timing pointer (TP). Refer to text for ignition timing adjustment.

nd reed valve assembly. Remove
crews retaining exhaust cover
(8 – Fig. MR16-20) and withdraw.
Crankcase halves can be separated after
removal of ten screws securing crankcase half (1) to cylinder block. Crankshaft and pistons are now accessible for
removal and overhaul as outlined in the
appropriate following paragraphs.

ASSEMBLY. Two-stroke engine design dictates that intake manifold and
crankcase are completely sealed against
both vacuum and pressure. Exhaust
manifold and cylinder head must be
sealed against water leakage and
pressure. Mating surfaces of water intake and exhaust areas between power
head and drive shaft housing must form
a tight seal.

Whenever the power head is disassembled, it is recommended that all gasket
surfaces of crankcase halves be carefully
checked for nicks, burrs or warped surfaces which might interfere with a tight
seal. The cylinder head, head end of
cylinder block, and the mating surfaces
of manifolds and crankcase may be
checked and lapped, if necessary, to provide a smooth surface. Do not remove
any more metal than is necessary to obtain a smooth finish. Thoroughly clean
the parts with new oil on a clean, soft
rag, then wash with soapsuds and clean
rags.

Mating surface of crankcase halves
may be checked on the lapping block,
and high spots or nicks removed, but
surfaces must not be lowered. If extreme care is used, a slightly damaged
crankcase can be salvaged in this manner. In case of doubt, renew the crankcase assembly.

The crankcase halves are positively
located during assembly by the use of
two dowel pins. Check to make sure that
dowel pins are not bent, nicked or
distorted and that dowel holes are clean
and true. When installing pins, make
certain they are fully seated, but do not
use excessive force.

The mating surfaces of the crankcase
halves must be sealed during reassembly
using a nonhardening type of gasket
sealer. Make certain that surfaces are
thoroughly cleaned of oil and old sealer
before making a fresh application. Apply
sealer evenly and use sparingly, so excess does not squeeze into crankcase
cavity. Cylinder head, gasket (8 – Fig.
MR16-20) and exhaust manifold gaskets
(15 and 17) should be coated with a good
grade of heat resistant gasket sealer.

Tighten the crankcase screws to
24.5-34 N·m (18-25 ft.-lbs.) following the
sequence shown in Fig. MR16-17.
Tighten the cylinder head screws to
24.5-34 N·m (18-25 ft.-lbs.) following the

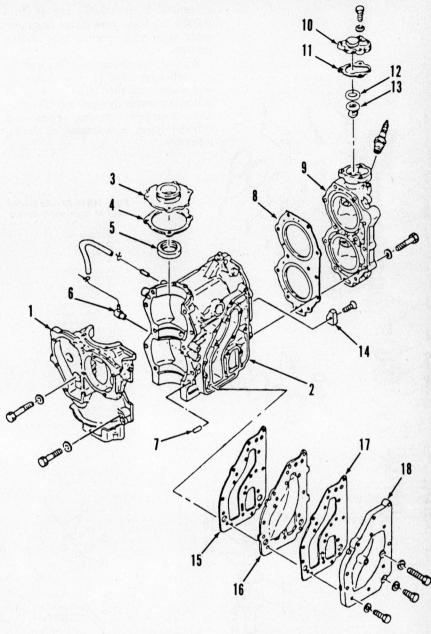

Fig. MR16-20—Exploded view of cylinder block assembly.

1. Crankcase	6. Check valve	10. Thermostat cover
2. Cylinder block	7. Dowel pin	11. Gasket
3. Oil seal housing	8. Gasket	12. Spacer
4. Gasket	9. Cylinder head	13. Thermostat
5. Oil seal		14. Anode
		15. Gasket
		16. Inner exhaust plate
		17. Gasket
		18. Exhaust cover

sequence shown in Fig. MR16-18. Refer
to CONDENSED SERVICE DATA section for general torquing specifications.

**PISTONS, PINS, RINGS AND
CYLINDERS.** Cylinder bore should be
measured in several different locations
to determine if an out-of-round or
tapered condition exists. Inspect
cylinder wall for scoring. If minor scoring is noted, cylinders should be honed
to smooth out cylinder wall.

**NOTE: Cylinder sleeves are cast into
the cylinder block. If cylinder is out-of-
round or tapered more than 0.54 mm (0.012
in.), or if excessive scoring is noted, the
cylinder block must be renewed.**

Recommended piston skirt to cylinder
clearance is 0.060-0.065 mm
(0.0024-0.0026 in.). Recommended
piston ring end gap is 0.2-0.4 mm
(0.008-0.016 in.) for both rings. The top
piston ring is semi-keystone shaped. The
recommended lower piston ring side

Illustrations Courtesy Mariner

clearance is 0.04-0.08 mm (0.0016-0.0032 in.). Make sure piston rings properly align with locating pins in ring grooves.

When reassembling, install new piston pin retaining clips (4 – Fig. MR16-22) and make sure that "UP" on dome of piston is towards flywheel end of engine. Coat bearings, pistons, rings and cylinder bores with engine oil during assembly.

CONNECTING RODS, CRANK-SHAFT AND BEARINGS. The crankshaft assembly should only be disassembled if the necesary tools and experience are available to service this type of crankshaft.

Maximum crankshaft runout measured at bearing outer races with crankshaft ends supported in lathe centers is 0.03 mm (0.0012 in.). Maximum connecting rod big end side clearance should be less than 0.8 mm (0.032 in.). Standard side-to-side shake of connecting rod small end measured as shown in Fig. MR16-23 should be 0.8 mm (0.03 in.) with a maximum of 2.0 mm (0.08 in.).

Crankshaft; connecting rods and center section components are available only as a unit assembly. Outer main bearings (17 and 24 – Fig. MR16-22) are available individually.

Thirty-four needle bearings (7) are used in each connecting rod small end. Rollers can be held in place with petroleum jelly while installing piston.

Lubricate bearings, pistons, rings and cylinders with engine oil prior to installation. Tighten crankcase and cylinder head screws as outlined in ASSEMBLY section.

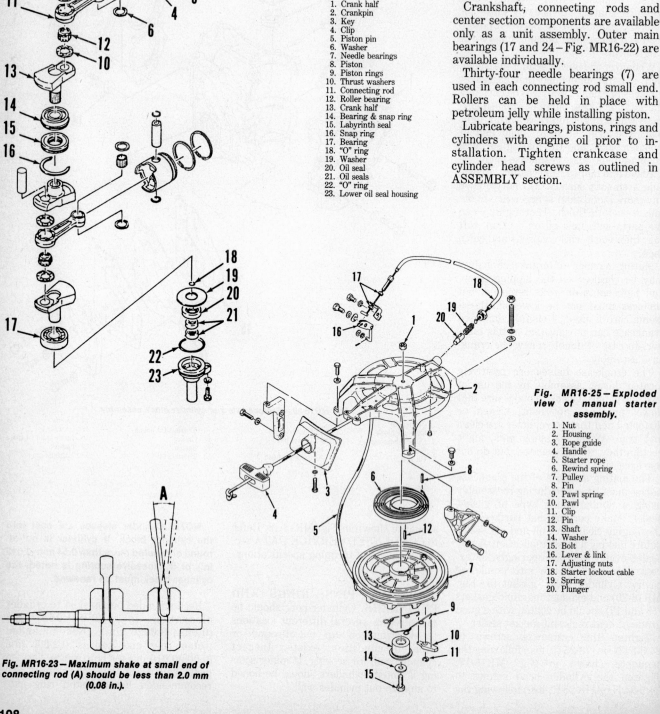

Fig. MR16-22 — Exploded view of crankshaft assembly.

1. Crank half
2. Crankpin
3. Key
4. Clip
5. Piston pin
6. Washer
7. Needle bearings
8. Piston
9. Piston rings
10. Thrust washers
11. Connecting rod
12. Roller bearing
13. Crank half
14. Bearing & snap ring
15. Labyrinth seal
16. Snap ring
17. Bearing
18. "O" ring
19. Washer
20. Oil seal
21. Oil seals
22. "O" ring
23. Lower oil seal housing

Fig. MR16-25 — Exploded view of manual starter assembly.

1. Nut
2. Housing
3. Rope guide
4. Handle
5. Starter rope
6. Rewind spring
7. Pulley
8. Pin
9. Pawl spring
10. Pawl
11. Clip
12. Pin
13. Shaft
14. Washer
15. Bolt
16. Lever & link
17. Adjusting nuts
18. Starter lockout cable
19. Spring
20. Plunger

Fig. MR16-23 — Maximum shake at small end of connecting rod (A) should be less than 2.0 mm (0.08 in.).

Fig. MR16-26 — View showing proper installation of pawl spring (9), pawl (10) and clip (11). Pulley hole (H) is used during pulley withdrawal. Refer to text.

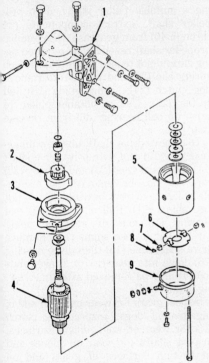

Fig. MR16-28 — Exploded view of electric starter assembly.

1. End frame
2. Drive assy.
3. Frame cover
4. Armature
5. Frame
6. Brush plate
7. Brush
8. Brush spring
9. End cover

Fig. MR16-30 — Exploded view of gearcase assembly.

1. Boot	13. Bearing	25. Pin	37. Key
2. Retainer	14. Shim	26. Spring clip	38. Bearing housing
3. "O" ring	15. Drive shaft tube	27. Shift plunger	39. Needle bearing
4. Lower shift rod	16. Needle bearing	28. Spring guide	40. Oil seals
5. Vent plug	17. Thrust washer	29. Spring	41. Tab washer
6. Water inlet cover	18. Pinion gear	30. Propeller shaft	42. Nut
7. Dowel	19. Nut	31. Thrust washer	43. Spacer
8. Oil level plug	20. Trim tab	32. Reverse gear	44. Spacer
9. Drain plug	21. Shim	33. Shim	45. Washer
10. Key	22. Taper roller bearing	34. Thrust washer	46. Nut
11. Drive shaft	23. Forward gear	35. "O" ring	47. Cotter pin
12. Oil seals	24. Clutch	36. Ball bearing	48. "O" ring

STARTER

MANUAL STARTER. When starter rope (5 – Fig. MR16-25) is pulled, pulley (7) will rotate. As pulley (7) rotates, drive pawl (10) moves to engage with the flywheel thus cranking the engine.

When starter rope (5) is released, pulley (7) is rotated in the reverse direction by force from rewind spring (6). As pulley (7) rotates, the starter rope is rewound and drive pawl (10) is disengaged from the flywheel.

Safety plunger (20) engages lugs on pulley (7) to prevent starter engagement when the gear shift lever is in the forward or reverse position.

To overhaul the manual starter, proceed as follows: Remove the engine top cover. Remove the screws retaining the manual starter to the engine. Remove starter lockout cable (18) at starter housing (2). Note plunger (20) and spring (19) located at cable end; care should be used not to lose components should they fall free. Withdraw the starter assembly.

Check pawl (10) for freedom of movement and excessive wear of engagement area or any other damage. Renew or lubricate pawl (10) with a suitable water-resistant grease and return starter to service if no other damage is noted.

To disassemble, remove clip (11) and withdraw pawl (10) and pawl spring (9). Untie starter rope (5) at handle (4) and allow the rope to wind into the starter. Remove bolt (15), washer (14) and shaft (13), then place a suitable screwdriver blade through hole (H–Fig. MR16-26) to hold rewind spring (6–Fig. MR16-25) securely in housing (2). Carefully lift pulley (7) with starter rope (5) from housing (2). BE CAREFUL when removing pulley (7) to prevent possible injury from rewind spring. Untie starter rope (5) and remove rope from pulley (7) if renewal is required. To remove rewind spring (6) from housing (2), invert hous-

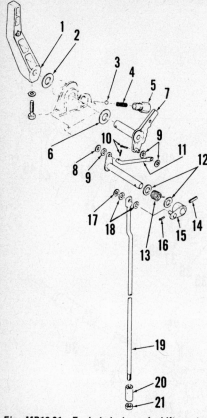

Fig. MR16-31 — Exploded view of shift control linkage.

1. Shift control handle	
2. Washer	12. Washers
3. Detent ball	13. Spring
4. Spring	14. Pin
5. Guide	15. Arm
6. Washer	16. Cotter pin
7. Cam	17. Washer
8. Washer	18. Washers
9. Washer	19. Upper shift rod
10. Pins	20. Coupler nut
11. Link	21. Locknut

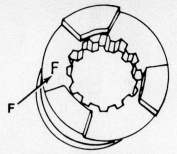

Fig. 16-32 — Install clutch so (F) mark is towards forward gear.

ing so it sits upright on a flat surface, then tap the housing top until rewind spring (6) falls free and uncoils.

Inspect all components for damage and excessive wear and renew if needed.

To reassemble, first apply a coating of a suitable water-resistant grease to rewind spring area of housing (2). Install rewind spring (6) in housing (2) so spring coils wind in a counterclockwise direction from the outer end. Make sure the spring outer hook is properly secured around starter housing pin (8). Wind starter rope (5) on to pulley (7) approximately 2½ turn counterclockwise when viewed from the flywheel side. Direct remaining starter rope (5) length through notch in pulley (7).

NOTE: Lubricate all friction surfaces with a suitable water-resistant grease during reassembly.

Assemble pulley (7) to starter housing making sure that pin (12) engages hook end in rewind spring (6). Install shaft (13), washer (14) and bolt (15). Apply Loctite 271 or 290, or an equivalent

thread fastening solution, on bolt (15) threads, then install nut (1) and securely tighten.

Thread starter rope (5) through starter housing (2), rope guide (3) and handle (4) and secure with a knot. Turn pulley (7) 2 to 3 turns counterclockwise when viewed from the flywheel side, then release starter rope (5) from pulley notch and allow rope to slowly wind onto pulley.

NOTE: Do not apply any more tension on rewind spring (6) than is required to draw starter handle (4) back into the proper released position.

Install spring (9), pawl (10) and clip (11) as shown in Fig. MR16-26. Remount manual starter assembly.

Adjust starter lockout assembly by turning adjusting nuts (17 – Fig. MR16-25) at cable (18) end so starter will engage when gear shift lever is in neutral position, but will not engage when gear shift lever is in forward or reverse position. Plunger (20) end should recess in starter housing (2) 1 mm (0.04 in.) when gear shift lever is in neutral position.

ELECTRIC STARTER. Some models are equipped with an electric starter motor. Refer to Fig. MR16-28 for an exploded view of the starter motor. Commutator undercut should be 0.5-0.8 mm (0.02-0.03 in.) with a minimum limit of 0.2 mm (0.008 in.). Minimum brush length is 10 mm (0.394 in.).

During reassembly, adjust shims so armature end play is 1.5-2.0 mm (0.06-0.08 in.).

LOWER UNIT

PROPELLER AND DRIVE HUB. Lower unit protection is provided by a cushion type hub in the propeller. Standard propeller rotates clockwise, has three blades and measures 251 mm (9-⅞ in.) in diameter and 286 mm (11¼ in.) in pitch.

R&R AND OVERHAUL. Most serv-

ice on lower unit can be performed after detaching gearcase from drive shaft housing. To remove gearcase, attach outboard motor to a suitable stand and remove vent and drain plugs in gearcase to allow lubricant to drain. Loosen locknut (21 – Fig. MR16-31) and remove coupler nut (20). Remove four bolts securing gearcase to drive shaft housing and carefully separate gearcase from drive shaft housing. Remove water pump being careful not to lose impeller key (10 – Fig. MR16-30). Remove propeller.

Disassemble gearcase by bending back locking tab of lockwasher (41), then remove nut (42) and lockwasher (41). Using a suitable puller attached to propeller shaft, extract components (24 through 40) from gearcase. Disassemble propeller shaft assembly as required being careful not to lose shims (33). Detach spring clip (26) and pin (25) to remove dog clutch (24), spring guide (28) and spring (29). Use a suitable puller to separate ball bearing (36) from reverse gear (32).

To remove drive shaft, unscrew pinion gear nut (19) and withdraw drive shaft (11). Forward gear (23) and bearing (22) cone may now be removed. Use a suitable puller to extract bearing cup; do not lose shims (21). Pull oil seals (12) and bearing (13) out of gearcase being careful not to lose shims (14). Remove drive shaft tube (15) then drive bearing (16) down into gear cavity. Lower shift rod (4) may be removed after unscrewing retainer (2).

Inspect gears for wear on teeth and in engagement dogs. Inspect dog clutch (24) for wear on engagement surfaces. Inspect shafts for wear on splines and on friction surfaces of gears and oil seals. Check shift cam for excessive wear on shift ramps. All seals and "O" rings should be renewed on each reassembly.

Assemble gearcase by reversing disassembly procedure. Install oil seals (12) with lips away from bearing (13). Install thrust washer (17) with grooved side facing pinion gear (18). Tighten pinion gear nut (19) to 34-38 N·m (25-28 ft.-lbs.). Forward gear backlash should be 0.2-0.5 mm (0.008-0.020 in.) and reverse gear backlash should be 0.7-1.0 mm (0.028-0.039 in.).

Install dog clutch (24) so "F" marked side (see Fig. MR16-32) is towards forward gear (23 – Fig. MR16-30). Shift plunger (27) is installed with round end towards cam on lower shift rod (4). Apply water resistant grease to drive shaft upper splines.

With gearcase assembled and installed, synchronize gear engagement with gear selector handle by turning shift rod adjusting coupler nut (20 – Fig. MR16-31), then tighten locknut (21).

MARINER 40 HP

CONDENSED SERVICE DATA

NOTE: Metric fasteners are used throughout outboard motor.

TUNE-UP

Hp/rpm	40/4500-5500
Bore	75 mm
	(2.95 in.)
Stroke	67 mm
	(2.64 in.)
Number of Cylinders	2
Displacement	592 cc
	(36.1 cu. in.)
Spark Plug – NGK	B8HS
Electrode Gap	0.6 mm
	(0.024 in.)
Ignition	See Text
Idle Speed (in gear)	850-950 rpm
Fuel:Oil Ratio	50:1

SIZES – CLEARANCES

Piston Ring End Gap	0.3-0.5 mm
	(0.012-0.020 in.)
Piston Skirt Clearance	0.050-0.055 mm
	(0.0020-0.0022 in.)

TIGHTENING TORQUES

Connecting Rod	31-34 N·m
	(23-25 ft.-lbs.)
Crankcase:	
6 mm	11-12 N·m
	(8-9 ft.-lbs.)
10 mm	37-41 N·m
	(27-30 ft.-lbs.)
Cylinder Head	27-31 N·m
	(20-23 ft.-lbs.)
Flywheel	149.6-170 N·m
	(110-125 ft.-lbs.)
Standard Screws:	
5 mm	3.4-5.3 N·m
	(30-47 in.-lbs.)
6 mm	5.9-9.3 N·m
	(52-82 in.-lbs.)
8 mm	13.6-21.8 N·m
	(10-16 ft.-lbs.)
10 mm	27.2-44.9 N·m
	(20-33 ft.-lbs.)
12 mm	35.4-50.3 N·m
	(26-37 ft.-lbs.)

LUBRICATION

The power head is lubricated by oil mixed with the fuel. Fuel should be regular leaded, low lead or unleaded gasoline with a minimum pump octane rating of 86. Recommended oil is Quicksilver Formula 50-D Outboard Lubricant. Normal fuel:oil ratio is 50:1, during engine break-in fuel:oil ratio should be 25:1.

Lower unit gears and bearings are lubricated by oil contained in the gearcase. Recommended oil is Mariner Super Duty Gear Lube. Lubricant is drained by removing vent and drain plugs in the gearcase. Refill through drain plug hole until oil has reached level of vent plug hole.

FUEL SYSTEM

SINGLE CARBURETOR MODELS. Use the standard carburetor jet sizes as recommended by the manufacturer for normal operation when used at altitudes of 2500 feet (762 m) or less. Main jet (13 – Fig. MR18-1) should be reduced from standard recommendation when the outboard motor is operated at higher altitudes.

Preliminary adjustment of idle mixture screw (6) is 1⅞ to 2⅜ turns out from a lightly seated position. Recommended idle speed is 850-950 rpm in gear with the engine at normal operating temperature.

To determine the float level, first note the numbers stamped on the top side of the carburetor mounting flange. Invert carburetor body (1 – Fig. MR18-2). On models with the numbers "67900" stamped on the flange, float (17) should be parallel (P) with carburetor base. On models with the numbers "67602" stamped on the flange, distance (D) from float (17) base to carburetor base should be 16.5-22.5 mm (21/32-7/8 in.). If correct setting is not obtained, renew inlet needle (15 – Fig. MR18-1) and seat (14) and/or float (17) as needed. Renew float bowl "O" ring (19).

FUEL FILTER. A fuel filter assembly (1 – Fig. MR18-5) is connected between fuel supply line (2) and fuel pump inlet line (3). With the engine stopped, periodically unscrew fuel filter

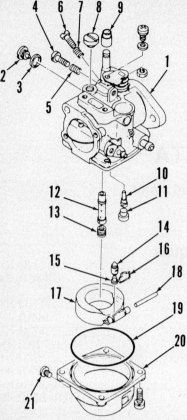

Fig. MR18-1 — Exploded view of carburetor used on single carburetor models.

1. Carburetor body
2. Plug
3. Washer
4. Idle speed screw
5. Spring
6. Idle mixture screw
7. Spring
8. Plug
9. Roller
10. Idle jet
11. Plug
12. Main nozzle
13. Main jet
14. Inlet seat
15. Inlet needle
16. Clip
17. Float
18. Pin
19. "O" ring
20. Float bowl
21. Drain plug

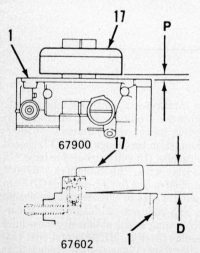

Fig. MR18-2 — Note the numbers on the carburetor mounting flange. Refer to the appropriate illustration and invert carburetor body (1) and note float (17) position. On carburetors with numbers "67900", float (17) should be parallel (P) with carburetor base. On carburetors with numbers "67602", base of float (17) should be a distance (D) of 16.5-22.5 mm (21/32-7/8 in.) from carburetor base.

cup (8) from filter base (4) and withdraw filter element (6), "O" ring (7) and gasket (5). Clean cup (8) and filter element (6) in a suitable solvent and blow dry with clean compressed air. Inspect filter element (6). If excessive blockage or damage is noted, renew filter element (6).

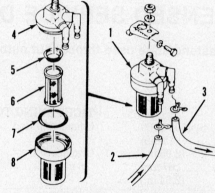

Fig. MR18-5 — Exploded view of cup type of fuel filter assembly (1).

1. Cup type fuel filter assy.
2. Inlet fuel line
3. Discharge fuel line
4. Filter base
5. Gasket
6. Filter element
7. "O" ring
8. Cup

Reassembly is reverse order of disassembly. Renew "O" ring (7) an gasket (5) during reassembly.

FUEL PUMP. The diaphragm typ fuel pump is located on the port side o the engine. Alternating pressure and vacuum pulsations in the crankcase ac tuates the diaphragm and check valve in the pump.

NOTE: Three different types of fue pump assemblies have been used. Show in Fig. MR18-7 and Fig. MR18-8 are fue pump assemblies using umbrella typ check valves. A third type fuel pump assembly is similar to the fuel pump assembly shown in Fig. MR18-8, excep reed type check valves are used instead o the umbrella type check valves (10). The reed valve type fuel pump assembly i identified by ribs on the inlet and outle nozzles.

Make certain that all gaskets, diaphragms and check valves are in good condtion when reassembling unit. Coat the mounting gasket with a non-hardening type gasket sealer making certain that passage in center is not blocked with gasket sealer.

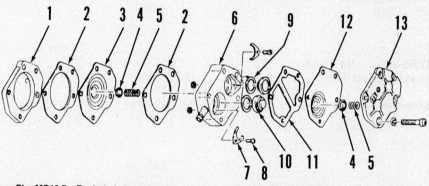

Fig. MR18-7 — Exploded view of diaphragm type fuel pump assembly used on some models.

1. Base
2. Gasket
3. Diaphragm
4. Spring plate
5. Spring
6. Body
7. Retainer
8. Screw
9. Gasket
10. Check valve
11. Gasket
12. Diaphragm
13. Cover

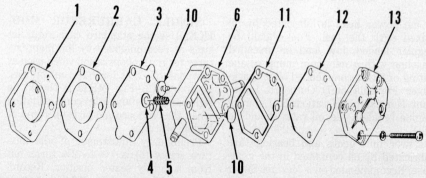

Fig. MR18-8 — Exploded view of diaphragm type fuel pump assembly used on some models. Some models are equipped with reed type check valves in place of umbrella type check valves (10). The reed valve type fuel pump assembly is identified by ribs on the inlet and outlet nozzles.

1. Base
2. Gasket
3. Diaphragm
4. Spring plate
5. Spring
6. Body
10. Check valves
11. Gasket
12. Diaphragm
13. Cover

Illustrations Courtesy Mariner

REED VALVES. Two "V" type reed alve assemblies mounted on a reed late and located between the intake anifold and crankcase are used on all ngines. Reed valves are accessible after emoving the intake manifold and reed late.

Reed valve seats must be smooth and lat. Renew reed valve if petals are bent, roken or otherwise damaged. Do not ttempt to straighten bent petals.

Reed valve petals may stand open a maximum of 0.3 mm (0.011 in.) at the ip. Reed valve stop setting (T – Fig. MR18-11) should be 4.8-5.2 mm 0.189-0.205 in.).

Individual components are not available. The reed valve must be serv-ced as a unit assembly.

CRANKCASE BREATHER. All models are equipped with a crankcase breather system to transfer puddled fuel and oil from lower crankcase to upper cylinder intake port for burning. A check valve assembly (5 – Fig. MR18-29) is installed in the crankcase area of the lower cylinder. Inspect breather hose (6) and renew if required.

SPEED CONTROL LINKAGE. Models With Breaker Point Type Igni-tion. To synchronize ignition and throt-tle control linkage, first make sure the ignition timing has been correctly ad-justed. When the twist grip is moved completely against the high speed stop, the carburetor throttle should be fully opened. MAKE SURE that the carbure-tor throttle does not reach the full open position before the ignition timing is ful-ly advanced.

To adjust the speed control linkage, proceed as follows: Move the magneto base plate to the full retard position. Detach magneto control rod (3 – Fig. MR18-13) from vertical control shaft (1). Rotate vertical control shaft (1) until pulley (8 – Fig. MR18-14) is positioned so bar (9) and pointer (10) are aligned as shown. Loosen locknut (4 – Fig. MR18-13) and adjust rod end (5) so it fits over the connecting ball joint without altering the position of the magneto base plate or pulley (8 – Fig. MR18-14). Tighten locknut to secure adjustment.

Bar (11) should align with pointer (10) when the throttle control is rotated to the full throttle position. If not, adjust the control cables length by rotating ad-justment collars (6 – Fig. MR18-13) until pointer (10 – Fig. MR18-14) and bar (11) are properly aligned. Recheck the full retard position setting. If not properly aligned, repeat adjustment procedures.

Models With CDI Type Ignition. To synchronize ignition and throttle control linkage, first make sure the ignition tim-ing is correctly adjusted as outlined in IGNITION section. When twist grip is moved completely against the high speed stop, the carburetor throttle should be fully opened. MAKE SURE that the carburetor throttle does not reach the full open position before the timing is fully advanced.

To adjust the speed control linkage, proceed as follows: Move the stator plate to the full retard position. Detach stator control rod (3 – Fig. MR18-15) from vertical control shaft (1). Rotate vertical control shaft (1) until pulley (9) is positioned so raised triangle (8) and pointer (10) are aligned. Loosen locknut (4) and adjust rod end (5) so it fits over the connecting ball joint without altering the position of the stator plate or pulley. Tighten locknut (4) to secure adjust-ment.

Triangle (11) should align with pointer (10) when the throttle control is rotated to the full throttle position. If not, adjust the control cables length by rotating ad-

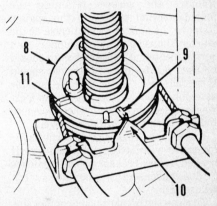

Fig. MR18-14 — View of control shaft pulley (8), bars (9 and 11) and pointer (10). Later models use arrows in place of bars (9 and 11). Refer to text for adjustment procedures.

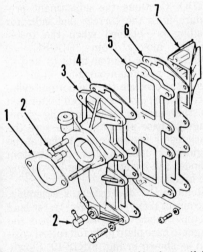

Fig. MR18-10 — Exploded view of intake manifold and reed plate assembly.

1. Gasket	
2. Check valve	5. Reed plate
3. Intake manifold	6. Gasket
4. Gasket	7. Reed valve

Fig. MR18-13 — View of speed control linkage used on models with breaker point type ignition system and equipped with a steering handle.

1. Vertical control shaft	5. Rod end
2. Throttle control rod	6. Adjustment collars
3. Magneto control rod	7. Magneto/throttle
4. Locknut	control rod

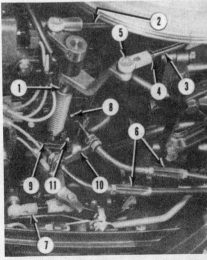

Fig. MR18-15 — View of speed control linkage used on models with CDI type ignition. Refer to text.

1. Vertical control shaft	7. Throttle/stator control rod
2. Throttle control rod	8. Raised triangle
3. Stator control rod	9. Pulley
4. Locknut	10. Pointer
5. Rod end	11. Triangle
6. Adjustment collars	

Fig. MR18-11 — Reed valve stop setting (T) should be 4.8-5.2 mm (0.189-0.205 in.).

justment collars (6) until pointer (10) and triangle (11) are properly aligned. Recheck the full retard position setting. If not properly aligned, repeat adjustment procedures.

IGNITION

Breaker Point Models

On early models a flywheel magneto ignition system is used with separate breaker points, condenser and secondary coil for each cylinder. A common primary coil is used.

The breaker point gap should be 0.30-0.40 mm (0.012-0.016 in.) and can be inspected and adjusted through the flywheel openings. Two breaker point assemblies (1 – Fig. MR18-17) and two condensers (2) are used. To inspect and, if needed, adjust the breaker point gap, first remove the engine top cover. Remove the screws retaining the manual rewind starter to the engine. Remove the starter lockout cable at the starter housing. Note plunger and spring located at cable end; care should be used not to lose components should they fall free. Withdraw the starter assembly. Remove the screws and lockwashers securing the flywheel cover to the flywheel, then withdraw cover.

Inspect the breaker point surfaces for excessive wear, pitting and damage. If needed, renew breaker point assemblies (1) and condensers (2) as outlined later in this section.

To clean the breaker point contact surfaces, rotate the flywheel until the breaker point contact surfaces are accessible through the opening in the flywheel. Use a point file or sandpaper with a grit rating of 400 to 600. After polishing, wipe the contact surfaces clean with a dry cloth and lightly grease the breaker point arm and lubricator with a suitable lubricant.

Turn the flywheel until the breaker point contact surfaces are at their widest position. Reach through the flywheel opening with a feeler gage of the appropriate size and check the

distance between the point surfaces. If the distance is not within the recommended limits, loosen the point set securing screw and adjust the point set until the correct gap is obtained. Tighten the point set securing screw and recheck the breaker point gap. Repeat the adjustment procedure, if needed, until the correct breaker point gap is obtained. Repeat the adjustment procedure on the other breaker point assembly.

To renew breaker point assemblies, remove flywheel from crankshaft using a suitable puller assembly. Renew breaker point assemblies (1) and condensers (2). Adjust the breaker point gap to the recommended setting as previously outlined. Make sure the securing screws are properly tightened. Be sure the flywheel key is properly positioned in the crankshaft keyway. Reinstall the flywheel and tighten flywheel securing nut to 150-170 N·m (110-125 ft.-lbs.).

To obtain the correct ignition timing, first adjust both breaker point assemblies (1) to the proper point gap as previously outlined. Remove the top spark plug and install a suitable dial indicator assembly into the spark plug hole. Properly synchronize the indicator

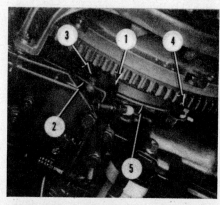

Fig. MR18-18 – View shows magneto base plate (5) in the full advance position. Refer to text for timing adjustment procedures.

1. Maximum advance stop bracket
2. Maximum advance stop
3. Bolt
4. Bolt
5. Magneto base plate

with the piston position at TDC. Use a point checker and attach the red tester lead to the grey wire coming from the magneto base plate (top cylinder low voltage coil lead). Connect the black tester lead to engine.

NOTE: A suitable continuity tester can be used.

Place the throttle control in the full throttle position. The magneto base plate (5 – Fig. MR18-18) is in the full advance position when stop (2) is against bracket (1). Slowly turn the flywheel counterclockwise until the tester pointer moves from "CLOSE" to "OPEN", then note dial indicator reading. Dial indicator should read 4.18-4.48 mm (0.165-0.177 in.) BTDC. If not, loosen bolts (3 and 4) and reposition maximum advance stop (2) until proper setting is obtained. Move stop (2) towards bracket (1) if dial indicator reads more than specified BTDC and away from bracket (1) if indicator reads less than specified BTDC. Continue the adjustment procedure until the correct dial indicator reading is obtained when the tester pointer moves from "CLOSE" to "OPEN", then tighten bolts (3 and 4) securing maximum advance stop (1). Repeat procedure for the bottom cylinder. Attach point checker red tester lead to the orange wire coming from magneto base plate (5). Make sure the black tester lead remains attached at the engine ground. Adjust the bottom cylinder full advance timing by varying the breaker point gap.

Remove the dial indicator assembly. Reconnect point checker red tester lead to top cylinder grey wire. Place the magneto base plate in its full retard position as shown in Fig. MR18-19. Slowly turn the flywheel counterclockwise until tester pointer moves from "CLOSE" to "OPEN", then note if pointer on maximum advance stop bracket (1 – Fig. MR18-18) is aligned with the 4° BTDC mark on the flywheel mounted timing decal. If not, loosen locknut (6 – Fig. MR18-19) and adjust screw (7) until the proper setting is obtained.

Fig. MR18-17 – View of breaker point assemblies (1) and condensers (2) used on breaker point type ignition systems.

Fig. MR18-19 – View shows the magneto base plate in the full retard position. Refer to text for timing adjustment procedures.

2. Stop
6. Locknut
7. Adjustment screw

When the ignition timing adjustment
is completed, check the speed control
linkage adjustment as outlined in the
previous SPEED CONTROL LINK-
AGE section.

CDI Models

Later models are equipped with a
capacitor discharge ignition (CDI)
system. If engine malfunction is noted
and the ignition system is suspected,
make sure the spark plugs and all electrical connections are tight before proceeding to troubleshooting the CD ignition system.

Proceed as follows to test CDI system
components: Refer to Fig. 18-21. To test
ignition coil, disconnect black wire (B)
and orange wire (O) at connectors and
spark plug boots from spark plugs. Use
a suitable ohmmeter and connect red
tester lead to orange wire (O) and black
tester lead to black wire (B). The
primary winding resistance reading
should be 0.08-0.10 ohms. Connect red
tester lead to terminal end in one spark
plug boot and black tester lead to terminal end in remaining spark plug boot.
The secondary winding resistance
reading should be 3,475-4.025 ohms. Use
a suitable coil tester or tester Model
9800 Magneto Analyzer to perform a
power test. Connect tester leads as
outlined in tester's handbook. A steady
spark should jump a 5 mm (13/64 in.) gap
when a current value of 1.7-2.1 amperes
is applied. A surface insulation test can
be performed using a suitable coil tester
or tester Model 9800 Magneto Analyzer
and following tester's handbook.

To check source (charge) coil, disconnect black wire (B) and brown wire (Br)
at connectors leading from magneto
base plate. Use a suitable ohmmeter and
connect red tester lead to brown wire
(Br) and black tester lead to black wire

**Fig. MR18-22 — Use chart
and values listed below to
test condition of CD ignition
module. Before making test
(J), connect CDI module's
orange wire and black wire
together. Then disconnect
wires and perform desired
test.**

A. Zero
B. Infinity
C. 9,000-19,000 ohms
D. 2,000-6,000 ohms
E. 80,000-160,000 ohms
F. 70,000-150,000 ohms
G. 33,000-63,000 ohms
H. 7,000-17,000 ohms
I. 15,000-35,000 ohms
J. Tester needle should show
deflection the return toward
infinite resistance

Red Test Lead \ Black Test Lead	CDI UNIT LEADS				
CDI UNIT LEADS	White	Black	Brown	White w/Red	Orange
White	A	B	B	B	B
Black	C	A	D	B	J
Brown	E	F	A	B	J
White w/Red	G	H	I	A	J
Orange	B	B	B	B	A

(B). DO NOT rotate flywheel while making test. The ohmmeter should read
121-147 ohms. Reconnect wires after
completing test.

To check pulser (trigger) coil, disconnect white wire with red tracer (W/R) at
connector leading from magneto base
plate and black wire (B) at back of CDI
unit. Use a suitable ohmmeter and connect red tester lead to white wire with
red tracer (W/R) and black tester lead to
black wire (B). DO NOT rotate flywheel
while making test. The ohmmeter
should read 12.6-15.4 ohms.

To test CDI module, first disconnect
all wires at connectors and remove CDI
module from outboard motor. Use a
suitable ohmmeter and refer to Fig.
MR18-22. With reference to chart, perform CDI module resistance tests.
Renew any components that are not
within the manufacturer's recommended limits.

To check ignition timing, proceed as
follows:

**NOTE: If position of flywheel timing
decal is suspect, install a dial indicator in
the number 1 (top) cylinder spark plug
hole and check top dead center piston
position. If dial indicator and timing decal
do not agree, reposition decal.**

Rotate flywheel (1 – Fig. MR18-23)
clockwise until 26° mark on timing decal
aligns with timing pointer (2). Rotate
stator plate (6) until stamped mark (7)
on plate aligns with TDC mark on timing
decal (3). Maximum advance stop (not
shown) on stop plate (5) should contact
timing pointer bracket (2). Loosen the
two stop plate retaining cap screws (4)
and reposition stop plate if required.
Cap screw retaining maximum advance
side of stop plate is not shown. With
maximum advance timing adjusted, hold
flywheel (1) at 26° BTDC and rotate
stator plate until maximum retard stop
on stop plate (5) contacts idle timing adjustment screw (8). At idle, stamped
mark (7) on stator plate (6) should align
with 22° BTDC mark on timing decal (3).
Rotate idle timing adjustment screw as
required to obtain desired setting.

When the ignition timing adjustment
is completed, check the speed control
linkage adjustment as outlined in the
previous SPEED CONTROL LINK-
AGE section.

COOLING SYSTEM

WATER PUMP. A rubber impeller
type water pump is mounted between
the drive shaft housing and gearcase.

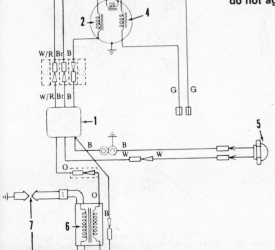

**Fig. MR18-21 — View identi-
fying CDI system com-
ponents.**

1. CDI module
2. Charge coil
3. Pulser coil
4. Lighting coil
5. Stop switch
6. Ignition coil
7. Spark plugs

**Fig. MR18-23 — View showing ignition timing
components on models with CDI type ignition.
Refer to text.**

1. Flywheel
2. Timing pointer
3. Timing decal
4. Cap screw
5. Stop plate
6. Stator plate
7. Stamped mark
8. Screw

Water pump impeller (6 – Fig. MR18-25) is driven by a key in the drive shaft.

When cooling system problems are encountered, first check water inlet for plugging or partial stoppage. Be sure thermostat located at top, front of cylinder head cover, operates properly. If the water pump is suspected defective, separate gearcase from drive shaft housing and inspect pump. Make sure all seals and mating surfaces are in good condition and water passages are unobstructed. Check impeller (6) and plate (8) for excessive wear. When reassembling, coat gasket surfaces with a thin coating of Perfect Seal.

POWER HEAD

R&R AND OVERHEAD. The power head can be removed for disassembly and overhaul as follows: Clamp outboard motor to a suitable stand and remove engine cowl and starter assembly. Disconnect speed control cables, fuel line and any wiring that will interfere with power head removal. Remove or disconnect any component that will interfere with power head removal.

Remove eight screws securing power head to drive shaft housing and lift power head free. Remove flywheel, ignition components, carburetor, intake manifold and reed valve assembly. Remove screws retaining exhaust cover (9 – Fig. MR18-30) and withdraw. Crankcase halves can be separated after removal of 15 screws securing crankcase half (1) to cylinder block. Crankshaft and pistons are now accessible for removal and overhaul as outlined in the appropriate following paragraphs.

ASSEMBLY. When reassembling, make sure all joint and gasket surfaces are clean and free from nicks, burrs, warped surfaces, hardened cement or carbon. The crankcase and intake manifolds must be completely sealed against both vacuum and pressure. Exhaust manifold and cylinder head must be sealed against water leakage and pressure.

The crankcase halves are positively located during assembly by the use of two dowel pins. Check to make sure that dowel pins are not bent, nicked or distorted and that dowel holes are clean and true. When installing pins, make certain they are fully seated, but do not use excessive force.

The mating surfaces of the crankcase halves must be sealed during reassembly using a nonhardening type of gasket sealer. Make certain that surfaces are thoroughly cleaned of oil and old sealer before making a fresh application. Apply sealer evenly and use sparingly, so excess does not squeeze into crankcase cavity.

Tighten the crankcase screws to torque specified in the CONDENSED SERVICE DATA following the sequence shown in Fig. MR18-27. Tighten the cylinder head screws to 27-31 N·m (20-23 ft.-lbs.) following the sequence shown in Fig. MR18-28. Refer to CONDENSED SERVICE DATA section for general torquing specifications.

PISTONS, PINS, RINGS AND CYLINDERS. Cylinder bore should be measured in several different locations to determine if an out-of-round or tapered condition exists. Inspect cylinder wall for scoring. If minor scoring is noted, cylinders should be honed to smooth out cylinder wall.

NOTE: Cylinder sleeves are cast into the cylinder block. If cylinder is out-of-round or tapered more than 0.54 mm (0.021 in.), or if excessive scoring is noted, the cylinder block must be renewed.

Recommended piston skirt to cylinder clearance is 0.050-0.055 mm (0.0020-0.0022 in.) Recommended piston ring end gap is 0.3-0.5 mm (0.012-0.020 in.) for both rings. Make sure piston rings properly align with locating pins in ring grooves.

When reassembling, install new piston pin retaining clips (18 – Fig. MR18-29) and make sure that "UP" on dome of piston is towards flywheel end of engine. Coat bearings, pistons, rings and cylinder bores with engine oil during assembly.

Fig. MR18-25 – Exploded view of water pump assembly.

1. Seal	
2. Housing	
3. Seal	7. Gasket
4. Liner	8. Plate
5. Key	9. Gasket
6. Impeller	10. Base
	11. Gasket

Fig. MR18-27 – Tighten crankcase screws to specified torque following sequence shown.

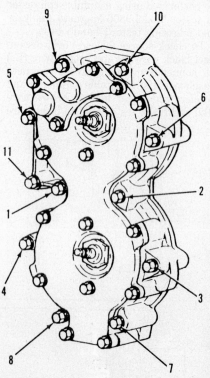

Fig. MR18-28 – Tighten cylinder head screws to 27-31 N·m (20-23 ft.-lbs.) following sequence shown.

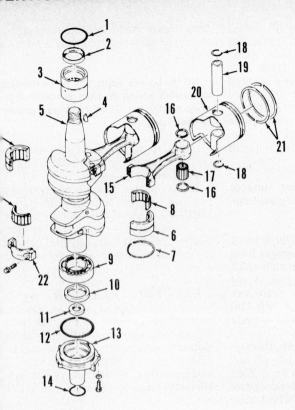

Fig. MR18-29 — Exploded view of crankshaft assembly.

1. "O" ring
2. Seal
3. Bearing
4. Key
5. Crankshaft
6. Bearing assy.
7. Snap ring
8. Cage & roller bearing assy.
9. Ball bearing
10. Seal
11. Seal
12. "O" ring
13. Oil seal housing
14. "O" ring
15. Connecting rod
16. Washers
17. Needle bearings
18. Clips
19. Piston pin
20. Piston
21. Piston rings
22. Rod cap

(7) will rotate. As pulley (7) rotates, drive pawl (10) moves to engage with the flywheel thus cranking the engine.

When starter rope (5) is released, pulley (7) is rotated in the reverse direction by force from rewind spring (6). As pulley (7) rotates, the starter rope is rewound and drive pawl (10) is disengaged from the flywheel.

Safety plunger (17) engages lugs on pulley (7) to prevent starter engagement when the gear shift lever is in the forward or reverse position.

To overhaul the manual starter, proceed as follows: Remove the engine top cover. Remove the screws retaining the manual starter to the engine. Remove starter lockout cable (19) at starter housing (2). Note plunger (17) and spring (18) located at cable end; care should be used not to lose components should they fall free. Withdraw the starter assembly.

CONNECTING RODS, CRANKSHAFT AND BEARINGS.

Before detaching connecting rods from crankshaft, make certain that rod and cap are properly marked for correct assembly to each other and in the correct cylinder. The needle rollers and cages at crankpin end of connecting rod should be kept with the assembly and not interchanged.

Bearing rollers and cages used in connecting rods and center main bearing are available only as a set which contains the cages and rollers for one bearing. Center main bearing outer races are held together by snap ring (7 – Fig. MR18-29). Be sure locating holes in upper and center main bearing outer races mate properly with locating dowels (4 – Fig. MR18-30) in cylinder block when installing crankshaft assembly.

Connecting rod and cap match marks must be on same side. Be sure cap is properly meshed with connecting rod. Twenty-eight needle bearings (17 – Fig. MR18-29) are used in each connecting rod small end. Rollers can be held in place with petroleum jelly while installing piston on connecting rod.

Lubricate bearings, pistons, rings and cylinders with engine oil prior to installation. Tighten crankcase and cylinder head screws as outlined in ASSEMBLY section.

STARTER

MANUAL STARTER.
When starter rope (5 – Fig. MR18-32) is pulled, pulley

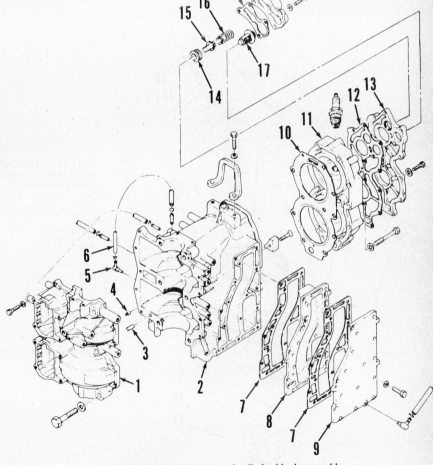

Fig. MR18-30 — Exploded view of cylinder block assembly.

1. Crankcase
2. Cylinder block
3. Dowel pin
4. Dowel pin
5. Check valve assy.
6. Breather hose
7. Gasket
8. Inner exhaust plate
9. Exhaust cover
10. Gasket
11. Cylinder head
12. Gasket
13. Cylinder head cover
14. Grommet
15. Pressure control valve
16. Spring
17. Thermostat
18. Gasket
19. Housing

Check pawl (10) for freedom of movement, excessive wear of engagement area and any other damage. Renew or lubricate pawl (10) with a suitable water-resistant grease and return starter to service if no other damage is noted.

To disassemble, remove clip (11) and withdraw pawl (10) and pawl spring (9). Untie starter rope (5) at handle (4) and allow the rope to wind into the starter. Remove bolt (16), washer (15) and shaft (14), then place a suitable screwdriver blade through hole (H – Fig. MR18-33) to hold rewind spring (6 – Fig. MR18-32) securely in housing (2). Carefully lift pulley (7) with starter rope (5) from housing (2). BE CAREFUL when removing pulley (7) to prevent possible injury from rewind spring. Untie starter rope (5) and remove rope from pulley (7) if renewal is required. To remove rewind spring (6) from housing (2), invert housing so its sits upright on a flat surface, then tap the housing top until rewind spring (6) falls free and uncoils.

Inspect all components for damage and excessive wear and renew if needed.

To reassemble, first apply a coating of a suitable water-resistant grease to rewind spring area of housing (2). Install rewind spring (6) in housing (2) so spring coils wind in a counterclockwise direction from the outer end. Make sure spring outer hook is properly secured over starter housing pin (8). Wind starter rope (5) onto pulley (7) approximately 2½ turns counterclockwise when viewed from the flywheel side. Direct remaining starter rope (5) length through notch in pulley (7).

NOTE: Lubricate all friction surfaces with a suitable water-resistant grease during reassembly.

Assemble pulley (7) to starter housing making sure that pin (12) engages hook end in rewind spring (6). Install shaft (14), washer (15) and bolt (16). Apply Loctite 271 or 290 or an equivalent thread fastening solution on bolt (16) threads, then install nut (1) and securely tighten.

Thread starter rope (5) through starter housing (2), rope guide (3) and handle (4) and secure with a knot. Turn pulley (7) 2 to 3 turns counterclockwise when viewed from the flywheel side, then release starter rope (5) from pulley notch and allow rope to slowly wind onto pulley.

NOTE: Do not apply any more tension on rewind spring (6) than is required to draw starter handle (4) back into proper released position.

Install spring (9), pawl (10) and clip (11) as shown in Fig. MR18-33. Remount manual starter assembly.

Adjust starter lockout assembly by turning adjusting nuts (N – Fig. MR18-34) at cable (19) end so starter will engage when gear shift lever is in neutral position, but will not engage when gear shift lever is in forward or reverse position.

ELECTRIC STARTER. Some models are equipped with an electric starter motor. Refer to Fig. MR18-36 for an exploded view of the starter motor. Commutator undercut should be 0.5-0.8 mm (0.02-0.03 in.) with a minimum limit of 0.2 mm (0.008 in.). Minimum brush length is 9.5 mm (0.374 in.).

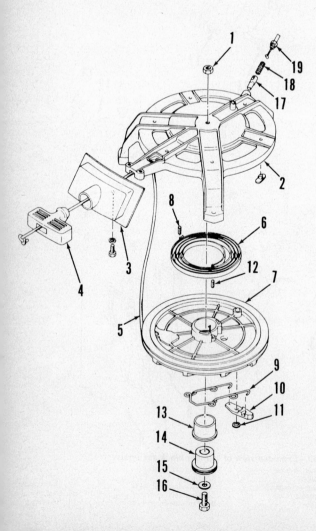

Fig. MR18-32 — Exploded view of manual rewind starter assembly.

1. Nut
2. Housing
3. Rope guide
4. Handle
5. Starter rope
6. Rewind spring
7. Pulley
8. Pin
9. Pawl spring
10. Pawl
11. Clip
12. Pin
13. Bushing
14. Shaft
15. Washer
16. Bolt
17. Plunger
18. Spring
19. Starter lockout cable

Fig. MR18-33 — View showing proper installation of pawl spring (9), pawl (10) and clip (11). Pulley hole (H) is used during pulley withdrawal. Refer to text.

Fig. MR18-34 — View showing starter lockout cable (19) and cable adjustment nuts (N). Refer to text.

Illustrations Courtesy Mariner

LOWER UNIT

Two types of gearcase assemblies
ave been used – an above prop exhaust
ype (Fig. MR18-38) and a through prop
xhaust type (Fig. MR18-40). Refer to
e appropriate following section for
ervice procedures.

bove Prop Exhaust Type
earcase

PROPELLER AND SHEAR PIN.
ower unit protection is provided by a
hear pin. Select a propeller that will
llow the engine at full throttle to reach
aximum operating range of 4500-5500
pm.

R&R AND OVERHAUL. Most lower
nit service may be performed after
eparating the gearcase from the drive
haft housing. The gearcase may be
emoved and disassembled as follows:
ttach outboard motor to a suitable
tand a remove both vent and drain
lugs in gearcase to allow lubricant to

drain. Loosen jam nut (46 – Fig.
MR18-38) and remove adjustment nut
(47). Remove six screws securing gearcase to drive shaft housing and carefully
separate gearcase from drive shaft
housing. Remove water pump using caution to prevent loss of key (5 – Fig.

MR18-25). Remove propeller and
unscrew the nine screws securing lower
gearcase housing (23 – Fig. MR18-38).
Propeller shaft (33), complete with gears
and bearings, can now be removed. Use
caution to prevent loss of cam follower
(24). Spring clip (28) retains drive pin
(30) in propeller shaft. Drive shaft may
be removed from gearcase after removal
of snap ring (20). Lower shift rod (50)
can be removed after removal of retainer (48).

Inspect gears for wear on teeth and in
engagement dogs. Inspect dog clutch
(29) for wear on engagement surfaces.
Inspect shafts for wear on splines and
on friction surfaces of gears and oil
seals. Check shift cam for excessive
wear on shift ramps. All seals and "O"
rings should be renewed on each
reassembly.

Backlash between pinion gear (19) and
drive gears (27 and 36) should be
0.05-0.15 mm (0.002-0.006 in.) and is adjusted by varying thickness of shims (26
and 37). Adjust gear mesh position by
varying thickness of shim (17).

Install dog clutch (29) on propeller
shaft (33) so "F" marked side faces forward gear (27).

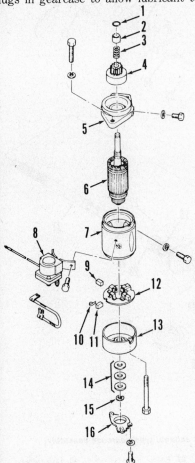

**Fig. MR18-36 – Exploded view of electric starter
motor.**

1. Retainer	9. Positive brush
2. Stop	10. Spring
3. Spring	11. Negative brush
4. Pinion	12. Brush plate
5. End plate	13. End cover
6. Armature	14. Washers
7. Frame	15. Snap ring
8. Solenoid	16. Dust cover

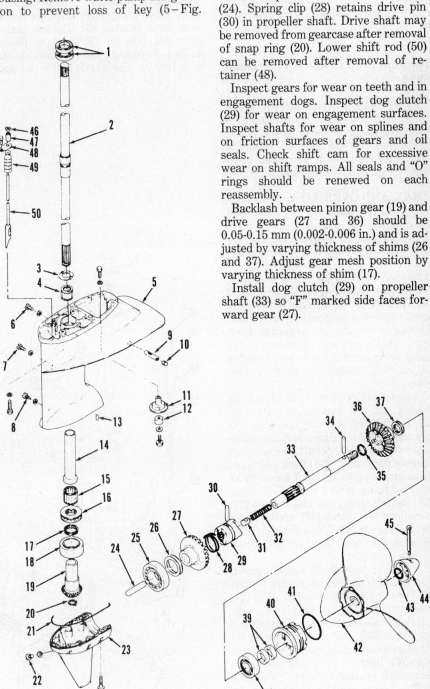

Fig. MR18-38 – Exploded view of above prop exhaust type gearcase assembly.

1. Seals	13. Dowel pin	25. Bearing	38. Bearing
2. Drive shaft	14. Sleeve	26. Shim	39. Seals
3. Thrust washer	15. Bearing	27. Forward gear	40. Bearing carrier
4. Bearing	16. Thrust bearing	28. Spring clip	41. "O" ring
5. Upper gearcase	17. Shim	29. Dog clutch	42. Propeller
housing	18. Bearing	30. Pin	43. Washer
6. Wash plug	19. Pinion gear	31. Spring guide	44. Spinner
7. Vent plug	20. Snap ring	32. Spring	45. Cotter pin
8. Shift limit screw	21. Seal	33. Propeller shaft	46. Jam nut
9. Screen	22. Drain plug	34. Shear pin	47. Adjustment nut
10. Plug	23. Lower gearcase	35. Thrust washer	48. Retainer
11. Water inlet cover	housing	36. Reverse gear	49. Boot
12. Anode	24. Cam follower	37. Shim	50. Lower shift rod

When reassembling gearcase, make sure all case mating surfaces are clean and free of nicks or burrs.

Shift linkage is set by pressing lower shift rod (50) down until cam is against stopper pin (8), then adjusting adjustment nut (47) until shift control lever is in "REVERSE" position. Secure adjustment with jam nut (46).

Through Prop Exhaust Type Gearcase

PROPELLER AND DRIVE HUB. Lower unit protection is provided by a cushion type hub in the propeller. Select a propeller that will allow the engine at full throttle to reach maximum operating range of 4500-5500 rpm.

R&R AND OVERHAUL. Most service on lower unit can be performed after detaching gearcase from drive shaft housing. To remove gearcase, attach outboard motor to a suitable stand and remove vent and drain plugs in gearcase to allow lubricant to drain. Loosen jam nut (48–Fig. MR18-40) and remove adjustment nut (49). Remove six screws securing gearcase to drive shaft housing and carefully separate from drive shaft housing. Remove water pump being careful not to lose impeller key (5–Fig. MR18-25). Remove propeller.

Disassemble gearcase by bending back locking tab of lockwasher (40–Fig. MR18-40), then remove nut (41) and lockwasher (40). Using a suitable puller attached to propeller shaft, extract components (26 through 43) from gearcase. Disassemble propeller shaft assembly as required being careful not to lose shims (34). Detach spring clip (26) and pin (27) to remove dog clutch (28), spring guide (29) and spring (30). Use a suitable puller to separate ball bearing (37) from reverse gear (33).

To remove drive shaft, unscrew pinion gear nut (18) and withdraw drive shaft (4). Forward gear (25) and bearing (24) cone many now be removed. Use a suitable puller to extract bearing cup; do not lose shims (23). Pull race of bearing (5) out of gearcase being careful not to lose shims (6). Remove drive shaft sleeve (7) then drive bearing (8) down into gear cavity. Lower shift rod (52) may be removed after unscrewing retainer (50).

NOTE: Manufacturer recommends renewing tapered roller bearing assembly (5) if removed from drive shaft.

Inspect gears for wear on teeth and in engagement dogs. Inspect dog clutch (28) for wear on engagement surfaces. Inspect shafts for wear on splines and on friction surfaces of gears and oil

seals. Check shift cam for excessive wear on shift ramps. All seals and "O" rings should be renewed on each reassembly.

Assemble gearcase by reversing disassembly procedure. Install oil seals (2) in water pump base with lips facing away from bearing (5). Tighten pinion gear nut (18) to 68-78 N·m (50-58 ft.-lbs.). Forward gear backlash should be 0.10-0.24 mm (0.004-0.009 in.) and

reverse gear backlash should be 0.40-0.54 mm (0.016-0.021 in.).

Install dog clutch (28) so "F" marked side is towards forward gear (25). Apply water-resistant grease to drive shaft upper splines.

With gearcase assembled and installed, synchronize gear engagement with gear selector handle by turning shift rod adjustment nut (49), then tighten jam nut (48).

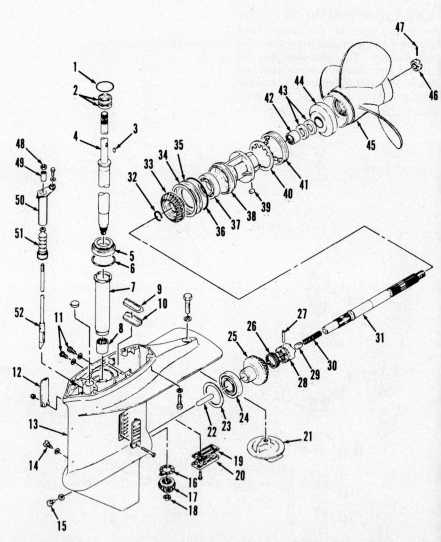

Fig. MR18-40 – Exploded view of through prop exhaust type gearcase assembly.

1. "O" ring	14. Shift limit screw	27. Pin	40. Lockwasher
2. Seals	15. Drain plug	28. Dog clutch	41. Cover nut
3. Key	16. Thrust washer	29. Spring guide	42. Bearing
4. Drive shaft	17. Pinion gear	30. Spring	43. Seals
5. Tapered roller bearing assy.	18. Nut	31. Propeller shaft	44. Thrust hub
6. Shim	19. Gasket	32. Thrust washer	45. Propeller
7. Sleeve	20. Plate	33. Reverse gear	46. Nut
8. Bearing	21. Trim tab	34. Shim	47. Cotter pin
9. Rubber seal	22. Cam follower	35. Thrust washer	48. Jam nut
10. Seal guide	23. Shim	36. "O" ring	49. Adjustment nut
11. Plugs	24. Bearing	37. Bearing	50. Retainer
12. Water inlet covers	25. Forward gear	38. Bearing carrier	51. Boot
13. Gearcase housing	26. Spring clip	39. Key	52. Lower shift shaft

MARINER 48 AND 60 (2 cyl.) HP

CONDENSED SERVICE DATA

NOTE: Metric fasteners are used throughout outboard motor.

TUNE-UP

Hp/rpm:
Model 48 . . . . .48/5500
Model 60 . . . . .60/5500
Bore . . . . .82 mm
(3.23 in.)
Stroke . . . . .72 mm
(2.83 in.)
Number of Cylinders 2
Displacement . . . . .760 cc
(46.4 cu. in.)
Spark Plug—NGK:
Model 48 . . . . .B7HS
Model 60 . . . . .B8HS
Spark Plug Electrode Gap . . . . .0.7 mm
(0.027 in.)
Ignition Type . . . . .CDI
Idle Speed (in gear) . . . . .750-850 rpm
Fuel:Oil Ratio 50:1

SIZES—CLEARANCES

Piston Ring End Gap . . . . .0.3-0.5 mm
(0.012-0.020 in.)
Piston Skirt Clearance . . . . .0.050-0.055 mm
(0.0019-0.0022 in.)
Crankshaft Bearings:
Top Main Bearing . . . . .Roller Bearing
Center Main Bearing . . . . .Roller Bearing
Lower Main Bearing . . . . .Ball Bearing
Crankpin . . . . .Roller Bearing

SIZES—CLEARANCES CONT.

Piston Pin Bearing In Rod . . . . .Loose Rollers
No. of Rollers (each rod) 28

TIGHTENING TORQUES

Connecting rod . . . . .31.4 N·m
(23 ft.-lbs.)
Crankcase:
M6 . . . . .5.9-9.3 N·m
(52-82 in.-lbs.)
M10 . . . . .39.2 N·m
(29 ft.-lbs.)
Cylinder head .27.4-31.4 N·m
(20-23 ft.-lbs.)
Flywheel . . . . .147 N·m
(108 ft.-lbs.)
Standard screws:
5 mm . . . . .4.9-5.4 N·m
(43-48 in.-lbs.)
6 mm . . . . .7.9-9.3 N·m
(70-82 in.-lbs.)
8 mm . . . . .14.7-19.6 N·m
(130-173 in.-lbs.)
10 mm . . . . .29.4-44.1 N·m
(22-32 ft.-lbs.)
12 mm . . . . .34.3-49.0 N·m
(25-36 ft.-lbs.)

LUBRICATION

The power head is lubricated by oil mixed with the fuel. Fuel should be regular leaded, low lead or unleaded gasoline with a minimum pump octane rating of 86. Recommended oil is Quicksilver Formula 50-D Outboard Lubricant. Normal fuel:oil ratio is 50:1; during engine break-in, fuel:oil ratio should be 25:1.

Lower unit gears and bearings are lubricated by oil contained in the gearcase. Recommended oil is Mariner Super Duty Gear Lube. Lubricant is drained by removing vent and drain plugs in the gearcase. Refill through drain plug hole until oil has reached level of vent hole. Lower unit oil capacity is 500 mL (16.9 oz.).

FUEL SYSTEM

CARBURETOR. Two carburetors are used. Refer to Fig. MR20-1 for an exploded view of carburetor. Main jet (13) size is 185 for 48 hp models and 180 for 60 hp models. Idle jet (2) size is 92 for 48 hp models and 100 for 60 hp models. Idle air jet (11) size is 105 for 48 hp models and 100 for 60 hp models. Main air jet (10) size is 160 for all models. Initial setting for idle mixture screw (5) is 1⅛ to 1⅜ turns out.

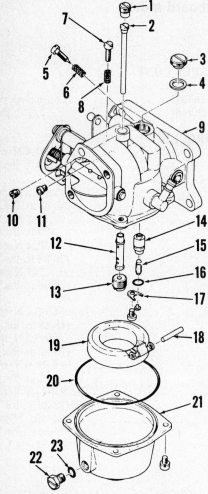

Fig. MR20-1 — Exploded view of carburetor.

1. Plug	13. Main jet
2. Pilot jet	14. Fuel inlet seat
3. Plug	15. Fuel inlet valve
4. Washer	16. "O" ring
5. Idle mixture screw	17. Retainer
6. Spring	18. Float pin
7. Idle speed screw	19. Float
8. Spring	20. "O" ring
9. Body	21. Float bowl
10. Main air jet	22. Drain screw
11. Idle air jet	23. "O" ring
12. Nozzle	

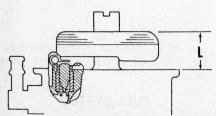

Fig. MR20-2 — Float level (L) should be 18 mm (0.7 in.). Adjust float level by bending float arm tang.

Float level is measured with float bowl removed and carburetor inverted as shown in Fig. MR20-2. Float level (L) should be 18 mm (0.7 in.) and is adjusted by bending float arm tang.

To synchronize upper and lower carburetors, detach one end of throttle connector rod (T – Fig. MR20-3) and back out idle speed screw on each carburetor so throttle valve is closed. Adjust length of throttle connector rod by turning rod ends and reattach. Adjust engine idle speed using idle speed screw of lower carburetor. Adjust choke rod clamp (C) so choke valves in carburetors operate uniformly.

SPEED CONTROL LINKAGE. Ignition timing advance and throttle opening must be synchronized so that throttle is opened as ignition timing is advanced.

To synchronize speed control linkage, first make certain that ignition timing is correctly set as outlined in IGNITION TIMING section. Rotate speed control handle so ignition timing is set at 3°-7° before top dead center (BTDC). Detach end of throttle rod (R – Fig. MR20-5) and adjust length of rod by turning rod

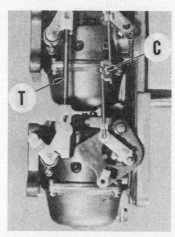

Fig. MR20-3 — View of carburetors. Synchronize carburetors using throttle connector rod (T) and choke rod clamp (C) as outlined in text.

Fig. MR20-5 — View of power head. Refer to text for synchronization of speed control linkage.

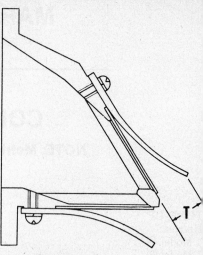

Fig. MR20-6 — Reed valve stop setting (T) should be 2.8-3.2 mm (0.11-0.12 in.) for 48 hp models and 9.7-10.1 mm (0.38-0.40 in.) for 60 hp models.

end so when rod end is reattached, cam follower roller (R) just contacts cam (C). Rotate speed control handle to close position, then recheck adjustment. When rotating speed control handle roller (R) should contact cam when ignition timing advances to 3°-7° BTDC.

Adjust throttle stop screw (S) so screw contacts boss just as throttle valve reach wide open position.

REED VALVES. A "V" type reed valve assembly located between the intake manifold and crankcase is used on all engines. Reed valves are accessible after removing the carburetors.

Reed valve seats must be smooth and flat. Renew reed valve if petals are bent, broken or otherwise damaged. Do not attempt to straighten bent petals.

Reed valve petals may stand open a maximum of 0.2 mm (0.008 in.) at the tip. Reed valve stop setting (T – Fig. MR20-6) should be 2.8-3.2 mm (0.11-0.12 in.) for 48 hp models and 9.7-10.1 mm (0.38-0.40 in.) for 60 hp models.

Individual components are not available. The reed valve must be serviced as a unit assembly.

CRANKCASE BREATHER. All models are equipped with a crankcase breather system to transfer puddled fuel and oil from lower crankcase to upper cylinder intake port for burning. A check valve (4 – Fig. MR20-7) is located in fitting (3). Some models are equipped with check valve (5) in the cylinder block. Inspect breather hose (1) and renew if required.

FUEL PUMP. All models are equipped with a diaphragm type fuel pump as shown in Fig. MR20-8. Inspect diaphragms (4) and renew if deformed

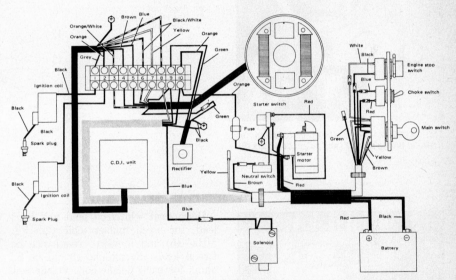

To adjust idle ignition timing, position flywheel at 4° ATDC on 48 hp models or 2° ATDC on 60 hp models. Move magneto base plate so mark (P–Fig. MR20-12) on top of pulser coil is aligned with flywheel mark (F). Turn idle timing screw (IT–Fig. MR20-13) so screw end just contacts magneto base plate boss.

To adjust full throttle ignition timing, position flywheel at 20° BTDC on 48 hp models or 26° BTDC on 60 hp models. Move magneto base plate so mark (P–Fig. MR20-12) on top of pulser coil is aligned with flywheel mark (F). Turn full throttle timing screw (FT–Fig. MR20-14) so screw end just contacts magneto base plate boss.

If flywheel timing decal is damaged or missing, flywheel position may be determined using a dial indicator in number 1 (upper) cylinder spark plug hole. Piston

Fig. MR20-7 – View showing location of crankcase breather valves (4 and 5).

1. Hose
2. Fitting
3. Elbow
4. & 5. Breather valves

torn or holed. Determine if check valves (10) operate properly. Renew springs (6 and 13) if damaged or distorted.

IGNITION SYSTEM

All models are equipped with a capacitor discharge ignition system. Ignition system components are accessible after removing flywheel. Refer to Fig. MR20-10 for a practical drawing of ignition system.

IGNITION TIMING. Ignition timing may be adjusted for idle and fuel throttle. If questioned, verify position of timing pointer and flywheel timing decal by installing a dial indicator in number 1 (upper) cylinder spark plug hole and determining piston top dead center. Before checking ignition timing, check length of magneto control rod which should be 52 mm (2-3/64 in.) as shown in Fig. MR20-11.

Fig. MR20-10 – Wiring diagram for 60 hp models. Ignition wiring is similar for 48 hp models.

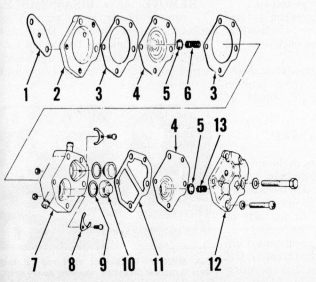

Fig. MR20-8 – Exploded view of fuel pump.

1. Gasket
2. Base
3. Gasket
4. Pump diaphragm
5. Spring plate
6. Spring
7. Body
8. Retainer
9. Gasket
10. Check valve
11. Gasket
12. Cover
13. Spring

Fig. MR20-11 – Magneto control and length should be 52 mm (2-3/64 in.) as shown. Adjust length by detaching and turning rod end.

position at idle should be 0.07-0.17 mm (0.003-0.007 in.) ATDC on 48 hp models or 0.001-0.005 mm (0.0004-0.002 in.) ATDC on 60 hp models. Piston position at full throttle should be 2.55-3.11 mm (0.099-0.121 in.) BTDC on 48 hp models or 4.39-4.99 mm (0.171-0.195 in.) BTDC on 60 hp models. Adjust timing screws as previously outlined.

After adjusting ignition timing, recheck speed control linkage adjustment.

TROUBLESHOOTING. If ignition system malfunction is suspected, check for spark at spark plugs. Check wiring and be sure all connections are clean and tight. Note the following specifications when inspecting electrical units.

Fig. MR20-12—View showing location of flywheel timing mark (F) and pulser coil mark (P).

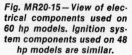
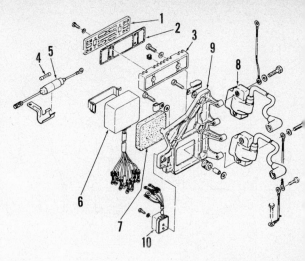

Fig. MR20-15—View of electrical components used on 60 hp models. Ignition system components used on 48 hp models are similar.

1. Cover
2. Gasket
3. Terminal plate
4. Fuse
5. Fuse holder
6. Ignition module (CDI)
7. Vibration damper
8. Ignition coil
9. Bracket
10. Rectifier
11. Cover
12. Nut
13. Washer
14. Flywheel
15. Timing pointer
16. Timing decal
17. Retainer
18. Lighting coil
19. Charge coil
20. Trigger coil
21. Magneto base plate
22. Pulser coils

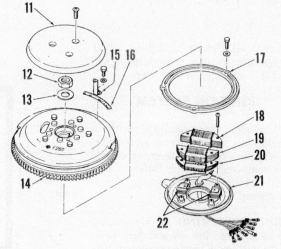

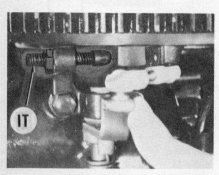

Fig. MR20-13—Adjust idle speed ignition timing by turning screw (IT). Refer to text.

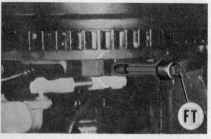

Fig. MR20-14—Adjust full throttle ignition timing by turning screw (FT). Refer to text.

Disconnect white/red lead and black lead for each pulser coil (22—Fig. MR20-15) and measure resistance between leads. Resistance should be 8.5 ohms for each pulser coil. Pulser coils are not available individually but must be obtained as a unit assembly with magneto base plate (21).

Disconnect brown lead and blue lead of charge coil (19). Resistance should be 23.5 ohms between charge coil leads.

Disconnect yellow trigger coil lead and measure resistance between yellow lead and ground. Resistance should be 2.2 ohms.

Ignition coil primary resistance should be approximately 0.25 ohms. Ignition coil secondary resistance should be 2000-3000 ohms.

COOLING SYSTEM

A thermostat is located in the cylinder head on 60 hp models while 48 hp models are not so equipped. All models are equipped with a rubber impeller type water pump mounted on top side of lower unit gearcase.

When cooling system problems are encountered, first check the thermostat, if so equipped, to see that it is operating

properly. Check the water inlet for plugging or partial stoppage, then if trouble is not corrected, remove the lower unit gearcase as outlined in LOWER UNIT section, and check the condition of water pump, water passages and sealing surfaces.

POWER HEAD

REMOVE AND DISASSEMBLE. To remove power head, proceed as follows: Remove flywheel. Disconnect manual choke linkage. Disconnect battery leads from starter then disconnect wires from starter solenoid. Disconnect

Fig. MR20-17—Disconnect shift rod (R) and detach bracket (B) before removing power head.

Illustrations Courtesy Mariner

interfering wires from terminal plate (3 – Fig. MR20-15) and remove electrical unit bracket (9). Disconnect fuel line and exhaust cover hose. Disconnect throttle and shift cables. Disconnect shift rod (R – Fig. MR20-17) and detach bracket (B). Remove bottom cowl covers by unscrewing four screws inside bottom cowl. Unscrew eight nuts securing power head to drive shaft housing and lift off power head.

For access to short block assembly, remove the fuel pump and fuel filter. Remove starter motor on 60 hp models. Remove magneto base plate assembly. Remove air cleaner, carburetors and reed valve assemblies. Remove tower shaft assembly shown in Fig. MR20-18. Remove any other components which interfere with intended service operation.

To disassemble power head, unscrew and remove cylinder head. Remove lower oil seal housing. Unscrew retaining nuts and screws and separate crankcase half from cylinder block. Crankshaft, pistons and bearings are now accessible for removal and overhaul as outlined in the appropriate following paragraphs. Assemble as outlined in the ASSEMBLY paragraph.

ASSEMBLY. When reassembling, make sure all joint and gasket surfaces are clean and free from nicks, burrs, warped surfaces, hardened cement or carbon. The crankcase and intake manifolds must be completely sealed against both vacuum and pressure. Exhaust manifold and cylinder head must be sealed against water leakage and pressure.

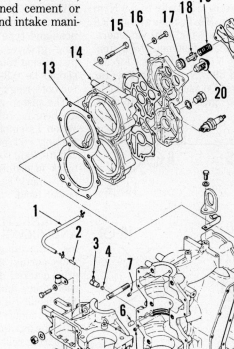

Fig. MR20-19 — Exploded view of cylinder block assembly. Breather valve (5) is not used on all models. Components (17 through 20) are used on 60 hp models.

1. Breather hose
2. Fitting
3. Elbow
4. Breather valve
5. Breather valve
6. Dowel
7. Bearing locator pin
8. Crankcase half
9. Cylinder block
10. Gasket
11. Exhaust cover
12. Anode
13. Gasket
14. Cylinder head
15. Gasket
16. Cover
17. Grommet
18. Water pressure relief valve
19. Spring
20. Thermostat
21. Gasket
22. Cover

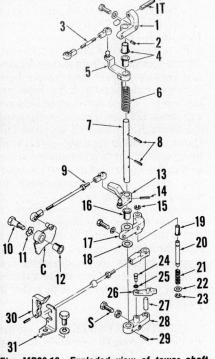

Fig. MR20-18 — Exploded view of tower shaft assembly.

1. Bracket
2. Roll pin
3. Magneto control rod
4. Bushings
5. Magneto control arm
6. Spring
7. Tower shaft
8. Pin
9. Throttle rod
10. Shoulder bolt
11. Wave washer
12. Bushing
13. Lever
14. Pin
15. "E" ring
16. Bushing
17. Bracket
18. Washer
19. Bushing
20. Pin
21. Spring
22. Washer
23. "E" ring
24. Pin
25. Wave washer
26. Retainer
27. Pin
28. Arm
29. Pin
30. Cable clamp
31. Cable bracket
C. Throttle cam
IT. Idle ignition timing screw
S. Throttle stop screw

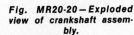

Fig. MR20-20 — Exploded view of crankshaft assembly.

1. "O" ring
2. Seal
3. Bearing
4. Thrust washer
5. Key
6. Center main bearing
7. Crankshaft
8. Rod bearing
9. Rod cap
10. Ball bearing
11. Seal
12. Seal
13. "O" ring
14. Seal housing
15. Clip
16. Connecting rod
17. Bearing rollers (28)
18. Thrust washer
19. Pin retainer clip
20. Piston pin
21. Piston
22. Lower piston ring
23. Upper piston ring

Reverse disassembly procedure for assembly. Apply engine oil to moving parts prior to assembly. Apply a non-hardening sealer to contact surfaces of crankcase half and cylinder block. Refer to Fig. MR20-21 for tightening sequence of crankcase nuts and screws. Tighten crankcase fasteners initially to 3.9 N·m (34 in.-lbs.) for M6 fasteners and 19.6 N·m (173 in.-lbs.) for M10 fasteners. Tighten crankcase fasteners to a final torque of 7.8 N·m (69 in.-lbs.) for M6 fasteners and 39.2 N·m (28 ft.-lbs.) for M10 fasteners. Do not apply sealant to cylinder head gasket. Refer to Fig.

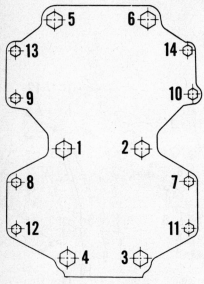

Fig. MR20-21—Use the tightening sequence shown above when tightening crankcase fasteners.

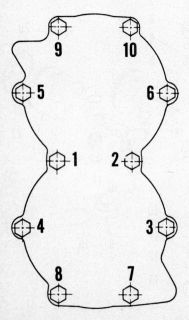

Fig. MR20-22—Use the tightening sequence shown above when tightening cylinder head screws.

MR20-22 for tightening sequence of cylinder head screws. Tighten cylinder head screws to 14.7 N·m (130 in.-lbs.) initially, then to a final torque of 29.4 N·m (22 ft.-lbs.).

PISTONS, PINS, RINGS AND CYLINDERS. Each piston is equipped with two piston rings with the top ring a headland type piston ring. Both piston ring grooves have a pin to prevent piston ring rotation. Piston ring end gap should be 0.3-0.5 mm (0.012-0.020 in.) for both rings.

The piston pin rides in 28 loose needle bearing rollers (17–Fig. MR20-20). When assembling piston, pin and connecting rod be sure oil hole (H–Fig. MR20-23) in rod is on same side as "UP" mark in piston crown. Install piston so "UP" mark is towards flywheel end of power head.

CONNECTING RODS, BEARINGS AND CRANKSHAFT. Before detaching connecting rods from crankshaft, make certain that rod and cap are properly marked for correct assembly to each other and in the correct cylinder. The needle rollers and cages at crankpin end of connecting rod should be kept with the assembly and not interchanged.

Bearing rollers and cages used in con-

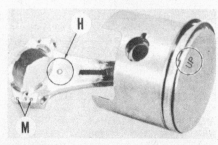

Fig. MR20-23—Assemble rod and piston so oil hole (H) is on same side as "UP" on piston crown. Be sure match marks (M) are on same side when installing cap on rod.

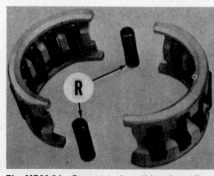

Fig. MR20-24—Be sure to install bearing rollers (R) when installing center main bearing.

necting rods and center main bearing are available only as a set which contains the cages and rollers for one bearing. Center main bearing outer races are held together by snap ring (15–Fig. MR20-20). Be sure locating holes in main bearing outer races mate properly with locating dowels (7–Fig. MR20-19 in cylinder block when installing crankshaft assembly.

When installing connecting rod on crankshaft, be sure loose bearing rollers (R–Fig. MR20-24) are installed between bearing cages. Connecting rod and cap match marks (M–Fig. MR20-23) must be on same side. Be sure cap is properly meshed with connecting rod.

STARTER

MANUAL STARTER. The rewind starter used on 48 hp models is shown in Fig. MR20-26. A starter interlock prevents operating manual starter when outboard is in forward or reverse gears. Cable (25) is connected to shift shaft (24) and actuates interlock pawl (3) which engages dogs on rope pulley (11). To adjust starter interlock, position shift lever in neutral position. Position cable (25) in clamps (7) so marks on pawl (3) and cam plate (6) are aligned.

To disassemble starter, detach shift interlock cable (25) from starter housing and remove starter from power head. Remove rope handle from rope and allow rope to wind into starter. Unscrew cap screw (22) and remove components (15 through 21) as well as pawl (13). Carefully remove rope pulley (11) while being careful not to allow rewind spring to uncoil uncontrolled as personal injury may result. Inspect components for damage and excessive wear.

Reverse disassembly procedure to assemble starter. Install rewind spring (10) with coils wound in counterclockwise direction from outer spring end. Apply a suitable grease to bushing (14). Wind rope in counterclockwise direction around pulley as viewed with pulley installed.

ELECTRIC STARTER. An electric starter is used on 60 hp models. Refer to Fig. MR20-27 for an exploded view of starter. Early models were equipped with a solenoid mounted on starter as shown while later models are equipped with a separate starter switch. A safety switch (N–Fig. MR20-28) prevents starter actuation when outboard is in forward or reverse gear.

Maximum no-load current draw should be 60 amperes at 12 volts with starter speed of 7000 rpm minimum. Minimum brush length is 11.5 mm (0.45 in.). Brush spring pressure should be 13.7-17.6 newtons (49-63 oz.). Starter motor pinion clearance in engaged position should be 0.3-1.5 mm (0.012-0.059 in.). Pinion to flywheel ring gear backlash should be 3-5 mm (0.118-0.197 in.)

PROPELLER

All models are equipped with a three-bladed, right-hand propeller. The propeller has an integral cushion hub to protect outboard driveline components. Optional propellers are available and should be selected to provide full throttle operation at 5000-5500 rpm.

LOWER UNIT

R&R AND OVERHAUL. Most service on lower unit can be performed by detaching gearcase from the drive shaft housing. To remove gearcase, drain lubricant, unscrew trim tab retaining screw (S – Fig. MR20-30), remove trim tab (50) and unscrew gearcase retaining screw (W) in gearcase trim tab cavity. Unscrew four nuts securing gearcase and separate gearcase from drive shaft housing.

Disassemble the gearcase after re-

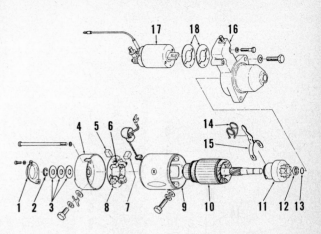

Fig. MR20-27 – Exploded view of electric starter used on 60 hp models. Later models are equipped with a separate starter switch instead of solenoid (17).

1. Dust cover
2. "E" ring
3. Washers
4. End cover
5. Neg. brush
6. Brush spring
7. Pos. brush
8. Brush plate
9. Frame
10. Armature
11. Drive assy.
12. Collar
13. Clip
14. Spring
15. Yoke
16. End frame
17. Solenoid
18. Washer

moving the propeller. Bend back locking tab of lockwasher, unscrew bearing housing nut (41) and remove lockwasher (40). Clamp the outer end of propeller shaft in a soft-jawed vise and remove the gearcase by tapping with a rubber mallet. Be careful not to lose key (37) or shims (32). Forward gear (49) will remain in gearcase. Withdraw the propeller shaft from bearing housing (36) and reverse gear (31).

Clamp bearing housing (36) in a soft-jawed vise and remove reverse gear (31) and bearing (34) using a suitable puller. Remove and discard seals (39).

To remove clutch (26) from propeller shaft, remove retaining ring (27). Insert cam follower (23) in hole in shaft and apply only enough pressure to cam follower end to relieve spring pressure so pin (28) can be driven out.

To disassemble drive shaft and associated parts, position gearcase with drive shaft pointing upwards. Remove water pump assembly. Unscrew pinion nut (22) and remove pinion (21), thrust washer (20), forward gear (49) and bearing (48) cone. Use a suitable puller to extract bearing (48) cup while being careful not to damage or lose shims (47). Withdraw drive shaft (14) along with bearing (16) cone. Using a suitable puller, remove bearing (16) cup while being careful not to damage or lose shims (17). Extract sleeve (18) then remove bearing (19) by driving down into gearcase. Shift components (53 through 60) may now be removed.

If gear wear was abnormal or if any parts that affect gear alignment were renewed, check and adjust gear mesh as follows: Install bearing (19) in gearcase. Install forward gear (49) and bearing (48) using originally installed shims (47). Position shims (17) that were originally installed at bottom of bearing bore, then install bearing (16) cup. Position pinion

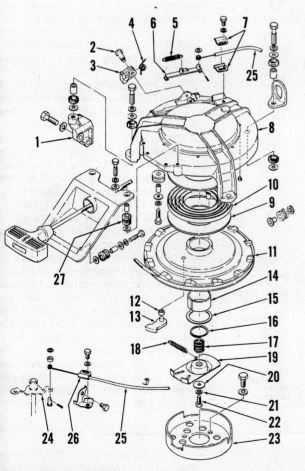

Fig. MR20-26 – Exploded view of manual starter used on 48 hp models.

1. Bracket
2. Pivot screw
3. Pawl
4. Spring
5. Spring
6. Cam plate
7. Cable clamp
8. Starter housing
9. Plate
10. Rewind spring
11. Rope pulley
12. Bushing
13. Pawl
14. Bushing
15. Washer
16. Clip
17. Spring
18. Spring
19. Drive plate
20. Washer
21. Lockwasher
22. Cap screw
23. Starter cap
24. Shift lever
25. Starter lockout cable
26. Cable clamp
27. Rope roller

Fig. MR20-28 – View showing location of neutral start switch (N) on 60 hp models.

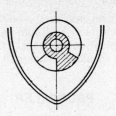

Fig. MR20-31—With lower unit gears in neutral install reverse cam (54—Fig. MR20-30) as shown.

gear (21) and thrust washer (20) in gear case—thrust washer grooves must be towards gear. Insert drive shaft (14) with bearing (16) cone, install nut (22) and tighten to 69-78 N·m (51-57 ft.-lbs.). Coat gears with gear paint or compound and check mesh position. It will be necessary to push down on end of drive shaft while checking mesh position. If gears do not mesh in center of teeth, add or remove shims (17) as necessary. After setting mesh position, check backlash between teeth of gears (21 and 49). Backlash should be 0.075-0.125 mm (0.003-0.005 in.). To increase backlash delete shims (47); add shims (47) to decrease backlash. After adjusting backlash, recheck gear mesh position. Install bearings (34 and 38) in bearing housing (36) then install reverse gear (31), shims (32), thrust washer (33) and bearing housing (36) in gearcase and check backlash between gears (21 and 31). If backlash is not 0.15-0.25 mm (0.006-0.010 in.), add or delete shims (32) as required. Adding shims will increase backlash.

When reassembling, long splines of shift rod (59) should be toward top. Install shift cam (60) with "UP" marked side towards top. Assemble shift parts (23 through 28) in propeller shaft. Pin (28) should pass through hole in slide (24). Install a new "O" ring (35) and seal (39) in bearing housing with seal lips facing out towards propeller. Tighten nut (41) to 118-137 N·m (87-100 ft.-lbs.).

Install oil seals (13) in water pump base (10) with seal lips facing up towards impeller. With gears shifted to neutral install reverse cam (54) as shown in Fig. MR20-31, then install shaft guide (53).

Before attaching gearcase to drive shaft housing, apply water resistant grease to upper drive shaft splines and water tube seals. Place water tube into position and be sure gearcase is in neutral gear and shift control lever on engine is in neutral. Complete remainder of assembly by reversing disassembly procedure. Tighten propeller nut to 29.4-39.2 N·m (22-28 ft.-lbs.).

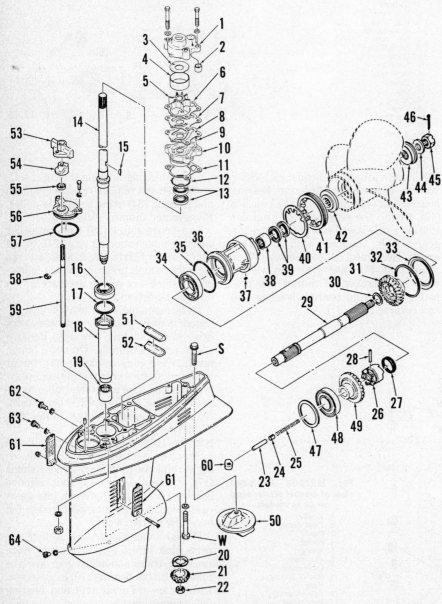

Fig. MR20-30—Exploded view of gearcase.

1. Water pump housing
2. Water tube seal
3. Plate
4. Liner
5. Impeller
6. Gasket
7. Plate
8. Gasket
9. Pin
10. Base
11. Gasket
12. "O" ring
13. Seals
14. Drive shaft
15. Key
16. Taper roller bearing
17. Shim
18. Sleeve
19. Needle bearing
20. Thrust washer
21. Pinion gear
22. Nut
23. Cam follower
24. Slide
25. Spring
26. Clutch
27. Clip
28. Pin
29. Propeller shaft
30. Thrust washer
31. Reverse gear
32. Shim
33. Thrust washer
34. Ball bearing
35. "O" ring
36. Bearing housing
37. Key
38. Needle bearing
39. Seals
40. Lockwasher
41. Nut
42. Thrust hub
43. Splined spacer
44. Washer
45. Nut
46. Cotter pin
47. Shim
48. Taper roller bearing
49. Forward gear
50. Trim tab
51. Seal
52. Seal plate
53. Reverse rod guide
54. Reverse cam
55. Seal
56. Shift rod guide
57. "O" ring
58. "E" ring
59. Shift rod
60. Shift cam
61. Water inlet cover
62. Vent plug
63. Oil level plug
64. Fill plug
S. Cap screw
W. Cap screw

MARINER 60 (3 cyl.) AND 70 HP
(Prior To 1986)

CONDENSED SERVICE DATA

TUNE-UP

Hp/rpm:
  Model 60 ....60/5000-5500
  Model 70 ....70/5000-5500
Bore.....................................2-7/8 in.
                                           (73 mm)
Stroke ....2-9/16 in.
                                           (65 mm)
Displacement ....49.8 cu. in.
                                          (816 cc)
Firing Order 1-3-2*
Compression at Cranking Speed ....†
Ignition ....Solid State
Spark Plugs ....See Text
Fuel:Oil Ratio 50:1
*On models prior to serial number 5579017, firing order is
1-2-3.
†Not more than 15 psi (103.5 kPa) variation between cylinders.

SIZES—CLEARANCES

Piston Rings:
  End Gap ....*
  Side Clearance......................................*
Piston Skirt Clearance ....*
Crankshaft Bearing Type:
  Top Main ....Ball Bearing
  Main Bearing (2) ....Loose Rollers
  No. of Rollers.........................56

SIZES—CLEARANCES CONT.

  Main Bearing (3) ....Loose Rollers
  No. of Rollers........................56
  Bottom Main Bearing ....Ball Bearing
  Crankpin ....Caged Roller
Piston Pin Bearing ....Loose Rollers
  No. of Rollers (each rod) 29
*Publication not authorized by manufacturer.

TIGHTENING TORQUES

Connecting Rods ....180 in.-lbs.
                                  (20.3 N·m)
Crankcase Screws ....200 in.-lbs.
                                  (22.6 N·m)
Cylinder Cover ....70 in.-lbs.
                                  (7.9 N·m)
Exhaust Cover
  1/4 inch ....115 in.-lbs.
                                    (13 N·m)
  5/16 inch ....200 in.-lbs.
                                    (22.6 N·m)
Flywheel Nut ....65 ft.-lbs.
                                  (88.4 N·m)
Reed Screws ....50 in.-lbs.
                                    (5.6 N·m)
Spark Plugs...........................20 ft.-lbs.
                                  (27.2 N·m)
Transfer Port Covers ....60 in.-lbs.
                                  (6.8 N·m)

LUBRICATION

The power head is lubricated by oil mixed with the fuel. Fuel should be regular leaded, low lead or unleaded gasoline with a minimum pump octane rating of 86. Recommended oil is Quicksilver Formula 50-D Outboard Lubricant. Normal fuel:oil ratio is 50:1; during engine break-in, fuel:oil ratio should be 25:1.

Lower unit gears and bearings are lubricated by oil contained in the gearcase. Recommended oil is Mariner Super Duty Gear Lube. Lubricant is drained by removing vent and drain plugs in the gearcase. Refill through drain plug hole until oil has reached level of vent plug opening, then allow 1 ounce (30 mL) of oil to drain from gearcase. Lower unit oil capacity is 12.5 fl.oz. (370 mL).

FUEL SYSTEM

CARBURETOR. Standard make of carburetor is a center bowl type Mercarb. Two carburetors are used. Note that these carburetors are equipped with an enrichment valve (24–Fig. MR22-1) in place of a choke plate. Standard main jet (10) size is 0.086 inch (2.18 mm) for operation below 2500 feet (762

m) altitude. Standard vent jet (4) size is 0.066 inch (1.68 mm) for operation below 2500 feet (762 m) altitude. Other jet sizes are available for adjusting the calibration for altitude or other special conditions. Preliminary adjustment of idle mixture screw (19) is 1 turn out from a lightly seated position. Recom-

mended idle speed is 650-750 rpm with engine at normal operating temperature and in gear.

When overhauling carburetor, drive float pins (16) and fuel inlet lever pin (18) out towards knurled end of pin. Insert plain end of pin first during assembly. Note that strong (0.034 in. dia. wire) throttle return spring must be used on top carburetor throttle shaft. Numbers on throttle plate (29) must face outwards at closed throttle. Be sure rubber insert in fuel inlet valve seat (6) is installed so flat end of insert is towards inlet valve.

To determine the final level, invert the carburetor body and measure distance (D – Fig. MR22-2) from the carburetor body to base of float (15). Distance (D) should be 11/16 inch (17.5 mm) and is adjusted by bending fuel inlet lever (17 – Fig. MR22-3) within area (A).

SPEED CONTROL LINKAGE. To synchronize ignition and carburetor opening, proceed as follows: On models with an adjustable timing pointer, a dial indicator must be installed in the top cylinder and the indicator synchronized with the piston position (dial indicator reads zero when piston is at top dead center.)

NOTE: To prevent accidental starting from flywheel rotation, remove all spark plugs and properly ground plug wires.

Rotate the flywheel counterclockwise approximately ¼ turn past the 0.46 inch (12 mm) BTDC reading, then rotate flywheel clockwise until indicator face reads 0.464 inch (12 mm) BTDC. Note position of the timing pointer and reposition if timing pointer (P – Fig. MR22-5) is not aligned with dot (D) on timing decal. Loosen screw (S) to reposition. Remove the dial indicator assembly from the top cylinder after adjustment is completed and reassemble.

Connect a power timing light to the number 1 (top) spark plug wire. With the lower unit properly immersed, start the engine and shift the outboard motor into the "Forward" gear. Run the engine at 5000-5500 rpm. Adjust maximum ignition advance screw (M – Fig. MR22-6) until the timing pointer is aligned with the 23° BTDC mark on the timing decal. Secure ignition advance screw position with the locknut. Stop the engine and remove the timing light.

Move the spark lever until maximum advance screw (M) just contacts the stop boss and adjust secondary pickup screw (W) so carburetor cluster pin (R – Fig. MR22-7) is located on throttle actuator cam (C) as shown.

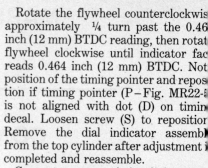

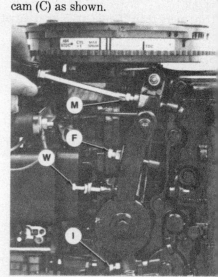

Fig. MR22-6 – View showing location of maximum ignition advance screw (M), full throttle stop screw (F), secondary pickup screw (W) and idle speed screw (I). Refer to text.

Fig. MR22-1 – Exploded view of center bowl type Mercarb carburetor.

1. Welch plug (9/16 inch)
2. Fuel inlet strainer
3. Body
4. Vent jet
5. Gasket
6. Inlet needle & seat assy.
7. Venturi
8. Nozzle
9. Gasket
10. Main jet
11. Main jet plug
12. Screw
13. Float bowl
14. Gasket
15. Float
16. Pin
17. Fuel inlet lever
18. Pin
19. Idle mixture screw
20. Spring
21. Spring
22. Flat washer
23. Rubber seal
24. Enrichment valve assy.
25. Screw & lockwasher
26. Welch plug (7/16 inch)
27. Gasket
28. Throttle shaft
29. Throttle plate
30. Screw

Fig. MR2-3 – Adjust float level by bending fuel inlet lever (17) within area (A).

Fig. MR22-5 – Timing pointer (P) must align with dot (D) on flywheel timing decal when the piston of the top cylinder is 0.464 inch (12 mm) BTDC. Loosen screw (S) to reposition pointer (P).

Fig. MR2-2 – To determine float level, invert the carburetor body and measure distance (D) from the carburetor body to base of float (15). Distance (D) should be 11/16 inch (17.5 mm).

Illustrations Courtesy Mariner

To prevent damage to the carburetor throttle plate at full throttle, adjust full throttle stop screw (F–Fig. MR22-6) so a clearance of 0.010-0.015 inch (0.25-0.38 mm) is between throttle actuator cam (C–Fig. MR22-8) and cluster pin (R) when throttle lever is moved to the wide open position.

Adjust idle speed screw (I–Fig. MR22-6) as outlined in the previous CARBURETOR section.

REED VALVES. The inlet reed valves are located on the intermediate main bearing assemblies. Two reed valve assemblies are used, one for each carburetor. The center cylinder receives a partial fuel:air charge from each reed valve and carburetor.

Reed petals (2–Fig. MR22-10) should be perfectly flat with no more than 0.007 inch (0.18 mm) clearance between free end of reed petal and seating surface of center main bearing. Reed stop height (A) should be 0.180 inch (4.57 mm). Bend reed stop (1) to adjust. Reed petal seating surface on bearing housing must be smooth and may be refinished on a lapping plate after removing reed stops, reed valves and dowels. Do not attempt to bend or straighten a reed petal to modify performance or to salvage a damaged reed. Never install a bent reed. Lubricate the reed valve units with "Quicksilver" Multipurpose Lubricant or a light distributor cam grease when reassembling.

Each valve unit has four reeds which are available only as a matched set. Crankshaft must be removed before reed valve units can be serviced.

Fig. MR22-7 – Adjust secondary pickup screw (W–Fig. MR22-6) so carburetor cluster pin (R) locates on throttle actuator cam (C) as shown when maximum ignition advance screw (M–Fig. MR22-6) just contacts the stop boss.

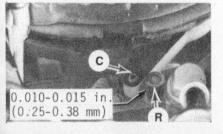

Fig. MR22-8 – Adjust full throttle stop screw (F–Fig. MR22-6) so there is 0.010-0.015 inch (0.25-0.38 mm) clearance between throttle actuator cam (C) and cluster pin (R) at full throttle.

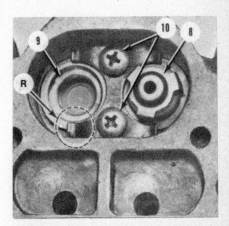

Fig. MR22-10 – View of intermediate main bearing housing and reed valve assembly. Height (A) of read stop should be 0.180 inch (4.57 mm).

FUEL PUMP. All models are equipped with a diaphragm type fuel pump mounted on the starboard side of power head. Fuel pressure at idle speed should be 2 psi (13.8 kPa) while fuel pressure at full throttle should be 4-5½ psi (27.6-37.9 kPa).

When assembling fuel pump install check valves as shown in Fig. MR22-12 with tips of retainer (R) pointing away from check valves.

IGNITION SYSTEM

All models are equipped with a "Thunderbolt" solid state capacitor discharge ignition system consisting of trigger coils, stator, switch box and ignition coils. The trigger coils are contained in a trigger ring module under the flywheel. Diodes, SCR's and capacitors are contained in the switch box. Switch box, trigger ring module and stator must be serviced as unit assemblies.

Check all valves and connections before troubleshooting ignition circuit. The following test specifications will aid troubleshooting. Resistance between red and blue stator leads should be 5400-6200 ohms. Resistance between red stator lead and ground should be 125-175 ohms. Resistance between white, violet or brown trigger coil leads and white/black trigger coil lead should be 1100-1400 ohms.

Recommended spark plugs are AC V40FFM or Champion L76V.

COOLING SYSTEM

WATER PUMP. The rubber impeller type water pump is housed in the gearcase housing. The impeller is mounted on and driven by the lower unit drive shaft.

When cooling system problems are encountered, first check the water inlet for plugging or partial stoppage, then if not corrected, remove the gearcase housing as outlined in LOWER UNIT section and examine the water pump, water tubes and seals.

Water pump housing is plastic. Refer to assembly notes, cautions and tightening torques listed in the LOWER UNIT section when assembling.

POWER HEAD

R&R AND DISASSEMBLE. To remove the power head assembly, first disconnect the battery and remove the top side cowling. Remove electric starter, then disconnect all interfering wires and linkage. Remove the stud nuts which secure the power head to lower unit, then jar power head on exhaust side to loosen gasket. Lift power head from lower unit and install on a suitable stand. Remove the flywheel, stator assembly, trigger plate assembly and the carburetors. Exhaust manifold cover, cylinder block cover and transfer port covers should be removed for cleaning and inspection.

Remove the upper and lower crankcase end caps by using a suitable puller attached to threaded holes in caps. Remove the main bearing locking bolts from front crankcase half, remove the flange bolts; then remove crankcase front half by inserting screwdriver in the recesses provided on side flanges. Use extra care not to spring the parts or

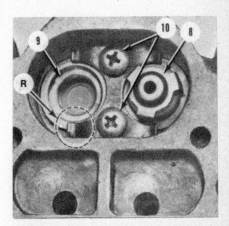

Fig. MR22-12 – View of fuel pump showing inlet (8) and discharge (9) check valves installed. Retainer (R) is secured by screws (10) and retainer tips must point away from check valves.

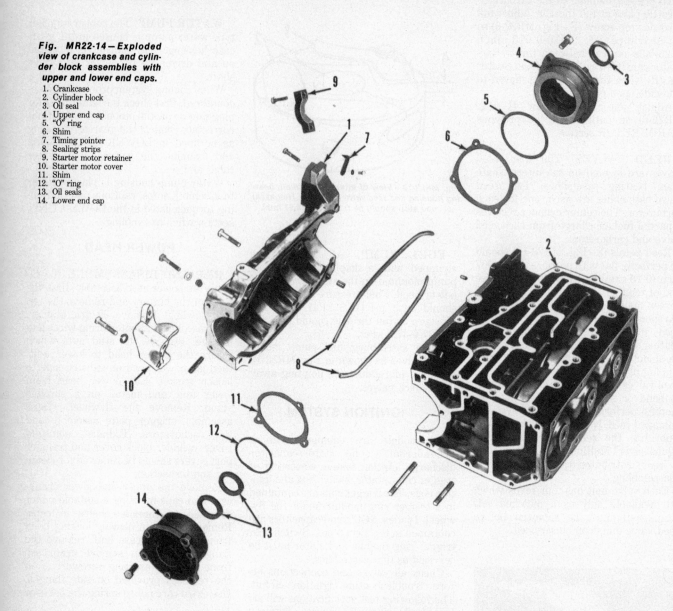

Fig. MR22-14 — Exploded view of crankcase and cylinder block assemblies with upper and lower end caps.

1. Crankcase
2. Cylinder block
3. Oil seal
4. Upper end cap
5. "O" ring
6. Shim
7. Timing pointer
8. Sealing strips
9. Starter motor retainer
10. Starter motor cover
11. Shim
12. "O" ring
13. Oil seals
14. Lower end cap

to mar the machined, mating surfaces. The crankcase half (1 – Fig. MR22-14 and cylinder block assembly (2) are matched and align bored, and are available only as an assembly.

Crankshaft, pistons, bearings and connecting rods may now be removed for service as outlined in the appropriate following paragraphs. When assembling, follow the procedures outlined in the ASSEMBLY paragraph.

ASSEMBLY. When assembling, the crankcase must be completely sealed against both vacuum and pressure. Exhaust manifold and water passages must be sealed against pressure leakage. Whenever power head is disassembled, it is recommended that all gasket surfaces and machined joints without gaskets be carefully checked for nicks and burrs which might interfere with a tight seal.

Lubricate all bearing and friction surfaces with engine oil. Loose needle bearings may be held in place during assembly using a light, nonfibrous grease.

After the crankshaft, connecting rods, pistons and main bearings are positioned in the cylinder, check the crankshaft end play. Temporarily install the crankshaft end caps (4 and 14 – Fig. MR22-14) omitting "O" rings (5 and 12), but using shims (6 and 11) that were originally installed. Tighten the end cap to cylinder retaining screws. Use a soft hammer to bump the crankshaft each way to seat bearings, then measure end play.

Bump the crankshaft toward top and measure clearance between the top crankshaft counterweight and the end cap as shown in Fig. MR22-18. Bump the crankshaft toward bottom and again measure clearance between counter-

weight and top end cap. Subtract the first (minimum) clearance from the second clearance which will indicate the amount of end play. If end play is not within limits of 0.004-0.012 inch (0.102-0.305 mm), add or remove shims (6 and 11 – Fig. MR22-14) as necessary, then recheck. The crankshaft should be centered by varying the amount of shims between upper (6) and lower (11) shim stacks. When centering the crankshaft, make certain that end play is correct.

Shims (6 and 11) are available in thicknesses of 0.002, 0.003, 0.005, 0.006, 0.008 and 0.010 inch.

All gaskets and sealing surfaces should be lightly and carefully coated with an impervious liquid sealer. Surface must be completely coated, using care that excess sealer does not squeeze out into bearings, crankcase or other passages.

Check the assembly by turning the crankshaft after each step to check for binding or locking which might indicate improper assembly. Remove the cause before proceeding. Rotate the crankshaft until each piston ring in turn appears in one of the exhaust or transfer ports, then check by pressing on ring with a blunt tool. Ring should spring back when released; if it does not, a broken or binding ring is indicated, and the trouble should be corrected.

Tighten the crankcase exhaust cover and cylinder cover cap screws by first tightening center screws, then tightening screws evenly working outward, away from center of crankcase. Tightening torques are given in the CONDENSED SERVICE DATA table.

Fig. MR22-18 — Refer to text for method of checking crankshaft end play. Position crankshaft so each crankpin is centered in cylinder.

PISTONS, PINS, RINGS AND CYLINDERS. Before detaching connecting rods from crankshaft, make sure that rod and cap are properly identified for correct assembly to each other and in the correct cylinder.

Piston rings are interchangeable in the ring grooves and are pinned in place.

Maximum allowable cylinder bore wear or out-of-round is 0.004 inch (0.102 mm). Excessively worn or slightly damaged, standard size cylinders may be repaired by boring and honing to fit an oversize piston. Pistons and rings are available in 0.015 inch (0.38 mm) oversize on early models and 0.015 inch (0.38 mm) and 0.030 inch (0.76 mm) oversizes on later models.

Piston pin is pressed in piston bosses and secured with retaining rings. The retaining rings should not be reused. Piston end of connecting rod is fitted with 29 loose needle rollers.

The piston pin needle rollers use the connecting rod bore and the piston pin as bearing races. When assembling, install bearing washers and needle bearings in piston end of connecting rod using light nonfibrous grease to hold them in place. A Mariner special tool may be used to hold needles in position while positioning piston for installation. Piston must be installed so sharp, vertical side of deflector will be to starboard (intake) side of cylinder bore. Heat piston to approximately 135°F (57°C) and press piston pin into place. Pin should be centered in piston. Use new piston pin retaining rings on each assembly.

CONNECTING RODS, BEARINGS AND CRANKSHAFT. Upper and lower ends of crankshaft are carried by ball bearings. The two center main bearings (18 – Fig. MR22-16) also contain the inlet reed valve assemblies. Two split type outer races (21) each contain 56 loose bearing rollers in two rows. The outer race is held together by a retaining ring (23). The reed valve assembly (18) fits around outer race (21).

The connecting rod uses 29 loose rollers at the piston end and a caged roller bearing at the crankpin end.

Check rod for alignment by placing rod on a surface plate and checking with a light. Rod is bent or distorted if a 0.002 inch (0.051 mm) feeler gage can be inserted between rod and surface plate.

If bearing surface of rod and cap is rough, scored, worn or shows evidence of overheating, renew the connecting rod. Inspect crankpin and main bearing journals. If scored, out-of-round or worn, renew the crankshaft. Check the crankshaft for straightness using a dial indicator and "V" blocks.

Inspect and adjust the reed valves as outlined in REED VALVE paragraph, and reassemble as outlined in ASSEMBLY paragraph.

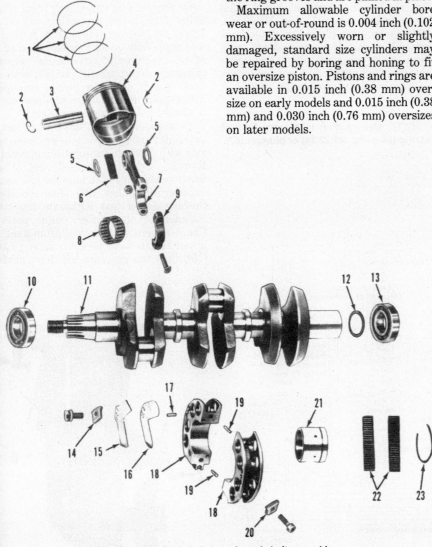

Fig. MR22-16 — Exploded view of crankshaft assembly.

1. Piston rings	7. Connecting rod	12. Shim	18. Reed plate & main bearing housing
2. Clips	8. Caged roller bearing	13. Ball bearing	19. Pin
3. Piston pin	9. Rod cap	14. Clamp nut	20. Nut
4. Piston	10. Ball bearing	15. Reed stop	21. Outer race
5. Thrust washers	11. Crankshaft	16. Reed petal	22. Needle bearings
6. Needle bearings		17. Locating dowel	23. Retaining ring

ELECTRICAL SYSTEM

Refer to Fig. MR22-20 for wiring diagram of electrical system. Before any servicing, refer to precautions listed in ignition paragraphs.

The rectifier assembly is designed to protect the ignition switch box if battery terminals or harness plug becomes loose with motor running. However, the rectifier assembly (Fig. MR22-21) will be damaged. If battery terminals are reversed, the rectifier and the ignition switch box will be damaged. The motor can be operated without rectifier if the two yellow/red wires (from the alternator) are disconnected from the rectifier and taped separately.

Refer to Fig. MR22-21 for correct rectifier connections.

LOWER UNIT

PROPELLER AND DRIVE CLUTCH. Protection for the motor is built into a special cushioning clutch in the propeller hub. No adjustment is possible on the propeller or clutch. Various pitch propellers are available and propeller should be selected for best performance under applicable conditions. Propellers other than those designed for the motor must not be used.

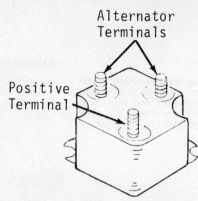

Fig. MR22-21 — Rectifier must be connected as shown or damage to the electrical system will result.

R&R AND OVERHAUL. Most service on lower unit can be performed by detaching the gearcase housing from drive shaft housing. To remove the housing, remove the plastic plug and Allen screw from location (1 – Fig. MR22-23). Remove trim tab (2) and stud nut from under trim tab. Remove stud nut from location (3), two stud nuts (4) from each side and stud nut (5) if so equipped, then withdraw the lower unit gearcase assembly.

NOTE: Use caution to prevent loss of spring (68 – Fig. MR22-24) or plunger (67).

Remove the housing plugs and drain the housing, then secure gearcase in vise between two blocks of soft wood with propeller up. Wedge a piece of wood between propeller and antiventilation plate, remove the propeller nut then remove propeller.

Disassemble the gearcase by removing the gearcase housing cover nut (61 – Fig. MR22-24). Clamp the outer end of propeller shaft in a soft jawed vise and remove the gearcase by tapping with a rubber mallet. Be careful not to lose key (56). Forward gear (43) will remain in housing. Withdraw the propeller shaft from bearing carrier (55) and reverse gear (51).

Clamp the bearing carrier (55) in a soft-jawed vise and remove reverse gear (51) and bearing (53) with an internal expanding puller and slide hammer. Remove and discard the propeller shaft rear seals (58 and 59).

To remove dog clutch (48) from propeller shaft, remove retaining ring (47). Insert cam follower (44) in hole in shaft and apply only enough pressure on end of cam follower to remove the spring pressure, then push out pin (49) with a small punch. The pin passes through drilled holes in dog clutch and operates in slotted holes in propeller shaft.

To disassemble the drive shaft and associated parts, reposition gearcase in vise with drive shaft projecting upward. Remove seal (16), splined seal (17), water pump body (23), impeller (25) and impeller drive key (26). Remove the flushing screw and withdraw the remainder of the water pump parts. Clamp upper end of drive shaft in a soft-jawed vise, remove pinion retaining nut (15); then tap gearcase off drive shaft.

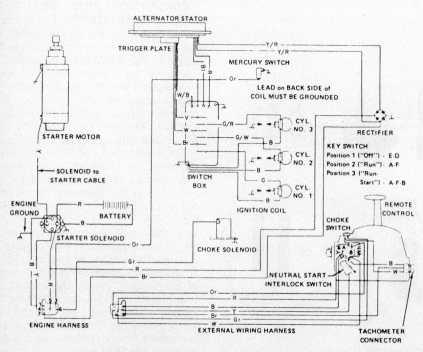

Fig. MR22-20 — Wiring schematic typical of all models.

B. Black		
R. Red	Bl. Blue	G/R. Green with red tracer
V. Violet	Br. Brown	
W. White	Gr. Gray	G/W. Green with white tracer
Y. Yellow	Or. Orange	

W/B. White with black tracer	
Y/R. Yellow with red tracer	

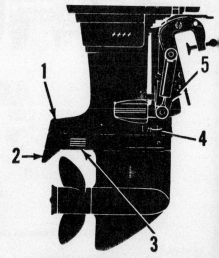

Fig. MR22-23 — To remove the lower unit gearcase assembly, remove the attaching screws and stud nuts from positions indicated.

and bearing. Note the position and thickness of shims (11) on drive shaft upper bearing. Mesh position of pinion is controlled by shims (11) placed underneath the bearing.

After drive shaft has been removed, the forward gear (43) and bearing cone can be withdrawn. Use an internal expanding type puller to withdraw bearing cup if removal is required. Remove and save the shim pack (40).

Shift shaft (7) and cam (39) can be removed after removing forward gear and unscrewing bushing (5) from gearcase housing.

If gear wear was abnormal or if any parts that affect gear alignment were renewed, check and adjust gear mesh as follows: Install forward gear (43) and bearing (41) using shims (40) that were originally installed. Position shims (11) that were originally installed at bottom of bearing bore. Install bearing assembly (10) in housing bore against shims (11). Position the drive pinion (14) in housing and insert drive shaft (9), with bearing assembly (10) installed, into housing, bearing (13) and gear (14). Install retaining nut (15). Coat gears (14 and 43) with bearing blue and check mesh position. Due to the spiral cut gears, it will be necessary to press down on end of drive shaft while checking position. If gears do not mesh in center of teeth, add or remove shims (11) under bearing as necessary. After setting mesh position, check backlash between teeth of gears (14 and 43). Backlash should be within limits of 0.003-0.005 inch (0.076-0.127 mm). To increase

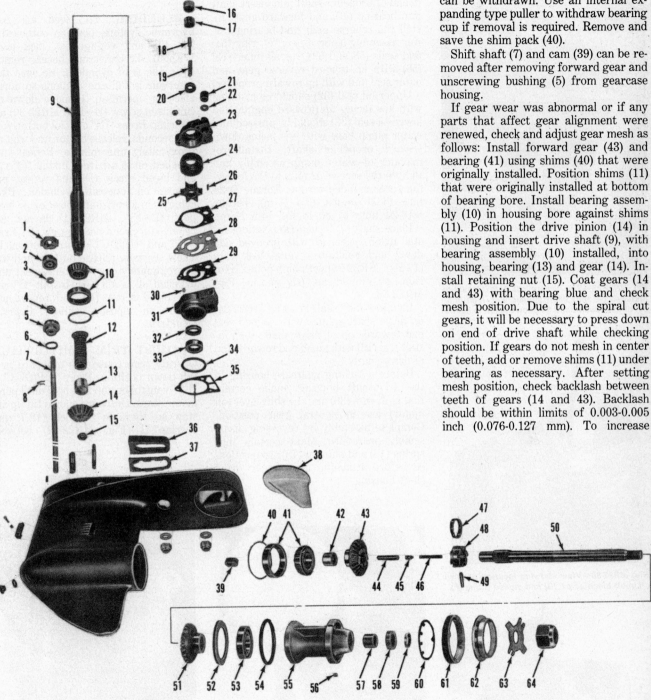

Fig. MR22-24 — Exploded view of gearcase assembly.

1. Reverse locking cam	11. Shim	22. Nylon washer
2. Spacer	12. Sleeve	23. Water pump body
3. Rubber washer	13. Bearing	24. Insert
4. Oil seal	14. Pinion gear	25. Impeller
5. Bushing	15. Nut	26. Drive key
6. "O" ring	16. Seal	27. Gasket
7. Shift shaft	17. Splined seal	28. Plate
8. Snap ring	18. Plunger	29. Gasket
9. Drive shaft	19. Spring	30. Dowel
10. Tapered roller bearing	20. Seal	31. Pump base
& cup	21. Seal	32. Oil seal

33. Oil seal	43. Forward gear	54. "O" ring
34. "O" ring	44. Cam follower	55. Bearing carrier
35. Gasket	45. Slide	56. Key
36. Exhaust tube seal	46. Spring	57. Bearing
37. Support plate	47. Retaining ring	58. Oil seal
38. Trim tab	48. Dog clutch	59. Oil seal
39. Shift cam	49. Pin	60. Washer
40. Shim	50. Propeller shaft	61. Gear housing cover
41. Tapered roller bearing	51. Reverse gear	62. Cupped washer
& cup	52. Thrust washer	63. Tab washer
42. Bearing	53. Ball bearing	64. Nut

clearance (backlash), remove part of shim stack (40) behind bearing cup. If gears are too loose, add shims. After changing thickness of shims (40), gears should be recoated with bearing blue and mesh position should be rechecked.

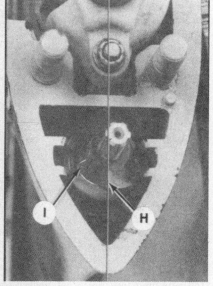

Fig. MR22-25 — The reverse lock cam (1) must be installed on shift shaft splines with high point (H) of cam positioned as shown when in neutral position.

Fig. MR22-30 — View showing location of down circuit bleed screw (D) and grease fitting (F).

Fig. MR22-31 — View showing location of up circuit bleed screw (U) and bleed port (P).

When reassembling, long splines on shift rod (7) should be toward top. Shift cam (39) is installed with notches up and toward rear. Assemble shifting parts (45, 46, 47, 48 and 49) into propeller shaft (50). Pin (49) should be through hole in slide (45). Position follower (44) in end of propeller shaft and insert shaft into bearing (42) and forward gear. Install the reverse gear and bearing carrier assembly using a new "O" ring (54) and seals (58 and 59). Install inner seal (58) with lip toward reverse gear and outer seal (59) with lip toward propeller.

Upper oil seal (32) should be installed with lips facing up (toward engine) and lower oil seal (33) should be pressed into water pump base with lips facing down toward propeller shaft. Install remainder of water pump assembly and tighten the screws or nuts to the following recommended torque. Torque 1/4-28 nuts to 30 in.-lbs. (3.4 N·m). Torque 5/16-24 nuts to 40 in.-lbs. (4.5 N·m).

Place shaft (7) in neutral position. Install nylon spacer (2) with grooved side down and position reverse lock cam (1 – Fig. MR22-25) with high point (H) of cam positioned as shown in Fig. MR22-25.

Install splined seal (17 – Fig. MR22-24) on drive shaft splines with splined seal end toward top of drive shaft, then install seal (16) with small end towards top of drive shaft.

Before attaching gearcase housing to the driveshaft housing, make certain that shift cam (39) and the shift lever (on motor) are in neutral gear position. Complete assembly by reversing disassembly procedure. Make certain that spring (19) and plunger (18) are positioned before attaching gearcase to drive shaft housing.

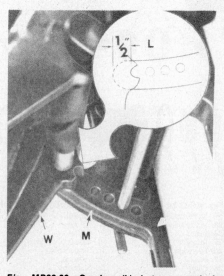

Fig. MR22-32 — Overlap (L) between swivel bracket flange (W) and clamp bracket flange (M) should be 1/2 inch (12.7 mm).

POWER TILT/TRIM

FLUID. Recommended fluid is SAE 10W-30 or 10W-40 automotive oil. With outboard in full up position, oil level should reach bottom of fill plug hole threads. Do not overfill.

BLEEDING. To bleed air from hydraulic system, position outboard at full tilt and engage tilt lock lever. Without disconnecting hoses, remove hydraulic trim cylinders. Be sure fluid reservoir is full and remains so during bleeding operation. Remove down circuit bleed screw (D – Fig. MR22-30) and "O" ring. Press "IN" control button for a few seconds, release button and wait approximately one minute. Repeat until expelled oil is air-free. Install "O" ring and bleed screw (D) and repeat procedure on opposite cylinder. Place cylinder in a horizontal position so bleed port (P – Fig. MR22-31) is up and remove up circuit bleed screw (U). Press "UP" and "UP/OUT" control buttons for a few seconds, release buttons and wait approximately one minute. Repeat until expelled oil is air-free. Install "O" ring and bleed screw (U) and repeat procedure on opposite cylinder. Reinstall cylinders.

ADJUST TRIM LIMIT SWITCH. Operate trim control so outboard is in full down position. Press "UP/OUT" or "UP" control button and hold until pump motor stops. Outboard should tilt up and stop so there is 1/2 inch (12.7 mm) overlap (L – Fig. MR22-32) between

Fig. MR22-33 — Loosen retainer screw (R) and turn trim limit adjusting nut (N) to adjust trim limit switch.

swivel bracket flange (W) and clamp bracket flange (M). Pull up on lower unit to remove slack when checking overlap (L). Note that if cylinder rods enter cylinders more than an additional ⅛ inch (3.17 mm), that hydraulic system should be bled of air as outlined in BLEEDING section. If overlap (L) is incorrect, loosen retainer screw (R – Fig. MR22-33) then turn adjusting nut (N) counterclockwise to increase overlap or clockwise to decrease overlap. Retighten retainer screw (R) and recheck adjustment.

PRESSURE TEST. To check hydraulic system pressure, disconnect four hoses attached to control valve as shown in Fig. MR22-34; small hoses are for up circuit while large hoses are for down circuit. Connect a pressure gage to one up circuit port (small) of control valve and another pressure gage to one down circuit port (large). Screw plugs

into remaining ports. Check fluid reservoir and fill if necessary. Operate trim control in up direction and note pressure gage reading. Minimum pressure should be 3500 psi (24.1 MPa) on new pumps with a red sleeve on wires or 3200-3500 psi (22.0-24.1 MPa) minimum on used pumps with reed sleeve on wires. Minimum pressure on all other new pumps is 3000 psi (20.7 MPa) while minimum pressure on all other used pumps is 2700-3000 psi (18.6-20.7 MPa). Release trim control button. Pressure will drop slightly after stabilizing but should not drop faster than 100 psi (690 kPa) every 15 seconds. Operate trim control in down direction and note pressure gage reading. Minimum pressure is 500-1000 psi (3.4-6.9 MPa). Release trim control button. Pressure will drop slightly after stabilizing but should not drop faster than 100 psi (690 kPa) every 15 seconds. If pressure is normal, inspect trim cylinders and hoses

for leakage. If pressure is abnormal, install a good control valve and recheck pressure. If pressure remains abnormal, install a new pump body.

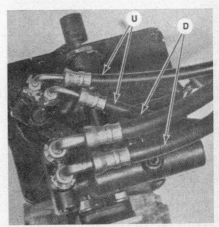

Fig. MR22-34—View of control valve showing location of up circuit hoses (U) and down circuit hoses (D).

MARINER 50, 75, 80 AND 85 HP
(PRIOR TO 1986)

CONDENSED SERVICE DATA

TUNE-UP
Hp/rpm:
Model 50 . . . . .50/4800-5500
Model 75 . . . . .75/5000-5500
Model 80 . . . . .80/4800-5500
Model 85 . . . . .85/4800-5500
Bore:
Model 50 . . . . .2-9/16 in.
(65.09 mm)
Models 75, 80 & 85 . . . . .2-7/8 in.
(73.03 mm)
Stroke:
Model 50 . . . . .2-1/8 in.
(53.97 mm)
Models 75, 80 & 85 . . . . .2-9/16 in.
(65.09 mm)
Displacement:
Model 50 . . . . .44 cu. in.
(721.6 cc)
Models 75, 80 & 85 . . . . .66.6 cu. in.
(1091 cc)
Firing Order 1-3-2-4
Compression at Cranking Speed . . . .*
Spark Plug . . . . .See Text
Ignition . . . . .See Text
Idle Speed . . . . .See Text
Fuel:Oil Ratio 50:1

*Not more than 15 psi (103.5 kPa) variation between cylinders.

SIZES—CLEARANCES
Piston Rings:
End Gap . . . .*
Side Clearance . . . .*
Piston Skirt Clearance . . . .*
Crankshaft Bearing Type:
Top Main Bearing . . . . .Ball Bearing
Main Bearing (2) . . . . .Bushing with Reed Valve
Center Main Bearing .Roller†
Main Bearing (4) . . . . .Bushing with Reed Valve

SIZES—CLEARANCES CONT.
Bottom Main Bearing . . . . .Ball Bearing
Crankpin . . . . .Roller†
Piston Pin Bearing . . . . .Roller†

*Publication not authorized by manufacturer.
†Refer to text for number of rollers at center main bearing, crankpin and piston pin.

TIGHTENING TORQUES
Connecting Rod . . . . .180 in.-lbs.
(20.3 N·m)
Crankcase Screws . . . . .200 in.-lbs.
(22.6 N·m)
Cylinder Cover:
Model 50 . . . . .70 in.-lbs.
(7.9 N·m)
Models 75, 80 & 85 .85 in.-lbs.
(9.6 N·m)
Exhaust Cover:
Model 50 . . . . .200 in.-lbs.
(22.6 N·m)
Models 75, 80 & 85 .250 in.-lbs.
(28.2 N·m)
Flywheel:
Model 50 . . . . .65 ft.-lbs.
(88.4 N·m)
Models 75, 80 & 85 .100 ft.-lbs.
(136 N·m)
Reed Screws:
Model 50 . . . . .30 in.-lbs.
(3.4 N·m)
Models 75, 80 & 85 .25 in.-lbs.
(2.8 N·m)
Spark Plugs . . . . .240 in.-lbs.
(27.1 N·m)
Transfer Port Covers:
Model 50 . . . . .60 in.-lbs.
(6.8 N·m)
Models 75, 80 & 85 .85 in.-lbs.
(9.6 N·m)

LUBRICATION

The power head is lubricated by oil mixed with the fuel. Fuel should be regular leaded, low lead or unleaded gasoline with a minimum pump octane rating of 86. Recommended oil is Quick-silver Formula 50-D Outboard Lubricant. Normal fuel:oil ratio is 50:1; during engine break-in, fuel:oil ratio should be 25:1.

Lower unit gears and bearings are lubricated by oil contained in the gearcase. Recommended oil is Mariner Super Duty Gear Lube. Lubricant is drained by removing vent and drain plugs in the gearcase. Refill through drain plug hole until oil has reached level of vent plug opening, then allow 1 ounce (30 mL) of oil to drain from gearcase. Lower unit oil capacity is 12.5 fl. oz. (370 mL) for 50 hp models or 21 fl. oz. (621 mL) for 75, 80 and 85 hp models.

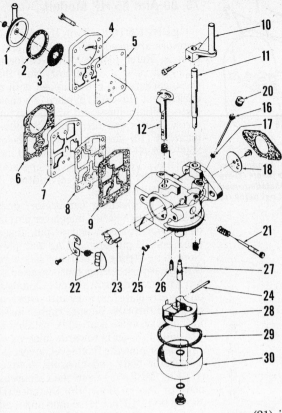

Fig. MR24-1—Exploded view of Mercarb type carburetor used on 50 hp models.

1. Inlet fitting
2. Gasket
3. Screen
4. Cover
5. Diaphragm
6. Gasket
7. Pump body
8. Check valve diaphragm
9. Gasket
10. Throttle lever
11. Throttle shaft
12. Choke shaft
16. Idle tube
17. Gasket
18. Throttle plate
19. Carburetor body
20. Plug
21. Idle mixture screw
22. Choke shutter plates
23. Boost venturi
25. Main jet
26. Inlet needle
27. Main nozzle
28. Float
29. Gasket
30. Float bowl

Open throttle until ignition timing is 7°-9° BTDC, loosen actuator plate screws (S–Fig. MR24-3) and rotate actuator plate (P) so primary pickup arm (A–Fig. MR24-4) just contacts primary cam (C). Retighten actuator plate screws. Open throttle and adjust maximum ignition advance screw (A–Fig. MR24-5) so ignition timing is 32° BTDC. Stop engine.

NOTE: Due to electronic characteristics of ignition system, maximum advance is set at 32° BTDC but ignition will retard to 30° BTDC at 5000 rpm.

Fig. MR24-3—View of actuator plate (P) and secondary pickup adjusting screw (W) on 50 hp models. See text for adjustment.

FUEL SYSTEM

50 HP Models

CARBURETOR. Fifty-horsepower models are equipped with two Mercarb carburetors. Refer to Fig. MR24-1 for exploded view of carburetor.

The carburetor uses a fixed main jet (25). Standard main jet size is 0.055 inch (1.40 mm) for operation below 2500 feet altitude. Initial setting of idle mixture

screw (21) is 1½ turns open. Turning idle mixture screw clockwise will lean the mixture.

To adjust fuel level, remove float bowl and invert carburetor. Measure distance from float to gasket surface as shown in Fig. MR24-2. Float level should be 15/64 to 17/64 inch (6-6.8 mm). Bend float tang (T) to adjust float level. Turn carburetor right side up and check float drop. Float drop should be 1/32 to 1/16 inch (0.8-1.6 mm) measured from float to highest point on main jet (25).

SPEED CONTROL LINKAGE. To synchronize ignition and carburetor opening, connect a power timing light to number 1 (top) spark plug wire. Run engine with outboard in forward gear.

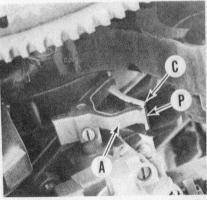

Fig. MR24-4—Primary pickup arm (A) should just contact primary cam (C) at point (P) with 7°-9° BTDC ignition timing.

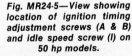

Fig. MR24-2—Float level should be 15/64 to 17/64 inch (6-6.8 mm) from float to gasket surface. Float drop is measured with carburetor upright from top of main jet (25) to float. See text.

Fig. MR24-5—View showing location of ignition timing adjustment screws (A & B) and idle speed screw (I) on 50 hp models.

Open throttle so maximum advance screw (A) just touches boss and adjust actuator plate secondary pickup screw (W – Fig. MR24-3) so screw just touches secondary pickup arm (R – Fig. MR24-6).

To prevent damage in carburetor throttle plate at full throttle, lightly hold carburetor throttle plate in full open position by turning secondary pickup arm (R). Adjust full throttle stop screw (B – Fig. MR24-5) so there is 0.010-0.015 inch (0.25-0.38 mm) clearance between secondary pickup screw (W – Fig. MR24-6) and pickup arm (R) when full throttle stop screw (B – Fig. MR24-5) just touches boss.

Turn idle speed screw (I) to obtain idle speed of 550-600 rpm in forward gear.

REED VALVES. The inlet reed valves are located on the crankshaft second and fourth main bearing assemblies. Each reed valve passes fuel mixture from one of the carburetors to the two adjoining cylinders. The crankshaft must be removed before reed valve units can be serviced.

Reed petals (2 – Fig. MR24-8) should be perfectly flat with no more than 0.007 inch (0.178 mm) clearance between free end of reed petal and seating surface of center main bearing. Reed stop height (A) should be 0.180 inch (4.57 mm). Reed petal seating surface on bearing housing must be smooth and may be refinished on a lapping plate after removing reed stops, reed valves and dowels. Do not attempt to bend or straighten reed petals. Renew petal locating pin if damaged.

When installing reed petals, place the reed petal with the cut-out notch (N) to the left as shown.

FUEL PUMP. A diaphragm type fuel pump is mounted on side of carburetor as shown in Fig. MR24-1. Inspect diaphragms and renew if damaged.

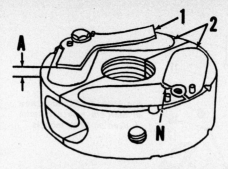

Fig. MR24-8—Intermediate main bearing and reed valve for 50 hp models. Reed petals (2) are right and left hand units. When installing reed petals, place the reed with the cut-out notch (N) on the left as shown.

75, 80 And 85 HP Models

CARBURETOR. Two Mercarb carburetors are used on 75, 80 and 85 h models. Refer to Fig. MR24-10 for a exploded view of carburetor. Note tha these carburetors are equipped with a enrichment valve (24) in place of a chok plate. Initial adjustment of idle mixtur screw (19) is one turn open. Standar main jet (10) size for operation belov 2500 feet (762 m) altitude is 0.090 inc (2.29 mm). Vent jet (4) size for operation below 2500 feet (762 m) altitude i 0.072 inch (1.83 mm).

When overhauling carburetor, driv float pins (16) and fuel inlet lever pin (18 out toward knurled end of pin. Inser plain end of pin first during assembly Note that strong (0.034 in. dia. wire throttle return spring must be used o top carburetor throttle shaft. Numbers on throttle plate (29) must face outwards at closed throttle. Be sure rubber insert in fuel inlet valve seat (6) is installed s flat end of insert is towards inlet valve.

To determine the float level, invert the carburetor body and measure distance (D – Fig. MR24-11) from the carburetor body to base of float (15). Distance (D) should be 11/16 inch (17.5 mm) and is adjusted by bending fuel inlet lever (17 – Fig. MR24-12) within area (A).

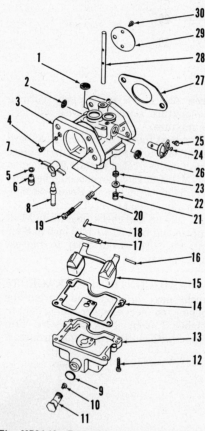

Fig. MR24-10—Exploded view of center bowl type Mercarb carburetor.

1. Welch plug (9/16 inch)
2. Fuel inlet strainer
3. Body
4. Vent jet
5. Gasket
6. Inlet needle & seat assy.
7. Venturi
8. Nozzle
9. Gasket
10. Main jet
11. Main jet plug
12. Screw
13. Float bowl
14. Gasket
15. Float
16. Pin
17. Fuel inlet lever
18. Pin
19. Idle mixture screw
20. Spring
21. Spring
22. Flat washer
23. Rubber seal
24. Enrichment valve assy.
25. Screw & lockwasher
26. Welch plug (7/16 inch)
27. Gasket
28. Throttle shaft
29. Throttle plate
30. Screw

Fig. MR24-11—To determine float level, invert the carburetor body and measure distance (D) from the carburetor body to base of float (15). Distance (D) should be 11/16 inch (17.5 mm).

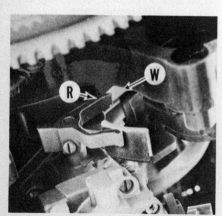

Fig. MR14-6—Adjust full throttle stop screw (B—Fig. MR24-5) so there is 0.010-0.015 inch (0.25-0.38 mm) clearance between secondary pickup arm (R) and screw (W) at full throttle.

Fig. MR24-12—Adjust float level by bending fuel inlet lever (17) within area (A).

Illustrations Courtesy Mariner

SPEED CONTROL LINKAGE.

Check ignition timing pointer alignment as follows: Install a dial indicator gage in number 1 (top) spark plug hole and turn flywheel clockwise until piston is 0.464 inch BTDC. Loosen retaining screw and position timing pointer so that it is aligned with ".464 BTDC" mark on flywheel.

Connect a power timing light to number 1 (top) spark plug wire. Run engine with outboard in forward gear and open throttle until primary cam (B – Fig. MR24-14) just touches throttle lever primary pin (A). Primary cam should contact primary pin at 2°-4° BTDC on models below serial number 4423112 or 2° BTDC to 2° ATDC on models after serial number 4423111. Turn pickup adjustment screw (W – Fig. MR24-15) to obtain desired pickup point. Open throttle and turn maximum advance adjustment screw (M) so spark arm (R) movement will stop at 27° BTDC. Stop engine.

Carburetor throttle plate must not act as stop for wide open throttle. To prevent damage to carburetor, lightly hold carburetor throttle plate in full open

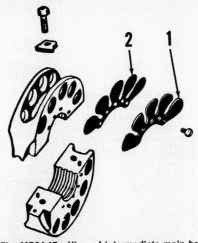

Fig. MR24-17—View of intermediate main bearing and reed valve assembly used on 75, 80 and 85 hp models.

position by turning upper carburetor throttle lever. Adjust full throttle stop screw (T) so there is 0.010-0.015 inch (0.25-0.38 mm) between throttle lever secondary pin (C – Fig. MR24-14) and secondary cam (D) when throttle arm (H – Fig. MR24-15) is in wide open position.

Idle speed should be 550-650 rpm with outboard in forward gear. Turn idle speed screw (1) to adjust idle speed.

REED VALVES. The inlet reed valves are located on the crankshaft second and fourth main bearing assemblies. Each reed valve unit passes fuel mixture from one of the carburetors to the two adjoining cylinders.

Reed petals (2 – Fig. MR24-17) should be perfectly flat with no more than 0.007 inch (0.178 mm) clearance between free end of reed petal and seating surface of

center main bearing. Reed stop height should be 0.162 inch (4.11 mm). If reed petals have indented reed block, then reed block should be renewed. Do not attempt to bend or straighten reed petals.

FUEL PUMP. All models are equipped with a diaphragm type fuel pump mounted on the starboard side of power head. Fuel pressure at idle speed should be 2½-3½ psi (17-24 kPa) while fuel pressure at full throttle should be 4¼-5½ psi (29-36 kPa).

When assembling fuel pump install check valves as shown in Fig. MR24-19 with tips of retainer (3) pointing away from check valves.

IGNITION SYSTEM

These models are equipped with a solid state capacitor discharge ignition system consisting of trigger coils, stator, switch box and ignition coils. The trigger coils are contained in a trigger ring module under the flywheel. Diodes, SCR's and capacitors are contained in the switch box. Switch box, trigger ring module and stator must be serviced as unit assemblies. A wiring diagram is shown in Fig. MR24-21.

Check all wires and connections before troubleshooting ignition circuit. The following test specifications will aid troubleshooting. Resistance between blue and blue/white stator leads should be 5700-8000 ohms. Resistance between red and red/white stator leads should be 56-76 ohms. Resistance between trigger coil brown and white/black leads or trigger coil white and violet leads should be 700-1000 ohms.

Recommended spark plugs are AC V40FFK or Champion L78V.

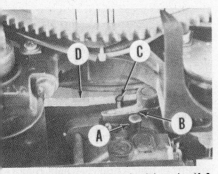

Fig. MR24-14—View of throttle pickup pins (A & C) and cams (B & D) used on 75, 80 and 85 hp models.

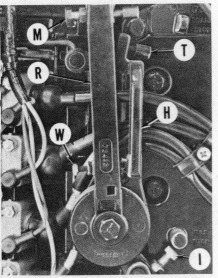

Fig. MR24-15—View of throttle (H) and spark (R) control arms on 75, 80 and 85 hp models.

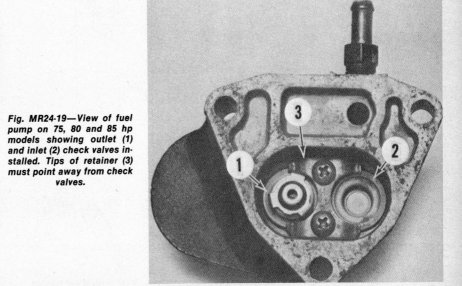

Fig. MR24-19—View of fuel pump on 75, 80 and 85 hp models showing outlet (1) and inlet (2) check valves installed. Tips of retainer (3) must point away from check valves.

COOLING SYSTEM

WATER PUMP. The rubber impeller type water pump is housed in the gearcase housing. The impeller is mounted on and driven by the lower unit drive shaft.

When cooling system problems are encountered, first check the water inlet for plugging or partial stoppage, then if not corrected, remove the gearcase as outlined in LOWER UNIT section and examine the water pump, water tubes and seals.

When assembling, observe the assembly notes, cautions and tightening torques listed in the LOWER UNIT section.

POWER HEAD

REMOVE AND DISASSEMBLE. To remove the power head assembly, first disconnect the battery and remove the top and side cowling. Remove electric starter, then disconnect fuel line, all interfering wires and linkage. Remove the stud nuts which secure the power

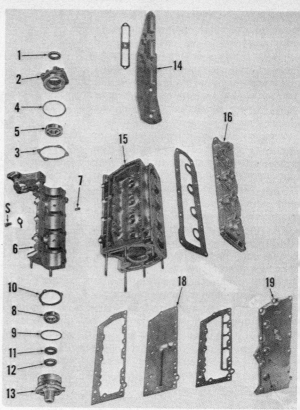

Fig. MR24-23—Exploded view of crankcase and associated parts used on 50 hp models.

S. Main bearing screw
1. Oil seal
2. End cap
3. Shim
4. "O" ring
5. Ball bearing
6. Crankcase half
7. Dowel pins
8. Ball bearing
9. "O" ring
10. Shim
11. Oil seal
12. Oil seal
13. End cap
14. Transfer port cover
15. Cylinder half
16. Cylinder cover
18. Exhaust plate
19. Exhaust cover

head to lower unit then jar power head on exhaust side to loosen gasket. Lift power head from lower unit and install on a suitable stand. Remove flywheel, ignition components, alternator and carburetors. Exhaust manifold cover, cylinder block cover and transfer port covers should be removed for cleaning and inspection.

Remove the main bearing locking bolts from front crankcase half, remove the flange bolts; then remove crankcase front half by inserting screwdriver in the recesses provided on side flanges. Use extra care not to spring the parts or to mar the machined, mating surfaces. Gently tap end caps off crankshaft. The crankcase half (6–Fig. MR24-23 or MR24-24) and cylinder assembly (15) are matched and align bored, and are available only as an assembly.

Crankshaft, pistons, bearings and connecting rods may now be removed for service as outlined in the appropriate following paragraphs. When assembling, follow the procedures outlined in the ASSEMBLY paragraph.

ASSEMBLY. When assembling, the crankcase must be completely sealed against both vacuum and pressure. Exhaust manifold and water passages must be sealed against pressure leakage. Whenever power head is disassembled, it is recommended that all gasket surfaces and machined joints without gaskets be carefully checked for nicks

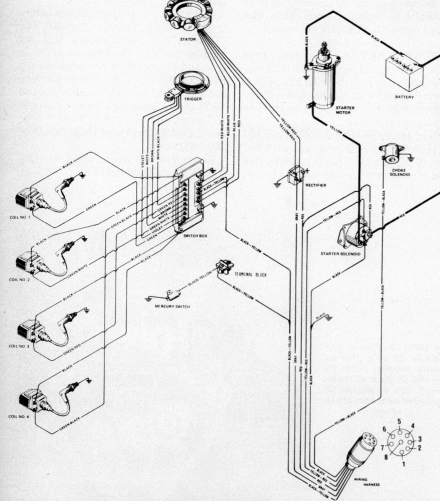

Fig. MR24-21—Wiring diagram for 75 hp and later 80 hp models. Other models are similar.

nd burrs which might interfere with a ight seal. On 75, 80 and 85 hp models, nake certain that threaded holes in ylinder for attaching water jacket over (20 – Fig. MR24-24) are cleaned.

Lubricate all bearing and friction suraces with engine oil. Loose needle bearngs may be held in place during ssembly using a light, nonfibrous rease.

After the crankshaft, connecting rods, istons and main bearings are positioned in the cylinder, check crankshaft nd play. Temporarily install crankshaft nd caps (2 and 13 – Fig. MR24-23 or MR24-24) omitting sealing rings (4 and), but using shims (3 and 10) that were riginally installed. Tighten end cap to ylinder retaining screws. Use a soft ammer to bump crankshaft each way o seat bearings, then measure end play.

To measure end play bump the crankhaft toward top, and measure clearance etween top crankshaft counterweight nd end cap as shown in Fig. MR24-26. Bump crankshaft toward bottom and gain measure clearance between ounterweight and end cap. Subtract irst (minimum) clearance from second learance which will indicate the amount of end play. If end play is not within imits of 0.004-0.012 inch (0.102-0.305 nm) on 75 hp models or 0.008-0.012 inch 0.203-0.305 mm) on all other models, dd or remove shims (3 or 10 – Fig. MR24-23 or MR24-24) as necessary, hen recheck. The crankshaft should be entered by varying the amount of shims etween upper (3) and lower (10) shims stacks. When centering crankshaft, nake certain that end play is correct.

On all models, all of the gasket and sealing surfaces should be lightly and carefully coated with an impervious liquid sealer. Surface must be completely coated, using care that excess sealer does not squeeze out into bearings, crankcase or other passages.

On 75, 80 and 85 hp models, clean the gasket surfaces and threaded holes of the water jacket cover (20 – Fig. MR24-24) and cylinder (15). Coat the first four threads of all screws (22) with Resiweld and allow to set for 10 minutes. Coat gasket surface of water jacket cover and mating surface of cylinder with gasket sealer, then install gasket (21) and water jacket cover (20). Tighten screws (22) evenly from the center outward to a torque of 200 in.-lbs. (22.6 N·m) on early models and 150 in.-lbs. (16.9 N·m) on later models.

On all models, check the assembly by turning the crankshaft after each step to check for binding or locking which might indicate improper assembly. Remove the cause before proceeding. Rotate the crankshaft until each piston ring in turn appears in one of the exhaust or transfer ports, then check by pressing on ring with a blunt tool. Ring should spring back when released; if it does not, a broken or binding ring is indicated, and the trouble should be corrected.

Tighten the crankcase, exhaust cover and cylinder cover cap screws beginning with screws in center of crankcase and working outward. Tightening torques are given in the CONDENSED SERVICE DATA table.

PISTONS, PINS, RINGS AND CYLINDERS. Before detaching connecting rods from crankshaft, make sure that rod and cap are properly identified for correct assembly to each other and in the correct cylinder.

Maximum allowable cylinder bore wear or out-of-round is 0.004 inch (0.102 mm). Worn or slightly damaged, standard size, cylinders may be repaired by boring and honing to fit an oversize piston. Pistons and rings are available in 0.015 inch (0.38 mm) oversize on early models and 0.015 inch (0.38 mm) and 0.030 inch (0.76 mm) oversizes on later models.

Piston rings are interchangeable in the ring grooves and are pinned in place.

Piston pin is pressed in piston bosses and secured with retaining rings. The retaining rings should not be reused. Two types of retaining rings have been used and must NOT be interchanged.

The 50 hp models use "G" rings, while 75, 80 and 85 hp models use "C" type retaining rings. Piston end of connecting rod is fitted with loose needle rollers. Refer to the CONNECTING RODS, BEARINGS AND CRANKSHAFT paragraphs for number of rollers used.

The piston pin needle rollers use the connecting rod bore and the piston pin as bearing races. When assembling, install bearing washers and needle bearings in piston end of connecting rod using light nonfibrous grease to hold them in place. Use a torch lamp or suitable equivalent to heat piston to approximately 135°F (57°C) on early models and 190°F (88°C) on late models, then install and center the piston pin. Special tools are available from manufacturer for installing and centering the piston pin. Piston must be installed so that sharp, vertical side of deflector will be to starboard (intake) side of cylinder block.

Assemble the connecting rod and piston assemblies, together with the main bearing units to the crankshaft; then install the complete assembly in cylinder half of block. Number 2 and number 3 piston should be started into cylinders first. Use the Mariner Ring Compressor Kit (C-91-47844A2), if available; or carefully compress each ring with the fingers if kit is not available. Thoroughly lubricate pistons and rings during assembly.

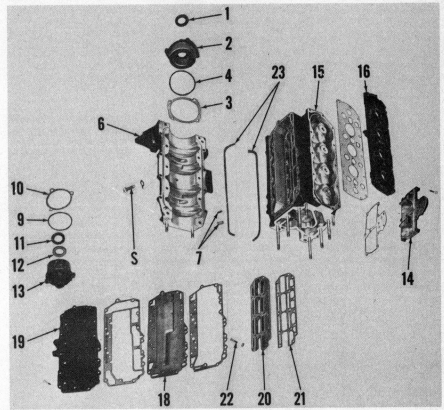

Fig. MR24-24—Exploded view of crankcase and associated parts used on 75, 80 and 85 hp models. Refer to Fig. MR24-23 for parts identification except for: 20. Water jacket cover; 21. Gasket; 22. Screw; 23. Seal strips.

CONNECTING RODS, BEARINGS AND CRANKSHAFT. Upper and lower ends of crankshaft are carried by ball bearings. The second and fourth main bearings (10 – Fig. MR24-25) also contain the inlet reed valves. The third main bearing (13) contains loose needle rollers (15) which ride in a split type outer race (14), held together by a retaining ring (16).

The 50 hp models use 27 loose needle rollers while 75, 80 and 85 hp models use 29 loose needle rollers in small connecting rod end. The crankpin end of connecting rod contains 25 loose needle rollers on 50 hp models. A caged roller bearing is used at crankpin end of connecting rod on 75, 80 and 85 hp models. The 50 hp models use 28 loose needle rollers on single row models and 56 loose needle rollers on double row models in main bearings. The 75, 80 and 85 hp models use 56 loose needle rollers in main bearings.

Check rod for alignment by placing rod on a surface plate and checking with a light. Rod is bent or distorted if 0.002 inch (0.051 mm) feeler gage can be inserted between rod and surface plate.

If bearing surface of rod and cap is rough, scored, worn or shows evidence of overheating, renew the connecting rod. Inspect crankpin and main bearing journals. If scored, out-of-round or worn, renew the crankshaft. Check the crankshaft for straightness using a dial indicator and "V" blocks.

Inspect and adjust the reed valves as outlined in REED VALVE paragraph, and reassemble as outlined in ASSEMBLY paragraph.

MANUAL STARTER

Refer to Fig. MR24-28 for the rewind starter used on manual starting 50 hp motors. Remove the top cowl and the recoil starter assembly from motor. Insert a screwdriver in slot in top of sheave shaft (19) and loosen the left hand thread nut (3). Allow the screwdriver and shaft (19) to turn clockwise until recoil spring unwinds. Pry anchor (22) out of starter handle and remove anchor and handle from rope. Remove nut (3), invert the assembly and remove the parts, making sure that recoil spring (7) remains in housing recess as pulley (10) is removed. Remove spring (7) and allow it to unwind slowly. Care must be taken during spring removal to prevent injury.

Lubricate the parts with Multipurpose Lubricant, and assemble by reversing the disassembly procedure. Install spring guide bushing (8) with chamfered end toward pulley (10). Make sure that pawls (12) are all installed the same way, with radius to outside and identification mark away from pulley (10). Install retainer (15) with cup end out and position washer (16) and wave washer (17) in cup. Make certain that tang on spring retainer (6) engages slot in sheave shaft (19). Position starter with end of shaft (19) through housing (5) and install lockwasher (4) and nut (3). Pull free end of recoil rope through starter housing and

Fig. MR24-26—Refer to text for method of checking crankshaft end play. The crankshaft should be centered in the cylinder block.

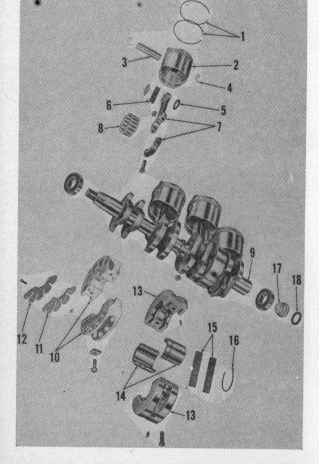

Fig. MR24-25—Exploded view of crankshaft and associated parts on 75, 80 and 85 hp models. Model 50 hp is similar.

1. Piston rings
2. Piston
3. Piston pin
4. Retainers
5. Bearing washers
6. Needle rollers
7. Connecting rod
8. Caged needle bearing
9. Crankshaft
10. Intermediate main bearing
11. Reed petals
12. Reed stop
13. Main bearing
14. Outer race
15. Needle rollers
16. Retaining ring
17. Seal retainer
18. Seal

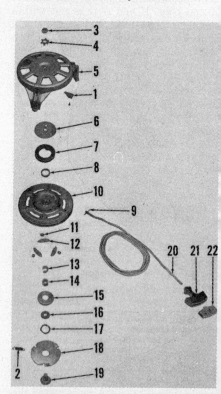

Fig. MR24-28—Exploded view of rewind starter assembly typical of the type used on 50 hp models.

1. Rope guide	12. Pawls
2. Spring	13. Bushing
3. Nut	14. Spacer
4. Lockwasher	15. Retainer
5. Starter housing	16. Washer
6. Retainer	17. Wave washer
7. Rewind spring	18. Plate
8. Bushing	19. Sheave shaft
9. Rope retaining pin	20. Rope
10. Pulley	21. Handle
11. Wave washers	22. Anchor

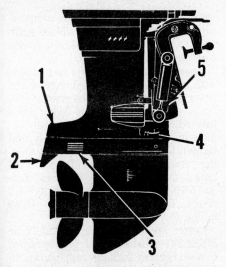

Fig. MR24-30—To remove the lower unit gearcase assembly, remove the attaching screws and stud nuts for position indicated.

install handle (21) and anchor (22). Turn pulley shaft (19) counterclockwise until handle is pulled against starter housing, plus an additional 1¼ turns; then tighten nut (3). Pull cord out and check for sticking and full turn.

ELECTRICAL SYSTEM

Refer to Fig. MR24-21 for a typical wiring diagram. Note the following cautions when servicing electrical components:

DO NOT reverse battery connections. Battery negative (−) terminal is grounded.

DO NOT "spark" battery connections to check polarity.

DO NOT disconnect battery cables while engine is running.

DO NOT crank engine if ignition switch boxes are not grounded to engine.

LOWER UNIT

PROPELLER AND DRIVE CLUTCH. Protection for the motor is built into a special cushioning clutch in the propeller hub. No adjustment is possible on the propeller or clutch. Various pitch propellers are available and propeller should be selected to provide full throttle engine operation within rpm range listed in CONDENSED SERVICE DATA table at the beginning of section. Propellers other than those designed for the motor must not be used.

R&R AND OVERHAUL. Most service on lower unit can be performed by detaching gearcase housing from driveshaft housing. To remove housing, remove plastic plug and Allen screw from location (1 – Fig. MR24-30).

Remove trim tab (2) and screw from under trim tab. Remove stud nut from location (3), and stud nut (5) if so equipped then withdraw the lower unit gearcase assembly.

NOTE: Do not lose plunger or spring (67 & 68—Fig. M24-32) on 50 hp models.

Remove plugs and drain oil from housing, then secure gearcase in a soft jawed vise, with propeller up. Wedge a piece of wood between propeller and antiventilation plate, remove propeller nut, then remove propeller.

Disassemble gearcase by removing gearcase housing cover nut (61 – Fig. MR24-32 or MR24-34). Clamp outer end of propeller shaft in a soft jawed vise and remove the gearcase by tapping with a rubber mallet. Be careful not to lose key (59) or shims (47). Forward gear (40) will remain in housing. Withdraw propeller shaft from bearing carrier (56) and reverse gear (46).

Clamp bearing carrier (56) in a soft jawed vise and remove reverse gear (46) and bearing (49) with an internal expanding puller and slide hammer. Remove and discard propeller shaft rear seals (58).

To remove dog clutch (43) from propeller shaft, remove retaining ring (44). Insert cam follower (8) in hole in shaft and apply only enough pressure on end of cam follower to remove spring pressure, then push out pin (42) with a small punch. The pin passes through drilled holes in dog clutch and operates in slotted holes in propeller shaft.

To disassemble the drive shaft and associated parts, reposition gearcase in vise with drive shaft projecting upward.

Remove rubber slinger (11), water pump body (16), impeller (19) and impeller drive key (20). Remove flushing screw and withdraw remainder of water pump parts. Clamp upper end of drive shaft in a soft jawed vise, remove pinion retaining nut or screw (37); then tap gearcase off drive shaft and bearing. Note position and thickness of shims (30 and 30A) on drive shaft upper bearing. On all models, mesh position of pinion is controlled by shims (30) placed underneath the bearing. On models with ball type upper bearing, shims (30A) control shaft end play. The shims are identical but should not be interchanged or mixed, except to adjust mesh position of drive pinion.

After drive shaft has been removed, forward gear (40) and bearing cone can be withdrawn. Use an internal expanding type puller to withdraw bearing cup if removal is required. Remove and save shim pack (38).

Shift shaft (5) and cam (7) can be removed after removing forward gear and unscrewing bushing (3) from gearcase housing.

If gear wear was abnormal or if any parts that affect gear alignment were renewed, check and adjust gear mesh as follows: Install forward gear (40 – Fig. MR24-32 or MR24-34) and bearing (39) using shims (38) that were originally installed. Position shims (30) that were originally installed at bottom of bearing bore. On 50 hp models (32 – Fig. MR24-32) install bearing cup (32) in housing bore against shims (30). On all models, position drive pinion (35 – Fig. MR24-32 or MR24-34) in housing and insert drive shaft (33), with bearing (32)

Fig. MR24-32—Exploded view of gearcase assembly used on 50 hp models. Components (63 & 65) are not used on later models. Two seals (58) are used on later models. Shim (47) is not used on later models. Refer to Fig. MR24-34 for parts identification.

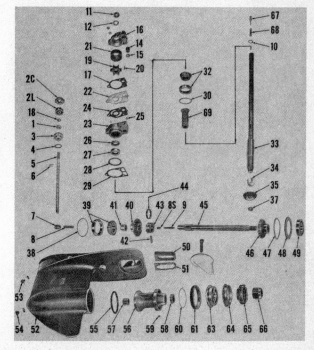

installed, into housing, bearing (34) and gear (35). On 75, 80 and 85 hp models, the ball bearing must be firmly seated in housing bore. On all models, install retaining screw or nut (37). Coat gears (35 and 40) with bearing blue and check mesh position. On 50 hp models, it will be necessary to push down on end of drive shaft while checking mesh position. On all models, if gears do not mesh in center of teeth, add or remove shims (30) under bearing as necessary. After setting mesh position, check backlash between teeth of gears (35 and 40). Backlash should be 0.003-0.005 inch (0.076-0.127 mm) for 50 hp models, 0.014-0.016 inch (0.356-0.406 mm) for 85 hp models and 0.008-0.012 inch (0.203-0.305 mm) for 75 and 80 hp models. To increase clearance (backlash), remove part of shim stack (38) behind bearing cup. If gears are too loose, add shims. After changing thickness of shims (38), gears should be recoated with bearing blue and mesh position should be rechecked. Install bearing (49), thrust washer (48) and reverse gear (46) in bearing carrier (56). To check reverse gear (46) backlash on all early models, install bearing carrier and gear assembly using shims (47) that

were originally installed. If backlash is not within limits of 0.003-0.005 inch (0.076-0.127 mm) for 50 hp models and 0.006-0.008 inch (0.152-0.203 mm) for 80 and 85 hp models, add or remove shims (47) as required. Adding shims at (47) increases backlash (clearance).

When reassembling, long splines on shift rod (5 – Fig. MR24-32 or MR24-34) should be toward top. Shift cam (7) is installed with notches up and toward rear. Assemble shifting parts (9, 8S, 43, 42 and 44) into propeller shaft (45). Pin (42) should be through hole in slide (8S). Position follower (8) in end of propeller shaft and insert shaft into bearing (41) and forward gear. Install the reverse gear and bearing carrier assembly using new seals (55 and 58). Lip of inner seal (58) should face in and lip of outer seal (58) should face propeller (out).

On 75, 80 and 85 hp models, install shims (30A) above bearing and position new gasket (29) and water pump base (23) on housing. Add shims (30A) until the water pump base stands out slightly from gasket, then measure clearance between gasket and water pump base with a feeler gage. Remove shims (30A) equal to 0.002-0.003 inch (0.051-0.076 mm) less than clearance measured. When

water pump is tightened down, compression of a new gasket (29) will be sufficient to hold bearing (32) in position with zero clearance.

Upper oil seal (26) should be installed with lips facing up (toward engine) and lower oil seal (27) should be pressed into water pump base with lips facing down toward propeller shaft. Install remainder of water pump assembly and tighten the screw or nuts to the following recommended torque. Torque 1/4-28 nuts to 24-30 in.-lbs. (2.7-3.4 N·m). Torque 5/16-24 nuts to 35-40 in.-lbs. (3.9-4.5 N·m). Torque 1/4-20 screws to 15-20 in.-lbs. (1.7-2.2 N·m).

Lower spacer (2L – Fig. MR24-32 or MR24-34) is installed with groove down. Install reverse locking cam shown in Fig. MR24-35 with high part of cam aligned as shown with unit in neutral. Push rod guide (2G – Fig. MR24-34) is located in drive shaft housing of all models.

Before attaching gearcase housing to the drive shaft housing, make certain that shaft cam (7 – Fig. MR24-32 or MR24-34) and the shift lever (on motor) are in forward gear position on early models and neutral position on late models. In forward gear position, shift shaft (5) should be in clockwise position (viewed from top end of shaft). Complete assembly by reversing disassembly procedure.

On 50 hp models, make certain that spring (68 – Fig. MR24-32) and plunger (67) are positioned before attaching gearcase to drive shaft housing.

POWER TILT/TRIM

Non-Integral Type

FLUID. Recommended fluid is SAE 10W-30 or 10W-40 automotive oil. With outboard in full up position, oil level should reach bottom of fill plug hole threads. Do not overfill.

BLEEDING. To bleed air from hydraulic system, position outboard at full tilt and engage tilt rock lever. Without disconnecting hoses, remove hydraulic trim cylinders. Be sure fluid reservoir is full and remains so during bleeding operation. Remove down circuit bleed screw (D – Fig. MR24-40) and "O" ring. Press "IN" control button for a few seconds, release button and wait approximately one minute. Repeat until expelled oil is air-free. Install "O" ring and bleed screw (D) and repeat procedure on opposite cylinder. Place cylinder in a horizontal position so bleed port (P – Fig. MR24-41) is up and remove up circuit bleed screw (U). Press "UP" and "UP/OUT" control buttons for a few seconds, release buttons and wait approx-

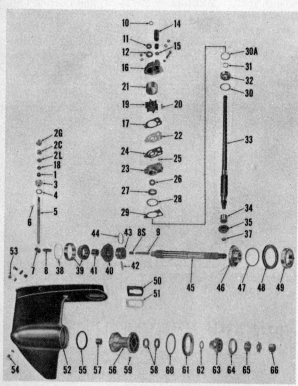

15. Nylon washer
16. Water pump body
17. Gasket
18. Rubber washer
19. Impeller
20. Drive key
21. Insert
22. Plate
23. Pump base
24. Gasket
25. Dowel
26. Oil seal
27. Spring loaded oil seal
28. "O" ring
29. Gasket
30 & 30A. Shims
31. Snap ring
32. Ball bearing
33. Drive shaft
34. Roller bearing
35. Drive pinion
37. Nut
38. Shim
39. Tapered roller bearing
40. Forward gear
41. Roller bearing
42. Cross pin
43. Dog clutch
44. Retaining ring
45. Propeller shaft
46. Reverse gear
47. Shim
48. Thrust washer
49. Ball bearing
50. Exhaust tube seal
51. Support plate
52. Gear housing
53. Vent screw
54. Filler screw
55. "O" ring
56. Bearing carrier
57. Roller bearing
58. Oil seals
59. Key
60. Washer
61. Gear housing cover
62. Thrust washer
63. Thrust hub
64. Cupped washer
65. Splined washer
66. Propeller nut

Fig. MR24-34 — Exploded view of gearcase assembly used on 75, 80 and 85 hp models. Shim (47) is not used on later models.

1. Oil seal
2C. Reverse locking cam
2G. Push rod guide
2L. Lower spacer
3. Bushing
4. "O" ring
5. Shift shaft
6. Snap ring
7. Shift cam
8. Cam follower
8S. Slide
9. Spring
10. "O" ring
11. Rubber ring (slinger)
12. Oil seal
14. Seal

mately one minute. Repeat until expelled oil is air-free. Install "O" ring and bleed screw (U) and repeat procedure on opposite cylinder. Reinstall cylinders.

ADJUST TRIM LIMIT SWITCH.

Operate trim control so outboard is in full down position. Press "UP/OUT" or "UP" control button and hold until pump motor stops. Outboard should tilt up and stop so there is ½ inch (12.7 mm) overlap (L–Fig. MR24-42) between swivel bracket flange (W) and clamp bracket flange (M). Pull up on lower unit to remove slack when checking overlap (L). Note that if cylinder rods enter cylinders more than an additional ⅛ inch (3.17 mm), that hydraulic system should be bled of air as outlined in BLEEDING section. If overlap (L) is incorrect, loosen retainer screw (R–Fig.

MR24-43) then turn adjusting nut (N) counterclockwise to increase overlap or clockwise to decrease overlap. Retighten retainer screw (R) and recheck adjustment.

PRESSURE TEST. To check hydraulic system pressure, disconnect four hoses attached to control valve as shown in Fig. MR24-44; small hoses are for up circuit while large hoses are for down circuit. Connect a pressure gage to one up circuit port (small) of control valve and another pressure gage to one down circuit port (large). Screw plugs into remaining ports. Check fluid reservoir and fill if necessary. Operate trim control in up direction and note pressure gage reading. Minimum pressure should be 3500 psi (24.1 MPa) on new pumps with a red sleeve on wires or 3200-3500 psi (22.0-24.1 MPa) minimum on used pumps with red sleeve on wires. Minimum pressure on all other new pumps is 3000 psi (20.7 MPa) while minimum

pressure on all other used pumps is 2700-3000 psi (18.6-20.7 MPa). Release trim control button. Pressure will drop slightly after stabilizing but should not drop faster than 100 psi (690 kPa) every 15 seconds. Operate trim control in down direction and note pressure gage reading. Minimum pressure is 500-1000 psi (3.4-6.9 MPa). Release trim control button. Pressure will drop slightly after stabilizing but should not drop faster than 100 psi (690 kPa) every 15 seconds. If pressure is normal, inspect trim cylinders and hoses for leakage. If pressure is abnormal, install a good control valve and recheck pressure. If pressure remains abnormal, install a new pump body.

Fig. MR24-43—Loosen retainer screw (R) and turn trim limit adjusting nut (N) to adjust trim limit switch.

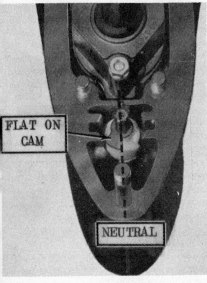

Fig. MR24-35—View of reverse lock cam with a single cam. Cam must be in position shown when lower unit (and shift shaft) is in neutral.

Fig. MR24-41—View showing location of up circuit bleed screw (U) and bleed port (P).

Fig. MR24-40—View showing location of down circuit bleed screw (D) and grease fitting (F).

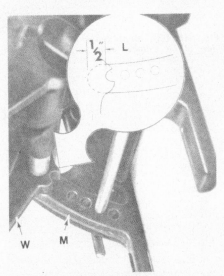

Fig. MR24-42—Overlap (L) between swivel bracket flange (W) and clamp bracket flange (M) should be ½ inch (12.7 mm).

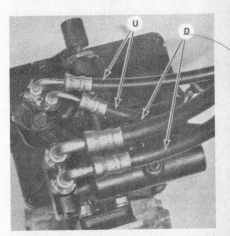

Fig. MR24-44—View of control valve showing location of up circuit hoses (U) and down circuit hoses (D).

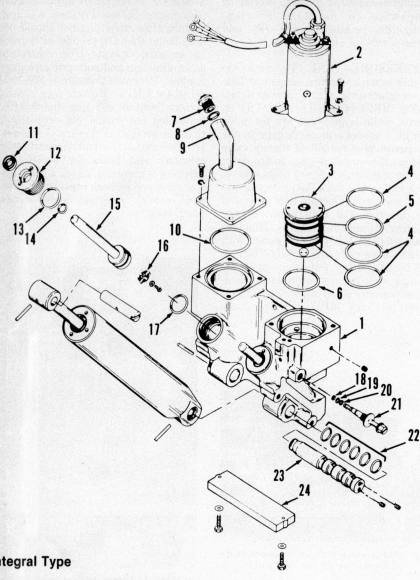

Fig. MR24-50—Exploded view of integral type power tilt/trim system

1. Manifold
2. Electric motor
3. Pump assy.
4. "O" rings (2.614 in. [66.40 mm] ID)
5. "O" rings (2.739 in. [69.57 mm] ID)
6. "O" rings (2.739 in. [69.57 mm] ID)
7. Fill plug
8. "O" ring (0.583 in. [14.81 mm] ID)
9. Reservoir cover
10. Seal ring
11. Seal
12. Cap
13. "O" ring (1.475 in. [37.47 mm] ID)
14. "O" ring (0.612 in. [15.54 mm] ID)
15. Trim piston & rod
16. Strainer
17. "O" ring (1.248 in. [31.70 mm] ID)
18. "O" ring (0.114 in. [2.90 mm] ID)
19. "O" ring (0.208 in. [5.28 mm] ID)
20. "O" ring (0.239 in. [6.07 mm] ID)
21. Manual release valve
22. "O" rings (0.989 in. [25.12 mm] ID)
23. Shaft
24. Anode plate

Integral Type

FLUID AND BLEEDING. Recommended fluid is Dexron II or Type AF automatic transmission fluid. Remove fill plug (7 – Fig. MR24-50) and fill reservoir until fluid is visible in fill tube with the outboard motor in the full-up position.

The hydraulic circuit is self-bleeding as the tilt/trim system is operated through several cycles. After servicing system, be sure to check reservoir level after filling and operating.

HYDRAULIC TESTING. The system can be checked by connecting a 5000 psi (34.5 MPa) test gage to the UP (U – Fig. MR24-52) and DOWN (D – Fig. MR24-53) ports. Prior to connecting test gage, place outboard motor in the full-up position and engage tilt lock lever. Unscrew reservoir fill plug and rotate manual release valve (21 – Fig. MR24-52) three to four turns counterclockwise to release pressure on system.

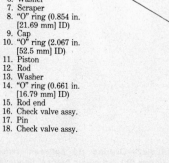

Fig. MR24-51—Exploded view of tilt cylinder components.

1. "O" ring (0.307 in. [7.79 mm] ID)
2. Cup
3. "O" ring (1.957 in. [49.71 mm] ID)
4. Cylinder
5. Circlip
6. Washer
7. Scraper
8. "O" ring (0.854 in. [21.69 mm] ID)
9. Cap
10. "O" ring (2.067 in. [52.5 mm] ID)
11. Piston
12. Rod
13. Washer
14. "O" ring (0.661 in. [16.79 mm] ID)
15. Rod end
16. Check valve assy.
17. Pin
18. Check valve assy.

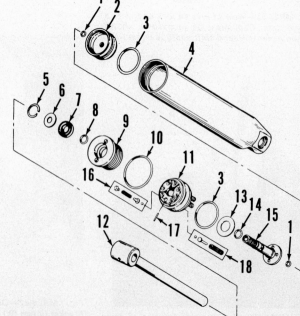

Remove UP or DOWN Allen head test port plug and connect test gage with suitable adapter and hose. Install fill plug and rotate manual release valve clockwise until seated. System pressure when testing at UP (U) port should be a minimum of 1300 psi (8.9 MPa). System pressure when testing at DOWN (D–Fig. MR24-53) port should be a minimum of 500 psi (3.5 MPa). Release pressure on system as previously outlined prior to removing test gage. Reinstall Allen head plug.

OVERHAUL. Refer to Fig. MR24-50 for an exploded view of manifold and trim cylinder components, and Fig. MR24-51 for an exploded view of tilt cylinder components. Special Mercury socket 91-44487A1 and a spanner wrench is required to service trim and tilt cylinders. Keep all components clean and away from contamination. Keep components separated and label if needed for correct reassembly. Note "O" ring sizes as stated in legends of Figs. MR24-50 and MR24-51. Lubricate all

Fig. MR24-52—Release pressure on system, then remove Allen head plug (U) and install a 5000 psi (34.5 MPa) test gage with a suitable adapter and hose to test system pressure when operated in the "UP" direction. View identifies location of manual release valve (21).

Fig. MR24-53—Release pressure on system, then remove Allen head plug (D) and install a 5000 psi (34.5 MPa) test gage with a suitable adapter and hose to test system pressure when operated in the "DOWN" direction.

"O" rings or seal lips with Dexron II or Type AF automatic transmission fluid during assembly.

MARINER 90, 115 AND 140 HP
(PRIOR TO 1986)

CONDENSED SERVICE DATA

TUNE-UP
Hp/rpm:
Model 90 ....90/4500-5000
Model 115 ....115/5000-5500
Model 140 ....140/5300-5800
Bore ....2-7/8 in.
(73.03 mm)
Stroke ....2-9/16 in.
(65.09 mm)
Displacement ....99.8 cu. in.
(1635 cc)
Compression at Cranking Speed ....*
Firing Order 1-4-5-2-3-6
Ignition Type ....Breakerless
Spark Plug ....See Text
Idle Speed:
Model 90 (in gear)...................500-600 rpm
Models 115 & 140 (in gear)..........550-600 rpm
Fuel:Oil Ratio 50:1

*Not more than 15 psi (103.5 kPa) variation between cylinders.

SIZES—CLEARANCES
Piston Rings:
End Gap...*
Side Clearance....................................*
Piston Skirt Clearance.............................*
Crankshaft Bearing Type:
Top Main Bearing ....Ball Bearing
Main Bearing (2) ....Bushing with Reed Valve
Main Bearing (3) ....Roller
Center Main Bearing ....Bushing with Reed Valve

SIZES—CLEARANCES CONT.
Main Bearing (5) ....Roller
Main Bearing (6) ....Bushing with Reed Valve
Bottom Main Bearing ....Ball Bearing
Crankpin ....Roller
Piston Pin Bearing:
Type ....Roller
Number of Rollers..........................29

**Publication not authorized by manufacturer.

TIGHTENING TORQUES
Connecting Rod ....180 in.-lbs.
(20.3 N·m)
Crankcase Screws ....200 in.-lbs.
(22.6 N·m)
Cylinder Cover ....85 in.-lbs.
(9.6 N·m)
Exhaust Cover ....250 in.-lbs.
(28.2 N·m)
Flywheel Nut ....100 ft.-lbs.
(136 N·m)
Reed Screws ....25 in.-lbs.
(2.8 N·m)
Spark Plugs ....240 in.-lbs.
(27.1 N·m)
Transfer Port Covers ....85 in.-lbs.
(9.6 N·m)
Water Jacket Cover:
Early Models ....200 in.-lbs.
(22.6 N·m
Late Models ....150 in.-lbs.
(16.9 N·m)

LUBRICATION

The power head is lubricated by oil mixed with the fuel. Fuel should be regular leaded, low lead or unleaded gasoline with a minimum pump octane rating of 86. Recommended oil is Quick-silver Formula 50-D Outboard Lubri-cant. Normal fuel:oil ratio is 50:1; during engine break-in, fuel:oil ratio should be 25:1.

Lower unit gears and bearings are lubricated by oil contained in the gear-case. Recommended oil is Mariner Super Duty Gear Lube. Lubricant is drained by removing vent and drain plugs in the gearcase. Refill through drain plug hole until oil has reached level of vent plug. Then allow 1 ounce (30 mL) to drain from gearcase.

FUEL SYSTEM

CARBURETOR. Three "Back Drag" type carburetors are used on all 6-cylinder motors. Refer to Fig. MR26-1

Illustrations Courtesy Mariner

or exploded view of caburetor typical of type used on all models. Initial setting for the idle mixture screw (12) is one turn open from the closed position. Run motor until operating temperature is reached, then shift to forward gear and allow motor to run at idle speed. Slowly turn idle mixture screw (12) out (counterclockwise) until motor runs unevenly (loads up). Turn needle in (clockwise) until motor picks up speed and again runs evenly and continue turning until motor slows down and misses. Needle should be set between the two extremes. Turning screw (12) in (clockwise) leans the mixture. Slightly rich idle mixture is more desirable than too lean.

NOTE: Mixture adjustment should not be attempted in neutral.

Standard main jet (13) size is 0.070 inch (1.78 mm) on 90 hp models, 0.072 inch (1.83 mm) on 115 hp models below serial number 5050763, 0.074 inch (1.88 mm) on 115 hp models serial number 5050763 and above, 0.080 inch (2.03 mm) on 140 hp models below serial number 5327663 and 0.074 inch (1.88 mm) on 140 hp models serial number 5327663 and above for operation below 2500 feet (762 m) altitude. Standard

vent jet (V – Fig. MR26-2) size is 0.092 inch (2.34 mm) on 90 hp models, 0.092 inch (2.34 mm) on 115 hp models below serial number 5050763, 0.096 inch (2.44 mm) on 115 hp models serial number 5050763 and above, 0.092 inch (2.34 mm) on 140 hp models below serial number 5327663 and 0.090 inch (2.29 mm) on 140 hp models serial number 5327663 and above for operation below 2500 feet (762 m) altitude. Other jet sizes are available for adjusting the calibration for altitude or other special conditions.

To determine the float level, invert bowl cover (1 – Fig. MR26-3) with inlet needle and seat (5) primary lever (6) and secondary lever (7) installed. Measure distance (A) from carburetor body surface to top of secondary lever (7). Distance (A) should be 13/32 inch (10.32 mm). Adjust distance (A) by bending curved end of primary lever (6). Turn bowl cover (1 – Fig. MR26-4) upright and measure distance (D) between primary lever (6) and end of secondary lever (7). Distance (D) should be ¼ inch (6.4 mm). Bend tab (T) to adjust. The contact spring located in center of float (9 – Fig. MR26-1) should extend 3/32 inch (2.38 mm) above top of float. Check to see if spring has been stretched or damaged.

SPEED CONTROL LINKAGE. The speed control linkage must be synchronized to advance the ignition timing and open the carburetor throttles in a precise manner. Because the two actions are interrelated, it is important to check the complete system following the sequence outlined in the following paragraphs.

Models With Distributor. Refer to the special precautions listed in the IGNITION section before servicing these motors. Incorrect servicing procedures can damage the ignition system.

NOTE: Do not disconnect any part of the ignition system while engine is running or while checking the speed control linkage adjustments.

Connect a power timing light to number 1 (top) spark plug wire. Mount motor in test tank and start engine with timing light installed. Slowly advance speed control until 4°-6° BTDC throttle pickup timing marks are aligned.

Timing grid is marked on cowl support bracket and three punch marks on flywheel are used as timing mark on these models. A white dot is painted on top side of flywheel adjacent to three timing dots.

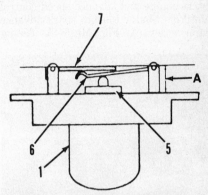

Fig. MR26-3—Distance (A) should be 13/32 inch (10.32 mm). Refer to text for adjustment procedure and Fig. MR26-1 for parts identification.

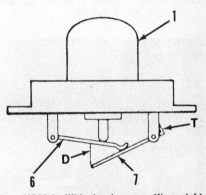

Fig. MR26-4—With bowl cover (1) upright, distance (D) between primary lever (6) and end of secondary lever (7) should be ¼ inch (6.4 m). Bend tab (T) to adjust.

Fig. MR26-6—View of throttle pickup cams and lever typical of models equipped with a distributor. Primary pickup should occur at (1) and secondary pickup at (2). Refer to text for adjustment.

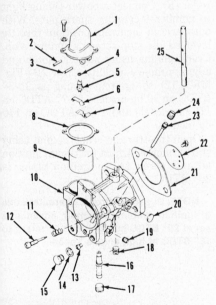

Fig. MR26-1—Exploded view of typical carburetor used on all models. A different cover (1) with a fuel strainer located under the cover is used on some early models.

1. Cover
2. Pin
3. Pin
4. Gasket
5. Inlet needle & seat
6. Primary lever
7. Secondary lever
8. Gasket
9. Float
10. Body
11. Spring
12. Idle mixture screw
13. Main jet
14. Gasket
15. Plug
16. Main nozzle
17. Plug
18. Spring
19. Plug
20. Welch plug
21. Gasket
22. Throttle plate
23. Idle tube
24. Plug
25. Throttle shaft

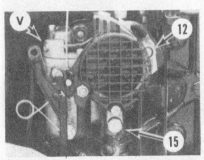

Fig. MR26-2—View showing vent jet (V), idle mixture screw (12) and main jet access plug (15).

The primary cam on the throttle pickup plate should just contact the primary pickup lever as shown at (1 – Fig. MR26-6) when the speed control is advanced to 4°-6° BTDC pickup position. If clearance at (1) is not 0-0.005 inch (0-0.13 mm), loosen the two attaching screws (P – Fig. MR26-7) and move the throttle pickup plate. Recheck pickup point after tightening the two attaching screws.

To check maximum spark advance, start engine and advance speed control until distributor touches spark advance stop screw (A – Fig. MR26-8). Timing

Fig. MR26-7—View of secondary pickup adjusting screws (S) and primary pickup plate attaching screws (P) typical of models equipped with a distributor.

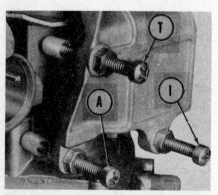

Fig. MR26-8—View showing location of maximum advance screw (A), idle speed screw (I) and throttle stop screw (T) on models equipped with a distributor.

Fig. MR26-9—View showing location of idle stabilizer module (M) used on some models.

light should indicate full spark advance at 21° BTDC. Turn spark advance stop screw to adjust full advance timing if necessary.

Secondary throttle pickup should be checked after maximum spark advance is adjusted. With engine stopped, advance speed controls until distributor is just touching spark advance stop screw. Secondary pickup on throttle cam should be just touching secondary pickup on carburetor cluster (2 – Fig. MR26-6) at this point. Turn throttle pickup screw (S – Fig. MR26-7) to adjust secondary throttle pickup.

Maximum throttle stop screw (T – Fig. MR26-8) should be adjusted so throttles are fully opened at maximum speed position of speed control. Linkage should have a small amount of free play at maximum speed position to prevent binding.

Adjust idle speed screw (I) so idle speed is 500-600 rpm on 90 hp models and 550-650 rpm on 115 and 140 hp models with outboard in gear.

Models Without Distributor. Refer to special precautions listed in the IGNITION section before servicing these motors. Incorrect servicing procedures can damage the ignition system.

Fig. MR26-10—View of idle speed screw (I) on models without a distributor.

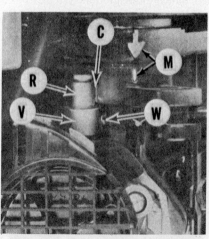

Fig. MR26-11—View of pickup cam (C) and throttle roller (R) on models without a distributor.

C. Pickup cam
M. Idle speed marks
R. Throttle roller
V. Carburetor lever
W. Screw

NOTE: Do not disconnect any part of the ignition system while engine is running or while checking the speed control linkage adjustment.

Check ignition timing pointer alignment as follows: Install a dial indicator gage in number 1 (top) spark plug hole and turn flywheel clockwise until piston is 0.464 inch (12 mm) BTDC. Loosen retaining screw and position timing pointer so it is aligned with ".464 BTDC" mark on flywheel.

If engine is equipped with an idle stabilizer module (M – Fig. MR26-9), disconnect white/black module wire from switch box terminal. Tape end of wire to prevent grounding. Reconnect other white/black wire between switch boxes to switch box terminal. Remove all spark plugs except number 1 (top) cylinder spark plug to prevent engine starting. Detach throttle cable barrel from retainer of cable anchor bracket. Adjust idle stop screw (I – Fig. MR26-10) so idle marks (M – Fig. MR26-11) on throttle cam and bracket are aligned as shown; retighten stop screw locknut. Loosen screw (W) in top carburetor lever (V). Hold idle stop screw (I – Fig. MR26-10) against stop then turn carburetor lever (V – Fig. MR26-11) so throttle valves are completely closed and cam (C) just contacts roller (R). Connect a power timing light to number 1 cylinder spark plug. With outboard in neutral, position throttle lever so idle stop screw is against stop. Crank engine using starter motor and adjust primary pickup screw (P – Fig. MR26-12) so ignition timing is 1°-3° BTDC on 90 hp models, 5°-7° ATDC on 115 hp models and 4°-6° ATDC on 140 hp models.

Open throttle and crank engine using starter motor. Adjust maximum ignition advance screw (A) so ignition timing is 20° BTDC.

NOTE: Due to electronic characteristics of ignition system, maximum advance is set at 20° BTDC but ignition will retard to 18° BTDC at high engine speed.

Fig. MR26-12—Adjust primary pickup screw (P) and maximum advance screw (A) on models without distributor as outlined in text.

Without engine running, move throttle lever to maximum throttle position and adjust full throttle stop screw (T–Fig. MR26-9) so there is 0.010-0.015 inch (0.25-0.38 mm) clearance between roller (R–Fig. MR26-11) and cam (C). Be sure carburetor throttle plates are not acting as stops.

Reconnect idle stabilizer module wire to switch box. Install throttle cable barrel in retainer while adjusting barrel so it fits into retainer and places a very light preload on throttle lever against idle speed screw. Excessive throttle cable preload will result in difficult shifting from forward to neutral.

Adjust idle speed screw (I–Fig. MR26-10) so idle speed is 500-600 rpm on 90 hp models and 550-650 rpm on 115 and 140 hp models with outboard in gear.

REED VALVES. The inlet reed valves are located on the crankshaft second, fourth and sixth main bearings. Each reed valve unit passes fuel mixture from one of the carburetors to the two adjoining cylinders.

Reed petals (2–Fig. MR26-14) should be perfectly flat and have no more than 0.007 inch (0.178 mm) clearance between free end of reed petal seating surface of center main bearing. The reed stop (1) must be carefully adjusted to 0.162 inch (4.11 mm). This clearance is measured between end of stop and seating surface of reed plate. Seating surface of bearing must be smooth and flat, and may be refinished on a lapping plate after removing reed stops, reed valves and dowels. Do not attempt to bend or straighten a reed petal to modify performance or to salvage a damaged reed. Never install a bent reed. Lubricate the reed valve units with "Quicksilver" Multipurpose Lubricant or a light distributor cam grease when reassembling.

FUEL PUMP. A diaphragm type fuel pump is used. Pressure and vacuum pulsations from the crankcases alternate to pull fuel from the supply tank and supply the carburetor. Most of the work is performed by the main supply chamber (5–Fig. MR26-16). Vacuum in the crankcase pulls the diaphragm (2) downward causing fuel to be drawn through inlet line (8), past inlet check valve (7) into main pump chamber (5). The alternate pressure forces diaphragm out and fuel leaves the chamber through outlet check valve (6). The booster pump chamber (3) serves to dampen the action of the larger, main pump chamber (5), and increase the maximum potential fuel flow.

When overhauling the fuel pump, renew all defective or questionable parts.

When assembling fuel pump, install check valves as shown in Fig. MR26-17 with tips of retainer (R) pointing away from check valves. Fuel pressure should be at least 2 psi (13.8 kPa) at carburetor when running motor at full throttle.

IGNITION SYSTEM

All models are equipped with a capacitor discharge ignition system. Refer to the appropriate following paragraphs for service.

Models With Distributor

This ignition is extremely durable in normal operation but can be easily damaged by improper testing or servicing procedures. Observe the following list of cautions and use **only** the approved methods for checking the system to prevent damage to the components.

1. DO NOT reverse battery terminals.
2. DO NOT check polarity of battery by sparking the lead wires.
3. DO NOT install resistor type spark plugs or lead wires other than those specified.
4. DO NOT disconnect **any** wires while engine is running.
5. DO NOT ground any wires to engine block when checking. Ground only to front cover plate or bottom cowl to which switch box is mounted as described.
6. DO NOT use tachometer except for those designed or approved for this system.

TROUBLESHOOTING. Use only approved procedures when testing to prevent damage to components.

SPARK TEST. Do not remove spark plug wire while motor is running. Cut off the ground electrode from a standard spark plug (such as Champion J4J or L4J) and connect one of the spark plug wires to the test plug. Ground the test plug to the support bracket using a clamp or jumper wire.

CAUTION: Do not hold spark plug or wire in hand.

Make certain that test plug is properly grounded, then crank motor with electric starter. If test plug fires but engine will not start, check for incorrect installation of timing belt as outlined in the following TRIGGER AND DISTRIBUTOR paragraphs. Fuel system problems can also prevent starting. If test plug does not fire, check wiring and connections.

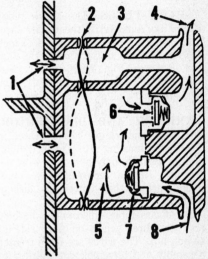

Fig. MR26-16—Schematic view of diaphragm type fuel pump. Pump body mounts on side of cylinder block and is ported to two crankcases as shown.

1. Pressure ports	5. Main fuel chamber
2. Diaphragm	6. Outlet check valve
3. Booster chamber	7. Inlet check valve
4. To carburetor	8. Fuel inlet

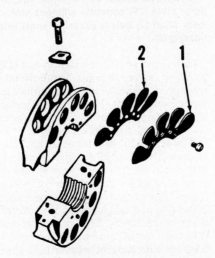

Fig. MR26-14—View of intermediate main bearing and reed valve assembly. Inspect reed stops (1) and reed petals (2) as outlined in text.

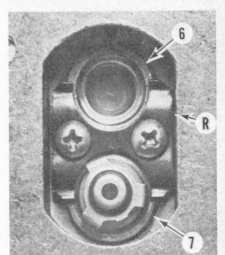

Fig. MR26-17—View showing installation of outlet check valve (6) and inlet check valve (7) in fuel pump body. Install retainer (R) so tips are away from check valves.

TRIGGER COIL AND SWITCH BOX
TEST. To check trigger coil and switch
box, manufacturer recommends use of
Thunderbolt Ignition Analyzer
(C-91-62563A1). Follow instructions ac-
companying tester.

COIL TEST. The ignition coil can be
checked using an ignition tester
available from several sources, including
the following:

GRAHAM TESTERS, INC.
4220 Central Ave. N.E.
Minneapolis, Minn. 55421

MERC-O-TRONIC
INSTRUMENTS CORP.
215 Branch St.
Almont, Mich. 48003

SPARK PLUGS. The spark plugs
should be removed if the center electrode is burned back more than 1/32 inch
(0.79 mm) below flat surface of the plug
end. Refer to Fig. MR26-19. AC type
V40FFM or Champion type L76V, surface gap spark plugs should be used.

TRIGGER AND DISTRIBUTOR.
The electronic trigger coil is located in
distributor housing (10 – Fig. MR26-20)
and is available only as a unit with the
housing. Before removing any wires,
make certain that battery is disconnected.

To disassemble, disconnect battery
and the three wires on port side of
switch box. The wires are from trigger
assembly and terminals are marked to
indicate correct wire connections. Remove cover (18), drive belt pulley (19)
and spacer (20). Bend tabs of washer
(23) away from nut (21), remove nut and
withdraw the distributor from adapter
and economizer (25 and 29). Remove
clamp (3) and cap (1). Carefully press
bearing (15) out of housing by working
through the two holes provided.

**NOTE: Do not damage nut (17) or shaft
when removing bearing.**

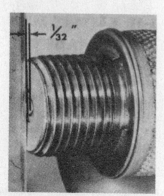

Fig. MR26-19—Surface gap plug should be renewed if center electrode is 1/32 inch (0.79 mm)
below the end of plug.

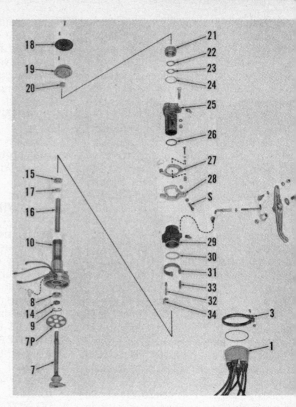

**Fig. MR26-20—Exploded
view of the ignition distributor and drive used on some
models.**

1. Distributor cap
3. Clamp
7. Rotor & shaft
7P. Timer plate
8. Ball bearing
9. Snap ring
10. Distributor housing
& trigger assy.
14. Spacer
15. Ball bearing
16. Spacer
17. Nut
18. Flange plate
19. Drive pulley
20. Spacer
21. Cap nut
22. Wave washer
23. Tang washer
24. Washer
25. Adapter
26. Washer
27. Throttle cam plate
(primary pickup)
28. Throttle cam (secondary
pickup)
29. Economizer collar
30. Washer
31. Spring
32. Spring anchor stud
33. Spring anchor pin
34. Spark advance stop

Remove nut (17) then bump the rotor
shaft (7) out of bearing (8). The shaft
should slide easily out of timer plate (7P)
and spacer (14). Bearing (8) can be removed after extracting snap ring (9).

When reassembling, install bearing (8)
and snap ring (9). Position spacer (14)
then insert the timer plate (7P) into the
trigger coil slot. Insert the rotor shaft
(7) through the timer plate (7P), spacer
(14) and bearing (8).

**CAUTION: Make certain that tab on
timer plate (7P) correctly engages slot in
rotor shaft (7) before pressing shaft into
bearing (8).**

Install spacer (16) and tighten nut (17)
to 75-80 in-lbs. (8.5-9.0 N·m). Rotate
rotor shaft and note any interference as
timer plate turns. If necessary, install
shims between bearing (8) and spacer
(14) to adjust timer plate height. Press
ball bearing (15) around shaft and into
housing (10). Install distributor cap (1)
and clamp (3). Joint of clamp should be
positioned under the trigger coil wires.
Assemble distributor to the economizer
collar (29) and adapter (25), then install
washers (22, 23 and 24). Tighten cap nut
(21), back nut off until the nearest notch
lines up with tang of washer (23), then
bend tang into notch. Install spacer (20)
and pulley (19) over the drive key. Firing
order is 1-4-5-2-3-6.

To renew the distributor drive belt, i
is first necessary to remove pulle
flange plate (18), disengage belt from
pulley, then remove flywheel. When in
stalling, position drive belt under alter
nator stator and around the crankshaft
Install flywheel being careful not to
damage the belt. Turn the flywheel an
distributor pulley as shown in (Fig
MR26-21) so timing dot (D) is aligne
with pulley arrow (A), then install driv
belt over the pulley. Recheck timing
marks after belt is installed. Marks mus
be on center line between crankshaf
and distributor shaft. Refer to SPEEI
CONTROL LINKAGE paragraphs fo
adjusting linkage and ignition timing.

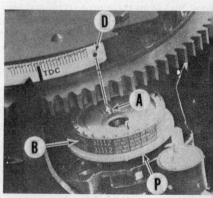

Fig. MR26-21—Distributor drive belt (B) shoule
be installed with cast arrow (A) on drive pulley (P
aligned with dot (D) on flywheel as shown.

Models Without Distributor

These models are equipped with a solid-state, capacitor discharge ignition system consisting of trigger coils, stator, switch boxes and ignition coils. The trigger coils are contained in a trigger ring module under the flywheel. Diodes, SCR's and capacitors are contained in the switch boxes. Switch boxes, trigger ring module and stator must be serviced as unit assemblies.

Check all wires and connections before troubleshooting ignition circuit. The following test specifications will aid troubleshooting.

STATOR

Tests	Ohms
Blue and red stator leads	5400-6200
Blue/white and red/white stator leads	5400-6200
Red stator lead and engine ground*	125-175
Red/white stator lead and engine ground*	125-175

*If stator has a black ground wire, be sure ground wire is properly connected to engine.

Note when testing the trigger module that yellow sleeves enclose wires from the trigger module to the lower switch box. The lower switch box serves the even-numbered cylinders while the upper switch box serves the odd-numbered cylinders.

TRIGGER MODULE

Tests	Ohms
Brown trigger lead (no yellow sleeve) and white trigger lead (with yellow sleeve)	1100-1400
White trigger lead (no yellow sleeve) and violet trigger lead (with yellow sleeve)	1100-1400
Violet trigger lead (no yellow sleeve) and brown trigger lead (with yellow sleeve)	1100-1400

COOLING SYSTEM

WATER PUMP. The rubber impeller type water pump is housed in the gearcase housing. The impeller is mounted on and driven by the lower unit drive shaft.

When cooling system problems are encountered, first check the water inlet for plugging or partial stoppage, then if not corrected, remove the gearcase housing as outlined in LOWER UNIT section and examine the water pump, water tubes and seals.

POWER HEAD

R&R AND DISASSEMBLE. To remove the power head assembly, first disconnect the battery and remove the top and side cowling. Remove electric starter, then disconnect all interfering wires and linkage. Remove the stud nuts which secure the power head to lower unit then jar power head on exhaust side to loosen gasket. Lift power head from lower unit and install on a suitable stand. Remove the flywheel, distributor, alternator-generator and the carburetors. Exhaust manifold cover, cylinder block cover and transfer port covers should be removed for cleaning and inspection.

Remove screws securing upper and lower crankcase end caps. Remove the main bearing locking bolts from front crankcase half, remove the flange bolts; then remove crankcase front half by inserting screwdriver in the recesses provided on side flanges. Use extra care not to spring the parts or to mar the machined, mating surfaces. Use a mallet or soft faced hammer to tap crankcase end caps from cylinder block assembly. Be careful not to damage adjustment shims on end caps. The crankcase half (6 – Fig. MR26-23) and cylinder assembly (15) are matched and align bored, and are available only as an assembly.

Crankshaft, pistons, bearings and connecting rods may now be removed for service as outlined in the appropriate following paragraphs. When assembling, follow the procedures outlined in the ASSEMBLY paragraph.

ASSEMBLY. When assembling, the crankcase must be completely sealed against both vacuum and pressure. Exhaust manifold and water passages must be sealed against pressure leakage.

Whenever power head is disassembled, it is recommended that all gasket surfaces and machined joints without gaskets be carefully checked for nicks and burrs which might interfere with a tight seal. Make certain that threaded holes in cylinder for attaching the water jacket cover (20 – Fig. MR26-23) are cleaned.

Lubricate all bearing and friction surfaces with engine oil. Loose needle bearings may be held in place during assembly using a light, nonfibrous grease.

After the crankcase, connecting rods, pistons and main bearings are positioned in the cylinder, check the crankshaft end play. Temporarily install the crankshaft end caps (2 and 13) omitting the sealing rings (4 and 9), but using the shims (3 and 10) that were originally installed. Tighten the end cap to cylinder retaining screws. Use a soft hammer to bump the crankshaft each way to seat bearings, then measure the end play.

Bump the crankshaft toward top, and measure clearance between the top crankshaft counterweight and the end cap as shown in Fig. MR26-24. Bump the crankshaft toward bottom and again measure clearance between counterweight and end cap. Subtract the first (minimum) clearance from the second clearance which will indicate the amount of end play. If end play is not within limits of 0.004-0.012 inch (0.102-0.305 mm), add or remove shims (3 or 10 – Fig. MR26-23) as necessary, then recheck. The crankshaft should be centered by varying the amount of shims between upper (3) and lower (10) shim stacks. When centering the crankshaft, make certain that end play is correct.

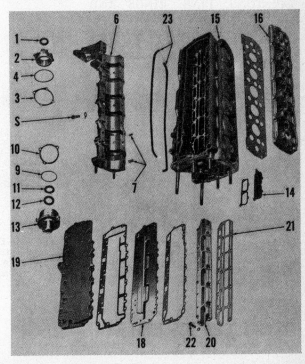

Fig. MR26-23—Exploded view of typical crankcase assembly.

S. Main bearing screw
1. Oil seal
2. End cap
3. Shim
4. "O" ring
6. Crankcase half
7. Dowel pins
9. "O" ring
10. Shim
11. Oil seal
12. Oil seal
13. End cap
14. Transfer port cover
15. Cylinder half
16. Cylinder cover
18. Exhaust plate
19. Exhaust cover
20. Water jacket cover
21. Gasket
22. Screws
23. Sealing strips

Gasket and sealing surfaces should be lightly and carefully coated with an impervious liquid sealer. Surface must be completely coated, using care that excess sealer does not squeeze out into bearings, crankcase or other passages.

Clean the gasket surfaces and threaded holes of water jacket cover (20) and cylinder (15). Coat the first four threads of all screws (22) with Resiweld and allow to set for 10 minutes. Coat gasket surface of water jacket cover and mating surface of cylinder with gasket sealer, then install gasket (21) and water jacket cover (20). Tighten the screws (22) evenly from the center outward to a torque of 200 in.-lbs. (22.6 N·m) on early models and 150 in.-lbs. (16.9 N·m) on late models.

Check the assembly by turning the crankshaft after each step to check for binding or locking which might indicate improper assembly. Remove the cause before proceeding. Rotate the crankshaft until each piston ring in turn appears in one of the exhaust or transfer ports, then check by pressing on ring with a blunt tool. Ring should spring back when released; if it does not, a broken or binding ring is indicated, and the trouble should be corrected.

Tighten the crankcase exhaust cover and cylinder cover cap screws by first tightening the center screws, then tightening screws evenly working toward top of power head. When upper half is tightened, again start at the center and tighten screws alternately toward bottom of power head. Tightening torques are given in the CONDENSED SERVICE DATA table.

PISTONS, PINS, RINGS AND CYLINDERS. Before detaching connecting rods from crankshaft, make sure that rod and cap are properly identified for correct assembly to each other and in the correct cylinder.

Maximum allowable cylinder bore wear or out-of-round is 0.004 inch (0.102 mm). Worn or slightly damaged standard size cylinders may be repaired by boring and honing to fit an oversize piston. Pistons and rings are available in 0.015 inch (0.38 mm) oversize on early models and 0.015 inch (0.38 mm) and 0.030 inch (0.76 mm) oversizes on later models.

Two or three piston rings are used on each piston. Piston rings are interchangeable in the ring grooves and are pinned to prevent rings from rotating in grooves.

Piston pin is pressed in piston bosses and secured with retaining rings. The retaining rings should not be reused. Two types of retaining rings (4–Fig. MR26-25) have been used and must NOT be interchanged. Some late models use "C" rings and other models use "G" type retaining rings. Piston end of connecting rod is fitted with loose needle rollers. Refer to the CONNECTING RODS, BEARINGS AND CRANKSHAFT paragraphs for number of rollers used. The piston pin needle rollers use the connecting rod bore and the piston pin as bearing races. When assembling, install bearing washers and needle bearings in piston end of connecting rod using light nonfibrous grease to hold them in place. A Mariner special tool may be used to hold needles in position while positioning piston for installation. Piston must be installed so sharp, vertical side of deflector will be to starboard (intake side of cylinder block. Heat piston to approximately 135°F (57°C) on early models and 190°F (88°C) on late models, then press piston pin into place. Pin should be centered in piston. Use new retaining rings on each reassembly of engine.

Assemble the connecting rod and piston assemblies, together with the main bearing units to the crankshaft, then install the complete assembly in cylinder half of block. Numbers 2 and 4 pistons should be started first. Use the Ring Compressor Kit (C-91-47844A2), if available; or carefully compress each ring with the fingers if kit is not available. Thoroughly lubricate pistons and rings during assembly.

CONNECTING RODS, BEARINGS AND CRANKSHAFT. Upper and lower ends of crankshaft are carried by ball bearings. The second, fourth and sixth main bearings (Fig. MR26-14) also contain the inlet reed valves. The third and fifth main bearings (13–Fig. MR26-25), contain loose needle rollers (15) which ride in a split type outer race (14), held together by a retaining ring (16).

The connecting rod uses 29 loose needle rollers at piston end. The crankpin end of connecting rod uses a caged needle bearing. Check rod for alignment by placing rod on a surface plate and checking with a light. Rod is bent or distorted if 0.002 inch (0.05 mm) feeler gage can be inserted between rod and surface plate.

If bearing surface of rod and cap is rough, scored, worn or shows evidence of overheating, renew the connecting rod. Inspect crankpin and main bearing journals. If scored, out-of-round or worn, renew the crankshaft. Check the crankshaft for straightness using a dial indicator and "V" blocks.

Inspect and adjust the reed valves as outlined in REED VALVE paragraph, and reassemble as outlined in ASSEMBLY paragraph.

ELECTRICAL SYSTEM

Refer to Fig. MR26-27 or MR26-28 for a typical wiring diagram. Note the following cautions when servicing electrical components:

DO NOT reverse battery connections. Battery negative (–) terminal is grounded.

DO NOT "spark" battery connections to check polarity.

DO NOT disconnect battery cables while engine is running.

DO NOT crank engine if ignition switch boxes are not grounded to engine.

Fig. MR26-24—Refer to text for method of checking crankshaft end play. The crankshaft should be centered in the cylinder block.

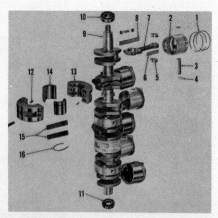

Fig. MR26-25—Exploded view of the crankshaft and associated parts typical of all models. Refer to Fig. MR26-14 for intermediate main bearings and reed valve assemblies.

1. Piston rings
2. Piston
3. Piston pin
4. Retainers
5. Bearing washers
6. Needle rollers
7. Connecting rod
8. Needle rollers
9. Crankshaft
10. Top main bearing
11. Bottom main bearing
12. Bearing alignment dowel
13. Bearing housing
14. Main bearing race
15. Needle rollers
16. Retaining ring

LOWER UNIT

PROPELLER AND DRIVE CLUTCH. Protection for the motor is built into a special cushioning clutch in the propeller hub. No adjustment is possible on the propeller or clutch. Various pitch propellers are available and propeller should be selected to provide full throttle engine operation within rpm range listed below. Propellers other than those designed for the motor must not be used.

Model	RPM Range
90 hp	4500-5000
115 hp	5000-5500
140 hp	5300-5800

R&R AND OVERHAUL. Most service on the lower unit can be performed by detaching the gearcase housing from the drive shaft housing. To remove housing, remove plastic plug and Allen head screw from location (1 – Fig. MR26-30). Remove trim tab (2) and screw from under trim tab. Remove stud nut from location (3), and stud nuts (4) on each side and stud nut (5), if so equipped then withdraw the lower unit gearcase assembly.

Remove plugs and drain oil from housing, then secure the gearcase in a soft jawed vise with propeller up. Wedge a piece of wood between propeller and antiventilation plate, remove propeller nut, then remove propeller.

Disassemble gearcase by removing gearcase housing cover nut (61 – Fig. MR26-31). Clamp the outer end of pro-

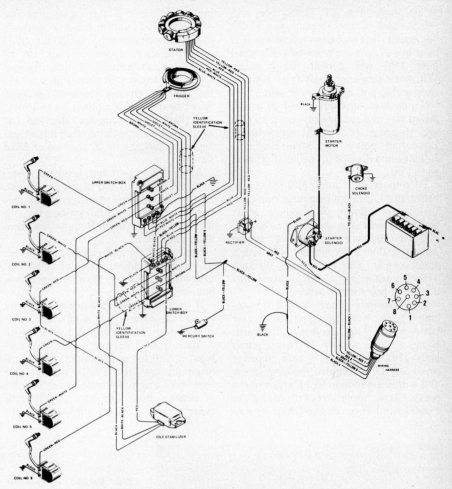

Fig. MR26-28—Wiring diagram typical of models not equipped with a distributor.

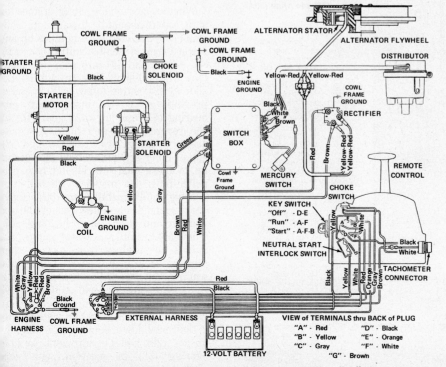

Fig. MR26-27—Wiring schematic for models equipped with a distributor.

VIEW of TERMINALS thru BACK of PLUG
"A" - Red   "D" - Black
"B" - Yellow   "E" - Orange
"C" - Gray   "F" - White
"G" - Brown

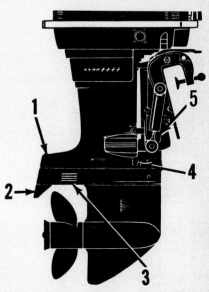

Fig. MR26-30—To remove the lower unit gearcase assembly, remove the attaching screws and stud nuts from positions indicated.

peller shaft in a soft jawed vise and remove gearcase by tapping with a rubber mallet. Be careful not to lose key (59) or shims (47) on early models. Forward gear (40) will remain in housing. Withdraw propeller shaft from bearing carrier (56) and reverse gear (46).

Clamp bearing carrier (56) in a soft jawed vise and remove reverse gear (46) and bearing (49) with an internal expanding puller and slide hammer. Remove and discard propeller shaft rear seals (58).

To remove dog clutch (43) from propeller shaft, remove retaining ring (44). Insert cam follower (8) in hole in shaft and apply only enough pressure on end of cam follower to remove spring pressure, then push out pin (42) with a small punch. The pin passes through drilled holes in dog clutch and operates in slotted holes in propeller shaft.

To disassemble drive shaft and associated parts, reposition gearcase in vise with drive shaft projecting upward. Remove rubber slinger (11), water pump body (16), impeller (19) and impeller drive key (20). Remove flushing screw and withdraw remainder of water pump parts. Clamp upper end of drive shaft in a soft jawed vise, remove pinion retain-

ing nut or screw (37); then tap gearcase off drive shaft and bearing. Note position and thickness of shims (30 and 30A) on drive shaft upper bearing. On all models, mesh position of pinion is controlled by shims (30) placed underneath the bearing. On models with ball type upper bearing, shims (30A) control shaft end play. The shims are identical but should not be interchanged or mixed, except to adjust the mesh position of drive pinion.

After drive shaft has been removed, forward gear (40) and bearing cone can be withdrawn. Use an internal expanding type puller to withdraw bearing cup if removal is required. Remove and save shim pack (38).

Shift shaft (5) and cam (7) can be removed after removing forward gear and unscrewing bushing (3) from gearcase housing.

If gear wear was abnormal or if any parts that affect gear alignment were renewed, check and adjust gear mesh as follows: Install forward gear (40) and bearing (39) using shims (38) that were originally installed. Position shims (30) that were originally installed at bottom of bearing bore. On late models with taper bearing (32) and spiral gear teeth,

install bearing cup (32) in housing bo against shims (30). On all models, po tion drive pinion (35) in housing and i sert drive shaft (33), with bearing (3 installed, into housing, bearing (34) a gear (35). On all models with ball ty upper bearing, the bearing must be fir ly seated in housing bore. On all mode install retaining screw or nut (37). Co gears (35 and 40) with bearing blue a check mesh position. On models wi straight-cut gears, pull up on drive sha gears to check mesh position. On mode with spiral gears, it will be necessary push down on end of drive shaft whi checking mesh position. On all models, gears do not mesh in center of teeth, ac or remove shims (30) under bearing necessary. After setting mesh positio check backlash between teeth of gear (35 and 40). Backlash should b 0.014-0.016 inch (0.356-0.406 mm). T increase clearance (backlash), remov part of shim stack (38) behind bearin cup. If gears are too loose, add shim After changing thickness of shims (38 gears should be recoated with bearin blue and mesh position should b rechecked. Install bearing (49), thru washer (48) and reverse gear (46) i bearing carrier (56). To check revers gear (46) backlash on all early mode with straight-cut gear teeth, install bea ing carrier and gear assembly usin shims (47) that were originally installe If backlash is not within limits 0.006-0.008 inch (0.152-0.203 mm), ad or remove shims (47) as required. Ad ing shims at (47) increases backlas (clearance). Reverse gear backlash is n adjustable on models with spiral gears

When reassembling, long splines o shift rod (5) should be toward top. Shif cam (7) is installed with notches up an toward rear. Assemble shifting parts (9 8S, 43, 42 and 44) into propeller shaf (45). Pin (42) should be through hole i slide (8S). Position follower (8) in end o propeller shaft and insert shaft int bearing (41) and forward gear. Instal the reverse gear and bearing carrie assembly using new seals (55 and 58) Lip of inner seal (58) should face in an lip of outer seal (58) should face pro peller (out). On models with ball typ bearing at (32), install shims (30A) abov bearing and position new gasket (29) an water pump base (23) on housing. Ad shims (30A) until the water pump bas stands out slightly from gasket, the measure clearance between gasket an water pump base with a feeler gage. Re move shims (30A) equal to 0.002-0.00 inch (0.051-0.076 mm) less tha clearance measured. When water pum is tightened down, compression of a ne gasket (29) will be sufficient to hol bearing (32) in position with zer clearance.

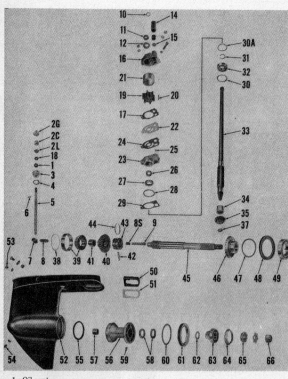

Fig. MR26-31—Exploded view of gearcase assembly typical of all models. Shim (47) is not used on later models. Some models use a tapered bearing in place of ball bearing (32), snap ring (31) and shim (30A).

25. Dowel
26. Oil seal
27. Spring loaded oil seal
28. "O" ring
29. Gasket
30. & 30A. Shims
31. Snap ring
32. Ball bearing
33. Drive shaft
34. Roller bearing
35. Drive pinion
37. Nut
38. Shim
39. Tapered roller bearing
40. Forward gear
41. Roller bearing
42. Cross pin
43. Dog clutch
44. Retaining ring
45. Propeller shaft
46. Reverse gear
47. Shim
48. Thrust washer
48. Ball bearing
50. Exhaust tube seal
51. Support plate
52. Gear housing
53. Vent screw
54. Filler screw
55. "O" ring
56. Bearing carrier
57. Roller bearing
58. Oil seals
59. Key
60. Washer
61. Housing cover nut
62. Thrust washer
63. Thrust hub
64. Cupped washer
65. Splined washer
66. Propeller nut

1. Oil seal
2C. Reverse locking cam
2G. Push rod guide
2L. Lower spacer
3. Bushing
4. "O" ring
5. Shift shaft
6. Snap ring
7. Shift cam
8. Cam follower
8S. Slide
9. Spring
10. "O" ring
11. Rubber ring (slinger)
12. Oil seal
14. Seal
15. Nylon washer
16. Water pump body
17. Gasket
19. Impeller
20. Key
21. Insert
22. Plate
23. Pump base
24. Gasket

Upper oil seal (26) should be installed with lips facing up (toward engine) and lower oil seal (27) should be pressed into water pump base with lips facing down toward propeller shaft. Install remainder of water pump assembly and tighten the screws or nuts to the following recommended torque. Torque ¼-28 nuts to 30 in.-lbs. (3.4 N·m). Torque 5/16-24 nuts to 40 in.-lbs. (4.5 N·m). Torque ¼-20 screws to 20 in.-lbs. (2.2 N·m).

The lower spacer (2L) should be installed with groove down. Reverse locking cam (2C) should be installed on shaft splines so flat on cam is in center toward front when shift shaft (5) is in reverse position. When in neutral, reverse locking cam should be positioned as shown in Fig. MR26-32. The push rod guide (2G–Fig. MR26-31) is located in the drive shaft housing.

Before attaching gearcase housing to the drive shaft housing, make certain that shift cam (7) and the shift lever (on motor) are in forward gear position on early models and neutral position on late models. In forward gear position, shift shaft (5) should be in clockwise position (viewed from top end of shaft). Complete assembly by reversing disassembly.

POWER TILT/TRIM

Non-Integral Type

FLUID. Recommended fluid is SAE 10W-30 or 10W-40 automotive oil. With outboard in full up position, oil level should reach bottom of fill plug hole threads. Do not overfill.

BLEEDING. To bleed air from hydraulic system, position outboard at full tilt and engage tilt lock lever. Without disconnecting hoses, remove hydraulic trim cylinders. Be sure fluid reservoir is full and remains so during bleeding operation. Remove down circuit bleed screw (D–Fig. MR26-35) and "O" ring. Press "IN" control button for a few seconds, release button and wait approximately one minute. Repeat until expelled oil is air-free. Install "O" ring and bleed screw (D) and repeat procedure on opposite cylinder. Place cylinder in a horizontal position so bleed port (P–Fig. MR26-36) is up and remove up circuit bleed screw (U). Press "UP" and "UP/OUT" control buttons for a few seconds, release buttons and wait approximately one minute. Repeat until expelled oil is air-free. Install "O" ring and bleed screw (U) and repeat procedure on opposite cylinder. Reinstall cylinders.

ADJUST TRIM LIMIT SWITCH. Operate trim control so outboard is in full down position. Press "UP/OUT" or "UP" control button and hold until pump motor stops. Outboard should tilt up and stop so there is ½ inch (12.7 mm) overlap (L–Fig. MR26-37) between swivel bracket flange (W) and clamp bracket flange (M). Pull up on lower unit to remove slack when checking overlap (L). Note that if cylinder rods enter cylinders more than an additional ⅛ inch (3.17 mm), that hydraulic system should be bled of air as outlined in BLEEDING section. If overlap (L) is incorrect, loosen retainer screw (R–Fig. MR26-38) then turn adjusting nut (N)

Fig. MR26-35—View showing location of down circuit bleed screw (D) and grease fitting (F).

Fig. MR26-36—View showing location of up circuit bleed screw (U) and bleed port (P).

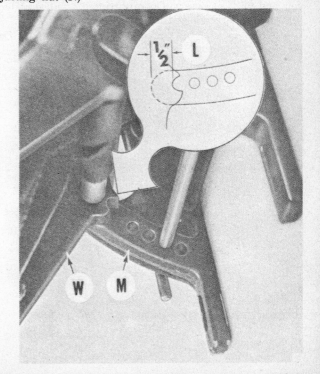

Fig. MR26-37—Overlap (L) between swivel bracket flange (W) and clamp bracket flange (M) should be ½ inch (12.7 mm).

FLAT ON CAM

NEUTRAL

Fig. MR26-32—The reverse locking cam must be in position shown when lower unit (and the shift shaft) are in neutral.

Fig. MR26-38—Loosen retainer screw (R) and turn trim limit adjusting nut (N) to adjust trim limit switch.

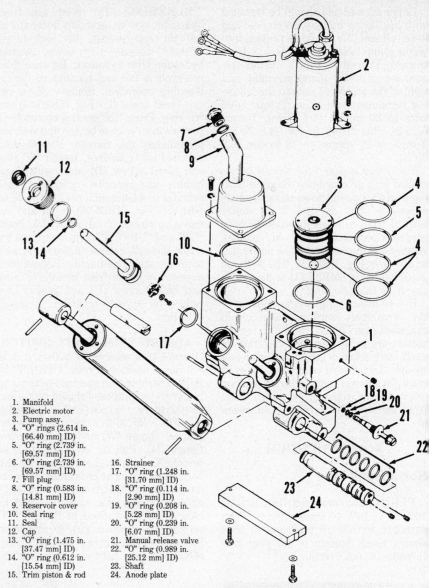

1. Manifold
2. Electric motor
3. Pump assy.
4. "O" rings (2.614 in. [66.40 mm] ID)
5. "O" ring (2.739 in. [69.57 mm] ID)
6. "O" ring (2.739 in. [69.57 mm] ID)
7. Fill plug
8. "O" ring (0.583 in. [14.81 mm] ID)
9. Reservoir cover
10. Seal ring
11. Seal
12. Cap
13. "O" ring (1.475 in. [37.47 mm] ID)
14. "O" ring (0.612 in. [15.54 mm] ID)
15. Trim piston & rod
16. Strainer
17. "O" ring (1.248 in. [31.70 mm] ID)
18. "O" ring (0.114 in. [2.90 mm] ID)
19. "O" ring (0.208 in. [5.28 mm] ID)
20. "O" ring (0.239 in. [6.07 mm] ID)
21. Manual release valve
22. "O" ring (0.989 in. [25.12 mm] ID)
23. Shaft
24. Anode plate

Fig. MR26-45—Exploded view of integral type power tilt/trim system.

counterclockwise to increase overlap or clockwise to decrease overlap. Retighten retainer screw (R) and recheck adjustment.

PRESSURE TEST. To check hydraulic system pressure, disconnect four hoses attached to control valve as shown in Fig. MR26-39; small hoses are for up circuit while large hoses are for down circuit. Connect a pressure gage to one up circuit port (small) of control valve and another pressure gage to one down circuit port (large). Screw plugs into remaining ports. Check fluid reservoir and fill if necessary. Operate trim control in up direction and note pressure

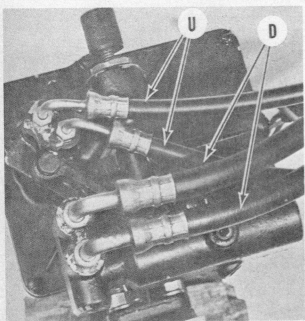

Fig. MR26-39—View of control valve showing location of up circuit hoses (U) and down circuit hoses (D).

gage reading. Minimum pressure should be 3500 psi (24.1 MPa) on new pumps with a red sleeve on wires or 3200-3500 psi (22.0-24.1 MPa) minimum on used pumps with red sleeve on wires. Minimum pressure on all other new pumps is 3000 psi (20.7 MPa) while minimum pressure on used pumps is 2700-3000 psi (18.6-20.7 MPa). Release trim control button. Pressure will drop slightly after stabilizing but should not drop faster than 100 psi (690 kPa) every 15 seconds. Operate trim control in down direction and note pressure gage reading. Minimum pressure is 500-1000 psi (3.4-6.9 MPa). Release trim control button. Pressure will drop slightly after stabilizing but should not drop faster than 100 psi (690 kPa) every 15 seconds. If pressure is normal, inspect trim cylinders and hoses for leakage. If pressure is abnormal, install a good control valve and recheck pressure. If

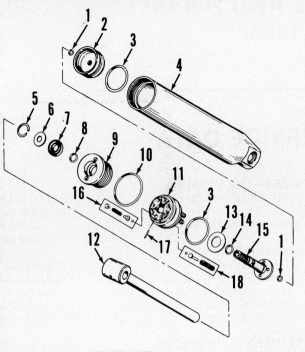

Fig. MR26-46—Exploded view of tilt cylinder components.

1. "O" ring (0.307 in. [7.79 mm] ID)
2. Cup
3. "O" ring (1.957 in. [49.71 mm] ID)
4. Cylinder
5. Circlip
6. Washer
7. Scraper
8. "O" ring (0.854 in. [21.69 mm] ID)
9. Cap
10. "O" ring (2.067 in. [52.5 mm] ID)
11. Piston
12. Rod
13. Washer
14. "O" ring (0.661 in. [16.79 mm] ID)
15. Rod end
16. Check valve assy.
17. Pin
18. Check valve assy.

Fig. MR26-47—Release pressure on system, then remove Allen head plug (U) and install a 5000 psi (34.5 MPa) test gage with a suitable adapter and hose to test system pressure when operated in the "UP" direction. View identifies location of manual release valve (21).

pressure remains abnormal, install a new pump body.

Integral Type

FLUID AND BLEEDING. Recommended fluid is Dexron II or Type AF automatic transmission fluid. Remove fill plug (7 – Fig. MR26-45) and fill reservoir until fluid is visible in fill tube with the outboard motor in the full-up position.

The hydraulic circuit is self-bleeding as the tilt/trim system is operated through several cycles. After servicing system, be sure to check reservoir level after filling and operating system.

HYDRAULIC TESTING. The system can be checked by connecting a 5000 psi (34.5 MPa) test gage to the UP (U – Fig. MR26-47) and DOWN (D – Fig. MR26-48) ports. Prior to connecting test gage, place outboard motor in the full-up position and engage tilt lock lever. Unscrew reservoir fill plug and rotate manual release valve (21 – Fig. MR26-47) three to four turns counterclockwise to release pressure on system. Remove UP

or DOWN Allen head test port plug and connect test gage with suitable adapter and hose. Install fill plug and rotate manual release valve clockwise until seated. System pressure when testing at UP (U) port should be a minimum of 1300 psi (8.9 MPa). System pressure when testing at DOWN (D – Fig. MR26-48) port should be a minimum of 500 psi (3.5 MPa). Release pressure on system as previously outlined prior to removing test gage. Reinstall Allen head plug.

OVERHAUL. Refer to Fig. MR26-45 for an exploded view of manifold and trim cylinder components, and Fig. MR26-46 for an exploded view of tilt cylinder components. Special socket 91-44487A1 and a spanner wrench is required to service trim and tilt cylinders. Keep all components clean and away from contamination. Keep components separated and label if needed for correct reassembly. Note "O" ring sizes as stated in legends of Figs. MR26-45 and MR26-46. Lubricate all "O" rings or seal lips with Dexron II or Type AF

automatic transmission fluid during reassembly.

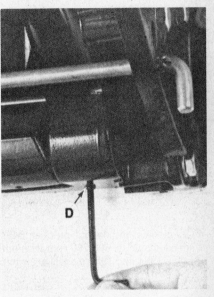

Fig. MR26-48—Release pressure on system, then remove Allen head plug (D) and install a 5000 psi (34.5 MPa) test gage with a suitable adapter and hose to test system pressure when operated in the "DOWN" direction.

MARINER 150, 175 AND 200 HP
(Prior To 1986)

CONDENSED SERVICE DATA

TUNE-UP

Hp/rpm:
Model 150 . . . . 150/5000-5500
Model 175 . . . . 175/5300-5800
Model 200 . . . . 200/5300-5800

Bore:
150 HP & 175 HP (prior to serial
no. 6618751) . . . . 3.125 in.
(79.38 mm)
175 HP (after serial no. 6618750) &
200 HP . . . . 3.375 in.
(85.72 mm)

Stroke . . . . 2.650 in.
(67.31 mm)

Displacement:
150 HP & 175 HP (prior to serial
no. 6618751) . . . . 122 cu. in.
(1999 cc)
175 HP (after serial no. 6618750) &
200 HP . . . . 142 cu. in.
(2327 cc)

Firing Order 1-2-3-4-5-6
Number System (top to bottom):
Port 2-4-6
Starboard 1-3-5
Spark Plug:
Models Prior to Serial No. 5464486 . . . . Champion – L76V
Models After Serial No. 5464485 . . . . NGK – BU8H
Idle Speed (in gear) . . . . 550-650 rpm*
Fuel:Oil Ratio . . . . 50:1†

*On models with serial number 5464486 and above, idle
speed should be 600-700 rpm with outboard motor in gear.
†Some 1984 and 1985 models are equipped with an oil injection system.

SIZES – CLEARANCES

Piston Rings End Gap . . . . 0.018-0.025 i
(0.457-0.635 m
Maximum Cylinder Tolerance . . . . 0.006 i
(0.152 m

Crankshaft Bearing Type:
Top Main Bearing . . . . Caged Roll
Center Main Bearing . . . . Caged Roll
Bottom Main Bearing . . . . Ball Beari
Crankpin . . . . Caged Roll
Piston Pin Bearing . . . . 29 Loose Rolle

TIGHTENING TORQUES

Connecting Rod . . . . 30 ft.-lb
(41 N·r
Crankcase Screws:
5/16 . . . . 200 in.-lb
(22.6 N·r
3/8 . . . . 35 ft.-lb
(47.6 N·r
Cylinder Head . . . . 30 ft.-lb
(40.8 N·r
Cylinder Head Cover . . . . 150 in.-lb
(16.9 N·r
End Cap:
Upper . . . . 150 in.-lb
(16.9 N·r
Lower . . . . 60 in.-lb
(6.7 N·r
Exhaust Cover . . . . 180 in.-lb
(20.3 N·r
Flywheel Nut . . . . 100 ft.-lb
(136 N·r
Reed Block Mounting Screws . . . . 60 in.-lb
(6.7 N·r
Spark Plugs . . . . 240 in.-lb
(27.1 N·r

LUBRICATION

The power head is lubricated by oil mixed with the fuel. Fuel should be regular leaded, low lead or unleaded gasoline with a minimum pump octane rating of 86. Recommended oil is Quicksilver Formula 50-D Outboard Lubricant. Normal fuel:oil ratio is 50:1; during engine break-in, fuel:oil ratio should be 25:1.

On some 1984 and 1985 models, an oil injection system is used. The fuel:oil ratio is varied from approximately 50:1 at full throttle up to approximately 100:1 at idle. The oil pump is synchronized with carburetor throttle opening via linkage. As the carburetor throttle opens or closes, the oil being supplied to the fuel pump is varied, thus matching the proper fuel:oil ratio to engine demand.

During oil injection system's first 30 hours of operation, the fuel in the fuel tank must be mixed at a fuel:oil ratio of 50:1 to ensure the engine of proper lubrication and the oil level in the remote oil tank monitored. If, after 30 hours of op-eration, oil level has dropped indicating the oil injection system is operating refill the remote oil tank and switch to straight fuel.

Lower unit gears and bearings are lubricated by oil contained in the gearcase Recommended oil is Mariner Super Duty Gear Lube. Lubricant is drained by removing vent and drain plugs in the gearcase. Refill through drain plug hole until oil has reached level of vent plug open-ing, then allow 1 ounce (30 mL) of oil to drain from gearcase. Lower unit oil capacity is 24¼ fl. oz. (717 mL)

Illustrations Courtesy Marine

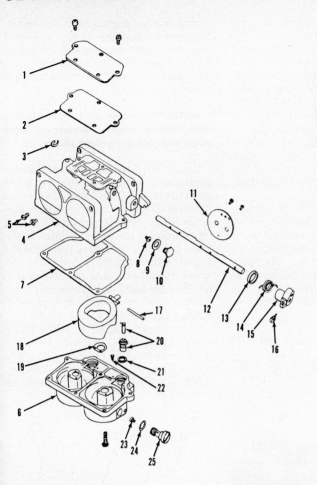

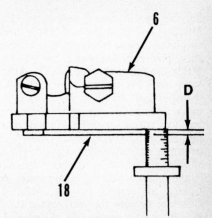

6

D

18

Fig. MR28-1 — Exploded view of carburetor used on all models. Note that idle jet components (8 through 10) and main jet components (23 through 25) are also located on the starboard side of carburetor.

1. Cover
2. Gasket
3. Clip
4. Body
5. Vent jets
6. Float bowl
7. Gasket
8. Idle jet
9. Gasket
10. Plug
11. Throttle plate
12. Throttle shaft
13. Spacer
14. Spring
15. Lever
16. Screw
17. Float pin
18. Float
19. Gasket
20. Inlet needle & seat
21. Gasket
22. Screw
23. Main jet
24. Gasket
25. Plug

Fig. MR28-2 — Invert float bowl (6) with needle and seat (20 — Fig. MR28-1) and float (18) installed. Distance (D) should be 1/16 inch (1.6 mm) for proper float setting.

FUEL SYSTEM

CARBURETOR. Three "dual float center bowl" type carburetors are used. Carburetor identification numbers are stamped on each carburetor mounting flange. Standard jet sizes are dependent upon the carburetor identification numbers. Use the standard carburetor jet sizes as recommended by the manufacturer for normal operation when used at altitudes of 2500 feet (762 m) and below. Main jets (23 – Fig. MR28-1) and vent jets (5) should be reduced in size by 0.002 inch (0.05 mm) at altitudes of 2500-5000 feet (762-1524 m). Idle jets (8) should be increased in size by 0.002 inch (0.05 mm) at altitudes of 2500-5000 feet (762-1524 m). Main jets (23) and vent jets (5) should be reduced in size by 0.004 inch (0.10 mm) at altitudes of 5000-7500 feet (1524-2286 m). Idle jets (8) should be increased in size by 0.004 inch (0.10 mm) at altitudes of 5000-7500 feet (1524-2286 m). Main jets (23) and vent jets (5) should be reduced in size by 0.006 inch (0.15 mm) at altitudes of 7500 feet (2286 m) and above. Idle jets (8) should be increased in size by 0.006 inch (0.15 mm) at altitudes of 7500 feet (2286 m) and above.

NOTE: Vent jets (5) are not used on some models. If vent jets are not noted, do not try to install jets.

No idle mixture screw adjustment is provided. Idle jet (8) size must be altered to change idle air:fuel ratio. Refer to CONDENSED SERVICE DATA for recommended idle speeds.

To measure float setting, invert float bowl (6) with inlet needle and seat (20) and float (18) installed. On each float chamber, measure distance (D – Fig. MR28-2) from float bowl surface to top of float (18). Distance (D) should be 1/16 inch (1.6 mm). Adjust distance (D) by bending tang at rear of float arm.

On some models, a choke plate containing choke valves is positioned in the air silencer. The choke valves are actuated by a solenoid mounted on the reed housing.

SPEED CONTROL LINKAGE (Model 175 HP). To synchronize ignition and carburetor opening, proceed as follows: To verify timing pointer alignment, a dial indicator must be installed in the number 1 (top, starboard) cylinder and the indicator synchronized with the

piston position (dial indicator reads zero when piston is at top dead center).

NOTE: To prevent accidental starting from flywheel rotation, remove all spark plugs and properly ground plug wires.

Rotate the flywheel counterclockwise approximately ¼ turn past the 0.462 inch (12 mm) BTDC reading, then rotate flywheel clockwise until indicator face reads 0.462 inch (12 mm) BTDC. Note the position of the timing pointer. Reposition pointer if the timing pointer is aligned with ".462 BTDC" mark on flywheel. Remove the dial indicator assembly from the number 1 cylinder after adjustment is completed and reinstall spark plug and plug lead.

Be sure link rod (L – Fig. MR28-4) protrudes 11/16 inch (17.46 mm) from link body as shown. If the engine is equipped with an idle stabilizer module (M-Fig. MR28-5), disconnect the white/black module wire from switch box terminal. Tape the end of the wire to prevent grounding. Be sure the other white/black wire remains connected to switch box terminal.

NOTE: To prevent engine from starting, make sure only the number 1 (top, starboard) spark plug is installed and is plug wire attached.

Disconnect the fuel tank supply hose at the outboard motor connector. Detach the throttle cable barrel from the retainer of the cable anchor bracket. Remove the choke knob and wing nuts, then withdraw the air intake cover from the front of the carburetors. Loosen carburetor synchronizing screws (S – Fig. MR28-4) and allow the carburetor throttle plates to close freely. With light pressure, hold cam follower roller (R – Fig. MR28-6) against throttle cam (T). At the same time, lift up on bottom carburetor throttle shaft (H – Fig. MR28-4) to remove slack in linkage components. Adjust idle speed screw (I) so short mark (M – Fig. MR28-6) on throttle cam (T) is centered on cam follower roller (R) as shown. Retighten stop screw locknut. While maintaining light pressure, retighten all screws (S – Fig. MR28-4). Check to be sure that carburetor throttle plates are completely closed when cam follower roller (R – Fig. MR28-6) is aligned with short mark (M) on throttle cam (T). Repeat adjustment procedure if setting is incorrect. Reinstall air intake cover.

Connect a power timing light to the number 1 cylinder spark plug lead. With the outboard motor in neutral, position throttle lever (C – Fig. MR28-4) so idle speed screw (I) is against stop. Crank the engine with the starter motor and adjust primary screw (P) so the ignition timing is 14° ATDC.

Open the throttle until the maximum spark advance screw (A) is against stop. Crank the engine with the starter motor and adjust maximum spark advance screw (A) so ignition timing is 20° BTDC.

NOTE. Due to electronic characteristics of the ignition system, maximum advance is set at 20° BTDC but ignition will retard to 18° BTDC at high engine speed.

The carburetor throttle plate must not act as the wide open throttle stop. To prevent damage to the carburetors, move speed control linkage to the maximum speed position and adjust maximum throttle stop screw (N) so a clearance (C – Fig. MR28-7) of 0.010-0.015 inch (0.25-0.38 mm) is between throttle cam (T) and cam follower roller (R).

Reconnect idle stabilizer module wire to switch box. Reinstall spark plugs, then adjust idle speed screw (I-Fig. MR28-4) as outlined in the CARBURETOR section.

Hold idle speed screw (I) against stop and install the throttle cable barrel in the retainer while adjusting throttle cable barrel so it fits into retainer and a very light preload between idle speed screw and its stop is established. Excessive throttle cable preload will result in difficult shifting from forward to neutral.

(Model 150 HP And Early 200 HP.) To synchronize ignition and carburetor opening, proceed as follows: To verify

Fig. MR28-5 — View showing location of idle stabilizer module (M) used on some models.

timing pointer alignment, a dial indicator must be installed in the number 1 (top, starboard) cylinder and the indicator synchronized with the piston position (dial indicator reads zero when piston is at top dead center).

NOTE: To prevent accidental starting from flywheel rotation, remove all spark plugs and properly ground plug wires.

Rotate the flywheel counterclockwise approximately ¼ turn past the 0.462 inch (12 mm) BTDC reading, then rotate flywheel clockwise until indicator face reads 0.462 inch (12 mm) BTDC. Note the position of the timing pointer. Reposition pointer if the timing pointer is not aligned with ".462 BTDC" mark on flywheel. Remove the dial indicator assembly from the number 1 cylinder after adjustment is completed and reinstall spark plug and plug lead.

Be sure link rod (L – Fig. MR28-4) protrudes 11/16 inch (17.46 mm) from link body as shown. If the engine is equipped with an idle stabilizer module (M – Fig. MR28-5), disconnect the white/black

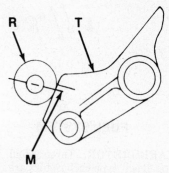

Fig. MR28-6 — Cam follower roller (R) should align with short mark (M) on throttle cam (T) when speed control linkage is set as outlined in text.

Fig. MR28-4 — View showing speed control linkage components used on 150, 175 and early 200 hp models. Refer to text for adjustment procedures.

A. Maximum spark advance screw
B. Maximum spark advance lever
C. Throttle lever
H. Throttle shaft
I. Idle speed screw
L. Link rod
N. Maximum throttle stop screw
P. Primary screw
S. Screws
T. Throttle cam

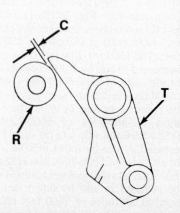

Fig. MR28-7 — Clearance (C) should exist between cam follower (R) and throttle cam (T) when speed control linkage is set as outlined in text.

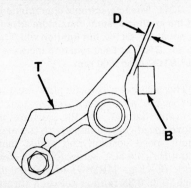

g. MR28-8 — Distance (D) should exist between rottle cam (T) and boss (B) when speed control linkage is set as outlined in text.

odule wire from switch box terminal. ape the end of the wire to prevent rounding. Be sure the other white/ lack wire remains connected to switch ox terminal.

NOTE: To prevent engine from starting, ake sure only the number 1 (top, star-oard) spark plug is installed and its plug ire attached.

Disconnect the fuel tank supply hose t the outboard motor connector. De-ach the throttle cable barrel from the etainer of the cable anchor bracket. Ad-ust idle speed screw (I – Fig. MR28-4) so ottom edge of throttle cam (T – Fig. R28-8) is a distance (D) of ⅛ inch (3.2 m) from top edge of mounting boss (B) or maximum throttle stop screw.

Withdraw the air intake cover from he front of the carburetors. Position hrottle lever (C – Fig. MR28-4) so idle peed screw (I) is against its stop. Loos-n carburetor synchronizing screws (S) nd allow the carburetor throttle plates o close freely. With light pressure, hold he cam follower roller against throttle am (T). At the same time, lift up on the ottom carburetor throttle shaft (H) to emove slack in linkage components. hen retighten screws (S). Check to be ure that carburetor throttle plates are ompletely closed and operate freely. Repeat adjustment procedure if setting s incorrect. Reinstall air intake cover.

Connect a power timing light to the number 1 cylinder spark plug lead. With the outboard motor in neutral, position hrottle lever (C) so idle speed screw (I) s against stop. Crank the engine with the starter motor and adjust primary screw (P) so the ignition timing is 11° ATDC on 150 hp models and 10° ATDC on 200 hp models.

Open the throttle until the maximum spark advance screw (A) is against stop. Crank the engine with the starter motor and adjust maximum spark advance

screw (A) so ignition timing is 18° BTDC on 150 hp models and 20° BTDC on 200 hp models.

NOTE: Due to electronic characteristics of the ignition system, maximum advance is set at 18° BTDC on 150 hp models and 20° BTDC on 200 hp models, but ignition will retard to 16° BTDC on 150 hp models and 18° BTDC on 200 hp models at high engine speed.

The carburetor throttle plate must not act as the wide open throttle stop. To prevent damage to the carburetors, move speed control linkage to the maxi-mum speed position and adjust maxi-mum throttle stop screw (N) so a clear-ance (C – Fig. MR28-7) of 0.010-0.015 inch (0.25-038 mm) is between throttle cam (T) and cam follower roller (R).

Reconnect idle stabilizer module wire to switch box. Reinstall spark plugs, then adjust idle speed screw (I – Fig. MR28-4) as outlined in the CARBURE-TOR section.

Hold idle speed screw (I) against stop and install the throttle cable barrel in the retainer while adjusting throttle ca-ble barrel so it fits into retainer and a very light preload between idle speed screw and its stop is established. Ex-cessive throttle cable preload will result in difficult shifting from forward to neutral.

(Late Model 200 HP). To synchronize ignition and carburetor opening, pro-ceed as follows: To verify timing pointer alignment, a dial indicator must be in-stalled in the number 1 (top, starboard) cylinder and the indicator synchronized with the piston position (dial indicator

reads zero when piston is at top dead center).

NOTE: To prevent accidental starting from flywheel rotation, remove all spark plugs and properly ground plug wires.

Rotate the flywheel counterclockwise approximately ¼ turn past the 0.462 inch (12 mm) BTDC reading, then rotate flywheel clockwise until indicator face reads 0.462 inch (12 mm) BTDC. Note the position of the timing pointer. Repo-sition pointer if the timing pointer is not aligned with ".462 BTDC" mark on fly-wheel. Remove the dial indicator assem-bly from the number 1 cylinder after ad-justment is completed and reinstall spark plug and plug lead.

Be sure link rod (L – Fig. MR28-9) pro-trudes 11/16 inch (17.46 mm) from link body as shown. A spark advance module is located above the top carburetor and is mounted to the air intake cover. If the module is equipped with four wires, no wires need to be disconnected to time the engine. But if the module is equipped with three wires, disconnect the white/ black module wire from switch box terminal. Tape the end of the wire to prevent grounding. Be sure the other white/black wire remains connected to switch box terminal.

NOTE: To prevent engine from starting, make sure only the number 1 (top, star-board) spark plug in installed and its plug wire attached.

Disconnect the fuel tank supply hose at the outboard motor connector. De-tach the throttle cable barrel from the retainer of the cable anchor bracket.

Fig. MR28-9 — View showing speed control linkage com-ponents used on late 200 hp models. Refer to text for ad-justment procedures.
A. Maximum spark advance screw
B. Maximum spark advance lever
L. Link rod
P. Primary screw

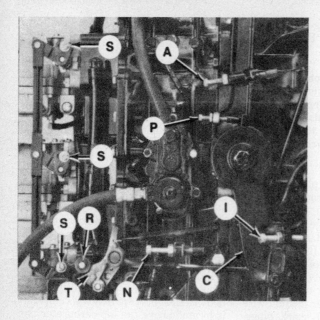

Fig. MR28-10 — View showing speed control linkage components used on late 200 hp models. Refer to text for adjustment procedures.

A. Maximum spark advance screw
C. Throttle lever
I. Idle speed screw
N. Maximum throttle stop screw
P. Primary screw
R. Cam follower roller
S. Screws
T. Throttle cam

NOTE: Due to electronic characteristi of the ignition system, maximum advance is set at 22° BTDC, but ignition will reta to 20° BTDC at 5400 rpm and increase 26° BTDC over 5600 rpm.

The carburetor throttle plate must n act as the wide open throttle stop. T prevent damage to the carburetor move speed control linkage to the max mum speed position and adjust max mum throttle stop screw (N) so a clea ance (C – Fig. MR28-7) of 0.010-0.01 inch (0.25-0.38 mm) is between thrott cam (T) and cam follower roller (R).

Reconnect spark advance module wir to switch box. Reinstall spark plug then adjust idle speed screw (I – Fi MR28-10) as outlined in the previou CARBURETOR section.

Hold idle speed screw (I) against sto and install the throttle cable barrel the retainer while adjusting throttle ca ble barrel so it fits into retainer and very light preload between idle scre and its stop is established. Excessiv throttle cable preload will result in diff cult shifting from forward to neutral.

REED VALVES. The fuel:air mix ture for each cylinder is directe through a reed valve assembly. Six ree valve assemblies are attached to the in take manifold. Reed block assemblie may be either mounted horizontally o vertically on intake manifold.

Reed petals shown in Fig. MR28-1 should be flat and have no more tha 0.007 inch (0.18 mm) clearance betwee free end of reed petal and seating sur face of reed block. On vertical mounte reed blocks, reed petals should not stan open more than 0.020 inch (0.51 mm Do not attempt to bend or straighten reed petal or turn reed petals around o reed block. Reed block seating surfac must be flat. Reed block should be re newed if indented by reed petals or dam aged. Reed petals are available in set for each reed block only.

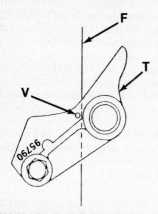

Fig. MR28-11 — A ⅛ inch (3 mm) diameter rod or drill bit must be installed in hole (V) on models with the numbers "95790" cast on throttle cam (T). The rod or drill bit should just contact edge of carburetor adapter flange (F) when speed control linkage is set and adjusted as outlined in text.

Install a ⅛ inch (3 mm) diameter rod or drill bit in hole (V – Fig. MR28-11) on models equipped with the casting numbers "95790" on throttle cam (T). Install a ⅛ inch (3 mm) diameter rod or drill bit in hole (V – Fig MR28-12) on models not equipped with numbers cast on throttle cam (T). While holding rod or drill bit perpendicular to throttle cam (T – Fig. MR28-11 or Fig. MR28-12), adjust idle speed screw (I – Fig. MR28-10) until rod or drill bit just contacts edge of carburetor adapter flange (F – Fig. MR28-11 or Fig. MR28-12).

Withdraw the air intake cover from the front of the carburetors. Position throttle lever (C – Fig. MR28-10) so idle speed screw (I) is against its stop. Loosen carburetor synchronizing screws (S) and allow the carburetor throttle plates to close freely. With light pressure, hold the cam follower roller (R) against throttle cam (T). At the same time, lift up on bottom carburetor throttle shaft to remove slack in linkage components. Then retighten screws (S). Check to be sure that carburetor throttle plates are completely closed and operate freely. Repeat adjustment procedure if setting is incorrect. Reinstall air intake cover.

Connect a power timing light to the number 1 cylinder spark plug lead. With the outboard motor in neutral, position throttle lever (C) so idle speed screw (I) is against stop. Crank the engine with the starter motor and adjust primary screw (P) so the ignition timing is 12° ATDC.

Open the throttle until the maximum spark advance screw (A) is against stop. Crank the engine with the starter motor and adjust maximum spark advance screw (A) so ignition timing is 22° BTDC.

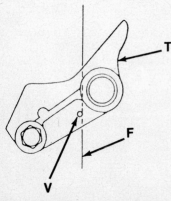

Fig. MR28-12 — A ⅛ inch (3 mm) diameter rod or drill bit must be installed in hole (V) on models with no numbers cast on throttle cam (T). The rod or drill bit should just contact edge of carburetor adapter flange (F) when speed control linkage is set and adjusted as outlined in text.

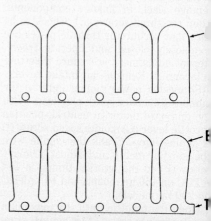

Fig. MR28-14 — View of "straight-cut" (A) and "teardrop" (B) reed petals. Note tang (T) on "teardrop" reed petals.

Note reed petal shapes in Fig. MR28-14. Early 150 hp engines are equipped with "straight-cut" reed petals (A) while late 150 and 200 hp engines are equipped with "teardrop" reed petals (B). Early 175 hp engines used both types of reed petals while later 175 hp engines are equipped with "teardrop" reed petals (B). Install reed blocks of early 175 hp engines so "teardrop" reed petals are towards center side of reed housing. When renewing reed petals on early 175 hp engines, always install a "teardrop" reed petal, even if the old reed was "straight-cut" type.

Reed stop setting is 0.200 inch (5.08 mm) for 150 hp models and 0.300 inch (7.62 mm) for 175 and 200 hp models. Measure from reed stop to reed petal seating surface as shown in Fig. MR28-15.

FUEL PUMP. A diaphragm type fuel pump is mounted on the intake manifold. Crankcase pulsations actuate the fuel pump diaphragm to pump fuel from tank to carburetors. Fuel pump pressure should be 4-5½ psi (28-38 kPa) at full throttle and 3 psi (21 kPa) at idle.

If the fuel pump malfunctions due to a split diaphragm on early 175 hp models, drill a 0.078 inch (1.98 mm) hole (B – Fig. MR28-17) through the pulse chamber so the hole is ⅜ inch (9.5 mm) from centerline of hole (A) as shown, and bevel edge of hole (A).

When overhauling the fuel pump, renew all defective or questionable parts. When assembling fuel pump, install check valves as shown in Fig. MR28-18 with tips of retainer (R) pointing away from check valves.

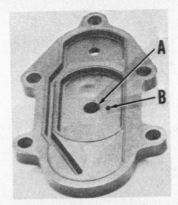

Fig. MR28-17—Modify the fuel pump on early 175 hp models with a split diaphragm as outlined in text.

OIL INJECTION SYSTEM. On some 1984 and 1985 models, an oil injection system is used. The fuel:oil ratio is varied from approximately 50:1 at full throttle up to approximately 100:1 at idle. The oil injection pump is synchronized with carburetor throttle opening via linkage. As the carburetor throttle opens or closes, the oil being supplied to the fuel pump is varied, thus matching the proper fuel:oil ratio to engine demand. The oil injection pump is driven by a gear secured to the engine crankshaft.

BLEEDING OIL INJECTION PUMP. Prior to engine start up, loosen bleed screw (B – Fig. MR28-20) 3 to 4 turns. Allow oil to drain from around bleed screw until no air bubbles are noticed, then retighten bleed screw (B).

THROTTLE ARM AND OIL INJECTION PUMP SYNCHRONIZATION. Place throttle linkage in idle position, then note if arm on oil injection pump aligns with mark (R) on casting. If not, adjust length of throttle arm (A) until marks properly align.

DRIVE GEAR. If a new oil injection pump drive gear is installed on crankshaft, the maximum allowable misalignment at split line of gear is 0.030 inch (0.76 mm). Tighten gear retaining Allen head screw to 8 in.-lbs. (0.9 N·m). Zero clearance should be noted at split line of gear.

CRANKCASE BLEED SYSTEM

A crankcase bleed system is used to remove unburned oil residue from the crankcase and lower main bearing and burn it or direct it to the three upper main bearings. See diagram in Fig. MR28-22 for a view of a typical crankcase bleed system. The number of hoses and hose routing may differ on some models. Check valves are located in intake manifold while fittings to cylinders are located in cylinder block. Hoses must be connected between fitting and check valve with same letter, i.e. a hose is connected between check valve "B" on reed valve housing and fitting "B" on cylinder

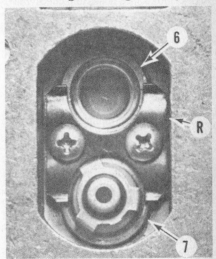

Fig. MR28-18 — View showing installation of outlet check valve (6) and inlet check valve (7) in fuel pump body. Install retainer (R) so tips are away from check valves.

Fig. MR28-15 — Reed stop setting (D) should be 0.200 inch (5.08 mm) for 150 hp models and 0.300 inch (7.62 mm) for 175 and 200 hp models.

Fig. MR28-20 — View showing oil injection pump used on some 1984 and 1985 models. Refer to text for adjustment procedures and identification of components.

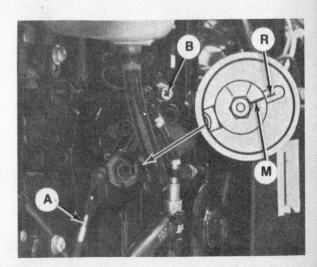

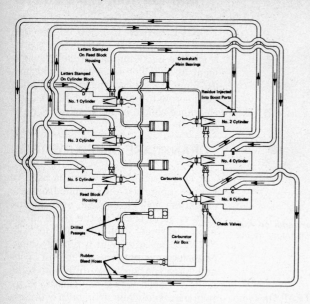

Fig. MR28-22—Diagram of typical crankcase bleed system.

COOLING SYSTEM

THERMOSTAT. All models are equipped with a thermostat in each cylinder head cover. Thermostat should begin to open at 140°-145°F (60°-63°C). A temperature sender is installed in the starboard cylinder head either below number one spark plug or in the outer portion of the cylinder head between number one and number three spark plug. The temperature sender will activate an alarm horn should engine overheating occur. Temperature sender may be checked with a continuity tester and a high temperature thermometer. Place sender and thermometer in water that is being heated. Sender positioned in the outer portion of the cylinder head should show a closed circuit when water tem-

block. Make sure hoses and check valves are properly identified prior to components being separated. Engine will not operate properly if hoses are connected incorrectly. Check operation of check valves.

IGNITION SYSTEM

All models are equipped with a solid state capacitor discharge ignition system consisting of trigger coils, stator switch box and ignition coils. The trigger coils are contained in a trigger ring module under the flywheel. Diodes, SCRs and capacitors are contained in the switch box. Switch box, trigger ring module and stator must be serviced as unit assemblies.

Check all wires and connections before troubleshooting ignition circuit. The following test specifications will aid troubleshooting. Resistance between blue and red stator leads or blue/white and red/white stator leads should be 5400-6200 ohms. Resistance between red stator lead and ground or red/white stator lead and ground should be 125-175 ohms. Resistance should be 1200-1400 ohms between the following trigger coil leads: between brown (in yellow sleeve) and violet (without yellow sleeve), between white (in yellow sleeve) and brown (without yellow sleeve), between violet (in yellow sleeve) and white (without yellow sleeve). Ignition coils may be checked using a suitable coil checker.

Recommended spark plugs are AC V40FFM or Champion L76V on models prior to serial number 5464486 or NGK-BU8H on models after serial number 5464485.

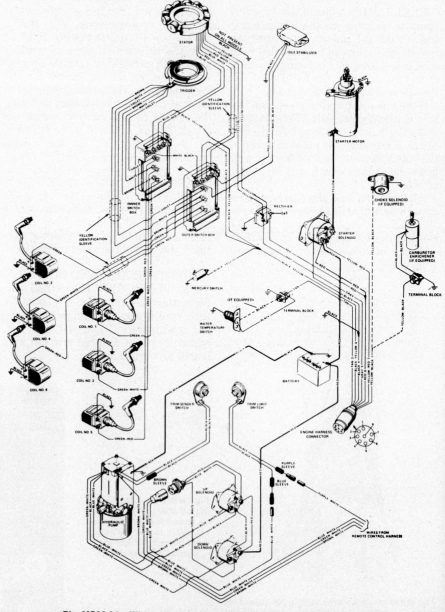

Fig. MR28-24 — Wiring diagram of later models. Early models are similar.

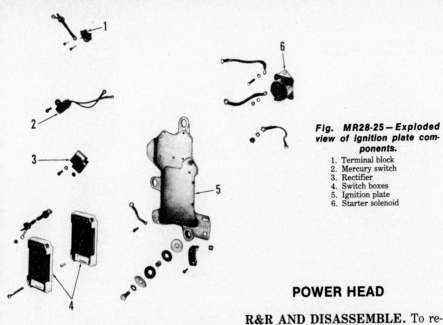

Fig. MR28-25 — Exploded view of ignition plate components.

1. Terminal block
2. Mercury switch
3. Rectifier
4. Switch boxes
5. Ignition plate
6. Starter solenoid

perature reaches 180°-200°F (82°-93°C) and then reopen when temperature drops to 160°-180°F (71°-82° C). Sender positioned below number one spark plug should show a closed circuit when water temperature reaches 230°-250°F (110°-121°C) and then reopen when temperature starts dropping below 230°F (110°C).

A water pressure relief valve is located on starboard side of cylinder block. Note cross section of valve shown in Fig. MR28-29. Diaphragm is renewable. Inspect components for nicks, cracks or other damage which may cause leakage.

WATER PUMP. The rubber impeller type water pump is housed in the gearcase housing. The impeller is mounted on and driven by the lower unit drive shaft. Water pump is accessible after separating gearcase housing from drive shaft housing as outlined in LOWER UNIT section.

POWER HEAD

R&R AND DISASSEMBLE. To remove power head assembly, disconnect all wires and hoses and remove all cowling which will interfere with power head separation from drive shaft housing. Detach shift rod from control cable bracket. Unscrew 10 locknuts securing power head to drive shaft housing and lift power head off drive shaft housing and install on a suitable stand. If equipped, remove oil injection pump reservoir and plug hose fittings. Remove flywheel, stator, trigger plate and starter motor. Remove choke solenoid, temperature sender, ignition coils, switch box plate assembly and speed control linkage. If equipped, remove oil injection pump. Re-

move fuel pump and disconnect and label interfering bleed hoses. Remove carburetors and airbox as an assembly. Remove intake manifold with reed valve assemblies, cylinder head cover, cylinder heads and exhaust manifold assembly.

Remove screws securing end caps to crankcase and loosen end cap to cylinder block screws. Remove crankcase mounting screws, then remove crankcase by using recesses under crankcase to pry against. Use extra care not to damage machined mating surfaces of cylinder block and crankcase. Mark connecting rods with cylinder numbers so they can be reinstalled in original cylinders and remove rod and piston assemblies. Unscrew end cap to cylinder block screws and remove end caps. Crankcase and cylinder block are matched and align bored and can be renewed as a set only.

Refer to following paragraphs to service pistons, rods, crankshaft and bearings. When assembling, follow the procedures outlined in the ASSEMBLY paragraphs.

ASSEMBLY. When assembling, the crankcase must be sealed against both vacuum and pressure. Exhaust manifold and water passage must be sealed against pressure leakage. Whenever power head is disassembled, it is recommended that all gasket surfaces and machined joints without gaskets be carefully checked for nicks and burrs which might interfere with a tight seal.

Install seals in lower end cap with lips down (away from cylinder block). Install seal in upper end cap with lip down (to-

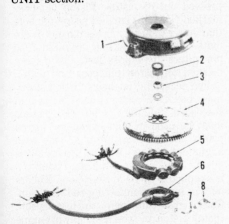

Fig. MR28-26 — View of flywheel and ignition components.

1. Flywheel cover	5. Stator
2. Plug	6. Trigger plate
3. Nut	7. Trigger plate link rod
4. Flywheel	8. Ball joint

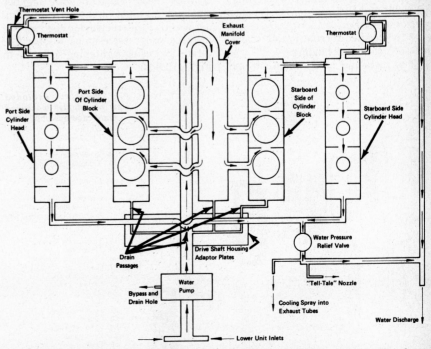

Fig. MR28-28 — Typical diagram of coolant flow. Refer to Fig. MR28-29 for cross section of water pressure relief valve.

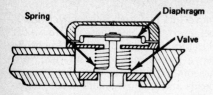

Fig. MR28-29 — Cross-sectional view of water pressure relief valve.

Fig. MR28-32 — Exploded view of crankshaft assembly.

1. Crankshaft
2. Roller bearing
3. Bearing race
4. Retaining ring
5. Seal rings
6. Ball bearing
7. Snap ring
8. Seal carrier
9. Oil seal
10. Piston rings
11. Piston pin
12. Piston
13. Retaining ring
14. Spacer
15. Bearing rollers (29)
16. Connecting rod
17. Rod cap
18. Roller bearing

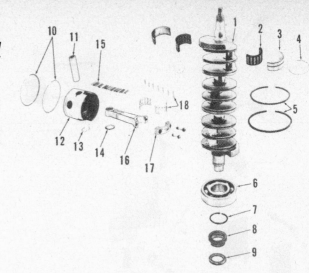

ward cylinder block). Be sure seal does not block bleed passage in end cap. Loctite 271 or 290 should be applied to seal bore of end caps. Lubricate all bearing and friction surfaces with engine oil. Loose needle bearings may be held in place during assembly using a light, nonfibrous grease.

Install pistons, rod and crankshaft assemblies as outlined in appropriate following paragraphs. End caps should be in place with screws installed but not tightened. Rotate crankshaft and check for binding. Cut gasket strips off flush with edge of crankcase bores. Apply a thin coat of sealer such as Permatex 2C-12 to mating surfaces of crankcase and cylinder block using care to prevent excess sealer from entering bearings, crankcase or passages.

Progressively tighten eight large crankcase screws until crankshaft seal rings are compressed and crankcase mates with cylinder block. Tighten eight large crankcase screws in three progressive steps to specified torque and using tightening sequence in Fig. MR28-33 for models prior to serial number 5464486 and Fig. MR28-34 for models after serial number 5464485. On early models, note location of long seal screw (B – Fig. MR28-33) and then tighten six smaller crankcase screws in three progressive steps to specified torque. Rotate crankshaft and check for binding.

When installing intake manifold and

Fig. MR28-33 — On models prior to serial number 5464486, use tightening sequence shown for large crankcase screws (C). Tighten small crankcase screws (S) next. Note position of long seal screw (B) used on early models.

exhaust manifold cover, tighten center screws first and work outward. Install cylinder head gaskets with number stamped in gasket up (away from cylinder block). Tighten cylinder head screws in three progressive steps to specified torque and using tightening sequence in Fig. MR28-35.

Fig. MR28-31 — Exploded view of cylinder block and crankcase assemblies.

1. Oil seal
2. Upper end cap
3. "O" ring
4. Roller bearing
5. Exhaust manifold cover
6. Gasket
7. Divider plate
8. Seal
9. Gasket
10. Cylinder block
11. Bearing locating dowel pins
12. Sealing strips
13. Crankcase
14. Thermostat housing
15. Thermostat
16. Cylinder head cover
17. Gasket
18. Cylinder head
19. Gasket
20. Oil seals
21. "O" ring
22. Lower end cap
23. Gasket
24. Reed petal stop
25. Reed petal
26. Reed block
27. Gasket
28. Intake manifold

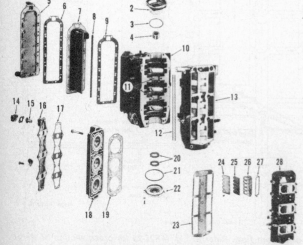

PISTONS, PINS, RINGS AND CYLINDERS. Before detaching connecting rods from crankshaft, make sure that rod and cap are marked so rods and caps are not interchanged and may be returned to original cylinders.

Piston pin is pressed into piston on all models. On early models, manufacturer recommends discarding piston if pin is pressed out of piston. Piston pin boss marked "UP" has smaller piston pin hole than other pin boss. Press pin out so pin exits "UP" boss first and press pin in so pin enters "UP" boss last. Pistons are marked on piston pin boss and piston crown according to their location in cylinder block. "S" pistons must be used in starboard cylinders while "P" pistons must be used in port cylinders. Install piston on connecting rods so side with alignment bumps (B – Fig. MR28-36) is nearer "UP" piston pin boss. Piston pin is supported by 29 loose rollers. Rollers may be held in connecting rod with nonfibrous grease during piston installation. Install piston and rod assembly in engine so "UP" pin boss is towards flywheel end of engine. Be sure piston ring ends are properly located around pins in ring grooves during installation.

On late models, the manufacturer recommends renewing piston pin needle bearings if piston pin is removed from ston. A torch lamp or suitable equivalent should be used to heat piston dome approximately 190°F (88°C) prior to removal or installation of piston pin. Piston pin is supported by 29 loose rollers. ollers may be held in connecting rod ith nonfibrous grease during piston installation. Use recommended Mariner ools or suitable equivalents when pressng piston pin in to or out of piston. Renew piston pin retaining clips during reassembly. Install piston and rod assemly in cylinder identified on rod during isassembly. Piston must be installed ith "UP" stamped on piston dome toard flywheel end of crankshaft. Pisons are marked "P" for port and "S" for tarboard on piston domes for correct istallation in port or starboard cylinder ank.

Maximum allowable cylinder tolerance is 0.006 inch (0.152 mm). Cylinders on 150 and 175 hp models can be bored to accommodate 0.015 inch (0.38 mm) or 0.030 inch (0.76 mm) oversize pistons. Cylinders on 200 hp models are chrome plated and no service other than renewal of cylinder block and crankcase assembly is recommended by the manufacturer.

CONNECTING RODS, BEARINGS AND CRANKSHAFT. Connecting rod has 29 loose rollers in small end and caged roller bearings in big end. Install piston on connecting rod so side with alignment bumps (B–Fig. MR28-36) is nearer "UP" piston pin boss on early models or bumps (B) and "UP" stamped on piston dome both face flywheel end of crankshaft on late models. Be sure alignment bumps (B) and marks (M) are correctly positioned when installing rod on crankshaft. Connecting rod big end is fractured type and rod and cap must be mated perfectly before tightening cap screws.

Inspect crankshaft crankpin and main bearing journal surfaces. If scored, out-of-round or worn, renew crankshaft. Check crankshaft for straightness. Do not interchange main bearings.

ELECTRICAL SYSTEM

Refer to Fig. MR28-24 for wiring diagram.

The rectifier may be checked by disconnecting wires to rectifier and using a continuity tester or ohmmeter as follows: Connect a tester lead to ground and then alternately connect other tester lead to alternator terminals of rectifier. Note reading then reverse tester leads. Tester should indicate a short or open circuit with first test and opposite reading when tester leads are reversed. Connect a tester lead to positive rectifier terminal and alternately connect other tester lead to alternator terminals of rectifier. Note reading then reverse tester leads. Tester should show opposite reading when tester leads are re-

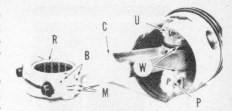

Fig. MR28-36 — View of piston and connecting rod assembly. Note location of alignment bumps (B), alignment marks (M), and washers (W) used on all models. "P" locating mark (P) and "UP" mark (U) are used on early models. "P" locating mark indicates port side piston while a starboard piston will have an "S" locating mark.

versed. Renew rectifier if testing indicates faulty circuits.

To check alternator stator, disconnect alternator leads from rectifier and connect an ohmmeter to alternator leads. Resistance reading should be approximately 0.75 ohms. There should be infinite resistance between either alternator lead or ground. Alternator output should be 7-9 amps.

LOWER UNIT

Two different lower units have been used and are identified by the gear shift mechanism. Cam-Shift lower units were used on early 150 and 175 hp models while E-Z Shift lower units are used on later 150 and 175 hp models and all 200 hp models. To externally determine which lower unit is being serviced, note the following: With lower unit attached to engine and in reverse gear, a Cam-Shift unit propeller will not ratchet when rotated counterclockwise while and E-Z Shift propeller will ratchet. With lower unit detached from engine, the Cam-Shift lower unit shift shaft will rotate 360° in a counterclockwise direction while E-Z Shift lower unit shift shaft will only rotate 30° in either direction.

After identifying lower unit, refer to appropriate following service section.

All Models

PROPELLER AND DRIVE CLUTCH. Protection for the motor is built into a special cushioning clutch in the propeller hub. No adjustment is possible on the propeller or clutch. Various pitch propellers are available and propeller should be selected to provide full throttle engine operation within rpm range listed in CONDENSED SERVICE DATA table at beginning of section. Propellers other than those designed for the motor must not be used.

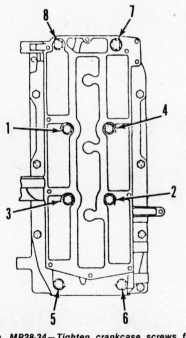

Fig. MR28-34 — Tighten crankcase screws following sequence shown on vertical and horizontal reed models after serial number 5464485.

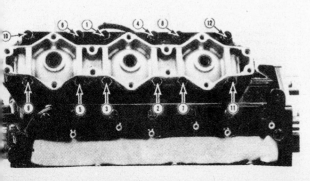

Fig. MR28-35 — Use sequence shown when tightening cylinder head screws.

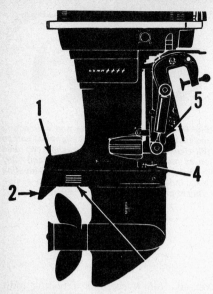

Fig. MR28-38—To remove the lower unit gear-case assembly, remove the attaching screws and stud nuts from positions indicated.

Cam-Shift Models

R&R AND OVERHAUL. Most service on the lower unit can be performed by detaching the gearcase from the drive shaft housing. To remove gearcase, remove plastic plug and Allen screw from location (1–Fig. MR28-38). Remove trim tab (2) and screw from under trim tab. Remove stud nuts from location (3), stud nuts (4) on each side and stud nut (5) then remove the lower unit gearcase assembly.

Remove the gearcase plugs and drain the gearcase lubricant, then secure the gearcase in a vise between two blocks of soft wood, with propeller up. Wedge a piece of wood between propeller and antiventilation plate, remove the propeller nut, then remove the propeller.

Disassemble gearcase by removing gearcase cover nut (55–Fig. MR28-39). Clamp outer end of propeller shaft in a soft-jawed vise and remove the gearcase by tapping with a rubber mallet. Be careful not to lose key (51). Forward gear (41) will remain in gearcase. Withdraw propeller shaft from bearing carrier (50) and reverse gear (46).

Clamp the bearing carrier (50) in a soft-jawed vise and remove reverse gear (46) and bearing (49) with an internal expanding puller and slide hammer. Remove and discard the propeller shaft rear seals (53).

To remove clutch (43) from propeller shaft, remove retaining ring (42). Insert cam follower (35) in hole in shaft and apply only enough pressure on end of cam follower to remove the spring pressure, then push out pin (44) with a small

punch. The pin passes through drilled holes in clutch and operates in slotted holes in propeller shaft.

To disassemble drive shaft and associated parts, reposition gearcase in vise with drive shaft projecting upward. Remove rubber slinger (5), water pump body (6), impeller (8) and impeller drive key (9). Remove flushing screw and

withdraw remainder of water pum parts. Clamp upper end of drive shaft a soft-jawed vise, remove pinion retaing nut (25); then tap gearcase off dri shaft and bearing. Note position a thickness of shims (21) on drive shaft uper bearing. Mesh position of pinion controlled by shims (21) placed unde neath the bearing.

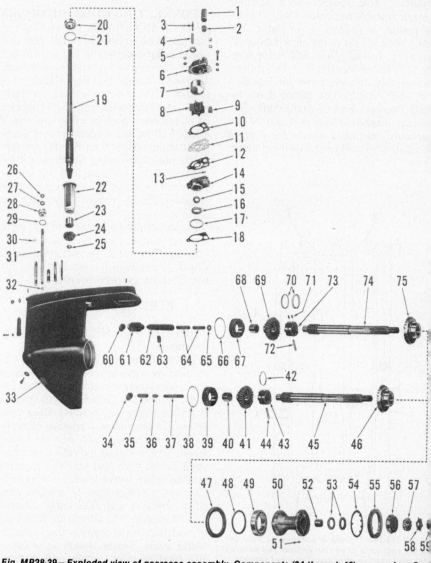

Fig. MR28-39—Exploded view of gearcase assembly. Components (34 through 46) are used on Cam Shift models while components (60 through 75) are used on E-Z Shift models. On late E-Z Shi models, a threaded bearing retainer located above bearing (20) is used on models not equipped wit preload pin (3) and spring (4).

1. Water tube guide	20. Bearing	39. Tapered roller	57. Thrust piece
2. Seal	21. Shim	bearing	58. Tab washer
3. Pin	22. Sleeve	40. Roller bearing	59. Nut
4. Spring	23. Roller bearing	41. Forward gear	60. Shift cam
5. Rubber ring (slinger)	24. Pinion gear	42. Spring clip	61. Cam follower
6. Water pump body	25. Nut	43. Dog clutch	62. Shift rod
7. Insert	26. Rubber washer	44. Pin	63. Pin
8. Impeller	27. Oil seal	45. Propeller shaft	64. Springs
9. Key	28. Bushing	46. Reverse gear	65. Shim
10. Gasket	29. "O" ring	47. Thrust washer	66. Shim
11. Plate	30. "E" ring	48. "O" ring	67. Tapered rolle
12. Gasket	31. Shift shaft	49. Ball bearing	bearing
13. Dowel pin	32. Circlip	50. Bearing carrier	68. Roller bearin
14. Pump base	33. Gearcase	51. Key	69. Forward gea
15. Oil seal	34. Shift cam	52. Roller bearing	70. Spring clips
16. Oil seal	35. Cam follower	53. Oil seals	71. Detent pins
17. "O" ring	36. Slide	54. Washer	72. Pin
18. Gasket	37. Spring	55. Nut	73. Dog clutch
19. Drive shaft	38. Shim	56. Thrust hub	74. Propeller sha
			75. Reverse gear

After drive shaft has been removed, forward gear (41) and bearing cone can be extracted. Use an internal expanding type puller to extract bearing cup if removal is required. Remove and save shim pack (38).

Shift shaft (31) and cam (34) can be removed after removing forward gear and unscrewing bushing (28) from gearcase.

If gear wear was abnormal or if any parts that affect gear alignment were renewed, install bearings on gears and drive shaft, and in gearcase (including shims 21 and 38). To determine gear mesh and forward gear backlash, proceed as follows: Install drive shaft components (19 through 25) and forward gear components (38 through 41). Tighten pinion nut (25) to 70 ft.-lbs (95 N·m). Install tool C-91-74776 in gear cavity of gearcase so it bottoms against shoulder of gearcase. Apply approximately 15 pounds (66.7 N) of downward pressure (toward pinion gear) and rotate drive shaft several times to seat drive shaft bearing. While maintaining downward pressure on drive shaft, measure clearance between pinion gear and tool. Clearance should be 0.025 inch (0.63 mm). Add or delete shims (21) to obtain desired clearance. Apply "Loctite" to drive shaft threads during final assembly.

With drive shaft and forward gear assemblies installed, install propeller shaft (without shift components) and bearing carrier (50), then install nut (55) until snug, but do not tighten. Attach a suitable puller to bearing carrier as shown in Fig. MR28-40 and apply 45 in.-lbs. (5.1 N·m) torque to puller screw. Rotate drive shaft several times to seat forward gear bearing. Install backlash measuring tool C-91-78473 on drive shaft as shown in Fig. MR28-41 and set up a dial indicator to read movement at "2" on backlash tool. Recheck torque on bearing carrier puller (45 in.-lbs. [5.1 N·m]). Measure forward gear backlash by applying downward pressure and turning drive shaft. Dial indicator should measure 0.008-0.013 inch (0.20-0.33 mm) backlash. Adjust backlash by adding or deleting shims (38 – Fig. MR28-39). Changing shim thickness by 0.001 inch (0.025 mm) will alter backlash by 0.0015 inch (0.038 mm).

When reassembling, long splines of shift shaft (31) should be toward top. Shift cam (34) is installed with long side on port side of gearcase. Assemble shifting parts (37, 36, 43, 44 and 42) into propeller shaft (45). Pin (44) should pass through hole in slide (36). Position follower (35) in end of propeller shaft and insert shaft into bearing (40) and forward gear. Install the reverse gear and bearing carrier assembly using new seals (48 and 53). Lip of inner seal (53)

should face in and lip of outer seal (53) should face propeller (out).

Upper oil seal (15) should be installed with lips facing up (toward engine) and lower oil seal (16) should be pressed into water pump base with lips facing down toward propeller shaft. Install remainder of water pump assembly and tighten the screws or nuts to the following recommended torque. Torque ¼-28 nuts to 25-30 in.-lbs. (2.8-3.4 N·m). Torque 5/16-24 nuts to 35-40 in.-lbs. (3.9-4.5 N·m). Torque ¼-20 screws to 15-20 in.-lbs. (1.7-2.2 N·m).

Do not apply excessive grease to drive shaft splines; there must not be grease on tops of drive shaft or shift shaft. Shift lower unit to forward gear and move guide block anchor pin on engine to forward gear position. Tighten gearcase fasteners with ⅜-16 threads to 55 ft.-lbs. (75 N·m) and fasteners with 7/16-20 threads to 65 ft.-lbs (88 N·m).

E-Z Shift Models

R&R AND OVERHAUL. Most service on the lower unit can be performed by detaching the gearcase from the drive shaft housing. To remove gearcase, shift outboard to neutral gear, then detach propeller and drain gearcase lubricant. Remove the plastic plug and Allen screw from location (1 – Fig. MR28-38). Remove trim tab (2) and stud nut from under trim tab. Remove stud

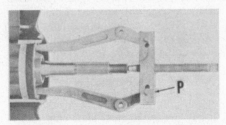

Fig. MR28-40 – Install a puller (P) as shown to preload forward gear bearing when determining gear backlash as outlined in text.

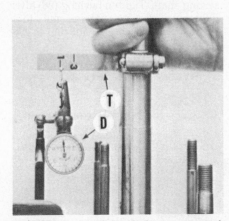

Fig. MR28-41 – Install backlash measuring tool C-91-78473 (T) and a dial indicator (D) set to read movement at number on tool as described in text.

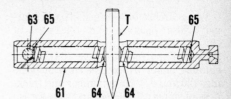

Fig. MR28-42 – Cross section of shift rod on E-Z Shift models. Center tool (T) using shims (64) as outlined in text.

nut from location (3), two stud nuts (4) from each side and stud nut (5) if so equipped, then withdraw the lower unit gearcase assembly.

To disassemble gearcase, remove rubber slinger (5 – Fig. MR28-39), water tube guide (1) and seal (2). Unscrew and remove water pump components (6 through 18). Position gearcase in a soft-jawed vise so propeller shaft is horizontal. Check and be sure gearcase is in neutral gear. Unscrew but do not remove shift shaft bushing (28) and withdraw shift shaft (31) from gearcase. DO NOT turn shift shaft during removal or gearcase may be shifted into forward or reverse gear position. Bend back lockwasher (54) tabs, unscrew nut (55) and use a suitable puller to remove bearing carrier (50).

NOTE: Do not apply side load or strike side of propeller shaft during or after removal of bearing carrier as shift rod (62) may break.

Withdraw propeller shaft from gearcase, but do not use excessive force or a puller. If shaft is lodged in gearcase proceed as follows: Push propeller shaft inward so it contacts forward gear, reinstall shift shaft and be sure gears are in neutral. Remove shift shaft and attempt to withdraw propeller shaft. If propeller shaft remains stuck, push shaft inward so it contacts forward gear. Reinstall bearing carrier and lay gearcase on its port side. Strike upper forward end of gearcase with a rubber mallet so shift cam (60) is dislodged and falls into a cavity in side of gearcase. Remove bearing carrier and propeller shaft.

To remove shift rod (62) from propeller shaft, remove spring clips (70) while being careful not to lose detent pins (71). Drive out pin (72) and remove shift rod (62) while being careful not to lose pin (63) which may fall from rod. Slide dog clutch (73) off shaft.

To disassemble drive shaft and associated parts, clamp upper end of drive shaft in a soft-jawed vise and remove pinion gear nut (25).

NOTE: On late models not equipped with pin (3) and spring (4), unscrew and remove bearing retainer above bearing assembly (20).

Tap gearcase off drive shaft and bearing. Note position and thickness of shims (21) and bearing. Remove pinion gear (24) and forward gear (69). Use a suitable puller to extract cups of bearings (20 and 67). Note number and thickness of shims (21 and 66) and save for reassembly. Pull out sleeve (22) then drive roller bearing (23) down into gear cavity for removal.

Inspect all components for excessive wear and damage. If water pump insert (7) must be renewed, use a punch and drive out old insert. It may be necessary to drill two holes in top of water pump body (6) to drive out insert – do not drill through insert. Apply RTV sealant to holes after installing the new insert.

Install bearings on gears and drive shaft, and in gearcase (including shims 21 and 66). To determine gear mesh and forward gear backlash, note number of pinion gear (24) teeth, then proceed as follows: Install drive shaft components (19 through 25) and forward gear components (66 through 69). Tighten bearing retainer above bearing assembly (20), if so equipped, to 100 ft.-lbs. (136 N·m) with side of retainer marked "OFF" facing toward top of gearcase housing. Tighten pinion nut (25) to 70 ft.-lbs. (95 N·m) on early models and 80 ft.-lbs. (109 N·m) on late models. Install tool C-91-74776 in gear cavity of gearcase so it bottoms against shoulder of gearcase. Apply approximately 15 pounds (67 N) of downward pressure (toward pinion gear) and rotate drive shaft several times to seat drive shaft bearing. While maintaining downward pressure on drive shaft, measure clearance between pinion gear and tool. Clearance should be 0.025 inch (0.64 mm). Add or delete shims (21) to obtain desired clearance. Apply Loctite to drive shaft threads during final assembly.

With drive shaft and forward gear assemblies installed, install propeller shaft (without shift components) and bearing carrier (50), then install nut (55) until snug, but do not tighten. Attach a suitable puller to bearing carrier as shown in Fig. MR28-40 and apply 45 in.-lbs. (5.1 N·m) torque to puller screw. Rotate drive shaft several times to seat forward gear bearing. Install backlash measuring tool C-91-78473 on drive shaft as shown in Fig. MR28-41 and set up a dial indicator to read movement at "1" on backlash tool for models with a 15-tooth pinion gear or at "2" for models with a 14-tooth pinion gear. Recheck torque on bearing carrier puller (45 in.-lbs. [5.1 N·m]). Measure forward gear backlash by applying downward pressure and turning drive shaft. Dial indicator should measure 0.008-0.013 inch (0.20-0.33 mm) backlash on models equipped with preload type drive shaft and 0.018-0.027 inch (0.46-0.69 mm) on models without preload type drive shaft. Adjust backlash by adding or deleting shims (66 – Fig. MR28-39). Changing shim thickness by 0.001 inch (0.025 mm) will alter backlash by 0.0015 inch (0.038 mm).

To properly adjust spring tension in shift rod (62), install springs (64) and pin (63) in shift rod. Insert tool C-91-86642, or an old pin (72) with a ground-down end, between springs as shown in Fig. MR28-42. Tool (T) or pin should be centered in shift rod slot within 1/64 inch (0.397 mm). Adjust tool position by installing shims (65) at ends of springs (64).

Assemble remainder of lower unit by reversing disassembly procedure while noting the following points: Install thrust washer (47) so larger diameter side is nearer reverse gear (75) then press bearing (49) on gear. Lip of inner seal (53) should face in and lip of outer seal (53) should face propeller (out). Install spring clips (70) so bent end of each spring engages the hole in one of the detent pins (71). Spring clips should be wound in opposite directions around dog clutch (73) and must not overlap. Use heavy grease to hold shift cam (60) in cam follower (61) with "UP" side facing up. Be sure "E" ring (30) and circlip (32) are seated on shift shaft (31) before inserting shaft. Tighten bushing (28) after tightening bearing carrier nut (55). Tighten bearing carrier nut (55) to 210 ft.-lbs. (284 N·m).

Upper oil seal (15) is installed with lips facing (toward engine) while lower oil seal (16) lips should face down towards gearcase. If reusing old impeller (8), install impeller so vanes rotate in same direction during previous operation. Be sure key (9) is properly installed. Tighten water pump fasteners to following torques: 1/4-28 nuts to 25-30 in.-lbs. (2.8-3.4 N·m), 5/16-24 nuts to 35-40 in.-lbs. (3.9-4.5 N·m) and 1/2-20 screws to 15-20 in.-lbs. (1.7-2.2 N·m).

Do not apply excessive grease to drive shaft splines; there must not be grease on tops of drive shaft or shift shaft. Shift lower unit to forward gear and move guide block anchor pin on engine to forward gear position. Tighten gearcase fasteners with 3/8-16 threads to 55 ft.-lbs. (75 N·m) and 7/16-20 threads to 65 ft.-lbs. (88 N·m).

POWER TILT/TRIM

Non-Integral Type

Two types of hydraulic power tilt/trim systems have been used. Early models are identified by the rectangular oil reservoir while later models use a circular fluid reservoir. Refer to the following sections for service.

Early Models

FLUID. Recommended fluid is SAE 10W-30 or 10W-40 automotive oil. With outboard in full down position, oil level should reach "Full" mark on dipstick. Do not overfill.

BLEEDING. Check fluid level in reservoir and fill if required. Operate trim system several times to purge air in system. Recheck fluid level and fill if required.

HYDRAULIC TESTING. Disconnect cylinder hoses from control valve and connect a pressure gage to outlets of control valve as shown in Fig. MR28-45. Note that large outlet is "up" circuit and small outlet is "down" circuit. Close appropriate pressure gage valve circuit. Make sure manual tilt valve (M) is tightly closed. Close and open appropriate pressure gage valves while operating system to check pressure in up and down circuits. Hydraulic pressure should be 3100 psi (21.4 MPa) minimum for up circuit and 1200 psi (8.3 MPa) minimum for down circuit. Pressure may drop slightly but should remain steady. If pressure is normal, inspect trim cylinders and hoses for leakage. If pressure is abnormal, install a good control valve and recheck pressure. If pressure remains abnormal, install a new pump body.

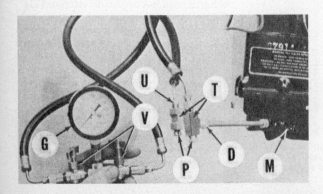

Fig. MR28-45 — Connect a pressure gage (G) as shown for hydraulic testing of non-integral type power tilt/trim.

D. "Down" line
G. Pressure gage
M. Manual tilt valve
P. Plugs
T. Tees
U. "Up" line
V. Valves

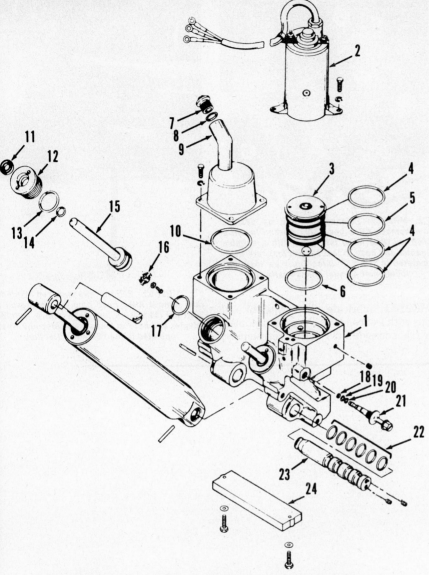

"UP" and "DOWN" ports. Note that the pump motor blue wire is the positive battery connection to pressurize the "UP" port and connecting the positive battery terminal to the pump motor green wire will pressurize the "DOWN" port. Pressure at the "UP" port should be 3100-3500 psi (21.4-24.1 MPa) and should not drop lower than 1500 psi (10.3 MPa) after pumping stops. Pressure at the "DOWN" port should be 1500-1900 psi (10.3-13.1 MPa) and should not drop lower than 750 psi (5.2 MPa) after pumping stops.

Integral Type

FLUID AND BLEEDING. Recommended fluid is Dexron II or Type AF automatic transmission fluid. Remove fill plug (7 – Fig. MR28-50) and fill reservoir until fluid is visible in fill tube with the outboard motor in the full-up position.

The hydraulic circuit is self-bleeding as the tilt/trim system is operated through several cycles. After servicing system, be sure to check reservoir level after filling and operating system.

HYDRAULIC TESTING. The system can be checked by connecting a 5000 psi (34.5 MPa) test gage to the UP (U – Fig. MR28-52) and DOWN (D – Fig. MR28-53) ports. Prior to connecting test gage, place outboard motor in the full-up position and engage tilt lock lever. Unscrew reservoir fill plug and rotate manual release valve (21 – Fig. MR28-52) three to four turns counterclockwise to release pressure on system. Remove UP

Fig. MR28-50 – Exploded view of integral type power tilt/trim system.

1. Manifold	9. Reservoir cover	18. "O" ring (0.114 in. [2.90 mm] ID)
2. Electric motor	10. Seal ring	19. "O" ring (0.208 in. [5.28 mm] ID)
3. Pump assy.	11. Seal	20. "O" ring (0.239 in. [6.07 mm] ID)
4. "O" rings (2.614 in. [66.40 mm] ID)	12. Cap	21. Manual release valve
5. "O" ring (2.739 in. [69.57 mm] ID)	13. "O" ring (1.475 in. [37.47 mm] ID)	22. "O" rings (0.989 in. [25.12 mm] ID)
6. "O" ring (2.739 in. [69.57 mm] ID)	14. "O" ring (0.612 in. [15.54 mm] ID)	23. Shaft
7. Fill plug	15. Trim piston & rod	24. Anode plate
8. "O" ring (0.583 in. [14.81 mm] ID)	16. Strainer	
	17. "O" ring (1.248 in. [31.70 mm] ID)	

ater Models

FLUID AND BLEEDING. Recommended fluid is SAE 10W-40 with an API rating of SE. Fill reservoir to FULL" mark on dipstick.

The hydraulic circuit is self-bleeding s the trim system is operated several imes. Be sure to check reservoir level fter filling and operating system after system has been serviced.

HYDRAULIC TESTING. The pump nay be checked by connecting a 5000 psi 34.5 MPa) test gage alternately to the

Fig. MR28-51 – Exploded view of tilt cylinder components.

1. "O" ring (0.307 in. [7.79 mm] ID)
2. Cup
3. "O" ring (1.957 in. [49.71 mm] ID)
4. Cylinder
5. Circlip
6. Washer
7. Scraper
8. "O" ring (0.854 in. [21.69 mm] ID)
9. Cap
10. "O" ring (2.067 in. [52.5 mm] ID)
11. Piston
12. Rod
13. Washer

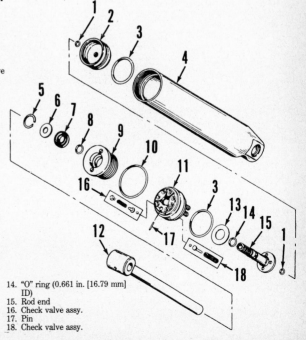

14. "O" ring (0.661 in. [16.79 mm] ID)
15. Rod end
16. Check valve assy.
17. Pin
18. Check valve assy.

or DOWN Allen head test port plug and connect test gage with suitable adapter and hose. Install fill plug and rotate manual release valve clockwise until seated. System pressure when testing at UP (U) port should be a minimum of 1300 psi (8.9 MPa). System pressure when testing at DOWN (D–Fig. MR28-53) port should be a minimum of 500 psi (3.5 MPa). Release pressure on system as previously outlined prior to removing test gage. Reinstall Allen head plug.

OVERHAUL. Refer to Fig. MR28-50 for an exploded view of manifold and trim cylinder components, and Fig. MR28-51 for an exploded view of tilt cylinder components. Special socket 91-44487A1 and a spanner wrench is required to service trim and tilt cylinders. Keep all components clean and away from contamination. Keep components separated and label if needed for correct reassembly. Note "O" ring sizes as stated in legends of Figs. MR28-50 and

Fig. MR28-52—Release pressure on system, then remove Allen head plug (U) and install a 5000 psi (34.5 MPa) test gage with a suitable adapter and hose to test system pressure when operated in the "UP" direction. View identifies location of manual release valve (21).

MR28-51. Lubricate all "O" rings or seal lips with Dexron II or Type AF automatic transmission fluid during reassembly.

Fig. MR28-53—Release pressure on system, then remove Allen head plug (D) and install a 5000 psi (34.5 MPa) test gage with a suitable adapter and hose to test system pressure when operated in the "DOWN" direction.

MERCURY

**Mercury Marine
Div. Brunswick Corp.
Fond du Lac, Wisconsin 54935**

TWO-CYLINDER MODELS

CONDENSED SERVICE DATA

TUNE-UP

Hp/rpm:
  Model 35 ....35/5400-6000
  Models 40, 400 & 402 ....40/5000-5500
Bore......................................2.870 in.
                                          (72.9 mm)
Stroke....................................2.562 in.
                                          (65.1 mm)
Displacement ....33.3 cu. in.
                                          (546 cc)
Compression At Cranking Speed ....*
Spark Plug:
  AC.......................................V40FFM†
  Champion...................................L76V
    Electrode Gap ....Surface Gap
Ignition:
  Type.................................Solid State
  Trigger Gap (Model 400) ....0.050-0.060 in.
                                       (1.27-1.52 mm)
  Carburetor Pickup Timing..................See Text
  Maximum Advance ....See Text
Fuel:Oil Ratio............................See Text

*Not more than 15 psi (103.5 kPa) variations between cylinders.
†AC type M40FFX spark plugs gapped at 0.030 inch (0.76 mm) are recommended for use on 1971 400 models if rough low speed operation is noted.

SIZES—CLEARANCES

Piston Rings:
  End Gap......................................*
  Side Clearance...............................*
Piston Skirt Clearance ....*

SIZES—CLEARANCES CONT.

Crankshaft Bearings:
  Top Main Bearing ....Roller or Ball Bearing
  Center Main Bearing ....Bushing With Reed Valve
  Lower Main Bearing ....Ball Bearing
  Crankpin ....Caged Rollers
Piston Pin Bearing In Rod ....Loose Rollers
  Number of Rollers Per Rod 29

*Publication not authorized by manufacturer.

TIGHTENING TORQUES

Connecting Rod ....180 in.-lbs.
                                        (20.3 N·m)
Crankcase Screws ....200 in.-lbs.
                                        (22.6 N·m)
Cylinder Cover:
  35 HP ....100 in.-lbs.
                                        (11.3 N·m)
  40 HP ....70 in.-lbs.
                                        (7.9 N·m)
Exhaust Cover ....200 in.-lbs.
                                        (22.6 N·m)
Flywheel Nut ....70-75 ft.-lbs.
                                        (95.2-102 N·m)
Reed Screws ....25 in.-lbs.
                                        (2.8 N·m)
Spark Plugs ....240 in.-lbs.
                                        (27.1 N·m)
Transfer Port Cover:
  35 HP ....50 in.-lbs.
                                        (5.6 N·m)
  40 HP ....60 in.-lbs.
                                        (6.8 N·m)

LUBRICATION

The engine is lubricated by oil mixed with the fuel. Fuel should be regular leaded, low lead or unleaded gasoline with a minimum pump octane rating of 86. Premium gasoline may be used if desired regular gasoline is not available. Recommended oil is Quicksilver Formula 50 or 50-D. A good quality BIA cer-

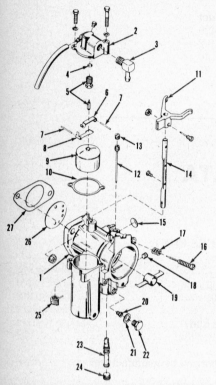

Fig. M10-1 — Exploded view of Mercarb "WMK" carburetor. Tillotson carburetor is similar.

1. Body
2. Bowl cover
3. Inlet fitting
4. Gasket
5. Inlet needle & seat
6. Primary lever
7. Pin
8. Secondary lever
9. Float
10. Gasket
11. Follower
12. Idle tube
13. Plug
14. Throttle shaft
15. Welch plug
16. Idle mixture screw
17. Spring
18. Plug
19. Venturi
20. Main jet
21. Gasket
22. Plug
23. Main nozzle
24. Plug
25. Spring

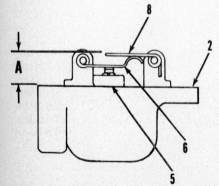

Fig. M10-2 — Distance (A) should be 13/32 inch (10.32 mm). Refer to text for adjustment procedure and Fig. M10-1 for parts identification.

tified TC-W oil may be used. Fuel:oil ratio should be 50:1 when using Formula 50 or 50-D oil. Follow fuel:oil ratio recommended by oil manufacturer if Formula 50 or 50-D is not used.

To break in new or overhauled motors, observe the following: If Quicksilver Formula 50 or 50D oil is used, vary throttle opening during first hour of operation while avoiding extended idling in cold water and prolonged full throttle operation.

The lower unit gears and bearings are lubricated by oil contained in the gearcase. Only Quicksilver Super Duty Gear Lubricant should be used. Gearcase is filled through the lower plug hole on port side of case, with motor in an upright position. The vent plug (located aft and above the fill plug) should be removed when filling. Lubricant should be maintained at level of vent plug.

FUEL SYSTEM

CARBURETOR. Standard make of carburetor is a Tillotson KD-5A on Model 400 prior to serial number 2979679. The standard make of carburetor on all other models is a Mercarb "WMK". Standard main jet (20 – Fig. M10-1) size on early models is 0.0785 (2 mm) and 0.072 inch (1.83 mm) on later models. Other main jet (20) sizes are available for adjusting the calibration for altitude or other special conditions. Preliminary adjustment of idle mixture screw (16) is 1 turn out from a lightly seated position. Recommended idle speed is 650-750 rpm on early models and 550-650 on later models with engine at normal operating temperature and in gear.

With the outboard motor properly mounted on a boat or suitable test tank, immerse the lower unit. Connect a tachometer and set it on the appropriate range scale. Start the engine and allow it to warm up to normal operating temperature. With the engine running at idle speed and forward gear engaged, turn idle mixture screw (16) until smooth engine operation is noted. Readjust engine idle speed screw (IS – Fig. M10-8, Fig. M10-13 or Fig. M10-14) to recommended idle speed if required.

To determine the float level, invert bowl cover (2 – Fig. M10-2) with inlet needle and seat (5), primary lever (6) and secondary lever (8) installed. Measure distance (A) from carburetor body surface to top of secondary lever (8). Distance (A) should be 13/32 inch (10.32 mm). Adjust distance (A) by bending curved end of primary lever (6). Turn bowl cover (2 – Fig. M10-3) upright and measure distance (D) between primary lever (6) and end of secondary lever (8). Distance (D) should be ¼ inch (6.4 mm).

Bend tab (T) to adjust. The contact spring located in center of float (9 – Fig. M10-1) should extend 3/32 inch (2.38 mm) above top of float. Check to see if spring has been stretched or damaged.

SPEED CONTROL LINKAGE. The speed controls change ignition timing and the amount of carburetor throttle opening. The timing and throttle opening must be correctly synchronized to provide proper operation. When checking, the complete system should be tested in sequence to ensure desired results. Speed control linkage used on 400 models is different from linkage used on 35, 40 and 402 models. Refer to the appropriate following paragraphs.

Model 400

Before attempting any test, check all linkage for free movement. Make certain that spark advance arm (Fig. M10-5) remains aligned with the throttle arm throughout its full movement, from idle until the spark control arm contacts the maximum advance stop screw. The spark advance arm is attached to the throttle arm with a spring which allows further movement of the throttle arm after ignition reaches maximum ad-

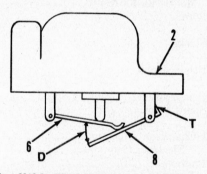

Fig. M10-3 — With bowl cover (2) upright, distance (D) between primary lever (6) and end of secondary lever (8) should be ¼ inch (6.4 mm). Bend tab (T) to adjust.

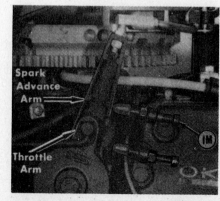

Fig. M10-5 — Merc 400 spark advance arm and throttle arm should be aligned as shown from idle until the spark advance arm contacts stop screw (IM). The throttle arm should still be able to move until carburetor throttle is completely open.

ance. Excessive friction in linkage, incorrect routing of pickup coil wires, etc., may prevent free movement and result in inaccurate checks and adjustments.

Check clearance between trigger pickup coil (C – Fig. M10-6) and trigger magnets in flywheel. Trigger gap (clearance) should be 0.050-0.060 inch (1.27-1.52 mm). If incorrect, loosen screws (S) and add or remove shims between plate (P) and starter housing. Make certain that trigger gap remains within limits throughout operating slot length. Screws (S) should be centered in elongated holes in plate (P).

Connect a suitable tachometer to the engine and a timing light to the top cylinder. Start the engine and shift into forward gear. Increase engine speed until the two ignition timing dots (D – Fig. M10-7) are in center of timing window. With controls set as outlined, the primary pickup edge of throttle plate should just contact throttle follower (11 – Fig. M10-8). If the primary pickup is not in contact with the follower or if the throttle is partially open, loosen the two screws that attach the throttle plate to the bottom of the actuator and move the throttle plate. Repeat the above procedure to confirm the proper adjustment.

Increase engine speed to 5000-5200 rpm and check maximum advance timing marks in window (W – Fig. M10-7). If the straight line timing mark is not in the center of the timing window, loosen locknut and turn ignition maximum advance stop screw (IM – Fig. M10-5) to stop movement of the spark advance arm when maximum advance timing is correct.

With the engine stopped, move speed controls slowly from idle toward fast position and stop just as the spark advance arm contacts ignition maximum advance stop screw (IM).

NOTE: It is important that maximum advance is correct before attempting this check. Just as the spark advance arm

touches stop screw (IM), the secondary throttle pickup should just contact the secondary arm of follower as shown in Fig. M10-9. If the secondary pickup is not yet touching or if the primary arm is away from cam at (X), carefully bend the secondary pickup until correct. If corrections are necessary, recheck by again moving speed controls from idle toward fast until spark advance arm just contacts stop screw (IM – Fig. M10-5).

Carefully move the speed controls toward maximum speed position while checking for play at the carburetor throttle follower. The throttle stop screw (Fig. M10-10) should stop movement of throttle arm just before all play is removed from the throttle and follower (11 – Fig. M10-9). With throttle arm against stop screw (Fig. M10-10), throttle follower (11 – Fig. M10-9) should have approximately 0.010-0.015 inch (0.25-0.38 mm) play to prevent damage. If speed controls are forced after throttle is completely open, the secondary pickup may be bent or other damage may result.

Idle speed is adjusted at stop screw (IS – Fig. M10-8). Refer to the CARBURETOR section for idle speed adjustment.

Models 35, 40 And 402

To synchronize ignition timing and throttle opening, proceed as follows: Connect a power timing light to the top cylinder spark plug lead and attach a suitable tachometer to the engine. With the engine running, shift into "Forward" gear. On manual start models, view window (A – Fig. M10-11) on all 35 and 40

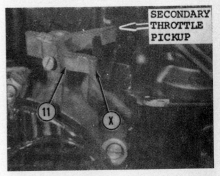

Fig. M10-9 – On Model 400, view of the throttle follower (11) attached to top of carburetor throttle shaft. Refer to text for checking the secondary throttle pickup.

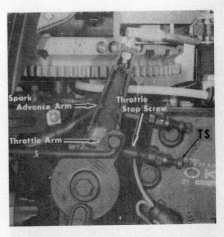

Fig. M10-10 – View of Model 400 control arms in maximum speed position. The spark advance arm contacts the ignition maximum advance screw before the throttle arm contacts the throttle stop screw (TS). Refer to text for adjustment.

Fig. M10-7 – View showing timing dots (D) and window (W) used on Model 400. Refer to text.

Fig. M10-8 – View showing throttle follower (11), idle mixture screw (16) and idle speed screw (IS) used on Model 400.

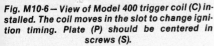

Fig. M10-6 – View of Model 400 trigger coil (C) installed. The coil moves in the slot to change ignition timing. Plate (P) should be centered in screws (S).

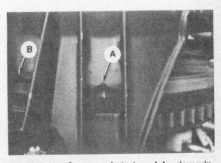

Fig. M10-11 – On manual start models, view window (A) on all 35 and 40 models and 402 models with serial number 4726798 and above, and window (B) on 402 models prior to serial number 4726798.

models and 402 models with serial number 4726798 and above, and window (B) on 402 models prior to serial number 4726798. On electric start models, refer to timing pointer and numbered degree marks on flywheel. Increase the engine speed until the two ignition timing dots (D–Fig. M10-12), on manual start models, are aligned with timing window notch (N). On electric start models, timing pointer should align with 2°-5° BTDC timing mark on flywheel. At this point, on 402 models and early 40 models, adjust turnbuckle (T–Fig. M10-13) so throttle cam just contacts follower (11) at point (P). On 35 models and late 40 models, adjust primary throttle pickup screw (PP–Fig. M10-14) so throttle cam just contacts follower (11–Fig. M10-13) at point (P).

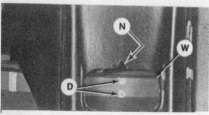

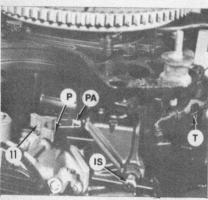

Fig. M10-12 — View showing timing dots (D), timing window (W) and notch (N) used on Models 35, 40 and 402 with manual start. Refer to text.

Fig. M10-13 — View of speed control components used on 402 models and early 40 models. Refer to text.

11. Throttle follower
P. Contact point
T. Turnbuckle
IS. Idle speed screw
PA. Secondary pickup arm

Fig. M10-14 — View of speed control components used on 35 models and late 40 models. Refer to text.

S. Spark advance arm
IM. Maximum advance stop screw
IS. Idle speed screw
PP. Primary throttle pickup screw
TP. Secondary throttle pickup screw
TS. Throttle stop screw

Increase engine speed to 5000-5500 rpm on 40 models and 5400-6000 rpm on 35 models and check maximum advance timing at timing pointer on electric start models and look for mark in window (W–Fig. M10-12) on manual start models. If the straight line timing mark is not aligned with notch (N) on manual start models or 27° BTDC mark on electric start models, loosen locknut and turn ignition maximum advance stop screw (IM–Fig. M10-4 or Fig. M10-15) to stop movement of the spark advance arm (S) when maximum advance timing is correct. Tighten locknut on screw.

Stop the engine and remove the timing light. Position spark advance arm (S) so it touches maximum advance stop screw (IM). Adjust throttle pickup screw (TP–Fig. M10-14 or Fig. M10-16) so it just contacts secondary pickup arm (PA–Fig. M10-13) on carburetor follower.

Move speed control to maximum speed position and check carburetor to make sure throttle valve is completely open. The throttle stop screw (TS–Fig. M10-14 or Fig. M10-15) should stop movement of throttle arm just before all play is removed from the throttle and follower (11–Fig. M10-13). With throttle arm against stop screw (TS–Fig. M10-14 or Fig. M10-15), throttle follower (11–Fig. M10-13) should have approximately 0.010-0.015 inch (0.25-0.38 mm) play to prevent damage.

Idle speed is adjusted at stop screw (IS–Fig. M10-13 or Fig. M10-14). Refer to the CARBURETOR section for idle speed adjustment.

REED VALVES. The inlet reed valves are located on the center main bearing assembly. The crankshaft must be removed before reed valves can be serviced.

Reed petals (18–Fig. M10-27) should be perfectly flat and have no more than 0.007 inch (0.18 mm) clearance between free end and seating surface of main bearing. The reed stop (17) must be carefully adjusted to provide 5/32 inch (3.97 mm) clearance between end of stop

and reed seating surface. Seating surface on bearing must be smooth and flat and may be refinished on a lapping plate after removing reed valves. Do not attempt to bend or straighten a reed petal and never install a bent petal. Reeds and reed plates are secured by either short screws threaded into main bearing or by screws extending through the bearing and having nuts on the ends. Lubricate reed valve before assembly. On models so equipped, install screws (21) with heads toward top and nuts (16) toward bottom to provide proper clearance for crankshaft.

FUEL PUMP. A diaphragm type fuel pump is used. Pressure and vacuum pulsations from the crankcase alternate to pull fuel from supply tank and fill carburetor float bowl. Most of the work is performed by the main supply chamber (5–Fig. M10-18). Vacuum in the crankcase pulls diaphragm (2) downward causing fuel to be drawn through inlet line (8), past inlet check valve (7) into main pump chamber (5). The alternate pressure forces diaphragm out and fuel leaves the chamber through outlet check valve (6). The booster pump chamber (3)

Fig. M10-15 — View identifying spark advance arm (S), maximum advance stop screw (IM) and throttle stop screw (TS) used on 402 models and early 40 models. Refer to text.

Fig. M10-16 — View identifying secondary throttle pickup screw (TP) used on 402 models and early 40 models. Refer to text for adjustment procedures.

Illustrations Courtesy Mercury

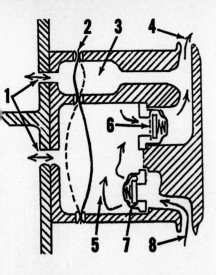

Fig. M10-18 — Schematic view of diaphragm type fuel pump. Pump body mounts on side of cylinder block and is ported to two crankcases as shown.

1. Pressure ports
2. Diaphram
3. Booster chamber
4. To carburetor
5. Main fuel chamber
6. Outlet check valve
7. Inlet check valve
8. Fuel inlet

serves to dampen the action of the larger, main pump chamber (5), and increase maximum potential fuel flow.

When overhauling fuel pump, renew all defective or questionable parts. Fuel pressure should be at least 2 psi (13.8 kPa) at carburetor with motor running at full speed.

IGNITION SYSTEM

Refer to Fig. M10-20 for Model 400 wiring diagram, Fig. M10-21 for early Model 40 and Model 402 wiring diagram and Fig. M10-22 for late Model 40 and Model 35 wiring diagram. All models are equipped with breakerless, solid state ignitions, however components, checks and adjustments are different. Schematics shown are for electric start models and include start motors and associated parts not used on manual start models. Ignition systems on manual start models are the same as those used on corresponding electric start models.

Refer to the appropriate SPEED CONTROL LINKAGE paragraphs in the FUEL SYSTEM section for checking and adjusting the ignition timing. Complete speed control linkage, including ignition, should be checked and adjusted if necessary, in a specific order.

Service to the ignition system consists of renewal of the faulty unit or repair of broken or shorted wires.

Recommended spark plug is AC V40FFM or Champion L76V. Champion QL76V may be used if radio noise suppression is required. Renew surface gap

plugs if the center electrode is more than 1/32 inch (0.79 mm) below flush with flat surface of plug end. If rough low speed operation is encountered on 1971 400 models, AC M40FFX or Champion L77J spark plugs gapped at 0.030 inch (0.76 mm) can be used.

COOLING SYSTEM

WATER PUMP. The rubber impeller type water pump is housed in the gearcase housing. The impeller is mounted on and driven by the lower unit drive shaft. Model 402 is equipped with a thermostat and a poppet type pressure relief valve (Fig. M10-24) mounted under the ignition coil bracket on top of the power head.

When cooling system problems are encountered, first check the water inlet for plugging or partial stoppage, then if not corrected, remove the gearcase housing as outlined in LOWER UNIT section and examine the water pump, water tubes and seals.

When assembling, observe the assembly notes, cautions and tightening torques listed in the LOWER UNIT section.

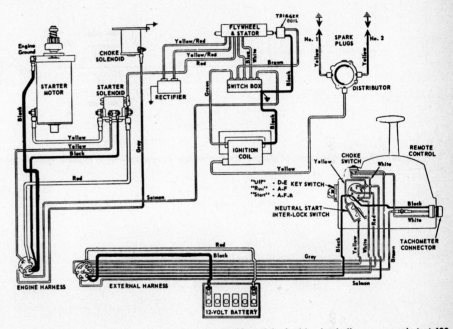

Fig. M10-20 — Wiring diagram of electric starting 400 models. Ignition is similar on manual start 400 models.

Fig. M10-21 — Wiring diagram of electric starting on early 40 models and 402 models. Ignition for manual start 40 and 402 is similar. External wiring harness in Fig. M10-20 is common to all electric start models.

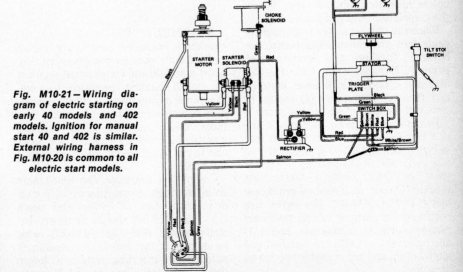

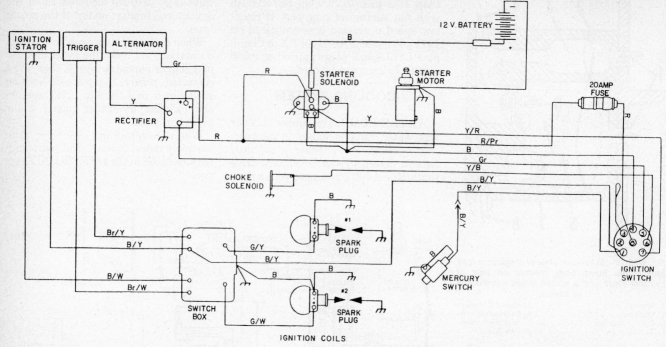

Fig. M10-22—Wiring diagram of electric starting on late 40 models and 35 models. Ignition system on manual start models is similar.

B. Black
R. Red
Y. Yellow
Gr. Gray
B/W. Black with white tracer

B/Y. Black with yellow tracer
G/W. Green with white tracer

G/Y. Green with yellow tracer
Y/B. Yellow with black tracer

Y/R. Yellow with red tracer
R/Pr. Red with purple tracer
Br/Y. Brown with yellow tracer

POWER HEAD

R&R AND DISASSEMBLE. To remove the power head assembly, first remove the top cowl and disconnect stop switch wire, speed control linkage and choke linkage. Remove nuts securing power head to lower unit; then lift off the complete power head assembly.

Place the unit on power head stand or equivalent and remove fuel pump, carburetor, flywheel and ignition components. Exhaust cover plate (1–Fig. M10-26), cylinder block cover plate (3) and transfer port cover (4) should be removed for inspection and cleaning.

Remove cap screws that retain top end cap (5). Remove screws (20) that secure lower end cap (16) on 35, 40 and 402 models and bearing retainer (10–Fig. M10-27) on 35, 40, 400 and 402 models. Unbolt and remove crankcase half (11–Fig. M10-26). Use extra care not to spring parts or to mar machined mating surfaces. Crankcase half (11) and cylinder block (13) are matched and align bored, and are available only as an assembly.

The crankshaft and bearings assembly, with pistons and connecting rods attached can now be lifted out of cylinder block for service or overhaul as outlined in the appropriate following paragraphs. Assemble by following the procedures outlined in the ASSEMBLY paragraph.

ASSEMBLY. When assembling, the crankcase must be completely sealed against both vacuum and pressure. Exhaust manifold and water passages must be sealed against pressure leakage. Whenever power head is disassembled, it is recommended that all gasket surfaces and machined joints without gaskets be carefully checked for nicks and burrs which might interfere with a tight seal.

Completely assemble the crankshaft main bearings, connecting rods, piston and rings. Lip of lower end seals (15–Fig. M10-26) should be down. Install screws (21–Fig. M10-27) with heads toward top. Install the crankshaft assembly by inserting pistons in lower end of cylinders. Two special Mercury

ring compressors should be used. If ring compressor kit is not available, two men must work together and use extreme care in installing the crankshaft and pistons assembly. Thoroughly lubricate the pistons, rings and bearings using new engine oil and make sure that ring end gaps are aligned with the locating pins in the ring grooves.

Make certain that end cap (5–Fig. M10-26) correctly engages dowel (10) and that retainer (10–Fig. M10-27) engages dowel (21–Fig. M10-26). Sealing strips (12) are used between halves of crankcase (11 and 13) on all models. Apply a thin bead of Permatex 2C-12 or a suitable equivalent to mating surface of crankcase half prior to installation. On models so equipped, seals (18) should be installed on the retainer attaching screws (20). After crankcase is assembled, turn the crankshaft until each piston ring has been visible in the exhaust and transfer ports and check for damage during assembly. Turn crankshaft several revolutions to make certain that all parts are free and do not bind.

PISTONS, PINS, RINGS AND CYLINDERS. Before detaching connecting rods from crankshaft assembly, make sure that rod and cap are properly identified for correct assembly to each other and in the correct cylinder.

Maximum allowable cylinder bore wear or out-of-round is 0.004 inch (0.102 mm) on 400, 402 and early 40 models and 0.006 inch (0.152 mm) on late 40 models and 35 models. Worn or slightly damaged, standard size cylinders may be repaired by boring and honing to accept an oversize piston. Pistons and rings are available in 0.015 inch (0.38 mm) oversize on 400, 401 and early 40 models and 0.015 inch (0.38 mm) and 030 inch (0.76 mm) on late 40 models and 35 models.

Piston pin is pressed in piston bosses and secured with retaining rings. Piston end of connecting rod is fitted with 29 loose bearing rollers which use the connecting rod bore and the piston pin as bearing races. Install bearing washers and needle bearings in piston end of connecting rod using light nonfibrous grease to hold them in place. Heat piston to 190°F (88°C), then install the piston pin using Mercury special tool (91-76159A1). Pistons must be installed so sharp vertical side of deflector will be toward intake side and long sloping side of piston will be toward exhaust port in cylinder. Thoroughly lubricate all friction surfaces during assembly.

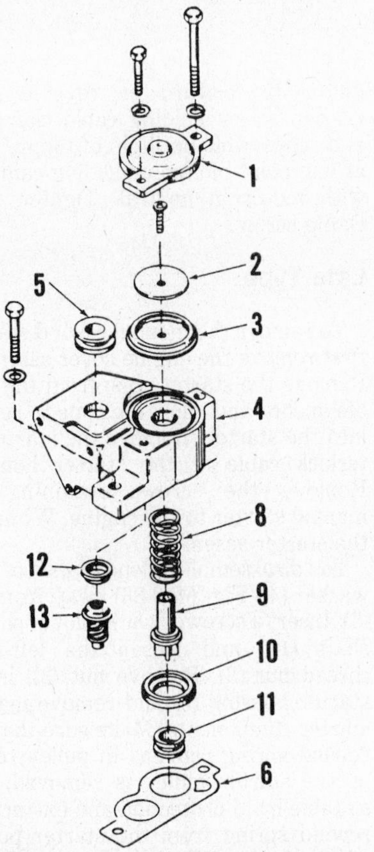

CONNECTING RODS, BEARINGS AND CRANKSHAFT. Upper end of crankshaft is carried by ball bearing (8 – Fig. M10-26). The unbushed center main bearing also contains the inlet reed valves. Lower main bearing (11 – Fig. M10-27) is not interchangeable with the upper ball bearing.

Each connecting rod rides on 29 loose bearing rollers (4) at piston pin end and caged rollers (5) at crankpin end. Check rod for alignment, using Mercury Alignment Tool C-91-2844A2, or by placing rod on a surface plate and checking with a light. Make certain that alignment marks on connecting rods are both on same side of rod during assembly.

Bearing surface in connecting rods and rod journals on crankshaft may be cleaned with #320 emery cloth if slight chatter marks are found. Inside diameter must not be increased nor outside diameter decreased by more than 0.001 inch (0.025 mm).

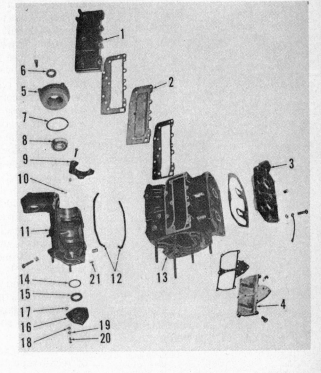

Fig. M10-26 — Exploded view of crankcase and cylinder block assembly typical of all models. Refer to text.

1. Exhaust cover
2. Exhaust baffle
3. Cylinder cover
4. Transfer port cover
5. Top end cap
6. Oil seal
7. "O" ring
8. Ball bearing
9. Starter motor bracket
10. Dowel
11. Crankcase half
12. Sealing strips
13. Cylinder block
14. "O" ring
15. Lower seal
16. Lower end cap
17. "O" ring
18. Seal
19. Washer
20. Screw
21. Dowel

Fig. M10-24 — Exploded view of typical thermostat and relief valve installation used on Model 402. Thermostat (13) is used on some 35 and 40 models.

1. Cover
2. Washer
3. Diaphragm
4. Coil mount bracket
5. Grommet
6. Gasket
8. Spring
9. Poppet valve
10. Washer
11. Grommet
12. Gasket
13. Thermostat

Fig. M10-27 — View of crankshaft and center main bearing assembly typical of the type used on all models. Bearing retainer (12) and spacer (13) are not used on early 402 models. Components (12 through 15) are not used on 400 models. Components (13 through 15) are not used on 35 and late 40 models.

1. Piston
2. Piston pin
3. Washer
4. Needles
5. Bearing cage
6. Connecting rod
7. Rod cap
8. Rod screw
9. Crankshaft
10. Bearing retainer
11. Ball bearing
12. Retainer ring
13. Retainer spacer
14. "O" ring carrier
15. "O" ring
16. Nut
17. Reed stop
18. Reeds
19. Center main bearing
20. Dowel pin
21. Reed stop screw
22. Bearing clamp screw

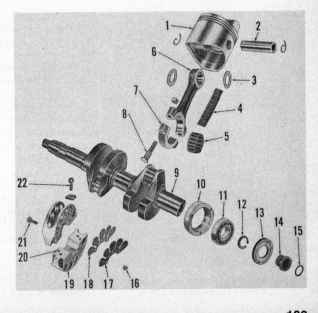

If bearing surface of rod and cap is rough, scored, worn, or shows evidence of overheating, renew the connecting rod. Inspect crankpin and main bearing journals. If scored, out-of-round, or worn, renew the crankshaft. Check the crankshaft for straightness using a dial indicator and "V" blocks.

Inspect and adjust the reed valves as outlined in REED VALVE paragraph, and reassemble as outlined in ASSEMBLY paragraph.

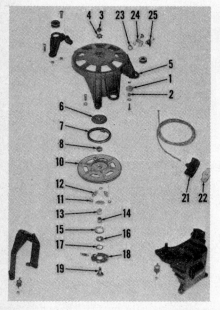

Fig. M10-30 — Exploded view of the recoil starter used on 400 models. Unit used on Models 40 and 402 is similar.

1. Pulley	14. Spacer
2. Spacer	15. Retainer
3. Nut	16. Washer
4. Lockwasher	17. Wave washer
5. Housing	18. Plate
6. Retainer	19. Sheave shaft
7. Rewind spring	21. Handle
8. Bushing	22. Anchor
10. Sheave	23. Spring
11. Wave washers	24. Lockout lever
12. Pawls	25. Cam
13. Bushing	

Fig. M10-31 — Refer to the text for adjusting the manual starter lockout cam.

MANUAL STARTER

Early Type

Refer to Fig. M10-30 for exploded view of rewind starter assembly. To disassemble, remove three stud nuts securing motor top cowl to power head, pry rope anchor (22) out of starter handle and remove top cowl. Tie a slip knot in start rope to keep it from winding into housing. Remove ignition trigger assembly on 400 models. Disconnect shift interlock cable (Fig. M10-32) on late 400 models and 40 and 402 models. Detach starter housing from top of motor. Insert a screwdriver in slot in top in sheave shaft (19 – Fig. M10-30) and loosen the left hand thread nut (3). Allow the screwdriver and shaft (19) to turn clockwise until recoil spring unwinds. Remove nut (3), invert the assembly and remove the parts, making sure that recoil spring (7) remains in housing recess as sheave (10) is removed. Protect hands with gloves or a cloth, grasp the recoil spring (7), remove spring and allow it to unwind slowly.

Lubricate the parts with Multipurpose Lubricant, and assemble by reversing the disassembly procedure. Install spring guide bushing (8) with chamfered end toward sheave (10). Make sure that pawls (12) are all installed the same way, with radius to outside and identification mark away from sheave (10). Install retainer (15) with cup end out and position washer (16) and wave washer (17) in cup. Make certain that tang on spring retainer (6) engages slot in sheave shaft (19). Position starter with end of shaft (19) through housing (15) and install lockwasher (4) and nut (3). Pull free end of recoil rope through cowl or starter housing and install handle (21) and anchor (22). Turn sheave shaft (19) counterclockwise until handle is pulled against cowl, plus an additional 1¼ turns; then tighten nut (3). Pull cord out and check for sticking and full return.

NOTE: When checking, it will be necessary to hold starter lock (24) up.

The starter lockout (23, 24 and 25) used on early 400 models prevents manual starter from being pulled at high speed throttle settings. To adjust, locate the locknut cam with ⅛ inch (3.175 mm) clearance as shown in Fig. M10-31. The top screw should be located at front of slot in cam. Adjustment is accomplished by moving cam on bottom screw. The ignition control rod should push the lockout cam and lever up at slow speed settings.

The shift interlock (Fig. M10-32) used on late 400 models and 40 and 402 models is used to prevent starting with

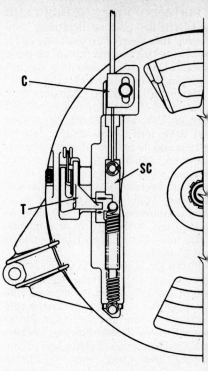

Fig. M10-32 — View of shift interlock used on early Model 40, Model 402 and late Model 400.

motor in forward or reverse gear. Loosen screw holding cable clamp (C) and move cable until pin of toggle (T) is at mid-point of cam on sliding cam (SC) with motor in neutral. Tighten cable clamp screw.

Late Type

To remove the manual rewind starter, first remove the engine cover assembly. Remove the starter rope from the handle anchor and allow the rope to rewind into the starter. Remove the starter interlock cable at the starter housing. Remove the screws retaining the manual starter to the engine. Withdraw the starter assembly.

To disassemble, bend tabs of tab washer (4 – Fig. M10-33) away from nut (3). Insert a screwdriver in slot of sheave shaft (19) and loosen the left-hand thread nut (3). Remove nut (3), invert starter housing (5) and remove manual starter components. Make sure that the rewind spring remains in pulley recess as the starter pulley is removed. Use suitable hand protection and extract the rewind spring from the starter pulley. Allow the rewind spring to uncoil in a safe area.

Inspect all components for damage and excessive wear and renew if needed.

NOTE: During reassembly, lubricate all friction surfaces with a suitable low temperature grease.

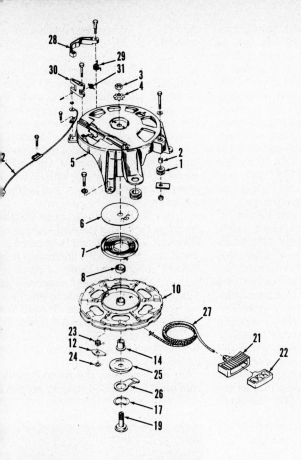

**Fig. M10-33 – Exploded view
of manual rewind starter
used on late Model 40 and
Model 35.**

1. Pulley
2. Spacer
3. Nut
4. Tab washer
5. Housing
6. Retainer
7. Rewind spring
8. Bushing
10. Sheave
12. Pawl
14. Spacer
17. Wave washer
19. Sheave shaft
21. Handle
22. Anchor
23. Spring
24. Clip
25. Washer
26. Lever
27. Starter rope
28. Interlock cam
29. Spring
30. Interlock actuator
31. Spring
32. Interlock cable

Assemble by reversing the disassembly procedure. Be sure that pawl (12) is installed with the radius toward the outside and the identification mark (dot) away from sheave (10). On early models, install washer (25) with cupped side facing away from sheave (10). Make certain that tab on spring retainer plate (6) properly engages rewind spring (7) loop during installation.

With the manual starter assembly properly assembled, install tab washer (4) and nut (3). Pull free end of starter rope (27) through housing (5) and secure with a knot approximately 1 foot (30 cm) from rope end. Place a suitable size screwdriver blade in sheave shaft (19) slot. Turn sheave shaft counterclockwise until starter rope knot is pulled against the rope guide, then continue to turn the sheave shaft an additional 2 full turns. Tighten nut (3) and bend tabs of tab washer (4) to secure nut (3) in place. Bend one tab on tab washer (4) into starter housing hole. Pull the starter out to full length while checking for freedom of travel, then allow the starter rope to rewind slowly onto the starter pulley.

Remount the manual starter assembly. Adjust starter lockout assembly by varying position of operation cable. Starter should engage when gear shift lever is in the neutral position,

but not engage when gear shift lever is in the forward or reverse position.

Install the engine cover assembly. Feed the starter rope through the engine cover opening and starter handle. Secure rope end with handle anchor.

LOWER UNIT

PROPELLER AND DRIVE CLUTCH. Protection for the motor is built into a special cushioning clutch in the propeller hub. No adjustment is possible on the propeller or clutch. Various pitch propellers are available and propeller should be selected for the best performance under applicable conditions. With speed control linkage correctly adjusted propeller should be selected to provide maximum speed of 5400-6000 rpm on 35 hp models and 5000-5500 rpm on 40 hp models. Propellers other than those designed for the motor must not be used.

R&R AND OVERHAUL. Most service on the lower unit can be performed by detaching the gearcase housing from the drive shaft housing. To remove the housing, remove the plastic plug and Allen head screw from location (1–Fig. M10-35). Remove trim tab (2) and stud nut from under trim tab. Remove the

stud nut from location (3) and the two stud nuts (4) from each side then withdraw the lower unit gearcase assembly.

NOTE: Do not lose plunger or spring (67 and 68—Fig. M10-36).

Remove the housing plugs and drain the housing, then secure the gearcase in a vise between two blocks of soft wood, with propeller up. Wedge a piece of wood between propeller and antiventilation plate, remove the propeller nut, then remove the propeller.

Disassemble the gearcase by removing the gearcase housing cover nut (61 – Fig. M10-36). Clamp the outer end of propeller shaft in a soft jawed vise and remove the gearcase by tapping with a rubber mallet. Be careful not to lose key (59) or shims (47) on early models. Forward gear (40) will remain in housing. Withdraw the propeller shaft from bearing carrier (56) and reverse gear (46).

Clamp the bearing carrier (56) in a soft-jawed vise and remove reverse gear (46) and bearing (49) with an internal expanding puller and slide hammer. Remove and discard the propeller shaft rear seal or seals (58).

To remove dog clutch (43) from propeller shaft, remove retaining ring (44). Insert cam follower (8) in hole in shaft and apply only enough pressure on end of cam follower to remove the spring pressure, then push out pin (42) with a small punch. The pin passes through drilled holes in dog clutch and operates in slotted holes in propeller shaft.

To disassemble the drive shaft and associated parts, reposition gearcase in vise with drive shaft projecting upward. Remove rubber slinger (11), water pump body (16), impeller (19) and impeller drive pin (20). Remove the flushing screw and withdraw the remainder of

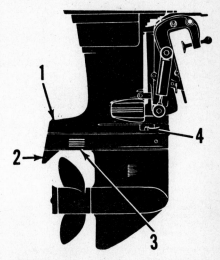

Fig. M10-35 – To remove the lower unit gearcase assembly, remove the Allen head screw and stud nuts from location indicated.

the water pump parts. Clamp upper end of drive shaft in a soft jawed vise, remove pinion retaining cap screw or nut (37); then tap gearcase off drive shaft and bearing. Note the position and thickness of shims (30) on drive shaft upper bearing. Mesh position of pinion is controlled by shims (30) placed underneath the bearing.

After drive shaft has been removed, the forward gear (40) and bearing cone can be withdrawn. Use an internal expanding type puller to withdraw bearing cup if removal is required. Remove and save the shim pack (38).

Shift shaft (5) and cam (7) can be removed after removing forward gear and unscrewing bushing (3) from gearcase housing.

If gear wear is abnormal or if any parts that affect gear alignment were renewed, check and adjust gear mesh as follows: Install forward gear (40) and bearing (39) using shims (38) that were originally installed. Position shims (30) that were originally installed at bottom of bearing bore, then install bearing cup (32) in housing bore against shims (30). Position the drive pinion in housing and insert drive shaft (33), with bearing (32) installed, into housing, bearing (34) and gear (35). Install the retaining nut (37).

Coat gears (35 and 40) with bearing blue and check mesh position. It will be necessary to push down on end of drive shaft while checking mesh position. If gears do not mesh in center of teeth, add or remove shims (30) under bearing as necessary. After setting mesh position, check backlash between teeth of gears (35 and 40). Backlash should be within limits of 0.003-0.005 inch (0.076-0.127 mm) on 400, 402 and early 40 models and 0.007-0.010 inch (0.178-0.254 mm) on 35 and late 40 models. To increase clearance (backlash), remove part of shim stack (38) behind bearing cup. If gears are too loose, add shims. After changing thickness of shims (38), gears should be recoated with bearing blue and mesh position should be rechecked. Install bearings (49), thrust washer (48) and reverse gear (46) in bearing carrier (56). Then, install bearing carrier and gear assembly using shims (47), on early models, that were originally installed and check backlash between gears (35 and 46). If backlash is not within the limits of 0.003-0.005 inch (0.076-0.127 mm), add or remove shims (47) as required. Adding shims (47) increases backlash (clearance).

When reassembling, long splines on shift rod (5) should be toward top. Shift

cam (7) is installed with notches up an toward rear. Assemble shifting parts (8S, 43, 42 and 44) into propeller sha (45). Pin (42) should be through hole slide (8S). Position follower (8) in end propeller shaft and insert shaft in bearing (41) and forward gear. Insta the reverse gear and bearing carrie assembly using new seals (55 and 58 Lip of seal (58) should face propell (out) on single seal models. On two se models, install inner seal with lip towar reverse gear and outer seal with l toward propeller.

Upper oil seal (26) should be installe with lips facing up (toward engine) an lower oil seal (27) should be pressed int water pump base with lips facing dow toward propeller shaft. Install r mainder of water pump assembly an tighten the screws or nuts to the follov ing recommended torque. Torque ¼-20 nuts to 25-30 in.-lbs. (2.8-3.4 N·m). To que 5/16-24 nuts to 35-40 in.-lbs. (3.9-4 N·m). Torque ¼-20 screws to 15-2 in.-lbs. (1.7-2.2 N·m).

On early models, the reverse lockin cam must be installed on shaft splines s

Fig. M10-37 – On early models, the reverse loc cam must be installed on shift splines as show when in forward gear position.

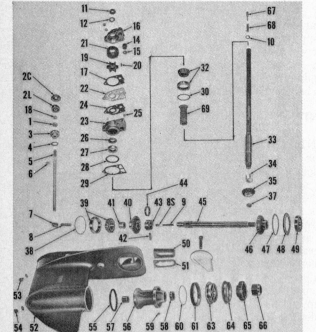

Fig. M10-36 – Exploded view of typical gearcase assembly. Two oil seals (1) are used on some models. Two seals (58) are used on later models. Shim (47) is not used on later models. On later models, a nylon washer replaces spacer (2L).

26. Oil seal
27. Spring loaded oil seal
28. "O" ring
29. Gasket
30. Shims
32. Tapered bearing
33. Drive shaft
34. Roller bearing
35. Drive pinion
37. Nut
38. Shim
39. Tapered roller bearing
40. Forward gear
41. Roller bearing
42. Cross pin
43. Dog clutch
44. Retaining ring
45. Propeller shaft
46. Reverse gear
47. Shim
48. Thrust washer
49. Ball bearing
50. Exhaust tube seal
51. Support plate
52. Gear housing
53. Vent screw
54. Filler screw
55. "O" ring
56. Bearing carrier
57. Roller bearing
58. Oil seal
59. Key
60. Washer
61. Housing cover nut
63. Thrust hub
64. Cupped washer
65. Spline washer
66. Propeller nut
67. Plunger
68. Spring
69. Lubrication sleeve

1. Oil seal
2C. Reverse locking cam
2L. Spacer
3. Bushing
4. "O" ring
5. Shift shaft
6. Snap ring
7. Shift cam
8. Cam follower
8S. Slide
9. Spring
10. "O" ring
11. Rubber ring (slinger)
12. Oil seal
14. Seal
15. Nylon washer
16. Water pump body
17. Gasket
18. Rubber washer
19. Impeller
20. Key
21. Insert
22. Plate
23. Pump base
24. Gasket
25. Dowel

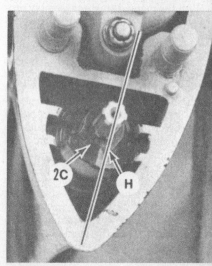

Fig. M10-38 – On later models, the reverse loc cam (2C) must be installed on shift splines wit high point (H) of cam positioned as shown whe in neutral position.

the two tabs are aligned with the left front stud when in FORWARD gear (clockwise) position. Refer to Fig. M10-37. On later models, place shift shaft (5 – Fig. M10-36) in neutral position. Install nylon washer with grooved side down and position reverse lock cam (2C – Fig. M10-38) with high point (H) of cam positioned as shown in Fig. M10-38.

Later models are equipped with two seals which fit over upper drive shaft splines. Install splined seal on drive shaft splines with splined seal end toward top of drive shaft, then install remaining seal with small end towards top of drive shaft.

Before attaching gearcase housing to the drive shaft housing, make certain that shift cam (7 – Fig. M10-36) and the shift lever (on motor) are in forward gear position on models with reverse locking cam shown in Fig. M10-37 and neutral position on models with reverse locking cam shown in Fig. M10-38. Complete assembly by reversing disassembly procedure.

Make certain that spring (68 – Fig. M10-36) and plunger (67) are positioned before attaching gearcase to drive shaft housing.

MERCURY
THREE-CYLINDER MODELS

Year Produced	Models
1972-1976	650
1977-1978	700
1979-1983	70
1984-1985	60

Letters after model number indicate equipment variations.
E – Electric starter and alternator
L – Long shaft
XS – High performance
PT – Power trim

CONDENSED SERVICE DATA

TUNE-UP
Hp/rpm:
Model 650 .... 65/4800-5300*
Models 700 & 70 .... 70/5000-5500
Model 60 .... 60/5000-5500
Bore .... 2⅞ in.
(73 mm)
Stroke .... 2-9/16 in.
(65 mm)
Displacement .... 49.8 cu. in.
(816 cc)
Firing Order .... 1-3-2†
Compression At Cranking Speed .... ‡
Ignition .... Solid State
Spark Plugs .... See Text
Fuel:Oil Ratio 50:1

*Model 650XS is rated 70 hp at 6000-7000 rpm.
†On models prior to serial number 5579017, firing order is 1-2-3.
‡Not more than 15 psi (103.5 kPa) variation between cylinders.

SIZES – CLEARANCES
Piston Rings:
End Gap .... *
Side Clearance .... *
Piston Skirt Clearance .... *
Crankshaft Bearing Type:
Top Main .... Ball Bearing
Main Bearing (2) .... Loose Rollers
No. of Rollers 56
Main Bearing (3) .... Loose Rollers
No. of Rollers 56
Bottom Main Bearing .... Ball Bearing
Crankpin .... Caged Roller

SIZES – CLEARANCES CONT.
Piston Pin Bearing .... Loose Rollers
No. of Rollers (each rod) 29

*Publication not authorized by manufacturer.

TIGHTENING TORQUES
Connecting Rods .... 180 in.-lbs.
(20.3 N·m)
Crankcase Screws .... 200 in.-lbs.
(22.6 N·m)
Cylinder Cover .... 70 in.-lbs.
(7.9 N·m)
Exhaust Cover:
¼ inch .... 115 in.-lbs.
(13 N·m)
5/16 inch .... 200 in.-lbs.
(22.6 N·m)
Flywheel Nut:
Model 650 .... 85 ft.-lbs.
(115.6 N·m)
All Other Models .... 65 ft.-lbs.
(88.4 N·m)
Reed Screws:
Model 650 .... 32 in.-lbs.
(3.6 N·m)
All Other Models .... 50 in.-lbs.
(5.6 N·m)
Spark Plugs:
Model 650 .... 17 ft.-lbs.
(23.1 N·m)
All Other Models .... 20 ft.-lbs.
(27.2 N·m)
Transfer Port Covers .... 60 in.-lbs.
(6.8 N·m)

LUBRICATION

The engine is lubricated by oil mixed with the fuel. Fuel should be regular leaded, low lead or unleaded gasoline with a minimum pump octane rating of 86. Premium gasoline may be used if desired regular gasoline is not available. Recommended oil is Quicksilver Formula 50 or 50-D. A good quality BIA certified TC-W oil may be used. Fuel:oil ratio should be 50:1 when using Formula 50 or 50-D oil. Follow fuel:oil ratio recommended by oil manufacturer if Formula 50 or 50-D is not used.

The lower unit gears and bearings are lubricated by oil contained in the gearcase. Only Quicksilver Super Duty Gear Lubricant should be used. Gearcase is filled through the lower filler plug hole until lubricant reaches the upper vent plug hole. Then allow 1 ounce (30 mL) of oil to drain from gearcase. On most models, both plugs are on port side of gearcase.

FUEL SYSTEM

CARBURETOR. Two WMK type carburetors (Fig. M11-1) are used on early 650 models; two Mercarb type carburetors (Fig. M11-5) are used on all 60, 70 and 700 and late 650 models. Refer to the appropriate following paragraphs for service information.

EARLY MODEL 650. Initial setting for idle mixture needle (A – Fig. M11-2) is one turn open from the closed position. Run motor until operating temperature is reached, then shift to forward gear and allow motor to run at idle speed. Slowly turn idle needle (A) out (counterclockwise) until motor runs unevenly (loads up). Turn needle in (clockwise) until motor picks up speed and again runs evenly and continue turning until motor slows down and misses. Needle should be set between the two extremes. Turning needle (A) in (clockwise) leans the idle mixture. Slightly rich idle mixture is more desirable than too lean.

NOTE: Mixture adjustment should not be attempted in neutral.

The high speed mixture may be adjusted for altitude or other special conditions by changing the size of the main jet (20 – Fig. M11-1). The standard 0.074 inch main jet should normally be correct for altitudes below 4000 feet.

NOTE: If main jet (20) is too small, high speed mixture will be too lean and may result in damage to power head.

To adjust the fuel level, remove inlet cover (2) and invert the cover assembly. Measure the distance (A – Fig. M11-3) between secondary lever (8) and gasket surface of bowl cover with inlet valve (5) closed. This distance should be 13/32 inch (10.32 mm). If incorrect, bend the

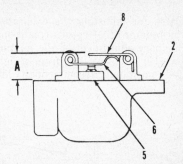

Fig. M11-3 – Distance (A) should be 13/32 inch (10.32 mm). Refer to text for adjustment procedure and Fig. M11-1 for parts identification.

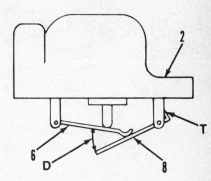

Fig. M11-4 – With bowl cover (2) upright, distance (D) between primary lever (6) and end of secondary lever (8) should be ¼ inch (6.4 mm). Bend tab (T) to adjust.

curved tang on primary lever (6) until correct measurement is obtained. Turn bowl cover (2 – Fig. M11-4) upright and measure distance (D) between primary lever (6) and end of secondary lever (8). Distance (D) should be ¼ inch (6.4 mm). Bend tab (T) to adjust. The contact spring located in center of float (9 – Fig. M11-1) should extend 3/32 inch (2.38 mm) above top of float. Check to see if spring has been stretched or damaged.

LATE 650, 60, 70 AND 700 MODELS. Standard make of carburetor is a center bowl type Mercarb. Two carburetors are used. Note that these carburetors are equipped with an enrichment valve (24 – Fig. M11-5) in place of a choke plate. Standard main jet (10) size is 0.080 inch (2.03 mm) for 650 short shaft models, 0.088 inch (2.23 mm) for 650 long shaft models and 0.086 inch (2.18 mm) for 60, 70, 650XS and 700 models. Standard vent jet (4) size is 0.072 inch (1.83 mm) for 650 short shaft models, 0.052 inch (1.32 mm) for 650 long shaft models and 0.066 inch (1.68 mm) for 60, 70, and 700 models. Standard main jet and vent jet sizes should be correct for operation below 2500 feet (762 m) altitude. Other jet sizes are

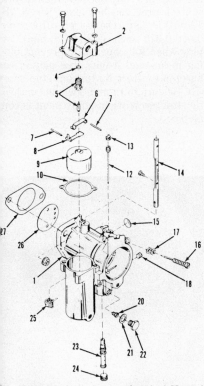

Fig. M11-1 – Exploded view of typical Mercarb "WMK" type carburetor.

1. Body	15. Welch plug
2. Bowl cover	16. Idle mixture screw
4. Gasket	17. Spring
5. Inlet needle & seat	18. Plug
6. Primary lever	20. Main jet
7. Pin	21. Gasket
8. Secondary lever	22. Plug
9. Float	23. Main nozzle
10. Gasket	24. Plug
12. Idle tube	25. Spring
13. Plug	26. Throttle plate
14. Throttle shaft	27. Gasket

Fig. M11-2 – Idle mixture needles (A) should be one turn out from a lightly seated position for initial adjustment.

available for adjusting the calibration for altitude or other special conditions. Preliminary adjustment of idle mixture screw (19) is 1 turn out from a light seated position. Recommended idle

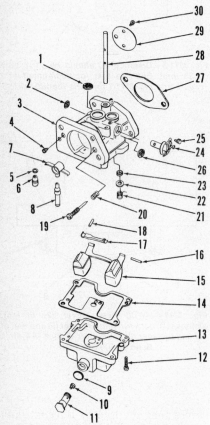

Fig. M11-5 — Exploded view of center bowl type Mercarb carburetor used on late 650, 700, 70 and 60 models.

1. Welch plug (9/16 inch)
2. Fuel inlet strainer
3. Body
4. Vent jet
5. Gasket
6. Inlet needle & seat assy.
7. Venturi
8. Nozzle
9. Gasket
10. Main jet
11. Main jet plug
12. Screw
13. Float bowl
14. Gasket
15. Float
16. Pin
17. Fuel inlet lever
18. Pin
19. Idle mixture screw
20. Spring
21. Spring
22. Flat washer
23. Rubber seal
24. Enrichment valve assy.
25. Screw & lockwasher
26. Welch plug (7/16 inch)
27. Gasket
28. Throttle shaft
29. Throttle plate
30. Screw

speed is 550-650 rpm on 650 models and 650-750 rpm on 60, 70 and 700 models with engine at normal operating temperature and in gear.

When overhauling carburetor, drive float pins (16) and fuel inlet lever pin (18) out towards knurled end of pin. Insert plain end of pin first during assembly. Note that strong (0.034 in. dia. wire) throttle return spring must be used on top carburetor throttle shaft. Numbers on throttle plate (29) must face outwards at closed throttle. Be sure rubber insert in fuel inlet valve seat (6) is installed so flat end of insert is towards inlet valve.

To determine the float level, invert the carburetor body and measure distance (D – Fig. M11-6) from the carburetor body to base of float (15). Distance (D) should be 11/16 inch (17.5 mm) and is adjusted by bending float inlet lever (17 – Fig. M11-7) within area (A).

SPEED CONTROL LINKAGE. The speed control linkage must be synchronized to advance the ignition timing and open the carburetor throttles in a precise manner. Because the two actions are interrelated, it is important to check the complete system in the sequence outlined in the appropriate following paragraphs.

Refer to the special precautions listed in the IGNITION section before servicing these motors. Incorrect servicing procedures can damage the ignition system.

NOTE: Do not disconnect any part of the ignition system while engine is running or while checking the speed control linkage adjustments.

MODEL 650 WITH DISTRIBUTOR. Disconnect the fuel tank and allow motor to run until all fuel is out of the carburetors. If any fuel remains, motor can start while checking the speed control linkage and may prevent accurate adjustments.

Connect an approved Mercury tachometer and timing light to the engine Slowly advance speed controls while cranking engine with electric starter. Throttle cam should just contact throttle lever (A – Fig. M11-10) as timing pointer aligns with specified primary pickup point on flywheel decal.

Primary pickup point is 0°-2° BTDC on models before serial number 355290 and 3°-5° BTDC on models after serial number 3552905. Adjust primary pickup point (initial contact of the throttle cam and lever) by turning adjustment screw (S). Be sure to tighten locknut on screw (S) when adjustment is complete.

To adjust maximum spark advance crank engine with electric starter and move speed controls toward full speed position. Timing pointer should align with 23° BTDC mark on flywheel decal as full advance stop screw (C – Fig M11-11) just touches spark control arm. If full advance is incorrect, loosen locknut on stop screw (C) and turn screw until timing light indicates full advance timing at 23° BTDC. Tighten locknut when adjustment is completed and recheck full advance timing.

Adjust stop screw (B) so carburetor throttles are fully opened when throttle control arm touches stop screw (B). Throttle shutters should have 0.010-0.015 inch (0.25-0.38 mm) free play when fully opened to prevent binding in linkage. Adjust free play in carburetor shutters by turning stop screw (B). Be sure to tighten locknut on throttle stop screw when adjustment is completed.

Fig. M11-6 — To determine float level, invert the carburetor body and measure distance (D) from the carburetor body to base of float (15). Distance (D) should be 11/16 inch (17.5 mm).

Fig. M11-7 — Adjust float level by bending fuel inlet lever (17) within area (A).

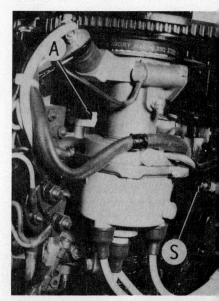

Fig. M11-10 — Primary pickup of throttle lever (A) should occur when ignition is advanced the specification listed in text. Refer to text for adjustment procedures.

MODEL 650 WITHOUT DISTRI-BUTOR. Disconnect fuel tank and run engine out of fuel to prevent engine starting while adjusting timing.

Connect a power timing light to number 1 (top) cylinder. Primary pickup point is 6°-8° BTDC. Crank engine with starter and position speed control so timing pointer and timing decal are aligned at 6°-8° BTDC. Turn pickup adjusting screw (P–Fig. M11-12) so carburetor throttle roller jsut contacts cam.

Crank engine with starter and position speed control so ignition timing advances to 28° BTDC. Turn stop screw (A) so screw just touches boss with ignition timing at 28° BTDC. Due to design of ignition system, maximum advance of 28° at cranking speed will provide a desired maximum advance of 23° BTDC at 5300 rpm.

Adjust stop screw (B) so carburetor throttle plates are fully opened with throttle arm stop screw (B) contacts boss. There should be 0.010-0.015 inch (0.25-0.38 mm) clearance between cam and carburetor throttle roller to prevent throttle plates from sticking in bores.

MODELS 60, 70 AND 700. To synchronize ignition and carburetor opening, proceed as follows: On models with an adjustable timing pointer, a dial indicator must be installed in the top cylinder and the indicator synchronized with the piston position.

Rotate the flywheel counterclockwise approximately ¼ turn past the 0.464 inch (12 mm) BTDC reading, then rotate flywheel clockwise until indicator face reads 0.464 inch (12 mm) BTDC. Note position of the timing pointer and reposition if timing pointer (P–Fig. M11-13) is not aligned with dot (D) on timing decal. Loosen screw (S) to reposition. Remove the dial indicator assembly from the top cylinder after adjustment is completed and reassemble.

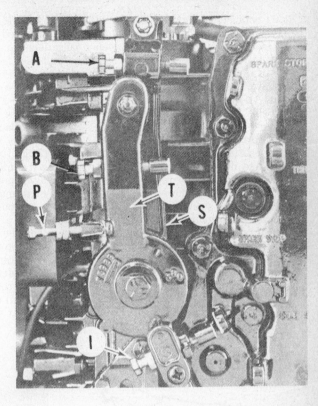

Fig. M11-12 — View of throttle and spark control linkage. Refer to text for adjustment.

A. Max. advance stop screw
B. Throttle stop screw
I. Idle speed screw
P. Pickup screw
S. Spark control lever
T. Throttle control arm

Connect a power timing light to number 1 (top) spark plug wire. With the lower unit properly immersed, start the engine and shift the outboard motor into the "Forward" gear. Run the engine at 5000-5500 rpm. Adjust maximum ignition advance screw (A–Fig. M11-12) until the timing pointer is aligned with the 23° BTDC mark on the timing decal. Secure screw position with locknut. Stop the engine and remove the timing light.

Move the spark lever until maximum advance screw (A) just contacts the stop boss and adjust secondary pickup screw (J) so carburetor cluster pin (R–Fig. M11-14) is located on throttle acutator cam (C) as shown. To prevent damage to the carburetor throttle plate at full throttle, adjust full throttle stop screw (B–Fig. M11-12) so a clearance of 0.010-0.015 inch (0.25-0.38 mm) is between throttle actuator cam (C–Fig. M11-14) and cluster pin (R) when throttle lever is moved to the wide open position.

Adjust idle speed screw (I–Fig. M11-12) as outlined in the previous CARBURETOR section.

REED VALVES. The inlet reed valves are located on the intermediate main bearing assemblies. Two reed valve assemblies are used, one for each carburetor. The center cylinder receives a partial fuel-air charge from each reed valve and carburetor.

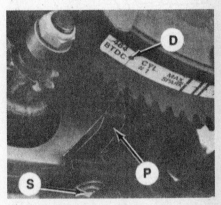

Fig. M11-13 — On models equipped with an adjustable timing pointer, timing pointer (P) must align with dot (D) on flywheel timing decal when the piston of the top cylinder is 0.464 inch (12 mm) BTDC. Loosen screw (S) to reposition pointer (P).

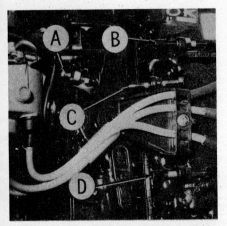

Fig. M11-11 — View of primary pickup screw (A), throttle stop screw (B), spark stop screw (C) and idle stop screw (D). Refer to text for adjustment procedures.

Fig. M11-14 — Adjust secondary pickup screw (P–Fig. M11-12) so carburetor cluster pin (R) is located on throttle actuator cam (C) as shown when maximum ignition advance screw (A–Fig. M11-12) just contacts the stop boss.

Illustrations Courtesy Mercury

Reed petals (19 – Fig. M11-28) should be perfectly flat and have no more than 0.007 inch (0.18 mm) clearance between free end of reed petal and seating surface of main bearing/reed block assembly. The reed stop (18) must be carefully adjusted to 0.180 inch (4.57 mm). This clearance is measured between end of stop and seating surface of reed plate as shown at (A – Fig. M11-16). Seating surface of bearing must be smooth and flat, and may be refinished on a lapping plate after removing reed stops, reed valves and dowels. Do not attempt to bend or straighten a reed petal to modify performance or to salvage a damaged reed. Never install a bent reed. Lubricate the reed valve units with "Quicksilver" Multipurpose Lubricant or a light distributor cam grease when reassembling.

Each valve unit has four reeds which are available only as a matched set. Crankshaft must be removed before reed valve units can be serviced.

FUEL PUMP. A diaphragm type fuel pump is used. Pressure and vacuum pulsations from the crankcase alternate to pull fuel from the supply tank and supply the carburetor. Most of the work is performed by the main supply chamber (5 – Fig. M11-18). Vacuum in the crankcase pulls the diaphragm (2) downward causing fuel to be drawn through inlet line (8), past inlet check valve (7) into main pump chamber (5). The alternate pressure forces diaphragm out and fuel leaves the chamber through outlet check valve (6). The booster pump chamber (3) serves to dampen the action of the larger, main pump chamber (5), and increase the maximum potential fuel flow.

When overhauling the fuel pump, renew all defective or questionable parts. Fuel pressure should be at least 2 psi (13.8 kPa) at carburetor when running motor at full throttle.

IGNITION SYSTEM

Models Equipped With Distributor

"Thunderbolt" electronic ignition used on three-cylinder 650 models uses an electronic triggering device and does not use breaker points. This ignition is extremely durable in normal operation but can be easily damaged by improper testing or servicing procedures.

Observe the following list of cautions and use only the approved methods for checking the system to prevent damage to the components.

1. DO NOT reverse battery terminals.
2. DO NOT check polarity of battery by sparking the lead wires.
3. DO NOT install resistor type spark plugs or lead wires other than those specified by the manufacturer.
4. DO NOT disconnect any wires while engine is running.
5. DO NOT ground any wire to engine block when checking. Ground only to front cover plate or bottom cowl to which switch box is mounted as described.
6. DO NOT use tachometer except those designed for this system.

TROUBLESHOOTING. Use only approved procedures when testing to prevent damage to components.

SPARK TEST. Do not remove spark plug wire while motor is running. Cut off the ground electrode from a standard 14 mm spark plug (not surface gap type) and connect one of the spark plug

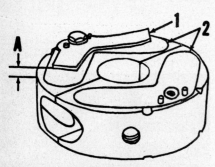

Fig. M11-16 – View of intermediate main bearing housing and reed valve assembly. Height (A) of reed stop should be 0.180 inch (4.57 mm).

Fig. M11-20 – Surface gap spark plugs should be renewed if center electrode is 1/32 inch (0.79 mm) below the end of plug.

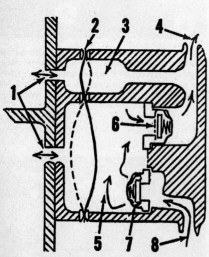

Fig. M11-18 – Schematic view of diaphragm type fuel pump. Pump body mounts on side of cylinder block and is ported to two crankcases as shown.

1. Pressure ports
2. Diaphragm
3. Booster chamber
4. To carburetor
5. Main fuel chamber
6. Outlet check valve
7. Inlet check valve
8. Fuel inlet

Fig. M11-21 – Exploded view of distributor drive and control components.

1. Screw
2. Flange
3. Key
4. Pin
5. Pulley
6. Spacer
7. Nut
8. Wave washer
9. Tab washer
10. Washer
11. Bolt
12. Ground strap
13. Adapter
14. Grease fitting
15. Locating pin
16. Nut
17. Washer
18. Distributor housing
19. Spark advance link
20. Washer
21. Primary pickup screw
22. Rubber cap
23. Spark advance lever
24. Return spring
25. Spring
26. Control lever bushing
27. Throttle control lever
28. Latch
29. Screw
30. Bushing
31. Throttle cam housing
32. Throttle cam
33. Link
34. Timing belt

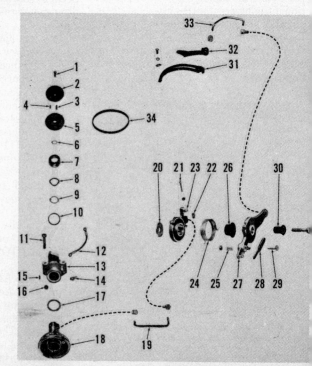

wires to the test plug. Ground the test plug to the support bracket using a clamp or jumper wire.

CAUTION: Do not hold spark plug or wire in hand.

Make certain that the test plug is properly grounded; then, crank motor with electric starter. If test plug fires but engine will not start, check for incorrect installation of timing belt as outlined in the following TRIGGER AND DISTRIBUTOR paragraph. Fuel system problems can also prevent starting. If test plug does not fire, check the wiring as follows.

WIRING AND CONNECTION TEST. Turn the key switch OFF. Connect one lead of voltmeter to red terminal of switch box (Fig. M11-33) and ground other lead to front cover plate. If red terminal is dead (no voltage), check battery, battery connections or for broken wiring harness. If red terminal has voltage, proceed as follows:

Connect one lead of voltmeter to white terminal and ground other lead to front cover plate. Turn key to the RUN position. If white terminal is dead (no voltage), key switch or wiring is defective. If white terminal has voltage, check the remaining components of system as follows:

Turn key switch OFF. Disconnect the black, white/black and blue trigger wires

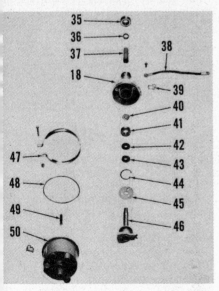

Fig. M11-22—Exploded view of distributor assembly. Refer to text for disassembly procedure.

18. Distributor housing
35. Upper ball bearing
36. Nut
37. Sleeve
38. Ground strap
39. Flame arrestor
40. Shim
41. Lower ball bearing
42. Shim

43. Spacer
44. Snap ring
45. Timing disc
46. Rotor & shaft assy.
47. Clamp
48. Gasket
49. Brush & spring
50. Distributor cap

from the distributor assembly and connect them to a distributor with a trigger that is known to be good. Disconnect the coil secondary lead from the distributor center terminal, then connect a test spark plug (or gap tester) to the coil secondary lead and ground the tester to the cowl support bracket. Turn the key switch to RUN position and rotate the test distributor by hand. If a spark jumps at test plug, the original trigger assembly is faulty and should be renewed. If spark does not jump at test plug, listen for "click" around area of the high tensions coil as the test distributor is turned. "Clicking" indicated shorted high tension coils or high tension (secondary) lead wire. If the lead wire is not shorted, the high tension coil should be checked further as outlined in the following paragraph. If spark does not jump the test plug and coil is not damaged, the switch box should be renewed.

NOTE: A faulty switch box is nearly always caused by reversing battery leads, which damages the rectifier and in turn damages the switch box.

If switch box is suspected, check rectifier before renewing the switch box. If tests indicate that rectifier is damaged, renew the rectifier and again test the ignition system.

NOTE: Before disconnecting any wires, make certain that motor is not running and disconnect battery.

COIL TEST. The ignition coil can be tested using an ignition tester available from several sources including the following:

GRAHAM TESTERS, INC.
4220 Central Ave. N.E.
Minneapolis, Minn. 55421

MERC-O-TRONIC
INSTRUMENTS CORP.
215 Branch St.
Almont, Mich. 48003

An alternate method of checking is possible as follows: Disconnect the coil secondary lead and the green lead to the switch box. Resistance between the CONV (green lead) terminal and the GRD (black lead) terminal should be 0 ohms on the Rx1 scale of an ohmmeter. Resistance between the GRD terminal and the secondary voltage tower should be 8-12 ohms on the Rx100 scale. If either of these resistances are incorrect, renew the high tension coil.

SPARK PLUGS. The spark plugs should be renewed if the center electrode is burned back more than 1/32 inch

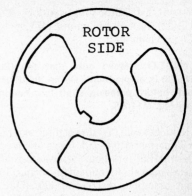

Fig. M11-23—Timing disc must be installed with side shown toward distributor cap (down).

(0.79 mm) below flat surface of the plug end. Refer to Fig. M11-20. Standard recommended spark plugs are Champion type L77V or AC type V40FFM surface gap spark plugs. Radio noise suppression, AC type, VR40FFM spark plug may also be used.

TRIGGER AND DISTRIBUTOR. The electronic trigger coil is located in the distributor housing (18—Fig. M11-21) and is available only as an assembly with the housing. Before removing any of the components or disconnecting any wires, make certain that battery is disconnected.

Disassemble as follows: Disconnect battery and trigger wires. Remove flange (2—Fig. M11-21), then unbolt and remove adapter (13). Pry pulley (5) off shaft, then remove key (3) and spacer (6). Bend tabs of washer (9) away from nut (7). Remove nut and withdraw distributor from adapter (13). Carefully press bearing (35—Fig. M11-22) out of housing by working through two holes provided. Use caution to prevent damage to nut (36) or to distributor rotor shaft (46). Remove nut (36) and bump distributor shaft out of bearing (41). Bearing (41) is retained by snap ring (44).

Inspect distributor parts, especially bearings for wear and cleanliness. Renew or clean and lubricate parts as necessary. Inspect distributor cap for cracks or evidence of corrosion or carbon build up. Renew distributor cap if cracked or if evidence of leakage is found.

When reassembling, install shim (40), bearing (41) and snap ring bearing retainer (44). Position shim (42) and spacer (43), then insert timing disc (45) as shown in Fig. M11-23.

NOTE: If the timing disc is installed incorrectly it will be impossible to set ignition timing.

Insert distributor rotor shaft (46 – Fig. M11-22) through timing disc (45), spacer (43) and shim (42).

CAUTION: Make sure that tab (Fig. M11-23) is aligned with slot in distributor shaft before pressing shaft into bearing (41 — Fig. M11-22).

Install sleeve (37) and tighten nut (36) to 70 in.-lbs. (7.9 N·m). Press upper ball bearing (35) into housing around shaft. Install gasket (48) and brush spring (49), then assemble distributor cap (50) to housing with clamp (47).

NOTE: Joint of clamp (47) should be positioned next to trigger wires coming out of distributor housing.

Place wave washer (17 – Fig. M11-21) on distributor housing (18) and insert housing in adapter (13). Install flat washer (10), tab washer (9) and washer (8) with raised portion next to nut (7). Install and tighten nut (7), back it out just enough to align tabs on tab washer (9), then bend tabs into slots in nut. Install spacer (6), then install pulley (5) over drive key (3).

Align BELT ALIGNING MARK on flywheel with plastic timing pointer on engine, then align cast timing point on pulley (5) with cast timing boss on adapter (13). Place distributor drive belt over pulley (5) and bolt adapter to engine while maintaining alignment of all marks. Make sure that locating pin

(15) is installed between engine block and adapter. Install flange (2) and secure in position with pin (4) and screw (1). Refer to SPEED CONTROL LINKAGE paragraphs for adjusting linkage and timing ignition.

Models Without Distributor

These models are equipped with a "Thunderbolt" solid state capacitor discharge ignition system consisting of trigger coils, stator, switch box and ignition coils. The trigger coils are contained in a trigger ring module under the flywheel. Diodes, SCR's and capacitors are contained in the switch box. Switch box, trigger ring module and stator must be serviced as unit assemblies.

Check all wires and connections before troubleshooting ignition circuit. The following test specifications will aid troubleshooting. Resistance between red and blue stator leads should be 5400-6200 ohms. Resistance between red stator lead and ground should be 125-175 ohms. Resistance between white, violet or brown trigger coil leads and white/black trigger coil lead should be 1100-1400 ohms.

Recommended spark plugs are AC V40FFM or Champion L76V.

COOLING SYSTEM

WATER PUMP. The rubber impeller type water pump is housed in the gearcase housing. The impeller is mounted

on and driven by the lower unit drive shaft.

When cooling system problems are encountered, first check the water inlet for plugging or partial stoppage, then if not corrected, remove the gearcase housing as outlined in LOWER UNIT section and examine the water pump, water tubes and seals.

Water pump housing is plastic. Refer to assembly notes, cautions and tightening torques listed in the LOWER UNIT section when assembling.

POWER HEAD

R&R AND DISASSEMBLE. To remove the power head assembly, first disconnect the battery and remove the top side cowling. Remove electric starter, then disconnect all interfering wires and linkage. Remove the stud nuts which secure the power head to lower unit, then jar power head on exhaust side to loosen gasket. Lift power head from lower unit and install on a suitable stand. Remove the flywheel, distributor, alternator-generator and the carburetors. Exhaust manifold cover, cylinder block cover and transfer port covers should be removed for cleaning and inspection.

Remove the upper and lower crankcase end caps by using a suitable puller attached to threaded holes in caps. Remove the main bearing locking bolts from front crankcase half, remove the flange bolts; then remove crankcase front half by inserting screwdriver in the recesses provided on side flanges. Use extra care not to spring the parts or to mar the machined, mating surfaces. The crankcase half (25 – Fig. M11-25 or Fig. M11-26) and cylinder assembly (6) are matched and align bored, and are available only as an assembly.

Crankshaft, pistons, bearings and connecting rods may now be removed for service as outlined in the appropriate following paragraphs. When assembling, follow the procedures outlined in the ASSEMBLY paragraph.

ASSEMBLY. When assembling, the crankcase must be completely sealed against both vacuum and pressure. Exhaust manifold and water passages must sealed against pressure leakage. Whenever power head is disassembled, it is recommended that all gasket surfaces and machined joints without gaskets be carefully checked for nicks and burrs which might interfere with a tight seal.

Lubricate all bearing and friction surfaces with engine oil. Loose needle bearings may be held in place during assembly using a light, nonfibrous grease.

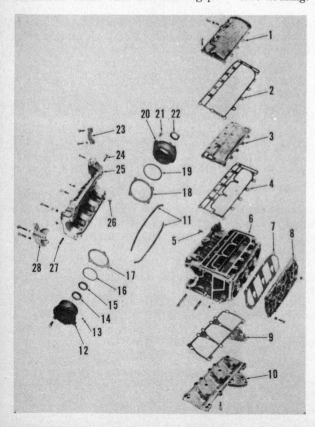

Fig. M11-25 — Exploded view of early type crankcase assembly.

1. Exhaust cover
2. Gasket
3. Baffle
4. Gasket
5. Dowel
6. Cylinder block
7. Gasket
8. Head cover
9. Gasket
10. Transfer cover
11. Sealing strips
12. Lower end cap
13. Check valve assy.
14. Oil seal
15. Oil seal
16. "O" ring
17. Shim
18. Shim
19. "O" ring
20. Upper end cap
21. Screw
22. Oil seal
23. Start motor retainer
24. Plastic timing pointer
25. Crankcase half
26. Dowel
27. Stud
28. Start motor cover

After the crankshaft, connecting rods, pistons and main bearings are positioned in the cylinder, check the crankshaft end play. Temporarily install the crankshaft end caps (20 and 12 – Fig. M11-25) omitting sealing rings (19 and 16), but using shims (18 and 17) that were originally installed. Tighten the end cap to cylinder retaining screws. Use a soft hammer to bump the crankshaft each way to seat bearings, then measure end play.

Bump the crankshaft toward top and measure clearance between the top crankshaft counterweight and the end cap as shown in Fig. M11-27. Bump the crankshaft toward bottom and again measure clearance between counterweight and top end cap. Subtract the first (minimum) clearance from the second clearance which will indicate the amount of end play. If end play is not within limits of 0.004-0.012 inch (0.102-0.305 mm), add or remove shims (18 and 17 – Fig. M11-25) as necessary, then recheck. The crankshaft should be centered by varying the amount of shims between upper (18) and lower (17) shim stacks. When centering the crankshaft, make certain that end play is correct.

Shims (18 and 17) are available in thicknesses of 0.002, 0.003, 0.005, 0.006, 0.008 and 0.010 inch.

All gaskets and sealing surfaces should be lightly and carefully coated with an impervious liquid sealer such as Mercury Gasket Sealer Compound (C-92-28804). Surface must be completely coated, using care that excess sealer does not squeeze out into bearings, crankcase or other passages.

Check the assembly by turning the crankshaft after each step to check for binding or locking which might indicate improper assembly. Remove the cause before proceeding. Rotate the crankshaft until each piston ring in turn appears in one of the exhaust or transfer ports, then check by pressing on ring with a blunt tool. Ring should spring back when released; if it does not, a broken or binding ring is indicated, and the trouble should be corrected.

Tighten the crankcase exhaust cover and cylinder cover cap screws by first tightening center screws, then tightening screws evenly working outward, away from center of crankcase. Tightening torques are given in the CONDENSED SERVICE DATA table.

PISTONS, PINS, RINGS AND CYLINDERS.

Before detaching connecting rods from crankshaft, make sure that rod and cap are properly identified for correct assembly to each other and in the correct cylinder.

Piston rings are interchangeable in the ring grooves and are pinned in place.

9. Grommet
30. Retainer
31. Relief valve grommet
32. Relief valve
33. Diaphragm
34. Washer
35. Screw
36. Spring
37. Gasket
38. Thermostat
39. Gasket

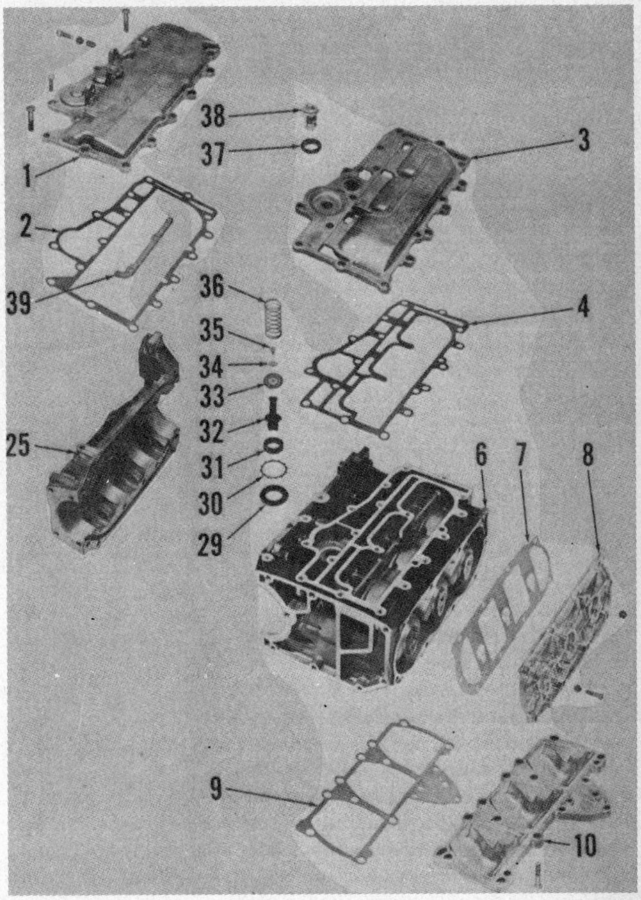

Fig. M11-26 — View of late type crankcase components with thermostat. Diaphragm components (33, 34 & 35) are not used on all models with thermostat in block assembly. Refer to Fig. M11-25 and the following for legend.

Maximum allowable cylinder bore wear or out-of-round is 0.004 inch (0.102 mm). Excessively worn or slightly damaged, standard size cylinders may be repaired by boring and honing to fit an oversize piston. Pistons and rings are available in 0.015 inch (0.38 mm) oversize on early models and 0.015 inch (0.38 mm) and 0.030 inch (0.76 mm) oversizes on later models.

Piston pin is pressed in piston bosses and secured with retaining rings. The retaining rings should not be reused. Piston end of connecting rod is fitted with 29 loose needle rollers.

The piston pin needle rollers use the connecting rod bore and the piston pin as bearing races. When assembling, install bearing washers and needle bearings in piston end of connecting rod using light nonfibrous grease to hold them in place. A Mercury special tool may be used to hold needles in position while positioning piston for installation. Piston must be installed so sharp, vertical side of deflector will be to starboard (intake) side of cylinder bore. Heat piston to approximately 135°F (57°C) and press piston pin into place. Pin

should be centered in piston. Use new piston retaining rings on each assembly.

CONNECTING RODS, BEARINGS AND CRANKSHAFT.

Upper and lower ends of crankshaft are carried by ball bearings. The two center main bearings (21 – Fig. M11-28) also contain the inlet reed valve assemblies. Two split type outer races (25) each contain 56 loose bearing rollers in two rows. The outer race is held together by a retaining ring (27). The reed valve assembly (21) fits around outer race (25).

The connecting rod uses 29 loose rollers at the piston end and a caged roller bearing at the crankpin end.

Check rod for alignment, using Mercury Alignment Tool, or by placing rod on a surface plate and checking with a light.

If bearing surface of rod and cap is rough, scored, worn or shows evidence of overheating, renew the connecting rod. Inspect crankpin and main bearing journals. If scored, out-of-round or worn, renew the crankshaft. Check the crankshaft for straightness using a dial indicator and "V" blocks.

Inspect and adjust the reed valves as outlined in REED VALVE paragraph, and reassemble as outlined in ASSEMBLY paragraph.

ELECTRICAL SYSTEM

Refer to Fig. M11-33 or M11-34 for wiring diagram of electrical system. Before any servicing, refer to precautions listed in ignition paragraphs.

The rectifier assembly is designed to protect the ignition switch box if battery terminals or harness plug becomes loose with motor running. However, the rectifier assembly (Fig. M11-35) will be damaged. If battery terminals are reversed, the rectifier and the ignition switch box will be damaged. The motor can be operated without rectifier if the two yellow/red wires (from the alternator) are disconnected from the rectifier and taped separately.

Refer to Fig. M11-35 for correct rectifier connections.

LOWER UNIT

PROPELLER AND DRIVE CLUTCH. Protection for the motor is built into a special cushioning clutch in the propeller hub. No adjustment is possible on the propeller or clutch. Various pitch propellers are available and propeller should be selected for best performance under applicable conditions. Propellers other than those designed for the motor must not be used.

R&R AND OVERHAUL. Most service on the lower unit can be performed by detaching the gearcase housing from the drive shaft housing. To remove the housing, remove the plastic plug and Allen head screw from location (1 – Fig. M11-38). Remove trim tab (2) and stud nut from under trim tab. Remove stud nut from location (3), two stud nuts (4)

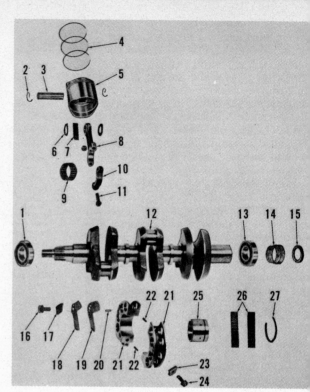

Fig. M11-28 — Exploded view of typical crankshaft assembly. On later models, a shim is used between crankshaft and ball bearing (13).

1. Ball bearing
2. Piston pin retaining clip
3. Piston pin
4. Piston rings
5. Piston
6. Side washer
7. Needle rollers
8. Connecting rod
9. Caged roller bearing
10. Rod cap
11. Screw
12. Crankshaft
13. Ball bearing
14. "O" ring carrier
15. "O" ring
16. Screw
17. Clamp nut
18. Reed stop
19. Reed petal
20. Locating dowel
21. Reed plate & main bearing housing
22. Pin
23. Nut
24. Screw
25. Outer race
26. Needle rollers
27. Outer race holding clip

from each side and stud nut (5) if so equipped, then withdraw the lower unit gearcase assembly.

NOTE: Use caution to prevent loss of spring (68 – Fig. M11-40) or plunger (67).

Remove the housing plugs and drain the housing, then secure the gearcase in

a vise between two blocks of soft wood, with propeller up. Wedge a piece of wood between propeller and anti-ventilation plate, remove the propeller nut, then remove the propeller.

Disassemble the gearcase by removing the gearcase housing cover nut (61 – Fig. M11-40). Clamp the outer end of propeller shaft in a soft jawed vise and

Fig. M11-27 — Refer to text for method of checking crankshaft end play. The crankshaft should be centered in the cylinder.

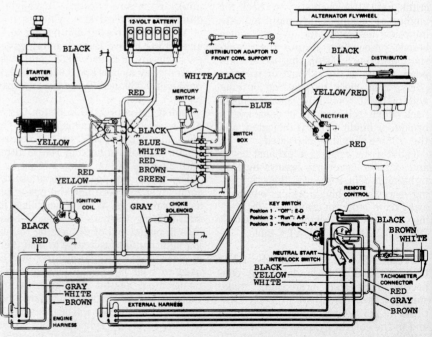

Fig. M11-33 — View of Model 650 wiring diagram. Refer to IGNITION section before attempting any checks.

Illustrations Courtesy Mercury

remove the gearcase by tapping with a rubber mallet. Be careful not to lose key (59) or shims (47) on early models. Forward gear (40) will remain in housing. Withdraw the propeller shaft from bearing carrier (56) and reverse gear (46).

Clamp the bearing carrier (56) in a soft jawed vise and remove reverse gear (46) and bearing (49) with an internal expanding puller and slide hammer. Remove and discard the propeller shaft rear seal or seals (58).

To remove dog clutch (43) from propeller shaft, remove retaining ring (44). Insert cam follower (8) in hole in shaft and apply only enough pressure on end of cam follower to remove the spring pressure, then push out pin (42) with a small punch. The pin passes through drilled holes in dog clutch and operates in slotted holes in propeller shaft.

To disassemble the drive shaft and associated parts, reposition gearcase in vise in drive shaft projecting upward. Remove rubber slinger (11), water pump body (16), impeller (19) and impeller drive pin (20). Remove the flushing screw and withdraw the remainder of the water pump parts. Clamp upper end of drive shaft in a soft jawed vise, remove pinion retaining nut (37); then tap gearcase off drive shaft and bearing. Note the position and thickness of shims (30) on drive shaft upper bearing. Mesh position of pinion is controlled by shims (30) placed underneath the bearing.

After drive shaft has been removed, the forward gear (40) and bearing cone can be withdrawn. Use an internal expanding type puller to withdraw bearing cup if removal is required. Remove and save the shim pack (38).

Shift shaft (5) and cam (7) can be removed after removing forward gear and unscrewing bushing (3) from gearcase housing.

If gear wear was abnormal or if any parts that affect gear alignment were renewed, check and adjust gear mesh as follows: Install forward gear (40) and bearing (39) using shims (38) that were originally installed. Position shims (30) that were originally installed at bottom of bearing bore. Install bearing assembly (32) in housing bore against shims (30). Position the drive pinion (35) in housing and insert drive shaft (33), with bearing assembly (32) installed, into housing, bearing (34) and gear (35). Install retaining nut (37). Coat gears (35 and 40) with bearing blue and check mesh position. Due to the spiral cut gears, it will be necessary to press down on end of drive shaft while checking position. If gears do not mesh in center of teeth, add or remove shims (30) under bearing as necessary. After setting mesh position of gears, check backlash between teeth of gears (35 and 40).

Backlash should be within limits of 0.003-0.005 inch (0.076-0.127 mm). To increase clearance (backlash), remove part of shim stack (38) behind bearing cup. If gears are too loose, add shims. After changing thickness of shims (38), gears should be recoated with bearing blue and mesh position should be rechecked. Install bearing (49), thrust washer (48) and reverse gear (46) in bearing carrier (56). Then, install bearing carrier and gear assembly using shims (47), on early models that were originally installed and check backlash between gears (35 and 46). If backlash is not within limits of 0.003-0.005 inch ((0.076-0.127 mm), add or remove shims (47) as required. Adding shims (47) increases backlash (clearance).

When reassembling, long splines on shift rod (5) should be toward top. Shift cam (7) is installed with notches up and toward rear. Assemble shifting parts (9, 8S, 43, 42 and 44) into propeller shaft (45). Pin (42) shoudl be through hole in slide (8S). Position follower (8) in end of propeller shaft and insert shaft into

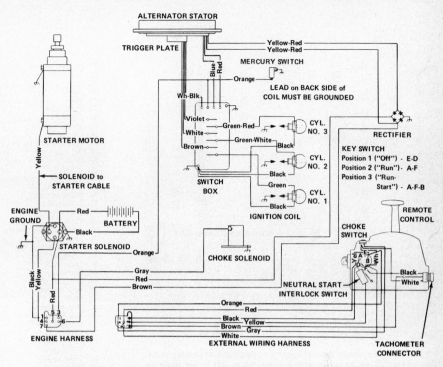

Fig. M11-34 – Wiring schematic for models not equipped with ignition distributor.

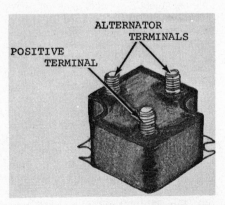

Fig. M11-35 – Rectifier must be connected as shown or damage to the electrical system will result.

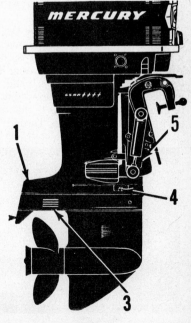

Fig. M11-38 – To remove the lower unit gearcase assembly, remove the attaching screws and stud nuts from positions indicated.

Illustrations Courtesy Mercury

197

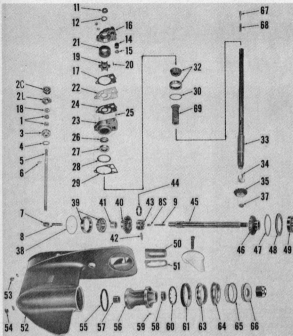

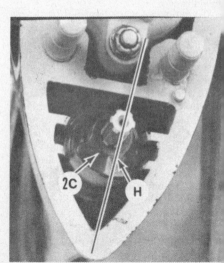

18. Rubber washer
19. Impeller
20. Key
21. Insert
22. Plate
23. Pump base
24. Gasket
25. Dowel
26. Oil seal
27. Spring loaded oil seal
28. "O" ring
29. Gasket
30. Shims
32. Taper roller bearing
33. Drive shaft
34. Roller bearing
35. Drive pinion
37. Nut
38. Shim
39. Tapered roller bearing
40. Forward gear
41. Roller bearing
42. Cross pin
43. Dog clutch
44. Retaining rings
45. Propeller shaft
46. Reverse gear
47. Shim
48. Thrust washer
49. Ball bearing
50. Exhaust tube seal
51. Support plate
52. Gear housing
53. Vent screw
54. Filler screw
55. "O" ring
56. Bearing carrier
57. Roller bearing
58. Oil seals
59. Key
60. Tab washer
61. Nut
63. Thrust hub
64. Cupped thrust washer
65. Cupped thrust washer
66. Thrust hub
67. Plunger
68. Spring

Fig. M11-40 — Exploded view of lower unit gearcase assembly used.
Two seals (58) are used on later models. Shim (47) is not used on
later models. On later models, a nylon washer replaces spacer (2L).
One oil seal (1) is used on later models.

1. Oil seals
2C. Reverse locking cam
2L. Lower spacer
3. Bushing
4. "O" ring
5. Shift shaft
6. Snap ring
7. Shift cam
8. Cam follower

8S. Slide
9. Spring
11. Rubber ring (slinger)
12. Oil seal
14. Seal
15. Nylon washer
16. Water pump body
17. Gasket

bearing (41) and forward gear. Install
the reverse gear and bearing carrier
assembly using new seals (55 and 58).
Lip of seal (58) should face propeller
(out) on single seal models. On two seal
models, install inner seal with lip toward
reverse gear and outer seal with lip
toward propeller.

Upper oil seal (26) should be installed
with lips facing up (toward engine) and
lower oil seal (27) should be pressed into
water pump base with lips facing down
toward propeller shaft. Install remainder of water pump assembly and
tighten the screws or nuts to the following recommended torque. Torque ¼-28

nuts to 30 in.-lbs (3.4 N·m). Torque
5/16-24 nuts to 40 in.-lbs. (4.5 N·m).

On early models, the reverse locking
cam (2C) must be installed on shaft
splines so the two tabs are aligned with
the left front stud when in forward gear
(full clockwise) position. Refer to Fig.
M11-42. On later models, place shift
shaft (5 – Fig. M11-40) in neutral position. Install nylon washer with grooved
side down and position reverse lock cam
(2L – Fig. M11-43) with high point (H) of
cam positioned as shown in Fig. M11-43.

Later models are equipped with two
seals which fit over upper drive shaft
splines. Install splined seal on drive
shaft splines with splined seal end
toward top of drive shaft, then install remaining seal with small end towards top
of drive shaft.

Before attaching gearcase housing to
the driveshaft housing, make certain
that shift cam (7 – Fig. M11-40) and the
shift lever (on motor) are in forward
gear position on models with reverse
locking cam shown in Fig. M11-42 and
neutral position on models with reverse
locking cam shown in Fig. M11-43. Complete assembly by reversing disassembly
procedure. Make certain that spring
(68 – Fig. M11-40) and plunger (67) are
positioned before attaching gearcase to
drive shaft housing.

POWER TILT/TRIM

FLUID. Recommended fluid is SAE
10W-30 or 10W-40 automotive oil. With
outboard in full up position, oil level
should reach bottom of fill plug hole
threads. Do not overfill.

BLEEDING. To bleed air from
hydraulic system, position outboard at
full tilt and engage tilt lock lever.
Without disconnecting hoses, remove
hydraulic trim cylinders. Be sure fluid
reservoir is full and remains so during
bleeding operation. Remove down circuit bleed screw (D – Fig. M11-50) and
"O" ring. Press "IN" control button for a
few seconds, release button and wait approximately one minute. Repeat until
expelled oil is air-free. Install "O" ring
and bleed screw (D) and repeat procedure on opposite cylinder. Place
cylinder in a horizontal position so bleed
port (P – Fig. M11-51) is up and remove
up circuit bleed screw (U). Press "UP"
and "UP/OUT" control buttons for a few
seconds, release buttons and wait approximately one minute. Repeat until
expelled oil is air-free. Install "O" ring
and bleed screw (U) and repeat procedure on opposite cylinder. Reinstall
cylinders.

ADJUST TRIM LIMIT SWITCH.
Operate trim control so outboard is in
full down position. Press "UP/OUT" or
"UP" control button and hold it until
pump motor stops. Outboard should tilt
up and stop so there is ½ inch (12.7 mm)
overlap (L – Fig. M11-52) between
swivel bracket flange (W) and clamp
bracket flange (M). Pull up on lower unit
to remove slack when checking overlap
(L). Note that if cylinder rods enter
cylinders more than an additional ⅛ inch

Fig. M11-42 — On early models, the reverse lock
cam must be installed on splines as shown
when in FORWARD gear position.

Fig. M11-43 — On later models, the reverse lock
cam (2C) must be installed on shift shaft splines
with high point (H) of cam positioned as shown
when in neutral position.

(3.17 mm), that hydraulic system should be bled of air as outlined in BLEEDING section. If overlap (L) is incorrect, loosen retainer screw (R–Fig. M11-53) then turn adjusting nut (N) counterclockwise to increase overlap or clockwise to decrease overlap. Retighten retainer screw (R) and recheck adjustment.

PRESSURE TEST. To check hydraulic system pressure, disconnect four hoses attached to control valve as shown in Fig. M11-54; small hoses are for up

circuit while large hoses are for down circuit. Connect a pressure gage to one up circuit port (small) of control valve and another pressure gage to one down circuit port (large). Screw plugs into remaining ports. Check fluid reservoir and fill if necessary. Operate trim control in up direction and note pressure gage reading. Minimum pressure should be 3500 psi (24.1 MPa) on new pumps with a red sleeve on wires or 3200-3500 psi (22.0-24.1 MPa) minimum on used pumps with red sleeve on wires. Minimum pressure on all other new pumps is 3000 psi (20.7 MPa) while minimum pressure on all other used pumps is 2700-3000 psi (18.6-20.7 MPa). Release trim control button. Pressure will drop slightly after stabilizing but should not drop faster than 100 psi (690 kPa) every 15 seconds. Operate trim control in down direction and note pressure gage reading. Minimum pressure is 500-1000 psi (3.4-6.9 MPa). Release trim control button. Pressure will drop slightly after stabilizing but should not drop faster than 100 psi (690 kPa) every 15 seconds. If pressure is normal, inspect trim cylinders and hoses

for leakage. If pressure is abnormal, install a good control valve and recheck pressure. If pressure remains abnormal, install a new pump body.

Fig. M11-53—Loosen retainer screw (R) and turn trim limit adjusting nut (N) to adjust trim limit switch.

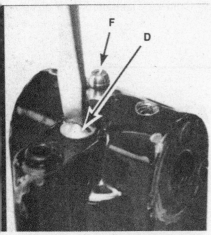

Fig. M11-50—View showing location of down circuit bleed screw (D) and grease fitting (F).

Fig. M11-51—View showing location of up circuit bleed screw (U) and bleed port (P).

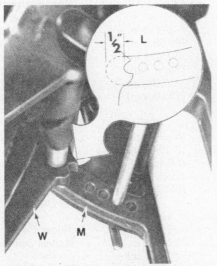

Fig. M11-52—Overlap (L) between swivel bracket flange (W) and clamp bracket flange (M) should be ½ inch (12.7 mm).

Fig. M11-54—View of control valve showing location of up circuit hoses (U) and down circuit hoses (D).

MERCURY
FOUR-CYLINDER MODELS (1969-1985)

<table>
<tr><td colspan="6">Year Produced</td></tr>
<tr><td>1969 . . . .</td><td>500</td><td>650</td><td>. . . .</td><td>800</td><td>. . . .</td></tr>
<tr><td>1970 . . . .</td><td>500</td><td>650</td><td>. . . .</td><td>800</td><td>. . . .</td></tr>
<tr><td>1971 . . . .</td><td>500</td><td>650</td><td>. . . .</td><td>800</td><td>. . . .</td></tr>
<tr><td>1972 . . . .</td><td>500</td><td>. . . .</td><td>. . . .</td><td>800</td><td>. . . .</td></tr>
<tr><td>1973 . . . .</td><td>500</td><td>. . . .</td><td>. . . .</td><td>. . . .</td><td>850</td></tr>
<tr><td>1974 . . . .</td><td>500</td><td>. . . .</td><td>. . . .</td><td>. . . .</td><td>850</td></tr>
<tr><td>1975 . . . .</td><td>500</td><td>. . . .</td><td>. . . .</td><td>. . . .</td><td>850</td></tr>
<tr><td>1976 . . . .</td><td>500</td><td>. . . .</td><td>. . . .</td><td>. . . .</td><td>850</td></tr>
<tr><td>1977 . . . .</td><td>500</td><td>. . . .</td><td>. . . .</td><td>. . . .</td><td>850</td></tr>
<tr><td>1978 . . . .</td><td>500</td><td>. . . .</td><td>. . . .</td><td>800</td><td>. . . .</td></tr>
<tr><td>1979 . . . .</td><td>50</td><td>. . . .</td><td>. . . .</td><td>80</td><td>. . . .</td></tr>
<tr><td>1980 . . . .</td><td>50</td><td>. . . .</td><td>. . . .</td><td>80</td><td>. . . .</td></tr>
</table>

<table>
<tr><td colspan="6">Year Produced</td></tr>
<tr><td>1981 . . . .</td><td>50</td><td>. . . .</td><td>. . . .</td><td>80</td><td>. . . .</td></tr>
<tr><td>1982 . . . .</td><td>50</td><td>. . . .</td><td>. . . .</td><td>80</td><td>. . . .</td></tr>
<tr><td>1983 . . . .</td><td>50</td><td>. . . .</td><td>. . . .</td><td>80</td><td>. . . .</td></tr>
<tr><td>1984 . . . .</td><td>50</td><td>. . . .</td><td>75</td><td>. . . .</td><td>. . . .</td></tr>
<tr><td>1985 . . . .</td><td>50</td><td>. . . .</td><td>75</td><td>. . . .</td><td>. . . .</td></tr>
</table>

Letter after model number indicates variation of equipment.

M – Manual starter, S – Electric starter without alternator, E – Electric starter and alternator, L – Long shaft, PT – Power trim, SS – Solid state ignition, XS – High performance.

CONDENSED SERVICE DATA

TUNE-UP

Hp/rpm:
Models 500 & 50 . . . . .50/4800-5500
Model 650 . . . . .65/4800-5300
Model 75 . . . . .75/5000-5500
Models 800 & 80 . . . . .80/4800-5500
Model 850 . . . . .85/4800-5500*
Bore:
Models 500 & 50 . . . . .2-9/16 in.
(65.09 mm)
Model 650 . . . . .2-15/16 in.
(74.61 mm)
Models 800, 850, 80 & 75 . . . .$2^7/8$ in.
(73.03 mm)
Stroke:
Models 500 & 50 . . . .$2^1/8$ in.
(53.97 mm)
Model 650 . . . . .2-19/64 in.
(58.42 mm)
Models 800, 850, 80 & 75 . . . . .2-9/16 in.
(65.09 mm)
Displacement:
Models 500 & 50 . . . . .44 cu. in.
(721.6 cc)
Model 650 . . . . .62.42 cu. in.
(1024 cc)
Models 800, 850, 80 & 75 . . . . .66.6 cu. in.
(1091 cc)
Firing Order 1-3-2-4
Compression At Cranking Speed . . . .†
Spark Plug . . . . .See Text
Ignition . . . . .See Text
Idle Speed . . . . .See Text
Fuel:Oil Ratio 50:1

*Rpm range is 4800-6000 on Model 850XS.
†Not more than 15 psi (103.5 kPa) variation between cylinders.

SIZES – CLEARANCES
Piston Rings:
End Gap . . . .*
Side Clearance . . . .*

SIZES – CLEARANCES CONT.
Piston Skirt Clearance . . . .*
Crankshaft Bearing Type:
Top Main Bearing . . . . .Ball Bearing
Main Bearing (2) . . . . .Bushing With Reed Valve
Center Main Bearing . . . . .Roller †
Main Bearing (4) . . . . .Bushing With Reed Valve
Bottom Main Bearing .Ball Bearing
Crankpin . . . . .Roller†
Piston Pin Bearing . . . . .Roller†

*Publication not authorized by manufacturer.
†Refer to text for number of rollers at center main bearing, crankpin and piston pin.

TIGHTENING TORQUES
Connecting Rod . . . . .180 in.-lbs.
(20.3 N·m)
Crankcase Screws:
Models 650 & 800 (Prior to 1973) . . . . .150 in.-lbs.
(16.9 N·m)
All Other Models . . . . .200 in.-lbs.
(22.6 N·m)
Cylinder Cover:
Models 500 & 50 . . . . .70 in.-lbs.
(7.9 N·m)
Models 650 & 800 (Prior to 1973) . . . . .100 in.-lbs.
(11.3 N·m)
Models 800 (After 1972), 850,
80 & 75 . . . . .85 in.-lbs.
(9.6 N·m)
Exhaust Cover:
Models 500 & 50 . . . . .200 in.-lbs.
(22.6 N·m)
Models 650 & 800 (Prior to 1973) . . . . .150 in.-lbs.
(16.9 N·m)
Models 800 (After 1972), 850,
80 & 75 . . . . .250 in.-lbs.
(28.2 N·m)
Flywheel:
Models 800 (After 1972), 850,
80 & 75 . . . . .100 ft.-lbs.
(136 N·m)

TIGHTENING TORQUES CONT.

All Other Models................65 ft.-lbs.
(88.4 N·m)

Reed Screws:
Models 500 & 50....................30 in.-lbs.
(3.4 N·m)

Models 650 & 800 (Prior to 1973)............35 in.-lbs.
(3.9 N·m)

Models 800 (After 1972), 850,
80 & 75.........................25 in.-lbs.
(2.8 N·m)

TIGHTENING TORQUES CONT.

Spark Plugs.....................240 in.-lbs.
(27.1 N·m)

Transfer Port Covers:
Models 800 (After 1972), 850,
80 & 75.........................85 in.-lbs.
(9.6 N·m)

All Other Models....................60 in.-lbs.
(6.8 N·m)

LUBRICATION

The engine is lubricated by oil mixed with the fuel. Fuel should be regular leaded, low leaded or unleaded gasoline with a minimum pump octane rating of 86. Premium gasoline may be used if desired regular gasoline is not available. Recommended oil is Quicksilver Formula 50 or 50-D. A good quality BIA certified TC-W oil may be used if Formula 50 or 50-D oil is not available.

Fuel:oil ratio when using Formula 50 or 50-D oil is 50:1 for normal operation. Follow fuel:oil ratio recommended by oil manufacturer if Formula 50 or 50-D is not used.

Fuel:oil ratio should be 25:1 during break-in. Do not operate engine above 2500-3500 rpm for first two hours when breaking-in a new or overhauled engine. Avoid sustained full throttle operation for first 10 hours of operation.

Lower unit gears and bearings are lubricated by oil in the gearcase. Recommended oil is Quicksilver Super Duty Gear Lubricant. Remove vent plug and fill gearcase through fill plug opening in lower end of gearcase until oil is expelled from vent plug opening, then allow 1 ounce (30 mL) of oil to drain from gearcase.

FUEL SYSTEM

CARBURETOR. ALL MODELS PRIOR TO 1976. Refer to Fig. M12-1 for exploded view of carburetor, typical of type used on models prior to 1976.

Initial setting for the idle mixture screw (14) is one turn open from the closed position. Run motor until operating temperature is reached, then shift to Forward gear and allow motor to run at idle speed. Slowly turn idle screw (14) out (counterclockwise) until motor runs unevenly (loads up). Turn needle in (clockwise) until motor picks up speed and again runs evenly and continue turning until motor slows down and misses. Needle should be set between the two extremes. Turning screw (14) in (clockwise) leans the idle mixture. Slightly rich idle mixture is more desirable than too lean.

NOTE: Mixture adjustment should not be attempted in neutral.

The high speed mixture may be adjusted for altitude or other special conditions by changing the size of main jet (16). The standard main jet should normally be correct for altitudes below 4000 feet (1220 m). Refer to the following for standard main jet size (diameter).

Model 500

Carburetor	Main Jet
KA-21A	0.057 in. (1.45 mm)
KA-21B	0.061 in. (1.55 mm)
KA-21C	0.065 in. (1.65 mm)
KA-21D & KA-24A	0.063 in. (1.60 mm)

Model 650

KC-5A	0.071 in. (1.80 mm)
KC-5B, KC-5C, KC-11A and KC-15A	0.061 in. (1.55 mm)

Model 800

KD-4A and WMK-2	0.074 in. (1.88 mm)

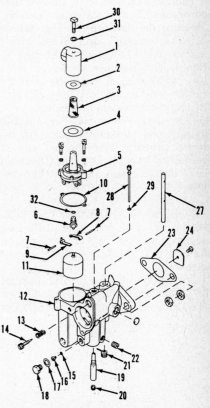

Fig. M12-1 — Exploded view of a Tillotson type carburetor. Mercarb "WMK" type carburetor is similar. Main jet (16) has a tapered seat and does not use gasket (15) on "KD" and "WMK" type carburetors.

1. Strainer cover
2. Gasket
3. Strainer
4. Gasket
5. Bowl cover
6. Inlet needle & seat
7. Pins
8. Primary lever
9. Secondary lever
10. Gasket
11. Float
12. Body
13. Spring
14. Idle mixture screw
15. Gasket
16. Main jet
17. Gasket
18. Plug
19. Main nozzle
20. Plug
21. Spring
22. Plug
23. Gasket
24. Throttle valve
25. Throttle shaft
26. Idle tube
27. Gasket
28. Cap screw
29. Gasket
30. Gasket

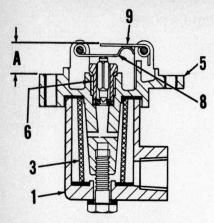

Fig. M12-2 — Float height is adjusted by bending primary lever (8) until distance (A) is 13/32 inch (10.32 mm) with inlet valve (6) closed.

NOTE: If main jet (16 – Fig. M12-1) is too small, high speed mixture will be too lean and may result in damage to power head.

To adjust the fuel level, remove bowl cover (5) and invert the cover assembly. Measure the distance (A – Fig. M12-2) between secondary lever (9) and gasket surface of bowl cover with inlet valve (6, closed. This distance should be 13/32 inch (10.32 mm). If incorrect, bend the curved tang on primary lever (8) until correct measurement is obtained.

Turn bowl cover (5 – Fig. M12-3) upright and measure distance (D) between primary lever (8) and end of secondary lever (9). Distance (D) should be ¼ inch (6.4 mm). Bend tab (T) to adjust.

MODELS 50 AND 500 AFTER 1975. Models 50 and 500 after 1975 are equipped with two Mercarb carburetors. Refer to Fig. M12-4 for exploded view of carburetor.

The carburetor uses a fixed main jet (24). Standard main jet size is 0.055 inch (1.40 mm) for operation below 2500 feet

Fig. M12-4 — Exploded view of Mercarb type carburetor used on Model 50 and Model 500 after 1975.

1. Inlet fitting
2. Gasket
3. Screen
4. Cover
5. Diaphragm
6. Gasket
7. Pump body
8. Check valve diaphragm
9. Gasket
10. Throttle lever
11. Throttle shaft
12. Choke shaft
13. Plug
16. Idle tube
17. Gasket
18. Throttle plate
19. Carburetor body
20. Welch plug
21. Idle mixture screw
22. Choke shutter plates
23. Boost venturi
24. Main jet
25. Float pin
26. Inlet needle
27. Main nozzle
28. Float
29. Gasket
30. Float bowl

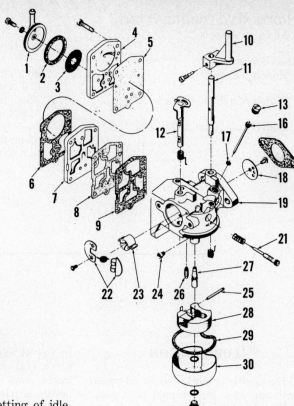

(762 m) altitude. Initial setting of idle mixture screw (21) is 1½ turns open. Turning idle mixture screw clockwise will lean the mixture.

To adjust fuel level, remove float bowl and invert carburetor. Measure distance from float to gasket surface as shown in Fig. M12-5. Float level should be 15/64 to 17/64 inch (6-6.8 mm). Turn carburetor right side up and check float drop. Float drop should be 1/32 to 1/16 inch (0.8-1.6 mm) measured from float to highest point on main jet (24).

MODELS 75, 80, 800 AND 850 AFTER 1975. Two Mercarb carburetors are used. Refer to Fig. M12-6 for an exploded view of carburetor. Note that these carburetors are equipped with an enrichment valve (24) in place of a choke plate. Initial adjustment of idle mixture screw (19) is one turn open. Standard main jet (10) size for operation below 2500 feet (762 m) altitude is 0.088 inch (2.23 mm) for units with serial number 4366802-4423111 and 0.090 inch (2.29 mm) for units with serial numbers above 4423111. Vent jet (4) size for operation below 2500 feet (762 m) altitude is 0.080 inch (2.03 mm) for units with serial number 4366802-4423111 and 0.072 inch (1.83 mm) for units with serial numbers above 4423111.

When overhauling carburetor, drive float pins (16) and fuel inlet drive lever pin (18) out toward knurled end of pin. Insert plain end of pin first during assembly. Note that strong (0.034 in. dia. wire) throttle return spring must be used on top carburetor throttle shaft.

Numbers on throttle plate (29) must face outwards at closed throttle. Be sure rubber insert in fuel inlet valve seat (6) is installed so flat end of insert is towards inlet drive.

To determine the float level, invert the carburetor body and measure distance (D – Fig. M12-7) from the carburetor

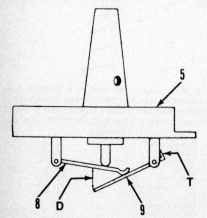

Fig. M12-3 — With bowl cover (5) upright, distance (D) between primary lever (8) and end of secondary lever (9) should be ¼ inch (6.4 mm). Bend tab (T) to adjust.

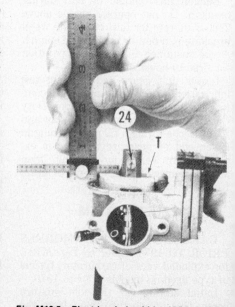

Fig. M12-5 — Float level should be 15/64 to 17/64 inch (6-6.8 mm) from float to gasket surface. Float drop is measured with carburetor upright from top of main jet (24) to float. Refer to text.

body to base of float (15). Distance (D) should be 11/16 inch (17.5 mm) and is adjusted by bending fuel inlet lever (17 – Fig. M12-8) within area (A).

SPEED CONTROL LINKAGE. The speed control linkage must be synchronized to advance the ignition timing and open the carburetor throttles in a precise manner. Because the two actions are interrelated, it is important to check the complete system in the sequence outlined in the appropriate following paragraphs. Examine the motor to establish which type of ignition is used. Original system application is listed in the IGNITION SYSTEM section.

Model 500 And Model 650 With "Thunderbolt" Ignition. Refer to special precautions listed in the "Thunderbolt" IGNITION section before servicing these motors. Incorrect service procedures can damage the ignition system.

NOTE: Do not disconnect any part of the ignition system while engine is running or while checking the speed control linkage.

Disconnect the fuel tank and allow motor to run until all fuel is used out of the carburetors. If any fuel remains, motor can start while checking the speed control linkage and prevent accurate adjustments.

Connect a power timing light (such as Mercury part C-91-35507) to the top (No. 1) spark plug.

Turn ignition key on and crank motor with electric starter. Advance the speed controls until timing light flashes when

the flywheel timing mark is aligned with the correct maximum advance degree mark (Fig. M12-14). Maximum ignition advance should be 35° BTDC for Model 500SS and should be 38° BTDC for Model 650SS. If maximum advance timing is incorrect, turn the stop screw (A – Fig. M12-13) to stop the ignition advance at correct position.

With the timing light still connected, synchronize the carburetor throttle opening to the ignition timing as follows: Crank motor with the electric starter and slowly advance speed control from the idle position. On Model 500SS, the timing light should flash when the flywheel mark passes the "CYL #1TDC" mark (Fig. M12-14). On Model 650SS,

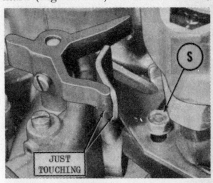

Fig. M12-11 – Refer to text for method of determining throttle pickup point. Two screws (S) retain the pickup plate.

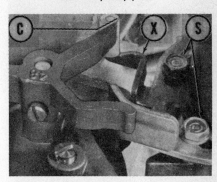

Fig. M12-12 – When adjusting clearance (C), refer to text. Clearance is adjusted by bending at (X).

Fig. M12-7 – To determine float level, invert the carburetor body and measure distance (D) from the carburetor body to base of float (15). Distance (D) should be 11/16 inch (17.5 mm).

Fig. M12-8 – Adjust float level by bending fuel inlet lever (17) within area (A).

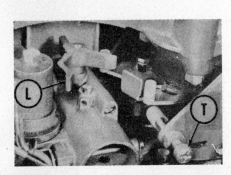

Fig. M12-10 – When controls are in maximum speed position, stop should be against screw (T) and lever (L) should have less than 1/64 inch (0.4 mm) free movement.

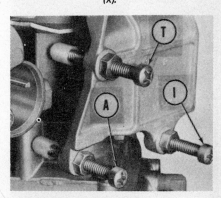

Fig. M12-13 – Maximum ignition advance is adjusted by stop screw (A); idle speed by screw (I); and throttle stop screw (T) prevents damage to linkage. Position of these three screws is similar for all models.

Fig. M12-6 – Exploded view of center bowl type Mercarb carburetor used on Models 75, 80, 800 and 850 after 1975.

1. Welch plug (9/16 inch)
2. Fuel inlet strainer
3. Body
4. Vent jet
5. Gasket
6. Inlet needle & seat assy.
7. Venturi
8. Nozzle
9. Gasket
10. Main jet
11. Main jet plug
12. Screw
13. Float bowl
14. Gasket
15. Float
16. Pin
17. Fuel inlet lever
18. Pin
19. Idle mixture screw
20. Spring
21. Spring
22. Flat washer
23. Rubber seal
24. Enrichment valve assy.
25. Screw & lockwasher
26. Welch plug (7/16 inch)
27. Gasket
28. Throttle shaft
29. Throttle plate
30. Screw

timing light should flash when flywheel mark passes the "PICKUP" mark (Fig. M12-14). With controls correctly set as outlined, the pickup tab should just contact the carburetor throttle lever as shown in Fig. M12-11. If throttle is partly open or if lever is not touching the tab, loosen the two screws (S–Fig. M12-12) and move the pickup plate in the elongated holes. Throttle pickup should be rechecked after tightening the pickup plate retaining screws (S).

Move the speed control handle to the maximum speed position until the throttle stop contacts the throttle stop screw (T–Fig. M12-10). The carburetor should be completely open. If the stop does not contact screw (T), turn the screw in to prevent damage to linkage. If throttle lever (L) has more than 1/64 inch (0.4 mm) free movement, turn the throttle stop screw (T) out.

Model 500 And Model 650 With "Lightening Energizer" Ignition. Refer to the special precautions listed under **"Lightning Energizer" IGNI-TION** before servicing these motors. Incorrect servicing procedures can damage the ignition system.

NOTE: It is important that an approved tachometer is used. Do NOT disconnect any part of the ignition system while engine is running or while checking the speed control linkage.

Use a Mercury timing light (part C-91-35507) or equivalent.

NOTE: A jumper wire (ground) must be connected from negative terminal of battery to the motor lower cowl or front cover plate on manual start motors.

Start engine and adjust the idle speed screw (I–Fig. M12-15) to provide 550-650 rpm in forward gear while holding the ignition unit at full retard. Advance the ignition until timing occurs between 7° and 9° BTDC. The throttle actuator plate should be just touching the carburetor primary pickup as shown at (1–Fig. M12-16). If throttle is slightly open or if pickup is not touching, loosen the two attaching screws (P–Fig. M12-17) and move throttle actuator plate so it just touches the primary pickup lever when ignition is set at 7°-9° BTDC.

With motor running at maximum speed, check the ignition timing. Ignition timing should be within the limits as follows for the operating rpm.

Model 500

RPM	Degrees BTDC
2000-4000	38-39
4000-4800	37-38
5200-5600	35

Model 650

2000-4000	41-42
4000-4800	40-41
4800-5200	38

If maximum ignition timing is incorrect, loosen the locknut and turn the advance stop screw (A–Fig. M12-13) until timing is correct for the rpm. After adjusting, be sure to recheck.

Fig. M12-14—Refer to text for method used for setting the speed control linkage before adjusting. Timing marks shown are typical.

Fig. M12-16—View of the throttle actuator plate just contacting the primary pickup lever (1). Refer to text.

Fig. M12-17—View of the secondary pickup lever just contacting the screw (2). Refer to text. The primary pickup lever should still be contacting cam at (1).

Fig. M12-15—Refer to text for adjusting speed control linkage on Models 500 and 650 with "Lightning Energizer" ignition system.

I. Idle stop screw   S. Secondary pickup screw

NOTE: It is important to know engine speed (rpm) when checking maximum ignition timing because of the characteristics of the electronic ignition. Timing may be checked on boat or test tank, but must be accomplished at maximum throttle opening.

To adjust the throttle secondary pickup, advance the ignition unit until it contacts the advance stop (A–Fig. M12-13).

NOTE: Do not move the economizer collar after the ignition unit contacts stop screw (A).

Check clearance at (2–Fig. M12-17) between secondary pickup lever and screw. The screw should be just contacting the secondary pickup lever and is adjusted by turning screw (S–Fig. M12-15). Make certain that the primary end of the throttle pickup lever is still against the primary pickup cam (1–Fig. M12-17).

To adjust the throttle stop screw (T–Fig. M12-13), move the speed control handle to maximum speed position. The carburetor throttles should be completely open when the throttle stop contacts screw (T). If the throttles are not completely open, turn stop screw (T) out. If the throttle stop does not contact screw (T), turn the screw in to prevent damage to linkage.

Model 800 And Model 850 (Below Ser. No. 386595). Refer to the special precautions listed in the **"Thunderbolt"** IGNITION section before servicing these motors. Incorrect servicing procedures can damage the ignition system.

NOTE: Do not synchronize any part of the ignition system while engine is running or while checking the speed control linkage adjustments.

Disconnect the fuel tank and allow motor to run until all fuel is used out of the carburetors. If any fuel remains, motor can start while checking the speed control linkage and may prevent accurate adjustments. Connect a power timing light to number 1 (top) spark plug wire.

To adjust the spark advance stop screw (A–Fig. M12-20), the speed control must be in the maximum speed position. Turn on the key switch, crank engine with starter and check the ignition timing. The timing mark on flywheel (dots) should be aligned with 23° BTDC mark when the timing light flashes. If incorrect, loosen the locknut and turn stop screw (A) as required to stop ignition advance at 23° BTDC. Recheck timing after tightening locknut.

The primary cam on the throttle pickup plate should just contact the primary pickup lever as shown at (1–Fig. M12-18) when the speed control lever is advanced to provide 5°-7° BTDC ignition timing. To check, crank engine with starter while checking ignition timing. Advance the speed control until the ignition timing is within 5°-7° BTDC, then check the throttle pickup at (1). If clearance is not 0-0.005 inch (0-0.13 mm), loosen the two attaching screws (P–Fig. M12-19) and move the throttle pickup plate. Recheck pickup point after moving plate and tightening the two attaching screws.

To adjust the secondary pickup, rotate the distributor against the maximum advance stop screw (A–Fig. M12-20) and check the secondary pickup between cam and throttle lever at (2–Fig. M12-18).

NOTE: Do not advance speed control past the point that distributor just touches stop screw (A — Fig. M12-20) when checking the secondary pickup. If the secondary pickup is not touching, loosen the locknut and turn screw (S — Fig. M12-19) in until secondary cam just touches throttle lever. If secondary cam is contacting the throttle lever, back screw (S) out until cam is away from lever, then readjust to make certain that cam is just touching.

Move the speed control to the maximum speed position unit throttle stop contacts screw (T–Fig. M12-20). The carburetor throttles should be completely open. If stop does not contact screw (T), turn the stop screw in to prevent damage to linkage. If throttles are not completely open, turn the stop screw (T) out.

Model 850 (Ser. No. 3865695-4366800). Refer to the special precautions listed in the **"Thunderbolt"** IGNITION section before servicing these motors. Incorrect servicing procedures can damage the ignition system.

NOTE: Do not disconnect any part of the ignition system while engine is running or while checking the speed control linkage adjustments.

Ignition timing pointer alignment may be checked as follows: Install a dial gage in number 1 (top) spark plug hole and turn flywheel clockwise until piston is 0.464 inch (12 mm). Before Top Dead Center. Loosen retaining screw and position timing pointer (P–Fig. M12-21) so it aligns with ".464 BTDC" mark on flywheel.

Connect a power timing light to number 1 (top) spark plug wire. The primary cam on the throttle pickup plate should just contact the primary pickup lever as shown at (1–Fig. M12-18) when

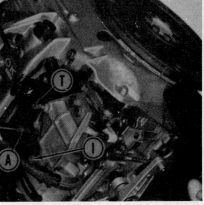

Fig. M12-20 – View of Model 800 showing location of ignition advance stop screw (A), idle speed stop screw (I) and throttle stop screw (T). Model 850 with distributor is similar.

Fig. M12-21 – View of flywheel and timing pointer (P) used on late 850 models.

Fig. M12-18 – View of throttle pickup cams and lever used on Models 800 and 850. Primary pickup should occur at (1) and secondary pickup at (2). Refer to text for adjusting.

Fig. M12-19 – View of secondary pickup adjusting screws (S) and primary pickup plate attaching screws (P) typical of Model 800 and Model 850 with distributor.

the speed control lever is advanced to provide BTDC ignition timing. To check, crank engine with starter while checking ignition timing. Advance the speed control until the ignition timing is within 3°-5° BTDC, then check the throttle pickup at (1). If clearance is not 0-0.005 inch (0-0.13 mm), loosen the two attaching screws (P—Fig. M12-19) and move the throttle pickup plate. Recheck pickup point after moving plate and tightening the two attaching screws.

To check maximum spark advance, start motor in test tank with timing light attached. Hold timing light on pointer (P—Fig. M12-21) and advance speed control until pointer is aligned with 27° mark on flywheel. Distributor should be just touching maximum advance stop screw (A—Fig. M12-20) at this point. To adjust, loosen locknut and turn screw (A) until it is just touching distributor with timing pointer and 27° mark on flywheel aligned. Recheck maximum spark advance after tightening locknut on adjustment screw.

To adjust the secondary pickup, rotate the distributor against the maximum advance stop screw (A—Fig. M12-20) and check the secondary pickup between cam and throttle lever at (2—Fig. M12-18).

NOTE: Do not advance speed control past the point that distributor just touches stop screw (A—Fig. M12-20) when checking the secondary pickup. If the secondary pickup is not touching, loosen the locknut and turn screw (S—Fig. M12-19) in until secondary cam just touches throttle lever. If secondary cam is contacting the throttle lever, back screw (S) out until cam is away from lever, then readjust to make certain that cam is just touching.

Move the speed control to the maximum speed position until throttle stop contacts screw (T—Fig. M12-20). The carburetor throttles should be completely open. If the stop does not contact screw (T), turn the stop screw in to prevent damage to linkage. If throttles are not completely open, turn the stop screw (T) out.

Models 50 And 500 (After Ser. No. 4357640). To synchronize ignition and carburetor opening, connect a power timing light (Mercury part 3-91-35507) to number 1 (top) spark plug wire. Run engine with outboard in forward gear. Open throttle until ignition timing is 7°-9° BTDC, loosen actuator plate screws (S—Fig. M12-22) and rotate actuator plate (P) so primary pickup arm (A—Fig. 12-23) just contacts primary cam (C). Retighten actuator plate screws. Open throttle and adjust maximum ignition advance screw (A—Fig. M12-24) so ignition timing is 32° BTDC. Stop engine.

NOTE: Due to electronic characteristics of ignition system, maximum advance is set at 32° BTDC but ignition will retard to 30° BTDC at 5000 rpm.

Open throttle so spark arm (S) just touches maximum advance screw (A) and adjust actuator plate secondary pickup screw (W—Fig. M12-22) so screw just touches secondary pickup arm as shown in Fig. M12-25.

To prevent damage to carburetor throttle plate at full throttle, lightly hold carburetor throttle plate in full open position by turning secondary pickup arm (R—Fig. M12-25). Adjust full throttle stop screw (B—Fig. M12-24) so there is 0.010-0.015 inch (0.25-0.38 mm) clearance between secondary pickup screw (W—Fig. M12-25) and pickup arm (R) when throttle arm (T—Fig. M12-24) just touches full throttle stop screw (B).

Turn idle speed screw (I) to obtain idle speed of 550-600 rpm in forward gear.

Models 75, 80, 800 And 850 (After Ser. No. 4366801). Check ignition timing pointer alignment as follows: Install a dial indicator gage in number 1 (top) spark plug hole and turn flywheel clockwise until piston is 0.464 inch (12 mm) BTDC. Loosen retaining screw and position timing pointer so that it is aligned with ".464 BTDC" mark on flywheel.

Connect a power timing light to number 1 (top) spark plug wire. Run engine with outboard in forward gear

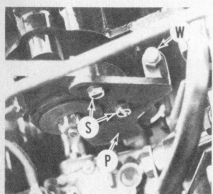

Fig. M12-22 — View of actuator plate (P) and secondary pickup adjusting screw (W) on Model 500 after serial number 4357640. Refer to text for adjustment.

Fig. M12-23 — Primary pickup arm (A) should just contact primary cam (C) at point (P) with 7°-9° BTDC ignition timing.

Fig. M12-24 — View of throttle (T) and spark (S) control arms on Model 500 after serial number 4357640. On models after 1977, screws (A, B & I) are located on arms (T and S).

Fig. M12-25 — Adjust full throttle stop screw (B—Fig. M12-24) so there is 0.010-0.015 inch (0.25-0.38 mm) clearance between secondary pickup arm (R) and screw (W) at full throttle.

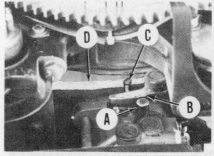

Fig. M12-26 — View of throttle pickup pins (A & C) and cams (B & D) used on Models 75, 80, 800 and 850 after serial number 4366801.

and open throttle until primary cam (B–Fig. M12-26) just touches throttle lever primary pin (A). Primary cam should contact primary pin at 2°-4° BTDC on models below serial number 4423112 or 2° BTDC to 2° ATDC on models after serial number 4423111. Turn pickup adjustment screw (A–Fig. M12-27) to obtain desired pickup point. Open throttle and turn maximum advance adjustment screw (M) so spark arm (R) movement will stop at 27°BTDC. Stop engine.

Carburetor throttle plate must not act as stop for wide open throttle. To prevent damage to carburetor, lightly hold carburetor throttle plate in full open position by turning upper carburetor throttle lever. Adjust full throttle stop screw (T) so there is 0.010-0.015 inch (0.25-0.38 mm) between throttle lever secondary pin (C–Fig. M12-26) and secondary cam (D) when throttle arm (B–Fig. M12-27) is in wide open position.

Idle speed should be 550-650 rpm with outboard in forward gear. Turn idle speed screw (I) to adjust idle speed.

REED VALVES. The inlet reed valves are located on the crankshaft second and fourth main bearing assemblies. Each reed valve unit supplies fuel mixture from one of the carburetors to the two adjoining cylinders.

Reed petals (2–Fig. M12-30 or M12-31) should be perfectly flat and have no more than 0.007 inch (0.178 mm) clearance between free end of reed petal and seating surface of center main bearing. The reed stop (1) must be carefully adjusted to 3/16 inch (4.76 mm) on 650 models, 0.180 inch (4.57 mm) on 50, 500 and 800 models and 0.162 inch

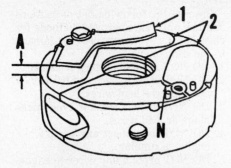

Fig. M12-30 — Intermediate main bearing and reed valve for Models 50, 500 and 650. Reed petals (2) are right and left hand units. When installing reed petals, place the reed with the cut-out notch (N) on the left as shown. Refer also to Fig. M12-31.

(4.11 mm) on 75, 80 and 850 models. This clearance is measured between end of stop and seating surface of reed plate as shown at (A–Fig. M12-30). Seating surface of bearing must be smooth and flat, and may be refinished on a lapping plate after removing reed stops, reed valves and dowels. Do not attempt to bend or straighten a reed petal to modify performance or to salvage a damaged reed. Never install a bent reed. Lubricate the reed valve units with "Quicksilver" Multipurpose Lubricant or a light distributor cam grease when reassembling.

On 50, 500 and 650 models, each valve unit has eight reeds which are right-hand and left-hand units, and are available only as a matched set. When installing reed valves, place the reed petal with the cut-out notch (N) to the left as shown. Crankshaft must be removed before reed valve units can be serviced.

FUEL PUMP. Diaphragm type fuel pumps are used. Pressure and vacuum pulsations from the crankcase alternate to pull fuel from the supply tank and supply the carburetor. Most of the work is performed by the main supply chamber (5–Fig. M12-32). Vacuum in the crankcase pulls the diaphragm (2) downward causing fuel to be drawn through inlet line (8), past inlet check valve (7) into main pump chamber (5). The alternate pressure forces diaphragm out and fuel leaves the chamber through outlet check valve (6). The booster pump chamber (3) serves to dampen the action of the larger, main pump chamber (5), and increase the maximum potential fuel flow.

When overhauling the fuel pump, renew all defective or questionable parts. Fuel pressure should be at least 2 psi (13.8 kPa) at carburetor when running motor at full throttle.

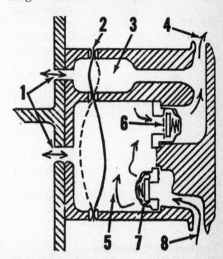

Fig. M12-32 — Schematic view of diaphragm type fuel pump. Pump body mounts on side of cylinder block and is ported to two crankcases as shown.

1. Pressure ports
2. Diaphragm
3. Booster chamber
4. To carburetor
5. Main fuel chamber
6. Outlet check valve
7. Inlet check valve
8. Fuel inlet

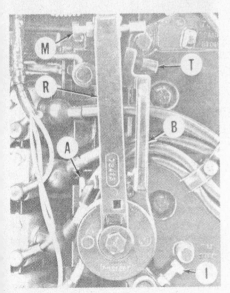

Fig. M12-27 — View of throttle (B) and spark (R) control arms on Models 75, 80, 800 and 850 after serial number 4366801.

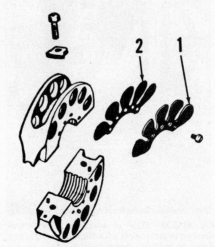

Fig M12-31 — View of intermediate main bearing and reed valve assembly used on Models 75, 80, 800 and 850. Later models use nuts and three bolts to secure reeds (2) and reed stops (1) to valve assembly.

Fig. M12-33 — Refer to text for timing instructions when installing drive belt or ignition unit. Dots (I) are marked on flywheels of some models that are timed by aligning straight line and arrow (TM). Be sure to use proper aligning marks.

IGNITION SYSTEM

Various types of ignition systems have been used. Make certain of type used, then refer to the appropriate following paragraphs for service. Original ignition system application is as follows:

MODEL	IGNITION TYPE
500 Ser. No. 251419-4357639	Lightening Energizer
50 and 500 after Ser. No. 4357639	Thunderbolt Without Distributor
650 Ser. No. 2503991-2803561	Lightning Energizer
650 Ser. No. 2803562-4382056	Thunderbolt With Distributor
650 After Ser. No. 4382056	Thunderbolt With Distributor
800 Prior To Ser. No. 4831999	Thunderbolt With Distributor
75, 80 and 800 After Ser. No. 4831998	Thunderbolt Without Distributor
850 Prior To Ser. No. 4366802	Thunderbolt With Distributor
850 After Ser. No. 4366801	Thunderbolt Without Distributor

Thunderbolt Models With Distributor

Models with Thunderbolt ignition and a distributor vary slightly. When variations in service procedures are necessary, notation will be made.

The Thunderbolt ignition system uses an electronic triggering device and does not use breaker points. This ignition is extremely durable in normal operation but can be easily damaged by improper testing or servicing procedures.

Fig. M12-34 — When installing ignition drive belt on 650 models with Thunderbolt or Lightning Energizer ignition, on late 800 models or on 850 models, the three ignition timing dots should be aligned with the arrow on pulley. Refer to text.

Observe the following list of cautions and use **only** the approved methods for checking the system to prevent damage to the components.

1. DO NOT reverse battery terminals.
2. DO NOT check polarity of battery by sparking the lead wires.
3. DO NOT install resistor type spark plugs or lead wires.
4. DO NOT disconnect **any** wires while engine is running.
5. DO NOT ground any wires to engine block when checking. Ground only to front cover plate or bottom cowl to which switch box is mounted as described.
6. DO NOT use tachometer except those designed for this system.

Fig. M12-36 — Surface gap plugs should be renewed if center electrode is 1/32 inch (0.79 mm) below the end of plug.

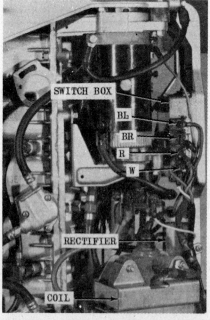

Fig. M12-37 — View of electrical connections used on most models with Thunderbolt ignition. Refer to text for motor identification. Six-cylinder motor is shown, however, four-cylinder models are similar.

BL. Black (green on some models)
BR. Brown
R. Red
W. White

TROUBLESHOOTING. Use only approved procedures when testing to prevent damage to components.

SPARK TEST. Do not remove spark plug wire **while motor is running.** Cut off the ground electrode from a standard spark plug (such as Champion J4J or L4J) and connect one of the spark plug wires to the test plug. Ground the test plug to the support bracket using a clamp or jumper wire.

CAUTION: Do not hold spark plug or wire in hand.

Make certain that test plug is properly grounded; then, crank motor with electric starter. If test plug fires but engine will not start, check for incorrect installation of timing belt as outlined in the appropriate following TRIGGER AND DISTRIBUTOR paragraph. Fuel system problems can also prevent starting. If test plug does not fire, check the wiring as follows.

WIRING AND CONNECTION TEST (Model 800 Ser. No. 3051041 through 3052380 and Model 800 Ser. No. 3144219 through 3192962 ONLY). Turn key switch "OFF." Make certain that all connections are tight. Make certain that all bonding straps are in position.

NOTE: Switch box damage will result if bonding strap from cylinder head to cowl is disconnected with engine running.

Connect one voltmeter lead to white wire terminal on high tension lead retainer and other lead to ground. Battery

Fig. M12-39 — Wires to port side of switch box and rectifiers must be connected as shown on motors with Thunderbolt ignition shown in Fig. M12-56.

BL. Black
BR. Brown
R. Red
W. White
Y. Yellow

voltage should be indicated with key switch in "RUN" position. Check wiring to switch, switch and battery if no voltage is found. If battery voltage is available, proceed as follows:

Turn key switch "OFF" and connect a test plug to top cylinder plug wire as described in SPARK TEST section. Turn engine by hand to place number 1 (top) piston in TDC position. Disconnect blue wire at switch box that comes from distributor. Attach a jumper wire to ground on motor and and turn key switch to "RUN" position. Hold jumper wire to blue terminal on switch box (Fig. M12-57). Spark plug firing when jumper is removed from blue terminal will indicate that trigger assembly is faulty. No spark when jumper is lifted will indicate a faulty high tension coil or a faulty switch box.

WIRING AND CONNECTION TEST ALL OTHER MOTORS WITH THUNDERBOLT IGNITION AND DISTRIBUTOR). Turn the key switch OFF. Connect one lead of voltmeter to red terminal of switch box (R-Fig. M12-37) and ground other lead to front cover plate. If red terminal is dead (no voltage), check battery, battery connections or for broken wire in wiring harness. If red terminal has voltage, proceed as follows:

Connect one lead of voltmeter to the white terminal (W-Fig. M12-37) and ground to other lead to front cover plate. Turn key switch ON. If white terminal is dead (no voltage), key switch or

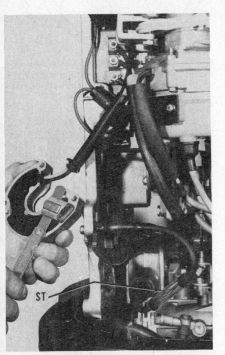

Fig. M12-40 — Refer to text when testing Thunderbolt ignition system. Spark tester is shown at (ST).

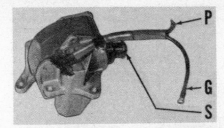

Fig. M12-41 — View of high tension ignition coil used on some Thunderbolt ignition motors. Primary lead (P) is green on late models, black on other models. Ground wire (G) is black on all models. The secondary (high tension) terminal is at (S).

wiring is defective. If white terminal has voltage, check the remaining components of system as follows:

Turn the key switch OFF. Disconnect the blace (BL-Fig. M12-39), white (W) and brown (BR) wires from switch box and connect the three wires from a trigger assembly that is known to be good. Refer to Fig. M12-40. Disconnect the coil secondary lead from the distributor center terminal, then connect a test spark plug (or gap tester) to the coil secondary lead.

NOTE: Spark plug or spark tester must also be grounded to engine.

Turn key switch ON, then pass a metal feeler gage through the trigger coil as shown. If a spark jumps at test plug, the original trigger assembly is faulty and should be renewed. If spark does not jump at test plug, listen for "click" around area of high tension coil as the feeler gage passes through the trigger coil. "Clicking" indicates shorted high tension coil or high tension (secondary) lead wire. If the lead wire is not shorted, the high tension coil should be checked further as outlined in the following paragraph. If spark does not jump the test plug and coil is not damaged, the switch box should be renewed.

NOTE: A faulty switch box is nearly always caused by reversing battery leads, which damages the rectifier and in turn damages the switch box.

If switch box is suspected, check rectifier before renewing the switch box. If tests indicate that rectifier is damaged, renew the rectifier and again test the ignition system.

NOTE: Before disconnecting any wires, make certain that motor is not running and disconnect battery.

COIL TEST. The ignition coil can be tested using an ignition tester available from several sources including the following:

GRAHAM TESTERS, INC.
4220 Central Ave., N.E.
Minneapolis, Minn. 55421

MERC-O-TRONIC
INSTRUMENTS CORP.
215 Branch St.
Almont, Mich. 48003

SPARK PLUGS. The spark plugs should be renewed if the center electrode is burned back more than 1/32 inch (0.79 mm) below flat surface of the plug end. Refer to Fig. M12-36. AC type V40FFM or radio noise suppression type VR40FFM surface gap spark plugs should be used.

TRIGGER AND DISTRIBUTOR (Model 650 After Ser. No. 2803561, Model 800 And Model 850). The electronic trigger coil (A-Fig. M12-43) is contained in the distributor housing (10) on Model 800 serial number 3051041 through 3052380 and 800 serial number 3144219 through 3192962. The trigger coil may be purchased separately for these motors. The trigger coil on other motors is built into the distributor housing (10-Fig. M12-42) and is available only as a unit with the housing. Before removing any of the components or disconnecting any wires, make certain that battery is disconnected.

To disassemble, disconnect battery, and the three wires that lead from distributor. Remove cover (18-Fig. M12-42), drive belt, pulley (19) and spacer (20). Bend tabs of washer (23) away from nut (21), remove nut and withdraw the distributor from adapter and economizer (25 and 29). Remove clamp (3) and cap (1). Carefully press bearing (15) out of housing by working through the two holes provided.

NOTE: Do not damage nut (17) or shaft when removing bearing.

Remove nut (17) then bump the rotor shaft (7) out of bearing (8). The shaft should slide easily out of timer plate (7P) or trigger wheel (B-Fig. M12-43) and spacer (14-Fig. M12-42). Bearing (8) can be removed after extracting snap ring (9).

When reassembling, install bearing (8) and snap ring (9). Position spacer (14) then insert the timer plate (7P) into the trigger coil slot. Make certain that the side of timer plate shown in Fig. M12-44 is out (toward distributor cap).

NOTE: If the timer plate is incorrectly installed it will be impossible to set ignition timing.

Insert the rotor shaft (7-Fig. M12-42) through the timer plate (7P), spacer (14) and bearing (8).

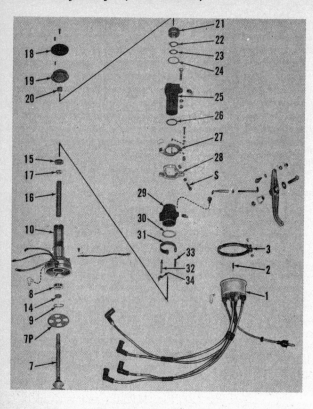

Fig. M12-42 – Exploded view of the Thunderbolt ignition distributor and drive used on Model 850 and most 800 models. Late 650 models are similar except for parts (27 & 28).

1. Distributor cap
2. Brush & spring
3. Clamp
7. Rotor & shaft
7P. Timer plate
8. Ball bearing
9. Snap ring
10. Distributor housing & trigger assy.
14. Spacer
15. Ball bearing
16. Spacer
17. Nut
18. Cover
19. Drive pulley
20. Spacer
21. Cap nut
22. Wave washer
23. Tang washer
24. Washer
25. Adapter
26. Washer
27. Throttle cam plate (primary pickup)
28. Throttle cam (secondary pickup)
29. Economizer collar
30. Washer
31. Spring
32. Spring anchor stud
33. Spring anchor pin
34. Spark advance stop

in a trigger ring module under the flywheel. Diodes, SCR's and capacitors are contained in the switch box. Switch box, trigger ring module and stator must be serviced as unit assemblies.

Check all wires and connections before troubleshooting ignition circuit. The following test specifications will aid troubleshooting. Resistance between blue and blue/white stator leads should be 5700-8000 ohms. Resistance between red and red/white stator leads should be 56-76 ohms. Resistance between trigger coil brown and white/black leads or trigger coil white and violet leads should be 700-1000 ohms.

Recommended spark plug for Model 500 before serial number 4576237 and Model 650 is AC V40FFM and Champion L76V. Recommended spark plug for Model 500 after serial number 4576236 and Models 50, 75, 80, 800 and 850 is AC V40FFK and Champion L78V.

"Lightning Energizer" Ignition

The "Lightning Energizer" ignition system consists of the drive unit, switch box and the high tension coil. Refer to

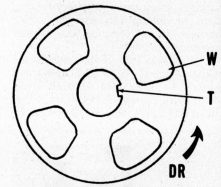

Fig. M12-44 – Install the timer plate with side shown, out toward the distributor cap. If the timer is installed incorrectly, it will be impossible to time the ignition.

T. Tab   W. Window

CAUTION: Make certain that tab (T – Fig. M12-44) correctly engages slot in rotor shaft before pressing shaft into bearing (8 – Fig. M12-42).

Install spacer (16) and tighten nut (17) to 75-80 in.-lbs. (8.5-9 N·m). Press ball bearing (15) around shaft and into housing (10). Install brush and spring (2), distributor cap (1) and clamp (3). Joint of clamp should be positioned under the trigger coil wires as shown in Fig. M12-45. Assemble distributor to the economizer collar (29 – Fig. M12-42) and adapter (25), then install washers (22, 23 and 24). Tighten cap nut (21), back nut off until the nearest notch lines up with tang of washer (23), then bend tang into notch. Install spacer (20) and pulley (19) over the drive key.

Turn the flywheel and distributor pulley until the index mark on flywheel is aligned with the arrow on distributor pulley.

Flywheel index mark on 800 models before serial number 2881082 is a straight white line (Fig. M12-33). Flywheel index mark on all other models is three dots (Fig. M12-34). Dots are on flywheel decal on late 850 models. When flywheel index mark and arrow on distributor pulley are aligned, install drive belt over the pulley.

Make certain that index marks on flywheel and arrow on distributor pulley are correctly aligned and on center line of crankshaft and distributor shaft. In-

stall cover (18 – Fig. M12-42) and tighten the retaining screw to 60 in.-lbs. (6.8 N·m). Refer to the SPEED CONTROL LINKAGE paragraphs for adjusting linkage and ignition timing.

Thunderbolt Models Without Distributor

These models are equipped with a Thunderbolt solid state capacitor discharge ignition system consisting of trigger coils, stator, switch box and ignition coils. The trigger coils are contained

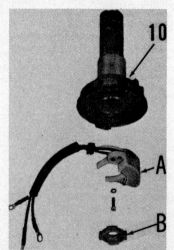

Fig. M12-43 – View of removable trigger coil (A) and trigger wheel (B) used on some Model 800 distributor housings. Refer to Fig. M12-42 for parts common to all motors.

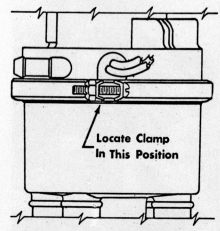

Fig. M12-45 – The joint of distributor cap clamp should be located below the wires from the timing coil.

Fig. M12-46. Electrical current for ignition is generated within driver unit (A). Wire (S) is connected to the ignition switch and is grounded to stop engine.

Observe the following cautions and use only approved methods for checking the system to prevent damage to the components.

1. DO NOT install incorrect spark plugs or lead wires.
2. DO NOT disconnect any wires while engine is running.
3. DO NOT use any tachometer except those approved for use with this system. (Mercury A-91-45294A3 or A-91-4816A6 with module A-52552A3 for boat or C-91-31591 for use while servicing.

TROUBLESHOOTING. Failure of one (or more) of the "Lightning Energizer" ignition components will normally prevent the motor from running at all. Some ignition problems that will cause an engine to lack performance are:

1. Incorrectly adjusted speed control linkage.
2. Faulty (or incorrect) spark plugs.
3. Faulty (or incorrect) high tension wires.
4. Intermittent short (ground) in the mercury safety switch (D–Fig. M12-46), ignition key switch, tachometer or ignition low tension wires (1 through 7).

If engine will not start, disconnect the salmon and brown wires (6 and 7) from the blue terminal of switch box (B).

NOTE: Leave blue wire (2) attached.

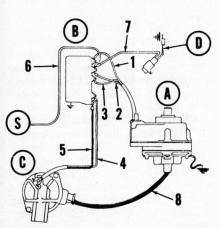

Fig. M12-46 – Schematic of components used on models with Lightning Energizer ignition system. Wire (S) is attached to the ignition switch and tachometer.

A. Ignition driver unit
B. Switch box
C. High tension coil
D. Mercury safety switch
1. Red
2. Blue
3. White
4. Green
5. Black
6. Salmon
7. Brown
8. High tension (secondary) wire

Attempt to start engine. If engine starts, grounding the blue switch box terminal to the cowl frame will stop engine and fault is in the disconnected wires, switches or tachometer. If engine will not start, proceed with remaining tests.

Disconnect red, white and blue wires (1, 2 and 3–M12-46) from switch box and check continuity using an ohmmeter. Resistance between red wire (1) and white wire (3) should be 4.1-4.3 ohms when tested on Rx100 scale of ohmmeter. Resistance between blue wire (2) and white wire (3) should be 10.0-11.0 ohms when tested on Rx100 scale. Test resistance between each of the three wires (1, 2 and 3) and housing of driver (A) using the Rx100 scale. Resistance should be infinite. If any resistance is incorrect, the driver unit (A) should be disassembled and tested further. If resistance is correct, check the high tension coil (C) as follows:

Disconnect the black and green wires (4 and 5) from switch box terminals and the coil secondary wire (8) from coil. The

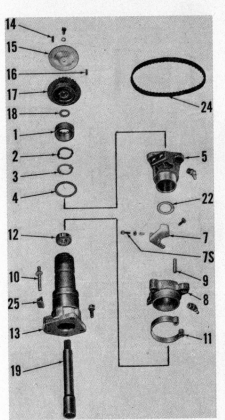

Fig. M12-47 – Exploded view of ignition drive and mounting bracket used on models with Lightning Energizer ignition system.

1. Cap nut
2. Wave washer
3. Tab washer
4. Thrust washer
5. Adapter
7. Throttle pickup
7S. Secondary pickup screw
8. Advance collar
9. Pin
10. Pin
11. Retard spring
12. Ball bearing
13. Pilot assy.
14. Pulley drive key
15. Pulley flange
16. Flange pin
17. Pulley
18. Thrust washer
19. Drive shaft
22. Washer
24. Drive belt
25. Ignition advance stop

resistance between the two leads (4 and 5) should be zero when tested on Rx1 ohmmeter scale. Resistance between one (either) of the leads (4 or 5) and the secondary terminal should be 3.0-3.6 ohms when tested on Rx1000 scale. Check resistance between each of the three leads (4, 5 and secondary terminal) to the coil bracket. Resistance should be infinite when checked on the Rx1000 scale. If any resistance is incorrect, the high tension coil should be renewed. If resistance tests of ignition driver (A) and coil (C) are correct, the switch box (B) should be renewed.

DRIVER UNIT. If resistance checks listed in the TROUBLESHOOTING section indicate that drive unit is faulty, proceed as follows:

Unbolt and remove driver from the pilot assembly (13–Fig. M12-47). Remove cap (1–Fig. M12-48), rotor (4) and cover (6). Remove the four retaining screws (15), clamp (17) and terminal block (14), then withdraw coils (12 and 13).

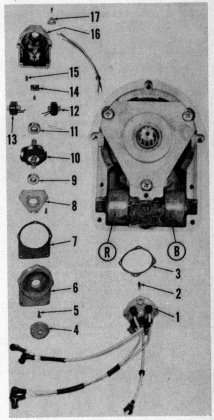

Fig. M12-48 – Exploded and partially assembled views of the Lightning Energizer ignition driver. The coils (12 & 13) are color coded and must be correctly assembled as shown in the partially assembled view. Refer to text.

B. Blue coil
R. Red coil
1. Cap
2. Brush & spring
3. Gasket
4. Rotor
5. Rotor clip
6. Cover
7. Gasket
8. Bearing cap
9. Bearing
10. Rotating magnet
11. Bearing
12. Blue coil
13. Red coil
14. Terminal block
15. Coil retaining screw
16. Housing
17. Wire retaining clamp

NOTE: The rotor (4) and the retaining screws (15) are installed with Loctite. The housing (16) should be heated slightly before attempting to remove screws (15).

The coils (12 and 13) can be checked and renewed (if necessary) individually after detaching wires from soldered connections of terminal block (14). Rotating magnet (10) and bearings (9 and 11) can be removed after removing bearing cap (8).

When assembling, Loctite should be used on the screws attaching bearing cap (8) to housing (16). After bearings (9 and (11), rotating magnet (10) and bearing cap (8) are assembled in housing (16), rotate the shaft to check for binding. When assembling coil, make certain that the RED coil (410-430 ohms

resistance) is installed at (R). The BLUE coil (10-11 ohms resistance) is installed at (B). Apply Loctite to the four coil retaining screws (15) and tighten to 22-25 in.-lbs. (2.5-2.8 N·m). After the coil wires are soldered to the terminal block, coat the terminals with liquid neoprene (Mercury C-92-25711-1). Cover gasket (7) should be renewed if damaged, before installing cover (6). Clean the splines of rotating magnet shaft (10) and make certain that clip (5) is pressed into bottom of rotor (4). Apply three drops of Loctite to bottom of hole in rotor and install on shaft. Check condition of brush and spring (2), cap (1) and gasket (3), before assembling. Mating splines on shafts (19 – Fig. M12-47) and (10 – Fig. M12-48) are provided with a blind spline to facilitate installation. Because of the

electronic timing characteristics, the speed control linkage adjustment should be checked after the ignition drive unit is repaired or renewed.

To remove the ignition drive belt (24 – Fig. M12-47), remove pulley flange (15) and disengage belt from pulley (17). Remove flywheel using a suitable puller and withdraw the belt. When installing, position drive belt under the alternator stator (if so equipped) and around crankshaft. Install flywheel being careful not to damage the belt. On Model 500, turn the flywheel and ignition driven pulley until the straight line on flywheel is aligned with arrow on driven pulley as shown in Fig. M12-33, then install drive belt over the pulley. On Model 650, turn the flywheel and driven pulley until the three ignition timing dots on flywheel are aligned with the arrow on ignition driven pulley as shown in Fig. M12-34, then install drive belt over the pulley. On all models, the correct mark on flywheel must be toward the arrow on pulley and both must be on center line between the crankshaft and ignition drive shaft as shown in Fig. M12-33 or M12-34 after belt is installed.

SPARK PLUGS. The spark plugs should be renewed if the center electrode is burned back more than 1/32 inch (0.79 mm) below flat surface of plug end. Refer to Fig. M12-36. AC type V40FFM or radio noise suppression type VR40FFM surface gap spark plugs should be used.

COOLING SYSTEM

WATER PUMP. The rubber impeller type water pump is housed in the gearcase housing. The impeller is mounted on and driven by the lower unit drive shaft.

When cooling system problems are encountered, first check the water inlet for plugging or partial stoppage, then if not corrected, remove the gearcase housing as outlined in LOWER UNIT section and examine the water pump, water tubes and seals.

Early models were originally equipped with aluminum water pump housings; however, on later models, the water pump housings are plastic. The later type pump can be installed on early models. When assembling, observe the assembly notes, cautions and tightening torques listed in the LOWER UNIT section.

POWER HEAD

R&R AND DISASSEMBLE. To remove the power head assembly, first disconnect the battery and remove the top and side cowling. Remove electric starter, then disconnect all interfering

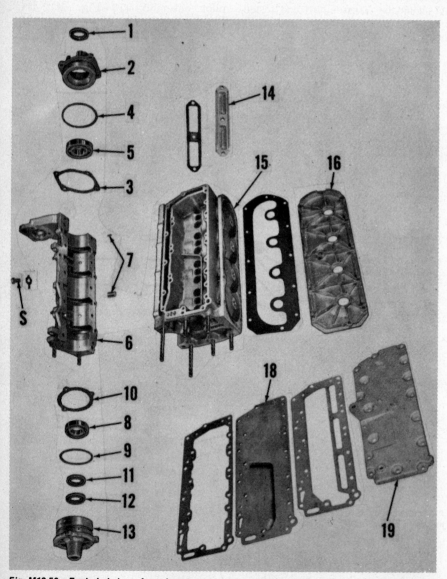

Fig. M12-50 — Exploded view of crankcase and associated parts used on Model 650; Models 50 and 500 are similar. Refer to Fig. M12-51.

S. Main bearing screw	5. Ball bearing	10. Shim
1. Oil seal	6. Crankcase half	11. Oil seal	15. Cylinder half
2. End cap	7. Dowel pins	12. Oil seal	16. Cylinder cover
3. Shim	8. Ball bearing	13. End cap	18. Exhaust plate
4. "O" ring	9. "O" ring	14. Transfer port cover	19. Exhaust cover

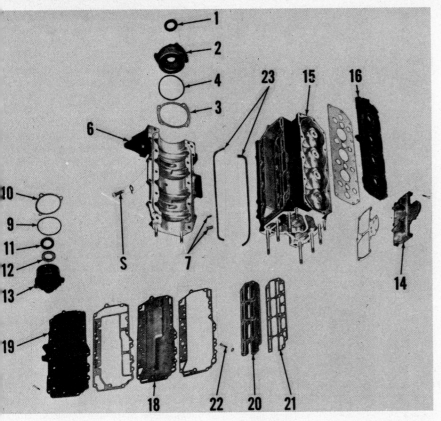

Fig. M12-51 — Exploded view of Model 800 prior to 1978 crankcase and associated parts showing the water jacket cover (20), gasket (21) and attaching screws (22). Sealing strips are shown at (23). Model 800 after 1977 and Models 75, 80 and 850 crankcase assembly have similar construction. Refer to Fig. M12-50 for parts identification.

ASSEMBLY. When assembling, the crankcase must be completely sealed against both vacuum and pressure. Exhaust manifold and water passages must be sealed against pressure leakage. Whenever power head is disassembled, it is recommended that all gasket surfaces and machined joints without gaskets be carefully checked for nicks and burrs which might interfere with a tight seal. On Models 75, 80, 800 and 850, make certain that threaded holes in cylinder for attaching the water jacket cover (20 – Fig. M12-51) are cleaned.

Lubricate all bearing and friction surfaces with engine oil. Loose needle bearings may be held in place during assembly using a light, nonfibrous grease.

After the crankshaft, connecting rods, pistons and main bearings are positioned in the cylinder, check crankshaft end play. Temporarily install crankshaft end caps (2 and 13 – Fig. M12-50 or M12-51) omitting sealing rings (4 and 9), but using shims (3 and 10) that were originally installed. Tighten end cap to cylinder retaining screws. Use a soft hammer to bump crankshaft each way to seat bearings, then measure end play.

To measure end play, (M12-50 or M12-51), bump the crankshaft toward top, and measure clearance between top crankshaft counterweight and end cap as shown in Fig. M12-53. Bump

wires and linkage. Remove the stud nuts which secure the power head to lower unit then jar power head on exhaust side to loosen gasket. Lift power head from lower unit and install on a suitable stand. Remove the flywheel, magneto or distributor, alternator-generator and the carburetors. Exhaust manifold cover, cylinder block cover and transfer port covers should be removed for cleaning and inspection.

Remove the main bearing locking bolts from front crankcase half, remove the flange bolts; then remove crankcase front half by inserting screwdriver in the recesses provided on side flanges. Use extra care not to spring the parts or to mar the machined, mating surfaces. Gently tap end caps off crankshaft. The crankcase half (6 – Fig. M12-50 or M12-51) and cylinder assembly (15) are matched and align bored, and are available only as an assembly.

Crankshaft, pistons, bearings and connecting rods may now be removed for service as outlined in the appropriate following paragraphs. When assembling, follow the procedures outlined in the ASSEMBLY paragraph.

Fig. M12-52 — Exploded view of Model 850 crankshaft and associated parts. Other motors are similar.

1. Piston rings
2. Piston
3. Piston pin
4. Retainers
5. Bearing washers
6. Needle rollers
7. Connecting rod
8. Caged needle bearing
9. Crankshaft
10. Intermediate main bearing
11. Reed petals
12. Reed stop
13. Main bearing
14. Outer race
15. Needle rollers
16. Retaining ring
17. Seal retainer
18. Seal

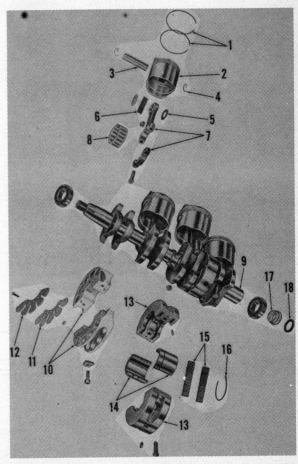

crankshaft toward bottom and again measure clearance between counterweight and end cap. Subtract first (minimum) clearance from second clearance which will indicate the amount of end play. If end play is not within limits of 0.004-0.012 inch (0.102-0.305 mm) on Model 75 or 0.008-0.012 inch (0.203-0.305 mm) on all other models, add or remove shims (3 or 10—Fig. M12-50 or M12-51) as necessary, then recheck. The crankshaft should be centered by varying the amount of shims between upper (3) and lower (10) shims stacks. When centering crankshaft, make certain that end play is correct. Shims are available in thicknesses of 0.005 and 0.010 inch for Models 50, 75 and 80. Shims (3) are available in thicknesses of 0.006, 0.008 and 0.010 inch for Models 800 and 850 and thicknesses of 0.002, 0.003, 0.005 and 0.010 inch for all other models.

On all models, all of the gasket and sealing surfaces should be lightly and carefully coated with an impervious liquid sealer. Surface must be completely coated, using care that excess sealer does not squeeze out into bearings, crankcase or other passages.

On Models 75, 80, 800 and 850, clean the gasket surfaces and threaded holes of the water jacket cover (20—Fig. M12-51) and cylinder (15). Coat the first four threads of all screws (22) with Resiweld and allow to set for 10 minutes. Coat gasket surface of water jacket cover and mating surface of cylinder with gasket sealer, then install gasket (21) and water jacket cover (20). Tighten screws (22) evenly from the center outward to a torque of 200 in.-lbs. (22.6 N·m) on early models and 150 in-lbs. (16.9 N·m) on later models.

On all models, check the assembly by turning the crankshaft after each step to check for binding or locking which might indicate improper assembly. Remove the cause before proceeding. Rotate the crankshaft until each piston ring in turn appears in one of the exhaust or transfer ports, then check by pressing on ring with a blunt tool. Ring should spring back when released; if it does not, a broken or binding ring is indicated, and the trouble should be corrected.

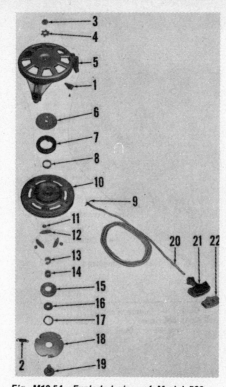

Fig. M12-54—Exploded view of Model 500 rewind starter assembly. Model 50 is similar.

1. Rope guide	12. Pawls
2. Spring	13. Bushing
3. Nut	14. Spacer
4. Lockwasher	15. Retainer
5. Starter housing	16. Washer
6. Retainer	17. Wave washer
7. Recoil spring	18. Plate
8. Bushing	19. Sheave shaft
9. Rope retaining pin	20. Rope
10. Sheave	21. Handle
11. Wave washers	22. Anchor

Tighten the crankcase, exhaust cover and cylinder cover cap screws beginning with screws in center of crankcase and working outward. Tightening torques are given in the CONDENSED SERVICE DATA table.

PISTONS, PINS, RINGS AND CYLINDERS. Before detaching connecting rods from crankshaft, make sure that rod and cap are properly identified for correct assembly to each other and in the correct cylinder.

Maximum allowable cylinder bore wear or out-of-round is 0.004 inch (0.102 mm). Worn or slightly damaged, standard size, cylinders may be repaired by boring and honing to fit an oversize piston. Pistons and rings are available in 0.015 inch (0.38 mm) oversize on early models and 0.015 inch (0.38 mm) and 0.030 inch (0.76 mm) oversizes on later models.

Piston rings are interchangeable in the ring grooves and are pinned in place.

Piston pin is pressed in piston bosses and secured with retaining rings. The retaining rings should not be reused. Two types of retaining rings have been used and must NOT be interchanged. Models 75, 80, 800 and 850 use "C" rings and other models use "G" type retaining rings. Piston end of connecting rod is fitted with loose needle rollers. Refer to the CONNECTING RODS, BEARINGS AND CRANKSHAFT paragraphs for number of rollers used.

The piston pin needle rollers use the connecting rod bore and the piston pin as bearing races. When assembling, install bearing washers and needle bearings in piston end of connecting rod using light nonfibrous grease to hold them in place. Use a torch lamp or suitable equivalent to heat piston to approx-

Fig. M12-53—Refer to text for method of checking crankshaft end play. The crankshaft should be centered in the cylinder block.

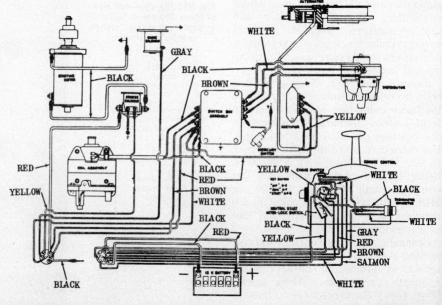

Fig. M12-56—Wiring diagram typical of most models with Thunderbolt ignition and a distributor.

Illustrations Courtesy Mercury

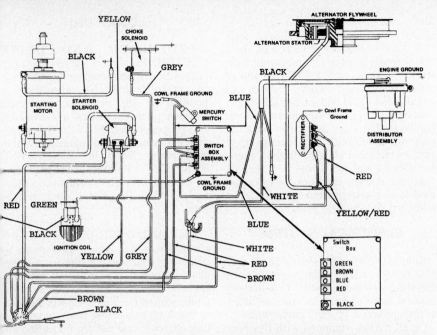

Fig. M12-57 — Wiring diagram of Thunderbolt ignition system with distributor used on some motors. Refer to text for particular motor serial numbers. Remote control unit in Fig. M12-56 is common to all Thunderbolt ignition models. Brown switch box terminal does not exist on some models and brown or orange wire from E and G ignition switch terminals connects to blue switch box terminal.

ROLLER MAIN BEARINGS

Model	No. of Rollers
50 and 500:	
Single Row	28
Double Row	56
All other models (each main bearing)	56

Check rod for alignment, using Mercury Alignment Tool, or by placing rod on a surface plate and checking with a light.

If bearing surface of rod and cap is rough, scored, worn or shows evidence of overheating, renew the connecting rod. Inspect crankpin and main bearing journals. If scored, out-of-round or worn, renew the crankshaft. Check the crankshaft for straightness using a dial indicator and "V" blocks.

Inspect and adjust the reed valves as outlined in REED VALVE paragraph, and reassemble as outlined in ASSEMBLY paragraph.

MANUAL STARTER

Refer to Fig. M12-54 for the rewind starter used on Models 50 and 500. Remove the top cowl and the recoil starter assembly from motor. Insert a screwdriver in slot in top of sheave shaft (19) and loosen the left hand thread nut (3). Allow the screwdriver and shaft (19) to turn clockwise until recoil spring unwinds. Pry anchor (22) out of starter handle and remove anchor and handle from rope. Remove nut (3), invert the assembly and remove the parts, making sure that recoil spring (7) remains in housing recess as sheave (10) is re-

mately 135°F (57°C) on early models and 190°F (88°C) on late models, then install and center the piston pin. Special tools are available from Mercury Marine for installing and centering the piston pin. Piston must be installed so that sharp, vertical side of deflector will be to starboard (intake) side of cylinder block.

Assemble the connecting rod and piston assemblies, together with the main bearing units to the crankshaft; then install the complete assembly in cylinder half of block. Number 2 and number 3 piston should be started into cylinders first. Use the Mercury Ring Compressor Kit (C-91-47844A2), if available; or carefully compress each ring with the fingers if kit is not available. Thoroughly lubricate pistons and rings during assembly.

PISTON PIN BEARINGS

Model	No. of Rollers
50 and 500	27
75, 80, 650, 800 and 850	29

CRANKPIN BEARINGS

Model	No. of Rollers
50 and 500	25
650	32
75, 80 and 800	Caged Rollers
850	Caged Rollers

CONNECTING RODS, BEARINGS AND CRANKSHAFT.
Upper and lower ends of crankshaft are carried by ball bearings. The second and fourth main bearings (10 – Fig. M12-52) also contain the inlet reed valves. The third main bearing (13) contains loose needle rollers (15) which ride in a split type outer race (14), held together by a retaining ring (16).

The connecting rod uses loose needle rollers at piston end. The crankpin end of connecting rod contains loose needle rollers in Models 50, 500 and 650. A caged roller bearing is used at crankpin end of connecting rod in Models 75, 80, 800 and 850. Refer to the following table of number of rollers used.

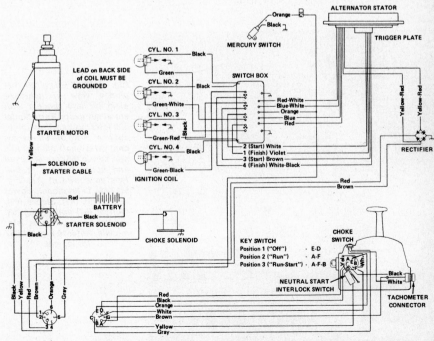

Fig. M12-58 — Wiring schematic for Model 800 (after 1977), Model 500 and Model 850 Thunderbolt models without a distributor. Models 50, 75 and 80 are similar.

moved. Remove spring (7) and allow it to unwind slowly. Care must be taken during spring removal to prevent injury.

Lubricate the parts with Multipurpose Lubricant, and assemble by reversing the disassembly procedure. Install spring guide bushing (8) with chamfered end toward pulley (10). Make sure that pawls (12) are all installed the same way, with radius to outside and identification mark away from sheave (10). Install retainer (15) with cup end out and position washer (16) and wave washer (17) in cup.

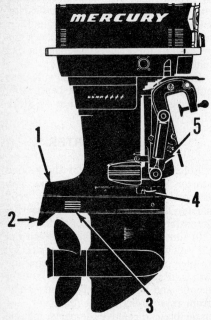

Fig. M12-60 — To remove the lower unit gearcase assembly, remove the attaching screws and stud nuts from position indicated.

Make certain that tang on spring retainer (6) engages slot in sheave shaft (19). Position starter with end of shaft (19) through housing (5) and install lockwasher (4) and nut (3). Pull free end of recoil rope through starter housing and install handle (21) and anchor (22). Turn sheave shaft (19) counterclockwise until handle is pulled against starter housing, plus an additional 1¼ turns; then tighten nut (3). Pull cord out and check for sticking and full turn.

Adjust starter interlock cable on 50 models so starter cannot operate unless outboard is in neutral gear.

ELECTRICAL SYSTEM

Refer to Figs. M12-56, M12-57 and M12-58 for wiring diagrams. Before servicing any motors with Thunderbolt ignition system, refer to cautions listed in the applicable ignition paragraphs.

On all motors equipped with flywheel alternator, the rectifier will be damaged if battery leads are disconnected while motor is running or leads are reversed.

On motors with Thunderbolt ignition and a distributor, the rectifier assembly is designed to protect the ignition switch box if battery terminals or harness plug becomes loose with motor running. However, the rectifier assembly will be damaged. If battery terminals are reversed, the rectifier and the ignition switch box will be damaged. The motor can be operated without rectifier if the two yellow or yellow/red wires (from the alternator) are disconnected from rectifier and taped separately.

LOWER UNIT

PROPELLER AND DRIVE CLUTCH. Protection for the motor is built into a special cushioning clutch in the propeller hub. No adjustment is possible on the propeller or clutch. Various pitch propellers are available and propeller should be selected to provide full throttle engine operation within rpm range listed in CONDENSED SERVICE DATA table at the beginning of section. Propellers other than those designed for the motor must not be used.

R&R AND OVERHAUL. Most service on lower unit can be performed by detaching gearcase housing from driveshaft housing. To remove housing, remove plastic plug and Allen screw from location (1 – Fig. M12-60). Remove trim tab (2) and screw from under trim tab. Remove stud nut from location (3), stud nuts (4) on each side and stud nut (5) if so equipped, then withdraw the lower unit gearcase assembly.

NOTE: On late models with spiral cut gears and tapered bearing, do not lose plunger or spring (67 & 68 — Fig. M12-61).

Remove plugs and drain oil from housing, then secure gearcase in a soft jawed vise, with propeller up. Wedge a piece of wood between propeller and antiventilation plate, remove propeller nut, then remove propeller.

Disassemble gearcase by removing gearcase housing cover nut (61 – Fig. M12-61 or M12-62). Clamp outer end of propeller shaft in a soft jawed vise and remove the gearcase by tapping with a rubber mallet. Be careful not to lose key (59) or shims (47) on early models. Forward gear (40) will remain in housing. Withdraw propeller shaft from bearing carrier (56) and reverse gear (46).

Clamp bearing carrier (56) in a soft jawed vise and remove reverse gear (46) and bearing (49) with an internal expanding puller and slide hammer. Remove and discard propeller shaft rear seals (58).

To remove dog clutch (43) from propeller shaft, remove retaining ring (44). Insert cam follower (8) in hole in shaft and apply only enough pressure on end of cam follower to remove spring pressure, then push out pin (42) with a small punch. The pin passes through drilled holes in dog clutch and operates in slotted holes in propeller shaft.

To disassemble the drive shaft and associated parts, reposition gearcase in vise with drive shaft projecting upward. Remove rubber slinger (11), water pump body (16), impeller (19) and impeller

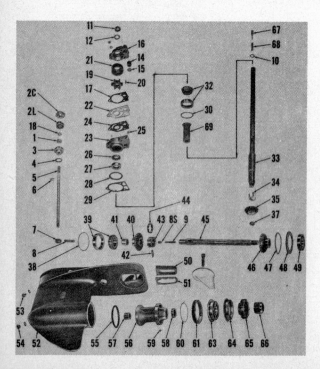

Fig. M12-61 — Typical exploded view of gearcase used on late models with spiral cut gears. Early Model 500 lower units with straight cut gear teeth are similar except drive shaft plunger (67) and spring (68) are not used and upper bearing is ball type as shown at (32 — Fig. M12-62). Later models do not use shims (47). Sleeve (69), plunger (67) and spring (68) are not used on some later models. Refer to Fig. M12-62 for legend.

drive key (20). Remove flushing screw and withdraw remainder of water pump parts. Clamp upper end of drive shaft in a soft jawed vise, remove pinion retaining nut or screw (37); then tap gearcase off drive shaft and bearing. Note position and thickness of shims (30 and 30A) on drive shaft upper bearing. On all models, mesh position of pinion is controlled by shims (30) placed underneath the bearing. On models with ball type upper bearing, shims (30A) control shaft end play. The shims are identical but should not be interchanged or mixed, except to adjust mesh position of drive pinion.

After drive shaft has been removed, forward gear (40) and bearing cone can be withdrawn. Use an internal expanding type puller to withdraw bearing cup if removal is required. Remove and save shim pack (38).

Shift shaft (5) and cam (7) can be removed after removing forward gear and unscrewing bushing (3) from gearcase housing.

If gear wear was abnormal or if any parts that affect gear alignment were renewed, check and adjust gear mesh as follows: Install forward gear (40 – Fig. M12-61 or M12-62) and bearing (39) using shims (38) that were originally installed. Position shims (30) that were originally installed at bottom of bearing bore. On models with taper bearing (32 – Fig. M12-61) and spiral gear teeth, install bearing cup (32) in housing bore against shims (30). On all models, position drive pinion (35 – Fig. M12-61 or M12-62) in housing and insert drive shaft (33), with bearing (32) installed, into housing, bearing (34) and gear (35). On all models with ball type bearing, the bearing must be firmly seated in housing bore. On all models, install retaining screw or nut (37). Coat gears (35 and 40) with bearing blue and check mesh position. On models with spiral gears, it will be necessary to push down on end of drive shaft while checking mesh position. On all models, if gears do not mesh in center of teeth, add or remove shims (30) under bearing as necessary. After setting mesh position, check backlash between teeth of gears (35 and 40). Backlash should be 0.003-0.005 inch (0.076-0.127 mm) for Models 50 and 500 with spiral cut gears and 0.006-0.008 inch (0.152-0.203 mm) for other 500, 650 and 800 models. Backlash should be 0.014-0.016 inch (0.356-0.406 mm) on 850 models and 0.008-0.012 inch (0.203-0.305 mm) on 75 and 80 models. To increase clearance (backlash), remove part of shim stack (38) behind bearing cup. If gears are too loose, add shims. After changing thickness of shims (38), gears should be recoated with bearing blue and mesh position

1. Oil seal
2C. Reverse locking cam
2G. Push rod guide
2L. Lower spacer
3. Bushing
4. "O" ring
5. Shift shaft
6. Snap ring
7. Shift cam
8. Cam follower
8S. Slide
9. Spring
10. "O" ring
11. Rubber ring (slinger)
12. Oil seal
14. Seal
15. Nylon washer
16. Water pump body
17. Gasket
18. Rubber washer
19. Impeller
20. Drive key
21. Insert
22. Plate
23. Pump base
24. Gasket
25. Dowel
26. Oil seal
27. Spring loaded oil seal
28. "O" ring
29. Gasket
30. & 30A. Shims
31. Snap ring
32. Ball bearing
33. Drive shaft
34. Roller bearing
35. Drive pinion
37. Nut
38. Shim
39. Tapered roller bearing
40. Forward gear
41. Roller bearing
42. Cross pin
43. Dog clutch
44. Retaining ring
45. Propeller shaft
46. Reverse gear
47. Shim
48. Thrust washer
49. Ball bearing
50. Exhaust tube seal
51. Support plate
52. Gear housing
53. Vent screw
54. Filler screw
55. "O" ring
56. Bearing carrier
57. Roller bearing
58. Oil seals
59. Key
60. Washer
61. Housing cover nut
62. Thrust washer
63. Thrust hub
64. Cupped washer
65. Splined washer
66. Propeller nut

Fig. M12-62 — Exploded view of gearcase assembly typical of Model 650 before serial number 2997339 and Model 800 before serial number 3059821.

should be rechecked. Install bearing (49), thrust washer (48) and reverse gear (46) in bearing carrier (56). To check reverse gear (46) backlash on all early models except Model 850 with spiral gears, install bearing carrier and gear assembly using shims (47) that were originally installed. If backlash is not within limits of 0.003-0.005 inch (0.076-0.127 mm) for Models 50 and 500 and 0.006-0.008 inch (0.152-0.203 mm) for other models, add or remove shims (47) as required. Add shims at (47) increases backlash (clearance). Reverse gear backlash is not adjustable on models with spiral gears.

When reassembling, long splines on shift rod (5 – Fig. M12-61 or M12-62) should be toward top. Shift cam (7) is installed with notches up and toward rear. Assemble shifting parts (9, 8S, 43, 42 and 44) into propeller shaft (45). Pin (42) should be through hole in slide (8S).

Fig. M12-63 — View of reverse lock cam with two tangs. The reverse lock cam must be installed on splines as shown when in forward gear position.

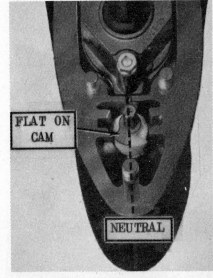

Fig. M12-64 — View of reverse lock cam with a single cam. Cam must be in position when lower unit (and shift-shaft) is in neutral.

Position follower (8) in end of propeller shaft and insert shaft into bearing (41) and forward gear. Install the reverse gear and bearing carrier assembly using new seals (55 and 58). Lip of inner seal (58) should face in and lip of outer seal (58) should face propeller (out). On models with ball type bearing at (32), install shims (30A) above bearing and position new gasket (29) and water pump base (23) on housing. Add shims (30A) until the water pump base stands out slightly from gasket, then measure clearance between gasket and water pump base with a feeler gage. Remove shims (30A) equal to 0.002-0.003 inch (0.051-0.076 mm) less than clearance measured. When water pump is tightened down, compression of a new gasket (29) will be sufficient to hold bearing (32) in position with zero clearance.

Upper oil seal (26) should be installed with lips facing up (toward engine) and lower oil seal (27) should be pressed into water pump base with lips facing down toward propeller shaft. Install remainder of water pump assembly and tighten the screw or nuts to the following recommended torque. Torque 1/4-28 nuts to 25-30 in.-lbs. (2.8-3.4 N·m). Torque 5/16-24 nuts to 35-40 in.-lbs.

(3.9-4.5 N·m). Torque 1/4-20 screws to 15-20 in.-lbs. (1.7-2.2 N·m).

Lower spacer (2L–Fig. M12-61 or M12-62) is installed with groove down. Note two types of reverse locking cam (2C) in Figs. M12-63 and M12-64. Two tabs of reverse locking cam shown in Fig. M12-63 must be aligned with left front stud when unit is in forward gear. Install reverse locking cam shown in Fig. M12-64 with high part of cam aligned as shown with unit in neutral. Push rod guide (2G–Fig. M12-62) is located in drive shaft housing.

Before attaching gearcase housing to the drive shaft housing, make certain that shift cam (7–Fig. M12-61 or M12-62) and the shift lever (on motor) are in forward gear position on early models and neutral position on late models. In forward gear position, shift shaft (5) should be in clockwise position (viewed from top end of shaft). Complete assembly by reversing disassembly procedure.

Later models are equipped with two seals which fit over upper drive shaft splines. Install splined seal on drive shaft splines with splined seal end toward top of drive shaft, then install remaining seal with small end towards top of drive shaft.

On models so equipped, make certain that spring (68–Fig. M12-61) and plunger (67) are positioned before attaching gearcase to drive shaft housing.

POWER TILT/TRIM

Non-Integral Type

FLUID. Recommended fluid is SAE 10W-30 or 10W-40 automotive oil. With outboard in full up position, oil level should reach bottom of fill plug hole threads. Do not overfill.

Fig. M12-73 — Loosen retainer screw (R) and tur trim limit adjusting nut (N) to adjust trim lim switch.

BLEEDING. To bleed air from hydraulic system, position outboard a full tilt and engage tilt lock lever Without disconnecting hoses, remove hydraulic trim cylinders. Be sure fluid reservoir is full and remains so during bleeding operation. Remove down cir cuit bleed screw (D–Fig. M12-70) and "O" ring. Press "IN" control button for a few seconds, release button and wait approximately one minute. Repeat until expelled oil is air-free. Install "O" ring and bleed screw (D) and repeat procedure on opposite cylinder. Place cylinder in a horizontal position so bleed port (P–Fig. M12-71) is up and remove up circuit bleed screw (U). Press "UP" and "UP/OUT" control buttons for a few seconds, release buttons and wait approximately one minute. Repeat until

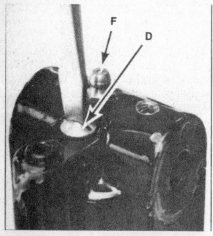

Fig. M12-70 — View showing location of down circuit bleed screw (D) and grease fitting (F).

Fig. M12-71 — View showing location of up circuit bleed screw (U) and bleed port (P).

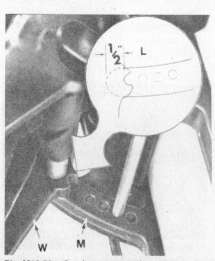

Fig. M12-72 — Overlap (L) between swivel bracket flange (W) and clamp bracket flange (M) should be 1/2 inch (12.7 mm).

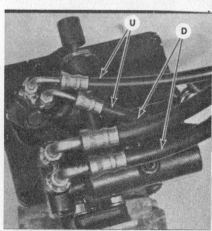

Fig. M12-74 — View of control valve showing location of up circuit hoses (U) and down circuit hoses (D).

expelled oil is air-free. Install "O" ring and bleed screw (U) and repeat procedure on opposite cylinder. Reinstall cylinders.

ADJUST TRIM LIMIT SWITCH. Operate firm control so outboard is in full down position. Press "UP/OUT" or "UP" control button and hold until pump motor stops. Outboard should tilt up and stop so there is ½ inch (12.7 mm) overlap (L–Fig. M12-72) between swivel bracket flange (W) and clamp bracket flange (M). Pull up on lower unit to remove slack when checking overlap (L). Note that if cylinder rods enter cylinders more than an additional ⅛ inch

(3.17 mm), that hydraulic system should be bled of air as outlined in BLEEDING section. If overlap (L) is incorrect, loosen retainer screw (R–Fig. M12-73) then turn adjusting nut (N) counterclockwise to increase overlap or clockwise to decrease overlap. Retighten retainer screw (R) and recheck adjustment.

PRESSURE TEST. To check hydraulic system pressure, disconnect four hoses attached to control valve as shown in Fig. M12-74; small hoses are for up circuit while large hoses are for down circuit. Connect a pressure gage to one up circuit port (small) of control

Fig. M12-78 — Release pressure on system, then remove Allen head plug (U) and install a 5000 psi (34.5 MPa) test gage with a suitable adapter and hose to test system pressure when operated in the "UP" direction. View identifies location of manual release valve (21).

valve and another pressure gage to one down circuit port (large). Screw plugs into remaining ports. Check fluid reservoir and fill if necessary. Operate trim control in up direction and note pressure gage reading. Minimum pressure should be 3500 psi (24.1 MPa) on new pumps with a red sleeve on wires or 3200-3500 psi (22.0-24.1 MPa) minimum on used pumps with red sleeve on wires. Minimum pressure on all other new pumps is 3000 psi (20.7 MPa) while minimum pressure on all other used pumps is 2700-3000 psi (18.6-20.7 MPa). Release trim control button. Pressure will drop slightly after stabilizing but should not drop faster than 100 psi (690 kPa) every 15 seconds. Operate trim control in down direction and note pressure gage reading. Minimum pressure is 500-1000 psi (3.4-6.9 MPa). Release trim control button. Pressure will drop slightly after stabilizing but should not drop faster than 100 psi (690 kPa) every 15 seconds. If pressure is normal, inspect trim cylinders and hoses for leakage. If pressure is abnormal, install a good control valve and recheck pressure. If pressure remains abnormal, install a new pump body.

Integral Type

FLUID AND BLEEDING. Recommended fluid is Dexron II or Type AF automatic transmission fluid. Remove fill plug (7–Fig. M12-77) and fill reservoir until fluid is visible in fill tube with the outboard motor in the full-up position.

The hydraulic circuit is self-bleeding as the tilt/trim system is operated through several cycles. After servicing system, be sure to check reservoir level after filling and operating system.

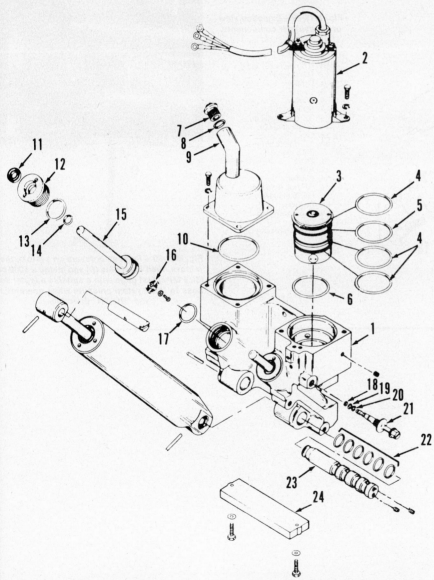

Fig. M12-77 — Exploded view of integral type power tilt/trim system.

1. Manifold	13. "O" ring (1.475 in. [37.47 mm] ID)
2. Electric motor	14. "O" ring (0.612 in. [15.54 mm] ID)
3. Pump assy.	15. Trim piston & rod
4. "O" rings (2.614 in. [66.40 mm] ID)	16. Strainer
5. "O" ring (2.739 in. [69.57 mm] ID)	17. "O" ring (1.248 in. [31.70 mm] ID)
6. "O" ring (2.739 in. [69.57 mm] ID)	18. "O" ring (0.114 in. [2.90 mm] ID)
7. Fill plug	19. "O" ring (0.208 in. [5.28 mm] ID)
8. "O" ring (0.583 in. [14.81 mm] ID)	20. "O" ring (0.239 in. [6.07 mm] ID)
9. Reservoir cover	21. Manual release valve
10. Seal ring	22. "O" rings (0.989 in. [25.12 mm] ID
11. Seal	23. Shaft
12. Cap	24. Anode plate

HYDRAULIC TESTING. The system can be checked by connecting a 5000 psi (34.5 MPa) test gage to the UP (U – Fig. M12-78) and DOWN (D – Fig. M12-80) ports. Prior to connecting test gage, place outboard motor in the full-up position and engage tilt lock lever. Unscrew reservoir fill plug and rotate manual release valve (21 – Fig. M12-78) three to four turns counterclockwise to release pressure on system. Remove UP or DOWN Allen head test port plug and connect test gage with suitable adapter and hose. Install fill plug and rotate manual release valve clockwise until seated. System pressure when testing at UP (U) port should be a minimum of 1300 psi (8.9 MPa). System pressure when testing at DOWN (D – Fig. M12-80) port should be a minimum of 500 psi (3.5 MPa). Release pressure on system as previously outlined prior to removing test gage. Reinstall Allen head plug.

OVERHAUL. Refer to Fig. M12-77 for an exploded view of manifold and trim cylinder components, and Fig. M12-79 for an exploded view of tilt cylinder components. Special Mercury socket 91-44487A1 and a spanner wrench is required to service trim and tilt cylinders. Keep all components clean and away from contamination. Keep components separated and label if needed for correct reassembly. Note "O" ring sizes as stated in legends of Figs. M12-77 and M12-79. Lubricate all "O" rings or seal lips with Dexron II or Type AF automatic transmission fluid during reassembly.

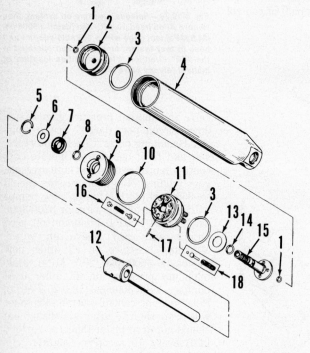

Fig. M12-79 — Exploded view of tilt cylinder components.
1. "O" ring (0.307 in. [7.79 mm] ID)
2. Cup
3. "O" ring (1.957 in. [49.71 mm] ID)
4. Cylinder
5. Circliip
6. Washer
7. Scraper
8. "O" ring (0.854 in. [21.69 mm] ID)
9. Cap
10. "O" ring (2.067 in. [52.5 mm] ID)
11. Piston
12. Rod
13. Washer
14. "O" ring (0.661 in. [16.79 mm] ID)
15. Rod end
16. Check valve assy.
17. Pin
18. Check valve assy.

Fig. M12-80 — Release pressure on system, then remove Allen head plug (D) and install a 5000 psi (34.5 MPa) test gage with a suitable adapter and hose to test system pressure when operated in the "DOWN" direction.

MERCURY IN-LINE
SIX-CYLINDER MODELS (1969-1985)

Year Produced	Model
1969	1000
	1250
1970	1150
	1350
1971	1150
	1350
1972	1150
	1400
1973	1150
	1500
1974	1150
	1500
1975	150
	1500
1976	1150
	1500
1977	1150
	1500
1978	900
	1150
	1400
	1500XS

Year Produced	Model
1979	90
	115
	140
1980	90
	115
	140
1981	90
	115
	140
1982	90
	115
1983	90
	115
1984	90
	115
1985	90
	115

Letter after model number indicates variation of equipment.
BP – Racing models, E – Electric starter and alternator, L – Long shaft,
SS – Solid state ignition, PT – Power trim, XS – High performance.

CONDENSED SERVICE DATA

TUNE-UP
Hp/rpm:
Models 90 & 900 ....90/4500-5000
Model 1000 ....100/4800-5300
Models 115 & 1150 ....115/5000-5500
Model 1250 ....125/4800-5300
Model 1350 ....135/4800-5300
Models 140 & 1400 ....140/5300-5800
Model 1500 ....150/5300-5800
Model 1500XS 155/5800-6300
Bore ....2⅞ in.
(73.03 mm)
Stroke:
Model 1000............................2.3 in.
(58.42 mm)
All Other Models.........................2-9/16 in.
(65.09 mm)

Displacement:
Model 1000............................89.6 cu. in.
(1469 cc)
All Other Models ....99.8 cu. in.
(1635 cc)

Compression At Cranking Speed ....*
Firing Order 1-4-5-2-3-6
Ignition Type ....Breakerless
Spark Plug *BS-V.H.Q.FFM. , CHAM - L77V* ....See Text
PCVR 40FFM, CHAM - GL76V or GL77V
Idle Speed:
Model 90 (in gear) ....500-600 rpm
All Other Models (in gear) ....550-600 rpm
Fuel:Oil Ratio 50:1
*Not more than 15 psi (103.5 kPa) variation between
cylinders.

SIZES – CLEARANCES
Piston Rings:
End Gap ....*
Side Clearance....................................*
Piston Skirt Clearance ....*
Crankshaft Bearing Type:
Top Main Bearing ....Ball Bearing
Main Bearing (2).............Bushing With Reed Valve
Main Bearing (3) ....Roller
Center Main Bearing ....Bushing With Reed Valve
Main Bearing (5) ....Roller
Main Bearing (6).............Bushing With Reed Valve
Bottom Main Bearing ....Ball Bearing
Crankpin ....Roller
Piston Pin Bearing ....Roller†
*Publication not authorized by manufacturer.
†Refer to text for number of piston pin rollers.

TIGHTENING TORQUES
Connecting Rod ....180 in.-lbs.
(20.3 N·m)
Crankcase Screws:
Models 1000 & 1250 ....150 in.-lbs.
(16.9 N·m)
All Other Models ....200 in.-lbs.
(22.6 N·m)
Cylinder Cover ....85 in.-lbs.
(9.6 N·m)

TIGHTENING TORQUES CONT.

Exhaust Cover:
Models 1000 & 1250 .150 in.-lbs.
(16.9 N·m)
All Other Models . . . . .250 in.-lbs.
(28.2 N·m)
Flywheel Nut . . . . .100 ft.-lbs.
(136 N·m)
Reed Screws . . . . .25 in.-lbs.
(2.8 N·m)

TIGHTENING TORQUES CONT.

Spark Plugs . . . . .240 in.-lbs
(27.1 N·m
Transfer Port Covers .85 in.-lbs
(9.6 N·m
Water Jacket Cover:
Early Models . . . . .200 in.-lbs
(22.6 N·m
Late Models . . . . .150 in.-lbs
(16.9 N·m

LUBRICATION

The engine is lubricated by oil mixed with the fuel. Fuel should be regular leaded, low lead or unleaded gasoline with a minimum pump octane rating of 86. Premium gasoline may be used if desired regular gasoline is not available. Recommended oil is Quicksilver Formula 50 or 50D. A good quality BIA certified TC-W oil may be used. Fuel:oil ratio should be 50:1 when using Formula 50 or 50-D oil. Follow fuel:oil ratio recommended by oil manufacturer if Formula 50 or 50-D is not used.

The lower unit gears and bearings are lubricated by oil contained in the gearcase. Only Quicksilver Super Duty Gear Lubricant should be used. Gearcase is filled through the lower filler plug hole until lubricant reaches the upper vent plug hole. Then allow 1 ounce (30 mL) to drain from gearcase. On most models, both plugs are on port side of gearcase.

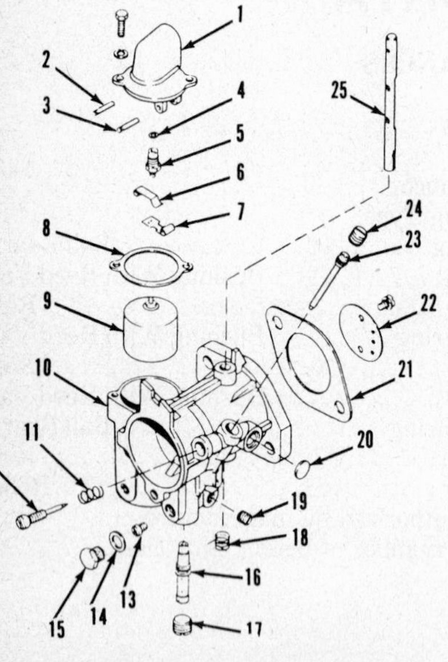

FUEL SYSTEM

CARBURETOR. Three "Back Drag" type carburetors are used. Refer to Fig. M14-1 for exploded view of carburetor, typical of type used on all models. Initial setting for the idle mixture screw (12) is one turn open from the closed position. Run motor until operating temperature is reached, then shift to forward gear and allow motor to run at idle speed. Slowly turn idle mixture screw (12) out (counterclockwise) until motor runs unevenly (loads up). Turn needle in (clockwise) until motor picks up speed and again runs evenly and continue turning until motor slows down and misses. Needle should be set between the two extremes. Turning screw (12) in (clockwise) leans the mixture. Slightly rich idle mixture is more desirable than too lean.

NOTE: Mixture adjustment should not be attempted in neutral.

Standard main jet (13) size is 0.070 inch (1.78 mm) on Model 90, 0.072 inch (1.83 mm) on Model 115 below serial number 5050763, 0.074 inch (1.88 mm) on Model 115 serial number 5050763 and above, 0.080 inch (2.03 mm) on Model 140 below serial number 5327663 and 0.074

inch (1.88 mm) on Model 140 serial number 5327663 and above for operation below 2500 feet (762 m) altitude. Standard vent jet (V – Fig. M14-2) size is 0.092 inch (2.34 mm) on Model 90, 0.092 inch (2.34 mm) on Model 115 below serial number 5050763, 0.096 inch (2.44 mm) on Model 115 serial number 5050763 and above, 0.092 inch (2.34 mm) on Model 140 below serial number 5327663 and 0.090 inch (2.29 mm) on Model 140 serial number 5327663 and above for operation below 2500 feet (762 m) altitude. Other jet sizes are available for adjusting the calibration for altitude or other special conditions.

Refer to the following for standard main jet (13 – Fig. M14-1) sizes on all early models operated below 4000 feet (1220 m).

Model 900

All Carburetors . . . . .0.070 in.
(1.78 mm)

Model 1000

KA-10A, KC-7B1 and
KC-14A . . . . .0.059 in.
(1.5 mm)

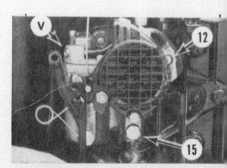

Fig. M14-1 — Exploded view of typical carburetor used on all models. A different cover (1) with a fuel strainer located under the cover is used on some early models.

1. Cover
2. Pin
3. Pin
4. Gasket
5. Inlet needle & seat
6. Primary lever
7. Secondary lever
8. Gasket
9. Float
10. Body
11. Spring
12. Idle mixture screw
13. Main jet
14. Gasket
15. Plug
16. Main nozzle
17. Plug
18. Spring
19. Plug
20. Welch plug
21. Gasket
22. Throttle plate
23. Idle tube
24. Plug
25. Throttle shaft

Fig. M14-2 — View showing vent jet (V), idle mixture screw (12) and main jet access plug (15).

Model 1150

KD-6A, KD-6B and WMK-3 . . .0.066 in.
(1.67 mm)
WMK-10 . . . . .0.072 in.
(1.83 mm)

Model 1250

KD-1A and KD-1B . . . . .0.082 in.
(2.08 mm)
KD-1BR1 . . . . .0.080 in.
(2.03 mm)
KD-2A . . . . .0.076 in.
(1.93 mm)

Model 1350

KD-7A, KD-7B and WMK-4 . .0.0785 in.
(1.99 mm)

Model 1400

(Serial no. 3293234-3295133 and
serial no. 3425632-345672)
Top carburetor . . . . .0.084 in.
(2.13 mm)
Lower and center carburetor . .0.082 in.
(2.08 mm)
(All 1400 models not included in
above serial numbers)
All carburetors . . . . .0.080 in.
(2.03 mm)

Model 1500

WMK-11 and WMK-14
Model 1500 . . . . .0.080 in.
(2.03 mm)
Model 1500XS . . . . .0.082 in.
(2.08 mm)

To determine the float level, invert bowl cover (1–Fig. M14-3) with inlet needle and seat (5), primary lever (6) and secondary lever (7) installed. Measure distance (A) from carburetor body surface to top of secondary lever (7). Distance (A) should be 13/32 inch (10.32 mm). Adjust distance (A) by bending curved end of primary lever (6). Turn bowl cover (1–Fig. M14-4) upright and measure distance (D) between primary lever (6) and end of secondary lever (7). Distance (D) should be ¼ inch (6.4 mm). Bend tab (T) to adjust. The contact spring located in center of float (9–Fig. M14-1) should extend 3/32 inch (2.38 mm) above top of float. Check to see if spring has been stretched or damaged.

SPEED CONTROL LINKAGE. The speed control linkage must be synchronized to advance the ignition timing and open the carburetor throttles in a precise manner. Because the two actions are interrelated, it is important to check the complete system following the sequence outlined in the appropriate following paragraphs.

Model 1000SS With "Thunderbolt Ignition." Refer to the special precautions listed in the **"Thunderbolt"** IGNITION section before servicing these motors. Incorrect service procedures can damage the ignition system.

NOTE: Do not disconnect any part of the ignition system while engine is running or while checking the speed control linkage.

Disconnect the fuel tank and allow motor to run until all fuel is used out of the carburetors. If any fuel remains, motor can start while checking the speed control linkage and may prevent accurate adjustments.

Connect a power timing light to the number 1 (top) spark plug. Turn ignition key on and crank motor with electric starter. Advance the speed controls until the timing light flashes when flywheel timing mark dots are aligned with the 36½° advance timing mark (Fig. M14-8). If advance timing is incorrect, turn the stop screw (A–Fig. M14-5) to stop the ignition advance at the correct position.

With the timing light still connected, synchronize the carburetor throttle opening to the ignition timing as follows: Crank motor with the electric starter and slowly advance speed control from idle position. The timing light should flash when dots on flywheel are between 5° and 7° BTDC.

With controls correctly set as outlined, the pickup tab should just contact the carburetor throttle lever. Refer to Fig. M14-9. If throttle is partly open or if lever is not touching the tab, loosen the two screws securing pickup plate and reposition plate for proper alignment.

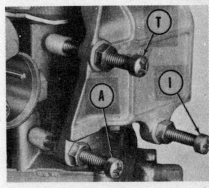

Fig. M14-5 — Maximum ignition advance is adjusted by stop screw (A) and idle speed by screw (I). Throttle stop screw (T) prevents damage to linkage.

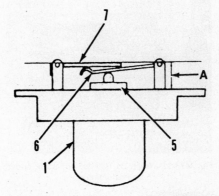

Fig. M14-3 — Distance (A) should be 13/32 inch (10.32 mm). Refer to text for adjustment procedure and Fig. M14-1 for parts identification.

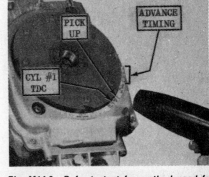

Fig. M14-8 — Refer to text for method used for setting the speed control linkage before adjusting.

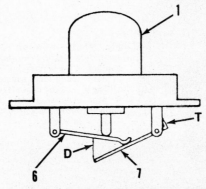

Fig. M14-4 — With bowl cover (1) upright, distance (D) between primary lever (6) and end of secondary lever (7) should be ¼ inch (6.4 mm). Bend tab (T) to adjust.

Fig. M14-9 — View of the throttle actuator plate just contacting the primary pickup lever (1). A four-cylinder motor is shown; however, Model 1000 is similar.

Throttle pickup should be rechecked after tightening the pickup plate retaining screws.

To adjust the throttle secondary pickup, advance the ignition distributor until it contacts the advance stop (A – Fig. M14-5).

NOTE: Do not move the economizer collar after the distributor contacts screw (A).

Check clearance at (2 – Fig. M14-10) between secondary pickup lever and screw. The screw should be just contacting the secondary pickup lever and is adjusted by turning screw (S – Fig. M14-11). Make certain that the primary end of the throttle pickup lever is still against the primary pickup cam (1 – Fig. M14-10).

To adjust the throttle stop screw (T – Fig. M14-5), move the speed control handle to maximum speed position. The carburetor throttles should be completely open when the throttle stop contacts screw (T). If the throttles are not completely open, turn stop screw (T) out. If the throttle stop does not contact screw (T), turn the screw in to prevent damage to linkage.

Model 1250. Refer to the special precautions listed in the **"Thunderbolt"** IGNITION section before servicing these motors. Incorrect servicing procedures can damage the ignition system.

NOTE: Do not disconnect any part of the ignition system while engine is running or while checking the speed control linkage adjustments.

Disconnect the fuel tank and allow motor to run until all fuel is used out of carburetors. If any fuel remains, motor can start while checking the speed control linkage and may prevent accurate adjustments.

Connect a power timing light to number 1 (top) spark plug wire. Back the throttle stop screw (T – Fig. M14-12) out and move the speed control to the maximum speed position until the carburetor throttle valves are completely open. Turn screw (T) in until it just touches the throttle stop, then turn the screw in an additional ¾ turn to prevent damage to the linkage.

To adjust the spark advance linkage, the speed control should be in the maximum speed position. Turn the key switch on, crank engine with starter and check the ignition timing. The mark on flywheel (dots) should be aligned with the correct degree mark when the timing light flashes. Advance timing should occur at 34° BTDC. If timing is incorrect, vary the length of link rod by turning nuts (N – Fig. M14-12). Make certain to recheck after nuts are tightened against the swivel.

Fig. M14-11 – Refer to text for adjusting speed control linkage.

The primary cam on the throttle pickup plate should just contact the primary pickup lever as shown at (1 – Fig. M14-13) when the speed control lever is advanced to provide 7°-9° BTDC ignition timing. To check, crank the engine with the starter while checking the ignition timing. Advance the speed control until the ignition timing is within 7°-9° BTDC, then check the throttle pickup at (1). If clearance at (1) is not 0-0.005 inch (0-0.13 mm), loosen the two attaching screws (P – Fig. M14-14) and move the throttle pickup plate. Recheck pickup point after moving plate and tightening the two attaching screws.

To adjust the secondary throttle pickup, move the speed control to maximum speed position, then turn screw (S – Fig. M14-14) until the carburetor throttles are fully open and the maximum speed stop contacts stop screw (T – Fig. M14-12). At maximum speed carburetor throttles should have slight play and should not bind, but all carburetor throttles should be fully open.

Fig. M14-12 – View of throttle stop screw (T) and idle stop screw (I) for 1250 models.

Fig. M14-10 – View of the secondary pickup lever just contacting the screw (2). The primary pickup lever should still be contacting cam at (1). A four cylinder motor is shown; however, Model 1000 is similar.

Fig. M14-13 – View of throttle pickup cams and lever typical of all models except Model 1000. Primary pickup should occur at (1) and secondary pickup at (2). Refer to text for adjusting.

Fig. M14-14—Typical view of secondary pickup adjusting screws (S) and primary pickup plate attaching screws (P) used on Models 900, 1150, 1250, 1350, 1400 and 1500.

Models 900, 1150, 1350, 1400 And 1500. Refer to the special precautions listed in the **"Thunderbolt"** IGNITION section before servicing these motors. Incorrect servicing procedures can damage the ignition system.

NOTE: Do not disconnect any part of the ignition system while engine is running or while checking the speed control linkage adjustments.

Connect a power timing light to number 1 (top) spark plug wire. Mount motor in test tank and start engine with timing light installed. Slowly advance speed control until proper throttle pickup timing marks are aligned. Refer to the following for throttle pickup timing specifications:

Model	Throttle Pickup Timing
900	4°-6° BTDC
1150 (Below Ser. No. 2928768)	5°-7° BTDC
1150 (Ser. No. 2928768-3761035)	2° BTDC-TDC
1150 (Above Ser. No. 3761035)	1°-3° BTDC
1350 (Below Ser. No. 2928768)	5°-7°BTDC
1350 (Above Ser. No. 2928767)	2° BTDC-TDC
1400 (1972)	2° BTDC-TDC
1400 (1978)	4°-6° BTDC
1500 (Below Ser. No. 3628318)	2° BTDC-TDC
1500 (Ser. No. 3628318-3751849)	2°-4° BTDC
1500 (Above Ser. No. 3751850)	4°-6° BTDC

Timing grid is marked on cowl support bracket on Model 1150 before serial number 3761035, Model 1350, Model 1400 and Model 1500 before serial number 3628318. Three punch marks on flywheel are used as timing mark on

these models. A white dot is painted on top side of flywheel adjacent to three timing dots.

A metal timing pointer is secured to engine and a timing decal is placed on flywheel of Model 900, late Model 1150 and late Model 1500.

The primary cam on the throttle pickup plate should just contact the primary pickup lever as shown at (1–Fig. M14-13) when the speed control is advanced to specified pickup position. If clearance at (1) is not 0-0.005 inch (0-0.13 mm), loosen the two attaching screws (P–Fig. M14-14) and move the throttle pickup plate. Recheck pickup point after tightening the two attaching screws.

To check maximum spark advance, start engine and advance speed control until distributor touches spark advance stop screw (A–Fig. M14-10). Timing light should indicate full spark advance at 21° BTDC. Turn spark advance stop screw to adjust full advance timing if necessary.

Secondary throttle pickup should be checked after maximum spark advance is adjusted. With engine stopped, advance speed controls until distributor is just touching spark advance stop screw. Secondary pickup on throttle cam should be just touching secondary pickup on carburetor cluster (2–Fig. M14-13) at this point. Turn throttle pickup screw (S–Fig. M14-11) to adjust secondary throttle pickup.

Maximum throttle stop screw (T–Fig. M14-10) should be adjusted so throttles are fully opened at maximum speed position of speed control. Linkage should have a small amount of free play at maximum speed position to prevent binding.

Models 90, 115 And 140. Refer to special precautions listed in the IGNITION section before servicing these motors. Incorrect servicing procedures can damage the ignition system.

NOTE: Do not disconnect any part of the ignition system while engine is running or while checking speed control linkage adjustments.

Check ignition timing pointer alignment as follows: Install a dial indicator gage in number 1 (top) spark plug hole and turn flywheel clockwise until piston is 0.464 inch (12 mm) BTDC. Loosen retaining screw and position timing pointer so it is aligned with ".464 BTDC" mark on flywheel.

If engine is equipped with an idle stabilizer module (M–Fig. M14-15), disconnect white/black module wire from switch box terminal. Tape end of wire to prevent grounding. Reconnect other white/black wire between switch

boxes to switch box terminal. Remove all spark plugs except number 1 (top) cylinder spark plug to prevent engine starting. Detach throttle cable barrel from retainer of cable anchor bracket. Adjust idle stop screw (I–Fig. M14-16) so idle marks (M–Fig. M14-17) on throttle cam and bracket are aligned as shown; retighten stop screw locknut. Loosen screw (W) in top carburetor lever (V). Hold idle stop screw (I–Fig. M14-16) against stop then turn carburetor lever (V–Fig. M14-17) so throttle valves are completely closed and cam (C) just contacts roller (R). Connect a power timing light to number 1 cylinder spark plug. With outboard in neutral, position throttle lever so idle stop screw is against stop. Crank engine using starter motor and adjust primary pickup screw (P–Fig. M14-18) so ignition timing is 1°-3° BTDC on Model 90, 5°-7° ATDC on Model 115 and 4°-6° ATDC on Model 140.

Open throttle and crank engine using starter motor. Adjust maximum ignition advance screw (A) so ignition timing is 20° BTDC.

NOTE: Due to electronic characteristics of ignition system, maximum advance is set at 20°BTDC but ignition will retard to 18° BTDC at high engine speed.

Fig. M14-15—View showing location of idle stabilizer module (M) used on some models.

Fig. M14-16—View of idle speed screw (I) on 90, 115 and 140 models.

Without engine running, move throttle lever to maximum throttle position and adjust full throttle stop screw (T – Fig. M14-15) so there is 0.010-0.015 inch (0.25-0.38 mm) clearance between roller (R – Fig. M14-17) and cam (C). Be sure carburetor throttle plates are not acting as stops.

Reconnect idle stabilizer module wire to switch box. Install throttle cable barrel in retainer while adjusting barrel so it fits into retainer and places a very light preload on throttle lever against idle speed screw. Excessive throttle cable preload will result in difficult shifting from forward to neutral.

Adjust idle speed screw (I – Fig. M14-16) so idle speed is 500-600 rpm on Model 90 and 550-600 rpm on Models 115 and 140 with outboard in gear.

REED VALVES. The inlet reed valves are located on the crankshaft second, fourth and sixth main bearings. Each reed valve unit supplies fuel mixture from one of the carburetors to the two adjoining cylinders.

Reed petals (2 – Fig. M14-19 or M14-20) should be perfectly flat and have no more than 0.007 inch (0.178 mm) clearance between free end of reed petal and seating surface of center main bearing. The reed stop (1) must be

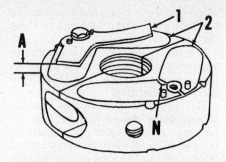

Fig. M14-19 – Intermediate main bearing and reed valve for 1000 models. Reed petals are right and left hand units. When installing reed petals, place reed with the cutout notch (N) on left as shown. Refer also to Fig. M14-20.

carefully adjusted to 3/16 inch (4.76 mm) on Model 1000; 5/32 inch on Models 1150, 1250, 1350 and 1400; and 0.162 inch (4.11 mm) on Models 90, 115, 140, 900, 1150 and 1500. This clearance is measured between end of stop and seating surface of reed plate as shown at (A – Fig. M14-19). Seating surface of bearing must be smooth and flat, and may be refinished on a lapping plate after removing reed stops, reed valves and dowels. Do not attempt to bend or straighten a reed petal to modify performance or to salvage a damaged reed. Never install a bent reed. Lubricate the reed valve units with "Quicksilver" Multipurpose Lubricant or a light distributor cam grease when reassembling.

On Model 1000, each reed valve unit has eight reeds which are right-hand and left-hand units, and are available only as a matched set. When installing reed valves, place the reed petal with the cutout notch (N) to the left as shown. Crankshaft must be removed before reed valve units can be serviced.

FUEL PUMP. Diaphragm type fuel pumps are used. Pressure and vacuum pulsations from the crankcase alternate to pull fuel from the supply tank and supply the carburetor. Most of the work is performed by the main supply chamber (5 – Fig. M14-21). Vacuum in the crankcase pulls the diaphragm (2) downward causing fuel to be drawn through inlet line (8), past inlet check valve (7) into main pump chamber (5). The alternate pressure forces diaphragm out and fuel leaves the chamber through outlet check valve (6). The booster pump chamber (3) serves to dampen the action of the larger, main pump chamber (5), and increase the maximum potential fuel flow.

When overhauling the fuel pump, renew all defective or questionable parts. Fuel pressure should be at least 2 psi (13.8 kPa) at carburetor when running motor at full throttle.

IGNITION SYSTEM

All models are equipped with Thunderbolt ignition system. Refer to the appropriate following paragraphs for service.

The breakerless Thunderbolt ignition system uses an electronic triggering device and does not use breaker points. This ignition is extremely durable in normal operation but can be easily damaged by improper testing or servicing procedures.

Observe the following list of cautions and use **only** the approved methods for checking the system to prevent damage to the components.

1. DO NOT reverse battery terminals.

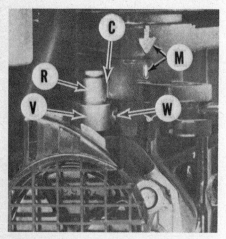

Fig. M14-17 – View of pickup cam (C) and throttle roller (R) on Merc 90, 115 and 140.

C. Pickup cam
M. Idle speed marks
R. Throttle roller
V. Carburetor lever
W. Screw

Fig. M14-18 – Adjust primary pickup screw (P) and maximum advance screw (A) 90, 115 and 140 models.

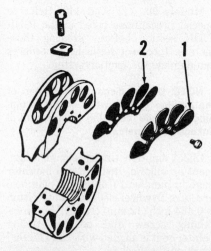

Fig. M14-20 – View of the intermediate main bearing and reed valve assembly use on 90, 115, 140, 900, 1500, 1250 and 1350 models. Reed petals are shown at (2) and reed stops at (1). In addition to small retaining screw shown, Models 90, 115 and 140, late Model 1150, Model 1400 and Model 1500 have through-bolts securing reed plates and petals to valve assemblies.

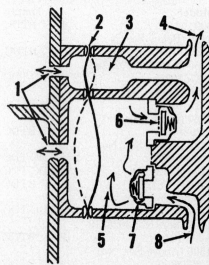

Fig. M14-21 – Schematic view of diaphragm type fuel pump. Pump body mounts on side of cylinder block and is ported to two crankcases as shown.

1. Pressure ports
2. Diaphragm
3. Booster chamber
4. To carburetor
5. Main fuel chamber
6. Outlet check valve
7. Inlet check valve
8. Fuel inlet

. DO NOT check polarity of battery by sparking the lead wires.

. DO NOT install resistor type spark plugs or lead wires other than those specified.

. DO NOT disconnect **any** wires while engine is running.

. DO NOT ground any wires to engine block when checking. Ground only to front cover plate or bottom cowl to which switch box is mounted as described.

. DO NOT use tachometer except for those designed for this system.

All Models Except Models 90, 115 And 140

TROUBLESHOOTING. Use only approved procedures when testing to prevent damage to components.

SPARK TEST. Do not remove spark plug wire while motor is running. Cut off the ground electrode from a standard spark plug (such as Champion J4J or L4J) and connect one of the spark plug wires to the test plug. Ground the test plug to the support bracket using a clamp or jumper wire.

CAUTION: Do not hold spark plug or wire in hand.

Make certain that test plug is properly grounded, then crank motor with electric starter. If test plug fires but engine will not start, check for incorrect installation of timing belt as outlined in the following TRIGGER AND DISTRIBUTOR paragraphs. Fuel system problems can also prevent starting. If test plug does not fire, check the wiring as follows.

WIRING AND CONNECTION TEST (Models Prior To 1976.) Turn the key switch OFF. Connect one lead of voltmeter to red terminal of switch box (R – Fig. M14-27) and ground other lead

to front cover plate. If red terminal is dead (no voltage), check battery, battery connections or for broken wire in wiring harness. If red terminal has voltage, proceed as follows:

Connect one lead of voltmeter to the white terminal (W) and ground other lead to front cover plate. Turn key switch ON. If white terminal is dead (no voltage), key switch or wiring is defective. If white terminal has voltage, check the remaining components of system as follows:

Turn the key switch OFF. Disconnect the black (BL – Fig. M14-29), white (W) and brown (BR) wires from switch box and connect the three wires from a trigger assembly that is known to be good. Refer to Fig. M14-30. Disconnect the coil secondary lead from the distributor center terminal, then connect a test spark plug (or gap tester) to the coil secondary lead.

NOTE: Spark plug or spark tester must also be grounded to engine.

Turn key switch ON, then pass a metal feeler gage through the trigger coil as shown in Fig. M14-30. If a spark jumps at test plug, the original trigger assembly is faulty and should be renewed. If spark does not jump at test plug, listen for "click" around area of the high tension coil as the feeler gage passes through the trigger coil. "Clicking" indicates shorted high tension coil or high tension (secondary) lead wire. If the lead wire is not shorted, the high tension coil should be checked further as outlined in the following paragraph. If spark does not jump the test plug and coil is not damaged, the switch box should be renewed.

NOTE: A faulty switch box is nearly always caused by reversing battery leads, which damages the rectifier and in turn damages the switch box.

If switch box is suspected, check rectifier before renewing the switch box. If tests indicate that rectifier is damaged, renew the rectifier and again test the ignition system.

NOTE: Before disconnecting any wires, make certain that motor is not running and disconnect battery.

Models After 1975. To check trigger coil and switch box, manufacturer recommends use of Thunderbolt Ignition Analyzer (C-91-62563A1). Follow instructions accompanying tester.

Fig. M14-26 – Surface gap plus should be renewed if center electrode is 1/32 inch (0.79 mm) below the end of plug.

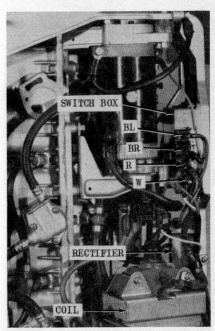

Fig. M14-27 – Wires to starboard side of switch box must be connected as shown on motors with breakerless Thunderbolt ignition.

BL. Black or green   R. Red
BR. Brown   W. White

Fig. M14-22 – Refer to text for timing instructions when installing drive belt or ignition unit. Straight line mark on flywheel is used as belt aligning mark on 1000 and 1250 models. Refer to Fig. M14-33 for belt aligning marks on later models.

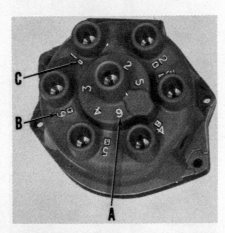

Fig. M14-23 – The distributor cap is marked for installation on several 6-cylinder motors. Inside numbers (A) are used for early 60 cu.-in. (983 cc) and 66 cu.-in. (1081 cc) motors. The outside numbers (B) are used for 76 cu.-in. (1245 cc) and larger motors except those with Thunderbolt ignition. Numbers (C) inside the squares are for early models (before 1970) with Thunderbolt ignition.

COIL TEST. The ignition coil can be checked using an ignition tester available from several sources, including the following:

GRAHAM TESTERS, INC.
4220 Central Ave. N.E.
Minneapolis, Minn. 55421

MERC-O-TRONIC
INSTRUMENTS CORP.
215 Branch St.
Almont, Mich. 48003

SPARK PLUGS. The spark plugs should be removed if the center electrode is burned back more than 1/32 inch

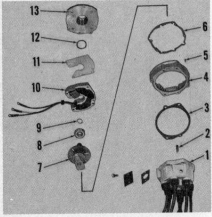

Fig. M14-28 — Exploded view of ignition distributor typical of breakerless Thunderbolt ignition models before 1970.

1. Distributor cap
2. Brush & spring
3. Gasket
4. Adapter
5. Dowel pin (2 used)
6. Gasket
7. Shaft, rotor & timer assy.
8. Ball bearing (2 used)
9. Snap ring (2 used)
10. Trigger assy.
11. Shims
12. Wave washer
13. Primary housing

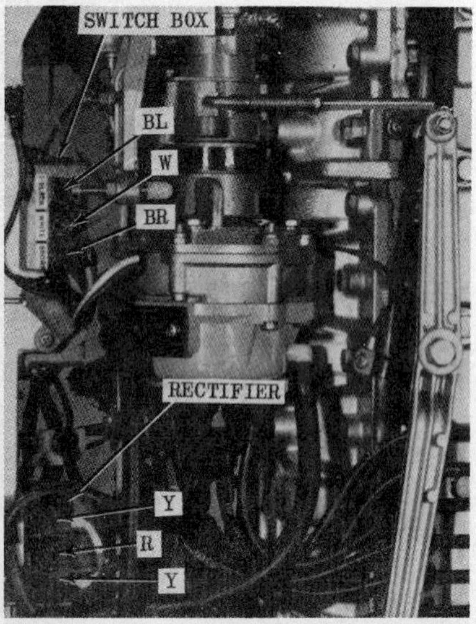

(0.79 mm) below flat surface of the plug end. Refer to Fig. M14-26. AC type V40FFM or Champion type L77V, surface gap spark plugs should be used. Radio noise suppression spark plugs, AC type VR40FFM or Champion types QL76V or QL77V, may also be used.

TRIGGER AND DISTRIBUTOR (Models 1000 and 1250). The electronic trigger assembly is mounted in the distributor assembly as shown in Fig. M14-28. Before disconnecting any wires, disconnect the battery. The three wires from the trigger assembly (10) are connected to three terminals on port side of the switch box. The three terminals are marked to indicate correct wire connections. When installing trigger assembly, install shims (11) between trigger housing (10) and primary housing (13) until the timer disc on rotor shaft (7) is centered in trigger slot. Recheck after trigger housing screws are tightened to make certain that timer disc is centered in slot.

NOTE: The rotor and timer disc cannot be removed from shaft.

Connect wires from trigger assembly to terminals on port side of switch box. Switch box terminals are marked for correct installation of wires as shown in Fig. M14-29.

To install the distributor to the drive pulley and housing, turn drive end of distributor shaft so tang is forward.

Firing order is 1-4-5-2-3-6. The distributor cap is marked for installing

Fig. M14-30 — Refer to text when testing Thunderbolt ignition system. Spark tester is shown at (ST).

spark plug wires. The numbers (C – Fig M14-23) inside the squares are for Thunderbolt ignition models.

To remove the distributor drive belt, i is first necessary to remove the pulley flange plate. Disengage belt from the distributor pulley, then remove flywheel using a suitable puller. When installing position drive belt under the alternator stator and around the crankshaft. In stall flywheel being careful not to damage to the belt. Turn the flywheel and distributor until the straight line or flywheel is aligned with the arrow or distributor pulley as shown in (TM – Fig M14-22), then install drive belt over the pulley.

NOTE: Do not use the ignition timing mark dots (I). Recheck marks (TM) after belt is installed. Marks must be on center line between crankshaft and distributor shaft.

TRIGGER AND DISTRIBUTOR (Models 900, 1150, 1350, 1400 and 1500). The electronic trigger coil is located in distributor housing (10 – Fig M14-32) and is available only as a unit with the housing. Before removing any wires, make certain that battery is disconnected.

To disassemble, disconnect battery and three wires on port side of switch box. The wires from trigger assembly and terminals are marked to indicate correct wire connections. Remove cover (18), drive belt pulley (19) and spacer (20). Bend tabs of washer (23) away from nut (21), remove nut and withdraw the distributor from adapter and economizer (25 and 29). Remove clamp (3) and cap (1). Carefully press bearing (15) out of housing by working through the two holes provided.

NOTE: Do not damage nut (17) or shaft when removing bearing.

Remove nut (17) then bump the rotor shaft (7) out of bearing (8). The shaft should slide easily out of timer plate (7P) and spacer (14). Bearing (8) can be removed after extracting snap ring (9).

When reassembling, install bearing (8) and snap ring (9). Position spacer (14) then insert the timer plate (7P) into the trigger coil slot. Insert the rotor shaft (7) through the timer plate (7P), spacer (14) and bearing (8).

CAUTION: Make certain that tab on timer plate (7P) correctly engages slot in rotor shaft (7) before pressing shaft into bearing (8).

Install spacer (16) and tighten nut (17) to 75-80 in.-lbs. (8.5-9.0 N·m). Rotate rotor shaft and note any interference as

Fig. M14-29 — Wires to port side of switch box and rectifier on models prior to 1976 must be connected as shown.

BL. Black
BR. Brown
R. Red
W. White
Y. Yellow

timer plate turns. If necessary, install shims between bearing plate (8) and spacer (14) to adjust timer plate height. Press ball bearing (15) around shaft and into housing (10). Install distributor cap (1) and clamp (3). Joint of clamp should be positioned under the trigger coil wires. Assemble distributor to the economizer collar (29) and adapter (25), then install washers (22, 23 and 24). Tighten cap nut (21), back nut off until the nearest notch lines up with tang of washer (23), then bend tang into notch. Install spacer (20) and pulley (19) over the drive key. Firing order is 1-4-5-2-3-6.

To renew the distributor drive belt, it is first necessary to remove pulley flange plate (18), disengage belt from pulley, then remove flywheel. When installing, position drive belt under alternator stator and around the crankshaft. Install flywheel being careful not to damage the belt. Turn the flywheel and distributor pulley as shown in (Fig. M14-33), then install drive belt over the pulley. Dots are punched into flywheel and painted white on early models. Recheck timing marks after belt is installed. Marks must be on center line between crankshaft and distributor shaft. Refer to SPEED CONTROL LINKAGE. Paragraphs for adjusting linkage and ignition timing.

Models 90, 115 And 140

These models are equipped with a solid-state, capacitor discharge ignition system consisting of trigger coils, stator, switch boxes and ignition coils. The trigger coils are contained in a trigger ring module under the flywheel. Diodes, SCR's and capacitors are contained in the switch boxes. Switch boxes trigger ring module and stator must be serviced as unit assemblies.

Check all wires and connections before troubleshooting ignition circuit. The following test specificatiosn will aid troubleshooting.

STATOR

Tests	Ohms
Blue and red stator leads	5400-6200
Blue/white and red/white stator leads	5400-6200
Red stator lead and engine ground*	125-175
Red/white stator lead and engine ground*	125-175

*If stator has a black ground wire, be sure ground wire is properly connected to engine.

Note when testing the trigger module that yellow sleeves enclose wires from the trigger module to the lower switch box. The lower switch box serves the even-numbered cylinders while the upper switch box serves the odd-numbered cylinders.

TRIGGER MODULE

Tests	Ohms
Brown trigger lead (no yellow sleeve) and white trigger lead (with yellow sleeve)	1100-1400
White trigger lead (no yellow sleeve) and violet trigger lead (with yellow sleeve)	1100-1400
Violet trigger lead (no yellow sleeve) and brown trigger lead (with yellow sleeve)	1100-1400

COOLING SYSTEM

WATER PUMP. The rubber impeller type water pump is housed in the gearcase housing. The impeller is mounted on and driven by the lower unit drive shaft.

When cooling system problems are encountered, first check the water inlet for plugging or partial stoppage, then if not corrected, remove the gearcase housing as outlined in LOWER UNIT section and examine the water pump, water tubes and seals.

Early models were originally equipped with aluminum water pump housings; however, on later models, the water pump housings are plastic. The later type pump can be installed on early models. When assembling, observe the assembly notes, cautions and tightening torques listed in the LOWER UNIT section.

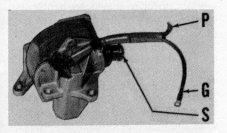

Fig. M14-31 – View of typical high tension ignition coil. Primary lead (P) may be green or black. Ground wire (G) is black on all models. The secondary (high tension) terminal is at (S).

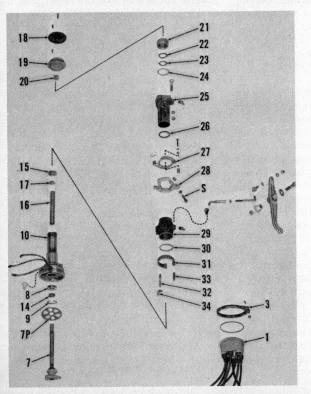

Fig. M14-32 – Exploded view of the Thunderbolt ignition distributor and drive used on 1970 and later models.

1. Distributor cap
3. Clamp
7. Rotor & shaft
7P. Timer plate
8. Ball bearing
9. Snap ring
10. Distributor housing & trigger assy.
14. Spacer
15. Ball bearing
16. Spacer
17. Nut
18. Flange plate
19. Drive pulley
20. Spacer
21. Cap nut
22. Wave washer
23. Tang washer
24. Washer
25. Adapter
26. Washer
27. Throttle cam plate (primary pickup)
28. Throttle cam (secondary pickup)
29. Economizer collar
30. Washer
31. Spring
32. Spring anchor stud
33. Spring anchor pin
34. Spark advance stop

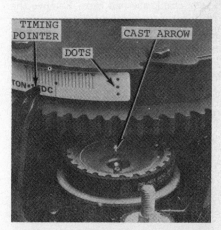

Fig. M14-33 – Distributor drive belt should be installed with cast arrow on drive pulley aligned with dots on flywheel of 900, 1150, 1350, 1400 and 1500 models. Dots are stamped into flywheel and painted white on early models not equipped with timing decal on flywheel.

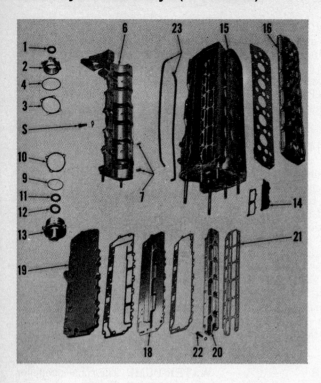

S. Main bearing screw
1. Oil seal
2. End cap
3. Shim
4. "O" ring
6. Crankcase half
7. Dowel pins
9. "O" ring
10. Shim
11. Oil seal
12. Oil seal
13. End cap
14. Transfer port cover
15. Cylinder half
16. Cylinder cover
18. Exhaust plate
19. Exhaust cover
20. Water jacket cover
21. Gasket
22. Screws
23. Sealing strips

POWER HEAD

R&R AND DISASSEMBLE. To remove the power head assembly, first disconnect the battery and remove the top and side cowling. Remove electric starter, then disconnect all interfering wire and linkage. Remove the stud nuts which secure the power head to lower unit then jar power head on exhaust side to loosen gasket. Lift power head from lower unit and install on a suitable stand. Remove the flywheel, distributor, alternator-generator and the carburetors. Exhaust manifold cover, cylinder block cover and transfer port covers should be removed for cleaning and inspection.

Remove screws securing upper and lower crankcase end caps. Remove the main bearing locking bolts from front crankcase half, remove the flange bolts;

Fig. M14-42 — Refer to text for method of checking crankshaft end play. The crankshaft should be centered in the cylinder block.

then remove crankcase front half by inserting screwdriver in the recesses provided on side flanges. Use extra care not to spring the parts or to mar the machined, mating surfaces. Use a mallet or soft faced hammer to tap crankcase end caps from cylinder block assembly. Be careful not to damage adjustment shims on end caps. The crankcase half (6 – Fig. M14-41) and cylinder assembly (15) are matched and align bored, and are available only as an assembly.

Crankshaft, pistons, bearings and connecting rods may now be removed for service as outlined in the appropriate following paragraphs. When assembling, follow the procedures outlined in the ASSEMBLY paragraph.

ASSEMBLY. When assembling, the crankcase must be completely sealed against both vacuum and pressure. Exhaust manifold and water passages must be sealed against pressure leakage. Whenever power head is disassembled, it is recommended that all gasket surfaces and machined joints without gaskets be carefully checked for nicks and burrs which might interfere with a tight seal.

On all models so equipped, make certain that threaded holes in cylinder for attaching the water jacket cover (20 – Fi.g M14-41) are cleaned.

Lubricate all bearing and friction surfaces with engine oil. Loose needle bearings may be held in place during assembly using a light, nonfibrous grease.

After the crankcase, connecting rods, pistons and main bearings are positioned in the cylinder, check the crank-

shaft end play. Temporarily install the crankshaft end caps (2 and 13) omitting the sealing rings (4 and 9), but using the shims (3 and 10) that were originally installed. Tighten the end cap to cylinder, retaining screws. Use a soft hammer to bump the crankshaft each way to seat bearings, then measure the end play.

Bump the crankshaft toward top, and measure clearance between the top crankshaft counterweight and the end cap as shown in Fig. M14-42. Bump the crankshaft toward bottom and again measure clearance between counterweight and end cap. Subtract the first (minimum) clearance from the second clearance which will indicate the amount of end play. If end play is not within limits of 0.004-0.012 inch (0.102-0.305 mm), add or remove shims (3 or 10 – Fig. M14-41) as necessary, then recheck. The crankshaft should be centered by varying the amount of shims between upper (3) and lower (10) shim stacks. When centering the crankshaft, make certain that end play is correct.

On all models, all of the gasket and sealing surfaces should be lightly and carefully coated with an impervious liquid sealer. Surface must be completely coated, using care that excess sealer does not squeeze out into bearings, crankcase or other passages.

On models so equipped, clean the gasket surfaces and threaded holes of water jacket cover (20) and cylinder (15). Coat the first four threads of all screws (22) with Resiweld (C-92-65150-1) and allow to set for 10 minutes. Coat gasket surface of water jacket cover and mating surface of cylinder with gasket sealer, then install gasket (21) and water jacket cover (20). Tighten the screws (22) evenly from the center outward to a torque of 200 in.-lbs. (22.6 N·m) on early models and 150 in.-lbs. (16.9 N·m) on late models.

On all models, check the assembly by turning the crankshaft after each step to check for binding or locking which might indicate improper assembly. Remove the cause before proceeding. Rotate the crankshaft until each piston ring in turn appears in one of the exhaust or transfer ports, then check by pressing on ring with a blunt tool. Ring should spring back when released; if it does not, a broken or binding ring is indicated, and the trouble should be corrected.

Tighten the crankcase exhaust cover and cylinder cover cap screws by first tightening the center screws, then tightening screws evenly working toward top of power head. When upper half is tightened, again start at the center and tighten screws alternately toward bottom of power head. Tightening torques are given in the CONDENSED SERVICE DATA table.

PISTONS, PINS, RINGS AND CYLINDERS.

Before detaching connecting rods from crankshaft, make sure that rod and cap are properly identified for correct assembly to each other and in the correct cylinder.

Maximum allowable cylinder bore wear or out-of-round is 0.004 inch (0.102 mm). Worn or slightly damaged standard size cylinders may be repaired by boring and honing to fit an oversize piston. Pistons and rings are available in 0.015 inch (0.38 mm) oversize on early models and 0.015 inch (0.38 mm) and 0.030 inch (0.76 mm) oversizes on later models.

Piston rings are interchangeable in the ring grooves and are pinned to prevent rings from rotating in grooves. Some motors use two rings on each piston while others use three rings.

Piston pin is pressed in piston bosses and secured with retaining rings. The retaining rings should not be reused. Two types of retaining rings (4 – Fig. M14-43) have been used and must NOT be interchanged. Some late models use "C" rings and other models use "G" type retaining rings. Piston end of connecting rod is fitted with loose needle rollers. Refer to the CONNECTING RODS, BEARINGS AND CRANKSHAFT paragraphs for number of rollers used. The piston pin needle rollers use the connecting rod bore and the piston pin as bearing races. When assembling, install bearing washers and needle bearings in piston end of connecting rod using light nonfibrous grease to hold them in place. A Mercury special tool may be used to hold needles in position while positioning piston for installation.

Piston must be installed so sharp, vertical side of deflector will be to starboard (intake) side of cylinder block. Heat piston to approximately 135°F (57°C) on early models and 190°F (88°C) on late models, then press piston pin into place. Pin should be centered in piston. Use new retaining rings on each reassembly of engine.

Assemble the connecting rod and piston assemblies, together with the main bearing units to the crankshaft; then install the complete assembly in cylinder half of block. Numbers 2 and 4 pistons should be started first. Use the Mercury Ring Compressor Kit (C-91-47844A2), if available; or carefully compress each ring with the fingers if kit is not available. Thoroughly lubricate pistons and rings during assembly.

CONNECTING RODS, BEARINGS AND CRANKSHAFT.

Upper and lower ends of crankshaft are carried by ball bearings. The second, fourth and sixth main bearings (Fig. M14-19 or M14-20) also contain the inlet reed valves. The third and fifth main bearings (13 – Fig. M14-43), contain both loose needle rollers (15) which ride in a split

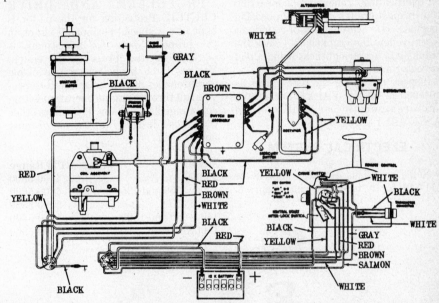

Fig. M14-47 – Wiring diagram typical of all models with breakerless Thunderbolt ignition prior to 1976.

Fig. M14-43 – Exploded view of the crankshaft and associated parts typical of all models. Refer to Fig. M14-19 or M14-20 for intermediate main bearings and reed valve assemblies.

1. Piston rings
2. Piston
3. Piston pin
4. Retainers
5. Bearing washers
6. Needle rollers
7. Connecting rod
8. Needle rollers
9. Crankshaft
10. Top main bearing
11. Bottom main bearing
12. Bearing alignment dowel
13. Bearing housing
14. Main bearing race
15. Needle rollers
16. Retaining ring

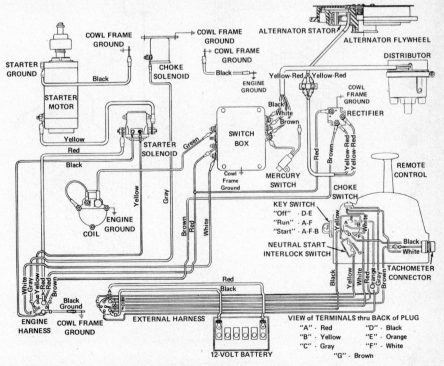

Fig. M14-48 – Wiring schematic for models between 1975 and 1979 equipped with Thunderbolt ignition.

type outer race (14), held together by a retaining ring (16).

The connecting rod uses 29 loose needle rollers at piston end. The crankpin end of connecting rod uses a caged needle bearing on all models except Model 1000. Model 1000 motors were equipped with 32 loose needle roller bearings at crankpin end of connecting rod.

Check rod for alignment using Mercury Alignment tool, or by placing rod on a surface plate and checking with a light.

If bearing surface of rod and cap is rough, scored, worn or shows evidence of overheating, renew the connecting rod. Inspect crankpin and main bearing journals. If scored, out-of-round or worn, renew the crankshaft. Check the crankshaft for straightness using a dial indicator and "V" blocks.

Inspect and adjust the reed valves as outlined in REED VALVE paragraph, and reassemble as outlined in ASSEMBLY paragraph.

ELECTRICAL SYSTEM

Refer to Figs. M14-47, M14-48 or M14-49 for a typical wiring diagram.

Note the following cautions when servicing electrical components:

DO NOT reverse battery connections. Battery negative (–) terminal is grounded.

DO NOT "spark" battery connections to check polarity.

DO NOT disconnect battery cables while engine is running.

DO NOT crank engine if ignition switch boxes are not grounded to engine.

LOWER UNIT

PROPELLER AND DRIVE CLUTCH. Protection for the motor is built into a special cushioning clutch in the propeller hub. No adjustment is possible on the propeller or clutch. Various pitch propellers are available and propeller should be selected to provide full throttle engine operation within rpm range listed below. Propellers other than those designed for the motor must not be used.

Model	RPM Range
90,900	4500-5000
1000, 1250 and 1350	4800-5300
115, 1150	5000-5500
140, 1400 and 1500	5300-5800
1500XS	5800-6300

R&R AND OVERHAUL. Most service on the lower unit can be performed by detaching the gearcase housing from the drive shaft housing. To remove housing, remove plastic plug and Allen screw from location (1–Fig. M14-51. Remove trim tab (2) and screw from under trim tab. Remove stud nut from location (3), stud nuts (4) on each side and stud nut (5), if so equipped, then withdraw the lower unit gearcase assembly.

Remove plugs and drain oil from housing, then secure the gearcase in a soft jawed vise with propeller up. Wedge a piece of wood between propeller and antiventilation plate, remove propeller nut, then remove propeller.

Disassemble gearcase by removing gearcase housing cover nut (61–Fig. M14-52). Clamp the outer end of propeller shaft in a soft jawed vise and remove gearcase by tapping with a rubber mallet. Be careful not to lose key (59) or shims (47) on early models. Forward gear (40) will remain in housing. Withdraw propeller shaft from bearing carrier (56) and reverse gear (46).

Clamp bearing carrier (56) in a soft jawed vise and remove reverse gear (46) and bearing (49) with an internal expanding puller and slide hammer. Remove and discard propeller shaft rear seals (58).

To remove dog clutch (43) from propeller shaft, remove retaining ring (44). Insert cam follower (8) in hole in shaft and apply only enough pressure on end of cam follower to remove spring pressure, then push out pin (42) with a small punch. The pin passes through drilled

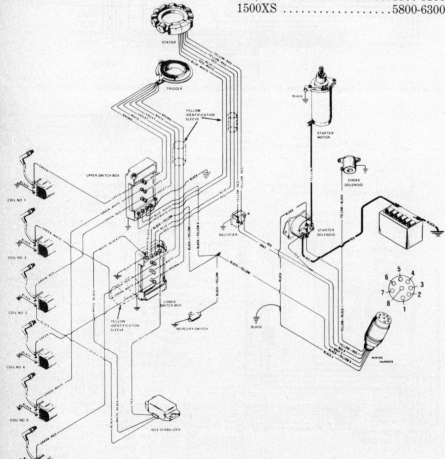

Fig. M14-49 — Wiring diagram typical of 90, 115 and 140 models.

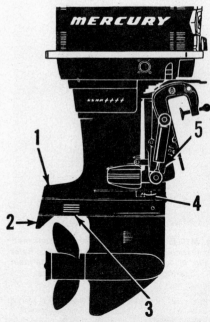

Fig. M14-51 — To remove the lower unit gearcase assembly, remove the attaching screws and stud nuts from positions indicated.

Illustrations Courtesy Mercury

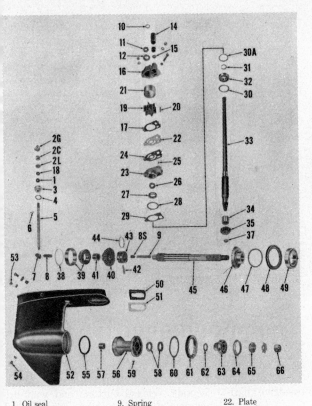

necessary. After setting mesh position, check backlash between teeth of gears (35 and 40). Backlash should be 0.014-0.016 inch (0.356-0.406 mm). To increase clearance (backlash), remove part of shim stack (38) behind bearing cup. If gears are too loose, add shims. After changing thickness of shims (38), gears should be recoated with bearing blue and mesh position should be rechecked. Install bearing (49), thrust washer (48) and reverse gear (46) in bearing carrier (56). To check reverse gear (46) backlash on all early models with straight-cut gear teeth, install bearing carrier and gear assembly using shims (47) that were originally installed. If backlash is not within limits of 0.006-0.008 inch (0.152-0.203 mm), add or remove shims (47) as required. Adding shims at (47) increases backlash (clearance). Reverse gear backlash is not adjustable on models with spiral gears.

When reassembling, long splines on shift rod (5) should be toward top. Shift cam (7) is installed with notches up and toward rear. Assemble shifting parts (9, 8S, 43, 42 and 44) into propeller shaft (45). Pin (42) should be through hole in slide (8S). Position follower (8) in end of propeller shaft insert shaft into bearing (41) and forward gear. Install the reverse gear and bearing carrier assembly using new seals (55 and 58). Lip of inner seal (58) should face in and lip of outer seal (58) should face propeller (out). On models with ball type bearing at (32), install shims (30A) above bearing and position new gasket (29) and water pump base (23) on housing. Add shims (30A) until the water pump base stands out slightly from gasket, then measure clearance between gasket and

Fig. M14-52 – Exploded view of gearcase assembly typical of all models. Shim (47) is not used on later models. Some models use a tapered bearing in place of ball bearing (32), snap ring (31) and shim (30A).

33. Drive shaft
34. Roller bearing
35. Drive pinion
37. Nut
38. Shim
39. Tapered roller bearing
40. Forward gear
41. Roller bearing
42. Cross pin
43. Dog clutch
44. Retaining ring
45. Propeller shaft
46. Reverse gear
47. Shim
48. Thrust washer
49. Ball bearing
50. Exhaust tube seal
51. Support plate
52. Gear housing
53. Vent screw
54. Filler screw
55. "O" ring
56. Bearing carrier
57. Roller bearing
58. Oil seals
59. Key
60. Washer
61. Housing cover nut
62. Thrust washer
63. Thrust hub
64. Cupped washer
65. Splined washer
66. Propeller nut

1. Oil seal
2C. Reverse locking cam
2G. Push rod guide
2L. Lower spacer
3. Bushing
4. "O" ring
5. Shift shaft
6. Snap ring
7. Shift cam
8. Cam follower
8S. Slide
9. Spring
10. "O" ring
11. Rubber ring (slinger)
12. Oil seal
14. Seal
15. Nylon washer
16. Water pump body
17. Seal
19. Impeller
20. Key
21. Insert
22. Plate
23. Pump base
24. Gasket
25. Dowel
26. Oil seal
27. Spring loaded oil seal
28. "O" ring
29. Gasket
30. & 30A. Shims
31. Snap ring
32. Ball bearing

holes in clutch and operates in slotted holes in propeller shaft.

To disassemble drive shaft and associated parts, reposition gearcase in vise with drive shaft projecting upward. Remove rubber slinger (11), water pump body (16), impeller (19) and impeller drive key (20). Remove flushing screw and withdraw remainder of water pump parts. Clamp upper end of drive shaft in a soft jawed vise, remove pinion retaining nut or screw (37); then tap gearcase off drive shaft and bearing. Note position and thickness of shims (30 and 30A) on drive shaft upper bearing. On all models, mesh portion of pinion is controlled by shims (30) placed underneath the bearing. On models with ball type upper bearing, shims (30A) control shaft end play. The shims are identical but should not be interchanged or mixed, except to adjust the mesh portion of drive pinion.

After drive shaft has been removed, forward gear (40) and bearing cone can be withdrawn. Use an internal expanding type puller to withdraw bearing cup if removal is required. Remove and save shim pack (38).

Shift shaft (5) and cam (7) can be removed after removing forward gear and unscrewing bushing (3) from gearcase housing.

If gear wear was abnormal or if any parts that affect gear alignment were renewed, check and adjust gear mesh as follows: Install forward gear (40) and bearing (39) using shims (38) that were originally installed. Position shims (30) that were originally installed at bottom of bearing bore. On late models with taper bearing (32) and spiral gear teeth, install bearing cup (32) in housing bore against shims (30). On all models, position drive pinion (35) in housing and insert drive shaft (33), with bearing (32) installed, into housing, bearing (34) and gear (35). On models with ball type bearing, the bearing must be firmly seated in housing bore. On all models, install retaining screw or nut (37). Coat gears (35 and 40) with bearing blue and check mesh position. On models with spiral gears, it will be necessary to push down on end of drive shaft while checking mesh position. On all models, if gears do not mesh in center of teeth, add or remove shims (30) under bearing as

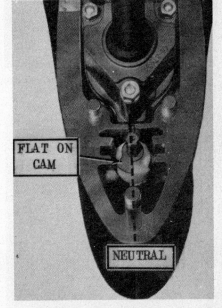

Fig. M14-53 – The reverse locking cam must be in position shown when lower unit (and the shift shaft) are in neutral.

water pump base with feeler gage. Remove shims (30A) equal to 0.002-0.003 inch (0.051-0.076 mm) less than clearance measured. When water pump is tightened down, compression of a new gasket (29) will be sufficient to hold bearing (32) in position with zero clearance.

Upper oil seal (26) should be installed with lips facing up (toward engine) and lower oil seal (27) should be pressed into water pump base with lips facing down toward propeller shaft. Install remainder of water pump assembly and tighten the screws or nuts to the following recommended torque. Torque ¼-28 nuts to 30 in.-lbs. (3.4 N·m). Torque 5/16-24 nuts to 40 in.-lbs. (4.5 N·m). Torque ¼-20 screws to 20 in.-lbs. (2.2 N·m).

The lower spacer (2L) should be installed with groove down. Reverse locking cam (2C) should be installed on shaft splines so flat on cam is in center toward front when shift shaft (5) is in reverse position. When in neutral, reverse locking cam should be positioned as shown in Fig. M14-53. The push rod guide (2G–

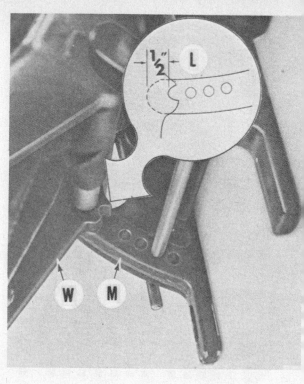

Fig. M14-57 — Overlap (L) between swivel bracket flange (W) and clamp bracket flange (M) should be ½ inch (12.7 mm).

Fig. M14-55 — View showing location of down circuit bleed screw (D) and grease fitting (F).

Fig. M14-56 — View showing location of up circuit bleed screw (U) and bleed port (P).

Fig. M14-52) is located in the drive shaft housing.

Before attaching gearcase housing to the drive shaft housing, make certain that shift cam (7) and the shift lever (on motor) are in forward gear position on early models and neutral position on late models. In forward gear position, shift shaft (5) should be in clockwise position (viewed from top end of shaft). Complete assembly by reversing disassembly.

POWER TILT/TRIM

Non-Integral Type

FLUID. Recommended fluid is SAE 10W-30 or 10W-40 automotive oil. With outboard in full up position, oil level should reach bottom of fill plug hole threads. Do not overfill.

BLEEDING. To bleed air from hydraulic system, position outboard at full tilt and engage tilt lock lever. Without disconnecting hoses, remove hydraulic trim cylinders. Be sure fluid reservoir is full and remains so during bleeding operation. Remove down circuit bleed screw (D – Fig. M14-55) and "O" ring. Press "IN" control button for a few seconds, release button and wait approximately one minute. Repeat until expelled oil is air-free. Install "O" ring and bleed screw (D) and repeat procedure on opposite cylinder. Place cylinder in horizontal position so bleed port (P – Fig. M14-56) is up and remove up circuit bleed screw (U). Press "UP" and "UP/OUT" control buttons for a few

seconds, release buttons and wait approximately one minute. Repeat until expelled oil is air-free. Install "O" ring and bleed screw (U) and repeat procedure on opposite cylinder. Reinstall cylinders.

ADJUST TRIM LIMIT SWITCH. Operate trim control so outboard is in full down position. Press "UP/OUT" or "UP" control button and hold until pump motor stops. Outboard should tilt up and stop so there is ½ inch (12.7 mm) overlap (L–Fig. M14-57) between swivel bracket flange (W) and clamp bracket flange (M). Pull up on lower unit to remove slack when checking overlap (L). Note that if cylinder rods enter cylinders more than an additional ⅛ inch (3.17 mm), that hydraulic system should be bled of air as outlined in BLEEDING section. If overlap (L) is incorrect, loosen retainer screw (R–Fig. M14-58) then turn adjusting nut (N) counterclockwise to increase overlap or clockwise to decrease overlap. Retighten retainer screw (R) and recheck adjustment.

PRESSURE TEST. To check hydraulic system pressure, disconnect four hoses attached to control valve as shown in Fig. M14-59; small hoses are for up circuit while large hoses are for down circuit. Connect a pressure gage to one up circuit port (small) of control valve and another pressure gage to one down circuit port (large). Screw plugs into remaining ports. Check fluid reservoir and fill if necessary. Operate trim control in up direction and note pressure gage reading. Minimum pressure should be 3500 psi (24.1 MPa) on new pumps with a red sleeve on wires or 3200-3500 psi (22.0-24.1 MPa) minimum on used pumps with red sleeve on wires. Minimum pressure on all other new pumps is 3000 psi (20.7 MPa) while minimum pressure on all other used pumps is 2700-3000 psi (18.6-20.7 MPa). Release trim control button. Pressure will drop slightly after stabilizing but should not drop faster than 100 psi (690 kPa) every 15 seconds. Operate trim control in down direction and note pressure gage reading. Minimum pressure is 500-1000 psi (3.4-6.9 MPa). Release trim control button. Pressure

Fig. M14-58—Loosen retainer screw (R) and turn trim limit adjusting nut (N) to adjust trim limit switch.

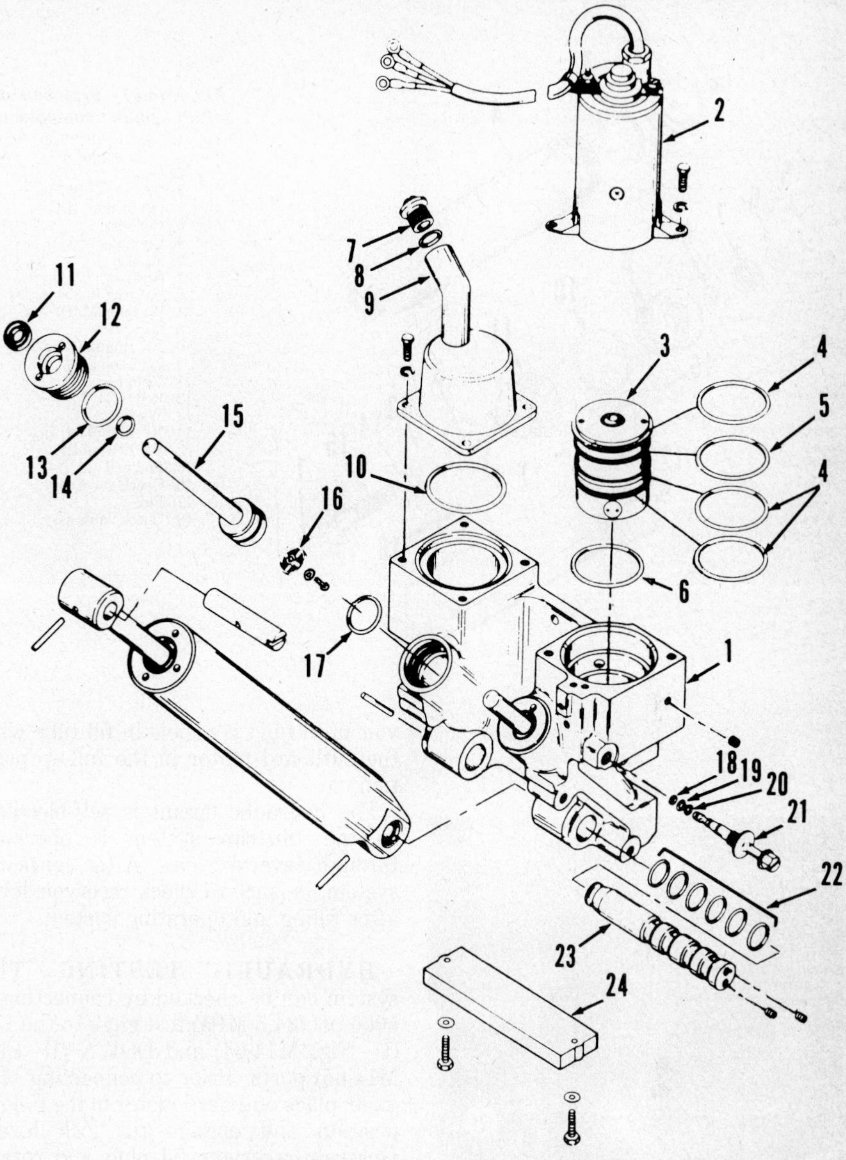

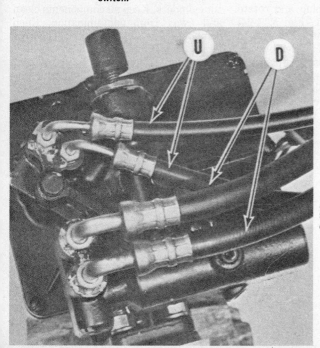

Fig. M14-59—View of control valve showing location of up circuit hoses (U) and down circuit hoses (D).

Fig. M14-62—Exploded view of integral type power tilt/trim system.

1. Manifold	9. Reservoir cover	
2. Electric motor	10. Seal ring	18. "O" ring (0.114 in. [2.90 mm] ID)
3. Pump assy.	11. Seal	
4. "O" rings (2.614 in. [66.40 mm] ID)	12. Cap	19. "O" ring (0.208 in. [5.28 mm] ID)
5. "O" rings (2.739 in. [69.57 mm] ID)	13. "O" ring (1.475 in. [37.47 mm] ID)	20. "O" ring (0.239 in. [6.07 mm] ID)
6. "O" ring (2.739 in. [69.57 mm] ID)	14. "O" ring (0.612 in. [15.54 mm] ID)	21. Manual release valve
7. Fill plug	15. Trim piston & rod	22. "O" rings (0.989 in. [25.12 mm] ID)
8. "O" ring (0.583 in. [14.81 mm] ID)	16. Strainer	23. Shaft
	17. "O" ring (1.248 in. [31.70 mm] ID)	24. Anode plate

will drop slightly after stabilizing but should not drop faster than 100 psi (690 kPa) every 15 seconds. If pressure is normal, inspect trim cylinders and hoses for leakage. If pressure is abnormal, install a good control valve and recheck pressure. If pressure remains abnormal, install a new pump body.

Integral Type

FLUID AND BLEEDING. Recommended fluid is Dexron II or Type AF automatic transmission fluid. Remove fill plug (7—Fig. M14-62) and fill reser-

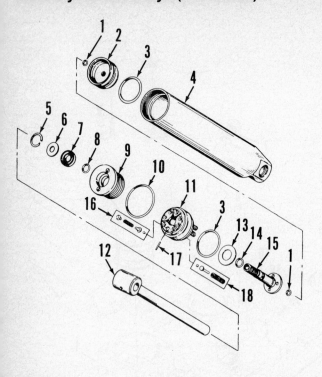

Fig. M14-65 — Release pressure on system, then remove Allen head plug (D) and install a 5000 psi (34.5 MPa) test gage with a suitable adapter and hose to test system pressure when operated in the "DOWN" direction.

Fig. M14-64 — Release pressure on system, then remove Allen head plug (U) and install a 5000 psi (34.5 MPa) test gage with a suitable adapter and hose to test system pressure when operated in the "UP" direction. View identifies location of manual release valve (21).

voir until fluid is visible in fill tube with the outboard motor in the full-up position.

The hydraulic circuit is self-bleeding as the tilt/trim system is operated through several cycles. After servicing system, be sure to check reservoir level after filling and operating system.

HYDRAULIC TESTING. The system can be checked by connecting a 5000 psi (34.5 MPa) test gage to the UP (U–Fig. M14-64) and DOWN (D–Fig. M14-65) ports. Prior to connecting test gage, place outboard motor in the full-up position and engage tilt lock lever. Unscrew reservoir fill plug and rotate manual release valve (21–Fig. M14-64) three to four turns counterclockwise to release pressure on system. Remove UP and DOWN Allen head test port plug and connect test gage with suitable adapter and hose. Install fill plug and rotate manual release valve clockwise until seated. System pressure when testing at

UP (U) port should be a minimum of 1300 psi (8.9 MPa). System pressure when testing at DOWN (D–Fig. M14-65) port should be a minimum of 500 psi (3.5 MPa). Release pressure on system as previously outlined prior to removing test gage. Reinstall Allen head plug.

OVERHAUL. Refer to Fig. M14-62 for an exploded view of manifold and trim cylinder components, and Fig. M14-63 for an exploded view of tilt cylinder components. Special Mercury socket 91-44487A1 and a spanner wrench is required to service trim and tilt cylinders. Keep all components clean and away from contamination. Keep components separated and label if needed for correct reassembly. Note "O" ring sizes as stated in legends of Figs. M14-62 and M14-63. Lubricate all "O" rings or seal lips with Dexron II or Type AF automatic transmission fluid during reassembly.

MERCURY V-6
(EXCEPT 300 AND 3.4L)

Year Produced	Model
1976	1750
1977	1750
1978	1500
	1750
	2000
1979	150
	175
	200
1980	150
	175
	200
1981	150
	175
	200
	225

Year Produced	Model
1982	150
	200
1983	150
	200
1984	150
	200
1985	150
	175
	200

Letter suffix indicates equipment variation: E – Electric starter and alternator, L – Long shaft, O – Oil injection and PT – Power trim.

CONDENSED SERVICE DATA

TUNE-UP

Hp/rpm:
 Models 150 & 1500 ....150/5000-5500
 Models 175 & 1750 ....175/5300-5800
 Models 200 & 2000 ....200/5300-5800
 Model 225 ....225/5300-5800

Bore:
 150 HP & 175 HP (prior to serial
  no. 6618751) ....3.125 in.
   (79.38 mm)
 175 HP (after serial no. 6618750),
  200 HP & 225 HP ....3.375 in.
   (85.72 mm)

Stroke ....2.650 in.
   (67.31 mm)

Displacement:
 150 HP & 175 HP (prior to serial
  no. 6618751) ....122 cu. in.
   (1999 cc)
 175 HP (after serial no. 6618750),
  200 HP & 225 HP ....142 cu. in.
   (2327 cc)

Firing Order 1-2-3-4-5-6
Number System (top to bottom):
 Port 2-4-6
 Starboard 1-3-5
Spark Plug:
 Models Prior To Serial No. 5464486 ...Champion – L76V
 Models After Serial No. 5464485 ....NGK – BU8H
Idle Speed (in gear) ....550-650 rpm*
Fuel:Oil Ratio ....50:1†

*On models with serial number 5464486 and above, idle speed should be 600-700 rpm with outboard motor in gear.
†Some 1984 and 1985 models are equipped with an oil injection system.

SIZES – CLEARANCES

Piston Ring End Gap ....0.018-0.025 in.
   (0.457-0.635 mm)
Maximum Cylinder Tolerance ....0.006 in.
   (0.152 mm)
Crankshaft Bearing Type:
 Top Main Bearing ....Caged Roller
 Center Main Bearings ....Caged Roller
 Bottom Main Bearing ....Ball Bearing
 Crankpin ....Caged Roller
Piston Pin Bearing ....29 Loose Rollers

TIGHTENING TORQUES

Connecting Rod ....30 ft.-lbs.
   (41 N·m)
Crankcase Screws:
 5/16 ....200 in.-lbs.
   (22.6 N·m)
 3/8 ....35 ft.-lbs.
   (47.6 N·m)
Cylinder Head ....30 ft.-lbs.
   (40.8 N·m)
Cylinder Head Cover ....150 in.-lbs.
   (16.9 N·m)
End Cap:
 Upper ....150 in.-lbs.
   (16.9 N·m)
 Lower ....60 in.-lbs.
   (6.7 N·m)
Exhaust Cover ....180 in.-lbs.
   (20.3 N·m)
Flywheel Nut ....100 ft.-lbs.
   (136 N·m)
Reed Block Mounting Screws ....60 in.-lbs.
   (6.7 N·m)
Spark Plugs ....240 in.-lbs.
   (27.1 N·m)

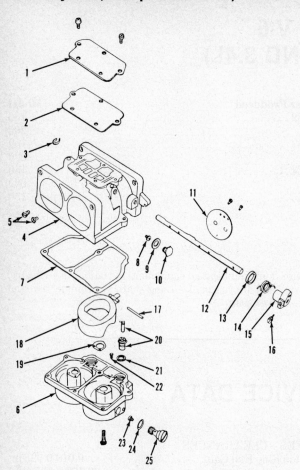

Fig. M15-1—Exploded view of carburetor used on all models. Note that idle jet components (8 through 10) and main jet components (23 through 25) are located on the carburetor starboard side.

1. Cover
2. Gasket
3. Clip
4. Body
5. Vent jets
6. Float bowl
7. Gasket
8. Idle jet
9. Gasket
10. Plug
11. Throttle plate
12. Throttle shaft
13. Spacer
14. Spring
15. Lever
16. Screw
17. Float pin
18. Float
19. Gasket
20. Inlet needle & seat
21. Gasket
22. Screw
23. Main jet
24. Gasket
25. Plug

mm) at altitudes of 2500-5000 feet (762-1524 m). Idle jets (8) should be increased in size by 0.002 inch (0.05 mm) at altitudes of 2500-5000 feet (762-1524 m). Main jets (23) and vent jets (5) should be reduced in size by 0.004 inch (0.10 mm) at altitudes of 5000-7500 feet (1524-2286 m). Idle jets (8) should be increased in size by 0.004 inch (0.10 mm) at altitudes of 5000-7500 feet (1524-2286 m). Main jets (23) and vent jets (5) should be reduced in size by 0.006 inch (0.15 mm) at altitudes of 7500 feet (2286 m) and above. Idle jets (8) should be increased in size by 0.006 inch (0.15 mm) at altitudes of 7500 feet (2286 m) and above.

NOTE: Vent jets (5) are not used on some models. If vent jets are not noted, do not try to install jets.

No idle mixture screw adjustment is provided. Idle jet (8) size must be altered to change idle air:fuel ratio. Refer to CONDENSED SERVICE DATA for recommended idle speeds.

To measure float setting, invert float bowl (6) with inlet needle and seat (20) and float (18) installed. On each float chamber, measure distance (D—Fig. M15-2) from float bowl surface to top of float (18). Distance (D) should be 1/16 inch (1.6 mm). Adjust distance (D) by bending tang at rear of float arm.

On some models, a separate choke plate containing choke valves is positioned in the air silencer. The choke valves are actuated by a solenoid mounted on the reed housing.

SPEED CONTROL LINKAGE (Model 175 HP). To synchronize ignition and carburetor opening, proceed as follows: To verify timing pointer alignment, a dial indicator must be installed in the number 1 (top, starboard) cylinder

LUBRICATION

The engine is lubricated by oil mixed with the fuel. Fuel should be regular leaded, low lead or unleaded gasoline with a minimum pump octane rating of 86. Premium gasoline may be used if desired gasoline is not available. Recommended oil is Quicksilver Formula 50 or 50-D. A good quality BIA certified TC-W oil may be used if Formula 50 or 50-D oil is not available.

Fuel:oil ratio when using Formula 50 or 50-D oil is 50:1 for normal operation. Follow fuel:oil ratio recommended by oil manufacturer if Formula 50 or 50-D is not used.

Fuel:oil ratio should be 25:1 during break-in. Do not operate engine above 2500-3500 rpm for first two hours when breaking-in a new or overhauled engine. Avoid sustained full throttle operation for first 10 hours of operation.

On some 1984 and 1985 models, an oil injection system is used. The fuel:oil ratio is varied from approximately 50:1 at full throttle up to approximately 100:1 at idle. The oil pump is synchronized with carburetor throttle opening via linkage. As the carburetor throttle opens or closes, the oil being supplied to the fuel pump is varied, thus matching the proper fuel:oil ratio to engine demand.

During oil injection system's first 30 hours of operation, the fuel in the fuel tank must be mixed at a fuel:oil ratio of 50:1 to ensure the engine of proper lubrication and the oil level in the remote oil tank monitored. If, after 30 hours of operation, oil level has dropped indicating the oil injection system is operating, refill the remote oil tank and switch to straight fuel.

Lower unit gears and bearings are lubricated by oil in the gearcase. Recommended oil is Quicksilver Super Duty Gear Lubricant. Remove vent plug and fill gearcase through fill plug opening in lower end of gearcase until oil is expelled from vent plug opening, then allow 2 ounce (30 mL) of oil to drain from gearcase.

FUEL SYSTEM

CARBURETOR. Three "dual float center bowl" type carburetors are used. Carburetor identification numbers are stamped on each carburetor mounting flange. Standard jet sizes are dependent upon carburetor identification numbers. Use the standard carburetor jet sizes as recommended by the manufacturer for normal operation when used at altitudes of 2500 feet (762 m) and below. Main jets (23–Fig. M15-1) and vent jets (5) should be reduced in size by 0.002 inch (0.05

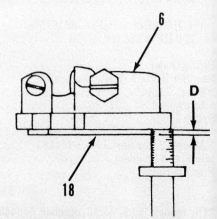

Fig. M15-2—Invert float bowl (6) with needle and seat (20—Fig. M15-1) and float (18) installed. Distance (D) should be 1/16 inch (1.6 mm) for proper float setting.

and the indicator synchronized with the piston position (dial indicator reads zero when piston is at top dead center).

NOTE: To prevent accidental starting from flywheel rotation, remove all spark plugs and properly ground plug wires.

Rotate the flywheel counterclockwise approximately ¼ turn past the 0.462 inch (12 mm) BTDC reading, then rotate flywheel clockwise until indicator face reads 0.462 inch (12 mm) BTDC. Note the position of the timing pointer and reposition if the timing pointer is not aligned with ".462 BTDC" mark on flywheel. Remove the dial indicator assembly from the number 1 cylinder after adjustment is completed and reinstall spark plug and plug lead.

Be sure link rod (L – Fig. M15-4) protrudes 11/16 inch (17.46 mm) from link body as shown. If the engine is equipped with an idle stabilizer module (M – Fig. M15-5), disconnect the white/black module wire from switch box terminal. Tape the end of the wire to prevent grounding. Be sure the other white/black wire remains connected to switch box terminal.

NOTE: To prevent engine from starting, make sure only the number 1 (top, starboard) spark plug is installed and its plug wire attached.

Disconnect the fuel tank supply hose at the connector. Detach the throttle cable barrel from the retainer of the cable anchor bracket. Remove the choke knob and wing nuts, then withdraw the air intake cover from the front of the

Fig. M15-5—View showing location of idle stabilizer module (M) used on some models.

carburetors. Loosen carburetor synchronizing screws (S – Fig. M15-4) and allow the carburetor throttle plates to close freely. With light pressure, hold cam follower roller (R – Fig. M15-6) against throttle cam (T). At the same time, lift up on bottom carburetor throttle shaft (H – Fig. M15-4) to remove slack in linkage components. Adjust idle speed screw (I) so short mark (M – Fig. M15-6) on throttle cam (T) is centered on follower roller (R) as shown. Retighten stop screw locknut. While maintaining light pressure, retighten all screws (S – Fig. M15-4). Check to be sure that carburetor throttle plates are completely closed when cam follower roller (R – Fig. M15-6) is aligned with short mark (M) on throttle cam (T). Repeat adjustment procedure if setting is incorrect. Reinstall air intake cover.

Connect a power timing light to number 1 cylinder spark plug lead. With the outboard motor in neutral, position throttle lever (C – Fig. M15-4) so idle speed screw (I) is against stop. Crank

the engine over with the starter motor and adjust primary screw (P) so the ignition timing is 14° ATDC.

Open the throttle until the maximum spark advance screw (A) is against stop. Crank the engine over with the starter motor and adjust maximum spark advance screw (A) so ignition timing is 20° BTDC.

NOTE: Due to electronic characteristics of the ignition system, maximum advance is set at 20° BTDC but ignition will retard to 18° BTDC at high engine speed.

The carburetor throttle plate must not act as the wide open throttle stop. To prevent damage to the carburetors, move speed control linkage to the maximum speed position and adjust maximum throttle stop screw (N) so a clearance (C – Fig. M15-7) of 0.010-0.015 inch (0.25-0.38 mm) is between throttle cam (T) and cam follower roller (R).

Reconnect idle stabilizer module wire to switch box. Reassemble and adjust idle speed screw (I – Fig. M15-4) as outlined in the CARBURETOR section.

Hold idle speed screw (I) against stop and install the throttle cable barrel in the retainer while adjusting barrel so it fits into retainer and a very light preload between idle speed screw and its stop is

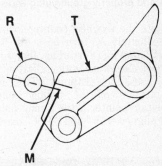

Fig. M15-6—Cam follower roller (R) should align with short mark (M) on throttle cam (T) when speed control linkage is set as outlined in text.

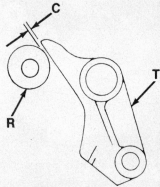

Fig. M15-7—Clearance (C) should exist between cam follower (R) and throttle cam (T) when speed control linkage is set as outlined in text.

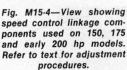

Fig. M15-4—View showing speed control linkage components used on 150, 175 and early 200 hp models. Refer to text for adjustment procedures.

A. Maximum spark advance screw
B. Maximum spark advance lever
C. Throttle lever
H. Throttle shaft
I. Idle speed screw
L. Link rod
N. Maximum throttle stop screw
P. Primary screw
S. Screws
T. Throttle cam

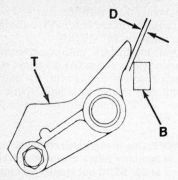

Fig. M15-8—Distance (D) should exist between throttle cam (T) and boss (B) when speed control linkage is set as outlined in text.

established. Excessive throttle cable preload will result in difficult shifting from forward to neutral.

(Models 150 HP And Early 200 HP). To synchronize ignition and carburetor opening, proceed as follows: To verify timing pointer alignment, a dial indicator must be installed in the number 1 (top, starboard) cylinder and the indicator zeroed when the piston is positioned at TDC.

NOTE: To prevent accidental starting from flywheel rotation, remove all spark plugs and properly ground plug wires.

Rotate the flywheel counterclockwise approximately ¼ turn past the 0.462 inch (12 mm) BTDC reading, then rotate flywheel clockwise until indicator face reads 0.462 inch (12 mm) BTDC. Note the position of the timing pointer. Reposition pointer if the timing pointer is not aligned with ".462 BTDC" mark on

flywheel. Remove the dial indicator assembly from the number 1 cylinder after adjustment is completed and reinstall spark plug and plug lead.

Be sure link rod (L–Fig. M15-4) protrudes 11/16 inch (17.46 mm) from link body as shown. If the engine is equipped with an idle stabilizer module (M–Fig. M15-5), disconnect the white/black module wire from switch box terminal. Tape the end of the wire to prevent grounding. Be sure the other white/black wire remains connected to switch box terminal.

NOTE: To prevent engine from starting, make sure only the number 1 (top, starboard) spark plug is installed and its plug wire attached.

Disconnect the fuel tank supply hose at the outboard motor connector. Detach the throttle cable barrel from the retainer of the cable anchor bracket. Adjust idle speed screw (I–Fig. M15-4) so bottom edge of throttle cam (T–Fig. M15-8) is a distance (D) of ⅛ inch (3.2 mm) from top edge of mounting boss (B) for maximum throttle stop screw.

Withdraw the air intake cover from the front of the carburetors. Position throttle lever (C–Fig. M15-4) so idle speed screw (I) is against its stop. Loosen carburetor synchronizing screws (S) and allow the carburetor throttle plates to close freely. With light pressure, hold the cam follower roller against throttle cam (T). At the same time, lift up on the bottom carburetor throttle shaft (H) to remove slack in linkage components. Then retighten screws (S). Check to be sure that carburetor throttle plates are completely closed and operate freely. Repeat ad-

Fig. M15-9 – View showing speed control linkage components used on late 200 hp and 225 hp models. Refer to text for adjustment procedures.

A. Maximum spark advance screw
B. Maximum spark advance lever
L. Link rod
P. Primary screw

justment procedure if setting is incorrect. Reinstall air intake cover.

Connect a power timing light to number 1 cylinder spark plug lead. With the outboard motor in neutral, position throttle lever (C) so idle speed screw (I) is against stop. Crank the engine over with the starter motor and adjust primary screw (P) so the ignition timing is 11° ATDC on 150 hp models and 10° ATDC on 200 hp models.

Open the throttle until the maximum spark advance screw (A) is against stop. Crank the engine over with the starter motor and adjust maximum spark advance screw (A) so ignition timing is 18° BTDC on 150 hp models and 20° BTDC on 200 hp models.

NOTE: Due to electronic characteristics of the ignition system, maximum advance is set at 18° BTDC on 150 hp models and 20° BTDC on 200 hp models, but ignition will retard to 16° BTDC on 150 hp models and 18° BTDC on 200 hp models at high engine speed.

The carburetor throttle plate must not act as the wide open throttle stop. To prevent damage to the carburetors, move speed control linkage to the maximum speed position and adjust maximum throttle stop screw (N) so a clearance (C–Fig. M15-7) of 0.010-0.015 inch (0.25-0.38 mm) is between throttle cam (T) and cam follower roller (R).

Reconnect idle stabilizer module wire to switch box. Reassemble and adjust idle speed screw (I–Fig. M15-4) as outlined in the CARBURETOR section.

Hold idle speed screw (I) against stop and install the throttle cable barrel in the retainer while adjusting barrel so it fits into retainer and a very light preload between idle speed screw and its stop is established. Excessive throttle cable preload will result in difficult shifting from forward to neutral.

(Late Models 200 HP And All 225 HP). To synchronize ignition and carburetor opening, proceed as follows: To verify timing pointer alignment, a dial indicator must be installed in the number 1 (top, starboard) cylinder and the indicator zeroed when the piston is positioned at TDC.

NOTE: To prevent accidental starting from flywheel rotation, remove all spark plugs and properly ground plug wires.

Rotate the flywheel counterclockwise approximately ¼ turn past the 0.462 inch (12 mm) BTDC reading, then rotate flywheel clockwise until indicator face reads 0.462 inch (12 mm) BTDC. Note the position of the timing pointer. Reposition pointer if the timing pointer is not aligned with ".462 BTDC" mark on flywheel. Remove the dial indicator assembly from the number 1 cylinder after adjustment is completed and reinstall spark plug and plug lead.

Be sure link rod (L – Fig. M15-9) protrudes 11/16 inch (17.46 mm) from link body as shown. A spark advance module is located above the top carburetor and is mounted to the air intake cover. If the module is equipped with four wires, no wires need to be connected to time the engine. But if the module is equipped with three wires, disconnect the white/black module wire from the switch box terminal. Tape the end of the wire to prevent grounding. Be sure the other white/black wire remains connected to switch box terminal.

NOTE: To prevent engine from starting, make sure only the number 1 (top, starboard) spark plug is installed and its plug wire attached.

Disconnect the fuel tank supply hose at the outboard motor connector. Detach the throttle cable barrel from the retainer of the cable anchor bracket.

Install a 1/8 inch (3 mm) diameter rod or drill bit in hole (V – Fig. M15-11) on models equipped with the casting numbers "95790" on throttle cam (T). Install a 1/8 inch (3 mm) diameter rod or drill bit in hole (V – Fig. M15-12) on models not equipped with numbers cast on throttle cam (T). While holding rod or drill bit perpendicular to throttle cam (T – Fig. M15-11 or Fig. M15-12), adjustable idle speed screw (I – Fig. M15-10) until rod or drill bit just contacts edge of carburetor adapter flange (F – Fig. M15-11 or Fig. M15-12).

Withdraw the air intake cover from the front of the carburetors. Position throttle lever (C – Fig. M15-10) so idle

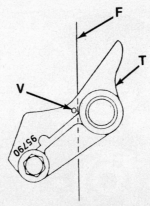

Fig. M15-11 – A 1/8 inch (3mm) diameter rod or drill bit must be installed in hole (V) on models with the numbers "95790" cast on throttle cam (T). The rod or drill bit should just contact edge of carburetor adapter flange (F) when speed control linkage is set and adjusted as outlined in text.

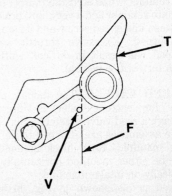

Fig. M15-12 – A 1/8 inch (3 mm) distance rod or drill bit must be installed in hole (V) on models with no numbers cast on throttle cam (T). The rod or drill bit should just contact edge of carburetor adapter flange (F) when speed control linkage is set and adjusted as outlined in text.

speed screw (I) is against its stop. Loosen carburetor synchronizing screws (S) and allow the carburetor throttle plates to close freely. With light pressure, hold cam follower roller (R) against throttle cam (T). At the same time, lift up on bottom carburetor throttle shaft to remove slack in linkage components. Then retighten screws (S). Check to be sure that carburetor throttle plates are completely closed and operate freely. Repeat adjustment procedure if setting is incorrect. Reinstall air intake cover.

Connect a power timing light to number 1 cylinder spark plug lead. With the outboard motor in neutral, position throttle lever (C) so idle speed screw (I) is against stop. Crank the engine over with the starter motor and adjust primary screw (P) so the ignition timing is 12° ATDC.

Open the throttle until the maximum spark advance screw (A) is against stop.

Crank the engine over with the starter motor and adjust maximum spark advance screw (A) so ignition timing is 22° BTDC.

NOTE: Due to electronic characteristics of the ignition system, maximum advance is set at 22° BTDC, but ignition will retard to 20° BTDC at 5400 rpm and increase to 26° BTDC over 5600 rpm.

The carburetor throttle plate must not act as the wide open throttle stop. To prevent damage to the carburetors, move speed control linkage to the maximum speed position and adjust maximum throttle stop screw (N) so a clearance (C – Fig. M15-7) of 0.010-0.015 inch (0.25-0.38 mm) is between throttle cam (T) and cam follower roller (R).

Reconnect spark advance module wire to switch box. Reassemble and adjust idle speed screw (I – Fig. M15-10) as outlined in the previous CARBURETOR section.

Hold idle speed screw (I) against stop and install the throttle cable barrel in

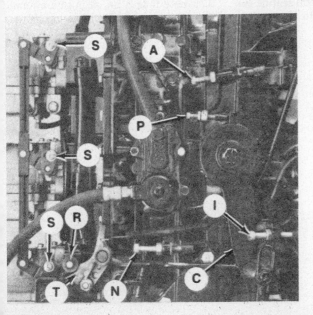

Fig. M15-10—View showing speed control linkage components used on late 200 hp and 225 hp models. Refer to text for adjustment procedures.

A. Maximum spark advance screw
C. Throttle lever
I. Idle speed screw
N. Maximum throttle stop screw
P. Primary screw
R. Cam follower roller
S. Screws
T. Throttle cam

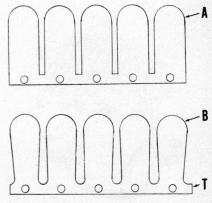

Fig. M15-14—View of "straight-cut" (A) and "teardrop" (B) reed petals. Note tang (T) on "teardrop" reed petals.

the retainer while adjusting barrel so it fits into retainer and a very light preload between idle speed screw and its stop is established. Excessive throttle cable preload will result in difficult shifting from forward to neutral.

REED VALVES. The fuel:air mixture for each cylinder is directed through a reed valve assembly. Six reed valve assemblies are attached to the intake manifold. Reed block assemblies may be either mounted horizontally or vertically on intake manifold.

Reed petals shown in Fig. M15-14 should be flat and have no more than 0.007 inch (0.18 mm) clearance between free end of reed petal and seating surface of reed block. On vertical mounted reed blocks, reed petals should not stand open more than 0.020 inch (0.51 mm). Do not attempt to bend or straighten a reed petal or turn reed petals around on reed block. Reed block seating surface

Fig. M15-18—View showing installation of outlet check valve (6) and inlet check valve (7) in fuel pump body. Install retainer (R) so tips are away from check valves.

must be flat. Reed block should be renewed if indented by reed petals or damaged. Reed petals are available in sets for each reed block only.

Note reed petal shapes in Fig. M15-14. Early 150 hp engines are equipped with "straight-cut" reed petals (A) while late 150, 200 and 225 hp engines are equipped with "teardrop" reed petals (B). Early 175 hp engines used both types of reed petals while later 175 hp engines are equipped with "teardrop" reed petals (B). Install reed blocks of early 175 hp engines so "teardrop" reed petals are towards center side of reed housing. When renewing reed petals on early 175 hp engines, always install a "teardrop" reed petal, even if the old reed was "straight-cut" type.

Reed stop setting is 0.200 inch (5.08 mm) for 150 hp models and 0.300 inch (7.62 mm) for all other models. Measure from reed stop to reed petal seating surface as shown in Fig. M15-15.

FUEL PUMP. A diaphragm type fuel pump is mounted on intake manifold. Crankcase pulsations actuate the fuel pump diaphragm to pump fuel from tank to carburetors. Fuel pump pressure should be 4-5½ psi (28-38 kPa) at full throttle and 3 psi (21 kPa) at idle.

If the fuel pump malfunctions due to a split diaphragm on early 175 hp models, drill a 0.078 inch (1.98 mm) hole (B–Fig. M15-17) through the pulse chamber so the hole is ⅜ inch (9.5 mm) from centerline of hole (A) as shown, and bevel edge of hole (A).

When overhauling the fuel pump, renew all defective or questionable parts. When assembling fuel pump, install check valves as shown in Fig. M15-18 with tips of retainer (R) pointing away from check valves.

OIL INJECTION SYSTEM. On some 1984 and 1985 models, an oil injection system is used. The fuel:oil ratio is varied from approximately 50:1 at full throttle up to approximately 100:1 at idle. The oil injection pump is synchronized with carburetor throttle opening via linkage. As the carburetor throttle opens or closes, the oil being supplied to the fuel pump is varied, thus matching the proper fuel:oil ratio to engine demand. The oil injection pump is driven by a gear secured to the engine crankshaft.

BLEEDING OIL INJECTION PUMP. Prior to engine start up, loosen bleed screw (B–Fig. M15-20) 3 to 4 turns. Allow oil to drain from around bleed screw until no air bubbles are noticed, then retighten bleed screw (B).

THROTTLE ARM AND OIL INJECTION PUMP SYNCHRONIZATION. Place throttle linkage in idle position, then note if arm on oil injection pump aligns with mark (R) on casting. If not,

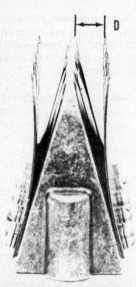

Fig. M15-15—Reed stop setting (D) should be 0.200 inch (5.08 mm) for 150 hp models and 0.300 inch (7.62 mm) for all other models.

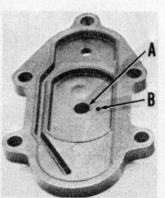

Fig. M15-17—Modify fuel pump on early 175 hp models with a split diaphragm as outlined in text.

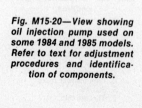

Fig. M15-20—View showing oil injection pump used on some 1984 and 1985 models. Refer to text for adjustment procedures and identification of components.

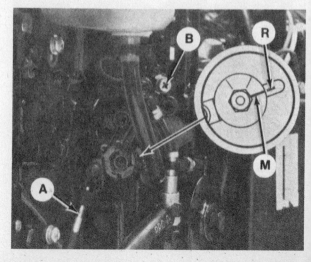

adjust length of throttle arm (A) until marks properly align.

DRIVE GEAR. If a new oil injection pump drive gear is installed on crankshaft, the maximum allowable misalignment at split line of gear is 0.030 inch (0.76 mm). Tighten gear retaining Allen head screw to 8 in.-lbs. (0.9 N·m). Zero clearance should be noted at split line of gear.

CRANKCASE BLEED SCREW

A crankcase bleed system is used to remove unburned oil residue from the crankcase and lower main bearing and burn it or direct it to the three upper main bearings. See diagram in Fig. M15-22 for a view of a typical crankcase bleed system. The number of hoses and hose routing may differ on some models. Check valves are located in intake manifold while fittings to cylinders are located in cylinder block. Hoses must be connected between fitting and check valve with same letter, **i.e.** a hose is connected between check valve "B" on reed valve housing and fitting "B" on cylinder block. Make sure hoses and check valves are properly identified prior to components being separated. Engine will not operate properly if hoses are connected incorrectly. Check operation of check valves.

IGNITION SYSTEM

All models are equipped with a Thunderbolt solid state capacitor discharge ignition system consisting of trigger coils, stator, switch box and ignition coils. The trigger coils are contained in a trigger ring module under the flywheel. Diodes, SCR's and capacitors are contained in the switch box. Switch box, trigger ring module and stator must be serviced as unit assemblies.

Check all wires and connections before troubleshooting ignition circuit. The following test specifications will aid troubleshooting. Resistance between blue and red stator leads or blue/white and red/white stator leads should be 5400-6200 ohms. Resistance between red stator lead and ground or red/white stator lead and ground should be 125-175 ohms. Resistance should be 1200-1400 ohms between the following trigger coil leads; between brown (in yellow sleeve) and violet (without yellow sleeve), between white (in yellow sleeve) and brown (without yellow sleeve), be-

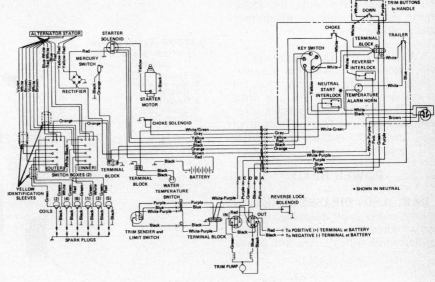

Fig. M15-24—Typical wiring diagram of models prior to 1980.

tween violet (in yellow sleeve) and white (without yellow sleeve). Ignition coils may be checked using a suitable coil checker.

Recommended spark plugs are AC V40FFM or Champion L76V on models prior to serial number 5464486 or NGK-BU8H on models after serial number 5464485.

COOLING SYSTEM

THERMOSTAT. All models are equipped with a thermostat in each cylinder head cover. Thermostat should begin to open at 140°-145°F (60°-63°C). A temperature sender is installed in the starboard cylinder head either below number one spark plug or in the outer portion of the cylinder head between number one and number three spark plug. The temperature sender will activate an alarm horn should engine overheating occur. Temperature sender may be checked with a continuity tester and a high temperature thermometer. Place sender and thermometer in water that is being heated. Sender positioned in the outer portion of the cylinder head should show a closed circuit when water temperature reaches 180°-200°F (82°-93°C) and then reopen when temperature drops to 160°-180°F (71°-82°C). Sender positioned below number one spark plug should show a closed circuit when water temperature reaches 230°-250°F (110°-121°C) and then reopen when temperature starts dropping below 230°F (110°C).

A water pressure relief valve is located on starboard side of cylinder block. Note cross section of valve shown

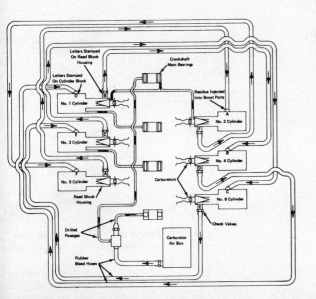

Fig. M15-22—Diagram of a typical crankcase bleed system.

in Fig. M15-30. Diaphragm is renewable. Inspect components for nicks, cracks or other damage which may cause leakage.

WATER PUMP. The rubber impeller type water pump is housed in the gearcase housing. The impeller is mounted on and driven by the lower unit drive shaft. Water pump is accessible after separating gearcase housing from drive shaft housing as outlined in LOWER UNIT section.

POWER HEAD

R&R AND DISASSEMBLE. To remove power head assembly, disconnect all wires and hoses and remove all cowling which will interfere with power

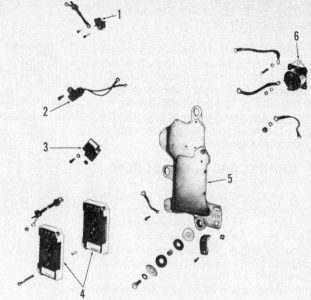

Fig. M15-26—Exploded view of ignition plate components.

1. Terminal block
2. Mercury switch
3. Rectifier
4. Switch boxes
5. Ignition plate
6. Starter solenoid

head separation from drive shaft housing. Detach shift rod from control cable bracket. Unscrew 10 locknuts securing power head to drive shaft housing and lift power head off drive shaft housing and install on a suitable stand. If equipped, remove oil injection pump reservoir and plug hose fittings. Remove flywheel, stator, trigger plate and starter motor. Remove choke solenoid, temperature sender, ignition coils, switch box plate assembly and speed control linkage. If equipped, remove oil injection pump. Remove fuel pump and disconnect and label interfering bleed hoses. Remove carburetors and airbox as an assembly. Remove intake manifold with reed valve assemblies, cylinder head cover, cylinder heads and exhaust manifold assembly.

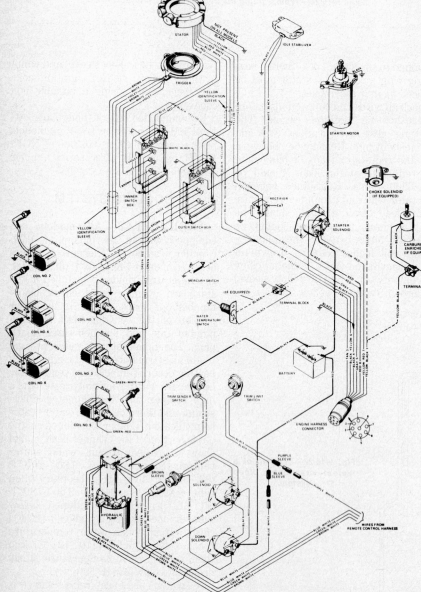

Fig. M15-25—Typical wiring diagram for all late models.

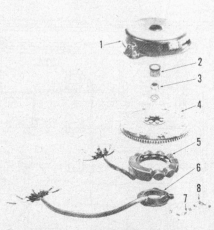

Fig. M15-27—View of flywheel and ignition components.

1. Flywheel cover
2. Plug
3. Nut
4. Flywheel
5. Stator
6. Trigger plate
7. Trigger plate link rod
8. Ball joint

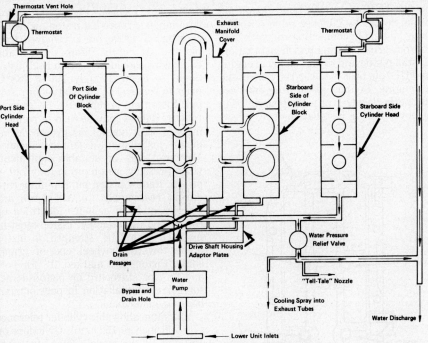

Fig. M15-29—Typical diagram of coolant flow. Refer to Fig. M15-30 for cross section of water pressure relief valve.

mended that all gasket surfaces and machined joints without gaskets be carefully checked for nicks and burrs which might interfere with a tight seal.

Install seals in lower end cap with lips down (away from cylinder block). Install seal in upper end cap with lip down (toward cylinder block). Be sure seal does not block bleed passage in end cap. Loctite 271 or 290 should be applied to seal bore of end caps. Lubricate all bearing and friction surfaces with engine oil. Loose needle bearings may be held in place during assembly using light, nonfibrous grease. Gaps of seal rings (5 – Fig. 15-34) must be towards crankcase.

Install piston, rod and crankshaft assemblies as outlined in appropriate following paragraphs. End caps should be in place with screws installed but not tightened. Rotate crankshaft and check for binding. Cut gasket strips off flush

Remove screws securing end caps to crankcase and loosen end cap to cylinder block screws. Remove crankcase mounting screws, then remove crankcase by using recesses under crankcase to pry against. Use extra care not to damage machined mating surfaces of cylinder block and crankcase. Mark connecting rods with cylinder numbers so they can be reinstalled in original cylinders and remove rod and piston assemblies. Unscrew end cap to cylinder block screws and remove end caps. Crankcase and cylinder block are matched and align bored and can be renewed as a set only.

Refer to following paragraphs to service pistons, rods, crankshaft and bearings. When assembling, follow the procedures outlined in the ASSEMBLY paragraphs.

ASSEMBLY. When assembling, the crankcase must be sealed against both vacuum and pressure. Exhaust manifold and water passage must be sealed against pressure leakage. Whenever power head is disassembled, it is recom-

Fig. M15-32—Exploded view of cylinder block and crankcase assemblies.

1. Oil seal
2. Upper end cap
3. "O" ring
4. Roller bearing
5. Exhaust manifold cover
6. Gasket
7. Divider plate
8. Seal
9. Gasket
10. Cylinder block
11. Bearing locating dowel pin
12. Sealing strips
13. Crankcase
14. Thermostat housing
15. Thermostat
16. Cylinder head cover
17. Gasket
18. Cylinder head
19. Gasket
20. Oil seals
21. "O" ring
22. Lower end gap
23. Gasket
24. Reed petal stop
25. Reed petal
26. Reed block
27. Gasket
28. Intake manifold

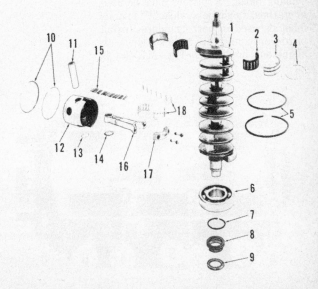

Fig. M15-34—Exploded view of crankshaft assembly.

1. Crankshaft
2. Roller bearing
3. Bearing race
4. Retaining ring
5. Seal rings
6. Ball bearings
7. Snap ring
8. Seal carrier
9. Oil seal
10. Piston rings
11. Piston pin
12. Piston
13. Retaining ring
14. Spacer
15. Bearing rollers (29)
16. Connecting rod
17. Rod cap
18. Roller bearing

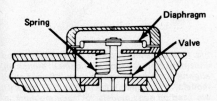

Fig. M15-30—Cross-sectional view of water pressure relief valve.

with edge of crankcase bores. Apply a thin coat of sealer such as Permatex 2C-12 to mating surfaces of crankcase and cylinder block using care to prevent excess sealer from entering bearings, crankcase or passages.

Progressively tighten eight large crankcase screws until crankshaft seal rings are compressed and crankcase mates with cylinder block. Tighten eight large crankcase screws in three progressive steps to specified torque and using tightening sequence in Fig. M15-35 for models prior to serial number 5464486 and Fig. M15-36 for models after serial number 5464485. On early models note location of long seal screw (B – Fig. M15-35) and then tighten six smaller crankcase screws in three progressive steps to specified torque. Rotate crankshaft and check for binding.

When installing intake manifold and exhaust manifold cover, tighten center screws first and work outward. Install cylinder head gaskets with number stamped in gasket up (away from cylinder block). Tighten cylinder head screws in three progressive steps to specified torque and using tightening sequence in Fig. M15-37.

PISTONS, PINS, RINGS AND CYLINDERS. Before detaching connecting rods from crankshaft, make sure that rod and cap are marked so rods and caps are not interchanged and may be returned to original cylinders.

Piston pin is pressed into piston on all models. On early models, manufacturer recommends discarding piston if pin is pressed out of piston. Piston pin boss marked "UP" has smaller piston pin hole than other pin boss. Press pin out so pin exits "UP" boss first and press pin in so pin enters "UP" boss last. Pistons are marked on piston pin boss and piston crown according to their location in cylinder block. "S" pistons must be used in starboard cylinders while "P" pistons must be used in port cylinders. Install piston on connecting rods so side with alignment bumps (B – Fig. M15-38) is

nearer "UP" piston pin boss. Piston pin is supported by 29 loose rollers. Rollers may be held in connecting rod with nonfibrous grease during piston installation. Install piston and rod assembly in engine so "UP" pin boss is towards flywheel end of engine. Be sure piston ring ends are properly located around pins in ring grooves during installation.

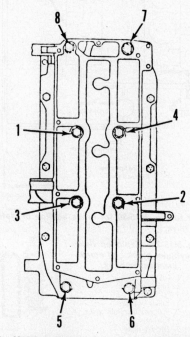

Fig. M15-36 – Tighten crankcase screws following sequence shown on vertical and horizontal reed models after serial number 5464485.

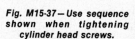

Fig. M15-37 – Use sequence shown when tightening cylinder head screws.

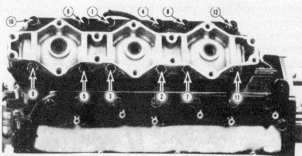

On late models, the manufacture recommends renewing piston pin needl bearings if piston pin is removed fror piston. A torch lamp or suitabl equivalent should be used to heat pisto dome to approximately 190°F (88°C prior to removal or installation of pisto pin. Piston pin is supported by 29 loos rollers. Rollers may be held in connecting rod with nonfibrous grease durin piston installation. Use recommende Mercury tools or suitable equivalent when pressing piston pin in to or out o piston. Renew piston pin retaining clip during reassembly. Install piston an rod assembly in cylinder identified or rod during disassembly. Piston must b installed with "UP" stamped on pisto dome toward flywheel end of crank shaft. Pistons are marked "P" for por and "S" for starboard on piston dome for correct installation in port or star board cylinder bank.

Maximum allowable cylinder toleranc is 0.006 inch (0.152 mm). Cylinders or 150 and 175 hp models can be bored to accomodate 0.015 inch (0.38 mm) or 0.030 inch (0.76 mm) oversize pistons Cylinders on 200 and 225 hp models are chrome plated and no service other than renewal of cylinder block and crankcase assembly is recommended by the manufacturer.

CONNECTING RODS, BEARINGS AND CRANKSHAFT. Connecting rod has 29 loose rollers in small end and caged roller bearings in big end. Install

Fig. M15-35 – On models prior to serial number 5464486, use tightening sequence shown for large crankcase screws (C). Reverse tightening sequence of screws one and three on 225 hp models. Tighten small crankcase screws (S) next. Note position of long seal screw (B) used on early models except 225 hp models.

Fig. M15-38 – View of piston and connecting rod assembly. Note location of alignment bumps (B), alignment marks (M) and washers (W) used on all models. "P" locating mark (P) and "UP" mark (U) are used on early models. "P" locating mark indicates port side while a starboard piston will have an "S" locating mark.

piston on connecting rod so side with alignment bumps (B–Fig. M15-38) is nearer "UP" piston pin boss on early models or bumps (B) and "UP" stamped on piston dome both face flywheel end of crankshaft on late models. Be sure alignment bumps (B) and marks (M) are correctly positioned when installing rod on crankshaft. Connecting rod big end is fractured type and rod cap must be mated perfectly before tightening cap screws.

Inspect crankshaft crankpin and main bearing journal surfaces. If scored, out-of-round or worn, renew crankshaft. Check crankshaft for straightness. Do not interchange main bearings.

ELECTRICAL SYSTEM

Refer to Fig. M15-24 or Fig. M15-25 for wiring schematic.

The rectifier may be checked by disconnecting wires to rectifier and using a continuity tester or ohmmeter as follows: Connect a tester lead to ground and then alternately connect other tester lead to alternator terminals of rectifier. Note reading then reverse tester leads. Tester should indicate a short or open circuit with first test and opposite reading when tester leads are reversed. Connect a tester lead to positive rectifier terminal and alternately connect other tester lead to alternator terminals of rectifier. Note reading then reverse tester leads. Tester should show

opposite reading when tester leads are reversed. Renew rectifier if testing indicates faulty circuits.

To check alternator stator, disconnect alternator leads from rectifier and connect an ohmmeter to alternator leads. Resistance reading should be approximately 0.75 ohms. There should be in-

finite resistance between either alternator lead and ground. Alternator output should be 7-9 amps.

LOWER UNIT

Two different lower units have been used and are identified by the gear shift

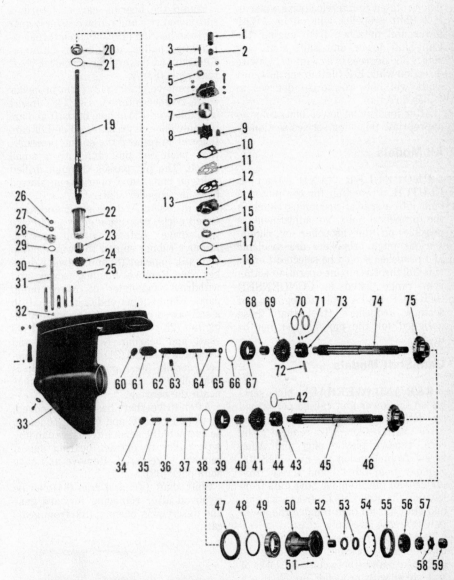

Fig. M15-41—Exploded view of gearcase assembly. Components (34 through 48) are used on Cam-Shift models while components (60 through 75) are used on E-Z Shift models. On late E-Z shift models, a threaded bearing retainer located above bearing (20) is used on models not equipped with preload pin (3) and spring (4).

1. Water tube guide	38. Shim	57. Thrust piece
2. Seal	39. Tapered roller bearing	58. Tab washer
3. Pin	40. Roller bearing	59. Nut
4. Spring	41. Forward gear	60. Shift cam
5. Rubber ring (slinger)	42. Spring clip	61. Cam follower
6. Water pump body	43. Dog clutch	62. Shift rod
7. Insert	44. Pin	63. Pin
8. Impeller	45. Propeller shaft	64. Springs
9. Key	46. Reverse gear	65. Shim
10. Gasket	47. Thrust washer	66. Shim
11. Plate	48. "O" ring	67. Tapered roller bearing
12. Gasket	49. Ball bearing	68. Roller bearing
13. Dowel pin	50. Bearing carrier	69. Forward gear
14. Pump base	51. Key	70. Spring clips
15. Oil seal	52. Roller bearing	71. Detent pins
16. Oil seal	53. Oil seals	72. Pin
17. "O" ring	54. Washer	73. Dog clutch
18. Gasket	55. Nut	74. Propeller shaft
19. Drive shaft	56. Thrust hub	75. Reverse gear
20. Bearing		
21. Shim		
22. Sleeve		
23. Roller bearing		
24. Pinion gear		
25. Nut		
26. Rubber washer		
27. Oil seal		
28. Bushing		
29. "O" ring		
30. "E" ring		
31. Shift shaft		
32. Circlip		
33. Gearcase		
34. Shift cam		
35. Cam follower		
36. Slide		
37. Spring		

Fig. M15-40 — To remove the lower unit gearcase assembly, remove the attaching screws and stud nuts from positions indicated.

mechanism. Cam-Shift lower units were used on early 150 and 175 hp models while E-Z Shift lower units are used on later 150 and 175 hp models and all 200 and 225 hp models. To externally determine which lower unit is being serviced, note the following: With lower unit attached to engine and in reverse gear, a Cam-Shift unit propeller will not ratchet when rotated counterclockwise while an E-Z Shift propeller will ratchet. With lower unit detached from engine, the Cam-Shift lower unit shift shaft will rotate 360 degrees in a counterclockwise direction while E-Z Shift lower unit shift shaft will only rotate 30 degrees in either direction.

After identifying lower unit, refer to appropriate following service section.

All Models

PROPELLER AND DRIVE CLUTCH. Protection for the motor is built into a special cushioning clutch in the propeller hub. No adjustment is possible on the propeller or clutch. Various pitch propellers are available and propeller should be selected to provide full throttle engine operation within rpm range listed in CONDENSED SERVICE DATA table at beginning of section. Propellers other than those designed for the motor must not be used.

Cam-Shift Models

R&R AND OVERHAUL. Most service on the lower unit can be performed by detaching the gearcase from the drive shaft housing. To remove gearcase, remove plastic plug and Allen screw from location (1–Fig. M15-40). Remove trim tab (2) and screw from under trim tab. Remove stud nuts from location (3), stud nuts (4) from each side and stud nut (5) then remove the lower unit gearcase assembly.

Remove the gearcase plugs and drain the gearcase lubricant, then secure the gearcase in a vise between two blocks of soft wood with propeller up. Wedge a piece of wood between propeller and antiventilation plate remove the propeller nut, then remove the propeller.

Disassemble gearcase by removing gearcase cover nut (55–Fig. M15-41). Clamp outer end of propeller shaft in a soft-jawed vise and remove the gearcase by tapping with a rubber mallet. Be careful not to lose key (51). Forward gear (41) will remain in gearcase. Withdraw propeller shaft from bearing carrier (50) and reverse gear (46).

Clamp the bearing carrier (50) in a soft-jawed vise and remove reverse gear (46) and bearing (49) with an internal expanding puller and slide hammer. Remove and discard the propeller shaft rear seals (53).

To remove clutch (43) from propeller shaft, remove retaining ring (42). Insert cam follower (35) in hole in shaft and apply only enough pressure on end of cam follower to remove the spring pressure, then push out pin (44) with a small punch. The pin passes through drilled holes in clutch and operates in slotted holes in propeller shaft.

To disassemble drive shaft and associated parts, reposition gearcase in vise with drive shaft projecting upward. Remove rubber slinger (5), water pump body (6), impeller (8) and impeller drive key (9). Remove flushing screw and withdraw remainder of water pump parts. Clamp upper end of drive shaft in a soft-jawed vise, remove pinion retaining nut (25); then tap gearcase off drive shaft and bearing. Note position and thickness of shims (21) on drive shaft upper bearing. Mesh position of pinion is controlled by shims (21) placed underneath the bearing.

After drive shaft has been removed, forward gear (41) and bearing cone can be extracted. Use an internal expanding type puller to extract bearing cup if removal is required. Remove and save shim pack (38).

Shift shaft (31) and cam (34) can be removed after removing forward gear and unscrewing bushing (28) from gearcase.

If gear wear is abnormal or if an parts that affect gear alignment wer renewed, install bearings on gears an drive shaft, and in gearcase (includin shims 21 and 38). To determine gea mesh and forward gear backlash, pro ceed as follows: Install drive shaft com ponents (19 through 25) and forwar gear components (38 through 41 Tighten pinion nut (25) to 70 ft.-lbs. (9 N·m). Install tool C-91-74776 in gea cavity of gearcase so it bottoms agains shoulder of gearcase. Apply approx imately 15 pounds (66.7 N) of downwar pressure (toward pinion gear) and rotat drive shaft several times to seat driv shaft bearing. While maintainin downward pressure on drive shaft measure clearance between pinion gea and tool. Clearance should be 0.025 inch (0.63 mm). Add or delete shims (21) t obtain desired clearance. Apply Loctite to drive shaft threads durin final assembly.

With drive shaft and forward gea assemblies installed, install propeller shaft (without shift components) and bearing carrier (50), then install nut (55 until snug, but do not tighten. Attach a suitable puller to bearing carrier as shown in Fig. M15-42 and apply 45 in.-lbs. (5.1 N·m) torque to puller screw. Rotate drive shaft several times to seat forward gear bearing. Install backlash measuring tool C-91-78473 on drive shaft as shown in Fig. M15-43 and set up a dial indicator to read movement at "2" on backlash tool. Recheck torque on bearing carrier puller (45 in.-lbs. [5.1 N·m]). Measure forward gear backlash by applying downward pressure and turning drive shaft. Dial indicator should measure 0.008-0.013 inch (0.20-0.33 mm) backlash. Adjust backlash by adding or deleting shims (38–Fig. M15-41). Changing shim thickness by 0.001 inch (0.025 mm) will alter backlash by 0.0015 inch (0.038 mm).

When reassembling, long splines of shift shaft (31) should be toward top. Shift cam (34) is installed with long side on port side of gearcase. Assemble shifting parts (37, 36, 43, 44 and 42) into propeller shaft (45). Pin (44) should pass through hole in slide (36). Position follower (35) in end of propeller shaft and insert shaft into bearing (40) and forward gear. Install the reverse gear and bearing carrier assembly using new seals (48 and 53). Lip of inner seal (53) should face in and lip of outer seal (53) should face propeller (out).

Upper oil seal (15) should be installed with lips facing up (toward engine) and lower oil seal (16) should be pressed into water pump base with lips facing down toward propeller shaft. Install re mainder of water pump assembly and

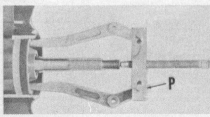

Fig. M15-42—Install a puller (P) as shown to preload forward gear bearing when determining gear backlash as outlined in text.

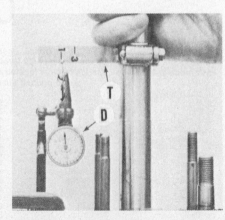

Fig. M15-43—Install backlash measuring tool C-91-78473 (T) and a dial indicator (D) set to read movement at number on tool as described in text.

tighten the screws or nuts to the following recommended torque. Torque 1/4-28 nuts to 24-30 in.-lbs. (2.7-3.4 N·m). Torque 5/16-24 nuts to 35-40 in.-lbs. (3.9-4.5 N·m). Torque 1/4-20 screws to 15-20 in.-lbs. (1.7-2.2 N·m).

Do not apply excessive grease to drive shaft splines; there must not be grease on tops of drive shaft or shift shaft. Shift power unit to forward gear and move guide block anchor pin on engine to forward gear position. Tighten gearcase fasteners with 3/8-16 threads to 55 ft.-lbs. (75 N·m) and fasteners with 7/16-20 threads to 65 ft.-lbs. (88 N·m).

E-Z Shift Models

R&R AND OVERHAUL. Most service on the lower unit can be performed by detaching the gearcase from the drive shaft housing. To remove gearcase, shift outboard to neutral gear, then detach propeller and drain gearcase lubricant. Remove the plastic plug and Allen screw from location (1 – Fig. M15-40). Remove trim tab (2) and stud nut from under trim tab. Remove stud nut from location (3), two stud nuts (4) from each side and stud nut (5) if so equipped, then withdraw the lower unit gearcase assembly.

To disassemble gearcase, remove rubber slinger (5 – Fig. M15-41), water tube guide (1) and seal (2). Unscrew and remove water pump components (6 through 18). Position gearcase in a soft-jawed vise so propeller shaft is horizontal. Check and be sure gearcase is in neutral gear. Unscrew but do not remove shift shaft bushing (28) and withdraw shift shaft (31) from gearcase. DO NOT turn shift shaft during removal or gearcase may be shifted into forward or reverse gear position. Bend back lockwasher (54) tabs, unscrew nut (55) and use a suitable puller to remove bearing carrier (50).

NOTE: Do not apply side load or strike side of propeller shaft during or after removal of bearing carrier as shift rod (62) may break.

Withdraw propeller shaft from gearcase, but do not use excessive force or a puller. If shaft is lodged in gearcase proceed as follows: Push propeller shaft inward so it contacts forward gear, reinstall shift shaft and be sure gears are in neutral. Remove shift shaft and attempt to withdraw propeller shaft. If propeller shaft remains stuck, push shaft inward so it contacts forward gear. Reinstall bearing carrier and lay gearcase on its port side. Strike upper forward end of gearcase with a rubber mallet so shift cam (6) is dislodged and falls into a cavi-

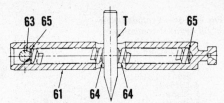

Fig. M15-44—Cross section of shift rod on E-Z Shift models. Center tool (T) using shims (64) as outlined in text.

ty in side of gearcase. Remove bearing carrier and propeller shaft.

To remove shift rod (62) from propeller shaft, remove spring clips (70) while being careful not to lose detent pins (71). Drive out pin (72) and remove shift rod (62) while being careful not to lose pin (63) which may fall from rod. Slide dog clutch (73) off shaft.

To disassemble drive shaft and associated parts, clamp upper end of drive shaft in a soft-jawed vise and remove pinion gear nut (25).

NOTE: On late models not equipped with pin (3) and spring (4), unscrew and remove bearing retainer above bearing assembly (20).

Tap gearcase off drive shaft and bearing. Note position and thickness of shims (21) and bearing. Remove pinion gear (24) and forward gear (69). Use a suitable puller to extract cups of bearings (20 and 67). Note number and thickness of shims (21 and 66) and save for reassembly. Pull out sleeve (22) then drive roller bearing (23) down into gear cavity for removal.

Inspect all components for excessive wear and damage. If water pump insert (7) must be renewed, use a punch and drive out old insert. It may be necessary to drill two holes in top of water pump body (6) to drive out insert – do not drill through insert. Apply RTV sealant to holes after installing the new insert.

Install bearings on gears and drive shaft, and in gearcase (including shims 21 and 66). To determine gear mesh and forward gear backlash, note number of pinion gear (24) teeth, then proceed as

follows: Install drive shaft components (19 through 25) and forward gear components (66 through 69). Tighten bearing retainer above bearing assembly (20), if so equipped, to 100 ft.-lbs. (136 N·m) with side of retainer marked "OFF" facing toward top of gearcase housing. Tighten pinion nut (25) to 70 ft.-lbs. (95 N·m) on early models and 80 ft.-lbs. (109 N·m) on later models. Install tool C-91-74776 in gear cavity of gearcase so it bottoms against shoulder of gearcase. Apply approximately 15 pounds (67 N) of downward pressure (toward pinion gear) and rotate drive shaft several times to seat drive shaft bearing. While maintaining downward pressure on drive shaft, measure clearance between pinion gear and tool. Clearance should be 0.025 inch (0.64 mm). Add or delete shims (21) to obtain desired clearance. Apply Loctite to drive shaft threads during final assembly.

With drive shaft and forward gear assemblies installed, install propeller shaft (without shift components) and bearing carrier (50), then install nut (55) until snug, but do not tighten. Attach a suitable puller to bearing carrier as shown in Fig. M15-42 and apply 45 in.-lbs. (5.1 N·m) torque to puller screw. Rotate drive shaft several times to seat forward gear bearing. Install backlash measuring tool C-91-78473 on drive shaft as shown in Fig. M15-43 and set up a dial indicator to read movement at "1" on backlash tool for models with a 15-tooth pinion gear or at "2" for models with a 14-tooth pinion gear. Recheck torque on bearing carrier puller (45 in.-lbs. [5.1 N·m]). Measure forward gear backlash by applying downward pressure and turning drive shaft. Dial indicator should measure 0.008-0.013 inch (0.20-0.33 mm) backlash on models equipped with preload type drive shaft and 0.018-0.027 inch (0.46-0.69 mm) on models without preload type drive shaft. Adjust backlash by adding or deleting shims (66 – Fig. M15-41). Changing shim thickness by 0.001 inch (0.025 mm) will alter backlash by 0.0015 inch (0.038 mm).

Fig. M15-50—Connect a pressure gage (G) as shown for hydraulic testing of non-integral type power tilt/trim.
D. "Down" line
G. Pressure gage
M. Manual tilt valve
P. Plugs
T. Tees
U. "Up" line
V. Valves

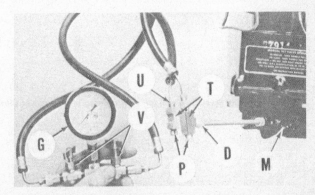

To properly adjust spring tension in shift rod (62), install springs (64) and pin (63) in shift rod. Insert tool C-91-86642, or an old pin (72) with a ground-down end, between springs as shown in Fig. M15-44. Tool (T) or pin should be centered in shift rod slot within 1/64 inch (0.397 mm). Adjust tool position by installing shims (65) at ends of springs (64).

Assemble remainder of lower unit by reversing disassembly procedure while noting the following points: Install thrust washer (47) so larger diameter side is nearer reverse gear (75) then press bearing (49) on gear. Lip of inner seal (53) should face in and lip of outer

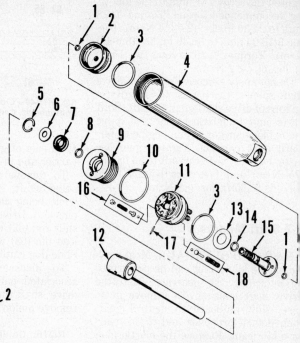

Fig. M15-56—Exploded view of tilt cylinder components.
1. "O" ring (0.307 in. [7.9 mm] ID)
2. Cup
3. "O" ring (1.957 in. [49.71 mm] ID)
4. Cylinder
5. Circlip
6. Washer
7. Scraper
8. "O" ring (0.854 in. [21.69 mm] ID)
9. Cap
10. "O" ring (2.067 in. [52.5 mm] ID)
11. Piston
12. Rod
13. Washer
14. "O" ring (0.661 in. [16.79 mm] ID)
15. Rod end
16. Check valve assy.
17. Pin
18. Check valve assy.

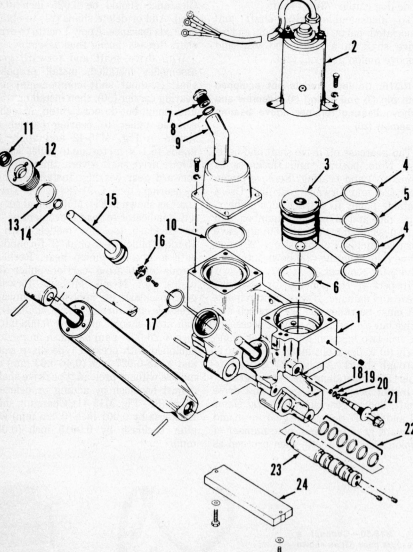

Fig. M15-55—Exploded view of integral type power tilt/trim system.

1. Manifold	7. Fill plug	14. "O" ring (0.612 in. (15.54 mm) ID)	19. "O" ring (0.208 in. [5.28 mm] ID)
2. Electric motor	8. "O" ring (0.583 in. [14.81 mm] ID)	15. Trim piston & rod	20. "O" ring (0.239 in. [6.07 mm] ID)
3. Pump assy.	9. Reservoir cover	16. Strainer	21. Manual release valve
4. "O" rings (2.614 in. [66.40 mm] ID)	10. Seal ring	17. "O" ring (1.248 in. [31.70 mm] ID)	22. "O" rings (0.989 in. [25.12 mm] ID)
5. "O" rings (2.739 in. [69.57 mm] ID)	11. Seal	18. "O" ring (0.114 in. [2.90 mm] ID)	23. Shaft
6. "O" ring (2.739 in. [69.57 mm] ID)	12. Cap		24. Anode plate
	13. "O" ring (1.475 in. (37.47 mm) ID)		

seal (53) should face propeller (out). Install spring clips (70) so bent end of each spring engages the hole in one of the detent pins (71). Spring clips should be wound in opposite directions around dog clutch (73) and must not overlap.

Use heavy grease to hold shift cam (60) in cam follower (61) with "UP" side facing up. Be sure "E" ring (30) and circlip (32) are seated on shift shaft (31) before installing shaft. Tighten bushing (28) after tightening bearing carrier nut (55). Tighten bearing carrier nut (55) to 210 ft.-lbs. (284 N·m).

Upper oil seal (15) is installed with lips facing up (toward engine) while lower oil seal (16) lips should face down towards gearcase. If reusing old impeller (8), install impeller so vanes rotate in same direction during previous operation. Be sure key (9) is properly installed. Tighten water pump fasteners to following torques: 1/4-28 nuts to 25-30 in.-lbs. (2.8-3.4 N·m), 5/16-24 nuts to 35-40 in.-lbs. (3.9-4.5 N·m) and 1/2-20 screws to 15-20 in.-lbs. (1.7-2.2 N·m).

Do not apply excessive grease to drive shaft splines; there must not be grease on tops of drive shaft or shift shaft. Shift lower unit to forward gear and move guide block anchor pin on engine to forward gear position. Tighten gearcase fasteners with 3/8-16 threads to 55 ft.-lbs. (75 N·m) and 7/16-20 threads to 65 ft.-lbs. (88 N·m).

POWER TILT/TRIM

Non-Integral Type

Two types of hydraulic power tilt/trim systems have been used. Early models re identified by the rectangular oil reservoir while later models use a circular fluid reservoir. Refer to the following sections for service.

Early Models

FLUID. Recommended fluid is SAE 10W-30 or 10W-40 automotive oil. With outboard in full down position, oil level should reach "Full" mark on dipstick. Do not overfill.

BLEEDING. Check fluid level in reservoir and fill if required. Operate trim system several times to purge air in system. Recheck fluid level and fill if required.

HYDRAULIC TESTING. Disconnect cylinder hoses from control valve and connect a pressure gage to oulets of control valve as shown in Fig. M15-50. Note that large outlet is "up" circuit and small outlet is "down" circuit. Close appropriate pressure gage valve circuit. Make sure manual tilt valve (M) is tightly closed. Close and open appropriate pressure gage valves while operating system to check pressure in up and down circuits. Hydraulic pressure should be 3100 psi (21.4 MPa) minimum for up circuit and 1200 psi (8.3 MPa) minimum for down circuit. Pressure may drop slightly but should remain steady. If pressure is normal, inspect trim cylinders and hoses for leakage. If pressure is abnormal, install a good control valve and recheck pressure. If pressure remains abnormal, install a new pump body.

Later Models

FLUID AND BLEEDING. Recommended fluid is SAE 10W-40 with an API rating of SE. Fill reservoir to "FULL" mark on dipstick.

The hydraulic circuit is self-bleeding as the trim system is operated several times. Be sure to check reservoir level after filling and operating system after system has been serviced.

HYDRAULIC TESTING. The pump may be checked by connecting a 5000 psi (34.5 MPa) test gage alternately to the "UP" and "DOWN" ports. Note that the pump motor blue wire is the postive battery connection to pressurize the "UP"

port and connecting the positive battery terminal to the pump motor green wire will pressurize the "DOWN" port. Pressure at the "UP" port should be 3100-3500 psi (21.4-24.1 MPa) and should not drop lower than 1500 psi (10.3 MPa) after pumping stops. Pressure at the "DOWN" port should be 1500-1900 psi (10.3-13.1 MPa) and should not drop lower than 750 psi (5.2 MPa) after pumping stops.

FLUID AND BLEEDING. Recommended fluid is Dexron II or Type AF automatic transmission fluid. Remove fill plug (7 – Fig. M15-55) and fill reservoir until fluid is visible in fill tube with the outboard motor in the full-up position.

The hydraulic circuit is self-bleeding as the tilt/trim system is operated through several cycles. After servicing system, be sure to check reservoir level after filling and operating system.

HYDRAULIC TESTING. The system can be checked by connecting a 5000 psi (34.5 MPa) test gage to the UP (U – Fig. M15-57) and DOWN (D – Fig. M15-58) ports. Prior to connecting test gage, place outboard motor in the full-up position and engage tilt lock lever. Unscrew reservoir fill plug and rotate manual release valve (21 – Fig. M15-57)

three to four turns counterclockwise to release pressure on system. Remove UP or DOWN Allen head test port plug and connect test gage with suitable adapter and hose. Install fill plug and rotate manual release valve clockwise until seated. System pressure when testing at UP (U) port should be a minimum of 1300 psi (8.9 MPa). System pressure when testing at DOWN (D – Fig. M15-58) port should be a minimum of 500 psi (3.5 MPa). Release pressure on system as previously outlined prior to removing test gage. Reinstall Allen head plug.

OVERHAUL. Refer to Fig. M15-55 for an exploded view of manifold and trim cylinder components, and Fig. M15-56 for an exploded view of tilt cylinder components. Special Mercury socket 91-44487A1 and a spanner wrench is required to service trim and tilt cylinders. Keep all components clean and away from contamination. Keep components separated and label if needed for correct reassembly. Note "O" ring sizes as stated in legends of Figs. M15-55 and M15-56. Lubricate all "O" rings or seal lips with Dexron II or Type AF automatic transmission fluid during assembly.

Fig. M15-57—Release pressure on system, then remove Allen head plug (U) and install a 5000 psi (34.5 MPa) test gage with suitable adapter and hose to test system pressure when operated in the "UP" direction. View identifies location of manual release valve (21).

Fig. M15-58—Release pressure on system, then remove Allen head plug (D) and install a 5000 psi (34.5 MPa) test gage with a suitable adapter and hose to test system pressure when operated in the "DOWN" direction.

MERCURY 300 AND 3.4L

Year Produced	Model
1980	300
1981	300
1982	...
1983	300
1984	3.4L
1985	3.4L

Letter suffix indicates equipment variation: E – Electric starter and alternator, L – Long shaft, XL – Extra long shaft and PT – Power trim.

CONDENSED SERVICE DATA

TUNE-UP

Hp/rpm:
Model 300	300/5300-5800
Model 3.4L	275/5300-5800
Bore	3.74 in.
	(95 mm)
Stroke	3.14 in.
	(80 mm)
Number of Cylinders	6
Displacement	207 cu. in.
	(3393 cc)
Firing Order	1-2-3-4-5-6

Number System (top to bottom):
Port	2-4-6
Starboard	1-3-5

Spark Plug:
Champion	L76V
AC	V40FFM
Electrode Gap	Surface Gap
Idle Speed (in gear)	550-600 rpm
Fuel:Oil Ratio	50:1

SIZES – CLEARANCES

Piston Ring End Gap	0.018-0.025 in.
	(0.457-0.635 mm)
Maximum Cylinder Tolerance	0.006 in.
	(0.152 mm)

SIZES – CLEARANCES CONT.

Crankshaft Bearing Type:
Top Main Bearing	Caged Rolle
Center Main Bearings	Caged Rolle
Bottom Main Bearing	Ball Bearin
Crankpin	Caged Rolle
Piston Pin Bearing	34 Loose Roller

TIGHTENING TORQUES

Carburetor Adapter Plate	150 in.-lbs
	(17 N·m)
Connecting Rod	See Tex
Crankcase Screws	30 ft.-lbs
	(40 N·m)
Cylinder Head	150 in.-lbs
	(17 N·m)
Lower End Cap	150 in.-lbs
	(17 N·m)
Exhaust Cover	150 in.-lbs
	(17 N·m)
Flywheel Nut	125 ft.-lbs
	(169 N·m)
Reed Block to Reed Plate Mounting Screws	60 in.-lbs
	(6.7 N·m)
Reed Plate to Carburetor Adapter Plate Mounting Screws	60 in.-lbs
	(6.7 N·m)
Spark Plugs	204 in.-lbs
	(17 N·m)

LUBRICATION

The engine is lubricated by oil mixed with the fuel. The fuel should be regular leaded, low lead or unleaded gasoline with a minimum pump octane rating of 86. Recommended oil is Quicksilver Formula 50-D Outboard Lubricant or a BIA certified TC-W motor oil. The recommended fuel:oil ratio for normal operation is 50:1. During engine break-in, the fuel:oil ratio should be increased to 25:1.

The lower unit gears and bearings are lubricated by oil contained in the gearcase. The recommended oil is Quicksilver Super Duty Gear Lubricant or a suitable EP90 outboard gear oil.

The gearcase should be refilled periodically and the lubricant renewed after every 30 hours of operation or more frequently if needed. The gearcase is drained and filled through the same plug port. An upper and lower oil level (vent) port are used in the gearcase filling procedure and to ease in oil drainage. Drain plug and level plugs are

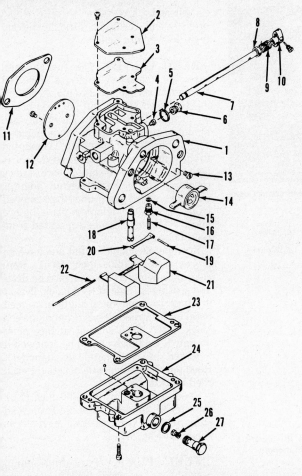

Fig. M17-1—Exploded view of carburetor.

1. Body
2. Cover plate
3. Gasket
4. Idle jet
5. Gasket
6. Plug
7. Throttle shaft
8. Spacer
9. Spring
10. Lever
11. Gasket
12. Throttle plate
13. Vent jet
14. Venturi
15. Gasket
16. Seat
17. Needle
18. Main nozzle
19. Pin
20. Inlet lever
21. Float
22. Pin
23. Gasket
24. Float bowl
25. Gasket
26. Main jet
27. Main jet plug

SPEED CONTROL LINKAGE. To synchronize ignition and carburetor opening, proceed as follows: To verify timing pointer alignment, a dial indicator must be installed in the number 1 (top, starboard) cylinder and the indicator synchronized with the piston position (dial indicator reads zero when piston is at top dead center).

NOTE: To prevent accidental starting from flywheel rotation, remove all spark plugs and properly ground plug wires.

Rotate the flywheel counterclockwise approximately ¼ turn past the 0.557 inch (14.15 mm) BTDC reading, then rotate flywheel clockwise until indicator face reads 0.557 inch (14.15 mm) BTDC. Note position of the timing pointer and reposition if the timing pointer is not

Fig. M17-2—To determine float level, invert the carburetor body and measure distance (D) from the carburetor body to base of float (21). Distance (D) should be 11/16 inch (17.5 mm).

located on starboard side of gearcase. To fill gearcase with oil, place the outboard motor in a vertical position. Add oil through drain plug opening until oil begins to overflow from lower oil level plug port. Reinstall lower oil level plug, then continue to add oil until the oil begins to overflow from upper oil level plug port. Allow 1 ounce (30 mL) to drain from gearcase, then reinstall upper oil level plug and drain plug.

FUEL SYSTEM

CARBURETOR. Standard make of carburetor is a center bowl type Mercarb. Six carburetors are used. For operation below 2500 feet (762 m) altitude, the standard jet sizes are as follows:

WO-3 Carburetor

Main jet . . . . .0.072 in.
              (1.83 mm)
Vent jet . . . . .0.080 in.
              (2.03 mm)
Idle jet . . . . .0.052 in.
              (1.32 mm)

WO-5 Carburetor

Main jet . . . . .0.076 in.
              (1.93 mm)
Vent jet . . . . .0.080 in.
              (2.03 mm)
Idle jet . . . . .0.062 in.
              (1.57 mm)

NOTE: Carburetor indentification letters and number are stamped on the top side of carburetor mounting flange.

Other jet sizes are available for adjusting the calibration for altitude or other special conditions. No idle mixture screw adjustment is provided. Idle jet (4–Fig. MY13-9) size must be altered to change idle air:fuel ratio. The idle jet meters air, therefore installing an idle jet with a smaller orifice will richen the idle air:fuel ratio and intstalling an idle jet with a larger orifice will lean the idle air:fuel ratio. Recommended idle speed is 550-600 rpm with engine at normal operating temperature and forward gear engaged. After engine idle speed adjustment, hold idle speed screw against stop and install the throttle cable barrel in the retainer while adjusting barrel so it fits into retainer and a very light preload between idle speed screw and its stop is established. Excessive throttle cable preload will result in difficult shifting from forward to neutral.

To determine the float level, invert the carburetor body and measure distance (D–Fig. MY13-10) from the carburetor body to base of float (21). Distance (D) should be 11/16 inch (17.5 mm) and is adjusted by bending fuel inlet lever (20–Fig. MY13-11) within area (A).

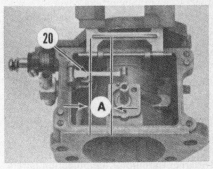

Fig. M17-3—Adjust float level by bending fuel inlet lever (20) within area (A).

Fig. M17-5—Link rod (L) should protrude 11/16 inch (17.46 mm) from link body. Refer to text for procedures to adjust maximum spark advance screw (A).

aligned with ".557 BTDC" mark on flywheel. Loosen the two cap screws retaining the timing pointer and reposition, if needed, then retighten cap screws. Remove the dial indicator assembly from the top cylinder after adjustment is completed and reinstall number 1 (top) spark plug and lead.

Be sure link rod (L – Fig. M17-5) protrudes 11/16 inch (17.46 mm) from link body as shown.

NOTE: To prevent engine from starting, make sure only the number 1 (top, starboard) spark plug is installed and its plug wire attached.

Disconnect the fuel tank supply hose at the outboard motor connector. Detach the throttle cable barrel from the retainer of the cable anchor bracket. Adjust idle speed screw (I – Fig. M17-6) so idle mark (M) on throttle cam (C) is in contact with roller (R) as shown.

Withdraw the air intake cover from the front of the carburetors. Position throttle lever (T) so idle speed screw (I) is against its stop. Loosen carburetor synchronizing screws (S) and allow the carburetor throttle plates to close freely. With light pressure, hold cam follower roller (R) against throttle cam (C). Then retighten screws (S). Check to be sure that carburetor throttle plates are completely closed and operate freely. Repeat adjustment procedure if setting is incorrect. Reinstall air intake cover.

Connect a suitable timing light to number 1 cylinder spark plug lead. With the outboard motor in neutral, position throttle lever (T) so idle speed screw (I) is against stop. Crank the engine with the electric starter and adjust primary screw (P) so the ignition timing is 7° ATDC on engines equipped with WO-5 carburetors and 13° ATDC on engines equipped with WO-3 carburetors.

NOTE: Carburetor identification letters and number are stamped on the top side of carburetor mounting flange.

Open the throttle until maximum spark advance screw (A – Fig. M17-5) is against stop. Crank the engine with the starter motor and adjust maximum spark advance screw (A) so ignition timing is 22° BTDC.

NOTE: Due to electronic characteristics of the ignition system, maximum advance is set at 22° BTDC, but ignition will retard to 20° BTDC at 5500 rpm.

The carburetor throttle plates must not act as the wide open throttle stop. To prevent damage to the carburetors, move speed control linkage to the max-

Fig. M17-6—View showing speed control components.

B. Maximum throttle stop screw
C. Throttle cam
I. Idle speed screw
M. Idle mark
P. Primary screw
R. Roller
S. Screw
T. Throttle lever

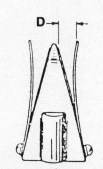

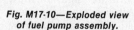

Fig. M17-8—Reed stop setting (D) should be 0.300 inch (7.62 mm) on all models.

imum speed position and adjust maximum throttle stop screw (B – Fig. M17-6) so a clearance of 0.010-0.015 inch (0.25-0.38 mm) is between throttle cam (C) and cam follower roller (R).

Reassemble and adjust idle speed screw (I) as outlined in the following CARBURETOR section.

Hold idle speed screw (I) against stop and install the throttle cable barrel in the retainer while adjusting barrel so it fits into retainer and a very light preload between idle speed screw and its stop is

established. Excessive throttle cable preload will result in difficult shifting from forward to neutral.

REED VALVES. The fuel:air mixture for each cylinder is directed through a reed plate assembly containing two reed blocks with 10 reed petals on each block. Reed plate assemblies are mounted to a carburetor adapter plate. The carburetor adapter plate is mounted to the crankcase. The upper reed block is retained to the reed plate by two screws reaching through carburetor adapter plate. The reed plate must be removed from carburetor adapter plate before lower reed block can be separated from reed plate.

Reed petals should be flat and have no more than 0.020 inch (0.51 mm) clearance between free end of reed petal and seating surface of reed block. Do not attempt to bend or straighten a reed petal or turn reed petals around on reed block. Reed block seating surface must be flat. Reed block should be renewed if indented by reed petals or damaged. Reed petals are available in sets for each reed block only.

Reed stop setting is 0.300 inch (7.62 mm) for all models. Measure from reed stop to reed petal seating surface as shown in Fig. M17-8.

FUEL PUMP. Two fuel pump assemblies are used. The fuel pumps operate in series, the starboard mounted fuel pump pumps fuel to the port mounted fuel pump, which pumps fuel to the carburetors.

Pulse hoses connected between the crankcase and fuel pump mounting plate (20 – Fig. M17-10) are used to transfer crankcase pulsating pressure. Make sure hoses are airtight and in good condition.

A booster chamber is used on pump discharge side to dampen the action of the larger main pump diaphragm, thus

Fig. M17-10—Exploded view of fuel pump assembly.

1. Cap screw
2. Plastic washer
3. Filter cover
4. "O" ring
5. Strainer
6. Housing
7. Gaskets
8. Inlet check valve
9. Discharge check valve
10. Retainer
11. Retainer
12. Spring
13. Cap
14. Gaskets
15. Diaphragm
16. Booster chamber
17. Gasket
18. Base
19. Gasket
20. Mounting plate

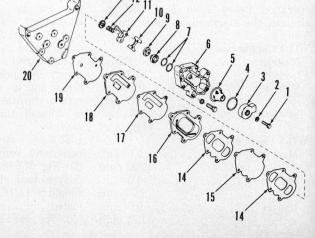

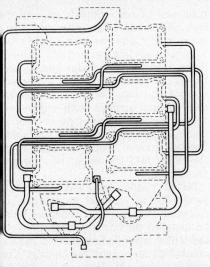

Fig. M17-12—View showing correct routing of crankcase bleed system hoses and fuel pump pulse hoses.

increasing the maximum potential fuel flow.

Spring (12) and cap (13) are used to load the diaphragm, thus allowing the diaphragm to respond more quickly to crankcase pressure changes.

When overhauling the fuel pump or pumps, renew all defective or questionable parts. When assembling fuel pump, retainer (10) must be installed with tips pointing away from the check valves.

CRANKCASE BLEED SYSTEM

A crankcase bleed system is used to remove unburned oil residue from the crankcase and lower main bearing and burn or direct the unburned oil residue to the three upper main bearings. Refer to Fig. M17-12 for the correct routing of crankcase bleed system hoses.

IGNITION SYSTEM

All models are equipped with a Thunderbolt solid state capacitor discharge ignition system consisting of trigger coils, stator, switch boxes and ignition coils. The trigger coils are contained in a trigger ring module under the flywheel. Diodes, SCR's and capacitors are contained in the switch boxes. Switch boxes, trigger ring module and stator must be serviced as unit assemblies.

Check all wires and connections before troubleshooting ignition circuit. The following test specifications will aid troubleshooting. Resistance between blue and red stator leads or blue/white and red/white stator leads should be 5400-6200 ohms. Resistance between red stator lead and ground or red/white stator lead and ground should be 125-175 ohms. Resistance should be 1200-1400 ohms between the following

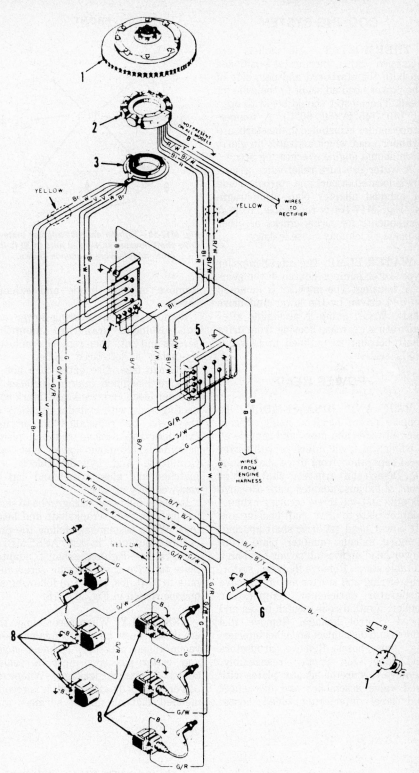

Fig. M17-14—Typical wiring diagram of ignition system used on all models.

1. Flywheel	7. Ignition switch	Y. Yellow	G/R. Green with red tracer
2. Stator	8. Ignition coils	Bl. Blue	
3. Trigger ring	B. Black	Br. Brown	G/W. Green with white tracer
4. Upper switch box	G. Green	B/W. Black with white tracer	
5. Lower switch box	R. Red		R/W. Red with white tracer
6. Mercury stop switch	V. Violet	B/Y. Black with white tracer	Bl/W. Blue with white tracer
	W. White		

trigger coil leads; between brown (in yellow sleeve) and violet (without yellow sleeve), between white (in yellow sleeve) and brown (without yellow sleeve), between violet (in yellow sleeve) and white (without yellow sleeve). Ignition coils may be checked using a suitable coil checker.

Recommended spark plugs are AC V40FFM or Champion L76V.

COOLING SYSTEM

THERMOSTAT. All models are equipped with a thermostat positioned on both the starboard and port side of the power head adjacent to the cylinder head. Thermostat should begin to open at 140°-145°F (60°-63°C). A temperature sender is installed in the starboard cylinder head which activates an alarm horn should engine overheating occur.

A water pressure relief valve assembly is located in port and starboard side of exhaust adapter plate. Diaphragm (4–Fig. M17-16) is renewable. Inspect components for nicks, cracks or other damage which may cause leakage.

WATER PUMP. The rubber impeller type water pump is housed in the gearcase housing. The impeller is mounted on and driven by the lower unit drive shaft. Water pump is accessible after separating gearcase housing from drive shaft housing as outlined in LOWER UNIT section.

POWER HEAD

R&R AND DISASSEMBLE. To remove power head assembly, disconnect all wires and hoses and remove all cowling which will interfere with power head separation from drive shaft housing. Detach shift arm from shift shaft at front of exhaust adapter plate. Remove six nuts and one screw securing exhaust adapter plate to drive shaft housing and lift power head off drive shaft housing. Remove exhaust adapter plate from power head and install power head on a suitable stand. Remove flywheel, stator, trigger ring and starter motor. Remove carburetor enrichener, temperature sender, ignition coils, switch boxes and speed control linkage. Remove fuel pumps and disconnect and label interfering pulse hoses. Remove carburetors and label for proper reassembly. Remove carburetor adapter plates with reed valve assemblies and disconnect and label interfering bleed hoses.

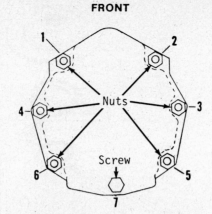

FRONT

Fig. M17-18 — Tighten exhaust adapter plate to drive shaft housing screw and nuts to 30 ft.-lbs. (40N·m) following sequence shown.

Remove cylinder heads and exhaust cover.

Remove screws securing lower end cap. Remove crankcase mounting screws and nut, then remove crankcase by using a soft-faced mallet to tap crankcase free. Use extra care not to damage machined mating surfaces of cylinder block and crankcase. Mark connecting rods with cylinder numbers so they can be reinstalled in original cylinders and remove rod and piston assemblies. Remove lower end cap. Crankcase and cylinder block are matched and align bored and can be renewed only as a set.

Refer to following paragraphs to service pistons, rods, crankshaft and bearings. When assembling, follow the procedures outlined in the ASSEMBLY paragraphs. Tighten exhaust adapter plate to drive shaft housing screw and nuts to 30 ft.-lbs. (40 N·m) following sequence shown in Fig. M17-18.

ASSEMBLY. When assembling, the crankcase must be sealed against both vacuum and pressure. Exhaust cover and water passages must be sealed against pressure leakage. Whenever power head is disassembled, it is recommended that all gasket surfaces and machined joints without gaskets be carefully checked for nicks and burrs which might interfere with a tight seal.

Install seals in lower end cap with lips down (away from cylinder block). Loctite 271 or 290 should be applied to seal bore of end cap. Lubricate all bearing and friction surfaces with engine oil. Loose needle bearings may be held in place during assembly using a light, nonfibrous grease. Gaps of seal rings (15–Fig. M17-19) must be towards crankcase.

Install piston, rod and crankshaft assemblies as outlined in appropriate following paragraphs. Crankcase must be installed on cylinder block prior to tightening lower end cap screws. Rotate crankshaft and check for binding. Cut gasket strips off flush with edge of crankcase bores. Apply a thin coat of sealer such as Permatex 2C-12 to mating surfaces of crankcase and cylinder block using care to prevent excess sealer from entering bearings, crankcase or passages.

Progressively tighten crankcase seven main bearing screws and one nut until crankshaft seal rings are compressed and crankcase mates with cylinder block. Tighten seven screws and one nut in three progressive steps to a final torque of 30 ft.-lbs. (40 N·m) using a criss-cross tightening sequence starting in center of crankcase and working out to ends. Tighten six crankcase flange screws in three progressive steps to 30 ft.-lbs. (40 N·m). Rotate crankshaft and check for binding.

Complete reassembly in reverse order of disassembly and tighten components to torque values shown in CONDENSED SERVICE DATA.

PISTONS, PINS, RINGS AND CYLINDERS. Before detaching connecting rods from crankshaft, make sure that rod and cap are marked so rods and caps are not interchanged and can be returned to original cylinders.

The manufacturer recommends renewing piston pin needle bearings if piston pin is removed from piston. Piston pin is supported by 34 loose needle bearings. Needle bearings can be held in connecting rod with nonfibrous grease during piston pin installation. Use recommended Mercury tools or suitable equivalents when installing or removing piston pin. Renew piston pin retaining clips during reassembly.

Piston rings must be installed on piston with dot side facing top of piston. Piston ring gap should be 0.018-0.025 inch (0.45-0.64 mm).

Install piston and rod assembly in cylinder identified on rod during disassembly. Piston must be installed with letter on piston dome toward

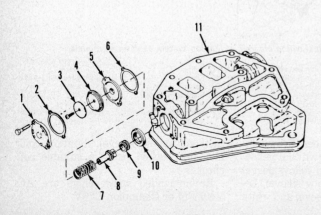

Fig. M17-16 — Exploded view of water pressure relief valve assembly located in port and starboard side of exhaust adapter plate.

1. Cover
2. Gasket
3. Washer
4. Diaphragm
5. Plate
6. Gasket
7. Spring
8. Relief valve
9. Carrier
10. Grommet
11. Exhaust adapter plate

flywheel end of crankshaft. Pistons are marked "P" for port and "S" for starboard on piston domes for correct installation in port or starboard cylinder bank.

Maximum allowable cylinder tolerance is 0.006 inch (0.152 mm). Cylinders are chrome plated and no service other than renewal of cylinder block and crankcase assembly is recommended by the manufacturer.

CONNECTING RODS, BEARINGS AND CRANKSHAFT.

Connecting rod has 34 loose needle bearings in small end and caged roller bearings in big end. Connecting rod big end is fractured type and rod and cap must be mated perfectly before tightening screws. Tighten 5/16-18 rod cap screws to 180 in.-lbs. (20.3 N·m), then rotate screws an additional ½ turn. Tighten ⅜-24 rod cap screws to 360 in.-lbs. (40.6 N·m), then rotate screws an additional ¼ turn.

Inspect crankshaft crankpin and main bearing journal surfaces; if scored, out-of-round or worn, renew crankshaft. Check crankshaft for straightness. Do not interchange main bearings.

ELECTRICAL SYSTEM

Refer to Fig. M17-14 for a typical wiring diagram of ignition and starter components for all models. Note the following cautions when servicing electrical components:

DO NOT reverse battery connections. Battery negative (–) terminal is grounded.

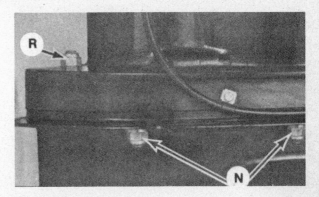

Fig. M17-21—Remove nut or screw (R) and two nuts (N) on each side of gearcase housing during removal of gearcase assembly. Refer to text.

DO NOT "spark" battery connections to check polarity.

DO NOT disconnect battery cables while engine is running.

DO NOT crank engine if ignition switch boxes are not grounded to engine.

The rectifier may be checked by disconnecting wires to rectifier and using a continuity tester or ohmmeter as follows: Connect a tester lead to ground and then alternately connect other tester lead to alternator terminals of rectifier. Note reading then reverse tester leads. Tester should indicate a short or open circuit with first test and opposite reading when tester leads are reversed. Connect a tester lead to positive rectifier terminal and alternately connect other tester lead to alternator terminals of rectifier. Note reading then reverse tester leads. Tester should show opposite reading when tester leads are reversed. Renew rectifier if testing indicated faulty circuits.

To check alternator stator, disconnect alternator leads from rectifier and connect an ohmmeter to alternator leads. Resistance reading should be approximately 0.30 ohms. There should be infinite resistance between either alternator lead and ground. Alternator output should be 13.5-15.5 amps.

LOWER UNIT

PROPELLER AND DRIVE CLUTCH. Protection for the motor is built into a special cushioning clutch in the propeller hub. No adjustment is possible on the propeller or clutch. Various pitch propellers are available and propeller should be selected to provide full throttle engine operation within range of 5300-5800 rpm. Propellers other than those recommended should not be used.

R&R AND OVERHAUL. Most service on the lower unit can be performed by detaching the gearcase from the drive shaft housing. To remove gearcase, shift outboard motor to neutral gear, then detach propeller and drain gearcase lubricant. Disconnect hydrasteer cables from rudder arm (26–Fig. M17-22) and remove rudder arm (26) and rudder (30). Remove anode plate (31) and nut under anode plate. Remove two screws from bottom of antiventilation plate. Remove nut or screw (R–Fig. M17-21) and two nuts (N) in equal increments from each side of gearcase. Disconnect speedometer hose, if needed, then withdrawn the lower unit gearcase assembly.

To disassemble gearcase, remove water tube guide (1–Fig. M17-22) and seal (2). Unscrew and remove water pump components (3 through 8). Use two water pump screws to extract seal carrier (9) with oil seal (10) and "O" ring (11). Position gearcase in a soft-jawed vise so propeller shaft is horizontal. Check and be sure gearcase is in neutral gear. Unscrew shift shaft bushing (20) and withdraw shift shaft (23) with bushing (20) from gearcase. DO NOT turn shift shaft during removal or gearcase may be shifted into forward or

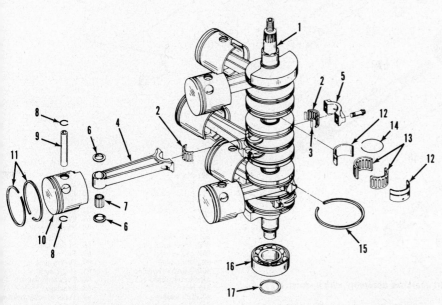

Fig. M17-19-Exploded view of crankshaft, connecting rod and piston assemblies.

1. Crankshaft	6. Spacers	10. Piston	14. Retaining ring
2. Bearing cage	7. Needle bearings	11. Piston rings	15. Seal ring
3. Roller	8. Clips	12. Bearing race	16. Ball bearing
4. Connecting rod	9. Piston pin	13. Bearing	17. Snap ring
5. Rod cap			

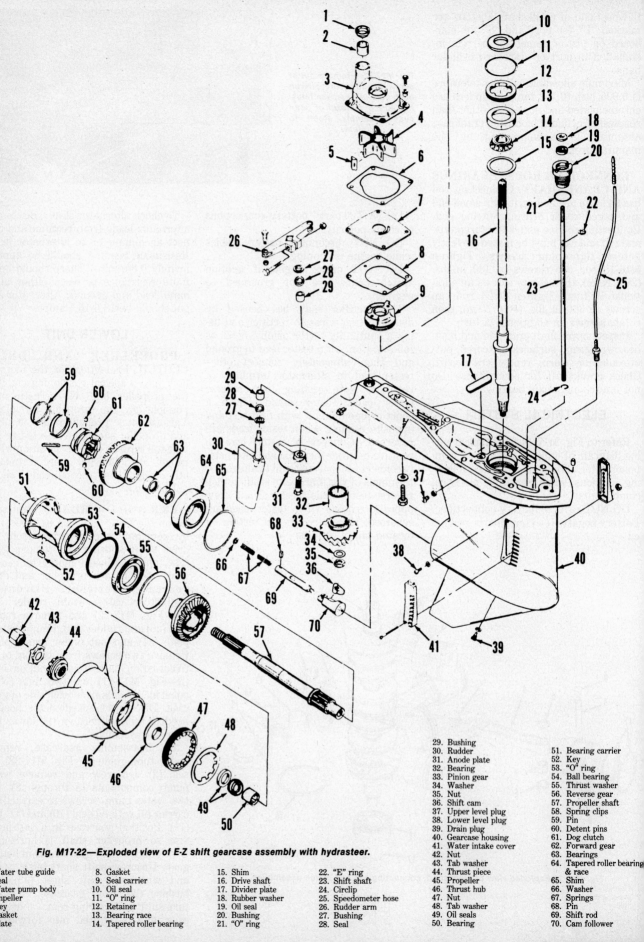

Fig. M17-22—Exploded view of E-Z shift gearcase assembly with hydrasteer.

1. Water tube guide	8. Gasket	15. Shim	22. "E" ring
2. Seal	9. Seal carrier	16. Drive shaft	23. Shift shaft
3. Water pump body	10. Oil seal	17. Divider plate	24. Circlip
4. Impeller	11. "O" ring	18. Rubber washer	25. Speedometer hose
5. Key	12. Retainer	19. Oil seal	26. Rudder arm
6. Gasket	13. Bearing race	20. Bushing	27. Bushing
7. Plate	14. Tapered roller bearing	21. "O" ring	28. Seal

29. Bushing	51. Bearing carrier
30. Rudder	52. Key
31. Anode plate	53. "O" ring
32. Bearing	54. Ball bearing
33. Pinion gear	55. Thrust washer
34. Washer	56. Reverse gear
35. Nut	57. Propeller shaft
36. Shift cam	58. Spring clips
37. Upper level plug	59. Pin
38. Lower level plug	60. Detent pins
39. Drain plug	61. Dog clutch
40. Gearcase housing	62. Forward gear
41. Water intake cover	63. Bearings
42. Nut	64. Tapered roller bearing
43. Tab washer	& race
44. Thrust piece	65. Shim
45. Propeller	66. Washer
46. Thrust hub	67. Springs
47. Nut	68. Pin
48. Tab washer	69. Shift rod
49. Oil seals	70. Cam follower
50. Bearing	

reverse gear position. Bend back tabs on tab washer (48) and unscrew nut (47), then use a suitable puller to remove bearing carrier (51).

NOTE: Do not apply side load or strike side of propeller shaft during or after removal of bearing carrier as shift rod (69) could break.

Withdraw propeller shaft from gearcase, but do not use excessive force or a puller. If shaft is lodged in gearcase, proceed as follows: Push propeller shaft inward so it contacts forward gear. Reinstall shift shaft and be sure gears are in neutral. Remove shift shaft and attempt to withdraw propeller shaft. If propeller shaft remains stuck, push shaft inward so it contacts forward gear. Reinstall bearing carrier and lay gearcase on its port side. Strike upper forward end of gearcase with a rubber mallet so shift cam (36) is dislodged and falls into a cavity in side of gearcase. Remove bearing carrier and propeller shaft.

To remove shift rod (69) from propeller shaft, remove spring clips (58) while being careful not to lose detent pins (60). Drive out pin (59) and remove shift rod (69) while being careful not to lose pin (68) which may fall from rod. Slide dog clutch (61) off shaft.

To disassemble drive shaft and associated parts, clamp upper end of drive shaft in a soft-jawed vise and remove retainer (12) and pinion gear nut (35). Tap gearcase off drive shaft and bearing. Note position and thickness of shims (15). Remove pinion gear (33) and forward gear (62). Use a suitable puller to extract cup of bearing (64). Note number and thickness of shims (65) and save for reassembly. Drive roller bearing (32) down into gear cavity for removal.

Inspect all components for excessive wear and damage. Install bearings on gears and drive shaft, and in gearcase including shims 15 and 65. To determine gear mesh and forward gear backlash, proceed as follows: Install drive shaft components (12 through 16 and 32 through 35) and forward gear components (62 through 65). Tighten retainer (12) to 55 ft.-lbs. (75 N·m) and pinion nut (25) to 70 ft.-lbs. (95 N·m). Install tool 91-74776 in gear cavity of gearcase so it bottoms against shoulder of gearcase. Apply approximately 15 pounds (67 N) of upward pressure on drive shaft and rotate drive shaft several times to seat drive shaft bearing. While maintaining upward pressure on drive shaft, measure clearance between pinion gear and tool. Clearance should be 0.025 inch (0.64 mm). Add or delete shims (15) to obtain desired clearance.

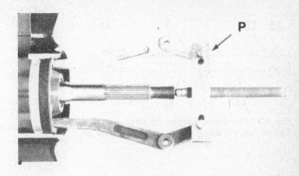

Fig. M17-23—Install a puller (P) as shown to preload forward gear bearing when determining gear backlash as outlined in text.

Apply Loctite 271 or 290 to drive shaft threads during final assembly.

With drive shaft and forward gear assemblies installed, install propeller shaft (without shift components) and bearing carrier (51), then install nut (47) until snug, but do not tighten. Attach a suitable puller to bearing carrier as shown in Fig. M17-23 and apply 45 in.-lbs. (5.1 N·m) torque to puller screw. Rotate drive shaft several times to seat forward gear bearing. Install backlash measuring tool 91-53459 on drive shaft as shown in Fig. M17-24 and set up a dial indicator to read movement at "I" on backlash tool. Recheck torque on bearing carrier puller (45 in.-lbs. [5.1 N·m]). Measure forward gear backlash by applying upward pressure and turning drive shaft. Dial indicator should measure 0.010-0.015 inch (0.25-0.38 mm) backlash. Adjust backlash by adding or deleting shims (65—Fig. M17-22). Changing shim thickness by 0.001 inch (0.025 mm) will alter backlash by 0.0015 inch (0.038 mm).

To properly adjust spring tension in shift rod (69), install springs (67) and pin (68) in shift rod. Insert tool 91-86642, or an old pin (59) with a ground-down end, between springs as shown in Fig. M17-25. Tool (T) or pin should be centered in shift rod slot within 1/64 inch (0.397 mm). Adjust tool position by installing washers (66) at ends of springs (67).

Assemble remainder of lower unit by reversing disassembly procedure while noting the following points: Install thrust washer (55—Fig. M17-22) so larger diameter side is nearer reverse gear (56), then press bearing (54) on gear. Lip of inner seal (49) should face in and lip of outer seal (49) should face propeller (out). Install spring clips (58) so bent end of each spring engages the hole in one of the detent pins (60). Spring clips should be wound in opposite directions around dog clutch (61) and must not overlap. Use heavy grease to hold shift cam (36) in cam follower (70) with "UP" side facing up. Be sure "E" ring (22) and circlip (24) are seated on shift shaft (23) before inserting shaft. Tighten

bushing (20) after tightening bearing carrier nut (47). Tighten bearing carrier nut (47) to 210 ft.-lbs. (284 N·m).

Assemble oil seal (10) to seal carrier (9) so spring end of oil seal is toward top of seal carrier. If reusing old impeller (4), install impeller so vanes rotate in same direction as previous operation. Be sure key (5) is properly installed. Tighten water pump screws to 30 in.-lbs. (3.4 N·m).

Do not apply excessive grease to drive shaft splines; there must not be grease on tops of drive shaft or shift shaft. Install splined seal on drive shaft splines with splined seal end towards top of drive shaft, then install remaining seal with small end towards top of drive shaft. Shift lower unit to forward gear and move shift lever on engine to forward gear position. Tighten gearcase fasteners to 40 ft.-lbs. (54 N·m).

POWER TILT/TRIM

FLUID AND BLEEDING. Recommended fluid is SAE 10W-30 or 10W-40. Fill reservoir to "FULL" mark on dipstick with the outboard motor in the full-down position.

Fig. M17-24—Install backlash measuring tool 91-53459 (T) and a dial indicator (D) using a suitable adapter kit (A). Position dial indicator pointer on the "I" line of tool (T). Proceed as outlined in text.

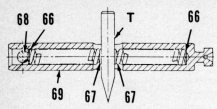

Fig. M17-25—Cross section of shift rod (69). Center tool (T) using washers (66) at ends of springs (67).

The hydraulic circuit is self-bleeding as the tilt/trim system is operated through several cycles. After servicing system, be sure to check reservoir level after filling and operating system.

HYDRAULIC TESTING. The pump can be checked by connecting a 5000 psi (34.5 MPa) test gage alternately to the UP (U – Fig. M17-27) and DOWN (D) pump ports. Note that the pump motor blue wire with white tracer is the positive battery connection to pressurize the UP (U) port and connecting the positive battery lead to the pump motor green wire with white tracer will pressurize the DOWN (D) port. Pressure at the UP (U) port should be 3100-3500 psi (21.4-24.1 MPa) and should not drop lower than 1500 psi (10.3 MPa) after pumping stops. Pressure at the DOWN (D) port should be 1500-1900 psi (10.3-13.1 MPa) and should not drop

lower than 750 psi (5.2 MPa) after pumping stops.

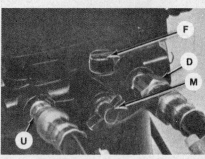

Fig. M17-27—View identifying reservoir fill screw (F), manual release valve (M), up port (U) and down port (D) on power tilt/trim pump.

OUTBOARD MARINE CORPORATION

EVINRUDE MOTORS
4143 N. 27th Street
Milwaukee, Wisconsin 53216

JOHNSON MOTORS
200 Sea-horse Drive
Waukegan, Illinois 60085

EVINRUDE AND JOHNSON
30 AND 35 HP (1976-1986)

EVINRUDE MODELS

Year Produced	30 HP	35 HP
1976..........	....	35602, 35603, *35652, *35653
1977..........	....	35702, 35703, *35752, *35753
1978..........	....	35802, 35803, *35852, *35853
1979..........	....	35902, 35903, *35952, *35953
1980..........	....	35RCS, 35RLCS, *35ECS, *35ELCS
1981..........	....	35RCI, 35RLCI, *35ECI, *35ELCI
1982..........	....	35RCN, 35RLCN, *35ECN, *35ELCN
1983..........	....	35RCT, 35RLCT, *35ECT, *35ELCT, *35TELCT
1984..........	*30ECR, *30ELCR	35RCR, 35RLCR, *35ECR, *35ELCR, *35TELCR
1985..........	30RCO, 30RLCO, *30ECO, *30ELCO, *30TECO, *30TELCO	....
1986..........	30RCD, 30RLCD, *30ECD, *30ELCD, *30TECD, *30TELCD	....

JOHNSON MODELS

Year Produced	30 HP	35 HP
1976...........	....	35602, 35603, *35652, *35653
1977...........	....	35702, 35703, *35752, *35753
1978...........	....	35802, 35803, *35852, *35853
1979...........	....	35902, 35903, *35952, *35953
1980...........	....	35RCS, 35RLCS, *35ECS, *35ELCS
1981...........	....	35RCI, 35RLCI, *35ECI, *35ELCI
1982...........	....	35RCN, 35RLCN, *35ECN, *35ELCN
1983...........	....	35RCT, 35RLCT, *35ECT, *35ELCT, *35TELCT
1984...........	*30ECR, *30ELCR	35RCR, 35RLCR, *35ECR, *35ELCR, *35TELCR
1985...........	30RCO, 30RLCO, *30ECO, *30ELCO, *30TECO, *30TELCO	....
1986...........	30RCD, 30RLCD, *30ECD, *30ELCD, *30TECD, *30TELCD	....

*Electric start models.

CONDENSED SERVICE DATA

TUNE-UP
Hp/rpm 30/4500-5500
              35/5200-5800
Bore...3.000 in.
          (76.2 mm)
Stroke...................................2.250 in.
         (57.15 mm)

Number of Cylinders 2
Displacement ....31.8 cu. in.
         (521 cc)
Spark Plug–Champion:
  1976 ....UL81J
    Electrode Gap ....0.030 in.
         (0.76 mm)

TUNE-UP CONT.

Spark Plug – Champion:
1977-1985 ....QL77J4*
   Electrode Gap ....0.040 in.
     (1.0 mm)
1986 ....QL77JC4*
   Electrode Gap ....0.040 in.
     (1.0 mm)

*A Champion QL78V is recommended for 1985 and 1986 models when used at sustained high speeds. Renew surface gap spark plug if center electrode is more than 1/32 inch (0.79 mm) below the flat surface of the plug end.

Ignition Type:
1976 ....Breaker Point
   Breaker Point Gap........................0.020 in.
     (0.51 mm)
1977-1986 ....CD
Carburetor Make ....Own
Idle Speed (in gear)......................650 rpm
Fuel:Oil Ratio ....50 – 1†

†On 1985 and 1986 models, a 100:1 ratio can be used when Evinrude or Johnson outboard lubricant formulated for 100:1 fuel mix is used.

SIZES – CLEARANCES

Piston Ring End Gap....................0.007-0.017 in.
   (0.18-0.43 mm)

Lower Piston Ring Side Clearance:
1976-1984......................0.0015-0.0040 in.
   (0.038-0.102 mm)
1985-1986 ....0.004 in. Max.
   (0.102 mm)

Piston Skirt Clearance:
1976-1978 ....0.0030-0.0050 in.
   (0.076-0.127 mm)
1979-1982 ....0.0035-0.0065 in.
   (0.089-0.165 mm)
1983-1984 ....0.0024-0.0044 in.
   (0.061-0.118 mm)
Maximum Cylinder Tolerance ....0.003 in.
   (0.076 mm)

Crankshaft Journal Diameters:
Top Main (1976 & 1977)..............1.2495-1.2500 in.
   (31.737-31.750 mm)
  (1978-1986) ....1.2510-1.2515 in.
   (31.775-31.788 mm)
Center Main (1976 & 1977)..........0.9995-1.0000 in.
   (25.387-25.400 mm)
  (1978-1982) ....1.1805-1.1810 in.
   (29.985-29.997 mm)
  (1983-1986) ....1.1833-1.1838 in.
   (30.06-30.07 mm)

SIZES – CLEARANCES CONT.

Bottom Main ....0.9842-0.9846 in.
   (25.00-25.01 mm)
Crankpin ....1.1823-1.1828 in.
   (30.03-30.04 mm)
Crankshaft End Play:
1976-1978 ....0.003-0.011 in.
   (0.08-0.28 mm)
1979-1984 ....0.000-0.025 in.
   (0.000-0.635 mm)
Lower Unit Diametral Clearances –
1976-1984:
  Propeller Shaft to Forward
   Gear Bushing ....0.0010-0.0020 in.
   (0.025-0.051 mm)
  Propeller Shaft to Reverse
   Gear Bushing ....0.0005-0.0015 in.
   (0.013-0.038 mm)
  Bushing to Reverse Gear ....0.0005-0.0020 in.
   (0.013-0.051 mm)

TIGHTENING TORQUES

Connecting Rod ....348-372 in.-lbs.
   (40-42 N·m)
Crankcase Halves:
  Six Main Bearing Screws ....168-192 in.-lbs.
   (19-22 N·m)
  Eight Outer Screws ....60-84 in.-lbs.
   (7-9 N·m)
Cylinder Head ....216-240 in.-lbs.
   (24-27 N·m)
Flywheel...........................100-105 ft.-lbs.
   (136-143 N·m)
Spark Plug ....216-240 in.-lbs.
   (24-27 N·m)
Standard Screws:
  No. 6 ....7-10 in.-lbs.
   (0.8-1.2 N·m)
  No. 8 ....15-22 in.-lbs.
   (1.6-2.4 N·m)
  No. 10 ....25-35 in.-lbs.
   (2.8-4.0 N·m)
  No. 12 ....35-40 in.-lbs.
   (4.0-4.6 N·m)
  ¼ Inch ....60-80 in.-lbs.
   (7-9 N·m)
  5/16 Inch ....120-140 in.-lbs.
   (14-16 N·m)
  ⅜ Inch ....220-240 in.-lbs.
   (24-27 N·m)
  7/16 Inch ....340-360 in.-lbs.
   (38-40 N·m)

LUBRICATION

The power head is lubricated by oil mixed with the fuel. The fuel should be regular leaded or unleaded gasoline with a minimum pump octane rating of 86.

NOTE: On 1981 and later models, the manufacturer permits the above fuel to be used at a minimum pump octane rating of 67.

On models prior to 1985, recommended oil is Evinrude or Johnson 50/1 Lubricant or a BIA certified two-stroke motor oil. The recommended fuel:oil ratio for normal operation and engine break-in is 50:1.

On 1985 and 1986 models, a fuel:oil ratio of 100:1 can be used when Evinrude or Johnson outboard lubricant formulated for 100:1 fuel mix is used. When any other BIA certified two-stroke motor oil is used or during engine break-in, the recommended fuel:oil ratio is 50:1.

The lower unit gears and bearings are lubricated by oil contained in the gearcase. The recommended oil is OMC HI-VIS Gearcase Lube. The gearcase oil level should be checked after every 50 hours of operation and the gearcase should be drained and filled with new oil every 100 hours or once each season, whichever occurs first.

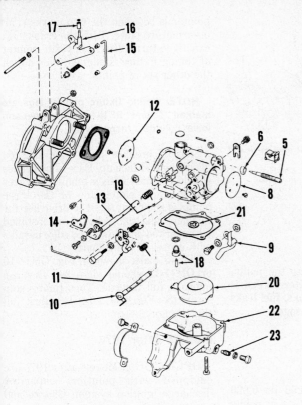

Fig. OM11-1—Exploded view of carburetor typical of all models. Choke components are not used on models after 1983.

5. Idle mixture needle
6. Retainer
8. Choke plate
9. Choke lever
10. Choke shaft
11. Choke bellcrank
12. Throttle plate
13. Throttle shaft
14. Throttle lever
15. Link
16. Follower
17. Follower roller
18. Inlet valve
19. Float pivot
20. Float
21. Nozzle gasket
22. Float chamber
23. Main jet

Fig. OM11-3. Loosen throttle shaft screw (S – Fig. OM11-5), hold throttle closed and retighten screw (S). Check to make certain that throttle begins to open as marks on cam (Fig. OM11-3) pass the follower roller when speed control is advanced. Adjust throttle control rod by shifting unit to forward gear then advance throttle so throttle lever is against cylinder stop. Push throttle control rod (R – Fig. OM11-6) to full open position and move collar (C) so it is against pivot block (B). Tighten collar screw.

The idle speed stop screw (Fig. OM11-7) should be set to provide an idle speed of approximately 650 rpm in forward gear.

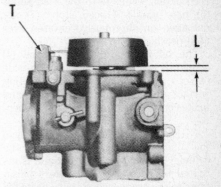

Fig. OM11-2 — Float level (L) should be parallel to carburetor body. Bend float tang (T) to adjust float level.

Fig. OM11-3 — Refer to text when checking the speed control linkage.

The gearcase oil is drained and filled through the same plug port. An oil level (vent) port is used to indicate the full level of the gearcase with oil and to ease oil drainage.

To drain the oil, place the outboard motor in a vertical position. Remove drain plug and oil level plug and allow the lubricant to drain into a suitable container.

To fill the gearcase with oil, place the outboard motor in a vertical position. Add oil through drain plug opening with an oil feeder until the oil begins to overflow from oil level plug port. Reinstall oil level plug with a new gasket, if needed, and tighten. Remove oil feeder, then reinstall drain plug with a new gasket, if needed, and tighten.

FUEL SYSTEM

CARBURETOR. A float type carburetor is used. Refer to Fig. OM11-1. To accurately set idle mixture, turn needle (5) in until it seats lightly, then back out one turn on 1976 models and 1¼ turn on later models. Start and run motor until it reaches normal operating temperature, then turn needle (5) to provide smoothest operation while idling in forward gear. Clockwise rotation of idle mixture needle leans the mixture. High speed mixture is controlled by size of main jet (23). Float should be parallel to carburetor body for correct float level (Fig. OM11-2). Bend tang to adjust float position.

The screws attaching throttle plate (12 – Fig. OM11-1) and choke plate (8) to shafts are staked after installation. Screws must be renewed if removed. Be sure to stake new screws after installing.

Some models prior to 1984 are optionally equipped with an electrically operated choke which uses a solenoid mounted on the carburetor to actuate the choke. To adjust, loosen the mounting band and move solenoid to provide correct operating range.

Models after 1983 use a manual primer system on tiller handle models, and an electric primer system on remote start models.

SPEED CONTROL LINKAGE. The speed control lever rotates the magneto armature plate and the carburetor throttle valve is synchronized to open as ignition timing is advanced. A cam attached to the bottom of the magneto armature plate moves cam follower (16 and 17 – Fig. OM11-1) which opens the throttle plate (12), via link (15) and lever (14). It is very important that the ignition timing and throttle plate opening be correctly synchronized to obtain satisfactory operation.

Before adjusting the speed control linkage, make certain that roller (17) is contacting the cam and that choke linkage is not holding throttle partially open. Turn the speed control grip until the cam follower roller is centered between the two index marks as shown in

Fig. OM11-5—Loosen throttle shaft screw (S) to adjust linkage as outlined in text.

REED VALVES. The reed type inlet valves (6 – Fig. OM11-8) and reed stops (7) are attached to reed plate (5). Reed plate assembly is attached to power head with screw (3).

The reed petals (6) should seat very lightly against reed plate (5) throughout the entire length of reed with the least possible tension. Renew reed petals if broken, cracked, warped or bent. Do not attempt to repair reed petals (6). Seating surface of reed plate (5) must be smooth and flat and reeds must be centered over inlet holes in plate. Alignment recesses are provided at one location for each set of reed petals to assist in centering the reed petals. Make certain that reed stops (7) are not damaged and that stops are centered behind the reed petals. Damage to the reed petals (6) may result if reed stops (7) are damaged or improperly centered over reed petals.

The oil drain valve reed petal (4) should be centered over hole on outside of reed plate. Check petal and seating surface of reed plate (5) carefully and make certain that hole is clean and open.

FUEL PUMP. The diaphragm type fuel pump is mounted on one of the cylinder transfer port covers and is actuated by vacuum and pressure pulsations in the crankcase. Service parts for the pump are not available and damage to the pump can be corrected only by renewing the pump and fuel filter

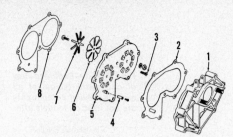

Fig. OM11-8—Exploded view of reed valve and inlet manifold.

1. Inlet manifold
2. Manifold to plate gasket
3. Plate retaining screw
4. Oil drain valve
5. Reed plate
6. Reed petals
7. Reed stop
8. Crankcase to plate gasket

assembly. Before renewing the pump, make certain that fuel filter screen is clean and check for air leaks, fuel leaks or restricted lines and passages.

IGNITION

Models Prior to 1977

Breaker point gap should be 0.020 inch (0.51 mm) and both sets of points should be synchronized so they open exactly 180° apart. The manufacturer provides a timing fixture (OMC part 386635) to be used for adjusting and synchronizing the breaker points. The fixture is installed on crankshaft in place of the flywheel as shown in Fig. OM11-9, and is used in conjunction with a timing light (with battery) or continuity meter.

To synchronize the points using the timing fixture and light, remove flywheel and install timing fixture, making sure it is properly fitted over flywheel key. Disconnect condenser and magneto coil leads from both sets of breaker points. Attach test light or meter to the opening set of breaker points and to a suitable ground. Bulb should light when points are opened. Turn crankshaft until fixture pointer rests midway between the two embossed armature plate timing marks shown in Fig. OM11-9. Adjust the gap until points just open when timing fixture

pointer is between the two marks (TM) on armature plate. Turn the crankshaft exactly ½ turn until the opposite pointer of timing fixture is aligned; then adjust the other set of points.

NOTE: Timing fixture pointer legs are marked "T" and "B" to indicate upper and lower cylinders respectively.

Side of breaker point cam marked "TOP" should face up. Face of coil shoes should be flush with machined surfaces on armature plate. One of the three points is shown at (F). The drive key for flywheel and cam should be installed with marked end down and edge parallel with center of crankshaft.

Timing mark shown in Fig. OM11-10 or OM11-11 should align 34° flywheel mark at full throttle. Turn timing stop screw (S – Fig. OM11-12) to adjust full throttle ignition timing.

Models After 1976

OPERATION. Models after 1976 are equipped with pointless capacitor discharge ignition system. Charge and sensor coils are located under flywheel. Two magnets in flywheel induce a current in the charge coil which is rectified and directed to a capacitor. The two flywheel magnets also induce current in the sensor coil to provide a positive charge on the gate of one of two silicon controlled rectifiers (SCR's). The positive charge opens the SCR and allows the charged capacitor to discharge through the SCR and primary circuit of the ignition coil. The rapid coil

Fig. OM11-6—Collar (C) should touch pivot block (B) when throttle control rod (R) is in full forward position. Refer to text.

Fig. OM11-7—Idle speed stop screw should be set to provide an idle speed of approximately 650 rpm.

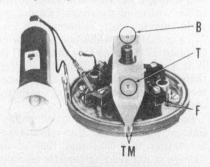

Fig. OM11-9—View showing timing fixture and timing test light attached. Refer to Text for setting breaker point gap.

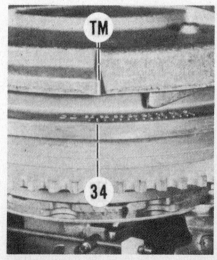

Fig. OM11-10—On manual rewind start models, timing mark (TM) should align with 34° mark on flywheel of 1976 models and 30°-31° degree mark on 1977 and later models. Thirty-four (34) degree mark is identified. Turn screw (S—Fig. OM11-12) to adjust timing.

field buildup induces a secondary voltage which fires the spark plug. The STOP button or key switch shorts the charge coil to ground to prevent capacitor charging thereby preventing ignition. Diodes, SCR's and capacitor are contained in the power pack assembly and are not available individually.

IGNITION TIMING. To check the ignition timing, first mount the outboard motor on a boat or a suitable test tank and immerse the lower unit. Connect a suitable timing light to the top cylinder (No. 1) spark plug lead. Start the engine and adjust the speed control until the engine is running at full throttle. On manual rewind start models, timing mark (TM – Fig. OM11-10) should align with 34° mark on flywheel of 1976 models and 30°-31° mark on 1977 and later models. On electric start models, timing mark (TM – Fig. OM11-11) should align with 34° mark on flywheel of 1976 models and 30°-31° mark on 1977 and later models. To adjust ignition timing on all models, turn timing stop screw (S – Fig. OM11-12). Each complete turn is equivalent to approximately one degree. Turning screw (S) clockwise retards the timing while turning screw counterclockwise advances the timing. Backfiring and popping may be due to improperly connected wiring. Note wiring schematic in Fig. OM11-13.

TROUBLESHOOTING. If ignition malfunction occurs, use the following procedures to determine faulty component. To check charge coil, disconnect four-wire connector and connect an ohmmeter to terminals A and D (Fig. OM11-13) in stator plate lead connector. Renew charge coil if resistance is not

Fig. OM11-12—View of ignition timing adjusting screw.

500-650 ohms. Connect negative ohmmeter lead to stator plate (ground) and positive ohmmeter lead to connector terminal A, then to connector terminal D. Infinite resistance should exist between A terminal and stator plate and D terminal and stator plate. If not, charge coil or charge coil lead is shorting to ground. To check charge coil output, use Merc-O-Tronic Model 781, Stevens Model CD77 or a suitable peak voltage tester. Connect black tester lead to stator lead connector terminal A and red tester lead to terminal D. Turn tester knobs to "NEG (–)" and "500." Crank engine while observing tester. Renew charge coil if meter reads below 230 volts.

To check sensor coil, connect an ohmmeter to terminals B and C in stator plate lead connector. Renew sensor coil if resistance is not 30-50 ohms. Connect negative ohmmeter lead to stator plate (ground) and positive ohmmeter lead to connector terminal B, then to connector terminal C. Infinite resistance should exist between B terminal and stator plate and C terminal and stator plate. If not, sensor coil or sensor coil lead is shorting to ground. To check sensor coil output, use Merc-O-Tronic Model 781, Stevens Model CD77 or a suitable peak voltage tester. Connect black tester lead to stator lead connector terminal C and red tester lead to terminal B. On Merc-O-Tronic Model 781, turn knobs to "POS (+)" and "5" and on Stevens Models CD77, turn knobs to "S" and "5." Crank engine while observing tester. Renew sensor coil if meter reads below 2 volts.

NOTE: Use OMC Coil Locating Ring (Tool 317001) to properly align charge coil and sensor coil on stator plate.

To check power pack output, first reconnect four-wire connector. Use Merc-O-Tronic Model 781, Stevens Model CD77 or a suitable peak voltage tester. Connect black tester lead to a suitable engine ground. Connect red tester lead to wire leading to either ignition coil. Turn tester knobs to "NEG(–)" and "500." Crank engine while observing tester. Repeat test on other lead. Renew power pack if readings are not at least 180 volts or higher.

Renew ignition coil or coils if no other ignition component is found faulty.

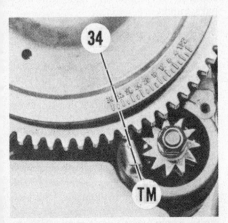

Fig. OM11-11—On electric start models, timing mark (TM) should align with 34° mark on flywheel of 1976 models and 30°-31° degree mark on 1977 and later models. Thirty-four (34) degree mark is identified. Turn screw (S—Fig. OM11-12) to adjust timing.

Fig. OM11-13—Typical wiring schematic of ignition circuit. Electric start models have a key switch in place of STOP button.

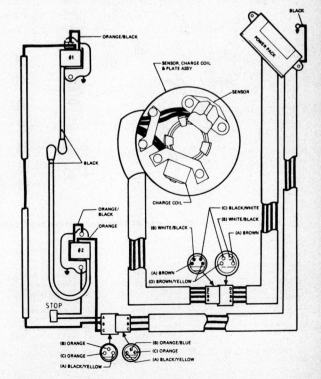

COOLING SYSTEM

A rubber impeller type water pump located around the drive shaft is used to circulate water to the power head.

When cooling system problems are encountered, first check water inlet for plugging or partial stoppage, then if not corrected, check water pump and thermostat.

WATER PUMP. To remove the water pump, refer to the LOWER UNIT section and remove the gearcase assembly. Water pump is located at top of gearcase as shown in Fig. OM11-25. Make certain water passages and tubes are not damaged or plugged. Refer to LOWER UNIT section for installation and assembly instructions.

THERMOSTAT. The thermostat is located behind cylinder head cover (4–Fig. OM11-15) at top of cylinder head. Operating temperature can be checked using "Thermomelt" sticks. With outboard motor operating in forward gear and under 1000 rpm, a 125°F (52°C) stick should melt but not melt a 163°F (73°C) stick for correct normal operating temperature.

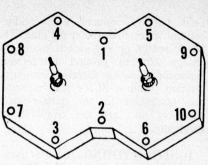

Fig. OM11-16—Cylinder head tightening sequence.

POWER HEAD

R&R AND DISASSEMBLE. It is usually desirable, depending upon work to be done, to remove the rewind starter (electric starter, if so equipped), magneto assembly, carburetor, inlet manifold, reed valves, fuel pump and covers before removing the power head. Remove the port and starboard starter mounting brackets, remove the power head attaching screws then lift power head off.

Unbolt and remove cylinder head (5–Fig. OM11-15), drive the taper aligning pin(s) (43) out of crankcase toward front (carburetor) side of motor. Remove armature support (10) and retainer (11), then unbolt and remove the crankcase front half (44).

NOTE: Two of the crankcase screws are accessible through intake passages in front of crankcase.

If crankcase half is stuck, tap it lightly with a soft hammer. DO NOT pry between crankcase and cylinders.

Pistons, rods and crankshaft are now accessible for removal and overhaul as outlined in the following paragraphs.

When assembling, follow the procedures outlined in the following paragraphs.

ASSEMBLY. Before assembling check all sealing surfaces of crankcase and covers making certain that all sealing surfaces are clean, smooth and flat. Small nicks or burrs may be polished out on a lapping plate, but sealing surfaces **MUST NOT** be lowered.

When reassembling crankcase, make sure mating surfaces of crankcase halves are completely clean and free of old cement, nicks and burrs. On 1976 models, install sealing strips and trim ends to extend approximately 1/32 inch (0.79 mm) into bearing bores, then sparingly apply OMC Adhesive "M" to cylinder half of crankcase only. On models after 1976, apply OMC Gel-Seal II to one crankcase mating surface. Do not use sealers which will harden and

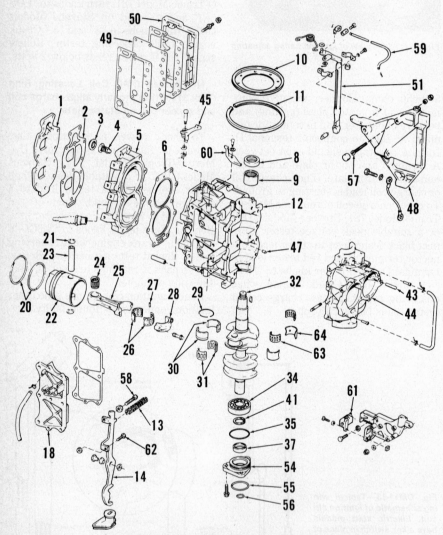

Fig. OM11-15—Exploded view of early model power head. Later models are similar.

1. Cover	21. Retaining rings	35. "O" ring
2. Gasket	22. Piston	37. Lower bearing seal
3. Seal	23. Piston pin	41. Snap ring
4. Thermostat	24. Needle bearing	43. Taper pin
5. Cylinder head	25. Connecting rod	44. Crankcase front half
6. Gasket	26. Bearing cage	45. Lockout assy.
8. Upper seal	27. Roller	47. Bearing retaining
9. Top main bearing	28. Rod cap	dowel
10. Support	29. Retaining ring	48. Starter bracket
11. Retainer	30. Center bearing	49. Exhaust inner cover
12. Cylinder	outer race	50. Outer cover
13. Spring	31. Center main	51. Speed control shaft
14. Shift lock	bearings & cage	54. Seal housing
18. Transfer port cover	32. Crankshaft	55. "O" ring
20. Piston rings	34. Lower main bearing	56. "O" ring

57. Timing adjusting	screw
58. Shifter lock adjusting	screw
59. Throttle control rod	
60. Lockout lever	
61. Electric start safety	switch
62. Safety switch	adjusting screw
63. Bearing	
64. Bearing race	

prevent contact between crankcase mating surfaces. Immediately assemble crankcase halves after applying sealer and position halves by installing locating taper pin; then install and tighten crankcase screws.

Refer to the CONDENSED SERVICE DATA tables for recommended tightening torques. Refer to Fig. OM11-16 for cylinder head bolt tightening sequence. Cylinder head screws should be retightened after motor has been test run and allowed to cool.

PISTONS, RINGS AND CYLINDERS.

Each piston is fitted with two rings. Top piston ring is semi-keystone shaped. If cylinder bore taper or out-of-round exceeds 0.003 inch (0.076 mm), cylinder should be renewed or rebored and fitted with oversize pistons and rings. Pistons and rings are available in 0.030 inch (0.76 mm) oversize. Refer to the CONDENSED SERVICE DATA table for recommended ring end gap, ring side clearance in groove and piston skirt clearance.

On models prior to 1978, one pin boss is press fit while the other is a slip fit. The loose pin boss is marked. When removing piston pin, remove both retaining rings (21 – Fig. OM11-15), heat piston and press pin out toward the tight piston pin boss. Install pin through loose side first. On all models, piston must be assembled to connecting rod with the long tapered side of piston head toward exhaust side of cylinder. And on models so equipped, oil hole (Fig. OM11-17) in connecting rod piston pin end or crankpin end, must face toward top. Thoroughly lubricate all friction surfaces during assembly.

CONNECTING RODS, BEARINGS AND CRANKSHAFT.

Before detaching connecting rods from crankshaft, make sure that rod, cap and piston are marked for correct assembly to each other and in the correct cylinder.

The piston pin end of connecting rod is fitted with needle bearing (24 – Fig. OM11-15) and crankpin end of rod uses split cage (26) and 16 bearing rollers (27). The connecting rod is used as outer race for both bearings. The piston and crankshaft crankpin are used for inner races. Check condition of bearings (24, 26 and 27) and bearing races and renew parts as necessary.

When assembling main bearings and seals to crankshaft on 1977 models, observe the following: Press lower main bearing (34 – Fig. OM11-15) onto crankshaft and install snap ring (41). Position center main bearing cage and rollers (31) around bearing journal, install outer race halves (30) with retaining ring groove toward bottom of crankshaft and hold bearing together with retaining ring (29). Install seal (8) with lip towards engine. Install seal (37) in seal housing (54) with lip towards engine. Be sure bearing (9) dowel pin engages cylinder block hole and cylinder block dowel pin (47) engages bearing race (30) hole when installing crankshaft in cylinder block.

Observe the following when assembling crankshaft components on models after 1977: Press lower main bearing (34) onto crankshaft and install snap ring (41). Install seal (37) in seal housing (54) with lip towards engine. Install seal (8) with lip towards engine. Install center main bearing race (64) with hole over dowel pin (47) and place caged bearing rollers (63) in race. Install crankshaft assembly in cylinder block being sure bearing (9) dowel pin is aligned with notch in cylinder block

mating surface. Install bearing (63) and race (64) being sure races (64) are properly mated.

When assembling connecting rods to crankpins, make certain of the following: all bearing rollers are installed in each rod; oil hole (Fig. OM11-17), if so equipped, is toward top; intake side of piston is toward transfer ports in cylinder and match marks (M) on rod and cap is aligned. Joint between connecting rod and cap is fractured and not machined. With the correct cap installed and properly aligned, the separation line between rod and cap should be nearly invisible. On 1985 and later models equipped with precision ground rods, OMC Alignment Fixture 396749 is recommended to properly align connecting rod with rod cap during tightening of connecting rod screws.

NOTE: Precision ground rods are identified by grind marks running ACROSS corners on ears of connecting rod and rod cap.

Coat all friction surfaces with oil while assembling. Refer to the CONDENSED SERVICE DATA table for recommended tightening torques. Refer to the ASSEMBLY paragraphs when joining the crankcase halves.

MANUAL STARTER

Fig. OM11-19 shows an exploded view of manual rewind starter typical of the type used on all models. When installing a new starter cord or spring, invert the removed starter assembly in a vise and wind the spring by turning the starter pulley counterclockwise until spring is completely wound. Reverse the pulley one turn and install the cord.

The starter is designed with an oval pulley (4), and a single pawl (7) which engages the flywheel at one of two points to apply additional leverage when pistons are passing over compression. The pawl (7) is extended and retracted by friction drag of spring (5) on a groove in spindle (9), whenever starter rope is pulled. Check to see that pawl does not bind, and properly extends when starter rope is released. Timing is automatic if unit is properly assembled.

To disassemble the starter, remove starter handle and allow recoil spring to completely unwind in housing. Remove pawl (7), links (6) and friction spring (5) as a unit. Remove the spindle screw and spindle (9), then carefully withdraw pulley (4) leaving recoil spring (3) in housing. When reassembling make sure recoil spring is installed as shown.

On models prior to 1981, turn screw (58 – Fig. OM11-15) so there is 0.03-0.06 inch gap between lockout lever (45) and

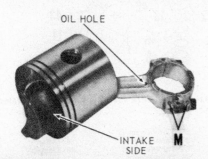

Fig. OM11-17—The piston and connecting rod must be assembled to each other with sharp deflector toward inlet side of cylinder. And on models so equipped, oil hole in connecting rod piston pin end or crankpin end, must face towards top. Match marks (M) on rod and cap must be aligned.

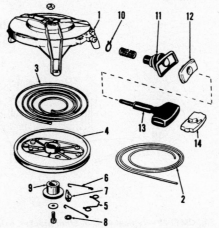

Fig. OM11-19—Exploded view of manual rewind starter typical of the type used on all models. Late type starters are equipped with two drive pawls (7). A spring washer, friction ring, friction plate, shim and bushing are located between spindle (9) and pulley (4) on later models.

1. Housing	8. Retainer
2. Rope	9. Spindle
3. Recoil spring	10. Clamp
4. Pulley	11. Cover
5. Spring	12. Cover
6. Link	13. Handle
7. Pawl	14. Anchor

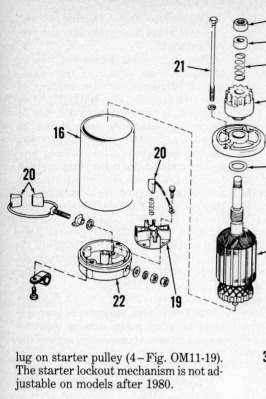

Fig. OM11-21—Exploded view of electric starter motor.

1. Stop nut
2. Pinion stop
3. Antidrift spring
7. Drive pinion
12. Head assy.
13. Thrust washer
15. Armature
16. Frame
19. Brush holder
20. Brush
21. Through-bolt

screw lower screw in shift rod connector (17–Fig. OM11-25). On models after 1979, detach water inlet screens (22–Fig. OM11-26) on both gearcase sides and unscrew upper shift rod connector (56). Note that keeper (57) under connector (56) may be dislodged when gearcase is removed. Unscrew fasteners retaining gearcase to exhaust housing and separate gearcase from exhaust housing.

To install gearcase, reverse removal procedure. Coat drive shaft splines with OMC Sea-Lube Moly Lube or equivalent but do not apply lubricant to end of shaft or drive shaft may not fully engage engine crankshaft. Coat gearcase retaining screws with sealing compound.

lug on starter pulley (4–Fig. OM11-19). The starter lockout mechanism is not adjustable on models after 1980.

ELECTRIC STARTER

Electric start models are equipped with the electric starter motor shown in Fig. OM11-21. Renew any components which are damaged or excessively worn.

All electric start models are equipped with a neutral safety switch which prevents electric starter usage except when outboard is in neutral. On models prior to 1981, turn adjusting screw (62–Fig. OM11-15) so engine will start in neutral but not in forward or reverse. On models after 1980, adjust position of neutral start switch, located adjacent to shift control, so engine will start in neutral but not in forward or reverse.

Starter no load test specifications should be as follows: With 12 volts applied to motor, maximum current draw should be 30 amps and motor speed should be 6500-7500 rpm.

LOWER UNIT

PROPELLER AND HUB. Protection for propeller and drive unit is provided by a cushioning hub built into the propeller. Service consists of propeller renewal if hub is damaged.

REMOVE AND REINSTALL. If water pump or gearcase service is required, remove engine cover and disconnect four wire connector. Drain lubricant and remove propeller if gearcase disassembly is necessary. On models prior to 1980 remove exhaust housing side cover (10–Fig. OM11-22) and un-

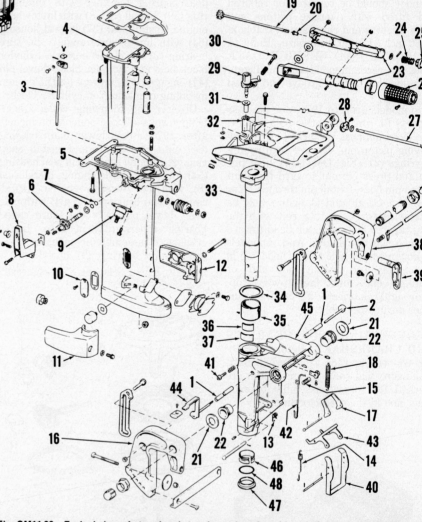

Fig. OM11-22—Typical view of stern bracket, exhaust housing, drive shaft housing and associated parts.

1. Bushings	26. Throttle grip	37. Plate
2. Tilt cam	27. Throttle shaft	38. Stern bracket
3. Shift rod	28. Throttle pinion	39. Clamp
4. Exhaust plate	29. Throttle gear	40. Link
5. Exhaust housing	30. Idle speed adjusting	41. Friction adjusting
6. Shifter shaft	screw	screw
7. "O" rings	31. Bushing	42. Link
8. Shift handle	32. Steering bracket	43. Link
9. Rubber mount	33. Pilot shaft	44. Tilt lever
10. Cover plate	34. Thrust washer	45. Swivel bracket
11. Lower mount	35. Liner	46. Bushing
12. Lower mount	36. Spacer	47. Thrust washer
13. Spring		48. "O" ring
14. Spring		
15. Spring		
16. Stern bracket		
17. Reverse lock		
18. Spring		
19. Throttle shaft		
20. Bushing		
21. Washer		
22. Bushing		
23. Steering handle		
24. Spring		
25. Friction block		

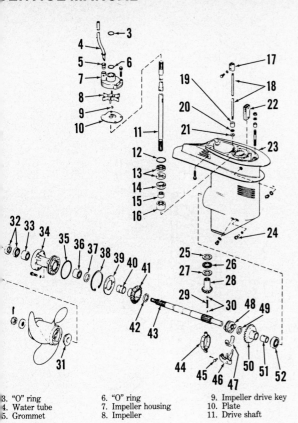

12. "O" ring
13. Seals
14. Bearing housing
15. Bearing
16. Bearing
17. Shift rod connector
18. Shift rod
19. Shift rod bushing
20. "O" ring
21. Washer
22. Intake screen
23. Gearcase
24. Pivot pin
25. Thrust washer
26. Thrust bearing
27. Thrust washer
28. Pinion gear
29. Spring
30. Detent balls
31. Thrust bearing
32. Seals
33. Bearing
34. Bearing housing
35. "O" ring
36. Bearing
37. Thrust washer
38. Snap ring
39. Retainer
40. Bushing
41. Reverse gear
42. Thrust washer
43. Propeller shaft
44. Shift yoke
45. Pin
46. Shift lever
47. Collar
48. Dog clutch
49. Thrust washer
50. Forward gear
51. Bushing
52. Bearing

3. "O" ring
4. Water tube
5. Grommet
6. "O" ring
7. Impeller housing
8. Impeller
9. Impeller drive key
10. Plate
11. Drive shaft

Check shift mechanism to be sure gearcase and shift control lever are synchronized. On models prior to 1981, place shift control lever in neutral and make certain that propeller turns freely. Rotate propeller by hand while moving shift handle slowly in each direction to the point where lower unit dog clutch engages gears. Mark shift handle location on shroud at point of engagement. Travel should be same distance each side of neutral position to point of engagement. If not, loosen clamp screw and adjustment screw, then move shift handle as required and retighten screws. There should be 0.03-0.06 inch (0.76-1.52 mm) gap (G–Fig. OM11-28) between shift lock (14–Fig. OM11-15) and stop on stator plate retainer with unit in reverse. Install spacers between shift control lever (8–Fig. OM11-22) and shifter shaft (6) to obtain desired gap.

Adjust shift mechanism on models after 1980 by adjusting shift control lever position so neutral in gearcase is synchronized with neutral on shift control detent plate.

WATER PUMP. Refer to previous section and remove gearcase. Unscrew pump housing screws and lift up pump housing (7–Fig. OM11-25 or Fig. OM11-26) and impeller (8) while holding drive shaft down. Remove and inspect remainder of water pump components.

To assemble water pump, apply OMC Adhesive "M" or equivalent to grommet (5) and install in pump housing. Apply GE Adhesive Sealant RTV or equivalent to bottom of impeller plate (10). Be sure sealant does not adhere to top of impeller plate. Install impeller key (9) on models prior to 1985 and drive cam on models after 1984. Drive cam must be installed with flat side against drive shaft and sharp edge pointing in a clockwise direction when viewed from crankshaft end of drive shaft. Install impeller (8). Lightly oil impeller tips and turn drive shaft clockwise while installing impeller housing. Apply sealing compound to impeller housing screws.

GEARCASE. Note: If OMC special tools are not used, exact position of seals and bearings should be noted during disassembly.

Remove water pump as previously outlined and withdraw drive shaft. Remove screws which retain housing (34–Fig. OM11-25 or Fig. OM11-26), then use OMC tool 378103 or other suitable puller to withdraw bearing housing (34) from gearcase. Remove snap ring (38) and retainer plate (39). Unscrew and remove shift rod (18). Remove shift yoke (44) and unscrew pivot pin (24). Withdraw propeller shaft assembly. Remove shift lever (46), pinion gear (28), thrust bearing (26),

thrust washers (25 and 27), forward gear (50) and bearing (52). Using a suitable puller, remove seals (13), bearing (15) and bearing and seal housing (14). Drive bearing or bearings (16) into propeller shaft cavity of gearcase and remove. Use a suitable puller to remove shift rod washer (21), "O" ring (20) and bushing (19). Remove "O" ring (55–Fig. OM11-26) on models after 1979. Using suitable pullers, remove bearing (52–Fig. OM11-25 or Fig. OM11-26) cup from gearcase and seals (32) and bearings (33 and 36) from bearing housing (34).

Inspect components for excessive wear or damage. Chipped or excessively rounded engagement surfaces of dog clutch dog (48) or gears (41 and 50) may cause shifting malfunction. Be sure gearcase and exhaust housing mating surfaces are flat and free of nicks.

To reassemble gearcase proceed as follows: Use OMC Gasket Sealing Compound or equivalent around outside of seals. Lubricate bearings, shafts and gears with recommended lubricant before assembly. Install shift rod washer (21), "O" ring (20) and bushing (19) using OMC Tool 304515. Install "O" ring (55–Fig. OM11-26) on models after 1979. Install pinion bearing or bearings (16–Fig. OM11-25 or Fig. OM11-26) into gearcase to correct depth with letter end of bearing up. OMC Tool 391257 can be used when assembled with correct spacer to install pinion bearing or bearings. Pinion bearing is at correct depth when plate bottoms against gearcase. Press bearing (15) into housing (14) so bearing is flush with housing. Using OMC Tool 322923, drive housing (14) into gearcase until plate bottoms against gearcase. Install seals (13) back-to-back in housing (14). Drive bearing (33) into bearing housing (34) with OMC Tool 321429 until tool abuts housing. Install seals (32) so inner seal lip is towards inside of bearing housing and outer seal lip is towards outside of housing. Drive bearing (36) into bearing housing with OMC Tool 321428 until tool abuts housing. Install bearing and cap (52) in gearcase. Place lower thrust washer (27) on pinion gear (28) with inner bevel towards gear. Install thrust bearing (26) and thrust washer (25) on pinion gear (28). External bevel on thrust washer (25) should be toward top of gearcase. Install pinion gear assembly in gearcase. Install forward gear (50), thrust washer (49)–models so equipped and shift lever (46) in gearcase. Place detent spring (29) and detent balls (30) in propeller shaft (43) and slide dog clutch (48) with groove towards propeller end of shaft onto shaft while making sure detent grooves in dog clutch are aligned with detent balls. Grease cradle (47) and

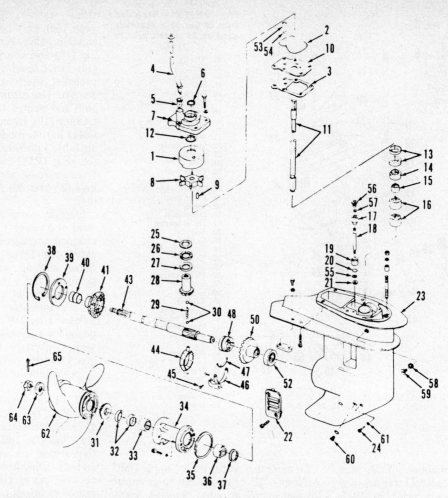

Fig. OM11-26 — Exploded view of gearcase assembly used on models after 1979. Shims (42 and 49 — Fig. OM11-25) are used on models prior to 1984. One bearing (16) is used on models prior to 1984. A gasket in place of seal (2) is used on models prior to 1983. An impeller key is used instead of drive cam (9) on models prior to 1985.

1. Liner
2. Seal
3. Gasket
4. Water tube
5. Grommet
6. "O" ring
7. Impeller housing
8. Impeller
9. Drive cam
10. Plate
11. Drive shaft

13. Seals
14. Bearing housing
15. Bearing
16. Bearings
17. Nut
18. Shift rod
19. Bushing
20. "O" ring
21. Washer
22. Water inlet screen

23. Gearcase
24. Pivot pin
25. Thrust washer
26. Thrust bearing
27. Thrust washer
28. Pinion gear
29. Spring
30. Detent balls
31. Spacer
32. Seals

33. Bearing
34. Bearing housing
35. "O" ring
36. Bearing
37. Thrust washer
38. Snap ring
39. Retainer
40. Bushing
41. Reverse gear
42. Propeller shaft

44. Shift yoke
45. Pin
46. Shift lever
47. Cradle
48. Dog clutch
50. Forward gear
52. Bearing
53. Bushing
54. "O" ring
55. "O" ring

56. Connector
57. Keeper
58. Gasket
59. Level plug
60. Drain plug
61. "O" ring
62. Propeller & drive hub
63. Spacer
64. Nut
65. Cotter pin

install on dog clutch (48). Install propeller shaft and dog clutch assembly in gearcase with slots in cradle (47) facing shift lever (46). Engage shift lever (46) fingers in cradle slots. Install thrust washers (42), models so equipped, and reverse gear (41).

Install shift yoke (44) with open end of hook towards gears and engage hook with shift lever pin (45). Thread shift rod (18) into yoke (44). Install pivot pin (24)

in shift lever (46) hole by moving shift rod (18). Remainder of assembly is evident after inspection of unit and referral to Fig. OM11-25 or Fig. OM11-26. On models after 1984, install drive cam (9 – Fig. OM11-26) with flat side against drive shaft and sharp edge pointing in a clockwise direction when viewed from crankshaft end of drive shaft. Install water pump, attach gearcase to exhaust housing and fill gearcase with lubricant.

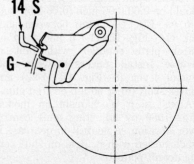

Fig. OM11-28 — Gap (G) should be 0.03-0.06 inch (0.76-1.52 mm) between shift lock (14) and stop (S) on stator plate retainer. Refer to text.

EVINRUDE AND JOHNSON

33 & 40 HP (1969-1976)

EVINRUDE Year Produced	33 HP	40 HP
1969	33902, 33903, 33952, 33953	40902, 40903, 40952, 40953, 40972, 40973
1970	33002, 33003, 33052, 33053	40002, 40003, 40052, 40053, 40072, 40073
1971	....	40102, 40103, 40152, 40153
1972	....	40202, 40203, 40252, 40253
1973	....	40304, 40305, 40354, 40355
1974	....	40404, 40405, 40454, 40455
1975	....	40504, 40505, 40554, 40555
1976	....	40604, 40605, 40654, 40655

JOHNSON Year Produced	33 HP	40 HP
1969	33R69, 33E69	40R69, 40E69, 40ES69
1970	33R70, 33E70	40R70, 40E70, 40E70
1971	....	40R71, 40RL71, 40E71, 40EL71
1972	....	40R72, 40RL72, 40E72, 40EL72
1973	....	40R73, 40RL73, 40E73, 40EL73
1974	....	40R74, 50RL74, 40E74, 40EL74
1975	....	40R75, 40RL75, 40E75, 40EL75
1976	....	40R76, 40RL76, 40E76, 40EL76

CONDENSED SERVICE DATA

TUNE-UP	33 HP	40 HP
Hp/rpm	33/4500	40/4500
Bore – Inches	3-1/16	3-3/16
Stroke – Inches	2¾	2¾
Number of Cylinders	2	2
Displacement – Cu. In.	40.5	43.9
Spark Plug:		
Champion	J4J	J4J**
Auto-Lite	A21X	....
AC	M42K	....
Electrode Gap	0.030	0.030
Magneto:		
Point Gap	0.020	0.020
Carburetor:		
Make	Own	Own
Fuel:Oil Ratio	50:1	50:1

SIZES – CLEARANCES	33 HP	40 HP
Piston Rings:		
End Gap	0.007-0.017	0.007-0.017
Side Clearance (1969-1970)	0.0045-0.007	0.002-0.0045
Side Clearance (1971-1976)	....	0.0015-0.004
Piston Skirt Clearance	0.003-0.0045	0.003-0.005
Crankshaft Bearing Diameters:		
Top Main Bearing	1.2495-1.250	1.4974-1.4979#
Center Main Bearing	0.9995-1.000	1.3748-1.3752#
Bottom Main Bearing	0.9995-1.000	1.1810-1.1815#
Crankpin	1.1823-1.1828	1.1823-1.1828
Crankshaft End Play	0.007-0.011	0.003-0.011

TIGHTENING TORQUES
(All Values In Inch-Pounds Unless Noted)

	33 HP	40 HP
Connecting Rod	348-372	348-372
Crankcase Halves:		
Center Screws	162-168	162-168
Flange Screws	150-170	150-170
Cylinder Head	168-192	168-192
Inlet Manifold	24-36	24-36
Exhaust Manifold	60-84	60-84
Flywheel (Ft.-Lbs.)	100-105	100-105
Spark Plug	240-246	240-246

**Champion L4J is used in 1974, 1975 and 1976 models.
\#Crankshaft bearing diameters on 40 hp models prior to 1974 are same as 33 hp models.

LUBRICATION

The power head is lubricated by oil mixed with the fuel. Use 1/6 pint of BIA certified TC-W outboard oil with each gallon of unleaded or low lead gasoline with octane rating on pump greater than 85 octane. Mix oil and gasoline thoroughly, using a separate container, before pouring mixture into fuel tank.

The lower unit of gears and bearings are lubricated by oil contained in the gearcase. Special OMC Sea-Lube Premium Blend Gearcase Lube should be used. This lubricant is supplied in a tube and filling procedures are as follows: Remove lower plug from gear case and attach tube. Remove upper (vent) plug from case and, with motor in an upright position, fill gearcase until lubricant reaches level of upper (vent) plug hole. Reinstall vent plug, then remove lubricant tube and reinstall lower plug. Tighten both plugs securely, using new gaskets if necessary, to assure a water-tight seal. Lower gear lubricant should be maintained at level of vent plug, and drained and renewed every 100 hours of operation or once a year.

FUEL SYSTEM

CARBURETOR. The carburetor used on 33 hp models is provided with both high speed and idle speed mixture adjustment needles. Inital setting is 3/8-1/4 turn open for the high speed needle (26–Fig. OM12-4) and 1¼ turns open for the idle mixture needle (20). Knob (23) and lever (25) must be disconnected before adjusting the mixture needles. The high speed needle must be adjusted to provide best operation at high speed

Fig. OM12-2—Idle speed stop screw (I) is located on port side of front motor cover on some 40 hp models. Refer also to Figs. OM12-1, OM12-2A, OM12-2B and OM12-2C.

(in forward gear) before adjusting the idle mixture needle. After needles are adjusted, attach knob (23) and lever (25) so that both knobs (22 and 23) are pointing up. Idle speed stop screw (I–Fig. OM12-1) should be adjusted to provide 650 rpm at minimum speed in forward gear.

The carburetor used on 40 hp models is provided with a 0.064 inch main jet (26A–Fig. OM12-5) on early models and a 0.067 inch main jet on later models. Initial setting for the idle mixture needle (20) is approximately 1-1/8 turns open. Adjustment is accomplished in forward gear after knob (23) is removed. After needle is adjusted, attach knob (23) so that it points up. Idle speed stop screw is located at (I–Fig. OM12-1, OM12-2, OM12-2A, OM12-2B or OM12-2C). Idle speed should be 650 rpm in forward gear.

To set the carburetor float level, remove the carburetor, then remove and invert the throttle body (5–Fig. OM12-4 or OM12-5) with float installed. With body inverted, nearest surface of float should be parallel and flush with gasket surface of carburetor body. If it is not, carefully bend float lever; then check after reassembly to be sure float does not stick or bind.

Fig. OM12-1—Idle speed screw (I) is located on throttle control gear on 33 hp and 40 hp (1972-1975) models.

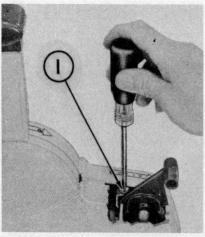

Fig. OM12-2A—On some 40 hp models, the idle speed stop screw (I) is located as shown in the remote control unit.

Fig. OM12-2B—On some late 40 hp motors, the idle speed stop screw (I) is located above the carburetor as shown.

To adjust the electric choke on 33 hp models so equipped, refer to Fig. OM12-6. Loosen band (A) securing solenoid housing to float chamber and pull out manual choke control until choke is fully closed. Push solenoid housing through band in direction indicated by arrow, until plunger bottoms in housing; then tighten band (A). Open the manual choke and check to see that choke operates properly when choke button is pressed.

On models with hot-air actuated automatic choke, a heat exchanger unit is built into the outer exhaust cover shown in Fig. OM12-7, and a vacuum passage (P – Fig. OM12-5) is built into carburetor body, gasket and intake manifold. When the engine is running, manifold vacuum draws air through the intake passage (11 – Fig. OM12-7) into the heat exchanger, then through the air transfer tube (10) to the choke housing, where engine heat controls the tension of the bimetal choke spring. The degree of choking action can be adjusted by loosening the three screws which secure cover (39 – Fig. OM12-5) to choke housing (41), then turning over counterclockwise to decrease choke action, or clockwise to increase choking. Service in addition to choke adjustment consists of making sure passages are kept open and clean and/or renewing choke parts. The air passage in manifold (at passage P – Fig. OM12-5) should be 0.020 and can be checked with a #76 drill.

NOTE: Do not enlarge hole.

In addition to the hot-air actuated bi-metal unit, the automatic choke contains a solenoid unit (32, 33, 34, 37, 43 and 44) which fully closes choke when key is turned to "START" position and returns

control to the bimetal strip when key is released to "ON" position. A toggle switch is locted on the control panel (adjacent to the key switch) which permits manual interruption of the solenoid circuit and thus prevents over-choking when attempting to start a warm motor. Service on the solenoid consists of checking the circuit and renewal of malfunctioning units. Make certain that plunger (33) moves freely in solenoid coil (34).

NOTE: Do not lubricate plunger or solenoid coil, because this will later cause plunger to stick. The solenoid coil (34) should have a resistance of 3 ohms.

SPEED CONTROL LINKAGE. The

carburetor throttle valve is synchronized to open as the ignition timing is advanced. It is important that ignition timing and throttle valve opening be checked and adjusted, if necessary.

To check the linkage, refer to Fig. OM12-8. Remove upper motor cover and move speed control lever until index on armature cam is aligned with index pointer on intake manifold as shown. With index marks aligned, all slack should be removed from throttle linkage with throttle plate just beginning to move from closed position. On 33 hp models, adjust by loosening the clamp screw (A – Inset), and turning the Nylon eccentric bushing (B) until slack is removed and throttle shaft just begins to move. On 40 hp models, adjust by

1. Throttle plate
2. Throttle shaft
3. Spring
4. Choke detent spring
5. Throttle body
6. Lever
7. Bellcrank
8. Spring
9. Choke shaft
10. Gasket
11. Fuel inlet valve
12. Float
13. Pivot pin
14. Nozzle
15. Float chamber
16. Choke rod
17. Choke plate
18. Packing
19. Nut
20. Idle mixture needle
21. Control panel
22. Knob
23. Knob
24. Link
25. Lever
26. High speed mixture needle
27. Nut
28. Packing
29. Stud
30. Choke bellcrank
31. Cover
32. Spring
33. Plunger
34. Solenoid cell
35. Clamp
36. Choke link

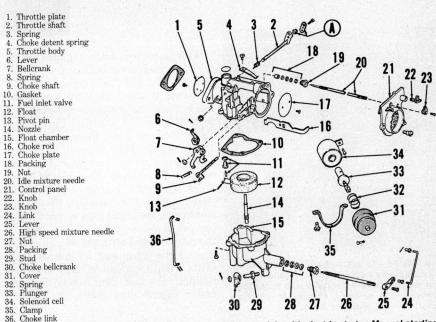

Fig. OM12-4—Exploded view of carburetor used on 33 hp models with electric starter. Manual starting models are similar except choke solenoid (29 through 36) is not used.

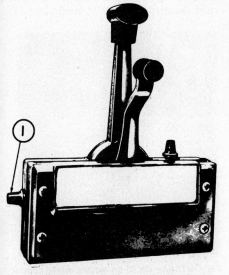

Fig. OM12-2C – On some control units, the idle speed stop screw (I) is located as shown.

Fig. OM12-5—Exploded view of carburetor and associated parts used on electric starting, 40 hp models. Hot air actuated choke and solenoid are not used on manual start models. Refer to Fig. OM12-4 for legend except for the following:

 A. Throttle arm
 B. Clamp screw
 P. Vacuum port
 26A. High speed jet
 27A. Plug
 37. Spring
 38. Air-transfer tube
 39. Cover
 40. Gasket
 41. Body
 42. Lever
 43. Washer
 44. Spring guide
 45. Sleeve

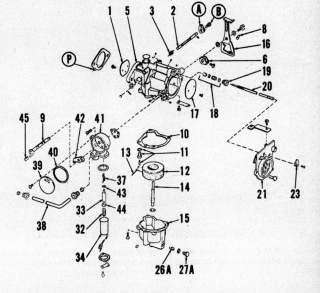

loosening clamp screw (B-Fig. OM12-8A) and moving throttle arm (A). On all models, retighten clamp screw when adjustment is correct.

All models are equipped with a fuel-saver linkage which permits partial throttle opening with full magneto advance. The linkage includes a spring which allows speed control lever to move in a slot after the armature plate reaches full advance position. Movement of the speed control after reaching full ignition advance, continues to open the carburetor throttle. To adjust the linkage first rotate the armature plate until plate contacts stop.

NOTE: Do not move the speed control linkage, rotate the armature plate only.

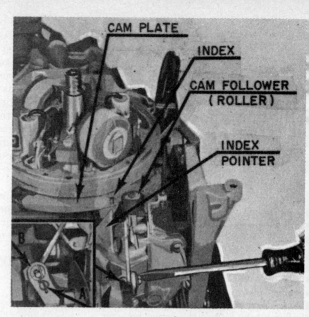

Fig. OM12-8 — On 33 hp motors, speed control linkage is adjusted by loosening clamp screw (A-inset) and turning eccentric bushing (B). Method of control is similar on all models. Refer to text.

Fig. OM12-6 — To adjust the choke solenoid on 33 hp motors so equipped, loosen band (A), pull out manual choke linkage and with choke fully closed, push solenoid housing in direction shown by arrow.

With advance plate against stop, measure clearance between moveable stop (C-Fig. OM12-10) and pivot (P). If clearance is not 1/32 inch, loosen the clamp screw in the moveable stop and reposition on the link (L). Tighten the clamp screw to retain the moveable stop 1/32 inch from pivot (P).

Electric starting models are equipped with a safety switch (22-Fig. OM12-11) which prevents starter actuation at wide-open throttle. To adjust the switch, disconnect the white lead at switch and connect a continuity meter or light to the disconnected terminal on switch and ground the other lead to bracket (21). With armature plate in fully retarded position, the test light should light or meter should show continuity. Slowly

move armature plate in direction indicated by arrow (advance direction) until the point where continuity is broken as indicated by meter or light. When continuity is broken, distance (D) between shifter lock bracket and cast stop on cylinder should measure 7/32-9/32 inch; if it does not, loosen clamp screw (A) and reposition bracket (21) and switch (22) until distance (D) is correct.

INLET REED VALVES. Two sets of reed valves (2-Fig. OM12-12) are used; one for each cylinder. Reed valve plate (1) is located between intake manifold and the power head crankcase, and should be checked whenever carburetor is removed for service. Reed petals (2) should seat very lightly against reed plate (1) throughout their entire length with the least possible tension. Do not attempt to straighten a bent reed or bend a reed in order to modify performance; always renew a bent or damaged reed. Seating surface of reed plate (1)

Fig. OM12-7 — On models with hot-air actuated automatic choke, a heat exchanger is inside the exhaust cover (4) and air is drawn through transfer tube (10) to choke housing. Make sure inlet port (11) is not plugged.

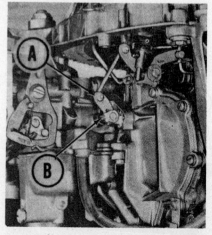

Fig. OM12-8A — On 40 hp motors, speed control linkage is adjusted by loosening clamp screw (B) and moving throttle arm (A),

should be smooth and flat and reed petals should be centered over ports. Reed stop (3) must center over reed petals.

FUEL PUMP. The diaphragm type fuel pump (Fig. OM12-13) is available only as an assembly which also contains the fuel filter (4 through 7). If fuel pump troubles are encountered, first remove and clean the filter (5) and check to be sure fuel lines are open and clean. If trouble is not corrected, renew the fuel pump assembly.

RECIRCULATING VALVE. Late model motors are equipped with a fuel

Fig. OM12-10— *When adjusting the fuel saver linkage, refer to text. The movable stop and the clamp screw on early models are shown at (C). Later models are similar.*

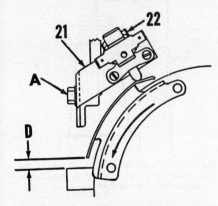

Fig. OM12-11— *Schematic view of safety switch and actuating linkage which interrupts starter current at fast throttle.*

A. Cap screw
D. Adjustment (see text)
21. Bracket
22. Switch

recirculating valve (Fig. OM12-14A). The recirculating valve allows liquid fuel or oil which may gather in the crankcase at slow operating speeds to be drawn back into the engine at the transfer port covers. Small passages in the bottom of each crankcase lead to the recirculating valve location at the bottom of the power head. Any condensed liquid accumulates in the bleed pocket and passage until the piston travels its downward stroke, when crankcase pressure forces the check valve off its seat and feeds the liquid back into the transfer cover of the same cylinder.

When engine is overhauled, passages to recirculating valve should be blown out with compressed air. Clean any accumulated gum or varnish from valve with solvent. Make certain that hoses to transfer covers are installed as per instructions on recirculating valve body.

CRANKCASE BLEEDER VALVE. All motors not equipped with a recirculating valve are equipped with a crankcase bleed valve as shown in Fig. OM12-14. The bleeder valve is designed to remove any liquid fuel or oil which might build up in crankcase, thus providing smoother operation at all speeds and lessening the possibility of spark plug fouling during slow-speed operation. There is a small passage leading

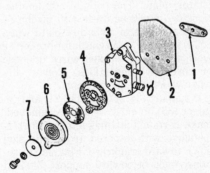

Fig. OM12-13—*Typical diaphragm type fuel pump showing filter exploded. Component parts of pump (3) are not serviced.*

1. Gasket
2. Plate
3. Fuel pump
4. Gasket
5. Filter
6. Cover
7. Washer

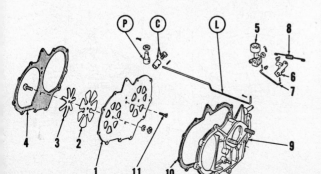

Fig. OM12-12—*Exploded view of the inlet reed valves, manifold and throttle linkage. Screw (11) attaches reed plate to crankcase. Economizer linkage (C, L & P) are shown in Fig. OM12-10.*

1. Reed plate
2. Reed petals
3. Stop
4. Gasket
5. Cam roller
6. Bellcrank
7. Link
8. Spring
9. Inlet manifold
10. Gasket

from the bottom of each crankcase to the bleeder valve location, at bottom of power head. Any condensed liquid accumulates in the bleeder pocket and passage until the piston travels its downward stroke, when crankcase pressure forces bleeder valve off its seat

Fig. OM12-14—*The crankcase bleeder valve may be serviced without disassembly of power head after removing the valve cover plate.*

1. Gasket
2. Screen retainer
3. Screen
4. Valve plate
5. Valve leaf
6. Leaf stop
7. Gasket
8. Cover plate

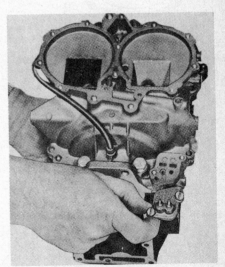

Fig. OM12-14A—*A recirculating valve is fitted to all late model 40 hp motors. Condensed liquid (gas or oil) is fed back into engine instead of overboard.*

and blows the accumulated liquid into the exhaust passage. When engine is overhauled, bleeder passages should be blown out with compressed air. Valve leaf petals should exert a slight pressure against seating surface of crankcase. Seating surface should be smooth and flat. Renew any parts which are badly worn, broken or otherwise damaged.

IGNITION

Breaker point gap should be 0.020 and both sets of points must be adjusted to open exactly 180° apart. Adjustment or inspection of points requires removal of flywheel.

The recommended method of breaker point adjustment and synchronization requires the use of a special timing fixture (OMC Part No. 378966 for models prior to 1974 or Part No. 386635 for later models) as shown in Fig. OM12-15, and a timing test light or continuity meter. To adjust the points using the special tools, first remove flywheel and disconnect the leads from both sets of points. Install the timing fixture and turn the crankshaft until either pointer is centered between the embossed timing marks (TM) on armature plate as shown. Attach the timing test light or meter to the insulated terminal of the opening set of points and to a suitable ground. Loosen the breaker point anchor screw and turn the adjusting screw until points are closed as indicated by the timing test light or meter; then, turn adjusting screw in the opposite direction until points barely open. Tighten the anchor screw and recheck by turning crankshaft, to be sure points open when timing pointer is midway between embossed timing marks (TM). Turn crankshaft ½ turn until opposite leg of timing fixture is properly aligned with timing marks, attach timing test light to the other set of points and adjust by following the same procedure.

Use Fig. OM12-16 or OM12-16A as a guide for overhaul of magneto armature (stator) plate. The ends of coil laminations (9) should be flush with machined mounting pads of armature plate when coil is installed. Also check for broken or worn insulation, broken wires or loose or corroded connections. Renew any parts which are questionable.

If support (34 – Fig. OM12-21) and retainer (33) on early models is removed, make certain that magneto retainer is installed with tapered (rounded) side down toward crankcase. Flat side of retainer must be toward support (34) and magneto armature plate.

When installing the flywheel, make sure that mating surfaces of flywheel and crankshaft are completely free from dirt, oil or grease. Remove any nicks or burrs which might interfere with flywheel seating. Outer edge of flywheel key must be parallel with centerline of crankshaft as shown in Fig. OM12-17 (not parallel with crankshaft taper). Tighten the flywheel retaining nut to a torque of 100-105 ft.-lbs.

AUTOMATIC CUT-OUT SWITCH. All motors are equipped with a vacuum actuated cut-out (overspeed) switch (S – Fig. OM12-18). The switch prevents erratic overspeed when motor is suddenly cut back from high speed to idle, with gear shift lever in neutral. One side of switch diaphragm is connected to intake manifold by vent tube (V) while a ground (kill) wire (3) leads from switch terminal to breaker terminal on one set of points. When overspeed occurs with throttle closed, high manifold vacuum momentarily closes the switch, shorting out one spark plug until engine speed again comes under control.

To service the automatic cut-out switch, refer to Fig. OM12-19. Check

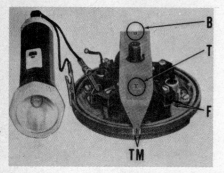

Fig. OM12-15—Timing fixture installed and aligned with armature plate timing marks (TM) for adjusting points. Refer to text.

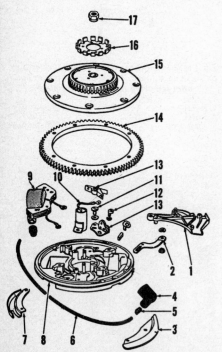

Fig. OM12-16—Exploded view of armature (stator) plate and associated parts used on models prior to 1971.

1. Anchor & pin
2. Link
3. Throttle cam
4. Cover
5. Terminal
6. Wire
7. Shift stop
8. Plate
9. Coil & lamination
10. Condenser
11. Screw
12. Adjusting screw
13. Point set
14. Ring gear
15. Flywheel
16. Starter cap
17. Nut

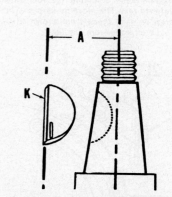

Fig. OM12-17—When installing flywheel, make sure outer edge of key (K) is parallel with centerline of crankshaft as shown at (A).

Fig. OM12-16A—Exploded view of magneto assembly used on models after 1970. Alternator stator (1) is only used on electric start models.

1. Alternator stator
2. Breaker points
3. Condenser
4. Armature plate
5. Ring
6. Plate support
7. Cam & link assy.
8. Ignition coil
9. Magneto coil
10. Nut
11. Starter cup
12. Flywheel

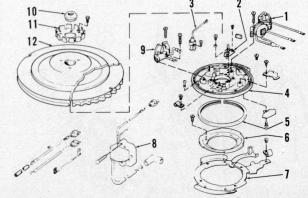

Fig. OM12-18—The vacuum actuated overspeed switch (S) grounds the ignition primary for the lower cylinder when throttle is closed suddenly.

. Overspeed switch	1. Wire from safety switch (T) to wire (2)
. Starting safety switch	2. Wire to starter solenoid
. Vacuum hose	

3. Wire to breaker points (lower cylinder)
4. Wire to ignition switch

5. Wire from breaker points (upper cylinder to ignition switch

electronically for grounds, if indicated, before disassembly. Disassemble the unit Fig. OM12-19 as a guide. Renew diaphragm (3) if leaks are apparent or if otherwise damaged. Make sure that terminal screw is tight and well insulated when reassembling, that diaphragm chamber is air-tight, and that breather passage is open to rear of diaphragm.

COOLING SYSTEM

WATER PUMP. All models are equipped with a rubber impeller type water pump. Impeller is mounted on and driven by the lower unit drive shaft. The main water inlet scoop is located below the exhaust outlet, above and behind the propeller as shown in Fig. OM12-20.

When cooling system problems are encountered, first check the water inlet for plugging or partial stoppage. On 40 hp models, check thermostat operation. If the trouble is not corrected, remove the lower unit gearcase as outlined in the appropriate section, and check the condition of water pump, water passages, gaskets and sealing surfaces.

THERMOSTAT. Forty horsepower models are equipped with a recirculating type thermostat as shown in Fig. OM12-20. Before coolant liquid reaches operating temperature, the main flow of coolant is recirculated through the return tube and water pump, as shown; little additional coolant water is introduced into the system. Thermostat (31) should open at a temperature of 130°-150°F; and spring (27) should maintain a pressure of approximately one psi in cooling system passages.

To service the thermostat, remove the motor cover and refer to Fig. OM12-21. Remove thermostat cover (32) and withdraw thermostat (31), housing (30), gasket (29), pressure valve (28) and spring (27). Renew any parts which are

damaged or questionable, and reassemble by reversing the disassembly procedure.

POWER HEAD

R&R AND DISASSEMBLE. To overhaul the power head, clamp the motor on a stand or support and remove the motor cover, rear exhaust housing cover, carburetor and intake manifold. Remove starter unit or units, flywheel, magneto armature plate and fuel pump.

Remove armature plate support (34–Fig. OM12-21) and retainer (33), speed control lever (39) and outer and inner exhaust covers (20 and 18). Remove cylinder head (24 or 24A) and port and starboard brackets (7 and 10), then unbolt and remove power head from lower unit.

Tap out the two tapered crankcase aligning pins (12), working from cylinder side of crankcase flange; then, unbolt and remove front crankcase half (8).

NOTE: The two center main bearing cap screws are accessible through intake ports, and must be removed.

Remove seal housing (29–Fig. OM12-23A) and snap ring (28) on 40 hp models after 1973.

Pistons, rods and crankshaft are now accessible for removal and overhaul as

Fig. OM12-19—Exploded view of vacuum actuated overspeed switch.

1. Adapter	7. Insulator
2. Gasket	8. Body
3. Diaphragm	9. Insulator washer
4. Spring	10. Washer
5. Screw	11. Wire
6. Insulator washer	12. Tube

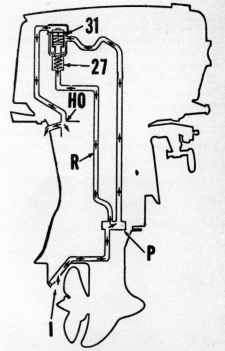

Fig. OM12-20—Schematic view of cooling system used on 40 hp models with recirculating type thermostat.

HO. Hot water oultet	R. Cold water return
I. Inlet	27. Spring
P. Water pump	31. Thermostat

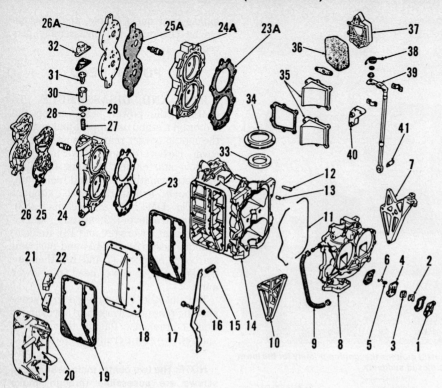

Fig. OM12-21 — Exploded view of crankcase and associated parts typical of all models.

1. Cover	12. Taper pin	22. Safety switch	32. Cover
2. Stop	13. Dowel	23. Gasket	33. Retainer
3. Bleeder valve	14. Cylinder half	24. Cylinder head	34. Support
4. Plate	15. Spring	25. Gasket	35. Transfer port cover
5. Screen	16. Lockout lever	26. Cover	36. Shield
6. Retainer	17. Gasket	27. Spring	37. Fuel pump
7. Bracket	18. Inner exhaust cover	28. Valve	38. Spring
8. Crankcase half	19. Gasket	29. Seal	39. Lever
9. Oil tube	20. Outer cover	30. Housing	40. Bracket
10. Bracket	21. Bracket	31. Thermostat	41. Pin
11. Seal strip			

Whenever power head is disassembled, it is recommended that all gasket surfaces and the mating surfaces of crankcase halves be carefully checked for nicks and burrs or warped surfaces which might interfere with at tight seal. The cylinder head, head end of cylinder block or mating surfaces of manifold and crankcase may be lapped if necessary, to provide a smooth surface. Do not remove any more metal than is necessary.

Mating surfaces of crankcase may be checked for smoothness on the lapping block, and high spots and nicks removed; but surfaces must not be lowered. If extreme care is used, a slightly damaged crankcase may be salvaged in this manner. In case of doubt, renew the crankcase.

The crankcase halves are positively located during assembly by the use of two tapered dowel pins. Check to make sure that the dowel pins are not bent, nicked or distorted, and that dowel pin holes are clean and true. When installing dowel pins, make sure they are fully seated, but do not use excessive force.

When reassembling the crankcase, install the sealing strips (11–Fig. OM12-21) and trim the ends to extend approximately 1/16 inch into bearing bores. Make sure mating surfaces of crankcase halves are completely clean and free from old cement or from nicks or burrs. Apply a non-hardening cement such as OMC Adhesive "M" to cylinder half of crankcase only. Apply cement sparingly and evenly, making sure entire surface is covered. Immediately install front half of crankcase and position

outlined in the appropriate following paragraphs. Remove crankcase bleeder valve (4) or recirculating valve if installed and oil line (9). Blow oil lines and passages out using compressed air. When reassembling, follow the procedures outlined in the ASSEMBLY paragraph which follows.

ASSEMBLY. Because of the two-stroke design, crankcase and intake manifold must be completely sealed against vacuum and pressure. The exhaust manifold and cylinder head must be sealed against water leakage and pressure. Mating surfaces of power head and exhaust housing must form a tight seal.

Fig. OM12-22—One piston boss is a slip fit for easier assembly and proper expansion control. Loose boss is marked as shown.

Fig. OM12-23—Exploded view of crankshaft, bearings, pistons, rings and associated parts used on models prior to 1974.

1. Snap ring
2. Retainer
3. Spring
4. Washer
5. Seal
6. Quad ring
7. "O" ring
8. Bearing
9. Crankshaft
10. Key
11. Bearing
12. Seal
13. "O" ring
14. Retaining ring
15. Bearing race
16. Bearing cage
17. Bearing roller
18. Rod bolt
19. Rod cap
20. Bearing cage
21. Bearing roller
22. Connecting rod
23. Bearing
24. Piston
25. Ring set
26. Piston pin
27. Retainer

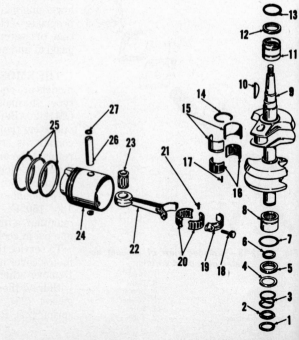

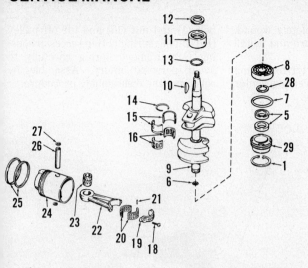

Fig. OM12-23A – Exploded view of crankshaft assembly used on models after 1973. Refer to Fig. OM12-23 for parts identification except for (28) snap ring; (29) seal housing.

on underneath side as shown in Fig. OM12-22. When servicing the piston or rod, press pin out or in, working through the "LOOSE" boss to keep from distorting piston. When assembling the piston to connecting rods, the oil hole (H – Fig. OM12-24) must be toward top of motor and the long tapering side of piston head toward exhaust side of motor.

When reassembling, all engine parts should be well coated with engine oil. Piston should be installed in cylinder with the long, tapering side of piston head toward exhaust port side of cylinder.

CONNECTING RODS, BEARINGS, AND CRANKSHAFTS. Before detaching connecting rods from crankshaft, make sure rods and pistons are properly marked for reinstallation in correct cylinder. Also note alignment marks on rod and and center main bearing cages.

Connecting rods are fitted with needle rollers in a two-piece bearing cage at crankpin end and a caged needle bearing at piston end. The bores at each end of the steel rod are hardened and ground to serve as the bearing outer race. All models are equipped with a cartridge type roller bearing at top main bearing and a split cage roller bearing for the center main bearing. Lower main bearing is a ball bearing on models after 1973 and a cartridge type roller bearing on all other models. The upper bearing on early models contains a recess for crankshaft upper seal. The center main bearing uses a split cage (16 – Fig. OM12-23

by installing the locating dowel pins; then install and tighten the crankcase screws.

Magneto retainer (33 – Fig. OM12-21) on early models must be installed with tapered (rounded) side down toward crankcase. Flat side is toward support (34) and magneto armature plate.

Install seals (5 – Fig. OM12-23A) back to back in seal housing (29) on 40 hp models after 1973.

When installing gaskets, check to make sure correct gasket is used and that ALL water passage holes are open. All gasket surfaces and cap screw threads must be sealed using a non-hardening cement such as OMC Gasket Sealing Compound. Tightening torques are given in the CONDENSED SERVICE DATA table. When installing the flywheel, refer to the special instructions given in IGNITION section.

PISTONS, PINS, RINGS AND CYLINDERS. Before detaching connecting rods from crankshaft, make sure that rod and cap are marked for

correct assembly to each other and in the proper cylinder.

Each aluminum piston on early models is fitted with three identical rings which are interchangeable and which may be installed either side up. Piston on later models has two piston rings which are not interchangeable. Piston and rings are available in standard size and over-sizes. Refer to CONDENSED SERVICE DATA for piston and ring specifications. Renew pistons, rings, and/or cylinder assembly if parts are scored or otherwise damaged, or if clearances are excessive.

Piston pin is a transition fit (0.0001-0.0006 clearance) in one piston pin boss and a press fit in other boss at room temperature. The looser boss is marked

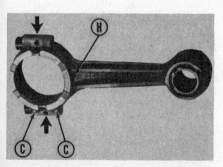

Fig. OM12-24 – Connecting rod is "fractured" at point of arrows. When installing cap, make sure correlation marks (C) are aligned, then work cap back and forth a slight amount until fracture lines match. Oil hole (H) must be toward top of motor.

Fig. OM12-25 – Exploded view of manual starter.

1. Screw
2. Washer
3. Spindle
4. Dowel
5. Wave washer
6. Friction ring
7. Bushing
8. Retainer
9. Pawl
10. Pulley
11. Recoil spring
12. Housing
13. Pin
14. Bushing
15. Spring
16. Ball
17. Nut
18. Guard
19. Rope
20. Lock
21. Spring
22. Anchor
23. Spring
24. Rod
25. Collar
26. Handle
27. Anchor

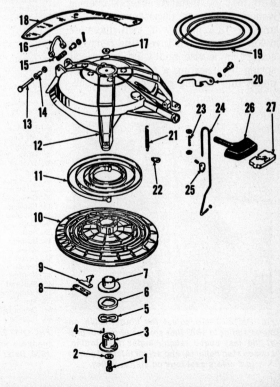

or OM12-23A) and outer race (15), held together at assembly by retaining ring (14).

When assembling the pistons to connecting rods, the oil hole (H – Fig. OM12-24) must be toward top of motor and the long tapering side of piston head toward exhaust side of motor.

The connecting rod is drilled and finished, then carefully fractured at points shown by arrows (Fig. OM12-24). The parting line is not machined, the uneven fractured surfaces serving to align rod and cap assembly. When installing the cap, align the index marks (C), then move rod cap back and forth slightly as rod screws are tightened, until uneven fracture lines mesh. Test the alignment after assembly, by scratching a fingernail across the parting line.

The main bearing outer races are prevented from turning in crankcase by locating dowels (13 – Fig. OM12-21) in cylinder half of bearing bore. The dowel must fit hole in bearing race. To renew the dowel, first center-punch end of dowel; then drill with a No. 25 drill. Tap the hole using a No. 10-24 thread tap and use a puller plate and jack screw to remove the dowel.

Thoroughly lubricate all friction surfaces during assembly, using engine oil. Use petroleum jelly or Lubriplate to retain the loose needle bearings. Renew all crankcases seals whenever motor is disassembled.

MANUAL STARTER

Figure OM12-25 shows an exploded view of the manual starter. A new starter cord may be installed after starter is removed without disassembly of the unit. A 73¾ inch, 7/32 inch diameter nylon cord is used. Invert the removed starter in a vise and wind the recoil spring by inserting a punch in hole in pulley and turning pulley counterclock-

wise until spring is completely wound. Reverse the pulley one turn and install the cord.

To disassemble the starter for spring renewal or other service, remove center bolt (1) and nut (17) and lift off pulley (10) leaving spring (11) in recess in housing (12). Remove spring carefully to avoid personal injury. Assemble by reversing the disassembly procedure.

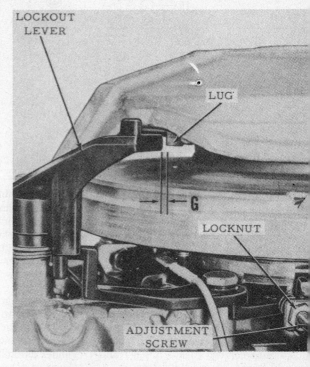

Fig. OM12-26A—Lockout lever on models after 1972 should be 0.030-0.060 inch (G) from lugs on starter pulley with outboard in neutral.

2. Drive shaft
3. Upper race
4. Thrust bearing
5. Lower race
6. Bearing
7. Drive pinion
8. Bearing cup
9. Bearing cone
10. Forward gear
11. Thrust washer
12. Shift lever
13. Pivot screw
14. Cradle
15. Dog clutch
16. Propeller shaft
17. Lower gearcase
18. Plug
19. Dowel
20. Seal strip
21. Thrust washer
23. Reverse gear
24. Thrust washer
25. Snap ring
26. Bearing
27. Seal
28. Housing
29. "O" ring
30. Propeller
31. Drive pin
32. Washer
33. Nut
34. Extension
35. Adapter
36. Grommet
37. Housing
38. Impeller
39. Plate
40. Seal
41. Bushing
42. Bearing
43. Gearcase
44. Screen
46. Bearing
47. Shift rod
48. Connector
53. Spring
54. Detent balls
55. Bushing

Fig. OM12-26—To adjust the starter latch on models prior to 1973 first set speed control grip at the fast speed recommended for starting. Loosen stop collar (A) and adjust latch (B) until it just clears cast lugs on starter pulley.

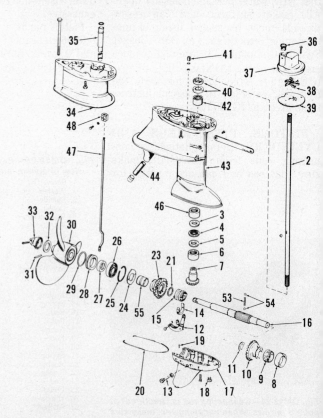

Fig. OM2-27—Exploded view of lower unit gearcase and associated parts used on models with manual shift. Snap ring (25) is not used on models after 1971. One seal (40) is used on models prior to 1974. Refer to Fig. OM12-27A for installation of detent balls (54) and spring (53). Pinion bearing (46) is not used on later models.

Models prior to 1973 are equipped with a starter latch which is mechanically linked to carburetor cam to prevent starting the motor when throttle is set for high speed. To adjust the starter latch, set shift lever in neutral position and the speed control lever to the fast limit (against neutral stop). Loosen the set screw in stop collar (A – Fig. OM12-26) and adjust the collar up or down on link until inner end of latch (B) just clears the cast lugs on starter pulley. Tighten the set screw (A) and check to make sure the latch disengages throughout the throttle range recommended for starting.

The starter lockout on models after 1972 is linked to the gearshift mechanism to prevent starter operation when outboard is in gear. To adjust starter lockout, place gearshift lever in neutral and turn adjustment screw shown in Fig. OM12-26A so that locknut lever is 0.030-0.060 inch from lugs (G) on starter pulley.

LOWER UNIT

Manual Shift Models

PROPELLER AND DRIVE PIN. Protection for the propeller and drive unit is provided by a cushion and slip clutch built into the propeller hub. Use only a propeller especially designed for the motor.

Propeller clutch slippage can be tested using a torque wrench and a suitable holding fixture and adapter. Slippage should occur at a torque of 185-225 ft.-lbs. Service consists of renewing the propeller. A 10½ inch diameter 3-blade 12 or 13 inch pitch propeller is normally used.

REMOVE AND REINSTALL. Most service on the lower unit can be performed by detaching the gearcase housing from exhaust housing. When servicing the lower unit, pay particular attention to water pump and water tubes with respect to air or water leaks. Leaky connections may interfere with proper cooling of the motor.

When overhauling the lower unit, use appropriate exploded views Fig. OM12-27 through OM12-30A as a guide, together with the special service information which follows. All gasket surfaces must be smooth, free from nicks and burrs, and assembled using a nonhardening sealer such as OMC Gasket Sealing Compound. All joints without gaskets must be smooth and free from nicks, burrs and old cement, and sealed with a nonhardening sealer such as OMC Adhesive "M." Refer to CONDENSED SERVICE DATA table for recommended tightening torques.

The propeller shaft (16 – Fig. OM12-27) and drive gears (10 and 23) can be removed after first draining lubricant from gear compartment, removing pivot screw (13), and unbolting and removing gearcase lower housing (17). The drive pinion (7) and bearings (3 through 6) can also be withdrawn.

Make certain that the two ¼ inch hardened steel balls (54) and spring (53) are not lost when dog clutch (15) is pulled from propeller shaft (16).

To separate gearcase from exhaust housing, first remove cover (36 – Fig. OM12-28) or covers (35 and 38 – Fig. OM-29) and remove the lower screw in shift rod clamp (48 – Fig. OM12-27). Gearcase can then be unbolted and separated from exhaust housing.

A slight difference will be noted in the two drive pinion thrust bearing races (3 and 5). The race with the larger hole should be installed above thrust bearing (4).

NOTE: Make certain that dog clutch (15 – Fig. OM12-27A) is correctly installed. If detent balls (54) do not exactly align with center of notches (N) turn dog clutch 180° and reinstall.

When reassembling gearcase, install a new sealing strip (20 – Fig. OM12-27) in lower housing groove and trim ends of strip evenly to extend approximately 1/16 inch beyond ends of seal groove. Coat mating surfaces of housings with a nonhardening cement such as OMC Adhesive "M."

Shift linkage must be adjusted to provide full engagement of shifter collar

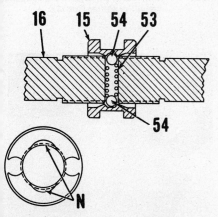

Fig. OM12-27A—The clutch is equipped with spring loaded detent balls as shown. When assembling, make certain that balls (54) are centered in notches (N).

| 15. Dog clutch | 53. Detent spring |
| 16. Propeller shaft | 54. Detent balls |

Fig. OM12-28—Exploded view of stern bracket, exhaust housing, swivel bracket and associated parts used on 33 hp and 40 hp (1971-1975) models.

1. Adjusting screw
2. Spring
3. Speed control gear
4. Bushing
5. Pinion
6. Connector
7. Steering bracket
8. Throttle cover
9. Throttle control
10. Tilt bolt
11. Stern bracket
12. Thrust washer
13. Liner
14. Pin
15. Adjusting screw
16. Friction plate
17. Bushing
18. Swivel bracket
19. Lever arm
20. Spring
21. Strap
22. Bumper
23. Link
24. Liner
25. "O" ring
26. Spacer
27. Detent
28. Stern bracket
29. Pin
30. Spring
31. Thrust rod
32. Tilt spring
33. Reverse lock
34. Spring
35. Lower mount
41. Lower mount
42. Mount
43. Bumper
44. Exhaust housing
45. Shift lever
36. Cover
37. Mount
38. Clevis
39. Shift rod
40. Water tube
46. Clamp screw
47. Shift arm
48. Deflector
49. Plate
50. Gasket

with the forward and reverse gears. To adjust the linkage, refer to Fig. OM12-30 or OM12-30A and proceed as follows: Loosen clamp screw (A) if necessary, and with lockout pin (P) setting in neutral detent as shown, adjust shift lever (L) to a vertical position. Tighten clamp screw and while turning propeller shaft by hand move shift lever in each direction and check to make sure that clutch dogs start to engage on high points of shifter lock (S) an equal distance from neutral detent.

On late models, neutral detent assembly (Fig. OM12-27A) in lower unit must be in neutral when pin (P–Fig. OM12-30 or OM12-30A) is in neutral position on shifter lock (S).

Steering tension can be adjusted by turning tension screw (15–Fig. OM12-28 or 5–Fig. OM12-29) until motor is easy to steer but will maintain a set course.

Electric Shift Models

PROPELLER AND DRIVE PIN. Protection for the propeller and drive unit is provided by a cushion and slip clutch built into the propeller hub. Use only a propeller especially designed for the motor.

Propeller clutch slippage can be tested using a torque wrench and a suitable holding fixture and adapter. Slippage should occur at a torque of 185-225 ft.-lbs. Service consists of renewing the propeller. A 10½ inch diameter 3-blade 12- or 13-inch pitch propeller is normally used.

REMOVE AND REINSTALL. Most service on the lower unit can be performed by detaching the gearcase housing from exhaust housing. When servicing the lower unit, pay particular attention to water pump and water tubes with respect to air or water leaks. Leaky connections may interfere with proper cooling of the motor.

When overhauling the lower unit, use appropriate exploded views Fig. OM12-32 through OM12-34 as a guide, together with the special service information which follows. All gasket surfaces must be smooth, free from nicks and burrs, and assembled using a nonhardening sealer such as OMC Gasket Sealing Compound. All joints without gaskets must be smooth and free from nicks, burrs and old cement, and sealed with a nonhardening sealer such as OMC "Adhesive M." Refer to CONDENSED SERVICE DATA table for

recommended tightening torques.

The driving mechanism of electric shift models consists of two driven gears which turn freely on the propeller shaft, two clutch coils, two clutch hubs splined to propeller shaft; and a forward drive and reverse drive electromagnet.

The clutch coils are anchored to their respective driven gears by three headless, Allen set screws, and the gear and clutch assembly secured to the splined clutch hub by snap ring. Energizing either of the electromagnets attracts the free end of the clutch coil, causing it to drag on friction surface of the splined clutch hub. The resultant friction causes the coil to wrap around hub, gripping it firmly and locking the propeller shaft to the selected drive gear. When the magnetic attraction is broken, the grip of the coil is released and both driven gears again turn independently of the propeller shaft.

Malfunction of the unit could result in clutch slippage in one or both directions of travel; complete loss of ability to engage in either or both of the gears;

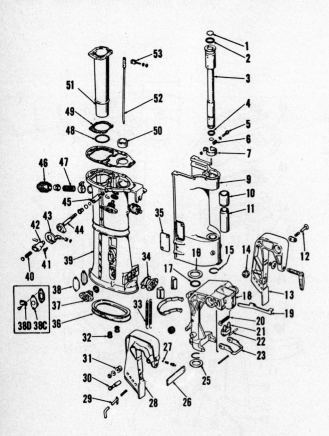

Fig. OM12-29—Exploded view of exhaust housing, drive shaft housing and mounting bracket used on 40 hp models prior to 1971.

1. Plug
2. "O" ring
3. Pivot shaft
4. "O" ring
5. Adjusting screw
6. Spring
7. Friction band
8. Exhaust cover
10. Bushing
11. Bushing
12. Tilt bolt
13. Stern clamp
14. Bushing
15. Snap ring
16. Thrust ring
17. "O" ring
18. Swivel bracket
19. Lever arm
20. Spring
21. Bumper
22. Shaft
23. Link
24. Thrust ring
25. Strap
27. Detent
28. Stern bracket
29. Thrust pad
30. Tilt lock pin
31. Spring
32. Grommet
33. Spring
34. Mount
35. Cover
36. Seal
37. Mount
38. Cover
38C. Cover for electric shift
38D. Clamp
39. Exhaust housing
40. Spring
41. Screw
42. Shift lever
43. Lockout lever
44. Shift shaft
45. Spacer
46. Boot
47. Spring
48. "O" ring
49. Gasket
50. Bushing
51. Inner housing
52. Shift rod
53. Yoke

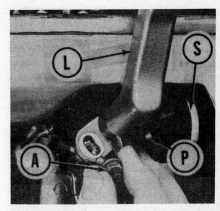

Fig. OM12-30—View of shift linkage for 33 hp and 40 hp (1971-1975) motors. Adjust so that lower unit is in neutral when pin (P) is in neutral detent or shifter lock (S).

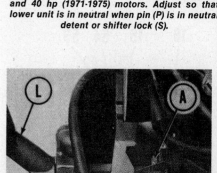

Fig. OM12-30A—View of shift linkage for manual shift of 40 hp motors prior to 1971. Refer to text for adjustment.

failure to release in one of the gears; or complete lock-up, in which drive shaft or propeller shaft could not be turned. Malfunction could be either electrical or mechanical in nature, and the cause should be determined as nearly as possible before disassembly is attempted.

The shift wiring consists of a hot wire leading from "A" terminal on starting switch to the remote control unit; the control switches; connecting wires leading from switches to the electromagnets; the electromagnets; and the ground running back through motor housings to the battery. Malfunction of an electrical nature usually results in failure of one or both clutch units to engage. Failure to disengage could be caused by malfunction of the control switch. Similar troubles could also be of a mechanical nature.

An electrical system test can be accomplished using an ohmmeter at the pins of the motor quick disconnect plug. The reverse shift wire is color coded light blue and the forward shift wire is light green. Attach one ohmmeter lead to motor ground and check resistance of each shift lead. Resistance should be approximately eight ohms. A zero ohms reading indicates a short circuit to ground while an infinite reading indicates an open circuit. An extremely high reading could indicate loose or corroded connections. To further check, connect one ohmmeter lead to the reverse shift wire and the other ohmmeter lead to the forward shift wire. Zero resistance indicates the two wires are shorted together, which will engage both clutches at the same time and lock up the lower end. If any case of unsatisfactory resistance is noted, the lower unit must be removed for further testing.

If a satisfactory reading was obtained, use a voltmeter to check continuity of circuits and available current with remote control unit and a battery connected. Current should flow at battery voltage from the proper shift wire to a suitable ground, when ignition switch is in "ON" position and control lever is moved to a forward or reverse operating position. There should be no current flow when switch is in "OFF" position or when control lever is in neutral or the opposite directional position.

To remove the lower unit, first remove the engine cover and the rear exhaust cover. Disconnect shift cable leads from motor wiring harness at the quick disconnects. Remove cover (35 – Fig. OM12-29) from the front exhaust cover (9). Remove the two attaching screws, then remove clamp (38D) and inner cover (38C).

NOTE: Apply oil or liquid soap to wires when withdrawing wires from cover (38C) and grommet. Be careful not to damage cable insulation. Refer to Fig. OM12-33.

After upper cable is free, remove propeller then unbolt upper gearcase assembly from exhaust housing. Remove gearcase while feeding cable through cable support opening. When installing, note that two series of ridges are molded into cable cover about five inches apart. When long shaft unit is installed, engage support in upper set of ridges. Engage support in lower rides on short shaft models, pulling slack into upper exhaust housing. The series of ridges form an exhaust gas seal.

To disassemble the gearcase, unbolt and remove the water pump and drive shaft, then remove and discard the two stud nuts (25 – Fig. OM12-32) retaining lower gearcase to upper housing. New self-locking nuts should be used when reassembling.

Invert the assembly and separate lower gearcase (35) from upper case (27). Tap lower gearcase lightly with a soft hammer, if necessary, to free lower case from its doweled position. Separate the housings 2-3 inches, then disconnect the two coil leads from upper shift cable (30). The connectors are covered by an insulating rubber sleeve which must first be pushed up the cable wires. After wiring is disconnected, the lower gearcase may be withdrawn.

Remove four screws from rear surface of gearcase head (41). Thread puller legs into both threaded holes and remove

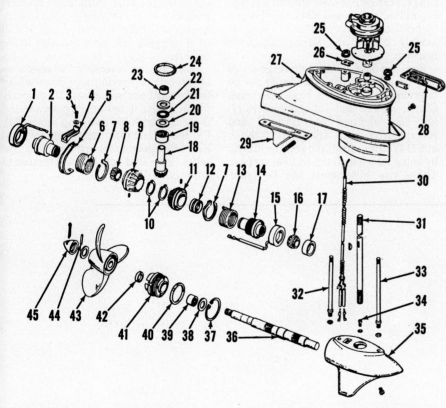

Fig. OM12-32 — Exploded view of gearcase and associated parts used on electric shift models.

1. Reverse electromagnet	12. Forward bushing	23. Needle bearing
2. Reverse hub	13. Clutch roll	24. "O" ring
3. Screw	14. Forward hub	25. Self-locking nut
4. Retainer	15. Forward electromagnet	26. Clip
5. Wire guard	16. Bearing cone	27. Upper housing
6. Clutch coil	17. Bearing cup	28. Water inlet
7. Spacer	18. Drive pinion	29. Water inlet
8. Needle bearing	19. Needle bearing	30. Upper wiring
9. Reverse gear	20. Washer (small holes)	31. Drive shaft
10. Snap ring	21. Thrust bearing	32. Stud
11. Forward gear	22. Washer (large hole)	33. Stud
		34. Clamp screw

35. Lower gearcase	40. "O" ring
36. Propeller shaft	41. Gearcase head
37. Snap ring	42. Seal
38. Thrust washer	43. Propeller
39. Needle bearing	44. Drive pin
	45. Propeller nut

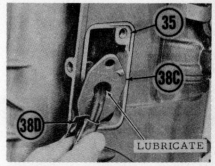

Fig. OM12-33 — Before lower unit can be removed, upper cable must be disconnected. Refer to text.

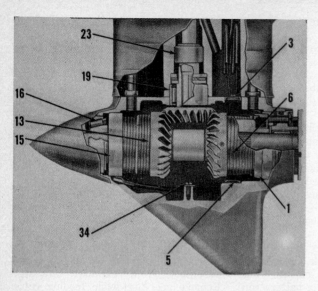

Fig. OM12-34 — Cross section of the assembled gearcase and associated parts used on electric shift models. Refer to Fig. OM12-32.

changed. The reverse driving gear (9) is fitted with a needle roller bearing (8), while forward gear contains a bushing (12). These must also be installed in the indicated positions.

The spacers (7) are wedge-shaped, and designed to fill up the space between the last winding of clutch coil and the pocket of the driving gear. The projecting lug of coil and spacer are placed side by side to completely fill the driving slot of gear. Apply one drop of Grade D "Loctite" to the threads of the retaining set screw, and tighten the screws to a torque of 15-20 inch-pounds, using a torque wrench and suitable adapter. Forward bushing (12) should have a diametral clearance of 0.0003-0.0011 on the hub (14) and in the bore of driving gear (11). Because of the close clearance, extreme care must be used in assembly. Make sure parts are absolutely clean, and do not use force. Perfect alignment is required when assembling the gear and hub unit. Use a light oil as a lubricant when assembling the forward gear and bushing assembly; and needle bearing assembly grease or equivalent, when assembling the reverse gear. If clutch coil tends to bind, turn gear counterclockwise while applying gentle pressure until gear is fully installed on hub. Install snap ring (10) with the sharp edge to the outside.

Assemble by reversing the disassembly procedure, making sure that the lead for forward electromagnet (15) properly fits in groove in bottom of gearcase and is secured with the retaining screw (34). Fit the guard (5) over tail of forward lead after gear units are installed. Use self-locking stud nuts (25) and tighten to a torque of 18-20 ft.-lbs.

gearcase head, using a suitable puller. Remove snap ring (37), clamp screw (3) and coil wire retaining clamp (4). Insert a small punch into drive pin hole in propeller shaft and tap lightly on side of punch, pulling propeller shaft out of gearcase enough to dislodge the reverse electromagnet (1); then remove the electromagnet, being careful not to damage the coil lead.

Withdraw propeller shaft (36) with the reverse gear and hub assembly remaining on shaft. Tilt the pinion gear (18) toward the rear and withdraw through rear opening of gearcase; then, tilt the gearcase and remove forward gear and hub assembly.

Reach down through drive pinion opening with a screwdriver and remove the screw (34) which retains the forward coil lead shield to bottom of gearcase. Refer to Fig. OM12-34. After the screw is removed, insert an internal expanding gear puller into bearing cone (16 – Fig. OM12-32), and pull the bearing cone and forward electromagnet (15). Bearing cup (17) can be removed with an internal expanding puller and slide hammer, or by heating the gearcase (35) to approximately 200°F. and jarring cup from housing.

Forward and reverse drive gears (9 and 11) are identical, but should not be interchanged once they have been used. Clutch coils (6 and 13) and spacers (7) are also identical for forward and reverse drive units. The forward clutch hub (14) differs from the reverse hub (2) by being knurled on the friction surface. These two hubs must not be inter-

EVINRUDE AND JOHNSON
TWO-CYLINDER MODELS

40 HP (1985 & 1986)

50 HP (1971-1975 & 1978-1986)

55 HP (1976-1981)

60 HP (1980-1985)

EVINRUDE

Year Produced	40 HP	50 HP	55 HP	60 HP
1971	....	50172, 50173	....	....
1972	....	50202, 50203, 50272, 50273	....	....
1973	....	50302, 50303, 50372, 50373	....	....
1974	....	50442, 50443, 50472, 50473	....	....
1975	....	50542, 50543, 50572, 50573	....	....
1976	....	....	55642, 55643, 55672, 55673	....
1977	....	....	55742, 55743, 55772, 55773	....
1978	....	50802, 50803	55874, 55875	....
1979	....	50902, 50903	55974, 55975	....
1980	....	50ECS, 50ELCS	55RCS, 55RLCS	60ECS, 60ELCS
1981	....	50BECI, 50BELCI	55RCI, 55RLCI	60ECI, 60ELCI, 60TLCI
1982	....	50BECN, 50BELCN	....	60ECN, 60ELCN, 60TLCN
1983	....	50BECT, 50BELCT, 50TELCT	....	60ECT, 60ELCT, 60TLCT
1984	....	50BECR, 50BELCR, 50TLCR, 50TELCR	....	60ECR, 60ELCR, 60TLCR
1985	40RCO, 40RLCO, 40ECO, 40ELCO, 40TECO, 40TELCO	50BECO, 50BELCO, 50TLCO, 50TELCO	....	60ECO, 60ELCO, 60TLCO
1986	40RCD, 40RLCD, 40ECD, 40ELCD, 40TECD, 40TELCD	50BECD, 50BELCD, 50TLCD, 50TELCD	....	....

JOHNSON

Year Produced	40 HP	50 HP	55 HP	60 HP
1971	...	50ES71, 50ESL71	....	....
1972	....	50ES72, 50ESL72, 50R72,50RL70	....	....
1973	....	50ES73, 50ESL73	....	....
1974	....	50ES74, 50ESL74	....	....
1975	....	50ES75, 50ESL75	....	....
1976	....	....	55E76, 55EL76	....
1977	....	....	55E77, 55EL77	....
1978	....	50MR78, 50MLR78	55E78, 55EL78	....
1979	....	50R79, 50RL79	55E79, 55EL79	....
1980	....	50ECS, 50ELCS	55RCS, 55RLCS	60ECS, 60ELCS
1981	....	50BECI, 50BELCI	55RCI, 55RLCI	60ECI, 60ELCI, 60TLCI
1982	....	50BECN, 50BELCN	55RCN, 55RLCN	60ECN, 60ELCN, 60TLCN
1983	....	50BECT, 50BELCT, 50TELCT	55RCT, 55RLCT	60ECT, 60ELCT, 60TLCT
1984	....	50BECR, 50BELCR, 50TLCR, 50TELCR	55RSF, 55RSLF	60ECR, 60ELCR, 60TLCR
1985	40RCO, 40RLCO, 40ECO, 40ELCO, 40TECO, 40TELCO	50BECO, 50BELCO, 50TLCO, 50TELCO,	....	60ECO, 60ELCO, 60TLCO
1986	40RCD, 40RLCD, 40ECD, 40ELCD, 40TECD, 40TELCD	50BECD, 50BELCD, 50TLCD, 50TELCD,	....	....

CONDENSED SERVICE DATA

Hp/rpm 40/5000
       50/5500 (prior to 1976)
       50/5000 (after 1977)
       55/5500 (prior to 1980)
       55/5000 (after 1979)
       60/5500
Bore .... 3.18 in.
       (80.9 mm)
Stroke .... 2.82 in.
       (71.6 mm)
Number of Cylinders 2
Displacement .... 45 cu. in.*
       (737 cc)

Spark Plug – Champion:
   1971-1985 .... L77J4†
     Electrode Gap .... 0.040 in.
       (1.0 mm)
   1986 .... QL77JC4†
     Electrode Gap .... 0.040 in.
       (1.0 mm)
Ignition Type .... CD
Carburetor Make .... Own
Idle Speed (in gear) .... 700-750 rpm
Fuel:Oil Ratio .... 50:1‡

*On 50 hp models prior to 1976, the bore is 3.06 inches (77.7 mm) making the displacement 41.5 cu. in. (680 cc).

†A Champion QL78V is recommended for 1985 and 1986 models when used at sustained high speeds. Renew surface gap spark plug if center electrode is more than 1/32 inch (0.79 mm) below the flat surface of the plug end.

‡On 1985 and 1986 models equipped with variable ratio oiling (VRO), the VRO pump meters the fuel:oil ratio from approximately 50:1 up to approximately 150:1 by sensing the engine power output. On recreational type 1985 and 1986 models without VRO, 100:1 ratio can be used when Evinrude or Johnson Outboard Lubricant formulated for 100:1 fuel mix is used.

SIZES – CLEARANCES

Piston Ring End Gap . . . . 0.007-0.017 in.
(0.18-0.43 mm)

Lower Piston Ring End Side Clearance:
1971-1984 . . . . 0.0015-0.0040 in.
(0.038-0.102 mm)
1985-1986 . . . . 0.004 in. Max.
(0.102 mm)

Piston Skirt Clearance:
1971-1978 . . . . 0.0045-0.0065 in.
(0.114-0.165 mm)
1979-1981 . . . . 0.0055-0.0095 in.
(0.140-0.241 mm)
1982-1984 . . . . 0.0018-0.0049 in.
(0.048-0.125 mm)

Maximum Cylinder Tolerance . . . . 0.003 in.
(0.076 mm)

Crankshaft Journal Diameters:
Top Main . . . . 1.4974-1.4979 in.
(38.03-38.04 mm)
Center Main . . . . 1.3748-1.3752 in.
(34.92-34.93 mm)
Bottom Main . . . . 1.1810-1.1815 in.
(30.00-30.11 mm)
Crankpin . . . . 1.1823-1.1828 in.
(30.03-30.04 mm)

SIZES – CLEARANCES CONT.

Crankshaft End Play:
1971-1981 . . . . 0.0006-0.0165 in.
(0.015-0.419 mm)

TIGHTENING TORQUES

Connecting Rod . . . . 348-372 in.-lbs.
(40-42 N·m)

Crankcase Halves:
Six Main Bearing Screws . . . . 216-240 in.-lbs.
(24-27 N·m)
Eight Outer Screws . . . . 60-84 in.-lbs.
(7-9 N·m)

Cylinder Head . . . . 216-240 in.-lbs.
(24-27 N·m)

Flywheel:
1978-1982 . . . . 80-85 ft.-lbs.
(110-115 N·m)
All Other Models . . . . 100-105 ft.-lbs.
(136-143 N·m)

Spark Plug . . . . 216-240 in.-lbs.
(24-27 N·m)

Standard Screws:
No. 6 . . . . 7-10 in.-lbs.
(0.8-1.2 N·m)
No. 8 . . . . 15-22 in-lbs.
(1.6-2.4 N·m)
No. 10 . . . . 25-35 in.-lbs.
(2.8-4.0 N·m)
No. 12 . . . . 35-40 in.-lbs.
(4.0-4.6 N·m)
¼ Inch . . . . 60-80 in.-lbs.
(7-9 N·m)
5/16 Inch . . . . 120-140 in.-lbs.
(14-16 N·m)
⅜ Inch . . . . 220-240 in.-lbs.
(24-27 N·m)
7/16 Inch . . . . 340-360 in.-lbs.
(38-40 N·m)

LUBRICATION

The engine is lubricated by oil mixed with the fuel. On 1971-1975 models, fuel should be regular leaded or premium leaded with a minimum pump octane rating of 89. On all models after 1975, the fuel should be regular leaded, regular unleaded, premium leaded or premium unleaded gasoline with a minimum pump octane rating of 86.

On models prior to 1985, recommended oil is Evinrude or Johnson 50/1 Lubricant or a BIA certified TC-W motor oil. The recommended fuel:oil ratio for normal operation and engine break-in is 50:1.

On 1985 and 1986 models equipped with variable ratio oiling (VRO), recommended oil is Evinrude or Johnson Outboard Lubricant, OMC 2 Cycle Motor Oil or a BIA certified TC-W motor oil. The VRO pump meters the fuel:oil ratio from approximately 50:1 up to approximately 150:1 by sensing the engine power output. During engine break-in, the fuel in the fuel tank must be mixed at a fuel:oil ratio of 50:1 to assure the engine of proper lubrication and the oil level in the VRO oil tank must be monitored. If, after engine break-in, oil level has dropped indicating the VRO system is operating, refill the VRO oil tank and switch to straight fuel.

On recreational type 1985 and 1986 models not equipped with VRO, a fuel:oil ratio of 100:1 can be used when Evinrude or Johnson Outboard Lubricant or a BIA certified TC-W motor oil formulated for 100:1 fuel mix is used. When any other outboard motor oil is used or during engine break-in, the recommended fuel:oil ratio is 50:1.

The lower unit gears and bearings are lubricated by oil contained in the gearcase. The recommended oil is OMC Sea-Lube Premium Blend Gearcase Lube on models prior to 1977 and OMC HI-VIS Gearcase Lube on models after 1976. The gearcase oil level should be checked after every 50 hours of operation and the gearcase should be drained and filled with new oil every 100 hours or once each season, whichever occurs first.

The gearcase is drained and filled through the same plug port. An oil level (vent) port is used to indicate the full oil level of the gearcase and to ease in oil drainage.

To drain the oil, place the outboard motor in a vertical position. Remove the drain plug and oil level plug and allow the lubricant to drain into a suitable container.

To fill the gearcase with oil, place the outboard motor in a vertical position. Add oil through the drain plug opening with an oil feeder until the oil begins to overflow from oil level plug port.

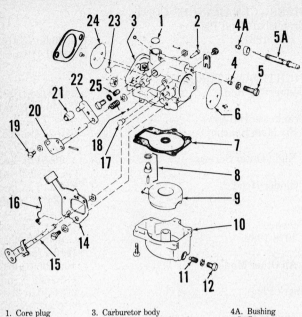

Fig. OM13-1—Exploded view of carburetor. Idle jet (4) is used on models after 1976 while idle mixture needle (5A) is used on models prior to 1977. On some later models, orifice (4) is the intermediate mixture jet and orifice (25) is the idle mixture jet. Choke components are not used on models after 1982. Refer to text.

5A. Idle mixture needle
6. Choke valve
7. Gasket
8. Inlet valve
9. Float
10. Float bowl
11. Main jet
12. Plug
14. Manual choke lever
15. Choke shaft
16. Override spring
17. Detent pin
18. Float pivot pin
19. Screw
20. Throttle shaft
21. Roller
22. Lever
23. Core plug
24. Throttle plate
25. Idle jet

1. Core plug
2. Fuel nipple
3. Carburetor body
4. Idle jet or intermediate jet
4A. Bushing
5. Screw

Reinstall oil level plug with a new gasket, if needed, and tighten. Remove oil feeder, then reinstall drain plug with a new gasket, if needed, and tighten.

FUEL SYSTEM

CARBURETOR. The carburetors used on motors prior to 1977 are equipped with a low speed mixture adjustment needle (5A–Fig. OM13-1), while models after 1976 are equipped with fixed idle mixture jet (4). On models after 1978 (except 1980 50 hp and 1985 and 1986 models), orifice (25) is the idle jet and orifice (4) is the intermediate mixture jet. High speed mixture for all models is controlled with a fixed jet (11). Initial position of idle mixture needle (5A) is ⅝ turn open on models prior to 1975 and 1⅛ turns open on 1975 models. Final adjustment should be done with motor running at normal operating temperature. Engine should be running at 700-800 rpm (idle) and lower unit should be in gear. If so equipped, arms should be detached from idle mixture needles before making individual ad-

justments. Reinstall arms so that levers are pointing straight to port when adjustment is finished.

Adjust idle speed stop screw (I–Fig. OM13-6 or Fig. OM13-8) to obtain idle speed of 700-750 rpm with motor in gear.

Float level of carburetor may be checked by dismounting carburetor and removing float bowl (10–Fig. OM13-1). With carburetor body inverted, float should be 1/16 inch (1.58 mm) from and parallel to installed gasket (7). Refer to Fig. OM13-4. Float lever arm may be bent to obtain proper adjustment. Make certain the float does not stick or bind when adjustment is completed.

Electric start models (prior to 1983) are provided with a choke solenoid (9–Fig. OM13-2). Solenoid is usually controlled by a thermo switch in exhaust cover, however, manual control is possible at motor. A switch is provided at the remote control box for additional choke control. Choke should be installed so top of plunger (11) is held 3/16 inch (4.76 mm) from top of solenoid (9) as shown in Fig. OM13-5. Choke spring (12–Fig. OM13-2) is installed on plunger 2½-3½ turns. Service to the choke solenoid consists of checking the circuit and renewal of malfunctioning parts. Make certain that plunger moves freely in solenoid coil.

NOTE: Do not lubricate plunger as eventual sticking will result.

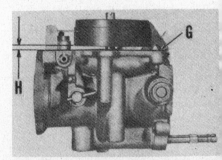

Fig. OM13-4—Float height (H) should be 1/16 inch (1.58 mm). Measurement is taken with gasket (G) installed.

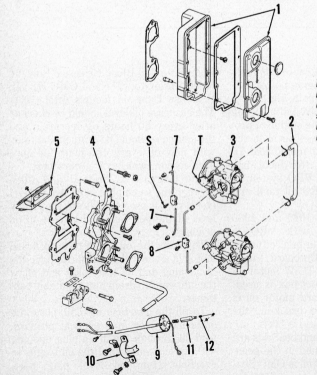

Fig. OM13-2—View of carburetor linkage. Screw (S) is used on early models while screw (T) is used on later models. Choke solenoid (9) is used on electric start models prior to 1983.

1. Silencer assy.
2. Fuel line
3. Carburetor
4. Intake manifold
5. Reed valve
7. Throttle links
8. Choke link fastener
9. Choke solenoid
10. Clamp
11. Plunger
12. Spring

Fig. OM13-5—Choke solenoid should be installed so plunger is 3/16 inch (4.76 mm) from casing.

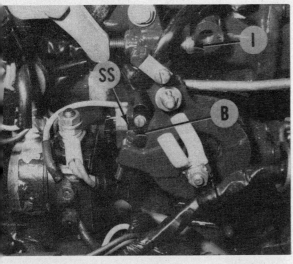

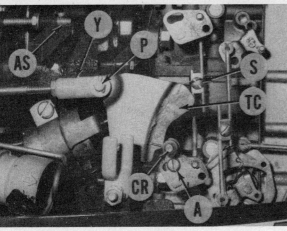

Fig. OM13-6—View of speed control linkage used on all models prior to 1984 and some 1984 models. Refer to text for identification of components and adjustment procedures.

speed control until throttle cam (TC) contacts cam roller (CR) and all slack is taken up. Lower mark on throttle cam should align with center of cam roller at this time. Loosen screw (A) to adjust cam roller. Connect a power timing light to top cylinder and start the engine. Turn idle speed screw (I) until spark advance at idle speed is 2°-4° BTDC. If necessary, stop the engine and remove pin (P) in throttle cam yoke. Turn yoke (Y) to realign mark on throttle cam with center of cam roller. Full advanced ignition timing should be 21° BTDC on 60 hp models and 18°-20° BTDC on all other models at a minimum of 3500 rpm. One clockwise turn of full advance stop screw (AS) will retard ignition timing approximately 1°. Stop the engine and check full throttle carburetor stop. Free play (A – Fig. OM13-7) between throttle cam and throttle cam roller should be 0.000-0.020 inch (0.00-0.50 mm) with speed controls in full speed position. Free play is adjusted by turning stop screw (B – Fig. OM13-6).

A safety starting switch (SS) is located on electric start models prior to 1976 to prevent starter operation with speed control set at high throttle settings. Switch is not adjustable but may be inspected with an ohmmeter or continuity light. Switch must show a closed circuit if throttle is set in the "START" position or below. On models after 1975, the safety start switch is located in the remote control.

Models after 1982 use a manual primer system on manual rewind start models, and an electric primer system on electric start models.

SPEED CONTROL LINKAGE

All Models Prior to 1984 And Some 1984 Models. The carburetor throttle valves are synchronized to open as the ignition is advanced. It is important that throttle valve opening and ignition timing synchronization be checked and adjusted if necessary.

The following procedure should be used to check and adjust synchronization of linkage. Move speed control to full stop position. Loosen set screw (S – Fig. OM13-6) on early models and screw located in top carburetor throttle shaft cam on later models and use a small amount of hand pressure to hold the throttle plates fully closed while screw is retightened. Slowly begin to advance

All 1985 And 1986 Models And Some 1984 Models. The carburetor throttle valves are synchronized to open as the ignition is advanced. It is important that throttle valve opening and ignition timing synchronization be checked and adjusted if necessary.

The following procedure should be used to check and adjust synchronization of linkage. Turn idle speed adjustment knob, located at the end of the steering handle, counterclockwise to complete slow speed position. While turning the twist grip from full closed position to full open position, check the clearance (C – Fig. OM13-8) between roller (1) and

Fig. OM13-7—Free play of throttle lever (A) should be 0.000-0.020 inch (0.00-0.50 mm) at full throttle position.

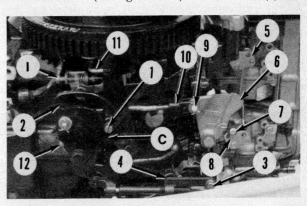

Fig. OM13-8—View of speed control linkage used on all 1985 and 1986 models and some 1984 models. Refer to text for identification of components and adjustment procedures.

Evinrude & Johnson 40 (1985 & 1986), 50, 55 & 60 HP 2 Cyl.

OUTBOARD MOTOR

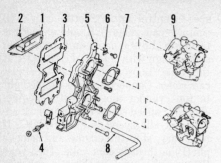

Fig. OM13-9—Carburetor and intake manifold typical of all models. Early type intake manifold (5) is shown.

1. Reed plate
2. Screw
3. Gasket
4. Pivot bolt
5. Manifold
6. Timing pointer
7. Gasket
8. Hose
9. Carburetor

Fig. OM13-10—View of non-VRO type fuel pump.

1. Screw
2. Cap
3. Screen
4. Gasket
5. Pump assy.
6. Pump to "T" fitting hose
7. Pump to manifold hose
8. Inlet hose

Fig. OM13-11—View of a VRO type fuel pump.

1. VRO fuel pump assy.
2. Oil inlet nipple
3. Fuel inlet nipple
4. Crankcase pulse nipple
5. Fuel mixture discharge nipple

end of slot in cam (2). Clearance should be ¼ inch (6.35 mm) at both ends of slot. If not, remove screw (3) and rotate connector (4) until the correct adjustment is obtained, then reinstall screw (3).

Rotate twist grip to closed position. Loosen the screw located in top carburetor throttle shaft cam (5). Use a small amount of hand pressure to hold the throttle plates fully closed and retighten screw (5). Rotate the twist grip until throttle cam (6) contacts cam roller (7) and all slack is taken up. Lower mark on throttle cam (6) should align with center of cam roller (7) just as throttle plates begin to open. Loosen screw (8) to adjust cam roller.

Connect a power timing light to engine top cylinder. Rotate the twist grip until the throttle plates just start to open. Start the engine and note the spark advance with the timing light. The spark advance at idle speed should be 2°-4° BTDC. If not, stop the engine and remove pin (9). Rotate yoke (10) clockwise to increase the pickup timing degrees and counterclockwise to decrease. One turn will equal approximately 2°.

Full advanced ignition timing should be 18°-20° BTDC on all models at a minimum of 3500 rpm. Spark advance rod (11) must be removed and the ends bent to adjust. The wide-open throttle adjustment screw (12) must be adjusted so the carburetor throttle shaft pins (port side of carburetor) are exactly vertical when throttle control is placed in full throttle position.

REED VALVES. Two sets of leaf (reed) valves (1–Fig. OM13-9) are used, one for each cylinder. The leaf plate assembly is located between the intake manifold and crankcase and should be inspected whenever the carburetors are removed for service. Leaf petals should seat lightly against leaf plate throughout their entire length with the least possible tension. Leaf petals should be

smooth, flat and completely free of gum or varnish. Unit may be disassembled for cleaning but no attempt should be made to straighten or repair a bent or damaged leaf petal. Tighten screws (2) uniformly to avoid warping leaf petals.

NON-VRO FUEL PUMP. The diaphragm type fuel pump (5–Fig. OM13-10) is available only as an assembly. If fuel system problems are encountered, renew filter element (3) and blow out fuel lines with compressed air before condemning fuel pump. If trouble persists, renew pump.

VRO TYPE FUEL PUMP. The VRO type fuel pump (1–Fig. OM13-11) meters the fuel:oil ratio from approximately 50:1 up to approximately 150:1 by sensing the engine power output. During engine break-in or after any procedure that permitted air to enter VRO system, the fuel in the fuel tank must be mixed at a fuel:oil ratio of 50:1 to ensure the engine of proper lubrication.

To check the VRO system for proper operation, first fill the VRO oil tank with a recommended two-stroke motor oil and note oil level for future reference. Install a fuel:oil mixture of 50:1 in the fuel tank. After the recommended engine break-in period or after a suitable test period for other conditions, note the oil level in the VRO oil tank. If the oil level has dropped indicating the VRO system is operating, refill the VRO oil tank and switch to straight fuel.

NOTE: When the VRO system is not used, the inlet nozzle at the outboard motor connector must be capped and clamped to prevent dirt or moisture from entering the fuel system. The fuel in the fuel tank must be mixed at a fuel:oil ratio of 50:1.

TESTING. Stop the engine. Disconnect fuel mixture discharge hose at VRO pump nipple (4–Fig. OM13-11). Connect

a tee fitting in hose end. Connect one end of a clear hose to one tee outlet and connect remaining hose end to pump discharge fitting. Connect a 0-15 psi (0-103 kPa) pressure gage to the remaining tee outlet. Start the engine and run at wide-open throttle. The VRO pump should develop between 3 psi (21 kPa) and 15 psi (103 kPa) at wide-open throttle. The fuel pressure will drop 1-2 psi (6.8-13.7 kPa) and a clicking sound should be heard with each oil discharge. A small squirt of oil should be noticed every time the pump pulses.

If fuel pump (1) malfunction is noted, the fuel pump must be renewed as a complete assembly.

MANUAL TYPE PRIMER. Some later models are equipped with a manually operated fuel primer pump to assist in cold-engine starting. Fuel can be pumped into the intake ports by actuating the primer pump knob located at front control panel. With the primer pump knob in the warm-up position, fuel can be sucked into the intake ports through the primer pump when the engine is operating to enrichen the fuel mixture during engine warm-up. Push primer pump knob in to full stop to shut off the primer pump.

The primer pump may be disassembled after removing the retaining clip. Inspect check valves and "O" rings and renew any component that is found to be faulty.

IGNITION SYSTEM

Models Prior To 1978

OPERATION. A breakerless capacitor discharge ignition system is used. Refer to Fig. OM13-12. The alternator produces approximately 300 volts which is stored in a capacitor (condenser). Sensor magnets induce a small

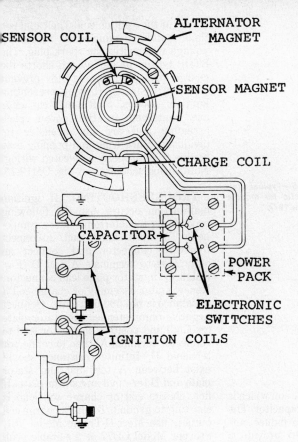

Fig. OM13-12—Schematic of ignition system on models prior to 1978. Charge coil is grounded to power head on later models.

current in the sensor coil which is used to trigger the electronic switches. When triggered the electronic switches (silicone controlled rectifier), release current stored in the capacitor to the ignition coil. The system is independent and requires no battery to operate.

This ignition system is extremely durable in normal use but can be easily damaged by improper operating, testing and servicing procedures. The following precautions should be observed:

1. Make certain that all wiring connections are clean and tightly joined.
2. Make certain that wires do not bind moving parts or touch metal edges where they may chafe through insulation.
3. DO NOT open or close any electrical circuits while engine is running.
4. DO NOT use an electric tachometer other than those recommended by the manufacturer.
5. DO NOT hold spark plug wires while checking for spark.

TROUBLESHOOTING. Use only approved methods to prevent damage to components. Before inspecting ignition system, make sure that trouble is not coming from contaminated fuel or improper carburetor adjustment.

CHECKING FOR SPARK. Disconnect spark plug leads at spark plugs and connect them to a needle point spark

checker as in Fig. OM13-13. Spark checker gap should be set at ½ inch (12.7 mm). Crank engine with ignition switch "ON" and observe spark checker.

A strong, steady spark firing one gap and then the other indicates system functioning correctly; suspect spark plugs, timing or improper wiring to coils to spark plugs.

Weak, inconsistent spark or spark from only one coil; suspect, sensor coil or ignition coil. Weak, inconsistent spark from both coils; suspect charge coils. No spark at all; suspect ignition switch or power pack.

WIRING. Engine missing, surging and failure to start or run can be caused by loose or corroded electrical connec-

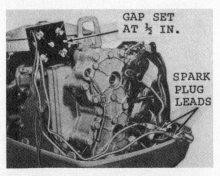

Fig. OM13-13—A spark checker may be used to check ignition output.

tions. Check all terminals and plug-in connectors for tight clean contact. Also check all wiring for short to ground.

SENSOR COIL. The sensor coil may be checked with an ohmmeter. Disconnect black/white lead wire from #6 terminals on power pack assembly (11–Fig. OM13-14) and tag them to avoid confusion. Meter should indicate 10-20 ohms resistance between sensor coil leads. Use ohmmeter to inspect sensor for short to groud. Sensor coil is not available separately, timer base (3) with sensor coil is renewed as an assembly.

CHARGE COILS. To inspect charge coils, disconnect light brown lead wire from #1 terminal on power pack. Resistance to ground through brown wire should be 800-950 ohms. Charge coils are renewed as an assembly with stator (2–Fig. OM13-14) after removal of the flywheel.

SHIFT DIODE (1971 & 1972 MODELS). Failure of the shift diode (5–Fig. OM13-14) on 1971 and 1972 models may cause the lower unit to shift into forward gear immediately after ignition switch is turned "OFF."

Shift diode may be inspected with an ohmmeter or a continuity light with no more than a 12 volt power source. Disconnect diode leads at terminal block (12). Connect tester leads to purple/green wire and to yellow wire from diode. Reverse connection. Tester

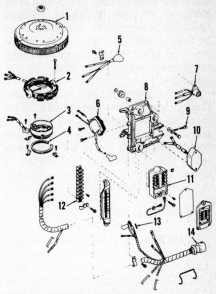

Fig. OM13-14—Component parts of ignition system used on models prior to 1978.

1. Flywheel	9. Ground strap
2. Stator	10. Voltage regulator
3. Timer base	(manual start models)
4. Retainer ring	11. Power pack
5. Diode	12. Terminal block
6. Ignition coil	13. Fuse (20 amp)
7. Rectifier	14. Connector
8. Bracket	

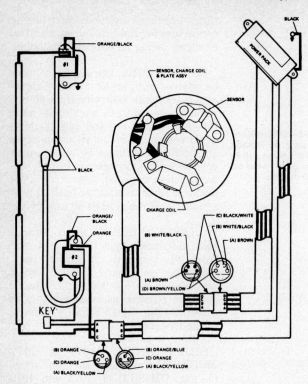

Fig. OM13-15—Typical ignition schematic for models after 1977.

circuit of the ignition coil. The rapid coil field buildup induces a secondary voltage which fires the spark plug. The STOP button or key switch shorts the charge coil to ground to prevent capacitor charging thereby preventing ignition. Diodes, SCR's and capacitor are contained in the power pack assembly and are not available individually. Backfiring and popping may be due to improperly connected wiring. Note wiring schematic in Fig. OM13-15.

TROUBLESHOOTING. If ignition malfunction occurs, use the following procedures to determine faulty component. To check charge coil, disconnect four-wire connector and connect an ohmmeter to terminals A and D (Fig. OM13-15) in stator plate lead connector. Renew stator assembly or charge coil if resistance is not 500-650 ohms. Connect negative ohmmeter lead to stator plate (ground) and positive ohmmeter lead to connector terminal A, then to connector terminal D. Infinite resistance should exist between A terminal and stator plate and D terminal and stator plate. If not, charge coil or charge coil lead is shorting to ground. To check charge coil output, use Merc-O-Tronic Model 781, Stevens Model CD77 or a suitable peak voltage tester. Connect black tester lead to stator lead connector terminal A and red tester lead to terminal D. Turn tester knobs to "NEG (–)" and "500." Crank engine while observing tester.

reading with a good shift diode will indicate infinite resistance with one connection and no resistance in other direction. Repeat this test with purple/green wire and yellow/gray wire. Again, diode should show no resistance in one direction and infinite resistance in other direction.

STATOR AND TIMER BASE ASSEMBLY. Stator (2–Fig. OM13-14) and timer base (3) may be serviced after removal of the flywheel. Stator assembly is secured to the power head by four screws. The timer base may be removed after the stator by removing the four screws and clips along the outside edge.

When reassembling unit, make certain that wiring does not restrict free movement of timer base. Inspect taper on crankshaft and taper in flywheel. Install flywheel key with flat of key parallel to center line of crankshaft NOT surface of taper. Torque flywheel nut to 100-105 ft.-lbs. (136-143 N·m).

Models After 1977

OPERATION. Models after 1977 are equipped with pointless capacitor discharge ignition system shown in Fig. OM13-15. Charge and sensor coils are located under flywheel. Ignition charge coil and sensor coil are incorporated in stator (2–Fig. OM13-16) on 1978-1983 models except 1980 and 1981 55 hp models. Components are mounted individually on stator plate (3) on 1980 and 1981 55 hp models and on all models after 1983. Two magnets in flywheel in-

duce a current in the charge coil which is rectified and directed to a capacitor. The two flywheel magnets also induce current in the sensor coil to provide a positive charge on the gate of one of two silicone controlled rectifiers (SCR's). The positive charge opens the SCR and allows the charged capacitor to discharge through the SCR and primary

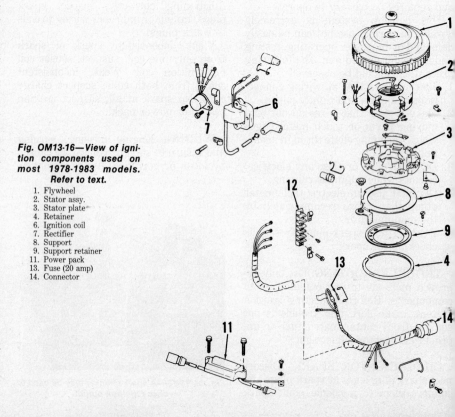

Fig. OM13-16—View of ignition components used on most 1978-1983 models. Refer to text.

1. Flywheel
2. Stator assy.
3. Stator plate
4. Retainer
6. Ignition coil
7. Rectifier
8. Support
9. Support retainer
11. Power pack
13. Fuse (20 amp)
14. Connector

Renew stator assembly or charge coil if meter reads below 230 volts.

To check sensor coil, connect an ohmmeter to terminals B and C in stator plate lead connector. Renew stator assembly or sensor coil if resistance is not 30-50 ohms. Connect negative ohmmeter lead to stator plate (ground) and positive ohmmeter lead to connector terminal B, then to connector terminal C. Infinite resistance should exist between B terminal and stator plate and C terminal and stator plate. If not, sensor coil or sensor coil lead is shorting to ground. To check sensor coil output, use Merc-O-Tronic Model 781, Stevens Model CD77 or a suitable peak voltage tester. Connect black tester lead to stator lead connector terminal C and red tester lead to terminal B. On Merc-O-Tronic Model 781, turn knobs to "POS (+)" and "5" and on Stevens Models CD77, turn knobs to "S" and "5." Crank engine while observing tester. Renew stator assembly or sensor coil if meter reads below 2 volts.

NOTE: On 1980 and 1981 55 hp models and on all models after 1983, use OMC Coil Locating Ring (Tool 317001) to properly align charge coil and sensor coil on stator plate.

To check power pack output, first reconnect four-wire connector. Use Merc-O-Tronic Model 781, Stevens Model CD77 or a suitable peak voltage tester. Connect black tester lead to a suitable engine ground. Connect red tester lead to wire leading to either ignition coil. Turn tester knobs to "NEG (−)" and "500." Crank engine while observing tester. Repeat test on other lead. Renew power pack if readings are not at least 180 volts or higher.

Renew ignition coil or coils if no other ignition component is found faulty.

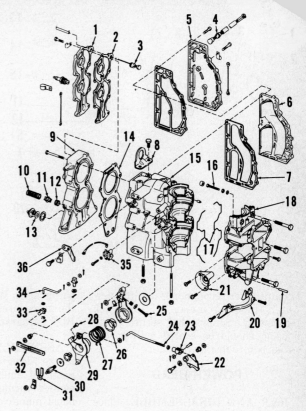

Fig. OM13-22 — Exploded view typical of crankcase and cylinder assembly used on all models. Sealing strips (17) are not used on later models.

1. Cylinder head cover
2. Gasket
3. Temperature switch
4. Thermo switch
5. Exhaust cover
6. Exhaust deflector
7. Gasket
8. Lifting ring
9. Cylinder head
10. Valve spring
11. Pressure relief valve
12. Grommet
13. Thermostat
14. Head gasket
15. Cylinder block
16. Spark advance stop screw
17. Sealing strip
18. Crankcase half
19. Locating dowel
20. Frame
21. Throttle lever bracket
22. Throttle cam
23. Yoke
24. Throttle rod
25. Idle adjustment screw
26. Bushing
27. Throttle lever spring
28. Throttle stop screw
29. Throttle lever
30. Lever screw
31. Cable clamp
32. Throttle link
33. Rod retainer
34. Rod
35. Safety starting switch
36. Idle adjustment stop

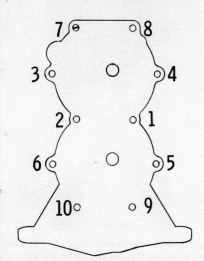

Fig. OM13-21—Cylinder head tightening sequence should be used to prevent head warpage.

COOLING SYSTEM

The cooling system is controlled by both temperature and pressure. At slow operating speeds, the thermostat opens when temperatures in the cooling system reaches approximately 145°F (63°C). At high operating speeds, water pump pressure forces pressure relief valve (11 – Fig. OM13-22) off its seat and allows cool water to circulate through the power head bypassing the thermostat. This allows the motor to run cooler at high operating speeds.

Cooling system operation can be checked by applying a heat sensitive stick such as "Markal Thermomelt Stik" to top of cylinder head. A 125°F (52°C) stick and a 163°F (73°C) stick will be needed. At speeds below 1000 rpm and in forward gear, 125°F (52°C) stick should melt and 163°F (73°C) stick should not. At engine speeds over 4000 rpm, 163°F (73°C) stick should not melt. If 125°F (52°C) stick does not melt at slow speeds, pressure relief valve or thermostat may be stuck open. Overheating may be caused by damaged thermostat, damaged relief valve, exhaust cover gaskets leaking, head gaskets leaking, water passages obstructed, water passages leaking or faulty water pump. A hot horn in remote control panel should sound when engine is overheated. Temperature switch (3) should close circuit to hot horm at 205°-217°F (96°-102°C).

Thermostat (13), pressure relief valve and temperature switch may be serviced after removing cylinder head cover. Install new gaskets when reassembling.

WATER PUMP. The water pump is mounted on top surface of gearcase housing. The rubber impeller is mounted on and driven by the drive shaft. Water pump may be serviced after separating the lower unit gearcase from the drive shaft/exhaust housing. Refer to Fig. OM13-40, Fig. OM13-48 or Fig. OM13-51 for exploded view of water pump. Seals (9 and 10) are identical. Install lower seal with lip down to prevent loss of gearcase grease and upper seal with lip up to prevent water from entering gearcase. Coat bottom of impeller plate (8) with OMC Adhesive "M" or equivalent before installation. On models prior to 1986, install key (7) in drive shaft. On 1986 models, install drive cam with flat side against drive shaft and sharp edge pointing in a clockwise direction when viewed from crankshaft end of drive shaft. Install impeller (6). Impeller may be installed with either side up if a new one is being used. Apply grease to impeller blades and rotate drive shaft in a clockwise direction while sliding pump housing (5) into position.

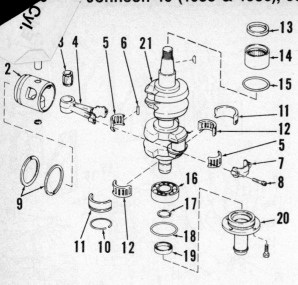

Fig. OM13-24 — Exploded view typical of crankshaft and related parts used on all models. On models after 1983, loose needle bearings and thrust washers are used in place of caged needle bearing (3).

1. Piston pin
2. Piston
3. Needle bearing
4. Connecting rod
5. Bearing cage
6. Bearing roller
7. Rod cap
8. Rod bolt
9. Piston rings
10. Bearing retainer
11. Bearing sleeve
12. Bearing cage
13. Seal
14. Needle bearing
15. "O" ring
16. Ball bearing
17. Snap ring
18. "O" ring
19. Seal
20. Seal housing

Manufacturer recommends use of a new water tube grommet (4) on each reassembly. Screws that secure pump housing should be coated with gasket sealer before installation.

POWER HEAD

R&R AND DISASSEMBLE. Place motor on a suitable stand and remove engine cover and forward and aft exhaust covers. Disconnect remote shift control wires on electric start models or shift rod screw (Fig. OM13-51) on all other models. Unscrew four nuts from each side of exhaust housing and single nut from aft stud. Power head and lower motor cover may be lifted from exhaust housing adapter as an assembly.

To disassemble power head, remove shift lever on manual start models and four bolts that secure lower motor cover on all models. Remove air intake, carburetors and starter assembly. Remove flywheel, stator and stator plate assembly. Note position of wires as they are disconnected and mark them if necessary to ensure proper replacement. Remove throttle linkage, spark advance linkage and choke solenoid (models prior to 1983). Remove lower main bearing seal housing (20 – Fig. OM13-24) and inspect seal (19) and "O" ring (18). Cylinder head (9 – Fig. OM13-22) may be removed without unbolting head cover (1). Removal of the head cover is necessary to service thermostat (13), pressure relief valve (11) and temperature switch (3).

Drive taper pin (19) out toward front of motor and remove fourteen screws securing lower crankcase half to cylinder block. Tap side of crankshaft with a rawhide mallet to break seal between crankcase sections.

Primary internal engine parts are now accessible for removal and overhaul as outlined in the appropriate following paragraphs. When reassembling, follow the procedures outlined in the ASSEMBLY paragraphs that follow.

ASSEMBLY. Because of the two-stroke design, crankcase and intake manifold must be completely sealed against vacuum and pressure. The exhaust manifold and cylinder head must be sealed against water leakage and pressure. Mating surfaces of power head and exhaust housing must form a tight seal.

Whenever power head is disassembled, it is recommended that all gasket surfaces and the mating surfaces of crankcase halves be carefully checked for nicks and burrs or warped surfaces which might interfere with a tight seal. The cylinder head, head end of cylinder block and mating surfaces of manifold and crankcase may be lapped if necessary, to provide a smooth surface. Do not remove any more metal than is necessary.

Mating surfaces of crankcase may be checked for smoothness on the lapping block, and high spots and nicks removed; but surfaces must not be lowered. If extreme care is used, a slightly damaged crankcase may be salvaged in this manner. In case of doubt, renew the crankcase.

The crankcase halves are positively located during assembly by the use of a tapered dowel pin (19 – Fig. OM13-22). Make sure that pin is not bent or distorted and that dowel pin hole is clean and true. Make certain that pin is fully seated on reinstallation.

When reassembling crankcase, make sure mating surfaces of crankcase halves are completely clean and free of old cement, nicks and burrs. On models prior to 1979, install sealing strips (17) and trim ends to extend approximately 1/32 inch (0.79 mm) into bearing bores, then sparingly apply OMC Adhesive "M"

to cylinder half of crankcase only. On models after 1978, apply OMC Gel-Seal II to one crankcase mating surface. Do not use sealers which will harden and prevent contact between crankcase mating surfaces. Immediately assemble crankcase halves after applying sealer and position halves by installing locating dowel pin; then install and tighten crankcase screws.

When installing gaskets, check to make sure correct gasket is used and that ALL water passage holes are open. All gasket surfaces and cap screw threads must be sealed using a non-hardening cement such as OMC Gasket Sealing Compound.

Tighten cylinder head screws to 216-240 in.-lbs. (24-27 N·m) using sequence shown in Fig. OM13-21 for initial tightening. After engine has been run up to normal operating temperature and allowed to cool, repeat tightening procedure. General tightening torques are given in the CONDENSED SERVICE DATA table. When installing the flywheel, make sure key is properly installed in crankshaft groove.

PISTONS, RINGS AND CYLINDERS. Before detaching connecting rods from crankshaft, make sure that rod and cap are marked for correct assembly to each other and in the proper cylinder.

Inspect cylinder walls for wear or damage. Cylinders worn 0.003 inch (0.076 mm) beyond standard or damaged should be bored oversize. Pistons and rings are available in standard and 0.030 inch (0.76 mm) oversize. Carefully

Fig. OM13-25 — Connecting rods must be reinstalled in original position, with oil hole up (models prior to 1985) and rod cap correctly installed.

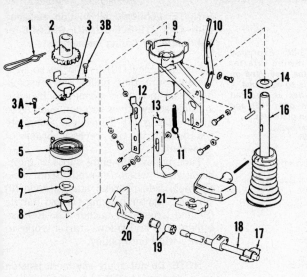

1. Drag spring
2. Pinion
3. Pinion latch
3A. Flat head screw
3B. Hex head screw
4. Spring cover
5. Rewind spring
6. Spring retainer
7. Thrust washer
8. Bushing
9. Starter bracket
10. Rope guide
11. Lockout spring
12. Lockout cam
13. Lockout link
14. Spring washer
15. Pinion pin
16. Rewind spool
17. Lever
18. Lever & shaft assy.
19. Bushings
20. Shift interlock cam

scrape all carbon accumulation from exhaust ports. Pistons should be checked for wear, roundness and carbon accumulation. Ring grooves should be cleaned of carbon and new piston rings installed on each reassembly. Check lower piston ring in ring groove for proper side clearance and piston rings for correct end gap. Refer to CONDENSED SERVICE DATA for specifications.

On all models except some 1982-1984 models, piston pins are a press fit in both pin bosses. Pistons should be heated in boiling water to ease removal from connecting rod. Pin should not be completely removed from piston as reassembly will be difficult. New pistons are supplied with a partially installed piston pin.

On some 1982-1984 models, one pin boss is press fit while the other is a slip fit. The loose pin boss is marked "L." When removing piston pin, remove both retaining rings, heat piston and press pin out toward the tight piston pin boss. Install pin through loose side first.

When assembling, oil hole in rod (models prior to 1985) must be turned toward top (Fig. OM13-25) and "UP" mark on piston head must be toward top side of power head. All parts should be well coated with engine oil during reassembly.

CONNECTING RODS, BEARINGS AND CRANKSHAFT. Before detaching connecting rods from crankshaft, make sure that rods and pistons are marked for reinstallation in correct cylinder. Also note alignment marks (M – Fig. OM13-25) on rods and rod caps.

Connecting rods are fitted with a two-piece roller bearing cage containing 16 rollers at crankpin end and a caged needle bearing at the piston end on models prior to 1984 and loose needle bearings and thrust washers on models after

1983. The split cage needle bearing at crankshaft center main may be disassembled for cleaning and inspection by working retaining ring (10 – Fig. OM13-24) out of groove and off end of retainers (11). Lower main bearing (16) may be removed with a bearing puller. Caged needle top main bearing will slide off shaft.

Assemble connecting rods on crankshaft with oil hole (Fig. OM13-25), models prior to 1985, toward threaded end of crankshaft (top).

On 1985 and later models equipped with precision ground rods, OMC Alignment Fixture 396749 is recommended to properly align connecting rod with rod cap during tightening of connecting rod screws.

NOTE: Precision ground rods are identified by grind marks running ACROSS corners on ears of connecting rod and rod cap.

Make certain that dowels in crankcase align with recesses in top and center main bearings.

Crankcase seals and "O" rings should be renewed at each reassembly. Lubricate all friction surfaces with engine oil on reassembly.

MANUAL STARTER

Early Type

Refer to Fig. OM13-28 for exploded view of early type manual rewind starter. Start rope may be renewed without disassembling starter. If rope has been broken, remove remnants and proceed as follows: Cut a new length of nylon starter rope 75¾ inches (192.4 cm) long and burn ends to facilitate reassembly and prevent fraying. Insert a suitable tool in top or rewind spool (16) and rewind spring until tight. Allow

spring to unwind far enough to gain access to rope hole in spool. Lift starter pinion (2) to engage flywheel teeth and place a wrench or other suitable tool beneath pinion to hold it in this position. Tie a knot in one end of start rope and thread it into hole in spool. Thread end of rope through lower motor cover, attach handle and allow rope to slowly rewind.

If start rope is not severed, simply pull rope all the way out, allow it to rewind far enough to gain access to rope hole in spool and lock pinion (2) as described previously. Rope may now be renewed as per previous instructions.

To disassemble starter for further service, remove air intake cover to gain access to two screws holding rope guide (10) and single screw holding bracket (9). Remove starter handle and allow rope to wind fully onto spool. Loosen lower screw in lock-out link (13) and release throttle cable from clamp. Do not disturb two smaller screws on lock-out link as readjustment will be required. Remove two remaining bolts securing starter bracket from port side and remove starter assembly.

NOTE: Safety glasses or goggles are recommended for further disassembly.

Use a punch to remove roll pin (15). Note position of drag spring (1) before removing pinion gear (2). Starter bracket should be mounted in a vise and recoil spring pulled out as far as possible (approximately 12 inches [30.5 cm]) before removing spring cover. Note position of latch (3) and flat head screw (3A). Slide spring retainer (6) up shaft to remove spring. Spool (16) may be pulled from bracket for access to bushing (8) in bracket or wave washer (14) between bracket and spool. When installing rewind spring, install spring cover and place a punch or other object through loop of spring inside spool to keep spring from pulling out while rewinding. Wedge a large screwdriver in spool with punch and rewind spring until end is seated in starter bracket. Use caution when releasing tension on screwdriver, make sure that end of spring is seated and will not snap back. Once spring is properly seated, remove cover and fill compartment with grease.

Adjust lock-out links (12 and 13) so starter pinion cannot engage flywheel in forward or reverse gear.

Late Type

A starter lockout slide (S – Fig. OM13-31) is used to prevent starter engagement when the gear shift lever is in the forward or reverse position.

To overhaul the manual starter, proceed as follows: Remove engine top

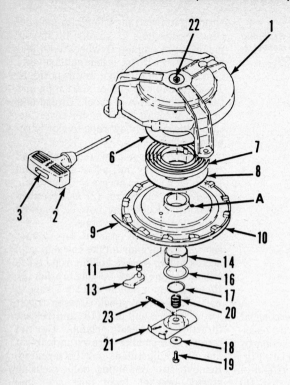

Fig. OM13-30 — Exploded view of rewind starter similar to the type used on later models so equipped. A wave washer is located under drive pawl (13) and friction plate (16).

1. Starter housing
2. Handle
3. Anchor
6. Plate
7. Rewind spring
8. Plate
9. Starter rope
10. Pulley
11. Bushing
13. Drive pawl
14. Bushing
16. Friction plate
17. Snap ring
18. Washer
19. Bolt
20. Spring
21. Pawl plate
22. Nut
23. Pawl return spring

NOTE: Lubricate all friction surfaces with OMC TRIPLE-GUARD GREASE or Lubriplate 777 during reassembly.

Install pulley (10) in starter housing making sure that pulley slot engages hook end in rewind spring (7). Insert a suitable screwdriver through hole (A) to guide spring (7) if needed. Complete reassembly in the reverse order of disassembly.

Turn pulley (10) eight turns counterclockwise when viewed from the flywheel side. Thread starter rope (9) through starter housing (1) and handle (2) and secure in anchor (3). Release pulley (10) and allow starter rope to slowly wind onto pulley.

NOTE: Do not apply any more tension on rewind spring (7) than required to draw starter handle (2) back into the proper released position.

Adjust starter lockout assembly by adjusting cable (L – Fig. OM13-31) so starter will engage when gear shift lever is in neutral position, but will not engage when gear shift lever is in forward or reverse position. Secure cable (L) by tightening cap screw (C).

PROPELLER

An aluminum, three-blade propeller with built-in cushion clutch is standard on most motors while some motors are equipped with a stainless steel propeller. Optional propellers are available. Only propellers designed for use on these motors should be used. Refer to CONDENSED SERVICE DATA for desired engine speed at full throttle.

LOWER UNIT

Electric Shift Lower Unit

REMOVE AND REINSTALL. An electric shift lower unit is used on 1971 and 1972 models with an electric starter. Most service of the lower unit can be accomplished after separating gearcase from exhaust housing.

Disconnect spark plug wires. Disconnect blade type connectors on remote shift wires and tie a length of string to loose wires as an assembly aid. Mark trim tab (22 – Fig. OM13-40) to ensure proper relocation and remove. Remove screw in trim tab cavity and screw just forward of trim tab area. Remaining two screws on port and two screws on starboard side secure gearcase to exhaust housing.

Reassemble gearcase to exhaust housing in following manner: Make sure that "O" ring (1) is in good condition and in place on the drive shaft. Coat mating

cover. Remove cap screw (C) and disconnect starter lockout cable (L) from lockout slide (S). Move lockout slide (S) to align with disassembly notches in starter housing and withdraw. Remove the screws retaining the manual starter to the engine. Withdraw the starter assembly.

Check pawl (13 – Fig. OM13-30) for freedom of movement, excessive wear of engagement area and damage. Renew or lubricate pawl (13) with OMC

TRIPLE-GUARD GREASE or Lubriplate 777 and reinstall the starter assembly if additional service is not required.

To disassemble, detach starter rope (9) at anchor (3) and allow the rope to wind into the starter. Remove nut (22), bolt (19), washer (18), pawl plate (21), pawl return spring (23), pawl (13), pawl wave washer and spring (20). Remove snap ring (17), friction plate (16) and wave washer. Insert a suitable screwdriver blade through hole (A) to hold rewind spring (7) securely in housing (1) Carefully lift pulley (10) with starter rope (9) from housing (1). BE CAREFUL when removing pulley (10) to prevent possible injury from rewind spring (7). Remove starter rope (9) from pulley (10) if renewal is required. To remove rewind spring (7) from housing (1), invert housing so it sets upright on a flat surface, then tap the housing top until rewind spring (7) falls free and uncoils.

Inspect all components from damage and excessive wear and renew if needed.

To reassemble, install plate (6) and apply a coating of OMC TRIPLE-GUARD GREASE or Lubriplate 777 to rewind spring area of housing (1). Install rewind spring (7) in housing (1) so spring coils wind in a counterclockwise direction from the outer end. Make sure spring outer hook is properly secured over starter housing pin. Install plate (8). If needed, a new starter rope (9) cut to a length of 96½ inches (245 cm) should be installed on pulley (10).

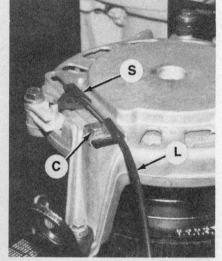

Fig. 13-31 — View showing starter lockout assembly used on later models.

C. Cap screw
L. Cable
S. Slide

surfaces of gearcase and exhaust housing with OMC Adhesive "M" or equivalent and run string tied to shift wires through exhaust housing into engine compartment. Make certain water tube enters pump grommet (4) and pull shift wires through exhaust housing and power head adapter. Drive shaft and crankshaft splines may be aligned by turning flywheel clockwise.

GEARCASE. Gearcase may be disassembled in the following manner: Drain lubricant and remove gearcase as described in previous section. Remove screws securing water pump housing (5–Fig. OM13-40); lift housing, impeller (6) and remove pump drive key. Remove plate (8) and bearing housing (11). Remove solenoid cover (24) and wave washer (27) then carefully lift out solenoid and plunger assembly. Dismount propeller and unscrew four screws holding bearing housing (69). Use a puller attached with two 8-inch long 5/16-18 bolts to remove bearing housing. Slide thrust washer (64) and thrust bearing (63) off shaft and remove retaining rings (66). Propeller shaft can now be removed with reverse gear (62), dog clutch (54) and associated parts. A special socket (OMC Special Tool 316612) is available to hold drive shaft so that nut securing pinion gear (18) can be removed. Drive shaft can be lifted free of gearcase and forward gear (52) removed after removing pinion gear. Use slide hammers and two 16-inch long rods with ¼-20 threads on the ends to remove oil pump (49).

Inspect drive shaft splines, bearing surfaces and seal surfaces for wear or damage. Damaged splines may be caused by striking a submerged object and bending the exhaust housing. Check parallelism of top and bottom surfaces if questionable. If surfaces are not parallel, renew housing, do not attempt to straighten it.

Lower drive shaft bearing (17) should only be removed if renewal is intended. Do not reinstall a used bearing. Removal and installation procedure varies between 1971 and 1972 models, refer to the following paragraphs for correct method: Bearing removal on 1971 models is accomplished by driving bearing out toward bottom of gearcase. OMC Special Tool 383173 (A–Fig. OM13-41) should be used to install new bearing. Assemble bearing and tool in gearcase with lettered side of bearing down and pull bearing up into case.

On 1972 models, bearing is held in position by a set screw (17A–Fig. OM13-40) as well as a press fit in gearcase. Set screw is located on starboard side in area of water intake. After removing set screw, install OMC Special

Tool 385546, with shouldered side of puller piece against bearing and pull bearing out of case toward top. New bearing is installed by assembling special tool with the sleeve provided and driving bearing into gearcase with lettered side of bearing up (Fig. OM13-42) and shouldered side of pusher piece

against bearing. Bearing will be properly positioned when plate of tool touches top of gearcase. Apply "Loctite" to set screw (17A–Fig. OM13-40) and install.

Shift solenoids (31 and 35) should be checked with an ohmmeter. Resistance should be 5-6 ohms when checked be-

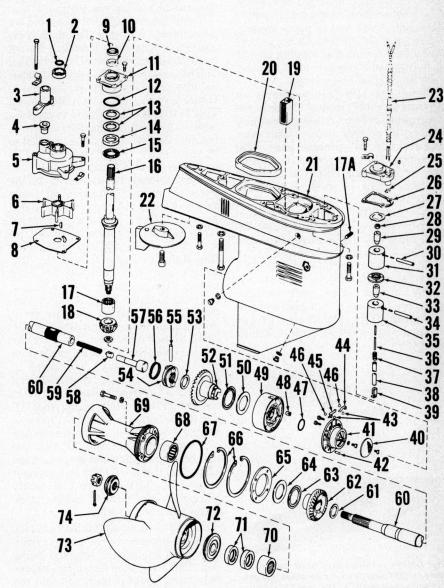

Fig. OM13-40—View of lower unit gearcase used on electric shift 50 hp models.

1. "O" ring	19. Water screen	56. Pin retaining spring
2. Grommet	20. Exhaust seal	38. Shift rod casing
3. Water tube bracket	21. Gearcase	39. Cap
4. Grommet	22. Trim tab	40. Oil screen
5. Impeller housing	23. Shift control wires	41. Valve housing
6. Impeller	24. Solenoid cover	42. Locating dowel
7. Drive key	25. Retainer	43. Shift valve balls
8. Plate	26. Gasket	44. Neutral lever
9. Seal	27. Wave washer	45. Reverse lever
10. Seal	28. Locknut	46. Valve seats
11. Bearing & housing assy.	29. Upper plunger	47. "O" ring
	30. Heat shrink tube	48. Plug
12. "O" ring	31. Upper solenoid	49. Oil pump assy.
13. Adjustment shims	32. Spacer	50. Thrust washer
14. Thrust washer	33. Lower plunger	51. Thrust bearing
15. Thrust bearing	34. Heat shrink tube	52. Forward gear
16. Drive shaft	35. Lower solenoid	53. Thrust washer
17. Needle bearing	36. Shift rod	54. Dog clutch
17A. Set screw	37. Lock screw	55. Pin
18. Pinion gear		

56. Pin retaining spring
57. Oil pump piston
58. Dog clutch retainer
59. Spring
60. Propeller shaft
61. Thrust washer
62. Reverse gear
63. Thrust bearing
64. Thrust washer
65. Retainer plate
66. Snap rings
67. "O" ring
68. Needle bearing
69. Bearing housing
70. Needle bearing
71. Seals
72. Thrust bushing
73. Propeller
74. Prop nut spacer

tween each of the wires and solenoid case. If solenoid or wires (23) are renewed, use new heat shrink insulating tubes (30 and 34) to seal wire connections.

The shift pump valve balls (43) and seats (46) for these balls can be renewed. The surfaces of rotor set in housing should be checked for wear and scoring. Renew complete pump assembly if any part of rotor set is damaged excessively. The front surfaces of rotor set should be flush with front face of pump housing, when parts (50, 51 and 52) are in position. Make certain that locating pin (42) is fully seated in recess in forward end of gear housing on reassembly.

Pinion gear (18) mesh position is not adjustable on 1971 models. The different arrangement of thrust bearing assembly (14 and 15) on 1972 models makes exact positioning of pinion gear (18) necessary. The mesh position is adjusted by varying shims (13). The following procedure may be used to determine proper shimming for 1972 models. Place pinion gear (18) on drive shaft and torque retaining nut to 40-45 ft.-lbs. Install shims (13) that were removed during disassembly and leave thrust washer (14) or thrust bearing (15) off shaft. Hold shim gage (OMC Special Tool 315767) firmly against shims and measure clearance between end of gage and pinion gear (Fig. OM13-44). Proper clearance is 0.000-0.002 inch (0.00-0.05 mm).

NOTE: If clearance appears to be 0, make certain that enough shims are installed for an accurate check.

Shims are available in thicknesses of 0.002 and 0.005 inch and may be used in any quantity to obtain proper clearance. Set the correct shims aside until drive shaft is installed.

Seals (9 and 10 – Fig. OM13-40) should be installed with lip of bottom seal (10) down and lip of top seal (9) up.

Needle bearings (68 and 70) should not be removed from propeller shaft housing unless renewal is intended. Do not install used bearings. OMC Special Tool 317061 should be used to press aft bearing into propeller shaft housing (69) to ensure proper positioning. OMC Special Tool 314641 should be used to properly position forward bearing (68) in bore of housing. Seals (71) should be installed so lip on aft seal is toward propeller and lip on forward seal is facing forward.

Gearcase may be assembled in the following manner: Position oil pump assembly (parts 40 through 49 and 57) in gearcase, making sure that locating pin (42) is fully seated in recess provided. Install drive shaft (16) and pinion gear (18). Refer to Fig. OM13-43 for 1971 motors and Fig. OM13-40 for 1972 motors. Torque pinion gear retaining nut to 40-45 ft.-lbs. (54-61 N·m). Assemble dog clutch (54) on propeller shaft, placing side of dog clutch marked "PROP END" toward rear. Place thrust washer (61), reverse gear (62) and retainer plate (65) on propeller shaft and install in gearcase. Install snap rings (66) and place thrust bearing parts (63 and 64) in position on shaft. Make certain that "O" ring (67) is correctly seated in groove of bearing housing (69) and is free of any nicks or tears. Lubricate "O" ring and slide bearing housing into gearcase making certain that "UP" mark on housing is toward top. Coat screws that secure bearing housing with a sealing compound and install them.

Install and adjust shift solenoids in the following manner: Screw plunger (with large hole) into tubular shift rod casing (Fig. OM13-45), then install and tighten lock screw. Insert plunger and shift rod

into reverse solenoid (blue wire) and push cap onto bottom of shift rod casing. Insert lower solenoid assembly into gearcase bore. Make sure end of shift rod is against the shift valve lever on pump and solenoid is against bottom of bore in housing. Check distance from top of plunger to top of solenoid. Top of plunger must be flush with top of solenoid. Adjustment is accomplished by removing assembly, loosening lock screw, and turning shift rod casing. The lock screw should be torqued to 9-11 in.-lbs. (1.0-1.2 N·m) when adjustment

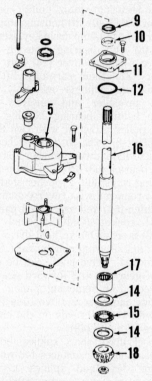

Fig. OM13-43 – Arrangement of thrust bearing parts (14 & 15) common to 1971 models. Refer to Fig. OM13-40 for legend.

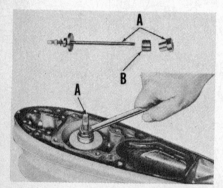

Fig. OM13-41—Lower drive shaft bearing (B) used on 1971 models should be pulled into position in gearcase with OMC Tool 383173 (A).

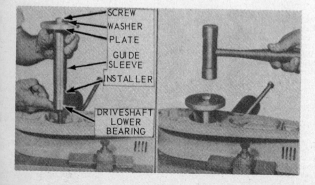

Fig. OM13-42 – Installer/removal tool (OMC Tool 385546) may be used to drive lower drive shaft bearing into gearcase of 1972 and some later models. Refer to text for procedure.

Fig. OM13-44—Shim gage (OMC Tool 315767) should be used to properly set mesh position of pinion gear on drive shaft. Refer to text for procedure.

SERVICE MANUAL

Evinrude & Johnson 40 (1985 & 1986), 50, 55 & 60 HP 2 Cyl.

is complete. Install lower solenoid assembly. Position spacer (32–Fig. OM13-40) on top of lower solenoid with flat side down. Assemble small shift rod (Fig. OM13-46), plunger with small hole and locknut. Position the plunger and shift rod in neutral (upper) solenoid. Insert the neutral solenoid and shift rod assembly into gearcase bore above the reverse shift assembly and spacer. Make sure end of rod is through hole in top valve lever (44–Fig. OM13-40) and solenoids are tight against bottom of bore. Check distance between top of plunger and top of solenoid. Top of plunger must be flush with top of solenoid. Adjustment is accomplished after loosening locknut and turning shift rod. Locknut should be torqued to 3-5 inch-pounds when adjustment is completed.

NOTE: Improper shifting will result if adjustment of shift rods and plungers is not correct.

Install solenoids and shift rods, position wave washer (27) on top of solenoids, coat both sides of gasket (26) with OMC Gasket Sealing Compound or equivalent and install cover (24). Apply OMC Adhesive "M" or equivalent to bottom of impeller plate (8), install key (7) in drive shaft and locate impeller (6) over key. Lubricate impeller, hold blades in and install water pump housing (5).

NOTE: Drive shaft can be rotated clockwise while assembling pump housing, but should never be turned backwards.

Coat screws attaching water pump housing with OMC Gasket Sealing Compound or equivalent before installing. Reinstall shift cable clamps in original position (aft, starboard screw in water pump housing and solenoid cover) and make certain that drive shaft "O" ring (1) is in position.

Hydraulic Shift Lower Unit

A hydraulically shifted lower unit is used on 1973 and 1974 models with an electric starter. To service lower unit, refer to following sections.

SHIFT LINKAGE ADJUSTMENT. Shift linkage is adjusted by disconnecting clevis (C–Fig. OM13-47) from bellcrank (R). Turn clevis (C) to obtain measurement (D) of 5-3/16 to 5-5/16 inches (13.18-13.49 cm) between center of bellcrank pin (P) and center of shift cable bracket (B).

REMOVE AND REINSTALL. To remove gearcase, disconnect spark plug leads, remove electric starter and detach upper end of shift rod by removing screw shown in Fig. OM13-52. Mark trim tab (22–Fig. OM13-48) to ensure proper relocation and remove trim tab. Remove screw in trim tab cavity and screw just forward of trim tab area. Unscrew two screws on port and starboard sides and separate gearcase from exhaust housing. Be careful not to bend shift rod during disassembly.

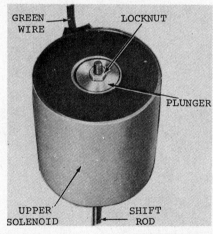

Fig. OM13-46 — View of upper (neutral) solenoid.

Reassemble gearcase to exhaust housing using following procedure: Make certain that "O" ring (1) is in good condition and in position on end of drive shaft. Check length of gear shift rod (27). With shifter in neutral, distance from mating surface of gearcase (21) to center of hole in top of shift rod should be 16-3/16 to 16¼ inches (41.12-41.27 cm) for standard models and 21-3/16 to 21¼ inches (53.82-53.97 cm) for long shaft models. Flattened area on end of shift rod should slant toward front on reassembly. Apply OMC Adhesive "M" or equivalent to mating surface of exhaust housing and gearcase. Install gearcase while observing proper alignment of water tube in water tube grommet on water pump. Turn flywheel clockwise to align crankshaft splines with those on drive shaft.

GEARCASE. To disassemble gearcase, drain lubricant, remove propeller and separate gearcase from exhaust housing as outlined in previous section. Remove water pump housing (5–Fig. OM13-48), impeller (6), key (7) and lower plate (8). Remove four screws holding propeller shaft bearing housing (69) and using a suitable puller, withdraw bearing housing from gearcase. Remove snap rings (66), thrust washer (64), thrust bearing (63) and shift rod cover (28). Remove shift rod and propeller shaft components by withdrawing shift rod (27) and propeller shaft simultaneously. Hold drive shaft with OMC Tool 316612 or another suitable tool and unscrew pinion nut. Remove pinion (18), unscrew bearing housing (11) screws and withdraw drive shaft and components from gearcase. Bearing in housing (11) is not renewable but must be obtained as a unit assembly with housing. Remove forward gear (53). Using a suitable puller and two 16 inch rods with ¼-20 threads, remove oil pump (43) from gearcase.

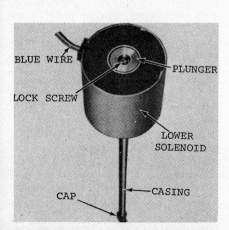

Fig. OM13-45 — View of lower (reverse) solenoid assembly. Refer to text for adjustment.

Fig. OM13-47 — View of gear shift mechanism on hydraulic shift models. Refer to text for adjustment.

To disassemble oil pump, unscrew four screws securing cover (42) and remove cover. Remove snap ring (48), plug (47), spring (46), guide (45) and pressure relief valve ball (44). Inspect pressure relief valve components and renew if worn or damaged. Inspect oil pump assembly for wear or damage. Dots on rotors must be up and surfaces of rotors and housing must be flat across ends when forward gear, thrust bearing and

washer are installed in pump. Rotors, housing and bearing are not available separately and must be renewed as a unit assembly.

Seals (9 and 10) should be installed with lip of bottom seal (10) down and lip of top seal (9) up.

Needle bearings (68 and 70) should not be removed from propeller shaft housing unless renewal is intended. Do not install used bearings. OMC Special Tool

317061 should be used to press aft bearing into propeller shaft housing (69) to ensure proper positioning. OMC Special Tool 314641 should be used to properly position forward bearing (68) in bore of housing. Seals (71) should be installed so that lip on aft seal is toward propeller and lip on forward seal is facing forward.

Thicknesses of shims (13) is varied to adjust mesh position of pinion gear (18) in forward and reverse gear. A shim gage, OMC Special Tool 315767, should be used to determine proper shimming.

Place pinion gear (18) on drive shaft and torque retaining nut to 40-45 ft.-lbs. (54-61 N·m). Install shims (13) that were removed during disassembly and leave thrust washer (14) and thrust bearing (15) off shaft. Hold shim gage firmly against shims and measure clearance between end of gage and pinion gear (Fig. OM13-44). Proper clearance is 0.000-0.002 inch (0.00-0.051 mm).

NOTE: If clearance appears to be 0, make certain that enough shims are installed for an accurate check.

Shims are available in thicknesses of 0.002 inch and 0.005 inch and may be installed in any quantity to obtain proper clearance. Set the correct shims aside until drive shaft is installed.

Inspect drive shaft splines, bearing surfaces and seal surfaces for wear or damage. Damaged splines may be caused by striking a submerged object and bending the exhaust housing. Check parallelism of top and bottom surfaces if questionable. If surfaces are not parallel, renew housing. Do not attempt to straighten it.

Lower drive shaft bearing (17–Fig. OM13-48) should only be removed if renewal is intended. Do not reinstall a used bearing. Drive shaft bearing is held in position by a set screw (17A) as well as a press fit in gearcase. Set screw is located on starboard side in area of water intake. After removing set screw, install OMC Special Tool 385546, with shouldered side of puller piece against bearing and pull bearing out of case toward top. New bearing is installed by assembling special tool with sleeve provided and puller piece turned over so that shouldered side will again be next to bearing. Drive bearing (with lettered side up) into case (Fig. OM13-42). Bearing will be properly positioned when plate of tool touches top of gearcase. Apply Loctite to set screw and install.

Hydraulic shift components (31 and 39–Fig. OM13-48) may be disassembled with OMC Tool 386112 by engaging pins on tool with holes in piston (37) and piston cap (31) and unscrewing cap from piston. Be careful not to bend or damage

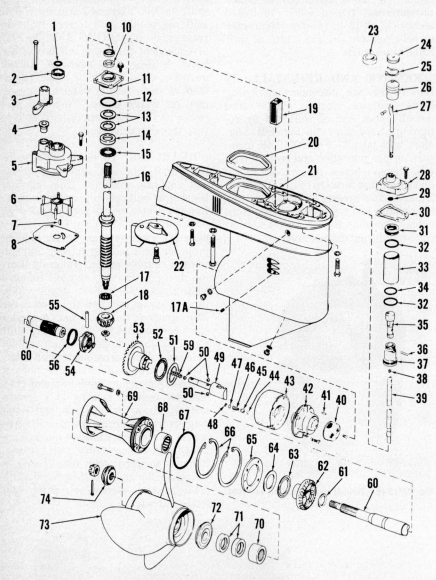

Fig. OM13-48—Exploded view of hydraulic shift lower unit used on 1973 models with electric starter and all 1974 models.

1. "O" ring	17A. Set screw	36. Pin
2. Grommet	18. Pinion gear	37. Piston
3. Water tube bracket	19. Water screen	38. Plug
4. Grommet	20. Exhaust seal	39. Push rod
5. Impeller housing	21. Gearcase	40. Screen
6. Impeller	22. Trim tab	41. Locating dowel
7. Drive key	23. Seal	42. Cover
8. Plate	24. Grommet	43. Oil pump & housing
9. Seal	25. Tie strap	44. Relief valve ball
10. Seal	26. Seal	45. Ball guide
11. Bearing & housing assy.	27. Shift rod	46. Spring
12. "O" ring	28. Shift rod cover	47. Plug
13. Shims	29. "O" ring	48. Snap ring
14. Thrust washer	30. Gasket	49. Shift plunger
15. Thrust bearing	31. Piston cap	50. Detent balls
16. Drive shaft	32. "O" ring	51. Thrust washer
17. Needle bearing	33. Cylinder	52. Thrust bearing
	34. "O" ring	53. Forward gear
	35. Valve	54. Dog clutch

55. Pin	
56. Retaining spring	
59. Spring	
60. Propeller shaft	
61. Thrust washer	
62. Reverse gear	
63. Thrust bearing	
64. Thrust washer	
65. Retainer plate	
66. Snap rings	
67. "O" ring	
68. Needle bearing	
69. Bearing housing	
70. Needle bearing	
71. Seals	
72. Thrust bushing	
73. Propeller	
74. Spacer	

push rod (39) during disassembly. Remove pin (36) to separate valve (35), piston (37) and push rod. Cap (31) should be tightened to 12-15 ft.-lbs. (16.3-20.4 N·m) during reassembly.

To assist in installing shift plunger components in propeller shaft, grind away the end of a 9/32-inch rod to form a long flat taper on one side. Rod should be approximately 2⅝ inches (66.67 mm) long. Position dog clutch (54–Fig. OM13-48) on propeller shaft with pin hole in dog clutch and slot in shaft aligned. Place three detent balls (50) and spring (59) in plunger (49) as shown in Fig. OM13-49 and install plunger in propeller shaft so detent balls match grooves in propeller shaft. Align holes in dog clutch (54–Fig. OM13-48) and shift plunger (48) and insert tapered end of tool through holes to properly position detent spring. Carefully push tool out with retaining pin (55) and install pin retaining spring (56) in outer groove of dog clutch. Coils of spring must not overlap.

To reassemble gearcase, install oil pump (43), forward gear (53), thrust bearing (52) and thrust washer (51) so that locating pin (41) aligns with pin hole in gearcase. Install drive shaft (16) and pinion gear (18) and tighten pinion nut to 40-45 ft.-lbs. (54-61 N·m). Lay gearcase on starboard side and install propeller shaft with flat side of shift plunger (49) up until propeller shaft is bottomed. Install hydraulic shift assembly with flat on end of push rod (39) down. Insert shift assembly until flats on push rod (39) and shift plunger (49) are engaged (push rod will not turn).

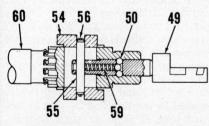

Fig. OM13-49—Cross-sectional view of shift plunger (49) and dog clutch (54) components. Refer to Fig. OM13-48 for parts identification.

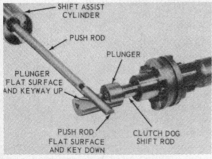

Fig. OM13-50—View showing relative positions of shift assemblies when installed in gearcase. Refer to text for installation.

Place light pressure against shift cylinder (33) and slowly withdraw propeller shaft until key on end of push rod meshes with keyway in shift plunger as shown in Fig. OM13-50. When key and keyway are meshed, push shift assembly and propeller shaft in to complete engagement. Complete remainder of assembly noting the following points: Install snap ring (66) with flat side out. Install bearing housing (69) with "UP" mark towards water pump. Apply OMC Gasket Sealing Compound to threads of screws securing retainer plate (65) and bearing housing (69).

Manual Shift Lower Unit

REMOVE AND REINSTALL. Most service of the lower unit can be accomplished after separating gearcase from exhaust housing. Gearcase may be removed in the following manner: Disconnect spark plug leads, remove manual starter (if equipped with early type) and remove shift rod screw (Fig. OM13-52).

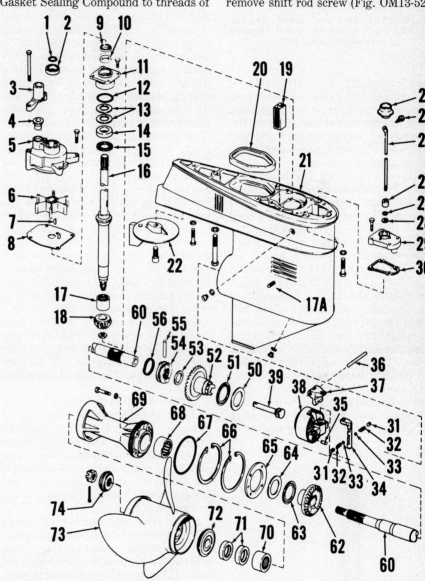

Fig. OM13-51—Typical exploded view of manual shift lower unit. Some models use tapered roller bearings in place of thrust bearings and washers (14, 15, 50 and 51). Later models do not use thrust washer (53).

1. "O" ring	16. Drive shaft	30. Gasket	55. Pin
2. Grommet	17. Needle bearing	31. Set screw	56. Pin retaining spring
3. Water tube bracket	17A. Set screw	32. Detent springs	60. Propeller shaft
4. Grommet	18. Pinion gear	33. Detent balls	62. Reverse gear
5. Impeller housing	18. Water screen	34. Detent	63. Thrust bearing
6. Impeller	19. Water screen	35. Locating dowel	64. Thrust washer
7. Drive key	20. Exhaust seal	36. Shift lever pin	65. Retainer plate
8. Plate	21. Gearcase	37. Shift lever	66. Snap rings
9. Seal	22. Trim tab	38. Bearing housing	67. "O" ring
10. Seal	23. Shift rod seal	39. Shift shaft	68. Needle bearing
11. Bearing & housing assy.	24. Shift rod screw	50. Thrust washer	69. Bearing housing
12. "O" ring	25. Shift rod	51. Thrust bearing	70. Needle bearing
13. Adjustment shims	26. Bushing	52. Forward gear	71. Seals
14. Thrust washer	27. "O" ring	53. Thrust washer	72. Thrust bushing
15. Thrust bearing	28. Gasket	54. Dog clutch	73. Propeller
	29. Shift rod cover		74. Prop nut spacer

Fig. OM13-52—Shift rod screw (24—Fig. OM13-51) must be removed before removing manual shift lower unit.

Mark trim tab (22–Fig. OM13-51) to ensure proper relocation and remove. Remove screw in trim tab cavity and screw just forward of trim tab area. Remaining two screws on port and two screws on starboard side secure gearcase to exhaust housing.

Reassemble gearcase to exhaust housing in the following manner: Make sure that "O" ring (1) is in good condition and in position on end of drive shaft. Check length of gear shift rod (25). With shifter in neutral, distance from mating surface of gearcase (21) to center of hole in top of shift rod on pre-1974 models should be 16-7/32 inches (41.19 cm) for standard models and 21-7/32 inches (53.89 cm) for long-shaft models. Shift rod height for 1975-1978 models should be set using OMC Tool 321200. Shift rod height for models after 1978 is 15-29/32 inches (40.4 cm) for standard models and 20-29/32 inches (53.1 cm) for long-shaft models. Flattened area on end of shift rod should slant toward drive shaft on reassembly. Apply OMC Adhesive "M" or equivalent to mating surface of

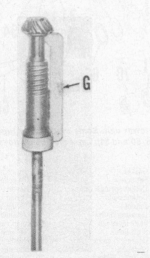

Fig. OM13-53—Measure gap between shift tool gage (G) and pinion gear to determine thickness of shims (13—Fig. OM13-53). Refer to text.

exhaust housing and gearcase. Install gearcase while observing proper alignment of water tube in water tube grommet on water pump. Turn flywheel clockwise to align crankshaft splines with those on drive shaft.

GEARCASE. Gearcase may be disassembled in the following manner: Remove propeller, drain lubricant and remove gearcase as described in previous section. Remove screws securing shift rod cover (29–Fig. OM13-51), unscrew shift rod (25) and remove shift rod and cover as an assembly. Remove water pump housing (5), impeller (6), key (7) and lower plate (8). Remove four screws holding propeller shaft bearing housing (69) and using a suitable puller, remove bearing housing. Discard seals (71) and "O" ring (67). Remove snap rings (66), thrust washer assembly (64 and 63) and slide reverse gear (62) off propeller shaft. A special socket (OMC Special Tool 316612) is available to hold drive shaft so nut securing pinion gear (18) can be removed. After pinion gear (18) retaining nut is removed, unscrew the four screws securing upper drive shaft bearing housing (11). Pull drive shaft and associated parts out of gearcase. A puller is necessary to remove drive shaft assembly on 1975 and later models. Bearing in housing (11) on models prior to 1974 is not renewable. If bearing is worn, renew entire housing. A taper roller bearing is used on 1975 and later model drive shaft. Propeller shaft (60) may now be pulled from gearcase complete with forward gear (52), forward bearing housing (38), and all associated parts.

Inspect drive shaft splines, bearing surfaces and seal surfaces for wear or damage. Damaged splines may be caused by striking a submerged object and bending the exhaust housing. Check parallelism of top and bottom surfaces if questionable. If surfaces are not parallel, renew housing. Do not attempt to straighten it.

Lower drive shaft bearing (17) should only be removed if renewal is intended. Do not reinstall a used bearing. Drive shaft bearing is held in position by a set screw (17A) as well as a press fit in gearcase. Set screw is located on starboard side in area of water intake. After removing set screw, use a suitable puller and pull bearing out of case toward top. New bearing is installed by assembling special tool with sleeve provided and puller piece turned over so shouldered side will again be next to drive bearing (with lettered side up) into case. Apply Loctite to set screw and install.

Forward gear (52) and propeller shaft (60) may be removed from propeller shaft bearing housing (38) after dislodg-

ing spring (56) and removing dog clutch assembly (55 and 54). Bearing housing and shifter mechanism assembly (38) may be disassembled by driving out shift lever pin (36) on all models and unscrewing set screws (31) on models prior to 1974.

Thickness of shims (13) is varied to adjust mesh position of pinion gear (18) in forward and reverse gears. An OMC shim tool should be used to determine proper shimming.

Place pinion gear (18) on drive shaft and torque retaining nut to 40-45 ft.-lbs. (54-61 N·m). On models prior to 1974, install shims (13) that were removed during disassembly and leave thrust washer (14) and thrust bearing (15) off shaft. On 1975 and later models, only pinion gear, nut, taper bearing cone and cup should be on drive shaft. Hold shim gage firmly against shims and measure distance between end of gage and pinion gear (Fig. OM13-53). Install shims (13) so there is zero clearance between shim tool and gear.

NOTE: On models prior to 1974, if clearance appears to be 0, make certain that enough shims are installed for an accurate check.

Shims are available in thicknesses of 0.002 inch and 0.005 inch for pre-1974 models and from 0.003 to 0.007 inch for 1975 and later models, and may be installed in any quantity to obtain proper clearance. Set the correct shims aside until drive shaft is installed.

Needle bearings (68 and 70–Fig. OM13-51) should not be removed from propeller shaft housing (69) unless renewal is intended. Do not reinstall used bearings. OMC Special Tool 317061 (pre-1974 models) or 320738 (1975 and later models) should be used to press aft bearing into propeller shaft housing to ensure proper positioning. OMC Special Tool 314641 (pre-1974 models) or 320669 (1975 and later models) should be used to position bearing (70) in forward bore of propeller shaft housing. Seals (71) should be installed so lip on aft seal is toward propeller and lip on forward seal is facing forward.

Assemble gearcase in the following manner: Renew all gaskets, seals and "O" rings. If lower drive shaft bearing (17) or propeller shaft bearings (68 and 70) have been removed, they too should be renewed. Assemble shift lever (37), shift detent (34) and shift shaft (39) in bearing housing (38). Install detent balls and springs, then apply Loctite to set screws (31) on pre-1974 models. Assemble forward gear (52) with bearing in bearing housing. Place thrust washer (53), on models so equipped, and dog clutch (54) on propeller shaft (60). Make sure that hole in dog clutch is

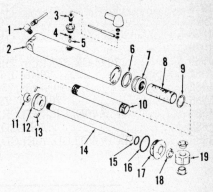

Fig. OM13-65—View identifying manual release valve screw (S) and reservoir fill plug (R) location.

aligned with slot in propeller shaft. Insert propeller shaft in forward gear and bearing housing assembly, then insert pin (55) through dog clutch propeller shaft and hole in shift shaft (39). Install pin retaining spring (56). Press shift detent (34) down and place propeller shaft, forward gear and bearing housing assembly (38) into position in gearcase. Make sure locating pin (35) is seated in recess provided in gearcase. Install shift rod (25) and shift rod cover (29) as an assembly. Thread shift rod fully into detent (34), pull rod to neutral (middle detent) and adjust for proper length. Refer to shift rod adjustment in LOWER UNIT REMOVE AND REINSTALL section for specifications. Pull rod up into forward gear position on completion of adjustment.

Pinion gear (18) may be positioned for reinstallation after turning gearcase upside down. Insert drive shaft (16). Install pinion gear retaining nut and torque it to 40-45 ft.-lbs. (54-61 N·m). Assemble thrust bearing (64 and 63) on reverse gear (62) and slide onto propeller shaft (60). Position bearing retainer plate (65) and install snap rings (66). Make sure that "O" ring (67) is fully seated in groove of bearing housing (69) and that seals (71) are properly installed. Lip of forward seal should be toward front and lip of aft seal should be toward propeller.

Installation of bearing housing (69) will be eased by using two guide pins 10 inches long with ¼-20 threads on one end. Thread guide pins into bearing retainer plate (65) and slide bearing housing (69) into position. Coat bearing housing screws with sealing compound and install. Turn gearcase right side up.

Install seals (9 and 10) in upper drive shaft bearing housing (11) with lip of lower seal (10) down and lip of upper seal (9) up. Place thrust bearing

assembly (14 and 15) on drive shaft of pre-1974 models and install previously selected shims or shims (13). Coat screws that secure bearing housing (11) with sealing compound and install. Bottom edge of impeller plate (8) should be coated with OMC Adhesive "M" or equivalent and placed in position. Install key (7), lubricate edges of impeller (6) and install on drive shaft. Drive shaft should be turned clockwise while installing water pump housing (5). Coat screws that secure water pump housing and water tube bracket with sealing compound and install.

POWER TILT AND TRIM

So Equipped Models After 1981

OPERATION. Some models after 1981 are equipped with a hydraulically actuated power tilt and trim system. An oil pump driven by a reversible electric motor provides oil pressure. One hydraulic cylinder trims the outboard motor while another hydraulic cylinder tilts the outboard motor. A rocker control switch determines motor and pump rotation thereby retracting or extending tilt and trim cylinders. The pump motor is equipped with a thermal overload switch which resets after approximately one minute. Turn slotted manual release valve screw (S–Fig. OM13-65) at bottom of pump to manually raise or lower outboard. Tighten manual release valve clockwise to operate hydraulic tilt and trim.

Hydraulic system contains approximately 25 oz. (740 mL) of oil. Recommended oil is OMC Power Trim and Tilt Fluid or DEXRON Automatic Transmission Fluid. Do not run pump without oil in reservoir. Fill plug (R) is located in side of pump reservoir. Oil level should reach fill plug hole threads with outboard tilted in full up position. Hydraulic tilt should be cycled several times and oil level rechecked if system has been drained or lost a large amount of oil.

TROUBLESHOOTING. The following specifications should be noted when a malfunction occurs in tilt and trim system. Current draw should be 45 amps when operating either up or down. Current draw with unit stalled in up or down position should be 55 amps. To check oil pressure, first momentarily cycle system "UP" and "DOWN" a few times. Remove manual release valve screw (S–Fig. OM13-65) and install OMC gage "A." Operate system in the "UP" direction and observe gage after system stalls out at full extension. Gage reading should not drop below 100-200 psi (700-1400 kPa). Install OMC gage

"B." Operate system in the "DOWN" direction and observe gage after system is fully retracted and stalls out. Gage reading should not drop below 100-200 psi (700-1400 kPa).

OVERHAUL. Oil pump must be serviced as a unit assembly. Motor components are available. Refer to Figs. OM13-66 and OM13-67 for exploded views of trim and cylinders. To check operation of trim gage sending unit, connect ohmmeter leads to sender (3–Fig. OM13-66) and elbow (1). Resistance should be 2.5-3.5 ohms with cylinder rod fully extended and 84-96 ohms with rod fully retracted.

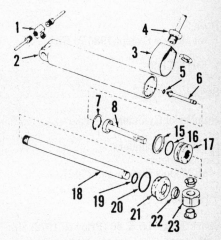

Fig. OM13-66—Exploded view of hydraulic trim cylinder.

1. Elbow	11. Stop
2. Trim cylinder	12. Carrier bearing
3. Sender	13. Sender ground
4. Spring	springs
5. Ball	14. Shaft
6. "O" ring	15. "O" ring
7. Piston	16. "O" ring
8. Sender bobbin	17. End cap
9. Retaining ring	18. Wiper
10. Piston carrier	19. Shaft end

Fig. OM13-67—Exploded view of hydraulic tilt cylinder.

1. Tee	16. "O" ring
2. Tilt cylinder	17. Piston
3. Band	18. Shaft
4. Oil line	19. "O" ring
5. "O" ring	20. "O" ring
6. Stem valve	21. End cap
7. Snap ring	22. Wiper
8. Relief valve assy.	23. Shaft end
15. Piston ring	

EVINRUDE AND JOHNSON
3-CYLINDER MODELS
55, 60, 65 70 AND 75 HP

EVINRUDE	
Year Produced	**Model**
1969	55972, 55973
1970	60072, 66073
1971	60172, 60173
1972	65272, 65273
1973	65372, 65373
1974	70442, 70443, 70472, 70473
1975	70572, 70573, 75542, 75543
1976	70673, 74642, 75643
1977	70773, 75742, 75743
1978	70873, 75842, 75843
1979	70973, 75942, 75943
1980	70ELCX, 75ERCS, 75ERLCS, 75TRLCS
1981	70ELCI, 75ERCI, 75TRLCI
1982	70ELCN, 75ERCN, 75TRLCN
1983	70ELCT, 75ERCT, 75TRLCT
1984	70ELCR, 70TLCR, 75ECR, 75TLCR
1985	70ELCO, 70TLCO, 75ECO
1986	60ELCD, 60TLCD, 70ELCD, 70TLCD, 75ECD

JOHNSON	
Year Produced	**Model**
1969	55ES69, 55ESL9
1970	60ES70, 60ESL70
1971	60ES71, 60ESL71
1972	65ES72, 65ESL72
1973	65ES73, 65ESL73, 65ESLR73
1974	70ES74, 70ESL74, 70ESLR74
1975	70ES75, 70ESL75, 74ERS75, 75ESLR75
1976	70EL76, 75ER76, 75ELR76
1977	70EL77, 75ER77, 75ELR77
1978	70EL78, 75ER78, 75ELR78
1979	70EL79, 75ER79, 75ELR79
1980	70ELCS, 75ERCS, 75ERLCS, 75TRLCS
1981	70ELCI, 75ERCI, 75TRLCI
1982	70ELCN, 75ERCN, 75TRLCN
1983	70ELCT, 75ERCT, 75TRLCT
1984	70ELCR, 70TLCR, 75ECR, 75TLCR
1985	70ELCO, 70TLCO, 75ECO
1986	60ELCD, 60TLCD, 70ELCD, 70TLCD, 75ECD

CONDENSED SERVICE DATA

TUNE-UP

Hp/rpm	55/5000
	60/5000‡
	65/5000
	70/5000*
	75/5500†
Bore:	
All Models Except 1986 70 Hp	3.0 in. (76.2 mm)
1986 70 HP	3.18 in. (80.9 mm)
Stroke	2.34 in. (59.5 mm)
Number of Cylinders	2.34 in. (59.5 mm)
Number of Cylinders	3
Displacement:	
All Models Except 1986 70 Hp	49.7 cu. in. (814 cc)
1986 70 Hp	56.1 cu. in. (913 cc)
Spark Plug—55 & 60 (Prior to 1972) Hp:	
AC	V40FF
Champion	L77V
Spark Plug—65 Hp (Prior to 1974):	
AC	VB40FFM
Champion	UL77V
Spark Plug—65 (After 1983), 70 & 75 (Prior to 1986) Hp:	
AC	M40FFX

TUNE-UP CONT.

Champion	QL77J4‡
Electrode Gap	0.040 in. (1.0 mm)
Spark Plug—All 1986 Models:	
Champion	QL77JC4‡
Electrode Gap	0.040 in. (1.0 mm)
Ignition—55 & 60 (Prior to 1972) Hp:	
Type	CDI—With Breaker Points
Point Gap	0.010 in. (0.25 mm)
Ignition—60 (1986), 65, 70 & 75 Hp:	
Type	CDI—Without Breaker Points
Carburetor Make	Own
Idle Speed (in gear)	750 rpm
Fuel:Oil Ratio	50:1§

*On 1986 70 hp models, the engine is rated at 5500 rpm.

†On 1978-1985 75 hp models, the engine is rated at 5200 rpm.

‡A Champion QL78V is recommended for 1985 and 1986 models when used at sustained high speeds. Renew surface gap spark plug if center electrode is more than 1/32 inch (0.79 mm) below the flat surface of the plug end.

§On 1985 and 1986 models equipped with variable ratio oiling (VRO), the VRO pump meters the fuel:oil ratio from approximately 50:1 up to approximately 150:1 by sensing the engine power output.

SIZES—CLEARANCES

Piston Ring End Gap . . . . 0.007-0.017 in.
(0.18-0.43 mm)

Piston Ring Side Clearance (1969-1984)*:
55 Hp (1969) . . . . 0.0045-0.0070 in.
(0.114-0.178 mm)
60 Hp (1970) . . . . 0.0015-0.0045 in.
(0.038-0.114 mm)
60 Hp (1971) . . . . 0.0015-0.0040 in.
(0.038-0.102 mm)
65, 70 & 75 Hp . . . . 0.0015-0.0040 in.
(0.038-0.102 mm)

Lower Piston Ring Side Clearance
(1985 & 1986) . . . . 0.004 in. Max.
(0.102 mm)

Piston Skirt Clearance:
55 Hp . . . . 0.0040-0.0055 in.
(0.102-0.140 mm)
1970-1978 . . . . 0.0035-0.0055 in.
(0.090-0.140 mm)
1979-1981 . . . . 0.0045-0.0065 in.
(0.114-0.165 mm)
1982-1984 . . . . 0.0045-0.0055 in.
(0.114-0.140 mm)

Maximum Cylinder Tolerance . . . . 0.003 in.
(0.076 mm)

Crankshaft Diameters:
Top Main . . . . 1.4974-1.4979 in.
(38.03-38.05 mm)
Center Mains . . . . 1.3748-1.3752 in.
(34.92-34.93 mm)
Lower Main . . . . 1.1810-1815 in.
(30.00-30.01 mm)
Crankpin . . . . 1.1823-1.1828 in.
(30.03-30.04 mm)

Crankshaft End Play:
55 Hp (1969) . . . . 0.00055-0.01635 in.
(0.0140-0.4153 mm)
60 Hp (1970 & 1971) . . . . 0.0006-0.0156 in.
(0.015-0.396 mm)
65, 70 & 75 Hp (Prior to 1982) . . . . 0.0006-0.0165 in.
(0.015-0.419 mm)

SIZES—CLEARANCES CONT.

Forward Gear Bushing to Propeller
Shaft Clearance (Prior to 1985) . . . . 0.001-0.002 in.
(0.03-0.05 mm)

*Ring side clearance is not applicable to semi-keystone type ring.

TIGHTENING TORQUES

Connecting Rod . . . . 348-372 in.-lbs.
(40-42 N·m)

Crankcase Halves:
Main Bearing Screws . . . . 216-240 in.-lbs.
(24-27 N·m)
Flange Screws . . . . 60-84 in.-lbs.
(7-9 N·m)

Cylinder Head . . . . 216-240 in.-lbs.
(24-27 N·m)

Flywheel:
1969-1971 . . . . 70-85 ft.-lbs.
(95-115 N·m)
All Other Models . . . . 100-105 ft.-lbs.
(136-143 N·m)

Spark Plug . . . . 216-240 in.-lbs.
(24-27 N·m)

Standard Screws:
No. 6 . . . . 7-10 in.-lbs.
(0.8-1.2 N·m)
No. 8 . . . . 15-22 in.-lbs.
(1.6-2.4 N·m)
No. 10 . . . . 25-35 in.-lbs.
(2.8-4.0 N·m)
No. 12 . . . . 35-40 in.-lbs.
(4.0-4.6 N·m)
¼ Inch . . . . 60-80 in.-lbs.
(7-9 N·m)
5/16 Inch . . . . 120-140 in.-lbs.
(14-16 N·m)
⅜ Inch . . . . 220-240 in.-lbs.
(24-27 N·m)
7/16 Inch . . . . 340-360 in.-lbs.
(38-40 N·m)

LUBRICATION

The engine is lubricated by oil mixed with the fuel. On 1969-1975 models, fuel should be regular unleaded or premium leaded with a minimum pump octane rating of 89. On all models after 1975, the fuel should be regular leaded, regular unleaded, premium leaded or premium unleaded gasoline with a minimum pump octane rating of 86.

On models prior to 1985, recommended oil is Evinrude or Johnson 50/1 Lubricant or a BIA certified TC-W motor oil. The recommended fuel:oil ratio for normal operation and engine break-in is 50:1.

On 1985 and 1986 models equipped with variable ratio oiling (VRO), recommended oil is Evinrude or Johnson Outboard Lubricant, OMC 2 Cycle Motor Oil or a BIA certified TC-W motor oil. The VRO pump meters the fuel:oil ratio from approximately 50:1 up to approximately 150:1 by sensing the engine power output. During engine break-in, the fuel in the fuel tank must be mixed at a fuel:oil ratio of 50:1 to ensure the engine of proper lubrication and the oil level in the VRO oil tank must be monitored. If, after engine break-in, oil level has dropped indicating the VRO system is operating, refill the VRO oil tank and switch to straight fuel.

On recreational type 1985 and 1986 models, when VRO system is not used, a fuel:oil ratio of 50:1 must be used in fuel tank.

The lower unit gears and bearings are lubricated by oil contained in the gearcase. The recommended oil is OMC Sea-Lube Premium Blend Gearcase Lube on models prior to 1977 and OMC HI-VIS Gearcase Lube on models after 1976. The gearcase oil level should be checked after every 50 hours of operation and the gearcase should be drained and filled with new oil every 100 hours or once each season, whichever occurs first.

The gearcase is drained and filled through the same plug port. An oil level

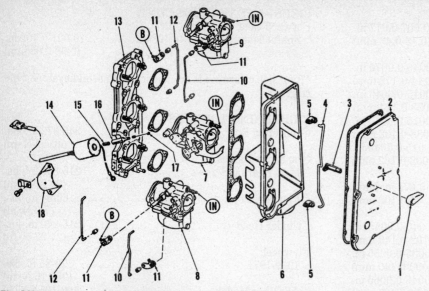

Fig. OM14-1 — View of early carburetors, inlet manifold and silencer. Later models are similar. Refer to Fig. OM14-2 for exploded view of carburetor.

B. Set screws (top & bottom carburetors only)
IN. Idle mixture needles
1. External adjustment knob
2. Cover
3. Lever for center carburetor
4. Link rod
5. Lever (top & bottom carburetors)
6. Silencer
7. Center carburetor
8. Bottom carburetor
9. Top carburetor
10. Choke links
11. Choke & throttle levers
12. Throttle links
13. Inlet manifold
14. Choke solenoid
15. Spring
16. Plunger
17. Connector spring
18. Retainer plate

(vent) port is used to indicate the full oil level of the gearcase and to ease in oil drainage.

To drain the oil, place the outboard motor in a vertical position. Remove the drain plug and oil level plug and allow the lubricant to drain into a suitable container.

To fill the gearcase with oil, place the outboard motor in a vertical position. Add oil through the drain plug opening with an oil feeder until the oil begins to overflow from oil level plug port. Reinstall oil level plug with a new gasket, if needed, and tighten. Remove oil feeder, then reinstall drain plug with a new gasket, if needed, and tighten.

FUEL SYSTEM

CARBURETORS. Three single-barrel, float type carburetors are used. Each carburetor provides fuel for one cylinder and each is equipped with low speed and high speed (main) metering components.

ADJUSTMENT. The idle mixture adjusting needles on models prior to 1976 are linked together and can be externally adjusted within a limited range by turning the adjustment knob behind the control panel door on front of motor. If further adjustment is necessary, remove the motor cover and proceed as follows: Pull knob (1 – Fig. OM14-1) off, then remove silencer cover (2). Pull levers (3 and 5) off idle mixture needles. Normal setting for idle needles (IN) is ⅝ turn open. Run motor until normal operating

temperature is reached, then adjust each of the three idle mixture needles to provide the smoothest operation at 700-750 rpm, in gear with motor on boat (or in test tank). After adjustment is complete, install levers (3 and 5) and connecting link (4) making certain that levers are horizontal and toward starboard.

NOTE: Make certain idle needles are not moved when installing levers.

Idle speed should be adjusted to 750 rpm in forward gear and is adjusted at

stop screw (I – Fig. OM14-3).

NOTE: If throttle valves are not synchronized to be open exactly the same amount, it may be impossible to obtain a smooth idle. If difficulty is encountered, close throttle and make certain that the follower roller (F) is not touching throttle cam (T). Loosen clamp screws (B) on throttle shafts of top and bottom carburetors, hold all three throttle shafts closed, then tighten screws (B).

Models in 1976-1978 are equipped with idle jet (8 or 22 – Fig. OM14-2). Models in 1985 and 1986 (except 75 hp) are equipped with idle jet (8). Change idle jet to alter idle mixture. On 1983-1986 75 hp models, idle mixture needle (IN) is used.

Models in 1979-1984 (except 1983 and 1984 75 hp) are equipped with an intermediate jet (8) and idle jet (22). Both jets (8 and 22) may be removed so another jet size can be installed to alter carburetor fuel mixture.

On models prior to 1983, the choke solenoid should be positioned so choke plates open and close fully. The solenoid plunger should protrude approximately ¼ inch (6.35 mm) as shown at (P – Fig. OM14-3). Make certain linkage is adjusted to close all three choke plates at the same time. The spring (17 – Fig. OM14-1) should be screwed onto the solenoid plunger 2½-3½ turns.

Models after 1982 are equipped with an electric primer system on recreational models.

R&R AND OVERHAUL. The carburetor can be removed after removing silencer (6 – Fig. OM14-1), linkage and fuel lines. The top and bottom car-

IN. Idle mixture needle
1. Fuel inlet valve
2. Float
3. Float pivot pin
4. Float bowl
5. Orifice plug
6. Gasket
7. Plug
8. Idle jet or intermediate jet
8A. Bearing
9. Retainer
10. Throttle plate
11. Throttle shaft
12. Follower lever
13. Follower roller
14. Screw
15. Choke manual control lever
16. Override spring
17. Choke shaft
18. Shoulder (pivot) screw
19. Spring washer
20. Washer
22. Idle jet
29. Roll pin
30. Washer

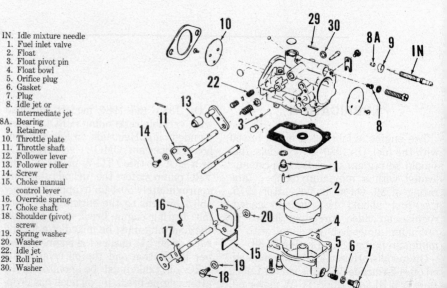

Fig. OM14-2 — Exploded view of carburetor. On early models, the top and bottom carburetors are the same; parts (11 through 20) are different for center carburetor. On early models note linkage for top and bottom carburetors in Fig. OM14-1. Choke components are not used on models after 1982.

buretors are the same; however, the center carburetor is equipped with different controls, linkage, choke shaft and throttle shaft. Disassembly procedure is self evident. The screws attaching choke and throttle plates are staked after assembly and should be renewed if removed from shafts.

NOTE: On models after 1979, the manufacturer does not recommend submerging the parts in carburetor or parts cleaning solutions. An aerosol type carburetor cleaner is recommended. The float and other components made of plastic and rubber should not be subjected to some cleaning solutions. Safety eyewear and solvent resistant gloves are recommended.

Float level is checked with carburetor body inverted. Float should be 1/16 inch (1.58 mm) (L–Fig. OM14-4) from gasket and parallel with gasket surface. Adjust float level by bending float arm.

The choke control lever (15–Fig. OM14-2) has three positions. When control is pushed up, the choke is manually off (open). When control is pushed down, choke is manually on (closed). The center position provides automatic operation. When in automatic position and ignition switch ON, battery current is supplied to the solenoid (14–Fig. OM14-1) via a thermal switch located at bottom of cylinder head. If motor is cool, current passes through the thermal switch, energizes the solenoid and closes the choke plates, but when motor reaches 145°F (63°C), the thermal switch should open and stop current flow to the solenoid.

Refer to ADJUSTMENT paragraphs after carburetors are assembled and installed.

SPEED CONTROL LINKAGE (Early Models). The carburetor throttle valves must be correctly synchronized to open as the ignition timing is advanced. To adjust the speed control linkage, it is necessary to first check (and adjust if required) the ignition maximum advance using a power timing light as outlined in the previous IGNITION SYSTEM section. Move the speed control to the idle position and make sure follower roller (F–Fig. OM14-3) is not touching throttle cam (T). Loosen top and bottom carburetor clamp screws (B) and make certain that all three throttle plates are closed, then tighten clamp screws (B). Move the speed control lever slowly from idle position toward fast position and note the point at which throttle cam (T) contacts follower roller (F). The cam should just contact roller (F) when throttle cam (T) lower alignment mark (T–Fig. OM14-5) is exactly centered with roller (F) as shown. If incorrect, loosen screw (14) and reposition the roller. Move the speed control lever to the maximum speed position and check the carburetor throttle plates. If the throttle plates are not completely open, reposition yoke (Y–Fig. OM14-3) on rod (R). Make sure the carburetor linkage cannot be damaged by attempting to open the throttle too far. Normally, length from end of rod (R) to the rear face of yoke (Y) should be 4-31/32 inches (126.2 mm).

Later Models. The carburetor throttle valves are synchronized to open as the ignition is advanced. It is important that throttle valve opening and ignition timing synchronization be checked and adjusted if necessary.

The following procedure should be used to check and adjust synchroniza-

tion of linkage. Move the speed control lever to the idle position and make sure follower roller (F–Fig. OM14-6) is not touching throttle cam (T). Loosen top and bottom carburetor lever screws (L) and make certain that all three throttle plates are closed, then tighten lever screws (L). Move the speed control lever slowly from the idle position toward the fast position and note the point at which throttle cam (T) contacts follower roller (F). The cam should just contact roller (F) when throttle cam (T) lower alignment mark is exactly centered with roller (F) as shown. If incorrect, loosen screw (14) and reposition the roller.

Connect a power timing light to engine top cylinder. Advance the speed control lever until the throttle plates just

Fig. OM14-4 — Clearance (L) between gasket and lower (when inverted) surface of float should be 1/16 inch (1.58 mm).

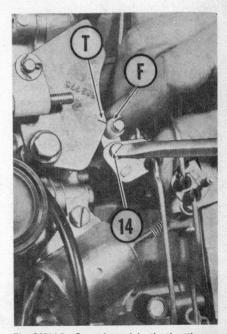

Fig. OM14-5 — On early models, the throttle cam should just contact roller (F) when throttle cam lower alignment mark (T) is exactly centered with the roller as shown. If incorrect, loosen screw (14) and reposition the roller.

Fig. OM14-3 — View of speed control linkage used on early models. Refer to text.

start to open. Start the engine and note the throttle pickup timing with the timing light. The throttle pickup timing should be 1° ATDC to 1° BTDC. If not, stop the engine and loosen locknut (N)), then rotate adjustment nut (A) clockwise (as viewed from the front of the engine) to increase the pickup timing degrees and counterclockwise to decrease. One complete turn will equal approximately 2°.

The wide-open throttle adjustment screw (W) must be adjusted so the carburetor throttle shaft pins (port side of carburetor) are exactly vertical when engine throttle lever is manually advanced top wide-open throttle.

NOTE: The throttle shaft pins must not go past vertical or damage to the carburetors may result.

REED VALVES. Three sets of leaf (reed) valves are used, one for each cylinder. The three valves are attached to the leaf plate base (3 – Fig. OM14-7). The leaf petals should seat very lightly against the valve block throughout their entire length with the least possible tension. The individual parts of the leaf valve assembly are not available separately. Renew the complete valve assembly if petals are broken, cracked, warped or bent.

NON-VRO FUEL PUMP. The fuel pump is operated by the pressure and vacuum pulsations in the crankcase. Repair parts for the fuel pump are not available. Complete pump must be renewed if unit fails. Make certain pump filter screen is clean and fuel lines, air lines and filter are not leaking air or fuel.

VRO TYPE FUEL PUMP. The VRO type fuel pump (1 – Fig. OM14-8) meters the fuel:oil ratio from approximately 50:1 up to approximately 150:1 by sensing the engine power output. During engine break-in or after any procedure that permitted air to enter VRO system,

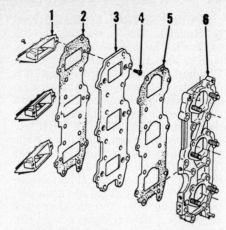

Fig. OM14-7 — Exploded view of the reed valves and inlet manifold. Base (3) and gasket (5) are not used on later models.

1. Leaf valve assy.
2. Gasket (leaf plate base to valves & crankcase)
3. Leaf plate base
4. Valve assy. retaining screw (6 used)
5. Gasket (inlet manifold to leaf plate base)
6. Inlet manifold

the fuel in the fuel tank must be mixed at a fuel:oil ratio of 50:1 to ensure the engine of proper lubrication.

To check the VRO system for proper operation, first fill the VRO oil tank with a recommended two-stroke motor oil and note oil level for future reference. Install a fuel:oil mixture of 50:1 in the fuel tank. After the recommended engine break-in period or after a suitable test period for other conditions, note the oil level in the VRO oil tank. If the oil level has dropped and the VRO system is operating properly, refill the VRO oil tank and switch to straight fuel.

NOTE: When the VRO system is not used, the inlet nozzle at the outboard motor connector must be capped and clamped to prevent dirt or moisture from entering the fuel system. The fuel in the fuel tank must be mixed at a fuel:oil ratio of 50:1.

TESTING. Stop the engine. Disconnect fuel mixture discharge hose at VRO

pump nipple (4 – Fig. OM14-8). Connect a tee fitting in hose end. Connect one end of a clear hose to one tee outlet and connect remaining hose end to pump discharge fitting. Connect a 0-15 psi (0-103 kPa) pressure gage to the remaining tee outlet. Start the engine and run at wide-open throttle. The VRO pump should develop between 3 psi (21 kPa) and 15 psi (103 kPa) at wide-open throttle. The fuel pressure will drop 1-2 psi (6.8-13.7 kPa) and a clicking sound should be heard with each oil discharge. A small squirt of oil should be noticed every time the pump pulses.

If fuel pump (1) malfunction is noted, the fuel pump must be renewed as a complete assembly.

IGNITION SYSTEM

A capacitor discharge ignition system is used on all models. The system used on 60 (1986), 65, 70 and 75 hp motors is breakerless. The system used on 55 and 60 (prior to 1972) hp models has breaker points. Refer to the appropriate following paragraphs.

Breaker Point Models

Two sets of breaker points operate against a cam at top of crankshaft to trigger the unit.

The ignition is extremely durable in normal operation, but can be easily damaged by improper operating, testing or servicing procedures. To prevent damage to the components, observe the following list of cautions and use only approved methods for checking and servicing the system.
1. DO NOT reverse battery terminals.
2. DO NOT disconnect battery while motor is running or attempt to start motor without a battery in the system.

Fig. OM14-6 — View of speed control linkage used on later models. Refer to text.

Fig. OM14-8 — View of a VRO type fuel pump.
1. VRO fuel pump assy.
2. Oil inlet nipple
3. Fuel inlet nipple
4. Crankcase pulse nipple
5. Fuel mixture discharge nipple

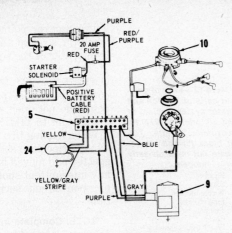

Spark gap must not be more than ³/₈ inch (9.5 mm). The coil wire is molded into coil and screwed into the distributor cap. Do not attempt to pull the coil wire out of either end.

If spark occurs at all three connected points of ignition tester, check ignition timing. Also check condition of the spark plugs and make certain that leads are connected to the correct spark plugs.

Fig. OM14-11 — View showing a spark tester connected to spark plug leads. A four prong tester is shown with only three being used.

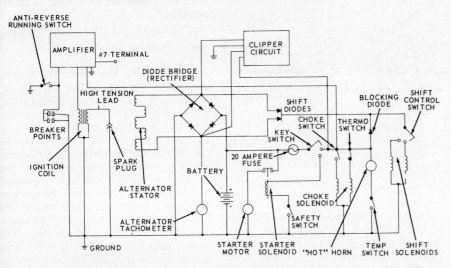

Fig. OM14-9 — Top view shows the basic parts of the ignition system used in 1971 60 hp motors. Lower view is a diagram of the complete system. Wiring is similar for 1970 motors except for the deletion of the clipper circuit. Refer to Fig. OM14-12 for legend.

3. DO NOT disconnect **any** wires while motor is running or while ignition switch is ON.

4. DO NOT use any tachometer except those approved for use with this system.

TROUBLESHOOTING. Use only approved procedures to prevent damage to the components. The fuel system should be checked first to make certain that faulty running is not caused by incorrect fuel mixture or contaminated fuel. If the motor continues to run after ignition switch is turned OFF, check the blocking diode as outlined in appropriate paragraphs.

CHECKING FOR SPARK. Connect a spark tester to the three spark plug leads as shown in Fig. OM14-11, attempt to start motor and check for spark at the tester.

NOTE: A neon spark tester or three conventional spark plugs with the ground electrode removed can be used in place of the tester shown.

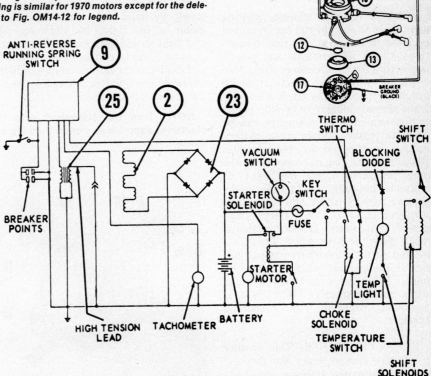

Fig. OM14-10 — The top view shows the basic parts of the capacitor discharge ignition system used in 55 hp motors. The lower view is schematic of the complete electrical system. Refer to Fig. OM14-12 for legend.

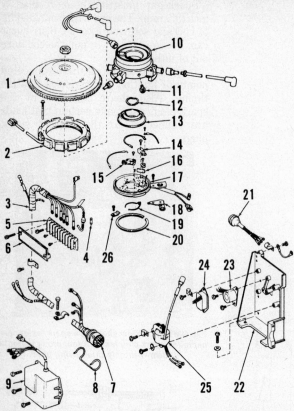

1. Flywheel
2. Stator
3. Wiring harness
4. Fuse (20 amp.)
5. Terminal block
6. Cover
7. Water tight connector
8. Clamp
9. Amplifier
10. Distributor cap assy.
11. Vent
12. Wave washer
13. Reverse cut off contact assy.
15. Breaker points
16. Oiler wick
17. Distributor base assy.
18. Clamp
19. Renerse cut off spring
20. Distributor base retainer
21. Shift diode
22. Bracket
23. Rectifier assy.
24. Clipper assy.
25. Ignition coil
26. Clips

The breaker points should just open when the straight "A" mark on flywheel is in center of the square mark on edge of ring gear guard as shown in Fig. OM14-15 (or 22° BTDC) if the speed control is in fast position. If breaker points do not open when timing marks align, refer to TIMING paragraphs.

When making this test, the black with white stripe wire should be carefully inspected and moved in an effort to locate any intermittent short circuit to ground or open circuit such as loose connections.

NOTE: Complete inspection will be impossible unless the distributor is disassembled.

If no malfunction is noted, proceed with remaining tests.

AMPLIFIER. Disconnect the plug-in connector from amplifier on 55 hp motors and connect jumper wires for the black/white stripe wire (breaker points) and the gray wire (tachometer lead). Connect a low reading ammeter across the purple wire terminals of connectors. On 60 hp motors, merely disconnect the purple lead wires at the terminal board and connect the low reading ammeter to the leads. With the ignition switch ON but motor not running, current draw should be 0.2 amperes. If possible, start motor and operate at 4500 rpm. Ammeter should indicate 1.5-3.0 amperes. Unsteady meter reading with motor running indicates trouble with breaker points. If current draw is steady but incorrect (either running or not running), the amplifier should be renewed.

NOTE: Use extreme caution to make certain that test connections are not disconnected or shorted. Clip on test connectors should not be used with motor running.

An alternate method of testing the amplifier is as follows: Connect one lead of a neon test light to the coil blue lead wire and ground other test light lead to the motor. Turn ignition switch ON, crank motor with electric starter and observe the neon bulb. If the bulb flickers while motor is cranking, the amplifier is operating correctly and the high tension coil, distributor cap, rotor, spark plug leads or spark plugs should be suspected. If the neon bulb does not light, disconnect the black/white wire (from breaker points to amplifier), turn ignition switch ON and ground the black/white wire (from amplifier) to the motor. When the black/white wire is lifted from contact with motor, the neon bulb should flicker. If the bulb lights, check condition of breaker points connecting wires and antireverse switch. If the neon test

If spark is erratic, check condition and gap of the breaker points.

If spark does not occur at any of the tester points, continue with remainder of tests.

WIRING. Engine missing, surging and failure to start or run can be caused by loose or corroded electrical connections. Check all terminals and plug-in connectors for tight clean contact. Also check all wiring for short circuit to ground, especially the black wire with white stripe leading from breaker points to the amplifier. A volt-meter can be used to make certain that battery voltage is supplied to the amplifier. Disconnect the plug-in connector to the amplifier and insert one lead of voltmeter into terminal of purple (power supply) wire. Ground other lead and turn ignition switch ON. Battery voltage should be indicated. If this terminal is dead, check the 20 amp fuse. The fuse is located on the wire which supplies current to the ignition switch (Battery terminal). If fuse is not faulty, check lead in wires and connectors. If current is available, proceed with remaining checks.

BREAKER POINTS. The breaker points are located under the flywheel and distributor cap; however, some tests can be accomplished without disassembly. Disconnect the plug-in connector from amplifier and insert an ohmmeter

or test light (with battery) lead into terminal for the black/white stripe wire. Ground the other ohmmeter or test light lead to the motor, remove the three spark plugs and move the speed control to the fast position. Turn the flywheel slowly by hand and observe the ohmmeter or test light. The ohmmeter or test light should indicate breaker points opening (infinite resistance or light off) and closing (near zero resistance or light on) three times during one revolution of the crankshaft (flywheel).

NOTE: Turn the crankshaft only in clockwise direction as viewed from top of motor.

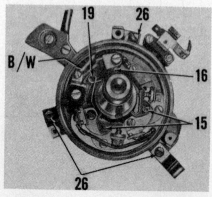

Fig. OM14-13 — View of breaker base with cap and rotor removed. Refer to Fig. OM14-12 for legend.

ight does not flicker, renew the amplifier.

COIL. The ignition high tension coil can be tested using an ignition tester available from several sources, including the following:

GRAHAM TESTERS, INC.
4220 Central Ave. N.E.
Minneapolis, Minn. 55421

MERC-O-TRONIC
INSTRUMENTS CORP.
215 Branch St.
Almont, Mich. 48003

Coil test procedures and specifications are available from the manufacturers of the tester.

NOTE: The high tension coil lead is molded into coil and screwed into distributor cap.

SHIFT DIODE. Failure of shift diode (21 – Fig. OM14-12) used on 60 hp motors may cause lower unit to shift to forward gear immediately after ignition switch is turned "OFF".

To check shift diode, disconnect yellow, yellow/gray and purple/green wires at terminal block that come from shift diode. Use a continuity light (with a battery of no more than 12 volts) or ohmmeter for checking. Attach one test light (or ohmmeter) lead to purple/green wire and other lead to yellow wire; then, reverse test leads. The test light or ohmmeter should indicate continuity witn one connection and NO continuity with leads reversed. Attach test leads similarly to yellow/gray wire and purple/green wire; then, reverse leads. Continuity should again exist with one connection; but not when test leads are reversed. If either of the two tests allow current to pass in both directions or prevent current from passing in either direction, renew shift diode.

CLIPPER. A clipper circuit is installed in all 1971 motors to prevent damage to CD ignition components in the event of an open circuit or intermittent battery current when engine is running.

Failure of the clipper unit (24 – Fig. OM14-12) should be suspected if any of the following occurs: Battery current is momentarily interrupted with motor running; charge low when charging system checks OK; CD amplifier inoperative; fuses blow repeatedly.

Clipper unit may be checked with an ohmmeter in the following manner: Disconnect **all** leads from the clipper to the terminal block before making any checks. Correct ohmmeter test lead polarity must be determined before in-

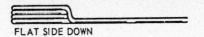

FLAT SIDE DOWN

Fig. OM14-14 — The antireverse spring should be installed with flat side down.

specting clipper unit. Ohmmeter polarity may be determined by connecting meter leads to yellow lead and purple/green lead of a good **shift diode.** Refer to SHIFT DIODE check in previous section. If ohmmeter shows little or no resistance through shift diode, lead attached to yellow wire will be ground lead for purposes of checking clipper. If resistance is high, opposite lead will be ground.

Depending on date of production, clipper units may have three or four wires attached. The fourth wire is black and is used to ground unit. Unit will ground through case if no ground wire is fitted.

To check clipper, momentarily touch the purple lead to the case of the clipper. Connect lead, which has been found to be the ohmmeter ground lead to ground (either the case of the black wire) of the clipper. Connect other ohmmeter lead to yellow wire of clipper. Renew clipper if reading is less than 300 ohms. If an infinite resistance reading is obtained, disconnect ohmmeter lead from yellow wire, momentarily short purple wire against case and connect ohmmeter to yellow/gray wire while retaining original ground connection. Renew clipper if reading is less than 300 ohms. If an infinite reading is obtained, remove lead from yellow/gray wire, momentarily short purple wire against case and connect ohmmeter lead to purple wire. If meter moves and then returns to infinity or registers less than 300 ohms, renew clipper. If an infinite resistance reading is obtained, disconnect ohmmeter, momentarily short purple wire against case, connect "ground lead" from ohmmeter to purple wire and other ohmmeter lead to ground of clipper. Clipper is good if meter swings toward zero and returns to infinity. Renew clipper if meter needle does not move or if meter needle moves to zero and stays.

BLOCKING DIODE. Failure of the blocking diode may allow motor to continue running after ignition switch is turned OFF. The blocking diode is located near the ignition switch and the purple wire is attached to the "IGNITION" terminal of switch. The purple with green stripe wire from diode is equipped with a quick release connector which attaches to a wire leading to the shift control switch.

To check the blocking diode, first remove the diode. Attach one lead of ohmmeter or continuity test light (with a battery of less than 12 volts) to each

wire from diode. Observe ohmmeter reading or test light, then reverse the test connections. Current should pass through diode with one connection (low resistance or light on) but should not pass current with leads reversed. If current passes both directions or does not pass in either direction, renew the blocking diode.

If the blocking diode checks OK but motor continues to run after switch is turned OFF and Forward gear is engaged until motor starts, check for open circuits or short circuits at switches, wires and connectors.

DISTRIBUTOR. To service components of the distributor, remove the flywheel (1 – Fig. OM14-12) and alternator stator (2). The distributor cap (10) is retained by the same three screws which attach alternator stator and these screws are coated with Loctite. The coil high tension wire and the spark plug wires are screwed into the distributor cap. Remove the wave washer (12) and rotor (13).

The antireverse spring (19) is clipped onto crankshaft and when crankshaft is turning in normal direction, the coiled projection is against the oiler felt (16). If the crankshaft turns in counterclockwise direction, the antireverse spring turns with the crankshaft until it grounds the ignition system through contact (14). When installing the antireverse spring, the crankshaft should be lubricated lightly and the flat side of spring should be down as shown in Fig. OM14-14.

Breaker point gap should be set at 0.010 0.25 mm) for used breaker points, or 0.012 (0.30 mm) if new breaker points are installed. After breaker point gap is correctly set, install rotor (13 – Fig. OM14-12) making certain that lug engages slot in crankshaft. Install wave washer (12), then position distributor cap (10) over breaker plate. Make cer-

Fig. OM14-15 — View of advance timing marks aligned. The straight mark on flywheel should be used. On 1970 motors, flywheel mark should align with 22° mark. The wedge shaped mark is not for use on these motors.

tain that coil high tension lead and spark plug wires are screwed into distributor cap and are correctly positioned. Locate the alternator stator (2) over distributor cap, coat the three retaining screws with Loctite and tighten screws to 48-60 in.-lbs. (5.4-6.7 N·m). Check ignition advance timing as outlined in TIMING paragraphs. Make certain that tapers in flywheel and on end of crankshaft are clean and dry before installing flywheel. The flywheel drive key should be parallel to crankshaft center line, NOT aligned with taper. Tighten the flywheel nut to 70-85 ft.-lbs. (95.2-115.6 N·m).

TIMING. Timing marks on flywheel of pre-1971 models and 1971 models with an "E" at the end of the model number consist of a straight line with an "A" or a triangle next to it. A timing mark or small timing grid will be on the ring gear guard of these models. Flywheels on later models (1971 motors with a "C" on the end of the model number) have a timing pointer attached to the intake manifold and a grid marked off in degrees on the flywheel. Timing procedure is basically the same for all

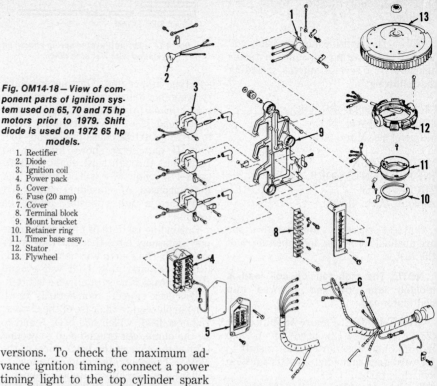

Fig. OM14-18 — View of component parts of ignition system used on 65, 70 and 75 hp motors prior to 1979. Shift diode is used on 1972 65 hp models.

1. Rectifier
2. Diode
3. Ignition coil
4. Power pack
5. Cover
6. Fuse (20 amp)
7. Cover
8. Terminal block
9. Mount bracket
10. Retainer ring
11. Timer base assy.
12. Stator
13. Flywheel

Fig. OM14-16 — View of flywheel with timing marks aligned properly for full advance ignition on 60 (prior to 1972) hp three-cylinder motors. This is a "C" type flywheel, refer to text.

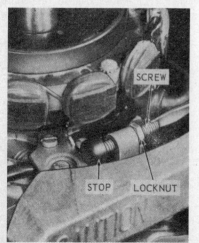

Fig. OM14-17 — View of the ignition advance stop screw. The flywheel is removed so screw can be easily seen. Removal of flywheel is not necessary for adjustment.

versions. To check the maximum advance ignition timing, connect a power timing light to the top cylinder spark plug and run motor at full speed in gear. The straight line on the flywheel of models so equipped, should be aligned with timing mark (22 degrees) on ring gear guard as shown in Fig. OM14-15. Timing pointer should align with 22° mark on flywheel of later models as shown in Fig. OM14-16. If timing is incorrect, loosen locknut and turn the spark advance stop screw (Fig. OM14-17) as required. Make certain that wires do not prevent free movement of base plate.

Breakerless Ignition Models Prior to 1979

The capacitor discharge ignition system used on 65, 70 and 75 hp motors prior to 1979 does not have breaker points. Magnets built into central portion of flywheel are used to trigger the ignition unit.

This ignition is extremely durable in normal operation, but can be easily damaged by improper operating, testing or servicing procedures. To prevent damage to components, observe the following list of precautions and use only approved methods for checking and servicing system.

DO NOT disconnect any wires while motor is running or while ignition switch is ON.

DO NOT use any tachometer except those approved for use with this system.

DO NOT hold spark plug wires while checking for spark.

DO make certain that all wiring connections are clean and tightly joined.

DO make certain that wires do not bind moving parts or touch metal edges where they may chafe through insulation.

TROUBLESHOOTING. Use only approved procedures to prevent damage to the components. The fuel system should be checked first to make certain that faulty running is not caused by incorrect mixture or contaminated fuel. If motor continues to run after ignition switch is turned OFF, check the blocking diode as outlined in appropriate paragraphs.

CHECKING FOR SPARK. Disconnect spark plug leads at spark plugs and connect them to a needle point spark checker, similar to unit in Fig. OM14-11, with three gaps used set at ½ inch (12.7 mm). Consistent, strong spark indicates ignition system functioning properly; suspect spark plugs, timing, improper wiring to ignition coils or to spark plugs.

Weak inconsistent spark or spark from only one or two ignition coils; suspect sensor coils or ignition coils. Weak, inconsistent spark from all three ignition coils; suspect charge coils. No spark at all; suspect power pack.

WIRING. Engine missing, surging and failure to start or run can be caused by loose or corroded electrical connections. Check all terminals and plug-in connectors for tight clean contact. Also check all wiring for short to ground.

SENSOR COILS. Sensor coils may be checked by disconnecting the white/

black lead wires from terminals #8, #9 and #10 (see Fig. OM14-19) and the common sensor lead (black/white wire) from terminal #11. Resistance between the common lead and each of the three sensor leads should be 7.5-9.5 ohms. Sensor coils should also be checked for a short to ground. Defective sensor coils are not renewable separately, timer base assembly (11 – Fig. OM14-18) must be renewed.

CHARGE COILS. Charge coils may be checked by reading resistance between brown wire attached to terminal #4 and brown/orange wire attached to terminal #5. Correct resistance is 870-930 ohms on models prior to 1976 and 555-705 ohms on models after 1975. Stator assembly (12 – Fig. 14-18) must be renewed if charge coils are defective.

IGNITION COILS. Ignition coils may be checked with standard ignition coil test equipment. Complete operating instructions and coil test specifications will be included with tester.

SHIFT DIODE. Failure of the shift diode (2 – Fig. OM14-18) on 1972 65 hp models may cause the lower unit to shift into forward gear immediately after ignition switch is turned "OFF".

Shift diode may be inspected with an ohmmeter or a continuity light with no more than a 12 volt power source. Disconnect diode leads at terminal block (8). Connect tester leads to purple/green wire and to yellow wire from diode.

Reverse connection. Tester reading with a good shift diode will indicate infinite resistance with one connection and no resistance in other direction. Repeat this test with purple/green wire and yellow/gray wire. Again, diode should show no resistance in one direction and infinite resistance in other direction.

STATOR AND TIMER BASE ASSEMBLY. Stator (12 – Fig. OM14-18) and timer base (11) may be serviced after removal of the flywheel. Stator assembly is secured to the power head by three screws. The timer base may be removed after the stator by removing the three screws and clips along the outside edge.

When reassembling unit, make certain that wiring does not restrict free movement of timer base. Inspect taper on crankshaft and taper in flywheel. Install flywheel key with flat of key parallel to center line of crankshaft. NOT surface of taper. Tighten flywheel nut to 100-105 ft.-lbs. (136-143 N·m).

TIMING. Connect a power timing light to number 1 (top) cylinder spark plug and note degree mark on flywheel with motor running at full speed in gear (Fig. OM14-21). Ignition should occur at 16° BTDC on all 75 hp models; 17° BTDC on 70 hp models after 1974; 20° BTDC on all 1974 hp models; 22° BTDC on all other models. Stop engine and turn spark advance stop screw (A – Fig. OM14-22) if timing is incorrect. Turning screw clockwise one full turn will retard

ignition timing approximately one degree.

Breakerless Ignition Models After 1978

All 70 and 75 hp models after 1978 and 60 hp (1986) are equipped with a capacitor discharge ignition system which is triggered by sensor coils on stator plate. To prevent damage to components, note the following list of precautions:

1. DO NOT disconnect any wires while motor is running or while ignition switch is ON.
2. DO NOT use any tachometer except those approved for use with this system.
3. DO NOT hold spark plug wires while checking for spark.
4. DO make certain that all wiring connections are clean and tightly joined.
5. DO make certain that wires do not bind moving parts or touch metal edges where they may chafe through insulation.

TROUBLESHOOTING. Use only approved procedures to prevent damage to

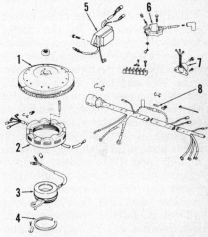

Fig. OM14-20 – View of igniton components typical of the type used on models after 1978.

1. Flywheel	4. Retainer ring		
2. Stator	5. Power pack	7. Rectifier	
3. Timer base	6. Ignition coil	8. Fuse (20 amp)	

Fig. OM14-19 – Simplified wiring diagram of CD magneto used on 65, 70 and 75 hp outboards prior to 1979.

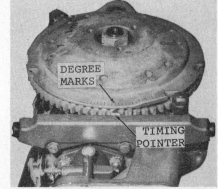

Fig. OM14-21 – Timing pointer should align with appropriate degree mark on flywheel at full advance.

the components. The fuel system should be checked first to make certain that faulty running is not caused by fuel starvation, incorrect mixture or contaminated fuel.

CHECKING FOR SPARK. Disconnect spark plug leads at spark plugs and connect them to a needle point spark checker, similar to unit in Fig. OM14-11, with three gaps used at ½ inch (12.7 mm). Consistent, strong spark indicates ignition system functioning properly; suspect spark plugs, timing, improper wiring to ignition coils or to spark plugs.

Weak, inconsistent spark or spark from only one or two ignition coils; suspect sensor coils or ignition coils. Weak, inconsistent spark from all three ignition coils; suspect charge coils. No spark at all; suspect power pack.

WIRING. Engine missing, surging and failure to start or run can be caused by loose or corroded electrical connections. Check all terminals and plug-in connectors for tight clean contact. Also check all wiring for short circuit to ground.

CHARGE COILS. The three charge coils are contained in the stator assembly. To check charge coils, disconnect the two-wire connector on models prior to 1985 and the three-wire connector on 1985 and 1986 models and connect an ohmmeter to terminals A and B (Fig. OM14-23) in connector leading to stator. Renew stator assembly if resistance is not 475-625 ohms on models prior to 1985 and 535-585 ohms on 1985 and 1986 models. Connect negative ohmmeter lead to an engine ground and positive ohmmeter lead to connector terminal A, then to connector terminal B. Infinite resistance should exist between A terminal and engine ground and B terminal and engine ground. If not, charge coil or charge coil lead is shorting to ground. To check charge coil output, use Merc-O-Tronic Model 781, Stevens Model CD77 or a

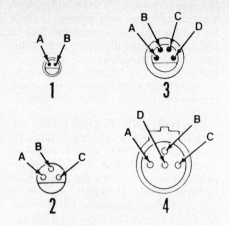

Fig. OM14-23 — View of ignition wire connectors and identification of terminals.

1. Two-wire connector used on models prior to 1985.
2. Three-wire connector used on 1985 and 1986 models.
3. Four-wire connector used on models prior to 1986.
4. Four-wire connector used on 1986 models.

suitable peak voltage tester. Connect black tester lead to terminal A in connector leading to stator and red tester lead to terminal B. Turn tester knobs to "NEG (−)" and "500." Crank engine while observing tester. Renew stator assembly if meter reads below 220 volts on models prior to 1985 and 250 volts on 1985 and 1986 models.

SENSOR COILS. The three sensor coils are contained in the timer base assembly. To check sensor coils, connect an ohmmeter to terminals A and D (Fig. OM14-23), then B and D, and then C and D in four-wire connector leading to timer base. Renew timer base if resistance readings are not 12-22 ohms. Connect negative ohmmeter lead to an engine ground and positive ohmmeter lead to connector terminal A, then B, then C and then D. Infinite resistance should exist between all terminal connections and engine ground. If not, sensor coil or sensor coil lead is shorting to ground. To check sensor coil output, use Merc-O-Tronic Model 781, Stevens Model CD77 or a suitable peak voltage tester. Connect black tester lead to timer base connector terminal D and red tester lead to terminal A. On Merc-O-Tronic Model 781, turn knobs to "POS" (+) and "5" and on Stevens Model CD77, turn knobs to "S" and "5." Crank engine while observing tester. Repeat test with black tester lead still connected to terminal D and connect red tester lead to terminal B and then to C. Renew sensor coil if meter reads below 0.4 volts on models prior to 1985 and 0.3 volts on 1985-1986 models.

POWER PACK. To check power pack output, first reconnect stator and timer base connectors. Use Merc-O-Tronic Model 781, Stevens Model CD77 or a

suitable peak voltage tester. Connect black tester lead to a suitable engine ground. Connect red tester lead to wire leading to one of the three ignition coils. Turn tester knobs to "NEG (−)" and "500." Crank engine while observing tester. Repeat test on other leads. Renew power pack if readings are not at least 230 volts or higher.

IGNITION COILS. Renew ignition coil or coils if no other ignition component is found faulty.

IGNITION TIMING. Timing pointer position is adjustable; be sure timing pointer is properly located if position is questioned.

Maximum ignition timing in full throttle operating range should be 19° BTDC. Adjust ignition timing by turning full advance timing stop screw (A – Fig. OM14-22).

COOLING SYSTEM

THERMOSTAT. A cooling system thermostat is used to maintain an even temperature of 130°-150°F. Temperature can be checked using heat sensitive sticks such as "Markal Thermomelt Stick." A 125°F (52°C) stick should melt, but a 163°F (73°C) stick should not melt, after engine reaches normal operating temperature. If the 125°F (52°C) stick does not melt, the thermostat may be stuck open. Overheating could be caused by damaged thermostat, damaged pressure contol valve, exhaust cover gaskets leaking, head gasket leaking, water passages obstructed, water passages leaking or water pump failure.

The thermostat is located at top of cylinder head under the small cover. When assembling thermostat and cover, use a new gasket and make certain that gasket is correctly positioned.

WATER PUMP. The water pump is mounted on top of the gearcase with the rubber impeller driven by the drive

Fig. OM14-22 — Full advance timing stop screw (A) may be turned after loosening locknut (B).

Fig. OM14-25 — View of bracket at front, port side of motor. Another bracket is similarly located on starboard side.

haft. Separate gearcase from exhaust housing for access to water pump.

Refer to Fig. OM14-37, Fig. OM14-40, Fig. OM14-43, Fig. OM14-47 and Fig. OM14-51 for an exploded view of water pump. On early models, install seal 16 – Fig. OM14-37 or 5 – Fig. OM14-40 and Fig. OM14-43) with lip towards top. Some later models are equipped with a renewable liner in the water pump housing. Later models are equipped with a gasket or "O" ring to seal between the pump housing and lower plate. On models after 1984, an impeller drive cam is used in place of drive key (7 – Fig. OM14-51). Install drive cam with flat side against drive shaft and sharp edge pointing in a clockwise direction when viewed from crankshaft end of drive shaft. Apply OMC Adhesive "M" or equivalent between pump housing and lower plate. Lubricate impeller and hold blades in while installing housing. Drive shaft can be rotated clockwise while assembling, but should not be turned backwards. Apply a suitable sealant to water pump screws.

POWER HEAD

R&R AND DISASSEMBLE. If so desired, remove carburetors, fuel pump or VRO pump, inlet manifold and reed valve assembly. On non-VRO equipped 1973 and later models, remove remote cables and disconnect shift rod from shift arm as shown in Fig. OM14-31. On VRO equipped models, remove remote cables and hairpin clip at base of shift lever (L – Fig. OM14-32). Push shift lever (L) towards power head, then slide shift rod off pin head of shift rod lever on port side of engine. Disconnect interfering wires and remove flywheel and ignition components. Remove starter and withdraw the red cable from crankcase web. Remove the two screws from the front brackets to the lower cover (Fig. OM14-25). Remove attaching screws, then remove the two halves of exhaust housing cover. Remove the six screws and one nut (Fig. OM14-26) and lift power head from lower unit.

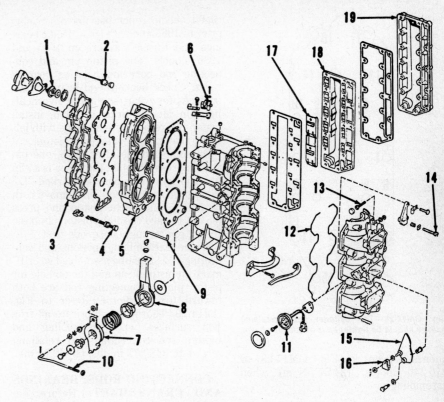

Fig. OM14-27 – Exploded view of early crankcase and associated parts. Later models are similar. Sealing strips (12) are not used on later models.

1. Thermostat
2. Temperature switch
3. Cylinder head cover
4. Automatic choke thermal switch
5. Cylinder head
6. Safety starting switch
7. Throttle lever
8. Spark advance lever
9. Ignition control link
10. Throttle control link
11. Vacuum switch
12. Sealing strips
13. Ignition advance stop screw
14. Idle speed stop screw
15. Throttle cam
16. Yoke
17. Exhaust deflector
18. Inner exhaust cover
19. Outer exhaust cover

To disassemble power head, remove the lower main bearing seal housing, cylinder head and exhaust cover. Drive taper pin out toward front and remove the screws and stud nuts attaching crankcase halves together. Do not damage crankcase when separating halves. Pistons, rods, rod caps, rod bearings and main bearings should be marked as they are removed for assembly in their original location.

ASSEMBLY. Refer to individual sections for checking and assembling pistons, rings, piston pins, connecting rods, crankshaft and bearings. Make certain that connecting rods are assembled to piston with "UP" mark on piston head and the oil hole in connecting rod at piston pin and both toward top.

Check all sealing surfaces of crankcase, cylinder head, exhaust covers for absolutely flat, smooth surfaces. Crankcase halves must seal both vacuum and pressure. The cylinder head and exhaust covers must seal against water leakage and pressure. Mating surface of crankcase and lower unit must form an exhaust and water tight seal.

Mating surfaces of crankcase halves may be checked on a lapping block and localized high spots or nicks removed, but surface must **NOT** be lowered. If ex-

treme care is used, a slightly damaged crankcase can be salvaged; however, crankcase should be renewed in case of doubt. Other surfaces of crankcase, cylinder head and exhaust cover can be lapped if necessary to provide a smooth, flat surface. Do not remove any more metal than absolutely necessary.

When reassembling crankcase, make sure mating surfaces of crankcase halves are completely clean and free of old cement or from nicks or burrs. On models prior to 1979, install sealing strips (12 – Fig. OM14-27) and trim ends to extend approximately 1/32 inch (0.79 mm) into bearing bores, then sparingly apply OMC Adhesive "M" to cylinder half of crankcase only. On models after 1978, apply OMC Gel-Seal II to one crankcase mating surface. Do not use sealers which will harden and prevent contact between crankcase mating surfaces. Immediately assemble crankcase halves after applying sealer and position halves by installing locating dowel pin; then install and tighten main bearing crankcase screws to 216-240 in.-lbs. (24-27 N·m) and flange screws to 60-84 in.-lbs. (7-9 N·m). Install the cylinder head, making certain that temperature indicator switch and choke control thermal unit are installed. Tighten the cylinder head screws in se-

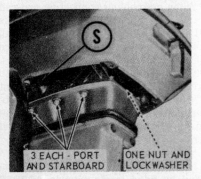

Fig. OM14-26 – View showing exhaust housing cover removed. Power head is attached by six screws (3 shown) and one nut.

3 EACH - PORT AND STARBOARD

ONE NUT AND LOCKWASHER

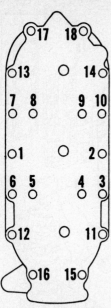

Fig. OM14-28—The cylinder head retaining screws should be tightened in sequence shown.

quence shown in Fig. OM14-28 to 216-240 in.-lbs. (24-27 N·m) when assembling.

NOTE: Retorque cylinder head screws after motor has been test run and motor has cooled completely.

Install the lower main bearing seal housing, using new seal and "O" rings. Securely tighten the four retaining screws.

PISTONS, PINS, RINGS AND CYLINDERS. Before detaching rods from crankshaft, be sure rod, cap and piston are all marked for correct assembly to each other and in correct cylinder. Separate bearings and cages for correct assembly to the original crankpin and connecting rod.

On 1969 models, each piston is fitted with three rings which are interchangeable and may be installed either side up. On 1970 and later models, the top ring of the semi-keystone type and the second ring is conventional type. When installing the top ring on these models, use caution not to damage ring groove in piston and install ring with beveled side toward top. On all models, pistons and rings are available in standard size and oversizes of 0.020 inch (0.51 mm) and 0.030 inch (0.76 mm). Refer to the CONDENSED SERVICE DATA table for recommended ring end gap, ring side clearance in groove and piston skirt clearance. Rebore cylinder bores or renew cylinder block if cylinder bore taper or out-of-round exceeds 0.003 inch (0.076 mm).

The piston pin is retained in piston by snap rings in piston pin bosses. Upper end of connecting rod is fitted with a caged needle roller bearing on models prior to 1985 and with loose needle bearings and thrust washers on 1985 and 1986 models. The piston pin and connecting rod bore are used as bearing races. Check bearing and bearing race surfaces for wear, scoring or overheating. On Models prior to 1976, install piston pin retaining snap rings with lettered side toward outside of piston.

On some models after 1975, one pin boss is press fit while the other is a slip fit. The loose pin boss is marked "L." When removing piston pin, remove both retaining rings, heat piston and press pin out toward the tight piston pin boss. Install pin through loose side first.

When reassembling, pistons and connecting rods must be assembled so "UP" mark on piston head and the oil hole for piston pin in connecting rod are both toward top of motor. Refer to Fig. OM14-29. Thoroughly lubricate all friction surfaces when assembling and tighten the connecting rod retaining screws to 348-372 in.-lbs. (40-42 N·m).

CONNECTING RODS, BEARINGS AND CRANKSHAFT. Before detaching connecting rods from crankshaft, make certain that piston, rod and cap are marked for correct assembly to each other and in original cylinder. Separate bearings and bearing cages for installation in original location.

Connecting rods ride on roller bearings at both ends. The lower bearing consists of 16 rollers located in a split retainer (cage). The piston pin bearing uses a one-piece cage on models prior to 1985 and loose needle bearings with thrust washers on 1985 and 1986 models. When assembling piston to connecting rods, make certain that "UP" mark on piston head and oil hole in connecting rod are both toward top of motor as shown in Fig. OM14-29.

The two center main bearings use a split retainer and a two-piece outer race.

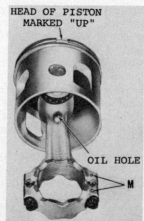

Fig. OM14-29—Connecting rods must be assembled to pistons with "UP" mark on piston head and oil hole toward top of motor.

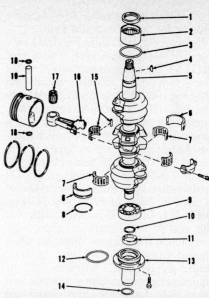

Fig. OM14-30—Exploded view of crankshaft, pistons, connecting rods and assembled parts. Two piston rings per piston are used on models after 1969. Loose needle bearings and thrust washers are used in place of caged piston pin bearing (17) on 1985 and 1986 models.

1. Top seal
2. Top main bearing
3. "O" ring
4. Flywheel key
5. Crankshaft
6. Center bearing outer race
7. Bearing retainer
8. Retainer ring
9. Lower bearing
10. Snap ring
11. Seal
12. "O" ring
13. Seal housing
14. "O" ring
15. Crankpin bearing & retainer
16. Connecting rod
17. Piston pin bearing
18. Snap ring
19. Piston pin

The outer race is held together by a retaining ring and is positioned in cylinder block by a dowel pin. The top main bearing is a roller type with rollers contained in the one-piece outer race. The outer race is also provided with a bore at top end to accept a lip type seal. The sealing "O" ring should be installed around top bearing. The ball type lower main bearing should be renewed if any looseness or roughness is detected.

When positioning crankshaft in main bearing bores, make certain that the top and two center main bearing races correctly engage locating dowel pins. Also make certain that "O" ring around top main bearing is aligned with groove in bearing bore.

When assembling connecting rod cap to rod, make certain that index marks (M – Fig. OM14-29) are aligned and all machined surfaces of rod and cap are smooth. Do not interchange rod caps. On 1985 and later models equipped with precision ground rods, OMC Alignment Fixture 396749 is recommended to properly align connecting rod with rod cap during tightening of connecting rod screws.

NOTE: Precision ground rods are identified by grind marks running ACROSS corners on ears of connecting rod and rod cap.

Refer to ASSEMBLY paragraphs for assembling the crankcase halves.

PROPELLER

An aluminum, three-blade propeller with built-in cushion clutch is standard on most motors while some motors are equipped with a stainless steel propeller. Optional propellers are available. Only propellers designed for use on these motors should be used. Refer to CONDENSED SERVICE DATA for desired engine speed at full throttle.

LOWER UNIT

REMOVE AND REINSTALL. Most service on the lower unit can be performed after detaching the gearcase housing from the drive shaft and exhaust housing. When servicing the lower unit pay particular attention to water pump and water tubes with respect to air or water leaks. Leaky connections may interfere with proper cooling and performance of motor.

To remove the gearcase, disconnect the two shift wires at connectors on side of power head exhaust cover on pre-1973 models. Disconnect shift rod from shift arm on non-VRO equipped 1973 and later models as shown in Fig. OM14-31. On VRO equipped models, remove hairpin clip at base of shift lever (L–Fig. OM14-32). Push shift lever (L) towards power head, then slide shift rod off pin head of shift rod lever on port side of engine. Remove the lower cover and drive shaft exhaust housing on pre-1973 models, apply liquid soap to cable sleeve (S–Fig. OM14-26) and push cables into exhaust housing. Mark location of trim tab to aid reassembly, then remove the trim tab. Remove the two screws from each side of gearcase and two screws at rear.

NOTE: One of the rear screws is under trim tab. Carefully withdraw the gearcase and drive shaft.

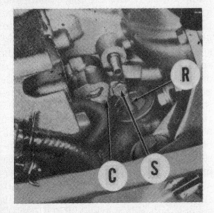

Fig. OM14-31 – Shift rod (R) on non-VRO equipped models after 1972 is disconnected from shift arm (C) by unscrewing screw (S).

Fig. OM14-32 – On VRO equipped models, remove hairpin clip at base of shift lever (L). Then push shift lever towards power head to allow removal of shift rod from shift rod lever.

CAUTION: Do not damage shift wires and do not lose the two plastic water tube guides.

When installing lower unit on models prior to 1973, renew "O" ring at top of drive shaft. Coat both gasket surfaces of gearcase and exhaust housing with OMC Adhesive "M" or equivalent. Insert a wire through hole (S–Fig. OM14-26) down through exhaust housing and attach to end of shift wires. Coat the shift wire grommet with liquid soap and slide the plastic water tube guides onto ends of water tubes. Install gearcase, while aligning water tube guides with pump grommets and pulling shift wires up through hole (S). Drive shaft splines can be aligned by turning flywheel clockwise. Dip the six attaching screws in OMC Gasket Sealing Compound or equivalent before installing. Make certain that shift cable grommet is through hole (S) and attach shift cable leads. Install trim tab, aligning the previously affixed marks.

To install lower unit on models after 1972, renew "O" ring at top of drive shaft. Coat both gasket surfaces of gearcase and exhaust housing with OMC Adhesive "M". Screw in shift rod (27–Fig. OM14-47 or 25–OM14-51) until seated then unscrew shift rod so offset at top of shift rod is located on port side of gearcase so it will mate with shift rod arm. On 1974 and later models, measure distance from gearcase mating surface to center of hole in upper shift rod and with gearcase in neutral. Distance for 1974 and 1975 models should be 16-11/32 inches (41.5 cm) for standard models and 21-11/32 inches (54.2 cm) for long shaft models. Distance should be 21-25/64 inches (54.3 cm) for long shaft 1976 and 1977 70 and 75 hp models, 21-23/32 inches (55.2 cm) for long shaft 1978 through 1986 60, 70 and 75 hp models and 16-13/32 inches (41.67 cm) for all standard 75 hp models. Install gearcase while aligning water tube guide with pump grommet and shift rod with grommet in lower motor cover. Turn engine clockwise to align crankshaft and drive shaft splines. Apply OMC Gasket Sealing Compound to six

gearcase screws. Install trim tab with marks aligned and connect upper end of shift rod to clevis. Move shift lever to forward gear while turning propeller shaft and check for full engagement of dog clutch with forward gear. On models prior to 1983, refer to Fig. OM14-33 or Fig. OM14-34 and check shift linkage adjustment. If distance is incorrect, remove clevis pin and turn clevis until desired distance is obtained.

Due to construction differences in the lower units used on 55, 60, 65, 70 and 75 hp motors, disassembly and overhaul of each unit will be covered separately.

55 HP GEARCASE. To disassemble, remove gearcase, drain lubricant, remove propeller (2–Fig. OM14-37) and detach shift cable (5) from clamps (6). Remove the four attaching screws, then withdraw pump housing (7), impeller (8), drive key (9) and plate (10). Remove screws attaching bearing housing (19) and solenoid cover (23). Remove solenoid and valve assembly (28 through 32). Remove the four screws (34) using a long ¼-inch Allen wrench, then pull bearing housing (35) out using a slide hammer puller with a hook. Remove the two snap rings (40) and withdraw propeller shaft (44). Remove nut (50), then lift drive shaft (55) and bearing housing (19) out top and gear (51), bearing (52) and thrust washer (53)

Fig. OM14-33 – Distance (D) between center of holes in shift arms should be 4-3/32 to 4-5/32 inches (10.4-10.5 cm) with lower unit in forward gear on models with manual shift lower unit. Turn clevis on shift link to obtain desired distance.

out bottom. Remove forward gear (56), thrust bearing (57) and washer (58), then remove snap ring (59). The oil pump (60 through 70) can now be withdrawn from

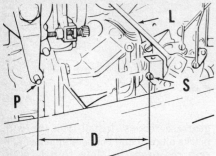

Fig. OM14-34 – Distance (D) between center of shift arm pin (P) and center of bracket screw (S) on hydraulic shift models should be 4¾ to 4⅞ inches (12.1-12.4 cm) with lower unit in forward gear. Turn clevis at upper end of shift link (L) until desired distance is obtained.

housing. If bearing (54) is to be renewed, drive the bearing down and remove from bottom.

Inspect drive shaft splines, bearing surfaces and seal surfaces for wear or damage. Damaged splines may be caused by striking a submerged object and bending a housing. Check parallelism of top and bottom gasket surfaces of the exhaust and drive shaft housing. If surfaces are not parallel, renew housing, do not attempt to straighten. Shift solenoids should be checked with an ohmmeter. Resistance should be 5-6 ohms when checked between each of the two wires and ground. If solenoids (28) or wires (5) are renewed, use new heat shrink insulating tubes (29). Before assembling oil pump, install the pump rotor set, bearing (62), thrust washer

(58), thrust bearing (57) and forward gear (56) in the pump housing (63). When checked with a straightedge as shown in Fig. OM14-38, the inner rotor, outer rotor and surface of housing should be flush. If the inner rotor is too high, inspect surface of thrust washer (58 – Fig. OM14-37), bearing (57) and forward gear (56). Also, make certain rotor is installed with correct side against drive lugs on gear.

NOTE: Most pumps have dots etched on sides of inner and outer rotors. If provided with these dots, they should both be toward cover (68).

Guide (65) should be on small end of spring (64) and ball (66) should be in open end of guide. Clearance between bushing in forward gear (56) and end of propeller shaft (44) should be 0.001-0.002 inch (0.025-0.051 mm). If clearances are excessive, renew propeller shaft and/or gears. When installing bearing (54), use special tool 383173 to pull bearing up into position. The lettered end of bearing should be down. Seals (20 and 21) should be installed with lip of bottom seal (21) down and lip of top seal (20) up. Seals (37) should be installed with lip of inside seal toward front (inside) and lip of outside seal toward rear (out).

To assemble the gearcase, position the oil pump (62 through 70) in forward end of gearcase.

NOTE: Make certain that dowel (69) engages hole in gearcase and pump is completely seated.

If pump is not correctly installed, plunger (31) will not fit into pump housing and solenoids will be impossible to install. Position screen (61) against pump with loops on screen toward rear (outside). Install snap ring (59) with flat side toward pump. Assemble thrust bearing (57) and washer (58) to forward gear (56) and insert into pump housing, making sure that lugs on gear engage lugs on pump rotor. Install the drive shaft and drive pinion (50, 51, 52, 53 and 55). The pinion nut (50) should be torqued to 40-45 ft.-lbs. (54.4-61.2 N·m) using special socket 312752 on the drive shaft splines. Position "O" ring (22) in groove of housing (19) and install housing in gearcase bore around drive shaft. Coat the four retaining screws with OMC Gasket Sealing Compound or equivalent before installing. If the clutch (49) has been removed from propeller shaft, insert spring (45) and retainer (46) into propeller shaft bore with hole in retainer aligned with hole in propeller shaft (at splines). Slide the clutch (49) on shaft splines with side marked "PROP END" toward rear and hole aligned with hole in propeller shaft. Compress retainer

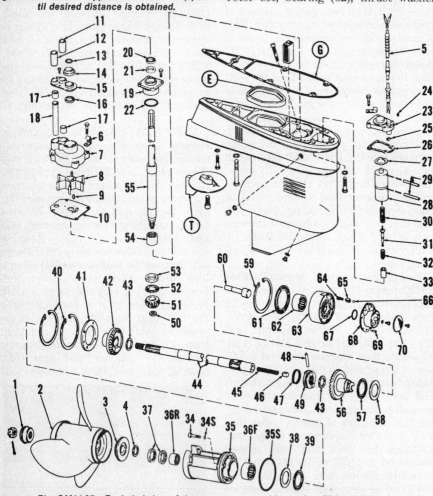

Fig. OM14-37 – Exploded view of the gearcase assembly used on 55 hp motors.

E. Exhaust seal	26. Gasket	55. Drive shaft
G. Gasket	27. Wave washer	56. Forward gear
T. Trim tab	28. Solenoid	57. Thrust bearing
1. Spacer	29. Heat shrink tubes (wire covers)	58. Thrust washer
2. Propeller	30. Spring	59. Snap ring
3. Thrust bushing sleeve	31. Valve	60. Shift plunger
4. Thrust washer	32. Spring	61. Screen
5. Shift cable	33. Sleeve	62. Bearing
6. Clamps	34. Allen screws	63. Pump housing & rotor set
7. Water pump housing	34S. Seal	64. Spring
8. Impeller	35. Bearing housing	65. Guide
9. Drive key	35S. "O" ring	66. Valve ball
10. Impeller plate	36F. Bearing	67. "O" ring
11. Short guide tube	36R. Bearing	68. Cover
12. Long guide tube	37. Seals	69. Dowel pin
13. Drive shaft "O" ring	38. Thrust washer	70. Screen
14. Seal	39. Thrust bearing	
15. Cover	40. Snap rings	
16. Seal	41. Retainer plate	
17. Grommets	42. Reverse gear	
18. Water tube	43. Thrust washers	
19. Bearing housing	44. Propeller shaft	
20. Upper seal	45. Spring	
21. Lower seal	46. Retainer	
22. "O" ring	47. Retainer spring	
23. Solenoid cover	48. Pin	
24. Wire connector clamp	49. Dog clutch	
25. Wire grommet retaining ring	50. Nut	
	51. Drive pinion	
	52. Thrust bearing	
	53. Thrust washer	
	54. Bearing	

(46) and spring (45) enough to align holes in retainer, propeller shaft and clutch, then insert pin (48). Wrap the retainer spring (47) around clutch to keep the pin in position. Install thrust washers (43) around propeller shaft and insert piston (60) in end of shaft. Carefully slide the propeller shaft (44) including parts (43, 45, 46, 47, 48 and 49) into the gearcase. Slide reverse gear (42) onto propeller shaft and position retaining plate (41) in housing. Install the two snap rings (40), then position thrust bearing (39) and thrust washer (38) over the reverse gear hub. Position retaining plate (41) in bearing housing (35) and lubricate outer edge of "O" ring . Slide bearing housing (35) into gearcase, with exhaust cut out toward top. The "Bottom" marking should be down. Coat the retaining Allen screws with OMC Gasket Sealing Compound or equivalent before installing and make certain that seals (34S) are correctly installed on screws.

NOTE: Installation of bearing housing will be easier if two long guide studs are used to locate holes in retainer plate (41) as the bearing housing is installed and the other two screws are installed.

Install solenoid assembly (27 through 33) making certain that valve plunger (31) enters hole in pump housing.

CAUTION: Do not attempt to force.

Position waver washer (27) on top of solenoids, coat both sides of gasket (26) with OMC Gasket Sealing Compound or equivalent and install cover (23). Apply OMC Adhesive "M' or equivalent to bottom of impeller plate (10), install key (9) in drive shaft and locate impeller (8) over key. Lubricate impeller, hold blades in and install water pump housing (7).

NOTE: Drive shaft can be rotated clockwise while assembling pump housing, but should not be turned backwards.

Coat the screws attaching water pump housing with OMC Gasket Sealing Compound or equivalent before installing. Refer to Fig. OM14-39 for location of clamps and routing of shift cable. The "O" ring for sealing the top splines of drive shaft is shown at (13–Fig. OM14-37).

60 HP GEARCASE. (Prior to 1972). To disassemble, remove propeller (79–Fig. OM14-40), drain lubricant and remove gearcase. Remove screws securing water pump housing (8) to gearcase, slide housing up off drive shaft, then remove impeller (9), key (10) and pump plate (11). Remove screws holding upper bearing housing (14). Remove screws in

solenoid cover (26), lift cover and remove wave washer (29) and then carefully lift solenoid assembly (24 through 40) out of gearcase. Remove propeller shaft bearing housing screws (73). Propeller shaft bearing housing (71) is used on models with "E" at end of the serial number. Housing may be removed with a pair of slide hammers with hooks on the ends. Models with "C" serial number suffix are equipped with housing (71A) which is provided with two 5/16-18 threaded holes in rear. A puller attached with two bolts approximately eight inches long may be used to remove housing (71A). On all models, slide thrust bearing assembly (66 and 65) off propeller shaft. Reverse gear (64), propeller shaft (62) and dog clutch assembly (56 through 61) can be removed after snap rings (68) are removed from gearcase. Remove nut (21), then lift drive shaft (16) and bearing housing (14) out top and pinion gear (20) and thrust bearing assembly (18 and 19) out bottom. Forward gear (54) and thrust bearing (52 and 53) may now be removed. Some models are equipped with a snap ring (51) which must be removed before oil pump assembly (41 through 50) can be pulled from gearcase. Bearing (17) should only be removed if renewal is intended. Drive bearing out of bore from top if renewal is necessary.

Inspect drive shaft splines, bearing surfaces and seal surfaces for wear or damage. Damaged splines may be caused by striking a submerged object and bending housing. Check parallelism of top and bottom gasket surfaces of the exhaust and drive shaft housing. If surfaces are not parallel, renew housing, do not attempt to straighten. Shift solenoids should be checked with an ohmmeter. Resistance should be 5-6 ohms when checked between each of the two wires and ground. If solenoids (32 or 36) or wires (24) are renewed, use new heat

shrink insulating tubes (33). Before assembling oil pump, install the rotor set, bearing assembly (52 and 53), forward gear (54) in the pump housing (50). When checked with a straightedge as shown in Fig. OM14-38, the inner rotor, outer rotor and surface of housing should be flush. If the inner rotor is too high, inspect surface of thrust washer (52 – Fig. OM14-40), bearing (53) and forward gear (54). Also, make certain rotor is installed with correct side against drive lugs on gear. Clearance between bushing in forward gear (54) and end of propeller shaft (62) should be 0.001-0.002 inch (0.025-0.051 mm). If clearance is excessive, renew propeller shaft and/or gear.

When installing new bearing (17), use OMC Special Tool 383173 to pull bearing up into position. The lettered end of bearing should be down. Bearings (70 and 74) should only be removed from propeller shaft bearing housing if renewal is intended. OMC Special Tools should be used to press new bearings into housing to ensure proper positioning. Use tool 314642 to install aft bearing (74) in housing (71) of "E" models. Use tool 314643 to install aft bearing (74) in housing (71A) of "C" models. Forward bearing (70) may be installed in either housing with tool 314641. Seals (75 and 76) should be installed with lip of forward seal toward front and lip of aft seal toward propeller.

Gearcase may be assembled in the following manner: Assemble oil pump (parts 41 through 50 and 59) and position in gearcase. Make sure that aligning dowel (42) is fully seated in recess provided in forward end of gearcase. Install snap ring (51), used on "E" models, with flat side of snap ring against oil pump. Position forward gear (54), thrust bearing (53) and thrust washer (52) in oil pump. Place drive shaft (16) in gearcase and assemble thrust washer (18), bearing (19) and pinion (20). Install retaining nut (21) and torque to 40-45 ft.-lbs. (54.4-61.2 N·m). Upper drive shaft bearing in housing (14) should be renewed if bearing is defective. Renew "O" ring (15)

Fig. OM14-38 – Refer to text when checking installation of pump rotor set. Note the dots on rotor set should both be up as shown.

THRUST WASHER AND BEARING NOT VISIBLE

FORWARD GEAR

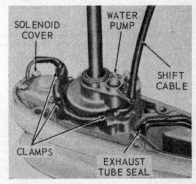

Fig. OM14-39 – View showing correct installation of the shift control cable and clamps.

SOLENOID COVER

WATER PUMP

SHIFT CABLE

CLAMPS

EXHAUST TUBE SEAL

and seals (12 and 13). Install lower seal (13) with lip down and upper seal (12) with lip toward top. Coat screws used to secure bearing housing (14) with sealing compound and install. Assemble propeller shaft and dog clutch components with side of dog clutch (56) marked "PROP END" toward rear. Place thrust washer (63), reverse gear (64) and retainer plate (67) on propeller shaft bearing housing (71) and oil the outer edge. Guide pins can be threaded into retainer plate (67) to ease alignment of bearing housing (71 or 71A) on installation.

Make certain that directional marking is positioned properly when installing bearing housing (71 or 71A). Coat screws (73) with sealing compound and secure housing in position.

Solenoid assembly (24 through 40) may be installed and adjusted in the following manner: Screw plunger (with large hole) into tubular shift rod casing (Fig. OM14-41), then install and tighten lock screw. Insert plunger and shift rod into reverse solenoid (blue wire) and push cap onto bottom of shift rod casing. Insert lower solenoid assembly into

gearcase bore. Make sure end of shift rod is against the shift valve lever on pump and solenoid is against bottom of bore in housing. Check distance from top of plunger to top of solenoid. Top of plunger must be flush to 1/64 inch (0.4 mm) below top of solenoid. Adjustment is accomplished by removing assembly, loosening lock screw, and turning shift rod casing. The lock screw should be torqued to 9-11 in.-lbs. (1.0-1.2 N·m) after adjustment is completed. Install lower solenoid assembly. Position spacer (34–Fig. OM14-40) on top of lower solenoid with flat side down. Assemble small shift rod (Fig. OM14-42), plunger with small hole and locknut. Position the plunger and shift rod in neutral (upper) solenoid. Insert the neutral solenoid and shift rod assembly into gearcase bore above the reverse shift assembly and spacer. Make sure end of rod is through hole in top valve lever (47–Fig. OM14-40) and solenoids are tight against bottom of bore. Check distance between top of plunger and top of solenoid. Top of plunger must be flush to 1/64 inch (0.4 mm) below top of solenoid. Adjustment is accomplished after loosening locknut and turning shift rod. Locknut should be torqued to 3-5 in.-lbs. (0.3-0.5 N·m) when adjustment is completed.

NOTE: Improper shifting will result if adjustment of shift rods and plungers is not correct.

Install solenoids and shift rods, position wave washer (29–Fig. OM14-40) on top of solenoids, coat both sides of gasket (28) with OMC Gasket Sealing Compound or equivalent and install cover (26). Apply OMC Adhesive "M" or equivalent to bottom of impeller plate (11), install key (10) in drive shaft and locate impeller (9) over key. Lubricate impeller, hold blades in and install water pump housing (8).

NOTE: Drive shaft can be rotated clockwise while assembling pump housing, but should never be turned backwards.

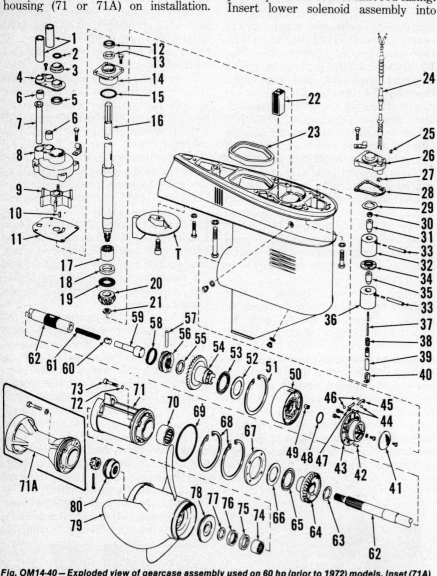

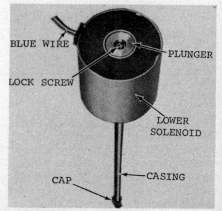

BLUE WIRE — PLUNGER
LOCK SCREW — LOWER SOLENOID
CAP — CASING

Fig. OM14-41 — View of lower (reverse) solenoid assembly. Refer to text for adjustment.

Fig. OM14-40 — Exploded view of gearcase assembly used on 60 hp (prior to 1972) models. Inset (71A) shows type of propeller shaft bearing housing used on late production units.

T. Trim tab	16. Drive shaft	33. Heat shrink tube
1. Water tube guides	17. Needle bearing	34. Spacer
2. "O" ring	18. Thrust washer	35. Lower plunger
3. Grommet	19. Thrust bearing	36. Lower (Reverse)
4. Cover	20. Pinion gear	solenoid
5. Seal	21. Retaining nut	37. Shift rod
6. Grommet	22. Water screen	38. Lock screw
7. Water tube	23. Exhaust gasket	39. Shift rod casing
extension	24. Shift wires	40. Cap
8. Impeller cover	25. Splice	41. Screen
9. Impeller	26. Solenoid cover	42. Locating dowel
10. Drive key	27. Retainer	43. Valve housing
11. Plate	28. Gasket	44. Shift valve balls
12. Seal	29. Wave washer	45. Neutral lever
13. Seal	30. Upper plunger	46. Shift valve seats
14. Bearing & housing	31. Upper plunger	47. Reverse lever
assy.	32. Upper (Neutral)	48. "O" ring
15. "O" ring	solenoid	49. Plug

50. Oil pump assy.	67. Retainer plate
51. Snap ring	68. Snap rings
52. Thrust washer	69. "O" ring
53. Thrust bearing	70. Needle bearing
54. Forward gear	71. Bearing housing
55. Thrust washer	("E" models)
56. Dog clutch	71A. Bearing housing
57. Pin	("C" models)
58. Pin retaining	72. Seal
spring	73. Screw
59. Shift shaft	74. Needle bearing
60. Dog clutch retainer	75. Seal
61. Spring	76. Seal
62. Propeller shaft	77. Thrust washer
63. Thrust washer	("E" models only)
64. Reverse gear	78. Thrust bearing
65. Thrust bearing	79. Propeller
66. Thrust washer	80. Prop nut spacer

Coat screws attaching water pump housing with OMC Gasket Sealing Compound or equivalent before installing. Make certain that drive shaft "O" ring (2) is in position.

65 HP GEARCASE (1972) MODELS). Gearcase may be disassembled as follows: Drain lubricant and remove gearcase. Remove screws securing water pump housing (8 – Fig. OM14-43); lift housing, impeller (9) and remove pump drive key. Remove plate (11) and bearing housing (14). Remove screws securing solenoid cover (26), remove wave washer (29) and carefully lift out solenoid and plunger assembly. Dismount propeller and unscrew four screws holding bearing housing (71). Use a puller attached with two 8-inch long 5/16-18 bolts to remove bearing housing. Slide thrust washer (66) and thrust bearing (65) off shaft and remove retaining rings (68). Propeller shaft can now be removed with reverse gear (64), dog clutch (56) and associated parts. A special socket (OMC Special Tool 316612) is available to hold drive shaft so that nut (21) securing pinion gear can be removed. Drive shaft can be lifted free of gearcase and forward gear (54) removed after removing pinion gear. Use slide hammers and two 16 inch long rods with 1/4-20 threads on the ends to remove oil pump (50).

Inspect drive shaft splines, bearing surfaces and seal surfaces for wear or damage. Damaged splines may be caused by striking a submerged object and bending the exhaust housing. Check parallelism of top and bottom surfaces if questionable. If surfaces are not parallel, renew housing, do not attempt to straighten it.

Lower drive shaft bearing (17) should only be removed if renewal is intended. Do not reinstall a used bearing. Lower drive shaft bearing is held in position by a set screw (17A – Fig. OM14-43) as well as a press fit in gearcase. Set screw is located on starboard side in area of

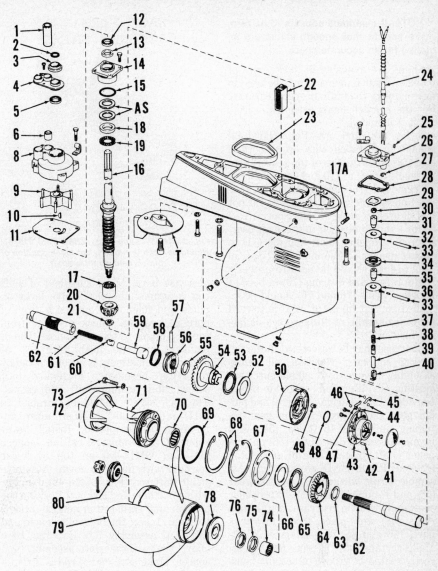

Fig. OM14-43-Exploded view of lower unit gearcase used on 1972 65 hp models. Drive shaft mesh position is adjusted by varying the number of shims (AS). Refer to Fig. OM14-40 for legend.

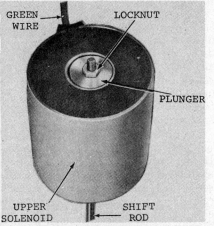

Fig. OM14-42 – View of upper (neutral) solenoid assembly.

water intake. After removing set screw, install OMC Special Tool 385546, with shouldered side of puller piece against bearing and pull bearing out of case toward top. New bearing is installed by assembling special tool with sleeve provided and driving bearing into gearcase with lettered side of bearing up (Fig. OM14-44) and shouldered side of pusher piece against bearing. Bearing will be properly positioned when plate of tool touches top of gearcase. Apply Loctite to set screw (17A – Fig. OM14-43) and install.

Shift solenoids (32 and 36) should be checked with an ohmmeter. Resistance should be 5-6 ohms when checked between each of the wires and case of solenoid. If solenoid wires (24) are renewed, use new heat shrink insulating tubes (33) to seal wire connections.

The shift pump valve balls (44 and 46) and seats can be renewed. The surfaces of rotor set in housing should be checked

for wear or scoring. Renew complete pump assembly if any part of rotor set is damaged excessively. The front surfaces of rotor set should be flush with front face of pump housing, when parts (54, 53 and 52) are in position. Make certain that locating pin (42) is fully seated in recess in forward end of rear housing on reassembly.

Mesh position of pinion gear (20) is determined by thickness of adjusting shims (AS). The following procedure may be used to determine proper shimming. Place pinion gear (20) on drive shaft and torque retaining nut to 40-45 ft.-lbs. (54.4-61.2 N·m). Install shims (AS) that were removed during disassembly without installing thrust washer (18) or thrust bearing (19). Hold shims gage (OMC Special Tool 315767) firmly against shims and measure clearance between end of gage and pinion gear (Fig. OM14-45). Proper clearance is 0.000-0.002 inch (0.00-0.051 mm).

NOTE: If clearance appears to be zero, make certain that enough shims are installed for an accurate check.

Shims are available in thicknesses of 0.002 and 0.005 inch and may be used in any quantity to obtain proper clearance. Set the correct shims aside until drive shaft is installed.

Seals (12 and 13–Fig. OM14-43) should be installed with lip of bottom seal (13) down and lip of top seal (12) up.

Needle bearings (70 and 74) should not be removed from propeller shaft housing unless renewal is intended. Do not install used bearings. OMC Special Tool 317061 should be used to press aft bearing into propeller shaft housing (71) to ensure proper positioning. OMC Special Tool 314641 should be used to properly position forward bearing (70) in bore of housing. Seals (76 and 75) should be installed so that lip on aft seal is toward propeller and lip on forward seal is facing forward.

Gearcase may be assembled in the following manner: Position oil pump assembly in gearcase, making sure that locating pin (42) is fully seated in recess provided. Install drive shaft (16) and pinion gear (20). Torque pinion gear retaining nut to 40-45 ft.-lbs. (54.4-61.2 N·m). Assemble dog clutch (56) on propeller shaft, placing side of dog clutch marked "PROP END" toward rear. Assemble thrust washer (63), reverse gear (64) and retainer plate (67) on propeller shaft and install in gearcase. Install snap rings (68) and place thrust bearings parts (66 and 65) in position on shaft. Make certain that "O" ring (69) is correctly seated in groove of bearing housing (71) and is free of any nicks or tears. Lubricate "O" ring and slide bearing housing into gearcase making certain that "UP" mark on housing is toward top. Coat bearing housing screws with sealing compound before installation.

Install and adjust shift solenoids in the following manner: Screw plunger (with large hole) into tubular shift rod casing (Fig. OM14-42), then install and tighten lock screw. Insert plunger and shift rod into reverse solenoid (blue wire) and push cap onto bottom of shift rod casing. Insert lower solenoid assembly into

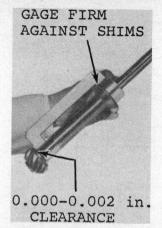

Fig. OM14-45–Shim gage (OMC Tool 315767) should be used to properly set mesh position of pinion gear on drive shaft.

gearcase bore. Make sure end of shift rod is against the shift valve lever on pump and solenoid is against bottom of bore in housing. Check distance from top of plunger to top of solenoid. Top of plunger must be flush with top of solenoid. Adjustment is accomplished by removing assembly, loosening lock screw, and turning shift rod casing. The lock screw should be torqued to 9-11 in.-lbs. (1.0-1.2 N·m) after adjustment is completed. Install lower solenoid assembly. Position spacer (34–Fig. OM14-43) on top of lower solenoid with flat side down. Assemble small shift rod (Fig. OM14-42), plunger with small hole and locknut. Position the plunger and shift rod in neutral (upper) solenoid. Insert the neutral solenoid and shift rod assembly into gearcase bore above the reverse shift assembly and spacer. Make sure end of rod is through hole in valve lever (47–Fig. OM14-43) and solenoids are tight against bottom of bore. Check distance between top of plunger and top of solenoid. Top of plunger must be flush with top of solenoid. Adjustment is accomplished after loosening locknut and turning shift rod. Locknut should be torqued to 3-5 in.-lbs. (0.3-0.5 N·m) when adjustment is completed.

NOTE: Improper shifting will result if adjustment of shift rods and plungers is not correct.

Install solenoids and shift rods, position wave washer (29–Fig. OM14-43) on top of solenoids, coat both sides of gasket (28) with OMC Gasket Sealing Compound or equivalent and install cover (26). Apply OMC Adhesive "M" or equivalent to bottom of impeller plate (11), install key (10) in drive shaft and locate impeller (9) over key. Lubricate impeller, hold blades in and install water pump housing (8).

NOTE: Drive shaft can be rotated clockwise while assembling pump housing, but should never be turned backwards.

Coat screws attaching water pump housing with OMC Gasket Sealing Compound or equivalent before installing. Reinstall shift cable clamps in original position and make certain that drive shaft "O" ring (2) is in position.

65 AND 70 HP WITH HYDRAULIC SHIFT GEARCASE. To disassemble gearcase, drain lubricant, remove propeller and separate gearcase from exhaust housing as outlined in previous section. Remove water pump housing (5–Fig. OM14-47), impeller (6), key (7) and lower plate (8). Remove four screws holding propeller shaft bearing housing (69) and using a suitable puller, withdraw bearing housing from gearcase. Remove snap rings (66), thrust washer (64), thrust bearing (63) and shift rod cover (28). Remove shift rod and propeller shaft components by withdrawing shift rod (27) and propeller shaft simultaneously. Hold drive shaft with OMC Tool 316612 or another suitable tool and unscrew pinion nut. Remove pinion (18), unscrew bearing housing (11) screws and withdraw drive shaft and components from gearcase. Bearing in housing (11) is not renewable but must be obtained as a unit assembly with housing. Remove forward gear (53). Using a suitable puller and two 16 inch long rods with ¼-20 threads, remove oil pump (43) from gearcase.

Inspect drive shaft splines, bearing surfaces and seal surfaces for wear or damage. Damaged splines may be caused by striking a submerged object and bending the exhaust housing. Check parallelism of top and bottom surfaces if questionable. If surfaces are not parallel, renew housing. Do not attempt to straighten it.

Lower drive shaft bearing (17) should only be removed if renewal is intended. Do not reinstall a used bearing. Drive shaft bearing is held in position by a set screw (17A) as well as a press fit in gearcase. Set screw is located on starboard side in area of water intake. After removing set screw, install OMC Special Tool 385546, with shouldered side of

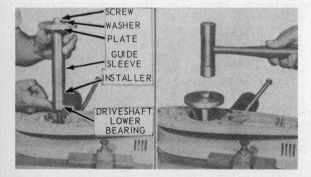

Fig. OM14-44–Installer/removal tool 385546 should be used to drive lower drive shaft bearing into gearcase. Refer to text for procedure.

puller piece against bearing and pull bearing out of case toward top. New bearing is installed by assembling special tool with sleeve provided and puller piece turned over so shouldered side will again be next to bearing. Drive bearing (with lettered side up) into case (Fig. OM14-44). Bearing will be properly positioned when plate of tool touches top of gearcase. Apply Loctite to set screw and install.

Hydraulic shift components (31 through 39 – Fig. OM14-47) may be disassembled with OMC Tool. 386112 by engaging pins on tool with holes in piston (37) and piston cap (31) and unscrewing cap from piston. Be careful not to bend or damage push rod (39) during disassembly. Remove pin (36) to separate valve (35), piston (37) and push rod. Cap (31) should be tightened to 12-15 ft.-lbs. (16.3-20.4 N·m) during reassembly.

To disassemble oil pump, unscrew four screws securing cover (42) and remove cover. Remove snap ring (48), plug (47), spring (46), guide (45) and pressure relief valve ball (44). Inspect pressure relief valve components and renew if worn or damaged. Inspect oil pump assembly for wear or damage. Dots on rotors must be up and surfaces of rotors and housing must be flat across ends when forward gear, thrust bearing and washer are installed in pump. Rotors, housing and bearing are not available separately and must be renewed as a unit assembly.

Seals (9 and 10 – Fig. OM14-47) should be installed with lip of bottom seal (10) down and lip of top seal (9) up.

Needle bearings (68 and 70) should not be removed from propeller shaft housing unless renewal is intended. Do not install used bearings. OMC Special Tool 317061 should be used to press aft bearing into propeller shaft housing (69) to ensure proper positioning. OMC Special Tool 314641 should be used to properly position forward bearing (68) in bore of housing. Seals (71) should be installed so that lip on aft seal is toward propeller and lip on forward seal is facing forward.

Thickness of shims (13) is varied to adjust mesh position of pinion gear (18) in forward and reverse gear. A shim gage, OMC Special Tool 315767, should be used to determine proper shimming.

Place pinion gear (18) on drive shaft and torque retaining nut to 40-45 ft.-lbs. (54.4-61.2 N·m). Install shims (13) that were removed during disassembly and leave thrust washer (14) and thrust bearing (15) off shaft. Hold shim gage firmly against shims and measure clearance between end of gage and pinion gear (Fig. OM14-45). Proper clearance is 0.000-0.002 inch. (0.000-0.05 mm).

NOTE: If clearance appears to be zero make certain that enough shims are installed for an accurate check.

Shims are available in thicknesses of 0.002 inch and 0.005 inch and may be installed in any quantity to obtain proper clearance. Set the correct shims aside until drive shaft is installed.

To assist in installing shift plunger components in propeller shaft, grind away the end of a 9/32 inch (7.14 mm) rod to form a long flat taper on one side. Rod should be approximately 2⅝ inches (6.67 cm) long. Position dog clutch (54 – Fig. OM14-47) on propeller shaft

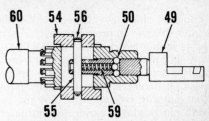

Fig. OM14-48 – Cross-sectional view of shift plunger (49) and dog clutch (54) components. Refer to Fig. OM14-47 for parts identification.

with pin hole in dog clutch and slot in shaft aligned. Place three shift balls (50) and spring (59) in plunger (49) as shown in Fig. OM14-48 and install plunger in

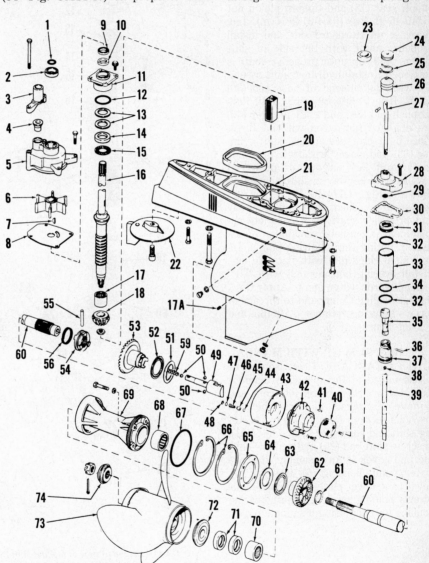

Fig. OM14-47 – Exploded view of hydraulic shift lower unit used on some 65 and 70 hp models.

1. "O" ring	15. Thrust bearing	29. "O" ring	44. Relief valve ball	61. Thrust washer
2. Grommet	16. Drive shaft	30. Gasket	45. Ball guide	62. Reverse gear
3. Water tube bracket	17. Needle bearing	31. Piston cap	46. Spring	63. Thrust bearing
4. Grommet	17A. Set screw	32. "O" ring	47. Plug	64. Thrust washer
5. Impeller housing	18. Pinion gear	33. Cylinder	48. Snap ring	65. Retainer plate
6. Impeller	19. Water screen	34. "O" ring	49. Shift plunger	66. Snap rings
7. Drive key	20. Exhaust seal	35. Valve	50. Detent balls	67. "O" ring
8. Plate	21. Gearcase	36. Pin	51. Thrust washer	68. Needle bearing
9. Seal	22. Tie tab	37. Piston	52. Thrust bearing	69. Bearing housing
10. Seal	23. Seal	38. Plug	53. Forward gear	70. Needle bearing
11. Bearing & housing assy.	24. Grommet	39. Push rod	54. Dog clutch	71. Seals
12. "O" ring	25. Tie strap	40. Screen	55. Pin	72. Thrust bushing
13. Shims	26. Seal	41. Locating dowel	56. Retaining spring	73. Propeller
14. Thrust washer	27. Shift rod	42. Cover	59. Spring	74. Spacer
	28. Shift rod cover	43. Oil pump & bearing	60. Propeller shaft	

propeller shaft so that detent balls match grooves in propeller shaft. Align holes in dog clutch (54 – Fig. OM14-47) and shift plunger (49) and insert tapered end of tool through holes to properly position detent spring. Carefully push tool out with retaining pin (55) and install pin retaining spring (56) in outer groove of dog clutch. Coils of spring must not overlap.

To reassemble gearcase, install oil pump (43), forward gear (53) and thrust bearing (52) and thrust washer (51) so that locating pin (41) aligns with pin hole in gearcase. Install drive shaft (16) and pinion gear (18) and tighten pinion nut to 40-45 ft.-lbs. (54.4-61.2 N·m). Lay gearcase on starboard side and install propeller shaft with flat side of shift plunger (49) up until propeller shaft is bottomed. Install hydraulic shift assembly with flat on end of push rod (39) down. Insert shift assembly until flats on push rod (39) and shift plunger (49) are engaged (push rod will not turn). Place light pressure against shift cylinder (33) and slowly withdraw propeller shaft until key on end of push rod meshes with keyway in shift plunger as shown in Fig. OM14-49. When key and keyway are meshed, push shift assembly and propeller shaft in to complete engagement. Complete remainder of assembly noting the following points: Install snap rings (66) with flat side out. Install bearing housing (69) with "UP" mark towards water pump. Apply OMC Gasket Sealing Compound to threads of screws securing retainer plate (65) and bearing housing (69).

60, 70 AND 75 HP WITH MANUAL SHIFT GEARCASE. Gearcase may be disassembled in the following manner: Remove propeller, drain lubricant and remove gearcase as described in previous section. Remove screws securing shift rod cover (29 – Fig. OM14-51), unscrew shift rod (25) and remove shift rod and cover as an assembly. Remove water pump housing (5), impeller (6), key (7) and lower plate (8). Remove four screws holding propeller shaft bearing housing (69) and using a suitable puller,

remove bearing housing. Discard seals (71) and "O" ring (67). Remove snap rings (66), thrust washer assembly (64 and 63) and slide reverse gear (62) off propeller shaft. A special socket is available to hold drive shaft so that nut securing pinion gear (18) can be removed. After pinion gear retaining nut is removed, unscrew the four screws securing upper drive shaft housing (11). Lift drive shaft and associated parts

from gearcase. A puller may be necessary to remove drive shaft assembly if drive shaft does not lift out easily. Upper drive shaft bearing on all models except standard length 75 hp models is contained in housing (11) and is not renewable. If bearing is worn, renew housing with bearing. A taper roller upper drive shaft bearing is used on standard length 75 hp models. Propeller shaft (60) may now be pulled from gearcase complete with forward gear (52), forward bearing housing (38) and all associated parts.

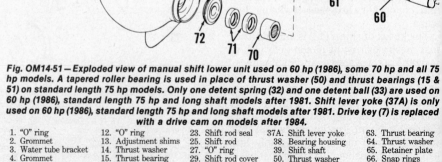

Fig. OM14-51 – Exploded view of manual shift lower unit used on 60 hp (1986), some 70 hp and all 75 hp models. A tapered roller bearing is used in place of thrust washer (50) and thrust bearings (15 & 51) on standard length 75 hp models. Only one detent spring (32) and one detent ball (33) are used on 60 hp (1986), standard length 75 hp and long shaft models after 1981. Shift lever yoke (37A) is only used on 60 hp (1986), standard length 75 hp and long shaft models after 1981. Drive key (7) is replaced with a drive cam on models after 1984.

1. "O" ring	12. "O" ring	23. Shift rod seal	37A. Shift lever yoke	63. Thrust bearing
2. Grommet	13. Adjustment shims	25. Shift rod	38. Bearing housing	64. Thrust washer
3. Water tube bracket	14. Thrust washer	27. "O" ring	39. Shift shaft	65. Retainer plate
4. Grommet	15. Thrust bearing	29. Shift rod cover	50. Thrust washer	66. Snap rings
5. Impeller housing	16. Drive shaft	30. Gasket	51. Thrust bearing	67. "O" ring
6. Impeller	17. Needle bearing	31. Set screw	52. Forward gear	68. Needle bearing
7. Drive key	17A. Set screw	32. Detent springs	54. Dog clutch	69. Bearing housing
8. Plate	18. Pinion gear	33. Detent balls	55. Pin	70. Needle bearing
9. Seal	19. Water screen	34. Detent	56. Pin retaining spring	71. Seals
10. Seal	20. Exhaust seal	35. Locating dowel	60. Propeller shaft	72. Thrust bushing
11. Bearing & housing assy.	21. Gearcase	36. Shift lever pin	61. Thrust washer	73. Propeller
	22. Trim tab	37. Shift lever	62. Reverse gear	74. Prop nut spacer

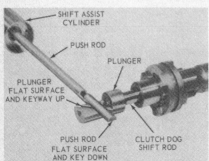

Fig. OM14-49 – View showing relative positions of shift assemblies when installed in gearcase. Refer to text for installation.

Inspect drive shaft splines, bearing surfaces and seal surfaces for wear or damage. Damaged splines may be caused by striking a submerged object and bending the exhaust housing. Check parallelism of top and bottom surfaces if questionable. If surfaces are not parallel, renew housing. Do not attempt to straighten it.

Lower drive shaft bearing (17) should only be removed if renewal is intended. Do not reinstall a used bearing. Drive shaft bearing is held in position by a set screw (17A) as well as a press fit in gearcase. Set screw is located on starboard side in area of water intake. After removing set screw, install a suitable puller or OMC special tool 391257 with correct adapter. Place shouldered side of puller adapter against bearing and pull bearing out of case toward top. New bearing is installed by properly assembling special tool 391257 and forcing bearing into gearcase. Install bearing with lettered side toward drive shaft housing end of gearcase. Apply OMC Gasket Sealing Compound to set screw and install.

Forward gear (52) and propeller shaft (60) may be removed from propeller shaft bearing housing (38) after dislodging spring (56) and removing dog clutch assembly (55 and 54). Bearing housing and shifter mechanism assembly (39) may be disassembled by driving out shift lever pin (36) on all models and unscrewing set screws (31) on models prior to 1982 except standard length 75 hp models.

Thickness of shims (13) is varied to adjust mesh position of pinion gear (18) in forward and reverse gear. A shim gage, OMC Special Tool 320739 for standard length 75 hp models or 315767 for all other models, should be used to determine proper shimming.

Place pinion gear (18) on drive shaft and torque retaining nut to 40-45 ft.-lbs. (54.4-61.2 N·m). On all models except standard length 75 hp models install shims (13) that were removed during disassembly and leave thrust washer (14) and thrust bearing (15) off shaft. On standard length 75 hp models, only pinion gear, nut, taper roller bearing cone and cup should be on drive shaft. Hold shim gage firmly against shims and measure clearance between end of gage and pinion gear (Fig. OM14-45). Proper clearance is 0.00-0.002 inch (0.00-0.05 mm) on models prior to 1977 and 0.000 inch (0.00 mm) on models after 1976.

NOTE: If clearance appears to be zero, make certain that enough shims are installed for accurate check.

Shims are available from 0.002 through 0.007 inch sizes for standard

length 75 hp models and 0.002 inch and 0.005 inch sizes for all other models. Set the correct shims aside until drive shaft is installed.

Needle bearings (68 and 70 – Fig. OM14-51) should not be removed from propeller shaft housing (69) unless renewal is intended. Do not reinstall used bearings. OMC special tools should be used to press bearings into propeller shaft housing to ensure proper positioning. Seals (71) should be installed so lip on aft seal is toward propeller and lip on forward seal is facing forward.

Assemble gearcase in the following manner: Renew all gaskets, seals and "O" rings. If lower drive shaft bearing

(17) or propeller shaft bearings (68 and 70) have been removed, they too should be renewed. Assemble shift lever (37), shift detent (34) and shift shaft (39) in bearing housing (38) on models prior to 1982 other than standard length 75 hp models. Install detent balls and springs, then apply Loctite to set screws (31) and install screws. On models after 1981 and on standard length 75 hp models, install detent spring (32) and detent ball (33) in blind hole of housing (38). Hold spring and ball in position while installing detent (34). Assemble shift shaft (39), shift lever yoke (37A), shift lever (37) and pin (36). On all models, assemble forward gear (52) with thrust bearing (51) and thrust washer (50), models so equipped, in bearing housing. Place dog clutch (54) on propeller shaft (60) making sure hole in dog clutch is aligned with slot in propeller shaft. Insert propeller shaft in forward gear and bearing housing assembly, then insert pin (55) through dog clutch propeller shaft and hole in shift shaft (39). Install pin retaining spring (56).

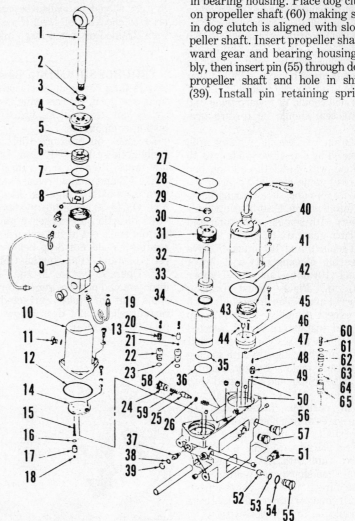

Fig. OM14-55 — Exploded view of hydraulic tilt and trim system used on models after 1979. A three-wire pump motor is used on 1980 and 1981 models.

1. Shaft	28. "O" ring	42. Oil pump filter
2. Wiper	29. Wiper	43. Drive coupling
3. "O" ring	30. "O" ring	44. Ball
4. End cap	31. End cap	45. Oil pump
5. "O" ring	32. Piston	46. "O" ring
6. Piston	33. Piston ring	47. Spring
7. "O" ring	34. Trim cylinder	48. Trim down pump
8. Band	35. Retaining ring	relief valve
9. Tilt cylinder	36. "O" ring	49. Seal
10. Reservoir	37. Manual release valve	50. Manifold
11. Fill plug	38. "O" ring	51. Separation valve
12. "O" ring	39. Snap ring	52. Valve piston
13. Needle	40. Pump motor	53. "O" ring
14. Plate	41. "O" ring	54. "O" ring
15. Screen		55. Impact letdown valve
16. "O" ring		56. Trim check valve
17. Check valve		57. Tilt check valve
18. Valve ball		58. Impact sensor valve
19. Spring		59. Spring
20. Spring seat		60. Spring
21. Ball		61. "O" ring
22. Trim up relief valve		62. Expansion relief valve core
23. "O" ring		63. "O" ring
24. Reverse lock check valve		64. "O" ring
25. Piston		65. Expansion relief valve seat
26. "O" ring		
27. Retaining ring		

Press shift detent (34) down and place propeller shaft, forward gear and bearing housing assembly (38) into position in gearcase. Make sure locating pin (35) is seated in recess provided in gearcase. Install shift rod (25) and shift rod cover (29) as an assembly. Thread shift rod fully into detent (34), pull rod to neutral (middle detent) and adjust for proper length. Refer to shift rod adjustment in LOWER UNIT REMOVE AND REINSTALL section for specifications. Pull rod up into forward gear position on completion of adjustment.

Pinion gear (18) may be positioned for reinstallation after turning gearcase upside down. Insert drive shaft (16). Install pinion gear retaining nut and torque it to 40-45 ft.-lbs. (54.4-61.2 N·m). Assemble thrust bearing (64 and 63) on reverse gear (62) and slide onto propeller shaft (60). Position bearing retainer plate (65) and install snap rings (66). Make sure that "O" ring (67) is fully seated in groove of bearing housing (69) and that seals (71) are properly installed. Lip of forward seal should be toward front and lip of aft seal should be toward propeller.

Installation of bearing housing (69) will be eased by using two guide pins 10 inches long with ¼-28 threads on one end. Thread guide pins into bearing retainer plate (65) and slide bearing housing (69) into position. Coat bearing housing screws with sealing compound and install. Turn gearcase right side up.

Install seals (9 and 10) in upper drive shaft bearing housing (11) with lip of lower seal (10) down and lip of upper seal (9) up. Place thrust bearing assembly (14 and 15) on drive shaft of all models except standard length 75 hp models and install previously selected shim or shims (13). Coat screws that secure bearing housing (11) with sealing compound and install. Bottom edge of impeller plate (8) should be coated with OMC Adhesive "M" or equivalent and placed in position. Install key (7), lubricate edges of impeller (6) and install on drive shaft. On models after 1984, key (7) is replaced with a drive cam. Install drive cam with flat side against drive shaft and sharp edge pointing in a clockwise direction when viewed from crankshaft end of drive shaft. Drive shaft should be turned clockwise while installing water pump housing (5). Coat screws that secure water pump housing and water tube bracket with sealing compound and install.

POWER TILT AND TRIM

So Equipped Models After 1979

OPERATION. A hydraulically actuated power tilt and trim system is used. Manifold (50 – Fig. OM14-55) contains valves, oil pump and trim cylinders. Oil pump motor, oil reservoir and tilt cylinder are attached to manifold. Electric oil pump motor is reversible and oil pump rotation is thereby changed to extend or retract trim and tilt cylinders. Note position of valves in Fig. OM14-55. Turn manual release valve counterclockwise to manually raise or lower outboard.

Hydraulic system contains approximately 25 fl. oz. (740 mL) of oil. Recommended oil is OMC Power Trim/Tilt Fluid or DEXRON II automatic transmission fluid. Do not run pump without oil in reservoir. Oil level should reach fill plug (11) hole threads when tilt and trim pistons are fully extended. System should be cycled several times prior to checking oil level if system has been drained or lost a large amount of oil.

TROUBLESHOOTING. Be sure battery is fully charged, electrical connections are good, oil reservoir is full and air is not trapped in system before testing components.

To check oil pressure, first momentarily cycle system "UP" and "DOWN" a few times. Remove snap ring (39 – Fig. OM14-55) and manual release valve (37), then install OMC gage "A" as shown in Fig. OM14-56. Operate system in the "UP" direction and observe gage after system stalls out at full extension. Gage reading should not drop below 100-200 psi (700-1400 kPa). Install OMC gage "B." Operate system in the "DOWN" direction and observe gage after system stalls out at fully retracted. Gage reading should not drop below 100-200 psi (700-1400 kPa).

To test check valves, screw each valve into OMC check valve tester 390063 (T – Fig. OM14-57). Use a suitable pressure tester (P) and apply 30 psi (207 kPa) of pressure to check valve. Check valve can be considered good if no pressure leakage is noted.

Refer to the following for a list of symptoms and probable causes:

Symptoms	Probable Causes
Tilt Leakdown	1, 2, 3, 4, 5 or 6
Trim and Tilt Both Leak	7, 8 or 9
Reverse Lock Does Not Hold	2, 3, 6, 10, 11 or 12
Will Not Trim Out Under Load or Will Not Tilt	1, 2, 7 or 9
Will Not Trim or Tilt Down	2, 8, 10, 11 or 13

Key to Probable Causes
1. Trim Up Relief Valve
2. Manual Release Valve
3. Tilt Cylinder Valve or Seals
4. Tilt Check Valve
5. Impact Letdown Valve
6. Oil Line
7. Trim Cylinders Sleeve "O" Rings or Piston Seals
8. Trim Check Valve
9. Expansion Relief Valve or "O" Rings
10. Filter Valve Seat
11. Impact Sensor Valve
12. Reverse Lock Check Valve
13. Trim Down Pump Relief Valve

OVERHAUL. Oil pump must be serviced as a unit assembly. Motor is not serviceable with the exception of brushes. Refer to Fig. OM14-55 for exploded view of trim and tilt cylinders and manifold components. Keep all components separated during disassembly and identify each component, if needed, to assure correct position during reassembly.

Fig. OM14-56 – Install OMC gage "A" or "B" into manual release valve (37 – Fig. OM14-55) port as shown to test system oil pressure. Refer to text.

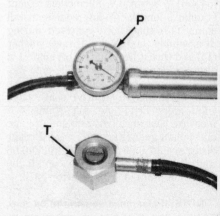

Fig. OM14-57 – Use OMC check valve tester 390063 (T) and a suitable pressure tester (P) to test check valves. Check valve can be considered good if no pressure leakage at approximately 30 psi (207 kPa) is noted.

EVINRUDE AND JOHNSON
4-CYLINDER MODELS
85, 90, 100, 110, 115, 120, 125, 135 and 140 HP

Year Produced	EVINRUDE	JOHNSON	Year Produced	EVINRUDE	JOHNSON	Year Produced	EVINRUDE	JOHNSON
1969	85993	85ESL69	1978	85890	85ML78	1982	90MLCN	90MLCN
	115983	115ESL69		85895	85ETLR78		90TLCN	90TLCN
1970	85093	85ESL70		85899	85TXLR78		90TXCN	90TXCN
	115083	115ESL70		115890	115ML78		115MLCN	115MLCN
1971	85193	85ESL71		115893	115ETL78		115TLCN	115TLCN
	100193	100ESL71		115899	115TXL78		115TXCN	115TXCN
	125183	125ESL71		140840	140ML78		140MLCN	140MLCN
1972	85293	85ESL72		140843	140TL78		140TRLCN	140TLCN
	100293	100ESL72		140883	140TXL78		140TRXCN	140TXCN
	125283	125ESL72	1979	85990	85ML79	1983	90MLCT	90MLCT
1973	85393	85ESL73		85995	85TL79		90TLCT	90TLCT
	115393	115ESL73		85999	85TXL79		90TXCT	90TXCT
	135383	135ESL73		100990	100ML79		115MLCT	115MLCT
1974	85493	85ESL74		100993	100TLR79		115TLCT	115TLCT
	115493	115ESL74		100999	100TXLR79		115TXCT	115TXCT
	135483	115ETL74		115990	115ML79		140TRLCT	140TRLCT
	135443	135ESL74		115993	115TL79		140TRXCT	140TRXCT
	135489	135ETL74		115999	115TXL79	1984	90MLCR	90MLCR
1975	85593	85ESL75		140940	140ML79		90TLCR	90TLCR
	115593	115ESL75		140943	140TL79		90TXCR	90TXCR
	135583	115ETL75		140983	140TXL79		115MLCR	115MLCR
	135543	135ESL75	1980	85MLCS	85MLCS		115TLCR	115TLCR
	135589	135ETL75		85TLCS	85TLCS		115TXCR	115TXCR
1976	85693	85EL76		85TXCS	85TXCS		140TLCR	140TLCR
	85699	85ETL76		100MLCS	100MLCS		140TXCR	140TXCR
	115693	115EL76		100TLCS	100TRLCS	1985	90MLCO	90MLCO
	115699	115ETL76		100TXCS	100TRXCS		90TLCO	90TLCO
	135643	135EL76		115MLCS	115MLCS		90TXCO	90TXCO
	135683	135ETL76		115TLCS	115TLCS		120TLCO	120TLCO
1977	85790	85EL77		115TXCS	115TXCS		120TXCO	120TXCO
	85793	85ETL77		140MLCS	140MLCS		140TLCO	140TLCO
	85799	85TXLR77		140TRLCS	140TLCS		140TXCO	140TXCO
	115790	115EL77		140TRXCS	140TXCS	1986	90MLCD	90MLCD
	115793	115ETL77	1981	90MLCI	90MLCI		90TLCD	90TLCD
	115799	115TXL77		90TLCI	90TLCI		90TXCD	90TXCD
	140740	140ML77		90TXCI	90TXCI		110MLCD	110MLCD
	140743	140TL77		115MLCI	115MLCI		110TLCD	110TLCD
	140783	140TXL77		115TLCI	115TLCI		120TLCD	120TLCD
				115TXCI	115TXCI		120TXCD	120TXCD
				140MLCI	140MLCI		140TLCD	140TLCD
				140TRLCI	140TLCI		140TXCD	140TXCD
				140TRXCI	140TXCI			

CONDENSED SERVICE DATA

TUNE-UP

Hp/rpm 85/5000
90/5000
100/5000
110/5000
115/5000
120/5500
125/5000
135/5000
140/5000 (Prior to 1985)
140/5500 (After 1984)

TUNE-UP CONT.

Bore:
85 HP (Prior to 1979) . . . . 3.375 in.
(85.73 mm)
100 HP (Prior to 1973) . . . . 3.375 in.
(85.73 mm)
115 HP (Prior to 1973) . . . . 3.438 in.
(87.33 mm)
All Other Models . . . . 3.500 in.
(88.90 mm)

TUNE-UP CONT.

Stroke:
120 and 140 HP (After 1984) ....2.860 in.
(72.60 mm)
All Other Models ....2.588 in.
(65.74 mm)
Number of Cylinders 4
Displacement:
85 HP (Prior to 1979) ....92.6 cu. in.
(1517 cc)
100 HP (Prior to 1973) ....92.6 cu. in.
(1517 cc)
115 HP (Prior to 1973) ....96.1 cu. in.
(1575 cc)
120 and 140 HP (After 1984) ....110 cu. in.
(1800 cc)
All Other Models ....99.6 cu. in.
(1632 cc)

Spark Plug – Champion:
85 HP and 90 HP (Prior to 1986) L77J4
90 HP (1986) QL77JC4*
100 HP L77V
110 HP QL77JC4*
115 HP L77J4
120 HP (Prior to 1986) L77J4*
120 HP (1986) QL77JC4*
125 HP L77V
135 HP UL77V
140 HP (Prior to 1985) UL77V
140 HP (1985) L77J4*
140 HP (1986) QL77JC4*
Ignition – 85 HP and 100 HP (1971):
Type ....CDI – With Breaker Points
Point Gap...............................0.010 in.
(0.25 mm)
Ignition – All Other Models:
Type...............CDI – Without Breaker Points
Carburetor Make ....Own
Idle Speed (in gear) ....600-650 rpm
Fuel:Oil Ratio ....50:1†

*A Champion QL78V is recommended when used at sustained high speeds. Renew surface gap spark plug if center electrode is more than 1/32 inch (0.79 mm) below the flat surface of the plug end.
†On 1984 and later models equipped with variable ratio oiling (VRO), the VRO pump meters the fuel:oil ratio from approximately 50:1 up to approximately 150:1 by sensing the engine power output.

SIZES – CLEARANCES

Piston Ring End Gap ....0.007-0.017 in.
(0.18-0.43 mm)
Piston Ring Side Clearance (1969-1984):
85, 100 and 115 HP (Prior to 1973) .....0.0045-0.0070 in.
(0.114-0.178 mm)
85, 100 and 115 HP (After 1972) ....0.002-0.004 in.
(0.051-0.102 mm)
90, 135 and 140 HP ....0.002-0.004 in.
(0.051-0.102 mm)
125 HP ....0.0045-0.0070 in.
(0.114-0.178 mm)
Lower Piston Ring Side Clearance
(1985 and 1986) ....0.004 in. Max.
(0.102 mm)
Piston Skirt Clearance:
125 HP ....0.0030-0.0045 in.
(0.076-0.114 mm)
135 and 140 HP (1973-1978) ....0.0035-0.0055 in.
(0.089-0.140 mm)

SIZES – CLEARANCES CONT.

All Other Models (1969-1978) ....0.0025-0.0040 in.
(0.063-0.102 mm)
All Models (1979-1984) ....0.0045-0.0075 in.
(0.114-0.190 mm)
Crankshaft Diameters:
Top Main (1969-1972) ....1.4975-1.4980 in.
(38.036-38.049 mm)
(After 1972) ....1.6199-1.6204 in.
(41.145-41.158 mm)
Center Main (1969-1978) ....1.3748-1.3752 in.
(34.920-34.930 mm)
(After 1978) ....2.1870-2.1875 in.
(55.550-55.562 mm)
Lower Main (1969-1972)..............1.1810-1.1815 in.
(29.997-30.010 mm)
(After 1972 Except 1985 and 1986
120 and 140 HP) ....1.3779-1.3784 in.
(34.998-35.011 mm)
(1985 and 1986 120 and 140 HP)......1.5747-1.5752 in.
(39.997-40.010 mm)
Crankpin (1969-1973) ....1.1823-1.1828 in.
(30.030-30.043 mm)
(After 1973 Except 1985 and 1986
120 and 140 HP) ....1.3757-1.3762 in.
(34.942-34.955 mm)
(1985 and 1986 120 and 140 HP)......1.4995-1.5000 in.
(38.087-38.100 mm)
Crankshaft End Play:
1969 and 1970 ....0.003-0.011 in.
(0.076-0.279 mm)
1971 and 1972 ....0.0006-0.0335 in.
(0.015-0.851 mm)
1973-1980 ....0.0017-0.0347 in.
(0.043-0.881 mm)
1981-1984 ....0.008-0.011 in.
(0.203-0.279 mm)
Forward Gear Bushing to Propeller
Shaft Clearance (Prior to 1985) ....0.001-0.002 in.
(0.03-0.05 mm)

TIGHTENING TORQUES

Connecting Rod:
All Models Except 1985 and 1986
120 and 140 HP ....348-372 in.-lbs.
(39-42 N·m)
1985 and 1986 120 and 140 HP ....504-528 in.-lbs.
(57-60 N·m)
Crankcase Halves:
Main Bearing Screws –
(1969-1972) ....162-168 in.-lbs.
(18-19 N·m)
After 1972 Except 1985 and
1986 120 and 140 HP) ....216-240 in.-lbs.
(24-27 N·m)
(1985 and 1986 120 and 140 HP)..........312-360 in.-lbs.
(35-41 N·m)
Flange Screws –
(1969-1972) ....144-168 in.-lbs.
(16-19 N·m)
(After 1972)........................60-84 in.-lbs.
(7-9 N·m)
Crankcase Head:
Upper –
(All Models Except 1985 and 1986
120 and 140 HP) ....120-144 in.-lbs.
(13-16 N·m)
(1985 and 1986 120 and 140 HP) ....72.96 in.-lbs.
(8-11 N·m)

TIGHTENING TORQUES CONT.

Lower Bearing Head –
(All Models Except 1985 and
1986 120 and 140 HP) . . . . 96-120 in.-lbs.
(11-13 N·m)
(1985 and 1986 120 and 140 HP) . . . . 72-96 in.-lbs.
(8-11 N·m)

Cylinder Head . . . . 216-240 in.-lbs.
(24-27 N·m)

Flywheel Nut:
1969-1971 . . . . 70-85 ft.-lbs.
(95-116 N·m)

After 1971 Except 1985 and 1986
120 and 140 HP . . . . 100-105 ft.-lbs.
(136-143 N·m)

1985 and 1986 120 and 140 HP . . . . 140-145 ft.-lbs.
(190-197 N·m)

Lower Main Bearing Retainer
Plate Screws . . . . 96-120 in.-lbs.
(11-13 N·m)

TIGHTENING TORQUES CONT.

Spark Plug . . . . 216-240 in.-lbs.
(24-27 N·m)

Standard Screws:
No. 6 . . . . 7-10 in.-lbs.
(0.8-1.2 N·m)

No. 8 . . . . 15-22 in.-lbs.
(1.6-2.4 N·m)

No. 10 . . . . 25-35 in.-lbs.
(2.8-4.0 N·m)

No. 12 . . . . 35-40 in.-lbs.
(4.0-4.6 N·m)

¼ Inch . . . . 60-80 in.-lbs.
(7-9 N·m)

5/16 Inch . . . . 120-140 in.-lbs.
(14-16 N·m)

⅜ Inch . . . . 220-240 in.-lbs.
(24-27 N·m)

7/16 Inch . . . . 340-360 in.-lbs.
(38-40 N·m)

LUBRICATION

The engine is lubricated by oil mixed with the fuel. On 1969-1975 models, fuel should be regular leaded or premium leaded with a minimum pump octane rating of 89. On 1976-1986 models except 1981-1984 140 hp models, fuel should be regular leaded or regular unleaded with a minimum pump octane rating of 86. On 1981-1984 140 hp models, fuel should be regular leaded or premium leaded with a minimum pump octane rating of 88.

On models prior to 1984, recommended oil is Evinrude or Johnson 50/1 Lubricant or a BIA certified TC-W motor oil. The recommended fuel:oil ratio for normal operation and engine break-in is 50:1.

On 1984 and later models equipped with variable ratio oiling (VRO), recommended oil is Evinrude or Johnson Outboard Lubricant, OMC 2 Cycle Motor Oil or a BIA certified TC-W motor oil. The VRO pump meters the fuel:oil ratio from approximately 50:1 up to approximately 150:1 by sensing the engine power output. During engine break-in, the fuel in the fuel tank must be mixed at a fuel:oil ratio of 50:1 to assure the engine of proper lubrication and the oil level in the VRO oil tank must be monitored. If, after engine break-in, oil level has dropped indicating the VRO system is operating, refill the VRO oil tank and switch to straight fuel.

On 1984 and later recreational models when VRO is not being used, the recommended fuel:oil ratio for normal operation and engine break-in is 50:1.

The lower unit gears and bearings are lubricated by oil contained in the gearcase. The recommended oil is OMC Sea-Lube Premium Blend Gearcase Lube on models prior to 1977 and OMC HI-VIS Gearcase Lube on models after 1976. The gearcase oil level should be checked after every 50 hours of operation and the gearcase should be drained and filled with new oil every 100 hours or once each season, whichever occurs first.

The gearcase is drained and filled through the same plug port. An oil level (vent) port is used to indicate the full oil level of the gearcase and to ease in oil drainage.

To drain the oil, place the outboard motor in a vertical position. Remove the drain plug and oil level plug and allow the lubricant to drain into a suitable container.

To fill the gearcase with oil, place the outboard motor in a vertical position. Add oil through the drain plug opening with an oil feeder until the oil begins to overflow from oil level plug port. Reinstall oil level plug with a new gasket, if needed, and tighten. Remove oil feeder, then reinstall drain plug with a new gasket, if needed, and tighten.

FUEL SYSTEM

All Models Except 1985 And 1986 120 And 140 HP Models

CARBURETORS. Two carburetors are used and each is of the two-barrel type with one (common) float chamber. Each of the four carburetor barrels provides fuel for one of the cylinders and is equipped with individual metering components.

Carburetors on models prior to 1980 are equipped with choke plates actuated by an electric solenoid through linkage. On models after 1979, additional fuel to aid starting is injected into the engine's transfer ports through tubes in the transfer port covers. A key-controlled, electric solenoid valve directs fuel from the fuel pump to the transfer port covers. The valve may be opened manually if rope starting is required.

Adjustment. Throttle valves must be synchronized for optimum performance. To synchronize throttle valves, close the throttle and make certain that follower roller (F – Fig. OM16-3 or OM16-7) is not touching throttle cam (T). Loosen clamp screw (B), hold both throttle shafts closed, then tighten screw (B).

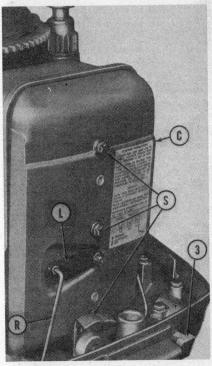

Fig. OM16-1 – The silencer cover (C) on early models is attached to base by the three screws (S). Rod (R) attaches the idle mixture external adjustment knob to the outer lever (L) on models prior to 1972.

High speed mixture on all models is controlled by high speed jets (30–Fig. OM16-5) located in opposite sides of the float bowl. On 1980 through early 1983 models an intermediate speed jet (31) is located just above high speed jet (30). On late 1983 and later models, intermediate speed jet (31) is mounted vertically in float bowl (29).

Idle mixture on models after 1971 is controlled by low speed jets (13) located in opposite sides of the carburetor. Models prior to 1972 are equipped with four idle mixture adjusting needles that are connected together with linkage and can be externally adjusted within a limited range by turning the adjustment knob at front of motor lower cover. If further adjustment is necessary, proceed as follows: Remove the motor top cover. Pull lever (L–Fig. OM16-1) off shaft, remove three screws (S) and lift the silencer cover (C). Pull the four levers from the idle mixture needles (N–Fig. OM16-2) and remove levers, linkage and bellcrank. Normal setting for idle mixture needles (N) is ⅞-turn

open. Run motor until normal oprating temperature is reached then adjust each of the four needles to provide the smoothest operation at 700-750 rpm, in gear with motor on boat (or in test tank). After adjustment is complete, install levers, links and bellcrank, making certain that needle setting is not changed and that levers are exactly horizontal as shown in Fig. OM16-2. After installing the silencer cover (C–Fig. OM16-1), install lever (L) so the external adjustment knob is in center of adjusting range.

NOTE: If throttle valves are not synchronized to open exactly the same amount, it may be impossible to adjust the idle mixture needles for a smooth idle.

Idle speed on all models should be adjusted to 600-650 rpm in gear and is adjusted by turning stop screw (I–Fig. OM16-3 or OM16-7).

Refer to SPEED CONTROL LINKAGE section for synchronizing carburetor throttle opening to the ignition timing.

The choke solenoid on models prior to 1980 should be positioned so choke plates open and close fully. The solenoid plunger (P–Fig. OM16-3) should protrude approximately 5/16 inch (7.9 mm). Make certain that the choke linkage is adjusted to close both choke plates at the same time. The spring should be screwed onto the solenoid plunger 2½-3½ turns.

Fig. OM16-2 — Each of the four idle mixture adjustment needles (N) on models prior to 1972 can be individually adjusted after removing connecting links.

Fig. OM16-3 — Idle speed is adjusted at stop screw (I) on early models. Refer to Fig. OM16-7 for linkage on later models.

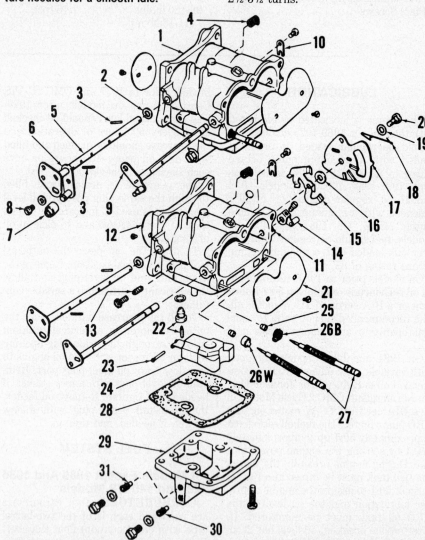

Fig. OM16-5 — Exploded view of carburetor typical of the type used on all models except 1985 and 1986 120 and 140 hp models. Carburetors on models after 1979 are not equipped with choke components. Low speed jets (13) are used on 1972-1979 models in place of idle mixture screws (27). Low speed jets are located in each carburetor barrel on models after 1979. On 1980 through early 1983 models, an intermediate speed jet (31) is located just above high speed jet (30). On late 1983 and later models, intermediate speed jet (31) is mounted vertically in float bowl (29).

1. Top carburetor	15. Detent spring	21. Choke plate	26W. White retainer
2. Washer	16. Washer	22. Fuel inlet valve	(Starboard)
3. Pins	9. Choke shaft (top)	17. Manual choke lever	23. Pivot pin	27. Idle mixture needle
4. Return spring	10. Choke shaft retainer	18. Manual choke spring	24. Float	28. Gasket
5. Throttle shaft	11. Body	19. Washer	25. Bushing	29. Float bowl
6. Cam follower lever	12. Throttle plate	20. Shoulder bolt	25B. Black retainer (Port)	30. High speed jet
7. Follower roller	13. Low speed jet			31. Intermediate jet
8. Set screw	14. Choke arm			

R&R And Overhaul. The carburetors can be removed after after removing the air silencer assembly and linkage. The top and bottom carburetors are slightly different as shown in Fig. OM16-5. Disassembly procedure is self-evident. The screws attaching choke and throttle plates are staked after assembly and should be renewed if removed from shafts.

The float should be parallel to carburetor body gasket surface as shown in Fig. OM16-6. The black retainers (26B – Fig. OM16-5) must be installed on port side and the white retainers (26W) must be on starboard as shown.

The fuel mixture on models prior to 1980 is enriched for starting using carburetor choke plates. The carburetor choke may be actuated manually by moving the choke control knob or lever, or by activating a solenoid controlled by the ignition key switch. On early models the solenoid regulates choke plate opening according to a signal from the thermal switch in the engine's water bypass cover. On later models the thermal switch is not used and the solenoid moves the choke plate to fully closed position when activated. Refer to ADJUSTMENT paragraphs for choke adjustment.

The fuel mixture on models after 1979 is enriched for starting using a key-controlled, electric solenoid valve which directs fuel from the fuel pump to the transfer port covers where fuel is injected into the transfer port passages. Inspect valve and renew any damaged components.

SPEED CONTROL LINKAGE. The carburetor throttle valves are synchronized to open as the ignition is advanced. It is important that throttle valve opening and ignition timing synchronization be checked and adjusted if necessary.

The following procedure should be used to check and adjust synchronization of linkage. Move the speed control lever to the idle position and make sure follower roller (F – Fig. OM16-3 or OM16-7) is not touching throttle cam (T).

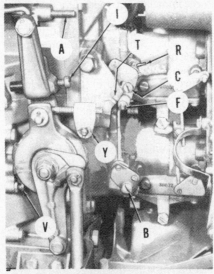

Fig. OM16-7 – View of speed control linkage typical of the type used on all later models except 1985 and 1986 120 and 140 hp models. Models after 1979 do not use the choke linkage. Refer to text.

Fig. OM16-8 – Lower mark (S) should be aligned with center of roller (F) when ignition advance screw just contacts maximum stop (A).

Loosen clamp screw (B) and make certain that throttle plates are closed, then tighten clamp screw (B). Move the speed control lever slowly from the idle position toward the fast position and note the point at which throttle cam (T) con-

tacts follower roller (F). The cam should just contact roller (F) when throttle cam (T) larger (upper) alignment mark is exactly centered with roller (F) as shown. If incorrect, loosen screw (C) and reposition the roller.

On models prior to 1971, move the speed control lever toward the fast position until the ignition advance just contacts the stop as shown at (A – Fig. OM16-8). The lower alignment mark (S) should be exactly aligned with the center of follower roller (F). If mark (S) is not in center of roller (F), reposition the throttle cam yoke on the rod.

On models after 1970 but prior to 1984, there should be 0.001-0.003 inch (0.02-0.07 mm) clearance between roll pin (R – Fig. OM16-7) and stop at wide-open throttle. Turn wide-open throttle stop screw (V) to obtain desired clearance.

On models after 1983, the wide-open throttle stop screw (V) must be adjusted so the carburetor throttle shaft pins are exactly vertical when engine throttle lever is manually advanced to wide-open throttle.

NOTE: The throttle shaft pin must not go past vertical or damage to the carburetors may result.

REED VALVES. Four sets of leaf (reed) valves are used, one for each cylinder. The four valves (15 – Fig. OM16-9) are attached to the intake manifold (14) with a gasket between each reed block and manifold. The leaf petals should seat very lightly against the valve block throughout their entire length with the least possible tension. The individual parts of the reed valve assembly are not available separately. Renew the reed valve assembly if petals are broken, cracked, warped or bent.

NON-VRO TYPE FUEL PUMP. The fuel pump is operated by the pressure and vacuum pulsations in the crankcase. Repair parts for the fuel pump (16 – Fig. OM16-9) are not available and the complete pump must be renewed if the unit fails. Make certain that filter screen (17)

Fig. OM16-6 – The float should be parallel to the gasket surface of carburetor body when fuel inlet valve is closed.

Fig. OM16-9 – Typical view of silencer, carburetors, fuel pump and intake manifold used on early models. Later models are similar.

1. Idle adjust lever
2. Silencer cover
3. Bushing
4. Spring
5. Bellcrank
6. Needle levers (4 used)
7. Bushing
8. Silencer base
9. Choke solenoid
10. Choke connecting link
11. Throttle connecting link
12. Top carburetor
13. Bottom carburetor
14. Intake manifold
15. Reed valve assy. (4 used)
16. Fuel pump
17. Fuel filter screen
18. Cover

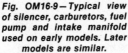

is clean and that fuel lines, air lines and filter are not leaking air or fuel.

VRO TYPE FUEL PUMP. The VRO type fuel pump (1–Fig. OM16-10) meters the fuel:oil ratio from approximately 50:1 up to approximately 150:1 by sensing the engine power output. During engine break-in or after any procedure that permitted air to enter VRO system, the fuel in the fuel tank must be mixed at a fuel:oil ratio of 50:1 to ensure the engine of proper lubrication.

To check the VRO system for proper operation, first fill the VRO oil tank with

Fig. OM16-10 – View of VRO type fuel pump.

1. VRO fuel pump assy.	4. Crankcase pulse
2. Oil inlet nipple	nipple
3. Fuel inlet nipple	5. Fuel mixature
	discharge nipple

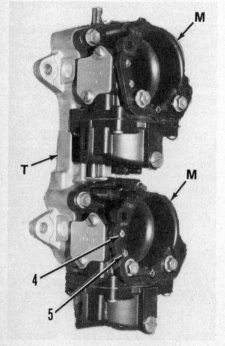

Fig. OM16-11 – View showing two-barrel type carburetors used on 1985 and 1986 120 and 140 hp models. A common throttle body assembly (T) with separate main body assemblies (M) are used. View identifies position of intermediate air bleed jet (4) and low speed air bleed jet (5). Refer to text.

a recommended two-stroke motor oil and note oil level for future reference. Install a fuel:oil mixture of 50:1 in the fuel tank. After the recommended engine break-in period or after a suitable test period for other conditions, note the oil level in the VRO oil tank. If the oil level has dropped and the VRO system is operating properly, refill the VRO oil tank and switch to straight fuel.

NOTE: When the VRO system is not used, the inlet nozzle at the outboard motor connector must be capped and clamped to prevent dirt or moisture from entering the fuel system. The fuel in the fuel tank must be mixed at a fuel:oil ratio of 50:1.

TESTING. Stop the engine. Disconnect fuel mixture discharge hose at VRO pump nipple (4–Fig. OM16-10). Connect a tee fitting in hose end. Connect one end of a clear hose to one tee outlet and connect remaining hose end to pump discharge fitting. Connect a 0-15 psi (0-103 kPa) pressure gage to the remaining tee outlet. Start the engine and run at wide open throttle. The VRO pump should develop between 3 psi (21 kPa) and 15 psi (103 kPa) at wide-open throttle. The fuel pressure will drop 1-2 psi (6.8-13.7 kPa) and a clicking sound should be heard with each oil discharge. A small squirt of oil should be noticed every time the pump pulses.

If fuel pump (1) malfunction is noted, the fuel pump must be renewed as a complete assembly.

1985 And 1986 120 And 140 HP Models

CARBURETOR. Two two-barrel type carburetors are used. Each carburetor assembly has a common throttle body assembly (T–Fig. OM16-11) with

Fig. OM16-12 – Exploded view of carburetor main body assembly used on 1985 and 1986 120 and 140 hp models.

1. Main body
2. Gasket
3. Plate
4. Intermediate air bleed jet
5. Low speed air bleed jet
6. Seal
7. Inlet needle & seat
8. Gasket
9. High speed jet
10. Gasket
11. Plug
12. Float bowl
13. Pin
14. Float

separate main body assemblies (M). Recommended low speed air bleed jet (5) size is #14 on 1985 120 and 140 hp models, #16 on 1986 120 hp models and #28 on 1986 140 hp models. Recommended intermediate air bleed jet (4) size is #43 on 1985 120 hp models, #40 on 1985 140 hp models, #45 on port carburetors on 1986 120 hp models, #42 on starboard carburetors on 1986 120 hp models, #20 on port carburetors on 1986 140 hp models and #16 on starboard carburetors on 1986 140 hp models. Recommended high speed jet (9–Fig. OM16-12) size is #57D on 1985 120 hp models, #59D on 1985 140 hp models and 1986 120 hp models and #61D on 1986 140 hp models.

NOTE: Starboard carburetors supply fuel to port cylinders and port carburetors supply fuel to starboard cylinders.

The main body assemblies are constructed of a nonmetallic type material. Care must be used when working with the main body assembly. DO NOT overtighten any screws. Tighten each screw in small increments using a criss-cross tightening sequence.

If service is performed, note the following: Keep carburetor components for each carburetor separate from the others. The manufacturer does not recommend submerging the parts in carburetor or parts cleaning solutions. An aerosol type carburetor cleaner is recommended. The float and other components made of plastic and rubber should not be subjected to some cleaning solutions. Safety eyewear and solvent resistant gloves are recommended.

To determine the float level, invert float bowl (12–Fig. OM16-13) with the fuel inlet valve and float installed. The float should be flush with the float bowl gasket surface. Use a straightedge as

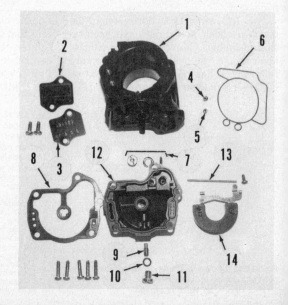

Fig. OM16-13 — With float bowl (12) inverted and fuel inlet valve and float installed, float should just touch straightedge (S). Refer to text.

shown in Fig. OM16-13 to check float setting. Remove the float and carefully bend the float tang to adjust.

Recommended idle speed is 600-650 rpm with the engine at normal operating temperature and forward gear engaged. Loosen nut (N–Fig. OM16-14) and turn screw (I) to adjust engine idle speed.

SPEED CONTROL LINKAGE. The carburetor throttle valves are synchronized to open as the ignition is advanced. it is important that throttle valve opening and ignition timing synchronization be checked and adjusted if necessary.

The following procedure should be used to check and adjust sychronization of linkage. Move the speed control lever to the idle position and make sure follower roller (F–Fig. OM16-14) is not touching throttle cam (T). Loosen follower roller screw (C) and move roller away from throttle cam (T). Loosen screw (S) two complete turns and make certain that throttle plates are closed, then tighten screw (S). Leave screw (C) loose. Hold follower roller (F) against throttle cam (T) and adjust throttle arm stop screw (D) until alignment mark (M) is centered with follower roller (F). Withdraw roller (F) away from throttle cam (T) enough to allow throttle plates to close at idle and tighten screw (C). Adjust wide-open throttle (WOT) stop screw (W) so WOT mark (0) on follower roller bracket points directly front-to-rear when the speed control lever is at WOT.

REED VALVES. Four sets of leaf (reed) valves are used, one for each cylinder. The four valves are positioned horizontally and are attached to the intake manifold with a gasket between each reed block and manifold. The leaf petals should seat very lightly against the valve block throughout their entire length with the least possible tension. The individual parts of the reed valve assembly are not available separately. Renew the reed valve assembly if petals are broken, cracked, warped or bent.

VRO TYPE FUEL PUMP. The VRO type fuel pump (1–Fig. OM16-10) meters the fuel:oil ratio from approximately 50:1 up to approximately 150:1 by sensing the engine power output. During engine break-in or after any procedure that permitted air to enter VRO system, the fuel in the fuel tank must be mixed at fuel:oil ratio of 50:1 to ensure the engine of proper lubrication.

To check the VRO system for proper operation, first fill the VRO oil tank with a recommended two-stroke motor oil and note oil level for future reference. Install a fuel:oil mixture of 50:1 in the fuel tank. After the recommended engine break-in period or after a suitable test period for other conditions, note the oil level in the VRO oil tank. If the oil level has dropped and the VRO system is operating properly, refill the VRO oil tank and switch to straight fuel.

NOTE: When the VRO system is not used, the inlet nozzle at the outboard motor connector must be capped and clamped to prevent dirt or moisture from entering the fuel system. The fuel in the fuel tank must be mixed at a fuel:oil ratio of 50:1.

Fig. OM16-14 — View of speed control linkage used on 1985 and 1986 120 and 140 hp models. Refer to text.

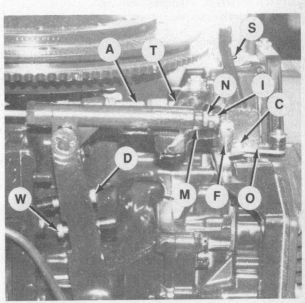

TESTING. Stop the engine. Disconnect fuel mixture discharge hose at VRO pump nipple (4–Fig. OM16-10). Connect a tee fitting in hose end. Connect one end of a clear hose to one tee outlet and connect remaining hose end to pump discharge fitting. Connect a 0-15 psi (0-103 kPa) pressure gage to the remaining tee outlet. Start the engine and run at wide-open throttle. The VRO pump should develop between 3 psi (21 kPa) and 15 psi (103 kPa) at wide-open throttle. The fuel pressure will drop 1-2 psi (6.8-13.7 kPa) and a clicking sound should be heard with each oil discharge. A small squirt of oil should be noticed every time the pump pulses.

If fuel pump (1) malfunction is noted, the fuel pump must be renewed as a complete assembly.

IGNITION SYSTEM

The ignition systems are of the capacitor discharge type; however, 85 hp models prior to 1973 and 1971 100 hp models use breaker points to trigger the ignition and all 90, 110, 115, 120, 125, 135 and 140 hp models and late 100 hp models are triggered by an electronic sensor. Refer to the appropriate following paragraphs when servicing.

BREAKER POINT MODELS

The capacitor discharge ignition is triggered by two sets of breaker points located in the distributor unit under the flywheel. The ignition is extremely durable in normal operation, but can be easily damaged by improper operating, testing or servicing procedures. To prevent damage to the components, observe the following list of cautions and use only approved methods for checking and servicing the system.

1. DO NOT reverse battery terminals.
2. DO NOT disconnect battery while motor is running or attempt to start motor without a battery in the system.
3. DO NOT disconnect any wires while motor is running or while ignition switch is ON.
4. DO NOT use any tachometer except those approved for use with this system.

TROUBLESHOOTING. Use only approved procedures to prevent damage to the components. The fuel system should be checked first to make certain that faulty running is not caused by incorrect fuel mixture or contaminated fuel. If the motor continues to run after ignition switch is turned OFF, check the blocking diode as outlined in the appropriate paragraphs.

CHECKING FOR SPARK. Connect a spark tester to the four plug leads as shown in Fig. OM16-15, attempt to start motor and check for spark at the tester.

NOTE: A neon spark tester or four conventional spark plugs with the ground electrodes removed can be used in place of the tester shown.

Spark gap must not be more than ⅜ inch (9.5 mm). The coil wire is molded into coil and screwed into the distributor cap. **Do not attempt to pull the coil wire out of either end.**

If spark occurs at all four points of ignition tester, check ignition timing. Also check condition of spark plugs and make certain the leads are connected to the correct spark plugs.

If spark occurs at only two of the four tester points, check condition and gap of the breaker points.

If spark does not occur at any of the four tester points, continue with remainder of tests.

WIRING. Engine missing, surging and failure to start or run can be caused by loose or corroded electrical connections. Check all terminals and plug-in connectors for tight clean contact. Also check all wiring for short circuit to ground, especially the black wire with white stripe leading from the breaker

Fig. OM16-15 — View showing a spark tester (T) connected to the spark plug leads. Refer to text for recommended gap.

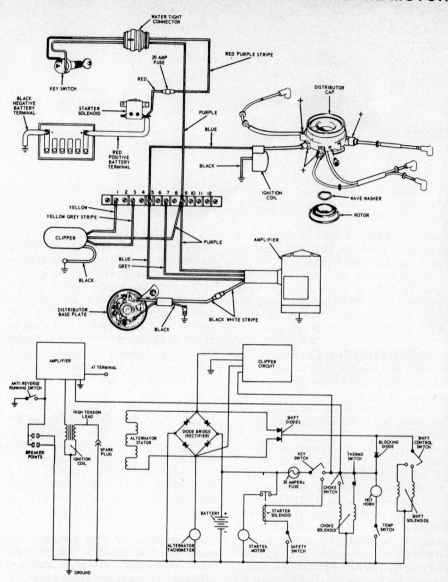

Fig. OM16-16 — The top shows the basic parts and color of connecting wires for ignition system used on breaker point ignition models. Lower view is a schematic of the complete electrical system. Early 85 hp motors were not equipped with a clipper, but wiring was otherwise the same.

points in distributor to the amplifier. Make certain that all wires are connected to the terminal block as shown in Fig. OM16-17 or Fig. OM16-18. A voltmeter or 12 volt test light can be used to check wiring. Connect one lead of voltmeter (or test light) to purple lead terminal (13, 13A, 14 or 15) and ground other lead. With ignition switch ON, battery voltage should be indicated. If this terminal is dead, check the 20 amp fuse located at (F—Fig. OM16-19), battery and all lead in wires and connectors.

NOTE: The fuse may be in a different location than shown.

If current is available, proceed with remaining checks.

BREAKER POINTS. The breaker points are located under the flywheel

and distributor cap; however, some tests can be accomplished without disassembly. Disconnect the plug-in connector (B—Fig. OM16-17) and attach one ohmmeter or test light (with battery) lead to the wire from the breaker points. Ground the other ohmmeter or test light lead to the motor, remove the four spark plugs and move the speed control to fast position. Turn flywheel slowly by hand and observe ohmmeter or test light. The ohmmeter or test light should indicate breaker points opening (infinite resistance or light off) and closing (near zero resistance or light on) four times during one revolution of the crankshaft (flywheel).

NOTE: Turn crankshaft only in clockwise direction as viewed from top of motor to prevent damage to water pump impeller.

The breaker points should just open when each of the two "B" marks on flywheel align with timing lug on lifting bracket if the speed control is in fast position. If breaker points open, but not when "B" marks align with timing lug, refer to the ignition timing paragraph.

When making this test, the black with white stripe wire should be carefully inspected and moved in an effort to locate any intermittent short circuit to ground or open circuit such as loose connections.

NOTE: Complete inspection will be impossible unless the distributor is disassembled.

If no malfunction is noted, proceed with remaining tests.

AMPLIFIER. Disconnect the purple wire (15–Fig. OM16-17) to the amplifier and attach a low reading ammeter between the disconnected wire (to amplifier) and power supply terminal (13). With ignition switch ON but motor not running, maximum current draw should be 0.2 amperes. If possible, start motor and operate at 4500 rpm. Ammeter should indicate 2.0-4.0 amperes. Unsteady meter reading with motor running indicates trouble with breaker points. If current draw is incorrect, either running or not running, the amplifier should be renewed.

NOTE: Use extreme caution to make certain that test connections are not disconnected or shorted. Clip on test connectors should not be used with motor running.

As an alternate method of testing the amplifier, connect one lead from a neon test light to terminal (8 and 9) and attach other lead from neon tester to motor ground. Turn ignition switch ON, crank motor with electric starter and observe the neon bulb. If the bulb flickers while motor is cranking, the amplifier is operating correctly and the high tension coil, distributor cap, rotor, spark plug leads or spark plugs should be suspected. If the neon bulb does not light, disconnect plug (B), turn ignition switch ON, and ground the amplifier end of connector (B) to the motor. When the connector (B) is lifted from contact with motor, the neon bulb should flicker. If the bulb lights, check condition of breaker points, connecting wires and antireverse switch. If the neon test light does not flicker, renew the amplifier.

COIL. The ignition high tension coil can be tested using an ignition tester available from several sources, including the following:

GRAHAM TESTERS INC.
4220 Central Ave. N.E.
Minneapolis, Minn. 55421

MERC-O-TRONIC
INSTRUMENTS CORP.
215 Branch St.
Almont, Mich. 48003

Coil test procedures and specifications are available from the manufacturers of the tester.

NOTE: The high tension coil lead is molded into coil and screwed into distributor cap.

SHIFT DIODE. Failure of the shift diode (D–Fig. OM16-17) may cause the lower unit to shift to forward gear immediately after ignition switch is turned OFF.

To check the shift diode, disconnect the yellow (3), yellow/gray (7) and purple/green (16) wires from the terminal block and remove the shift diode (D). Use a continuity light (with battery of less than 12 volts) or ohmmeter for checking. Attach one test light (or ohmmeter) lead to the purple/green wire and other lead to the yellow wire; then, reverse the test leads. The test light or ohmmeter should indicate continuity with one connection and NO continuity with leads reversed. Attach test leads similarly to the yellow/gray wire and the purple/green wire; then, reverse leads. Continuity should again exist with one connection; but not when leads are reversed. If either of the two tests allow current to pass in both directions or prevent current from passing in either direction, renew the shift diode.

CLIPPER. Models produced after 1970 were equipped with a clipper circuit to prevent damage to CD ignition components in the event of an open circuit or intermittent battery current when engine is running.

Failure of the clipper unit (C–Fig. OM16-17) should be suspected if any of the following occurs: Battery current is momentarily interrupted with motor running; battery charge low when charging system check OK; CD amplifier inoperative; fuses blow repeatedly.

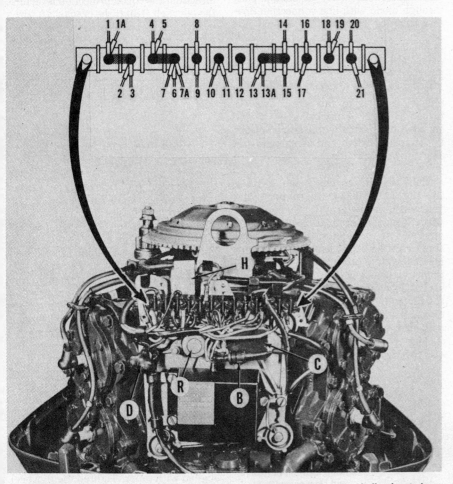

Fig. OM16-17— Rear view of 1972 85 hp motor. Other breaker timed motors are similar. Inset shows location of wires on terminal block.

1, 1A, 2 & 3. Yellow		13, 13A, 14 & 15. Purple
4 & 5. Yellow/gray stripe	8 & 9. Blue	16 & 17. Purple/green stripe
6. Gray	10 & 11. Red	18 & 19. Purple/yellow stripe
7 & 7A. Yellow/gray stripe	12. Gray	20 & 21. Purple/white stripe

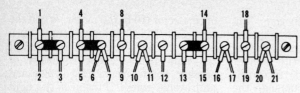

Fig. OM16-18—View of terminal block showing location of wires used on early 85 hp motors.

1, 2 & 3. Yellow
4 & 5. Yellow/gray stripe
6. Gray
7. Yellow/gray stripe
8 & 9. Blue
10 & 11. Red
12. Gray
13, 14 & 15. Purple
16 & 17. Purple/green stripe
18 & 19. Purple/yellow stripe
20 & 21. Purple/white stripe

Clipper unit may be checked with an ohmmeter in the following manner: Disconnect **all** leads from clipper to terminal block before making any checks. Correct ohmmeter test lead polarity must be determined before inspecting clipper unit. Ohmmeter polarity may be determined by connecting meter leads to the yellow lead and the purple/green lead of a good **shift diode**. Refer to Shift Diode check in previous section. If ohmmeter shows little or no resistance through shift diode, lead attached to yellow wire will be "ground lead" for purposes of checking clipper. If resistance is high, opposite lead will be ground.

To check clipper, momentarily touch the purple lead to the case of the clipper. Connect the ohmmeter "ground lead" to ground (either the case or the black wire) of the clipper. Connect other ohmmeter lead to yellow wire of clipper. Renew clipper if reading is less than 300 ohms. If an infinite resistance reading is obtained, disconnect ohmmeter lead from yellow wire, momentarily short purple wire against case and connect ohmmeter to yellow/gray wire while retaining original ground connection. Renew clipper if reading is less than 300 ohms. If an infinite reading is obtained, remove lead from yellow/gray wire, momentarily short purple wire against case and connect ohmmeter lead to purple wire. If meter moves and then returns to infinity or registers less than 300 ohms, renew clipper unit. If an infinite reading is obtained, disconnect ohmmeter, momentarily short purple wire against case, connect "ground lead" from ohmmeter to purple wire and other ohmmeter lead to ground of clipper. Clipper is good if meter swings toward zero and returns to infinity. Renew clipper if meter needle does not move or if meter needle moves to zero and stays.

BLOCKING DIODE. Failure of the blocking diode may allow motor to continue running after ignition switch is turned OFF or the lower unit may remain in Forward gear until after motor starts.

The blocking diode is located near the ignition switch and the purple wire is attached to "IGNITION" terminal of switch. The purple/green wire from diode is equipped with a quick release connector which attaches to a wire leading to the shift control switch.

To check the blocking diode, first remove the diode. Attach one lead of ohmmeter or continuity test light (with a battery of less than 12 volts) to each wire from diode. Observe ohmmeter reading or test light, then reverse the test connections. Current should pass through diode with one connection (low resistance or light on) but should not pass current with leads reversed. If current passes both directions or does not pass in either direction, renew the blocking diode.

If the blocking diode checks OK but motor continues to run after switch is turned OFF or Forward gear is not engaged until after motor starts, check the switches, wires and connectors for short or open circuits.

RECTIFIER. To check the rectifier (R – Fig. OM16-17), disconnect the yellow (2), yellow/gray (5) and red (10) wires from the terminal block. Connect one lead of ohmmeter to yellow wire from rectifier and attach other ohmmeter lead to motor ground. Check continuity, then reverse the ohmmeter leads. The ohmmeter should indicate low resistance (near zero) with one connection and high resistance (near infinity) with leads reversed. Repeat this test (including reversing the ohmmeter leads) at the ground connection and

yellow/gray lead; between the yellow ane red leads; then, between the red and yellow/gray leads.

If any of the tests indicate near zero resistance in both directions or near infinite resistance in both directions, renew the rectifier.

NOTE: A continuity test light (with battery of less than 12 volts) can be used to check condition of rectifier instead of ohmmeter. Light should glow with one connection, but should not when leads are reversed.

DISTRIBUTOR. To service components of the distributor, remove the flywheel (24 – Fig. OM16-20) and alternator stator (23). The distributor cap is retained by the same three screws which attach the alternator stator and these screws are coated with Loctite. The coil high tension wire and the spark plug wires are screwed into the distributor cap. Remove the spring washer (22) and rotor (4).

The antireverse spring (16 – Fig. OM16-21) is clipped onto crankshaft and when crankshaft is turning in normal direction, the coiled projection is against the oiler felt (18). If the crankshaft turns in counterclockwise direction, the antireverse spring turns with the crankshaft until it grounds the ignition system through contact (17). When installing the antireverse spring, the crankshaft should be lubricated lightly and the flat side of spring should be down as shown in Fig. OM16-22.

Breaker point gap should be set at 0.010 inch (0.25 mm) for used breaker points, or 0.012 inch (0.30 mm) if new breaker points are installed. After breaker point gap is correctly set, install rotor (4 – Fig. OM16-20) making certain that lug engages slot in crankshaft. Install spring washer (22), then position distributor cap (5) over breaker plate. Make certain that coil high tension lead and spark plug wires are screwed into distributor cap and are correctly positioned. Locate the alternator stator (23) over distributor cap, coat the three retaining screws with Loctite and tighten screws to 48-60 in.-lbs. (5.4-6.7 N·m) torque. Initial timing can be set using the timing marks shown in Fig. OM16-23; however, a power timing light and the flywheel timing marks should be used for final setting. Refer to TIMING paragraphs. Make certain that tapers in flywheel (and top of crankshaft) are clean and dry before installing flywheel. The flywheel drive key should be parallel with crankshaft center line, NOT aligned with taper. Tighten the flywheel retaining nut to 70-85 ft.-lbs. (95-116 N·m) torque.

Fig. OM16-19—View of port side of late model engine showing location of fuse (F) and start solenoid (S).

IGNITION TIMING. To check the

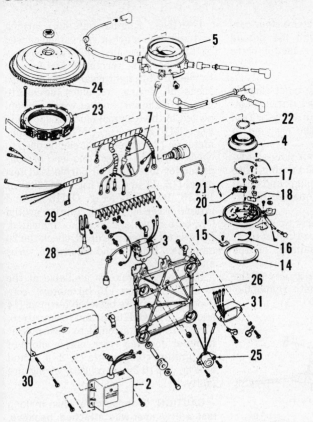

Fig. OM16-20 – Exploded view of the ignition and alternator system components used on breaker point ignition 85 and 100 hp models. Ignition cam is part of crankshaft. Clipper (31) is used on 1971 and later models only.

1. Distributor base plate
2. Amplifier
3. High tension coil
4. Rotor
5. Distributor cap
7. Fuse (20 amp)
14. Retaining ring
15. Clip
16. Antireverse spring
17. Antireverse contact
18. Oiler felt
20. Breaker points
21. Ground wire
22. Wave washer
23. Alternator stator
24. Flywheel
25. Rectifier
26. Bracket
28. Shift diodes
29. Terminal block
30. Cover
31. Clipper

in gear and running at 4500 rpm. If timing is incorrect, loosen locknut and turn the spark advance adjustment screw (Fig. OM16-23). One turn of the screw clockwise will retard ignition approximately one degree.

BREAKERLESS IGNITION

Models Prior to 1973

All 125 hp motors, 1972 100 hp motors and 115 hp motors prior to 1971 are equipped with breakerless capacitor ignition systems which use a distributor. The systems used are primarily the same. Testing and trouble-shooting procedures will be the same except when special note is made.

The capacitor discharge ignition is triggered electronically by a sensor coil located in the distributor unit under the flywheel. The ignition system is extremely durable in normal operation, but can be easily damaged by improper operating, testing or servicing procedures. To prevent damage to the components, observe the following list of cautions and use only approved methods for checking and servicing the system.

1. DO NOT reverse battery terminals.
2. DO NOT disconnect battery while motor is running or attempt to start motor without a battery in the system.

maximum advance ignition timing, connect a power timing light to number 1 (top starboard) cylinder spark plug and run motor at 4500 rpm in forward gear. Different flywheels were used on motors built in 1969 and 1970 than those used on later models. Refer to Fig. OM16-24, Fig. OM16-25 and the appropriate following paragraphs.

1969 And 1970 Models. The "B" timing mark with straight line must align with timing lug on hoisting bracket as shown in Fig. OM16-24. If timing is incorrect, loosen locknut and turn the spark advance adjustment screw (Fig. OM16-23) as required. Make certain that

wires do not prevent free movement of base plate.

The timing light can be attached to the number 2 (top port) cylinder spark plug to check timing of that cylinder. The light should flash as the "B" mark with wedge aligns with timing lug when motor is running at 4500 rpm. If timing is correct for number 1 cylinder but not for number 2, the breaker point gap should be rechecked.

1971 And Later Models. Timing pointer (A – Fig. OM16-25) must align with 28° mark on flywheel with engine

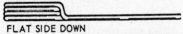

FLAT SIDE DOWN

Fig. OM16-22 – The antireverse spring should be clipped onto crankshaft with the flat side down as shown.

Fig. OM16-24 – When timing light flashes, the "B" mark on flywheel used on 1969 and 1970 models should be aligned with lug on hoisting bracket. Ignition timing is at maximum advance. The "A" mark is not used on these motors.

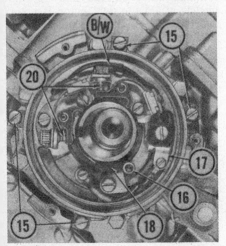

Fig. OM16-21 – View of breaker base with cap and rotor removed. Refer to Fig. OM16-20 for legend.

Fig. OM16-23 – View of maximum advance adjustment screw and initial timing marks. Speed control should be in fast position with base plate lever against stop screw.

Fig. OM16-25 – View of flywheel used after 1970. Full advanced ignition timing should occur when engine speed is above 4500 rpm.

3. DO NOT disconnect **any** wires while motor is running or while ignition switch is ON.

4. DO NOT use any tachometer except those approved for use with this system.

TROUBLE-SHOOTING. Use only approved procedures to prevent damage to the components. The fuel system should be checked first to make certain that faulty running is not caused by incorrect fuel mixture or contaminated fuel. If the motor continues to run after ignition switch is turned OFF, check the blocking diode as outlined in the appropriate paragraphs.

CHECKING FOR SPARK. Connect a spark tester to the four spark plug leads as shown in Fig. OM16-15, attempt to start motor and check for spark at the tester.

NOTE: A neon spark tester or four conventional spark plugs with the ground electrodes removed can be used in place of the tester shown.

Spark gap must not be more than ⅜ inch (9.5 mm). The coil wire is molded into coil and screwed into distributor cap. Do not attempt to pull the wire out of either end.

If spark occurs at all four points of ignition tester, check ignition timing. Also check condition of spark plugs and make certain that leads are connected to correct spark plugs.

If spark occurs regularly at some of the points and irregularly or not at all at other points, check condition of the spark plug leads.

If spark does not occur at any of the tester points, continue with remainder of tests.

WIRING. Engine missing, surging and failure to start or run can be caused by loose or corroded electrical connections. Check all terminals and plug-in connectors for tight clean contact. Also check all wiring for short circuit to ground. Make certain that wires are connected to the terminal block as shown in Fig. OM16-28 or Fig. OM16-29. A voltmeter or 12 volt test light can be used to check wiring. Connect one lead of voltmeter (or test light) to purple lead terminal (16, 17 and 18 – Fig. OM16-28 or 14, 15, 16 and 17 – Fig. OM16-29) and ground other lead. With ignition switch ON, battery voltage should be indicated. If these terminals are dead, check the 20 amp fuse, battery and all lead in wires and connectors.

If battery voltage is available at the terminal block on 115 hp motors, connect a jumper wire between terminal (14 and 15 – Fig. OM16-28) and terminal (16, 17 and 18), then attempt to start motor. If motor does not start, one or more of the ignition components (1, 2, 3, 4 and 5 – Fig. OM16-26 or related wiring are faulty.

CAUTION: Exercise care when making test with jumper wire attached; because, motor may start immediately before lower unit is in Neutral.

If the motor starts and runs properly with jumper wire connected (safety circuit bypassed), the ignition system is OK and one or more of the following components or connecting wires are faulty: Ignition safety circuit (9 – Fig. OM16-26), rectifier, shift diodes, alternator stator, tachometer or flywheel magnets. The ignition safety circuit is actuated by alternator output. Refer to the appropriate paragraphs for further testing of charging system and ignition safety circuit.

If battery voltage is available at the terminal block on 125 and 100 hp models, attempt to start motor. If motor does not start, any of the following components may be at fault; power pack, sensor, ignition coil, distributor cap, rotor or related wiring. Refer to the following paragraphs for inspection of individual components.

SENSOR. The sensor is used to actuate (trigger) the ignition circuit in much the same way as the breaker points of a standard ignition system. Any difficulty with the sensor or connecting wires will affect ignition of this system in a way similar to malfunctions of breaker points.

The air gap between the sensor and the trigger wheel should be 0.028 inch (0.71 mm) as checked in the DISTRIBUTOR paragraphs. To set the air gap, the flywheel, alternator stator,

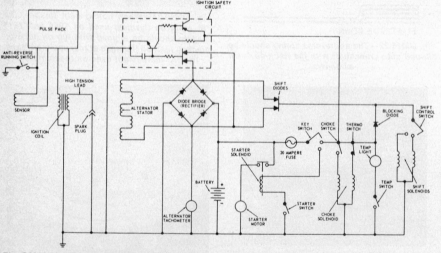

Fig. OM16-26 — The top view shows the basic parts and color of connecting wires for ignition system used on 1969 and 1970 115 hp motors. Lower view is schematic of complete electrical system.

1. Sensor unit	3. High tension coil	5. Distributor cap	7. Fuse (20 amp)
2. Amplifier	4. Rotor	6. Starter solenoid	8. Ignition switch
			9. Ignition safety circuit

distributor cap and rotor must be removed.

After sensor air gap is correctly set, disconnect sensor wires at connector plug (S – Fig. OM16-28 or Fig. OM16-29) and attach one ohmmeter lead to each of the two connectors (2 – Fig. OM16-30). The resistance through the sensor should be 4-6 ohms.

NOTE: Move the speed control linkage and the sensor wires while testing resistance to check for intermittent open circuit.

If resistance is within 4-6 ohms, detach one ohmmeter lead from connector plug and attach to ground. The test should indicate infinite resistance to ground.

NOTE: Move the wires and speed control linkage to check for short circuit to ground.

If the resistance through sensor is not 4-6 ohms or sensor circuit is shorted to ground, carefully check all wiring. If wires are not faulty, renew the sensor unit. Also, check the condition of the antireverse spring and the ground wire between distributor base and motor.

The ignition system can be triggered for test purposes by opening and closing the connection at (S – Fig. OM16-28 or Fig. OM16-29).

If the sensor circuit is not faulty, proceed with remaining tests.

POWER PACK. The power pack may be inspected with a low reading ammeter. Disconnect the 12 volt wire which provides power to the power pack. This wire will be purple with black stripe (15 – Fig. OM16-28) on 115 hp motors or purple (14, 15, 16 or 17 – Fig. OM16-29) on 100 and 125 hp motors.

NOTE: Wire to power pack may be at any one of the four locations (14, 15, 16 or 17) and must be isolated before detaching.

On all models, attach ammeter between terminal and disconnected wire. On 115 hp motors it is necessary to attach a jumper wire between terminal (14 and 15 – Fig. OM16-28) and terminal (16, 17 and 18) in order to bypass the ignition safety circuit. On all models, maximum current draw should be 0.7 amperes with key switch "ON." Current draw should be between 1.5 and 2.5 amperes with engine running at 4500 rpm. Do not attempt to run motor with clip-on type connectors holding ammeter in circuit as possible poor connection may damage ignition units. Unsteady meter reading indicates faulty sensor, incorrect distributor base ground or faulty sensor wires. If current draw is higher or lower than specified, power pack is defective.

NOTE: Use extreme caution to make sure that test connections are not disconnected or shorted while power is "ON".

As an alternate method for testing the power pack, first make certain that the sensor circuit is checked completely as previously outlined. Remove blue lead (11 – Fig. OM16-28 or Fig. OM16-29) from terminal and connect one lead from a neon test light to wire and other test light lead to motor ground. Turn the ignition switch ON, crank motor with electric starter and observe the neon bulb. If the bulb flickers while motor is cranking, the power pack is operating correctly and the high tension coil, distributor cap, rotor, spark plug leads or spark plugs should be suspected. If the neon bulb does not light, disconnect the high tension leads from spark plugs and proceed as follows:

Connect a jumper wire between terminal (14 and 15 – Fig. OM16-28) and terminal (16, 17 and 18) if working on a 115 hp motor. On all models, keep the neon light connected and ignition switch "ON"; open and close connector plug (S – Fig. OM16-28 or Fig. OM16-29) several times while observing the neon test light. If the neon bulb flickers, check the sensor air gap and the ignition safety circuitry on models so equipped. Renew power pack if the neon test light still does not glow and the sensor is known to be OK.

COIL. The ignition high tension coil can be tested usning an ignition tester available from several sources, including the following:

GRAHAM TESTERS, INC.
4220 Central Ave. N.E.
Minneapolis, Minn. 55421

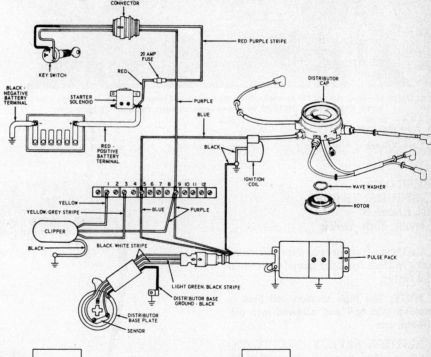

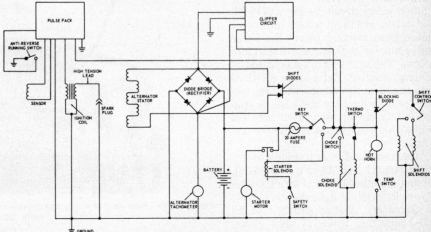

Fig. OM16-27 — The top view shows the basic parts and color of connecting wires for ignition system used on 125 hp motors. Lower view is schematic of complete electrical system.

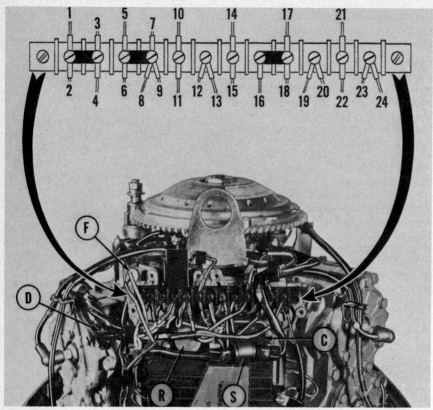

Fig. OM16-28 — Rear view of 115 hp motor showing location of terminal block. Inset shows location of wires. Refer to Fig. OM16-29 for wiring used on early 100 and 125 hp motors.

1, 2, 3 & 4. Yellow	10 & 11. Blue	16, 17 & 18. Purple
5. Yellow/gray stripe	12. Red	19 & 20. Purple/green stripe
6. Gray	13. Red/yellow stripe	21 & 22. Purple/yellow stripe
7, 8 & 9. Yellow/gray stripe	14 & 15. Purple/black stripe	23 & 24. Purple/white stripe

MERC-O-TRONIC
INSTRUMENTS CORP.
215 Branch St.
Almont, Mich. 48003

Coil test procedures and specifications are available from the manufacturers of the tester.

NOTE: The high tension coil lead is molded into coil and screwed into distributor cap.

IGNITION SAFETY CIRCUIT. The ignition safety circuit (9 – Fig. OM16-26) is installed on 115 hp motors to prevent motor from starting before the lower unit is supplied with current to shift into neutral. The safety circuit is actuated by alternator output. Refer to the WIRING paragraphs in this trouble-shooting section for a preliminary check of the ignition safety circuit using a 12 volt test bulb with wires for attaching to the test points.

Attach one lead from test light to terminal (16, 17 and 18–Fig. OM16-28), ground the other lead and turn the ignition switch ON. If light does not glow, check battery, ignition switch, fuse (F) and connecting wires. If light glows, proceed with remaining tests.

Attach one lead from test light to ter-

minal (14 and 15) and ground other lead. If light glows only when motor is being cranked, the ignition safety circuit is operating correctly. If the light does not glow, proceed with remaining tests.

Attach one test light lead to ground and other lead to terminal (1, 2, 3 and 4), then attempt to start motor. Disconnect lead from terminal (1, 2, 3 and 4) and attach to terminal (5, 6, 7, 8 and 9). Attempt to start motor again. If the light glows when attached to terminal (1, 2, 3 and 4) and terminal (5, 6, 7, 8 and 9); but does not glow when attached to terminal (14 and 15), the ignition safety circuit unit (C) is faulty and should be renewed. If the test light glows only when attached to terminal 16, 17 and 18) and does not glow when attached as described in other tests, check alternator stator, shift diodes and rectifier.

Disconnect the purple with black stripe wire (15) which leads to the ignition safety circuit (C). Attach one lead from test light to the disconnected wire and ground other lead. Turn the ignition switch ON. If the light glows, without cranking motor, disconnect the yellow wire to rectifier (2), yellow/gray to rectifier (8), yellow wire to shift diode (3). If the test light glows when ignition switch is turned on after wires are disconnected, renew the ignition safety circuit (C). If the test light does not glow after wires (2, 3 and 8) are disconnected, the shift diode (D) or rectifier (R) is faulty and

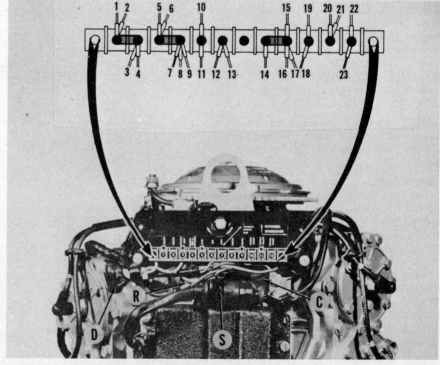

Fig. OM16-29 — Rear view of wiring and ignition system components common to 125 hp models and early 100 hp models.

1, 2, 3 & 4. Yellow	9. Yellow/gray stripe	
5, 6 & 7. Yellow/gray stripe	10 & 11. Blue	18 & 19. Purple/green stripe
8. Gray	12 & 13. Red	20 & 21. Purple/yellow stripe
	14, 15, 16 & 17. Purple	22 & 23. Purple/white stripe

should be checked as outlined in the following paragraphs.

SHIFT DIODE. Failure of the shift diode (D – Fig. OM16-28 or Fig. OM16-29) may prevent motor from starting or may cause the lower unit to shift to forward gear immediately after ignition switch is turned OFF.

To check the shift diode, disconnect the wires (yellow, yellow/gray stripe and purple/green) from terminal block, then remove diode (D). Use a continuity light (with a battery of less than 12 volts) or ohmmeter for checking. Attach one test light (or ohmmeter) lead to the purple/green wire and other lead to the yellow wire; then, reverse the test leads. The test light or ohmmeter should indicate continuity with one connection and NO continuity with leads reversed. Attach test leads similarly to the yellow/gray wire and the purple/green wire; then, reverse leads. Continuity should again exist with one connection; but not when leads are reversed. If either of the two tests allow current to pass in both directions or prevent current from passing in either direction, renew the shift diode.

CLIPPER. Failure of the clipper unit (31 – Fig. OM16-32) should be suspected if any of the following occur: Battery current is momentarily interrupted with motor running; battery charge is low and charging system checks OK; CD power pack inoperative; fuses blow repeatedly.

Clipper unit may be checked with an ohmmeter in the following manner: Disconnect **all** leads from clipper to terminal block before making any checks. Correct ohmmeter test lead polarity must be determined by connecting meter leads to the yellow lead and the purple/green lead of a good **shift diode.** Refer to Shift Diode check in previous section. If ohmmeter shows little or no

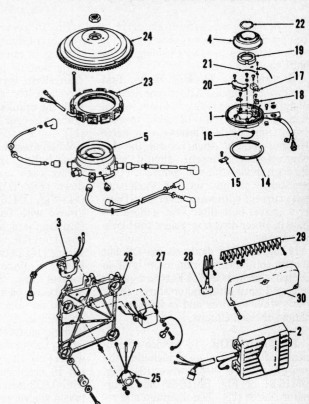

Fig. OM16-31 – Exploded view of the ignition and alternator system components used on 1969 and 1970 115 hp motors.

1. Distributor base plate
2. Amplifier
3. High tension coil
4. Rotor
5. Distributor cap
14. Retainer ring
15. Clip
16. Antireverse spring
17. Antireverse contact
18. Stop
19. Trigger wheel
20. Sensor
21. Sensor leads
22. Wave washer
23. Alternator stator
24. Flywheel
25. Rectifier
26. Bracket
27. Ignition safety circuit
28. Shift diode
29. Terminal block
30. Cover

resistance through shift diode, lead attached to yellow wire will be "ground lead" for purposes of checking clipper. If resistance is high, opposite lead will be ground.

To check clipper, momentarily touch the purple lead to the case of the clipper. Connect the ohmmeter "ground lead" to ground (either the case or the black wire) of the clipper. Connect other ohmmeter lead to yellow wire of clipper. Renew clipper if reading is less than 300 ohms. If an infinite resistance reading is obtained, disconnect ohmmeter lead from yellow wire, momentarily short purple wire against case and connect ohmmeter to yellow/gray wire while retaining original ground connection. Renew clipper if reading is less than 300 ohms. If an infinite reading is obtained, remove lead from yellow/gray wire, momentarily short purple wire against case and connect ohmmeter lead to purple wire. If meter moves and then returns to infinity or registers less than 300 ohms, renew clipper unit. If an infinite resistance reading is obtained, disconnect ohmmeter, momentarily short purple wire against case, connect "ground lead" from ohmmeter to purple wire and other ohmmeter lead to ground of clipper. Clipper is good if meter swings toward zero and returns to infinity. Renew clipper if meter needle does not move or if meter needle moves to zero and stays.

RECTIFIER. Failure of the rectifier should prevent motor from starting

unless the ignition safety circuit is bypassed.

To check the rectifier (R – Fig. OM16-28 or Fig. OM16-29), disconnect wires at terminal block from rectifier (yellow, yellow/gray, and red/yellow). Connect one lead of ohmmeter to yellow wire from rectifier and attach other ohmmeter lead to motor ground. Check continuity, then reverse the ohmmeter leads. The ohmmeter should indicate low resistance (near zero) with one connection and high resistance (near infinity) with leads reversed. Repeat this test (including reversing the ohmmeter leads) at the ground connection and yellow/gray lead; between the yellow and red/yellow leads; then, between red/yellow and yellow/gray leads.

If any of the tests indicate near zero resistance in both directions or near infinite resistance in both directions, renew the rectifier.

NOTE: A continuity test (with a battery of less than 12 volts) can be used to check condition of rectifier instead of ohmmeter. Light should glow with one connection, but should not when leads are reversed.

BLOCKING DIODE. Failure of the blocking diode may allow motor to continue running after ignition switch is turned OFF or the lower unit may remain in forward gear until after motor starts.

The blocking diode is located near the ignition switch with the purple wire attached to the "IGN." terminal of switch.

Fig. OM16-30 – The sensor circuit can be checked at terminals (2) using an ohmmeter.

The purple/green wire from diode is equipped with a quick release connector which attaches to a wire leading to the shift control switch.

To check the blocking diode, first remove the diode. Attach one lead of ohmmeter or continuity test light (with a battery of less than 12 volts) to each wire from diode. Observe ohmmeter reading or light, then reverse the test connections. Current should pass through diode with one connection (low resistance or light on) but should not pass current with leads reversed. If current passes both directions or does not pass in either direction, renew the blocking diode.

If the blocking diode checks OK but motor continues to run after ignition switch is turned OFF or Forward gear is engaged until after motor starts, check the switches, wires and connectors for shorts or open circuits.

DISTRIBUTOR. To service components of the distributor, including the sensor, remove the flywheel (24 – Fig. OM16-31 or Fig. OM16-32) and alternator stator (23). The distributor is retained by the same three screws which attach alternator stator with these screws are coated with Loctite. The coil high tension wire and the spark plug wires are screwed into distributor cap. Remove the spring washer (22) and rotor (4). If the trigger wheel (19) is to be removed, carefully pry unit off crankshaft using two screwdrivers. Remainder of disassembly will be self-evident.

The antireverse spring (16) is clipped onto crankshaft and when crankshaft is turning in normal direction, the coiled projection is against stop (18). If the crankshaft turns in counterclockwise direction, the antireverse spring turns with the crankshaft until it grounds the ignition sensor system through contact (17).

When assembling, lubricate the crankshaft lightly, then clip the antireverse spring onto crankshaft with flat side down (Fig. OM16-22). Install retainer (14 – Fig. OM16-31 or Fig. OM16-32) in groove with flat side toward base (1). Position base assembly around crankshaft with coil or antireverse spring (16) between stop (18) and contact (17). Make certain that the speed control link can be connected to distributor base. Install the clips (15) and be sure that base rotates freely with no binding. The base retainer (14) and bushing surface of base (1) can be oiled lightly before assembling. Install trigger wheel (19) with notch aligned with drive pin in crankshaft. Install sensor (20) with 0.028 inch (0.71 mm) clearance between sensor surface and trigger wheel (19). Make certain that sensor wires are correctly positioned and not shorted or broken.

Install rotor (4) making certain that lug engages notch in crankshaft. Install wave washer (22), then position distributor cap (5) and alternator stator over the distributor base plate. Make certain that the coil high tension lead and spark plug wires are screwed into cap and correctly positioned. Coat the three alternator stator and distributor cap retaining screws with Loctite and tighten the

screws evenly to 48-60 in.-lbs. (5.4-6.7 N·m) torque. Initial timing can be set using the timing marks shown in Fig. OM16-23; however, a power timing light and the flywheel timing marks should be used for final setting. Refer to TIMING paragraphs. Make certain that tapers in flywheel and on crankshaft are clean and dry before installing flywheel. The flywheel drive key should be parallel with crankshaft center line, NOT aligned with taper. Flywheel nut on all 1972 models should be torqued to 100-105 ft.-lbs. (136-143 N·m). Flywheel nut on all earlier models should be torqued to 70-85 ft.-lbs. (95-116 N·m).

IGNITION TIMING. To check the maximum advance ignition timing, connect a power timing light to the number 1 (top starboard) cylinder spark plug and run motor at 4500 rpm in forward gear.

When timing 1969 and 1970 motors, the "B" timing mark with straight line must align with timing lug on hoisting bracket as shown in Fig. OM16-24. If timing is incorrect, loosen locknut and turn the spark advance adjusting screw (Fig. OM16-23) as required. Make certain that wires do not prevent free movement of base plate. When timing 1971 and 1972 motors, the 28° mark on the flywheel must align with timing pointer (A – Fig. OM16-25). If timing is incorrect, loosen locknut and turn spark advance adjusting screw (Fig. OM16-23). One turn of screw will retard ignition approximately one degree. Make certain that wires do not prevent free movement of distributor base plate.

1973-1977 Models

The capacitor discharge ignition system used on motors from 1973 to 1977 does not have a distributor or breaker points. Magnets built into central portion of flywheel and two sensor coils are used to trigger the ignition unit.

This ignition is extremely durable in normal operation, but can be easily damaged by improper operating, testing or servicing procedures. To prevent damage to components, observe the following list of precautions and use only approved methods for checking and servicing system.

1. DO NOT disconnect any wires while motor is running or while ignition switch is ON.
2. DO NOT use any tachometer except those approved for use with this system.
3. DO NOT hold spark plug wires while checking for spark.
4. DO make certain that all wiring connections are clean and tightly joined.

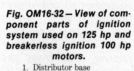

Fig. OM16-32 – View of component parts of ignition system used on 125 hp and breakerless ignition 100 hp motors.

1. Distributor base
2. Amplifier
3. Ignition coil
4. Rotor assy.
5. Distributor cap assy.
14. Distributor base retainer
15. Clip
16. Reverse cut off spring
17. Antireverse contact
18. Stop
19. Trigger wheel
20. Sensor
21. Sensor leads
22. Spring washer
23. Stator
24. Flywheel
25. Rectifier
26. Mount bracket
28. Shift diode
29. Terminal block
30. Cover
31. Clipper
32. Fuse (20 amp)

5. DO make certain that wires do not bind moving parts or touch metal edges where they may chafe through insulation.

TROUBLE-SHOOTING. Use only approved procedures to prevent damage to the components. The fuel system should be checked first to make certain that faulty running is not caused by incorrect mixture or contaminated fuel.

CHECKING FOR SPARK. Disconnect spark plug leads at spark plugs and connect them to a needle point spark checker, similar to unit in Fig. OM16-15, with four gaps used set at 7/16 inch (11.1 mm). Consistent, strong spark indicates ignition system functioning properly; suspect spark plugs, timing, improper wiring to ignition coils or to spark plugs.

Weak, inconsistent spark or spark from only one or two ignition coils; suspect sensor coils or ignition coils. Weak, inconsistent spark from all four ignition coils; suspect charge coils. No spark at all; suspect power pack.

WIRING. Engine missing, surging and failure to start or run can be caused by loose or corroded electrical connections. Check all terminals and plug-in connectors for tight clean contact. Also check all wiring for short to ground.

SENSOR COILS. Two sensor coils (1 and 2–Fig. OM16-34) are used to trigger ignition at each cylinder. Sensor coil 1/3 (1) controls ignition for cylinders 1 and 3 while sensor 2/4 (2) controls ignition for cylinders 2 and 4. Sensor coils may be checked by disconnecting the white/black and black/white lead wires from terminal #2, #4, #9 and #12 (see Fig. OM16-34). Resistance between the leads of sensor coils 1/3 or sensor coil 2/4 should be 6.5-10.5 ohms. Sensor coils should also be checked for a short to ground. Defective sensor coils are not renewable separately, timer base assembly (7–Fig. OM16-33) must be renewed.

CHARGE COILS. Charge coils may be checked by reading resistance between brown wire attached to terminal #7 and brown/yellow wire attached to terminal #8. Correct resistance is 555-705 ohms. There must also be infinite resistance between either lead and ground. Stator assembly (6–Fig. OM16-33) must be renewed if charge coils are defective.

IGNITION COILS. Ignition coils may be checked with standard ignition coil test equipment. Complete operating instructions and coil test specifications will be included with tester.

POWER PACK. Power pack contains storage capacitor, rectifier and SCR (silicone controlled rectifiers) switches for ignition operation. Misfire in one or more cylinders or complete ignition system failure may be caused by malfunction of power pack components. If power pack is suspected cause of ignition trouble, install a power pack known to be good in ignition system and check operation. Power pack is available only as a unit assembly.

STATOR AND TIMER BASE ASSEMBLY. Stator (6–Fig. OM16-33) and timer base (7) may be serviced after removal of the flywheel. Stator assembly is secured to the power head by four screws. The timer base may be removed after the stator by removing the four screws and clips along the outside edge.

When reassembling unit, make certain that wiring does not restrict free movement of timer base. Inspect taper on crankshaft and taper in flywheel. Install flywheel key with flat of key parallel to center line of crankshaft, NOT surface of taper. Tighten flywheel nut to 100-105 ft.-lbs. (136-143 N·m) torque.

IGNITION TIMING. Connect a power timing light to number 1 (top) cylinder spark plug. Timing pointer should align with appropriate degree mark on flywheel with motor running at full speed in gear (Fig. OM16-25). Stop engine and turn spark advance stop screw (A–Fig. OM16-8) if timing is incorrect. Turning screw clockwise one full turn will retard ignition timing approximately one degree.

Refer to following table for full advance ignition timing:

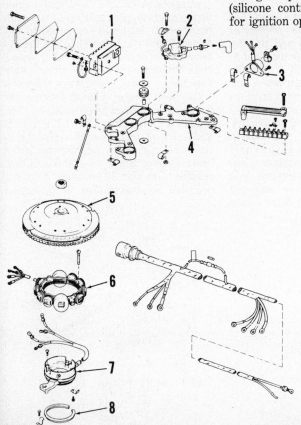

Fig. OM16-33 – Exploded view of ignition components used on models from 1973 through 1977.

1. Power pack
2. Ignition coils
3. Rectifier
4. Bracket
5. Flywheel
6. Stator
7. Timer base assy.
8. Retainer ring

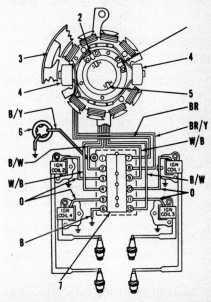

Fig. OM16-34 – Schematic of breakerless ignition system used on 1973-1977 models.

1. Sensor coil 1/3	7. Power pack
2. Sensor coil 2/4	B. Black
3. Charge magnet	BR. Brown
4. Charge coils	O. Orange
5. Sensor magnet	W. White
6. Ignition switch	Y. Yellow

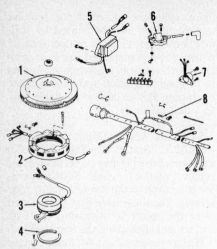

Fig. OM16-35 — View of ignition components typical of the type used on models after 1977.

1. Flywheel
2. Stator
3. Timer base
4. Retainer ring
5. Power pack
6. Ignition coil
7. Rectifier
8. Fuse (20 amp)

Models	Degrees BTDC
85 hp	
1973, 1974	28
1975, 1976, 1977	26
115 hp	
1973, 1974	26
1975, 1976	24
1977	28
135 and 140 hp	
1973, 1974	22
1975, 1976	20
1977	28

Models After 1977

All models are equipped with a capacitor discharge ignition system which is triggered by sensor coils on stator plate. To prevent damage to components, note the following list of precautions:

1. DO NOT disconnect any wires while motor is running or while ignition switch is ON.
2. DO NOT use any tachometer except those approved for use with this system.
3. DO NOT hold spark plug wires while checking for spark.
4. DO make certain that all wiring connections are clean and tightly joined.
5. DO make certain that wires do not bind moving parts or touch metal edges where they may chafe through insulation.

TROUBLE-SHOOTING. Use only approved procedures to prevent damage to the components. The fuel system should be checked first to make certain that faulty running is not caused by fuel starvation, incorrect mixture or contaminated fuel.

CHECKING FOR SPARK. Disconnect spark plug leads at spark plugs and connect them to a needle point spark checker, similar to unit in Fig. OM16-15, with four gaps used set at ½ inch (12.7 mm). Consistent, strong spark indicates ignition system functioning properly; suspect spark plugs, timing, improper wiring to ignition coils or to spark plugs.

Weak, inconsistent spark or spark from only one or two ignition coils; suspect sensor coils or ignition coils. Weak, inconsistent spark from all four ignition coils; suspect charge coils. No spark at all; suspect power pack.

WIRING. Engine missing, surging and failure to start or run can be caused by loose or corroded electrical connections. Check all terminals and plug-in connectors for tight clean contact. Also check all wiring for short circuit to ground.

CHARGE COILS. Models after 1977 except 1985 and 1986 120 and 140 hp models use two charge coils contained in the stator assembly. Models with 120 and 140 hp in 1985 and 1986 use one charge coil contained in the stator assembly. To check charge coil or coils, disconnect the two-wire connector (one per bank of cylinders on two charge coil models) and connect an ohmmeter to terminals A and B (Fig. OM16-36) in connector leading to stator. Renew stator assembly if resistance is not 485-635 ohms on two charge coil models and 535-585 ohms on one charge coil models. Connect negative ohmmeter lead to an engine ground and positive ohmmeter lead to connector terminal A, then to connector terminal B. Infinite resistance should exist between A terminal and engine ground and B terminal and engine ground. If not, charge coil or charge coil lead is shorting to ground. To check charge coil output, use Merc-O-Tronic Model 781, Stevens Model CD77 or a suitable peak voltage tester. Connect black tester lead to terminal A in connector leading to stator and red tester lead to terminal B. Turn tester

knobs to "NEG (−)" and "500." Crank engine while observing tester. Repeat test on other charge coil on two charge coil models. Renew stator assembly if meter reads below 160 volts on either coil test on two charge coil models and 175 volts on one charge coil models.

SENSOR COILS. Models after 1977 except 1985 and 1986 120 and 140 hp models use two sensor coils contained in the timer base assembly. Models with 120 and 140 hp in 1985 and 1986 use four sensor coils contained in the timer base assembly. To check sensor coils on two sensor coil models, connect an ohmmeter to terminals A and B (Fig. OM16-36) and then A and C in four-wire connector leading to timer base. Repeat test on other sensor coil connection. Renew timer base if resistance readings are not 30-50 ohms. Connect negative ohmmeter lead to an engine ground and positive ohmmeter lead to connector terminal A, then B and then C. Repeat test on other sensor coil connection. Infinite resistance should exist between all terminal connections and engine ground. If not, sensor coil or sensor coil lead is shorting to ground. To check sensor coil output, use Merc-O-Tronic Model 781, Stevens Model CD77 or a suitable peak voltage tester. Connect black tester lead to timer base connector terminal A and red tester lead to terminal B. On Merc-O-Tronic Model 781, turn knobs to "POS (+)" and "5" and on Stevens Model CD77, turn knobs to "S" and "5." Crank engine while observing tester. Repeat test with black tester lead still connected to terminal A and connect red tester lead to terminal C. Repeat test on other sensor coil connection. Renew timer base assembly if meter reads below 0.3 volts.

To check sensor coils on four sensor coil models, connect an ohmmeter to terminals A and E (Fig. OM16-37), then B and E, then C and E and then D and E in five-wire connector leading to timer base. Renew timer base if resistance readings are not 30-50 ohms. Connect negative ohmmeter lead to an engine

Fig. OM16-36 — Ignition wiring schematic for models after 1977 except 1985 and 1986 120 and 140 hp models. Models 120 and 140 in 1985 and 1986 use only one power pack (2). First letter indicates connector terminal while letters after dash denote wire color, i.e., A−BR/Y indicates terminal A is connected to a brown/yellow wire.

1. Stator
2. Power packs
3. Ignition switch
4. Ignition coils
B. Black
BL. Blue
BR. Brown
G. Green
O. Orange
W. White
Y. Yellow

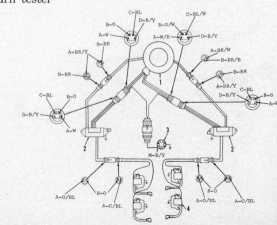

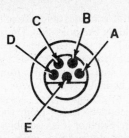

Fig. OM16-37—View identifying wire terminals in timer base assembly connector on 1985 and 1986 120 and 140 hp models.

ground and positive ohmmeter lead to connector terminal A, then B, then C, then D and then E. Infinite resistance should exist between all terminal connections and engine ground. If not, sensor coil or sensor coil lead is shorting to ground. To check sensor coil output, use Merc-O-Tronic Model 781, Stevens Model CD77 or a suitable peak voltage tester. Connect black tester lead to timer base connector terminal E and red tester lead to terminal A. On Merc-O-Tronic Model 781, turn knobs to "POS (+)" and "5" and on Stevens Model CD77, turns knobs to "S" and "5." Crank engine while observing tester. Repeat test with black tester lead still connected to terminal E and connect red tester lead to terminal B, then C and then to D. Renew timer base if meter reads below 0.3 volts.

POWER PACK. To check power pack output, first reconnect stator and timer base connectors. Use Merc-O-Tronic Model 781, Stevens Model CD77 or a suitable peak voltage tester. Connect black tester lead to a suitable engine ground. Connect red tester lead to wire leading to one of the four ignition coils. Turn tester knobs to "NEG (–)" and "500." Crank engine while observing tester. Repeat test on other leads. Renew power pack on 1985 and 1986 120 and 140 hp models if readings are not at least 175 volts or higher. Renew power pack or packs on all other models

Fig. OM16-40—View of starting safety switch (S) on models prior to 1973, and speed control lever (L). Refer to text for adjustment.

Fig. OM16-41—Exploded view of the thermostat and pressure relief valve components. Components in (A) are used on all models after 1976 (except 1985 and 1986 120 and 140 hp models). Components in (B) are used on all models prior to 1973. Components in (C) are used on all 1973-1976 models.

1. Cover
2. Thermostat spring
3. Pressure relief valve spring
4. Thermostat
5. Pressure relief valve
6. Gasket
7. Plate
8. Gasket
9. Thermostat control unit
10. Housing
11. Grommet

if readings are not at least 170 volts or higher.

NOTE: Power pack on 120 and 140 hp models marked "CDL" have an internal device to limit engine speed to 6100 rpm.

IGNITION COILS. Renew ignition coil or coils if no other ignition component is found faulty.

IGNITION TIMING. The timing pointer is adjustable. If the timing pointer or intake manifold has been disturbed, a dial indicator must be used to verify the timing pointer alignment with flywheel TDC mark when the number 1 (top, starboard) cylinder piston is at TDC. Remove the number 1 cylinder spark plug and install a dial indicator so indicator plunger extends through the plug opening and into the cylinder. Position the number 1 cylinder piston at TDC. Align timing pointer with TDC (0°) mark on the flywheel and secure the pointer position. Remove the dial indicator and reassemble.

To check the maximum advance ignition timing, connect a power timing light to the number 1 cylinder spark plug lead. Start the engine and shift into "FORWARD" gear, then accelerate to full throttle. Note the flywheel marks when the timing light flashes. Ignition should occur at 26° BTDC on 85 hp models and 28° BTDC on all other models prior to 1983. On models after 1982, consult the engine decal for maximum spark advance specifications. Ignition should occur at 22° BTDC on 1985 120 and 140 hp models and 17°-19° BTDC on 1986 120 and 140 hp models. Stop the engine and turn spark advance stop screw (A–Fig. OM16-7 or Fig.

OM16-14) if timing is incorrect. Turning screw (A) clockwise one full turn will retard ignition timing approximately one degree.

On all models except 1985 and 1986 120 and 140 hp models, check pickup timing as follows: Connect a power timing light to number 1 cylinder spark plug lead. Advance the speed control lever until the throttle plates just start to open. Start the engine and note the throttle pickup timing with the timing light. The throttle pickup timing should be 0°-3° BTDC on 115 and 140 hp models prior to 1979 and 5° BTDC on all other models. If not, stop the engine and adjust the position of yoke (Y). One complete turn will equal approximately 2°.

STARTING SAFETY SWITCH

The starting safety switch on models prior to 1973 prevents the motor from being started at advanced throttle. The switch (S – Fig. OM16-40) is actuated by a cam on the speed control lever (L) and should close at approximtely midpoint on the cam slope. Continuity should exist through the switch during the low speed section of lever movement and should open as the speed control lever passes the starting position. Adjust by loosening the screws (2) and repositioning the switch.

COOLING SYSTEM

THERMOSTAT. A cooling system thermostat is used to maintain an even temperature of 130°-150°F (54°-65°C). Later models have two thermostats as shown in Fig. OM16-41 and Fig. OM16-42. Temperatures can be checked using heat sensitive sticks such as "Markal Thermomelt Stik." A 125°F (52°C) stick should melt, but a 163°F (73°C). stick should not melt, after engine reaches normal operating temperature. If the 125°F (52°C) stick does not melt, the thermostat may be stuck open. Overheating could be caused by damaged thermostat, damaged pressure control valve, exhaust cover gaskets leaking, head gaskets leaking, water passages obstructed, water passages leaking or water pump failure. The control panel on 1969 and 1970 motors is fitted with a temperature warning light, later motors are fitted with a "hot horn." Either of these, when operating, indicates an overheated condition in the power head. A temperature sensing switch (16 – Fig. OM16-45) located in the starboard cylinder head on early models and in both cylinder heads on later models is used to activate these warning devices. Temperature switch operation may be checked with a continuity tester and a high temperature thermometer. Place switch and thermometer in oil that is being heated. Switch should show a closed circuit at 205°-217°F (96°-102°C) and should open again at 168°-182°F (75°-83°C).

On all models except 1985 and 1986 120 and 140 hp models, the thermostat housing is located at rear of adapter plate attaching power head to low unit, below the ignition power pack and bracket. Refer to Fig. OM16-41. On 1985 and 1986 120 and 140 hp models, a thermostat assembly is located at the top of each cylinder head. Refer to Fig. OM16-42.

On later 85, 115 and 140 (prior to 1985) hp models, check valves (3 – Fig. OM16-41) open at high engine rpm when high water pump impeller speed increases water pressure. On all other models, check valve (3) closes when ther-

mostat opens to expel water and prevent return of hot water to water pump. Check valve is open when thermostat is closed so water will circulate through engine until water reaches opening temperature of thermostat.

WATER PUMP. The water pump is mounted on top surface of gearcase housing. The rubber impeller is mounted on and driven by the drive shaft. To remove the water pump, separate the lower unit (gearcase) from the drive shaft and exhaust housing.

Lip of seal (16 – Fig. OM16-51, 9 – Fig. OM16-59 and 4 – Fig. OM16-66) should be down. Screws attaching water pump housing and cover should be coated with OMC Gasket Sealing Compound or equivalent. Apply OMC Adhesive M or equivalent to bottom of impeller plate before installing. Lubricate impeller and hold blades in while installing housing. The drive shaft can be rotated clockwise while assembling, but should not be turned backwards.

POWER HEAD

R&R AND DISASSEMBLE. Remove the flywheel and ignition and charging components if needed. Mark wires for identification, disconnect interfering wires, then remove the bracket (26 – Fig. OM16-20) on pre-1973 models and electrical components on all models. Mark wires for identification, then disconnect wires from starter solenoid, starting safety switch, starter motor, temperature switch, choke solenoid and shift cables on models prior to 1973. Disconnect upper end of shift rod shown in Fig. OM16-43 on 1973 through 1977 models or Fig. OM16-64 on all models after 1977 except 1985 and 1986 120 and 140 hp models. On 1985 and 1986 120 and 140 hp models, remove threaded pin

from shift cam located at base of intake manifold on the port side. On models so equipped or as needed, proceed as follows: Remove air silencer, carburetors and fuel pump. Remove exhaust housing rear cover, remove screws attaching motor lower covers and disconnect hoses from thermostat housing. Further disassembly may be desirable depending upon type of repairs. On all models except 1985 and 1986 120 and 140 hp models, remove four nuts and eight screws (Fig. OM16-44), then lift power head from lower unit. On 1985 and 1986 120 and 140 hp models, remove four screws and one nut from each side of upper end of drive shaft housing and two screws and one nut at rear of upper end of drive shaft housing. Lift power head from lower unit.

The transfer port covers, exhaust covers, cylinder heads and inlet manifold should be carefully removed, by loosening screws evenly, to prevent warpage. Remove screws attaching crankcase heads (23 and 27 – Fig. OM16-46) to crankcase. Drive the crankcase aligning taper pin or pins out toward front, then unbolt and remove the forward crankcase half.

NOTE: Be sure to remove the four Allen head screws located in the inlet passages before attempting to separate crankcase halves.

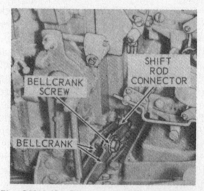

Fig. OM16-43 – Disconnect shift rod connector from bellcrank on 1973 through 1977 models to separate power head and lower unit.

Fig. OM16-44 – View identifying screws and nuts for removal of power head on all models except 1985 and 1986 120 and 140 hp models. Refer to text.

Fig. OM16-42 – On 1985 and 1986 120 and 140 hp models, a thermostat assembly is located behind cover (T) on both the port and starboard cylinder heads. The thermostat and pressure relief valve are a single unit.

Pistons, rods and crankshaft are now accessible for removal and overhaul as outlined in the appropriate following paragraphs. When assembling, follow procedure outline in the ASSEMBLY paragraphs.

ASSEMBLY. When assembling, the crankcase and inlet manifold must be completely sealed against both vacuum and pressure. Exhaust manifold and cylinder heads must be sealed against water leakage and pressure. Mating surfaces of water intake and exhaust areas between lower unit and power head must form a tight seal. It is recommended that all mating surfaces (including joints using gaskets) be carefully inspected for nicks, burrs, erosion and warpage which might interfere with a

tight seal. All of these surfaces may be lapped if necessary to provide a smooth, flat surface, but DO NOT remove any more metal than absolutely necessary. The mating surfaces between the crankcase halves (9 and 15 – Fig. OM16-45) **MUST NOT** be lowered, but can be polished to remove imperfections only.

The crankcase halves are positively located during assembly by the use of a tapered dowel pin or pins. Check to make certain that the dowel pin or pins are not bent, nicked or distorted and that dowel pin hole or holes are clean and true. When installing dowel pin or pins, make sure that pin or pins are fully seated, but do not use excessive force.

On models prior to 1979, the mating surfaces of crankcase halves are sealed by means of the sealing strips (14) which fit in grooves in face of front crankcase half (15). When installing these strips, first make certain that the complete surface, including the grooves, is absolutely clean and free from old cement, nicks or foreign matter. Position the crankshaft (32 – Fig. OM16-46) with top main bearing (22 through 25), center main bearing (34 and 35), lower main bearing (26 through 31) and sealing rings (33) assembled into block.

NOTE: The four bearing retainer plate screws (31S) should be installed loosely and should not be tightened until assembly is completed.

Install the piston and connecting rod assemblies to the crankshaft.

NOTE: Make certain that center main bearing outer race is seated correctly on the retaining dowel pin.

When reassembling crankcase, make sure mating surfaces of crankcase halves are completely clean and free of old cement, nicks and burrs. On models

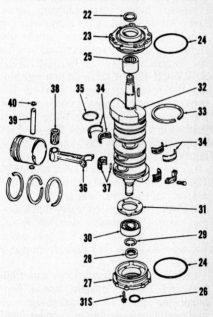

Fig. OM16-46 — Exploded view of the crankshaft and associated parts. Bearing (25) and head (23) are a one-piece unit on models after 1972. Two piston rings are used on later models. Two "O" rings (24) for top and bottom are used on 1985 and 1986 120 and 140 hp models. On 1986 90 and 110 hp models, loose needle bearings and two thrust washers are used in place of caged bearing (38).

22. Seal	
23. Crankcase upper bearing head	31S. Attaching screws
24. "O" rings	32. Crankshaft
25. Top main bearing	33. Seal rings (6 used)
26. "O" ring	34. Center main bearing
27. Crankcase lower bearing head	35. Retaining ring
28. Seal	36. Connecting rod
29. Snap ring	37. Crankpin bearing & cage
30. Lower main bearing	38. Piston pin bearing
31. Bearing retainer plate	39. Piston pin
	40. Snap ring

Fig. OM16-45 — Exploded view of early crankcase and associated parts. Later models, except for 1985 and 1986 120 and 140 hp models, are similar. Sealing strips (14) are not used on models after 1978. ON 1985 and 1986 120 and 140 hp models, covers (1) and cylinder heads (2) are one piece. Exhaust cover (4) and transfer port covers (10) are cast into cylinder block (9). Refer to Fig. OM16-46 for exploded view of crankshaft and related parts.

1. Cylinder head covers	7. Choke thermo unit	12. Throttle control rod	17. Ignition control lever
2. Cylinder heads	8. Hose to thermostat housing	13. Ignition control rod	18. Spring
3. Water passage cover	9. Cylinder block	14. Sealing strips	19. Throttle cam
4. Exhaust cover	10. Transfer port covers	15. Crankcase front half	20. Bushing
5. Exhaust inner cover	11. Speed control lever	16. Temperature warning switch	21. Bushing
6. Hoisting bracket			

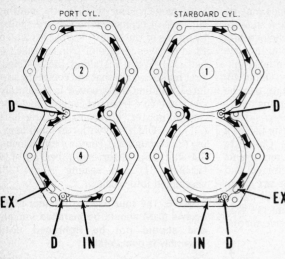

PORT CYL. STARBOARD CYL.

Fig. OM16-47 — On all models except 1985 and 1986 120 and 140 hp models, water deflectors (D) must be installed in locations shown for proper water flow around cylinders.

prior to 1979, install sealing strips (14) and trim ends to extend approximately 1/32 inch (0.79 mm) into bearing bores, then sparingly apply OMC Adhesive "M" to cylinder half of crankcase only. On models after 1978, apply OMC Gel-Seal II to one crankcase mating surface. Do not use sealers which will harden and prevent contact between crankcase mating surfaces. Immediately assemble crankcase halves after applying sealer and position halves by installing locating taper pin or pins; then install and tighten crankcase retaining screws to the torque listed in the CONDENSED SERVICE DATA table. When tightening the retaining screws, start in the center and work toward ends. Tighten the lower main bearing plate screws (31S – Fig. OM16-46) to the correct torque and check the crankshaft for binding.

On all models except 1985 and 1986 120 and 140 hp models, note location of water deflectors shown in Fig. OM16-47. Deteriorated water deflectors may cause overheating and hot spots. Deflectors are not as tall as water passages so water may drain from water jacket.

On all models except 1985 and 1986 120 and 140 hp models, use a non-hardening sealer on all gasket surfaces and complete assembly of cylinder head and covers. Threads of screws should be coated with nonhardening sealer to prevent water damage to threads, especially on motors operated in salt water. On 1985 and 1986 120 and 140 hp models, install cylinder head gaskets and intake manifold gasket without a sealer.

PISTONS, PINS, RINGS AND CYLINDERS. Before detaching connecting rods from crankshaft, mark piston, rod and cap for correct assembly to each other and for installation into the same cylinder from which they are removed. Separate bearing cages and rollers (37 – Fig. OM16-46) for assembly

into same location if they are to be reinstalled.

Pistons and rings are available in standard size and oversize. Pistons in early models are equipped with three piston rings while later models have two rings. Refer to the CONDENSED SERVICE DATA table for recommended ring end gap, ring side clearance and piston skirt clearance. Rebore cylinder bores or renew cylinder block if cylinder bore taper or out-of-round exceeds 0.003 inch (0.08 mm) on models prior to 1977 and 0.004 inch (0.10 mm) on models after 1976.

The piston pin is retained in piston by snap rings in piston pin bosses. On some models, one piston pin boss is tight on piston pin and the other has slight clearance. When removing or installing piston pin, always press pin from side marked "LOOSE" toward the tight side to prevent damage to piston. The upper end of connecting rod is fitted with a caged needle roller bearing on all models except 1986 90 and 110 hp models. On 1986 90 and 110 hp models, loose needle bearings and two thrust washers are used. The piston pin and connecting rod bore are used as bearing races. Check bearing rollers, cage and bearing race surfaces for wear, scoring or overheating. When assembling, pistons should be heated slightly to facilitate installation of piston pins. The pistons on port side are installed to connecting rods

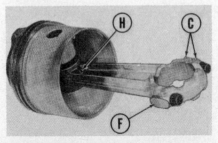

Fig. OM16-48 — The oil hole (H) should be toward top of motor and index marks (C) should be aligned.

differently than for starboard units. The oil hole in side of rod at piston pin end should be up on all connecting rods. On all models except 1985 and 1986 120 and 140 hp models, the long sloping side of pistons must be toward center of cylinder block "V" (exhaust ports). On 1985 and 1986 120 and 140 hp models, the stamping "Exhaust Side" on top of pistons must face cylinder bore exhaust ports. Thoroughly lubricate all bearing surfaces before assembling.

CONNECTING RODS, BEARINGS AND CRANKSHAFT. Before detaching connecting rods from crankshaft, mark rod and cap for correct assembly to each other and in original cylinder. Separate bearing cages and rollers for assembly to original crankpin if units are not renewed.

Connecting rods ride on roller bearings at both ends. The lower bearing consists of a split retainer (cage) and 16 rollers on pre-1974 models and 18 rollers on 1974 and later models except 1985 and 1986 120 and 140 hp models. Sixteen roller bearings per crankpin bearing set are used on 1985 and 1986 120 and 140 hp models. The crankpin end of rod is drilled and finished, then carefully fractured to separate the cap from the rod. The parting line should be nearly invisible. When assembling, make certain that index marks (C – Fig. OM16-48) are aligned, oil hole (H) is toward top of motor and long sloping side or stamping "Exhaust Side" of piston head is toward center of "V." The machined sides (F) of connecting rod and cap should be smooth when assembled. On 1985 and later models equipped with precision ground rods, OMC Alignment Fixture 396749 is recommended to properly align connecting rod with rod cap during tightening of connecting rod screws.

NOTE: Precision ground rods are identified by grind marks running ACROSS corners on ears of connecting rod and rod cap where the components join.

Crankshaft seal rings (33 – Fig. OM16-46) should have 0.0015-0.0025 inch (0.038-0.063 mm) side clearance in crankshaft groove on all models prior to 1985. Seal rings are available in four thicknesses: 0.1565-0.1570 inch (3.975-3.988 mm), 0.1575-0.1580 inch (4.000-4.013 mm), 0.1585-0.1590 inch (4.026-4.039 mm) and 0.1605-0.1610 inch (4.077-4.089 mm). On models after 1984, seal ring (33) should be renewed if thickness is less than 0.154 inch (3.91 mm).

The upper main bearing (25) on models prior to 1973, and seal (22) on all models are located in the upper main bearing head (23). The bearing should be

LOWER UNIT

Models Prior to 1973

pressed into bearing head with the lettered end of bearing out (toward bottom). Bearing and head (23) are a one-piece assembly on models after 1972 and must be serviced as a unit. Lip of seal (22) should be toward inside and should be pressed in until flush with top surface of bearing head.

The center main bearing (34 and 35) is a split-cage needle bearing. The two-piece outer race is held together with retaining ring (35) and is positioned in cylinder block by a dowel pin. When assembling, make certain that dowel pin in cylinder block bore engages hole in center bearing outer race.

The ball type lower main bearing (30) is located in the lower bearing head (27). The bearing outer race is clamped to the bearing head with retainer plate (31) and screws (31S). To disassemble the lower bearing assembly, remove screws (31S) and pull bearing head (27) from bearing (30). Remove snap ring (29), then remove bearing from crankshaft lower end using a suitable puller. The lower bearing should allow crankshaft end play within the limits specified in the CONDENSED SERVICE DATA table. When assembling, position retainer (31) around crankshaft, then press bearing (30) onto journal and install snap ring (29). Press seal (28) into bore in bearing head using special OMC tool to locate seal at correct depth in the bore. Install new "O" ring or "O" rings (24) in groove or grooves of bearing head and press bearing head onto outer race of bearing. Install screws (31S) into retainer (31), but do not tighten these screws until crankcase is assembled.

Refer to the CONDENSED SERVICE DATA table for dimensional data and recommended torque values. Refer to ASSEMBLY paragraphs for assembling the crankcase halves.

PROPELLER

PROPELLER. An aluminum, three-blade propeller with built in cushion clutch is standard on all motors. Alternates include both two and three blade units with a range in diameter from 12¾

inches (32.4 cm) to 14 inches (35.6 cm) and a range in pitch from 11 inches (27.9 cm) to 23 inches (58.4 cm). Bronze and stainless steel propellers are available in some sizes.

Only propellers designed for use on these motors should be used. Propellers should be selected to place full throttle operation in 5000-6000 rpm range on 1985 and 1986 120 and 140 hp models and 4500-5500 rpm range on all other models.

REMOVE AND REINSTALL. Most service on the lower unit can be performed after detaching the gearcase housing from the exhaust and drive shaft housing. When servicing the lower unit pay particular attention to water pump and water pump tubes with respect to air or water leaks. Leaky con-

Fig. OM16-50 — View of starboard side of power head showing location of connections for shift wires.

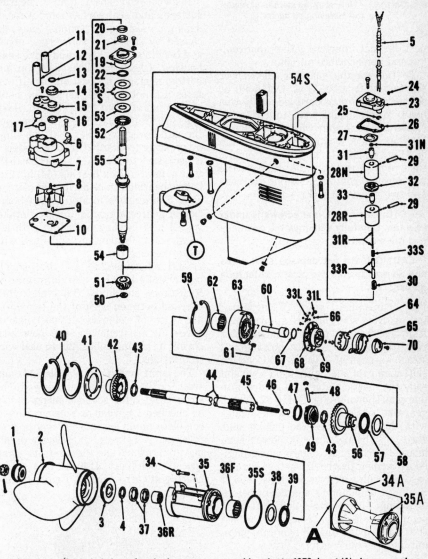

Fig. OM16-51 — Exploded view of typical gearcase assembly prior to 1973. Inset (A) shows rear bearing housing used on 1971 and 1972 motors. Snap ring (59) is used only on 1969 and 1970 motors and set screw (54S) is used only on 1972 motors.

T. Trim tab	19. Bearing housing	31L. Neutral valve lever	37. Seals
1. Spacer	20. Upper seal	31N. Locknut	38. Thrust washer
2. Propeller	21. Lower seal	31R. Neutral shift rod	39. Thrust bearing
3. Thrust bearing & sleeve	22. "O" ring	32. Spacer	40. Snap rings
4. Thrust washer	23. Solenoid cover	33. Reverse solenoid plunger	41. Retainer plate
5. Shift cable	24. Wiring connector clamps	33L. Reverse valve lever (with hole)	42. Reverse gear
6. Clamp	25. Wire grommet retaining ring	33R. Reverse shift rod (tube)	43. Thrust washers
7. Water pumphousing	26. Gasket	33S. Lock screw	44. Propeller shaft
8. Impeller	27. Wave washer	34. Allen screws	45. Spring
9. Drive key	28N. Neutral solenoid	34A. Hex head screws	46. Retainer
10. Impeller plate	28R. Reverse solenoid	35. Bearing housing	47. Retainer spring
11. Short guide tube	29. Heat shrink tubes (wire covers)	35A. Bearing housing	48. Pin
12. Long guide tube	30. Cap	35S. "O" ring	49. Dog clutch
13. Drive shaft "O" ring	31. Neutral solenoid plunger	36F. Bearing	50. Nut
14. Seal		36R. Bearing	51. Drive pinion
15. Cover			52. Thrust bearing
16. Seal			53. Thrust washer
17. Grommets			53S. Shims
			54. Bearing
			54S. Set screw
			55. Drive shaft
			56. Forward gear
			57. Thrust bearing
			58. Thrust washer
			59. Snap ring
			60. Shift plunger
			61. Plug
			62. Bearing
			63. Pump housing & rotor set
			64. Band
			65. Seal
			66. Valve seats & balls
			67. "O" ring
			68. Cover
			69. Dowel pin
			70. Screen

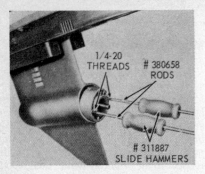

Fig. OM16-52 — View showing method of removing and installing oil pump.

nections may interfere with proper cooling and performance of motor.

To remove the gearcase, disconnect the two shift wires (Fig. OM16-50) at connectors on starboard side of power head. Apply liquid soap to the cable sleeve and push shift wires into exhaust housing. Mark location of the trim tab (T – Fig. OM16-51) to aid reassembly, then remove the trim tab. Remove the two screws from each side of gearcase and two screws at rear.

NOTE: One of the rear screws is under trim tab. Carefully withdraw the gearcase and drive shaft.

CAUTION: Do not damage shift wires and do not lose the two plastic water tube guides.

When installing, renew "O" ring (13) at top of drive shaft. Insert a wire down from the hole in power head adapter plate through the exhaust housing and attach to ends of shift wires. Coat the shift wire grommet with liquid soap and slide the plastic water tube guides onto pump as shown in Fig. OM16-57. Install gearcase while aligning plastic guides with the water tubes and pulling shift wires up through hole in power head adapter. Drive shaft splines can be aligned by turning flywheel. Dip the six gearcase attaching screws in OMC Gasket Sealing Compound or equivalent before installing. Make certain that shift cable grommet is through hole, then attach shift cable leads. Install trim tab, aligning the previously affixed marks.

GEARCASE. To disassemble, remove gearcase, drain lubricant, remove propeller (2 – Fig. OM16-51) and detach shift cable from clamps (6). Remove the attaching screws, then withdraw water pump housing (7), impeller (8), drive key (9) and plate (10). Remove screws attaching bearing housing (19) and solenoid cover (23). Remove solenoid assembly (23 through 33). Remove the four screws (34) using a long ¼ inch Allen wrench, then pull bearing housing (35) out using a slide hammer puller with a hook. Remove the

two snap rings (40) and withdraw propeller shaft (44). Remove nut (50), then lift out drive shaft (55), bearing housing (19), thrust washer (52 and 53) and shims (53S) out top and gear (51) out bottom. Remove forward gear (56), thrust bearing (57) and washer (58), then remove snap ring (59) if fitted. The oil pump (60 through 70) can now be withdrawn from housing using two slide hammer pullers as shown in Fig. OM16-52.

Inspect drive shaft splines, bearing surfaces and seal surfaces for wear or damage. Damaged splines may be caused by striking a submerged object and bending the exhaust and drive shaft housing. Check parallelism of top and bottom surfaces if questionable. If surfaces are not parallel, renew the housing, do not attempt to straighten. Bearing (54 – Fig. OM16-51) is removed through lower (propeller shaft) opening, by pressing from top. On 1972 models it is necessary to remove a set screw (54S) that is used to lock bearing (54) in place before bearing can be driven out of gearcase. Set screw is located on starboard side of gearcase in area of water intake. Install new bearing from top, with lettered end of bearing up and flush with top of bearing bore.

Shift solenoids (28N and 28R) should be checked with an ohmmeter. Resistance should be 5-6 ohms when checked between each of the two wires and case of solenoid. If solenoids or wires (5) are renewed, use new heat shrink insulating tubes (29) to seal wire connections.

The shift pump valve balls (66) and seats for these balls can be renewed. The surfaces of rotor set in housing should be checked for wear or scoring. Renew complete pump assembly if any part of rotor set is damaged excessively. Bearing (62) should be pressed in using special tool (part 314641) to position bearing at correct depth. Before install-

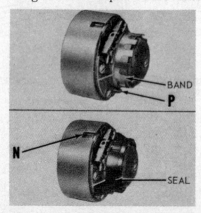

Fig. OM16-53 — Views of gear shift pump. Top view shows installation of band and lower view shows alignment of lug on seal. The control lever with hole should be on top and located on starboard side as shown.

ing cover (68), install pump rotor set in housing with drive lugs on pump inner rotor toward cover (68), install pump rotor set in housing with drive lugs on pump inner rotor toward cover (68).

NOTE: Most pumps have dots etched on sides of inner and outer rotors. If provided with these dots, they should both be toward cover (68).

If installation of rotors is questioned, assemble thrust bearing (57), washer (58) and forward gear (56), then insert into pump housing. If rotor is incorrectly installed, the inner rotor will be pushed out of pump housing. The front surfaces of rotor set should be flush with front face of pump housing, when parts (56, 57 and 58) are in position. Clearance between bushing in forward gear (56) and propeller shaft (44) should be 0.001-0.002 inch (0.03-0.05 mm). If clearances are excessive, renew propeller shaft and/or gears. Refer to Fig. OM16-53 for assembly of control levers, band and seal.

A gage block (part 315767) is required to determine the thickness of shims (53S – Fig. OM16-51) that should be installed. Remove thrust bearing (52) and washer (53) from drive shaft (55). Install pinion gear (51) on end of shaft and tighten nut (50) to 60-65 ft.-lbs (82-88 N·m). Install shims (53S) that were removed against shoulder on drive shaft. Position gage block against shims and surface of pinion gear as shown in Fig. OM16-54. With gage block tight against shims, clearance between end of gage block and top surface of pinion gears should be 0.000 to 0.002 inch (0.00-0.05 mm). If clearance is zero, make certain that enough shims are installed to provide an accurate check. Set the correct shims aside until drive shaft is installed.

Seals (20 and 21 – Fig. OM16-51) should be installed with lip of bottom seal (21) down to prevent gearcase oil from entering water pump and lip of top seal (20) should be up to prevent water from entering gearcase. Special tool (part 315945) should be used to install rear propeller shaft bearing (36R) so

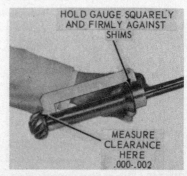

Fig. OM16-54 — View showing use of gage block for determining thickness of drive shaft shims.

bearing is at correct depth. The inner (first) seal (37) should be installed with lip in and outer seal should be installed with lip out.

Refer to the following for assembling the gearcase. Position the oil pump in gearcase, with notch (N – Fig. OM16-53) up and pin (P) correctly engaging hole in gearcase.

NOTE: Use slide hammers as shown in Fig. OM16-52 and make certain that pump is correctly seated.

Snap ring (59 – Fig. OM16-51) used in 1969 and 1970 motors only should be installed with flat side toward pump. Position thrust bearing (57) and washer (58) on forward gear (56), then slide gear into pump. Carefully engage drive lugs on gear with lugs on pump rotor. Position gear (51) and drive shaft (55) in housing and install nut (50). Position thrust bearing (52), washer (53) and shims (53S) over drive shaft and install bearing housing (19). Coat the four screws attaching bearing housing (19) with OMC Gasket Sealing Compound or equivalent before installing. The pinion nut (50) should be tightened to 60-65 ft.-lbs. (82-88 N·m) using special socket (part 312752) on the drive shaft splines. If the dog clutch (49) has been removed from propeller shaft, insert spring (45) and retainer (46) into propeller shaft bore with hole in retainer aligned with hole in propeller shaft (at splines). Slide the dog clutch (49) on shaft splines with the three ramp side toward front (forward gear) and hole aligned with hole in propeller shaft. Compress retainer (46) and spring (45) enough to align holes in retainer, propeller shaft and dog clutch, then insert pin (48). Wrap retainer spring (47) around dog clutch to keep pin in position. Install thrust washers (43) on each end and insert propeller shaft (44) including parts (43, 45, 46, 47, 48

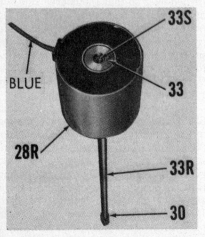

Fig. OM16-55 – View of the reverse shift solenoid and associated parts. Similar parts for neutral shift are shown in Fig. OM16-56.

30. Cap
33. Plunger
33R. Reverse shift rod
33S. Lock screw

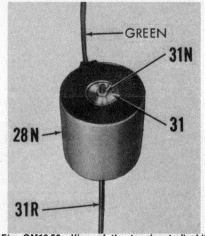

Fig. OM16-56 – View of the top (neutral) shift solenoid and associated parts.

31. Plunger
31N. Locknut
31R. Neutral shift rod

and 49) into the gearcase. Slide reverse gear (42) onto propeller shaft and position retainer plate (41) in housing. Install two snap rings (40), then position thrust bearing (39) and washer (38) over reverse gear hub. Position new "O" ring in groove of bearing housing (35) and lubricate outer edge of "O" ring. Slide bearing housing (35) into gearcase with exhaust cut out toward top. The "BOTTOM" marking should be down. Coat the retaining Allen screws (34) with OMC Gasket Sealing Compound or equivalent before installing.

NOTE: Installation of bearing housing will be easier if two long guide studs are used to locate the holes in retainer plate (41) as the bearing housing is installed and the other two screws are installed.

Install and adjust solenoids as follows: Screw plunger (with large hole) onto tubular shift rod (33R – Fig. OM16-55), then install and tighten lock screw (33S). Insert plunger and shift rod into reverse solenoid (blue wire) and push cap (30) onto bottom of shift rod. Insert the lower solenoid assembly into gearcase bore. Make sure end of shift rod is against the shift valve lever on pump and solenoid is against bottom of bore in housing. Measure distance between top of plunger and top of solenoid. If plunger is not 1/64 inch (0.4 mm) below, to flush with top of solenoid, remove the assembly and adjust by loosening lock screw (33S) and turning shift rod (33R). The lock screw should be torqued to 9-11 in.-lbs. (1-1.2 N·m) after adjustment is correct. Install the lower (reverse) solenoid and shift assembly after adjustment is complete. Position spacer (32 – Fig. OM16-51) on top of the lower solenoid with raised center section toward top. Assemble the small shift rod (31R – Fig. OM16-56), plunger with small hole (31) and locknut (31N). Position the plunger and shift rod in neutral

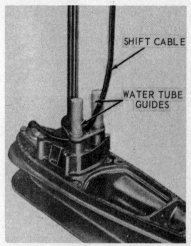

Fig. OM16-57 – View showing position of shift cable and installation of the plastic water tube guides.

solenoid (28N) which has a green wire. Insert the upper solenoid and shift rod assembly into gearcase bore above the reverse shift assembly and spacer. Make sure end of rod is through hole in top valve lever (33L – Fig. OM16-51) and solenoids are tight against bottom of bore. Measure distance between top of plunger and top of upper solenoid. If plunger is not 1/64 inch (0.4 mm) below, to flush with top of solenoid, loosen locknut and turn shift rod. The locknut (31N – Fig. OM16-56) should be tightended to 3-5 in.-lbs. (0.3-0.5 N·m) after adjustment is complete.

NOTE: Improper shifting will result if adjustment of shift rods and plungers is not correct.

Install solenoids and shift rods after adjustment is complete. Position wave washer (27 – Fig. OM16-51) on top of solenoids, coat both sides of gasket (26) with OMC Gasket Sealing Compound or equivalent and install cover (23). Apply OMC Adhesive "M" or equivalent to bottom of impeller plate (10), install key (9) in drive shaft and locate impeller (8) over key. Lubricate impeller, hold blades in and install water pump housing (7).

NOTE: Drive shaft can be rotated clockwise while assembling pump housing, but should never be turned backwards.

Coat screws attaching water pump housing with OMC Gasket Sealing Compound or equivalent before installing. Refer to Fig. OM16-57 for routing or shift cable. The "O" ring for sealing the top splines of drive shaft is shown at (13 – Fig. OM16-51).

1973-1977 Models

REMOVE AND REINSTALL. To remove gearcase, disconnect upper end of shift rod as shown in Fig. OM16-43,

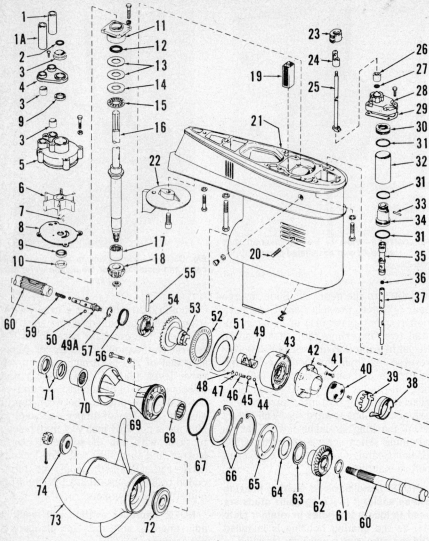

Fig. OM16-59 — Exploded view of hydraulic shift lower unit used on 1973-1977 models. Shift rod (49A) are one-piece on models after 1973. Seal (38) and band (39) are not used on some models.

1. Short water tube guide
1A. Long water tube guide
2. "O" ring
3. Grommet
4. Cover
5. Impeller cover
6. Impeller
7. Drive key
8. Plate
9. Seal
10. Seal
11. Bearing & housing assy.
12. "O" ring
13. Shims
14. Thrust washer
15. Thrust bearing
16. Drive shaft
17. Needle bearing
18. Pinion gear
19. Water screen
20. Set screw
21. Gearcase
22. Trim tab
23. Seal
24. Shift rod connector
25. Shift rod
26. Seal
27. "O" ring
28. Cover
29. Gasket
30. Piston cap
31. "O" ring
32. Cylinder
33. Pin
34. Piston
35. Valve
36. Plug
37. Push rod
38. Seal
39. Band
40. Screen
41. Locating dowel
42. Pump cover
43. Oil pump & bearing
44. Relief valve ball
45. Ball guide
46. Spring
47. Plug
48. Snap ring
49. Shift plunger
49A. Shift rod
50. Detent balls
51. Thrust washer
52. Thrust bearing
53. Forward gear
54. Dog clutch
55. Pin
57. Retaining spring
57. Snap ring
59. Spring
60. Propeller shaft
61. Thrust washer
62. Reverse gear
63. Thrust bearing
64. Thrust washer
65. Retainer plate
66. Snap rings
67. "O" ring
68. Needle bearing
69. Bearing housing
70. Needle bearing
71. Seals
72. Thrust bushing
73. Propeller
74. Spacer

using a suitable puller, withdraw bearing housing from gearcase. Remove snap rings (66), thrust washer (64), thrust bearing (63), shift rod cover (28) and shift rod (25). Remove hydraulic shift and propeller shaft components by withdrawing push rod (37) and propeller shaft simultaneously. Hold drive shaft with OMC Tool 311875 or another suitable tool and unscrew pinion nut. Remove pinion (18), unscrew bearing housing (11) screws and withdraw drive shaft and components from gearcase. Bearing in housing (11) is not renewable but must be obtained as a unit assembly with housing. Remove forward gear (53). Using a suitable puller and two 16 inch long rods with ¼-20 threads, remove oil pump (43) from gearcase. A two-piece shift plunger (49 and 49A) is used on 1973 models which may be separated by removing snap ring (57). Shift rod (49A) and plunger (49) are one-piece on later models.

Inspect drive shaft splines, bearing surfaces and seal surfaces for wear or damage. Damaged splines may be caused by striking a submerged object and bending the exhaust housing. Check parallelism of top and bottom surfaces if questionable. If surfaces are not parallel, renew housing. Do not attempt to straighten it.

Lower drive shaft bearing (17) should only be removed if renewal is intended. Do not reinstall a used bearing. Drive shaft bearing is held in position by a set screw (20) as well as a press fit in gearcase. Set screw is located on starboard side in area of water intake. To remove bearing (17) except on 140 hp and 85790 and 115790 models, install OMC Special Tool 385447, with shouldered side of removal piece against bearing and drive bearing down out of case. New bearing is installed by assembling special tool with sleeve provided and removal piece turned over so that shouldered side will again be next to bearing. Pull bearing (with lettered side against puller) into case (Fig. OM16-60). Bearing will be properly positioned when plate of tool is touching top of gearcase and bolt is tight. Do not overtighten bolt. Apply Loctite to set screw and install.

To remove bearing (17) on 140 hp and 85790 and 115790 models, pull bearing up and out using OMC Special Tool 385546 or other suitable puller. To install bearing, drive bearing down into gearcase with lettered end up using OMC Special Tools 385546 and 321518 assembled as shown in Fig. OM16-61. Bearing is correctly positioned when plate of tool contacts gearcase. Apply Loctite to set screw (20).

Hydraulic shift components (30 through 37—Fig. OM16-59) may be disassembled with OMC Tool 386112 by

remove propeller and drain lubricant from gearcase. Mark location of trim tab (22—Fig. OM16-59) to aid during reassembly and remove trim tab. Remove two screws on each side of gearcase and two screws at rear.

NOTE: One rear screw is in trim tab cavity.

Separate gearcase from exhaust housing being careful not to bend shift rod or lose water tube guides (1 and 1A).

To install gearcase, reverse removal procedure. Install a new "O" ring in end of drive shaft and coat splines with

a suitable antiseize compound. Apply OMC Adhesive "M" to gearcase and exhaust housing gasket surfaces. Be sure water tube guides and water tube are installed properly. Apply OMC Gasket Sealing Compound to threads of gearcase screws.

GEARCASE. To disassemble gearcase, separate gearcase from exhaust housing as outlined in previous section. Remove water pump housing (5—Fig. OM16-59), impeller (6), key (7) and lower plate (8). Remove four screws holding propeller shaft bearing housing (69) and

engaging pins on tool with holes in piston (34) and piston cap (30) and unscrewing cap from piston. Be careful not to bend or damage push rod (37) during disassembly. Remove pin (33) to separate valve (35), piston (34) and push rod. Cap (30) should be tightened to 12-15 ft.-lbs. (16-20 N·m) during reassembly.

To disassemble oil pump, unscrew four screws securing cover (42) and remove cover. Remove snap ring (48), plug (47), spring (46), guide (45) and pressure relief valve ball (44). Inspect pressure relief valve components and renew if worn or damaged. Inspect oil pump assembly for wear or damage. Dots on rotors must be up and surfaces of rotors and housing must be flat across ends when forward gear, thrust bearing and washer are installed in pump. Rotors, housing and bearing are not available separately and must be renewed as a unit assembly.

Seals (9 and 10 – Fig. OM16-59) should be installed with lip of bottom seal (10) down and lips of seals (9) up.

Needle bearings (68 and 70) should not be removed from propeller shaft housing unless renewal is intended. Do not install used bearings. OMC Special Tool 317061 should be used to press aft bearing into propeller shaft housing (69) to ensure proper positioning except on 140 hp and 85790 and 115790 models which should use tool 321517. OMC Special Tool 314641 should be used to properly position forward bearing (68) in bore of housing. Seals (71) should be installed so that lip on aft seal is toward propeller and lip on forward seal is facing forward.

Thickness of shims (13) is varied to adjust mesh position of pinion gear (18) in forward and reverse gear. A shim gage should be used to determine proper shimming. Use OMC shim gage 321520 on 140 hp and 85790 and 115790 models and shim gage 315767 for all other models.

Place pinion gear (18) on drive shaft and torque retaining nut to 60-65 ft.-lbs. (82-88 N·m). Install shims (13) that were removed during disassembly and leave thrust washer (14) and thrust bearing (15) off shaft. Hold shim gage firmly against shims and measure clearance between end of gage and pinion gear (Fig. OM16-54). Clearance should be zero between gear and gage.

NOTE: Make certain that enough shims are installed for an accurate check.

Shims are available in thicknesses of 0.002 inch and 0.005 inch and may be installed in any quantity to obtain proper clearance. Set the correct shims aside until drive shaft is installed.

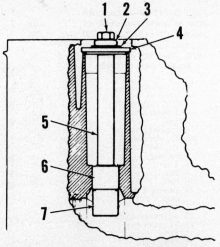

Fig. OM16-60 – View showing arrangement of OMC Tool 385447 for installation of pinion bearing (17 – Fig. OM16-59). Lettered end of bearing must be against puller.

1. Cap screw
2. Thrust bearing
3. Washer
4. Step washer
5. Spacer tube
6. Pinion bearing
7. Puller

To assist in installing shift plunger components in propeller shaft, grind away the end of a 9/32 inch (7.14 mm) rod to form a long flat taper on one side. Rod should be approximately 2⅝ inches (66.67 mm) long. Position dog clutch (54 – Fig. OM16-59) on propeller shaft with pin hole in dog clutch and slot in shaft aligned. "Prop end" stamped on dog clutch of 1977 models must be towards propeller end of shaft. Place three shift balls (50) and spring (59) in plunger (49) as shown in Fig. OM16-62 and install plunger in propeller shaft so detent balls match grooves in propeller shaft. Align holes in clutch dog (54 – Fig. OM16-59) and shift plunger (49) and insert tapered end of tool through holes to properly position detent spring. Carefully push tool out with retaining pin (55) and install pin retaining spring (56) in outer groove of dog clutch. Coils of spring must not overlap.

To reassemble gearcase, install oil pump (43), forward gear (53), thrust bearing (52) and thrust washer (51) so locating pin (41) aligns with pin hole in gearcase. Install drive shaft (16) and pinion gear (18) and tighten pinion nut to 60-65 ft.-lbs. (82-88 N·m). Lay gearcase on starboard side and install propeller shaft with flat side of shift plunger (49) up until propeller shaft is bottomed. Install hydraulic shift assembly with flat on end of push rod (37) down. Insert shift assembly until flats on push rod (37) and shift plunger (49) are engaged (push rod will not turn). Place light pressure against shift cylinder (32) and slowly withdraw propeller shaft until key on end of push rod meshes with keyway in shift plunger as shown in Fig. OM16-63. When key and keyway are meshed, push shift assembly and pro-

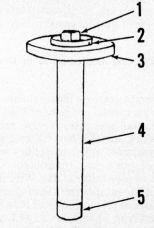

Fig. OM16-61 – View of pinion bearing installation tool.

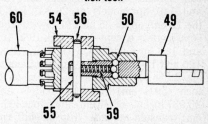

Fig. OM16-62 – Cross-sectional view of shift plunger (49) and dog clutch (54) components. Refer to Fig. OM16-59 for parts identification.

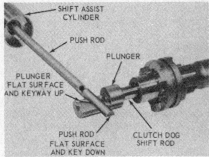

Fig. OM16-63 – View showing relative positions of shift assemblies when installed in gearcase. Refer to text for installation.

peller shaft in to complete engagement. Complete remainder of assembly noting the following points: Install snap rings (66 – Fig. OM16-59) with flat side out. Install bearing housing (69) with "UP" mark towards water pump. Apply OMC Gasket Sealing Compound to threads of screws securing retainer plate (65) and bearing housing (69).

Models After 1977

REMOVE AND REINSTALL. To remove gearcase, disconnect upper end of shift rod shown in Fig. OM16-64 on all models except 1985 and 1986 120 and 140 hp models. On 1985 and 1986 120 and 140 hp models, remove threaded pin from shift cam located at base of intake manifold on the port side. Remove propeller and drain lubricant from gearcase. Mark location of trim tab (22 – Fig. OM16-66) to aid during reassembly and remove trim tab. Remove two screws on each side of gearcase and two screws at rear.

NOTE: One rear screw is in trim tab cavity.

Separate gearcase from exhaust housing being careful not to bend shift rod.

To install gearcase, reverse removal procedure. Install a new "O" ring in end of drive shaft and coat splines with a suitable antiseize compound. Check length of gear shift rod (25). With shifter in neutral, distance from mating surface of gearcase (21) to center of hole in top of shift rod should be 21.843 inches (55.46 cm) on all 20 inch (50.8 cm) transom models except 1985 and 1986 120 and 140 hp models or 26.843 inches (68.16 cm) on all 25 inch (63.5 cm) transom models except 1985 and 1986 120 and 140 hp models. On 1985 and 1986 120 and 140 hp models, shift rod length should be 21.937 inches (55.73 cm) on 20 inch (50.8 cm) transom models and 26.937 inches (68.43 cm) on 25 inch (63.5 cm) transom models. Top of shift rod should slant forward. Apply OMC Adhesive "M" to gearcase and exhaust housing gasket surfaces. Be sure water tube guides and water tube are installed properly. Apply OMC Gasket Sealing Compound to threads of gearcase screws.

GEARCASE. Gearcase may be disassembled in the following manner: Remove propeller, drain lubricant and remove gearcase as described in previous section. Remove screws securing shift rod cover (29–Fig. OM16-66), unscrew shift rod (25) and remove shift rod and cover as an assembly. Remove water pump housing (5), impeller (6), impeller

Fig. OM16-66 — Exploded view of lower unit used on models after 1977. Shim (33) is used on models prior to 1979. Seal (4) is used on models prior to 1983.

1. "O" ring
2. Grommet
2A. Grommet
3. Water tube bracket
3A. Impeller housing
4. Seal
5. Impeller plate
5A. Impeller lining
6. Impeller
7. "O" ring
8. Plate
9. Seal
10. Seal
11. Bearing & housing assy.
12. "O" ring
13. Adjustment shims
14. Thrust washers
15. Thrust bearing
16. Drive shaft
17. Needle bearing
17A. Set screw
18. Pinion gear
19. Water screen
20. Magnet & spring
21. Gearcase
22. Trim tab
23. Shift rod seal
25. Shift rod
29. Shift rod cover
30. Gasket
31. Detent ball
32. Detent spring
33. Shim
34. Detent
35. Locating dowel
36. Shift lever pin
37. Gear housing
38. Shift lever
39. Shift yoke
40. Shift dog shaft
41. Spring
50. Thrust washer
51. Thrust bearing
52. Forward gear
54. Dog clutch
55. Pin
56. Pin retaining spring
60. Propeller shaft
62. Reverse gear
63. Thrust bearing
64. Thrust washer
65. Retainer plate
66. Snap rings
67. "O" ring
68. Needle bearing
69. Bearing housing
70. Needle bearing
71. Seals
72. Thrust bushing
73. Propeller bushing

key and lower plate (8). Remove four screws holding propeller shaft bearing housing (69) and using a suitable puller, remove bearing housing. Discard seals (71) and "O" ring (67). Remove snap rings (66), thrust washer assembly (64 and 63) and slide reverse gear (62) off propeller shaft. A special socket is available to hold drive shaft so nut securing pinion gear (18) can be removed. After pinion gear retaining nut is removed, unscrew the four screws securing upper drive shaft bearing housing (11). Pull drive shaft and associated parts out of gearcase. A puller may be necessary. Propeller shaft (60) may now be pulled from gearcase complete with forward gear (52), forward gear housing (37) and all associated parts.

Inspect drive shaft splines, bearing surfaces and seal surfaces for wear or damage. Damaged splines may be caused by striking a submerged object and bending the exhaust housing. Check parallelism of top and bottom surfaces if questionable. If surfaces are not parallel, renew housing. Do not attempt to straighten it.

Lower drive shaft bearing (17) should only be removed if renewal is intended. Do not reinstall a used bearing. Drive shaft bearing is held in position by a set screw (17A) as well as a press fit in gearcase. Set screw is located on starboard

side in area of water intake. After removing set screw, use OMC Special Tool 318117 or OMC Special Tool 391257 to renew bearing (17). To use OMC Special Tool 318117, place shouldered side of tool against bearing and drive bearing down into propeller shaft cavity. New bearing is installed by assembling special tool with sleeve provided and removal piece turned over so shouldered side will again be next to bearing. Pull bearing (with lettered side against puller) into case (Fig. OM16-67). Bearing will be properly positioned when plate of tool is touching top of gearcase and bolt is tight. Do not overtighten bolt. Apply Loctite to set screw and install.

Forward gear (52–Fig. OM16-66) and propeller shaft (60) may be removed from propeller shaft gear housing (37) after dislodging spring (56) and removing dog clutch assembly (55 and 54). Bearing housing and shifter mechanism assembly (38) may be disassembled by driving out shift lever pin (36).

Thickness of shims (13) is varied to adjust mesh position of pinion gear (18) in forward and reverse gear. An OMC shim gage should be used to determine proper shimming.

Place pinion gear (18) on drive shaft and torque retaining nut to 60-65 ft.-lbs. (82-88 N·m). Install shims (13) that were removed during disassembly and leave

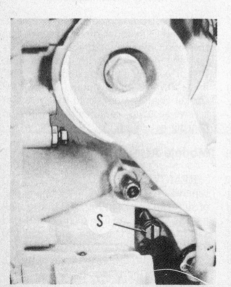

Fig. OM16-64 — View showing location of shift rod screw (S) used on all models after 1977 except 1985 and 1986 120 and 140 hp models.

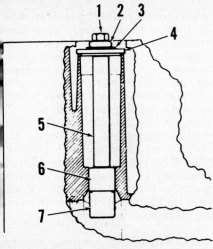

Fig. OM16-67 — View showing arrangement of OMC Tool 318117 for installation of pinion bearing (17 — Fig. OM16-66). Lettered end of bearing should be against puller.

1. Cap screw
2. Thrust bearing
3. Washer
4. Step washer
5. Spacer tube
6. Pinion bearing
7. Puller

thrust washer (14) and thrust bearing (15) off shaft. Hold shim gage firmly against shims and measure clearance between end of gage and pinion gear (Fig. OM16-54). Install or remove shims to obtain zero clearance between gear and gage.

NOTE: Make certain that enough shims are installed for accurate check.

Shims are available in 0.002, 0.003, 0.004 and 0.005 inch sizes. Set the correct shims aside until drive shaft is installed.

Needle bearings (68 and 70 — Fig. OM16-66) should not be removed from propeller shaft housing (69) unless renewal is intended. Do not reinstall used bearings. OMC Special Tool 321517 or Special Tool 326562 should be used to press aft bearing into propeller shaft housing to ensure proper positioning. OMC Special Tool 314641 should be used to position bearing (70) in forward bore of propeller shaft housing. Seals (71) should be installed so lip on aft seal is toward propeller and lip on forward seal is facing forward.

To determine thickness of shims (33) on models prior to 1979, install thrust bearing (51) and washer (50) on face of gear housing (37). Place gear housing (37) on a surface plate with thrust bearing (51) against plate. Position OMC Tool 324797 over housing so step marked "1.902" is directly over outer edge of gear housing and measure gap between tool and housing as shown in Fig. OM16-68. Install shims (33) equal to measured gap.

Assemble gearcase in the following manner: Renew all gaskets, seals and "O" rings. If lower drive shaft bearing (17) or propeller shaft bearings (68 and

Fig. OM16-68 — On models prior to 1979, measure gap between OMC Tool 324797 and bearing housing as outlined in text to determine thickness of shims (33 — Fig. OM16-66).

70) have been removed, they too should be renewed. Install detent spring (32) and detent ball (31) in blind hole of housing (37). Hold spring and ball in position while installing detent (34). Assemble shift dog shaft (40), shift lever yoke (39), shift lever (38) and pin (36). Assemble forward gear (52) with thrust bearing (51 and 50) and shims (33), on models prior to 1979, in gear housing. Place dog clutch (54) on propeller shaft (60) making sure that hole in dog clutch is aligned with slot in propeller shaft and splined dogs are towards forward gear. Insert propeller shaft in forward gear and bearing housing assembly, then insert pin (55) through dog clutch propeller shaft and hole in shift dog shaft (40). Install pin retaining spring (56). Press shift detent (34) down and place propeller shaft, forward gear and gear housing assembly (37) into position in gearcase. Make sure locating pin (35) is seated in recess provided in gearcase.

Insert drive shaft (16). Install pinion gear retaining nut and tighten to 60-65 ft.-lbs. (82-88 N·m). Install shift rod (25) and shift rod cover (29) as an assembly. Thread shift rod fully into detent (34), back off two turns, pull rod to neutral (middle detent) and adjust for proper length. Refer to shift rod adjustment in REMOVE AND REINSTALL section for specifications.

Assemble thrust bearing (64 and 63)

on reverse gear (62) and slide onto propeller shaft (60). Position bearing retainer plate (65) and install snap rings (66). Make sure "O" ring (67) is fully seated in groove of bearing housing (69) and that seals (71) are properly installed. Lip of forward seal should be toward front and lip of aft seal should be toward propeller.

Installation of bearing housing (69) will be eased by using two guide pins 10 inches long with ¼-20 threads on one end. Thread guide pin into bearing retainer plate (65) and slide bearing housing (69) into position. Coat bearing housing screws with sealing compound and install.

Install seals (9 and 10) in upper drive shaft bearing housing (11) with lip of lower seal (10) down and lip of upper seal (9) up. Place thrust bearing assembly (14 and 15) on drive shaft and install previously selected shim or shims (13). Coat screws that secure bearing housing (11) with sealing compound and install. Bottom edge of impeller plate (8) should be coated with OMC Adhesive "M" or equivalent and placed in position. Install impeller key, lubricate edges of impeller (6) and install on drive shaft. On models after 1984, impeller key is replaced with a drive cam. Install drive cam with flat side against drive shaft and sharp edge pointing in a clockwise direction when viewed from crankshaft end of drive shaft. Drive shaft should be turned clockwise while installing water pump housing (5). Coat screws that secure water pump housing and water tube bracket with sealing compound and install.

POWER TILT AND TRIM

All Models Prior to 1978 Except 85790, 85TXLR77, 115790, 115TXL77 And 140 Hp

OPERATION. These models are equipped with a hydraulically actuated power tilt and trim system. An oil pump

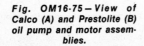

Fig. OM16-75 — View of Calco (A) and Prestolite (B) oil pump and motor assemblies.

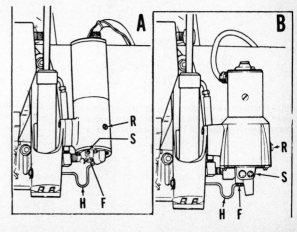

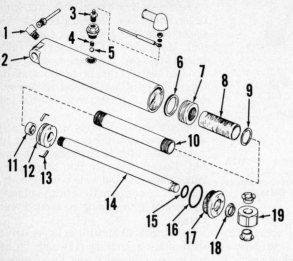

1. Elbow
2. Trim cylinder
3. Sender
4. Spring
5. Ball
6. "O" ring
7. Piston
8. Sender bobbin
9. Retaining ring
10. Piston carrier
11. Stop
12. Carrier bearing
13. Sender ground springs
14. Shaft
15. "O" ring
16. "O" ring
17. End cap
18. Wiper
19. Shaft end

when operating either up or down. Current draw with unit stalled in up or down position should be 45-55 amps. Torque required to turn oil pump shaft should not exceed 10 in.-ozs. (2.8 N). To check oil pressure, remove fill port plug (F–Fig. OM16-75) and connect a 2000 psi (13.8 MPa) gage to fill port. Oil pressure should be 200 psi (1.4 MPa) when trimming out and 300 psi (2.1 MPa) when tilting up. With 2000 psi (13.8 MPa) gage connected to fill port, disconnect high pressure line (H) from pump and plug hole. Oil pressure should be at least 1450 psi (10 MPa) with unit in tilt position for five seconds.

OVERHAUL. Oil pump must be serviced as a unit assembly and must be matched to Calco or Prestolite motor. Motor components are available. Refer to Fig. OM16-76 and Fig. OM16-77 for exploded views of trim and tilt cylinders. Tighten stem valve (6–Fig. OM16-77) to 10 in.-lbs. (1.1 N·m). Do not overtighten. To check operation of trim gage sending unit, connect ohmmeter leads to sender (3–Fig. OM16-76) and elbow (1). Resistance should be 0-3 ohms with

driven by a reversible electric motor provides oil pressure. One hydraulic cylinder trims the outboard motor while another hydraulic cylinder tilts the outboard. A rocker control switch determines motor and pump rotation thereby retracting extending tilt and trim cylinders. The pump motor is equipped with a thermal overload switch which resets after approximately one minute. Turn slotted manual valve screw (S–Fig. OM16-75) at bottom of pump to manually raise or lower outboard. Tighten manual valve screw clockwise to operate hydraulic tilt and trim.

Hydraulic system contains approximately ¾ pint (355 mL) of oil. Recommended oil is OMC Sea-Lube Power Trim/Tilt Fluid. Do not run pump without oil in reservoir. Fill plug (R) is located in side of pump reservoir. Oil level should reach fill plug hole threads with outboard tilted in full up position.

Hydraulic tilt should be cycled several times and oil level rechecked if system has been drained or lost a large amount of oil.

TROUBLE-SHOOTING. The following specifications should be noted when a malfunction occurs in tilt and trim system. Current draw should be 40-45 amps

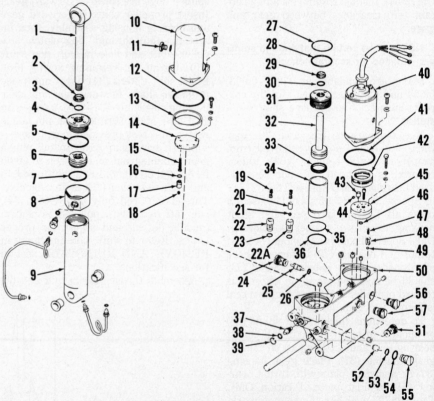

Fig. OM16-77 — Exploded view of tilt cylinder used on models identified in text. Relief valve components (8 through 14) are available as a unit only.

1. Tee	9. Valve seat
2. Tilt cylinder	10. Ball
3. Band	11. Piston
4. Oil line	12. Spring
5. "O" ring	13. Washer
6. Stem valve	14. Snap ring
7. Snap ring	15. Piston ring
8. Relief valve stem	16. "O" ring
17. Piston	
18. Shaft	
19. "O" ring	
20. "O" ring	
21. End cap	
22. Wiper	
23. Shaft end	

Fig. OM16-78 — Exploded view of hydraulic tilt and trim system used on models identified in text.

1. Shaft	13. Sleeve	24. Valve	35. Retaining ring	46. "O" ring
2. Wiper	14. Plate	25. Piston	36. "O" ring	47. Spring
3. "O" ring	15. Screen	26. "O" ring	37. Manual release valve	48. Pump relief valve
4. End cap	16. "O" ring	27. Retaining ring	38. "O" ring	49. Seal
5. "O" ring	17. Check valve	28. "O" ring	39. Snap ring	50. Manifold
6. Piston	18. Valve ball	29. Wiper	40. Pump motor	51. Valve
7. "O" ring	19. Spring	30. "O" ring	41. "O" ring	52. Valve piston
8. Band	20. Spring seat	31. End cap	42. Oil pump filter	53. "O" ring
9. Tilt cylinder	21. Ball	32. Piston	43. Drive coupling	54. "O" ring
10. Reservoir	22. Relief valve	33. Piston ring	44. Ball	55. Valve
11. Fill plug	22A. Impact relief valve	34. Trim cylinder	45. Oil pump	56. Valve
12. "O" ring	23. "O" ring			57. Valve

22 55 22A

10

37

45 57

52

56

25

24

34

6

9

51

Fig. OM16-79 — Schematic of hydraulic tilt and trim system. Refer to Fig. OM16-78 for parts identification.

TILT AND TRIM CYLINDERS. Tilt and trim system malfunction may be due to leaking "O" rings, seals and fittings in cylinders. Blocked oil lines may cause improper operation. Leaking valves in tilt cylinder piston (6 – Fig. OM16-78) may allow unit to leakdown.

OVERHAUL. Filter valve seat (17 – Fig. OM16-78) will be damaged if removed. Valves (24, 55, 56 and 57) are identical and may be interchanged. Valve (51) is taller than other valves and must not be interchanged. Motor must be serviced as a unit assembly. Apply OMC Nut Lock to piston shaft (1) threads and install piston (6) on shaft with small holes in piston up.

cylinder rod fully extended and 84-96 ohms with rod fully retracted. Sender ground springs (13) should extend 1/16 inch (1.58 mm) past edge of carrier bearing (12). Apply OMC Nut Lock to stop (11) and bearing (12) threads.

1978 Models And 85790, 85TXLR77, 115790, 115TXL77 And All 140 HP Models Prior to 1979

OPERATION. These models are equipped with a hydraulically actuated power tilt and trim system. Manifold (50 – Fig. OM16-78) contains valves, oil pump and trim cylinders. Oil pump motor, oil reservoir and tilt cylinder are attached to manifold. Electric oil pump motor is reversible and oil pump rotation is thereby changed to extend or retract trim and tilt cylinders. Note position of valves in Fig. OM16-78 and Fig. OM16-79. Turn manual release valve (37 – Fig. OM16-78) to manually raise or lower outboard.

Hydraulic system contains 25 fl. oz. (740 mL) of oil. Recommended oil is OMC Sea-Lube Power Trim/Tilt Fluid. Do not run pump without oil in reservoir. Oil level should reach fill plug (11) hole threads. Tilt should be recycled several times and oil level rechecked if system has been drained or lost a large amount of oil.

TROUBLE-SHOOTING. Be sure battery is fully charged, electrical connections are good, oil reservoir is full and air is not trapped in system before testing components.

OIL PUMP AND MOTOR. To check oil pump, unscrew plug (1 – Fig. OM16-80) and install a 2000 psi (13.8 MPa) pressure gage. Oil pressure should be 1300-1600 psi (9-11 MPa) with outboard tilted in full up position. Oil pressure less than specified may indicate

leakage, faulty pressure relief valve (22A – Fig. OM16-78) directional valve (56), oil pump or pump motor. Motor must operate properly in both directions.

VALVES. Faulty valves will cause system malfunction. Note function of valves and carefully inspect valve components which may cause malfunction. Valves (24 and 56 – Fig. OM16-78 or Fig. OM16-79) and valve piston (25) direct oil to tilt and trim cylinders from oil pump. Valve (57) directs oil to bottom of tilt cylinder when tilting outboard up and also directs oil to relief valve (22) which relieves system pressure at approximately 1500 psi (10.3 MPa). Valve (22A) relieves pressure during outboard impact and directs oil pressure to letdown valve piston (52) which allows oil to escape from bottom of tilt cylinder so top portion of tilt cylinder can be refilled after impact. Valves in tilt cylinder piston (6) allow oil to transfer from top to bottom of tilt cylinder during outboard impact. Valve (51) allows oil to flow from bottom of tilt cylinder during tilting down operation. Manual release valve (37) allows manual movement of outboard when valve is open.

Models After 1978

OPERATION. A hydraulically actuated power tilt and trim system is used. Manifold (50 – Fig. OM16-82) contains valves, oil pump and trim cylinders. Oil pump motor, oil reservoir and tilt cylinder are attached to manifold. Electric oil pump motor is reversible and oil pump rotation is thereby changed to extend or retract trim and tilt cylinders. Note position of valves in Fig. OM16-82. Turn manual release valve counterclockwise to manually raise or lower outboard.

Hydraulic system contains approximately 25 fl. oz. (740 mL) of oil. Recommended oil is OMC Power Trim/Tilt Fluid or DEXRON II automatic transmission fluid. Do not run pump without oil in reservoir. Oil level should reach fill plug (11) hole threads when tilt and trim pistons are fully extended. System should be cycled several times prior to checking oil level if system has been drained or lost a large amount of oil.

TROUBLE-SHOOTING. Be sure battery is fully charged, electrical connections are good, oil reservoir is full and air is not trapped in system before testing components.

To check oil pressure, first momentarily cycle system "UP" and "DOWN" a few times. Remove snap rings (39 – Fig. OM16-82) and manual release valve (37), then install OMC gage "A" as shown in Fig. OM16-83 Operate system in the "UP" direction and observe gage after system stalls out at full extension. Gage reading should drop below 100-200 psi (700-1400 kPa). Install OMC gage "B." Operate system in the "DOWN" direction and observe gage after system stalls out at fully retracted. Gage reading should not drop below 100-200 psi (700-1400 kPa).

To test check valves, screw each valve into OMC check valve tester 390063

1

2

3

Fig. OM16-80 — View of oil pressure reading points.

(T – Fig. OM16-84). Use a suitable pressure tester (P) and apply 30 psi (207 kPa) of pressure to check valve. Check valve can be considered good if no pressure leakage is noted.

Refer to the following for a list of symptoms and probable causes:

Symptoms	Probable Causes
Tilt Leakdown	1, 2, 3, 4, 5 or 6
Trim and Tilt Both Leak	7, 8 or 9

Reverse Lock
  Does Not Hold . . . . 2, 3, 6, 10, 11 or 12
Will Not Trim Out Under
  Load or Will Not Tilt . . . . . . 1, 2, 7 or 9
Will Not Trim or
  Tilt Down . . . . 2, 8, 10, 11, or 13

Key to Probable Causes
1. Trim Up Relief Valve
2. Manual Release Valve
3. Tilt Cylinder Valve or Seals
4. Tilt Check Valve
5. Impact Letdown Valve
6. Oil Line
7. Trim Cylinders Sleeve "O" Rings or Piston Seals
8. Trim Check Valve
9. Expansion Relief Valve or "O" Rings
10. Filter Valve Seat
11. Impact Sensor Valve
12. Reverse Lock Check Valve
13. Trim Down Pump Relief Valve

OVERHAUL. Oil pump must be serviced as a unit assembly. Motor is not serviceable with the exception of brushes. Refer to Fig. OM16-82 for exploded view of trim and tilt cylinders and manifold components. Keep all components separated during disassembly and identify each component, if needed, to assure correct position during reassembly.

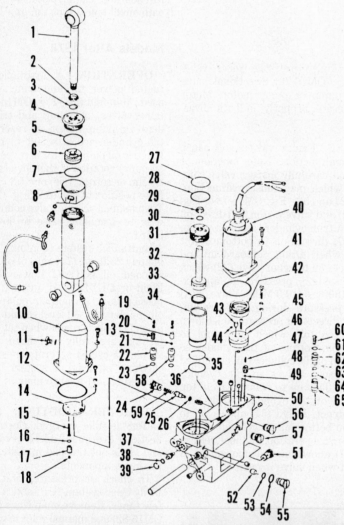

Fig. OM16-83 – Install OMC gage "A" or "B" into manual release valve (37 – Fig. OM16-82) port as shown in test system oil pressure. Refer to text.

Fig. OM16-82 – Exploded view of hydraulic tilt and trim system used on models after 1978. A three-wire pump motor is used on 1979 and 1980 models.

1. Shaft	18. Valve ball	35. Retaining ring	51. Separation valve
2. Wiper	19. Spring	36. "O" ring	52. Valve piston
3. "O" ring	20. Spring seat	37. Manual release valve	53. "O" ring
4. End cap	21. Ball	38. "O" ring	54. "O" ring
5. "O" ring	22. Trim up relief valve	39. Snap ring	55. Impact letdown valve
6. Piston	23. "O" ring	40. Pump motor	56. Trim check valve
7. "O" ring	24. Reverse lock check valve	41. "O" ring	57. Tilt check valve
8. Band	25. Piston	42. Oil pump filter	58. Impact sensor valve
9. Tilt cylinder	26. "O" ring	43. Drive coupling	59. Spring
10. Reservoir	27. Retaining ring	44. Ball	60. Spring
11. Fill plug	28. "O" ring	45. Oil pump	61. "O" ring
12. "O" ring	29. Wiper	46. "O" ring	62. Expansion relief
13. Needle	30. "O" ring	47. Spring	valve core
14. Plate	31. End cap	48. Trim down pump	63. "O" ring
15. Screen	32. Piston	relief valve	64. "O" ring
16. "O" ring	33. Piston ring	49. Seal	65. Expansion relief
17. Check valve	34. Trim cylinder	50. Manifold	valve seat

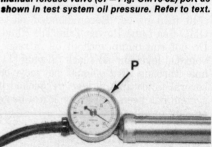

Fig. OM16-84 – Use OMC check valve tester 390063 (T) and a suitable pressure tester (P) to test check valves. Check valve can be considered good if no pressure leakage at approximately 30 psi (207 kPa) is noted.

EVINRUDE AND JOHNSON
6-CYLINDER MODELS

Year Produced	Evinrude Models	Johnson Models
1976...............	200640, 200649	200TL76, 200TXL76
1977...............	175740, 175749	175TL77, 175TXL77
	200740, 200749	200TL77, 200TXL77
1978...............	150849	150TL78
	175840, 175849	175TL78, 175TXL78
	200840, 200849	200TL78, 200TXL78
	235840, 235849	235TL78, 235TXL78
1979...............	150940, 150949	150TL79, 150TXL79
	175940, 175949	175TL79, 175TXL79
	200940, 200949	200TL79, 200TXL79
	235940, 235949	235TL79, 235TXL79
1980...............	150TRLCS, 150TRXCS	150TLCS, 150TXCS
	175TRLCS, 175TRXCS	175TLCS, 175TXCS
	200TRLCS, 200TRXCS	200TLCS, 200TXCS
	235TRLCS, 235TRXCS	235TRLCS, 235TXCS
1981...............	150TRLCI, 150TRXCI	150TLCI, 150TXCI
	175TRLCI, 175TRXCI	175TLCI, 175TXCI
	200TRLCI, 200TRXCI	200TLCI, 200TXCI
	235TRLCI, 235TRXCI	235TLCI, 235TXCI
1982...............	150TRLCN, 150TRXCN	150TLCN, 150TXCN
	175TRLCN, 175TRXCN	175TLCN, 175TXCN
	200TRLCN, 200TRXCN	200TLCN, 200TXCN
	235TRLCN, 235TRXCN	235TLCN, 235TXCN
1983...............	150TRLCT, 150TRXCT	150TRLCT, 150TRXCT
	175TRLCT, 175TRXCT	175TRLCT, 175TRXCT
	200TRLCT, 200TRXCT	200TRLCT, 200TRXCT
	235TRLCT, 235TRXCT	235TRLCT, 235TRXCT
1984...............	150TLCR, 150TXCR	150TLCR, 150TXCR
	150STLCR	150STLCR
	185TLCR, 185TXCR	185TLCR, 185TXCR
	235TLCR, 235TXCR	235TLCR, 235TXCR
	235STLCR	235STLCR
1985...............	150TLCO, 150TXCO	150TLCO, 150TXCO
	150STLCO	150STLCO
	185TLCO, 185TXCO	185TLCO, 185TXCO
	235TLCO, 235TXCO	235TLCO, 235TXCO
	235STLCO	235STLCO
1986...............	150TLCD, 150TXCD	150TLCD, 150TXCD
	150STLCD	150STLCD
	175TLCD, 175TXCD	175TLCD, 175TXCD
	200STLCD, 200TXCD	200STLCD, 200TXCD
	225TLCD, 225TXCD	225TLCD, 225TXCD
	225PTLCD, 225PTXCD	225PTLCD, 225PTXCD

CONDENSED SERVICE DATA

TUNE-UP

Hp/rpm....................................150/5000
175/5000 (Prior to 1984)
175/5250 (1986)
185/5250
200/5250 (1984)
200/5500 (1986)
225/5500
235/5250

Bore:
175 HP (1986) And
235 HP (After 1979) ....3.625 in.
(92.07 mm)

All Other Models ....149.4 cu. in.
(88.90 mm)

TUNE-UP CONT.

Stroke:
200 HP (1986) And 225 HP..................2.860 in.
(72.64 mm)

All Other Models ....2.588 in.
(65.74 mm)

Number of Cylinders 6

Displacement:
175 HP (1986) And
235 HP (After 1979)....................160.3 cu. in.
(2627 cc)

200 HP (1986) And 225 HP................165.1 cu. in.
(2705 cc)

All Other Models ....149.4 cu. in.
(2448 cc)

TUNE-UP CONT.

Spark Plug–Champion:
    200 HP (1986) And 225 HP QL77JC4*
        Electrode Gap . . . . 0.040 in.
                                                    (1.0 mm)
    All Other Models UL77V
Ignition Type . . . . CDI
Carburetor Make . . . . Own
Idle Speed (in gear) . . . . 650 rpm
Fuel:Oil Ratio . . . . 50:1†

*A Champion QL78V is recommended for 1986 200 hp and 225 hp models when used at sustained high speeds. Renew surface gap spark plug if center electrode is more than 1/32 inch (0.79 mm) below the flat surface of the plug end.
†On 1984 and later models equipped with variable ration oiling (VRO), the VRO pump meters the fuel:oil ratio from approximately 50:1 up to approximately 150:1 by sensing the engine power output.

SIZES–CLEARANCES

Piston Ring End Gap . . . . 0.007-0.017 in.
                                            (0.18-0.43 mm)
Lower Piston Ring Side
    Clearance:
    1976-1984 . . . . 0.002-0.004 in.
                                        (0.0051-0.102 mm)
    1985-1986 . . . . 0.004 in. Max.
                                            (0.102 mm)
Piston Skirt Clearance:
    1976-1978 . . . . 0.0055-0.0075 in.
                                        (0.140-0.190 mm)
    1979-1984 . . . . 0.0045-0.0075 in.
                                        (0.114-0.190 mm)
Maximum Cylinder Tolerance . . . . 0.004 in.
                                            (0.102 mm)
Crankshaft Diameters:
    Top Main . . . . 1.6199-1.6204 in.
                                        (41.15-41.16 mm)
    Center Mains . . . . 2.1870-2.1875 in.
                                        (55.55-55.56 mm)
    Bottom Main:
        200 HP (1986) And 225 HP . . . . 1.5747-1.5752 in.
                                        (40.00-40.01 mm)
        All Other Models . . . . 1.3779-1.3784 in.
                                        (35.00-35.01 mm)
Crankpin:
    200 HP (1986) And 225 HP . . . . 1.4995-1.5000 in.
                                        (38.09-38.10 mm)
    All Other Models . . . . 1.3757-1.3762 in.
                                        (34.94-34.95 mm)
Crankshaft End Play (Prior to
    1985) . . . . 0.008-0.011 in.
                                            (0.20-0.28 mm)

SIZES–CLEARANCES CONT.

Forward Gear Bushing to Propeller
    Shaft Clearance (Prior to 1985) . . . . 0.001-0.002 in.
                                            (0.03-0.05 mm)

TIGHTENING TORQUES

Connecting Rod:
    200 HP (1986) And 225 HP . . . . 504-528 in.-lbs.
                                            (57-60 N·m)
    All Other Models . . . . 348-372 in.-lbs.
                                            (39-42 N·m)
Crankcase Halves:
    Main Bearing Screws–
        200 HP (1986) And 225 HP . . . . 312-360 in.-lbs.
                                            (35-41 N·m)
        All Other Models . . . . 216-240 in.-lbs.
                                            (24-27 N·m)
    Flange Screws . . . . 60-84 in.-lbs.
                                            (7-9 N·m)
Crankcase Head . . . . 72-96 in.-lbs.
                                            (8-11 N·m)
Cylinder Head:
    175 HP (1986) And 235 HP
    (After 1979) . . . . 240-264 in.-lbs.
                                            (27-30 N·m)
    All Other Models . . . . 216-240 in.-lbs.
                                            (24-27 N·m)
Flywheel Nut . . . . 140-145 ft.-lbs.
                                            (190-197 N·m)
Lower Main Bearing
    Retainer Plate Screws . . . . 96-120 in.-lbs.
                                            (11-13 N·m)
Spark Plug . . . . 216-240 in.-lbs.
                                            (24-27 N·m)
Standard Screws:
    No. 6 . . . . 7-10 in.-lbs.
                                            (0.8-1.2 N·m)
    No. 8 . . . . 15-22 in.-lbs.
                                            (1.6-2.4 N·m)
    No. 10 . . . . 25-35 in.-lbs.
                                            (2.8-4.0 N·m)
    No. 12 . . . . 35-40 in.-lbs.
                                            (4.0-4.6 N·m)
    ¼ Inch . . . . 60-80 in.-lbs.
                                            (7-9 N·m)
    5/16 Inch . . . . 120-140 in.-lbs.
                                            (14-16 N·m)
    ⅜ Inch . . . . 220-240 in.-lbs.
                                            (24-27 N·m)
    7/16 Inch . . . . 340-360 in.-lbs.
                                            (38-40 N·m)

LUBRICATION

The engine is lubricated by oil mixed with the fuel. On 1976-1985 models, fuel should be regular leaded or premium leaded with a minimum pump octane rating of 88. On 1986 models, fuel should be regular leaded, regular unleaded, premium leaded or premium unleaded with a minimum pump octane rating of 86.

On models prior to 1984, recommended oil is Evinrude or Johnson 50/1 Lubricant or a BIA certified TC-W motor oil. The recommended fuel:oil ratio for normal operation and engine break-in is 50:1.

On 1984 and later models equipped with variable ratio oiling (VRO), recommended oil is Evinrude or Johnson Outboard Lubricant, OMC 2 Cycle Motor Oil or a BIA certified TC-W motor oil. The

VRO pump meters the fuel:oil ratio from approximately 50:1 up to approximately 150:1 by sensing the engine power output. During engine break-in, the fuel in the fuel tank must be mixed at a fuel:oil ratio of 50:1 (25:1 on 2.6 GT and XP models and 200STLCD [XP/GT] models) to ensure the engine of proper lubrication and the oil level in the VRO oil tank must be monitored. If, after engine break-in, oil level has dropped indicating the VRO system is operating, refill the VRO oil tank and switch to straight fuel.

NOTE: On 2.6 GT and XP models and 200STLCD (XP/GT) models, a premix of 50:1 must be used in fuel tank if VRO system is used and a premix of 25:1 must be used in fuel tank if VRO system is not used to assure engine of proper lubrication.

On 1984 and later recreational models (except 2.6 GT and XP models and 200STLCD [XP/GT] models) when VRO is not being used, the recommended fuel:oil ratio for normal operation and engine break-in is 50:1.

The lower unit gears and bearings are lubricated by oil contained in the gearcase. The recommended oil is OMC HI-VIS Gearcase Lube. The gearcase oil level should be checked after every 50 hours of operation and the gearcase should be drained and filled with new oil every 100 hours or once each season, whichever occurs first.

The gearcase is drained and filled through the same plug port. An oil level (vent) port is used to indicate the full oil level of the gearcase and to ease in oil drainage.

To drain the oil, place the outboard motor in a vertical position. Remove the drain plug and oil level plug and allow the lubricant to drain into a suitable container.

To fill the gearcase with oil, place the outboard motor in a vertical position. Add oil through the drain plug opening with an oil feeder until the oil begins to overflow from oil level plug port. Reinstall oil level plug with a new

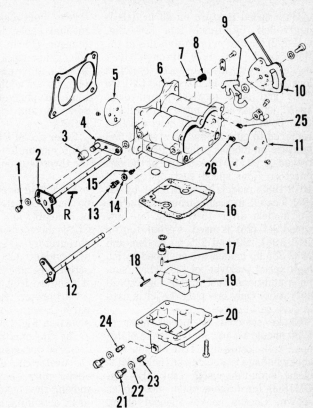

Fig. OM18-2 – Exploded view of typical carburetor used on all models except for 1986 200 and 225 hp models. Throttle and choke components will vary.

R. Throttle stop pin
1. Follower screw
2. Throttle shaft
3. Follower roller
4. Follower lever
5. Throttle plate
6. Body
7. Return spring pin
8. Return spring
9. Detent lever
10. Manual choke lever
11. Choke plate
12. Choke shaft
13. Plug
14. Washer
15. Idle mixture orifice
16. Gasket
17. Fuel needle & seat
18. Float pin
19. Float
20. Float bowl
21. Plug
22. Washer
23. High speed mixture orifice
24. Intermediate orifice
25. Low speed air orifice
26. High speed pullover orifice

gasket, if needed, and tighten. Remove oil feeder, then reinstall drain plug with a new gasket, if needed, and tighten.

FUEL SYSTEM

All Models Except 1986 200 And 225 HP Models

CARBURETORS. Three carburetors are used and each is a two-barrel carburetor with a single float. Each carburetor barrel provides fuel for one engine cylinder and is equipped with individual metering components.

Choke plates on models prior to 1980 may be operated manually or by activating choke solenoid. Turn choke control lever on front of outboard to "ON" position to manually close choke plates. Turn choke control lever to "OFF" on 1977 and 1978 models and push ignition key into ignition switch to activate choke solenoid. Turn choke control lever to "Automatic" on 1976 models and push choke switch on control panel to activate choke solenoid.

On models after 1979, additional fuel to aid starting is injected into the engine's transfer ports through tubes in the transfer port covers. A key-controlled, electric solenoid valve directs fuel from the fuel pump to the transfer port covers on early models and intake manifold on later models. The valve may be opened manually if rope starting is required.

Adjustment. Throttle valves must be synchronized for optimum performance. To synchronize throttle valves, close throttle and make sure follower roller (F – Fig. OM18-1) is not touching throttle cam (9). Loosen carburetor throttle arm screws (5) on upper and lower carburetors and allow throttle return springs to close throttle plates. Tighten screws (5).

Fig. OM18-1 – Exploded view of early carburetor and intake manifold assembly. Later models, except for 1986 200 and 225 hp models, are similar.

F. Follower roller
1. Ignition timing adjusting screw
2. Reed valve assy. (6 used)
3. Intake manifold
4. Throttle adjusting lever
5. Screw
6. Throttle link
7. Choke rods
8. Couplers
9. Throttle cam
10. Filler block
11. Choke solenoid
12. Spring
13. Plunger
14. Link
15. Hose
16. Silencer base
17. Silencer cover

High speed mixture on all models is controlled by fixed jets (23–Fig. OM18-2) located in opposite sides of the float bowl. On 1979 through 1982 models, an intermediate speed jet (24) is located just above high speed jet (23). On 1983 and later models, intermediate speed jet (24) is mounted vertically in float bowl (20). The float bowl must be removed to gain access. Low speed fuel mixture on models prior to 1979 is controlled by jet (15) on each side of the carburetor. Low speed fuel mixture on 1979-1983 models is controlled by jet (25) located in each carburetor barrel. On models after 1983, only one low speed jet (25) is used. Carburetor on 1979-1981 200 and 235 hp models and 1982 235 hp models are equipped with a high speed pullover jet (26) which supplies additional fuel during high speed operation. Only one pullover jet is used in each carburetor.

Choke solenoid on models prior to 1980 should be adjusted so choke plates open and close fully. Make certain that choke linkage is adjusted so choke plates close simultaneously. Link (L–Fig. OM18-3) must have open ends up as shown. Loosen choke solenoid clamp

screws and close choke plates with manual choke lever. Bottom solenoid plunger (P) in solenoid and position solenoid so slack is removed in solenoid link (L). Move choke solenoid away from plunger an additional 0.016 inch (0.41 mm) so plunger is not bottomed in solenoid and tighten solenoid clamp screws.

Refer to SPEED CONTROL LINKAGE section for synchronizing carburetor throttle opening to ignition timing.

R&R And Overhaul. Carburetors can be removed after removing air silencer assembly and disconnecting linkage. Choke mechanism is slightly different on carburetors. Disassembly procedure is self-evident. Choke and throttle plate screws are staked and must be renewed if removed from shaft.

Carburetor float level should be parallel with body gasket surface as shown in Fig. OM18-4.

The fuel mixture on models prior to 1980 is enriched for starting using carburetor choke plates. The carburetor choke may be actuated manually by moving the choke control knob or lever, or by activating a solenoid controlled by the ignition key switch. On early models the solenoid regulates choke plate opening according to a signal from the thermal switch in the engine's water bypass cover. On later models the thermal switch is not used and the solenoid moves the choke plate to fully closed position when activated. Refer to ADJUSTMENT paragraphs for choke adjustment.

The fuel mixture on models after 1979 is enriched for starting using a key-controlled, electric solenoid valve. On early models, fuel is directed from the fuel pump to the transfer port covers

where fuel is injected into the transfer port passages. On later models, fuel is injected directly into intake manifold. Inspect valve and renew any damaged components.

SPEED CONTROL LINKAGE. The carburetor throttle valves must be correctly synchronized to open as the ignition timing is advanced to obtain satisfactory performance. Synchronize throttle valves as previously outlined. Move speed control lever slowly from idle toward fast position and note point of contact between throttle cam and follower roller (F–Fig. OM18-5). Cam should just contact roller when first mark on cam is exactly in center of roller. If incorrect, loosen screw (S) and reposition roller. Refer to IGNITION SYSTEM and adjust ignition timing. Move speed control lever to full throttle. On models prior to 1984, there should be 0.001-0.003 inch (0.02-0.07 mm) clearance between roll pin (R–Fig. OM18-2) and stop at full throttle. Turn full throttle stop screw (T–Fig. OM18-5) to obtain desired clearance. On models after 1983, the full throttle stop screw (T) must be adjusted so the carburetor throttle shaft pins (R–Fig. OM18-2) are exactly vertical when the engine throttle lever is manually advanced to full throttle.

NOTE: The throttle shaft pins must not go past vertical or damage to the carburetors may result.

REED VALVES. Six sets of reed valves are used, one for each cylinder. The reed valves are attached to the intake manifold as shown in Fig. OM18-1. Reed petals should seat very lightly against reed seat throughout entire length. Individual reed components are not available on models prior to 1985. Renew reed valve assembly if petals are broken, cracked, warped or bent. Individual components are available on 1985 and 1986 models. Filler block (10) is not used on 1986 models.

NON-VRO FUEL PUMP. All models are equipped with two fuel pumps mounted adjacent to carburetors. On 1976 models, both fuel pumps transfer fuel from fuel tank to carburetors; on 1977 and 1978 models, the lower fuel pump transfers fuel from the fuel tank to the upper fuel pump which pumps fuel to the carburetors; on models after 1978, the upper fuel pump supplies the lower fuel pump which pumps fuel to the carburetors. Fuel pumps on all models are operated by crankcase pulsations. Fuel pressure to carburetors should be 2½-6 psi (17.2-41.4 kPa). Fuel pump must be serviced as a unit assembly.

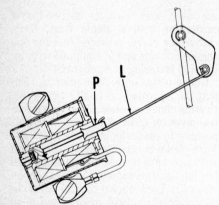

Fig. OM18-3–Cross-sectional view of choke solenoid used on models prior to 1980. Refer to text to correctly position solenoid.

Fig. OM18-4–Carburetor float (F) should be parallel (P) with gasket surface (G). Bend float arm (A) to adjust float.

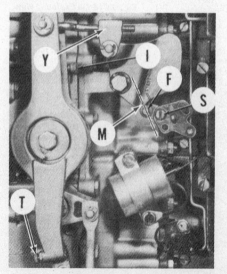

Fig. OM18-5–View of throttle control linkage. Refer to text for adjustment.

VRO TYPE FUEL PUMP. The VRO type fuel pump (1–Fig. OM18-6) meters the fuel:oil ratio from approximately 50:1 up to approximately 150:1 by sensing the engine power output. During engine break-in or after any procedure that permitted air to enter the VRO system, the fuel in the fuel tank must be mixed at a fuel:oil ratio of 50:1 to ensure the engine of proper lubrication. On 2.6 GT and XP models, a fuel:oil ratio of 25:1 must be used during testing of system.

To check the VRO system for proper operation, first fill the VRO oil tank with a recommended two-stroke motor oil and note oil level for future reference. Install correct fuel:oil mixture in the fuel tank. After the recommended engine break-in period or after a suitable test period for other conditions, note the oil level in the VRO oil tank. If the oil level has dropped indicating the VRO system is operating, refill the VRO oil tank and switch to straight fuel or recommended fuel mixture.

NOTE: When the VRO system is not used, the inlet nozzle at the outboard motor connector must be capped and clamped to prevent dirt or moisture from entering the fuel system. The fuel in the fuel tank must be mixed at correct fuel:oil ratio. Refer to LUBRICATION section.

TESTING. Stop the engine. Disconnect fuel mixture discharge hose at VRO pump nipple (4–Fig. OM18-6). Connect a tee fitting in hose end. Connect one end of a clear hose to one tee outlet and connect remaining hose to pump discharge fitting. Connect a 0-15 psi (0-103 kPa) pressure gage to the remaining tee outlet. Start the engine and run at wide-open throttle. The VRO pump should develop between 3 psi (21 kPa) and 15 psi (103 kPa) at wide-open throt-

Fig. OM18-7 — View showing two two-barrel type carburetors and two one-barrel type carburetors used on 1986 200 and 225 hp models. The top two port and starboard carburetor assemblies have a common throttle body assembly (T) with separate main body assemblies (M). View identifies position of intermediate air bleed jet (4) and low speed air bleed jet (5). Refer to text.

tle. The fuel pressure will drop 1-2 psi (6.8-13.7 kPa) and a clicking sound should be heard with each oil discharge. A small squirt of oil should be noticed every time the pump pulses.

If fuel pump (1) malfunction is noted, the fuel pump must be renewed as a complete assembly.

1986 200 And 225 HP Models

CARBURETOR. The two-barrel type carburetors and two one-barrel type carburetors are used. The top two port and starboard carburetor assemblies have a common throttle body assembly (T–Fig. OM18-7) with separate main body assemblies (M). Recommended low speed air bleed jet (5) size is #26 on Model 200TXCD and #20 on all other models. Recommended intermediate air bleed jet (4) size is #43 on Model 200TXCD, #42 on Model 200STLCD and #14 on all 225 hp models. Recommended high speed jet (9–Fig. OM18-8) size is #57D on Model 200TXCD, #76D on Model 200STLCD and #65D on all 225 hp models.

NOTE: Starboard carburetors supply fuel to port cylinders and port carburetors supply fuel to starboard cylinders.

The main body assemblies are constructed of a nonmetallic type material. Care must be used when working with the main body assembly. DO NOT overtighten any screws. Tighten each screw in small increments using a criss-cross tightening sequence.

If service is performed, note the following: Keep carburetor components for each carburetor separate from the others. The manufacturer does not recommend submerging the parts in carburetor or parts cleaning solutions. An aerosol type carburetor cleaner is recommended. The float and other components made of plastic and rubber should not be subjected to some cleaning solutions. Safety eyewear and solvent resistant gloves are recommended.

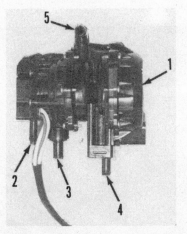

Fig. OM18-6 — View of a VRO type fuel pump.
1. VRO fuel pump assy.
2. Oil inlet nipple
3. Fuel inlet nipple
4. Crankcase pulse nipple
5. Fuel mixture discharge nipple

Fig. OM18-8 — Exploded view of carburetor main body assembly used on 1986 200 and 225 hp models.
1. Main body
2. Gasket
3. Plate
4. Intermediate air bleed jet
5. Low speed air bleed jet
6. Seal
7. Inlet needle & seat
8. Gasket
9. High speed jet
10. Gasket
11. Plug
12. Float bowl
13. Pin
14. Float

Fig. OM18-9 — With float bowl (12) inverted and fuel inlet valve and float installed, float should just touch straightedge (S). Refer to text.

To determine the float level, invert float bowl (12 – Fig. OM18-9) with the fuel inlet valve and float installed. The float should be flush with the float bowl gasket surface. Use a straightedge as shown in Fig. OM18-9 to check float setting. Remove the float and carefully bend the float tang to adjust.

Recommended idle speed is 650 rpm with the engine at normal operating temperature and forward gear engaged. Loosen nut (N – Fig. OM18-10) and turn screw (I) to adjust engine idle speed.

SPEED CONTROL LINKAGE. The carburetor throttle valves are synchronized to open as the ignition is advanced. It is important that throttle valve opening and ignition timing synchronization be checked and adjusted if necessary.

The following procedure should be used to check and adjust synchronization of linkage. Move the speed control lever to the idle position and make sure follower roller (F – Fig. OM18-10) is not touching throttle cam (T). Loosen follower roller screw (C) and move roller

away from throttle cam (T). Loosen screw (S) two complete turns and make certain that throttle plates are closed, then tighten screw (S). Leave screw (C) loose. Hold follower roller (F) against throttle cam (T) and adjust throttle arm stop screw (D) until alignment mark (M) is centered with follower roller (F). Withdraw roller (F) away from throttle cam (T) enough to allow throttle plates to close at idle and tighten screw (C). Adjust wide-open throttle (WOT) stop screw (W – Fig. OM18-11) so WOT mark (O – Fig. OM18-10) on follower roller bracket points directly front-to-rear when the speed control lever is at WOT.

REED VALVES. Six sets of leaf (reed) valves are used, one for each cylinder. The six valves are positioned horizontally and are attached to the upper and lower intake manifolds with a gasket between each reed block and manifold. The leaf petals should seat very lightly against the valve block throughout their entire length with the least possible tension. The individual parts of the reed valve assembly are not

available separately. Renew the reed valve assembly if petals are broken, cracked, warped or bent.

VRO TYPE FUEL PUMP. The VRO type fuel pump (1 – Fig. OM18-6) meters the fuel:oil ratio from approximately 50:1 up to approximately 150:1 by sensing the engine power output. During engine break-in or after any procedure that permitted air to enter VRO system, the fuel in the fuel tank must be mixed at a fuel:oil ratio of 50:1 to ensure the engine of proper lubrication. On 200STLCD (XP/GT) models, a fuel:oil ratio of 25:1 must be used during testing of system.

To check the VRO system for proper operation, first fill the VRO oil tank with a recommended two-stroke motor oil and note oil level for future reference. Install the correct fuel:oil mixture in the fuel tank. After the recommended engine break-in period or after a suitable test period for other conditions, note the oil level in the VRO oil tank. If the oil level has dropped and the VRO system is operating properly, refill the VRO oil tank and switch to straight fuel or recommended fuel mixture.

NOTE: When the VRO system is not used, the inlet nozzle at the outboard motor connector must be capped and clamped to prevent dirt or moisture from entering the fuel system. The fuel in the fuel tank must be mixed at correct fuel:oil ratio. Refer to LUBRICATION section.

TESTING. Stop the engine. Disconnect fuel mixture discharge hose at VRO pump nipple (4 – Fig. OM18-6). Connect a tee fitting in hose end. Connect one end of a clear hose to one tee outlet and connect remaining hose end to pump discharge fitting. Connect a 0-15 psi (0-103 kPa) pressure gage to the remaining tee outlet. Start the engine and run

Fig. OM18-10 — View of speed control linkage used on 1986 200 and 225 hp models. Refer to text.

Fig. OM18-11 — View identifying wide-open throttle (WOT) stop screw (W) and shift interrupter switch (SI) on 1986 200 and 225 hp models.

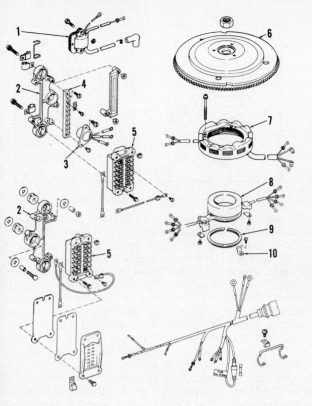

Fig. OM18-13 — Exploded view of early type ignition system.

1. Ignition coil (6 used)
2. Bracket
3. Rectifier
4. Terminal strip
5. Power pack
6. Flywheel
7. Stator
8. Timer base & sensor assy.
9. Retainer
10. Clips (4 used)

ohms on models prior to 1979, 475-625 ohms on 1979-1984 models, 535-585 ohms on 1985 models with 6 and 10 amp charging systems, 575-625 ohms on 1985 models with 35 amp charging systems, 535-585 ohms on 1986 models with 9 amp charging systems and 955-985 ohms on 1986 200 and 225 hp models and 1986 models with 35 amp charging systems. Connect negative ohmmeter lead to an engine ground and positive ohmmeter lead to each wire connector or terminal end leading to stator. Infinite resistance should exist between each wire connector or terminal end and

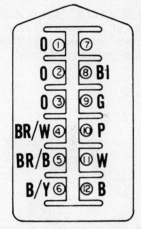

Fig. OM18-14 — Refer to following legend for starboard power pack wire connections on models prior to 1979.

1. Orange – #1 ign. coil
2. Orange – #3 ign. coil
3. Orange – #5 ign. coil
4. Brown/white – charge coil
5. Brown/black – charge coil
6. Black/yellow – ign. switch
7. Vacant
8. Blue – #1 sensor coil
9. Green – #3 sensor coil
10. Purple – #5 sensor coil
11. White – Common sensor coil
12. Black – ground

Fig. OM18-15 — Refer to following legend for port power pack wire connections on models prior to 1979.

1. Orange – #6 ign. coil
2. Orange – #4 ign. coil
3. Orange – #2 ign. coil
4. Brown – charge coil
5. Brown/yellow – charge coil
6. Black/yellow – ign. switch
7. Vacant
8. Purple – #6 sensor coil
9. Green – #4 sensor coil
10. Blue – #2 sensor coil
11. White – Common sensor coil
12. Black – ground

at wide-open throttle. The VRO pump should develop between 3 psi (21 kPa) and 15 psi (103 kPa) at wide-open throttle. The fuel pressure will drop 1-2 psi (6.8-13.7 kPa) and a clicking sound should be heard with each oil discharge. A small squirt of oil should be noticed every time the pump pulses.

If fuel pump (1) malfunction is noted, the fuel pump must be renewed as a complete assembly.

IGNITION SYSTEM

All models are equipped with a capacitor discharge ignition system which is triggered by sensor coils on stator plate. To prevent damage to components, note the following list of precautions:

1. DO NOT disconnect any wires while motor is running or while ignition switch is on.
2. DO NOT use any tachometer except those approved for use with this system.
3. DO NOT hold spark plug wires while checking for spark.
4. DO make certain that all wiring connections are clean and tightly joined.
5. DO make certain that wires do not bind moving parts or touch metal edges where they may chafe through insulation.

TROUBLE-SHOOTING. Use only approved procedures to prevent damage to the components. The fuel system should be checked first to make certain

that faulty running is not caused by fuel starvation, incorrect mixture or contaminated fuel.

CHECKING FOR SPARK. Disconnect spark plug leads at spark plugs and connect them to a needle point spark checker with six gaps set at 7/16 inch (11 mm). Consistent, strong spark indicates ignition system functioning properly; suspect spark plugs, timing, improper wiring to ignition coils or to spark plugs.

Weak, inconsistent spark or spark from only one or two ignition coils; suspect sensor coils or ignition coils. Weak, inconsistent spark from all six ignition coils; suspect charge coils. No spark at all; suspect power pack.

WIRING. Engine missing, surging and failure to start or run can be caused by loose or corroded electrical connections. Check all terminals and plug-in connectors for tight clean contact. Also check all wiring for short to ground.

CHARGE COILS. All models are equipped with two charge coils contained in the stator assembly. To check charge coils, proceed as follows: On models prior to 1979, disconnect charge coil wires as identified in Figs. OM18-14 and OM18-15 from power packs. On models after 1978, disconnect the two-wire connector (one per bank of cylinders). Connect an ohmmeter to wire connectors or terminal ends in connector leading to stator. Renew stator assembly if resistance is not 220-320

engine ground. If not, charge coil or charge coil lead is shorting to ground. To check charge coil output on models after 1978, use Merc-O-Tronic Model 781, Stevens Model CD77 or a suitable peak voltage tester. Connect black tester lead to terminal A in connector leading to stator and red tester lead to terminal B. Turn tester knobs to "NEG (−)" and "500." Crank engine while observing tester. Repeat test on other charge coil. Renew stator assembly if meter reads below 160 volts on 1979-1984 models, 200 volts on 1985 models, 130 volts on 1986 200 and 225 hp models and 200 volts on all other 1986 models.

SENSOR COILS. All models are equipped with six sensor coils contained in the timer base assembly. To check sensor coils, proceed as follows:

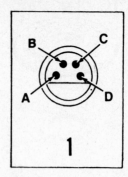
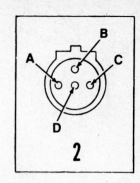

Fig. OM18-18 — View "1" identifies terminal ends in timer base connector on 1979-1985 models and view "2" identifies terminal ends in timer base connector on 1986 models.

On models prior to 1979, disconnect sensor coil wires as identified in Figs. OM18-14 and OM18-15 from power packs. Connect an ohmmeter between white common wire and each sensor wire for one bank of cylinders. Repeat test on other bank of cylinders. Renew timer base if resistance readings are not 13-23 ohms. Connect negative ohmmeter lead to an engine ground and positive ohmmeter lead to each sensor wire connector for one bank of cylinders. Repeat test on other bank of cylinders. Infinite resistance should exist between all terminal connections and engine ground. If not, sensor coil or sensor coil lead is shorting to ground. To check sensor coil output, use Merc-O-Tronic Model 781, Stevens Model CD77 or a suitable peak voltage tester. Connect black tester lead to common wire for one bank of cylinders and red tester lead to one of three sensor wires. On Merc-O-Tronic Model 781, turn knobs to "POS (+)" and "5" and on Stevens Model CD77, turn knobs to "S" and "5." Crank engine while observing tester. Repeat test with black tester lead still connected to common (white) wire and connect red tester lead to one of two remaining sensor wires and then to remaining sensor wire. Repeat test on other bank of cylinders. Renew timer base if meter reads below 0.3 volts.

On models after 1978, disconnect the four-wire connector (one per bank of cylinders). Connect an ohmmeter to terminals D and A (Fig. OM18-18), then D and B and then D and C in four-wire connector leading to timer base. Repeat test on other sensor coil connection. Renew timer base if resistance readings are not 35-45 ohms on 1986 200 and 225 hp models and 12-22 ohms on all other models. Connect negative ohmmeter lead to an engine ground and positive ohmmeter lead to connector terminal A, then B, then C and then D. Repeat test on other sensor coil connection. Infinite resistance should exist between all terminal connections and engine ground. If not, sensor coil or sensor coil lead is shorting to ground. To check sensor coil output, use Merc-O-Tronic Model 781,

Stevens Model CD77 or a suitable peak voltage tester. Connect black tester lead to timer base connector terminal D and red tester lead to terminal A. On Merc-O-Tronic Model 781, turn knobs to "POS (+)" and "5" and on Stevens Model CD77, turn knobs to "S" and "5." Crank engine while observing tester. Repeat test with black tester lead still connected to terminal D and connect red tester lead to terminal B and then to terminal C. Repeat test on other sensor coil connection. Renew timer base assembly if meter reads below 0.3 volts on 1986 200 and 225 hp models and 0.2 volts on all other models.

POWER PACKS. To check power pack output, first reconnect stator and timer base connectors. Use Merc-O-Tronic Model 781, Stevens Model CD77 or a suitable peak voltage tester. Connect black tester lead to suitable engine ground. Connect red tester lead to wire leading to one of the six ignition coils. Turn tester knobs to "NEG (−)" and "500." Crank engine while observing tester. Repeat test on other leads. Renew power pack or packs on 1986 200 and 225 hp models if readings are not at least 100 volts or higher. Renew power pack or packs on 1985 and 1986 models (except 200 and 225 hp models) if readings are not at least 175 volts or higher. Renew power pack or packs on all other models if readings are not at least 170 volts or higher.

NOTE: Power pack on 1986 200 and 225 hp models marked "CDL" have an internal device to limit engine speed to 6100 rpm.

IGNITION COILS. Renew ignition coil or coils if no other component is found faulty.

SHIFT INTERRUPTER SWITCH. On 1986 200 and 225 hp models, shift interrupter switch (SI-Fig. OM18-11) is used to interrupt power supply to starboard power pack during gearcase directional changes. This prevents firing of starboard cylinders, thus lowering engine rpm to allow easier engagement

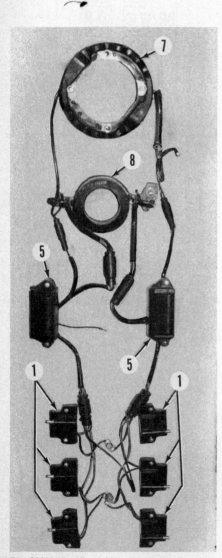

Fig. OM18-17 — View of late type ignition system.

1. Ignition coils   7. Stator
5. Power packs   8. Timer base & sensor assy.

and disengagement of shift components. To check shift interrupter switch (SI), use a suitable ohmmeter placed on a high ohms scale. Disconnect the single-wire connector at starboard power pack. Connect black tester lead to a suitable engine ground and red tester lead to terminal end in connector leading to shift interrupter switch (SI). An infinite meter reading should be noted. Activate shift interrupter switch (SI) and note ohmmeter. A low meter reading should be noted. Disconnect shift interrupter switch remaining single-wire connector. Connect ohmmeter leads between single-wire connectors of switch, note ohmmeter then reverse tester leads. Infinite resistance should be noted on one test and zero resistance should be noted on other test. Renew shift interrupter switch (SI) if previous test results are not noted.

IGNITION TIMING. Connect a power timing light to number 1 (top, starboard) cylinder spark plug, start and run engine at 4300-4600 rpm in gear on models prior to 1984 or 5000 rpm in gear on models after 1983 and note timing. Stop engine. On all models except 1986 200 and 225 hp models, repeat procedure with timing light connected to number 2 (top, port) cylinder. Note which cylinder had higher ignition timing and adjust ignition timing stop screw (1 – Fig. OM18-1) to obtain ignition timing noted in following table.

Model	Degrees BTDC
150 Hp	
1979	26
1980	28
1981	
Timer base with black sleeves	28
Timer base with red sleeves	32
1982	28
175 Hp	
1978, 1979, 1980	28
1981	
Timer with black sleeves	28
Timer with red sleeves	32
1982	28
200Hp	
1976, 1977, 1978, 1979	28
1980	26
1981	
Timer base with black sleeves and model suffix "H"	26
Timer base with black sleeves and model suffix "A, B, or M"	28
Timer base with red sleeves	30
1982	28
235 Hp	
1978, 1979	28
1980, 1981, 1982	30

On models after 1982, consult the engine decal for maximum spark ad-

vance specifications. Ignition should occur at 13°-15° BTDC on 1986 200STLCD (XP/GT) models and 17°-19° BTDC on all other 1986 200 and 225 hp models. Stop the engine and turn spark advance stop screw (1 – Fig. OM18-1 or A – Fig. OM18-10) if timing is incorrect. Turning spark advance stop screw clockwise one full turn will retard ignition timing approximately one degree.

On all models except 1986 200 and 225 hp models, adjust throttle cam as outlined in SPEED CONTROL LINKAGE section. Connect a power timing light to number 1 cylinder and start engine. Ignition timing should be 5° BTDC on 175 and 200 hp models prior to 1980, or 6°-8° BTDC on all other models, when "START" mark on throttle cam is centered on cam follower roller. Stop engine and adjust position of cam yoke (Y – Fig. OM18-5) to align mark and follower roller. On later models, an adjustment nut is used to adjust position of cam yoke (Y).

COOLING SYSTEM

THERMOSTAT. A cooling system thermostat is used in each cylinder head to maintain a water temperature of approximately 145°F (63°C). A relief valve adjacent to each thermostat opens at high engine speed when water pump impeller speed increases water pressure. On 1986 200 and 225 hp models, the relief valve is located within each thermostat assembly. Engine temperature

can be checked using heat sensitive sticks such as Markal Thermomelt Stik. A 163°F (73°C) stick should not melt, but a 125°F (52°C) stick should melt, after engine reaches operating temperature. The remote control box is equipped with a "hot horn" which is activated by either temperature sensing switch in each cylinder head. Temperature switch operation may be checked with a continuity tester and a high temperature thermometer. Place switch and thermometer in oil that is being heated. Switch should show a closed circuit at 205°-217°F (96°-102°C) and should open again at 168°-182°F (75°-83°C).

WATER PUMP. The water pump is mounted on top of the gearcase. Rubber impeller is driven by the drive shaft. Separate gearcase from exhaust housing for access to water pump.

Apply OMC Adhesive M to "O" ring (7 – Fig. OM18-26 or OM18-35) groove in impeller housing (4) and OMC Gasket Sealing Compound to bottom of impeller plate (8). Lubricate impeller (6) and hold blades in while installing housing.

POWER HEAD

R&R AND DISASSEMBLE. Remove electric starter solenoid, electric starter, flywheel, stator and timer base. Remove air silencer, carburetors and fuel pumps or VRO pump. Disconnect and mark interfering wires. Loosen

Fig. OM18-20 – Exploded view of typical cylinder block and associated parts used on all models except for 1986 200 and 225 hp models. Sealing strips (27) are not used on models after 1978. On 1986 200 and 225 hp models, covers (20) and cylinder heads (22) are one piece. Exhaust cover (1) and transfer port covers (8) are cast into cylinder block (26). Refer to Fig. OM18-21 for view of crankshaft and piston assemblies.

1. Exhaust cover
2. Gasket
3. Exhaust inner cover
4. Gasket
5. Water passage cover
6. Voltage regulator
7. Gasket
8. Transfer port covers
9. Thermostat cover
10. Gasket
11. Thermostat
12. Grommet
13. Relief valve spring
14. Spring seat
15. Seal
16. Relief valve
17. Valve seat
18. Washer
19. Temperature warning switch
20. Cylinder head cover
21. Gasket
22. Cylinder head
23. Gasket
24. Water deflector
25. Main bearing dowel pin
26. Cylinder block
27. Sealing strip
28. Crankcase
29. Taper pin
30. Bellcrank
31. Ignition advance rod
32. Ignition control lever
33. Speed control lever
34. Throttle lever link
35. Yoke
36. Shift rod
37. Shift lever

bellcrank (30 – Fig. OM18-20) screw on models prior to 1979 and disengage lower unit shift rod from bellcrank. Disconnect upper end of shift rod on models after 1978. On all models except 1986 200 and 225 hp models, remove exhaust housing rear cover (six screws) and then unbolt exhaust housing front cover and allow front cover to rest against exhaust housing. Remove two front rubber mount screws. Unscrew two engine to adapter stud nuts below exhaust cover. Unscrew nuts, two short screws and six long screws shown in Fig. OM18-22 retaining engine to adapter and lift engine off drive unit. On 1986 200 and 225 hp models, remove four screws and one nut from each side of upper end of drive shaft housing and two screws and one nut at rear of upper end of drive shaft housing. Lift power head from lower unit.

Transfer port covers should be marked before removal as all transfer port covers are not identical. Remove transfer port covers, exhaust covers, cylinder heads and inlet manifold should be carefully removed by loosening

screws evenly to prevent warpage. Remove upper and lower crankcase head (2 and 11 – Fig. OM18-21) screws. Taper pin or pins (29 – Fig. OM18-20) must be driven out towards front. Loosen but do not remove center four screws in lower crankcase head (11 – Fig. OM18-21) which hold retainer plate (7). Unscrew crankcase retaining screws and separate crankcase (28 – Fig. OM18-20) from cylinder block (26).

Pistons, rods and crankshaft are now accessible for removal and overhaul as outlined in the appropriate following paragraphs.

ASSEMBLY. When assembling, the crankcase and inlet manifold must be completely sealed against both vacuum and pressure. Exhaust manifold and cylinder heads must be sealed against water leakage and pressure. Mating surfaces of water intake and exhaust areas between lower unit and power head must form a tight seal. It is recommended that all mating surfaces be carefully inspected for nicks, burrs, corrosion and warpage which might interfere with a tight seal. All of these surfaces may be lapped if necessary to provide a smooth, flat surface. DO NOT remove any more metal than is necessary. Mating surfaces of crankcase and cylinder block MUST NOT be lowered, but can be polished to remove imperfections.

Cylinder block and crankcase are positively located by a tapered dowel pin or pins. Dowel pin or pins must not be nicked, bent or distorted and dowel pin hole or holes must be clean and true. When installing dowel pin or pins, make sure that pin or pins are fully seated, but do not use excessive force.

Crankcase and cylinder block mating surfaces on models prior to 1979 are

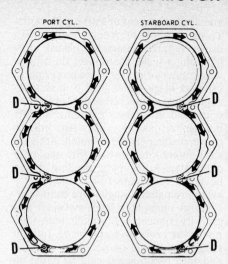

Fig. OM18-23 – On all models except 1986 200 and 225 hp models, water deflectors (D) must be installed in locations shown for proper water flow around cylinders.

sealed by rubber sealing strips (27 – Fig. OM18-20) which fit in grooves of crankcase mating surface. Make certain that grooves and mating surface are absolutely clean and free from old cement, nicks or foreign matter.

Refer to subsequent sections for assembly of piston, rod and crankshaft components. Install piston and rod assemblies in cylinder block with bearing in rod but do not install cap and bearing. Install lower head assembly (6 through 11 – Fig. OM18-21) on crankshaft but do not tighten four bearing retainer plate (7) screws. Install top bearing head assembly (1, 2 and 3) and seal rings (4) on crankshaft. Install center main bearings (13 and 14) on crankshaft as outlined in CRANKSHAFT section. Install crankshaft assembly in cylinder block making certain that holes in center main bearings align with dowel pins in cylinder block. Position connecting rods on crankshaft and install rod bearings (21 and 22) and rod caps (23).

When reassembling crankcase, make sure mating surfaces of crankcase halves are completely clean and free of old cement, nicks and burrs. On models prior to 1979, install sealing strips (27 – Fig. OM18-20) and trim ends to extend approximately 1/32 inch (0.79 mm) into bearing bores, then sparingly apply OMC Adhesive "M" to cylinder half of crankcase only. On models after 1978, apply OMC Gel-Seal II to one crankcase mating surface. Do not use sealers which will harden and prevent contact between crankcase mating surfaces. Immediately assemble crankcase halves after applying sealer and position halves by installing tapered locating dowel pin or pins; then install and tighten crankcase retaining screws to the torque listed in the CONDENSED SERVICE DATA table. When tightening the re-

Fig. OM18-21 — Exploded view of crankshaft and piston assemblies. Two "O" rings (3 and 6) and two seals (10) are used on 1986 200 and 225 hp models. On 1985 and 1986 models, except 200 and 225 hp models, loose needle bearings and two thrust washers are used in place of caged bearing (19).

1. Seal	
2. Upper crankcase head & bearing	13. Main bearing outer race
3. "O" ring	14. Roller bearing
4. Seal ring (9 used)	15. Piston rings
5. Crankshaft	16. Piston
6. "O" ring	17. Piston pin
7. Retainer plate	18. Snap ring
8. Ball bearing	19. Roller bearing
9. Snap ring	20. Connecting rod
10. Seal	21. Bearing cage
11. Lower crankcase head	22. Bearing rollers
12. Retaining ring	23. Rod cap

Fig. OM18-22 – On all models except 1986 200 and 225 hp models, remove nut (N), short screw (S) and long screws (L) from each side of outboard when removing power head.

taining screws, start in the center and work toward ends. Tighten the lower main bearing retainer plate (7 – Fig. OM18-21) screws to the correct torque and check the crankshaft for binding.

On all models except 1986 200 and 225 hp models, note location of water deflectors shown at (D – Fig. OM18-23). Deteriorated water deflectors may cause overheating and hot spots. Deflectors are not as tall as water passages so water may drain from water jacket.

On all models except 1986 200 and 225 hp models, use a nonhardening sealer on all gasket surfaces and complete assembly of cylinder head and covers. Threads of screws should be coated with nonhardening sealer to prevent water damage to threads, especially on motors operated in salt water. On 1986 200 and 225 hp models, install cylinder head gaskets and intake manifold gaskets without a sealer.

PISTONS, PINS, RINGS AND CYLINDERS. Before detaching connecting rods from crankshaft, mark piston, rod and cap for correct assembly to each other and for installation into the same cylinder from which they are removed. Separate bearing cages and rollers (21 and 22 – Fig. OM18-21) for assembly into same location if they are to be reinstalled.

Pistons and rings are available in standard and oversize. Refer to the CONDENSED SERVICE DATA table for recommended ring end gap, ring side clearance and piston skirt clearance. Rebore cylinder bores or renew cylinder block if cylinder bore taper or out-of-round exceeds 0.004 inch (0.102 mm).

The piston pin is retained in piston by snap rings in piston pin bosses. On some models, one piston pin boss is tight on piston pin and the other has slight clearance. When removing or installing piston pin, always press pin from side marked "L" toward the tight side to prevent damage to piston. The upper end of connecting rod is fitted with a caged needle roller bearing on all models prior to 1985 and 1986 200 and 225 hp models. On all other models after 1985, loose needle bearings and two thrust washers are used. The piston pin and connecting rod bore are used as bearing races. Check bearing rollers, cage and bearing race surfaces for wear, scoring or overheating. When assembling, pistons should be heated slightly to facilitate installation of piston pins. The pistons on port side are installed to connecting rods differently than for starboard units. The oil hole in side of rod at piston pin and should be up on all connecting rods. On all models except 1986 200 and 225 hp models, the long sloping side of pistons should be toward center of cylinder

block "V" (exhaust ports). On 1986 200 adn 225 hp models, the stamping "Exhaust Side" on top of pistons must face cylinder bore exhaust ports. Thoroughly lubricate all bearing surfaces before assembling.

CONNECTING RODS, BEARINGS AND CRANKSHAFT. Individual connecting rod and piston assemblies may be removed after removing crankcase (28 – Fig. OM18-20) and appropriate cylinder head (22). Before detaching connecting rods from crankshaft, mark rod and cap for correct assembly to each other and in original cylinder. Separate bearing cages and rollers for assembly to original crankpin if units are not renewed.

Connecting rods ride on roller bearings at both ends. The lower bearing consists of a split retainer (cage) and 18 rollers on all models except 1986 200 and 225 hp models. Sixteen roller bearings per crankpin bearing set are used on 1986 200 and 225 hp models. The crankpin end of rod is drilled and finished, then carefully fractured to separate the cap from the rod. The parting line is not machined and when correctly assembled, the uneven parting line should be nearly invisible. When assembling, make certain that index marks (M – Fig. OM18-24) are aligned, oil hole (H) is toward top of motor and long sloping side or stamping "Exhaust Side" of piston head is toward center of "V". The machined sides of connecting rod and cap should be smooth when assembled. On 1985 and later models equipped with precision ground rods, OMC Alignment Fixture 396749 is recommended to properly align connecting rod with rod cap during tightening of connecting rod screws.

NOTE: Precision ground rods are identified by grind marks running ACROSS

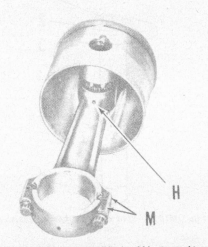

Fig. OM18-24 — Oil hole (H) should be toward top of motor and index marks (M) should be aligned.

corners on ears of connecting rod and rod cap.

Crankshaft seal rings (4 – Fig. OM18-21) should have 0.00015-0.0025 inch (0.038-0.063 mm side clearance in crankshaft groove on all models prior to 1985. Seal rings are available in four thicknesses: 0.1565-0.1570 inch (3.975-3.988 mm), 0.1575-0.1580 inch (4.000-4.013 mm), 0.1585-0.1590 inch (4.026-4.039 mm) and 0.1605-0.1610 inch (4.077-4.089 mm). On models after 1984, seal ring (4) should be renewed if thickness is less than 0.154 inch (3.91 mm).

Bearing and head (2) are a one-piece assembly and must be serviced as a unit. Lip of seal (1) should be toward inside and should be pressed in until flush with top surface of bearing head.

The center main bearings are split-cage needle bearings. The two-piece outer race is held together with retaining ring (12) and is positioned in cylinder block by a dowel pin. Install bearing races (13) with ring groove towards bottom of crankshaft. When assembling, make certain that dowel pin in cylinder block bore engages hole in center bearing outer race.

The ball type lower main bearing (8) is located in lower bearing head (11). The bearing outer race is clamped to the bearing head with retainer plate (7). To disassemble lower bearing assembly, remove retainer plate screws and pull bearing head (11) from bearing (8). Remove snap ring (9), then remove bearing from crankshaft lower end using a suitable puller. The lower bearing should allow crankshaft end play within the limits specified in the CONDENSED SERVICE DATA table. When assembling, position retainer (7) around crankshaft, then press bearing (8) onto journal and install snap ring (9). Press seals (10) on 1986 200 and 225 hp models into bore in bearing head using OMC special tool 325453 and seal (10) into bore in bearing head on all other models using OMC special tool 318619 or 326567 to locate seal at correct depth in the bore. Install new "O" ring or "O" rings (6) in bearing head groove or grooves and press bearing head onto outer race of bearing. Install screws into retainer (7), but do not tighten these screws until crankcase is assembled.

Refer to the CONDENSED SERVICE DATA table for dimensional data and recommended torque values. Refer to ASSEMBLY paragraphs for assembling the crankcase halves.

PROPELLER

An aluminum, three-blade propeller with built-in cushion clutch is standard on most motors while some motors are equipped with a stainless steel propeller. Optional propellers are available. Only propellers designed for use on these motors should be used. Refer to CONDENSED SERVICE DATA for desired engine speed at full throttle.

LOWER UNIT

Models Prior To 1979

REMOVE AND REINSTALL. To remove gearcase, disconnect upper end of shift rod from bellcrank (30–Fig. OM18-20), remove propeller and drain lubricant from gearcase. Mark location of trim tab (22–Fig. OM18-26) to aid during reassembly and remove trim tab. Remove two screws on each side of gearcase and two screws at rear.

NOTE: One rear screw is in trim tab cavity.

Separate gearcase from exhaust housing being careful not to bend shift rod.

To install gearcase, reverse removal procedure. Install a new "O" ring in end of drive shaft and coat splines with a suitable antiseize compound. Connector (24) bolt hole must be forward. Check length of gear shift rod (25). With shifter in neutral, distance from mating surface of gearcase (21) to center of hole in top of shift rod connector (24) should be 21 3/8–21-7/16 inches (54.29-54.45 cm) on 1976 standard length models or 26 3/8–26-7/16 inches (66.99-67.15 cm) on 1976 long leg models. Distance should be 21-9/16–21 5/8 inches (54.77-54.93 cm) for 1977 and 1978 standard length models and 26-9/16–26 5/8 inches (67.47-67.63 cm) for 1977 and 1978 long leg models. Distance for models after 1978 is 22-1/32–22-3/32 inches (55.96-56.12 cm) for standard length models and 27-1/32–27-3/32 inches (68.66-68.82 cm) for long leg models.

Apply OMC Adhesive "M" to gearcase and exhaust housing gasket surfaces. Be sure water tube is installed properly. Apply OMC Gasket Sealing Compound to threads of gearcase screws.

GEARCASE. To disassemble gearcase, separate gearcase from exhaust housing as outlined in previous section. Remove water pump housing (4–Fig. OM18-26), impeller (6), key and lower plate (8). Remove four screws holding propeller shaft bearing housing (69) and using a suitable puller, withdraw bearing housing from gearcase. Remove snap rings (66), thrust washer (64), thrust bearing (63), shift rod cover (28) and shift rod (25). Remove hydraulic shift and propeller shaft components by withdrawing push rod (37) and propeller shaft simultaneously. Hold drive shaft with OMC Tool 311875 or another suitable tool and unscrew pinion nut.

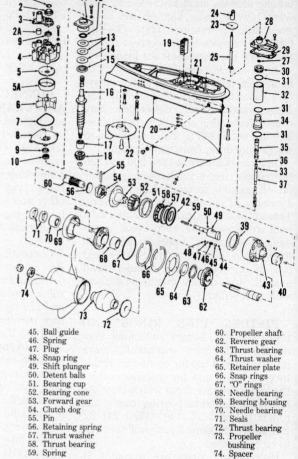

Fig. OM18-26 — Exploded view of lower unit used on models prior to 1979. Components (39, 42, 57 and 58) are used on models after 1977 in place of components (51 and 52) used on 1976 and 1977 models.

1. "O" ring
2. Grommet
2A. Grommet
3. Cover
4. Impeller housing
5. Plate
5A. Impeller liner
6. Impeller
7. "O" ring
8. Plate
9. Seal
10. Seal
11. Bearing & housing assy.
12. "O" ring
13. Shims
14. Thrust washer
15. Thrust bearing
16. Drive shaft
17. Needle bearing
18. Pinion gear
19. Water screen
20. Set screw
21. Gearcase
22. Trim tab
23. Seal
24. Shift rod connector
25. Shift rod
27. "O" ring
28. Cover
29. Gasket
30. Piston cap
31. "O" ring
32. Cylinder
33. Pin
34. Piston
35. Valve
36. Plug
37. Push rod
39. Bearing
40. Screen
42. Shim
43. Oil pump
44. Relief valve ball
45. Ball guide
46. Spring
47. Plug
48. Snap ring
49. Shift plunger
50. Detent balls
51. Bearing cup
52. Bearing cone
53. Forward gear
54. Clutch dog
55. Pin
56. Retaining spring
57. Thrust washer
58. Thrust bearing
59. Spring
60. Propeller shaft
62. Reverse gear
63. Thrust bearing
64. Thrust washer
65. Retainer plate
66. Snap rings
67. "O" rings
68. Needle bearing
69. Bearing housing
70. Needle bearing
71. Seals
72. Thrust bearing
73. Propeller bushing
74. Spacer

Remove pinion (18), unscrew bearing housing (11) screws and withdraw drive shaft and components from gearcase. Bearing in housing (11) is not renewable but must be obtained as a unit assembly with housing. Remove forward gear (53) and oil pump (43). Do not lose 25 loose rollers in bearing (39) on models after 1977.

Inspect drive shaft splines, bearing surfaces and seal surfaces for wear or

damage. Damaged splines may be caused by striking a submerged object and bending the exhaust housing. Check parallelism of top and bottom surfaces if questionable. If surfaces are not parallel, renew housing. Do not attempt to straighten it.

To remove bearing (17), pull bearing up and out using OMC Special Tool 385546 or other suitable puller. To install bearing, drive bearing down into gearcase with lettered end up using OMC Special Tools 385546 and 321518 assembled as shown in Fig. OM18-27. Bearing is correctly positioned when plate of tool contacts gearcase. Apply Loctite to set screw (20).

Hydraulic shift components (30 through 37–Fig. OM18-26) may be disassembled with OMC Tool 386112 by engaging pins on tool with holes in piston (34) and piston cap (30) and unscrewing cap from piston. Be careful not to bend or damage push rod (37). Remove pin (33) to separate valve (35), piston (34) and push rod. Cap (30) should be tightened to 12-15 ft.-lbs. (16.3-20.4 N·m).

Oil pump (43) is available as a unit assembly only. If necessary on models after 1977, remove and renew bearing (39). Bearing contains 25 loose rollers. Oil pump cover must be removed for ac-

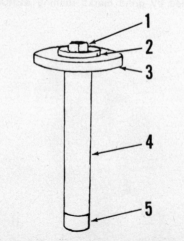

Fig. OM18-27 — View of pinion bearing installation tool.

1. Screw
2. Washer
3. Tool 385546 plate
4. Tool 321518
5. Bearing

cess to pressure relief valve components (44 through 48) or to drive bearing cup (51) out of pump housing. Round sides of plug (47) and snap ring (48) must be together. Surfaces of rotors and housing must be flat.

Needle bearings (68 and 70) should not be removed from propeller shaft housing unless renewal is intended. Do not install used bearings. OMC Special Tool 321517 should be used to press aft bearing into bearing housing (69) to ensure proper positioning. OMC Special Tool 314641 should be used to properly position forward bearing (68) in bore of housing. Seals (71) should be installed so that lip on aft seal is toward propeller and lip on forward seal is facing forward.

Install seals (9 and 10) with bottom seal (10) lip down and upper seal (9) lip up.

Thickness of shims (13) is varied to adjust mesh position of pinion gear (18) in forward and reverse gear. A shim gage, OMC Special Tool 321520, should be used to determine proper shimming.

Place pinion gear (18) on drive shaft and tighten retaining nut to 60-65 ft.-lbs. Install shims (13) that were removed during disassembly and leave thrust washer (14) and thrust bearing (15) off shaft. Hold shim gage firmly against shims and measure clearance between end of gage and pinion gear (Fig. OM18-28). There should be zero clearance between shims and gage.

NOTE: Make certain that enough shims are installed for an accurate check.

Shims are available in thicknesses of 0.002 inch and 0.005 inch and may be installed in any quantity to obtain proper clearance. Set the correct shims aside until drive shaft is installed.

To determine thickness of shims (42 – Fig. OM18-26) on models after 1977, install thrust bearing (58) and

washer (57) on face of gear housing (43). Place gear housing (43) on a surface plate with thrust bearing (58) against plate. Position OMC Tool 324797 over housing so step marked "1.862" is directly over outer edge of gear housing and measure gap between tool and housing as shown in Fig. OM18-29. Install shims (42 – Fig. OM18-26) equal to measured gap.

To assist in installing shift plunger components in propeller shaft, grind away the end of a 9/32 inch (7.14 mm) rod to form a long flat taper on one side. Rod should be approximately 4 inches (10.16 cm) long. Position clutch (54) on propeller shaft with pin hole in clutch and slot in shaft aligned. "PROP END" stamped on clutch must be towards propeller end of shaft. Place three shift balls (50) and spring (59) in plunger (49) as shown in Fig. OM18-30 and install plunger in propeller shaft so detent balls match grooves in propeller shaft. Align holes in clutch (54 – Fig. OM18-26) and shift plunger (49) and insert tapered end of tool through holes to properly position detent spring. Carefully push tool out with retaining pin (55) and install pin retaining spring (56) in outer groove of clutch. Coils of spring must not overlap.

To reassemble gearcase, install oil pump (43), forward gear (53), thrust washer (57) and thrust bearing (58) on models after 1977. On models prior to 1978, install bearing (52) in place of thrust bearing and washer. Locating pin in oil pump (43) must align with pin hole in gearcase. Install drive shaft (16) and pinion gear (18) and tighten pinion nut to 60-65 ft.-lbs. (81.6-88.4 N·m). Lay gearcase on starboard side and install propeller shaft with flat side of shift plunger (49) up until propeller shaft is bottomed. Install hydraulic shift assembly with flat on end of push rod (37) down. Insert shift assembly until flats on push rod (37) and shift plunger (49) are engaged (push rod will not turn). Place light pressure against shift cylinder (32) and slowly withdraw propeller shaft until key on end of push rod meshes with keyway in shift plunger as shown in Fig. OM18-31. When key and

keyway are meshed, push shift assembly and propeller shaft in to complete engagement. Complete remainder of assembly noting the following points: Install snap rings (66 – Fig. OM18-26) with flat side out. Install bearing housing (69) with "UP" mark toward water pump. Apply OMC Gasket Sealing Compound to threads of screws securing retainer plate (65) and bearing housing (69).

Models After 1978

REMOVE AND REINSTALL. To remove gearcase, disconnect upper end of shift rod then remove propeller and drain lubricant from gearcase. Mark location of trim tab (22 – Fig. OM18-35) to aid during reassembly and remove trim tab. Remove two screws on each side of gearcase and two screws at rear.

NOTE: One rear screw is in trim tab cavity.

Separate gearcase from exhaust housing being careful not to bend shift rod.

To install gearcase, reverse removal procedure. Install a new "O" ring in end of drive shaft and coat splines with a suitable antiseize compound. Check length of gear shift rod (25). With shifter in neutral, distance from mating surface of gearcase (21) to center of hole in top of shift rod should be 22.06 inches (56.03 cm) on all 20 inch (50.8 cm) transom models except 1986 200 and 225 hp models or 27.06 inches (68.73 cm) on all 25 inch (63.5 cm) transom models except 1986 200 and 225 hp models. On 1986 200 and 225 hp models, shift rod length should be 21.937 inches (55.73 cm) on 20

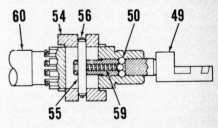

Fig. OM18-30 – Cross-sectional view of shift plunger (49) and dog clutch (54) components. Refer to Fig. OM18-26 for parts identification.

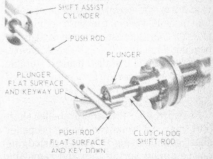

Fig. OM18-31 – View showing relative positions of shift assemblies when installed in gearcase. Refer to text for installation.

Fig. OM18-28 – View showing use of shim gage tool (G) as outlined in text.

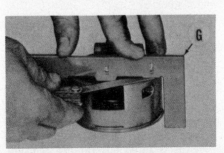

Fig. OM18-29 – Measure gap between OMC Tool 324797 and bearing housing as outlined in text to determine thickness of shims (42 – Fig. OM18-26).

inch (50.8 cm) transom models and 26.937 inches (68.43 cm) on 25 inch (63.5 cm) transom models. Top of shift rod should slant forward. Apply OMC Adhesive "M" to gearcase and exhaust housing gasket surfaces. Be sure water tube guides and water tubes are installed properly. Apply OMC Gasket Sealing Compound to threads of gearcase screws.

GEARCASE. Gearcase may be disassembled in the following manner: Remove propeller, drain lubricant and remove gearcase as described in previous section. Remove screws securing shift rod cover (29–Fig. OM18-35), unscrew shift rod (25) and remove shift rod and cover as an assembly. Remove water pump housing (5), impeller (6), impeller key and lower plate (8). Remove four screws holding propeller shaft bearing housing (69) and using a suitable puller, remove bearing housing. Discard seals (71) and "O" ring (67). Remove snap rings (66), thrust washer assembly (64 and 63) and slide reverse gear (62) off propeller shaft. A special socket from OMC is available to hold drive shaft so nut securing pinion gear (18) can be removed. After pinion gear retaining nut is removed, unscrew the four screws securing upper drive shaft bearing housing (11). Pull drive shaft and associated parts out of gearcase. A puller may be necessary. Propeller shaft (60) may now be pulled from gearcase complete with forward gear (52), forward gear housing (37) and all associated parts.

Inspect drive shaft splines, bearing surfaces and seal surfaces for wear or damage. Damaged splines may be caused by striking a submerged object and bending the exhaust housing. Check parallelism of top and bottom surfaces if questionable. If surfaces are not parallel, renew housing. Do not attempt to straighten it.

Lower drive shaft bearing (17) should only be removed if renewal is intended. Do not reinstall a used bearing. Drive shaft bearing is held in position by a set screw (17A) as well as a press fit in gearcase. Set screw is located on starboard side in area of water intake. After removing set screw, install a suitable tool or OMC special tool with shouldered side of tool against bearing, and drive bearing down into propeller shaft cavity. New bearing is installed using a suitable tool or OMC special tool with lettered end of bearing down. Apply Loctite to set screw (17A) and install.

Forward gear (52) and propeller shaft (60) may be removed from propeller shaft gear housing (37) after dislodging pin retaining spring (56) and removing dog clutch assembly (55 and 54). Bearing housing and shifter mechanism assem-

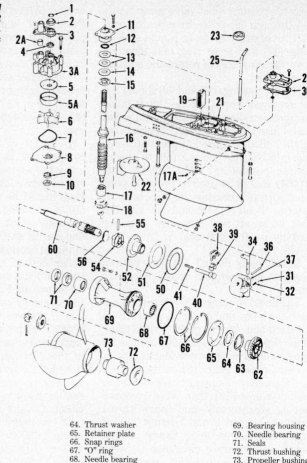

Fig. OM18-35 — Exploded view of typical lower unit used on models after 1978. Seal (4) is used on models prior to 1983.

1. "O" ring
2. Grommet
2A. Grommet
3. Water tube bracket
3A. Impeller housing
4. Seal
5. Impeller plate
5A. Impeller lining
6. Impeller
7. "O" ring
8. Plate
9. Seal
10. Seal
11. Bearing & housing assy.
12. "O" ring
13. Adjustment shims
14. Thrust washers
15. Thrust bearing
16. Drive shaft
17. Needle bearing
17A. Set screw
18. Pinion gear
19. Water screen
21. Gearcase
22. Trim tab
23. Shift rod seal
25. Shift rod
29. Shift rod cover
30. Gasket
31. Detent ball
32. Detent spring
34. Detent
36. Shift lever pin
37. Gear housing
38. Shift lever
39. Shift yoke
40. Shift shaft
41. Spring
50. Thrust washer
51. Thrust bearing
52. Forward gear
54. Dog clutch
55. Pin
56. Pin retaining spring
60. Propeller shaft
62. Reverse gear
63. Thrust bearing
64. Thrust washer
65. Retainer plate
66. Snap rings
67. "O" ring
68. Needle bearing
69. Bearing housing
70. Needle bearing
71. Seals
72. Thrust bushing
73. Propeller bushing

bly (38) may be disassembled by driving out shift lever pin (36).

Thickness of shims (13) is varied to adjust mesh position of pinion gear (18) in forward and reverse gear. A shim gage, OMC Special Tool 321520 or 315767, should be used to determine proper shimming.

Place pinion gear (18) on drive shaft and torque retaining nut to 60-65 ft.-lbs. (82-88 N·m). Install shims (13) that were removed during disassembly and leave thrust washer (14) and thrust bearing (15) off shaft. Hold shim gage firmly against shims and measure clearance between end of gage (G–Fig. OM18-28) and pinion gear. Install or remove shims to obtain zero clearance between gear and gage.

NOTE: Make certain that enough shims are installed for accurate check.

Shims are available in 0.002, 0.003, 0.004 and 0.005 inch sizes. Set the correct shims aside until drive shaft is installed.

Needle bearings (68 and 70–Fig. OM18-35) should not be removed from propeller shaft housing (69) unless renewal is intended. Do not reinstall used bearings. OMC special tools or suitable tools are used to install bearings in housing (69). Seals (71) should be in-

stalled so lip on aft seal is towards propeller and lip on forward seal is facing forward.

Assemble gearcase in the following manner: Renew all gaskets, seals and "O" rings. If lower drive shaft bearing (17) or propeller shaft bearings (68 and 70) have been removed, they too should be renewed. Install detent spring (32) and detent ball (31) in blind hole of housing (37). Hold spring and ball in position while installing detent (34). Assemble shift shaft (40), shift lever yoke (39), shift lever (38) and pin (36). Assemble forward gear (52) with thrust bearing (51 and 50) in gear housing. Place dog clutch (54) on propeller shaft (60) making sure hole in dog clutch is aligned with slot in propeller shaft and splined dogs are toward forward gear. Insert propeller shaft in forward gear and bearing housing assembly, then insert pin (55) through dog clutch propeller shaft and hole in shift shaft (40). Install pin retaining spring (56). Press shift detent (34) down and place propeller shaft, forward gear and gear housing assembly (37) into position in gearcase. Make sure locating pin (35) is seated in recess provided in gearcase.

Insert drive shaft (16). Install pinion gear retaining nut and tighten to 60-65 ft.-lbs. (82-88 N·m). Install shift rod (25)

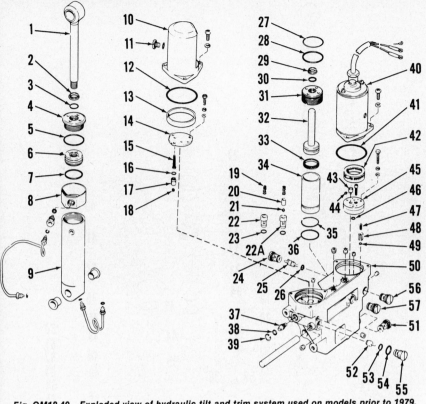

Fig. OM18-40 – Exploded view of hydraulic tilt and trim system used on models prior to 1979.

1. Shaft	16. "O" ring	30. "O" ring
2. Wiper	17. Check valve	31. End cap
3. "O" ring	18. Valve ball	32. Piston
4. End cap	19. Springs	33. Piston ring
5. "O" ring	20. Spring seat	34. Trim cylinder
6. Piston	21. Ball	35. Retaining ring
7. "O" ring	22. Relief valve	36. "O" ring
8. Band	22A. Impact relief valve	37. Manual release
9. Tilt cylinder	23. "O" ring	valve
10. Reservoir	24. Valve	38. "O" ring
11. Fill plug	25. Piston	39. Snap ring
12. "O" ring	26. "O" ring	40. Pump motor
13. Sleeve	27. Retaining ring	41. "O" ring
14. Plate	28. "O" ring	42. Oil pump filter
15. Screen	29. Wiper	

43. Drive coupling	
44. Ball	
45. Oil pump	
46. "O" ring	
47. Spring	
48. Pump relief valve	
49. Seal	
50. Manifold	
51. Valve	
52. Valve piston	
53. "O" ring	
54. "O" ring	
55. Valve	
56. Valve	
57. Valve	

and shift rod cover (29) as an assembly. Thread shift rod fully into detent (34), back off two turns, pull rod to neutral (middle detent) and adjust for proper length. Refer to shift rod adjustment in REMOVE AND REINSTALL section for specifications.

Assemble thrust bearing (64 and 63) on reverse gear (62) and slide onto propeller shaft (60). Position bearing retainer plate (65) and install snap rings (66). Make sure that "O" ring (67) is fully seated in groove of bearing housing (69) and that seals (71) are properly installed. Lip of forward seal should be toward front and lip of aft seal should be toward propeller.

Installation of bearing housing (69) will be eased by using two guide pins, 10-inches long. Thread guide pin into bearing retainer plate (65) and slide bearing housing (69) into position. Coat bearing housing screws with sealing compound and install.

Install seals (9 and 10) in upper drive shaft bearing housing (11) with lip of lower seal (10) down and lip of upper

seal (9) up. Place thrust bearing assembly (14 and 15) on drive shaft and install previously selected shim or shims (13). Coat screws that secure bearing housing (11) with sealing compound and install. Bottom edge of impeller plate (8) should

Fig. OM18-41 – Schematic of hydraulic tilt and trim system. Refer to Fig. OM18-40 for parts identification.

be coated with OMC Adhesive "M" or equivalent and placed in position. Install impeller key, lubricate edges of impeller (6) and install on drive shaft. On models after 1984, impeller key is replaced with a drive cam. Install drive cam with flat side against drive shaft and sharp edge pointing in a clockwise direction when viewed from crankshaft end of drive shaft. Drive shaft should be turned clockwise while installing water pump housing (5). Coat screws that secure water pump housing and water tube bracket with sealing compound and install.

POWER TILT AND TRIM

Models Prior to 1979

OPERATION. All models are equipped with a hydraulically actuated power tilt and trim system. Manifold (50 – Fig. OM18-40) contains valves, oil pump and trim cylinders. Oil pump motor, oil reservoir and tilt cylinder are attached to manifold. Electric oil pump motor is reversible and oil pump rotation is thereby changed to extend or retract trim and tilt cylinders. Note position of valves in Figs. OM18-40 and OM18-41. Turn manual release valve (37 – Fig. OM18-40) to manually raise or lower outboard.

Hydraulic system contains 25 ft. oz. (740 mL) of oil. Recommended oil is OMC Sea-Lube Power Trim/Tilt Fluid. Do not run pump without oil in reservoir. Oil level should reach fill plug (11) hole threads with outboard tilted in full up position. Hydraulic tilt should be recycled several times and oil level rechecked if system has been drained or lost a large amount of oil.

TROUBLE-SHOOTING. Be sure battery is fully charged, electrical connections are good, oil reservoir is full and air is not trapped in system before testing components.

OIL PUMP AND MOTOR. To check oil pump, unscrew plug (1–Fig. OM18-42) and install a 2000 psi (13.8 MPa) pressure gage. Oil pressure should be 1300-1600 psi (9-11 MPa) with outboard tilted in full up position. Oil pressure less than specified may indicate leakage, faulty pressure relief valve (22A–Fig. OM18-40), directional valve (56), oil pump or pump motor. No-load current draw of pump motor should not exceed 18 amps. Motor must operate properly in both directions.

VALVES. Faulty valves will cause system malfunction. Note function of valves and carefully inspect valve components which may cause malfunction. Valves (24 and 56–Fig. OM18-40 or OM18-41) and valve piston (25) direct oil to tilt and trim cylinders from oil pump. Valve (57) directs oil to bottom of tilt cylinder when tilting outboard up and also directs oil to relief valve (22) which relieves system pressure at approximately 1500 psi (10.3 MPa). Valve (22A) relieves pressure during outboard impact and directs oil pressure to letdown valve piston (52) which allows oil to escape from bottom of tilt cylinder so top portion of tilt cylinder can be refilled after impact. Valves in tilt cylinder piston (6) allow oil to transfer from top to bottom of tilt cylinder during outboard impact. Valve (51) allows oil to flow from bottom of tilt cylinder during tilting down operation. Manual release valve (37) allows manual movement of outboard when valve is open.

TILT AND TRIM CYLINDERS. Tilt and trim system malfunction may be due to leaking "O" rings, seals and fittings in cylinders. Blocked oil lines may cause improper operation. Leaking valves in tilt cylinder piston (6–Fig. OM18-40) may allow unit to leakdown.

OVERHAUL. Filter valve seat (17–Fig. OM18-40) will be damaged if removed. Valves (24, 55, 56 and 57) are

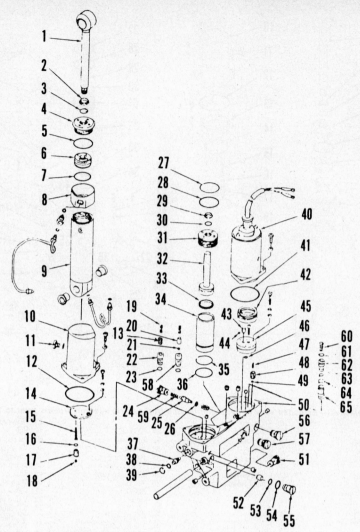

Fig. OM18-45 – Exploded view of hydraulic tilt and trim system used on models after 1978. A three-wire pump motor is used on 1979 and 1980 models.

1. Shaft	19. Spring	35. Retaining ring	51. Separation valve
2. Wiper	20. Spring seat	36. "O" ring	52. Valve piston
3. "O" ring	21. Ball	37. Manual release valve	53. "O" ring
4. End cap	22. Trim up relief valve	38. "O" ring	54. "O" ring
5. "O" ring	23. "O" ring	39. Snap ring	55. Impact letdown valve
6. Piston	24. Reverse lock check	40. Pump motor	56. Trim check valve
7. "O" ring	valve	41. "O" ring	57. Tilt check valve
8. Band	25. Piston	42. Oil pump filter	58. Impact sensor valve
9. Tilt cylinder	26. "O" ring	43. Drive coupling	59. Spring
10. Reservoir	27. Retaining ring	44. Ball	60. Spring
11. Fill plug	28. "O" ring	45. Oil pump	61. "O" ring
12. "O" ring	29. Wiper	46. "O" ring	62. Expansion relief valve
13. Needle	30. "O" ring	47. Spring	core
14. Plate	31. End cap	48. Trim down pump	63. "O" ring
15. Screen	32. Piston	relief valve	64. "O" ring
16. "O" ring	33. Piston ring	49. Seal	65. Expansion relief valve
17. Check valve	34. Trim cylinder	50. Manifold	seat
18. Valve ball			

identical and may be interchanged. Valve (51) is taller than other valves and must not be interchanged. Motor must be serviced as a unit assembly. Apply OMC Nut Lock to piston shaft (1) threads and install piston (6) on shaft with small holes in piston up.

POWER TILT AND TRIM

Models After 1978

OPERATION. A hydraulically actuated power tilt and trim system is used. Manifold (50–Fig. OM18-45) con-

tains valves, oil pump and trim cylinders. Oil pump motor, oil reservoir and tilt cylinder are attached to manifold. Electric oil pump motor is reversible and oil pump rotation is thereby changed to extend or retract trim and tilt cylinders. Note position of valves in Fig. OM18-45. Turn manual release valve counterclockwise to manually raise or lower outboard.

Hydraulic system contains approximately 25 fl. oz. (740 mL) of oil. Recommended oil is OMC Power Trim/Tilt Fluid or DEXRON II automatic transmission fluid. Do not run pump without

Fig. OM18-42 – View of oil pressure reading points.

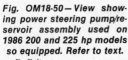

Fig. OM18-50—View show-ing power steering pump/re-servoir assembly used on 1986 200 and 225 hp models so equipped. Refer to text.

B. Bolts
F. Fill plug
I. Idler pulley
N. Nuts
P. Plug
S. Power steering pump/reser-voir assy.

Fig. OM18-46—Install OMC gage "A" or "B" into manual release valve (37—Fig. OM18-46) port as shown to test system oil pressure. Refer to text.

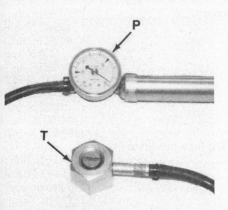

Fig. OM18-47—Use OMC check valve tester 390063 (T) and a suitable pressure tester (P) to test check valves. Check valve can be con-sidered good if no pressure leakage at approx-imately 30 psi (207 kPa) is noted.

oil in reservoir. Oil level should reach fill plug (11) hole threads when tilt and trim pistons are fully extended. System should be cycled several times prior to checking oil level if system has been drained or lost a large amount of oil.

TROUBLE-SHOOTING. Be sure bat-tery is fully charged, electrical connec-tions are good, oil reservoir is full and air is not trapped in system before test-ing components.

To check oil pressure, first momen-tarily cycle system "UP" and "DOWN" a few times. Remove snap ring (39—Fig. OM18-45) and manual release valve (37), then install OMC gage "A" as shown in Fig. OM18-46. Operate system in the "UP" direction and observe gage after system stalls out at full extension. Gage reading should not drop below 100-200

psi (700-1400 kPa). Install OMC gage "B." Operate system in the "DOWN" direction and observe gage after system stalls out at fully retracted. Gage read-ing should not drop below 100-200 psi (700-1400 kPa).

To test check valves, screw each valve into OMC check valve tester 390063 (T—Fig. OM18-47). Use a suitable pres-sure tester (P) and apply 30 psi (207 kPa) of pressure to check valve. Check valve can be considered good if no pressure leakage is noted.

Refer to the following for a list of symptoms and probable causes:

Symptoms	Probable Causes
Tilt Leakdown	1, 2, 3, 4, 5 or 6
Trim and Tilt Both Leak	7, 8 or 9
Reverse Lock Does Not Hold	2, 3, 6, 10, 11 or 12
Will Not Trim Out Under Load or Will Not Tilt	1, 2, 7 or 9
Will Not Trim or Tilt Down	2, 8, 10, 11 or 13

Key to Probable Causes
1. Trim Up Relief Valve
2. Manual Release Valve
3. Tilt Cylinder Valve or Seals
4. Tilt Check Valve
5. Impact Letdown Valve
6. Oil Line
7. Trim Cylinders Sleeve "O" Rings or Piston Seals
8. Trim Check Valve
9. Expansion Relief Valve or "O" Rings
10. Filter Valve Seat
11. Impact Sensor Valve
12. Reverse Lock Check Valve
13. Trim Down Pump Relief Valve

OVERHAUL. Oil pump must be serv-iced as a unit assembly. Motor is not serviceable with the exception of brushes. Refer to Fig. OM18-45 for ex-ploded view of trim and tilt cylinders and manifold components. Keep all com-ponents separated during disassembly and identify each component, if needed, to assure correct position during reassembly.

POWER STEERING

1986 200 And 225 HP Models So Equipped

DRIVE BELT TENSION ADJUST-MENT. Loosen idler housing bolts (B—Fig. OM18-50) and rotate nuts (N) clockwise to reduce tension on drive belt and counterclockwise to increase ten-sion on drive belt. Drive belt tension should be 25-30 pounds (111-133 N). Check belt tension using a suitable ten-sion gage positioned midway between idler pulley (I) and flywheel pulley.

PRESSURE TEST. Remove plug (P—Fig. OM18-50) and install OMC Pressure Gage 983975 or a suitable 2000 psi (13.8 MPa) pressure gage. Remove fill plug (F) and install OMC Power Trim and Tilt fluid or Dexron II in reservoir until fluid level is even with groove around base of dipstick with plug end of dipstick resting on top of fill hole. Install plug (P) and tighten. Start engine and operate at 1000 rpm. Completely extend or retract cylinder rod and observe pres-sure gage. The pump relief pressure should be 850-1000 psi (5861-6895 kPa).

EVINRUDE AND JOHNSON 8-CYLINDER MODELS

Year Produced	Evinrude Models	Johnson Models
1985	275TLCO, 275TXCO, 300TLCO	275TLCO, 275TXCO, 300TLCO
1986	275PTLCD, 275PTXCD, 300PTLCD	275PTLCD, 275PTXCD, 300PTLCD

CONDENSED SERVICE DATA

TUNE-UP

Hp/rpm	275/5500
	300/6000
Bore	3.50 in.
	(88.9 mm)
Stroke	2.86 in.
	(72.6 mm)
Number of Cylinders	8
Displacement	220 cu. in.
	(3608 cc)
Spark Plug – Champion:	
Standard	QL77JC4
Electrode Gap	0.040 in.
	(1.0 mm)
Sustained High Speeds	QL78V
Electrode Gap	Fixed
Ignition Type	CDI
Carburetor Make	Own
Idle Speed (in gear)	650 rpm
Fuel:Oil Ratio	VRO

SIZES – CLEARANCES

Piston Ring End Gap	0.005-0.018 in.
	(0.13-0.46 mm)
Lower Piston Ring Side Clearance	0.004 in. Max.
	(0.102 mm)
Maximum Cylinder Tolerance	0.004 in.
	(0.102 mm)
Crankshaft Diameters:	
Top Main	1.6199-1.6204 in.
	(41.15-41.16 mm)
Center Mains	2.1870-2.1875 in.
	(55.55-55.56 mm)
Bottom Main	1.5747-1.5752 in.
	(40.00-40.01 mm)
Crankpin	1.4995-1.5000 in.
	(38.09-38.10 mm)

TIGHTENING TORQUES

Connecting Rod	504-528 in.-lbs.
	(57-60 N·m)
Crankcase Halves:	
Main Bearing Screws	312-360 in.-lbs.
	(35-41 N·m)
Flange Screws	60-84 in.-lbs.
	(7.9 N·m)
Crankcase Head	72-96 in.-lbs.
	(8-11 N·m)
Cylinder Head	261-240 in.-lbs.
	(24.27 N·m)
Flywheel Nut	140-150 ft.-lbs.
	(190-204 N·m)
Lower Main Bearing Retainer Plate	
Screws	96-120 in.-lbs.
	(11-13 N·m)
Spark Plug	216-240 in.-lbs.
	(24-27 N·m)
Standard Screws:	
No. 6	7-10 in.-lbs.
	(0.8-1.2 N·m)
No. 8	15-22 in.-lbs.
	(1.6-2.4 N·m)
No. 10	25-35 in.-lbs.
	(2.8-4.0 N·m)
No. 12	(35-40 N·m)
	(4.0-4.6 N·m)
¼ Inch	60-80 in.-lbs.
	(7-9 N·m)
5/16 Inch	120-140 in.-lbs.
	(14-16 N·m)
⅜ Inch	220-240 in.-lbs.
	(24-27 N·m)
7/16 Inch	340-360 in.-lbs.
	(38-40 N·m)

LUBRICATION

The engine is lubricated by oil mixed with the fuel. Fuel should be regular leaded, regular unleaded, premium leaded or premium unleaded with a minimum pump octane rating of 86.

All models are equipped with variable ratio oiling (VRO). Two VRO pumps are used. Recommended oil is Evinrude or Johnson Outboard Lubricant, OMC 2 Cycle Motor Oil or a BIA certified TC-W motor oil. The VRO pump meters the fuel:oil ratio from approximately 50:1 up to approximately 150:1 by sensing the engine power output. During engine break-in, the fuel in the fuel tank must be mixed at a fuel:oil ratio of 50:1 (25:1 on 3.6 GT and XP models) to ensure the engine of proper lubrication and the oil level in the VRO oil tank must be monitored. If, after engine break-in, oil level has dropped indicating the VRO system is operating, refill the VRO oil tank and switch to straight fuel.

NOTE: On 3.6 GT and XP models when operated under high performance conditions, a premix of 50:1 must be used in fuel tank if VRO system is used and a premix of 25:1 must be used in fuel tank if VRO system is not used to ensure engine of proper lubrication.

On all recreational models when VRO system is not being used, the recommended fuel:oil ratio for normal operation and engine break-in is 50:1.

The lower unit gears and bearings are lubricated by oil contained in the gearcase. The recommended oil is OMC HI-VIS Gearcase Lube. The gearcase oil level should be checked after every 50 hours of operation and the gearcase should be drained and filled with new oil every 100 hours or once each season, whichever occurs first.

The gearcase is drained and filled through the same plug port. An oil level (vent) port is used to indicate the full oil level of the gearcase and to ease in oil drainage.

To drain the oil, place the outboard motor in a vertical position. Remove the drain plug and oil level plug and allow the lubricant to drain into a suitable container.

To fill the gearcase with oil, place the outboard motor in a vertical position. Add oil through the drain plug opening with an oil feeder until the oil begins to overflow from oil level plug port. Reinstall oil level plug with a new gasket, if needed, and tighten. Remove oil feeder, the reinstall drain plug with a new gasket, if needed, and tighten.

FUEL SYSTEM

CARBURETOR. Four two-barrel type carburetors are used. Each carburetor assembly has a common throttle body assembly (T–Fig. OM20-1) with separate main body assemblies (M). Recommended low speed air bleed jet (5) size is #33 on all models. Recommended intermediate air bleed jet (4) size is #29 on 275 hp models and #22 on 300 hp models. Recommended high speed jet (9–Fig. OM20-2) size is #62D on 275 hp models and #80D on 300 hp models.

NOTE: Starboard carburetors supply fuel to port cylinders and port carburetors supply fuel to starboard cylinders.

The main body assemblies are constructed of a nonmetallic type material. Care must be used when working with the main body assembly. DO NOT overtighten any screws. Tighten each screw in small increments using a criss-cross tightening sequence.

If service is performed, note the following: Keep carburetor components for each carburetor separate from the others. The manufacturer does not recommend submerging the parts in carburetor or parts cleaning solutions. An aerosol type carburetor cleaner is recommended. The float and other components made of plastic and rubber should not be subjected to some cleaning solutions. Safety eyewear and solvent resistant gloves are recommended.

To determine the float level, invert float bowl (12–Fig. OM20-3) with the fuel inlet valve and float installed. The float should be flush with the float bowl

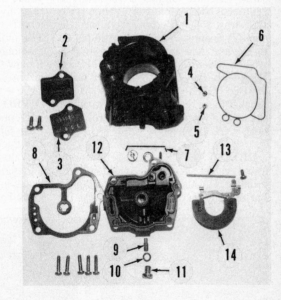

Fig. OM20-2—Exploded view of carburetor main body assembly.
1. Main body
2. Gasket
3. Plate
4. Intermediate air bleed jet
5. Low speed air bleed jet
6. Seal
7. Inlet needle & seat
8. Gasket
9. High speed jet
10. Gasket
11. Plug
12. Float bowl
13. Pin
14. Float

Fig. OM20-1—View showing two-barrel type carburetors. A common throttle body assembly (T) with separate main body assemblies (M) are used. View identifies position of intermediate air bleed jet (4) and low speed air bleed jet (5). Refer to text.

Fig. OM20-3—With float bowl (12) inverted and fuel inlet valve and float installed, float should just touch straightedge (S). Refer to text.

gasket surface. Use a straightedge as shown in Fig. OM20-3 to check float setting. Remove the float and carefully bend the float tank to adjust.

Recommended idle speed is 650 rpm with the engine at normal operating temperature and forward gear engaged. Loosen nut (N–Fig. OM20-5) and turn screw (I) to adjust engine idle speed.

SPEED CONTROL LINKAGE. The carburetor throttle valves are synchronized to open as the ignition is advanced. It is important that throttle valve opening and ignition timing synchronization be checked and adjusted if necessary.

The following procedure should be used to check and adjust synchronization of linkage. Move the speed control lever to the idle position and make sure follower roller (F–Fig. OM20-5) is not touching throttle cam (T). Loosen follower roller screw (C) and move roller away from throttle cam (T). Loose screw (S) two complete turns and make certain that throttle plates are closed, then tighten screw (S). Leave screw (C) loose. Hold follower roller (F) against throttle cam (T) and adjust throttle cam stop screw (D) until alignment mark (M) is centered with follower roller (F). Withdraw roller (F) away from throttle cam (T) enough to allow throttle plates to close at idle and tighten screw (C). Adjust wide-open throttle (WOT) stop screw (W–Fig. OM20-6) so WOT mark (0–Fig. OM20-5) on follower roller bracket faces directly front to rear with the engine when the speed control lever is at WOT.

REED VALVES. Eight sets of leaf (reed) valves are used, one for each cylinder. The eight valves are positioned horizontally and are attached to the in-

Fig. OM20-6 – Adjust wide-open throttle (WOT) stop screw (W) as outlined in text.

take manifold with a gasket between each reed block and mainfold. The leaf petals should seat very lightly against the valve block throughout their entire length with the least possible tension. The individual parts of the reed valve assembly are not available separately. Renew the reed valve assembly if petals are broken, cracked, warped or bent.

VRO TYPE FUEL PUMP. Two VRO fuel pumps are used. The VRO type fuel pump (1–Fig. OM20-8) meters the fuel:oil ratio from approximately 50:1 up to approximately 150:1 by sensing engine power output. During engine break-in or after any procedure that permitted air to enter VRO system, the fuel

in the fuel tank must be mixed at a fuel:oil ratio of 50:1 to ensure the engine of proper lubrication. On 3.6 GT and XP models, a fuel:oil ratio of 25:1 must be used during testing of system if operated under high performance conditions.

To check the VRO system for proper operation, first fill the VRO oil tank with a recommended two-stroke motor oil and note oil level for future reference. Install the correct fuel:oil mixture in the fuel tank. After the recommended engine break-in period or after a suitable test period for other conditions, note the oil level in the VRO oil tank. If the oil level has dropped and the VRO system is operating properly, refill the VRO oil tank and switch to straight fuel or recommended fuel mixture.

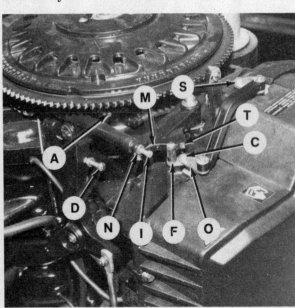

Fig. OM20-5 – View of speed control linkage. Refer to text.

Fig. OM20-8 – View of VRO type fuel pump.
1. VRO fuel pump assy.
2. Oil inlet nipple
3. Fuel inlet nipple
4. Crankcase pulse nipple
5. Fuel mixture discharge nipple

NOTE: When the VRO system is not used, the inlet nozzle at the outboard motor connector must be capped and clamped to prevent dirt or moisture from entering the fuel system. The fuel in the fuel tank must be mixed at correct fuel:oil ratio. Refer to LUBRICATION section.

TESTING. Stop the engine. Disconnect fuel mixture discharge hose at VRO pump nipple (4 – Fig. OM20-8). Connect a tee fitting in hose end. Connect one end of a clear hose to one tee outlet and connect remaining hose end to pump discharge fitting. Connect a 0-15 psi (0-103 kPa) pressure gage to the remaining tee outlet. Start the engine and run at wide-open throttle. The VRO pump should develop between 3 psi (21 kPa) and 15 psi (103 kPa) at wide-open throttle. The fuel pressure will drop 1-2 psi (6.8-13.7 kPa) and a clicking sound should be heard with each oil discharge. A small squirt of oil should be noticed every time the pump pulses.

If fuel pump (1) malfunction is noted, the fuel pump must be renewed as a complete assembly.

IGNITION SYSTEM

All models are equipped with a capacitor discharge ignition system which is triggered by sensor coils contained in timer base. To prevent damage to components, note the following list of precautions:

1. DO NOT disconnect any wires while motor is running or while ignition switch is ON.
2. DO NOT use any tachometer except those approved for use with this system.
3. DO NOT hold spark plug wires while checking for spark.
4. DO make certain that all wiring connections are clean and tightly joined.
5. DO make certain that wires do not bind moving parts or touch metal edges where they may chafe through insulation.

TROUBLE-SHOOTING. Use only approved procedures to prevent damage to the components. The fuel system should be checked first to make certain that faulty running is not caused by fuel starvation, incorrect mixture or contaminated fuel.

WIRING. Engine missing, surging and failure to start or run can be caused by loose or corroded electrical connections. Check all terminals and plug-in connectors for tight clean contact. Also check all wiring for short circuit to ground.

CHARGE COILS. All models use two charge coils contained in the stator assembly. To check charge coils, disconnect the two-wire connector (one for cylinders 1 through 4 and one for cylinders 5 through 8) and connect an ohmmeter to terminals A and B (Fig. OM20-11) in connector leading to stator. Renew stator assembly if resistance is not 955-985 ohms. Connect negative ohmmeter lead to an engine ground and positive ohmmeter lead to connector terminal A, then to connector terminal B. Infinite resistance should exist between A terminal and engine ground and B terminal and engine ground. If not, charge coil or charge coil lead is shorting to ground. Repeat previous tests on other two-wire connector leading to stator assembly. To check charge coil output, use Merc-O-Tronic Model 781, Stevens Model CD77 or a suitable peak voltage tester. Connect black tester lead to terminal A in connector leading to stator and red tester lead to terminal B. Turn tester knobs to "NEG (–)" and "500." Crank engine while observing tester. Repeat test on other charge coil. Renew

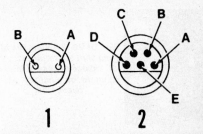

Fig. OM20-11 — View "1" identifies terminal ends in stator assembly connector and view "2" identifies terminal ends in timer base connector.

stator assembly if meter reads below 130 volts on either coil test.

SENSOR COILS. All models use eight sensor coils contained in the timer base assembly. To check sensor coils, disconnect one five-wire connector and connect and ohmmeter to terminals A and E (Fig. OM20-11), then B and E, then C and E and then D and E in five-wire connector leading to timer base. Renew timer base if resistance readings are not 35-45 ohms. Connect negative ohmmeter lead to an engine ground and positive ohmmeter lead to connector terminal A, then B, then C, then D and then E. Infinite resistance should exist between all terminal connections and engine ground. If not, sensor coil or sensor coil lead is shorting to ground. Repeat previous tests on other five-wire connector leading to timer base. To check sensor coil output, use Merc-O-Tronic Model 781, Stevens Model CD77 or a suitable peak voltage tester. Connect black tester lead to timer base connector terminal E and red tester lead to terminal A. On Merc-O-Tronic Model 781, turn knobs to "POS (+)" and "5" and on Stevens Models CD77, turn knobs to "S" and "5." Crank engine while observing tester. Repeat test with black tester lead still connected to terminal E and connect red tester lead to terminal B, then C and then to D. Repeat previous tests on other five-wire connector leading to timer base. Renew timer base if meter reads below 0.3 volts.

POWER PACKS. Two power packs are used, one power pack supplies cylinders 1 through 4 and the other power pack supplies cylinders 5 through 8. To check power pack output, first reconnect stator and timer base connectors. Use Merc-O-Tronic Model 781, Stevens Model CD77 or a suitable peak voltage tester. Connect black tester lead to a suitable engine ground. Connect red tester lead to wire leading to one of the eight ignition coils. Turn tester knobs to "NEG (–)" and "500." Crank engine while observing tester. Repeat test on other leads. Renew power pack or packs if readings are not at least 100 volts or higher.

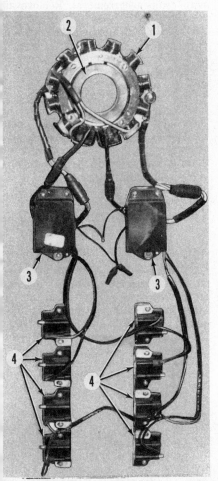

Fig. OM20-10 — View identifying stator assembly (1), timer base (2), power packs (3) and ignition coils (4) in CDI system.

Fig. OM20-12 — View identifying shift interrupter switch (SI) located at base of intake manifold on engine's starboard side.

NOTE: Power packs marked "CDL" have an internal device to limit engine speed to 6100 rpm on 275 hp models and 6700 rpm on 3.6 GT and XP models.

IGNITION COILS. Renew ignition coil or coils if no other ignition component is found faulty.

SHIFT INTERRUPTER SWITCH. Shift interrupter switch (SI – Fig. OM20-12) is used to interrupt power supply to starboard power pack during gearcase directional changes. This prevents firing of cylinders, 5 through 8 thus lowering engine rpm to allow easier engagement and disengagement of shift components. To check shift interrupter switch (SI), use a suitable ohmmeter placed on a high ohms scale. Disconnect the single-wire connector at starboard power pack. Connect black tester lead to a suitable engine ground and red tester lead to terminal end in connector leading to shift interrupter switch (SI). An infinite meter reading should be noted. Activate shift interrupter switch (SI) and note ohmmeter. A low meter reading should be noted. Disconnect shift interrupter switch remaining single-wire connector. Connect ohmmeter leads between single-wire connectors of switch, note ohmmeter then reverse tester leads. Infinite resistance should be noted on one test and zero resistance should be noted on other test. Renew shift interrupter switch (SI) if previous test results are not noted.

IGNITION TIMING. Connect a power timing light to number 1 (top, starboard) cylinder spark plug, then start and run engine at 4500-5000 rpm in gear and note timing. Stop engine. Ignition should occur at 18° BTDC on 275 hp models and 16° BTDC on 300 hp models. To adjust, turn spark advance stop screw (A – Fig. OM20-5). Turning screw (A) clockwise one full turn will retard ignition timing approximately one degree.

COOLING SYSTEM

THERMOSTAT. A cooling system thermostat is used in each cylinder head to maintain a water temperature of approximately 145°F (63°C). A relief valve within each thermostat opens at high engine speed when water pump impeller speed increases water pressure. Engine temperature can be checked using heat sensitive sticks such as Markal Thermomelt Stik. A 163°F (73°C) stick should not melt, but a 125°F (52°C) stick should melt, after engine reaches operating temperature. The remote control box is equipped with a "hot horn" which is activated by either temperature sensing switch in each cylinder head. Temperature switch operation may be checked with a continuity tester and a high temperature thermometer. Place switch and thermometer in oil that is being heated. Switch should show a closed circuit at 205°-217°F (96°-102°C) and should open again at 168°-182°F (75°-83°C).

WATER PUMP. The water pump is mounted on top of the gearcase. Rubber impeller is driven by the drive shaft. Separate gearcase from exhaust housing for access to water pump.

Apply OMC Adhesive M to "O" ring (7 – Fig. OM20-20) groove in impeller housing (4) and OMC Gasket Sealing

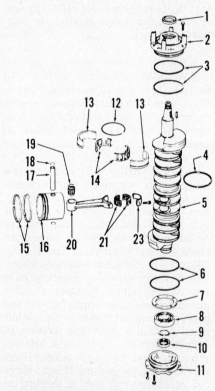

Fig. OM20-15 — Exploded view of crankshaft and piston assemblies.

1. Seal
2. Upper crankcase head & bearing
3. "O" rings
4. Seal ring (12 used)
5. Crankshaft
6. "O" rings
7. Retainer plate
8. Ball bearing
9. Snap ring
10. Seals
11. Lower crankcase head
12. Retaining ring
13. Main bearing outer race
14. Roller bearings & cages
15. Piston rings
16. Piston
17. Piston pin
18. Snap ring
19. Roller bearing
20. Connecting rod
21. Roller bearings & cages
23. Rod cap

Compound to bottom of impeller plate (8). Lubricate impeller (6) and hold blades in while installing housing.

POWER HEAD

R&R AND DISASSEMBLE

Remove lower engine covers. Remove six screws attaching flywheel to power steering pump drive pulley. Remove flywheel nut, then withdraw flywheel. Remove stator assembly screws to allow access to three power steering pump reservoir mounting screws. Remove screws then detach pump/reservoir from cylinder block and place to the side along with cooler and filter without disconnecting hoses. Disconnect and mark interfering wires. Disconnect upper end of shift rod. Remove five screws and one nut from each side of upper end of drive shaft housing and two screws and one nut at rear of upper end of drive shaft housing. Lift power head from lower unit.

Remove stator assembly, power steering drive pulley, timer base, power packs, tilt and trim junction box, rectifier/regulator assembly, electric starter and any wiring that will interfere with component removal. Remove air silencer, carburetors and VRO fuel pumps. Remove lower intake manifold, then remove upper intake manifold. Remove torsional damper at base of crankshaft. Remove upper and lower crankcase head (2 and 11 – Fig. OM20-15) screws. Cylinder block and crankcase aligning taper pin must be driven out towards front. Loosen but do not remove center four screws in lower crankcase head (11) which hold retainer plate (7). Unscrew crankcase retaining screws and separate crankcase from cylinder block.

Pistons, rods and crankshaft are now accessible for removal and overhaul as outlined in the approprite following paragraphs.

ASSEMBLY. When assembling, the crankcase and inlet manifold must be completely sealed against both vacuum and pressure. Cylinder heads must be sealed against water leakage and pressure. Mating surfaces of water intake and exhaust areas between lower unit and power head must form a tight seal. It is recommended that all mating surfaces be carefully inspected for nicks, burrs, corrosion and warpage which might interefere with a tight seal. All of these surfaces may be lapped if necessary to provide a smooth, flat surface. DO NOT remove any more metal than is necessary. Mating surfaces of crankcase and cylinder block MUST NOT be lowered, but can be polished to remove imperfections.

Cylinder block and crankcase are positively located by a tapered dowel pin. Dowel pin must not be nicked, bent or distorted and dowel pin hole must be clean and true. When installing dowel pin, make sure that pin is fully seated, but do not use excessive force.

Refer to subsequent sections for assembly of piston, rod and crankshaft components. Install piston and rod assemblies in cylinder block with bearing in rod but do not install cap and bearing. Install lower head assembly (6 through 11 – Fig. OM20-15) on crankshaft but do not tighten four bearing retainer plate (7) screws. Install top bearing head assembly (1, 2 and 3) and seal rings (4) on crankshaft. Face all seal ring gaps toward intake manifold side of crankcase. Install center main bearings (13 and 14) on crankshaft as outlined in CONNECTING RODS, BEARINGS AND CRANKSHAFT section. Install crankshaft assembly in cylinder block making certain that holes in center main bearings align with dowel pins in cylinder block. Position connecting rods on crankshaft and install rod bearings (21 and 22) and rod caps (23).

When reassembling crankcase, make sure mating surfaces of crankcase halves are completely clean and free of old cement, nicks and burrs. Apply OMC Gel-Seal II to one crankcase mating surface. Do not use sealers which will harden and prevent contact between crankcase mating surfaces. Immediately assemble crankcase halves after applying sealer and position halves by installing tapered locating dowel pin. Then install and tighten crankcase retaining screws to the torque listed in the CONDENSED SERVICE DATA table. When tightening the retaining screws, start in the center and work toward ends. Tighten the lower main bearing retainer plate (7) screws to the correct torque and check the crankshaft for binding.

Complete remainder of reassembly in reverse order of disassembly. Install cylinder head gaskets and intake manifold gaskets without a sealer. Install upper intake manifold first, then install lower intake manifold.

PISTONS, PINS, RINGS AND CYLINDERS. Before detaching connecting rods from crankshaft, mark piston, rod and cap for correct assembly to each other and for installation into the same cylinder for which they are removed. Separate bearing cages and rollers (21 and 22 – Fig. OM20-15) for assembly into same location if they are to be reinstalled.

Pistons and rings are available in standard and 0.030 inch (0.76 mm) oversize. Top piston ring is semi-keystone.

Refer to the CONDENSED SERVICE DATA table for recommended ring end gap and lower ring side clearance. Rebore cylinder bores or renew cylinder block if cylinder bore taper or out-of-round exceeds 0.004 inch (0.102 mm).

The piston pin is retained in piston by snap rings in piston pin bosses. The upper end of connecting rod is fitted with a caged needle roller bearing. The piston pin and connecting rod bore are used as bearing races. Check bearing rollers, cage and bearing race surfaces for wear, scoring and overheating. When assembling, pistons can be heated slightly to facilitate installation of piston pins. The pistons on port side are installed to connecting rods differently than for starboard units. The stamping "Exhaust Side" on top of pistons must face cylinder bore exhaust ports. Connecting rod oil hole (H – Fig. OM20-16) must face flywheel end of crankshaft when connecting rod is assembled to crankshaft. Thoroughly lubricate all bearing surfaces before assembling.

CONNECTING RODS, BEARINGS AND CRANKSHAFT. Individual connecting rod and piston assemblies can be removed after removing crankcase and appropriate cylinder head. Before detaching connecting rods from crankshaft, mark rod and cap for correct assembly to each other and in original cylinder. Separate bearing cages and rollers for assembly to original crankpin if units are not renewed.

Connecting rods ride on roller bearings at both ends. The crankpin end of rod is drilled and finished, then carefully fractured to separate the cap from the rod. The parting line is not machined and when correctly assembled, the uneven parting line should be nearly invisible. When assembling, make certain that alignment dot on connecting rod and rod cap are aligned, oil hole (H – Fig. OM20-16) is toward top of motor and stamping "Exhaust Side" on piston head is toward cylinder bore exhaust ports. The machined sides of connecting rod and cap should be smooth when assembled. OMC Alignment Fixture 396749 is recommended to properly align connecting rod with rod cap during tightening of connecting rod screws.

Crankshaft seal rings (4 – Fig. OM20-15) should be renewed if thickness is less than 0.154 inch (3.91 mm).

Bearing and head (2) are a one-piece assembly and must be serviced as a unit. Lip of seal (1) should be toward inside and should be pressed in until flush with top surface of bearing head.

The center main bearings are split-cage roller bearings. The two-piece outer race is held together with retaining ring (12) and is positioned in cylinder

block by a dowel pin. Install bearing races (13) with ring groove towards bottom of crankshaft. When assembling, make certain that dowel pin in cylinder block bore engages hole in center bearing outer race.

The ball type lower main bearing (8) is pressed onto crankshaft lower end. The bearing outer race is clamped to the bearing head with retainer plate (7). To disassemble lower bearing assembly, remove retainer plate screws and pull bearing head (11) from bearing (8). Remove snap ring (9), then remove bearing using a suitable puller. The lower bearing should be renewed whenever removed. Press a new bearing onto crankshaft until inner bearing race is seated against crankshaft shoulder. Press seals (10) into bore in bearing head using OMC special tool 325453 to locate seals at correct depth in the bore. Install new "O" rings (6) in bearing head grooves, then slide bearing head onto outer race of bearing using guide pins. Install screws in to retainer (7) but do not tighten these screws until crankcase is assembled.

Refer to the CONDENSED SERVICE DATA table for dimensional data and recommended torque values. Refer to ASSEMBLY paragraphs for assembling the crankcase halves.

PROPELLER

Only stainless steel propellers can be used. Select a propeller that will allow the engine at full throttle to reach maximum operating rpm of 5000-6000 rpm on 275 hp models and 5500-6000 rpm on 300 hpm models.

REMOVE AND REINSTALL. To remove gearcase, disconnect upper end of shift rod then remove propeller and drain lubricant from gearcase. Mark location of trim tab (22 – Fig. OM20-20) to aid during reassembly and remove trim tab. Remove two screws on each side of gearcase and two screws at rear.

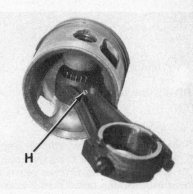

Fig. OM20-16 – Connecting rod oil hole (H) must face flywheel end of crankshaft when connecting rod is assembled to crankshaft.

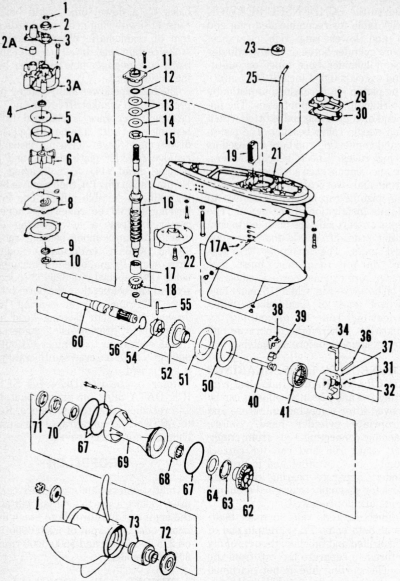

Fig. OM20-20—Exploded view of typical lower unit.

1. "O" ring	29. Shift rod cover	54. Dog clutch
2. Grommet	30. Gasket	55. Pin
2A. Grommet	31. Detent ball	56. Pin retaining screw
3. Water tube bracket	32. Detent spring	60. Propeller shaft
3A. Impeller housing	34. Detent	62. Reverse gear
4. "O" ring	36. Shift lever pin	63. Thrust bearing
5. Impeller plate	37. Gear housing	64. Thrust washer
5A. Impeller lining	38. Shift lever	67. "O" ring
6. Impeller	39. Shift yoke	68. Needle bearing
7. "O" ring	40. Shift shaft	69. Bearing housing
8. Plate	41. Bearing	70. Needle bearing
9. Seal	50. Thrust washer	71. Seals
10. Seal	51. Thrust bearing	72. Thrust bushing
11. Bearing & housing	52. Forward gear	73. Propeller bushing
assy.	12. "O" ring	
13. Adjustment shims		
14. Thrust washer		
15. Thrust bearing		
16. Drive shaft		
17. Needle bearing		
17A. Set screw		
18. Pinion gear		
19. Water screen		
21. Gearcase		
22. Trim tab		
23. Shift rod seal		
25. Shift rod		

NOTE: One rear screw is in trim tab cavity.

Separate gearcase from exhaust housing being careful not to bend shift rod.

To install gearcase, reverse removal procedure. Install a new "O" ring in end of drive shaft and coat splines with a suitable antiseize compound. Check length of gear shift rod (25). With shifter in neutral, distance from mating surface of gearcase (21) to center of hole in top of shift rod should be 22.41 inches (56.92 cm) on 20 inch (50.8 cm) transom models or 27.41 inches (69.62 cm) on 25 inches (63.5 cm) transom models. Top of shift rod should slant forward. Apply OMC Adhesive "M" to gearcase and exhaust housing gasket surfaces. Be sure water tube guides and water tube are installed properly. Apply OMC Gasket Sealing Compound to threads of gearcase screws.

GEARCASE. Gearcase may be disassembled in the following manner: Remove propeller, drain lubricant and remove gearcase as described in previous section. Remove screws securing shift rod cover (29–Fig. OM20-20), unscrew shift rod (25) and remove shift rod and cover as an assembly. Remove water pump housing (5), impeller (6), impeller key and lower plate (8). Remove four screws holding propeller shaft bearing housing (69) and using a suitable puller, remove bearing housing. Discard seals (71) and "O" ring (67). Remove snap rings (66), thrust washer assembly (64 and 63) and slide reverse gear (62) off propeller shaft. A special socket from OMC is available to hold drive shaft so nut securing pinion gear (18) can be removed. After pinion gear retaining nut is removed, unscrew the four screws securing upper drive shaft bearing housing (11). Pull drive shaft and associated parts out of gearcase. A puller may be necessary. Propeller shaft (60) may now be pulled from gearcase complete with forward gear (52), forward gear housing (37) and all associated parts.

Inspect drive shaft splines, bearing surfaces and seal surfaces for wear or damage. Damage splines may be caused by striking a submerged object and bending the exhaust housing. Check parallelism of top and bottom surfaces if questionable. If surfaces are not parallel, renew housing. Do not attempt to straighten it.

Lower drive shaft bearing (17) should only be removed if renewal is intended. Do not reinstall a used bearing. Drive shaft bearing is held in position by a set screw (17A) as well as a press fit in gearcase. Set screw is located on starboard side in area of water intake. After removing set screw, install a suitable tool or OMC special tool with shouldered side of tool against bearing, and drive bearing down into propeller shaft cavity. New bearing is installed using a suitable tool or OMC special tool with lettered end of bearing down. Apply Loctite to set screw (17A) and install.

Forward gear (52) and propeller shaft (60) may be removed from propeller shaft gear housing (37) after dislodging spring (56) and removing dog clutch assembly (55 and 54). Bearing housing and shifter mechanism assembly (38) may be disassembled by driving out shift lever pin (36).

Thickness of shims (13) is varied to adjust mesh position of pinion gear (18) in forward and reverse gear. A shim gage, OMC Special Tool 393185, should be used to determine proper shimming.

Place pinion gear (18) on drive shaft and torque retaining nut to 70-75 ft.-lbs. (95-102 N·m). Install bearing and housing assembly (11), thrust washer (14) and thrust bearing (15). Position drive shaft assembly in special tool as shown in Fig. OM20-21. Tighten preload screw (S–Fig. OM20-21) until groove around circumference of plunger (P) is even with end of preload screw (S), then tighten retaining nut (N). Position OMC Shim Gage 330224 (G) on guide pins of tool base and abut end with bearing and housing assembly (11–Fig. OM20-20). Use a selection of feeler gages (F–Fig. OM20-21) and measure clearance between end of gage 330224 and pinion gear. Rotate bearing and housing assembly (11–Fig. OM20-20) in ¼-turn increments and retake clearance measurement. Subtract the average clearance measurement from 0.030 inch (0.76 mm) to determine the correct shim (13) thickness. Shims (13) are available in 0.003, 0.004 and 0.005 inch thicknesses.

Needle bearings (68 and 70) should not be removed from propeller shaft housing (69) unless renewal is intended. Do not reinstall used bearings. OMC special tools or suitable tools are used to install bearings in housing (69). Seals (71) should be installed so lip on aft seal is towards propeller and lip on forward seal is facing forward.

Assemble gearcase in the following manner: Renew all gaskets, seals and "O" rings. If lower drive shaft bearing (17) or propeller shaft bearings (68 and 70 have been removed, they too should be renewed. Install detent spring (32) and detent ball (31) in blind hole of housing (37). Hold spring and ball in position while installing detent (34). Assemble shift shaft (40), shift lever yoke (39), shift lever (38) and pin (36). Assemble forward gear (52) with thrust bearing (51 and 50) in gear housing. Place clutch (54) on propeller shaft (60) making sure hole in dog clutch is aligned with slot in

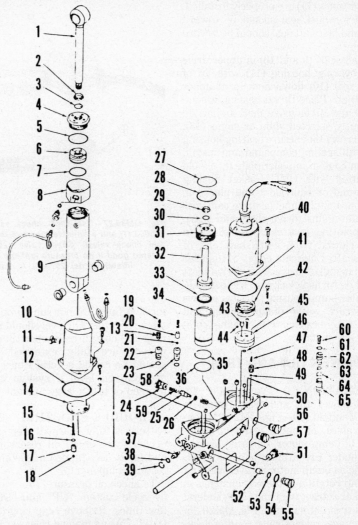

Fig. OM20-25 – Exploded view of hydraulic tilt and trim system.

1. Shaft	19. Spring	35. Retaining ring	51. Separation valve
2. Wiper	20. Spring seat	36. "O" ring	52. Valve piston
3. "O" ring	21. Ball	37. Manual release valve	53. "O" ring
4. End cap	22. Trim up relief valve	38. "O" ring	54. "O" ring
5. "O" ring	23. "O" ring	39. Snap ring	55. Impact letdown valve
6. Piston	24. Reverse lock check	40. Pump motor	56. Trim check valve
7. "O" ring	valve	41. "O" ring	57. Tilt check valve
8. Band	25. Piston	42. Oil pump filter	58. Impact sensor valve
9. Tilt cylinder	26. "O" ring	43. Drive coupling	59. Spring
10. Reservoir	27. Retaining ring	44. Ball	60. Spring
11. Fill plug	28. "O" ring	45. Oil pump	61. "O" ring
12. "O" ring	29. Wiper	46. "O" ring	62. Expansion relief valve
13. Needle	30. "O" ring	47. Spring	core
14. Plate	31. End cap	48. Trim down pump	63. "O" ring
15. Screen	32. Piston	relief valve	64. "O" ring
16. "O" ring	33. Piston ring	49. Seal	65. Expansion relief valve
17. Check valve	34. Trim cylinder	50. Manifold	seat
18. Valve ball			

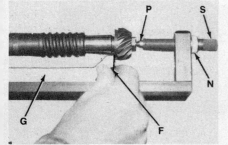

Fig. OM20-21 – View showing drive shaft positioned in OMC Shim Gage 393185. Refer to text for identification of components and procedure for measuring for correct thickness of shims (13–Fig. OM20-20).

propeller shaft and splined dogs are toward forward gear. Insert propeller shaft in forward gear and bearing housing assembly, then insert pin (55) through dog clutch propeller shaft and hole in shift shaft (40). Install pin retaining spring (56). Press shift detent (34) down and place propeller shaft, forward gear and gear housing assembly (37) into position in gearcase. Make sure locating pin (35) is seated in recess provided in gearcase.

Insert drive shaft (16). Install pinion gear retaining nut and tighten to 70-75

ft.-lbs. (90-102 N·m). Install shift rod (25) and shift rod cover (29) as an assembly. Thread shift rod fully into detent (34), back off two turns, pull rod to neutral (middle detent) and adjust for proper length. Refer to shift rod adjustment in REMOVE AND REINSTALL section for specifications.

Assemble thrust bearing (64 and 63) on reverse gear (62) and slide onto propeller shaft (60). Position bearing retainer plate (65) and install snap rings (66). Make sure that "O" ring (67) is fully seated in groove of bearing housing (69) and that seals (71) are properly installed. Lip of forward seal should be toward front and lip of aft seal should be toward propeller.

Install seals (9 and 10) in upper drive shaft bearing housing (11) with lip of lower seal (10) down and lip of upper seal (9) up. Place thrust bearing assembly (14 and 15) on drive shaft and install previously selected shim or shims (13). Coat screws that secure bearing housing (11) with sealing compound and install. Bottom edge of impeller plate (8) should be coated with OMC Gasket Sealing Compound or equivalent and placed in position. Install impeller drive cam with flat side against drive shaft and sharp edge pointing in a clockwise direction when viewed from crankshaft end of drive shaft. Lubricate edges of impeller (6) and install on drive shaft. Drive shaft should be turned clockwise while installing water pump housing (5). Coat screws that secure water pump housing and water tube bracket with sealing compound and install.

POWER TILT AND TRIM

OPERATION. A hydraulically actuated power tilt and trim system is used. Manifold (50 – Fig. OM20-25) contains valves, oil pump and trim cylinders. Oil pump motor, oil reservoir and tilt cylinder are attached to manifold. Electric oil pump motor is reversible and oil pump rotation is thereby changed to extend or retract trim and tilt cylinders. Note position of valves in Fig. OM20-25. Turn manual release valve counterclockwise to manually raise or lower outboard.

Hydraulic system contains approximately 25 fl. oz. (740 mL) of oil. Recommended oil is OMC Power Trim/Tilt Fluid or DEXRON II automatic transmission fluid. Do not run pump without oil in reservoir. Oil level should reach fill plug (11) hole threads when tilt and trim pistons are fully extended. System should be cycled several times prior to checking oil level if system has been drained or lost a large amount of oil.

TROUBLE-SHOOTING. Be sure battery is fully charged, electrical connections are good, oil reservoir is full and air is not trapped in system before testing components.

To check oil pressure, first momentarily cycle system "UP" and "DOWN" a few times. Remove snap ring (39 – Fig. OM20-25) and manual release valve (37), then install OMC gage "A" as shown in Fig. OM20-26. Operate system in the "UP" direction and observe gage after system stalls out at full extension. Gage reading should not drop below 100-200 psi (700-1400 kPa). Install OMC gage "B." Operate system in the "DOWN" direction and observe gage after system stalls out at fully retracted. Gage

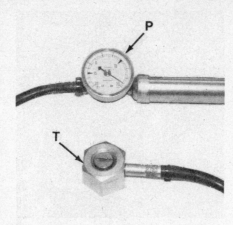

Fig. OM20-27 – Use OMC check valve tester 390063 (T) and a suitable pressure tester (P) to test check valves. Check valve can be considered good if no pressure leakage at approximately 30 psi (207 kPa) is noted.

reading should not drop below 100-200 psi (700-1400 kPa).

To check valves, screw each valve into OMC check valve tester 390063 (T – Fig. OM20-27). Use a suitable pressure tester (P) and apply 30 psi (207 kPa) of pressure to check valve. Check valve can be considered good if no pressure leakage is noted.

Refer to the following for a list of symptoms and probable causes:

Symptoms	Probable Causes
Tilt Leakdown	1, 2, 3, 4, 5 or 6
Trim and Tilt Both Leak	7, 8 or 9
Reverse Lock Does Not Hold	2, 3, 6, 10, 11 or 12
Will Not Trim Out Under Load or Will Not Tilt	1, 2, 7 or 9
Will Not Trim or Tilt Down	2, 8, 10, 11, or 13

Key To Probable Causes
1. Trim Up Relief Valve
2. Manual Release Valve
3. Tilt Cylinder Valve or Seals
4. Tilt Check Valve
5. Impact Letdown Valve
6. Oil Line
7. Trim Cylinders Sleeve "O" Rings or Piston Seals
8. Trim Check Valve
9. Expansion Relief Valve or "O" Rings
10. Filter Valve Seat
11. Impact Sensor Valve
12. Reverse Lock Check Valve
13. Trim Down Pump Relief Valve

OVERHAUL. Oil pump must be serviced as a unit assembly. Motor is not serviceable with the exception of brushes. Refer to Fig. OM20-25 for exploded view of trim and tilt cylinders and manifold components. Keep all components separated during disassembly and identify each component, if needed, to ensure correct position during reassembly.

Fig. OM20-26 – Install OMC gage "A" or "B" into manual release valve (37 – Fig. OM20-25) port as shown to test system oil pressure. Refer to text.

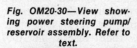

Fig. OM20-30 – View showing power steering pump/reservoir assembly. Refer to text.

  B. Bolts
  F. Fill plug
  I. Idler pulley
  N. Nuts
  P. Plug
  S. Power steering pump/reservoir assy

POWER STEERING

DRIVE BELT TENSION ADJUSTMENT. Loosen idler housing bolts (B – Fig. OM20-30) and rotate nuts (N) clockwise to reduce tension on drive belt and counterclockwise to increase tension on drive belt. Drive belt tension should be 25-30 pounds (111-113 N).

Check belt tension using a suitable tension gage positioned midway between idler pulley (I) and flywheel pulley.

PRESSURE TEST. Remove plug (P – Fig. OM20-30) and install OMC Pressure Gage 983975 or a suitable 2000 psi (13.8 MPa) pressure gage. Remove fill plug (F) and install OMC Power Trim and Tilt fluid or Dexron II in reservoir until fluid level is even with groove around base of dipstick with plug end of dipstick resting on top of fill hole. Install plug (P) and tighten. Start engine and operate at 1000 rpm. Completely extend or retract cylinder rod and observe pressure gage. The pump relief pressure should be 850-1000 psi (5861-6895 kPa).

SEA KING

MONTGOMERY WARD
619 West Chicago Avenue
Chicago, Illinois 60607

SEA KING 35, 45 & 55 HP

Year Produced	35 HP	45 HP	55 HP
1969	27935	27945	27955
	27936	27946	27956
1970	27035	.....	27055
1971	27035	.....	27055
	27036		27056
1972	27235	.....	27256
1973	27435	.....	27456
1974	52035	.....	52056
	52036		
1975	52035	.....	52056
	52036		
1976	52035	.....	52056
	52036		
1977	52035	.....	52056
	52036		
1979	52135	.....	.....
1980	52037	.....	.....

CONDENSED SERVICE DATA

TUNE-UP	35 HP	45 HP	55 HP
Hp/rpm	35/4750	45/4750	55/5250
Bore—Inches	3	3-1/8	3-3/16
Stroke—Inches	2.54	2.75	2.80
Number of Cylinders	2	2	2
Displacement—Cu. In.	35.9	42:18	44.7
Compression at Cranking Speed (Average)	95-105 psi	115-125 psi	145-155 psi
Spark Plug:			
Champion	L4J	L4J*	L4J*
Electrode Gap (Inch)	0.030	0.030*	0.030*
Ignition:			
Point Gap (Inch)	0.020§	0.020§	0.020§
Timing	See Text	See Text	See Text
Carburetor:			
Make	Tillotson	Tillotson	Tillotson
Model	OM or WB	OM or WB	WB
Fuel:Oil Ratio	**50:1	**50:1	**50:1

*A surface gap UL-18V Champion spark plug is used on models with capacitor discharge ignition.
**Use 24:1 fuel for first 10 hours and for severe service.
§Breaker point gap should be 0.015 on models with battery ignition.

SIZES—CLEARANCES (All Values In Inch)	35 HP	45 HP	55 HP
Piston Rings:			
End Gap	0.008-0.015	0.008-0.015	0.008-0.015
Side Clearance	0.002-0.003	0.002-0.003	0.002-0.003
Piston to Cylinder Clearance	0.005	0.005	0.005
Piston Pin Diameter	0.6875-0.68765	0.6875-0.68765	0.6875-0.68765
Crankshaft Bearing Clearance	Roller Bearing	Roller Bearing	Roller Bearing

TIGHTENING TORQUES (All Values In Inch-Pounds Unless Noted)	35 HP	45 HP	55 HP
Connecting Rod	150	150	150
Cylinder Head	270***	270***	270***
Flywheel Nut	75 Ft.-Lbs.	80 Ft.-Lbs.	70 Ft.-Lbs.
Main Bearing Bolts	270	270	270
Standard Screws:			
6-32	9	9	9
10-24	30	30	30
10-32	35	35	35
12-24	45	45	45
¼-20	70	70	70
5/16-18	160	160	160
3/8-16	270	270	270

***Refer to text for tightening cylinder head screws.

LUBRICATION

The power head is lubricated by oil mixed with the fuel. One-third (⅓) pint of two-stroke of Outboard Motor Oil should be mixed with each gallon of gasoline. The amount of oil in the fuel may be reduced after the first 10 hours of operation (motor is broken in), provided the highest quality SAE30 Outboard Motor Oil is used and motor is subjected to normal service only. The minimum recommended fuel:oil ratio is 50:1.

Manufacturer recommends using no-lead automotive gasoline in motors with less than 55 hp although regular or premium gasoline with octane rating of 85 or greater may also be used. Regular or premium automotive gasoline with octane rating of 85 or greater must be used in motors with more than 54 hp.

The lower unit gears and bearings are lubricated by oil contained in the gearcase. A non-corrosive, leaded, Extreme Pressure SAE 90 Gear Oil, should be used. DO NOT use a hypoid type lubricant. The gearcase should be drained and refilled every 100 hours or once each year, and fluid maintained at the level of upper (vent) plug opening.

To fill the gearcase, have motor in an upright position and fill through lower plug hole on starboard side of gearcase until lubricant reaches level of upper vent plug opening. Reinstall and tighten both plugs, using new gaskets if necessary, to assure a water tight seal.

FUEL SYSTEM

CARBURETOR. Tillotson type WB carburetors are used. Refer to Fig. SK6-1). Normal initial setting is one turn open for idle mixture adjustment needle (12). Fixed jet (3) controls high speed mixture. The carburetor model number is stamped on the mounting flange. Float level is 13/32 inch from float to gasket surface. Care must be used in selecting the high speed fixed jet (3). A fixed jet which is too small will result in a lean mixture and possible damage to power head. Jet may be identified by the diameter (in thousandths of an inch) stamped on the visible end of installed jet. Optional jets are available which will improve performance when motor is used in high-altitude locations; optional jet sizes and recommended altitudes are as follows:

35 HP (WB-3A)

Altitude	Jet Size	Part Number
Standard	0.084	014302

35 HP (WB-3C)

Altitude	Jet Size	Part Number
Sea Level-1250 ft.	0.0785	014306
1250-3750 ft.	0.070	013430
3750-6250 ft.	0.068	013967
6250-8250 ft.	0.062	014187

35 HP (WB-12A)

Altitude	Jet Size	Part Number
Sea Level-1250 ft.	0.074	014303
1250-3750 ft.	0.072	015026
3750-6250 ft.	0.070	013430
6250-8250 ft.	0.068	013967

35 HP (WB-12B)

Altitude	Jet Size	Part Number
Sea Level-1250 ft.	0.074	014303
1250-3750 ft.	0.072	015026
3750-6250 ft.	0.070	013430
6250-8250 ft.	0.068	013967

35 HP (WB-17A)

Altitude	Jet Size	Part Number
Sea Level-1250 ft.	0.090	015406
1250-3750 ft.	0.088	013193
3750-6250 ft.	0.086	013949
6250-8250 ft.	0.084	014302

35 HP (WB-17A with "X" stamped on mount flange)

Altitude	Jet Size	Part Number
Standard	0.098	014152

35 HP (WB-17C)

Altitude	Jet Size	Part Number
Sea Level-1250 ft.	0.090	015406
1250-3750 ft.	0.088	013193
3750-6250 ft.	0.086	013949
6250-8250 ft.	0.084	014302

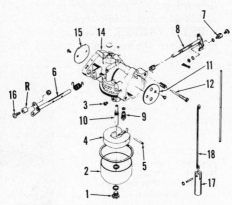

Fig. SK6-1—Exploded view of Tillotson WB type carburetor.

R. Roller
1. Bowl retaining screw
2. Fuel bowl
3. High speed jet
4. Float
5. Float pivot shaft
6. Throttle shaft
7. Connector
8. Choke shaft
9. Inlet needle & seat
10. Main nozzle
11. Choke plate
12. Idle mixture needle
13. Throttle body
14. Throttle body
15. Throttle plate
16. Eccentric screw
17. Choke solenoid plunger
18. Rod

45 HP (WB-4A)

Altitude	Jet Size	Part Number
Standard	0.096	012947

45 HP (WB-4C)

Altitude	Jet Size	Part Number
Sea Level-1250 ft.	0.086	013949
1250-3750 ft.	0.0785	014306
3750-6250 ft.	0.074	014303
6250-8250 ft.	0.068	013967

45 HP (WB-11A)

Altitude	Jet Size	Part Number
Sea Level-1250 ft.	0.082	014109
1250-3750 ft.	0.080	013194
3750-6250 ft.	0.0785	014306
6250-8250 ft.	0.076	013191

55 HP (WB-5A)

Altitude	Jet Size	Part Number
Standard	0.089	013367

55 HP (WB-5B)

Altitude	Jet Size	Part Number
Sea Level-1250 ft.	0.092	014152
1250-3750 ft.	0.084	014302
3750-6250 ft.	0.076	013191
6250-8250 ft.	0.074	014303

55 HP (WB-7A and WB-7B)

Altitude	Jet Size	Part Number
Sea Level-1250 ft.	0.086	013949
1250-3750 ft.	0.084	014302
3750-6250 ft.	0.082	014109
6250-8250 ft.	0.080	013194

55 HP (WB-15A)

Altitude	Jet Size	Part Number
Sea Level-1250 ft.	0.088	013193
1250-3750 ft.	0.086	013949
3750-6250 ft.	0.084	014302
6250-8250 ft.	0.082	014109

55 HP (WB-15A with "X" stamped on mount flange)

Altitude	Jet Size	Part Number
Standard	0.090	015406

55 HP (WB-15C)

Altitude	Jet Size	Part Number
Sea Level-1250 ft.	0.0937	014191
1250-3750 ft.	0.092	014190
3750-6250 ft.	0.090	015406
6250-8250 ft.	0.088	013193

55 HP (WB-27A)

Altitude	Jet Size	Part Number
Sea Level-1250 ft.	0.066	014188
1250-3750 ft.	0.064	014108
3750-6250 ft.	0.062	014187
6250-8250 ft.	0.060	014186

NOTE: Be sure that proper jet is installed before motor is used at a lower altitude.

The position of choke plunger rod (18) should be adjusted in connector (7) so that choke plate (11) is 0.010-0.040 inch open when choke is engaged and plunger (17) is bottomed in solenoid. Make certain that choke plate is free and returns to full open position.

SPEED CONTROL LINKAGE. On all models, ignition timing advance and throttle opening must be synchronized so that throttle is opened as timing is advanced.

To synchronize the linkage, first make certain that ignition timing is correctly set as outlined in IGNITION TIMING paragraph. Shift to forward gear and disconnect link (L—Fig. SK6-3) from tower shaft (T). With carburetor throttle closed, turn the eccentric screw (16) until roller (R) is exactly centered over the scribed line (S). Move the tower shaft (T) to full advance position and move the throttle cam until carburetor throttle is completely open. Vary the length of link (L) until the ball joint connector will just attach. Snap the ball joint connector onto ball stud and check maximum speed in neutral. If maximum rpm in neutral is not 1800-2500 rpm, it may be necessary to readjust speed control linkage.

Idle speed should be 700-800 rpm in forward gear (800-900 rpm in neutral) and is adjusted at idle screw (I).

REED VALVES. "Vee" type intake reed valves are used on all models. The reed plate is located between intake manifold and crankcase.

To remove the reed plate assembly after carburetor is removed, first remove the starter assembly and the screws retaining the intake manifold; then lift off manifold and the reed plate assembly. Refer to Fig. SK6-4.

Reed valve must be smooth and even with no sharp bends or broken reeds. Assembled reeds may stand open a maximum of 0.010 inch at tip end. Check seating visually.

Reed stop setting should be 9/32-inch when measured as shown in Fig. SK6-4. Renew reeds if petals are broken, cracked, warped or bent. Never attempt to bend a reed petal in an effort to improve performance; nor attempt to straighten a damaged reed. Never install a bent or damaged reed. Seating surface of reed plate should be smooth and flat. When installing reed petals and stops, proceed as follows: Install reed petals, stop, and the four retaining screws leaving screws loose. Slide the reed petals as far as possible toward mounting flange of reed plate and reed stops out toward tip of "Vee" as far as possible as indicated by arrows in Fig. SK6-6. Position reed petals and reed stops as outlined to provide maximum overlap; then, tighten the retaining screws.

PUDDLE DRAIN VALVES. All models are equipped with a puddle drain system designed to remove any liquid fuel or oil which might build up in the crankcase; thus providing smoother operation at all speeds and lessening the possibility of spark plug fouling during slow speed operation.

The puddle drain valve housing is located on the starboard side of power head, and can be removed as shown in Fig. SK6-5. The reed-type puddle drain valve petals must seat lightly and evenly against valve plate. Reed stops

Fig. SK6-3—Throttle linkage typcial of all 35-55 hp models. Refer to text for method of checking and adjusting.

A. High speed stop
I. Idle stop
L. Throttle link
N. Neutral stop
R. Roller
S. Scribed line
T. Tower shaft
16. Eccentric screw

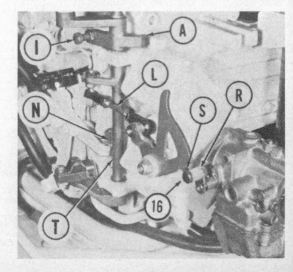

should be adjusted to 0.017-0.023 inch clearance at the tip. Blow out drain passages with compressed air while housing is off.

Later models are equipped with a recirculating puddle drain system. Fluid accumulated in puddle drain during slow speed operation is reintroduced to the cylinders once engine is returned to cruising speed. Inspect hoses and check valves when unit is disassembled.

FUEL PUMP. All models are equipped with a diaphragm type fuel pump which is actuated by pressure and vacuum pulsations from both crankcases as shown in Fig. SK6-6. The two stages operate alternately as shown.

NOTE: Either stage operating independently may permit the motor to run, but not at peak performance.

Most fuel pump service can be performed without removing the assembly from power head. Disconnect the pulse hoses and remove the retaining cap screws; then lift off the pump cover and diaphragm. Remove the sediment

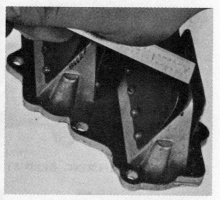

Fig. SK6-4—Reed stop setting should be 9/32 inch when measured as shown. Holes in stops and petals are elongated and should be positioned as shown by arrows for maximum overlap.

Fig. SK6-5—View of puddle drain housing removed showing the two screens.

bowl and strainer. First stage inlet check valve can be driven out from below, using a ½-inch diameter drift. First stage outlet check valve can be lifted out after removing the retaining screws. The check valves must be installed to permit fuel to flow in the proper direction as shown. To renew the second stage outlet check valve, it is first necessary to remove pump body from power head, remove outlet fuel elbow and drive the check valve out from below. Check valve will be damaged, and a new unit must be installed. DO NOT remove the valve unless renewal is indicated. Install new valve carefully, using an 11/16-inch diameter punch.

Renew the diaphragm if cracked or torn, or badly distorted. Install check valves carefully to prevent damage, and reassemble by reversing the disassembly procedure.

IGNITION SYSTEM

Thirty-five horsepower models are equipped with either a battery or magneto ignition system. Forty-five hp models may be equipped with magneto ignition, battery ignition with a flywheel mounted alternator or capacitor discharge ignition. Fifty-five hp models may be equipped wtih magneto ignition, battery ignition or capacitor discharge ignition. Refer to the appropriate following paragraphs after determining type of ignition used.

All Models

R&R FLYWHEEL. A special puller (T-8931) is used to remove the flywheel on late model units. Pulling bosses are provided on the flywheel for puller installation.

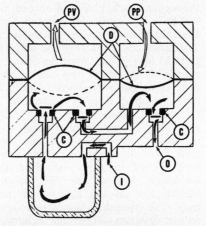

Fig. SK6-6—Cross-sectional view of the two stage fuel pump. Broken lines indicate position of diaphragm when pulse pressure and vacuum are reversed.

C. Check valves	O. Fuel outlet
D. Diaphragm	PP. Pulse pressure
I. Fuel inlet	PV. Pulse vacuum

NOTE: Models with alternators must have the three screws that secure the emergency starter collar removed, as well as the emergency starter collar. Make certain that aligning marks on flywheel and emergency starter collar are matched when reassembling.

Flywheel may be removed from models without puller bosses by using a special knockout nut (T-2910). Install the tool and apply upward pressure to rim of flywheel, then bump the tool sharply with a hammer to loosen flywheel from tapered portion of crankshaft.

The manufacturer recommends that mating surfaces of flywheel and crankshaft be lapped before flywheel is reinstalled. If evidence of working exists proceed as follows:

Remove the flywheel key and apply a light coating of valve grinding or lapping compound to tapered portion of crankshaft. Install the flywheel without the key or crankshaft nut and rotate flywheel gently back and forth about ¼-turn. Move flywheel 90° and repeat the operation. Lift off the flywheel, wipe off excess lapping compound and carefully examine crankshaft. A minimum of 90% surface contact should be indicated by the polished surface; continue lapping only if insufficient contact is evident. Thoroughly clean the crankshaft and flywheel bore to remove all traces of lapping compound, then clean both surfaces with a nonoily solvent.

Reinstall crankshaft key and flywheel, then tighten flywheel nut to torque indicated in CONDENSED SERVICE DATA table.

POINT ADJUSTMENT. Breaker point gap should be 0.020 inch for models with magneto ignition and 0.015 inch for all other models. Both sets of points must be adjusted as nearly alike as possible.

NOTE: A variation of 0.0015-inch in point adjustment will change ignition timing one degree.

To adjust the points, first remove the flywheel as previously outlined. Turn crankshaft clockwise until the rub block on one set of points is resting on high point of breaker cam approximately 10° from first point of maximum opening. Mark the exact location of rub block contact for use in adjusting the other set of points. Loosen breaker point mounting screws and adjust point gap until a slight drag exists using a 0.020-inch feeler gage for models with magneto ignition and 0.015 feeler gage for all other models.

Turn crankshaft until the previously installed mark on breaker cam is aligned with the rub block on the other set of points and adjust the other set of points in the same manner.

NOTE: If mid-range of breaker plate movement is used, final positioning can be made by moving the speed control handle to correctly position the rub block at the same point of breaker cam.

Magneto Ignition

IGNITION TIMING. If ignition points are carefully adjusted as previously outlined and advance timing marks align when speed control linkage contacts the maximum advance stop, timing can be assumed to be correct. A punch mark on stator plate should align with the crankcase parting line on PORT side of power head at maximum ignition advance.

If maximum advance timing marks do not align, shorten or lenghten the timing advance link (L—Fig. SK6-7).

If advance timing marks are not present or if timing is in doubt, the manufacturer makes a special tool available for checking advance timing position. Refer to Fig. SK6-8 and the following paragraphs.

Two different timing tools are used. Special tool T-8938 is used to time 35 hp Manual Tiller models after Ser. No. 3001 and 45 hp Manual Tiller models after Ser. No. 3001. Special tool TA-2937-1 is used to time all other models.

To check the timing using the special tool, first make sure ignition points are properly adjusted as previously outlined. Remove upper spark plug and thread the tool body into spark plug opening. Turn crankshaft until upper piston is at TDC, then insert gage rod

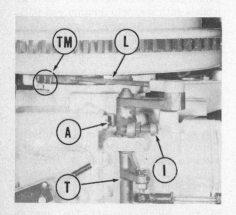

Fig. SK6-7—Timing advance linkage for motors equipped with battery ignition. Models equipped with magneto are similar except for location of timing marks (TM).

A. Advance stop
I. Idle stop
L. Link
T. Tower shaft
TM. Timing marks

into tool bore, 25 to 55 hp end out, until rod end contacts piston crown. With piston at extreme TDC, thread tool body in or out if necessary, until inner scribe line on gage rod is aligned with end of tool body; then turn crankshaft clockwise almost one complete revolution while applying pressure to end of gage rod, until outer scribe line aligns with tool body. Crankshaft should now be at correct position BTDC for maximum ignition advance.

NOTE: Crankshaft should not be rotated counterclockwise.

With crankshaft correctly positioned and breaker points properly adjusted, turn stator plate counterclockwise until points just open, and affix the maximum advance timing punch mark on stator plate.

Battery Ignition

IGNITION TIMING. If ignition breaker point gap is carefully adjusted as previously outlined and advance timing marks align when speed control linkage contacts maximum advance stop, timing can be assumed to be correct. A scribed line on breaker plate should align with a similar mark on starboard side of the upper bearing cage (TM—Fig. SK6-7) at maximum ignition advance.

If maximum advance timing marks do not align, shorten or lengthen the timing advance link (L).

If advance marks are not present or if timing is in doubt, the manufacturer makes a special tool available for checking ignition advance timing. Refer to Fig. SK6-8 and the following paragraph.

To check timing using the special timing tool, first make certain that ignition breaker point gap is correctly adjusted as previously outlined. Remove the upper spark plug and thread the tool body into spark plug opening. Turn crankshaft until upper piston is at TDC, then insert the gage rod with the 25 to 55 hp end out. With the piston at exactly TDC, thread the timing gage body in or out as necessary until the inner scribed line on gage rod is aligned with end of tool body. After gage body is correctly positioned, turn crankshaft clockwise almost one complete revolution while applying pressure to end of gage rod. Stop the crankshaft just as the first (outer) scribed line on rod aligns with tool body. The crankshaft should now be at correct position BTDC for maximum ignition advancement.

NOTE: Crankshaft should not be rotated counterclockwise.

With crankshaft correctly positioned and breaker point gap properly ad-

justed, turn the ignition breaker plate counterclockwise until the breaker points just open. Scribe the maximum advance timing marks on starboard side of breaker plate and upper bearing cage as shown at (TM—Fig. SK6-7).

Capacitor Discharge Ignition

IGNITION TIMING. To adjust ignition timing, remove the flywheel and carefully adjust breaker point gap for both breaker points as previously outlined. Remove both spark plugs and thread body of special timing gage TA-2937-1 into top spark plug opening. Insert the gage rod into tool body, rotate the crankshaft and carefully position top piston at exactly TDC.

NOTE: Gage rod should be installed with 25 to 55 hp end out.

With the top piston at TDC, thread timing tool body in or out as necessary until the inner scribed line on gage rod is aligned with end of tool body. After gage body is correctly positioned, turn the crankshaft clockwise almost one complete revolution while applying pressure to end of gage rod. Stop the crankshaft just as the first (outer) scribed line on rod aligns with tool body. The crankshaft should be at correct positon BTDC for maximum ignition advance timing.

NOTE: Crankshaft should not be rotated counterclockwise.

With the crankshaft correctly positioned and breaker point gap properly adjusted, connect one lead from timing test light (with battery) or ohmmeter to the breaker point terminal for white/brown wire and ground other test lead to motor. Move the speed control from slow toward fast (maximum advance) speed position and observe the test light or ohmmeter. The breaker points should just open (test light goes off or ohmmeter registers infinite resistance) when the speed control reaches maximum ignition advance. If the breaker points do not open, shorten link (L—Fig. SK6-7). If breaker points open too soon, lengthen link (L). If desired, the other set of breaker points can be synchronized using the timing gage (Fig. SK6-8) in the lower spark plug opening. Method of locating crankshaft for checking lower cylinder timing is similar. Timing test light or ohmmeter

Fig. SK6-8—Special tool is available for positioning piston at correct timing position. Refer to text for proper tool usage.

should be connected to breaker point terminal with brown wire. Synchronize the breaker points to open at correct time by varying the breaker point gap.

TROUBLESHOOTING. Use only approved procedures when testing to prevent damage to components. The fuel system should be checked to make certain that faulty running is not caused by incorrect fuel mixture or contaminated fuel.

CHECKING FOR SPARK. Remove the spark plugs and attach spark plug leads to a spark gap tester. With all wiring attached, attempt to start motor using the electric starter.

NOTE: Two conventional spark plugs (such as Champion L4J) with ground electrodes removed can be used to check for spark. Make certain that test plug shell is grounded against power head when checking.

If good regular spark occurs at tester (or test plugs), check fuel system and spark plugs. Also, make certain that wires from breaker points (1 and 2—Fig. SK6-9) to C-D unit (3), from C-D unit to ignition coils (4 and 5) and from coils to spark plugs are correct to provide spark to the proper cylinder.

If spark does not occur at tester (or test plugs), make certain that the small black wires on ignition coils (4 and 5) are attached to the negative (-) terminals and are securely grounded to the coil clamp screws. Also check continuity of the spark plug wires. If test plugs still do not spark, proceed with following checks.

WIRING. Engine missing, surging or failure to start can be caused by loose connections, corroded connections or short circuits. Electrical system components may also be damaged by faulty connections or short circuits.

Attach one lead of voltmeter to the terminal (10—Fig. SK6-9) where the blue wires are attached. Ground the other test lead to the metal case (housing) of the C-D unit (3). Turn the ignition switch ON and observe the test light or voltmeter. If the test light glows, current is available to the C-D unit. If checking with a voltmeter, voltage should be the same as available at the battery.

If test light does not glow or voltmeter indicates zero or low voltage, check the circuit breaker (6). If the circuit breaker is not faulty, check for broken wires, loose connections, faulty ignition switch or improper ground. Make certain that C-D unit (3) is properly grounded. Mounting surfaces on bracket and C-D unit must be free of all paint and the mounting bracket to motor ground wire must provide a good ground connection. Check the ground strap between power head and support plate. Before proceeding with remaining tests, make certain current is available to the C-D unit.

BREAKER POINTS. The breaker points are used to trigger the ignition system. Failure of breaker points to make contact (open circuit) or failure to break contact (short circuit) will prevent ignition just as in conventional magneto or battery ignition systems.

Remove the flywheel and check condition and gap of the breaker points as outlined in the preceding POINT ADJUSTMENT paragraphs. Check condition of all wires, making certain that ground wire from breaker plate to the alternator stator has good contact, especially at the stator end. Varnish should be scraped from stator before attaching ground wire. Check the BROWN and the WHITE/BROWN wires for short circuit to ground, for loose connections and for broken wire. Refer to IGNITION TIMING paragraphs and Fig. SK6-9. Make certain that breaker point wires and coil wires are properly connected to provide spark to the correct cylinder.

IGNITION COILS AND C-D UNIT. If the preceding checks do not indicate any malfunctions, the ignition coils can be tested using an ignition tester available from the following sources:

GRAHAM-LEE ELECTRONICS, INC.
4220 Central Ave. N.E.
Minneapolis, Minn. 55421

MERC-O-TRONIC INSTRUMENTS
CORP.
215 Branch St.
Almont, Mich. 48003

Fig. SK6-9—Wiring diagram for 55 hp motors with capacitor discharge ignition system. Yellow wires are for starting system, purple for charging, white for tachometer, green for choke, orange for heat indicator, red for battery positive, blue for ignition and black for ground.

1. Breaker points for top cylinder
2. Breaker points for bottom cylinder
3. Ignition capacitor discharge unit
4. Coil for top cylinder
5. Coil for bottom cylinder
6. Circuit breaker
7. Ignition and start switch
8. Alternator and stator
9. Rectifier
10. Terminal block at motor
11. Terminal block at dashboard
12. Alternator ground
13. Battery
14. Neutral interlock switch
15. Starter solenoid
16. Starter motor
17. Choke solenoid

Illustrations Courtesy Montgomery Ward

An alternate method of checking is possible as follows:

Connect one lead of a 12 volt test light to each of the two primary terminals of one ignition coil. Turn ignition switch to the ON position, attempt to start motor with the electric starter and observe the test light.

NOTE: After checking one of the ignition coils, connect the 12 volt test light to the primary terminals of the other coil and check the coil.

If the 12 volt test light flashes but spark did not occur at the test plug as tested in the CHECKING FOR SPARK paragraphs, the coil or attaching wires are faulty.

NOTE: The test plug connected to the high tension spark plug wire will not fire with test light connected across the primary terminals. Inspect the black ground wire from negative (-) terminal of coil to the coil clamp screw and the high tension spark plug wire.

If the 12 volt test light does not flash, when connected to the coil primary terminals, make certain that current is available to the C-D unit as outlined in WIRING paragraphs. Make certain that breaker points and associ-ated wires are not faulty as outlined in the BREAKER POINTS paragraphs in the TROUBLESHOOTING section. If current is still not available to the coil primary terminals, the C-D unit should be renewed.

COOLING SYSTEM

THERMOSTAT. The thermostat is located beneath a separate housing on top, rear face of cylinder head as shown in Fig. SK6-10. When installing the thermostat, position with "Vee" slot in visible end up as shown. Power head will overheat if run without thermostat installed.

WATER PUMP. All motors are equipped with a rubber impeller type water pump. Refer to Figs. SK6-11, SK6-18 and SK6-19. The water pump is mounted in the lower unit drive shaft housing (upper gearcase).

When cooling system problems are encountered, first check the thermostat to see that it is operating properly. Check the water inlet for plugging or partial stoppage, then if trouble is not corrected, remove the lower unit gearcase as outlined in LOWER UNIT section, and check the condition of water pump, water passages and sealing surfaces.

POWER HEAD

REMOVE AND DISASSEMBLE. To overhaul the power head, clamp the motor on a stand or support and remove the engine cover (shroud) and motor leg covers. Remove the starter, flywheel and magneto or alternator; fuel pump, carburetor and intake manifold. Disconnect all interfering wiring and linkage. Remove the cylinder head, and transfer port and exhaust covers if major repairs are required. Remove the power head attaching screws and lift off the cylinder block, crankshaft and associated parts as a unit.

NOTE: One of the power head attaching screws is located underneath the rear exhaust cover as shown in Fig. SK6-12. Cover must be removed for access to the screw.

To disassemble the power head, unbolt and remove the upper bearing cage; then unbolt and remove the crankcase front half. Pry slots are provided adjacent to retaining dowels for separating the crankcase; DO NOT pry on machined mating surfaces of cylinder block and crankcase front half.

Crankshaft, pistons and bearings are now accessible for removal and overhaul as outlined in the appropriate following paragraphs. Assemble as outlined in the ASSEMBLY paragraph.

ASSEMBLY. When reassembling, make sure all joint and gasket surfaces are clean, free from nicks and burrs, warped surfaces or hardenend cement or carbon. The crankcase and inlet manifolds must be completely sealed against both vacuum and pressure. Exhaust manifold and cylinder head must be sealed against water leakage and pressure. Mating surfaces of exhaust areas between power head and motor leg must form a tight seal.

Use a thin coating of Loctite, Grade "D" on upper and lower bearing bores of both halves of crankcase; and No. 1 Permatex on cap screw threads. The crankshaft upper seal should be installed with LOWER edge 0.150 inch from bearing counterbore as shown at (B – Fig. SK6-13).

Apply 3M-EC750 Sealer to mating surfaces of crankcase and to center main bearing bore; and install crankcase front half immediately. Tighten main bearing bolts to a torque of 270 inch-pounds. Make sure crankshaft turns freely before proceeding with assembly.

When installing cylinder head, coat the first ¾-inch of screw threads with "Permatex #2" or equivalent. Tighten the retaining screws progressively from the center outward. First to 100-125 inch-pounds torque, then to an even torque of 265-275 inch-pounds. After motor has been test run and cooled, retorque screws to 265-275 inch-pounds.

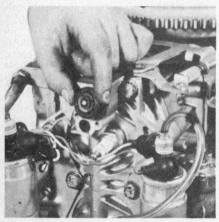

Fig. SK6-10—Removing thermostat from cylinder head. "Vee" slot should point up when thermostat is installed.

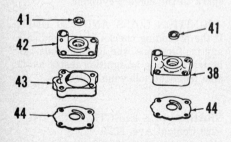

Fig. SK6-11—Variations of water pump bodies used on some models. Refer also to Figs. SK6-18 and SK6-19.

38. Water pump body
41. Seal
42. Cover
43. Pump housing
44. Back plate

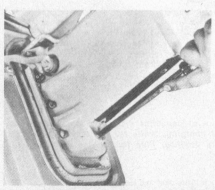

Fig. SK6-12—Rear exhaust cover must be removed from motor leg for access to power head rear attaching screw.

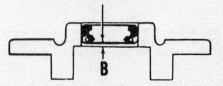

Fig. SK6-13—Cross-sectional view of crankshaft upper bearing cage showing correct seal location. Clearance (B) should be 0.150 inch.

PISTONS, PINS, RINGS & CYLINDERS. Piston on all models except late 55 hp models are fitted with three rings, while late 55 hp model pistons have two piston rings. Piston rings should be installed with the bevelled inner edge toward closed end of piston. Rings are pinned in place to prevent rotation in ring grooves.

The piston pin on early models is a tight press fit in connecting rod and a floating fit in piston bores. The special tool, Part No. T2990, should be used to install piston pin. Piston pin on later models rides in roller bearing in connecting rod. When assembling piston, pin and connecting rod, make sure long, tapering side of piston is assembled for installation toward exhaust side of cylinder and correlation marks (M—Fig. SK6-14) and lubrication hole (H) toward top (flywheel) end of crankshaft. Piston pin must be centered in connecting rod bore so that neither end of pin will extend through piston boss as rod is moved from side to side. All friction surfaces should be lubricated with new engine oil when assembling.

Pistons are available in standard sizes on all models and in oversizes on some models.

CONNECTING RODS, BEARINGS AND CRANKSHAFT. Before detaching connecting rods from crankshaft, make certain that rod and cap are properly marked for correct assembly to each other and in the correct cylinder. The needle rollers and cages at crankpin end of connecting rod should be kept with the assembly and not interchanged.

The bearing rollers and cages used in the two connecting rods and center main bearings are available only as a set which contains the rollers and cage halves for one bearing. The complete assembly should be installed whenever renewal is indicated. Bearing cages have bevelled match marks as shown by arrow, Fig. SK6-15. Match marks must be installed together and toward top (flywheel) end of crankshaft.

Upper main bearing is available only as an assembly with the crankshaft; bearing should not be removed from crankshaft when power head is being overhauled.

A non-fibrous grease can be used to hold loose needle bearing in position during assembly. All friction surfaces should be lubricated with new engine oil. Check frequently as power head is being assembled, for binding or locking of the moving parts. If binding occurs, remove the cause before proceeding with the assembly. When assembling, follow the procedures outlined in the ASSEMBLY paragraphs. Tightening torques are given in the CONDENSED SERVICE DATA tables.

Fig. SK6-15—When installing needle bearing cages, make sure bevelled ends (arrow) are together and to the top.

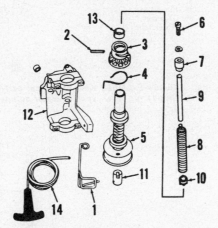

Fig. SK6-16—Exploded view of recoil starter assembly. Pinion (3) meshes with teeth on flywheel.

1. Rope guide
2. Drive pin
3. Pinion
4. Pinion spring
5. Starter spool
6. Lock screw
7. Spring drive
8. Recoil spring
9. Guide post
10. Retainer
11. Retainer extension
12. Mounting bracket
13. Interlock guide
14. Rope

MANUAL STARTER

Fig. SK6-16 shows an exploded view of the recoil starter assembly. Starter pinion (3) engages a starter ring gear on the flywheel.

To disassemble the starter, first remove the engine cover, then remove screw (6) in top of starter shaft.

NOTE: This screw locks pin (2) in place.

Thread the special tool (Part No. T-3139-1) in threaded hole from which screw (6) was removed. Tighten the tool until it bottoms; then turn tool handle slightly counterclockwise to relieve recoil spring tension, and push out pin (2). Allow the tool and spring drive (7) to turn clockwise to unwind the recoil spring (8). Pull up on tool to remove the recoil spring and components. Guide post (9) and spring retainer (10) can be lifted out after recoil spring is removed.

Recoil spring, pinion (3) or associated parts can be renewed at this time. To renew the starter rope, remove clamps (12) then remove the spool. Thread rope through hole in lower end of spool (5) and install the rope retainer approximately ½-inch from end of rope. Pull tight, then fully wind the rope onto spool and reinstall assembly. Make certain that retainer extension (11) is in place. With recoil spring and drive pinion (3) installed, use the special tool to wind the recoil spring counterclockwise eight turns. Align the holes in pinion (3), spool (5) and spring drive (7); then install the drive pin (2). Remove the tool and secure the pin with the locking screw (6). Recoil spring cavity should be partially filled with Lubriplate or similar grease when reassembling.

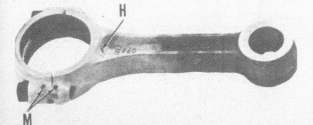

Fig. SK6-16A—View showing tool (T3139) used to pre-load the recoil spring.

Fig. SK6-14—Correlation marks (M) and oil hole (H) should be toward the top when connecting rod is installed.

PROPELLER

The propellers for normal use have three blades and are protected by a cushioning-slip clutch. Various propellers are available and should be selected to provide full throttle operation within the recommended limits of 4500-5000 rpm for 1969 fifty-five hp motors; 5000-5500 rpm for 1970 and later fifty-five hp motors; 3000-4000 rpm for 35 hp and 45 hp Manual Tiller motors after serial number 3001; 4400-5100 rpm for all other 35 and 45 hp motors. Propellers other than those designed for the motor should not be used.

LOWER UNIT

R&R AND OVERHAUL. To remove the lower unit gearcase and drive shaft housing on early style lower unit shown in Fig. SK6-18, first remove the motor leg covers and disconnect the shift rod coupler as shown in Fig. SK6-17, remove the screws securing drive shaft housing to motor leg and remove the complete lower unit drive assembly.

To remove lower unit on later style lower unit shown in Fig. SK6-19, remove motor leg covers and unbolt lower unit from motor leg. Remove pin (43) connecting intermediate shift rod (1) and lower shift rod (10). Separate lower unit from motor leg.

Drain the gearcase and secure gearcase skeg in a vise. Disassemble and remove the drive shaft and water pump assembly (32 through 38—Fig. SK6-18 or SK6-19). Remove propeller nut, pin (30) and propeller (29). Carefully clean exposed end of propeller shaft and remove the two screws securing propeller shaft bearing cage (27) to gearcase. Rotate the bearing cage approximately ½-turn until tabs

are accessible from the sides; then using a soft hammer, gently tap the bearing cage rearward out of gearcase. Remove the gearcase rear retaining stud nut working through propeller shaft opening as shown in Fig. SK6-20.

Remove shift rod (1—Fig. SK6-18 or SK6-19), nut (2—Fig. SK6-18) and the gearcase front retaining stud nut, then lift off drive shaft housing.

Withdraw drive pinion (31) from top of gearcase and propeller shaft and

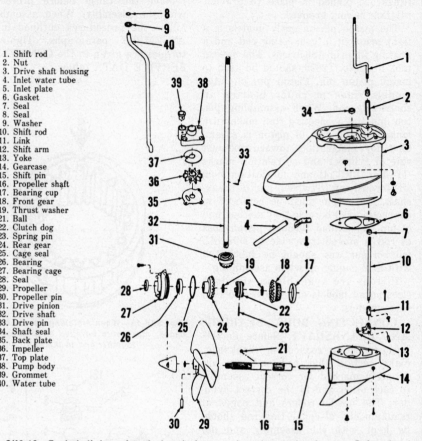

1. Shift rod
2. Nut
3. Drive shaft housing
4. Inlet water tube
5. Inlet plate
6. Gasket
7. Seal
8. Seal
9. Washer
10. Shift rod
11. Link
12. Shift arm
13. Yoke
14. Gearcase
15. Shift pin
16. Propeller shaft
17. Bearing cup
18. Front gear
19. Thrust washer
21. Ball
22. Clutch dog
23. Spring pin
24. Rear gear
25. Cage seal
26. Bearing
27. Bearing cage
28. Seal
29. Propeller
30. Propeller pin
31. Drive pinion
32. Drive shaft
33. Drive pin
34. Shaft seal
35. Back plate
36. Impeller
37. Top plate
38. Pump body
39. Grommet
40. Water tube

Fig. SK6-18—Exploded view of typical early lower unit and associated parts. Refer also to Fig. SK6-11 for other types of water pumps. Refer to Fig. SK6-19 for later type lower unit.

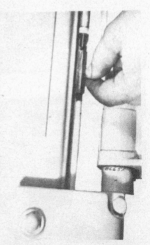

Fig. SK6-17—Disconnect the shift rod coupler before attempting to remove gearcase.

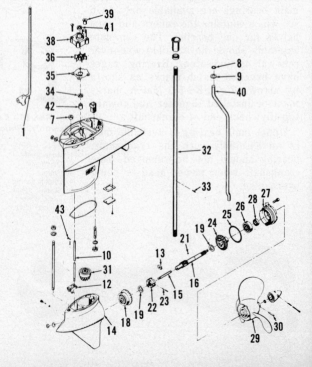

Fig. SK6-19—Exploded view of lower unit used on later models. Refer to Fig. SK6-18 for parts identification except for: 41. Drive shaft seal; 42. Upper drive shaft bearing; 43. Pin.

associated parts through rear opening. Withdraw front and rear gears from propeller shaft. Remove spring pin (23), clutch dog (22) and shift pin (15).

The drive shaft seal (34) should be installed with spring loaded lip toward top (power head). Propeller shaft seal (28) should be installed with spring loaded lip toward outside of bearing cage (27).

Drive gear backlash and bearing preload are fixed and not adjustable. Assemble by reversing the disassembly procedure. Make sure that hole in clutch dog (22) is aligned with slot in propeller shaft (16) and hole in shift pin (15); then, insert spring pin (23).

When reinstalling shift rod (1—Fig. SK6-18) refer to Fig. SK6-21. Upper end of shift rod must point to rear, starboard, so that angle (A) from housing centerline is approximately 28 degrees; and bend of rod must clear pump housing (B) approximately 1/16 inch, when shifted to lowermost (forward detent) position.

After early stage lower unit is installed, refer to Fig. SK6-22 and adjust the shift linkage coupling as follows: Using the shift lever, move the linkage through "Forward," "Neutral" and "Reverse" detent positions and mark the intermediate shift link where it emerges from motor leg as shown at (F, N & R). If marks are not equally spaced (caused by interference in linkage), adjust by means of the turnbuckle connector (C) until interference is removed.

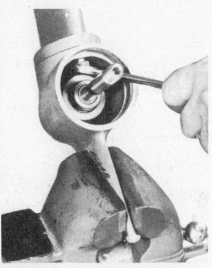

Fig. SK6-20—Gearcase rear nut is accessible through propeller shaft opening as shown.

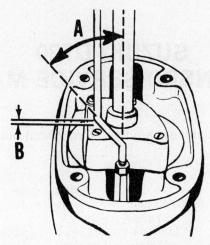

Fig. SK6-21—Before tightening shift rod locknut on early units, angle (A) should be 28° and minimum clearance (B) of 1/16-inch. Refer to text.

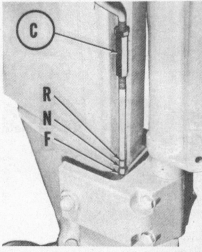

Fig. SK6-22—Check the shift linkage adjustment by marking detent positions as shown. Refer to text.

SUZUKI

SUZUKI AMERICA CORPORATION
3251 E. Imperial Highway
P.O. Box 1000
Brea, California 92621

SUZUKI DT30
CONDENSED SERVICE MANUAL

NOTE: Metric fasteners are used throughout outboard motor.

TUNE-UP

Hp/rpm 30/4800-5500
Bore . . . . .71 mm
　　　　　　　　　　　　　　　　(2.80 in.)
Stroke . . . . .63 mm
　　　　　　　　　　　　　　　　(2.48 in.)
Number of Cylinders 2
Displacement . . . . .499 cc
　　　　　　　　　　　　　　　　(30.45 cu. in.)
Spark Plug:
　NGK BR7HS
　Electrode Gap . . . . .0.9-1.0 mm
　　　　　　　　　　　　　　　　(0.035-0.039 in.)
Ignition Type . . . . .CDI
Carburetor Make . . . . .Mikuni
Idle Speed (in gear) . . . . .650-700 rpm
Fuel:Oil Ratio 50:1

SIZES—CLEARANCES

Piston Ring End Gap .0.2-0.4 mm
　　　　　　　　　　　　　　　　(0.008-0.016 in.)
Piston to Cylinder Clearance . . . . .0.067-0.082 mm
　　　　　　　　　　　　　　　　(0.0026-0.0032 in.)
Piston Pin Diameter . . . . .17.995-18.000 mm
　　　　　　　　　　　　　　　　(0.7085-0.7087 in.)
Max. Crankshaft Runout at Main
　Bearing Journal . . . . .0.05 mm
　　　　　　　　　　　　　　　　(0.002 in.)
Max. Connecting Rod Small End
　Side Shake . . . . .5.0 mm
　　　　　　　　　　　　　　　　(0.020 in.)

TIGHTENING TORQUES

Power Head Mounting Screws . . . . .15-20 N·m
　　　　　　　　　　　　　　　　(11-14 ft.-lbs.)
Crankcase:
　6 mm . . . . .8-12 N·m
　　　　　　　　　　　　　　　　(6-8 ft.-lbs.)
　8 mm . . . . .20-26 N·m
　　　　　　　　　　　　　　　　(14-19 ft.-lbs.)

TIGHTENING TORQUES CONT.

Flywheel Nut . . . . .130-150 N·m
　　　　　　　　　　　　　　　　(94-108 ft.-lbs.)
Cylinder Head Screws:
　6 mm . . . . .8-12 N·m
　　　　　　　　　　　　　　　　(6-8 ft.-lbs.)
　8 mm . . . . .20-26 N·m
　　　　　　　　　　　　　　　　(14-19 ft.-lbs.)
Gearcase Pinion Nut .18-22 N·m
　　　　　　　　　　　　　　　　(13-16 ft.-lbs.)
Propeller Shaft Nut . . . . .27-30 N·m
　　　　　　　　　　　　　　　　(19-21 ft.-lbs.)
Standard Screws:
　Unmarked or Marked "4"
　　5 mm . . . . .2-4 N·m
　　　　　　　　　　　　　　　　(2-3 ft.-lbs.)
　　6 mm . . . . .4-7 N·m
　　　　　　　　　　　　　　　　(3-5 ft.-lbs.)
　　8 mm . . . . .10-16 N·m
　　　　　　　　　　　　　　　　(7-12 ft.-lbs.)
　　10 mm . . . . .22-35 N·m
　　　　　　　　　　　　　　　　(16-26 ft.-lbs.)
　Stainless Steel
　　5 mm . . . . .2-4 N·m
　　　　　　　　　　　　　　　　(2-3 ft.-lbs.)
　　6 mm . . . . .6-10 N·m
　　　　　　　　　　　　　　　　(5-7 ft.-lbs.)
　　8 mm . . . . .15-20 N·m
　　　　　　　　　　　　　　　　(11-15 ft.-lbs.)
　　10 mm . . . . .34-41 N·m
　　　　　　　　　　　　　　　　(25-30 ft.-lbs.)
　Marked "7" or SAE Grade 5
　　5 mm . . . . .3-6 N·m
　　　　　　　　　　　　　　　　(2-5 ft.-lbs.)
　　6 mm . . . . .8-12 N·m
　　　　　　　　　　　　　　　　(6-9 ft.-lbs.)
　　8 mm . . . . .18-28 N·m
　　　　　　　　　　　　　　　　(13-20 ft.-lbs.)
　　10 mm . . . . .40-60 N·m
　　　　　　　　　　　　　　　　(29-44 ft.-lbs.)

LUBRICATION

The power head is lubricated by oil mixed with the fuel. Fuel:oil ratios should be 30:1 during break-in of a new or rebuilt engine and 50:1 for normal service when using a BIA certified two-stroke engine oil or Suzuki BIA oil. Manufacturer recommends regular or no-lead automotive gasoline having an 85-95 octane rating. Gasoline and oil should be thoroughly mixed.

The lower unit gears and bearings are lubricated by approximately 230 mL (7.77 ozs.) of SAE 90 hypoid outboard gear oil. Reinstall vent and fill plugs securely using a new gasket, if necessary, to ensure a water tight seal.

FUEL SYSTEM

CARBURETOR. A Mikuni B32-28 is used. Refer to Fig. SZ11-1 for exploded view. Initial setting of pilot air screw (6) from a lightly seated position should be 1¼-1¾ turns. Final carburetor adjustment should be made with engine at normal operating temperature and running in forward gear. Adjust idle speed screw (2) so engine idles at approximately 650-700 rpm. Adjust pilot air screw so engine idles smooth and will accelerate cleanly without hesitation. If necessary, readjust idle speed screw to obtain 650-700 rpm idle speed.

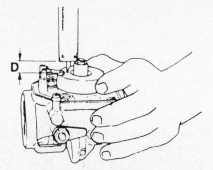

Fig. SZ11-2—Distance (D) for correct float level should be 10-12 mm (0.394-0.472 in.).

Main fuel metering is controlled by main jet (10). Standard main jet size for normal operation is #160. Standard pilot jet (4) size is #77.5.

To check float level, remove float bowl (14) and invert carburetor body (1). Distance (D–Fig. SZ11-2) between main jet and bottom of float should be 10-12 mm (0.394-0.472 in.). Adjust float level by bending float tang.

FUEL FILTER. A fuel filter assembly is used to filter the fuel prior to entering the fuel pump assembly. Periodically unscrew cup (5–Fig. SZ11-3) from base (1) and withdraw filter element (4). Clean cup (5) and filter element (4) in a suitable solvent and blow dry with clean compressed air. Inspect filter element (4). If excessive blockage or damage is noted, then the element must be renewed.

Reassembly is reverse order of disassembly. Renew "O" ring (3) and, if needed, seal (2) during reassembly.

FUEL PUMP. A diaphragm fuel pump (Fig. SZ11-4) is mounted on the side of power head cylinder block and is actuated by pressure and vacuum pulsations from the engine crankcase.

When servicing pump, scribe reference marks across pump body to aid in reassembly. Defective or questionable parts should be renewed. Diaphragm should be renewed if air leaks or cracks are found, or if deterioration is evident.

REED VALVES. The reed valves are located on a reed plate that is located behind the intake manifold. The intake manifold must be removed in order to remove reed plate and service reed valves.

Renew reed valves (2–Fig. SZ11-5) if petals are broken, cracked, warped, rusted or bent. Tip of reed petal must not stand open more than 0.2 mm (0.008 in.) from contact surface. Reed stop opening (0) should be 6.0-6.4 mm (0.24-0.25 in.).

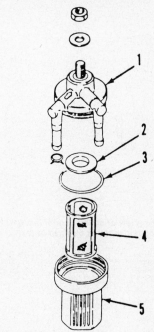

Fig. SZ11-3—Exploded view of fuel filter assembly.

1. Base	
2. Seal	4. Element
3. "O" ring	5. Cup

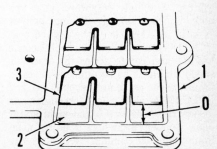

Fig. SZ11-4—Exploded view of diaphragm type fuel pump.

1. Cover	
2. Diaphragm	
3. Gasket	6. Gasket
4. Valve body	7. Spring
5. Plate	8. Spring seat
	9. Check valve

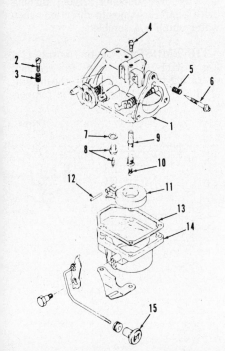

Fig. SZ11-1—Exploded view of Mikuni B32-28 carburetor.

1. Body	
2. Idle speed screw	
3. Spring	9. Main nozzle
4. Pilot jet	10. Main jet
5. Spring	11. Float
6. Pilot air screw	12. Pin
7. Gasket	13. Gasket
8. Needle & seat	14. Float bowl
	15. Choke knob

Fig. SZ11-5—View identifying reed plate (1), reed valves (2) and reed stops (3). Reed stop opening (0) should be 6.0-6.4 mm (0.24-0.25 in.).

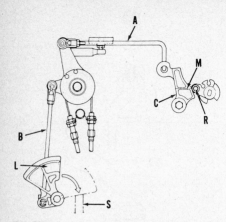

Fig. SZ11-6—View of speed control linkage. Adjust components as outlined in text.

A. Rod
B. Rod
C. Throttle cam
L. Throttle limiter
M. Mark
R. Roller
S. Stopper

SPEED CONTROL LINKAGE.

Place twist grip in the full closed position. Stator plate stopper (P – Fig. SZ11-8) should be in contact with cylinder block boss (D). Adjust rod (A – Fig. SZ11-6) length until mark (M) on throttle cam (C) is centered with roller (R). Rotate twist grip to the full throttle position. Stator plate stopper should be in contact with cylinder block boss. Adjust rod (B) length until throttle limiter (L) contacts stopper (S) on bottom engine cover.

IGNITION

A breakerless, capacitor discharge ignition system is used. Refer to Fig. SZ11-7 for wiring diagram.

Full throttle and full ignition advance should occur simultaneously. The ignition timing is mechanincally advanced and must be synchronized with throttle opening.

To check ignition timing, first immerse lower unit of outboard motor in water. Connect a suitable tachometer to the engine. Connect a power timing light to upper spark plug. Start the engine and warm up to normal operating temperature. Shift into "Forward" gear and note ignition timing. Timing pointer (T – Fig. SZ11-8) should be aligned with 2° ATDC mark (A) on flywheel. Loosen locknut and rotate screw (S) until idle speed timing is as recommended. Maximum advance timing should be 25° BTDC (M) at 5000 rpm. Stop engine and loosen cap screws (C) and slide stator plate stopper (P) in slots to adjust maximum advance timing. Retighten cap screws (C) after recommended maximum advance timing is obtained. Reset idel speed timing as previously recommended.

If ignition malfunction occurs, check condition of spark plugs, all wires and connections before trouble-shooting ignition circuit. Using Suzuki pocket tester 09900-25002 or a suitable ohmmeter, refer to the following test specifications and procedures to aid trouble-shooting.

To check secondary coil resistance of CDI unit, detach spark plug wires at spark plugs. Connect a tester lead to terminal end of each spark plug wire. Secondary coil resistance should be 2136-3204 ohms at 20°C (68°F).

Remove top cover of electrical parts holder for access to wire connectors. Remove top three-wire coupler and separate. To check charge coil (Fig. SZ11-7), connect a tester lead to black wire with red tracer and black wire of three-wire connector leading to stator plate. Charge coil can be considered satisfactory if resistance reading is within the limits of 102-154 ohms at 20°C (68°F).

To check pulser coil, connect a tester lead to red wire with white tracer and black wire of three-wire connector leading to stator plate. Pulser coil can be considered satisfactory if resistance reading is within the limits of 27.9-41.9 ohms at 20°C (68°F).

Check condition of battery lighting coil by separating connectors of yellow wire and red wire. Connect a tester lead to terminal end of wires leading to stator plate. Lighting coil can be considered satisfactory if resistance reading is within the limits of 0.24-0.36 ohms at 20°C (68°F).

If no component is found faulty in the previous tests, then the CDI unit must be renewed.

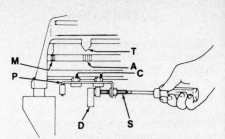

Fig. SZ11-8—Adjust idle speed timing and maximum advance timing as outlined in text.

A. 2° ATDC mark
C. Cap screws
D. Cylinder block boss
M. 25° BTDC mark
P. Stator plate stoppe
S. Idle speed timing adjustment screw
T. Timing pointer

COOLING SYSTEM

WATER PUMP. A rubber impeller type water pump is mounted between the drive shaft housing and gearcase. A key in the drive shaft is used to turn the pump impeller. If cooling system problems are encountered, check water intakes for plugging or partial stoppage. If water intakes are clear, remove gearcase as outlined under LOWER UNIT and check condition of the water pump, water passages and sealing surfaces.

When water pump is disassembled, check condition of impeller (8 – Fig. SZ11-19) and plate (9) for excessive wear. Turn drive shaft clockwise (viewed from top) while placing pump housing over impeller. Avoid turning drive shaft in opposite direction when water pump is assembled.

THERMOSTAT. A thermostat (7 – Fig. SZ11-14) is used to regulate operating temperature. The thermostat should start to open with the temper-

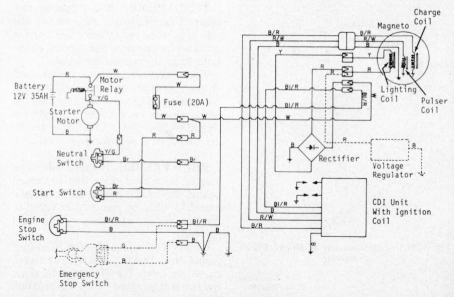

Fig. SZ11-7—Wiring diagram of electrical system on models with electric starter.

B. Black	W. White	Br. Brown	
G. Green	Y. Yellow	B/R. Black with red tracer	R/W. Red with white tracer
R. Red	Bl. Blue	Bl/R. Blue with red tracer	Y/G. Yellow with green tracer

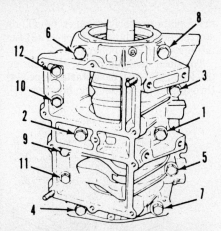

Fig. SZ11-9—Tighten crankcase screws in the sequence shown. Refer to CONDENSED SERVICE DATA for screw torques.

ature range of 48.5°-5.15°C (119°-125°F). Thermostat can be removed for inspection or renewal by removing cylinder head cover (6).

POWER HEAD

REMOVE AND REINSTALL. To remove the power head, first remove engine's top cover. Disconnect throttle cables, throttle limiting rod, fuel inlet hose at lower engine cover connector, choke knob and wires which will interfere with power head removal. Label wires, if needed, for later reference. Remove and carburetor's air intake cover, carburetor, rewind starter, starter motor relay and electric starter motor. Remove eight screws which secure power head assembly to drive shaft housing and lift off power head.

Before reinstalling power head, make certain drive shaft splines are clean then coat them with a light coating of water resistant grease. Install power head on drive shaft housing. Coat threads of retaining cap screws with silicone sealer and tighten screws to 15-20 N·m (11-14 ft.-lbs.). The remainder of installation is the reverse of removal procedure. Refer to SPEED CONTROL LINKAGE for synchronizing throttle opening with ignition advance.

DISASSEMBLY. Disassembly and inspection may be accomplished in the following manner. Remove electric starter bracket, exhaust tube, fuel filter and fuel pump. Remove flywheel and key, stator plate with pulser, charge and lighting coils. Remove electrical parts holder, speed control linkage, upper oil seal housing and stator retainer ring. Remove intake manifold, reed valve plate, exhaust cover and exhaust plate with gaskets. Remove cylinder head and cover with gaskets. Remove the twelve crankcase cap screws, then separate

crankcase from cylinder block. Lift crankshaft assembly with pistons and connecting rod assemblies from cylinder block.

Engine components are now accessible for overhaul as outlined in the appropriate following paragraphs. Clean carbon from cylinder head and combustion chambers and remove any foreign material accumulation in water passages. Inspect components for damage and renew if needed. Refer to the following section for assembly procedure.

ASSEMBLY. Refer to specific service sections when assembling the crankshaft, connecting rods, pistons and reed valves. Make sure all joint and gasket surfaces are clean and free from nicks and burrs. Make sure all carbon, salt, dirt and sand are cleaned from the combustion chambers, exhaust ports and water passages.

Lubricate crankpin bearings and cylinder walls of cylinder block with Suzuki BIA oil or a suitable BIA certified two-stroke engine oil. Install crankshaft assembly in crankcase. Make sure flange of lower oil seal (7 – Fig. SZ11-12) and middle labyrinth seal (5) fits properly in crankcase grooves. Make sure bearing pins engage notches in crankcase. Spread a coat of Suzuki Bond No. 1215 or a suitable equivalent on the mating surfaces of the crankcase and the cylinder block. Position crankcase half on cylinder block and tighten the crankcase screws in the sequence shown in Fig. SZ11-9 to torques shown in CONDENSED SERVICE DATA. Tighten the cylinder head screws in the sequence

shown in Fig. SZ11-10 to torques shown in CONDENSED SERVICE DATA. Tighten the intake manifold screws in the sequence shown in Fig. SZ11-11.

PISTONS, PINS, RINGS AND CYLINDERS. Each piston is fitted with two piston rings. Piston ring end gap should be 0.2-0.4 mm (0.008-0.016 in.) with a maximum allowable ring end gap of 0.8 (0.031 in.). Piston rings are retained in position by locating pins. Standard piston pin diameter is 17.995-18.000 mm (0.7085-0.7087 in.). Install marked side of piston ring toward top of piston. Piston to cylinder

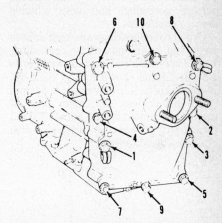

Fig. SZ11-11—Securely tighten intake manifold screws in sequence shown.

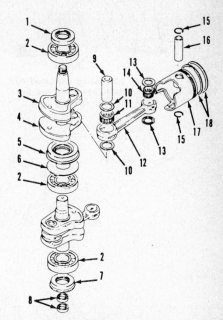

Fig. SZ11-12—Exploded view of piston and crankshaft assembly.

1. Seal	10. Thrust washers
2. Ball bearings	11. Roller bearing
3. Crank half	12. Connecting rod
4. Crank half	13. Thrust washers
5. Labyrinth seal	14. Roller bearing
6. Washer	15. Circlips
7. Seal	16. Piston pin
8. Seals	17. Piston
9. Crank pin	18. Piston rings

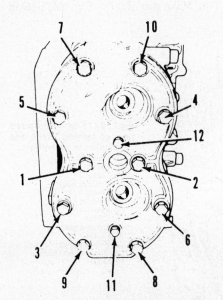

Fig. SZ11-10—Tighten cylinder head screws in sequence shown. Refer to CONDENSED SERVICE DATA for screw torques.

Suzuki DT30

wall clearance should be 0.067-0.082 mm (0.0026-0.0032 in.). Piston and rings are available in standard size as well as 0.25 mm (0.010 in.) and 0.50 mm (0.020 in.) oversizes. Cylinders should be bored to an oversize if either of the cylinders is out-of-round or taper exceeds 0.10 mm (0.004 in.). Install pistons on connecting rods so arrow on piston crown points toward exhaust port side of cylinder bore.

CONNECTING RODS, BEARINGS AND CRANKSHAFT.

Connecting rods, bearings and crankshaft are a press together unit. Crankshaft should be disassembled ONLY by experienced service personnel and with suitable service equipment.

Caged roller bearings are used at both large and small ends of the connecting rods. Determine rod bearing wear from side to side as shown in Fig. SZ11-13. Normal side to side movement is 5.0 mm (0.20 in.) or less. Maximum limit of crankshaft runout is 0.05 mm (0.002 in.) measured at bearing surfaces with crankshaft ends supported.

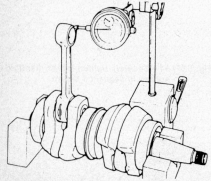

Fig. SZ11-13—Move connecting rod small end side to side to determine connecting rod, bearing and crank pin wear. Refer to text.

Apply Suzuki Super Grease "A" or a suitable high temperature grease to lip portion of lower crankshaft seal prior to installation.

MANUAL STARTER

Refer to Fig. SZ11-15 for an exploded view of manual starter assembly. Starter may be removed as a complete unit by detaching the neutral start cable and removing the three cap screws securing starter assembly to power head. To disassemble starter, proceed as follows: Remove starter handle (16–Fig. SZ11-15) and allow starter rope (14) to slowly wind onto pulley (4). Detach neutral start components. Invert starter housing (1) and remove cap screw (17). Withdraw plate (10) and spring (9).

Remove drive pawl (6) and return spring (5). Remove snap ring (8). Lift pulley (4) with starter rope (14) from starter housing. Use suitable hand and eye protection, and withdraw rewind spring (2) from starter housing (1). Be careful when removing rewind spring (2); a rapidly uncoiling starter spring could cause serious injury.

To reassemble, coat rewind spring area of starter housing (1) with a suitable water resistant grease. Install rewind spring (2) in starter housing. Rewind spring (2) must wind in a counterclockwise direction from the outer end. Wrap starter rope (14) in a clockwise direction 2½ turns onto pulley (4) when viewed from the flywheel side. Reassemble starter assembly by reversing disassembly procedure making certain rewind spring's hook properly engages groove in pulley (4). Apply water resistant grease to friction side of drive plate (10). Make sure slot (S–Fig. SZ11-16) in

drive plate properly engages tab (T) on starter housing boss and spring (9) fits into groove (G) in pulley (4).

To place tension on rewind spring (2–Fig. SZ11-15), pass starter rope (14) through rope outlet in housing (1),

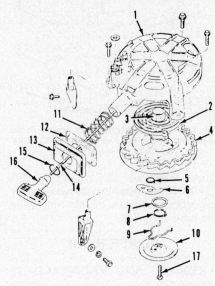

Fig. SZ11-15—Exploded view of manual starter assembly.

1. Housing
2. Rewind spring
3. Bushing
4. Pulley
5. Return spring
6. Drive pawl
7. Spacer
8. Snap ring
9. Spring
10. Plate
11. Spring
12. Rope guide
13. Rubber plate
14. Starter rope
15. Clip
16. Handle
17. Cap screw

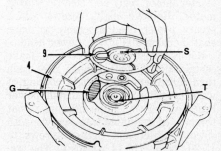

Fig. SZ11-16—During reassembly, slot (S) in drive plate must properly engage tab (T) on starter housing boss and spring (9) must fit into groove (G) in pulley (4).

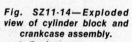

Fig. SZ11-14—Exploded view of cylinder block and crankcase assembly.

1. Crankcase
2. Cylinder block
3. Gasket
4. Cylinder head
5. Gasket
6. Cylinder head cover
7. Thermostat
8. Gasket
9. Exhaust plate
10. Gasket
11. Exhaust cover
12. Upper oil seal housing
13. Gasket

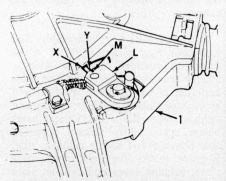

Fig. SZ11-17—For proper neutral start cable adjustment, mark (M) in lever (L) must be between marks (X and Y) on starter housing (1) when gear shift lever is in "Forward" or "Reverse" position.

Illustrations Courtesy Suzuki America Corp.

spring (11), rope guide (12), rubber plate (13) and install rope handle (16). With starter rope (14) inserted in slot of pulley (4), rotate pulley 4 turns counter-clockwise when viewed from the fly-wheel side. Secure pulley, then release starter rope (14) from slot in pulley and allow starter rope to slowly wind onto pulley. Do not place any more tension on rewind spring (2) than is necessary to draw rope handle up against housing.

Remount manual starter assembly and reassemble neutral start cable and associated components. With the gear shift lever in the "Forward" or "Reverse" position, mark (M–Fig. SZ11-17) in lever (L) must be between marks (X and Y) on starter housing (1). Adjust the length of the neutral start cable to obtain the correct adjustment.

ELECTRIC STARTER

Some models are equipped with electric starter shown in Fig. SZ11-18. Disassembly is evident after inspection of unit and reference to exploded view. Standard commutator outside diameter is 30 mm (1.18 in.) and should be renewed if worn to a diameter of 29 mm (1.14 in.) or less. Starter brushes have a

standard length of 12.5 mm (0.492 in.) and should be renewed if worn to 9 mm (0.354 in.) or less. During reassembly, make sure upper and lower alignment marks on frame (6–Fig. SZ11-18) align with notches in frame head (5) and frame end (12). After reassembly, bench test starter before installing on power head.

LOWER UNIT

PROPELLER AND RUBBER DAMPER.
A ratchet hub (50–Fig. SZ11-19) is used to provide shock protection for lower unit gears and shafts. Three-bladed propellers are used. Standard propeller has a 260.3 mm (10¼ in.) diameter and a 304.8 mm (12 in.)

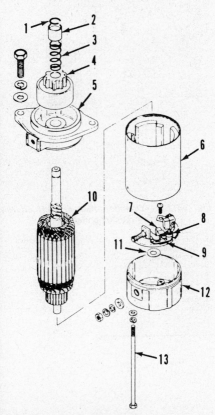

Fig. SZ11-18—Exploded view of electric start motor.

1. Retainer
2. Stop
3. Spring
4. Drive
5. Frame head
6. Frame
7. Brush
8. Spring
9. Brush holder
10. Armature
11. Thrust washer
12. Frame end
13. Through-bolt

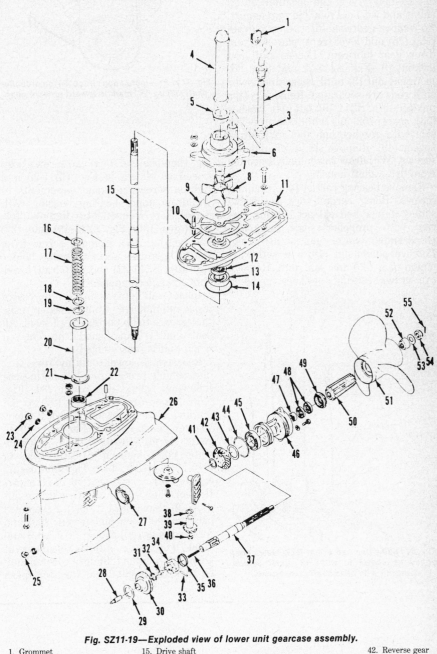

Fig. SZ11-19—Exploded view of lower unit gearcase assembly.

1. Grommet	15. Drive shaft	29. Shim	42. Reverse gear
2. Water tube	16. Washer	30. Forward gear	43. Shim
3. Grommet	17. Spring	31. Shim	44. "O" ring
4. Seal tube	18. Thrust washer	32. Spring guide	45. Bearing
5. Grommet	19. Washer	33. Pin	46. Bearing carrier
6. Water pump housing	20. Collar	34. Dog clutch	47. Bearing
7. Key	21. Snap ring	35. Retainer	48. Seals
8. Impeller	22. Bearing	36. Spring	49. Spacer
9. Plate	23. Retainer	37. Propeller shaft	50. Ratchet hub
10. Gasket	24. Gasket	38. Shim	51. Propeller
11. Upper bearing housing	25. Drain plug	39. Pinion gear	52. Spacer
12. Seal	26. Housing	40. Nut	53. Washer
13. Bearing	27. Bearing	41. Shim	54. Nut
14. "O" ring	28. Rod		55. Cotter pin

pitch on short shaft models and 279.4 mm (11 in.) pitch on long shaft models. Optional propellers are available from the manufacturer and should be selected to provide full throttle operation within the recommended limits of 4800-5500 rpm.

R&R AND OVERHAUL. Refer to Fig. SZ11-19 for exploded view of lower unit gearcase assembly. During disassembly, note the location of all shims and washers to aid in reassembly. To remove gearcase, first remove drain plug (25) and level (vent) plug (23) and drain gear lubricant. Loosen shift rod locknut (9–Fig. SZ11-22 and turn adjustment nut (8) until upper and lower shift rods are separated. Remove cotter pin (55–Fig. SZ11-19), nut (54), washer (53), spacer (52) and withdraw propeller (51) with ratchet hub (50). Withdraw spacer (49). Remove six lower unit cap screws. Withdraw lower unit assembly from drive shaft housing.

Remove bearing carrier (46) retaining screws. Being careful, use a suitable slide hammer and extract bearing carrier with propeller shaft assembly. Disassemble water pump assembly. Remove pinion nut (40) and withdraw pinion gear (39) and shim (38). Remove cap screws securing upper bearing hous-

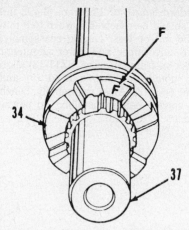

Fig. SZ11-21—Install dog clutch (34) on propeller shaft (37) so "F" mark is toward forward gear.

ing, then use two 6mm cap screws positioned as shown in Fig. SZ11-20 and tighten screws in equal increments to withdraw upper bearing housing with drive shaft components. Remove forward gear (30–Fig. SZ11-19) shim (29) and bearing (27). Remove screw from side of gearcase securing guide holder (13–Fig. SZ11-22) and withdraw lower shift linkage components.

Inspect all components for excessive wear and damage. Apply a water resistant grease to lip portion of all seals. All seals and "O" rings should be renewed when unit is reassembled.

Reassemble lower unit by reversing disassembly procedure while noting the following: Install dog clutch (34–Fig. SZ11-21) on propeller shaft (37) so "F" marked side is toward forward gear. Tighten pinion nut (40–Fig. SZ11-19) to 18-22 N·m (13-16 ft.-lbs.). Tighten water pump housing (6) cap screws to 6-10 N·m (4-7 ft.-lbs.). Tighten bearing carrier (46) cap screws to 6-10 N·m (4-7 ft.-lbs.). Tighten propeller retaining nut to 27-30 N·m (19-21 ft.-lbs.). Assembled backlash between pinion gear (39) and forward gear (30) should be 0.1-0.2 mm (0.004-0.008 in.). Adjust thickness of shim (38) or shim (29) until recommended backlash is obtained. Recheck mesh

pattern between pinion gear and forward gear to determine if correct tooth contact is being made. Adjust pinion gear shim (38) or forward gear shim (29), if needed, to obtain correct mesh pattern. Assembled propeller shaft end play should be 0.2-0.4 mm (0.008-0.016 in.). Adjust thickness of shim (41) until recommended end play is obtained. Apply silicone sealer to lower unit and drive shaft housing mating surfaces. Tighten lower unit cap screws to 15-20 N·m (11-15 ft.-lbs.).

Adjust shift rod adjustment nut (8–Fig. SZ11-22) until the proper engagement of "Forward," "Neutral" and "Reverse" is obtained. Tighten locknut (9) to secure adjustment nut (8) position. Fill gearcase with approximately 230 mL (7.77 ozs.) of SAE 90 hypoid outboard gear oil.

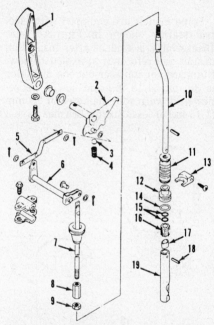

Fig. SZ11-22—Exploded view of shift control linkage components.

1. Shift lever	11. Dust seal
2. Cam	12. Rod guide
3. Detent ball	13. Guide holder
4. Detent spring	14. "O" ring
5. Rod	15. "O" rings
6. Shaft	16. Guide
7. Upper shift rod	17. Spacer
8. Adustment nut	18. Pin
9. Locknut	19. Shift cam
10. Lower shift rod	

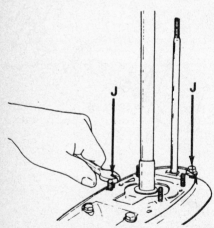

Fig. SZ11-20—Use two 6 mm jackscrews positioned as shown to withdraw upper bearing housing with drive shaft components.

SUZUKI DT40
(Prior To 1984)

CONDENSED SERVICE DATA

NOTE: Metric fasteners are used throughout outboard motor.

TUNE-UP	DT40
Hp	40
Bore	76 mm
Stroke	68 mm
Number of Cylinders	2
Displacement	617 cc
Spark Plug:	
NGK	B8HS
Electrode Gap	0.8-0.9 mm
Magneto:	
Breaker Point Gap	Breakerless
Carburetor:	
Make	Mikuni
Model	B401-32
Fuel:Oil Ratio	50:1

SIZES—CLEARANCES

Piston Ring End Gap	0.2-0.4 mm
Piston Pin Diameter	17.995-18.000 mm
Piston to Cylinder Wall	
Clearance	0.061-0.082 mm
Max. Crankshaft Runout at	
Main Bearing Journal	0.05 mm
Max. Con. Rod Small	
End Side Shake	5.0 mm

TIGHTENING TORQUES	
Cylinder Head:	
6 mm	8-10 N·m
8 mm	20-23 N·m
Crankcase:	
6 mm	8-12 N·m
10 mm	40-60 N·m
Exhaust Cover	8-10 N·m
Flywheel Nut	200 N·m
Gearcase Pinion Nut	35 N·m
Propeller Shaft Nut	50 N·m
Standard Screws:	
Unmarked or Marked "4"	
5 mm	2-4 N·m
6 mm	4-7 N·m
8 mm	10-16 N·m
10 mm	22-35 N·m
Marked "7"	
5 mm	3-6 N·m
6 mm	8-12 N·m
8 mm	18-28 N·m
10 mm	40-60 N·m

LUBRICATION

The power head is lubricated by oil mixed with the fuel. Fuel:oil ratios should be 30:1 during break-in of a new or rebuilt engine and 50:1 for normal service when using a BIA certified two-stroke engine oil or Suzuki "CCI" oil. When using any other type of two-stroke engine oil, fuel:oil ratios should be 20:1 during break-in and 30:1 for normal service. Manufacturer recommends regular or no-lead automotive gasoline having an 85-95 octane rating. Gasoline and oil should be thoroughly mixed.

The lower unit gears and bearings are lubricated by oil contained in the gearcase. SAE 90 hypoid outboard gear oil should be used. The gearcase should be drained and refilled after every 50 hours of use with 480 mL of gear oil. Reinstall vent and fill plugs securely, using a new gasket if necessary, to ensure a water tight seal.

FUEL SYSTEM

CARBURETOR. A Mikuni, type B401-32 carburetor is used. Refer to Fig. SZ12-1 for exploded view. Initial setting of pilot air screw (6) should be two turns out from a lightly seated position. Final carburetor adjustment should be made with engine at normal operating temperature and running in forward gear. Adjust throttle stop screw (4) so engine idles at approximately 650-700 rpm. Adjust pilot air screw so engine idles smoothly and will accelerate cleanly without hesitation. If necessary, readjust throttle stop screw to obtain 650-700 rpm idle speed.

Main fuel metering is controlled by main jet (10). Standard main jet size for normal operation is #200 on all models.

To check float level, remove float bowl and invert carburetor. Distance (A – Fig. SZ12-2) between main jet and bottom of float should be 16.7-18.7 mm. Adjust float level by bending float arm tang.

SPEED CONTROL LINKAGE. Ignition timing advance and throttle opening must be synchronized so that throttle is opened as timing is advanced.

To synchronize the linkage, first make certain that ignition timing is correctly set as outlined in IGNITION TIMING

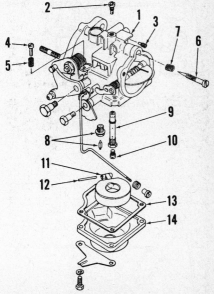

Fig. SZ12-1 – Exploded view of Mikuni carburetor typical of all models.

1. Body	8. Inlet valve
2. Pilot jet	9. Main nozzle
3. Air jet	10. Main jet
4. Throttle stop screw	11. Float
5. Spring	12. Float pin
6. Pilot air screw	13. Gasket
7. Spring	14. Float bowl

section. Determine type of ignition system used, as noted in IGNITION section, then refer to Fig. SZ12-3 and adjust the length of stator link (S), carburetor link (C) and lower link (L) using values listed in the following table. Measure link rod lengths between adjusting nuts as shown on lower link (L).

Independent Ignition	Rod Length
Stator rod (S)	30 mm
Carburetor rod (C)	155.5 mm
Lower rod (L)	91 mm

Simultaneous Ignition	Rod Length
Stator rod (S)	37 mm
Carburetor rod (C)	155 mm
Lower rod (L)	92 mm

REED VALVES. The inlet reed valves are located on a reed plate between inlet manifold and crankcase. The reed petals should seat very lightly against the reed plate throughout their entire length with the least possible tension. Tip of reed petal must not stand open more than 0.2 mm from contact surface. Reed stop opening should be 9.9 mm.

Renew reeds if petals are broken, cracked, warped, rusted or bent. Never attempt to bend a reed petal or to

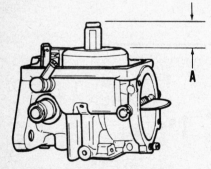

Fig. SZ12-2 — Float level (A) should be 16.7-18.7 mm.

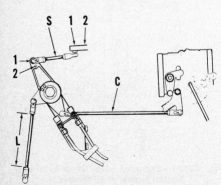

Fig. SZ12-3 — View of speed control linkage. Stator link (S) should be installed at position (1) for independent ignition and position (2) for simultaneous ignition. Refer to text for adjustment procedure.

straighten a damaged reed. Never install a bent or damaged reed. Seating surface of reed plate should be smooth and flat. When installing reeds or reed stop, make sure that petals are centered over the inlet holes in reed plate, and that the reed stops are centered over reed petals.

FUEL PUMP. A diaphragm type fuel pump is mounted on the side of power head cylinder block and is actuated by pressure and vacuum pulsations from the engine crankcases. Refer to Fig. SZ12-5 for exploded view of fuel pump assembly.

When servicing pump, scribe reference marks across pump body to aid in reassembly. Defective or questionable parts should be renewed. Diaphragm should be renewed if air leaks or cracks are found, or if deterioration is evident.

IGNITION

All models are equipped with either an independent or simultaneous, pointless electronic ignition system. One ignition coil is used on models with a simultaneous ignition system while two ignition coils are used on models with an independent ignition system. Refer to Fig. SZ12-6 for wiring diagram used on independent ignition models. Models with simultaneous ignition systems are similar.

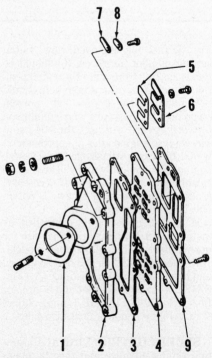

Fig. SZ12-4 — Exploded view of intake manifold and reed valve assembly.

1. Gasket
2. Manifold
3. Gasket
4. Reed plate
5. Reed petals
6. Reed stop
7. Lubrication valve
8. Valve stop
9. Gasket

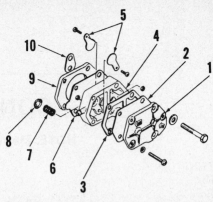

Fig. SZ12-5 — Exploded view of diaphragm type fuel pump assembly.

1. Cover
2. Diaphragm
3. Gasket
4. Body
5. Pump plates
6. Diaphragm
7. Spring
8. Spring seat
9. Base
10. Gasket

IGNITION TIMING. On independent ignition models, ignition timing should be 6° ATDC at 1000 rpm and 25° BTDC at 5000 rpm. On simultaneous ignition models, ignition timing should be 2° ATDC at 1000 rpm and 25° BTDC at 5000 rpm. On all models, initial setting of ignition timing may be accomplished by centering mark (M – Fig. SZ12-7) on stator plate with crankcase and cylinder block mating surfaces then adjust stator plate stop (S) so tab (T) just contacts boss on cylinder block.

Final ignition timing check can be made using a suitable power timing light. Immerse outboard in water and connect timing light to upper spark plug. Set engine throttle at full retard position and start engine. Refer to ignition timing specifications stated previously and check alignment of flywheel timing marks with index mark on flywheel cover. To check advance ignition timing, run engine at wide open throttle and note timing marks. Reposition stator plate stop to adjust ignition timing.

TROUBLE-SHOOTING. If ignition malfunction occurs, check and make sure malfunction is not due to spark plug, wiring or wiring connection failure. If spark is absent at both cylinders, first check neutral start interlock (NSI) operation. Check neutral switch adjustment; switch should depress at least 1 mm when shift linkage is in neutral position. Check condition of neutral switch (17 – Fig. SZ12-6) using Suzuki pocket tester number 09900-25002 or a suitable ohmmeter. Separate the wire connectors between switch (17) and NSI module (16) and attach a tester lead to each wire connected to switch. With shift linkage in neutral position, tester should read zero resistance. Moving shift linkage to "F" or "R" positions

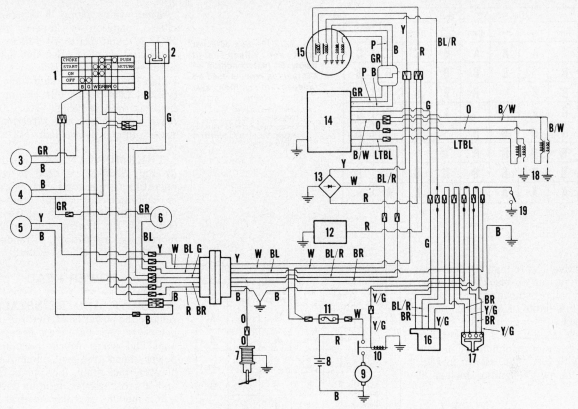

Fig. SZ12-6—Typical wiring diagram for DT40 models with independent ignition. Other models are similar.

1. Ignition switch
2. Emergency stop switch
3. Hour meter
4. Volt meter
5. Tachometer
6. Overheat buzzer
7. Choke solenoid
8. Battery
9. Starter motor
10. Starter relay
11. 20 amp fuse
12. Regulator
13. Rectifier
14. CD ignition module
15. Stator
16. NSI module
17. Neutral switch
18. Spark plugs
19. Overheat sensor

B. Black
BL. Blue
BR. Brown
G. Green
GR. Gray
Lt.Bl. Light blue
O. Orange
R. Red
W. White
Y. Yellow

should cause tester to read infinite resistance. Renew neutral switch if required.

To check condition of NSI module, use tester or ohmmeter in conjunction with test chart shown in Fig. SZ12-8. Renew NSI module if required.

Trouble-shoot ignition circuit using Suzuki pocket tester number 09900-25002 or ohmmeter as follows:

Independent Ignition Models. On independent ignition models, check condition of capacitor charge coil (2—Fig. SZ12-9) by separating the blue/red wire connector and black wire connector at stator and attach a tester lead to each

wire. Charge coil may be considered satisfactory if resistance reading is within the limits of 225-275 ohms.

Check condition of pulser coils (4) by separating the gray wire connector, pink wire connector and black wire connector at stator and attach tester positive lead to black wire. Attach negative lead to gray wire and note tester reading and then to pink wire and note tester reading. Resistance reading for each pulser coil should be within the limits of 180-220 ohms.

Check condition of each ignition coil as follows: Separate the orange wire connector and black/white wire connector at coil for top cylinder, then attach a tester lead to each wire and note tester reading. Separate light blue wire connector and black/white wire connector at coil for bottom cylinder, then attach a tester lead to each wire and note tester reading. Primary coil resistance reading should be within the limits of 0.87-1.17 ohms for each coil. Disconnect high tension wires from spark plugs. Attach

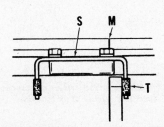

Fig. SZ12-7—Set ignition timing statically by centering mark (M) on stator plate with crankcase and cylinder block mating surface. Refer to text.

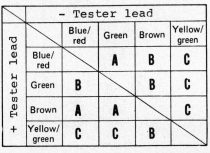

		− Tester lead		
		Blue/red	Green	Brown	Yellow/green
+ Tester lead	Blue/red		A	B	C
	Green	B		B	C
	Brown	A	A		C
	Yellow/green	C	C	B	

Fig. SZ12-8—Use chart shown above and values listed below to test condition of NSI module.

A. 200k ohms or less
B. 200k ohms or more
C. Tester needle should show deflection then return toward infinite resistance

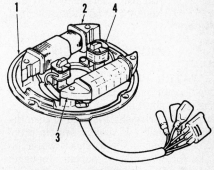

Fig. SZ12-9—View of independent ignition stator plate components.

1. Stator plate
2. Capacitor charge coil
3. Lighting coil
4. Pulser coil

	Green	Grey	Pink	Black	Blue/red	Orange	Light blue	Black/white
Green		A	A	A	B	C	C	C
Grey	B		B	B	B	B	B	B
Pink	B	B		B	B	B		
Black	C	A	A		A	C	C	C
Blue/red	B	B	B	B			B	B
Orange	B	B	B	B	B		B	B
Light blue	B	B	B	B	B	B		B
Black/white	A	A	A	A		A	A	

(Left: **– Tester lead** across top; **Tester lead +** down side)

Fig. SZ12-10—Use adjacent chart and values listed below to test condition of CD ignition module used on independent ignition systems.

A. 100k ohms or less
B. 100k ohms or more
C. Tester needle should show deflection then return toward infinite resistance

tester positive lead to high tension wire and negative lead to black/white wire. Secondary coil resistance reading should be within the limits of 5000-6800 ohms for each coil.

To check condition of CD ignition module, use tester or ohmmeter in conjunction with test chart shown in Fig. SZ12-10. Renew CD ignition module if required.

Simultaneous Ignition Models. On simultaneous ignition models, check condition of capacitor charge coil by separating the blue/red wire connector and gray wire connector at stator and attach a tester lead to each wire. Charge coil may be considered satisfactory if resistance reading is within the limits 135-165 ohms.

To check condition of ignition coil, separate the black/white wire connector at coil and remove high tension wires from spark plugs. Attach tester positive lead to black/white wire and negative lead to coil ground. Primary coil resistance reading should be within the limits of 0.08-0.10 ohms. Attach a tester lead to each high tension wire. Secondary coil resistance reading should be within the limits of 3000-4000 ohms.

To check condition of CD ignition module, use tester or ohmmeter in conjunction with test chart shown in Fig. SZ12-11. Renew CD ignition module if required.

COOLING SYSTEM

WATER PUMP. A rubber impeller type water pump is mounted between the drive shaft housing and gearcase. A key in the drive shaft is used to turn the pump impeller. If cooling system problems are encountered, check water intake for plugging or partial stoppage, then if not corrected, remove gearcase as outlined in LOWER UNIT section and check condition of the water pump, water passages and sealing surfaces.

	Green	Grey	Black/White	Blue/Red	Black
Green		A	B	B	A
Grey	C		A	B	A
Black/White	C	C		B	C
Blue/Red	A	B	B		B
Black	C	A	A	B	

(Top: **– Tester lead**; Side: **Tester lead +**)

Fig. SZ12-11 — Use chart shown above and values listed below to test condition of CD ignition module used on simultaneous ignition systems.

A. 100K ohms or less
B. 100K ohms or more
C. Tester needle should show deflection then return toward infinite resistance

When water pump is disassembled, check condition of impeller (4–Fig. SZ12-12) and plate (5) for excessive wear and damage. Reinstall plate (5) with side marked "UP" towards impeller. Turn drive shaft clockwise (viewed from top) while placing pump housing over impeller. Avoid turning drive shaft in opposite direction when water pump is assembled.

THERMOSTAT. A thermostat (3–Fig. SZ12-13) is used to regulate operating temperature. The thermostat is calibrated to control temperature within the range of 48.5°-51.5°C (119°-125°F). Thermostat can be removed for inspection or renewal by removing cylinder head cover.

POWER HEAD

REMOVE AND REINSTALL. To remove the power head, first remove upper cover and disconnect linkage, fuel lines and wires which interfere with power head removal. Remove carburetor, fuel filter, fuel pump, electric and/or recoil starter, ignition coil(s), ignition module, rectifier, neutral safety interlock switch, interlock rod, flywheel, and stator assembly before detaching power head from lower unit. Disconnect shift linkage at shift handle and at shift rod connector located below lower drive shaft housing mount (15–Fig. SZ12-15).

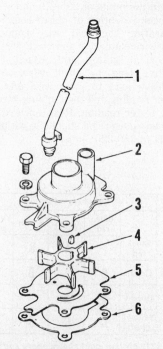

Fig. SZ12-12—Exploded view of water pump assembly.

1. Water tube
2. Pump housing
3. Key
4. Impeller
5. Plate
6. Gasket

Fig. SZ12-13—Exploded view of crankcase assembly typical of all models.

1. Cylinder head cover
2. Gasket
3. Thermostat
4. Cylinder head
5. Head gasket
6. Cylinder block
7. Crankcase
8. Outer exhaust cover
9. Gasket
10. Inner exhaust cover
11. Gasket
12. Upper seal housing
13. Gasket
14. Upper crankshaft seal
15. Lower crankshaft seal

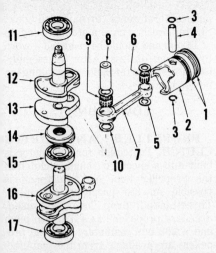

Fig. SZ12-14 — Exploded view of crankshaft assembly typical of all models.

1. Piston rings
2. Piston
3. Piston pin clip
4. Piston pin
5. Thrust washer
6. Needle bearing
7. Connecting rod
8. Crankpin
9. Needle bearing
10. Thrust washer
11. Ball bearing
12. Top crank half
13. Crank half
14. Labyrinth seal
15. Ball bearing
16. Lower crankshaft assembly
17. Ball bearing

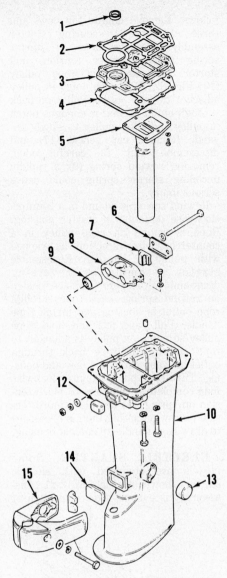

Fig. SZ12-15 — Exploded view of drive shaft housing and related components.

1. Drive shaft seal
2. Gasket
3. Seal housing
4. Gasket
5. Exhaust tube
6. Plate
7. Upper thrust mount
8. Upper mount housing
9. Rubber mount
10. Drive shaft housing
12. Reverse thrust mount
13. Side mount
14. Lower thrust mount
15. Lower mount cover

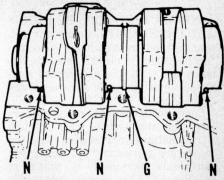

Fig. SZ12-16 — View of installed crankshaft assembly showing labyrinth seal locating groove (G) and main bearing locating notches (N).

Remove screws securing power head assembly to lower unit and lift off power head.

Before reinstalling power head, check condition of drive shaft seal (1–Fig. SZ12-15). If seal renewal is required, apply a suitable high temperature grease to lip portion of seal and install into seal housing (3) with open side towards drive shaft housing (10). Make certain drive shaft splines are clean then coat them with a light coating of water resistant grease. Apply a suitable sealer to mating surfaces of power head and lower unit and install a new gasket. The remainder of installation is the reverse of removal procedure.

DISASSEMBLY. Disassembly and inspection may be accomplished in the following manner. Remove upper oil seal housing, exhaust cover, intake manifold and reed valves. Remove cylinder head and clean carbon from combustion chamber and any foreign material accumulation in water passages. Crankcase (7–Fig. SZ12-13) may be separated from cylinder block (6) and crankshaft and piston assembly removed after removal of crankcase retaining cap screws.

Engine components are now ready for overhaul as outlined in the appropriate following paragraphs. Refer to the following section for assembly procedure.

ASSEMBLY. Refer to specific service sections when assembling the crankshaft, connecting rod, piston and

reed valves. Make sure all joint and gasket surfaces are clean, free from nicks and burrs and hardened cement or carbon.

Whenever the power head is disassembled, it is recommended that all gasket surfaces and mating surfaces without gaskets be carefully checked for nicks, burrs and warped surfaces which might interfere with a tight seal. Cylinder head, head end of cylinder block and some mating surfaces of manifold and crankcase should be checked on a surface plate and lapped if necessary to provide a smooth surface.

Do not remove any more metal than is necessary.

When assembling power head, first lubricate all friction surfaces and bearings with engine oil. Install crankshaft assembly. Make certain labyrinth seal engages groove (G–Fig. SZ12-16) and main bearing locating pins engage notches (N) in cylinder block. Apply a coat of Suzuki Bond No. 4 or a suitable sealer to mating surfaces of cylinder block and crankcase and position crankcase on cylinder block. Using a crossing pattern, tighten the 10 mm crankcase screws to 40-60 N·m and the 6 mm crankcase screws to 8-12 N·m. Cylinder head gasket should be installed with gasket sealer. Position cylinder head and gasket on cylinder block and tighten head screws in sequence shown in Fig. SZ12-17 to 20-23 N·m. Cylinder head cover cap screws (C) should be tightened to 8-10 N·m.

Install crankshaft seal (14–Fig. SZ12-13) into upper seal housing (12) with open side towards cylinder block. Apply a suitable high temperature grease to lip portion of crankshaft seals (14 and 15), then install upper seal housing and lower crankshaft seal in cylinder block assembly.

RINGS, PISTONS AND CYLINDERS. The piston is fitted with two piston rings. Rings are interchangeable in grooves but must be installed with manufacturers marking toward closed end of piston. Piston ring end gap should be 0.2-0.4 mm with a maximum allowable ring end gap of 0.8 mm. Piston to cylinder wall clearance should be 0.061-0.082 mm. Pistons and rings are available in standard size as well as 0.25 mm and 0.50 mm oversizes. Cylinder should be bored to an oversize if cylinder is out-of-round or taper exceeds 0.10 mm. Install piston on connecting rod so arrow on piston crown will point towards exhaust port when piston is in cylinder.

CONNECTING ROD, BEARINGS AND CRANKSHAFT. Connecting rod, bearings and crankshaft are a pressed together unit. Crankshaft should be disassembled ONLY by experienced service personnel and with suitable service equipment.

Caged roller bearings are used at both large and small ends of the connecting rod. Determine rod bearing wear by measuring connecting rod small end side-to-side movement as shown at (A – Fig. SZ12-18). Normal side-to-side movement is 5 mm or less. Maximum allowable crankshaft runout is 0.5 mm measured at bearing surfaces with crankshaft ends supported.

When installing crankshaft, lubricate pistons, rings, cylinders and bearings with engine oil as outlined in ASSEMBLY section.

STARTERS

MANUAL STARTER. Refer to Fig. SZ12-20 for exploded view of overhead type manual starter assembly. Starter may be disassembled for overhaul or renewal of individual components as

follows: Remove engine top cowl and three cap screws securing starter assembly to power head. If starter spring remains under tension, pull starter rope and hold rope pulley (10 – Fig. SZ12-20) with notch in pulley adjacent to rope outlet. Pull rope back through outlet so that it engages notch in pulley and allow pulley to slowly unwind. Remove cap screw (17) and disassemble unit. Be careful when removing rewind spring (9); a rapidly uncoiling starter spring could cause serious injury.

Rewind spring is wound in a counterclockwise direction in starter housing. Rope is wound on rope pulley in a counterclockwise direction as viewed with pulley in housing. Reassemble starter assembly by reversing disassembly procedure. To place tension on rewind spring, pass rope through rope outlet in housing and install rope handle. Pull rope out and hold rope pulley so notch on pulley is adjacent to rope outlet. Pull rope back through outlet between notch in pulley and housing. Turn rope pulley counterclockwise four complete revolutions to place tension on spring. Do not place more tension on rewind spring than is necessary to draw rope handle up against housing.

ELECTRIC STARTER. Some models are equipped with electric starter shown in Fig. SZ12-21. Disassembly is evident after inspection of

unit and reference to exploded view. Starter brushes have a standard length of 14 mm and should be renewed if worn to 9.5 mm or less. After reassembly, bench test starter before installing on power head.

LOWER UNIT

PROPELLER AND DRIVE CLUTCH. Protection for the motor is built into a special cushioning clutch in the propeller hub. No adjustment is possible on the propeller or clutch. Three-bladed propellers are used. Standard propeller has a 330 mm pitch and a 292 mm diameter. Optional propellers are available from the manufacturer and should be selected to provide full throttle operation within the recommended limits of 4800-5500 rpm.

R&R AND OVERHAUL. Refer to Fig. SZ12-22 for exploded view of lower unit gearcase assembly used on all

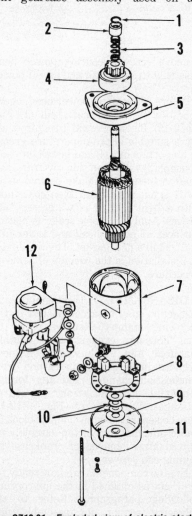

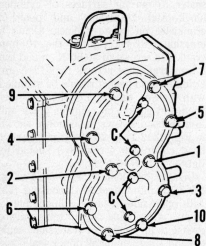

Fig. SZ12-17 – Cylinder head cap screws should be tightened in the sequence shown above. Refer to text.

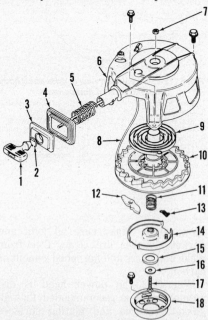

Fig. SZ12-20 – Exploded view of overhead starter assembly.

1. Rope handle	10. Rope pulley
2. Retainer	11. Spring
3. Rope guide	12. Pawl
4. Grommet	13. Spring
5. Spring	14. Drive plate
6. Starter housing	15. Spacer
7. Nut	16. Washer
8. Rope	17. Cap screw
9. Rewind spring	18. Starter cup

Fig. SZ12-21 – Exploded view of electric starter motor.

1. "C" ring	7. Frame
2. Stop	8. Brush assy.
3. Spring	9. Thrust washers
4. Drive	10. Shims
5. Frame head	11. Brush cover
6. Armature	12. Starter solenoid

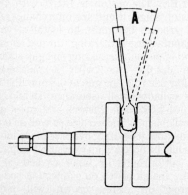

Fig. SZ12-18 – Maximum side-to-side shake (A) at small end of connecting rod should be 5.0 mm or less.

Illustrations Courtesy Suzuki America Corp.

models. During disassembly, note the location of all shims and thrust washers to aid in reassembly. To remove gearcase, first unscrew plug (30) and drain gear lubricant. Disconnect shift linkage at connector (2) located externally on the drive shaft housing. Remove the cap screws securing gearcase to drive shaft housing and separate gearcase assembly from drive shaft housing. Remove water pump assembly (Fig. SZ12-12). Remove propeller with related components from propeller shaft. Unscrew two bolts retaining gearcase end cap (50 – Fig. SZ12-22), then attach a suitable puller to propeller shaft (44) and withdraw propeller shaft assembly with gearcase end cap. Unscrew pinion nut (33) and remove pinion gear (32), then extract forward gear (36). Drive shaft (20) and related components may be withdrawn from gearcase after removal of bearing housing (13). Unscrew shift cam retaining screw (12) from gearcase to remove lower shift rod assembly.

Inspect gears for wear on teeth and on engagement dogs. Inspect clutch (40) for wear on engagement surfaces. Inspect shafts for wear on splines and on friction surfaces of gears and oil seals. Check shift cam (11) and shift pin (38) for excessive wear. Check condition of shift spring (43). Spring free length should be 69 mm with a minimum length of 67 mm. All seals and "O" rings should be renewed when unit is reassembled.

Backlash between pinion gear (32) and drive gears (36 and 46) should be 0.05-0.30 mm and is adjusted by varying thickness of shims (35) and thrust washer (47). Propeller shaft end play should be 0.05-0.30 mm and is adjusted by increasing or decreasing the thickness of thrust washers (37 and 45).

Reassemble gearcase by reversing disassembly procedure while noting the following: Install clutch (40) on propeller shaft (44) so "F" marked side (see Fig. SZ12-23) is towards forward gear (36 – Fig. SZ12-22). Tighten pinion nut (33) to 35 N·m. Apply water-resistant grease to mating surfaces of gearcase end cap (50) and gearcase. Apply silicone

sealer to gearcase and bearing housing (13) mating surfaces and to bearing housing and drive shaft housing mating surfaces.

With gearcase assembly installed, adjust shift linkage by first ensuring gearcase is in neutral. Adjust shift rod connector (2) so shift control handle is exactly between "F" and "R" positions, then tighten jam nut (1). Fill gearcase with outboard gear oil as outlined in LUBRICATION section.

Fig. SZ12-22 – Exploded view of lower unit gearcase assembly used on all models.

1. Nut
2. Connector
3. Dust seal
4. Rod guide
5. "O" ring
6. "O" ring
7. Lower shift rod
8. Magnet
9. Magnet holder
10. Pin
11. Shift cam
12. Cam retaining screw
13. Bearing housing
14. Seal
15. Needle bearing
16. Bearing race
17. Shim
18. Thrust bearing race
19. Thrust bearing
20. Drive shaft
21. Pin
22. Spring
23. Collar
24. Thrust washer
25. Washer
26. Needle bearings
27. Gearcase
28. Vent plug
29. Oil level plug
30. Drain plug
31. Strip seal
32. Pinion gear
33. Pinion nut
34. Taper bearing
35. Shim
36. Forward gear
37. Thrust washer
38. Shift pin
39. Spring guide
40. Clutch
41. Pin
42. Pin retainer
43. Shift spring
44. Propeller shaft
45. Thrust washer
46. Reverse gear
47. Thrust washer
48. "O" ring
49. Ball bearing
50. End cap
51. Needle bearings
52. Seal
53. Spacer
54. Washer
55. Propeller
56. Spacer
57. Lockwasher
58. Propeller nut

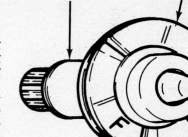

Fig. SZ12-23 – Install clutch (40) on propeller shaft (44) with "F" marked side towards forward gear.

SUZUKI DT50, DT60 AND DT65
(Prior To 1983)

CONDENSED SERVICE DATA

NOTE: Metric fasteners are used throughout outboard motor.

TUNE-UP
Hp/rpm:
DT50 . . . . .50/4800-5500
DT60 . . . . .60/4800-5500
DT65 . . . . .65/4800-5500
Bore:
DT50 (Prior to 1984) .80 mm
(3.15 in.)
DT50 (1984), DT60 & DT65 . . . . .84 mm
(3.31 in.)
Stroke . . . . .72 mm
(2.83 in.)
Number of Cylinders 2
Displacement:
DT50 (Prior to 1984) . . . . .723 cc
(44.12 cu. in.)
DT50 (1984), DT60 & DT65 . . . . .798 cc
(48.69 cu. in.)
Spark Plug:
NGK B8HS*
Electrode Gap . . . . .0.8-0.9 mm
(0.031-0.035 in.)
Ignition Type . . . . .Breakerless
Carburetor:
Make . . . . .Mikuni
Model B40-32
Fuel:Oil Ratio . . . . .50:1†
*1984 DT50 models use NGK B8HS-10 spark plugs with an
electrode gap of 1 mm (0.040 in.).
†1984 DT50 and 1983 and 1984 DT60 models are equipped
with oil injection.

SIZES–CLEARANCES
Piston Ring End Gap . . . . .0.2-0.4 mm
(0.008-0.016 in.)
Piston Pin Diameter . . . . .19.995-20.000 mm
(0.7872-0.7874 in.)
Piston to Cylinder Wall Clearance:
DT50 (Prior to 1984) . . . . .0.097-0.112 mm
(0.0038-0.0044 in.)
DT50 (1984), DT60 & DT65 . . . . .0.112-0.127 mm
(0.0044-0.0050 in.)
Max. Crankshaft Runout at Main
Bearing Journal . . . . .0.05 mm
(0.002 in.)
Max. Connecting Rod Small End
Side Shake . . . . .5.0 mm
(0.20 in.)

TIGHTENING TORQUES
Cylinder Head:
6 mm . . . . .8-12 N·m
(6-9 ft.-lbs.)
10 mm . . . . .40-60 N·m†
(29-44 ft.-lbs.)
Crankcase . . . . .40-60 N·m†
(29-44 ft.-lbs.)
Exhaust Cover . . . . .8-12 N·m
(6-9 ft.-lbs.)
Flywheel Nut . . . . .200-210 N·m
(145-152 ft.-lbs.)
Gearcase Pinion Nut .30-40 N·m
(22-29 ft.-lbs.)
Propeller Shaft Nut . . . . .50-60 N·m
(36-44 ft.-lbs.)
Standard Screws:
Unmarked or Marked "4":
5 mm . . . . .2-4 N·m
(2-3 ft.-lbs.)
6 mm . . . . .4-7 N·m
(3-5 ft.-lbs.)
8 mm . . . . .10-16 N·m
(7-12 ft.-lbs.)
10 mm . . . . .22-35 N·m
(16-26 ft.-lbs.)
Stainless Steel
5 mm . . . . .2-4 N·m
(2-3 ft.-lbs.)
6 mm . . . . .6-10 N·m
(5-7 ft.-lbs.)
8 mm . . . . .15-20 N·m
(11-15 ft.-lbs.)
10 mm . . . . .34-41 N·m
(25-30 ft.-lbs.)
Marked "7" or SAE Grade 5
5 mm . . . . .3-6 N·m
(2-5 ft.-lbs.)
6 mm . . . . .8-12 N·m
(6-9 ft.-lbs.)
8 mm . . . . .18-28 N·m
(13-20 ft.-lbs.)
10 mm . . . . .40-60 N·m
(29-44 ft.-lbs.)

†Torque values should be 46-54 N·m (34-39 ft.-lbs.) on DT50
(1984) and DT60 models.

LUBRICATION

The power head is lubricated by oil mixed with the fuel. On models without oil injection, fuel:oil ratios should be 30:1 during break-in of a new or rebuilt engine and 50:1 for normal service when using a BIA certified two-stroke engine oil or Suzuki "CCI" oil. When using any other type of two-stroke engine oil, fuel:oil ratios should be 20:1 during break-in and 30:1 for normal service. On models equipped with oil injection, for the first 5 hours of operation, mix fuel with oil in fuel tank at a ratio of 50:1 if Suzuki "CCI" oil or a BIA certified two-stroke oil is used. Mix fuel:oil at a ratio of 30:1 if any other type of two-stroke oil is used. Switch to straight fuel in fuel tank at the completion of the 5 hour break-in period. Manufacturer recommends regular or no-lead automotive gasoline having an 85-95 octane rating. Gasoline and oil should be thoroughly mixed in fuel tank when used on models without oil injection and when used during break-in period on models equipped with oil injection.

The lower unit gears and bearings are lubricated by oil contained in the gearcase. SAE 90 hypoid outboard gear oil

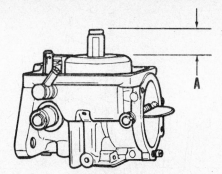

Fig. SZ14-2—Refer to text for float level (A) specifications.

should be used. Gearcase capacity is approximately 650 mL (22 oz.) of gear oil and should be drained and refilled after the first 10 hours of use and then after every 50 hours of use. Reinstall vent and fill plugs securely, using a new gasket if needed, to ensure a watertight seal.

FUEL SYSTEM

CARBURETOR. Mikuni type B40-32 carburetors are used on all models. Refer to Fig. SZ14-1 for exploded view. Initial setting of pilot air screw (7) from a lightly seated position should be $1\frac{3}{4}$ to $2\frac{1}{4}$ turns on DT50 models prior to 1984 and DT65 models and $1\frac{5}{8}$ to $2\frac{1}{8}$ turns on 1984 DT50 models and DT60 models. Final carburetor adjustment should be made with engine at normal operating temperature and running in forward gear. Rotate timing adjustment screw (B—Fig. SZ14-11) in small increments until engine idles at approximately 650-700 rpm. Adjust pilot air screw so engine idles smoothly and will accelerate cleanly without hesitation. If necessary, readjust timing adjustment screw to obtain 650-700 rpm idle speed.

Main fuel metering is controlled by main jet (10). Standard main jet size for normal operation is number 165 on DT50 models prior to 1984, number 155 on 1984 DT50 models, number 160 on DT60 models and number 167.5 on DT65 models.

To check float level, remove float bowl and invert carburetor. Distance (A—Fig. SZ14-2) between main jet and bottom of float should be 16.5-18.5 mm (0.65-0.75 in.) on DT50 models prior to 1984 and DT65 models, 16.5-18 mm (0.65-0.71 in.) on 1984 DT50 models and 16-18 mm (0.63-0.71 in.) on DT60 models. Adjust float level by bending float tang.

To synchronize throttle plate opening of top carburetor with bottom carburetor, use Suzuki carburetor balancer 09913-13121 or equivalent and make adjustment at throttle shaft connector (5—Fig. SZ14-1).

SPEED CONTROL LINKAGE. The carburetor throttle valves must be correctly synchronized to open as the ignition is advanced to obtain optimum performance. To adjust the speed control linkage, it is necessary to first check (and adjust if required) the ignition maximum advance as outlined in the IGNITION TIMING section. Disconnect carburetor link (C—Fig. SZ14-11) and rotate speed control lever (L) toward maximum speed position until it contacts maximum speed stop. Set carburetor throttle plates completely open then vary the length of carburetor link (C) until ball joint connector will just attach. Move speed control lever to full retard position. Clearance (A) at carburetor throttle shaft actuating levers should be 0.5-1.0 mm (0.020-0.040 in.).

REED VALVES. The inlet reed valves (Fig. SZ14-3) are located on a reed plate between inlet manifold and crankcase. The reed petals should seat very lightly against the reed plate throughout their entire length with the least possible tension. Tip of reed petal must not stand open more than 0.2 mm (0.008 in.) from contact surface. Reed stop opening should be 7.6-8.0 mm (0.30-0.31 in.) on DT50 models and 7.55-7.95 mm (0.30-0.31 in.) on DT60 and DT65 models.

Renew reeds if petals are broken, cracked, warped, rusted or bent. Never attempt to bend a reed petal or to straighten a damaged reed. Never install a bent or damaged reed. Seating surface of reed plate should be smooth

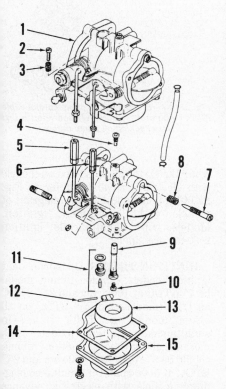

Fig. SZ14-1—Exploded view of Mikuni carburetors typical of all models.

1. Body
2. Throttle stop screw
3. Spring
4. Pilot jet
5. Throttle shaft connector
6. Choke shaft connector
7. Pilot air screw
8. Spring
9. Main nozzle
10. Main jet
11. Inlet valve
12. Float pin
13. Float
14. Gasket
15. Float bowl

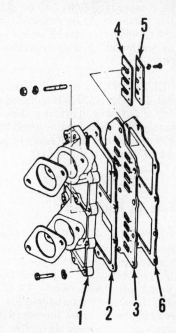

Fig. SZ14-3—Exploded view of intake manifold and reed valve assembly.

1. Manifold
2. Gasket
3. Reed plate
4. Reed petals
5. Reed stop
6. Gasket

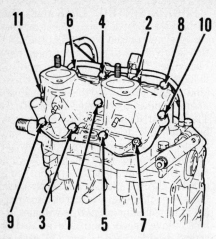

Fig. SZ14-4 — Inlet manifold cap screws should be tightened in the sequence shown above.

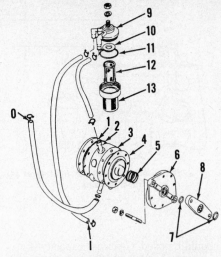

Fig. SZ14-5 — Exploded view of diaphragm type fuel pump and fuel filter assemblies.

1. Cover
2. Diaphragm
3. Body
4. Diaphragm
5. Spring
6. Body
7. "O" rings
8. Insulator block
9. Fuel filter body
10. Packing
11. "O" ring
12. Filter
13. Bowl
I. Inlet
O. Outlet

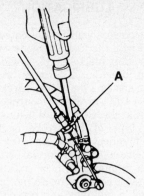

Fig. SZ14-6 — Use oil pump air bleed screw (A) to bleed trapped air from oil supply line or pump.

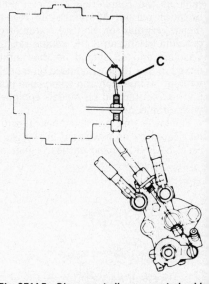

Fig. SZ14-7 — Disconnect oil pump control cable (C) at carburetor throttle lever and refer to text for checking oil pump output.

and flat. When installing reeds or reed stop, make sure that petals are centered over the inlet holes in reed plate, and that the reed stops are centered over reed petals. Apply a suitable high temperature grease to inlet manifold cap screw threads, then using sequence shown in Fig. SZ14-4 tighten cap screws.

FUEL PUMP. A diaphragm type fuel pump is mounted on the side of power head cylinder block and is actuated by pressure and vacuum pulsations from the engine crankcases. Refer to Fig. SZ14-5 for exploded view of fuel pump assembly.

When servicing pump, scribe reference marks across pump body to aid in reassembly. Defective or questionable parts should be renewed. Diaphragm should be renewed if air leaks or cracks are found, or if deterioration is evident.

FUEL FILTER. A fuel filter (9 through 13 – Fig. SZ14-5) is mounted on the side of power head cylinder block on all models. Filter should be disassembled and cleaned after every 50 hours of use. Renew "O" ring (11) if required.

OIL INJECTION

Models So Equipped

BLEEDING PUMP. To bleed trapped air from oil supply line or pump, first make sure outboard motor is in an upright position and oil tank is full. Open oil pump air bleed screw (A – Fig. SZ14-6) three or four turns to allow oil to seep out around screw threads. After five seconds or when no air bubbles are noticed, close air bleed screw (A).

CHECKING OIL PUMP OUTLET. Start engine and allow to warm-up for

approximately five minutes, then stop engine. Disconnect oil pump control cable (C – Fig. SZ14-7) at carburetor throttle lever. Detach oil supply line at oil tank outlet. Connect oil gage 09900-21602 to oil supply line. Fill oil gage with a recommended two-stroke oil unit even with an upper reference mark. With oil pump control cable (C) in released position, start engine and maintain engine speed at 1500 rpm. Allow engine to run for five minutes. After five minutes, stop the engine and observe oil gage. Recommended oil consumption is 2.7-3.5 mL (0.09-0.12 oz.) in five minutes at 1500 rpm.

To check oil pump at maximum output position, repeat previous procedure except use a suitable tool and hold oil pump control cable (C) in fully extended position. Recommended oil consumption is 4.6-5.6 mL (0.16-0.19 oz.) in five minutes at 1500 rpm.

If the obtained oil consumption measurements are not within the recommended limits, then oil pump must be renewed.

IGNITION

All models are equipped with either an independent or simultaneous pointless electronic ignition system. Simultaneous ignition system models are identified by the use of one ignition coil while two ignition coils are used on models with an independent ignition system. Simultaneous ignition models may have mechanical or electronic advance. Stator plate is movable on simultaneous ignition models with mechanical advance

while the stator plate is fixed on models with electronic advance. Refer to Fig. SZ14-8 for a typical wiring diagram of models with independent ignition. Models with simultaneous ignition systems are similar.

IGNITION TIMING. On independent ignition models, ignition timing should be 4° ATDC at 1000 rpm and 21° BTDC on DT60 models and 25° BTDC on all other models at 5000 rpm. On simultaneous ignition models with mechanical advance, ignition timing should be 3° ATDC at 1000 rpm and 25° BTDC at 5000 rpm. On simultaneous ignition models with electronic advance (fixed stator plate), ignition timing should be 8° BTDC at 1000 rpm and 25° BTDC at 5000 rpm.

Initial setting of ignition timing on all models with mechanical advance may be accomplished as follows: Set throttle at full advance position, then align mark

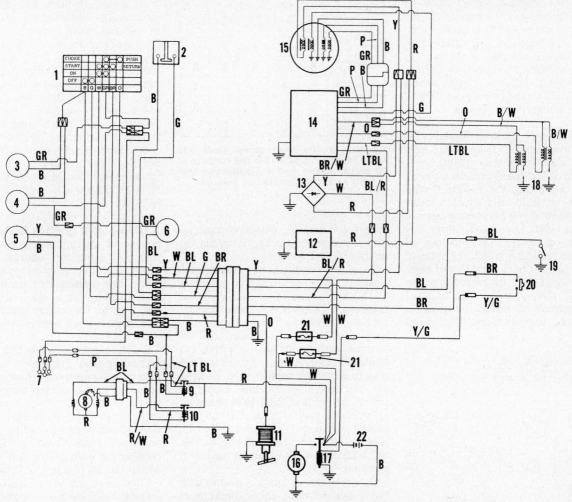

Fig. SZ14-8—Typical wiring diagram for models with independent ignition. Other models are similar.

1. Ignition switch
2. Emergency stop switch
3. Hour meter
4. Volt meter
5. Tachometer
6. Overheat buzzer
7. Tilt and trim switch
8. Tilt and trim motor
9. "Up" solenoid
10. "Down" solenoid
11. Choke solenoid
12. Regulator
13. Rectifier
14. CD ignition module
15. Stator
16. Starter motor
17. Starter solenoid
18. Spark plugs
19. Overheat sensor
20. Neutral switch
21. 20 amp fuse
22. Battery

GR. Gray
LtBl. Light blue
O. Orange
P. Pink
R. Red
W. White
Y. Yellow
B. Black
BL. Blue
BR. Brown
G. Green

(M – Fig. SZ14-9) on stator plate with stationary mark (S) on upper seal housing. Loosen nut (N) on stator plate link to reposition stator plate.

Initial setting of ignition timing on all models with electronic advance may be accomplished by aligning mark (M – Fig. SZ14-10) on stator plate with center of stator plate retaining screw hole (H).

Final ignition timing check can be made using a suitable power timing light. Immerse lower unit of outboard motor in water and connect timing light to upper spark plug. Set engine throttle at full retard position and start engine. Refer to ignition timing specifications stated previously and check alignment of flywheel timing marks with index mark on electric starter cap on models with mechanical advance or with index mark on flywheel housing on models with electronic advance. To check ad-

vance ignition timing, run engine at wide open throttle and note timing marks.

On models with mechanical advance, full retard timing may be adjusted by turning bolt (B – Fig. SZ14-11) in or out as required and full advance timing may be adjusted by loosening nut (N) and

repositioning stator plate. On models with electronic advance, reposition stator plate to adjust ignition timing.

TROUBLE-SHOOTING. If ignition malfunction occurs, use only approved procedures to prevent damage to the

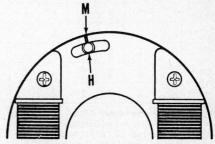

Fig. SZ14-9 – On models with mechanical advance, set ignition timing statically by aligning mark (M) on stator plate with stationary mark (S) when throttle is in the full advance position.

Fig. SZ14-10 – On models with electronic advance, set ignition timing statically by aligning mark (M) on stator plate with center of screw hole (H).

components. The fuel system should be checked first to make certain that faulty running is not caused by incorrect mixture or contaminated fuel. Make sure malfunction is not due to spark plug, wiring or wiring connection failure. Trouble-shoot ignition circuit using Suzuki pocket tester number 09900-25002 or ohmmeter as follows:

Simultaneous Ignition Models. On simultaneous ignition models with electronic advance (fixed stator plate), check condition of low-speed capacitor charge coil by separating the red/black wire connector at stator and attach a tester lead. Attach the other tester lead to engine ground. Low-speed charge coil may be considered satisfactory if resistance reading is within the limits of 112-149 ohms. Check condition of high-speed charge coil by separating the red/black wire connector and blue/red wire connector at stator and attach a tester lead to each wire. High-speed

−Tester lead ＼ +Tester lead		Charge	Pulser	Ground	Stop	Ignition
		Blue/Red	White/Red	Black	Blue/Red	Black/White
Charge	Blue/Red		A	A	A	A
Pulser	White/Red	B		B	B	B
Ground	Black	C	A		C	A
Stop	Blue/Red	A	A	A		A
Ignition	Black/White	C	C	C	C	

Fig. SZ14-13—Use chart shown above and values listed in Fig. SZ14-12 to test condition of CD ignition module used on simultaneous ignition models with mechanical advance.

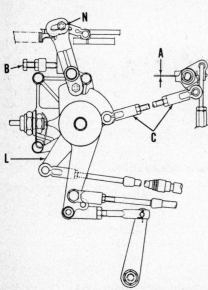

Fig. SZ14-11—View of speed control linkage used on models with mechanical advance. Models with electronic advance (fixed stator plate) are similar.

−Tester lead ＼ +Tester lead		Charge & pulser	Charge	Ground	Ignition	Stop
		Blue/Red	Red/Black	Black	White/Black	Blue/Red
Charge & pulser	Blue/Red		B	A	A	A
Charge	Red/Black	C		A	A	A
Ground	Black	C	B		A	A
Ignition	White/Black	C	B	C		C
Stop	Blue/Red	A	B	A	A	

Fig. SZ14-12—Use chart shown above and values listed below to test condition of CD ignition module used on simultaneous ignition models with electronic advance.

A. 100k ohms or less
B. 100k ohms or more
C. Tester needle should show deflection then return toward infinite resistance

charge coil may be considered satisfactory if resistance reading is within the limits of 1.62-1.98 ohms.

To check condition of ignition coil, separate the white/black wire connector at coil and remove high tension wires from spark plugs. Attach tester positive lead to white/black wire and negative lead to coil ground. Primary coil resistance reading should be within the limits of 0.28-0.38 ohms. Attach a tester lead to each high tension wire. Secondary coil resistance reading should be within the limits of 2980-4030 ohms.

To check condition of CD ignition module, use tester or ohmmeter in conjunction with test chart shown in Fig. SZ14-12. Renew CD ignition module if required.

On simultaneous ignition models with mechanical advance, check condition of capacitor charge coil by separating the blue/red connector and black wire connector at stator and attach a tester lead to each wire. Charge coil may be considered satisfactory if resistance reading is within the limits of 135-165 ohms.

Check condition of pulser coil by separating the white/red wire connector and black wire connector at stator and attach a tester lead to each wire. Pulser coil may be considered satisfactory if resistance reading is within the limits of 7.29-8.91 ohms.

Fig. SZ14-14—Use chart adjacent and values listed in Fig. SZ14-12 to test condition of CD ignition module used on independent ignition models.

To check condition of ignition coil, separate the black/white wire connector at coil and remove high tension wires from spark plugs. Attach tester positive lead to black/white wire and negative lead to coil ground. Primary coil resistance reading should be within the limits of 0.076-0.104 ohms. Attach a tester lead to each high tension wire. Secondary coil resistance reading should be within the limits of 2980-4030 ohms.

To check condition of CD ignition module, use tester or ohmmeter in conjunction with test chart shown in Fig. SZ14-13. Renew CD ignition module if required.

Independent Ignition Models. On independent ignition models, check condition of capacitor charge coil by separating the green wire connector and black wire connector at stator and attach a tester lead to each wire. Charge coil may be considered satisfactory if resistance reading is within the limits of 225-275 ohms.

Check condition of pulser coils by separating the gray wire connector, pink wire connector and black wire connector at stator. Attach tester positive lead to black wire. Attach negative lead to gray wire and note tester reading, then attach negative lead to pink wire and note tester reading. Resistance reading for each pulser coil should be within the limits of 180-220 ohms.

Check condition of each ignition coil as follows: Separate the orange wire connector and black/white wire connector at coil for top cylinder, then attach a tester lead to each wire and note tester reading. Separate light blue wire connector and black/white wire connector at coil for bottom cylinder, then attach a tester lead to each wire and note tester reading. Primary coil resistance reading should be within the limits of 0.87-1.17 ohms for each coil. Disconnect high tension wires from spark plugs. Attach tester positive lead to high tension wire and negative lead to black/white wire.

−Tester lead ＼ +Tester lead		Charge	Pulser		Ground	Stop	Ignition		
		Green	Gray	Pink	Black	Blue/Red	Orange	Light blue	Black/White
Charge	Green		A	A	A	B	C	C	C
Pulser	Gray	B		B	B	B	B	B	B
Pulser	Pink	B	B		B	B	B	B	B
Ground	Black	C	A	A		A	C	C	C
Stop	Blue/Red	B	B	B	B		B	B	B
Ignition	Orange	B	B	B	B	B			B
Ignition	Light blue	B	B	B	B	B			B
Ignition	Black/White	A	A	A	A	B	A	A	

Illustrations Courtesy Suzuki America Corp.

Secondary coil resistance reading should be within the limits of 5020-6790 ohms for each coil.

To check condition of CD ignition module, use tester or ohmmeter in conjunction with test chart shown in Fig. SZ14-14. Renew CD ignition module if required.

COOLING SYSTEM

WATER PUMP. A rubber impeller type water pump is mounted between the drive shaft housing and gearcase. A key in the drive shaft is used to turn the pump impeller. If cooling system problems are encountered, check water intake for plugging or partial stoppage, then if not corrected, remove gearcase as outlined in the appropriate section and check condition of the water pump, water passages and sealing surfaces.

When water pump is disassembled, check condition of impeller (4–Fig. SZ14-15) and plate (5) for excessive wear. Turn drive shaft clockwise (viewed from top) while placing pump housing over impeller. Avoid turning drive shaft in opposite direction when water pump is assembled.

THERMOSTAT. A thermostat (4–Fig. SZ14-16) is used to regulate operating temperature. The thermostat should start to open within the temperature range of 40°-44° C (104°-111°F). Thermostat can be removed for inspection or renewal by removing cylinder head cover.

POWER HEAD

REMOVE AND REINSTALL. To remove the power head, first remove up-

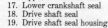

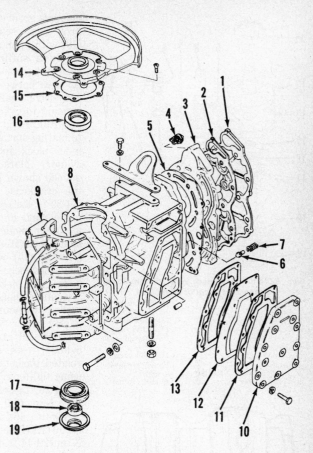

Fig. SZ14-16 — Exploded view of crankcase assembly typical of all models.

1. Cylinder head cover
2. Gasket
3. Cylinder head
4. Thermostat
5. Head gasket
6. Valve
7. Spring
8. Cylinder block
9. Crankcase
10. Outer exhaust cover
11. Gasket
12. Inner exhaust cover
13. Gasket
14. Upper seal housing
15. Gasket
16. Upper crankshaft seal
17. Lower crankshaft seal
18. Drive shaft seal
19. Drive shaft seal housing

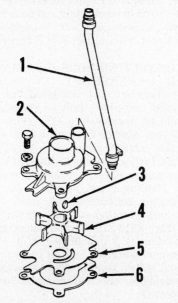

Fig. SZ14-15 — Exploded view of water pump assembly.

1. Water tube
2. Pump housing
3. Key
4. Impeller
5. Plate
6. Gasket

per cover and disconnect linkage, fuel lines and wires which interfere with power head removal. Remove carburetors and electric choke solenoid. Remove plug from side of lower cover to obtain access to shift linkage. Unscrew nuts retaining shift arm (2–Fig. SZ14-25) to shaft (4), then disengage shaft (4) from shift rod (9). Remove screws securing power head assembly to lower unit and lift off power head.

Before reinstalling power head, check condition of drive shaft seal (18–Fig. SZ14-16). If seal renewal is required, it will be necessary to separate crankcase (9) and cylinder block (8) as outlined in the appropriate following paragraphs. Apply a suitable high temperature grease to lip portion of seal and install seal into seal housing (19) with open side towards lower unit. Make certain drive shaft splines are clean then coat them with a light coating of water resistant grease. Apply a suitable sealer to mating surfaces of power head and lower unit and install a new gasket. Coat power head to lower unit retaining cap screws adjacent to cap screw heads with silicone sealer. The remainder of installation is the reverse of removal procedure.

DISASSEMBLY. Disassembly and inspection may be accomplished in the following manner. Remove electric or

recoil starter. Remove wiring connection cover plate located above exhaust cover (10–Fig. SZ14-16) on cylinder block and separate all wire connections. Remove ignition module, ignition coil(s), fuel pump, fuel filter, shift and speed control linkage, flywheel and stator plate assembly. Remove upper oil seal housing (14), outer exhaust cover (10), inner exhaust cover (12), intake manifold and reed valves. Remove cylinder head cover (1) and cylinder head (3), then clean carbon from combustion chamber and any foreign material accumulation in water passages. Withdraw spring (7) and valve (6) from cylinder block. Unscrew crankcase retaining screws and separate crankcase (9) from cylinder block (8). Remove lower oil seal housing (19). Crankshaft and piston assembly may now be removed from cylinder block.

Engine components are now ready for overhaul as outlined in the appropriate following paragraphs. Refer to the following section for assembly procedure.

ASSEMBLY. Refer to specific service sections when assembling the crankshaft, connecting rod, piston and reed valves. Make sure all joint and gasket surfaces are clean, free from nicks and burrs and hardened cement or carbon. Whenever the power head is disassembled, it is recommended that all gasket

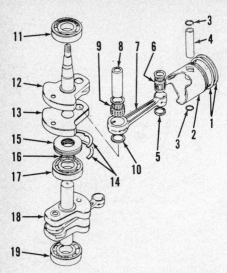

Fig. SZ14-17—Exploded view of crankshaft assembly typical of all models.

1. Piston rings
2. Piston
3. Piston pin clip
4. Piston pin
5. Thrust washer
6. Needle bearing
7. Connecting rod
8. Crankpin
9. Needle bearing
10. Thrust washer
11. Ball bearing
12. Top crank half
13. Crank half
14. Thrust rings
15. Labyrinth seal
16. "O" ring
17. Ball bearing
18. Lower crankshaft assy.
19. Ball bearing

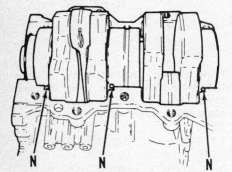

Fig. SZ14-18—View of installed crankshaft assembly showing main bearing locating notches (N).

surfaces and mating surfaces without gaskets be carefully checked for nicks, burrs and warped surfaces which might interfere with a tight seal. Cylinder head, head end of cylinder block and some mating surfaces of manifold and crankcase should be checked on a surface plate and lapped if necessary to provide a smooth surface. Do not remove any more metal than is necessary.

When assembling power head, first lubricate all friction surfaces and bearings with engine oil. Place thrust rings (14–Fig. SZ14-17) in cylinder block, then install crankshaft assembly. Make certain main bearing locating pins engage notches (N–Fig. SZ14-18) in cylinder block. Apply a suitable high temperature grease to lip portion of crankshaft and drive shaft seals, then install lower crankshaft seal (17–Fig. SZ14-16) ensuring seal flange properly

engages groove in cylinder block. Install drive shaft seal (18) into seal housing (19) with open side towards lower unit. Apply a sufficient amount of water-resistant grease to seal housing (19) to fill area between lower crankshaft seal and drive shaft seal, then install seal housing to cylinder block. Apply a coat of Suzuki Bond No. 4 or a suitable sealer to mating surfaces of crankcase and cylinder block and position crankcase on cylinder block. Using tightening sequence shown in Fig. SZ14-19, tighten the crankcase screws to 46-54 N·m (34-39 ft.-lbs.) on DT50 (1984) and DT60 models and 40-60 N·m (29-44 ft.-lbs.) on all other models. Install upper crankshaft seal (16–Fig. SZ14-16) into seal housing (14) with open side towards cylinder block, then install seal housing to cylinder block assembly.

Cylinder head gasket should be installed without the application of a gasket sealer. With valve (6) and spring (7) installed in cylinder block, position cylinder head, cylinder head cover and related gaskets on cylinder block then using tightening sequence shown in Fig. SZ14-20, tighten the 6 mm screws to 8-12 N·m (6-9 ft.-lbs.) and the 10 mm screws to 46-54 N·m (34-39 ft.-lbs.) on DT50 (1984) and DT60 models and 40-60 N·m (29-44 ft.-lbs.) on all other models.

RINGS, PISTONS AND CYLINDERS. The pistons are fitted with two piston rings. Piston rings are interchangeable in grooves but must be installed with manufacturers marking toward closed end of piston. Piston ring end gap should be 0.2-0.4 mm (0.008-0.016 in.) with a maximum allowable ring end gap of 0.8 mm (0.031 in.). Piston to cylinder wall clearance should be 0.097-0.112 mm (0.0038-0.0044 in.) on DT50 models prior to 1984 and 0.112-0.127 mm (0.0044-0.0050 in.) on all other models. Pistons and rings are available in standard size as well as 0.25

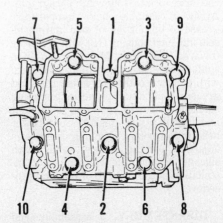

Fig. SZ14-19—Crankcase cap screws should be tightened in the sequence shown above.

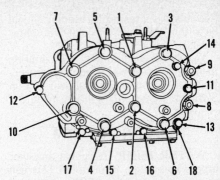

Fig. SZ14-20—Cylinder head cap screws should be tightened in the sequence shown above. Refer to text for tightening torque specifications.

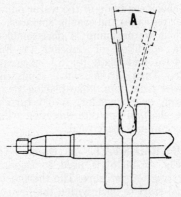

Fig. SZ14-21—Maximum side-to-side shake (A) at small end of connecting rod should be 5 mm (0.20 in.) or less.

mm (0.010 in.) and 0.50 mm (0.020 in.) oversizes. Cylinder should be bored to an oversize if cylinder is out-of-round or taper exceeds 0.10 mm (0.004 in.). Install piston on connecting rod so arrow on piston crown will point towards exhaust port when piston is in cylinder.

CONNECTING RODS, BEARINGS AND CRANKSHAFT. Connecting rods, bearings and crankshaft are a pressed together unit. Crankshaft should be disassembled ONLY by experienced service personnel and with suitable service equipment.

Caged roller bearings are used at both large and small ends of the connecting rod. Determine rod bearing wear by measuring connecting rod small end side-to-side movement as shown at (A–Fig. SZ14-21). Normal side-to-side movement is 5 mm (0.20 in.) or less. Maximum allowable limit of crankshaft runout is 0.05 mm (0.002 in.) measured at bearing surfaces with crankshaft ends supported.

When installing crankshaft, lubricate pistons, rings, cylinders and bearings with engine oil as outlined in ASSEMBLY section.

Illustrations Courtesy Suzuki America Corp.

STARTERS

MANUAL STARTER. Refer to Fig. SZ14-22 for exploded view of overhead type manual starter assembly used on some DT50 models. Starter may be disassembled for overhaul or renewal of individual components as follows: Remove engine top cowl and three cap screws securing starter assembly to power head. If starter spring remains under tension, pull starter rope and hold rope pulley (10) with notch in pulley adjacent to rope outlet. Pull rope back through outlet so that it engages notch in pulley and allow pulley to slowly unwind. Remove cap screw (21) and disassemble unit. Be careful when removing rewind spring (8); a rapidly uncoiling starter spring could cause serious injury.

Rewind spring is wound in a counterclockwise direction in starter housing. Rope is wound on rope pulley in a counterclockwise direction as viewed with pulley in housing. Reassemble starter assembly by reversing disassembly procedure. To place tension on rewind spring, pass rope through rope outlet in housing and install rope handle. Pull rope out and hold rope pulley so notch on pulley is adjacent to rope outlet. Pull rope back through outlet between notch in pulley and housing. Turn rope pulley counterclockwise four complete revolutions to place tension on spring. Do not place more ten-

sion on rewind spring than is necessary to draw rope handle up against housing.

ELECTRIC STARTER. Some models are equipped with electric starter shown in Fig. SZ14-23. Disassembly is evident after inspection of unit and reference to exploded view. Starter brushes have a standard length of 16 mm (0.63 in.) and should be renewed if worn to 9.5 mm (0.37 in.) or less. After reassembly, bench test starter before installing on power head.

LOWER UNIT

PROPELLER AND DRIVE CLUTCH. Protection for the motor is built into a special cushioning clutch in the propeller hub. No adjustment is possible on the propeller or clutch. Three-bladed propellers are used. Propellers are available from the manufacturer in various diameters and pitches and should be selected to provide optimum performance at full throttle within the recommended limits of 4800-5500 rpm.

R&R AND OVERHAUL. Refer to Fig. SZ14-24 for exploded view of lower unit gearcase assembly used on all models. During disassembly, note the location of all shims and thrust washers

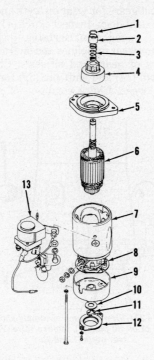

Fig. SZ14-23 — Exploded view of electric starter motor.

1. "C" ring
2. Stop
3. Spring
4. Drive
5. Frame head
6. Armature
7. Frame
8. Brush assy.
9. Brush cover
10. Thrust washer
11. "E" clip
12. End cap
13. Starter solenoid

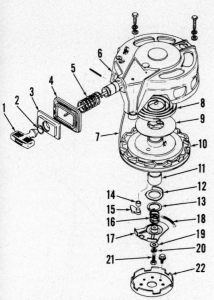

Fig. SZ14-22 — Exploded view of overhead starter assembly used on some models.

1. Rope handle
2. Retainer
3. Rope guide
4. Grommet
5. Spring
6. Starter housing
7. Rope
8. Rewind spring
9. Plate
10. Rope pulley
11. Bushing
12. Guide
13. Retainer
14. Bushing
15. Pawl
16. Spring
17. Cover plate
18. Spring
19. Washer
20. Lockwasher
21. Cap screw
22. Starter cup

Fig. SZ14-24 — Exploded view of lower unit gearcase assembly used on all models.

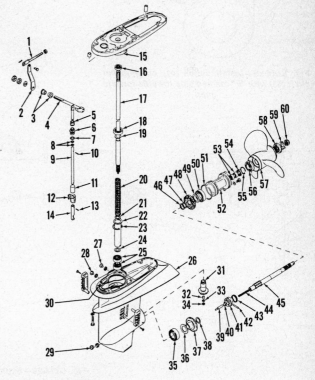

1. Link
2. Shift arm
3. Bushings
4. Shift shaft
5. Dust seal
6. Rod guide
7. "O" ring
8. "O" ring
9. Shift rod
10. Pin
11. Magnet
12. Magnet holder
13. Pin
14. Shift cam
15. Bearing housing
16. Seal
17. Drive shaft
18. Bearing
19. Thrust washer
20. Spring
21. Washer
22. Collar
23. Snap ring
24. Shim
25. Needle bearings
26. Gearcase
27. Vent plug
28. Oil level plug
29. Drain plug
30. Strip seal
31. Pinion gear
32. Collar
33. Washer
34. Pinion nut
35. Taper bearing
36. Shim
37. Forward gear
38. Thrust washer
39. Shift pin
40. Spring guide
41. Clutch
42. Pin
43. Pin retainer
44. Shift spring
45. Propeller shaft
46. Shim
47. Thrust washer
48. Reverse gear
49. Shim
50. Bearing
51. "O" ring
52. End cap
53. Needle bearings
54. Seal
55. Snap ring
56. Spacer
57. Propeller
58. Spacer
59. Lockwasher
60. Propeller nut

to aid in reassembly. To remove gearcase, first unscrew plug (29) and drain gear lubricant. Remove plug from side of lower engine cover to obtain access to shift linkage. Unscrew nuts retaining shift arm (2) to shaft (4), then disengage shaft (4) from shift rod (9). Remove the cap screws securing gearcase to drive shaft housing and separate gearcase assembly from drive shaft housing. Remove water pump assembly (Fig. SZ14-15). Remove propeller with related components from propeller shaft. Unscrew two screws retaining gearcase end cap (52–Fig. SZ14-24), then attach a suitable puller to propeller shaft (45) and withdraw propeller shaft assembly with gearcase end cap. Unscrew pinion nut (34) and remove pinion gear (31), then extract forward gear (37). Drive shaft (17) and related components may be withdrawn from gearcase after removal of bearing housing (15).

Inspect gears for wear on teeth and on engagement dogs. Inspect clutch (41) for wear on engagement surfaces. Inspect shafts for wear on splines and on friction surfaces of gears and oil seals. Check shift cam (14) and shift pin (39) for excessive wear. Check condition of shift

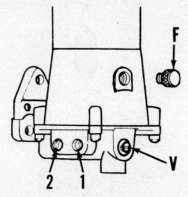

Fig. SZ14-27 — View of pump assembly showing location of oil fill plug (F), release valve (V) and test ports (1 and 2).

spring (44). Spring free length should be 69 mm (2.72 in.) with a minimum length of 67 mm (2.64 in.). All seals and "O" rings should be renewed when unit is reassembled.

Backlash between pinion gear (31) and drive gears (37 and 48) should be 0.05-0.30 mm (0.002-0.012 in.) and is adjusted by varying thickness of shims (36 and 49). Propeller shaft end play should be 0.05-0.30 mm (0.002-0.012 in.) and is adjusted by increasing or decreasing the thickness of thrust washers (38 and 47) and shims (46).

Reassemble gearcase by reversing disassembly procedure while noting the following: Install clutch (41) on propeller shaft (45) so "F" marked side (see Fig. SZ14-25) is towards forward gear (37–Fig. SZ14-24). Tighten pinion nut (34) to 30-40 N·m (22-29 ft.-lbs.). Apply water-resistant grease to "O" ring (51). Apply silicone sealer to gearcase and bearing housing (15) mating surfaces and to bearing housing and drive shaft housing mating surfaces. Coat retaining cap screws adjacent to cap screw heads with silicone sealer.

With gearcase assembly installed, adjust shift linkage as follows: Set shift arm (2) exactly between "F" and "R" positions, then adjust link (1) so protrusion (P–Fig. SZ14-26) on shift lever (L) is centered over neutral safety interlock switch. Fill gearcase with outboard gear oil as outlined in LUBRICATION section.

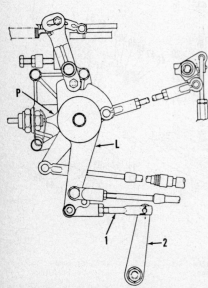

Fig. SZ14-25 — Install clutch (41) on propeller shaft (44) with "F" marked side towards forward gear.

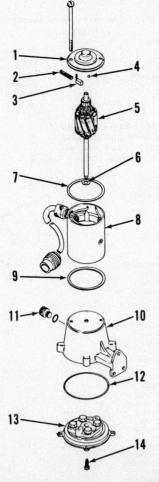

Fig. SZ14-28 — Exploded view of power tilt and trim electric motor and pump assembly.

1. End cap	8. Frame
2. Spring	9. Gasket
3. Brush	10. Reservoir
4. Ball	11. Fill plug
5. Armature	12. "O" ring
6. Thrust washer	13. Pump assy.
7. Gasket	14. Cap screw

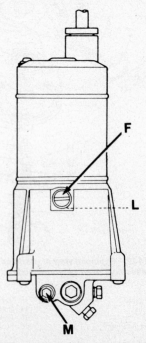

Fig. SZ14-29 — View identifying manual release valve (M), fill plug (F) and recommended reservoir oil level (L) on power tilt and trim pump used on models DT50 (1984) and DT60 (1983-1984).

Fig. SZ14-26 — Protrusion (P) on shift lever (L) should be centered on neutral safety switch when lower unit is in neutral.

POWER TILT AND TRIM

Some models are equipped with a hydraulically actuated power tilt and trim system. An oil pump driven by a reversible electric motor provides oil pressure. A rocker control switch determines motor and pump rotation thereby retracting or extending tilt and trim cylinders. The pump is equipped with an automatic and manual release valve (V – Fig. SZ14-27) that when set in the manual position (vertical) enables movement of trim and tilt cylinders if the electric motor malfunctions.

Recommended oil is SAE 20W or SAE 30W motor oil or Dexron automatic transmission fluid. Do not run pump without oil in reservoir. Fill plug (F) is located in side of pump reservoir. Oil level should reach fill plug hole threads with outboard motor in a vertical position. Hydraulic tilt should be cycled several times and oil level rechecked if system has been drained or lost a large amount of oil.

If a malfunction occurs in tilt and trim system, first make sure malfunction is not due to wiring, wiring connection or electric motor failure. To check oil pressure, connect a 20.7 MPa (3000 psi) gage to port "1" on pump and operate pump. Hydraulic oil pressure at port "1" should be within the limits of 6.9-17.25 MPa (1000-2500 psi). Connect test gage to port "2" and operate pump. Hydraulic oil pressure should be within the limits of 1.66-5.52 MPa (240-800 psi). Oil pressure less than specified may indicate leakage, faulty pressure relief valves or check valves.

If electric motor and pump assembly is disassembled for repair or renewal of individual components, upon reassembly use Ingilis Company EP630548 flat black neobase or equivalent to provide a watertight seal.

NOTE: On models DT50 (1984) and DT60 (1983-1984), the pump is equipped with manual release valve (M – Fig. SZ14-29) that when rotated two turns counterclockwise enables movement of trim and tilt cylinders if the electric motor malfunctions.

Recommended oil is SAE 20W, SAE 10W30 or SAE 10W40 motor oil or Dexron automatic transmission fluid. Oil level (L) should reach fill plug (F) hole threads with outboard motor in a vertical position. Do not run pump without oil in reservoir.

SUZUKI DT55 AND DT65
(After 1984)

CONDENSED SERVICE DATA

NOTE: Metric fasteners are used throughout outboard motor.

TUNE-UP
Hp/rpm:
DT55 ....55/4800-5500
DT65 ....65/4800-5500
Bore ....73 mm
(2.9 in.)
Stroke ....71 mm
(2.8 in.)
Number of Cylinders 3
Displacement ....891 cc
(54.4 cu. in.)
Spark Plug:
NGK B8HS
Electrode Gap ....0.9-1.0 mm
(0.035-0.040 in.)
Ignition Type ....Breakerless
Carburetor Make ....Mikuni

SIZES—CLEARANCES
Piston Ring End Gap ....0.2-0.4 mm
(0.008-0.016 in.)
Piston Pin Diameter ....19.995-20.000 mm
(0.7872-0.7874 in.)
Piston to Cylinder Wall Clearance ....0.112-0.127 mm
(0.0044-0.0050 in.)
Max. Crankshaft Runout at Main
Bearing Journal ....0.05 mm
(0.002 in.)
Max. Connecting Rod Small End Side
Shake ....5.0 mm
(0.20 in.)

TIGHTENING TORQUES
Cylinder Head Cover ....8-12 N·m
(6-9 ft.-lbs.)
Cylinder Head..........................20-26 N·m
(14-19 ft.-lbs.)
Crankcase:
6 mm ....8-12 N·m
(6-9 ft.-lbs.)

10 mm ....46-54 N·m
(34-39 ft.-lbs.)
Exhaust Cover ....8-10 N·m
(6-7 ft.-lbs.)
Flywheel Nut ....200-210 N·m
(145-152 ft.-lbs.)
Gearcase Pinion Nut ....30-40 N·m
(22-29 ft.-lbs.)
Propeller Shaft Nut ....50-60 N·m
(36-44 ft.-lbs.)
Standard Screws:
Unmarked or Marked "4"
5 mm ....2-4 N·m
(2-3 ft.-lbs.)
6 mm ....4-7 N·m
(3-5 ft.-lbs.)
8 mm ....10-16 N·m
(7-12 ft.-lbs.)
10 mm ....22-35 N·m
(16-26 ft.-lbs.)
Stainless Steel
5 mm ....2-4 N·m
(2-3 ft.-lbs.)
6 mm ....6-10 N·m
(5-7 ft.-lbs.)
8 mm ....15-20 N·m
(11-15 ft.-lbs.)
10 mm ....34-41 N·m
(25-30 ft.-lbs.)
Marked "7" or SAE Grade 5
5 mm ....3-6 N·m
(2-5 ft.-lbs.)
6 mm ....8-12 N·m
(6-9 ft.-lbs.)
8 mm ....18-28 N·m
(13-20 ft.-lbs.)
10 mm ....40-60 N·m
(29-44 ft.-lbs.)

LUBRICATION

The power head is lubricated by oil mixed with the fuel. Models DT55 and DT65 are equipped with oil injection. The manufacturer recommends using Suzuki BIA or a BIA certified two-stroke oil in oil injection tank. During break-in of a new or rebuilt engine, proceed as follows: For the first 15 hours of operation, mix fuel with oil in fuel tank at a ratio of 50:1 if Suzuki BIA oil or a BIA certified two-stroke oil is used. Mix fuel:oil at a ratio of 30:1 if any other type of two-stroke oil is used. Switch to straight fuel in fuel tank at the completion of the 15 hour break-in period. Manufacturer recommends regular or no-lead automotive gasoline having a minimum octane rating of 85. Gasoline and oil should be thoroughly mixed in fuel tank when used during break-in period.

The lower unit gears and bearings are lubricated by oil contained in the gearcase. Suzuki Outboard Motor Gear Oil should be used. Gearcase capacity is approximately 650 mL (22 oz.) of gear oil and should be drained and refilled after the first 10 hours of use and then after

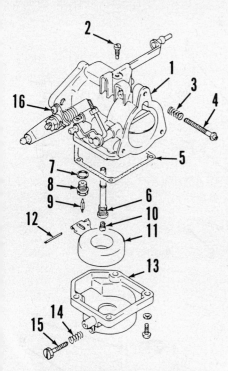

Fig. SZ15-1—Exploded view of Mikuni carburetor typical of all models.

1. Body	9. Needle
2. Pilot jet	10. Main jet
3. Spring	11. Float
4. Pilot air screw	12. Pin
5. Gasket	13. Float bowl
6. Main nozzle	14. Spring
7. Gasket	15. Drain plug
8. Seat	16. Screw

every 50 hours of use. Reinstall vent and fill plugs securely, using a new gasket if needed, to ensure a water tight seal.

FUEL SYSTEM

CARBURETOR. Mikuni type BV32-24 carburetors are used on DT55 models and Mikuni type BV40-32 carburetors are used on DT65 models. Three carburetors are used. Refer to Fig. SZ15-1 for exploded view. Initial setting of pilot air screw (4) from a slightly seated position should be 1⅛-1⅝ turns on DT55 models and 1½-2 turns on DT65 models. Final carburetor adjustment should be made with engine at normal operating temperature and running in forward gear. Adjust idle speed control knob (I–Fig. SZ15-2) so engine idles at 650-700 rpm in forward gear. Within the recommended limits, adjust pilot air screws (4–Fig. SZ15-1) so engine idles smoothly and will accelerate cleanly without hesitation. If necessary, readjust idle speed control knob (I–Fig. SZ15-2) so engine idle speed is 650-700 rpm.

Main fuel metering is controlled by main jet (10–Fig. SZ15-1). Standard main jet size for normal operation is number 117.5 on DT55 models and number 147.5 on DT65 models.

To check float level, remove float bowl and invert carburetor. Distance (D–Fig. SZ15-3) between main jet and bottom of float should be 11-12 mm (0.43-0.47 in.) on DT55 models and 17-19 mm (0.67-0.75 in.) on DT65 models. Adjust float level by bending tang (T) on float lever.

To synchronize throttle plate opening of all three carburetors, first detach rod between throttle shaft lever on middle carburetor and throttle control lever. Loosen screw or screws (16–Fig. SZ15-1) on top and bottom carburetors. Throttle lever return spring pressure should cause respective throttle plate to close. Visually verify all throttle plates are closed, then retighten screw or screws (16) of top and bottom carburetors. Reconnect rod between throttle shaft lever on middle carburetor and throttle control lever, then verify synchronization of throttle plates between all three carburetors.

SPEED CONTROL LINKAGE. The throttle plates of all three carburetors must be properly synchronized as outlined in the previous CARBURETOR section. A throttle plate switch assembly is used to register middle carburetor throttle plate position. An idle switch and an acceleration switch make up throttle plate switch assembly. Each

Fig. SZ15-2—Adjust idle speed control knob (I) to set engine idle speed.

Fig. SZ15-3—Distance (D) for correct float level should be 11-12 mm (0.43-0.47 in.) on DT55 models and 17-19 mm (0.67-0.75 in.) on DT65 models. Bend tank (T) on float lever to adjust.

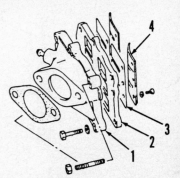

Fig. SZ15-4—Exploded view of intake manifold and reed valve assembly.

1. Intake manifold	3. Reed petals
2. Reed plate	4. Reed stop

switch has a roller mounted on a lever that contacts the throttle shaft cam mounted on the middle carburetor. As the cam is rotated, the lever on each switch activates a plunger, thus sending an electrical signal to the CDI unit by which the ignition timing is altered to match throttle plate opening for optimum performance. When the throttle plate is fully closed, the idle switch is turned "ON" and the acceleration switch is turned "OFF." When the throttle plate is opened, the idle switch is turned "OFF" and the acceleration switch is turned "ON."

NOTE: Throttle shaft cam used on Model DT55 differs from throttle shaft cam used on Model DT65. Backside of throttle shaft cam is identified by a "B" on DT55 models and by an "A" on DT65 models. Make sure correct cam is used.

REED VALVES. The inlet reed valves (Fig. SZ15-4) are located on a reed plate between intake manifold and crankcase. Each cylinder is fitted with a reed plate that contains two reed valve assemblies. The reed petals should seat very lightly against the reed plate throughout their entire length with the least possible tension. Tip of reed petal must not stand open more than 0.2 mm (0.008 in.) from contact surface. Reed stop opening should be 7.6-8.0 mm (0.30-0.31 in.).

Renew reeds if petals are broken, cracked, warped, rusted or bent. Never attempt to bend a reed petal or to straighten a damaged reed. Never install a bent or damaged reed. Seating surface of reed plate should be smooth and flat. When installing reeds or reed stop, make sure that petals are centered over the inlet holes in reed plate, and that the reed stops are centered over reed petals. Apply Thread Lock "1342" or a suitable equivalent to threads of reed stop screws prior to installation.

FUEL PUMP. A diaphragm type fuel pump is mounted on the side of power

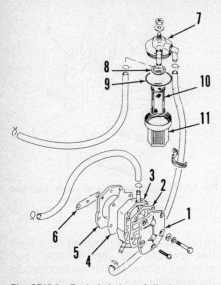

Fig. SZ15-5—Exploded view of diaphragm type fuel pump and fuel filter assemblies.

1. Cover
2. Gasket
3. Body
4. Diaphragm
5. Inner plate
6. Gasket
7. Filter base
8. Gasket
9. "O" ring
10. Filter element
11. Cup

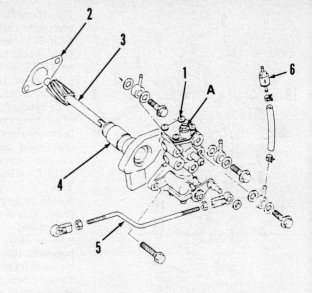

Fig. SZ15-6—Exploded view of oil injection pump and related components.

A. Air bleed screw
1. Pump assy.
2. Gasket
3. Driven gear
4. Retainer
5. Control rod
6. Check valve

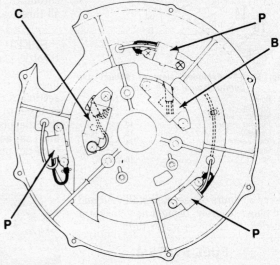

Fig. SZ15-7—View identifying location of pulser coils (P), condenser charging coil (C) and battery charging (B) on stator plate.

head cylinder block and is actuated by pressure and vacuum pulsations from the engine crankcase. Refer to Fig. SZ15-5 for exploded view of fuel pump assembly.

Defective or questionable parts should be renewed. Diaphragm should be renewed if air leaks or cracks are found, or if deterioration is evident.

FUEL FILTER. Fuel filter (7 through 11 – Fig. SZ15-5) is mounted on the side of power head cylinder block. Filter should be disassembled and cleaned after every 50 hours of use. Renew "O" ring (9) if required.

OIL INJECTION

BLEEDING PUMP. To bleed trapped air from oil supply line or pump, first make sure outboard motor is in upright position. Detach supply line from oil tank and plug oil tank outlet. Open oil pump air bleed screw (A – Fig. SZ15-6) three or four turns. Hold oil filter level with outlet side on top. Pour oil through oil supply line until oil seeps out around screw threads. After five seconds or when no air bubbles are noticed, close air bleed screw (A) and reconnect oil supply line to oil tank outlet.

CHECKING OIL PUMP OUTPUT. Start engine and allow to warm-up for approximately five minutes, then stop engine. Disconnect oil pump control rod (5 – Fig. SZ15-6) from bottom carburetor throttle shaft lever. Detach oil supply line at oil tank outlet and plug oil tank outlet. Connect oil gage 09900-

21602 to oil supply line. Fill oil gage with a recommended two-stroke oil until even with an upper reference mark. With oil pump control rod (5) in released position, start engine and maintain engine speed at 1500 rpm. Allow engine to run for five minutes. After five minutes, stop the engine and observe oil gage. Recommended oil consumption is 2.0-3.1 mL (0.067-0.105 oz.) on DT55 models and 2.0-3.2 mL (0.067-0.108 oz.) on DT65 models in five minutes at 1500 rpm.

To check oil pump at maximum output position, repeat previous procedure except hold oil pump control rod (5) in fully extended position. Recommended oil consumption is 3.4-5.1 mL (0.115-0.172 oz.) on DT55 models and 4.0-5.9 mL (0.135-0.199 oz.) on DT65 models in five minutes at 1500 rpm.

If the obtained oil consumption measurements are not within the recommended limits, then oil pump must be renewed.

NOTE: Oil pump used on DT55 models is identified by blue paint on top cover of pump. Oil pump used on DT65 models is not painted.

IGNITION

A capacitor discharge ignition (CDI) system is used. If engine malfunction is noted and the ignition system is suspected, make sure the spark plugs and all electrical wiring are in good condition and all electrical connections are tight before trouble-shooting the CD ignition system.

The standard spark plug is NGK B8HS with an electrode gap of 0.9-1.0 mm (0.036-0.040 in.).

TESTING CDI SYSTEM AND BATTERY CHARGING COIL. Refer to Fig. SZ15-7 and Fig. SZ15-8 and the following individual sections for testing CDI components and battery charging coil. Use Suzuki pocket tester

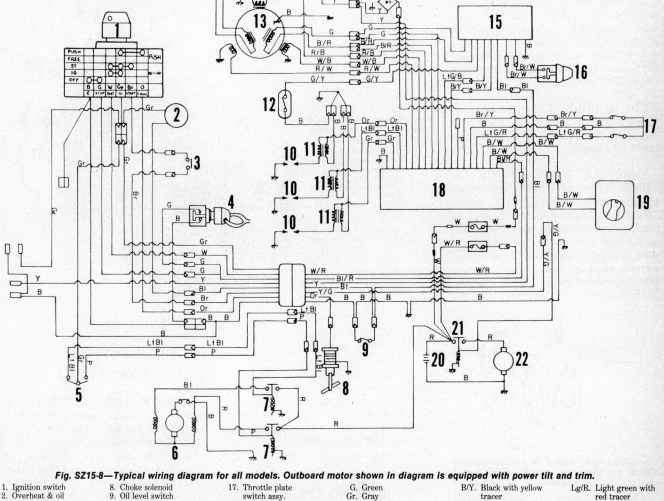

Fig. SZ15-8—Typical wiring diagram for all models. Outboard motor shown in diagram is equipped with power tilt and trim.

1. Ignition switch	8. Choke solenoid	17. Throttle plate	G. Green
2. Overheat & oil	9. Oil level switch	switch assy.	Gr. Gray
warning buzzer	10. Spark plugs	18. CDI module	Lt.Bl. Light blue
3. Neutral switch	11. Ignition coils	19. Idle speed control	O. Orange
4. Emergency stop	12. Cooling water	switch	P. Pink
switch	sensor	20. Battery	R. Red
5. Power tilt & trim	13. Stator plate assy.	21. Starter motor	W. White
switch	14. Rectifier	relay	Y. Yellow
6. Power tilt & trim	15. Low oil warning	22. Starter motor	B/R. Black with red
motor	reset unit	B. Black	tracer
7. Power tilt & trim	16. Oil warning reset	Bl. Blue	B/W. Black with white
motor relays	switch	Br. Brown	tracer

B/Y. Black with yellow tracer	Lg/R. Light green with red tracer
Bl/R. Blue with red tracer	R/B. Red with black tracer
Br/W. Brown with white tracer	R/W. Red with white tracer
Br/Y. Brown with yellow tracer	W/B. White with black tracer
G/Y. Green with yellow tracer	W/R. White with red tracer
Lg/B. Light green with black tracer	Y/G. Yellow with green tracer

09900-25002 or a suitable ohmmeter unless otherwise stated to test components. Renew the component or components if not within the recommended limits.

CONDENSER CHARGING COIL. Unplug wires at connectors leading from condenser charging coil. Attach one tester lead to green wire connector and remaining tester lead to connector of black wire with read tracer. Tester should show 190-270 ohms. Leave tester lead connected to green wire connector and attach remaining tester lead to coil's core. Tester should show an infinite reading.

PULSER COIL. Three pulser coils are used. Unplug wires at connectors leading from pulser coils. Attach one tester lead to black ground wire and remaining tester lead to connector leading to pulser coil. Tester should show 170-250 ohms. Repeat test for each pulser coil. Disconnect tester leads and attach one tester lead to mounting ear on pulser coil and remaining tester lead to connector leading to pulser coil. Tester should show an infinite reading.

BATTERY CHARGING COIL. Unplug wires at connectors leading from battery charging coil. Attach one tester lead to red wire connector and re-

maining tester lead to connector of yellow wire. Tester should show 0.2-0.6 ohms. Leave tester lead connected to red wire connector and attach remaining tester lead to coil's core. Tester should show an infinite reading.

IGNITION COILS. Three ignition coils are used. Unplug wires at connectors leading from ignition coils and secondary coil lead from spark plug. Attach one tester lead to black wire connector and remaining tester lead to orange wire connector for number one cylinder, light blue wire conductor for number two cylinder and gray wire connector for number three cylinder. Tester should show 0.5-0.8 ohms. Disconnect tester leads and attach one tester lead to spark plug end of secondary coil lead and remaining tester lead to orange wire connector for number one cylinder, light blue wire connector for number two cylinder and gray wire connector for number three cylinder. Tester should show 4700-7000 ohms.

CDI MODULE. Either Suzuki tool 09930-99810 or tool 09930-99830 with test cord 09930-89450 must be used to test CDI module.

THROTTLE PLATE SWITCH AS-SEMBLY. Unplug wires at connectors leading from throttle plate switch assembly. Attach one tester lead to black wire connector and remaining tester lead to connector of light green wire with red tracer. With lever on idle switch (I–Fig. SZ15-9) depressed, tester should show an infinite reading. With lever released, tester should show

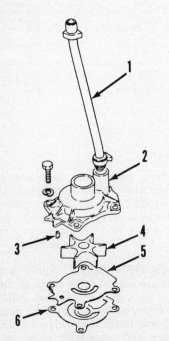

Fig. SZ15-9—Idle switch (I) and acceleration switch (A) make up throttle plate switch assembly.

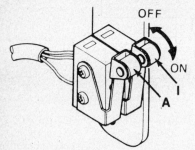

Fig. SZ15-10—Exploded view of water pump assembly.

1. Water tube	4. Impeller
2. Pump housing	5. Plate
3. Key	6. Gasket

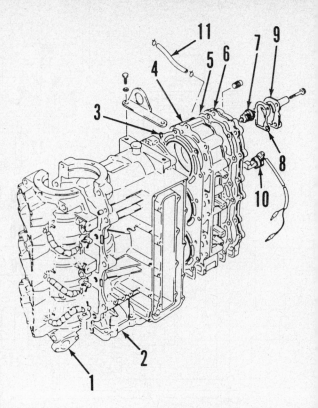

Fig. SZ15-11—Exploded view of cylinder block assembly.

1. Crankcase half
2. Cylinder block
3. Cylinder head gasket
4. Cylinder head
5. Cylinder head cover gasket
6. Cylinder head cover
7. Thermostat
8. Gasket
9. Thermostat housing
10. Cooling water sensor
11. Pilot discharge water hose

a zero ohm reading. Leave the tester lead attached to the black wire connector and connect remaining tester lead to connector of brown wire with yellow tracer to test acceleration switch (A). Previous test values should be obtained when previous test procedures are followed.

COOLING SYSTEM

WATER PUMP. A rubber impeller type water pump is mounted between the drive shaft housing and gearcase. A key in the drive shaft is used to turn the pump impeller. If cooling system problems are encountered, check water intake for plugging or partial stoppage, then if not corrected, remove gearcase as outlined in the appropriate section and check condition of the water pump, water passages and sealing surfaces.

When water pump is disassembled, check condition of impeller (4–Fig. SZ15-10) and plate (5) for excessive wear. Turn drive shaft clockwise (viewed from top) while placing pump housing over impeller. Avoid turning drive shaft in opposite direction when water pump is assembled.

THERMOSTAT. A thermostat (7–Fig. SZ15-11) is used to regulate operating temperature. The thermostat should start to open within the temperature range of 40°-44°C (104°-111°F). Thermostat can be removed for inspection or renewal by removing thermostat housing.

POWER HEAD

REMOVE AND REINSTALL. To remove the power head, first remove engine cover. Disconnect wiring to oil tank. Remove oil supply line from oil tank outlet and plug. Remove cap screws to withdraw oil tank. On models equipped with power tilt and trim, remove relays from side of cylinder head. Remove CDI module. Detach wiring from electric starter and starter relay that will interfere with power head removal. Remove engine flywheel. Disconnect fuel supply line from connector in bottom engine cover. Disconnect shift linkage and throttle linkage. Remove pilot discharge water hose (11–Fig. SZ15-11) from fitting in bottom engine cover. Remove cover to expose power head retaining cap screws. Remove the nine cap screws and lift power head assembly with related engine components from lower unit assembly.

Before reinstalling power head, check condition of drive shaft seals (25–Fig. SZ15-12). If renewal of seals is required, it is necessary to separate crankcase (1–Fig. SZ15-11) from cylinder block (2) as outlined in the appropriate following paragraphs. Apply a suitable water-resistant grease to lip portion of seals and install seals into seal housing (26–Fig. SZ15-12) with open side of seals towards lower unit. Make certain drive shaft splines are clean then coat them with a light coating of water-resistant grease. Apply a suitable sealer to mating surfaces of power head and lower unit and install a new gasket. Coat power head to lower unit retaining cap screws adjacent to cap screw heads with silicone sealer. Tighten the nine power head retaining cap screws to 18-28 N·m (13-20 ft.-lbs.). The remainder of installation is the reverse of removal procedure.

DISASSEMBLY. Disassembly and inspection can be accomplished in the following manner. Remove ignition coils, electric starter and bracket and idle speed adjusting switch and bracket. Remove throttle control arm and lever and clutch control arm. Remove stator plate assembly. Remove oil injection pump (1 – Fig. SZ15-6), retainer (4) and driven gear (3). Remove fuel pump and fuel filter assembly. Remove carburetors and electric choke solenoid. Remove intake manifolds and reed valve assemblies. Remove outer and inner exhaust covers. Remove cooling water sensor. Remove thermostat housing and withdraw thermostat. Remove spark plugs, cylinder head cover and cylinder head, then clean carbon from combustion chamber and any foreign material accumulation in water passages. Unscrew crankcase retaining screws and separate crankcase (1 – Fig. SZ15-11) from cylinder block (2). Crankshaft and piston assembly can now be removed from cylinder block.

Engine components are now accessible for overhaul as outlined in the appropriate paragraphs. Refer to the following section for assembly procedures.

ASSEMBLY. Refer to specific service sections when assembling the crankshaft, connecting rod, piston and reed valves. Make sure all joint and gasket surfaces are clean, free from nicks and burrs and hardened cement or carbon.

Whenever the power head is disassembled, it is recommended that all gasket surfaces and mating surfaces without gaskets be carefully checked for nicks, burrs and warped surfaces which might interfere with a tight seal. Cylinder head, head end of cylinder block and some mating surfaces of manifold and crankcase should be checked on a surface plate and lapped if necessary to provide a smooth surface. Do not remove any more metal than is necessary.

When assembling power head, first lubricate all friction surfaces and bearings with engine oil. Apply a suitable high temperature grease to lip portion of crankshaft seal. Apply a suitable water-resistant grease to lip portion of drive shaft seals and install seals into seal housing (26 – Fig. SZ15-12) with open side of seals towards lower unit.

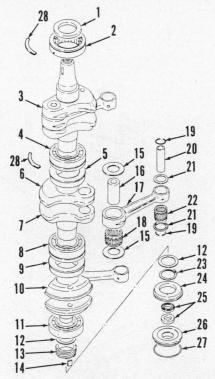

Fig. SZ15-12 — Exploded view of crankshaft assembly.

1. Seal	13. Oil injection pump drive gear
2. Roller bearing	14. Key
3. Upper crankshaft assy.	15. Thrust washers
4. Ball bearing	16. Crank pin
5. Labyrinth seal	17. Connecting rod
6. Middle crankshaft upper half	18. Needle bearing
7. Middle crankshaft lower half	19. Piston pin clips
8. Ball bearing	20. Piston pin
9. Labyrinth seal	21. Thrust washers
10. Lower crankshaft assy.	22. Needle bearing
11. Ball bearing	23. Snap ring
12. Thrust washers	24. Seal
	25. Seals
	26. Housing
	27. Seal
	28. Thrust rings

Place thrust rings in cylinder block, then install crankshaft assembly. Make certain main bearing locating pins engage notches in cylinder block. Flanges of labyrinth seals (5 and 9), seal (24) and housing (26) must fit securely in grooves of cylinder block. Apply a coat of Suzuki Bond No. 4 or a suitable sealer to mating surfaces of crankcase and cylinder block and position crankcase on cylinder block. Using tightening sequence shown

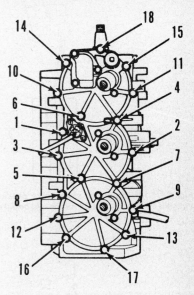

Fig. SZ15-14 — Tighten cylinder head cap screws in sequence shown to 20-26 N·m (14-19 ft.-lbs.).

in Fig. SZ15-13, tighten the 6 mm crankcase screws to 8-12 N·m (6-9 ft.-lbs.) and the 10 mm screws to 46-54 N·m (34-39 ft.-lbs.). Tighten cylinder head cap screws in sequence shown in Fig. SZ15-14 to 20-26 N·m (14-19 ft.-lbs.).

RINGS, PISTONS AND CYLINDERS. The pistons are fitted with two piston rings. The top piston ring is chrome plated. Piston rings must be installed with manufacturer's marking toward top end of piston. Rings are pinned in place to prevent rotation in ring grooves. Piston ring end gap should be 0.2-0.4 mm (0.008-0.016 in.) with a maximum allowable ring end gap of 0.8 mm (0.031 in.) Piston to cylinder wall clearance should be 0.112-0.127 mm (0.0044-0.0050 in.). Pistons and rings are available in standard size as well as 0.25 mm (0.010 in.) and 0.50 mm (0.020 in.) oversizes. Cylinder should be bored to an oversize if cylinder is out-of-round or taper exceeds 0.10 mm (0.004 in.). Install piston on connecting rod so arrow on piston crown will point towards exhaust port when piston is in cylinder.

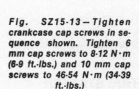

Fig. SZ15-13 — Tighten crankcase cap screws in sequence shown. Tighten 6 mm cap screws to 8-12 N·m (6-9 ft.-lbs.) and 10 mm cap screws to 46-54 N·m (34-39 ft.-lbs.)

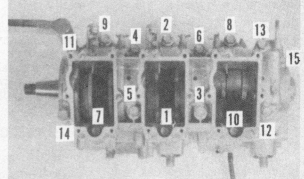

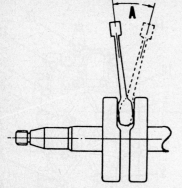

Fig. SZ15-15—Maximum side-to-side shake (A) at small end of connecting rod should be 5.0 mm (0.20 in.) or less.

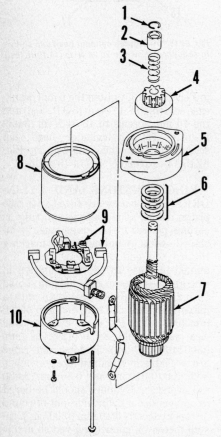

Fig. SZ15-16—Exploded view of electric starter motor.

1. "C" ring
2. Stop
3. Spring
4. Drive
5. Frame head
6. Thrust washers
7. Armature
8. Frame
9. Brush assy.
10. End housing

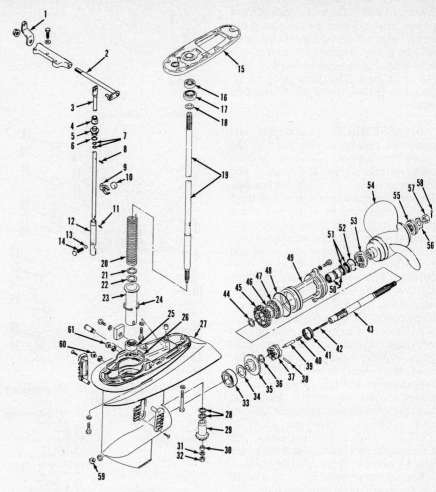

Fig. SZ15-17—Exploded view of lower unit gearcase assembly used on all models.

1. Shift arm
2. Shift shaft
3. Shift rod
4. Dust seal
5. Rod guide
6. "O" ring
7. "O" rings
8. Pin
9. Magnet holder
10. Magnet
11. Pin
12. Shift cam
13. Detent ball
14. Spring
15. Bearing housing
16. Seal
17. Bearing
18. Thrust washer
19. Drive shaft
20. Spring
21. Thrust washer
22. Washer
23. Collar
24. Snap ring
25. Needle bearing
26. Seal
27. Gearcase
28. Shims
29. Pinion gear
30. Collar
31. Washer
32. Nut
33. Bearing
34. Shim
35. Forward gear
36. Thrust washer
37. Dog clutch
38. Pin
39. Shift pin
40. Spring guide
41. Pin retainer
42. Shift spring
43. Propeller shaft
44. Thrust washer
45. Reverse gear
46. Shim
47. Bearing
48. "O" ring
49. End cap
50. Needle bearings
51. Seals
52. Snap ring
53. Spacer
54. Propeller
55. Spacer
56. Tab washer
57. Nut
58. Cotter pin
59. Drain plug
60. Level plug
61. Vent plug

are used in the middle and bottom end of crankshaft. Determine rod bearing wear by measuring connecting rod small end side-to-side movement as shown at (A—Fig. SZ15-15). Normal side-to-side movement is 5 mm (0.20 in.) or less. Maximum allowable limit of crankshaft runout is 0.05 mm (0.002 in.) measured at bearing surfaces with crankshaft ends supported.

When installing crankshaft, lubricate pistons, rings, cylinders and bearings with engine oil as outlined in ASSEMBLY section.

ELECTRIC STARTER

Models are equipped with electric starter shown in Fig. SZ15-16. Disas-

sembly is evident after inspection of unit and reference to exploded view. Starter brushes have a standard length of 16 mm (0.63 in.) and should be renewed if worn to 11.5 mm (0.45 in.) or less. After reassembly, bench test starter before installing on power head.

LOWER UNIT

PROPELLER AND DRIVE CLUTCH. Protection for the motor is built into a special cushioning clutch in the propeller hub. No adjustment is possible on the propeller or clutch. Three-bladed propellers are used. Propellers are available from the manufacturer in various diameters and pitches

CONNECTING RODS, BEARINGS AND CRANKSHAFT. Connecting
rods, bearings and crankshaft are a pressed-together unit. Crankshaft should be disassembled ONLY by experienced service personnel and with suitable service equipment.

Caged roller bearing is used at top end of crankshaft and caged ball bearings

and should be selected to provide optimum performance at full throttle within the recommended limits of 4800-5500 rpm.

R&R AND OVERHAUL. Refer to Fig. SZ15-17 for exploded view of lower unit gearcase assembly used on all models. During disassembly, note the location of all shims and thrust washers to aid in reassembly. To remove gearcase, first unscrew plug (59) and drain gear lubricant. Remove engine cover. Unscrew nut retaining shift arm (1) to shaft (2), then disengage shaft (2) from shift rod (3). Remove the cap screws securing gearcase to drive shaft housing and separate gearcase assembly from drive shaft housing. Remove water pump assembly (Fig. SZ15-10). Remove propeller with related components from propeller shaft. Unscrew two screws retaining gearcase end cap (49 – Fig. SZ15-17), then attach a suitable puller to propeller shaft (43) and withdraw propeller shaft assembly with gearcase end cap. Unscrew pinion nut (32) and remove pinion gear (29), then extract forward gear (35). Drive shaft (19) and related components can be withdrawn from gearcase after removal of bearing housing (15).

Inspect gears for wear on teeth and on engagement dogs. Inspect dog clutch (37) for wear on engagement surfaces. Inspect shafts for wear on splines and on friction surfaces of gears and oil seals. Check shift cam (12) and shift pin (39) for excessive wear. Check condition of shift spring (42). Spring free length should be 73 mm (2.9 in.) with a minimum length of 71 mm (2.8 in.). All seals and "O" rings should be renewed when unit is reassembled.

Backlash between pinion gear (29) and drive gears (35 and 45) should be 0.1-0.2 mm (0.004-0.008 in.) and is adjusted by varying thickness of shims (34 and 46). Propeller shaft end play should be 0.2-0.4 mm (0.008-0.016 in.) and is adjusted by increasing or decreasing the thickness of thrust washer (44).

Reassemble gearcase by reversing disassembly procedure while noting the following: Install dog clutch (37) on propeller shaft (43) so "REV" marked side is towards reverse gear (45). Tighten pinion nut (32) to 30-40 N·m (21-29 ft.-lbs.). Apply water-resistant grease to "O" ring (48). Apply silicone sealer to gearcase and bearing housing (15) mating surfaces and to bearing housing and drive shaft housing mating surfaces. Coat retaining cap screws adjacent to cap screw heads with silicone sealer.

Engage shift shaft (2) in shift rod (3) eyelet and attach shift arm (1). Secure with nut. Fill gearcase with outboard gear oil as outlined in LUBRICATION section.

POWER TILT AND TRIM

Some models are equipped with a hydraulically actuated power tilt and trim system. An oil pump driven by a reversible electric motor provides oil pressure. A rocker control switch determines motor and pump rotation thereby

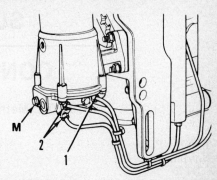

Fig. SZ15-19—View of pump assembly identifying test ports (1 and 2) and manual release valve (M). Refer to text.

retracting or extending tilt and trim cylinders. The pump is equipped with manual release valve (M – Fig. SZ15-19) that when rotated two turns counterclockwise enables movement of trim and tilt cylinders if the electric motor malfunctions.

Recommended oil is SAE 20W, SAE 10W30 or SAE 10W40 motor oil or Dexron automatic transmission fluid. Do not run pump without oil in reservoir. Fill plug (5 – Fig. SZ15-18) is located in side of pump reservoir. Oil level should reach fill plug hole threads. Hydraulic tilt should be cycled several times and oil level rechecked if system has been drained or lost a large amount of oil.

If a malfunction occurs in tilt and trim system, first make sure malfunction is not due to wiring, wiring connection or electric motor failure. To check oil pressure, connect a 34.5 MPa (5000 psi) gage to port "1" (Fig. SZ15-19) on pump and operate pump in the "UP" direction. Hydraulic oil pressure at port "1" should be within limits of 12.7-16.5 MPa (1850-2400 psi). Connect test gage to port "2" and operate pump in the "DOWN" direction. Hydraulic oil pressure should be within the limits of 23.4-31.4 MPa (3400-4550 psi). Oil pressure less than specified may indicate leakage, faulty pressure relief valves or check valves. The manufacturer recommends renewing pump and valve body assembly to service low pressure readings.

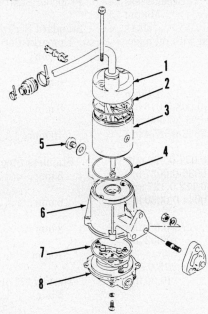

Fig. SZ15-18—Exploded view of power tilt and trim electric motor and pump assembly.

1. End cap
2. Gasket
3. Electric motor assy.
4. Gasket
5. Fill plug
6. Reservoir
7. "O" ring
8. Pump & valve body assy.

SUZUKI DT75 AND DT85

CONDENSED SERVICE DATA

NOTE: Metric fasteners are used throughout outboard motor.

TUNE-UP
Hp/rpm:
DT75 . . . . .75/4800-5500
DT85 . . . . .85/4800-5500
Bore . . . . .84 mm
(3.31 in.)
Stroke . . . . .72 mm
(2.83 in.)
Number of Cylinders .3
Displacement . . . . .1197 cc
(73.04 cu. in.)
Spark Plug:
NGK B8HS
Electrode Gap . . . . .0.8-0.9 mm
(0.031-0.035 in.)
Ignition Type .Breakerless
Carburetor Make .Mikuni
Fuel:Oil Ratio 50:1*
*Some DT75 and DT85 models are equipped with oil injection.

SIZES—CLEARANCES
Piston Ring End Gap . . . . .0.2-0.4 mm
(0.008-0.016 in.)
Piston Pin Diameter . . . . .19.995-20.000 mm
(0.7872-0.7874 in.)
Piston to Cylinder Wall Clearance:
DT75 . . . . .0.077-0.093 mm
(0.0030-0.0037 in.)
DT85 . . . . .0.112-0.127 mm
(0.0044-0.0050 in.)
Max. Crankshaft Runout at Main
Bearing Journal . . . . .0.05 mm
(0.002 in.)
Max. Connecting Rod Small End
Side Shake . . . . .5.0 mm
(0.20 in.)

TIGHTENING TORQUES
Cylinder Head (Prior to 1983):
6 mm . . . . .8-12 N·m
(6-9 ft.-lbs.)
10 mm . . . . .40-60 N·m
(29-44 ft.-lbs.)
Cylinder Head (After 1982) . . . . .46-54 N·m
(34-39 ft.-lbs.)

TIGHTENING TORQUES CONT.
Crankcase:
Prior to 1983 . . . . .40-60 N·m
(29-44 ft.-lbs.)
After 1982 . . . . .46-54 N·m
(34-39 ft.-lbs.)
Exhaust Cover . . . . .8-12 N·m
(6-9 ft.-lbs.)
Flywheel Nut .200-210 N·m
(145-152 ft.-lbs.)
Gearcase Pinion Nut:
Prior to 1983 . . . . .60-70 N·m
(43-50 ft.-lbs.)
After 1982 . . . . .70-80 N·m
(50-58 ft.-lbs.)
Propeller Shaft Nut . . . . .50-60 N·m
(36-44 ft.-lbs.)
Standard Screws:
Unmarked or Marked "4"
5 mm . . . . .2-4 N·m
(2-3 ft.-lbs.)
6 mm . . . . .4-7 N·m
(3-5 ft.-lbs.)
8 mm . . . . .10-16 N·m
(7-12 ft.-lbs.)
10 mm . . . . .22-35 N·m
(16-26 ft.-lbs.)
Stainless Steel
5 mm . . . . .2-4 N·m
(2-3 ft.-lbs.)
6 mm . . . . .6-10 N·m
(5-7 ft.-lbs.)
8 mm . . . . .15-20 N·m
(11-15 ft.-lbs.)
10mm . . . . .34-41 N·m
(25-30 ft.-lbs.)
Marked "7" or SAE Grade 5
5 mm . . . . .3-6 N·m
(2-5 ft.-lbs.)
6 mm . . . . .8-12 N·m
(6-9 ft.-lbs.)
8 mm . . . . .18-28 N·m
(13-20 ft.-lbs.)
10 mm . . . . .40-60 N·m
(29-44 ft.-lbs.)

LUBRICATION

The power head is lubricated by oil mixed with the fuel. On models without oil injection, fuel:oil ratios should be 30:1 during break-in of a new or rebuilt engine and 50:1 for normal service when using a BIA certified two-stroke engine oil or Suzuki "CCI" oil. When using any other type of two-stroke engine oil, fuel:oil ratios should be 20:1 during break-in and 30:1 for normal service. On models equipped with oil injection, for the first 5 hours of operation, mix fuel with oil in fuel tank at a ratio of 50:1 if Suzuki "CCI" oil or a BIA certified two-stroke oil is used. Mix fuel:oil at a ratio of 30:1 if any other type of two-stroke oil is used. Switch to straight fuel in fuel tank at the completion of the 5 hour break-in period. Manufacturer recommends regular or no-lead automotive gasoline having an 85-95 octane rating. Gasoline and oil should be thoroughly mixed in fuel tank when used on models without oil injection and when used during break-in period on models equipped with oil injection.

The lower unit gears and bearings are lubricated by oil contained in the gearcase. Suzuki Outboard Motor Gear Oil or a SAE 90 hypoid outboard gear oil should be used. Gearcase capacity is approximately 700 mL (23.7 oz.) of gear oil and should be drained and refilled after the first 10 hours of use and then after every 50 hours of use. Reinstall vent and fill plugs securely, using a new gasket if needed, to ensure a watertight seal.

FUEL SYSTEM

CARBURETOR. Mikuni type B32-28 carburetors are used on DT75 models and Mikuni type B40-32 carburetors are used on DT85 models. Refer to Fig. SZ16-1 for exploded view. Initial setting of pilot air screw (3) from a lightly

Fig. SZ16-2—Distance (D) for correct float level should be 12.5-14.5 mm (0.49-0.57 in.) on DT75 models and 17.5-19.5 mm (0.69-0.77 in.) on DT85 models. Bend tang (T) on float lever to adjust.

seated position should be 1-1½ turns on DT75 models and 1¼-1¾ turns on DT85 models. Final carburetor adjustment should be made with engine at normal operating temperature and running in forward gear. Rotate timing adjustment screw (B–Fig. SZ16-3) in small increments until engine idles at approximately 600-700 rpm. Adjust pilot air screw so engine idles smoothly and will accelerate cleanly without hesitation. If necessary, readjust timing adjustment screw to obtain 600-700 rpm idle speed.

Main fuel metering is controlled by main jet (5). Standard main jet size for normal operation is number 140 on DT75 models and number 162.5 on DT85 models.

To check float level, remove float bowl and invert carburetor. Distance (D–Fig. SZ16-2) between main jet and bottom of float should be 12.5-14.5 mm (0.49-0.57 in.) on DT75 models and 17.5-19.5 mm (0.69-0.77 in.) on DT85 models. Adjust float level by bending float tang (T).

To synchronize throttle plate opening of all three carburetors, use Suzuki carburetor balancer 09913-13121 or equivalent and make adjustment at throttle shaft connectors (14–Fig. SZ16-1) with engine running at 1000 rpm.

SPEED CONTROL LINKAGE. The carburetor throttle plates must be correctly synchronized to open as the ignition is advanced to obtain optimum performance. To adjust the speed control linkage, it is necessary to first check (and adjust if required) the ignition maximum advance as outlined in the IGNITION TIMING section. Disconnect carburetor link (C–Fig. SZ16-3) and rotate speed control lever (L) toward maximum speed position until it contacts maximum speed stop. Set carburetor throttle plates completely open then vary the length of carburetor link (C) until ball joint connector will just attach. Move speed control lever to full retard position. Clearance (A) at carburetor throttle shaft actuating levers should be 0-1 mm (0-0.039 in.).

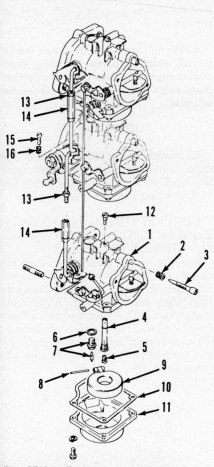

Fig. SZ16-1—Exploded view of Mikuni carburetors typical of all models.

1. Body	9. Float
2. Spring	10. Gasket
3. Pilot air screw	11. Float bowl
4. Main nozzle	12. Pilot jet
5. Main jet	13. Jam nut
6. Gasket	14. Connector
7. Needle & seat	15. Throttle stop screw
8. Pin	16. Spring

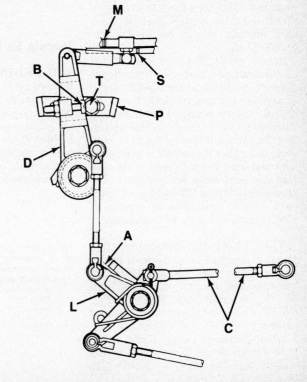

Fig. SZ16-3—View of speed control linkage typical of all models. Refer to text for indentification of components and servicing procedures.

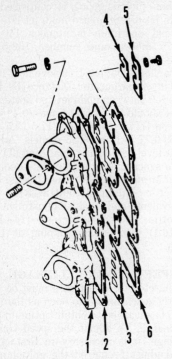

Fig. SZ16-4—Exploded view of intake manifold and reed valve assembly.

1. Manifold
2. Gasket
3. Reed plate
4. Reed petals
5. Reed stop
6. Gasket

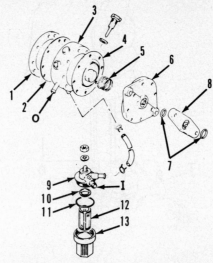

Fig. SZ16-5—Exploded view of diaphragm type fuel pump and fuel filter assemblies.

1. Cover
2. Diaphragm
3. Body
4. Diaphragm
5. Spring
6. Body
7. "O" rings
8. Insulator block
9. Fuel filter body
10. Packing
11. "O" ring
12. Filter
13. Bowl
I. Inlet
O. Outlet

REED VALVES.

REED VALVES. The inlet reed valves (Fig. SZ16-4) are located on a reed plate between intake manifold and crankcase. The reed petals should seat very lightly against the reed plate throughout their entire length with the least possible tension. Tip of reed petal must not stand open more than 0.2 mm (0.008 in.) from contact surface. Reed stop opening should be 7.6-8.0 mm (0.30-0.31 in.).

Renew reeds if petals are broken cracked, warped, rusted or bent. Never attempt to bend a reed petal or to straighten a damaged reed. Never install a bent or damaged reed. Seating surface of reed plate should be smooth and flat. When installing reeds or reed stop, make sure that petals are centered over the inlet holes in reed plate, and that the reed stops are centered over reed petals. Apply Thread Lock "1342" or a suitable equivalent to threads of reed stop screws prior to installation.

FUEL PUMP. A diaphragm type fuel pump is mounted on the side of power head cylinder block and is actuated by pressure and vacuum pulsations from the engine crankcases. Refer to Fig. SZ16-5 for exploded view of fuel pump assembly.

When servicing pump, scribe reference marks across pump body to aid reassembly. Defective or questionable parts should be renewed. Diaphragm should be renewed if air leaks or cracks are found, or if deterioration is evident.

FUEL FILTER. A fuel filter (9 through 13—Fig. SZ16-5) is mounted on the side of power head cylinder block on all models. Filter should be disassembled and cleaned after every 50 hours of use. Renew "O" ring (11) if required.

OIL INJECTION

Models So Equipped

BLEEDING PUMP. To bleed trapped air from oil supply line or pump, first make sure outboard motor is in an upright position and oil tank is full. Open oil pump air bleed screw (A—Fig. SZ16-6) three or four turns to allow oil to seep out around screw threads. After five seconds or when no air bubbles are noticed, close air bleed screw (A).

CHECKING OIL PUMP OUTPUT. Start engine and allow to warm-up for approximately five minutes, then stop engine. Disconnect oil pump control rod (5—Fig. SZ16-6) from bottom carburetor throttle shaft lever. Detach oil supply line at oil tank outlet and plug oil tank outlet. Connect oil gage 09900-21602 to oil supply line. Fill gage with a recommended two-stroke oil until even with an upper reference mark. With oil pump control rod (5) in released position, start engine and maintain engine speed at 1500 rpm. Allow engine to run for five minutes. After five minutes, stop the engine and observe oil gage. Recommended oil consumption is 4.0-5.0 mL (0.135-0.169 oz.) in five minutes at 1500 rpm.

To check oil pump at maximum output position, repeat previous procedure except hold oil pump control rod (5) in fully extended position. Recommended oil consumption is 6.5-7.9 mL (0.220-0.267 oz.) in two minutes at 1500 rpm.

If the obtained oil consumption measurements are not within the recommended limits, then oil pump must be renewed.

IGNITION

All models are equipped with an independent breakerless electronic ignition system. Refer to Fig. SZ16-7 for typical wiring diagram on all models.

IGNITION TIMING. Ignition timing should be 7° ATDC at 1000 rpm and 21.5° BTDC at 5000 rpm.

Initial setting of ignition timing on all models can be accomplished as follows: Set throttle at full advance position, then align mark (M—Fig. SZ16-3) on stator plate with stationary mark (S) on upper seal housing. Loosen two screws (T) on maximum advance stop plate (P) and position plate to lightly contact advance lever (D).

Fig. SZ16-6—Exploded view of oil injection pump and related components used on all models so equipped.

A. Air bleed screw
1. Pump assy.
2. Gasket
3. Driven gear
4. Retainer
5. Control rod

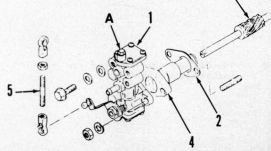

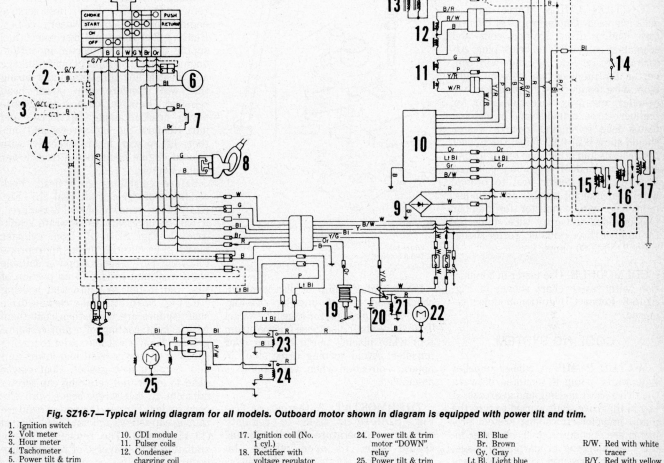

Fig. SZ16-7—Typical wiring diagram for all models. Outboard motor shown in diagram is equipped with power tilt and trim.

1. Ignition switch
2. Volt meter
3. Hour meter
4. Tachometer
5. Power tilt & trim switch
6. Overheat & oil warning buzzer
7. Neutral switch
8. Emergency stop switch
9. Rectifier

10. CDI module
11. Pulser coils
12. Condenser charging coil
13. Battery charging coil
14. Overneat switch
15. Ignition coil (No. 3 cyl.)
16. Ignition coil (No. 2 cyl.)

17. Ignition coil (No. 1 cyl.)
18. Rectifier with voltage regulator
19. Choke solenoid
20. Battery
21. Starter motor relay
22. Starter motor
23. Power tilt & trim motor "UP" relay

24. Power tilt & trim motor "DOWN" relay
25. Power tilt & trim motor

Bl. Black
G. Green
P. Pink
R. Red
W. White
Y. Yellow

Bl. Blue
Br. Brown
Gy. Gray
Lt Bl. Light blue
Or. Orange
B/R. Black with red tracer
B/W. Black with white tracer
G/Y. Green with yellow tracer

R/W. Red with white tracer
R/Y. Red with yellow tracer
W/R. White with red tracer
Y/G. Yellow with green tracer
Y/R. Yellow with red tracer

Final ignition timing check can be made using a suitable power timing light. Immerse lower unit of outboard motor in water and connect timing light to upper spark plug. Set engine throttle at full retard position and start engine. Refer to ignition timing specifications stated previously and check alignment of flywheel timing marks with index mark on electric starter cap. To check advance timing, run engine at wide-open throttle and note timing marks.

Full retard timing can be adjusted by turning screw (B) in or out as required. Note idle speed while making adjustment. Vary full retard timing to obtain recommended idle speed of 600-700 rpm.

TROUBLE-SHOOTING. If ignition malfunction occurs, use only approved procedures to prevent damage to the components. The fuel system should be checked first to make certain that faulty running is not caused by incorrect mixture or contaminated fuel. Make sure malfunction is not due to spark plug, wiring or wiring connection failure. Trouble-shoot ignition circuit using Suzuki pocket tester 09900-25002 or a suitable ohmmeter as follows:

CONDENSER CHARGING COIL. Unplug wires at connectors leading from condenser charging coil. Attach one tester lead to connector of black wire with red tracer and remaining tester lead to connector of red wire with white tracer. Tester should show 680-831 ohms. Leave tester lead attached to connector of red wire with white tracer and attach remaining tester lead to black wire. Tester should show 114-140 ohms.

PULSER COIL. Two pulser coils are used. Unplug wires at connectors leading from pulser coils. Attach one tester lead to green wire connector and remaining tester lead to connector of yellow wire with red tracer. Tester should show 320-391 ohms. Repeat test on other coil. Connect one tester lead to pink wire connector and remaining tester lead to connector of white wire with red tracer. Tester should show 320-391 ohms.

BATTERY CHARGING COIL. Unplug wires at connectors leading from battery charging coil. Attach one tester lead to red wire connector and remaining tester lead to connector of yellow wire. Tester should show 0.54-0.66 ohms. Leave tester lead connected to red wire connector and attach remaining tester lead to connector of red wire with yellow tracer. Tester should show 0.36-0.44 ohms.

IGNITION COILS. Three ignition coils are used. Unplug wires at connectors leading from ignition coils and secondary coil lead from spark plug. Attach one tester lead to orange wire connector for number one cylinder, light blue wire connector for number two cylinder and gray wire connector for number three cylinder and remaining tester lead to engine ground. Tester should show 0.21-0.29 ohms. Disconnect tester leads and attach one tester lead to spark plug end of secondary coil lead and remaining tester lead to orange wire connector for number one cylinder, light blue wire connector for number two cylinder and gray wire connector for number three cylinder. Tester should show 2130-2880 ohms.

CDI MODULE. Use tester in conjunction with tester chart shown in Fig. SZ16-8. Renew CD ignition module if required.

COOLING SYSTEM

WATER PUMP. A rubber impeller type water pump is mounted between the drive shaft housing and gearcase. A key in the drive shaft is used to turn the pump impeller. If cooling system problems are encountered, check water intake for plugging or partial stoppage, then if not corrected, remove gearcase as outlined in the appropriate section and check condition of the water pump, water passages and sealing surfaces.

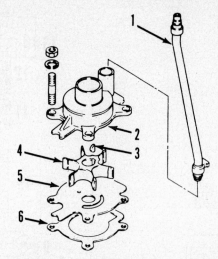

Fig. SZ16-9—Exploded view of water pump assembly.

1. Water tube
2. Pump housing
3. Key
4. Impeller
5. Plate
6. Gasket

When water pump is disassembled, check condition of impeller (4–Fig. SZ16-9) and plate (5) for excessive wear. Turn drive shaft clockwise (viewed from top) while placing pump housing over impeller. Avoid turning drive shaft in opposite direction when water pump is assembled.

THERMOSTAT. A thermostat (7– Fig. SZ16-10 is used to regulate operating temperature. The thermostat should start to open within the temperature range of 40°-44°C (104°-111°F). Thermostat can be removed for inspection or renewal by removing thermostat housing.

POWER HEAD

REMOVE AND REINSTALL. To remove the power head, first remove engine cover. Detach battery cables. Remove fuel filter and disconnect fuel supply line from connector in bottom engine cover. Disconnect shift linkage and throttle linkage. Detach any wiring that will interfere with power head removal. Remove covers to expose power head retaining cap screws and nut. Remove the cap screws and nut, then lift power head assembly with related engine components from lower unit assembly.

Before reinstalling power head, check condition of drive shaft seal (15–Fig. SZ16-11). If renewal of seal is required, it will be necessary to separate crankcase (1–Fig. SZ16-10) from cylinder block (2) as outlined in the appropriate following paragraphs. Apply a suitable water-resistant grease to lip portion of seal and install seal into seal housing (16–Fig. SZ16-11). Make certain drive shaft splines are clean then coat them with a light coating of water-resistant grease. Apply a suitable sealer to mating surfaces of power head and lower unit and install a new gasket. Coat power head to lower unit retaining cap screws adjacent to cap screw heads with silicone sealer. Tighten the power head retaining cap screws and nut to 15-20 N·m (11-15 ft.-lbs.). The remainder of installation is the reverse of removal procedure.

DISASSEMBLY. Disassembly and inspection can be accomplished in the following manner. On models equipped with oil injection, disconnect wiring to oil tank. Remove oil supply line from oil tank outlet and plug. Remove cap screws to withdraw oil tank. On models equipped with power tilt and trim, remove relays from side of cylinder block. Remove carburetors and electric choke solenoid. Remove fuel pump assembly. Remove oil injection pump (1–Fig. SZ16-6), retainer (4) and driven gear (3). Remove ignition coils, electric starter, starter motor relay, rectifier and CDI module. Remove speed control linkage. Remove flywheel and stator plate assembly. Remove electric starter motor bracket and any remaining wiring that will interfere with cylinder block and crankcase separation. Remove intake manifolds and reed valve assemblies. Remove outer and inner exhaust covers. Remove thermostat housing and withdraw thermostat. Remove spark plugs, cylinder head, spring (7–Fig. SZ16-10) and valve (8), then clean carbon from combustion chamber and any foreign material accumulation in water passages. Unscrew crankcase retaining

(−) TESTER LEAD / TESTER LEAD (+)	CHARGE			PULSER				IGNITION			STOP
	Black/Red	Red/White	Black	Green	Pink	White/Red	Yellow/Red	Orange	Light Blue	Grey	Black/White
CHARGE Black/Red		A	A	A	A	A	A	B	B	B	A
Red/White	B		B	B	B	B	B	B	B	B	B
Black	B	B		A	A	A	A	C	C	C	B
PULSER Green	B	B	A		A	A	A	C	C	C	B
Pink	B	B	B	B		B	B	B	B	B	B
White/Red	B	B	A	A	A		A	C	C	C	B
Yellow/Red	B	B	A	A	A	A		C	C	C	B
IGNITION Orange	C	C	C	B	B	C	C		B	B	C
Light Blue	C	C	C	B	B	C	C	B		B	C
Grey	C	C	C	B	B	C	C	B	B		C
STOP Black/White	A	A	A	A	A	A	A	C	C	C	

Fig. SZ16-8—Use above chart and values listed below to test condition of CD ignition module.

A. 100k ohms or less
B. 100k ohms or more
C. Tester needle should deflection then return toward infinite resistance

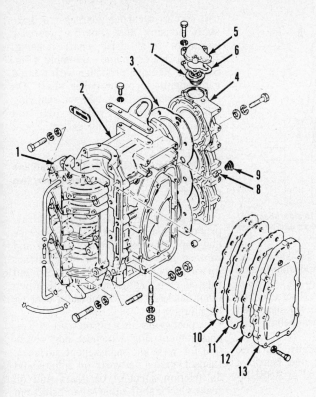

ing rings (8) and labyrinth seal rings (9) into cylinder block, then install crankshaft assembly. Make certain main bearing locating pins engage notches in cylinder block. Apply a coat of Suzuki Bond No. 4 or a suitable sealer to mating surfaces of crankcase and cylinder block and position crankcase on cylinder block. Using tightening sequence shown in Fig. SZ16-12, tighten crankcase screws to values shown in CONDENSED SERVICE DATA. Tighten cylinder head cap screws in sequence shown in Fig. SZ16-13 to values shown in CONDENSED SERVICE DATA.

RINGS, PISTONS AND CYLINDERS. The pistons are fitted with two piston rings. Piston rings must be installed with manufacturer's marking toward top end of piston. Rings are pinned in place to prevent rotation in ring grooves. Piston ring end gap should be 0.2-0.4 mm (0.008-0.016 in.) with a maximum allowable ring end gap of 0.8 mm (0.031 in.). Piston to cylinder wall clearance should be 0.077-0.093 mm (0.0030-0.0037 in.) on DT75 models and 0.112-0.127 mm (0.0044-0.0050 in.) on DT85 models. Pistons and rings are

Fig. SZ16-10—Exploded view of cylinder block assembly typical of all models.

1. Crankcase half
2. Cylinder block
3. Gasket
4. Cylinder head
5. Thermostat housing
6. Gasket
7. Thermostat
8. Valve
9. Spring
10. Gasket
11. Inner exhaust cover
12. Gasket
13. Outer exhaust cover

screws and separate crankcase (1) from cylinder block (2). Crankshaft and piston assembly can now be removed from cylinder block.

Engine components are now accessible for overhaul as outlined in the appropriate following paragraphs. Refer to the following section for assembly procedures.

ASSEMBLY. Refer to specific service sections when assembling the crankshaft, connecting rod, piston and reed valves. Make sure all joint and gasket surfaces are clean, free from nicks and burrs and hardened cement or carbon.

Whenever the power head is disassembled, it is recommended that all gasket surfaces and mating surfaces without gaskets be carefully checked for nicks, burrs and warped surfaces which might interfere with a tight seal. Cylinder head, head end of cylinder block and some mating surfaces of manifold and crankcase should be checked on a surface plate and lapped if necessary to provide a smooth surface. Do not remove any more metal than is necessary.

When assembling power head, first lubricate all friction surfaces and bearings with engine oil. Apply a suitable high temperature grease to lip portion of crankshaft seal. Apply a suitable water-resistant grease to lip portion of drive shaft seal and install seal into seal housing (16—Fig. SZ16-11). Place bear-

Fig. SZ16-11—Exploded view of crankshaft assembly typical of all models.

1. Seal
2. Roller bearing
3. Pin
4. Top crankshaft upper half
5. Top crankshaft lower half
6. Roller bearing
7. "O" ring
8. Bearing ring
9. Labyrinth seal ring
10. Labyrinth seal
11. Middle crankshaft half
12. Lower crankshaft half
13. Roller bearing
14. Seal
15. Seal
16. Seal housing
17. Crankpin
18. Thrust washer
19. Needle bearing
20. Connecting rod
21. Thrust washers
22. Needle bearing
23. Piston
24. Piston pin clips
25. Piston pin
26. Piston rings

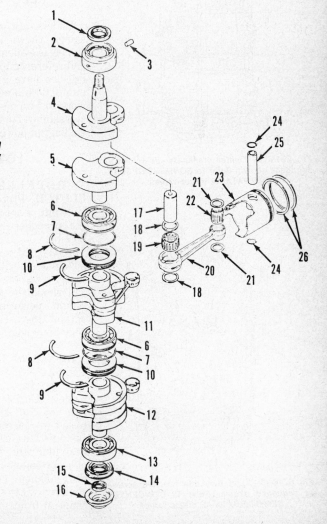

available in standard size as well as 0.25 mm (0.010 in.) and 0.50 mm (0.020 in.) oversizes. Cylinder should be bored to an oversize if cylinder is out-of-round or taper exceeds 0.10 mm (0.004 in.). Install piston on connecting rod so arrow on piston crown will point towards exhaust port when piston is in cylinder.

CONNECTING RODS, BEARINGS AND CRANKSHAFT. Connecting rods, bearings and crankshaft are a pressed-together unit. Crankshaft should be disassembled ONLY by experienced service personnel and with suitable service equipment.

Caged roller bearing is used at top end of crankshaft and caged ball bearings are used in the middle and bottom end of crankshaft. Determine rod bearing wear by measuring connecting rod small end

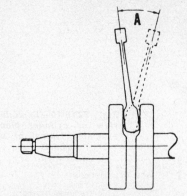

Fig. SZ16-14—Maximum side-to-side shake (A) at small end of connecting rod should be 5 mm (0.20 in.) or less.

side-to-side movement is shown at (A–Fig. SZ16-14). Normal side-to-side movement is 5 mm (0.20 in.) or less. Maximum allowable limit of crankshaft runout is 0.05 mm (0.002 in.) measured at bearing surfaces with crankshaft ends supported.

When installing crankshaft, lubricate pistons, rings, cylinders and bearings with engine oil as outlined in ASSEMBLY section.

ELECTRIC STARTER

Models are equipped with electric starter shown in Fig. SZ16-15. Disassembly is evident after inspection of unit and reference to exploded view. Starter brushes have a standard length of 16 mm (0.63 in.) and should be renewed if worn to 11.5 mm (0.45 in.) or less. After reassembly, bench test starter before installing on power head.

LOWER UNIT

PROPELLER AND DRIVE CLUTCH. Protection for the motor is built into a special cushioning clutch in the propeller hub. No adjustment is possible on the propeller or clutch. Three-bladed propellers are used. Propellers are available from the manufacturer in various diameters and pitches and should be selected to provide optimum performance at full throttle within the recommended limits of 4800-5500 rpm.

R&R AND OVERHAUL. Refer to Fig. SZ16-16 for exploded view of lower unit gearcase assembly used on all models. During disassembly, note the location of all shims and thrust washers to aid in reassembly. To remove gearcase, first unscrew plug (34) and drain gear lubricant. Remove plug from side of lower engine cover to obtain access to shift linkage. Unscrew nuts retaining shift arm (2) to shaft (4), then disengage shaft (4) from shift rod (5). Remove the

cap screws securing gearcase to drive shaft housing and separate gearcase assembly from drive shaft housing. Remove water pump assembly (Fig. SZ16-9). Remove propeller with related components from propeller shaft. On models prior to 1983, remove seal ring (65–Fig. SZ16-16), washer (64) and snap ring (63) retaining gearcase end cap (58).

NOTE: On models after 1982, gearcase end cap (58) is retained to gearcase by two cap screws.

Use a suitable puller and withdraw propeller shaft assembly with gearcase end cap. Unscrew pinion nut (50) and remove pinion gear (49), then extract forward gear (41). Drive shaft (20) and related components can be withdrawn from gearcase after removal of bearing housing (18).

Inspect gears for wear on teeth and on engagement dogs. Inspect dog clutch (45) for wear on engagement surfaces. Inspect shafts for wear on splines and on friction surfaces of gears and oil seals. Check shift cam (14) and shift pin (43) for excessive wear. Check condition

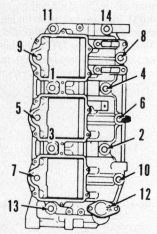

Fig. SZ16-12—Tighten crankcase cap screws in sequence shown. Refer to CONDENSED SERVICE DATA for torque values.

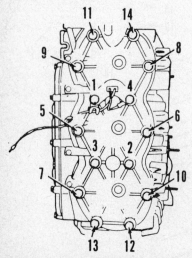

Fig. SZ16-13—Tighten cylinder head cap screws in sequence shown. Refer to CONDENSED SERVICE DATA for torque values.

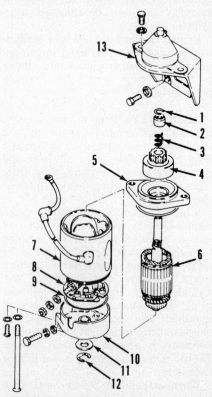

Fig. SZ16-15—Exploded view of electric starter motor.

1. "C" ring
2. Stop
3. Spring
4. Drive
5. Frame head
6. Armature
7. Frame
8. Brush assy.
9. Gasket
10. End housing
11. Thrust washer
12. "E" clip
13. Bracket

of shift spring (48). All seals and "O" rings should be renewed when unit is reassembled.

Backlash between pinion gear (49) and drive gears (41 and 53) should be 0.05-0.30 mm (0.002-0.012 in.) on models prior to 1983 and 0.1-0.2 mm (0.004-0.008 in.) on models after 1982. Backlash is adjusted by varying thickness of shims (40 and 54). Propeller shaft end play should be 0.05-0.30 mm (0.002-0.012 in.) on models prior to 1983 and 0.2-0.4 mm (0.008-0.016 in.) on models after 1982. Propeller shaft end play is adjusted by increasing or decreasing the thickness of shim (51).

Reassemble gearcase by reversing disassembly procedure while noting the following: Install dog clutch (45) on propeller shaft (56) so "F" marked side (Fig. SZ16-17) is towards forward gear (41 – Fig. SZ16-16). Tighten pinion nut to 60-70 N·m (44-51 ft.-lbs.) on models prior to 1983 and 70-80 N·m (51-58 ft.-lbs.) on models after 1982. Apply water-resistant grease to "O" ring (57). Apply silicone sealer to gearcase and bearing housing (18) mating surfaces and to bearing housing and drive shaft housing mating surfaces. Coat retaining cap screws adjacent to cap screw head with silicone sealer.

Engage shift shaft (4) in shift rod (5) eyelet and attach shift arm (2). Secure with nuts. Fill gearcase with outboard gear oil as outlined in LUBRICATION section.

POWER TILT AND TRIM

Some models are equipped with a hydraulically actuated power tilt and trim system. An oil pump driven by a reversible electric motor provides oil pressure. A rocker control switch determines motor and pump rotation thereby retracting or extending tilt and trim cylinders.

Early Type

The pump is equipped with an automatic and manual release valve (V – Fig. SZ16-18) that when set in the manual position (vertical) enables movement of trim and tilt cylinders if the electric motor malfunctions.

Recommended oil is SAE 20W or SAE 30W motor oil or Dexron automatic transmission fluid. Do not run pump without oil in reservoir. Fill plug (F) is located in side of pump reservoir. Oil level should reach fill plug hole threads with outboard motor in a vertical posi-

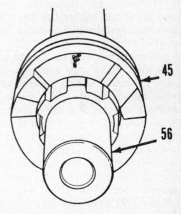

Fig. SZ16-17—Install dog clutch (45) on propeller shaft (56) with "F" marked side towards forward gear.

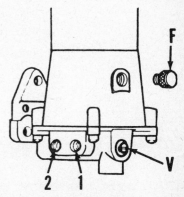

Fig. SZ16-18—View of early type pump assembly showing location of oil fill plug (F), release valve (V) and test ports (1 and 2).

Fig. SZ16-16—Exploded view of typical lower unit gearcase assembly used on all models. On models after 1982, gearcase end cap (58) is retained to gearcase by two cap screws.

1. Link	19. Bearing	36. Pin	53. Reverse gear
2. Shift arm	20. Drive shaft	37. Bearing	54. Shim
3. Grommets	21. Pin	38. Thrust bearing	55. Bearing
4. Shift shaft	22. Shim	39. Thrust washer	56. Propeller shaft
5. Shift rod	23. Thrust washer	40. Shim	57. "O" ring
6. Pin	24. Thrust bearing	41. Forward gear	58. End cap
7. Dust seal	25. Spring	42. Thrust washer	59. Pin
8. "O" ring	26. Collar	43. Shift pin	60. Needle bearing
9. Rod guide	27. Thrust washer	44. Spring guide	61. Seal
10. "O" ring	28. Thrust washer	45. Dog clutch	62. Snap ring
11. "O" ring	29. Needle bearings	46. Pin	63. Snap ring
12. Magnet	30. Vent plug	47. Pin retainer	64. Washer
13. Magnet holder	31. Seal ring	48. Shift spring	65. Seal ring
14. Shift cam	32. Level plug	49. Pinion gear	66. Spacer
15. Pins	33. Gearcase housing	50. Nut	67. Propeller
16. Snap ring	34. Drain plug	51. Shim	68. Spacer
17. Seal	35. Gasket	52. Thrust washer	69. Tab washer
18. Bearing housing			70. Nut

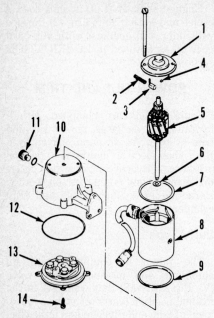

Fig. SZ16-19—Exploded view of early type power tilt and trim electric motor and pump assembly.

1. End cap	8. Frame
2. Spring	9. Gasket
3. Brush	10. Reservoir
4. Ball	11. Fill plug
5. Armature	12. "O" ring
6. Thrust washer	13. Pump assy.
7. Gasket	14. Cap screw

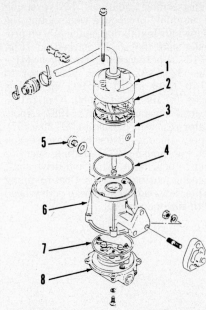

Fig. SZ16-20—Exploded view of late type power tilt and trim electric motor and pump assembly.

1. End cap	
2. Gasket	
3. Electric motor assy.	6. Reservoir
4. Gasket	7. "O" ring
5. Fill plug	8. Pump & valve body assy.

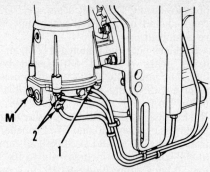

Fig. SZ16-21—View of late type pump assembly identifying test ports (1 and 2) and manual release valve (M). Refer to text.

tion. Hydraulic tilt should be cycled several times and oil level rechecked if system has been drained or lost a large amount of oil.

If malfunction occurs in tilt and trim system, first make sure malfunction is not due to wiring, wiring connection or electric motor failure. To check oil pressure, connect a 20.7 MPa (3000 psi) gage to port "1" on pump and operate pump. Hydraulic oil pressure at port "1" should be within the limits of 6.9-17.25 MPa (1000-2500 psi). Connect test gage to port "2" and operate pump. Hydraulic oil pressure should be within the limits of 1.66-5.52 MPa (240-800 psi). Oil pres-

sure less than specified may indicate leakage, faulty pressure relief valves or check valves.

If electric motor and pump assembly is disassembled for repair or renewal of individual components, upon reassembly use Ingilis Company EP630548 flat black neobase or equivalent to provide a watertight seal.

Late Type

The pump is equipped with manual release valve (M–Fig. SZ16-21) that when rotated two turns counterclockwise enables movement of trim and tilt cylinders if the electric motor malfunctions.

Recommended oil is SAE 20W, SAE 10W30 or SAE 10W40 motor oil or Dexron automatic transmission fluid. Do not run pump without oil in reservoir. Fill plug (5 – Fig. SZ16-20) is located in side of pump reservoir. Oil level should reach fill plug hole threads. Hydraulic tilt should be cycled several times and oil level rechecked if system has been drained or lost a large amount of oil.

If malfunction occurs in tilt and trim system, first make sure malfunction is not due to wiring, wiring connection or electric motor failure. To check oil pressure, connect a 34.5 MPa (5000 psi) gage to port "1" (Fig. SZ16-21) on pump and operate pump in the "UP" direction. Hydraulic oil pressure at port "1" should be within the limits of 12.7-16.5 MPa (1850-2400 psi). Connect test gage to port "2" and operate pump in the "DOWN" direction. Hydraulic oil pressure should be within the limits of 23.4-31.4 MPa (3400-4550 psi). Oil pressure less than specified may indicate leakage, faulty pressure relief valves or check valves. The manufacturer recommends renewing pump and valve body assembly to service low pressure readings.

SUZUKI DT115 AND DT140
(Prior To 1986)

CONDENSED SERVICE DATA

NOTE: Metric fasteners are used throughout outboard motor.

TUNE-UP
Hp/rpm:
  DT115 . . . . .115/4800-5500
  DT140 . . . . .140/4800-5500
Bore . . . . .84 mm
  (3.31 in.)
Stroke . . . . .80 mm
  (3.15 in.)
Number of Cylinders 4
Displacement . . . . .1773 cc
  (108.20 cu. in.)
Spark Plug:
  NGK B8HS
  Electrode Gap . . . . .0.8-0.9 mm
  (0.031-0.035 in.)
Ignition Type . . . . .Breakerless
Carburetor Make . . . . .Mikuni

SIZES—CLEARANCES
Piston Ring End Gap . . . . .0.2-0.4 mm
  (0.008-0.016 in.)
Piston Pin Diameter . . . . .21.995-22.000 mm
  (0.8659-0.8661 in.)
Piston to Cylinder Wall Clearance . . . . .0.112-0.127 mm
  (0.0044-0.0050 in.)
Max. Crankshaft Runout at Main
  Bearing Journal . . . . .0.05 mm
  (0.002 in.)
Max. Connecting Rod Small End
  Side Shake . . . . .5.0 mm
  (0.20 in.)

TIGHTENING TORQUES
Cylinder Head:
  6 mm . . . . .8-12 N·m
  (6-9 ft.-lbs.)
  10 mm . . . . .40-60 N·m
  (29.44 ft.-lbs.)

TIGHTENING TORQUES CONT.
Crankcase:
  8 mm . . . . .18-28 N·m
  (13-20 ft.-lbs.)
  10 mm . . . . .40-60 N·m
  (29-44 ft.-lbs.)
Connecting Rod . . . . .30-35 N·m
  (22-26 ft.-lbs.)
Exhaust Cover . . . . .8-12 N·m
  (6-9 ft.-lbs.)
Flywheel Nut . . . . .240-260 N·m
  (174-188 ft.-lbs.)
Gearcase Pinion Nut . . . . .80-90 N·m
  (58-65 ft.-lbs.)
Propeller Shaft Nut . . . . .50-60 N·m
  (36-44 ft.-lbs.)
Standard Screws:
  Unmarked or Marked "4"
  5 mm . . . . .2-4 N·m
  (2-3 ft.-lbs.)
  6 mm . . . . .4-7 N·m
  (3-5 ft.-lbs.)
  8 mm . . . . .10-16 N·m
  (7-12 ft.-lbs.)
  10 mm . . . . .22-35 N·m
  (16-26 ft.-lbs.)
Marked "7" or SAE Grade 5
  5 mm . . . . .3-6 N·m
  (2-5 ft.-lbs.)
  6 mm . . . . .8-12 N·m
  (6-9 ft.-lbs.)
  8 mm . . . . .18-28 N·m
  (13-20 ft.-lbs.)
  10 mm . . . . .40-60 N·m
  (29-44 ft.-lbs.)

LUBRICATION

The power head is lubricated by oil mixed with the fuel. Model DT115 and Model DT140 are equipped with oil injection. The manufacturer recommends using Suzuki "CCI" or a BIA certified two-stroke oil in oil injection tank. During break-in of a new or rebuilt engine, proceed as follows: For the first 5 hours of operation, mix fuel with oil in fuel tank at a ratio of 50:1 if Suzuki "CCI" oil or a BIA certified two-stroke oil is used. Mix fuel:oil at a ratio of 30:1 if any other type of two-stroke oil is used. Switch to straight fuel in fuel tank at the completion of the 5 hour break-in period. Manufacturer recommends regular or no-lead automotive gasoline having a minimum octane rating of 85. Gasoline and oil should be thoroughly mixed in fuel tank when used during break-in period.

The lower unit gears and bearings are lubricated by oil contained in the gearcase. Suzuki Outboard Motor Gear Oil or a SAE 90 hypoid outboard motor gear oil should be used. Gearcase capacity is approximately 1100 mL (37.2 oz.) of gear oil and should be drained and refilled after the first 10 hours of use and then after every 50 hours of use. Reinstall vent and fill plugs securely, using a new gasket if needed, to ensure watertight seal.

FUEL SYSTEM

CARBURETOR. Mikuni type B32-28 carburetors are used on DT115 and Mikuni type B40-32 carburetors are used on DT140 models. Refer to Fig. SZ17-1 for exploded view. Initial setting of pilot air screw (3) from a lightly seated position should be 1-1½ turns on DT115 models and 1⅛-1⅝ turns on DT140 models. Final carburetor adjustment should be made with engine at normal operating temperature and runnning in forward gear. Rotate timing adjustment screw (B–Fig. SZ17-3) in small increments until engine idles at approximately. 600-700 rpm. Adjust pilot air screw so engine idles smoothly and will

accelerate cleanly without hesitation. If necessary, readjust timing adjustment screw to obtain 600-700 rpm idle speed.

Main fuel metering is controlled by main jet (5). Standard main jet size for normal operation is number 135 on DT115 models and number 160 on DT140 models.

To check float level, remove float bowl and invert carburetor. Distance (D–Fig. SZ17-2) between main jet and bottom of float would be 10.4-12.4 mm (0.41-0.49 in.) on DT115 models and 17-19 mm (0.67-0.75 in.) DT140 models. Adjust float level by bending float tang (T).

To synchronize throttle plate opening of all four carburetors, loosen throttle shaft nuts and throttle lever screws. Visually verify that throttle plates on all four carburetors are closed, then retighten throttle lever screw and throttle shaft nuts.

SPEED CONTROL LINKAGE. The carburetor throttle plates must be correctly synchronized to open as the ignition is advanced to obtain optimum performance. To adjust the speed control linkage, it is necessary to first check (and adjust if required) the ignition maximum advance as outlined in the IGNITION TIMING section. Rotate speed control lever (L–Fig. SZ17-3) to align TDC mark (T) on stator plate with mark on upper end of cyliner block. With speed control lever (L) held in this position, mark (M) on throttle cam (C) should align with center of carburetor throttle lever roller (R). If not, loosen jam nuts (N) and rotate carburetor link (A) until correct setting is obtained then tighten jam nuts (N).

REED VALVES. The inlet reed valves (Fig. SZ17-4) are mounted on four reed plate assemblies located between intake manifold and crankcase. The reed petals should seat very lightly against the reed plate throughout their entire length with the least possible tension. Tip of reed petal must not stand open more than 0.2 mm (0.008 in.) from contact surface. Reed stop opening should be 7.9-8.3 mm (0.31-0.33 in.).

Renew reeds if petals are broken, cracked, warped, rusted or bent. Never attempt to bend a reed petal or to straighten a damaged reed. Never install a bent or damaged reed. Seating surface of reed plate should be smooth and flat. When installing reeds or reed

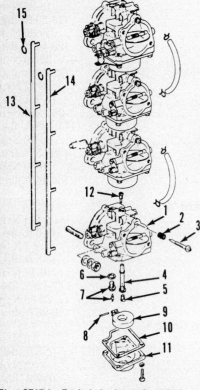

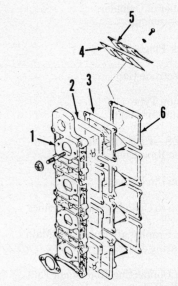

Fig. SZ17-4 — Exploded view of intake manifold and reed valve assembly.

1. Manifold	4. Reed petals
2. Gasket	5. Reed stop
3. Reed plate	6. Gasket

Fig. SZ17-1 — Exploded view of typical carburetor setup used on all models. Mikuni type B40-32 carburetors are shown. Mikuni type B32-28 carburetors are similar.

1. Body	10. Gasket
2. Spring	11. Float bowl
3. Pilot air screw	12. Pilot jet
4. Main nozzle	13. Throttle lever
5. Main jet	synchronizing plate
6. Gasket	14. Choke lever
7. Needle & seat	synchronizing plate
8. Pin	15. Clip
9. Float	

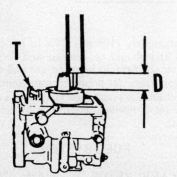

Fig. SZ17-2 — Distance (D) for correct float level should be 10.4-12.4 mm (0.41-0.49 in.) on DT115 models and 17-19 mm (0.67-0.75 in.) on DT140 models. Bend tang (T) on float lever to adjust.

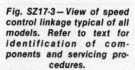

Fig. SZ17-3 — View of speed control linkage typical of all models. Refer to text for identification of components and servicing procedures.

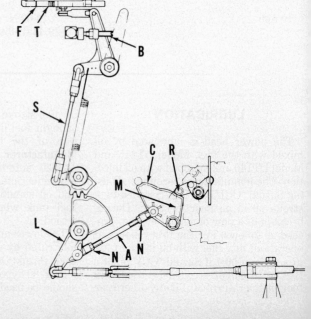

stop, make sure that petals are centered over the inlet holes in reed plate, and that the reed stops are centered over reed petals.

FUEL PUMP. A diaphragm type fuel pump is mounted on the side of power head cylinder block and is actuated by pressure and vacuum pulsations from the engine crankcases. Refer to Fig. SZ17-5 for exploded view of fuel pump assembly.

When servicing pump, scribe reference marks across pump body to aid in reassembly. Defective or questionable parts should be renewed. Diaphragm should be renewed if air leaks or cracks are found, or if deterioration is evident.

FUEL FILTER. A fuel filter (9 through 13 – Fig. SZ17-5) is mounted on the side of power head cylinder block on all models. Filter should be disassembled and cleaned after every 50 hours of use. Renew "O" ring (11) if required.

OIL INJECTION

BLEEDING PUMP. To bleed trapped air from oil supply line or pump, first make sure outboard motor is in an upright position and oil tank is full. Open oil pump air bleed screw (A – Fig. SZ17-6) three or four turns to allow oil to seep out around screw threads. After five seconds or when no air bubbles are noticed, close air bleed screw (A).

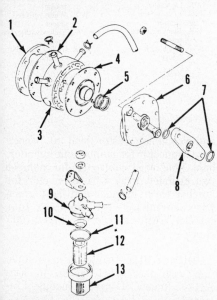

Fig. SZ17-5 – Exploded view of diaphragm type fuel pump and fuel filter assemblies.

1. Cover
2. Diaphragm
3. Body
4. Diaphragm
5. Spring
6. Body
7. "O" rings
8. Insulator block
9. Fuel filter body
10. Packing
11. "O" ring
12. Filter
13. Bowl

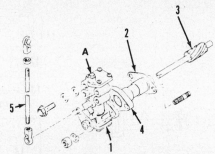

Fig. SZ17-6 – Exploded view of oil injection pump and related components.

A. Air bleed screw
1. Pump assy.
2. Gasket
3. Driven gear
4. Retainer
5. Control rod

CHECKING OIL PUMP OUTPUT. Start engine and allow to warm-up for approximately five minutes, then stop engine. Disconnect oil pump control rod (5 – Fig. SZ17-6) from throttle shaft lever on actuating carburetor. Detach oil supply line at oil tank outlet and plug oil tank outlet. Connect oil gage 09900-21602 to oil supply line. Fill oil gage with a recommended two-stroke oil until even with an upper reference mark. With oil pump control rod (5) in released position, start engine and maintain engine speed at 1500 rpm. Allow engine to run for three minutes. After three minutes, stop the engine and observe oil gage. Recommended oil consumption is 3.6-4.4 mL (0.122-0.149 oz.) in three minutes at 1500 rpm.

To check oil pump at maximum output position, repeat previous procedure except hold oil pump control rod (5) in fully extended position. Recommended oil consumption is 5-6 mL (0.169-0.203 oz.) in one minute at 1500 rpm.

If the obtained oil consumption measurements are not the recommended limits, the oil pump must be renewed.

NOTE: Index mark (I—Fig. SZ17-7) on oil injection pump must align with mark (M) on actuating lever when lever is in the released position.

IGNITION

All models are equipped with an independent breakerless electronic ignition system. Refer to Fig. SZ17-8 for typical wiring diagram on all models.

IGNITION TIMING. Ignition timing should be 3° ATDC at 1000 rpm and 23° BTDC at 5000 rpm.

Initial setting of ignition timing on all models can be accomplished as follows: Set throttle at full advance position,

then note if mark (F – Fig. SZ17-3) on stator plate aligns with mark on upper end of cylinder block. If not, loosen jam nuts and adjust length of rod (S) until correct static ignition timing is obtained then tighten jam nuts.

Final ignition timing check can be made using a suitable power timing light. Immerse lower unit of outboard motor in water and connect timing light to upper spark plug. Set engine throttle at full retard position and start engine. Refer to ignition timing specifications stated previously and check alignment of flywheel timing marks with timing pointer. To check advance timing, run engine at wide-open throttle and note timing marks.

Full retard timing can be adjusted by turning screw (B) in or out as required. Note idle speed while making adjustment. Vary full retard timing to obtain recommended idle speed of 600-700 rpm.

TROUBLE-SHOOTING. If ignition malfunction occurs, use only approved procedures to prevent damage to the components. The fuel system should be checked first to make certain that faulty running is not caused by incorrect mixture or contaminated fuel. Make sure malfunction is not due to spark plug, wiring or wiring connection failure. Trouble-shoot ignition circuit using Suzuki pocket tester 09900-25002 or a suitable ohmmeter as follows:

CONDENSER CHARGING COIL. Unplug wires at connectors leading from condenser charging coil. Attach one tester lead to connector of black wire with red tracer and remaining tester lead to connector of white wire with black tracer. Tester should show 600-900 ohms. Attach one tester lead to connector of red wire with white tracer and remaining tester lead to brown wire connector. Tester should show 100-150 ohms.

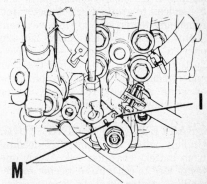

Fig. SZ17-7 – Index mark (I) on oil injection pump must align with mark (M) on actuating lever when lever is in the released position.

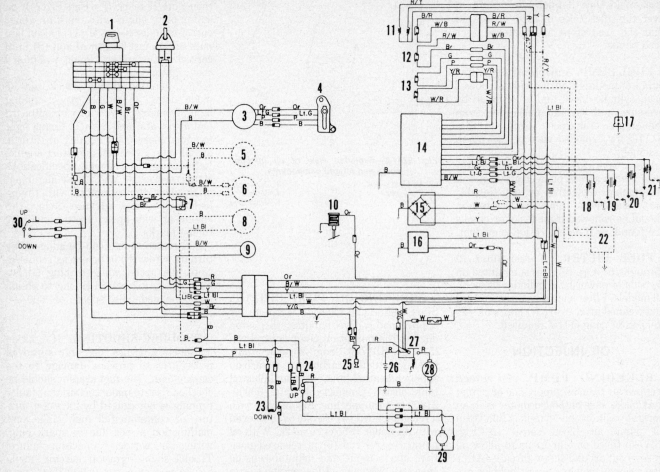

Fig. SZ17-8 — Typical wiring diagram for all models.

1. Ignition switch
2. Emergency stop switch
3. Trim meter
4. Trim sender
5. Volt meter
6. Hour meter
7. Neutral switch
8. Tachometer
9. Overheat & oil warning buzzer
10. Choke solenoid
11. Battery charging coil
12. Condenser charging coil
13. Pulser coils
14. CDI module
15. Rectifier
16. Buzzer check unit
17. Overheat sensor
18. Ignition coil (No. 4 cyl.)
19. Ignition coil (No. 3 cyl.)
20. Ignition coil (No. 2 cyl.)
21. Ignition coil (No. 1 cyl.)
22. Rectifier with voltage regulator
23. Power tilt & trim motor "DOWN" relay
24. Power tilt & trim motor "UP" relay
25. Oil level switch
26. Battery
27. Starter motor relay
28. Starter motor
29. Power tilt & trim motor
30. Power tilt & trim switch
B. Black
G. Green
P. Pink
R. Red

W. White
Y. Yellow
Br. Brown
Gr. Gray
LtBl. Light blue
LtG. Light green
Or. Orange
B/R. Black with red tracer
B/W. Black with white tracer

R/W. Red with white tracer
R/Y. Red with yellow tracer
W/B. White with black tracer
W/R. White with red tracer
Y/G. Yellow with green tracer
Y/R. Yellow with red tracer

PULSER COIL. Two pulser coils are used. Unplug wires at connectors leading from pulser coils. Attach one tester lead to green wire connector and remaining tester lead to pink wire connector. Tester should show 290-420 ohms. Connect one tester lead to connector of yellow wire with red tracer and remaining tester lead to connector of white wire with red tracer. Tester should show 290-420 ohms.

BATTERY CHARGING COIL. Unplug wires at connectors leading from battery charging coil. Attach one tester lead to red wire connector and remaining tester lead to connector of yellow wire. Tester should show 0.4-0.8 ohms. Leave tester lead connected to

red wire connector and attach remaining tester lead to connector of red wire with yellow tracer. Tester should show 0.2-0.6 ohms.

IGNITION COILS. Four ignition coils are used. Unplug wires at connectors leading from ignition coils and secondary coil lead from spark plug. Attach one tester lead to orange wire connector for number one cylinder, light blue wire connector for number two cylinder, gray wire connector for number three cylinder and light green connector for number four cylinder and remaining tester lead to engine ground. Tester should show 0.2-0.5 ohms. Disconnect tester leads and attach one tester lead to spark plug end of secondary coil lead

and remaining tester lead to orange wire connector for number one cylinder, light blue wire connector for number two cylinder, gray wire connector for number three cylinder and light green wire connector for number four cylinder. Tester should show 4700-7000 ohms.

CDI MODULE. Use tester in conjunction with test chart shown in Fig. SZ17-9. Renew CD ignition module if required.

COOLING SYSTEM

WATER PUMP. A rubber impeller type water pump is mounted between the drive shaft housing and gearcase. A

Tester Lead (−) / Tester Lead (+)	B/R	R/W	W/B	Br	G	P	Y/R	W/R	Or	Lt Bl	Gr	Lt G	B/W	B
B/R		A	B	B	B	B	B	B	B	B	B	B	B	A
R/W	B		B	A	B	B	B	B	B	B	B	B	A	A
W/B	B	B		A	B	B	B	B	B	B	B	B	B	A
Br	B	A	B		B	B	B	B	B	B	B	B	A	A
G	B	A	B	A		B	B	B	B	B	B	B	A	A
P	B	A	B	A	B		B	B	B	B	B	B	A	A
Y/R	B	A	B	A	B	B		B	B	B	B	B	A	A
W/R	B	A	B	A	B	B	B		B	B	B	B	A	A
Or	B	A	B	A	A	B	B	B		B	B	B	A	A
Lt Bl	B	A	B	A	B	A	B	B	B		B	B	A	A
Gr	B	A	B	A	B	B	A	B	B	B		B	A	A
Lt G	B	A	B	A	B	B	B	A	B	B	B		A	A
B/W	B	B	B	B	A	A	A	A	B	B	B	B		A
B	B	A	B	A	A	A	A	A	B	B	B	B	A	

Fig. SZ17-9 — Use above chart and values listed below to test condition of CD ignition module.

A. 100k ohms or less

B. More than 100k ohms

key in the drive shaft is used to turn the pump impeller. If cooling system problems are encountered, check water intake for plugging or partial stoppage, then if not corrected, remove gearcase as outlined in the appropriate section and check condition of the water pump, water passages and sealing surfaces.

When water pump is disassembled, check condition of impeller (6 – Fig. SZ17-10) and plate (7) for excessive wear. Turn drive shaft clockwise (viewed from top) while placing pump housing over impeller. Avoid turning drive shaft in opposite direction when water pump is assembled.

THERMOSTAT. A thermostat (7 – Fig. SZ17-11) is used to regulate operating temperature. The thermostat should start to open within the temperature range of 48°-52°C (118°-126°F).

Thermostat can be removed for inspection or renewal by removing cylinder head cover.

POWER HEAD

REMOVE AND REINSTALL. To remove the power head, first remove engine cover. Detach battery cables. Disconnect wiring to oil tank. Remove oil supply line from oil tank outlet and plug. Remove nut securing oil tank retaining band and withdraw oil tank. Remove rod used by oil tank retaining band to secure oil tank. Disconneect fuel supply line and water inspection hose from connectors in bottom engine cover. Disconnect shift linkage and throttle linkage. Detach any wiring that will interfere with power head removal. Remove covers to expose power head retaining cap screws and nuts. Remove cap screws and nuts, then lift power head assembly with related engine components from lower unit assembly.

Before reinstalling power head, make certain drive shaft splines are clean then coat them with a light coating of water-resistant grease. Apply a suitable sealer to mating surfaces of power head and lower unit and install a new gasket. Apply Thread Lock "1342" to power head retaining cap screws and nuts, then tighten to 34-41 N·m (25-30 ft.-lbs.). The remainder of installation is the reverse of removal procedure.

DISASSEMBLY. Disassembly and inspection can be accomplished in the following manner. Remove electric starter. Remove junction box cover and four cap screws retaining electrical components holding plate to side of cylinder block. Unplug any connector that will interfere with holding plate removal, then remove holding plate. Remove electric

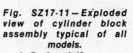

Fig. SZ17-11 — Exploded view of cylinder block assembly typical of all models.

1. Crankcase half
2. Cylinder block
3. Gasket
4. Cylinder head
5. Gasket
6. Cylinder head cover
7. Thermostat
8. Gasket
9. Inner exhaust cover
10. Gasket
11. Outer exhaust cover
12. Cylinder head connector
13. Small crankcase plug (No. 1 cyl.)
14. Large crankcase plug (No. 2, 3 & 4 cyls.)

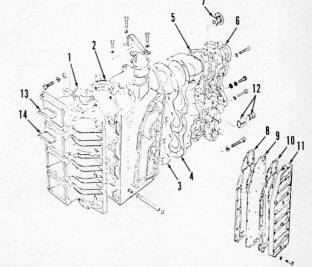

Fig. SZ17-10 — Exploded view of water pump assembly.

1. Pump housing
2. Top plate
3. Liner
4. Seal ring
5. Key
6. Impeller
7. Plate
8. Gasket
9. Grommet
10. Tube guide
11. Water tube

choke solenoid. Remove fuel pump assembly. Remove oil injection pump (1–Fig. SZ17-6), retainer (4) and driven gear (3). Remove speed control linkage. Remove flywheel and stator plate assembly. Remove electric starter motor bracket and any remaining wiring that will interfere with cylinder block and crankcase separation. Remove intake manifold with carburetor assemblies. Remove reed valve assemblies. Remove outer and inner exhaust covers. Remove spark plugs, cylinder head cover, cylinder head and thermostat, then clean carbon from combustion chamber and any foreign material accumulation in water passages. Unscrew crankcase retaining screws and separate crankcase (1–Fig. SZ17-11) from cylinder block (2). Remove connecting rod caps, then lift crankshaft from cylinder block. Push piston and connecting rod assemblies out cylinder head end of cylinder block.

Engine components are now accessible for overhaul as outlined in the appropriate following paragraphs. Refer to the following section for assembly procedures.

ASSEMBLY. Refer to specific service sections when assembling the crankshaft, connecting rod, piston and reed valves. Make sure all joint and gasket surfaces are clean, free from nicks and burrs and hardened cement or carbon.

Whenever the power head is disassembled, it is recommended that all gasket surfaces and mating surfaces without gaskets be carefully checked for nicks, burrs and warped surfaces which might interfere with a tight seal. Cylinder head, head end of cylinder block and some mating surfaces of manifold and crankcase should be checked on a surface plate and lapped if necessary to provide a smooth surface. Do not remove any more metal than is necessary.

When assembling power head, first lubricate all friction surfaces and bearings with engine oil. Apply a suitable high temperature grease to lip portion of crankshaft seal. Apply a suitable water-resistant grease to lip portion of drive shaft seal and install seal into seal housing (15–Fig. SZ17-12). Place bearing ring (8) into cylinder block, then install crankshaft assembly. Make certain main bearing locating pins engage notches in cylinder block. Apply a coat of Suzuki Bond No. 4 or a suitable sealer to mating surfaces of crankcase and cylinder block and position crankcase on cylinder block. Using tightening sequence shown in Fig. SZ17-13, tighten crankcase screws to values shown in CONDENSED SERVICE DATA. Tighten cylinder head cap screws in sequence shown in Fig. SZ17-14 to values shown in CONDENSED SERVICE DATA.

RINGS, PISTONS AND CYLINDERS. The pistons are fitted with two piston rings. Piston rings must be installed with manufacturer's marking toward top end of piston. Rings are pinned in place to prevent rotation in ring grooves. Piston ring end gap should be 0.2-0.4 mm (0.008-0.016 in.) with a maximum allowable ring end gap of 0.8 mm (0.031 in.). Piston to cylinder wall clearance should be 0.112-0.127 mm (0.0044-0.0050 in.). Pistons and rings are available in standard size as well as 0.25 mm (0.010 in.) and 0.50 mm (0.020 in.) oversizes. Cylinder should be bored to an oversize if cylinder is out-of-round or taper exceeds 0.10 mm (0.004 in.). Install piston on connecting rod so arrow on piston crown will point towards exhaust port when piston is in cylinder.

CONNECTING RODS, BEARINGS AND CRANKSHAFT. Before detaching connecting rods from crankshaft, mark rod and cap for correct assembly to each other and in original cylinder. Separate bearing cages and rollers for assembly to original crankpin if units are not renewed. Connecting rod must be installed in cylinder with "UP" side on connecting rod and dot on rod cap ear facing toward flywheel end of crankshaft. Tighten connecting rod screws to 30-35 N·m (22-26 ft.-lbs.).

Determine rod bearing wear by measuring connecting rod small end side-to-side movement as shown at (A–Fig. SZ17-15). Normal side-to-side movement is 5 mm (0.20 in.) or less. Maximum allowable limit of crankshaft runout is 0.05 mm (0.002 in.) measured at bearing surfaces with crankshaft ends supported.

When installing crankshaft, lubricate pistons, rings, cylinders and bearings with engine oil as outlined in ASSEMBLY section.

Fig. SZ17-12—Exploded view of crankshaft assembly typical of all models.

1. Seal
2. Roller bearing
3. Pin
4. Crankshaft
5. Upper balance weight
6. Lower balance weight
7. Oil injection pump drive gear
8. Bearing ring
9. Ball bearing
10. Washer
11. Snap ring
12. Seal
13. "O" ring
14. Seal
15. Seal housing
16. Bearing
17. Pin
18. Connecting rod
19. Rod cap
20. Needle bearing
21. Piston pin clips
22. Thrust washers
23. Needle bearing
24. Piston pin
25. Piston
26. Piston rings

Fig. SZ17-13—Tighten crankcase cap screws in sequence shown. Refer to CONDENSED SERVICE DATA for torque values.

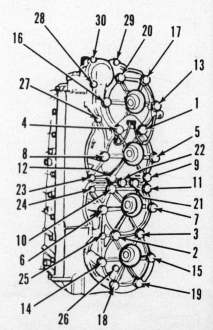

Fig. SZ17-14—Tighte cylinder head cap screws in sequence shown. Refer to CONDENSED SERVICE DATA for torque values.

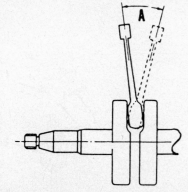

Fig. SZ17-15 — Maximum side-to-side shake (A) at small end of connecting rod should be 5 mm (0.20 in.) or less.

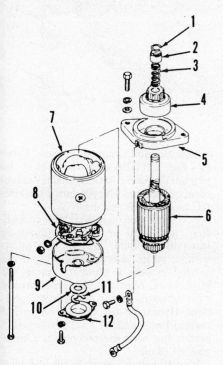

Fig. SZ17-16 — Exploded view of electric starter motor.

1. "C" ring	7. Frame
2. Stop	8. Brush assy.
3. Spring	9. End housing
4. Drive	10. Thrust washer
5. Frame head	11. "E" clip
6. Armature	12. Bracket

Fig. SZ17-17 — Exploded view typical of lower unit gearcase assembly used on all models.

1. Shift arm	20. Magnet holder	39. Bearing	57. Dog clutch
2. Caps	21. Magnet	40. Vent plug	58. Pin
3. Snap ring	22. Pin	41. Gasket	59. Pin retainer
4. Upper shift rod	23. Pin	42. Level plug	60. Shift spring
5. Clip	24. Shift cam	43. Drain plug	61. Propeller shaft
6. Connector	25. Ball	44. Gearcase housing	62. Thrust washers
7. Pin	26. Spring	45. Trim tab	63. Reverse gear
8. Shift rod guide housing	27. Seal	46. Forward gear bearing	64. Shim
9. Gasket	28. Bearing housing	housing	65. Bearing
10. Seal	29. "O" ring	47. Bearing	66. "O" ring
11. Washer	30. Bearing	48. Shim	67. End cap
12. "O" ring	31. Shim	49. Thrust washer	68. Bearings
13. Guide	32. Thrust washer	50. Thrust bearing	69. Seal
14. "O" ring	33. Thrust bearing	51. Forward gear	70. Snap ring
15. Snap ring	34. Drive shaft	52. Pinion gear	71. Spacer
16. Lower shift rod	35. Spring	53. Nut	72. Propeller
17. Pin	36. Thrust washer	54. Thrust washer	73. Spacer
18. Spring	37. Thrust washer	55. Shift pin	74. Tab washer
19. Collar	38. Collar	56. Spring guide	75. Nut

ELECTRIC STARTER

Models are equipped with electric starter shown in Fig. SZ17-16. Disassembly is evident after inspection of unit and reference to exploded view. Starter brushes should be renewed if worn to two-thirds or below their original manufactured length. After reassembly, bench test starter before installing on power head.

LOWER UNIT

PROPELLER AND DRIVE CLUTCH. Protection for the motor is built into a special cushioning clutch in the propeller hub. No adjustment is possible on the propeller or clutch. Three-bladed propellers are used. Propellers are available from the manufacturer in various diameters and pitches and should be selected to provide optimum performance at full throttle within the recommended limits of 4800-5500 rpm.

R&R AND OVERHAUL. Refer to Fig. SZ17-17 for exploded view of lower unit gearcase assembly used on all models. During disassembly, note the location of all shims and thrust washers to aid in reassembly. To remove gearcase, first unscrew plug (43) and drain gear lubricant. Remove drive shaft housing cover to obtain access to shift linkage. Pull out cotter pin, then withdraw pin (7) from connector (6). Remove the cap screws securing gearcase to drive shaft housing and separate gearcase assembly from drive shaft

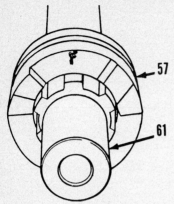

Fig. SZ17-18—Install dog clutch (57) on propeller shaft (61) with "F" marked side towards forward gear.

Fig. SZ17-20—Exploded view of power tilt and trim electric motor and pump assembly.

1. End cap
2. Spring
3. Brush
4. Ball
5. Armature
6. Thrust washer
7. Gasket
8. Frame
9. Gasket
10. Reservoir
11. Fill plug
12. "O" ring
13. Reservoir
14. Pump & valve body assy.

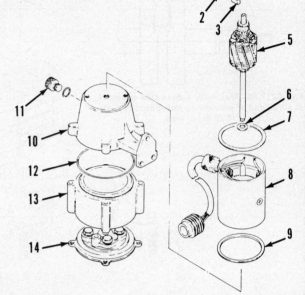

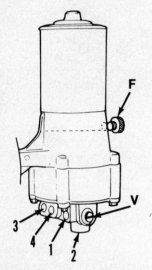

Fig. SZ17-19—View of pump assembly showing location of oil fill plug (F), release valve (V) and test ports (1, 2, 3 and 4).

housing. Remove water pump assembly (Fig. SZ17-10). Remove propeller with related components from propeller shaft. Unscrew two screws retaining gearcase end cap (67—Fig. SZ17-17), then attach a suitable puller to propeller shaft (61) and withdraw propeller shaft assembly with gearcase end cap. Unscrew pinion nut (53) and remove pinion gear (52), then extract forward gear (51). Drive shaft (34) and related components can be withdrawn from gearcase after removal of bearing housing (28).

Inspect gears for wear on teeth and on engagement dogs. Inspect dog clutch (57) for wear on engagement surfaces. Inspect shafts for wear on splines and on friction surfaces of gears and oil seals. Check shift cam (24) and shift pin (55) for excessive wear. Check condition of shift spring (60). All seals and "O" rings should be renewed when unit is reassembled.

No adjustment to forward gear shim (48) or reverse gear shim (64) is required unless forward gear or reverse gear is renewed. If a gear is renewed, shim adjustment should be made by comparing the values stamped on each gear. Thrust play of drive shaft (34) should be 0.25-0.40 mm (0.010-0.016 in.) and is adjusted by varying thickness of shim (31). Propeller shaft end play should be 0.2-0.4 mm (0.008-0.016 in.). Propeller shaft end play is adjusted by increasing or decreasing the thickness of thrust washers (62).

Reassemble gearcase by reversing disassembly procedure while noting the following: Install dog clutch (57) on propeller shaft (61) so "F" marked side (Fig. SZ17-18) is towards forward gear (51—Fig. SZ17-17). Tighten pinion nut to 80-90 N·m (58-65 ft.-lbs.). Apply water-resistant grease to "O" ring (66). Apply silicone sealer to gearcase and bearing housing (28) mating surfaces. Coat threads of gearcase retaining cap screws with Thread Lock "1342."

Install pin (7) through connector (6) and eyelet of lower shift rod (16), then retain with a new cotter pin. Fill gearcase with outboard gear oil as outlined in LUBRICATION section.

POWER TILT AND TRIM

Models are equipped with a hydraulically actuated power tilt and trim system. An oil pump driven by a reversible electric motor provides oil pressure. A rocker control switch determines motor and pump rotation thereby retracting or extending tilt and trim cylinders. The pump is equipped with an automatic and manual release valve (V—Fig. SZ17-19) that when set in the manual position (vertical) enables movement of trim and tilt cylinders if the electric motor malfunctions.

Recommended oil is SAE 20W or SAE 30W motor oil or Dexron automatic transmission fluid. Do not run pump without oil in reservoir. Fill plug (F) is located in side of pump reservoir. Oil level should reach fill plug hole threads with outboard motor in a vertical position. Hydraulic tilt should be cycled several times and oil level rechecked if system has been drained or lost a large amount of oil.

If malfunction occurs in tilt and trim system, first make sure malfunction is not due to wiring, wiring connection or electric motor failure. To check oil pressure, connect a 20.7 MPa (3000 psi) gage to port "1" on pump and operate pump. Hydraulic oil pressure at port "1" should be within the limits of 10.4-17.25 MPa (1500-2500 psi). Repeat the test for port "2." Connect test gage to port "3" and operate pump. Hydraulic oil pressure should be within the limits of 2.76-5.52 MPa (400-800 psi). Repeat test for port "4." Oil pressure less than specified may indicate leakage, faulty pressure relief valves or check valves.

If electric motor and pump assembly is disassembled for repair or renewal of individual components, upon reassembly use Inglis Company EP630548 flat black neobase or equivalent to provide a watertight seal.

SUZUKI DT150, DT150SS AND DT200

CONDENSED SERVICE DATA

NOTE: Metric fasteners are used throughout outboard motor.

TUNE-UP

Hp/rpm:
DT150 & DT150SS 150/5000-5600
DT200 .... 200/5000-5600
Bore .... 84 mm
(3.31 in.)
Stroke .... 81 mm
(3.2 in.)
Number of Cylinders 6
Displacement .... 2693 cc
(164.3 cu. in.)
Spark Plug:
DT150 & DT200 .... NGK B8HS-10
Electrode Gap .... 0.9-1.0 mm
(0.035-0.039 in.)
DT150SS .... NGK B8HS
Electrode Gap .... 0.6-0.7 mm
(0.024-0.028 in.)
Ignition Type .... Breakerless
Carburetor Make .... Mikuni

SIZES — CLEARANCES

Piston Ring End Gap .... 0.2-0.4 mm
(0.008-0.016 in.)
Piston Pin Diameter .... 21.995-22.000 mm
(0.8659-0.8661 in.)
Piston to Cylinder Wall Clearance ...... 0.100-0.110 mm
(0.0039-0.0043 in.)
Max. Crankshaft Runout at Main
Bearing Journal .... 0.05 mm
(0.002 in.)
Max. Connecting Rod Small End
Side Shake .... 5.0 mm
(0.20 in.)

TIGHTENING TORQUES

Cylinder Head:
6 mm .... 8-12 N·m
(6-9 ft.-lbs.)
8 mm .... 28-32 N·m
(20-23 ft.-lbs.)
Cylinder .... 46-54 N·m
(34-40 ft.-lbs.)

TIGHTENING TORQUES CONT.

Crankcase:
8 mm .... 21-25 N·m
(15-18 ft.-lbs.)
10 mm .... 46-54 N·m
(34-40 ft.-lbs.)
Exhaust Cover .... 8-12 N·m
(6-9 ft.-lbs.)
Flywheel Nut .... 250-260 N·m
(181-188 ft.-lbs.)
Gearcase Pinion Nut .... 140-150 N·m
(102-109 ft.-lbs.)
Propeller Shaft Nut .... 50-62 N·m
(36-45 ft.-lbs.)
Water Pump .... 15-20 N·m
(11-15 ft.-lbs.)
Standard Screws:
Unmarked or Marked "4"
5 mm .... 2.4 N·m
(2-3 ft.-lbs.)
6 mm .... 4-7 N·m
(3-5 ft.-lbs.)
8 mm .... 10-16 N·m
(7-12 ft.-lbs.)
10 mm .... 22-35 N·m
(16-26 ft.-lbs.)
Stainless Steel
5 mm .... 3-6 N·m
(2-3 ft.-lbs.)
6 mm .... 6-10 N·m
(5-7 ft.lbs.)
8 mm .... 15-20 N·m
(11-15 ft.-lbs.)
10 mm .... 34-41 N·m
(25-30 ft.-lbs.)
Marked "7" or SAE Grade 5
5 mm .... 3-6 N·m
(2-5 ft.-lbs.)
6 mm .... 8-12 N·m
(6-9 ft.-lbs.)
8 mm .... 18-28 N·m
(13-20 ft.-lbs.)
10 mm .... 40-60 N·m
(29-44 ft.-lbs.)

LUBRICATION

The power head is lubricated by oil mixed with the fuel. All models are equipped with oil injection. The manufacturer recommends using Suzuki BIA or a BIA certified two-stroke oil in oil injection tank. During break-in of a new or rebuilt engine, proceed as follows: For the first 5 hours of operation, mix fuel with oil in fuel tank at a ratio of 50:1. Switch to straight fuel in fuel tank at the completion of the 5 hour break-in period. Manufacturer recommends regular or no-lead automotive gasoline having a minimum octane rating of 85. Gasoline and oil should be thoroughly mixed in fuel tank when used during break-in period.

The lower unit gears and bearings are lubricated by oil contained in the gearcase. Suzuki Outboard Motor Gear Oil should be used. Gearcase capacity is approximately 1050 mL (35½ oz.) of gear oil and should be drained and refilled after the first 10 hours of use and then after every 100 hours of use. Reinstall drain and level plugs securely, using a new gasket if needed, to ensure a water-tight seal.

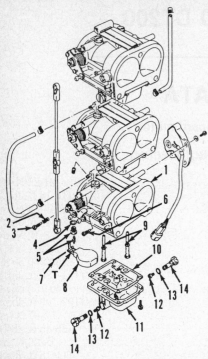

Fig. SZ20-1—Exploded view of Mikuni type BW40-28 carburetor used on all models.

1. Body
2. Spring
3. Pilot air screw
4. Gasket
5. Needle & seat
6. Pilot jet
7. Pin
8. Float
9. High speed nozzles
10. Gasket
11. Float bowl
12. Main jet
13. Gasket
14. Main jet holder
T. Tang

FUEL SYSTEM

CARBURETOR. Mikuni type BW40-28 carburetors are used on all models and 1½-2 turns on DT200 Refer to Fig. SZ20-1 for exploded view. Initial setting of pilot air screw (3) from a lightly seated position should be 1¼-1¾ turns on DT150 and DT150SS models and 1½-2 turns on DT200 models. Final carburetor adjustment should be made with engine at normal operating temperature and running in forward gear. Adjust idle speed control knob (I–Fig. SZ20-2) so engine idles at 600-700 rpm in forward gear. Within the recommended limits, adjust pilot air screws (3–Fig. SZ20-1) so engine idles smoothly and will accelerate cleanly without hesitation. If necessary, readjust idle speed control knob (I–Fig. SZ20-2) so engine idle speed is 600-700 rpm.

Main fuel metering is controlled by main jet (12–Fig. SZ20-1). Standard main jet size for normal operation is number 157.5 on DT150 models, number 147.5 on DT150SS models and number 167.5 on DT200 models.

To check float level, remove float bowl and invert carburetor. Distance (D–Fig. SZ20-3) between bottom of float and float bowl mating surface on carburetor body should be 9.5-11.5 mm (0.37-0.45 in.). Adjust float level by bending tang (T–Fig. SZ20-1) on float lever.

To synchronize throttle plate opening of all three carburetors, first detach rod (R–Fig. SZ20-4). Loosen screws (S) on top and middle carburetors. Throttle lever return spring pressure should cause respective throttle plates to close. Visually verify all throttle plates are closed, then retighten screws (S) of top and middle carburetors. Reconnect rod (R), then verify synchronization of throttle plates between all three carburetors.

SPEED CONTROL LINKAGE. The throttle plates of all three carburetors must be properly synchronized as outlined in the previous CARBURETOR section. A throttle plate switch assembly is used to register bottom carburetor throttle plate position. With throttle plates fully closed, continuity between light green wire with red tracer and black wire on throttle plate switch should be noted. There should be no continuity between brown wire with yellow tracer and black wire. When the throttle plates start opening, continuity between brown wire with yellow tracer and black wire should be noted.

REED VALVES. The inlet reed valves (Fig. SZ20-5) are located on a vee-shaped reed plate between intake manifold and crankcase. Each cylinder is fitted with a reed plate that contains four reed petals on DT150 models, six reed petals on DT150SS models and eight reed petals on DT200 models. The reed petals should seat very lightly against the reed plate throughout their entire length with the least possible tension. Tip of reed petal must not stand open more than 0.2 mm (0.008 in.) from contact surface. Reed stop opening should be 7.4 mm (0.29 in.) on DT150 models, 6.0 mm (0.24 in.) on DT150SS models and 10.9 mm (0.43 in.) on DT200 models.

Renew reeds if petals are broken, cracked, warped, rusted or bent. Never attempt to bend a reed petal or to straighten a damaged reed. Never install a bent or damaged reed. Seating surface or reed plate should be smooth and flat. When installing reeds or reed stop, make sure that petals are centered over the inlet holes in reed plate, and that reed stops are centered over reed petals. Apply Thread Lock "1342" or a suitable equivalent to threads of reed stop screws prior to installation.

FUEL PUMP. Two diaphragm type fuel pumps are mounted on the side of power head cylinder block and are ac-

Fig. SZ20-2—Adjust idle speed control knob (I) to set engine idle speed. View identifies electrical parts holder cover (C).

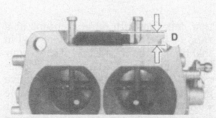

Fig. SZ20-3—Distance (D) for correct float level should be 9.5-11.5 mm (0.37-0.45 in.). Bend tang (T—Fig. SZ20-1) on float lever to adjust.

Fig. SZ20-4—Refer to text to synchronize throttle plate openings on all three carburetors. View identifies screws (S) and rod (R).

Illustrations Courtesy Suzuki America Corp.

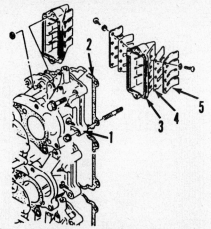

Fig. SZ20-5—Exploded view of intake manifold and reed valve assembly.

1. Intake manifold
2. Gasket
3. Reed plate
4. Reed petals
5. Reed stop

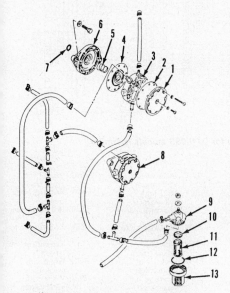

Fig. SZ20-6—Exploded view of diaphragm type fuel pump and fuel filter assemblies.

1. Cover
2. Diaphragm
3. Body
4. Diaphragm
5. Spring
6. Inner plate
7. "O" ring
8. Fuel pump assy.
9. Filter base
10. Packing
11. Filter element
12. "O" ring
13. Cup

tuated by pressure and vacuum pulsations from the engine crankcase. Refer to Fig. SZ20-6 for exploded view of fuel pump assembly.

Defective or questionable parts should be renewed. Diaphragm should be renewed if air leaks or cracks are found, or if deterioration is evident.

FUEL FILTER. A fuel filter (9 through 13—Fig. SZ20-6) is mounted on the side of power head cylinder block. Filter should be disassembled and cleaned after every 50 hours of use. Renew "O" ring (12) if required.

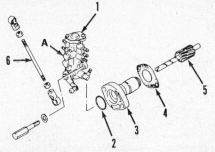

Fig. SZ20-7—Exploded view of oil injection pump and related components.

A. Air bleed screw
1. Pump assy.
2. "O" ring
3. Retainer
4. Gasket
5. Driven gear
6. Control rod

OIL INJECTION

BLEEDING PUMP. To bleed trapped air from oil supply line or pump, first make sure outboard motor is in upright position and oil tank is full. Mix fuel in fuel tank with a recommended oil to a ratio of 50:1. Open oil pump air bleed screw (A—Fig. SZ20-7) three or four turns. Submerge lower unit of outboard motor in a suitable test tank. Start engine and allow to idle until all trapped air is expelled out around screw threads. When no air bubbles are noticed, stop engine and close air bleed screw (A).

CHECKING OIL PUMP OUTPUT. Start engine and allow to warm-up for approximately five minutes, then stop engine. Disconnect oil pump control rod (6—Fig. SZ20-7) from bottom carburetor throttle shaft lever. Detach oil supply line at oil tank outlet and plug oil tank outlet. Connect oil gage 09941-68710 to oil supply line. Fill oil gage with recommended two-stroke oil until even with an upper reference mark. With oil pump control rod (6) in released position, start engine and maintain engine speed at 1500 rpm. Allow engine to run for five minutes. After five minutes, stop the engine and observe oil gage. Recommended oil consumption is 4.7-87 mL (0.159-0.294 oz.) in five minutes at 1500 rpm.

To check oil pump at maximum output position, repeat previous procedure except hold oil pump control rod (6) in fully extended position. Recommended oil consumption is 11.5-17.2 mL (0.389-0.582 oz.) on DT150 and DT150SS models and 13.3-18.0 mL (0.450-0.609 oz.) on DT200 models in two minutes at 1500 rpm.

If the obtained oil consumption measurements are not within the recommended limits, then oil pump must be renewed.

OIL FLOW SENSOR. An oil flow sensor is connected in-line between oil

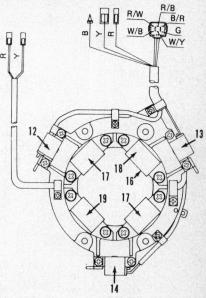

Fig. SZ20-8—View showing location of stator plate components.

12. Pulser coil (No. 1)
13. Pulser coil (No. 2)
14. Pulser coil (No. 3)
16. Battery charging coil (No. 1)
17. Battery charging coils (No. 2 & 3)
18. IC power source cell
19. Condenser charging coil

tank and oil pump. The oil flow sensor serves two functions: A filter for contaminates in oil and a sensor for unsatisfactory oil flow. Should oil flow become unsatisfactory, the sensor's circuit will open causing a decrease in engine rpm, warning buzzer to sound and warning light to glow.

IGNITION

A capacitor discharge ignition (CDI) system is used. If engine malfunction is noted and the ignition system is suspected, make sure the spark plugs and all electrical wiring are in good condition and all electrical connections are tight before trouble-shooting the CD ignition system.

The standard spark plug is NGK B8HS-10 on DT150 and DT200 models with an electrode gap of 0.9-1.0 mm (0.035-0.039 in.). The standard spark plug is NGK B8HS on DT150SS models with an electrode gap of 0.6-0.7 mm (0.024-0.028 in.).

TESTING CDI SYSTEM AND BATTERY CHARGING COILS. Refer to Fig. SZ20-8 and Fig. SZ20-9 and the following individual sections for testing CDI components and battery charging coil. Use Suzuki pocket tester 09900-25002 or a suitable ohmmeter. Renew the component or components if not within the recommended limits.

CONDENSER CHARGING COIL. Unplug connector leading from condenser charging coil. Attach one tester lead to green wire terminal and remain-

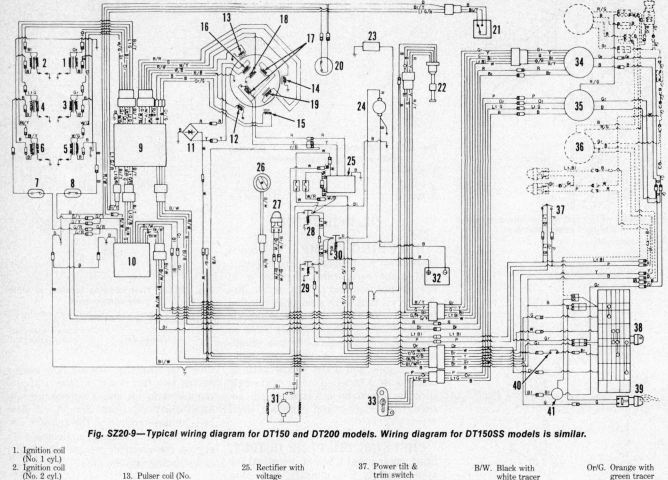

Fig. SZ20-9—Typical wiring diagram for DT150 and DT200 models. Wiring diagram for DT150SS models is similar.

1. Ignition coil (No. 1 cyl.)
2. Ignition coil (No. 2 cyl.)
3. Ignition coil (No. 3 cyl.)
4. Ignition coil (No. 4 cyl.)
5. Ignition coil (No. 5 cyl.)
6. Ignition coil (No. 6 cyl.)
7. Cooling water sensor (port side)
8. Cooling water sensor (starboard side)
9. CDI module
10. Low oil warning reset unit
11. Rectifier
12. Pulser coil (No. 1)
13. Pulser coil (No. 2)
14. Pulser coil (No. 3)
15. Counter coil
16. Battery charging coil (No. 1)
17. Battery charging coil (No. 2 & 3)
18. IC power source coil
19. Condenser charging coil
20. Oil flow sensor
21. Throttle plate sensor
22. Oil level switch
23. Starter valve
24. Starter motor
25. Rectifier with voltage regulator
26. Idle speed control knob
27. Oil warning reset switch
28. Power tilt & trim motor "UP" relay
29. Power tilt & trim motor "DOWN" relay
30. Starter motor relay
31. Power tilt & trim motor
32. Battery
33. Trim sender
34. Monitor
35. Trim meter
36. Tachometer
37. Power tilt & trim switch
38. Ignition switch
39. Emergency stop switch
40. Neutral switch
41. Overheat & oil warning buzzer

B. Black
G. Green
P. Pink
R. Red
W. White
Y. Yellow
Bl. Blue
Br. Brown
Gr. Gray
Lt Bl. Light blue
Lt G. Light green
Or. Orange
B/R. Black with red tracer

B/W. Black with white tracer
B/Y. Black with yellow tracer
Bl/R. Blue with red tracer
Bl/W. Blue with white tracer
Bl/Y. Blue with yellow tracer
Br/W. Brown with white tracer
Br/Y. Brown with yellow tracer
G/R. Green with red tracer
G/Y. Green with yellow tracer
Lt. G/B. Light green with black tracer
Lt. G/R. Light green with red tracer

Or/G. Orange with green tracer
R/B. Red with black tracer
R/G. Red with green tracer
R/W. Red with white tracer
R/Y. Red with yellow tracer
W/B. White with black tracer
W/G. White with green tracer
W/R. White with red tracer
W/Y. White with yellow tracer
Y/B. Yellow with black tracer
Y/G. Yellow with green tracer

ing tester lead to terminal of black wire with red tracer. Tester should show 180-260 ohms.

PULSER COIL. Three pulser coils are used. Unplug connector leading from pulser coils. Attach one tester lead to a suitable engine ground and remaining tester lead to terminal end of red wire with black tracer for number one coil, white wire with black tracer for number two coil and red wire with white tracer for number three coil. Tester should show 160-240 ohms. Repeat test for

each pulser coil.

COUNTER COIL. Unplug wires at connectors leading from counter coil. Attach one tester lead to black wire and remaining tester lead to connector of orange wire with green tracer. Tester should show 160-240 ohms.

IC POWER SOURCE COIL. Unplug connector leading from IC power source coil. Attach one tester lead to a suitable engine ground and remaining tester lead to terminal of white wire and yellow

tracer. Tester should show 210-310 ohms.

BATTERY CHARGING COILS. Three battery charging coils are used. Unplug wires at connectors leading from battery charging coils. Attach one tester lead to red wire connector and remaining tester lead to connector of yellow wire. Tester should show 0.05-0.2 ohms for number one coil and 0.1-0.04 ohms for number two and number three coils.

IGNITION COILS. Six ignition coils are used. Unplug wires at connectors leading from ignition coils and secondary coil lead from spark plug. Attach one tester lead to black wire connector and remaining tester lead to orange wire connector for number one cylinder, blue wire connector for number two cylinder, gray wire connector for number three cylinder, light green connector for number four cylinder, white wire with green tracer for number five cylinder and blue wire with yellow tracer for number six cylinder. Tester should show 0.3-0.5 ohms on DT150 and DT200 models and 0.05-0.15 ohms on DT150SS models. Disconnect tester leads and attach one tester lead to spark plug end of secondary coil lead and remaining tester lead to orange wire connector for number one cylinder, blue wire connector for number two cylinder, gray wire connector for number three cylinder, light green wire connector for number four cylinder, white wire with green tracer for number five cylinder and blue wire with yellow tracer for number six cylinder. Tester should show 14,000-21,000 ohms on DT150 and DT200 models and 11,000-16,000 ohms on DT150SS models.

CDI MODULE. No tests are provided for CDI module. If no components are found defective in previous tests, then renewal of CDI module is required.

THROTTLE PLATE SWITCH ASSEMBLY. Unplug connector leading from throttle plate switch assembly. With throttle plates fully closed, continuity between light green wire with red tracer and black wire should be noted. There should be no continuity between brown wire with yellow tracer and black wire. When the throttle plates start opening, continuity between brown wire with yellow tracer and black wire should be noted.

COOLING SYSTEM

WATER PUMP. A rubber impeller type water pump is mounted between the drive shaft housing and gearcase. A key in the drive shaft is used to turn the pump impeller. If cooling system problems are encountered, check water intake plugging or partial stoppage, then if not corrected, remove gearcase as outlined in the appropriate section and check condition of the water pump, water passages and sealing surfaces.

When water pump is disassembled, check condition of impeller (1–Fig. SZ20-10) and plate (3) for excessive wear. Turn drive shaft clockwise (viewed from top) while placing pump housing over impeller. Avoid turning

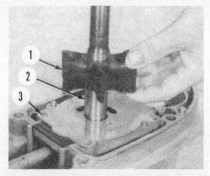

Fig. SZ20-10—View identifying water pump impeller (1), drive key (2) and plate (3).

drive shaft in opposite direction when water pump is assembled.

THERMOSTAT. A thermostat located at top of each cylinder is used to regulate operating temperature. The thermostat should start to open within the temperature range of 40°-44°C (104°-111°F). Thermostat can be removed for inspection or renewal by removing thermostat housing.

POWER HEAD

REMOVE AND REINSTALL. To remove the power head, first remove engine cover. Detach battery cables. Remove electrical parts holder cover (C–Fig. SZ20-2). Disconnect battery cables from starter motor and power tilt and trim motor relays. Remove fuel supply line from fuel filter inlet. Remove electrical parts holder cover located between cylinder head covers. Disconnect any wiring that will interfere with power head removal. Remove the five cap screws located at base of removed electrical parts holder. Remove the two cap screws to withdraw front power head retaining screws cover. Remove the four cap screws from the engine side to withdraw rear power head retaining screws cover. Disconnect water inspection hose from connector in bottom engine cover. Remove cotter pin and clevis pin connecting upper shift rod to connector of lower shift assembly.

Remove ten power head retaining cap screws, then lift power head high enough to expose shift linkage. Detach clutch lever rod connector (R–Fig. SZ20-11) and upper shift rod (U) from clutch shaft (S). Lift power head assembly with related engine components from lower unit assembly.

Before installing power head, make certain drive shaft splines are clean then coat them with a light coating of water-resistant grease. Reconnect clutch lever rod connector (R) and upper shift rod (U) to shift shaft (S) prior to power head installation. Coat power head to lower unit retaining cap screws adjacent to cap screw heads with silicone sealer. Tighten 8 mm power head retaining screws to 15-20 N·m (11-15 ft.-lbs.) and 10 mm screws to 34-41 N·m (25-30 ft.-lbs.). The remainder of installation is the reverse of removal procedure.

DISASSEMBLY. Disassembly and inspection can be accomplished in the following manner. Disconnect wiring to oil tank. Remove oil supply line from oil tank outlet and plug. Remove cap screws to withdraw oil tank. Remove flywheel, stator plate assembly and counter coil. Remove electrical parts holder beneath electric starter. Disconnect spark plug leads and remove electrical parts holder located between cylinder heads. Remove electric starter and bracket assembly. Remove fuel filter and fuel pump assemblies. Remove starter valve. Disconnect throttle control rod (R–Fig. SZ20-4) from bottom carburetor throttle lever, then remove carburetor assemblies. Remove oil injection pump, hoses (label for reassembly reference) and oil flow sensor. Remove speed control linkage. Remove outer and inner exhaust covers. Remove spark plugs, then remove cylinder heads with cylinder head covers. Remove the eleven cap screws and withdraw lower oil seal housing. Remove the eight cylinder retaining cap screws for each cylinder, then remove cylinders. Separate pistons from connecting rods. Remove intake manifolds and reed valve assemblies. Unscrew crankcase retaining screws

Fig. SZ20-11—Detach clutch lever rod connector (R) and upper shift rod (U) from clutch shaft (S) during power head removal. Refer to text.

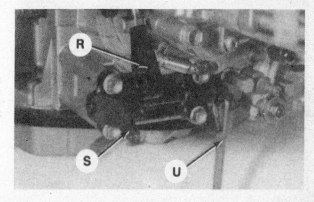

and separate crankcase from cylinder block. Crankshaft assembly can now be removed from cylinder block.

Engine components are now accessible for overhaul as outlined in the appropriate following paragraphs. Refer to the following section for assembly procedures.

ASSEMBLY. Refer to specific service sections when assembling the crankshaft, connecting rod, piston and reed valves. Make sure all joint and gasket surfaces are clean, free from nicks and burrs and hardened cement or carbon.

Whenever the power head is disassembled, it is recommended that all gasket surfaces and mating surfaces without gaskets be carefully checked for nicks, burrs and warped surfaces which might interfere with a tight seal. Cylinder heads, cylinders, head end of cylinder block and some mating surfaces of manifolds and crankcase should be checked on a surface plate and lapped if necessary to provide a smooth surface. Do not remove any more metal than is necessary.

When assembling power head, first lubricate all friction surfaces and bearings with engine oil. Apply a suitable high temperature grease to lip portion of upper crankshaft seal. Apply a suitable water-resistant grease to lip portion of drive shaft seal and install seal into lower oil seal housing. Place main bearing locating pins into crankcase portion of cylinder block, then install crankshaft assembly. Make certain bearing locating pins engage main bearings and upper crankshaft seal fits in cylinder block groove. Make certain lower main bearing locating pin engages notch in cylinder block and "C" ring fits into cylinder block groove. End gaps on all crankshaft seal rings must face towards crankcase cover. Apply a coat of Suzuki Bond 1207B or a suitable sealer to mating surfaces of crankcase and cylinder block and position crankcase on cylinder block. Using tightening sequence shown in Fig. SZ20-12, tighten crankcase screws to the values shown in

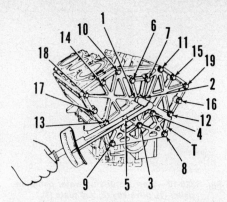

Fig. SZ20-13—Use Suzuki special tool (T) 09912-68710 and tighten cap screws in sequence shown to values listed in text for aligning cylinders on cylinder block.

CONDENSED SERVICE DATA. Install cylinders and lightly tighten retaining screws. Use Suzuki special tool 09912-68710 and attach to cylinders and cylinder block tightening screws in sequence shown in Fig. SZ20-13. Tighten 8 mm screws to 18-28 N·m (13-20 ft.-lbs.) and 10 mm screws to 40-60 N·m (29-44 ft.-lbs.). Tighten cylinder retaining screws to 46-54 N·m (34-40 ft.-lbs.). Remove Suzuki special tool 09912-68710 and install lower oil seal housing tightening 8 mm screws to 18-28 N·m (13-20 ft.-lbs.) and 10 mm screws to 40-60 N·m (29-44 ft.-lbs.). Tighten cylinder head cap screws in sequence shown in Fig.

Fig. SZ20-14—Tighten cylinder head cap screws in sequence shown. Refer to CONDENSED SERVICE DATA for torque values.

SZ20-14 to values shown in CONDENSED SERVICE DATA.

RINGS, PISTONS AND CYLINDERS. The pistons are fitted with two piston rings. Piston rings must be installed with manufacturer's marking toward top end of piston. Rings are pinned in place to prevent rotation in ring grooves. Piston ring end gap should be 0.2-0.4 mm (0.008-0.016 in.) with a maximum allowable ring end gap of 0.8 mm (0.031 in.). Piston to cylinder wall clearance should be 0.100-0.110 mm (0.0039-0.0043 in.). Pistons and rings are available in standard size as well as 0.25 mm (0.010 in.) and 0.50 mm (0.020 in.) oversizes. Cylinder should be bored to an oversize if cylinder is out-of-round or taper exceeds 0.10 mm (0.004 in.). Install piston on connecting rod so arrow on piston crown will point towards exhaust port when piston is in cylinder. Install piston pin with closed end facing toward flywheel side of crankshaft.

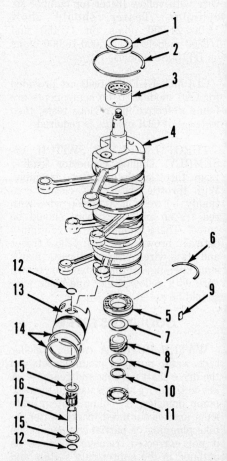

Fig. SZ20-15—Exploded view of crankshaft assembly typical of all models.

1. Seal
2. Snap ring
3. Roller bearing
4. Crankshaft assy.
5. Ball bearing
6. Bearing ring
7. Thrust washer
8. Oil injection pump drive gear
9. Key
10. Snap ring
11. Seal
12. Piston pin clips
13. Piston
14. Piston rings
15. Thrust washers
16. Needle bearing
17. Piston pin

Fig. SZ20-12—Tighten crankcase cap screws in sequence shown. Refer to CONDENSED SERVICE DATA for torque values.

Illustrations Courtesy Suzuki America Corp.

CONNECTING RODS, BEARINGS AND CRANKSHAFT.

Connecting rods, bearings and crankshaft are a pressed-together unit. Crankshaft should be disassembled ONLY by experienced service personnel and with suitable service equipment.

Caged roller bearings are used in middle and top end of crankshaft. A caged ball bearing is used at bottom end of crankshaft. Determine rod bearing wear by measuring connecting rod small end side-to-side movement as shown at

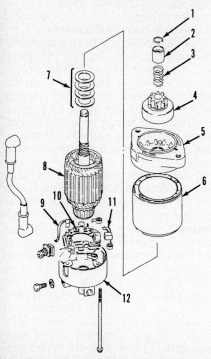

Fig. SZ20-16—Maximum side-to-side shake (A) at small end of connecting rod should be 5 mm (0.20 in.) or less.

(A–Fig. SZ20-16). Normal side-to-side movement is 5 mm (0.20 in.) or less. Maximum allowable limit of crankshaft

runout is 0.05 mm (0.002 in.) measured with crankshaft ends supported.

When installing crankshaft, lubricate pistons, rings, cylinders and bearings with engine oil as outlined in ASSEMBLY section.

ELECTRIC STARTER

Models are equipped with electric starter shown in Fig. SZ20-17. Disassembly is evident after inspection of unit and reference to exploded view. Starter brushes have a standard length of 16 mm (0.63 in.) and should be renewed if worn to 11.5 mm (0.45 in.) or less. After reassembly, bench test starter before installing on power head.

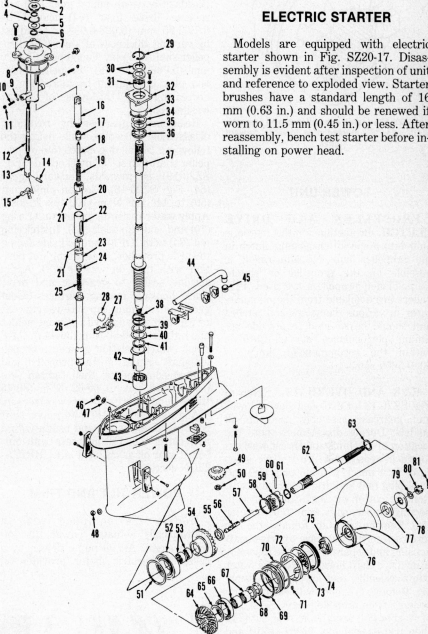

Fig. SZ20-18—Exploded view of lower unit gearcase assembly used on all models.

Fig. SZ20-17—Exploded view of electric starter motor.

1. "C" ring
2. Stop
3. Spring
4. Drive
5. Frame head
6. Frame
7. Thrust washers
8. Armature
9. Brush (+)
10. Brush holder
11. Brush (–)
12. End housing

1. Seal
2. Guide
3. "O" ring
4. "O" ring
5. Washer
6. Spacer
7. Housing
8. "O" ring
9. Ball
10. Spring
11. Screw
12. Pivot rod
13. Pivot shaft
14. Pin
15. Shifter yoke
16. Connector
17. Reverse plunger
18. Rod
19. Spring
20. Reverse sleeve
21. Lock ball
22. Lock sleeve
23. Forward sleeve
24. Forward plunger
25. Spring
26. Vertical slider
27. Magnet holder
28. Magnet
29. Snap ring
30. Seals
31. Bearing
32. Bearing housing
33. "O" ring
34. Shim
35. Thrust washer
36. Thrust bearing
37. Drive shaft
38. Spring
39. Thrust washer
40. Thrust washer
41. Protector
42. Collar
43. Bearing
44. Water tube
45. Grommet
46. Level plug
47. Gasket
48. Drain plug
49. Pinion gear
50. Nut
51. Shim
52. Bearing
53. Bearings
54. Forward gear
55. Spacer
56. Horizontal slider
57. Connector pin
58. Pin retainer
59. Dog clutch
60. Pin
61. Spacer
62. Propeller shaft
63. Thrust washer
64. Reverse gear
65. Shim
66. Bearing
67. Bearings
68. Seals
69. Spacer
70. "O" ring
71. Key
72. End cap
73. Tab washer
74. Ring nut
75. Spacer
76. Propeller
77. Spacer
78. Splined washer
79. Washer
80. Nut
81. Cotter pin

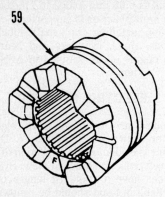

Fig. SZ20-19—Install dog clutch (59) on propeller shaft with "F" marked side towards forward gear.

LOWER UNIT

PROPELLER AND DRIVE CLUTCH. Protection for the motor is built into a special cushioning clutch in the propeller hub. No adjustment is possible on the propeller or clutch. Three-bladed propellers are used. Propellers are available from the manufacturer in various diameters and pitches and should be selected to provide optimum performance at full throttle within the recommended limits of 5000-5600 rpm.

R&R AND OVERHAUL. Refer to Fig. SZ20-18 for exploded view of lower unit gearcase assembly used on all models. During disassembly, note the location of all shims and thrust washers to aid in reassembly. To remove gearcase, first unscrew drain plug (48) and level plug (46) and drain gear lubricant. Remove cotter pin and clevis pin connecting upper shift rod to connector (16). Remove trim tab. Remove the cap screws securing gearcase to drive shaft housing and separate gearcase assembly from drive shaft housing. Remove water pump assembly and lower shift assembly. Remove propeller with related components from propeller shaft. Bend tabs of washer (73) away from ring nut (74), then use special tool 09951-18710 and unscrew ring nut (74). Remove ring nut (74) and tab washer (73). Use a suitable puller and withdraw propeller shaft assembly with gearcase end cap (72). Unscrew pinion nut (50) and remove pinion gear (49), then extract forward gear (54). Drive shaft (37) and related components can be withdrawn from gearcase after removal of bearings housing (32).

Inspect gears for wear on teeth and on engagement dogs. Inspect dog clutch (59) for wear on engagement surfaces. Inspect shafts for wear on splines and on friction surfaces of gears and oil

seals. All seals and "O" rings should be renewed when unit is reassembled.

Backlash between pinion gear (49) and forward drive gear (54) should be 0.50-0.65 mm (0.020-0.026 in.). Adjust by varying thickness of shim (51). Backlash between pinion gear (49) and reverse drive gear (64) should be 0.70-0.85 mm (0.028-0.033 in.). Adjust by varying thickness of shim (65). Propeller shaft end play should be 0.05-0.20 mm (0.002-0.008 in.). Propeller shaft end play is adjusted by increasing or decreasing the thickness of thrust washer (63).

Reassemble gearcase by reversing disassembly procedure while noting the following: Install dog clutch (59) on propeller shaft (62) so "F" marked side (Fig. SZ20-19) is towards forward gear (54–Fig. SZ20-18). Tighten pinion nut (50) to 140-150 N·m (102-109 ft.-lbs.). Apply water-resistant grease to "O" ring (70) and end cap seals (68). Install ring nut (74) with "OFF" marked side facing towards propeller. Secure ring nut position with tabs on washer (73). Apply silicone sealer to gearcase and drive shaft housing mating surfaces. Coat gearcase retaining cap screws adjacent to cap screw heads with silicone sealer and tighten to 50-60 N·m (36-44 ft.-lbs.). Apply water-resistant grease to propeller shaft splines. Install propeller and related components, then tighten propeller shaft nut to 50-62 N·m (36-45 ft.-lbs.) and secure with a new cotter pin.

Align connector (16) with upper shift rod. Install clevis pin and retain with a new cotter pin. Fill gearcase with outboard gear oil as outlined in LUBRICATION section.

POWER TILT AND TRIM

Models are equipped with a hydraulically actuated power tilt and trim system. An oil pump driven by a reversible electric motor provides oil

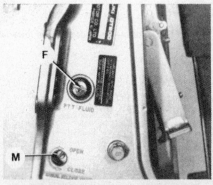

Fig. SZ20-20—View identifying location of power tilt and trim reservoir fill plug (F) and manual release valve (M). Manual release valve has left-hand threads.

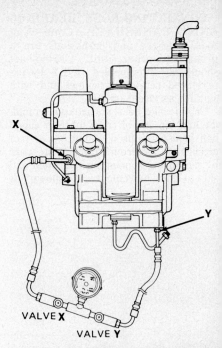

Fig. SZ20-21—Connect a 13.8 MPa (2000 psi) gage as shown in test pump pressure. Refer to text.

pressure. A rocker control switch determines motor and pump rotation thereby retracting or extending tilt and trim cylinders. The pump is equipped with a manual release valve (M–Fig. SZ20-20) that when rotated two turns clockwise enables movement of the tilt cylinder if the electric motor malfunctions.

Recommended oil is Dexron automatic transmission fluid. Do not run pump without oil in reservoir. Fill plug (F) is located in side of pump reservoir. Oil level should reach fill plug hole threads with outboard motor in full tilt position. Hydraulic tilt should be cycled several times and oil level rechecked if system has been drained or lost a large amount of oil.

If malfunction occurs in tilt and trim system, first make sure malfunction is not due to wiring, wiring connection or electric motor failure. To test pump pressure, proceed as follows: Tilt outboard motor to full up position and lower tilt lock lever. Connect a 13.8 MPa (2000 psi) gage between ports (X and Y–Fig. SZ20-21). Close (X) side of gage and open (Y) side. Operate rocker control switch in the "UP" direction. Oil pressure at port (Y) should be 8.83 MPa (1280-1700 psi). Close (Y) side of gage and open (X) side. Operate rocker control switch in the "DOWN" direction. Oil pressure at port (X) should be 2.76-5.52 MPa (400-800 psi). Renew pump and valve body assembly if pressure readings are not within recommended limits.

TOHATSU

TOHATSU U.S.A.
1211 Avenue of the Americas
New York, NY 10036

TOHATSU 30 HP

CONDENSED SERVICE DATA

NOTE: Metric fasters are used throughout outboard motor.

TUNE-UP

Hp/rpm	30/4800-5500
Bore	68 mm
	(2.68 in.)
Stroke	59 mm
	(2.32 in.)
Number of Cylinders	2
Displacement	430 cc
	(26.2 cu. in.)

Spark Plug:
  Model M30A
    Champion L82
    NGK B7HS
      Electrode Gap . . . . 0.6-0.7 mm
      (0.024-0.028 in.)
  Model M30A2
    Champion L82C10
    NGK B7HS-10
      Electrode Gap . . . . 0.9-1.0 mm
      (0.035-0.040 in.)
Ignition Type . . . . Breakerless CD
Ignition Timing . . . . 25° BTDC
Fuel:Oil Ratio 50:1

SIZES—CLEARANCES

Piston Ring End Gap . . . . 0.33-0.48 mm
  (0.013-0.019 in.)
Piston Ring Side Clearance:
  Top . . . . 0.05-0.09 mm
  (0.0020-0.0035 in.)
  Bottom . . . . 0.02-0.06 mm
  (0.0008-0.0024 in.)
Piston Clearance . . . . 0.06-0.10 mm
  (0.0024-0.0040 in.)
Piston Pin Clearance in Piston . . . . 0.001-0.013 mm
  (0.00004-0.00051 in.)

SIZES—CLEARANCES CONT.

Connecting Rod Side Clearance:
  Standard . . . . 0.3-0.5 mm
  (0.012-0.020 in.)
  Limit . . . . 0.7 mm
  (0.027 in.)
Crankshaft Runout . . . . 0.05 mm
  (0.002 in.)

TIGHTENING TORQUES

Crankcase . . . . 23.5-25.4 N·m
  (208-225 in.-lbs.)
Cylinder Head:
  M30A . . . . 32.4-37.2 N·m
  (287-329 in.-lbs.)
  M30A2 . . . . 23.5-25.4 N·m
  (208-225 in.-lbs.)
Flywheel Nut . . . . 118-137 N·m
  (87-101 ft.-lbs.)
Spark Plug . . . . 24.5 N·m
  (217 in.-lbs.)
Standard Screws:
  No. 3 . . . . 0.6-0.8 N·m
  (5-7 in.-lbs.)
  No. 4 . . . . 1.5-2 N·m
  (13-17 in.-lbs.)
  No. 5 . . . . 2.4-3.4 N·m
  (22-30 in.-lbs.)
  No. 6 . . . . 4.9-6.4 N·m
  (43-56 in.-lbs.)
  No. 8 . . . . 11.3-15.2 N·m
  (100-135 in.-lbs.)
  No. 10 . . . . 22.6-30.9 N·m
  (200-273 in.-lbs.)

LUBRICATION

The power head is lubricated by oil mixed with the fuel. Recommended oil is Tohatsu outboard motor oil mixed at a fuel:oil ratio of 50:1. During engine break-in the fuel:oil ratio should be 20:1 for a period of 10 operating hours.

Lower unit gears and bearings are lubricated by oil contained in the gearcase. Recommended oil is Tohatsu gear oil or a SAE 80 gear oil. Gearcase oil capacity is 410 mL (13.8 oz.) on M30A models and 250 mL (8.5 oz.) on M30A2 models. Oil should be changed after initial 10 hours of operation and every 200 hours of operation thereafter.

FUEL SYSTEM

CARBURETOR. Refer to Fig. T8-1 for an exploded view of carburetor. Standard main jet (9) size on Model M30A2 for normal operation is #175. Initial setting of idle mixture screw (3) is approximately 1¼ turns open on Model M30A and ⅝-1⅛ turns open on Model M30A2. Adjust idle mixture and idle speed after motor temperature has normalized. Idle speed screw (1) should be adjusted so engine idles at 900-950 rpm with gearcase engaged in forward gear.

Adjust float level so float is parallel to gasket surface with carburetor inverted and fuel bowl removed. Note clip (14) which secures inlet valve to float.

Illustrations Courtesy Tohatsu

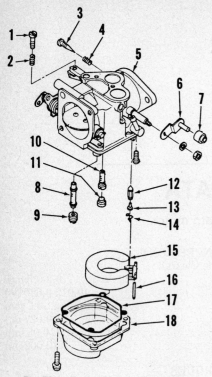

Fig. T8-1—Exploded view of carburetor.

1. Idle speed screw	10. Slow jet
2. Spring	11. Rubber cap
3. Idle mixture screw	12. Fuel inlet valve
4. Spring	13. Pin
5. Body	14. Clip
6. Lever	15. Float
7. Roller	16. Float pin
8. Main fuel nozzle	17. "O" ring
9. Main jet	18. Fuel bowl

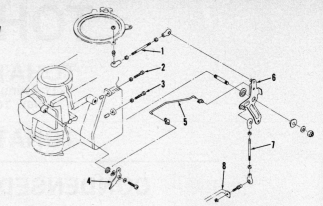

Fig. T8-2—View of speed control linkage.

1. Stator control link
2. Maximum timing screw
3. Idle timing screw
4. Throttle cam
5. Link
6. Bellcrank
7. Lower link
8. Control rod

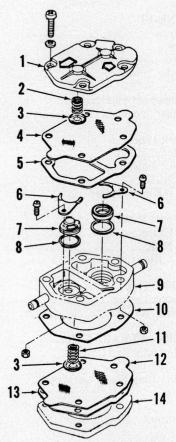

Fig. T8-3—Exploded view of fuel pump used on Model M30A.

1. Cover	8. Gasket
2. Spring	9. Body
3. Spring seat	10. Gasket
4. Diaphragm	11. Spring
5. Gasket	12. Diaphragm
6. Retainer	13. Gasket
7. Check valve	14. Base

SPEED CONTROL LINKAGE. Carburetor throttle opening and ignition timing are synchronized by the speed control linkage so the carburetor throttle valve is opened as the ignition timing is advanced.

To adjust speed control linkage, disconnect lower link (7–Fig. T8-2) and rotate bellcrank so "S" mark on throttle cam (4) is aligned with center of throttle lever roller (7–Fig. T8-1). Rotate speed control grip to "START" position. Adjust length of lower link (7–Fig. T8-2) by turning link ends so link can be attached to bellcrank and speed control rod (8) without disturbing position of bellcrank or speed control rod. Recheck adjustment and refer to IGNITION TIMING section and check ignition timing.

All models are equipped with a reverse speed limiting rod (24–Fig. T8-12) and lever (21) which prevents excessive engine speed when motor is in reverse gear. With motor in reverse gear, adjust length of rod (24) by turning rod ends (15) so mark "R" on throttle cam (4–Fig. T8-2) is aligned with center of throttle roller.

FUEL PUMP. A diaphragm type fuel pump is mounted on the starboard side of the cylinder block. The pump is operated by crankcase pulsations. Refer to Fig. T8-3 for an exploded view of fuel pump used on Model M30A and Fig. T8-4 for an exploded view of fuel pump used on Model M30A2.

REED VALVES. The reed valves are attached to a plate which is located between the intake manifold and the crankcase as shown in Fig. T8-5. Inspect reed valves and renew if cracked, bent or otherwise damaged. Do not attempt to straighten a reed valve petal. Reed valve seating surface of reed plate should be flat. Reed valve is available only as an assembly consisting of reed plate, reed petals and reed stops.

IGNITION

All models are equipped with a breakerless, capacitor discharge ignition system. The ignition exciter and trigger coils as well as the lighting coil are located under the flywheel. The flywheel nut has left-hand threads. Tighten flywheel nut to 118-137 N·m (87-101 ft.-lbs.).

The following checks using an ohmmeter can be made to locate faulty ignition system components. Disconnect three-wire connector between stator plate and CD ignition module, then connect one ohmmeter lead to stator plate. Connect remaining ohmmeter lead to red stator lead to check exciter coil. Ohmmeter reading should be 290 ohms. With ohmmeter leads connected to stator plate and blue stator lead to check trigger coil, ohmmeter reading should be 20 ohms. To check the CD ignition module, disconnect module leads and refer to chart in Fig. T8-7 for desired ohmmeter readings.

IGNITION TIMING. To adjust ignition timing, first refer to SPEED CONTROL LINKAGE section and check adjustment of speed control linkage, then proceed as follows:

Rotate speed control grip to full throttle position. The 25° BTDC mark on the stator plate (5–Fig. T8-6) should be aligned with the mating surface line of the crankcase and cylinder block. If not, turn maximum ignition timing adjustment screw (2–Fig. T8-2). Rotate speed control grip to fully closed position. The 2° ATDC mark on the stator plate should be aligned with the mating surface line of the crankcase and cylinder block. If not, turn idle speed ignition timing adjustment screw (3). It may be necessary to adjust length of upper link

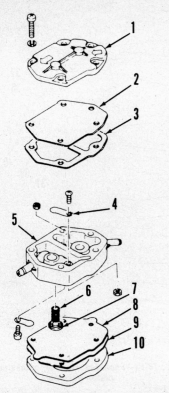

Fig. T8-4—Exploded view of fuel pump used on Model M30A2.

1. Cover
2. Diaphragm
3. Gasket
4. Check valve
5. Body
6. Spring
7. Spring seat
8. Diaphragm
9. Gasket
10. Base

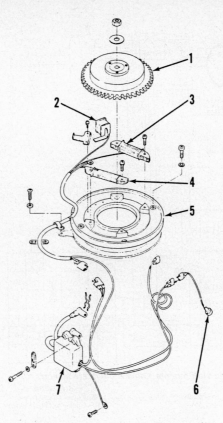

Fig. T8-6—Exploded view of ignition system.

1. Flywheel
2. Trigger coil
3. Lighting coil
4. Exciter coil
5. Stator plate
6. Ignition switch
7. Ignition module

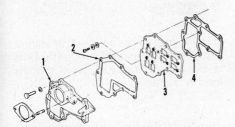

Fig. T8-5—View of reed valve assembly.

1. Intake manifold
2. Gasket
3. Reed valve assy.
4. Gasket

(1) to set ignition timing for full throttle and idle speed. Recheck ignition timing if upper link (1) is detached.

COOLING SYSTEM

THERMOSTAT. A thermostat (25–Fig. T8-9) is located in the cylinder head. Thermostat should begin opening at 50°-54° C (122°-129° F) and be fully open at 65° C (149° F). Thermostat opening at maximum opening should be 3.0 mm (0.118 in.).

WATER PUMP. A rubber impeller type water pump is mounted on the gearcase between the drive shaft housing and gearcase. The impeller is driven by a Woodruff key in the drive shaft.

Whenever cooling problems are encountered, check water inlet for plug-

ging or partial stoppage and the thermostat for proper operation, then if not corrected, remove gearcase and check condition of the water pump, water passages and sealing surfaces.

When water pump is disassembled, check condition of impeller (4–Fig. T8-16), liner (3) and plate (5). Turn drive shaft clockwise (viewed from top) while placing pump housing over impeller. Avoid turning drive shaft in opposite direction when water pump is assembled. Tighten pump housing screws in a crossing pattern.

POWER HEAD

REMOVE AND REINSTALL. To remove power head, remove upper motor cover and disconnect ignition wires. Detach speed control lower link (7–Fig. T8-2). Detach starter lockout rod from shift shaft, disconnect fuel

hoses and disengage choke control. Unscrew power head retaining screws and lift power head off drive shaft housing.

To install power head, reverse removal procedure. Apply water resistant grease to ends of crankshaft and drive shaft.

DISASSEMBLY. To disassemble power head, disconnect fuel lines and remove carburetor, fuel filter and fuel pump. Remove electric starter, if so equipped. Remove manual starter, disconnect ignition wires and remove ignition module. Detach speed control linkage. Remove flywheel, stator plate assembly, retainer (1–Fig. T8-9) and magneto ring (2). Remove exhaust cover (20) and cylinder head (22). Remove intake manifold and reed valve. Remove upper and lower seal housings (3 and 15). Unscrew labyrinth seal locating screw (8) and crankcase retaining screws. Separate crankcase from cylinder block and lift crankshaft assembly out of cylinder block. Individual components may now be serviced as outlined in following service sections.

ASSEMBLY. Before reassembling engine, be sure all joints and gasket surfaces are clean, free from nicks and burrs and hardened cement or carbon. Mating surfaces may be lapped to remove high spots or nicks, however, only a minimum amount of metal should be removed.

All friction surfaces and bearings should be thoroughly lubricated with engine oil during reassembly. Coat mating surfaces with a nonhardening gaset sealer.

Note the following points when assembling power head: Position lower bearing retainer (11–Fig. T8-9) in cylinder block groove before installing crankshaft; position inner bearing retainer (10) in cylinder block groove after crankshaft has been installed. Be sure piston rings properly mate with piston ring groove pins and locating pins in bearings and labyrinth seal engage holes or notches in cylinder block when installing crankshaft assembly in cylinder block. Tighten crankcase screws in steps to 23.5-25.4 N·m (208-255 in.-lbs.) torque using a crossing pattern; tighten the center screws first. Install seals (4 and 12) in

Fig. T8-7—An ohmmeter should indicate the readings in the adjacent chart when testing the CD ignition module.

Connection of Tester Leads and Ident. of CD Module Leads		Tester (+) Lead			
		BROWN	RED	BLUE	BLACK
Tester (−) Lead	BROWN		Infinity	Infinity	Infinity
	RED	Small deflection and soon returns			Zero
	BLUE	300Ω - 1000Ω	Infinity		Infinity
	BLACK	Small deflection and soon returns	Zero	Infinity	

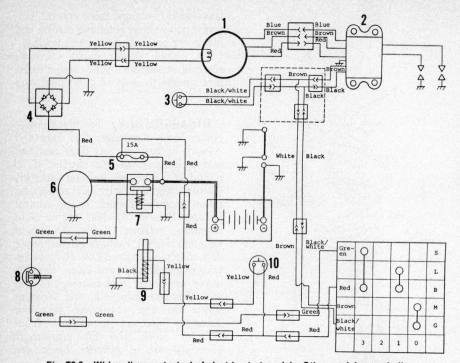

Fig. T8-8—Wiring diagram typical of electric start models. Other models are similar.

1. Stator plate
2. Ignition module
3. Starter safety switch
4. Rectifier
5. Fuse
6. Electric starter motor
7. Solenoid
8. Neutral switch
9. Choke solenoid
10. Choke solenoid switch

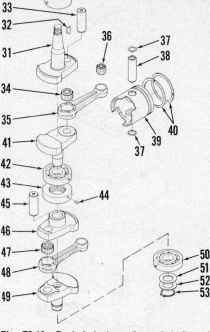

Fig. T8-10—Exploded view of crankshaft and piston assembly.

30. Bearing		42. Bearing	
31. Crankshaft half		43. Labyrinth seal	
32. Key		44. Pin	
33. Crankpin		45. Crankpin	
34. Roller bearing		46. Crankshaft half	
35. Connecting rod		47. Roller bearing	
36. Roller bearing		48. Connecting rod	
37. Circlip		49. Crankshaft half	
38. Piston pin		50. Bearing	
39. Piston		51. Shim	
40. Piston rings		52. Spacer	
41. Crankshaft half		53. Snap ring	

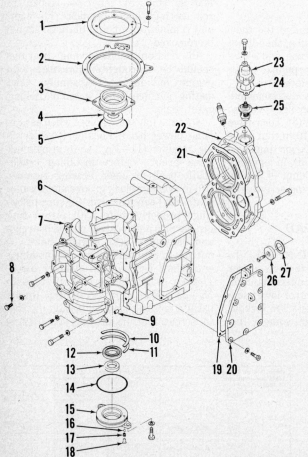

Fig. T8-9—Exploded view of crankcase and cylinder block assemblies.

1. Retainer
2. Magneto ring
3. Seal housing
4. Seal
5. "O" ring
6. Cylinder block
7. Crankcase
8. Labyrinth seal locating screw
9. Dowel pin
10. & 11. Bearing retaining ring
12. Seal
13. Seal
14. "O" ring
15. Seal housing
16. Check ball
17. Spring
18. Plug
19. Gasket
20. Exhaust cover
21. Gasket
22. Cylinder head
23. Thermostat cover
24. Gasket
25. Thermostat
26. Anode
27. Gasket

seal housings so lips are towards engine. Install seal (13) in seal housing (15) so lip is away from engine. Tighten cylinder head retaining screws to 32.4-37.2 N·m (287-329 in.-lbs.) on M30A models and 23.5-25.4 N·m (208-225 in.-lbs.) on M30A2 models using the tightening sequence shown in Fig. T8-11.

PISTONS, PINS, RINGS AND CYLINDERS. The cylinders are equipped with an iron liner which may be bored to accept oversize pistons. Pistons and piston rings are available in standard size and 0.5 mm (0.020 in.) oversize. Each piston ring is located in the piston ring groove by a pin in each ring groove.

The piston pin is retained by circlips (37 – Fig. T8-10) which should be renewed if removed. The piston pin rides in a roller bearing in rod small end. Install piston on connecting rod so arrow on piston crown will point towards exhaust port.

CRANKSHAFT AND CONNECTING RODS. Crankshaft, connecting rods, crankpins and bearings are assembled as a pressed-together unit. Disassembly and assembly of crankshaft should be performed by a shop ex-

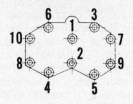

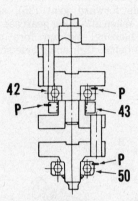

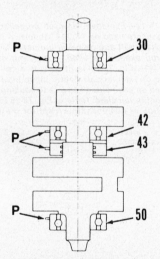

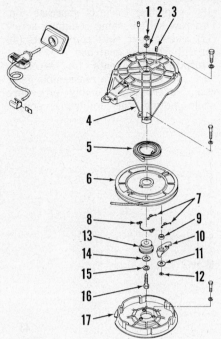

Fig. T8-12—When reassembling crankshaft on M30A models, install bearings (42 and 50) and labyrinth seal (43) so locating pins (P) are positioned as shown.

Fig. T8-13—When reassembling crankshaft on M30A2 models, install bearings (30, 42 and 50) and labyrinth seal (43) so locating pins (P) are positioned as shown.

Fig. T8-14—Exploded view of manual starter.

1. Nut
2. Washer
3. Pin
4. Starter housing
5. Rewind spring
6. Rope pulley
7. Spring links
8. Spring
9. Bushing
10. Pawl
11. Washer
12. "E" ring
13. Shaft
14. Washer
15. Lockwasher
16. Screw
17. Starter cup

Fig. T8-15—Exploded view of starter lockout and reverse speed limiting mechanism.

1. Pin
2. Cotter pin
3. Washer
4. Spring
5. Pawl
6. "E" ring
7. Collar
8. Cotter pin
9. Rod
10. Rod end
11. Shift shaft detent plate
12. Rod end
13. Rod
14. Locknut
15. Rod end
16. Washer
17. Lever
18. Wave washer
19. Bushing
20. Washer
21. Pivot arm
22. Magneto ring
23. Pivot stud
24. Reverse speed limiting rod

perienced in repair of this type crankshaft. Individual crankshaft components are available. Refer to Fig. T8-12 for M30A models and Fig. T8-13 for M30A2 models for correct installation of crankshaft bearings and labyrinth seal so locating pins are on correct side.

MANUAL STARTER

Refer to Fig. T8-14 for an exploded view of manual starter. The starter may be disassembled after removing motor cover, detaching starter lock-out linkage and removing starter from power head. Remove rope handle and allow rope to wind into starter. Remove screw (16) and shaft (13), then carefully lift pulley (6) out of housing while being careful not to disturb rewind spring (5). If rewind spring must be removed care should be used not to allow spring to uncoil uncontrolled. Inspect pawl (10) for wear and freedom of movement. Renew and grease pawl if required.

When assembling starter, wind rewind spring in housing in a counterclockwise direction from outer end. Wind rope around rope pulley in a counterclockwise direction as viewed with pulley in housing. Pawl spring (8) must engage groove in shaft (13). Rotate pulley three turns counterclockwise before passing rope through rope outlet to preload rewind spring.

A starter lockout mechanism (Fig. T8-15 is used to prevent starter usage when motor is in forward or reverse gear. Adjust length of lockout rod (13) by turning rod end so starter will operate with motor in neutral gear but not in forward or reverse gear.

ELECTRIC STARTER

Some models are equipped with an electric starter. Models equipped with an electric starter are also equipped with a battery charging system. Refer to Fig. T8-8 for a wiring diagram. Starter drive pinion and on some models, brush assembly, are only components serviceable on starter.

LOWER UNIT

PROPELLER AND SHEAR PIN. Lower unit protection is provided by a shear pin (32–Fig. T8-16) on M30A models. Be sure correct shear pin is installed for maximum protection to lower unit. Lower unit protection is provided by a clutch in propeller (55–Fig. T8-17) on M30A2 models.

The standard propeller has three blades and rotates clockwise. Various propellers are available to obtain best performance depending on outboard usage. Desired operating range at maximum engine speed is 4800-5500 rpm.

R&R AND OVERHAUL. To remove gearcase, disconnect shift rod coupler (44–Fig. T8-16) from lower shift rod (46) by driving out lower pin (45). Unscrew five cap screws securing gearcase to drive shaft housing and remove gearcase. Drain lubricant from gearcase and remove propeller. On Model M30A, remove shear pin. Remove water pump assembly. Remove bearing housing (38) and withdraw propeller shaft assembly. Drive out pin (29) to separate clutch (28) and spring (30) from propeller shaft. Unscrew pinion gear nut (22) and pull drive shaft (11) from gearcase. Pinion gear (21) and forward gear (25) with bearing may now be removed. Use a suitable puller and remove roller bearing (13) by pulling towards gearcase top. Unscrew shift bushing retaining screw (17) and remove shift components (46 through 52) from gearcase.

Inspect components for excessive wear and damage. To reassemble gearcase, reverse disassembly procedure while noting the following points:

Lubricate all "O" rings and seals prior to assembly. Backlash between pinion gear and forward or reverse gear should be 0.08-0.13 mm (0.003-0.005 in.) and is adjusted by varying thickness of shim (9). Apply Loctite during final assembly and tighten pinion gear nut (22) to 23.5-25.4 N·m (208-225 in.-lbs.). Install clutch (28) on propeller shaft so grooved end is towards forward gear (25); see Fig. T8-18. When attaching gearcase to drive shaft housing, tighten fore and aft screws before tightening side screws.

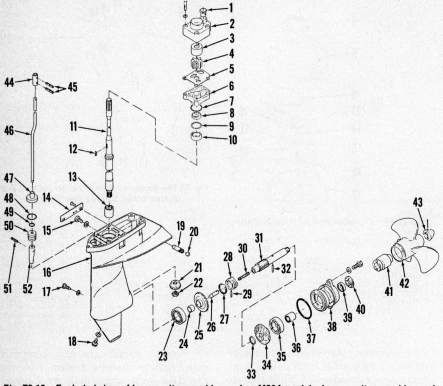

Fig. T8-16—Exploded view of lower unit assembly used on M30A models. Lower unit assembly used on M30A2 models is similar except for components noted in Fig. T8-17.

1. Bushing
2. Water pump housing
3. Liner
4. Impeller
5. Plate
6. Pump base
7. "O" ring
8. Seal
9. Shim
10. Bearing
11. Drive shaft
12. Key
13. Bearing
14. Water inlet cover
15. Vent plug
16. Gearcase
17. Shift bushing retaining screw
18. Fill plug
19. Screen
20. Plug
21. Pinion gear
22. Nut
23. Bearing
24. Bushing
25. Forward gear
26. Shift plunger
27. Wire retainer
28. Clutch
29. Pin
30. Spring
31. Propeller shaft
32. Shear pin
33. Thrust washer
34. Reverse gear
35. Bearing
36. Bearing
37. "O" ring
38. Bearing housing
39. Seal
40. Spacer
41. Hub
42. Propeller
43. Nut
44. Coupler
45. Pin
46. Lower shift rod
47. Guide
48. "O" ring
49. "O" ring
50. Bushing
51. Pin
52. Shift cam

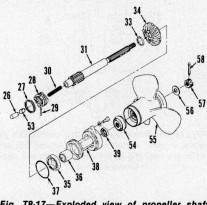

Fig. T8-17—Exploded view of propeller shaft components used on M30A2 models. A splined propeller shaft and propeller are used. Through-the-prop exhaust is used. Lower end of drive shaft (11—Fig. T8-16) is fitted with a collar and spring on later models. Water pump intakes are located on each side of gearcase housing below antiventilation plate. Refer to Fig. T8-16 for identification of components except for the following:

53. Spring holder
54. Thrust holder
55. Propeller
56. Washer
57. Nut
58. Cotter pin

Fig. T8-18—Install clutch so end with groove (G) is towards forward gear end of propeller shaft.

TOHATSU 35 AND 40 HP

CONDENSED SERVICE DATA

NOTE: Metric fasteners are used throughout outboard motor.

TUNE-UP

Hp/rpm 35/5700
            40/5800
Bore . . . . .70 mm
            (2.76 in.)
Stroke. . . . . .64 mm
            (2.52 in.)
Number of Cylinders 2
Displacement . . . . .493 cc
            (30.1 cu. in.)
Spark Plug:
   35 HP
      Champion L81Y
      NGK B7HS
         Electrode Gap .0.6-0.7 mm
            (0.024-0.028 in.)
   40 HP
      Champion L82YC
      NGK. B7HS-10
         Electrode Gap .0.9-1.0 mm
            (0.035-0.040 in.)
Ignition Type .Breakerless CD
Ignition Timing . . . . .25° BTDC
Fuel:Oil Ratio. 50:1

SIZES—CLEARANCES

Piston Ring End Gap:
   35 HP. . . . . .0.2-0.4 mm
            (0.008-0.016 in.)
   40 HP . . . . .0.25-0.4 mm
            (0.010-0.016 in.)
   Bottom Ring . . . . .0.2-0.4 mm
            (0.008-0.016 in.)
Piston Ring Side Clearance:
   35 HP
      Top Ring . . . . .0.05-0.09 mm
            (0.0020-0.0035 in.)
      Bottom Ring .0.02-0.06 mm
            (0.0008-0.0024 in.)
   40 HP
      Top Ring . . . . .Semi-Keystone
      Bottom Ring .0.02-0.06 mm
            (0.0008-0.0024 in.)
Piston Clearance:
   35 HP. . . . . .0.05-0.10 mm
            (0.0020-0.0040 in.)

SIZES—CLEARANCES CONT.

Piston Clearance:
   40 HP . . . . .0.08-0.13 mm
            (0.0031-0.0051 in.)
Piston Pin Clearance In Piston:
   35 HP . . . . .0.001-0.009 mm
            (0.00004-0.00035 in.)
   40 HP . . . . .0.007-0.010 mm
            (0.0003-0.0004 in.)
Connecting Rod Side Clearance . . . . .0.28-0.65 mm
            (0.011-0.026 in.)
Connecting Rod Small End Shake:
   Standard . . . . .1.0 mm
            (0.040 in.)
   Limit . . . . .2.0 mm
            (0.079 in.)
Crankshaft Runout . . . . .0.05 mm
            (0.002 in.)

TIGHTENING TORQUES

Crankcase . . . . .23.5-25.4 N·m
            (208-225 in.-lbs.)
Cylinder Head. . . . . .32.4-37.2 N·m
            (287-329 in.-lbs.)
Flywheel Nut . . . . .118-137 N·m
            (87-101 ft.-lbs.)
Pinion Gear Screw . . . . .23.5-25.4 N·m
            (208-225 in.-lbs.)
Propeller Nut . . . . .29.4-39.2 N·m
            (260-347 in.-lbs.)
Spark Plug . . . . .24.5-29.4 N·m
            (217-260 in.-lbs.)
Standard Screws:
   No. 3 . . . . .0.6-0.8 N·m
            (5-7 in.-lbs.)
   No. 4 . . . . .1.3-1.8 N·m
            (11-15 in.-lbs.)
   No. 5 . . . . .2.6-3.5 N·m
            (23-31 in.-lbs.)
   No. 6 . . . . .4.6-6.3 N·m
            (41-55 in.-lbs.)
   No. 8. . . . . .11.2-15.1 N·m
            (99-133 in.-lbs.)
   No. 10. . . . . .22.6-30.6 N·m
            (200-270 in.-lbs.)

LUBRICATION

The power head is lubricated by oil mixed with the fuel. Recommended oil is Tohatsu outboard motor oil mixed at a fuel:oil ratio of 50:1. During engine break-in the fuel:oil ratio should be 20:1 for a period of 10 operating hours.

Lower unit gears and bearings are lubricated by oil contained in the gearcase. Recommended oil is Tohatsu gear oil or a SAE 80 gear oil. Gearcase oil capacity is approximately 460 mL (15.5 oz.). Oil should be changed after initial 10 hours of operation and after every 200 hours of operation thereafter.

FUEL SYSTEM

CARBURETOR. Refer to Fig. T9-1 for an exploded view of carburetor. Initial setting of idle mixture screw (5) is 1¼ turns out from a lightly seated position. Adjust idle mixture and idle speed screws after motor temperature has normalized. Idle speed should be 900-950 rpm with motor engaged in forward gear.

To determine float height invert fuel bowl and measure float height as shown in Fig. T9-2. Float height should be 17-19 mm (0.67-0.75 in.) and is adjusted by bending float arm tang. Note clip (20) which secures fuel inlet valve to float arm.

Main jet (13 – Fig. T9-1) size for normal operation should be #220. Main air jet (10) size should be #120 and slow air jet (11) size should be #110.

SPEED CONTROL LINKAGE. Carburetor throttle opening and ignition timing are synchronized by the speed control linkage so the carburetor throttle valve is opened as the ignition timing is advanced.

(Model 35 HP). Prior to speed control linkage adjustment, refer to IGNITION TIMING section and check ignition timing. Detach lower link (7 – Fig. T9-3) and rotate bellcrank (4) so it is against advance speed stop screw (1). Throttle roller (9 – Fig. T9-1) should be against throttle cam stop (S – Fig. T9-4). Detach and adjust length of rod (5 – Fig. T9-3) by turning rod ends so throttle roller and cam are properly positioned. Adjust length of lower link (7) by turning ends so idle and full throttle markings on speed control grip are synchronized with idle and full throttle positions of bellcrank (4).

All models are equipped with a reverse speed stop (2 – Fig. T9-24) which prevents excessive engine speed when motor is in reverse gear. With motor in reverse gear, turn reverse speed adjusting screw (1) so mark (M – Fig. T9-4) on throttle cam is aligned with the center of throttle roller (9).

(Model 40 HP). To adjust speed control linkage, disconnect lower link (7 – Fig. 9-3) and rotate bellcrank so "S" mark on throttle cam (6) is aligned with center of throttle lever roller (9 – Fig. T9-1). Rotate speed control grip to "START" position. Adjust length of lower link (7 – Fig. T9-3) by turning link ends so link can be attached to bellcrank and speed control rod (8) without disturbing position of bellcrank or speed

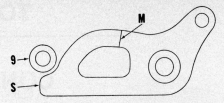

Fig. T9-4—On 35 hp models, throttle roller (9) should be against throttle cam stop (S) at maximum throttle. Throttle roller centerline should be aligned with throttle cam mark (M) when motor is in reverse gear. Refer to text for adjustment.

control rod. Recheck adjustment and refer to IGNITION TIMING section and check ignition timing.

All models are equipped with a reverse speed stop (2 – Fig. T9-24) which prevents excessive engine speed when motor is in reverse gear. With motor in reverse gear, turn reverse speed adjusting screw (1) so mark "R" on throttle cam (6 – Fig. T9-3) is aligned with the center of throttle roller (9 – Fig. T9-1).

FUEL PUMP. A diaphragm type fuel pump is mounted on the port side of the cylinder block. The pump is operated by crankcase pulsations. Refer to Fig. T9-5 for an exploded view of fuel pump used on 35 hp models and Fig. T9-6 for an exploded view of fuel pump used on 40 hp models.

REED VALVES. Two vee type reed valve assemblies (one for each cylinder) are located between the intake manifold and crankcase. Remove intake manifold and reed plate (4 – Fig. T9-7) for access to reed assemblies (6).

Renew reeds if petals are broken, cracked, warped or bent. Do not attempt to bend or straighten reeds. Reed seating surface on reed blocks should be smooth and flat. Reed stop setting should be 6.0-6.2 mm (0.236-0.244 in.) when measured as shown in Fig. T9-8.

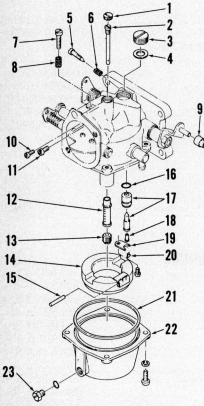

Fig. T9-1—Exploded view of carburetor.

1. Plug	13. Main jet
2. Slow jet	14. Float
3. Plug	15. Float pin
4. Gasket	16. Gasket
5. Idle mixture screw	17. Fuel inlet valve
6. Spring	18. Pin
7. Idle speed screw	19. Retainer
8. Spring	20. Clip
9. Throttle roller	21. "O" ring
10. Main air jet	22. Fuel bowl
11. Slow air jet	23. Drain screw
12. Main nozzle	

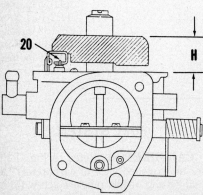

Fig. T9-2—Float height (H) should be 17-19 mm (0.67-0.75 in.). Clip (20) should secure float arm to fuel inlet valve.

Fig. T9-3—Exploded view of speed control linkage.

1. Maximum advance timing screw
2. Idle speed timing screw
3. Magneto control rod
4. Bellcrank
5. Throttle control rod
6. Throttle cam
7. Lower speed control link
8. Speed control rod

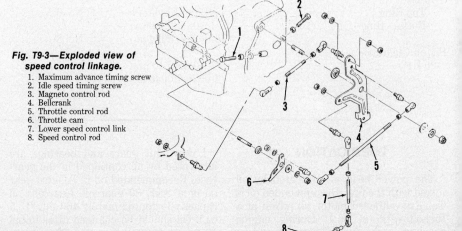

IGNITION

All models are equipped with a breakerless, capacitor discharge ignition system. The ignition exciter and trigger coils as well as the lighting coil are located under the flywheel. The flywheel nut has left-hand threads. Tighten flywheel nut to 118-137 N·m (87-101 ft.-lbs.).

The following checks using an ohmmeter may be made to locate faulty ignition system components. On 35 hp models, note if flywheel is equipped with two or four magnetic poles. Flywheel and stator plate using two poles are designated IIDA DENKI FS417114; flywheel and stator plate using four poles are designated IIDA DENKI FS412114. To check stator plate components, disconnect the three-wire connector between stator plate and ignition module, then connect one ohmmeter lead to stator plate. Connect remaining ohmmeter lead to red stator lead to check exciter coil. Ohmmeter reading should be 264-396 ohms on two-pole units, 240-360 ohms on four-pole units

and 232-348 ohms on 40 hp models. Disconnect ohmmeter lead from red stator lead and connect ohmmeter lead to blue stator lead to check trigger coil. Ohmmeter reading should be 16-24 ohms for either two- or four-pole ignitions and 40 hp models. Disconnect ohmmeter leads from blue stator lead and stator plate. Connect ohmmeter leads to yellow and white stator wires on 35 hp models and two yellow wires on 40 hp models to check lighting coil. Ohmmeter reading should be 0.56-0.84 ohms on two-pole ignitions, 0.8-1.2 ohms on four-pole ignitions and 0.27-0.41 ohms on 40 hp models. To check igntion module, disconnect module wire leads and using an ohmmeter refer to Fig. T9-12 for 35 hp models and Fig. T9-13 for 40 hp

models for a chart of desired ohmmeter readings. Use a tester which uses a testing voltage of three volts or less to prevent possible ignition module damage.

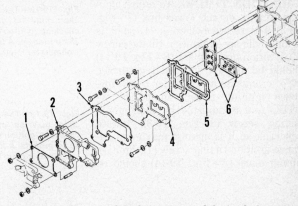

Fig. T9-7—Exploded view of reed valve and intake manifold assembly.

1. Gasket
2. Intake manifold
3. Gasket
4. Plate
5. Gasket
6. Reed valve assy.

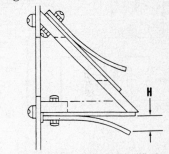

Fig. T9-8—Reed valve stop height (H) should be 6.0-6.2 mm (0.236-0.244 in.).

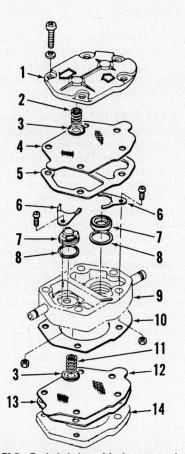

Fig. T9-5—Exploded view of fuel pump used on 35 hp models.

1. Cover	8. Gasket
2. Spring	9. Body
3. Spring seat	10. Gasket
4. Diaphragm	11. Spring
5. Gasket	12. Diaphragm
6. Retainer	13. Gasket
7. Check valve	14. Base

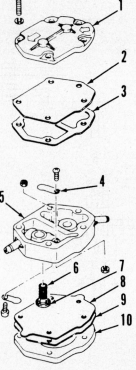

Fig. T9-6—Exploded view of fuel pump used on 40 hp models.

1. Cover	6. Spring
2. Diaphragm	7. Spring seat
3. Gasket	8. Diaphragm
4. Check valve	9. Gasket
5. Body	10. Base

Fig. T9-9—Exploded view of ignition system.

1. Flywheel	
2. Trigger coil	
3. Lighting coil	5. Stator plate
4. Exciter coil	6. Ignition switch
	7. Ignition module

IGNITION TIMING. To adjust ignition timing, detach lower link (7 – Fig. T9-3) and rotate bellcrank (4) so it is against idle speed ignition timing screw (2). Ignition timing mark (B – Fig. T9-14) should be aligned with mating surface (S) of crankcase and cylinder block. Idle speed ignition timing should be 2° BTDC and is adjusted by turning adjusting screw (2 – Fig. T9-3). Rotate bellcrank so it is against maximum advance ignition timing screw (1). Ignition timing mark (A – Fig. T9-14) should be

Fig. T9-12 – The adjacent chart may be used when checking ignition module on 35 hp models. A low-voltage ohmmeter must be used.

Fig. T9-13 – The adjacent chart may be used when checking ignition module on 40 hp models. A low-voltage ohmmeter must be used.

Connection of Tester Leads and Ident. of CD Module Leads		Tester (+) Lead			
		BROWN	RED	BLUE	BLACK
Tester (−) Lead	BROWN		Infinity	Infinity	Infinity
	RED	Small deflection and soon returns			Zero
	BLUE	160 Ω	Infinity		Infinity
	BLACK	Small deflection and soon returns	Zero	Infinity	

Connection of Tester Leads and Ident. of CD Module Leads		Tester (+) Lead			
		BROWN	RED	BLUE	BLACK
Tester (−) Lead	BROWN		Infinity	Infinity	Infinity
	RED	Small deflection and soon returns			Zero
	BLUE	300 Ω - 1000 Ω	Infinity		Infinity
	BLACK	Small deflection and soon returns	Zero	Infinity	

aligned with mating surface (S) of crankcase and cylinder block. Maximum advance ignition timing should be 25° BTDC and is adjusted by turning adjusting screw (1 – Fig. T9-3). Adjust length of rod (3) if adjustment is not possible using screws (1 and 2). Reconnect lower link (7) and adjust speed control linkage if necessary.

COOLING SYSTEM

THERMOSTAT. A thermostat (27 – Fig. T9-17) is located in the cylinder head. Thermostat should begin opening at 50°-54° C (122°-129° F) and be fully open at 65° C (149° F). Thermostat opening at maximum opening should be 3.0 mm (0.118 in.).

WATER PUMP. A rubber impeller type water pump is mounted on the gearcase between the drive shaft housing and gearcase. The impeller is driven by a Woodruff key in the drive shaft.

Whenever cooling problems are encountered, check water inlet for plugging or partial stoppage and the thermostat for proper operation, then if not corrected, remove gearcase and check condition of the water pump, water passages and sealing surfaces. Note that water inlet covers on some models are marked "R" and "L" as shown in Fig. T9-16 and are interchangeable. Install water inlet cover on starboard side so "R" end is up and install water inlet cover on port side so "L" end is up.

When water pump is disassembled, check condition of impeller (8 – Fig. T9-15), liner (7) and plate (9). When installing liner in pump housing note that

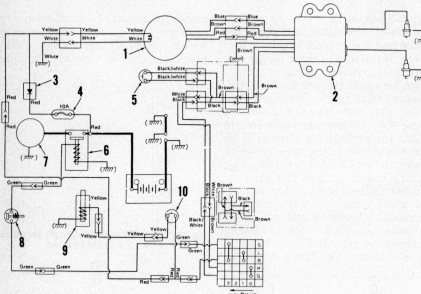

Fig. T9-10 – Typical wiring diagram for 35 hp models.

1. Stator plate	4. Fuse	8. Neutral switch
2. Ignition module	5. Ignition switch	9. Choke solenoid
3. Rectifier	6. Starter solenoid	10. Choke solenoid switch
	7. Starter motor	

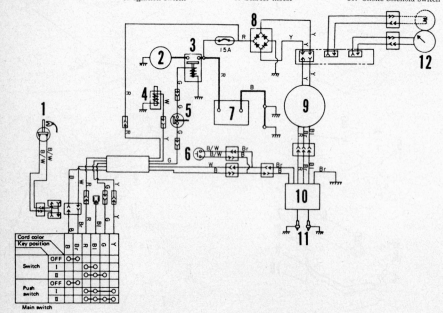

Fig. T9-11 – Typical wiring diagram for 40 hp models.

1. Safety switch	7. Battery	12. Tachometer	Y. Yellow
2. Starter motor	8. Rectifier	B. Black	Bl. Blue
3. Starter solenoid	9. Flywheel magneto	G. Green	Br. Brown
4. Choke solenoid	10. CD module	R. Red	B/W. Black with white
5. Neutral switch	11. Spark plugs	W. White	tracer
6. Stop switch			

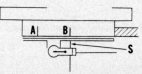

Fig. T9-14 – View showing location of full throttle timing mark (A) and idle speed timing mark (B). Refer to text for ignition timing adjustment.

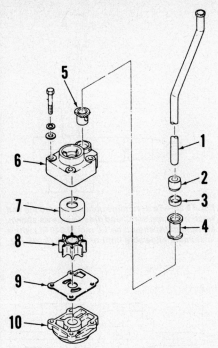

Fig. T9-15—Exploded view of water pump. Refer also to Fig. T9-25.

1. Water tube
2. Seal
3. Set ring
4. Grommet
5. Grommet
6. Pump housing
7. Liner
8. Impeller
9. Plate
10. Pump base

locating knob on upper end of liner must index with a corresponding indentation in housing. Turn drive shaft clockwise (viewed from top) while placing pump housing over impeller. Avoid turning drive shaft in opposite direction when water pump is assembled. Tighten pump housing screws in a crossing pattern.

POWER HEAD

REMOVE AND REINSTALL. To remove power head, remove upper motor cover and disconnect ignition wires and fuel hoses. Detach speed control link (7 – Fig. T9-3), starter interlock link (13 – Fig. T9-24) and choke rod. Unscrew engine mounting screws and lift power head off drive shaft housing.

To install power head, reverse removal procedure. Apply water resistant grease to ends of crankshaft and drive shaft.

DISASSEMBLY. To disassemble power head, disconnect fuel lines and remove carburetor, fuel filter and fuel pump. Remove electric starter, if so equipped. Remove manual starter, disconnect ignition wires and remove ignition module. Detach speed control linkage. Remove flywheel, stator plate assembly, retainer (1 – Fig. T9-17) and magneto ring (3). Remove exhaust cover (29) and cylinder head. Remove intake manifold and reed valve. Remove oil seal

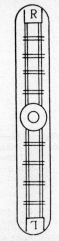

Fig. T9-16—On some models the water inlet cover is marked "R" and "L" at ends. Install cover so marked end which is up corresponds to gearcase side. The water inlet cover shown would be installed on starboard side of gearcase with "R" end up.

housing (4) retaining screws but do not remove seal housing. Remove crankcase retaining screws and separate crankcase from cylinder block. Lift crankshaft assembly out of cylinder block. Individual components may now be serviced as outlined in following service sections.

ASSEMBLY. Before reassembling engine, be sure all joints and gasket surfaces are clean, free from nicks and burrs and hardened cement or carbon.

Fig. T9-17—Exploded view of cylinder block assembly. Sacrificial anode assembly shown, components (17 through 22), are used on 35 hp models. Anode assembly is mounted in exhaust cover (29) on early 40 hp models and in base of cylinder block on later 40 hp models.

1. Retainer
2. Seal ring
3. Magneto ring
4. Seal housing
5. Seal
6. "O" ring
7. Bleeder hose
8. Check valve
9. Fitting
10. Main bearing locating pin
11. Crankcase
12. Check valve
13. Dowel pin
14. Retainer
15. Seal
16. Cylinder block
17. Anode cover
18. Stud
19. "O" ring
20. Gasket
21. Anode
22. Nylon nut
23. Gasket
24. Cylinder head
25. Cover
26. Gasket
27. Thermostat
28. Gasket
29. Exhaust cover

Mating surfaces may be lapped to remove high spots or nicks, however, only a minimum amount of metal should be removed.

All friction surfaces and bearings should be thoroughly lubricated with engine oil during reassembly. Coat mating surfaces with a nonhardening gasket sealer.

Note the following points when assembling power head: Install seal housing (4 – Fig. T9-17) on crankshaft prior to installation of crankshaft assembly. Be sure piston rings properly mate with piston ring groove pins when inserting pistons into cylinder block. Bearing and labyrinth seal locating pins must engage hole or notches in cylinder block. Bearing retainer (34 – Fig. T9-18) must engage cylinder block groove. Install oil seal retainer (14 – Fig. T9-17) in cylinder block groove. Note location of short and long crankcase screws in Fig. T9-19. Tighten all crankcase screws to 23.5-24.5 N·m (208-225 in.-lbs.) following sequence shown in Fig. T9-20.

PISTONS, PINS, RINGS AND CYLINDERS.

The cylinders are equipped with an iron liner which may be bored to accept oversize pistons. Pistons and piston rings are available in standard size and 0.5 mm (0.020 in.) oversize. The piston rings are located in the piston ring groove by a pin in each ring groove. Piston rings are not interchangeable. On 35 hp models, top ring is marked "T.TP" while bottom ring is

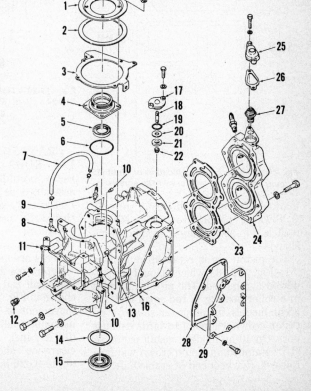

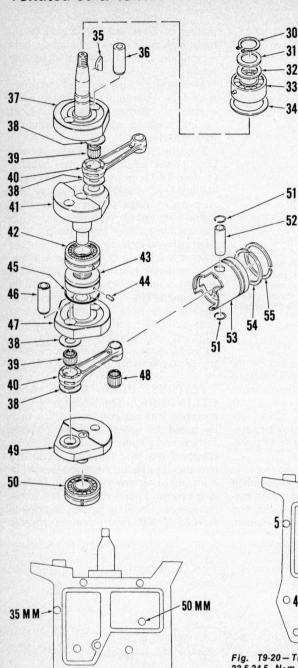

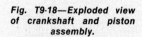

Fig. T9-18—Exploded view of crankshaft and piston assembly.

30. Snap ring
31. Washer
32. Shim
33. Ball bearing
34. Retainer
35. Woodruff key
36. Crankpin
37. Crank half
38. Thrust washer
39. Roller bearing
40. Connecting rod
41. Crank half
42. Roller bearing
43. Labyrinth seal
44. Locating pin
45. "O" ring
46. Crankpin
47. Crank half
48. Roller bearing
49. Crank half
50. Roller bearing
51. Circlip
52. Piston pin
53. Piston
54. Bottom piston ring
55. Top piston ring

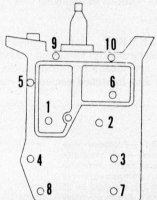

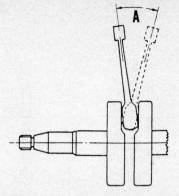

Fig. T9-21—To determine connecting rod big end wear, move rod small end side to side as shown. Movement (A) should be 1.0 mm (0.040 in.) with a maximum allowable limit of 2.0 mm (0.079 in.).

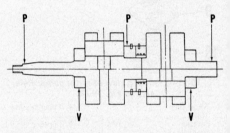

Fig. T9-22—With outer crankshaft main bearings supported in vee blocks (V), crankshaft runout measured at points (P) must not exceed 0.05 mm (0.002 in.).

Fig. T9-19—View showing location of short (35 mm) and long (50 mm) crankcase screws.

Fig. T9-20—Tighten crankcase screws to 23.5-24.5 N·m (208-225 in.-lbs.) following sequence shown.

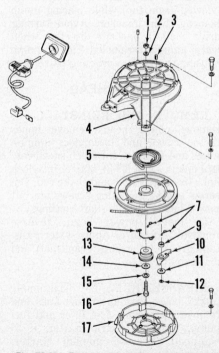

Fig. T9-23—Exploded view of manual starter.

1. Nut
2. Washer
3. Pin
4. Starter housing
5. Rewind spring
6. Rope pulley
7. Spring links
8. Spring
9. Bushing
10. Pawl
11. Washer
12. "E" ring
13. Shaft
14. Washer
15. Lockwasher
16. Screw
17. Starter cup

marked "T." Install piston ring so mark is towards piston crown. On 40 hp models, top piston ring is semi-keystone shaped.

The piston pin is retained by circlips (51–Fig. T9-18) which should be renewed if removed. The piston pin rides in a roller bearing in rod small end. On 35 hp models, install piston so arrow on piston crown will point towards exhaust port. On 40 hp models, install piston so "UP" stamped on piston crown will face towards flywheel end of crankshaft.

CRANKSHAFT AND CONNECTING RODS. Crankshaft, connecting rods, crankpins and bearings are assembled as a pressed-together unit. Disassembly and assembly of crankshaft should be performed by a shop experienced in repair of this type crankshaft. Individual crankshaft components are available.

Determine rod bearing wear by moving small rod end from side-to-side as shown in Fig. T9-21. Normal side to side movement is 1.0 mm (0.040 in.) while maximum allowable limit is 2.0 mm (0.079 in.). Connecting rod side clearance should be 0.28-0.65 mm (0.011-0.026 in.).

Check crankshaft runout by supporting outer main bearings in vee blocks. Maximum allowable crankshaft runout measured at points (P – Fig. T9-22) is 0.05 mm (0.002 in.).

MANUAL STARTER

Refer to Fig. T9-23 for an exploded view of manual starter. The starter may be disassembled after removing motor cover, detaching starter lockout linkage and removing starter from power head. Remove rope handle and allow rope to wind into starter. Remove screw (16) and shaft (13), then carefully lift pulley (6) out of housing while being careful not to disturb rewind spring (5). If rewind spring must be removed care should be used not to allow spring to uncoil uncontrolled. Inspect pawl (10) for wear and freedom of movement. Renew and grease pawl if required.

When assembling starter, wind rewind spring in housing in a counterclockwise direction from outer end. Wind rope around rope pulley in a counterclockwise direction as viewed with pulley in housing. Pawl spring (8) must engage groove in shaft (13). Rotate pulley three turns counterclockwise before passing rope through rope outlet to preload rewind spring.

A starter lockout mechanism (Fig. T9-24) is used to prevent starter usage when motor is in forward or reverse gear. Adjust length of lockout rod (13) by turning rod end so starter will operate with motor in neutral gear but not in forward or reverse gear.

ELECTRIC STARTER

Some models are equipped with an electric starter. Models equipped with an electric starter are also equipped with a battery charging system. Refer to Fig. T9-10 or T9-11) for a wiring diagram. Starter drive pinion and on some models, brush assembly, are only components serviceable on starter.

LOWER UNIT

PROPELLER AND DRIVE HUB.
The propeller is equipped with a splined cushion type hub to protect the lower unit. Propeller hub is not serviceable. Rotation of the three-blade propeller is clockwise. Various propellers are available to obtain best performance depending on outboard usage. Desired operating range at maximum engine speed is 5200-5900 rpm.

R&R AND OVERHAUL.
To remove gearcase, disconnect shift rod coupler (20 – Fig. T9-25) from lower shift rod (21) by driving out lower pin (19). Unscrew six cap screws securing gearcase to drive shaft housing and remove

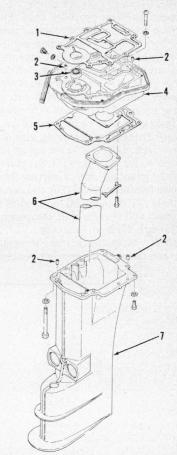

Fig. T9-26—Exploded view of drive shaft housing.

1. Gasket	
2. Dowel pin	5. Gasket
3. Seal	6. Exhaust tube
4. Base	7. Drive shaft housing

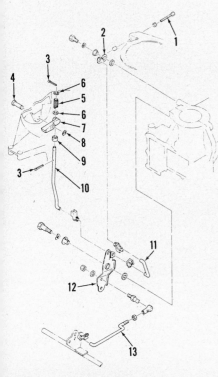

Fig. T9-24— Exploded view of starter lockout linkage. A cap nut is used in place of cotter pin (3) on later 40 hp models.

1. Reverse speed screw	
2. Stop	8. "E" ring
3. Cotter pin	9. Collar
4. Pin	10. Rod
5. Spring	11. Link
6. Washer	12. Bellcrank
7. Pawl	13. Rod

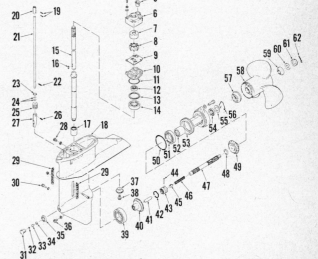

Fig. T9-25—Exploded view of gearcase. Components (31 through 35) are not used on 40 hp models.

5. Grommet	
6. Water pump housing	
7. Liner	
8. Impeller	
9. Plate	
10. Pump base	
11. "O" ring	
12. Seal	
13. Shim	
14. Bearing	
15. Drive shaft	
16. Woodruff key	
17. Bearing	
18. Gearcase	
19. Pin	
20. Coupler	
21. Lower shift rod	
22. Pin	
23. "O" ring	
24. "O" ring	
25. Bushing	
26. Pin	
27. Shift cam	
28. Vent plug	
29. Water inlet	
30. Shift bushing retainer screw	
31. Detent plug	
32. Spring	
33. Spacer	
34. Detent ball	
35. Seal	
36. Fill plug	43. Clutch	53. Bearing housing
37. Pinion gear	44. Pin	54. Seal
38. Screw	45. Spring guide	55. Washer
39. Bearing	46. Spring	56. Clip
40. Forward gear	47. Propeller shaft	57. Spacer
41. Shift plunger	48. Thrust washer	58. Propeller
42. Retainer	49. Reverse gear	59. Spacer
	50. "O" ring	60. Washer
	51. Bearing	61. Nut
	52. Bearing	62. Cotter pin

gearcase. Remove propeller then drain gearcase lubricant. Remove water pump assembly. Remove bearing housing (53) and withdraw propeller shaft assembly. Drive out pin (44) to separate clutch (43), spring guide (45) and spring (46) from propeller shaft. Unscrew pinion gear retaining screw (38) and pull drive shaft (15) from gearcase. Pinion gear (37) and forward gear (40) with bearing may now be removed. Use a suitable puller and remove roller bearing (17) by pulling towards gearcase top. Unscrew shift bushing retaining screw (30) and detent assembly (31 through 34), on models so equipped, and remove shift components (21 through 27) from gearcase.

Inspect components for excessive wear and damage. Inner roller bearings in forward and reverse gears (40 and 49) are available only as a unit with gear. Clutch spring (46) length should be 90 mm (3.54 in.); renew spring if length is less than 88 mm (3.46 in.). Clutch spring pressure should be 48.02 newtons (10.79 lbs.) at 71.5 mm (2.81 in.) on 35 hp models and 51 newtons (11.46 lbs.) at 71.5 mm (2.81 in.) on 40 hp models. Propeller shaft diameter at forward gear bearing contact surfaces should be 19.987-20.000 mm (0.7868-0.7874 in.) with a wear limit of 19.975 mm (0.7864 in.). Propeller shaft diameter at contact surface for bearing housing roller bearing (52) should be 21.987-22.000 mm (0.8656-0.8661 in.) with a wear limit of 21.975 mm (0.8651 in.). Propeller shaft runout must be less than 0.2 mm (0.0079 in.). Drive shaft diameter at contact surface for roller bearing (17) should be 21.987-22.000 mm (0.8656-0.8661 in.) with a wear limit of 21.975 mm (0.8651 in.). Drive shaft runout must be less than 0.5 mm (0.0197 in.).

To reassemble gearcase, reverse disassembly procedure while noting the following points: Lubricate all "O" rings and seals prior to installation. Backlash between pinion gear and forward or reverse gear should be 0.15-0.25 mm (0.006-0.010 in.) and is adjusted by varying thickness of shim (13). Apply Loctite during final assembly and tighten pinion gear retaining screw (38) to 23.5-25.4 N·m (208-225 in.-lbs.). Install clutch (43) so end closest to pin (44) groove is towards forward gear (40).

TOHATSU 55 AND 70 HP

CONDENSED SERVICE DATA

NOTE: Metric fasteners are used throughout outboard motor.

TUNE-UP

Hp/rpm 55/4500-5500
 70/5000-5500

Bore:
  55 HP . . . . .81 mm
  (3.19 in.)
  70 HP . . . . .86 mm
  (3.38 in.)

Stroke . . . . .72.7 mm
  (2.86 in.)

Number of Cylinders 2

Displacement:
  55 HP . . . . .749 cc
  (45.7 cu. in.)
  70 HP . . . . .845 cc
  (51.6 cu. in.)

Spark Plug:
  55 HP (M55A)
    Champion. L78
    NKG B8HS
      Electrode Gap . . . . .1.0 mm
      (0.040 in.)
  55 HP (M55B) and 70 HP
    Champion L78C10
    NGK B8HS10
      Electrode Gap . . . . .1.0 mm
      (0.040 in.)

Ignition Type . . . . .Breakerless CD
Ignition Timing . . . . .See Text
Fuel:Oil Ratio 50:1

SIZES—CLEARANCES

Piston Ring End Gap . . . . .0.25-0.4 mm
  (0.010-0.016 in.)
Piston Ring Side Clearance:
  Top Ring. . . . . .Semi-Keystone

SIZES—CLEARANCES CONT.

Piston Ring Side Clearance:
  Bottom Ring . . . . .0.04-0.08 mm
  (0.0015-0.0031 in.)
Piston Clearance . . . . .0.08-0.13 mm
  (0.0031-0.0051 in.)
Piston Pin Clearance In Piston . . . . .Interference-0.010 mm
  (Interference-0.0004 in.)
Crankshaft Runout . . . . .0.05 mm
  (0.002 in.)

TIGHTENING TORQUES

Crankcase. . . . . .23.5-25.4 N·m
  (208-225 in.-lbs.)
Cylinder Head . . . . .32.4-37.2 N·m
  (287-329 in.-lbs.)
Flywheel Nut . . . . .137-157 N·m
  (101-116 ft.-lbs.)
Pinion Gear Nut. . . . . .59 N·m
  (43 ft.-lbs.)
Spark Plug . . . . .24.5-29.4 N·m
  (217-260 in.-lbs.)
Standard Screws:
  No. 3 . . . . .0.6-0.8 N·m
  (5-7 in.-lbs.)
  No. 4 . . . . .1.3-1.8 N·m
  (11-15 in.-lbs.)
  No. 5 . . . . .2.6-3.5 N·m
  (23-31 in.-lbs.)
  No. 6 . . . . .4.6-6.3 N·m
  (41-55 in.-lbs.)
  No. 8 . . . . .11.2-15.1 N·m
  (99-133 in.-lbs.)
  No. 10 . . . . .22.6-30.6 N·m
  (200-270 in.-lbs.)

LUBRICATION

The power head is lubricated by oil mixed with the fuel. Recommended oil is Tohatsu outboard motor oil mixed at a fuel:oil ratio of 50:1. During engine break-in the fuel:oil ratio should be 20:1 for a period of 10 operating hours.

Lower unit gears and bearings are lubricated by oil contained in the gearcase. Recommended oil is Tohatsu gear oil or a SAE 80 gear oil. Oil should be changed after initial 10 hours of operation and every 200 hours of operation thereafter. Gearcase oil capacity is approximately 920 mL (31.1 oz.).

FUEL SYSTEM

CARBURETOR. The power head is equipped with two carburetors which are not interchangeable. Refer to Fig. T10-1 for an exploded view of carburetor. Before adjusting idle speed, back out idle speed screw (1) and note if throttle plates for both carburetors are closed. If not, adjust throttle link between carburetors. Check choke plate movement of both carburetors and if not synchronized adjust length of link between choke levers of carburetors. Adjust idle mixture and idle speed screws after motor temperature has normalized.

Adjust float level so float is parallel to gasket surface with carburetor inverted

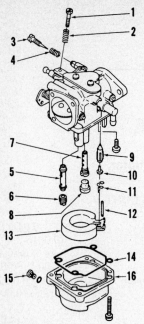

Fig. T10-1—Exploded view of carburetor.

1. Idle speed screw
2. Spring
3. Idle mixture screw
4. Spring
5. Main nozzle
6. Main jet
7. Slow jet
8. Rubber cap
9. Fuel inlet valve
10. Pin
11. Clip
12. Float pin
13. Float
14. Gasket
15. Drain plug
16. Fuel bowl

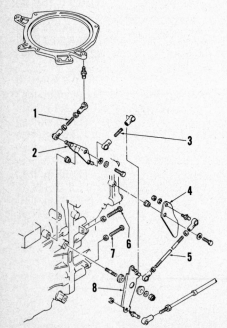

Fig. T10-2—View of speed control linkage.

1. Magneto control rod
2. Lever
3. Intermediate rod
4. Throttle cam
5. Throttle link
6. Idle speed timing screw
7. Maximum advance ignition timing screw
8. Bellcrank

and fuel bowl removed. Note clip (11) which secures inlet valve to float.

Standard main jet size is #165 and tonhard slow jet size is #75 on early 55 hp models. Standard main jet size is

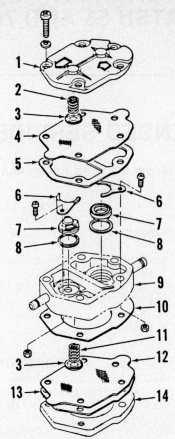

Fig. T10-3—Exploded view of fuel pump.

1. Cover
2. Spring
3. Spring seat
4. Diaphragm
5. Gasket
6. Retainer
7. Check valve
8. Gasket
9. Body
10. Gasket
11. Spring
12. Diaphragm
13. Gasket
14. Base

#160 and standard slow jet size is #80 on late 55 hp models. Standard main jet size is #175 and standard slow jet size is #80 on 70 hp models.

SPEED CONTROL LINKAGE. Carburetor throttle opening and ignition timing are synchronized by the speed control linkage so the carburetors are opened as the ignition timing is advanced.

Before adjusting carburetor throttle link, refer to IGNITION TIMING section and be sure ignition timing is set correctly. Adjust length of throttle link (5–Fig. T10-2) by turning ends so carburetors are fully open when bellcrank (8) contacts maximum advance screw (7), and when throttle roller just contacts throttle cam (4) as bellcrank contacts idle speed timing screw (6).

FUEL PUMP. A diaphragm type fuel pump is mounted on the port side of the engine. The pump is operated by crankcase pulsations. Refer to Fig. T10-3 for an exploded view of fuel pump

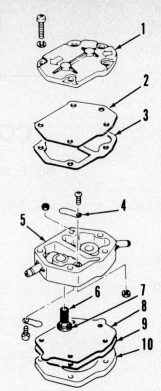

Fig. T10-4—Exploded view of fuel pump used on late 55 hp models and 70 hp models.

1. Cover
2. Diaphragm
3. Gasket
4. Check valve
5. Body
6. Spring
7. Spring seat
8. Diaphragm
9. Gasket
10. Base

used on early 55 hp models and Fig. T10-4 for an exploded view of fuel pump used on late 55 hp models and 70 hp models.

REED VALVES. Two vee type reed valve assemblies (one for each cylinder) are located between the intake manifold and crankcase. Remove intake manifold for access to reed valve assemblies. Refer to Fig. T10-5 for an exploded view of reed valve.

Renew reeds if petals are broken, cracked, warped or bent. Do not attempt to bend or straighten reeds. Reed seating surface on reed blocks should be smooth and flat. Reed stop setting should be 9 mm (0.35 in.) on early 55 hp models and 10.0-10.2 mm (0.39-0.40 in.) on late 55 hp models and 70 hp models when measured as shown in Fig. T10-6.

IGNITION

All models are equipped with a breakerless, capacitor discharge ignition system. The ignition exciter and trigger coils as well as the battery charging coil are located under the flywheel. An ignition cutout switch (9–Fig. T10-9) is used to prevent engine overspeeding. Tighten flywheel nut to 137-157 N·m (101-116 ft.-lbs.).

The following checks using an ohmmeter can be made to locate faulty ignition system components. Disconnect three-wire connector between stator plate and CD ignition module, then connect one ohmmeter lead to stator plate. Connect remaining ohmmeter lead to red stator lead to check exciter coil.

Ohmmeter reading should be 290 ohms. With ohmmeter leads connected to stator plate and blue stator lead to check trigger coil, ohmmeter reading should be 20 ohms. Connect ohmmeter leads to yellow and white stator wires to check battery charging coil. Ohmmeter reading should be 0.34 ohm. To check

the CD ignition module, disconnect module leads and refer to chart in Fig. T10-10 for desired ohmmeter readings.

IGNITION TIMING. Before adjusting ignition timing, detach magneto control rod (1 – Fig. T10-2) and intermediate rod (3) and measure distance

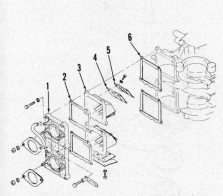

Fig. T10-5—Exploded view of intake manifold and reed valve assembly.

1. Intake manifold	4. Reed petals
2. Gasket	5. Reed stop
3. Reed body	6. Gasket

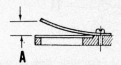

Fig. T10-6—Reed valve stop height (A) should be 9 mm (0.35 in.) on early 55 hp models and 10.0-10.2 mm (0.39-0.40 in.) on late 55 hp models and 70 hp models.

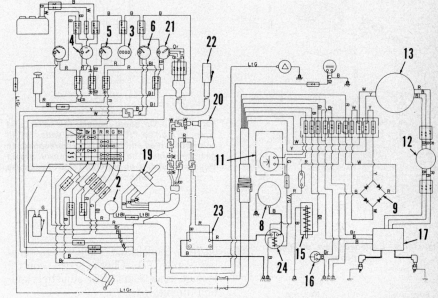

Fig. T10-8—Typical wiring schematic for 55 hp models with engine number 11804 and later and 70 hp models with engine number 10911 and later.

B. Black			17. CDI module
G. Green	Lt. G. Light green	6. Tachometer	19. Power tilt & trim switch
P. Pink	Lt. Bl. Light blue	8. Starter motor	
R. Red	Y/G. Yellow with	9. Rectifier	20. Power tilt & trim motor
W. White	green tracer	11. Neutral switch	21. Trimmeter
Y. Yellow	2. Overheat buzzer	12. Overspeed switch	22. Trim sensor
Bl. Blue	3. Hour meter	13. Stator plate	23. Battery
Br. Brown	4. Fuel gage	15. Choke solenoid	24. Starter solenoid
Or. Orange	5. Speedometer	16. Stop switch	

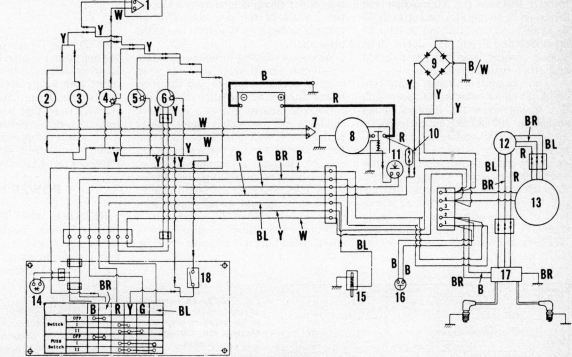

B. Black
BL. Blue
BR. Brown
G. Green
R. Red
W. White
Y. Yellow
1. Fuel Sensor
2. Overheat buzzer
3. Hour meter
4. Fuel gage
5. Speedometer
6. Tachometer
7. Starter sensor
8. Starter motor
9. Rectifier
10. Fuse
11. Neutral switch
12. Overspeed switch
13. Stator plate
14. Safety switch
15. Choke solenoid
16. Stop switch
17. Ignition module
18. Lamp switch

Fig. T10-7—Typical wiring schematic for 55 hp models prior to engine number 11804 and 70 hp models prior to engine number 10911.

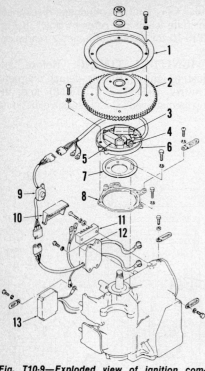

Fig. T10-9—Exploded view of ignition components.

1. Rope pulley
2. Flywheel
3. Exciter coil
4. Trigger coil
5. Battery charging coil
6. Stator plate
7. Retainer
8. Magneto control ring
9. Overspeed switch
10. Cover
11. Terminal block
12. Ignition module
13. Rectifier

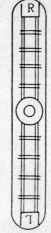

Fig. T10-11—On some models, the water inlet cover is marked "R" and "L" at ends. Install cover so marked end which is up corresponds to gearcase side. The water inlet cover shown would be installed on starboard side of gearcase with "R" end up.

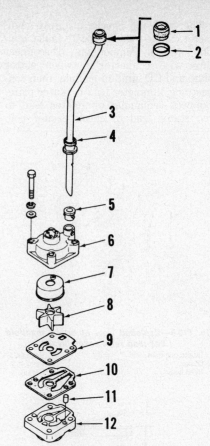

Fig. T10-12—Exploded view of water pump. Refer also to Fig. T10-19.

1. Grommet
2. Retainer
3. Water tube
4. Grommet
5. Seal
6. Pump housing
7. Liner
8. Impeller
9. Plate
10. Gasket
11. Dowel pin
12. Pump base

between rod end centers of each rod. Distance for magneto control rod (1) should be 55 mm (2.16 in.) on early 55 hp models, 57 mm (2.24 in.) on later 55 hp models and 50 mm (1.97 in.) on 70 hp models. Distance for intermediate rod (3) should be 40 mm (1.57 in.) on early 55 hp models, 43 mm (1.69 in.) on later 55 hp models and 45 mm (1.77 in.) on 70 hp models. Adjust length by turning rod ends, then reattach both rods.

To adjust ignition timing, rotate bellcrank (8) so it contacts idle speed ignition timing screw (6). Ignition timing should be 10° ATDC on early 55 hp models and TDC on later 55 hp and 70 hp models as indicated by timing mark on stator plate aligned with crankcase and cylinder block mating surfaces. Turn idle ignition timing screw (6) to adjust timing. Rotate bellcrank so it contacts maximum advance ignition timing screw (7). Ignition timing should be 25° BTDC on 55 hp models and 22.5° BTDC

on 70 hp models and is adjusted by turning screw (7). Check speed control linkage adjustment after adjusting ignition timing.

COOLING SYSTEM

THERMOSTAT. A thermostat (3 – Fig. T10-13) is located in the cylinder head. Thermostat should begin opening at 60° C (140° F).

WATER PUMP. A rubber impeller type water pump is mounted on the upper surface of the gearcase. The impeller is driven by a Woodruff key in the drive shaft.

Whenever cooling problems are encountered, check water inlet for plugging or partial stoppage and the thermostat for proper operation, then if not corrected, remove gearcase and check condition of the water pump, water passages and sealing surfaces. Note that water inlet covers on some models are marked "R" and "L" as shown in Fig. T10-11 and are interchangeable. Install water inlet cover on starboard side so "R" end is up and install water inlet cover on port side so "L" end is up.

When water pump is disassembled, check condition of impeller (8 – Fig.

Fig. T10-10—An ohmmeter should indicate the readings in the adjacent chart when testing the CD ignition module.

T10-12), liner (7) and plate (9). When installing liner in pump housing note that locating knob on upper end of liner must index with a corresponding indentation in housing. Turn drive shaft clockwise (viewed from top) while placing pump housing over impeller. Avoid turning drive shaft in opposite direction after pump is assembled. Tighten pump housing screws in a crossing pattern.

POWER HEAD

REMOVE AND REINSTALL. To remove power head, remove upper motor cover and disconnect fuel hose and interfering wires. Detach remote control wires. Unscrew engine mounting screws and lift power head off drive shaft housing.

To install power head, reverse removal procedure. Apply water resistant grease to ends of crankshaft and drive shaft. Apply sealer to engine base gasket except in shaded area shown in Fig. T10-15.

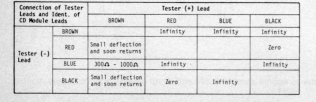

Connection of Tester Leads and Ident. of CD Module Leads		Tester (+) Lead			
		BROWN	RED	BLUE	BLACK
Tester (-) Lead	BROWN		Infinity	Infinity	Infinity
	RED	Small deflection and soon returns			Zero
	BLUE	300Ω - 1000Ω	Infinity		Infinity
	BLACK	Small deflection and soon returns	Zero	Infinity	

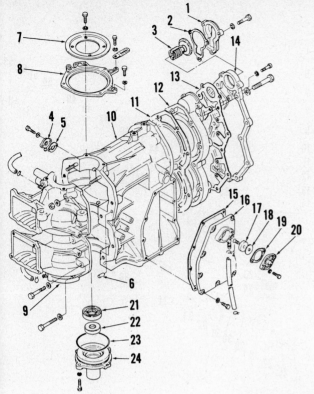

Fig. T10-13—Exploded view of crankcase.

1. Thermostat cover
2. Gasket
3. Thermostat
4. Fitting
5. Breather valve
6. Dowel pin
7. Retainer
8. Magneto control ring
9. Crankcase
10. Cylinder block
11. Gasket
12. Cylinder head
13. Gasket
14. Cover
15. Gasket
16. Exhaust cover
17. Anode
18. Gasket
19. Gasket
20. Cover
21. Seal
22. Seal
23. "O" ring
24. Seal housing

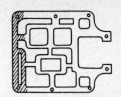

Fig. T10-15 — Do not apply sealer to shaded area of engine base gasket.

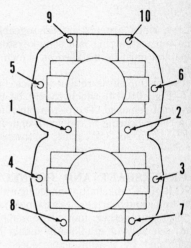

Fig. T10-16-Tighten crankcase screws to 23.5-25.4 N·m (208-225 in.-lbs.) following sequence shown.

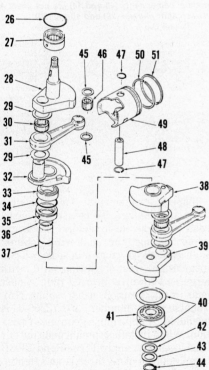

Fig. T10-14 — Exploded view of crankshaft and piston assembly.

26. "O" ring
27. Roller bearing
28. Crank half
29. Roller bearing
30. Roller bearing
31. Connecting rod
32. Crank half
33. Roller bearing
34. "O" ring
35. Labyrinth seal
36. Circlip
37. Center crankshaft journal
38. Crank half
39. Crank half
40. Retainer
41. Ball bearing
42. Shim
43. Washer
44. Snap ring
45. Thrust washer
46. Roller bearing
47. Circlip
48. Piston pin
49. Piston
50. Piston ring
51. Piston ring

DISASSEMBLY. To disassemble power head, disconnect fuel hoses and remove air cleaner, carburetors, fuel filter and fuel pump. Disconnect wire leads then remove electric starter and electrical components. Remove flywheel and stator plate (6 – Fig. T10-9). Detach speed control linkage. Remove retainer (7) and magneto ring (8). Remove exhaust cover (16 – Fig. T10-13), cylinder head cover (14) and cylinder head (12). Remove intake manifold and reed valve assembly. Remove oil seal housing (24) retaining screws but do not remove housing. Unscrew crankcase retaining screws and separate crankcase from cylinder block. Lift crankshaft assembly out of cylinder block. Individual components are now accessible for service as outlined in following service sections.

ASSSEMBLY. Before reassembling engine, be sure all joints and gasket surfaces are clean, free from nicks and burrs and hardened cement or carbon. Mating surfaces may be lapped to remove high spots or nicks, however, only a minimum amount of metal should be removed.

All friction surfaces and bearings should be thoroughly lubricated with engine oil during reassembly. Coat mating surfaces with a nonhardening gasket sealer.

Note the following points when assembling power head: Be sure piston rings properly mate with piston ring groove pins when inserting pistons into cylinder block. Labyrinth seal and bearings must

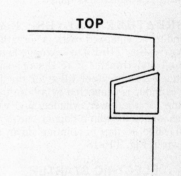

Fig. T10-17 — Install top piston ring so beveled side is toward top of piston.

engage locating pins in cylinder block. Bearing retaining rings (40 – Fig. T10-14) must engage grooves in cylinder block and crankcase. Install seal (22 – Fig. T10-13) in seal housing (24) so lip will point away from engine and install seal (21) so lip will point towards engine. Tighten crankcase screws to 23.5-25.4 N·m (208-225 in.-lbs.) following sequence shown in Fig. T10-16.

PISTON, PIN, RINGS AND CYLINDER. The cylinders are equipped with an iron liner which may be bored to accept oversize pistons. Piston and piston rings are available in standard size and 0.5 mm (0.020 in.) oversize.

Piston rings are located in the piston ring groove by a pin in each ring groove.

Fig. T10-18—Install breather valve (5—Fig. T10-13) so flap (F) points down.

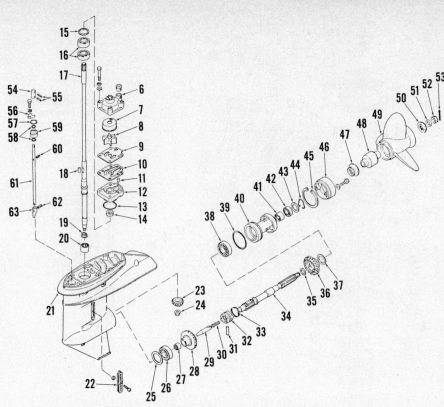

Fig. T10-19—Exploded view of gearcase. On later models, components (43 and 44) are not used. A clutch ball and spring holder are located between shift plunger (29) and spring (30).

6. Water pump housing	21. Gearcase	36. Reverse gear
7. Liner	22. Water inlet cover	37. Shim
8. Impeller	23. Pinion gear	38. Ball bearing
9. Plate	24. Nut	39. "O" ring
10. Gasket	25. Shim	40. Bearing housing
11. Dowel pin	26. Taper roller bearing	41. Roller bearing
12. Pump base	27. Roller bearing	42. Seal
13. "O" ring	28. Forward gear	43. Washer
14. Seal	29. Shift plunger	44. Retainer
15. Shim	30. Spring	45. Snap ring
16. Ball bearings	31. Pin	46. Cap
17. Drive shaft	32. Clutch	47. Thrust piece
18. Impeller drive key	33. Spring retainer	48. Hub
19. Spring	34. Propeller shaft	49. Propeller
20. Roller bearing	35. Thrust washer	50. Thrust washer

51. Washer
52. Nut
53. Cotter pin
54. Coupler
55. Pin
56. Retainer
57. "O" ring
58. "O" ring
59. Bushing
60. Pin
61. Shift rod
62. Pin
63. Shift cam

Piston rings are not interchangeable. The top piston ring is a semi-keystone type and must be installed as shown in Fig. T10-17.

The piston pin is retained by circlips (47—Fig. T10-14) which should be renewed if removed. The piston pin rides in a roller bearing in rod small end. Install piston so "UP" mark is towards flywheel.

CRANKSHAFT AND CONNECTING ROD.
Crankshaft, connecting rods, crankpins and bearings are assembled as a pressed-together unit. Disassembly and assembly of crankshaft should be performed by a shop experienced in repair of this type crankshaft. Individual crankshaft components are available. Refer to Fig. T10-14 for an exploded view of crankshaft assembly.

BREATHER VALVES.
Each cylinder is equipped with a breather valve (5—Fig. T10-13) to scavenge liquid fuel/oil and transfer it to the opposite cylinder. The breather valve for the upper cylinder is connected by a hose to a fitting for the lower cylinder, and vice versa. When installing flapper valve, install valve so flap is pointing down as shown in Fig. T10-18.

ELECTRIC STARTER

All models are equipped with an electric starter. Starter brushes, drive and relay are available. Refer to Fig. T10-7 or Fig. T10-8 for a wiring diagram.

LOWER UNIT

PROPELLER AND DRIVE HUB.
The propeller is equipped with a cushion type hub to protect the lower unit. Propeller hub is not available separately from propeller. Rotation of the three-blade propeller is clockwise. Various propellers are available to obtain best performance depending on outboard usage. Desired operating range at maximum engine speed is 4500-5500 rpm for 55 hp models and 5000-5500 rpm for 70 hp models.

R&R AND OVERHAUL.
To remove gearcase, disconnect shift rod coupler

(54—Fig. T10-19) from lower shift rod (61) by driving out lower pin (55). Unscrew six cap screws securing gearcase to drive shaft housing and remove gearcase. Remove propeller then drain gearcase lubricant. Remove water pump assembly. Unscrew and remove cap (46). Remove snap ring (45) then use a suitable puller to remove bearing housing (40). Withdraw propeller shaft assembly. Remove retainer spring (33) and drive out pin (31) to separate shift plunger (29), spring (30) and clutch (32) from propeller shaft. Unscrew pinion gear retaining nut (24) and pull drive shaft (17) from gearcase. Pinion gear (23) and forward gear (28) with bearing may now be removed from gearcase. If necessary, use a suitable puller to extract bearing (26) cup from gearcase while being careful not to lose or damage shims (25). Use a suitable puller and remove roller bearing (20). Remove retainer (56) and remove shift components (57 through 63).

Inspect components for excessive wear and damage. To reassemble gearcase, reverse disassembly procedure while noting the following points: Lubricate all "O" rings and seals prior to installation. Install spring (19) with large end towards bearing (20). Adjust gear mesh position using shims (15). Tohatsu tool number 353-72250-0 is available to determine gear mesh position. When installing pinion gear nut for final assembly, apply Three Bond 1303B or an equivalent to threads and tighten nut to 59 N·m (43 ft.-lbs.). Backlash between pinion gear and forward or reverse gear should be 0.08-0.26 mm (0.003-0.010 in.) and is adjusted by varying thickness of shims (25 and 37). Tohatsu tool number 353-72255-0 is available to determine gear backlash. Install clutch (32) so grooved end is nearer forward gear. Install seal (42) so open side is towards bearing housing (40). Install seal (14) so open side is away from pump base (12).

YAMAHA

YAMAHA MOTOR CORPORATION U.S.A.
Marine Division
6555 Katella Avenue
Cypress, CA 90630

YAMAHA 30 HP

CONDENSED SERVICE DATA

NOTE: Metric fasteners are used throughout outboard motor.

TUNE-UP

Hp/rpm	30/4500-5500
Bore	72 mm
	(2.84 in.)
Stroke	61 mm
	(2.40 in.)
Number of Cylinders	2
Displacement	496 cc
	(30.3 cu. in.)
Spark Plug—NGK	B7HS
Electrode Gap	0.5-0.6 mm
	(0.020-0.024 in.)
Ignition	CDI
Idle Speed (in gear)	750-850 rpm
Fuel:Oil Ratio	100:1

SIZES—CLEARANCES

Piston Ring End Gap	0.2-0.4 mm
	(0.008-0.016 in.)
Lower Piston Ring Side Clearance	0.04-0.08 mm
	(0.0016-0.0032 in.)
Piston Skirt Clearance	0.060-0.065 mm
	(0.0024-0.0026 in.)
Crankshaft Runout—Max.	0.03 mm
	(0.0012 in.)

SIZES—CLEARANCES CONT.

Connecting Rod Small End Shake:

Standard	0.8 mm
	(0.03 in.)
Limit	2.0 mm
	(0.08 in.)

TIGHTENING TORQUES

Crankcase	27 N·m
	(19 ft.-lbs.)
Cylinder Head	27 N·m
	(19 ft.-lbs.)
Flywheel	160 N·m
	(115 ft.-lbs.)

Standard Screws:

5 mm	5 N·m
	(44 in.-lbs.)
6 mm	8 N·m
	(71 in.-lbs.)
8 mm	18 N·m
	(13 ft.-lbs.)
10 mm	36 N·m
	(25 ft.-lbs.)
12 mm	43 N·m
	(31 ft.-lbs.)

LUBRICATION

The power head is lubricated by oil mixed with the fuel. Fuel should be regular leaded, low lead or unleaded gasoline with a minimum pump octane rating of 84. Recommended oil is YAMALUBE 100/1 Two-Cycle Lubricant. Normal fuel:oil ratio is 100:1. During the first 10 hours of operation, the fuel:oil ratio should be increased to 25:1.

Lower unit gears and bearings are lubricated by oil contained in the gearcase. Recommended oil is YAMALUBE Gearcase Lube. Lubricant is drained by removing vent and drain plugs in the gearcase. Refill through drain plug hole until oil has reached level of vent plug hole.

FUEL SYSTEM

CARBURETOR. Refer to Fig. Y16-1 for an exploded view of carburetor. Recommended standard main jet (15 – Fig. Y16-1) size is #135 and recommended standard pilot jet (6) size is #54. Main jet (15) size should be reduced from standard recommendation by one size for altitudes of 2500 to 5000 feet (750 to 1500 m), two sizes for altitudes of 5000 to 7500 feet (1500 to 2250 m) and three

sizes for altitudes of 7500 feet (2250 m) and up. Initial adjustment of idle mixture screw (21) is 1¼ to 1¾ turns out from a lightly seated position. Recommended idle speed is 750-850 rpm (in gear) with the engine at normal operating temperature.

To determine the float level, remove the carburetor and float bowl)14). Invert carburetor body (1) and slowly raise float (11). Note whether float (11) is parallel with surface of carburetor body when needle of fuel inlet valve (10) just breaks contact with float (11) tang. If not, adjust float (11) tang until proper float level is obtained.

Fig. Y16-1 — Exploded view of carburetor.

1. Body
2. Bushing
3. Clip
4. Cam follower roller
5. Cam follower
6. Pilot jet
7. Washer
8. Clip
9. Spring
10. Fuel inlet valve
11. Float
12. Pin
13. Gasket
14. Float bowl
15. Main jet
16. Main nozzle
17. Screw
18. Throttle arm
19. Link
20. Link keeper
21. Idle mixture screw
22. Spring
23. Throttle shaft
24. Spring
25. Choke shaft
26. Spring
27. Idle speed screw

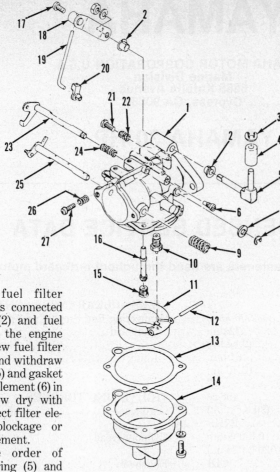

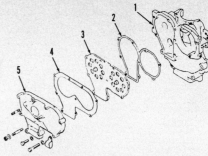

Fig. Y16-6 — Exploded view of reed valve and intake manifold assembly.

1. Crankcase half
2. Gasket
3. Reef valve assy.
4. Gasket
5. Intake manifold

FUEL FILTER.

A fuel filter assembly (1 – Fig. Y16-3) is connected between fuel supply line (2) and fuel pump inlet line (3). With the engine stopped, periodically unscrew fuel filter cup (7) from filter base (4) and withdraw filter element (6), "O" ring (5) and gasket (8). Clean cup (7) and filter element (6) in a suitable solvent and blow dry with clean compressed air. Inspect filter element (6). If excessive blockage or damage is noted, rewew element.

Reassembly is reverse order of disassembly. Renew "O" ring (5) and gasket (8) during reassembly.

FUEL PUMP.

The diaphragm type fuel pump is located on the port side of the engine. Refer to Fig. Y16-4 for an exploded view of fuel pump. Alternating pressure and vacuum pulsations in the crankcase actuates the diaphragm and check valves in the pump. Fuel pump assembly uses reed valve type check valves.

Make certain that all gaskets, diaphragms and check valves are in good condition when reassembling unit. Coat fuel pump mounting with a nonhardening type gasket sealer making certain that passage in center is not blocked with gasket sealer.

REED VALVE.

The reed valve assembly is located between the intake manifold and crankcase. Refer to Fig. Y16-6 for a view of reed valve assembly.

Cracked, warped, chipped or bent reed petals will impair operation and should be renewed. Do not attempt to straighten or repair bent or damaged reed petals. Reed petals should seat smoothly against reed plate along their entire length. Make sure reed petals are centered over reed plate passages. Height of reed stop should be 5.4 mm (0.21 in.). Renew reed stop if height adjustment is 0.3 mm (0.012 in.) more or less than specified, or damage is noted.

SPEED CONTROL LINKAGE.

To synchronize ignition and throttle control linkage, first make sure the ignition timing has been correctly adjusted. Detach magneto base plate control rod (3 – Fig. Y16-9) from throttle control lever. Place magneto base plate in full advanced position. Rotate twist grip to full throttle position. Adjust length of control rod (3) until rod end slides onto throttle lever ball socket without disturbing position of throttle lever.

With the twist grip held in full throttle position, blockout lever (2) should contact bottom cowling stopper. If not, readjust blockout lever control rod (1) until the proper adjustment is obtained.

With wide-open mark on throttle cam centered on carburetor throttle cam roller (4 – Fig. Y16-1), make sure carburetor throttle plate is in wide-open position. If not, loosen screw (17) and adjust rod (19) to alter throttle plate opening.

Fig. Y16-3 — Exploded view of fuel filter assembly, fuel hoses and mounting brackets.

1. Fuel filter assy.
2. Fuel supply line
3. Fuel pump inlet line
4. Filter base
5. "O" ring
6. Filter element
7. Cup
8. Gasket

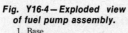

Fig. Y16-4 — Exploded view of fuel pump assembly.

1. Base
2. Gasket
3. Diaphragm
4. Check valves
5. Spring plate
6. Spring
7. Body
8. Gasket
9. Diaphragm
10. Cover

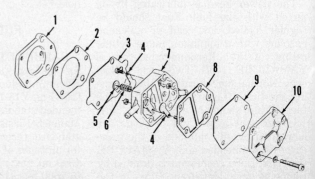

IGNITION

All models are equipped with a capacitor discharge ignition (CDI) system. If engine malfunction is noted and the ignition system is suspected, make sure the spark plugs and all electrical connections are tight before proceeding to trouble-shooting the CD ignition system.

Proceed as follows to test CDI system components: Refer to Fig. Y16-11. To test ignition coil, disconnect black wire (B) and orange wire (O) at connectors and spark plug boots from spark plugs. Use a suitable ohmmeter and connect red tester lead to orange wire (O) and black tester lead to black wire (B). The primary winding resistance reading should be 0.08-0.10 ohms. Connect red tester lead to terminal end in one spark plug boot and black tester lead to terminal end in remaining spark plug boot. The secondary winding resistance reading should be 2,975-4,025 ohms. Use a suitable coil tester or Yamaha tester YU-33261 to perform a power test. Connect tester leads as outlined in tester's handbook. On Yamaha tester YU-33261, a steady spark should jump a 8 mm (0.31 in.) gap with voltage selector switch in "CDI" position. A surface insulation test can be performed using a suitable coil tester or Yamaha tester YU-33261 and following tester's handbook.

To check source (charge) coil, disconnect black wire (B) and brown wire (Br) at connectors leading from magneto base plate. Use a suitable ohmmeter and connect red tester lead to brown wire (Br) and black tester lead to black wire (B). DO NOT rotate flywheel while mak-

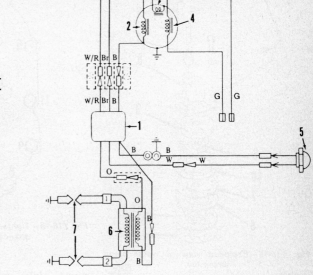

Fig. Y16-11 — View identifying CDI system components.

1. CDI module
2. Charge coil
3. Pulser coil
4. Lighting coil
5. Stop switch
6. Ignition coil
7. Spark plugs

ing test. The ohmmeter should read 121-147 ohms. Reconnect wires after completing test.

To check pulser (trigger) coil, disconnect white wire with red tracer (W/R) at connector leading from magneto base plate and black wire (B) at back of CDI unit. Use a suitable ohmmeter and connect red tester lead to white wire with red tracer (W/R) and black tester lead to black wire (B). DO NOT rotate flywheel while making test. The ohmmeter should read 12.6-15.4 ohms.

To test CDI module, first disconnect all wires at connectors and remove CDI module from outboard motor. Use a suitable ohmmeter and refer to Fig. Y16-12. With reference to chart, perform CDI module resistance tests.

Renew any components that are not within the manufacturer's recommended limits.

To check ignition timing, rotate flywheel so timing pointer (TP–Fig. Y16-13) is aligned with 25° BTDC mark on flywheel. Rotate magneto base plate

Fig. Y16-9 — View of blockout lever control rod (1), blockout lever (2) and stator base plate control rod (3). Locknuts (N) and adjuster (A) are used to adjust cable slack. Refer to text.

Fig. Y16-12 — Use adjacent chart and values listed below to test condition of CD ignition module. Before making test (J), connect CDI module's orange wire and black wire together. Then disconnect wires and perform test.

A. Zero
B. Infinity
C. 9,000-19,000 ohms
D. 2,000-6,000 ohms
E. 80,000-160,000 ohms
F. 70,000-150,000 ohms
G. 33,000-63,000 ohms
H. 7,000-17,000 ohms
I. 15,000-35,000 ohms
J. Tester needle should show deflection then return toward infinite resistance.

	Black Test Lead / Red Test Lead	CDI UNIT LEADS				
		White	Black	Brown	White w/Red	Orange
C D I U N I T L E A D S	White	A	B	B	B	B
	Black	C	A	D	B	J
	Brown	E	F	A	B	J
	White w/Red	G	H	I	A	J
	Orange	B	B	B	B	A

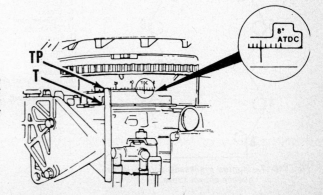

Fig. Y16-13 — Full advance occurs when stop bracket tab (T) contacts timing pointer (TP). Refer to text for ignition timing adjustment.

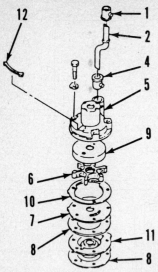

Fig. Y16-15 — Exploded view of water pump assembly.

1. Seal	7. Plate
2. Water tube	8. Gasket
4. Seal	9. Liner
5. Pump housing	10. Gasket
6. Impeller	11. Base
	12. Spacer

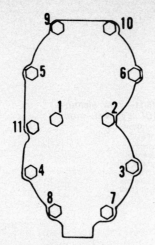

Fig. Y16-18 — Tighten cylinder head screws in sequence shown above.

so stop bracket tab (T) is against timing pointer. The stamped mark on the magneto base plate should be aligned with 0° (TDC) mark on flywheel. Adjust timing by loosening stop bracket retaining screws and relocating bracket.

COOLING SYSTEM

WATER PUMP. A rubber impeller type water pump is mounted between the drive shaft housing and gearcase. Water pump impeller (6 – Fig. Y16-15) is driven by a key in the drive shaft.

When cooling system problems are encountered, first check water inlet for plugging or partial stoppage. Be sure thermostat located in cylinder head operates properly. If the water pump is suspected defective, separate gearcase from drive shaft housing and inspect

pump. Make sure all seals and mating surfaces are in good condition and water passages are unobstructed. Check impeller (6) and plate (7) for excessive wear. When reassembling, coat gasket surfaces with a thin coating of Yamaha Bond No. 4.

POWER HEAD

R&R AND OVERHAUL. The power head can be removed for disassembly and overhaul as follows: Clamp outboard motor to a suitable stand and remove engine cowl and starter assembly. Disconnect speed control cables, fuel line and any wiring that will interfere with power head removal. Remove or

disconnect any component that will interfere with power head removal. Remove six screws securing power head to drive shaft housing and lift power head free. Remove flywheel, ignition components, carburetor, intake manifold and reed valve assembly. Remove screws retaining exhaust cover (18 – Fig. Y16-20) and withdraw. Crankcase halves can be separated after removal of ten screws securing crankcase half (1) to cylinder block. Crankshaft and pistons are now accessible for removal and overhaul as outlined in the appropriate following paragraphs.

ASSEMBLY. Two-stroke engine design dictates that intake manifold and crankcase are completely sealed against both vacuum and pressure. Exhaust manifold and cylinder head must be sealed against water leakage and pressure. Mating surfaces of water intake and exhaust areas between power head and drive shaft housing must form a tight seal.

Whenever the power head is disassembled, it is recommended that all gasket surfaces of crankcase halves be carefully checked for nicks, burrs or warped surfaces which might interfere with a tight seal. The cylinder head, head end of cylinder block, and the mating surfaces of manifolds and crankcase may be checked and lapped, if necessary, to provide a smooth surface.

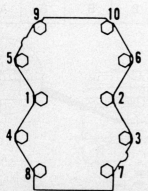

Fig. Y16-17 — Tighten crankcase screws in sequence shown above.

Fig. Y16-20 — Exploded view of cylinder block assembly.

1. Crankcase
2. Cylinder block
3. Oil seal housing
4. Gasket
5. Oil seal
6. Check valve
7. Dowel pin
8. Gasket
9. Cylinder head
10. Thermostat cover
11. Gasket
12. Spacer
13. Thermostat
14. Anode
15. Gasket
16. Inner exhaust plate
17. Gasket
18. Exhaust cover

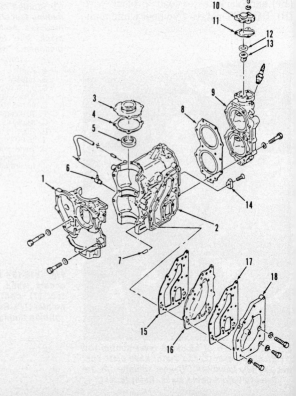

Do not remove any more metal than is necessary to obtain a smooth finish. Thoroughly clean the parts with new oil on a clean, soft rag, then wash with soapsuds and clean rags.

Mating surface of crankcase halves may be checked on the lapping block, and high spots or nicks removed, but surfaces must not be lowered. If extreme care is used, a slightly damaged crankcase can be salvaged in this manner. In case of doubt, renew the crankcase assembly.

The crankcase halves are positively located during assembly by the use of two dowel pins. Check to make sure that dowel pins are not bent, nicked or distorted and that dowel holes are clean and true. When installing pins, make certain they are fully seated, but do not use excessive force.

The mating surfaces of the crankcase halves must be sealed during reassembly using a Yamaha Bond No. 4 or a nonhardening type of gasket sealer. Make certain that surfaces are thoroughly cleaned of oil and old sealer before making a fresh application. Apply sealer evenly and use sparingly, so excess does not squeeze into crankcase cavity.

Tighten the crankcase screws to 27 N·m (19 ft.-lbs.) following the sequence shown in Fig. Y16-17. Tighten the cylinder head screws to 27 N·m (19 ft.-lbs.) following the sequence shown in Fig. Y16-18. Refer to CONDENSED SERVICE DATA section for general torquing specifications.

PISTONS, PINS, RINGS AND CYLINDERS. Cylinder bore should be measured in several different locations to determine if an out-of-round or tapered condition exists. Inspect cylinder wall for scoring. If minor scoring is noted, cylinders should be honed to smooth out cylinder wall.

Recommended piston skirt to cylinder clearance is 0.060-0.065 mm (0.0024-0.0026 in.). Recommended piston ring end gap is 0.2-0.04 mm (0.008-0.016 in.) for both rings. The top piston ring is semi-keystone shaped. The recommended lower piston ring side clearance is 0.04-0.08 mm (0.0016-0.0032 in.). Make sure piston rings properly align with locating pins in ring grooves.

When reassembling, install new piston pin retaining clips (4 – Fig. Y16-22) and make sure that "UP" on dome of piston is towards flywheel end of engine. Coat bearings, pistons, rings and cylinder bores with engine oil during assembly.

CONNECTING RODS, CRANKSHAFT AND BEARINGS. The crankshaft assembly should only be disassembled if the necessary tools and experience are available to service this type of crankshaft.

Maximum crankshaft runout measured at bearing outer races with crankshaft ends supported in lathe centers is 0.03 mm (0.0012 in.). Maximum connecting rod big end side clearance should be less than 0.3 mm (0.012 in.). Side-to-side shake of connecting rod small end measured as shown in Fig. Y16-23 should be a maximum of 2.0 mm (0.08 in.).

Crankshaft, connecting rods and center section components are available only as a unit assembly. Outer main bearings (17 and 24 – Fig. Y16-22) are available individually.

Thirty-four needle bearings (7) are used in each connecting rod small end. Rollers can be held in place with petroleum jelly while installing piston.

Lubricate bearings, pistons, rings and cylinders with engine oil prior to installation. Tighten crankcase and cylinder head screws as outlined in ASSEMBLY section.

STARTER

MANUAL STARTER. When starter rope (5 – Fig. Y16-25) is pulled, pulley (7) will rotate. As pulley (7) rotates, drive

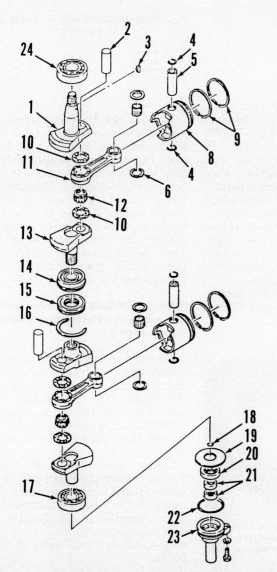

Fig. Y16-22 – Exploded view of crankshaft assembly.

1. Crank half
2. Crankpin
3. Key
4. Clip
5. Piston pin
6. Washer
7. Needle bearings
8. Piston
9. Piston rings
10. Thrust washers
11. Connecting rod
12. Roller bearing
13. Crank half
14. Bearing & snap ring
15. Labyrinth seal
16. Snap ring
17. Bearing
18. "O" ring
19. Washer
20. Oil seal
21. Oil seals
22. "O" ring
23. Lower oil seal housing

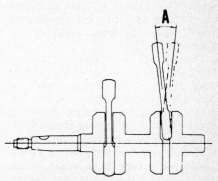

Fig. Y16-23 – Maximum shake at small end of connecting rod (A) should be less than 2.0 mm (0.08 in.).

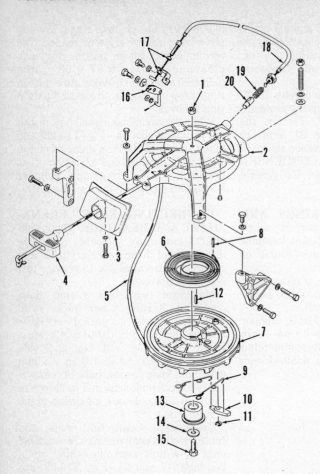

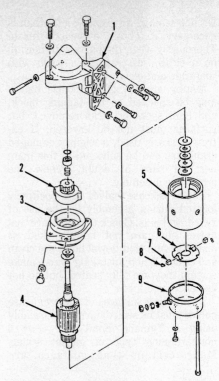

Fig. Y16-25—Exploded view of manual starter assembly.

1. Nut
2. Housing
3. Rope guide
4. Handle
5. Starter rope
6. Rewind spring
7. Pulley
8. Pin
9. Pawl spring
10. Pawl
11. Clip
12. Pin
13. Shaft
14. Washer
15. Bolt
16. Lever & link
17. Adjusting nuts
18. Starter lockout cable
19. Spring
20. Plunger

Fig. Y16-28—Exploded view of electric starter assembly.

1. End frame
2. Drive assy.
3. Frame cover
4. Armature
5. Frame
6. Brush plate
7. Brush
8. Brush spring
9. End cover

pawl (10) moves to engage with the flywheel thus cranking the engine.

When starter rope (5) is released, pulley (7) is rotated in the reverse direction by force from rewind spring (6). As pulley (7) rotates, the starter rope is rewound and drive pawl (10) is disengaged from the flywheel.

Safety plunger (20) engages lugs on pulley (7) to prevent starter engagement when the gear shift lever is in the forward or reverse position.

To overhaul the manual starter, proceed as follows: Remove the engine top cover. Remove the screws retaining the manual starter to the engine. Remove starter lockout cable (18) at starter housing (2). Note plunger (20) and spring (19) located at cable end; care should be used not to lose components should they fall free. Withdraw the starter assembly.

Check pawl (10) for freedom of movement and excessive wear of engagement area or any other damage. Renew or lubricate pawl (10) with a suitable water-resistant grease and return starter to service if no other damage is noted.

To disassemble, remove clip (11) and withdraw pawl (10) and pawl spring (9). Untie starter rope (5) at handle (4) and allow the rope to wind into the starter. Remove bolt (15), washer (14) and shaft (13), then place a suitable screwdriver

blade through hole (H–Fig. Y16-26) to hold rewind spring (6–Fig. Y16-25) securely in housing (2). Carefully lift pulley (7) with starter rope (5) from housing (2). BE CAREFUL when removing pulley (7) to prevent possible injury from rewind spring (6). Untie starter rope (5) and remove rope from pulley (7) if renewal is required. To remove rewind spring (6) from housing (2), invert housing so it sits upright on a flat surface, then tap the housing top until rewind spring (6) falls free and uncoils.

Inspect all components for damage and excessive wear and renew if needed.

Fig. Y16-26—View showing proper installation of pawl spring (9), pawl (10) and clip (11). Pulley hole (H) is used during pulley withdrawal. Refer to text.

To reassemble, first apply a coating of a suitable water-resistant grease to rewind spring area of housing (2). Install rewind spring (6) in housing (2) so spring coils wind in a counterclockwise direction from the outer end. Make sure the spring outer hook is properly secured around starter housing pin (8). Wind starter rope (5) onto pulley (7) approximately 2½ turns counterclockwise when viewed from the flywheel side. Direct remaining starter rope (5) length through notch in pulley (7).

NOTE: Lubricate all friction surfaces with a suitable water-resistant grease during reassembly.

Assemble pulley (7) to starter housing making sure that pin (12) engages hook end in rewind spring (6). Install shaft (13), washer (14) and bolt (15). Apply Loctite 271 or 290 or an equivalent thread fastening solution, on bolt (15) threads, then install nut (1) and securely tighten.

Thread starter rope (5) through starter housing (2), rope guide (3) and handle (4) and secure with a knot. Turn pulley (7) 2 to 3 turns counterclockwise when viewed from the flywheel side, then release starter rope (5) from pulley notch and allow rope to slowly wind onto pulley.

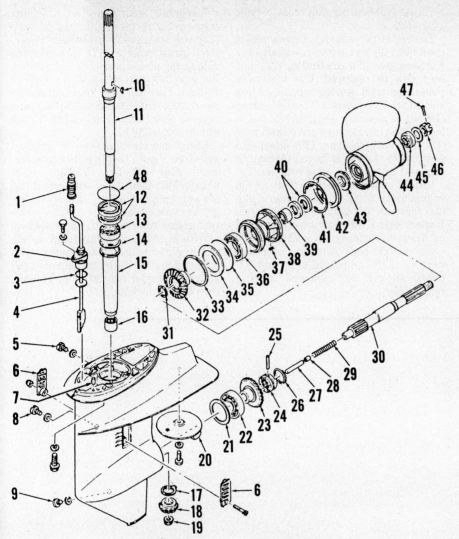

Fig. Y16-30—Exploded view of gearcase assembly.

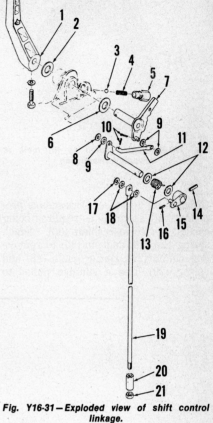

Fig. Y16-31—Exploded view of shift control linkage.

1. Shift control handle	
2. Washer	12. Washers
3. Detent ball	13. Spring
4. Spring	14. Pin
5. Guide	15. Arm
6. Washer	16. Cotter pin
7. Cam	17. Washer
8. Washer	18. Washers
9. Washer	19. Upper shift rod
10. Pins	20. Coupler nut
11. Link	21. Locknut

1. Boot	13. Bearing	25. Pin	37. Key
2. Retainer	14. Shim	26. Spring clip	38. Bearing housing
3. "O" ring	15. Drive shaft tube	27. Shift plunger	39. Needle bearing
4. Lower shift rod	16. Needle bearing	28. Spring guide	40. Oil seals
5. Vent plug	17. Thrust washer	29. Spring	41. Tab washer
6. Water inlet cover	18. Pinion gear	30. Propeller shaft	42. Nut
7. Dowel	19. Nut	31. Thrust washer	43. Spacer
8. Oil level plug	20. Trim tab	32. Reverse gear	44. Spacer
9. Drain plug	21. Shim	33. Shim	45. Washer
10. Key	22. Taper roller bearing	34. Thrust washer	46. Nut
11. Drive shaft	23. Forward gear	35. "O" ring	47. Cotter pin
12. Oil seals	24. Dog clutch	36. Ball bearing	48. "O" ring

NOTE: Do not apply any more tension on rewind spring (6) than is required to draw starter handle (4) back into the proper released position.

Install spring (9), pawl (10) and clip (11) as shown in Fig. Y16-26. Remount manual starter assembly.

Adjust starter lockout assembly by turning adjusting nuts (17–Fig. Y16-25) at cable (18) end so starter will engage when gear shift lever is in neutral position, but will not engage when gear shift lever is in forward or reverse position. Plunger (20) end should recess in starter housing (2) 1 mm (0.04 in.) when gear shift lever is in neutral position.

ELECTRIC STARTER. Some models are equipped with an electric starter motor. Refer to Fig. Y16-28 for an exploded view of the starter motor. Commutator undercut should be 0.5-0.8 mm (0.02-0.03 in.) with a minimum limit of 0.2 mm (0.008 in.). Minimum brush length is 10 mm (0.394 in.).

During reassembly, adjust shims so armature end play is 1.5-2.0 mm (0.06-0.08 in.).

LOWER UNIT

PROPELLER AND DRIVE HUB.
Lower unit protection is provided by a cushion type hub in the propeller. Stand-

ard propeller that will allow the engine at full throttle to reach maximum operating range or 4500-5500 rpm.

R&R AND OVERHAUL. Most service on lower unit can be performed after detaching gearcase from drive shaft housing. To remove gearcase, attach outboard motor to a suitable stand and remove vent and drain plugs in gearcase to allow lubricant to drain. Loosen locknut (21–Fig. Y16-31) and remove coupler nut (20). Remove four bolts securing gearcase to drive shaft housing and carefully separate gearcase from drive shaft housing. Remove water pump being careful not to lose impeller key (10–Fig. Y16-30). Remove propeller.

Disassemble gearcase by bending back locking tab of lockwasher (41), then remove nut (42) and lockwasher (41). Using a suitable puller attached to propeller shaft, extract components (24

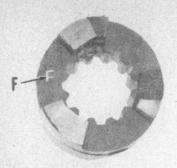

Fig. Y16-32 — Install clutch so (F) mark is towards forward gear.

through 40) gearcase. Disassemble propeller shaft assembly as required being careful not to lose shims (33). Detach spring clip (26) and pin (25) to remove dog clutch (24), spring guide (28) and spring (29). Use a suitable puller to separate ball bearing (36) from reverse gear (32).

To remove drive shaft, unscrew pinion gear nut (19) and withdraw shaft (11). Forward gear (23) and bearing (22) cone may now be removed. Use a suitable puller to extract bearing cup; do not lose shims (21). Pull oil seals (12) and bearing (13) out of gearcase being careful not to lose shims (14). Remove drive shaft tube (15) then drive bearing (16) down into gear cavity. Lower shift rod (4) may be removed after unscrewing retainer (2).

Inspect gears for wear on teeth and in engagement dogs. Inspect dog clutch (24) for wear on engagement surfaces. Inspect shafts for wear on splines and on friction surfaces of gears and oil seals. Check shift cam for excessive wear on shift ramps. All seals and "O" rings should be renewed during reassembly.

Assemble gearcase by reversing disassembly procedure. Install oil seals (12) with lips away from bearing (13). Install thrust washer (17) with grooved side facing pinion gear (18). Tighten pinion gear nut (19) to 34-38 N·m (25-28 ft.-lbs.). Forward gear backlash should be 0.2-0.5 mm (0.008-0.020 in.) and reverse gear backlash should be 0.7-1.0 mm (0.028-0.039 in.).

Install dog clutch (24) so "F" marked side (see Fig. Y16-32) is towards forward gear (23–Fig. Y16-30). Shift plunger (27) is installed with round end towards cam on lower shift rod (4). Apply Yamaha Grease A or a water resistant grease to drive shaft upper splines.

With gearcase assembled and installed, synchronize gear engagement with gear selector handle by turning shift rod adjusting coupler nut (20–Fig. Y16-31), then tighten locknut (21).